Blackstone's Statutes on

Commercial & Consumer Law

31st edition

edited by

F. D. Rose

PhD, LLD, DCL, of Gray's Inn, Barrister-at-Law

Senior Research Fellow, Commercial Law Centre, Harris Manchester College, University of Oxford

OXFORD

UNIVERSITY PRESS

OXFORD
UNIVERSITY PRESS

Great Clarendon Street, Oxford, OX2 6DP,
United Kingdom

Oxford University Press is a department of the University of Oxford.
It furthers the University's objective of excellence in research, scholarship,
and education by publishing worldwide. Oxford is a registered trade mark of
Oxford University Press in the UK and in certain other countries

This selection © F. D. Rose 2023

The moral rights of the author have been asserted

First published by Blackstone Press 1989

Twenty-eighth edition 2019
Twenty-ninth edition 2020
Thirtieth edition 2021
Thirty-first edition 2023

Public sector information reproduced under Open Government Licence v3.0
(http://www.nationalarchives.gov.uk/doc/open-government-licence/open-government-licence.htm)

Published in the United States of America by Oxford University Press
198 Madison Avenue, New York, NY 10016, United States of America

British Library Cataloguing in Publication Data
Data available

ISBN 978–0–19–285856–6

Printed in the UK by
Bell & Bain Ltd., Glasgow

For Josephine

Blackstone's Statutes
Unsurpassed in authority, reliability, and accuracy

The titles in the Blackstone's Statutes series are a collection of carefully reviewed and selected unannotated legislative material and official documents.

We make every effort to ensure titles in the series meet the needs of their target market. They are reviewed by lecturers to match university courses closely and are expertly edited to be manageable in size, whilst retaining their comprehensive coverage.

The editors only include material that will be valuable to students and lecturers and it is therefore abridged where necessary.

Every effort has been made to trace and contact copyright holders prior to publication. Where this has not proved possible, if notified, the publisher will undertake to rectify any errors or omissions at the earliest opportunity.

Conventions used in *Blackstone's Statutes on Commercial & Consumer Law*

The material in this book is reproduced in its most up-to-date form and all amendments are incorporated within square brackets. Occasional omissions are indicated by ellipses . . .

Supplementary notes and details of amending provisions are generally not included.

All statutes have received royal assent but some legislation may not yet be in force.

Contents

Part I	Statutes	1

Alphabetical contents

Chronological contents

Editor's preface

As in previous editions, this book sets out to present the principal legislative materials in the conventionally central areas of commercial and consumer law (including particularly relevant topics of general common law) but (in order to keep the collection manageable and its price reasonable) generally omitting more specialist subjects. This, of course, is more easily said than done. Commercial activity is infinitely varied and the pace of change continues to accelerate. For their part, our law makers (of which there are an increasing number) are engaged in responding to, facilitating and promoting such changes. Legislation, both primary and secondary, is subject to constant expansion, revision and complication. And it is increasingly difficult to find in an easily accessible form, for even electronic databases are dependent on fallible human masters, and even the best programmers have to grapple with an overabundance of unimplemented legislative amendments, some of which never have effect. These elements, coupled with the volume of new material each year, make revision of this book both challenging and exciting. They also require increased selectivity in combining the core features of our commercial law with a flavour of its diversity, particularly given the tension between its more obviously commercial and its consumer protection aspects.

Commercial and consumer law and statutes have in common that they are all in a permanent state of flux, making it essential continually to update this collection of materials. The book therefore has the usual range of necessary amendments to existing legislative provisions together with recent innovations.

We have now passed the end of the implementation period leading up to the United Kingdom's exit from the European Union and the consequent tidying up which that has entailed but much work continues towards removing EU-based law from our legislation with many of its fruits remaining to be seen. Alongside this, the Law Commission continues with its work in modernising the law, with a good prospect that its draft Electronic Trade Documents Bill, currently before Parliament, will soon be enacted, with or without minor amendment.

I continue to be grateful to my wife, Lynda, for her contribution to revision of these materials. As always, I am happy to acknowledge the holders' rights in copyright materials. Also, I continue to be grateful for suggestions as to possible revisions of this collection of materials. Given the diversity of components of, and courses in, commercial and consumer law, plus the requirement to restrain the size of this book, it is, to say the least, a challenging task to select an appropriate range of materials. The task is not made easier by the number of, often conflicting, suggestions as to what ought to be omitted and/or included. However, all suggestions are carefully considered and revisited. They will continue to be welcomed.

Francis Rose
1 April 2023

New to this edition

The 31st edition of *Blackstone's Statutes on Commercial & Consumer Law* has been fully revised and updated to incorporate all relevant original and amending legislation and materials up to April 2023, including:

- Financial Services Act 2021
- Consumer Rights (Transfer of Ownership under Sales Contracts) Bill 2021
- Electronic Trade Documents Bill 2022

Amendments have been made to the following materials:

- Consumer Protection from Unfair Trading Regulations 2008
- Payment Services Regulations 2017

Part I

Statutes

Life Assurance Act 1774

(14 Geo. III, c. 48)

1 No insurance to be made on lives, etc., by persons having no interest, etc.
From and after the passing of this Act no insurance shall be made by any person or persons, bodies politick or corporate, on the life or lives of any person or persons, or on any other event or events whatsoever, wherein the person or persons for whose use, benefit, or on whose account such policy or policies shall be made, shall have no interest, or by way of gaming or wagering; and that every assurance made contrary to the true intent and meaning hereof shall be null and void to all intents and purposes whatsoever.

2 No policies on lives without inserting the names of persons interested, etc.
And [...] it shall not be lawful to make any policy or policies on the life or lives of any person or persons, or other event or events, without inserting in such policy or policies the person or persons name or names interested therein, or for whose use, benefit, or on whose account such policy is so made or underwrote.

3 How much may be recovered where the insured hath interest in lives
And [...] in all cases where the insured hath interest in such life or lives, event or events, no greater sum shall be recovered or received from the insurer or insurers than the amount of value of the interest of the insured in such life or lives, or other event or events.

4 Not to extend to insurances on ships, goods, etc.
Provided, always, that nothing herein contained shall extend or be construed to extend to insurances bona fide made by any person or persons on ships, goods, or merchandises, but every such insurance shall be as valid and effectual in the law as if this Act had not been made.

Bills of Sale Act 1878

(41 & 42 Vict., c. 31)

3 Application
This Act shall apply to every bill of sale executed on or after the first day of January one thousand eight hundred and seventy-nine (whether the same be absolute, or subject or not subject to any

trust) whereby the holder or grantee has power, either with or without notice, and either immediately or at any future time, to seize or take possession of any personal chattels comprised in or made subject to such bill of sale.

4   Interpretation of terms

In this Act the following words and expressions shall have the meanings in this section assigned to them respectively, unless there be something in the subject or context repugnant to such construction; (that is to say),

The expression 'bill of sale' shall include bills of sale, assignments, transfers, declarations of trust without transfer, inventories of goods with receipt thereto attached, or receipts for purchase moneys of goods, and other assurances of personal chattels, and also powers of attorney, authorities, or licenses to take possession of personal chattels as security for any debt, and also any agreement, whether intended or not to be followed by the execution of any other instrument, by which a right in equity to any personal chattels, or to any charge or security thereon, shall be conferred, but shall not include the following documents; that is to say, assignments for the benefit of the creditors of the person making or giving the same, marriage settlements, transfers or assignments of any ship or vessel or any share thereof, transfers of goods in the ordinary course of business of any trade or calling, bills of sale of goods in foreign parts or at sea, bills of lading, India warrants, warehouse-keepers' certificates, warrants or orders for the delivery of goods, or any other documents used in the ordinary course of business as proof of the possession or control of goods, or authorising or purporting to authorise, either by indorsement or by delivery, the possessor of such document to transfer or receive goods thereby represented:

The expression 'personal chattels' shall mean goods, furniture, and other articles capable of complete transfer by delivery, and (when separately assigned or charged) fixtures and growing crops, but shall not include chattel interests in real estate, nor fixtures (except trade machinery as hereinafter defined), when assigned together with a freehold or leasehold interest in any land or building to which they are affixed, nor growing crops when assigned together with any interest in the land on which they grow, nor shares or interests in the stock, funds, or securities of any government, or in the capital or property of incorporated or joint stock companies, nor choses in action, nor any stock or produce upon any farm or lands which by virtue of any covenant or agreement or of the custom of the country ought not to be removed from any farm where the same are at the time of making or giving of such bill of sale:

Personal chattels shall be deemed to be in the 'apparent possession' of the person making or giving a bill of sale, so long as they remain or are in or upon any house, mill, warehouse, building, works, yard, land, or other premises occupied by him, or are used and enjoyed by him in any place whatsoever, notwithstanding that formal possession thereof may have been taken by or given to any other person:

'Prescribed' means prescribed by rules made under the provisions of this Act.

5   Application of Act to trade machinery

From and after the commencement of this Act trade machinery shall, for the purposes of this Act, be deemed to be personal chattels, and any mode of disposition of trade machinery by the owner thereof which would be a bill of sale as to any other personal chattels shall be deemed to be a bill of sale within the meaning of this Act.

For the purposes of this Act—

'Trade machinery' means the machinery used in or attached to any factory or workshop;

1st.   Exclusive of the fixed motive-powers, such as the water-wheels and steam-engines, and the steam-boilers, donkey-engines, and other fixed appurtenances of the said motive-powers; and

2nd.   Exclusive of the fixed power machinery, such as the shafts, wheels, drums, and their fixed appurtenances, which transmit the action of the motive-powers to the other machinery, fixed and loose; and,

3rd.   Exclusive of the pipes for steam gas and water in the factory or workshop.

The machinery or effects excluded by this section from the definition of trade machinery shall not be deemed to be personal chattels within the meaning of this Act.

'Factory or workshop' means any premises on which any manual labour is exercised by way of trade, or for purposes of gain, in or incidental to the following purposes or any of them; that is to say,

(a) In or incidental to the making of any article or part of an article; or

(b) In or incidental to the altering repairing ornamenting finishing of any article; or

(c) In or incidental to the adapting for sale of any article.

6   Certain instruments giving powers of distress to be subject to this Act

Every attornment instrument or agreement, not being a mining lease, whereby a power of distress is given or agreed to be given by any person to any other person by way of security for any present future or contingent debt or advance, and whereby any rent is reserved or made payable as a mode of providing for the payment of interest on such debt or advance, or otherwise for the purpose of such security only, shall be deemed to be a bill of sale, within the meaning of this Act, of any personal chattels which may be seized or taken under such power of distress.

Provided, that nothing in this section shall extend to any mortgage of any estate or interest in any land tenement or hereditament which the mortgagee, being in possession, shall have demised to the mortgagor as his tenant at a fair and reasonable rent.

7   Fixtures or growing crops not to be deemed separately assigned when the land passes by the same instrument

No fixtures or growing crops shall be deemed, under this Act, to be separately assigned or charged by reason only that they are assigned by separate words, or that power is given to sever them from the land or building to which they are affixed, or from the land on which they grow, without otherwise taking possession of or dealing with such land or building, or land, if by the same instrument any freehold or leasehold interest in the land or building to which such fixtures are affixed, or in the land on which such crops grow, is also conveyed or assigned to the same persons or person.

The same rule of construction shall be applied to all deeds or instruments, including fixtures or growing crops, executed before the commencement of this Act, and then subsisting and in force, in all questions arising under any bankruptcy liquidation assignment for the benefit of creditors, or execution of any process of any court, which shall take place or be issued after the commencement of this Act.

8   Avoidance of unregistered bills of sale in certain cases

Every bill of sale to which this Act applies shall be duly attested and shall be registered under this Act, within seven days after the making or giving thereof, and shall set forth the consideration for which such bill of sale was given, otherwise such bill of sale, as against all trustees or assignees of the estate of the person whose chattels, or any of them, are comprised in such bill of sale under the law relating to bankruptcy or liquidation, or under any assignment for the benefit of the creditors of such person, and also as against all sheriffs officers and other persons seizing any chattels comprised in such bill of sale, in the execution of any process of any court authorising the seizure of the chattels of the person by whom or of whose chattels such bill has been made, and also as against every person on whose behalf such process shall have been issued, shall be deemed fraudulent and void so far as regards the property in or right to the possession of any chattels comprised in such bill of sale which, at or after the time of [making the bankruptcy application or] filing the petition for bankruptcy or liquidation, or of the execution of such assignment, or of executing such process (as the case may be), and after the expiration of such seven days are in the possession or apparent possession of the person making such bill of sale (or of any person against whom the process has issued under or in the execution of which such bill has been made or given, as the case may be).

9 Avoidance of certain duplicate bills of sale

Where a subsequent bill of sale is executed within or on the expiration of seven days after the execution of a prior unregistered bill of sale, and comprises all or any part of the personal chattels comprised in such prior bill of sale, then, if such subsequent bill of sale is given as a security for the same debt as is secured by the prior bill of sale, or for any part of such debt, it shall, to the extent to which it is a security for the same debt or part thereof, and so far as respects the personal chattels or part thereof comprised in the prior bill, be absolutely void, unless it is proved to the satisfaction of the court having cognizance of the case that the subsequent bill of sale was bona fide given for the purpose of correcting some material error in the prior bill of sale, and not for the purpose of evading this Act.

10 Mode of registering bills of sale

A bill of sale shall be attested and registered under this Act in the following manner:

(1) The execution of every bill of sale shall be attested by a solicitor of the [Senior Courts], and the attestation shall state that before the execution of the bill of sale the effect thereof has been explained to the grantor by the attesting solicitor.

(2) Such bill, with every schedule or inventory thereto annexed or therein referred to, and also a true copy of such bill and of every such schedule or inventory, and of every attestation of the execution of such bill of sale, together with an affidavit of the time of such bill of sale being made or given, and of its due execution and attestation, and a description of the residence and occupation of the person making or giving the same (or in case the same is made or given by any person under or in the execution of any process, then a description of the residence and occupation of the person against whom such process issued), and of every attesting witness to such bill of sale, shall be presented to and the said copy and affidavit shall be filed with the registrar within seven clear days after the making or giving of such bill of sale, in like manner as a warrant of attorney in any personal action given by a trader is now by law required to be filed:

(3) If the bill of sale is made or given subject to any defeasance or condition, or declaration of trust not contained in the body thereof, such defeasance, condition, or declaration shall be deemed to be part of the bill, and shall be written on the same paper or parchment therewith before the registration, and shall be truly set forth in the copy filed under this Act therewith and as part thereof, otherwise the registration shall be void.

In case two or more bills of sale are given, comprising in whole or in part any of the same chattels, they shall have priority in the order of the date of their registration respectively as regards such chattels.

A transfer or assignment of a registered bill of sale need not be registered.

11 Renewal of registration

The registration of a bill of sale, whether executed before or after the commencement of this Act, must be renewed once at least every five years, and if a period of five years elapses from the registration or renewed registration of a bill of sale without a renewal or further renewal (as the case may be), the registration shall become void.

The renewal of a registration shall be effected by filing with the registrar an affidavit stating the date of the bill of sale and of the last registration thereof, and the names, residences, and occupations of the parties thereto as stated therein, and that the bill of sale is still a subsisting security.

Every such affidavit may be in the form set forth in the Schedule (A) to this Act annexed.

A renewal of registration shall not become necessary by reason only of a transfer or assignment of a bill of sale.

12   Form of register

The registrar shall keep a book (in this Act called 'the register') for the purposes of this Act, and shall, upon the filing of any bill of sale or copy under this Act, enter therein in the form set forth in the second schedule (B) to this Act annexed, or in any other prescribed form, the name residence and occupation of the person by whom the bill was made or given (or in case the same was made or given by any person under or in the execution of process, then the name residence and occupation of the person against whom such process was issued, and also the name of the person or persons to whom or in whose favour the bill was given), and the other particulars shown in the said schedule or to be prescribed under this Act, and shall number all such bills registered in each year consecutively, according to the respective dates of their registration.

Upon the registration of any affidavit of renewal the like entry shall be made, with the addition of the date and number of the last previous entry relating to the same bill, and the bill of sale or copy originally filed shall be thereupon marked with the number affixed to such affidavit of renewal.

The registrar shall also keep an index of the names of the grantors of registered bills of sale with reference to entries in the register of the bills of sale given by each such grantor.

Such index shall be arranged in divisions corresponding with the letters of the alphabet, so that all grantors whose surnames begin with the same letter (and no others) shall be comprised in one division, but the arrangement within each such division need not be strictly alphabetical.

13   The registrar

The masters of the [Senior Courts] attached to the Queen's Bench Division of the High Court of Justice, or such other officers as may for the time being be assigned for this purpose under the provisions of the Supreme Court of Judicature Acts 1873 and 1875, shall be the registrar for the purposes of this Act, and any one of the said masters may perform all or any of the duties of the registrar.

14   Rectification of register

Any judge of the High Court of Justice on being satisfied that the omission to register a bill of sale or an affidavit or renewal thereof within the time prescribed by this Act, or the omission or mis-statement of the name residence or occupation of any person, was accidental or due to inadvertence, may in his discretion order such omission or mis-statement to be rectified by the insertion in the register of the true name residence or occupation, or by extending the time for such registration on such terms and conditions (if any) as to security, notice by advertisement or otherwise, or as to any other matter, as he thinks fit to direct.

15   Entry of satisfaction

Subject to and in accordance with any rules to be made under and for the purposes of this Act, the registrar may order a memorandum of satisfaction to be written upon any registered copy of a bill of sale, upon the prescribed evidence being given that the debt (if any) for which such bill of sale was made or given has been satisfied or discharged.

16   Copies may be taken, etc.

Any person shall be entitled to have an office copy or extract of any registered bill of sale, and affidavit of execution filed therewith, or copy thereof, and of any affidavit filed therewith, if any, or registered affidavit of renewal, upon paying for the same at the like rate as for office copies of judgments of the High Court of Justice, and any copy of a registered bill of sale, and affidavit purporting to be an office copy thereof, shall in all courts and before all arbitrators or other persons, be admitted as prima facie evidence thereof, and of the fact and date of registration as shown thereon [...].

20 Order and disposition

Chattels comprised in a bill of sale which has been and continues to be duly registered under this Act shall not be deemed to be in the possession, order, or disposition of the grantor of the bill of sale within the meaning of the Bankruptcy Act 1869.

21 Rules

Rules for the purposes of this Act may be made and altered from time to time by the like persons and in the like manner in which rules and regulations may be made under and for the purposes of the Supreme Court of Judicature Acts 1873 and 1875.

22 Time for registration

When the time for registering a bill of sale expires on a Sunday, or other day on which the registrar's office is closed, the registration shall be valid if made on the next following day on which the office is open.

SCHEDULES

Section 11   ## SCHEDULE (A)

I [*A.B.*]   of   do swear that a bill of sale, bearing date the   day of   18 [*insert the date of the bill*], and made between [*insert the names and descriptions of the parties in the original bill of sale*] and which said bill of sale [*or,* and a copy of which said bill of sale, *as the case may be*] was registered on the   day of   18 [*insert date of registration*], is still a subsisting security.

Sworn, &c.

SCHEDULE (B)

Satisfaction entered	No	By whom given (or against whom process issued)			To whom given	Nature of Instrument	Date	Date of Registration	Date of Registration of affidavit of renewal
		Name	Residence	Occupation					

Bills of Exchange Act 1882

(45 & 46 Vict., c. 61)

PART I   PRELIMINARY

2   Interpretation of terms

In this Act, unless the context otherwise requires,—

'Acceptance' means an acceptance completed by delivery or notification.

'Action' includes counter claim and set off.

'Banker' includes a body of persons whether incorporated or not who carry on the business of banking.

'Bankrupt' includes any person whose estate is vested in a trustee or assignee under the law for the time being in force relating to bankruptcy.

'Bearer' means the person in possession of a bill or note which is payable to bearer.

'Bill' means bill of exchange, and 'note' means promissory note.

'Delivery' means transfer of possession, actual or constructive, from one person to another.

'Holder' means the payee or indorsee of a bill or note who is in possession of it, or the bearer thereof.

'Indorsement' means an indorsement completed by delivery.

'Issue' means the first delivery of a bill or note, complete in form to a person who takes it as a holder.

'Person' includes a body of persons whether incorporated or not.

['postal operator' has the meaning given by section 125(1) of the Postal Services Act 2000.]

'Value' means valuable consideration.

'Written' includes printed, and 'writing' includes print.

PART II   BILLS OF EXCHANGE

Form and interpretation

3   Bill of exchange defined

(1) A bill of exchange is an unconditional order in writing, addressed by one person to another, signed by the person giving it, requiring the person to whom it is addressed to pay on demand or at a fixed or determinable future time a sum certain in money to or to the order of a specified person, or to bearer.

(2) An instrument which does not comply with these conditions, or which orders any act to be done in addition to the payment of money, is not a bill of exchange.

(3) An order to pay out of a particular fund is not unconditional within the meaning of this section; but an unqualified order to pay, coupled with (a) an indication of a particular fund out of which the drawee is to re-imburse himself or a particular account to be debited with the amount, or (b) a statement of the transaction which gives rise to the bill, is unconditional.

(4) A bill is not invalid by reason—

(a) That it is not dated;

(b) That it does not specify the value given, or that any value has been given therefor;

(c) That it does not specify the place where it is drawn or the place where it is payable.

4   Inland and foreign bills

(1) An inland bill is a bill which is or on the face of it purports to be (a) both drawn and payable within the British Islands, or (b) drawn within the British Islands upon some person resident therein. Any other bill is a foreign bill.

For the purposes of this Act 'British Islands' means any part of the United Kingdom of Great Britain and Ireland, the islands of Man, Guernsey, Jersey, Alderney, and Sark, and the islands adjacent to any of them being part of the dominions of Her Majesty.

(2) Unless the contrary appear on the face of the bill the holder may treat it as an inland bill.

5   Effect where different parties to bill are the same person

(1) A bill may be drawn payable to, or to the order of, the drawer; or it may be drawn payable to, or to the order of, the drawee.

(2) Where in a bill drawer and drawee are the same person, or where the drawee is a fictitious person or a person not having capacity to contract, the holder may treat the instrument, at his option, either as a bill of exchange or as a promissory note.

6   Address to drawee

(1) The drawee must be named or otherwise indicated in a bill with reasonable certainty.

(2) A bill may be addressed to two or more drawees whether they are partners or not, but an order addressed to two drawees in the alternative or to two or more drawees in succession is not a bill of exchange.

7   Certainty required as to payee

(1) Where a bill is not payable to bearer, the payee must be named or otherwise indicated therein with reasonable certainty.

(2) A bill may be made payable to two or more payees jointly, or it may be made payable in the alternative to one of two, or one or some of several payees. A bill may also be made payable to the holder of an office for the time being.

(3) Where the payee is a fictitious or non-existing person the bill may be treated as payable to bearer.

8   What bills are negotiable

(1) When a bill contains words prohibiting transfer, or indicating an intention that it should not be transferable, it is valid as between the parties thereto, but is not negotiable.

(2) A negotiable bill may be payable either to order or to bearer.

(3) A bill is payable to bearer which is expressed to be so payable, or on which the only or last indorsement is an indorsement in blank.

(4) A bill is payable to order which is expressed to be so payable, or which is expressed to be payable to a particular person, and does not contain words prohibiting transfer or indicating an intention that it should not be transferable.

(5) Where a bill, either originally or by indorsement, is expressed to be payable to the order of a specified person, and not to him or his order, it is nevertheless payable to him or his order at his option.

9   Sum payable

(1) The sum payable by a bill is a sum certain within the meaning of this Act, although it is required to be paid—

   (a) With interest.
   (b) By stated instalments.
   (c) By stated instalments, with a provision that upon default in payment of any instalment the whole shall become due.
   (d) According to an indicated rate of exchange or according to a rate of exchange to be ascertained as directed by the bill.

(2) Where the sum payable is expressed in words and also in figures, and there is a discrepancy between the two, the sum denoted by the words is the amount payable.

(3) Where a bill is expressed to be payable with interest, unless the instrument otherwise provides, interest runs from the date of the bill, and if the bill is undated from the issue thereof.

10   Bill payable on demand

(1) A bill is payable on demand—

(a) Which is expressed to be payable on demand, or at sight, or on presentation; or

(b) In which no time for payment is expressed.

(2) Where a bill is accepted or indorsed when it is overdue, it shall, as regards the acceptor who so accepts, or any indorser who so indorses it, be deemed a bill payable on demand.

11   Bill payable at a future time

A bill is payable at a determinable future time within the meaning of this Act which is expressed to be payable—

(1) At a fixed period after date or sight.

(2) On or at a fixed period after the occurrence of a specified event which is certain to happen, though the time of happening may be uncertain.

An instrument expressed to be payable on a contingency is not a bill, and the happening of the event does not cure the defect.

12   Omission of date in bill payable after date

Where a bill expressed to be payable at a fixed period after date is issued undated, or where the acceptance of a bill payable at a fixed period after sight is undated, any holder may insert therein the true date of issue or acceptance, and the bill shall be payable accordingly.

Provided that (1) where the holder in good faith and by mistake inserts a wrong date, and (2) in every case where a wrong date is inserted, if the bill subsequently comes into the hands of a holder in due course the bill shall not be avoided thereby, but shall operate and be payable as if the date so inserted had been the true date.

13   Ante-dating and post-dating

(1) Where a bill or an acceptance or any indorsement on a bill is dated, the date shall, unless the contrary be proved, be deemed to be the true date of the drawing, acceptance, or indorsement, as the case may be.

(2) A bill is not invalid by reason only that it is ante-dated or post-dated, or that it bears date on a Sunday.

14   Computation of time of payment

Where a bill is not payable on demand the day on which it falls due is determined as follows:

[(1) The bill is due and payable in all cases on the last day of the time of payment as fixed by the bill or, if that is a non-business day, on the succeeding business day.]

(2) Where a bill is payable at a fixed period after date, after sight, or after the happening of a specified event, the time of payment is determined by excluding the day from which the time is to begin to run and by including the day of payment.

(3) Where a bill is payable at a fixed period after sight, the time begins to run from the date of the acceptance if the bill be accepted, and from the date of noting or protest if the bill be noted or protested for non-acceptance, or for non-delivery.

15   Case of need

The drawer of a bill and any indorser may insert therein the name of a person to whom the holder may resort in case of need, that is to say, in case the bill is dishonoured by non-acceptance or non-payment. Such person is called the referee in case of need. It is in the option of the holder to resort to the referee in case of need or not as he may think fit.

16   Optional stipulations by drawer or indorser

The drawer of a bill, and any indorser may insert therein an express stipulation—

(1) Negativing or limiting his own liability to the holder:

(2) Waiving as regards himself some or all of the holder's duties.

17   Definition and requisites of acceptance

(1) The acceptance of a bill is the signification by the drawee of his assent to the order of the drawer.

(2) An acceptance is invalid unless it complies with the following conditions, namely:

    (a) It must be written on the bill and be signed by the drawee. The mere signature of the drawee without additional words is sufficient.

    (b) It must not express that the drawee will perform his promise by any other means than the payment of money.

18   Time for acceptance

A bill may be accepted—

(1) before it has been signed by the drawer, or while otherwise incomplete:

(2) When it is overdue, or after it has been dishonoured by a previous refusal to accept, or by non-payment:

(3) When a bill payable after sight is dishonoured by non-acceptance, and the drawee subsequently accepts it, the holder, in the absence of any different agreement, is entitled to have the bill accepted as of the date of first presentment to the drawee for acceptance.

19   General and qualified acceptance

(1) An acceptance is either (a) general or (b) qualified.

(2) A general acceptance assents without qualification to the order of the drawer. A qualified acceptance in express terms varies the effect of the bill as drawn.

In particular an acceptance is qualified which is—

    (a) conditional, that is to say, which makes payment by the acceptor dependent on the fulfilment of a condition therein stated:

    (b) partial, that is to say, an acceptance to pay part only of the amount for which the bill is drawn:

    (c) local, that is to say, an acceptance to pay only at a particular specified place: An acceptance to pay at a particular place is a general acceptance, unless it expressly states that the bill is to be paid there only and not elsewhere:

    (d) qualified as to time:

    (e) the acceptance of some one or more of the drawees, but not of all.

20   Inchoate instruments

(1) Where a simple signature on a blank [...] paper is delivered by the signer in order that it may be converted into a bill, it operates as a prima facie authority to fill it up as a complete bill for any amount [...] using the signature for that of the drawer, or the acceptor, or an indorser; and, in like manner, when a bill is wanting in any material particular, the person in possession of it has a prima facie authority to fill up the omission in any way he thinks fit.

(2) In order that any such instrument when completed may be enforceable against any person who became a party thereto prior to its completion, it must be filled up within a reasonable time, and strictly in accordance with the authority given. Reasonable time for this purpose is a question of fact.

Provided that if any such instrument after completion is negotiated to a holder in due course it shall be valid and effectual for all purposes in his hands and he may enforce it as if it had been filled up within a reasonable time and strictly in accordance with the authority given.

21   Delivery

(1) Every contract on a bill, whether it be the drawer's, the acceptor's, or an indorser's is incomplete and revocable, until delivery of the instrument in order to give effect thereto.

Provided that where an acceptance is written on a bill, and the drawee gives notice to or according to the directions of the person entitled to the bill that he has accepted it, the acceptance then becomes complete and irrevocable.

(2) As between immediate parties, and as regards a remote party other than a holder in due course, the delivery—

> (a) in order to be effectual must be made either by or under the authority of the party drawing, accepting, or indorsing, as the case may be:
> (b) may be shown to have been conditional or for a special purpose only, and not for the purpose of transferring the property in the bill.

But if the bill be in the hands of a holder in due course a valid delivery of the bill by all parties prior to him so as to make them liable to him is conclusively presumed.

(3) Where a bill is no longer in the possession of a party who has signed it as drawer, acceptor, or indorser, a valid and unconditional delivery by him is presumed until the contrary is proved.

Capacity and authority of parties

22 Capacity of parties

(1) Capacity to incur liability as a party to a bill is coextensive with capacity to contract. Provided that nothing in this section shall enable a corporation to make itself liable as drawer, acceptor, or indorser of a bill unless it is competent to it so to do under the law for the time being in force relating to corporations.

(2) Where a bill is drawn or indorsed by an infant, minor, or corporation having no capacity or power to incur liability on a bill, the drawing or indorsement entitles the holder to receive payment of the bill, and to enforce it against any other party thereto.

23 Signature essential to liability

No person is liable as drawer, indorser, or acceptor of a bill who has not signed it as such: Provided that

(1) Where a person signs a bill in a trade or assumed name, he is liable thereon as if he had signed it in his own name:

(2) The signature of the name of a firm is equivalent to the signature by the person so signing of the names of all persons liable as partners in that firm.

24 Forged or unauthorised signature

Subject to the provisions of this Act, where a signature on a bill is forged or placed thereon without the authority of the person whose signature it purports to be, the forged or unauthorised signature is wholly inoperative, and no right to retain the bill or to give a discharge therefor or to enforce payment thereof against any party thereto can be acquired through or under that signature, unless the party against whom it is sought to retain or enforce payment of the bill is precluded from setting up the forgery or want of authority.

Provided that nothing in this section shall affect the ratification of an unauthorised signature not amounting to a forgery.

25 Procuration signatures

A signature by procuration operates as notice that the agent has but a limited authority to sign, and the principal is only bound by such signature if the agent in so signing was acting within the actual limits of his authority.

26 Person signing as agent or in representative capacity

(1) Where a person signs a bill as drawer, indorser, or acceptor, and adds words to his signature, indicating that he signs for or on behalf of a principal, or in a representative character, he is not personally liable thereon; but the mere addition to his signature of words describing him as an agent, or as filling a representative character, does not exempt him from personal liability.

(2) In determining whether a signature on a bill is that of the principal or that of the agent by whose hand it is written, the construction most favourable to the validity of the instrument shall be adopted.

The consideration for a bill

27 Value and holder for value

(1) Valuable consideration for a bill may be constituted by,—

    (a) Any consideration sufficient to support a simple contract;

    (b) An antecedent debt or liability. Such a debt or liability is deemed valuable consideration whether the bill is payable on demand or at a future time.

(2) Where value has at any time been given for a bill the holder is deemed to be a holder for value as regards the acceptor and all parties to the bill who became parties prior to such time.

(3) Where the holder of a bill has a lien on it, arising either from contract or by implication of law, he is deemed to be a holder for value to the extent of the sum for which he has a lien.

28 Accommodation bill or party

(1) An accommodation party to a bill is a person who has signed a bill as drawer, acceptor, or indorser, without receiving value therefor, and for the purpose of lending his name to some other person.

(2) An accommodation party is liable on the bill to a holder for value; and it is immaterial whether, when such holder took the bill, he knew such party to be an accommodation party or not.

29 Holder in due course

(1) A holder in due course is a holder who has taken a bill, complete and regular on the face of it, under the following conditions, namely,

    (a) That he became the holder of it before it was overdue, and without notice that it had been previously dishonoured, if such was the fact:

    (b) That he took the bill in good faith and for value, and that at the time the bill was negotiated to him he had no notice of any defect in the title of the person who negotiated it.

(2) In particular the title of a person who negotiates a bill is defective within the meaning of this Act when he obtained the bill, or the acceptance thereof, by fraud, duress or force and fear, or other unlawful means, or for an illegal consideration, or when he negotiates it in breach of faith, or under such circumstances as amount to a fraud.

(3) A holder (whether for value or not), who derives his title to a bill through a holder in due course, and who is not himself a party to any fraud or illegality affecting it, has all the rights of that holder in due course as regards the acceptor and all parties to the bill prior to that holder.

30 Presumption of value and good faith

(1) Every party whose signature appears on a bill is prima facie deemed to have become a party thereto for value.

(2) Every holder of a bill is prima facie deemed to be a holder in due course; but if in an action on a bill it is admitted or proved that the acceptance, issue, or subsequent negotiation of the bill is affected with fraud, duress, or force and fear, or illegality, the burden of proof is shifted, unless and until the holder proves that, subsequent to the alleged fraud or illegality, value has in good faith been given for the bill.

Negotiation of bills

31 Negotiation of bill

(1) A bill is negotiated when it is transferred from one person to another in such a manner as to constitute the transferee the holder of the bill.

(2) A bill payable to bearer is negotiated by delivery.

(3) A bill payable to order is negotiated by the indorsement of the holder completed by delivery.

(4) Where, the holder of a bill payable to his order transfers it for value without indorsing it, the transfer gives the transferee such title as the transferor had in the bill, and the transferee in addition acquires the right to have the indorsement of the transferor.

(5) Where any person is under obligation to indorse a bill in a representative capacity, he may indorse a bill in such terms as to negative personal liability.

32   Requisites of a valid indorsement

An indorsement in order to operate as a negotiation must comply with the following conditions, namely:—

(1) It must be written on the bill itself and signed by the indorser. The simple signature of the indorser on the bill, without additional words, is sufficient.

An indorsement written on an allonge or a 'copy' of a bill issued or negotiated in a country where 'copies' are recognised, is deemed to have been written on the bill itself.

(2) It must be an indorsement of the entire bill. A partial indorsement, that is to say, an indorsement which purports to transfer to the indorsee a part only of the amount payable, or which purports to transfer the bill to two or more indorsees severally, does not operate as a negotiation of the bill.

(3) Where a bill is payable to the order of two or more payees or indorsees who are not partners all must indorse, unless the one indorsing has authority to indorse for the others.

(4) Where, in a bill payable to order, the payee or indorsee is wrongly designated, or his name is mis-spelt, he may indorse the bill as therein described, adding, if he think fit, his proper signature.

(5) Where there are two or more indorsements on a bill, each indorsement is deemed to have been made in the order in which it appears on the bill, until the contrary is proved.

(6) An indorsement may be made in blank or special. It may also contain terms making it restrictive.

33   Conditional indorsement

Where a bill purports to be indorsed conditionally the condition may be disregarded by the payer, and payment to the indorsee is valid whether the condition has been fulfilled or not.

34   Indorsement in blank and special indorsement

(1) An indorsement in blank specifies no indorsee, and a bill so indorsed becomes payable to bearer.

(2) A special indorsement specifies the person to whom, or to whose order, the bill is to be payable.

(3) The provisions of this Act relating to a payee apply with the necessary modifications to an indorsee under a special indorsement.

(4) When a bill has been indorsed in blank, any holder may convert the blank indorsement into a special indorsement by writing above the indorser's signature a direction to pay the bill to or to the order of himself or some other person.

35   Restrictive indorsement

(1) An indorsement is restrictive which prohibits the further negotiation of the bill or which expresses that it is a mere authority to deal with the bill as thereby directed and not a transfer of ownership thereof, as, for example, if a bill be indorsed 'Pay D. only', or 'Pay D. for the account of X.,' or 'Pay D. or order for collection.'

(2) A restrictive indorsement gives the indorsee the right to receive payment of the bill and to sue any party thereto that his indorser could have sued, but gives him no power to transfer his rights as indorsee unless it expressly authorise him to do so.

(3) Where a restrictive indorsement authorises further transfer, all subsequent indorsees take the bill with the same rights and subject to the same liabilities as the first indorsee under the restrictive indorsement.

36   Negotiation of overdue or dishonoured bills

(1) Where a bill is negotiable in its origin it continues to be negotiable until it has been (a) restrictively indorsed or (b) discharged by payment or otherwise.

(2) Where an overdue bill is negotiated, it can only be negotiated subject to any defect of title affecting it at its maturity, and thenceforward no person who takes it can acquire or give a better title than that which the person from whom he took it had.

(3) A bill payable on demand is deemed to be overdue within the meaning and for the purposes of this section, when it appears on the face of it to have been in circulation for an unreasonable length of time. What is an unreasonable length of time for this purpose is a question of fact.

(4) Except where an indorsement bears date after the maturity of the bill, every negotiation is prima facie deemed to have been effected before the bill was overdue.

(5) Where a bill which is not overdue has been dishonoured any person who takes it with notice of the dishonour takes it subject to any defect of title attaching thereto at the time of dishonour, but nothing in this sub-section shall affect the rights of a holder in due course.

37   Negotiation of bill to party already liable thereon
Where a bill is negotiated back to the drawer, or to a prior indorser or to the acceptor, such party may, subject to the provisions of this Act, reissue and further negotiate the bill, but he is not entitled to enforce payment of the bill against any intervening party to whom he was previously liable.

38   Rights of the holder
The rights and powers of the holder of a bill are as follows:

(1) He may sue on the bill in his own name:

(2) Where he is a holder in due course, he holds the bill free from any defect of title of prior parties, as well as from mere personal defences available to prior parties among themselves, and may enforce payment against all parties liable on the bill:

(3) Where his title is defective (a) if he negotiates the bill to a holder in due course, that holder obtains a good and complete title to the bill, and (b) if he obtains payment of the bill the person who pays him in due course gets a valid discharge for the bill.

General duties of the holder

39   When presentment for acceptance is necessary
(1) Where a bill is payable after sight, presentment for acceptance is necessary in order to fix the maturity of the instrument.

(2) Where a bill expressly stipulates that it shall be presented for acceptance, or where a bill is drawn payable elsewhere than at the residence or place of business of the drawee, it must be presented for acceptance before it can be presented for payment.

(3) In no other case is presentment for acceptance necessary in order to render liable any party to the bill.

(4) Where the holder of a bill, drawn payable elsewhere than at the place of business or residence of the drawee, has not time, with the exercise of reasonable diligence, to present the bill for acceptance before presenting it for payment on the day that it falls due, the delay caused by presenting the bill for acceptance before presenting it for payment is excused, and does not discharge the drawer and the indorsers.

40   Time for presenting bill payable after sight
(1) Subject to the provisions of this Act, when a bill payable after sight is negotiated, the holder must either present it for acceptance or negotiate it within a reasonable time.

(2) If he do not do so, the drawer and all indorsers prior to that holder are discharged.

(3) In determining what is a reasonable time within the meaning of this section, regard shall be had to the nature of the bill, the usage of trade with respect to similar bills, and the facts of the particular case.

41   Rules as to presentment for acceptance and excuses for non-presentment
(1) A bill is duly presented for acceptance which is presented in accordance with the following rules:

  (a) The presentment must be made by or on behalf of the holder to the drawee or to some person authorised to accept or refuse acceptance on his behalf at a reasonable hour on a business day and before the bill is overdue:

(b) Where a bill is addressed to two or more drawees, who are not partners, presentment must be made to them all, unless one has authority to accept for them all, then presentment must be made to him only:

(c) Where the drawee is dead presentment may be made to his personal representative:

(d) Where the drawee is bankrupt, presentment may be made to him or to his trustee:

(e) Where authorised by agreement or usage, a presentment through [a postal operator] is sufficient.

(2) Presentment in accordance with these rules is excused, and a bill may be treated as dishonoured by non-acceptance—

(a) Where the drawee is dead or bankrupt, or is a fictitious person or a person not having capacity to contract by bill:

(b) Where, after the exercise of reasonable diligence, such presentment cannot be effected:

(c) Where although the presentment has been irregular, acceptance has been refused on some other ground.

(3) The fact that the holder has reason to believe that the bill, on presentment, will be dishonoured does not excuse presentment.

42   Non-acceptance

(1) When a bill is duly presented for acceptance and is not accepted within the customary time, the person presenting it must treat it as dishonoured by non-acceptance. If he do not, the holder shall lose his right of recourse against the drawer and indorsers.

43   Dishonour by non-acceptance and its consequences

(1) A bill is dishonoured by non-acceptance—

(a) when it is duly presented for acceptance, and such an acceptance as is prescribed by this Act is refused or cannot be obtained; or

(b) when presentment for acceptance is excused and the bill is not accepted.

(2) Subject to the provisions of this Act when a bill is dishonoured by non-acceptance an immediate right of recourse against the drawer and indorsers accrues to the holder, and no presentment for payment is necessary.

44   Duties as to qualified acceptances

(1) The holder of a bill may refuse to take a qualified acceptance, and if he does not obtain an unqualified acceptance may treat the bill as dishonoured by non-acceptance.

(2) Where a qualified acceptance is taken, and the drawer or an indorser has not expressly or impliedly authorised the holder to take a qualified acceptance, or does not subsequently assent thereto, such drawer or indorser is discharged from his liability on the bill.

The provisions of this sub-section do not apply to a partial acceptance, whereof due notice has been given. Where a foreign bill has been accepted as to part, it must be protested as to the balance.

(3) When the drawer or indorser of a bill receives notice of a qualified acceptance, and does not within a reasonable time express his dissent to the holder he shall be deemed to have assented thereto.

45   Rules as to presentment for payment

Subject to the provisions of this Act a bill must be duly presented for payment. If it be not so presented the drawer and indorsers shall be discharged.

A bill is duly presented for payment which is presented in accordance with the following rules:—

(1) Where the bill is not payable on demand, presentment must be made on the day it falls due.

(2) Where the bill is payable on demand then, subject to the provisions of this Act, presentment must be made within a reasonable time after its issue in order to render the drawer liable, and within a reasonable time after the indorsement, in order to render the indorser liable.

In determining what is a reasonable time, regard shall be had to the nature of the bill, the usage of trade with regard to similar bills, and the facts of the particular case.

(3) Presentment must be made by the holder or by some person authorised to receive payment on his behalf at a reasonable hour on a business day, at the proper place as hereinafter defined, either to the person designated by the bill as payer, or to some person authorised to pay or refuse payment on his behalf if with the exercise of reasonable diligence such person can there be found.

(4) A bill is presented at the proper place:—

(a) Where a place of payment is specified in the bill and the bill is there presented.

(b) Where no place of payment is specified, but the address of the drawee or acceptor is given in the bill, and the bill is there presented.

(c) Where no place of payment is specified and no address given, and the bill is presented at the drawees or acceptor's place of business if known, and if not, at his ordinary residence if known.

(d) In any other case if presented to the drawer or acceptor wherever he can be found, or if presented at his last known place of business or residence.

(5) Where a bill is presented at the proper place, and after the exercise of reasonable diligence no person authorised to pay or refuse payment can be found there, no further presentment to the drawee or acceptor is required.

(6) Where a bill is drawn upon, or accepted by two or more persons who are not partners, and no place of payment is specified, presentment must be made to them all.

(7) Where the drawee or acceptor of a bill is dead, and no place of payment is specified, presentment must be made to a personal representative, if such there be, and with the exercise of reasonable diligence he can be found.

(8) Where authorised by agreement or usage a presentment through [a postal operator] is sufficient.

46 Excuses for delay or non-presentment for payment

(1) Delay in making presentment for payment is excused when the delay is caused by circumstances beyond the control of the holder, and not imputable to his default, misconduct, or negligence. When the cause of delay ceases to operate presentment must be made with reasonable diligence.

(2) Presentment for payment is dispensed with,—

(a) Where, after the exercise of reasonable diligence presentment, as required by this Act, cannot be effected.

The fact that the holder has reason to believe that the bill will, on presentment, be dishonoured, does not dispense with the necessity for presentment.

(b) Where the drawee is a fictitious person.

(c) As regards the drawer where the drawee or acceptor is not bound, as between himself and the drawee, to accept or pay the bill, and the drawer has no reason to believe that the bill would be paid if presented.

(d) As regards an indorser, where the bill was accepted or made for the accommodation of the indorser, and he has no reason to expect that the bill would be paid if presented.

(e) By waiver of presentment, expressed or implied.

47 Dishonour by non-payment

(1) A bill is dishonoured by non-payment (a) when it is duly presented for payment and payment is refused or cannot be obtained, or (b) when presentment is excused and the bill is overdue and unpaid.

(2) Subject to the provisions of this Act, when a bill is dishonoured by non-payment, an immediate right of recourse against the drawer and indorsers accrues to the holder.

48 Notice of dishonour and effect of non-notice

Subject to the provisions of this Act, when a bill has been dishonoured by non-acceptance or by non-payment, notice of dishonour must be given to the drawer and each indorser, and any drawer or indorser to whom such notice is not given is discharged; Provided that—

(1) Where a bill is dishonoured by non-acceptance, and notice of dishonour is not given, the rights of the holder in due course subsequent to the omission, shall not be prejudiced by the omission.

(2) Where a bill is dishonoured by non-acceptance and due notice of dishonour is given, it shall not be necessary to give notice of a subsequent dishonour by non-payment unless the bill shall in the meantime have been accepted.

49 Rules as of notice of dishonour

Notice of dishonour in order to be valid and effectual must be given in accordance with the following rules:—

(1) The notice must be given by or on behalf of the holder, or by or on behalf of an indorser who, at the time of giving it, is himself liable on the bill.

(2) Notice of dishonour may be given by an agent either in his own name, or in the name of any party entitled to give notice whether that party be his principal or not.

(3) Where the notice is given by or on behalf of the holder, it enures for the benefit of all subsequent holders and all prior indorsers who have a right of recourse against the party to whom it is given.

(4) Where notice is given by or on behalf of an indorser entitled to give notice as herein-before provided, it enures for the benefit of the holder and all indorsers subsequent to the party to whom notice is given.

(5) The notice may be given in writing or by personal communication, and may be given in any terms which sufficiently identify the bill, and intimate that the bill has been dishonoured by non-acceptance or non-payment.

(6) The return of a dishonoured bill to the drawer or an indorser is, in point of form, deemed a sufficient notice of dishonour.

(7) A written notice need not be signed, and an insufficient written notice may be supplemented and validated by verbal communication. A misdescription of the bill shall not vitiate the notice unless the party to whom the notice is given is in fact misled thereby.

(8) Where notice of dishonour is required to be given to any person, it may be given either to the party himself, or to his agent in that behalf.

(9) Where the drawer or indorser is dead, and the party giving notice knows it, the notice must be given to a personal representative if such there be, and with the exercise of reasonable diligence he can be found.

(10) Where the drawer or indorser is bankrupt, notice may be given either to the party himself or to the trustee.

(11) Where there are two or more drawers or indorsers who are not partners, notice must be given to each of them, unless one of them has authority to receive such notice for the others.

(12) The notice may be given as soon as the bill is dishonoured and must be given within a reasonable time thereafter.

In the absence of special circumstances notice is not deemed to have been given within a reasonable time, unless—

(a) where the person giving and the person to receive notice reside in the same place, the notice is given or sent off in time to reach the latter on the day after the dishonour of the bill.

(b) where the person giving and the person to receive notice reside in different places, the notice is sent off on the day after the dishonour of the bill, if there be a post at a convenient hour on that day, and if there be no such post on that day then by the next post thereafter.

(13) Where a bill when dishonoured is in the hands of an agent, he may either himself give notice to the parties liable on the bill, or he may give notice to his principal. If he gives notice to his principal, he must do so within the same time as if he were the holder, and the principal upon receipt of such notice has himself the same time for giving notice as if the agent had been an independent holder.

(14) Where a party to a bill receives due notice of dishonour, he has after the receipt of such notice the same period of time for giving notice to antecedent parties that the holder has after the dishonour.

(15) Where a notice of dishonour is duly addressed and posted, the sender is deemed to have given due notice of dishonour, notwithstanding any miscarriage by the [postal operator concerned].

50   Excuses for non-notice and delay

(1) Delay in giving notice of dishonour is excused where the delay is caused by circumstances beyond the control of the party giving notice, and not imputable to his default, misconduct, or negligence. When the cause of delay ceases to operate the notice must be given with reasonable diligence.

(2) Notice of dishonour is dispensed with—

(a) When, after the exercise of reasonable diligence, notice as required by this Act cannot be given to or does not reach the drawer or indorser sought to be charged:

(b) By waiver express or implied. Notice of dishonour may be waived before the time of giving notice has arrived, or after the omission to give due notice:

(c) As regards the drawer in the following cases, namely, (1) where drawer and drawee are the same person, (2) where the drawee is a fictitious person or a person not having capacity to contract, (3) where the drawer is the person to whom the bill is presented for payment, (4) where the drawee or acceptor is as between himself and the drawer under no obligation to accept or pay the bill, (5) where the drawer has countermanded payment:

(d) As regards the indorser in the following cases, namely (1) where the drawee is a fictitious person or a person not having the capacity to contract and the indorser was aware of the fact at the time he indorsed the bill, (2) where the indorser is the person to whom the bill is presented for payment, (3) where the bill was accepted or made for his accommodation.

51   Noting or protest of bill

(1) Where an inland bill has been dishonoured it may, if the holder think fit, be noted for non-acceptance or non-payment, as the case may be; but it shall not be necessary to note or protest any such bill in order to preserve the recourse against the drawer or indorser.

(2) Where a foreign bill, appearing on the face of it to be such, has been dishonoured by non-acceptance it must be duly protested for non-acceptance and where such a bill, which has not been previously dishonoured by non-acceptance, is dishonoured by non-payment it must be duly protested for non-payment. If it be not so protested the drawer and indorsers are discharged. Where a bill does not appear on the face of it to be a foreign bill, protest thereof in the case of dishonour is unnecessary.

(3) A bill which has been protested for non-acceptance may be subsequently protested for non-payment.

(4) Subject to the provisions of this Act, when a bill is noted or protested, [it may be noted on the day of its dishonour and must be noted not later than the next succeeding business day]. When a bill has been duly noted, the protest may be subsequently extended as of the date of the noting.

(5) Where the acceptor of the bill becomes bankrupt or insolvent or suspends payment before it matures, the holder may cause the bill to be protested for better security against the drawer and indorsers.

(6) A bill must be protested at the place where it is dishonoured: Provided that—

(a) When a bill is presented through [a postal operator], and returned by post dishonoured, it may be protested at the place to which it is returned and on the day of its return if received during business hours, and if not received during business hours, then not later than the next business day;

(b) When a bill drawn payable at the place of business or residence of some person other than the drawee, has been dishonoured by non-acceptance, it must be protested for non-payment at the place where it is expressed to be payable, and no further presentment for payment to, or demand on, the drawee is necessary.

(7) A protest must contain a copy of the bill, and must be signed by the notary making it, and must specify—

(a) The person at whose request the bill is protested:

(b) The place and date of protest, the cause or reason for protesting the bill, the demand made, and the answer given, if any, or the fact that the drawee or acceptor could not be found.

[(7A) In subsection (7) 'notary' includes a person who, for the purposes of the Legal Services Act 2007, is an authorised person in relation to any activity which constitutes a notarial activity (within the meaning of that Act).]

(8) Where a bill is lost or destroyed, or is wrongly detained from the person entitled to hold it, protest may be made on a copy or written particulars thereof.

(9) Protest is dispensed with by any circumstance which would dispense with notice of dishonour. Delay in noting or protesting is excused when the delay is caused by circumstances beyond the control of the holder, and not imputable to his default, misconduct, or negligence. When the cause of delay ceases to operate the bill must be noted or protested with reasonable diligence.

52 Duties of holder as regards drawee or acceptor

(1) When a bill is accepted generally presentment for payment is not necessary in order to render the acceptor liable.

(2) When by the terms of a qualified acceptance presentment for payment is required, the acceptor, in the absence of an express stipulation to that effect, is not discharged by the omission to present the bill for payment on the day that it matures.

(3) In order to render the acceptor of a bill liable it is not necessary to protest it, or that notice of dishonour should be given to him.

(4) [Subject to Part 4A (presentment by electronic means),] Where the holder of a bill presents it for payment, he shall exhibit the bill to the person from whom he demands payment, and when a bill is paid the holder shall forthwith deliver it up to the party paying it.

Liabilities of parties

53 Funds in hands of drawee

(1) A bill, of itself, does not operate as an assignment of funds in the hands of the drawee available for the payment thereof, and the drawee of a bill who does not accept as required by this Act is not liable on the instrument. This sub-section shall not extend to Scotland.

54 Liability of acceptor

The acceptor of a bill, by accepting it—

(1) Engages that he will pay it according to the tenor of his acceptance:

(2) Is precluded from denying to a holder in due course:

(a) The existence of the drawer, the genuineness of his signature, and his capacity and authority to draw the bill;

(b) In the case of a bill payable to drawer's order, the then capacity of the drawer to indorse, but not the genuineness or validity of his indorsement;

(c) In the case of a bill payable to the order of a third person, the existence of the payee and his then capacity to indorse, but not the genuineness or validity of his indorsement.

55 Liability of drawer or indorser

(1) The drawer of a bill by drawing it—

(a) Engages that on due presentment it shall be accepted and paid according to its tenor, and that if it be dishonoured he will compensate the holder or any indorser who is compelled to pay it, provided that the requisite proceedings on dishonour be duly taken;

(b) Is precluded from denying to a holder in due course the existence of the payee and his then capacity to indorse.

(2) The indorser of a bill by indorsing it—

(a) Engages that on due presentment it shall be accepted and paid according to its tenor, and that if it be dishonoured he will compensate the holder or a subsequent indorser who is compelled to pay it, provided that the requisite proceedings on dishonour be duly taken;

(b) Is precluded from denying to a holder in due course the genuineness and regularity in all respects of the drawer's signature and all previous indorsements;

(c) Is precluded from denying to his immediate or a subsequent indorsee that the bill was at the time of his indorsement a valid and subsisting bill, and that he had then a good title thereto.

56 Stranger signing bill liable as indorser

Where a person signs a bill otherwise than as drawer or acceptor, he thereby incurs the liabilities of an indorser to a holder in due course.

57 Measure of damages against parties to dishonoured bill

Where a bill is dishonoured, the measure of damages, which shall be deemed to be liquidated damages, shall be as follows:

(1) The holder may recover from any party liable on the bill, and the drawer who has been compelled to pay the bill may recover from the acceptor, and an indorser who has been compelled to pay the bill may recover from the acceptor or from the drawer, or from a prior indorser—

(a) The amount of the bill:

(b) Interest thereon from the time of presentment for payment if the bill is payable on demand, and from the maturity of the bill in any other case:

(c) The expenses of noting, or, when protest is necessary, and the protest has been extended, the expenses of protest.

[...]

(3) Where by this Act interest may be recovered as damages, such interest may, if justice require it, be withheld wholly or in part, and where a bill is expressed to be payable with interest at a given rate, interest as damages may or may not be given at the same rate as interest proper.

58 Transferor by delivery and transferee

(1) Where the holder of a bill payable to bearer negotiates it by delivery without indorsing it, he is called a 'transferor by delivery.'

(2) A transferor by delivery is not liable on the instrument.

(3) A transferor by delivery who negotiates a bill thereby warrants to his immediate transferee being a holder for value that the bill is what it purports to be, that he has a right to transfer it, and that at the time of the transfer he is not aware of any fact which renders it valueless.

Discharge of bill

59 Payment in due course

(1) A bill is discharged by payment in due course by or on behalf of the drawee or acceptor. 'Payment in due course' means payment made at or after the maturity of the bill to the holder thereof in good faith and without notice that his title to the bill is defective.

(2) Subject to the provisions herein-after contained, when a bill is paid by the drawer or an indorser it is not discharged; but

(a) Where a bill payable to, or to the order of, a third party is paid by the drawer, the drawer may enforce payment thereof against the acceptor, but may not re-issue the bill.

(b) Where a bill is paid by an indorser, or where a bill payable to drawer's order is paid by the drawer, the party paying it is remitted to his former rights as regards the acceptor or antecedent parties, and he may, if he thinks fit, strike out his own and subsequent indorsements, and again negotiate the bill.

(3) Where an accommodation bill is paid in due course by the party accommodated the bill is discharged.

60 Banker paying demand draft whereon indorsement is forged

When a bill payable to order on demand is drawn on a banker, and the banker on whom it is drawn, pays the bill in good faith and in the ordinary course of business, it is not incumbent on the banker to show that the indorsement of the payee or any subsequent indorsement was made by or under the authority of the person whose indorsement it purports to be, and the banker is deemed to have paid the bill in due course, although such indorsement has been forged or made without authority.

61 Acceptor the holder at maturity

When the acceptor of a bill is or becomes the holder of it at or after its maturity, in his own right, the bill is discharged.

62 Express waiver

(1) When the holder of a bill at or after its maturity absolutely and unconditionally renounces his rights against the acceptor the bill is discharged.

The renunciation must be in writing, unless the bill is delivered up to the acceptor.

(2) The liabilities of any party to a bill may in like manner be renounced by the holder before, at, or after its maturity; but nothing in this section shall affect the rights of a holder in due course without notice of the renunciation.

63 Cancellation

(1) Where a bill is intentionally cancelled by the holder or his agent, and the cancellation is apparent thereon, the bill is discharged.

(2) In like manner any party liable on a bill may be discharged by the intentional cancellation of his signature by the holder or his agent. In such case any indorser who would have had a right of recourse against the party whose signature is cancelled, is also discharged.

(3) A cancellation made unintentionally, or under a mistake, or without the authority of the holder is inoperative; but where a bill or any signature thereon appears to have been cancelled the burden of proof lies on the party who alleges that the cancellation was made unintentionally, or under a mistake, or without authority.

64 Alteration of bill

(1) Where a bill or acceptance is materially altered without the assent of all parties liable on the bill, the bill is avoided except as against a party who has himself made, authorised, or assented to the alteration, and subsequent indorsers.

Provided that,

Where a bill has been materially altered, but the alteration is not apparent, and the bill is in the hands of a holder in due course, such holder may avail himself of the bill as if it had not been altered, and may enforce payment of it according to its original tenour.

(2) In particular the following alterations are material, namely, any alteration of the date, the sum payable, the time of payment, the place of payment, and where a bill has been accepted generally, the addition of a place of payment without the acceptor's assent.

Acceptance and payment for honour

65 Acceptance for honour supra protest

(1) Where a bill of exchange has been protested for dishonour by non-acceptance, or protested for better security, and is not overdue, any person, not being a party already liable thereon, may, with the consent of the holder, intervene and accept the bill *supra protest,* for the honour of any party liable thereon, or for the honour of the person for whose account the bill is drawn.

(2) A bill may be accepted for honour for part only of the sum for which it is drawn.

(3) An acceptance for honour supra protest in order to be valid must—

(a) be written on the bill, and indicate that it is an acceptance for honour;

(b) be signed by the acceptor for honour:

(4) Where an acceptance for honour does not expressly state for whose honour it is made, it is deemed to be an acceptance for the honour of the drawer.

(5) Where a bill payable after sight is accepted for honour, its maturity is calculated from the date of the noting for non-acceptance, and not from the date of the acceptance for honour.

66   Liability of acceptor for honour

(1)   The acceptor for honour of a bill by accepting it engages that he will, on due presentment, pay the bill according to the tenor of his acceptance, if it is not paid by the drawee, provided it has been duly presented for payment, and protested for non-payment, and that he receives notice of these facts.

(2)   The acceptor for honour is liable to the holder and to all parties to the bill subsequent to the party for whose honour he has accepted.

67   Presentment to acceptor for honour

(1)   Where a dishonoured bill has been accepted for honour supra protest, or contains a reference in case of need, it must be protested for non-payment before it is presented for payment to the acceptor for honour, or referee in case of need.

(2)   Where the address of the acceptor for honour is in the same place where the bill is protested for non-payment, the bill must be presented to him not later than the day following its maturity; and where the address of the acceptor for honour is in some place other than the place where it was protested for non-payment, the bill must be forwarded not later than the day following its maturity for presentment to him.

(3)   Delay in presentment or non-presentment is excused by any circumstances which would excuse delay in presentment for payment or non-presentment for payment.

(4)   When a bill of exchange is dishonoured by the acceptor for honour it must be protested for non-payment by him.

68   Payment for honour supra protest

(1)   Where a bill has been protested for non-payment any person may intervene and pay it *supra protest* for the honour of any party liable thereon, or for the honour of the person for whose account the bill is drawn.

(2)   Where two or more persons offer to pay a bill for the honour of different parties, the person whose payment will discharge most parties to the bill shall have the preference.

(3)   Payment for honour *supra protest,* in order to operate as such and not as a mere voluntary payment, must be attested by a notarial act of honour which may be appended to the protest or form an extension of it.

(4)   The notarial act of honour must be founded on a declaration made by the payer for honour, or his agent in that behalf, declaring his intention to pay the bill for honour, and for whose honour he pays.

(5)   Where a bill has been paid for honour, all parties subsequent to the party for whose honour it is paid are discharged, but the payer for honour is subrogated for, and succeeds to both the rights and duties of, the holder as regards the party for whose honour he pays, and all parties liable to that party.

(6)   The payer for honour on paying to the holder the amount of the bill and the notarial expenses incidental to its dishonour is entitled to receive both the bill itself and the protest. If the holder do not on demand deliver them up he shall be liable to the payer for honour in damages.

(7)   Where the holder of a bill refuses to receive payment *supra protest* he shall lose his right of recourse against any party who would have been discharged by such payment.

Lost instruments

69   Holder's right to duplicate of lost bill

Where a bill has been lost before it is overdue, the person who was the holder of it may apply to the drawer to give him another bill of the same tenor, giving security to the drawer if required to indemnify him against all persons whatever in case the bill alleged to have been lost shall be found again.

If the drawer on request as aforesaid refuses to give such duplicate bill, he may be compelled to do so.

70   Action on lost bill

In any action or proceeding upon a bill, the court or a judge may order that the loss of the instrument shall not be set up, provided an indemnity be given to the satisfaction of the court or judge against the claims of any other person upon the instrument in question.

Bill in a set

71   Rules as to sets

(1) Where a bill is drawn in a set, each part of the set being numbered and containing a reference to the other parts, the whole of the parts constitute one bill.

(2) Where the holder of a set indorses two or more parts to different persons, he is liable to every such part, and every indorser subsequent to him is liable on the part he has himself indorsed as if the said parts were separate bills.

(3) Where two or more parts of a set are negotiated to different holders in due course, the holder whose title first accrues is as between such holders deemed the true owner of the bill; but nothing in this sub-section shall affect the rights of a person who in the course accepts or pays the part first presented to him.

(4) The acceptance may be written on any part, and it must be written on one part only.

If the drawee accepts more than one part, and such accepted parts get into the hands of different holders in due course, he is liable on every such part as if it were a separate bill.

(5) When the acceptor of a bill drawn in a set pays it without requiring the part bearing the acceptance to be delivered up to him, and that part at maturity is outstanding in the hands of a holder in due course, he is liable to the holder thereof.

(6) Subject to the preceding rules, where any one part of a bill drawn in a set is discharged by payment or otherwise, the whole bill is discharged.

Conflict of laws

72   Rules where laws conflict

Where a bill drawn in one country is negotiated, accepted, or payable in another, the rights, duties, and liabilities of the parties thereto are determined as follows:

(1) The validity of a bill as regards requisites in form is determined by the law of the place of issue, and the validity as regards requisites in form of the supervening contracts, such as acceptance, or indorsement, or acceptance supra protest, is determined by the law of the place where such contract was made.

Provided that—

(a) Where a bill is issued out of the United Kingdom it is not invalid by reason only that it is not stamped in accordance with the law of the place of issue:

(b) Where a bill, issued out of the United Kingdom, conforms, as regards requisites in form, to the law of the United Kingdom, it may, for the purpose of enforcing payment thereof, be treated as valid as between all persons who negotiate, hold, or become parties to it in the United Kingdom.

(2) Subject to the provisions of this Act, the interpretation of the drawing, indorsement, acceptance, or acceptance supra protest of a bill, is determined by the law of the place where such contract is made.

Provided that where an inland bill is indorsed in a foreign country the indorsement shall as regards the payer be interpreted according to the law of the United Kingdom.

(3) The duties of the holder with respect to presentment for acceptance or payment and the necessity for or sufficiency of a protest or notice of dishonour, or otherwise, are determined by the law of the place where the act is done or the bill is dishonoured.

[...]

(5) Where a bill is drawn in one country and is payable in another, the due date thereof is determined according to the law of the place where it is payable.

PART III CHEQUES ON A BANKER

73 Cheque defined
A cheque is a bill of exchange drawn on a banker payable on demand. Except as otherwise provided in this Part, the provisions of this Act applicable to a bill of exchange payable on demand apply to a cheque.

74 Presentment of cheque for payment
Subject to the provisions of this Act—

(1) Where a cheque is not presented for payment within a reasonable time of its issue, and the drawer or the person on whose account it is drawn had the right at the time of such presentment as between him and the banker to have the cheque paid and suffers actual damage through the delay, he is discharged to the extent of such damage, that is to say, to the extent to which such drawer or person is a creditor of such banker to a larger amount than he would have been had such cheque been paid.

(2) In determining what is a reasonable time regard shall be had to the nature of the instrument, the usage of trade and of bankers, and the facts of the particular case.

(3) The holder of such cheque as to which such drawer or person is discharged shall be a creditor, in lieu of such drawer or person, of such banker to the extent of such discharge, and entitled to recover the amount from him.

[74A Presentment of cheque for payment: alternative place of presentment
Where the banker on whom a cheque is drawn—

(a) has by notice published in the London, Edinburgh and Belfast Gazettes specified an address at which cheques drawn on him may be presented, and

(b) has not by notice so published cancelled the specification of that address, the cheque is also presented at the proper place if it is presented there.]

75 Revocation of banker's authority
The duty and authority of a banker to pay a cheque drawn on him by his customer are determined by—

(1) Countermand of payment:

(2) Notice of the customer's death.

Crossed cheques

76 General and special crossings defined
(1) Where a cheque bears across its face an addition of—

(a) The words 'and company' or any abbreviation thereof between two parallel transverse lines either with or without the words 'not negotiable'; or

(b) Two parallel transverse lines simply, either with or without the words 'not negotiable'; that addition constitutes a crossing, and the cheque is crossed generally.

(2) Where a cheque bears across its face an addition of the name of a banker, either with or without the words 'not negotiable', that addition constitutes a crossing, and the cheque is crossed specially and to that banker.

77 Crossing by drawer or after issue
(1) A cheque may be crossed generally or specially by the drawer.

(2) Where a cheque is uncrossed, the holder may cross it generally or specially.

(3) Where a cheque is crossed generally the holder may cross it specially.

(4) Where a cheque is crossed generally or specially, the holder may add the words 'not negotiable.'

(5) Where a cheque is crossed specially, the banker to whom it is crossed may again cross it specially to another banker for collection.

(6) Where an uncrossed cheque, or a cheque crossed generally is sent to a banker for collection, he may cross it specially to himself.

78   Crossing a material part of cheque

A crossing authorised by this Act is a material part of the cheque; it shall not be lawful for any person to obliterate or except as authorised by this Act, to add to or alter the crossing.

79   Duties of banker as to crossed cheques

(1) Where a cheque is crossed specially to more than one banker except when crossed to an agent for collection being a banker, the banker on whom it is drawn shall refuse payment thereof.

(2) Where the banker on whom a cheque is drawn which is so crossed nevertheless pays the same, or pays a cheque crossed generally otherwise than to a banker, or if crossed specially otherwise than to the banker to whom it is crossed, or his agent for collection being a banker, he is liable to the true owner of the cheque for any loss he may sustain owing to the cheque having been so paid.

Provided that where a cheque is presented for payment which does not at the time of presentment appear to be crossed, or to have had a crossing which had been obliterated, or to have been added to or altered otherwise than as authorised by this Act, the banker paying the cheque in good faith and without negligence shall not be responsible or incur any liability, nor shall the payment be questioned by reason of the cheque having been crossed, or of the crossing having been obliterated on having been added to or altered otherwise than as authorised by this Act, and of payment having been made otherwise than to a banker or to the banker to whom the cheque is or was crossed, or to his agent for collection being a banker as the case may be.

80   Protection to banker and drawer where cheque is crossed

Where the banker, on whom a crossed cheque [(including a cheque which under section 81A below or otherwise is not transferable)] is drawn in good faith and without negligence pays it, if crossed generally to a banker, and if crossed specially, to the banker to whom it is crossed, or his agent for collection being a banker the banker paying the cheque, and, if the cheque has come into the hands of the payee, the drawer, shall respectively be entitled to the same rights and be placed in the same position as if payment of the cheque had been made to the true owner thereof.

81   Effect of crossing on holder

Where a person takes a crossed cheque which bears on it the words 'not negotiable,' he shall not have and shall not be capable of giving a better title to the cheque than that which the person from whom he took it had.

[81A   Non-transferable cheques

(1) Where a cheque is crossed and bears across its face the words 'account payee' or 'a/c payee', either with or without the words 'only', the cheque shall not be transferable, but shall only be valid as between the parties thereto.

(2) A banker is not to be treated for the purposes of section 80 above as having been negligent by reason only of his failure to concern himself with any purported indorsement of a cheque which under subsection (1) above or otherwise is not transferable.]

PART IV PROMISSORY NOTES

83   Promissory note defined

(1) A promissory note is an unconditional promise in writing made by one person to another signed by the maker, engaging to pay, on demand or at a fixed or determinable future time, a sum certain in money, to, or to the order of, a specified person or to bearer.

(2) An instrument in the form of a note payable to maker's order is not a note within the meaning of this section unless and until it is indorsed by the maker.

(3) A note is not invalid by reason only that it contains also a pledge of collateral security with authority to sell or dispose thereof.

(4) A note which is, or on the face of it purports to be, both made and payable within the British Islands is an inland note. Any other note is a foreign note.

84 Delivery necessary

A promissory note is inchoate and incomplete until delivery thereof to the payee or bearer.

85 Joint and several notes

(1) A promissory note may be made by two or more makers, and they may be liable thereon jointly, or jointly and severally according to its tenour.

(2) Where a note runs 'I promise to pay' and is signed by two or more persons it is deemed to be their joint and several note.

86 Note payable on demand

(1) Where a note payable on demand has been indorsed, it must be presented for payment within a reasonable time of the indorsement. If it be not so presented the indorser is discharged.

(2) In determining what is a reasonable time, regard shall be had to the nature of the instrument, the usage of trade, and the facts of the particular case.

(3) Where a note payable on demand is negotiated, it is not deemed to be overdue for the purpose of affecting the holder with defects of title of which he had no notice, by reason that it appears that a reasonable time for presenting it for payment has elapsed since its issue.

87 Presentment of note for payment

(1) Where a promissory note is in the body of it made payable at a particular place, it must be presented for payment at that place in order to render the maker liable. In any other case, presentment for payment is not necessary to render the maker liable.

(2) Presentment for payment is necessary in order to render the indorser of a note liable.

(3) Where a note is in the body of it made payable at a particular place, presentment at that place is necessary in order to render an indorser liable; but when a place of payment is indicated by way of memorandum only, presentment at that place is sufficient to render the indorser liable, but a presentment to the maker elsewhere, if sufficient in other respects, shall also suffice.

[(4) This section is subject to Part 4A (presentment by electronic means).]

88 Liability of maker

The maker of a promissory note by making it—

(1) Engages that he will pay it according to its tenour;

(2) Is precluded from denying to a holder in due course the existence of the payee and his then capacity to indorse.

89 Application of Part II to notes

(1) Subject to the provisions in this part and, except as by this section provided, the provisions of this Act relating to bills of exchange apply, with the necessary modifications, to promissory notes.

(2) In applying those provisions the maker of a note shall be deemed to correspond with the acceptor of a bill, and the first indorser of a note shall be deemed to correspond with the drawer of an accepted bill payable to drawer's order.

(3) The following provisions as to bills do not apply to notes; namely, provisions relating to—

    (a) Presentment for acceptance;

    (b) Acceptance;

    (c) Acceptance supra protest;

    (d) Bills in a set.

(4) Where a foreign note is dishonoured, protest thereof is unnecessary.

[PART 4A PRESENTMENT OF CHEQUES AND OTHER INSTRUMENTS BY ELECTRONIC MEANS]

[89A Presentment of instruments by electronic means

(1) Presentment for payment of an instrument to which this section applies may be effected by provision of an electronic image of both faces of the instrument, instead of by presenting the physical instrument, if the person to whom presentment is made accepts the presentment as effective.

This is subject to regulations under subsection (2) and to section 89C.

(2) The Treasury may by regulations prescribe circumstances in which subsection (1) does not apply.

(3) Regulations under subsection (2) may in particular prescribe circumstances by reference to—

(a) descriptions of instrument;

(b) arrangements under which presentment is made;

(c) descriptions of persons by or to whom presentment is made;

(d) descriptions of persons receiving payment or on whose behalf payment is received.

(4) Where presentment for payment is made under subsection (1)—

(a) any requirement—

(i)   that the physical instrument must be exhibited, presented or delivered on or in connection with presentment or payment (including after presentment or payment or in connection with dishonour for non-payment), or

(ii) as to the day, time or place on or at which presentment of the physical instrument may be or is to be made, and

(b) any other requirement which is inconsistent with subsection (1),

does not apply.

(5) Subsection (4) does not affect any requirement as to the latest time for presentment.

(6) References in subsections (4) and (5) to a requirement are to a requirement or prohibition, whether imposed by or under any enactment, by a rule of law or by the instrument in question.

(7) Where an instrument is presented for payment under this section—

(a) any banker providing the electronic image,

(b) any banker to whom it is provided, and

(c) any banker making payment of the instrument as a result of provision of the electronic image,

are subject to the same duties in relation to collection and payment of the instrument as if the physical instrument had been presented.

This is subject to any provision made by or under this Part.]

[89B Instruments to which section 89A applies

(1) Subject to subsection (2), section 89A applies to—

(a) a cheque, or

(b) any other bill of exchange or any promissory note or other instrument—

(i)   which appears to be intended by the person creating it to enable a person to obtain payment from a banker indicated in it of the sum so mentioned,

(ii) payment of which requires the instrument to be presented, and

(iii) which, but for section 89A, could not be presented otherwise than by presenting the physical instrument.

(2) Section 89A does not apply to any banknote (within the meaning given in section 208 of the Banking Act 2009).

(3) The reference in subsection (1) to the person creating an instrument is—

(a) in the case of a bill of exchange, a reference to the drawer;

(b) in the case of a promissory note, a reference to the maker.

(4) For the purposes of subsection (1)(b)(i) an indication may be by code or number and need not indicate that payment is intended to be obtained from the banker.]

[89C   Banker's obligation in relation to accepting physical instrument for presentment

Provision of an electronic image of an instrument does not constitute presentment of the instrument under section 89A if the arrangements between—

(a) the banker authorised to collect payment of the instrument on behalf of a customer, and

(b) that customer,

do not permit the customer to pay in the physical instrument but instead require an electronic image to be provided (whether to that banker or to any other person).]

[89D   Copies of instruments and evidence of payment

(1) The Treasury may by regulations make provision for—

(a) requiring a copy of an instrument paid as a result of presentment under section 89A to be provided, on request, to the creator of the instrument by the banker who paid the instrument;

(b) a copy of an instrument provided in accordance with the regulations to be evidence of receipt by a person identified in accordance with the regulations of the sum payable by the instrument.

(2) Regulations under subsection (1)(a) may in particular—

(a) prescribe the manner and form in which a copy is to be provided;

(b) require the copy to be certified to be a true copy of the electronic image provided to the banker making the payment on presentment under section 89A;

(c) provide for the copy to be accompanied by prescribed information;

(d) require any copy to be provided free of charge or permit charges to be made for the provision of copies in prescribed circumstances.

(3) The reference in subsection (1)(a) to the creator of the instrument is—

(a) in the case of a bill of exchange, a reference to the drawer;

(b) in the case of a promissory note, a reference to the maker.]

[89E   Compensation in cases of presentment by electronic means

(1) The Treasury may by regulations make provision for the responsible banker to compensate any person for any loss of a kind specified by the regulations which that person incurs in connection with electronic presentment or purported electronic presentment of an instrument.

(2) In this section 'electronic presentment or purported electronic presentment of an instrument' includes—

(a) presentment of an instrument to which section 89A applies under that section;

(b) presentment of any other instrument by any means involving provision of an electronic image by which it may be presented for payment;

(c) purported presentment for payment by any means involving provision of an electronic image of an instrument that may not be presented for payment in that way;

(d) provision, in purported presentment for payment, of—

(i)   an electronic image that purports to be, but is not, an image of a physical instrument (including an image that has been altered electronically), or

(ii) an electronic image of an instrument which has no legal effect; or

(e) provision, in presentment or purported presentment for payment, of an electronic image which has been stolen.

(3) In this section, the 'responsible banker', in relation to electronic presentment or purported electronic presentment of an instrument, means—

(a) the banker who is authorised to collect payment of the instrument on a customer's behalf, or

(b) if the holder of the instrument is a banker, that banker.

(4) In this section—

(a) references to an instrument include references to an instrument which has no legal effect (whether because it has been fraudulently altered or created, or because it has been discharged, or otherwise);

(b) in relation to an electronic image which is not an image of a physical instrument, references to the instrument are to a purported instrument (of which it purports to be an image); and

(c) in relation to an instrument which is not a bill of exchange or promissory note, references to the holder are to the payee or indorsee of the instrument who is in possession of it or, if it is payable to bearer, the person in possession of it.

(5) Regulations under this section may in particular make provision for—

(a) the responsible banker to be required to pay compensation irrespective of fault;

(b) the amount of compensation to be reduced by virtue of anything done, or any failure to act, by the person to whom compensation is payable.

(6) Nothing in this section or regulations under it is to be taken to—

(a) prevent the responsible banker claiming a contribution from any other person, or

(b) affect any remedy available to the responsible banker in contract or otherwise.

(7) Except so far as regulations under this section provide expressly, nothing in this section or regulations under it is to be taken to affect any liability of the responsible banker which exists apart from this section or any such regulations.]

[89F   Supplementary

(1) Regulations under this Part may—

(a) include incidental, supplementary and consequential provision;

(b) make transitory or transitional provision or savings;

(c) make different provision for different cases or circumstances or for different purposes;

(d) make provision subject to exceptions.

(2) The power to make regulations under this Part is exercisable by statutory instrument.

(3) An instrument containing—

(a) regulations under section 89A or 89D, or

(b) the first regulations to be made under section 89E,

may not be made unless a draft of the instrument has been laid before, and approved by resolution of, each House of Parliament.

(4) An instrument containing any other regulations under section 89E is subject to annulment in pursuance of a resolution of either House of Parliament.

(5) For the purposes of this Part, a banker collects payment of an instrument on behalf of a customer by—

(a) receiving payment of the instrument for the customer, or

(b) receiving payment of the instrument for the banker (but not as holder), having—

(i)   credited the customer's account with the amount of the instrument, or

(ii)   otherwise given value to the customer in respect of the instrument.

(6) Section 89E(4) applies for the purposes of subsection (5) in its application to section 89E.]

PART V   SUPPLEMENTARY

90   Good faith

A thing is deemed to be done in good faith, within the meaning of this Act, where it is in fact done honestly, whether it is done negligently or not.

91   Signature

(1) Where, by this Act, any instrument or writing is required to be signed by any person, it is not necessary that he should sign it with his own hand, but it is sufficient if his signature is written thereon by some other person by or under his authority.

(2) In the case of a corporation, where, by this Act, any instrument or writing is required to be signed, it is sufficient if the instrument or writing be sealed with the corporate seal.

But nothing in this section shall be construed as requiring the bill or note of a corporation to be under seal.

92   Computation of time

Where, by this Act, the time limited for doing any act or thing is less than three days, in reckoning time, non-business days are excluded.

'Non-business days' for the purposes of this Act mean—

(a)   [Saturday], Sunday, Good Friday, Christmas Day:

(b)   A bank holiday under [the Banking and Financial Dealings Act 1971.]

(c)   A day appointed by Royal proclamation as a public fast or thanksgiving day.

[(d)   a day declared by an order under section 2 of the Banking and Financial Dealings Act 1971 to be a non-business day.]

Any other day is a business day.

93   When noting equivalent to protest

For the purposes of this Act, where a bill or note is required to be protested within a specified time or before some further proceeding is taken, it is sufficient that the bill has been noted for protest before the expiration of the specified time or the taking of the proceeding; and the formal protest may be extended at any time thereafter as of the date of the noting.

94   Protest when notary not accessible

[(1)]   Where a dishonoured bill or note is authorised or required to be protested, and the services of a notary cannot be obtained at the place where the bill is dishonoured, any householder, or substantial resident of the place may, in the presence of two witnesses, give a certificate, signed by them, attesting to the dishonour of the bill, and the certificate shall in all respects operate as if it were a formal protest of the bill.

The form given in Schedule I to this Act may be used with necessary modifications, and if used shall be sufficient.

[(2)   In subsection (1), 'notary' includes a person who, for the purposes of the Legal Services Act 2007, is an authorised person in relation to any activity which constitutes a notarial activity (within the meaning of that Act).]

95   Dividend warrants may be crossed

The provisions of this Act as to crossed cheques shall apply to a warrant for payment of dividend.

97   Savings

(1)   The rules in bankruptcy relating to bills of exchange, promissory notes, and cheques, shall continue to apply thereto notwithstanding anything in this Act contained.

(2)   The rules of common law including the law merchant, save in so far as they are inconsistent with the express provisions of this Act, shall continue to apply to bills of exchange, promissory notes, and cheques—

(3)   Nothing in this Act or in any repeal effected thereby shall affect—

(a)   [...] any law or enactment for the time being in force relating to the revenue;

(b)   The provisions of the Companies Act, 1862, or Acts amending it, or any Act relating to joint stock banks or companies:

(c)   The provisions of any Act relating to or confirming the privileges of the Bank of England or the Bank of Ireland respectively:

(d)   The validity of any usage relating to dividend warrants, or the indorsements thereof.

99   Construction with other Acts, etc.

Where any Act or document refers to any enactment repealed by this Act, the Act or document shall be construed, and shall operate as if it referred to the corresponding provisions of this Act.

SCHEDULES

Section 94　　　　　　**FIRST SCHEDULE**

Form of protest which may be used when the services of a notary cannot
be obtained.

Know all men that I, *A. B.* householder, of　　　in the county of
in the United Kingdom, at the request of *C. D.*, there being no notary
public available, did on the　　　day of　　　188　　at ————————
demand payment [*or* acceptance] of the bill of exchange hereunder written, from *E. F*, to which
demand he made answer [state answer, if any] wherefore I now, in the presence of *G. H.* and *J. K.* do
protest the said bill of exchange.

(Signed)　A.　B.

G.　H.
　　　　　　} *Witnesses*
J.　K.

N.B.—The bill itself should be annexed, or a copy of the bill and all that is written thereon should
be underwritten.

Bills of Sale Act (1878) Amendment Act 1882

(45 & 46 Vict., c. 43)

1　Short title
This Act may be cited for all purposes as the Bills of Sale Act (1878) Amendment Act 1882; and
this Act and the Bills of Sale Act 1878 may be cited together as the Bills of Sale Acts 1878 and
1882.

3　Construction of Act
The Bills of Sale Act 1878 is herein-after referred to as 'the principal Act', and this Act shall,
so far as is consistent with the tenor thereof, be construed as one with the principal Act; but
unless the context otherwise requires shall not apply to any bill of sale duly registered before
the commencement of this Act so long as the registration thereof is not avoided by non-renewal
or otherwise.

　The expression 'bill of sale', and other expressions in this Act, have the same meaning as in the
principal Act, except as to bills of sale or other documents mentioned in section four of the principal
Act, which may be given otherwise than by way of security for the payment of money, to which last-
mentioned bills of sale and other documents this Act shall not apply.

4　Bill of sale to have schedule of property attached thereto
Every bill of sale shall have annexed thereto or written thereon a schedule containing an inventory
of the personal chattels comprised in the bill of sale; and such bill of sale, save as herein-after mentioned, shall have effect only in respect of the personal chattels specifically described in the said
schedule; and shall be void, except as against the grantor, in respect of any personal chattels not so
specifically described.

5　Bill of sale not to affect after acquired property
Save as herein-after mentioned, a bill of sale shall be void, except as against the grantor, in respect
of any personal chattels specifically described in the schedule thereto of which the grantor was not
the true owner at the time of the execution of the bill of sale.

6   Exception as to certain things

Nothing contained in the foregoing sections of this Act shall render a bill of sale void in respect of any of the following things; (that is to say,)

(1) Any growing crops separately assigned or charged where such crops were actually growing at the time when the bill of sale was executed.

(2) Any fixtures separately assigned or charged, and any plant, or trade machinery where such fixtures, plant, or trade machinery are used in, attached to, or brought upon any land, farm, factory, workshop, shop, house, warehouse, or other place in substitution for any of the like fixtures, plant, or trade machinery specifically described in the schedule to such bill of sale.

7   Bill of sale with power to seize except in certain events to be void

Personal chattels assigned under a bill of sale shall not be liable to be seized or taken possession of by the grantee for any other than the following causes:—

(1) If the grantor shall make default in payment of the sum or sums of money thereby secured at the time therein provided for payment, or in the performance of any covenant or agreement contained in the bill of sale and necessary for maintaining the security;

(2) If the grantor shall become a bankrupt, or suffer the said goods or any of them to be distrained [or taken control of using the power in Schedule 12 to the Tribunals, Courts and Enforcement Act 2007,] for rent, rates, or taxes;

(3) If the grantor shall fraudulently either remove or suffer the said goods, or any of them, to be removed from the premises;

(4) If the grantor shall not, without reasonable excuse, upon demand in writing by the grantee, produce to him his last receipts for rent, rates, and taxes;

(5) If execution shall have been levied against the goods of the grantor under any judgment at law:

Provided that the grantor may within five days from the seizure or taking possession of any chattels on account of any of the above-mentioned causes, apply to the High Court, or to a judge thereof in chambers, and such court or judge, if satisfied that by payment of money or otherwise the said cause of seizure no longer exists, may restrain the grantee from removing or selling the said chattels, or may make such other order as may seem just.

[7A   Defaults under consumer credit agreements

(1) Paragraph (1) of section 7 of this Act does not apply to a default relating to a bill of sale given by way of security for the payment of money under a regulated agreement to which section 87(1) of the Consumer Credit Act 1974 applies—

(a) unless the restriction imposed by section 88(2) of that Act has ceased to apply to the bill of sale; or

(b) if, by virtue of section 89 of that Act, the default is to be treated as not having occurred.

(2) Where paragraph (1) of section 7 of this Act does apply in relation to a bill of sale such as is mentioned in subsection (1) of this section, the proviso to that section shall have effect with the substitution of 'county court' for 'High Court'.]

8   Bill of sale to be void unless attested and registered

Every bill of sale shall be duly attested, and shall be registered under the principal Act within seven clear days after the execution thereof, or if it is executed in any place out of England then within seven clear days after the time at which it would in the ordinary course of post arrive in England if posted immediately after the execution thereof; and shall truly set forth the consideration for which it was given; otherwise such bill of sale shall be void in respect of the personal chattels comprised therein.

9   Form of bill of sale

A bill of sale made or given by way of security for the payment of money by the grantor thereof shall be void unless made in accordance with the form in the schedule to this Act annexed.

10   Attestation

The execution of every bill of sale by the grantor shall be attested by one or more credible witness or witnesses, not being a party or parties thereto...

11   Local registration of contents of bills of sale

Where the affidavit (which under section ten of the principal Act is required to accompany a bill of sale when presented for registration) describes the residence of the person making or giving the same or of the person against whom the process is issued to be in some place outside [the London insolvency district] or where the bill of sale describes the chattels enumerated therein as being in some place outside [the London insolvency district], the registrar under the principal Act shall forthwith and within three clear days after registration in the principal registry, and in accordance with the prescribed directions, transmit an abstract in the prescribed form of the contents of such bill of sale to the county court registrar in whose district such places are situate, and if such places are in the districts of different registrars to each such registrar.

Every abstract so transmitted shall be filed, kept, and indexed by the registrar of the county court in the prescribed manner, and any person may search, inspect, make extracts from, and obtain copies of the abstract so registered in the like manner and upon the like terms as to payment or otherwise as near as may be as in the case of bills of sale registered by the registrar under the principal Act.

12   Bill of sale under £30 to be void

Every bill of sale made or given in consideration of any sum under thirty pounds shall be void.

13   Chattels not to be removed or sold

All personal chattels seized or of which possession is taken [...] under or by virtue of any bill of sale (whether registered before or after the commencement of this Act), shall remain on the premises where they were so seized or so taken possession of, and shall not be removed or sold until after the expiration of five clear days from the day they were so seized or so taken possession of.

14   Bill of sale not to protect chattels against poor and parochial rates

A bill of sale to which this Act applies shall be no protection in respect of personal chattels included in such bill of sale which but for such bill of sale would have been liable to distress under a warrant[, or subject to a warrant of control,] for the recovery of taxes and poor and other parochial rates.

15   Repeal of part of Bills of Sale Act 1878

...All...enactments contained in the principal Act which are inconsistent with this Act are repealed...

16   Inspection of registered bills of sale

...Any person shall be entitled at all reasonable times to search the register, on payment of a fee of [5p], or such other fee as may be prescribed, and subject to such regulations as may be prescribed, and shall be entitled at all reasonable times to inspect, examine, and make extracts from any and every registered bill of sale without being required to make a written application, or to specify any particulars in reference thereto, upon payment of [5p] for each bill of sale inspected, and such payment shall be made by a judicature stamp. Provided that the said extracts shall be limited to the dates of execution, registration, renewal of registration, and satisfaction, to the names, addresses, and occupations of the parties, to the amount of the consideration, and to any further prescribed particulars.

17   Debentures to which Act not to apply

Nothing in this Act shall apply to any debentures issued by any mortgage, loan, or other incorporated company [or by any limited liability partnership], and secured upon the capital stock or goods, chattels, and effects of such company [or a limited liability partnership].

Section 9 ## SCHEDULE

FORM OF BILL OF SALE

This Indenture made the   day of   between *A.B.* of   of the one part, and *C.D.*
of   of the other part, witnesseth that in consideration of the sum of £   now paid to *A.B.*
by *C.D.*, the receipt of which the said *A.B.* hereby acknowledges [*or whatever else the consideration
may be*], he the said *A.B.* doth hereby assign unto *C.D.*, his executors, administrators, and assigns, all
and singular the several chattels and things specifically described in the schedule hereto annexed
by way of security for the payment of the sum of £   and interest thereon at the rate of   per
cent per annum [*or whatever else may be the rate*]. And the said *A.B.* doth further agree and declare
that he will duly pay to the said *C.D.* the principal sum aforesaid, together with the interest then
due, by equal payments of £   on the   day of   [*or whatever else may be the stipulated times
or time of payment*]. And the said *A.B.* doth also agree with the said *C.D.* that he will [*here insert
terms as to insurance, payment of rent, or otherwise, which the parties may agree to for the maintenance
or defeasance of the security*].

   Provided always, that the chattels hereby assigned shall not be liable to seizure or to be taken possession of by the said *C.D.* for any cause other than those specified in section seven of the Bills of Sale
Act (1878) Amendment Act 1882.

In witness, &c.

   Signed and sealed by the said *A.B.* in the presence of me *E.F.* [*add witness' name, address, and
description*].

Factors Act 1889

(52 & 53 Vict., c. 45)

Preliminary

1 Definitions
For the purposes of this Act—

   (1) The expression 'mercantile agent' shall mean a mercantile agent having in the customary
course of his business as such agent authority either to sell goods or to consign goods for the purpose
of sale, or to buy goods, or to raise money on the security of goods:

   (2) A person shall be deemed to be in possession of goods or of the documents of title to goods,
where the goods or documents are in the actual custody or are held by any other person subject to
his control or for him or on his behalf:

   (3) The expression 'goods' shall include wares and merchandise:

   (4) The expression 'document of title' shall include any bill of lading, dock warrant, warehouse-
keeper's certificate, and warrant or order for the delivery of goods, and any other document used
in the ordinary course of business as proof of the possession or control of goods, or authorising or
purporting to authorise, either by endorsement or by delivery, the possessor of the document to
transfer or receive goods thereby represented:

   (5) The expression 'pledge' shall include any contract pledging, or giving a lien or security on,
goods, whether in consideration of an original advance or of any further or continuing advance or
of any pecuniary liability:

   (6) The expression 'person' shall include any body of persons corporate or unincorporate.

Dispositions by mercantile agents

2 Powers of mercantile agent with respect to disposition of goods
   (1) Where a mercantile agent is, with the consent of the owner, in possession of goods or of
the documents of title to goods, any sale, pledge, or other disposition of the goods, made by him

when acting in the ordinary course of business of a mercantile agent, shall, subject to the provisions of this Act, be as valid as if he were expressly authorised by the owner of the goods to make the same; provided that the person taking under the disposition acts in good faith, and has not at the time of the disposition notice that the person making the disposition has not authority to make the same.

(2) Where a mercantile agent has, with the consent of the owner, been in possession of goods or of the documents of title to goods, any sale, pledge, or other disposition, which would have been valid if the consent had continued, shall be valid notwithstanding the determination of the consent; provided that the person taking under the disposition has not at the time thereof notice that the consent has been determined.

(3) Where a mercantile agent has obtained possession of any documents of title to goods by reason of his being or having been, with the consent of the owner, in possession of the goods represented thereby, or of any other documents of title to the goods, his possession of the first-mentioned documents shall, for the purposes of this Act, be deemed to be with the consent of the owner.

(4) For the purposes of this Act the consent of the owner shall be presumed in the absence of evidence to the contrary.

3   Effect of pledges of documents of title

A pledge of the documents of title to goods shall be deemed to be a pledge of the goods.

4   Pledge for antecedent debt

Where a mercantile agent pledges goods as security for a debt or liability due from the pledgor to the pledgee before the time of the pledge, the pledgee shall acquire no further right to the goods than could have been enforced by the pledgor at the time of the pledge.

5   Rights acquired by exchange of goods or documents

The consideration necessary for the validity of a sale, pledge, or other disposition of goods, in pursuance of this Act, may be either a payment in cash, or the delivery or transfer of other goods, or of a document of title to goods, or of a negotiable security, or any other valuable consideration; but where goods are pledged by a mercantile agent in consideration of the delivery or transfer of other goods, or of a document of title to goods, or of a negotiable security, the pledgee shall acquire no right or interest in the goods so pledged in excess of the value of the goods, documents, or security when so delivered or transferred in exchange.

6   Agreements through clerks, &c.

For the purposes of this Act an agreement made with a mercantile agent through a clerk or other person authorised in the ordinary course of business to make contracts of sale or pledge on his behalf shall be deemed to be an agreement with the agent.

7   Provisions as to consignors and consignees

(1) Where the owner of goods has given possession of the goods to another person for the purpose of consignment or sale, or has shipped the goods in the name of another person, and the consignee of the goods has not had notice that such person is not the owner of the goods, the consignee shall, in respect of advances made to or for the use of such person, have the same lien on the goods as if such person were the owner of the goods, and may transfer any such lien to another person.

(2) Nothing in this section shall limit or affect the validity of any sale, pledge, or disposition, by a mercantile agent.

Dispositions by sellers and buyers of goods

8   Disposition by seller remaining in possession

Where a person, having sold goods, continues, or is, in possession of the goods or of the documents of title to the goods, the delivery or transfer by that person, or by a mercantile agent acting for him, of the goods or documents of title under any sale, pledge, or other disposition thereof, or under any agreement for sale, pledge, or other disposition thereof, to any person receiving the same in good faith and without notice of the previous sale, shall have the same effect as if the person making the delivery or transfer were expressly authorised by the owner of the goods to make the same.

9 Disposition by buyer obtaining possession

Where a person, having bought or agreed to buy goods, obtains with the consent of the seller possession of the goods or the documents of title to the goods, the delivery or transfer, by that person or by a mercantile agent acting for him, of the goods or documents of title under any sale, pledge, or other disposition thereof, or under any agreement for sale, pledge, or other disposition thereof, to any person receiving the same in good faith and without notice of any lien or other right of the original seller in respect of the goods, shall have the same effect as if the person making the delivery or transfer were a mercantile agent in possession of the goods or documents of title with the consent of the owner.

[For the purposes of this section—

   (i)   the buyer under a conditional sale agreement shall be deemed not to be a person who has bought or agreed to buy goods, and

   (ii) 'conditional sale agreement' means an agreement for the sale of goods which is a consumer credit agreement within the meaning of the Consumer Credit Act 1974 under which the purchase price or part of it is payable in instalments, and the property in the goods is to remain in the seller (notwithstanding that the buyer is to be in possession of the goods) until such conditions as to the payment of instalments or otherwise as may be specified in the agreement are fulfilled.]

10 Effect of transfer of documents on vendor's lien or right of stoppage in transitu

Where a document of title to goods has been lawfully transferred to a person as a buyer or owner of the goods, and that person transfers the document to a person who takes the document in good faith and for valuable consideration, the last-mentioned transfer shall have the same effect for defeating any vendor's lien or right of stoppage in transitu as the transfer of a bill of lading has for defeating the right of stoppage in transitu.

Supplemental

11 Mode of transferring documents

For the purposes of this Act, the transfer of a document may be by endorsement, or, where the document is by custom or by its express terms transferable by delivery or makes the goods deliverable to the bearer, then by delivery.

12 Saving for rights of true owner

(1) Nothing in this Act shall authorise an agent to exceed or depart from his authority as between himself and his principal, or exempt him from any liability, civil or criminal, for so doing.

(2) Nothing in this Act shall prevent the owner of goods from recovering the goods from any agent or his trustee in bankruptcy at any time before the sale or pledge thereof, or shall prevent the owner of goods pledged by an agent from having the right to redeem the goods at any time before the sale thereof, on satisfying the claim for which the goods were pledged, and paying to the agent, if by him required, any money in respect of which the agent would by law be entitled to retain the goods or the documents of title thereto, or any of them, by way of lien as against the owner, or from recovering from any person with whom the goods have been pledged any balance of money remaining in his hands as the produce of the sale of the goods after deducting the amount of his lien.

(3) Nothing in this Act shall prevent the owner of goods sold by an agent from recovering from the buyer the price agreed to be paid for the same, or any part of that price, subject to any right of set off on the part of the buyer against the agent.

13 Saving for common law powers of agent

The provisions of this Act shall be construed in amplification and not in derogation of the powers exercisable by an agent independently of this Act.

Marine Insurance Act 1906

(6 Edw. 7, c. 41)

Marine insurance

1 Marine insurance defined

A contract of marine insurance is a contract whereby the insurer undertakes to indemnify the assured, in manner and to the extent thereby agreed, against marine losses, that is to say, the losses incident to marine adventure.

2 Mixed sea and land risks

(1) A contract of marine insurance may, by its express terms, or by usage of trade, be extended so as to protect the assured against losses on inland waters or on any land risk which may be incidental to any sea voyage.

(2) Where a ship in course of building, or the launch of a ship, or any adventure analogous to marine adventure, is covered by a policy in the form of a marine policy, the provisions of this Act, in so far as applicable, shall apply thereto; but, except as by this section provided, nothing in this Act shall alter or affect any rule of law applicable to any contract of insurance other than a contract of marine insurance as by this Act defined.

3 Marine adventure and maritime perils defined

(1) Subject to the provisions of this Act, every lawful marine adventure may be the subject of marine insurance.

(2) In particular there is a marine adventure where—

    (a) Any ship goods or other moveables are exposed to maritime perils. Such property is in this Act referred to as 'insurable property';

    (b) The earning or acquisition of any freight, passage money, commission, profit, or other pecuniary benefit, or the security for any advances, loan or disbursements, is endangered by the exposure of insurable property to maritime perils;

    (c) Any liability to a third party may be incurred by the owner of, or other person interested in or responsible for, insurable property, by reason of maritime perils.

'Maritime perils' means the perils consequent on, or incidental to, the navigation of the sea, that is to say, perils of the seas, fire, war perils, pirates, rovers, thieves, captures, seisures, restraints, and detainments of princes and peoples, jettisons, barratry, and any other perils, either of the like kind or which may be designated by the policy.

Insurable interest

4 Avoidance of wagering or gaming contracts

(1) Every contract of marine insurance by way of gaming or wagering is void.

(2) A contract of marine insurance is deemed to be a gaming or wagering contract—

    (a) Where the assured has not an insurable interest as defined by this Act, and the contract is entered into with no expectation of acquiring such an interest; or

    (b) Where the policy is made 'interest or no interest,' or 'without further proof of interest than the policy itself,' or 'without benefit of salvage to the insurer,' or subject to any other like term:

Provided that, where there is no possibility of salvage, a policy may be effected without benefit of salvage to the insurer.

5   Insurable interest defined

(1) Subject to the provisions of this Act, every person has an insurable interest who is interested in a marine adventure.

(2) In particular a person is interested in a marine adventure where he stands in any legal or equitable relation to the adventure or to any insurable property at risk therein, in consequence of which he may benefit by the safety or due arrival of insurable property, or may be prejudiced by its loss, or damage thereto, or by the detention thereof, or may incur liability in respect thereof.

6   When interest must attach

(1) The assured must be interested in the subject-matter insured at the time of the loss though he need not be interested when the insurance is effected:

Provided that where the subject-matter is insured 'lost or not lost,' the assured may recover although he may not have acquired his interest until after the loss, unless at the time of effecting the contract of insurance the assured was aware of the loss, and the insurer was not.

(2) Where the assured has no interest at the time of the loss, he cannot acquire interest by any act or election after he is aware of the loss.

7   Defeasible or contingent interest

(1) A defeasible interest is insurable, as also is a contingent interest.

(2) In particular, where the buyer of goods has insured them, he has an insurable interest, notwithstanding that he might, at his election, have rejected the goods, or have treated them as at the seller's risk, by reason of the latter's delay in making delivery or otherwise.

8   Partial interest

A partial interest of any nature is insurable.

9   Re-insurance

(1) The insurer under a contract of marine insurance has an insurable interest in his risk, and may re-insure in respect of it.

(2) Unless the policy otherwise provides, the original assured has no right or interest in respect of such re-insurance.

10   Bottomry

The lender of money on bottomry or respondentia has an insurable interest in respect of the loan.

11   Master's and seamen's wages

The master or any member of the crew of a ship has an insurable interest in respect of his wages.

12   Advance freight

In the case of advance freight, the person advancing the freight has an insurable interest, in so far as such freight is not repayable in case of loss.

13   Charges of insurance

The assured has an insurable interest in the charges of any insurance which he may effect.

14   Quantum of interest

(1) Where the subject-matter insured is mortgaged, the mortgagor has an insurable interest in the full value thereof, and the mortgagee has an insurable interest in respect of any sum due or to become due under the mortgage.

(2) A mortgagee, consignee, or other person having an interest in the subject-matter insured may insure on his own behalf and for the benefit of other persons interested as well as for his own benefit.

(3) The owner of insurable property has an insurable interest in respect of the full value thereof, notwithstanding that some third person may have agreed, or be liable, to indemnify him in case of loss.

15   Assignment of interest

Where the assured assigns or otherwise parts with his interest in the subject-matter insured, he does not thereby transfer to the assignee his rights under the contract of insurance, unless there be an express or implied agreement with the assignee to that effect.

But the provisions of this section do not affect a transmission of interest by operation of law.

Insurable value

16   Measure of insurable value

Subject to any express provision or valuation in the policy, the insurable value of the subject-matter insured must be ascertained as follows:—

(1) In insurance on ship, the insurable value is the value, at the commencement of the risk, of the ship, including her outfit, provisions and stores for the officers and crew, money advanced for seamen's wages, and other disbursements (if any) incurred to make the ship fit for the voyage or adventure contemplated by the policy, plus the charges of insurance upon the whole:

The insurable value, in the case of a steamship, includes also the machinery, boilers, and coals and engine stores if owned by the assured, and, in the case of a ship engaged in a special trade, the ordinary fittings requisite for that trade:

(2) In insurance on freight, whether paid in advance or otherwise, the insurable value is the gross amount of freight at the risk of the assured, plus the charges of insurance:

(3) In insurance on goods or merchandise, the insurable value is the prime cost of the property insured, plus the expenses of and incidental to shipping and the charges of insurance upon the whole:

(4) In insurance on any other subject-matter, the insurable value is the amount at the risk of the assured when the policy attaches, plus the charges of insurance.

Disclosure and representations

17   Insurance is uberrimae fidei

A contract of marine insurance is a contract based upon the utmost good faith, [...]

21   When contract is deemed to be concluded

A contract of marine insurance is deemed to be concluded when the proposal of the assured is accepted by the insurer, whether the policy be then issued or not; and, for the purpose of showing when the proposal was accepted, reference may be made to the slip or covering note or other customary memorandum of the contract, [...]

The policy

22   Contract must be embedded in policy

Subject to the provisions of any statute, a contract of marine insurance is inadmissible in evidence unless it is embodied in a marine policy in accordance with this Act. The policy may be executed and issued either at the time when the contract is concluded or afterwards.

23   What policy must specify

A marine policy must specify—

(1) The name of the assured, or of some person who effects the insurance on his behalf:

[...]

24   Signature of insurer

(1) A marine policy must be signed by or on behalf of the insurer, provided that in the case of a corporation the corporate seal may be sufficient, but nothing in this section shall be construed as requiring the subscription of a corporation to be under seal.

(2) Where a policy is subscribed by or on behalf of two or more insurers, each subscription, unless the contrary be expressed, constitutes a distinct contract with the assured.

25 Voyage and time policies

(1) Where the contract is to insure the subject-matter 'at and from', or from one place to another or others, the policy is called a 'voyage policy', and where the contract is to insure the subject-matter for a definite period of time the policy is called a 'time policy'. A contract for both voyage and time may be included in the same policy.

[...]

26 Designation of subject-matter

(1) The subject-matter insured must be designated in a marine policy with reasonable certainty.

(2) The nature and extent of the interest of the assured in the subject-matter insured need not be specified in the policy.

(3) Where the policy designates the subject-matter insured in general terms, it shall be construed to apply to the interest intended by the assured to be covered.

(4) In the application of this section regard shall be had to any usage regulating the designation of the subject-matter insured.

27 Valued policy

(1) A policy may be either valued or unvalued.

(2) A valued policy is a policy which specifies the agreed value of the subject-matter insured.

(3) Subject to the provisions of this Act, and in the absence of fraud, the value fixed by the policy is, as between the insurer and the assured, conclusive of the insurable value of the subject intended to be insured, whether the loss be total or partial.

(4) Unless the policy otherwise provides, the value fixed by the policy is not conclusive for the purpose of determining whether there has been a constructive total loss.

28 Unvalued policy

An unvalued policy is a policy which does not specify the value of the subject-matter insured, but, subject to the limit of the sum insured, leaves the insurable value to be subsequently ascertained, in the manner herein-before specified.

29 Floating policy by ship or ships

(1) A floating policy is a policy which describes the insurance in general terms, and leaves the name of the ship or ships and other particulars to be defined by subsequent declaration.

(2) The subsequent declaration or declarations may be made by indorsement on the policy, or in other customary manner.

(3) Unless the policy otherwise provides, the declarations must be made in the order of dispatch or shipment. They must, in the case of goods, comprise all consignments within the terms of the policy, and the value of the goods or other property must be honestly stated, but an omission or erroneous declaration may be rectified even after loss or arrival, provided the omission or declaration was made in good faith.

(4) Unless the policy otherwise provides, where a declaration of value is not made until after notice of loss or arrival, the policy must be treated as an unvalued policy as regards the subject-matter of that declaration.

30 Construction of terms in policy

(1) A policy may be in the form in the First Schedule to this Act.

(2) Subject to the provisions of this Act, and unless the context of the policy otherwise requires, the terms and expressions mentioned in the First Schedule to this Act shall be construed as having the scope and meaning in that schedule assigned to them.

31 Premium to be arranged

(1) Where an insurance is effected at a premium to be arranged, and no arrangement is made, a reasonable premium is payable.

(2) Where an insurance is effected on the terms that an additional premium is to be arranged in a given event, and that event happens but no arrangement is made, then a reasonable additional premium is payable.

Double insurance

32   Double insurance

(1) Where two or more policies are effected by or on behalf of the assured on the same adventure and interest or any part thereof, and the sums insured exceed the indemnity allowed by this Act, the assured is said to be over-insured by double insurance.

(2) Where the assured is over-insured by double insurance—

(a) The assured, unless the policy otherwise provides, may claim payment from the insurers in such order as he may think fit, provided that he is not entitled to receive any sum in excess of the indemnity allowed by this Act;

(b) Where the policy under which the assured claims is a valued policy, the assured must give credit as against the valuation for any sum received by him under any other policy without regard to the actual value of the subject-matter insured;

(c) Where the policy under which the assured claims is an unvalued policy he must give credit, as against the full insurable value, for any sum received by him under any other policy.

(d) Where the assured receives any sum in excess of the indemnity allowed by this Act, he is deemed to hold such sum in trust for the insurers, according to their right of contribution among themselves.

Warranties, etc.

33   Nature of warranty

(1) A warranty, in the following sections relating to warranties, means a promissory warranty, that is to say, a warranty by which the assured undertakes that some particular thing shall or shall not be done, or that some condition shall be fulfilled, or whereby he affirms or negatives the existence of a particular state of facts.

(2) A warranty may be express or implied.

(3) A warranty, as above defined, is a condition which must be exactly complied with, whether it be material to the risk or not. [...]

35   Express warranties

(1) An express warranty may be in any form of words from which the intention to warrant is to be inferred.

(2) An express warranty must be included in, or written upon, the policy, or must be contained in some document incorporated by reference into the policy.

(3) An express warranty does not exclude an implied warranty, unless it be inconsistent therewith.

36   Warranty of neutrality

(1) Where insurable property, whether ship or goods, is expressly warranted neutral, there is an implied condition that the property shall have a neutral character at the commencement of the risk, and that, so far as the assured can control the matter, its neutral character shall be preserved during the risk.

(2) Where a ship is expressly warranted 'neutral' there is also an implied condition that, so far as the assured can control the matter, she shall be properly documented, that is to say, that she shall carry the necessary papers to establish her neutrality, and that she shall not falsify or suppress her papers, or use simulated papers. If any loss occurs through breach of this condition, the insurer may avoid the contract.

37   No implied warranty of nationality

There is no implied warranty as to the nationality of a ship, or that her nationality shall not be changed during the risk.

38   Warranty of good safety

Where the subject-matter insured is warranted 'well' or 'in good safety' on a particular day, it is sufficient if it be safe at any time during that day.

39   Warranty of seaworthiness of ship

(1) In a voyage policy there is an implied warranty that at the commencement of the voyage the ship shall be seaworthy for the purpose of the particular adventure insured.

(2) Where the policy attaches while the ship is in port, there is also an implied warranty that she shall, at the commencement of the risk, be reasonably fit to encounter the ordinary perils of the port.

(3) Where the policy relates to a voyage which is performed in different stages, during which the ship requires different kinds of or further preparation or equipment, there is an implied warranty that at the commencement of each stage the ship is seaworthy in respect of such preparation or equipment for the purposes of that stage.

(4) A ship is deemed to be seaworthy when she is reasonably fit in all respects to encounter the ordinary perils of the seas of the adventure insured.

(5) In a time policy there is no implied warranty that the ship shall be seaworthy at any stage of the adventure, but where, with the privity of the assured, the ship is sent to sea in an unseaworthy state, the insurer is not liable for any loss attributable to unseaworthiness.

40   No implied warranty that goods are seaworthy

(1) In a policy on goods or other moveables there is no implied warranty that the goods or moveables are seaworthy.

(2) In a voyage policy on goods or other moveables there is an implied warranty that at the commencement of the voyage the ship is not only seaworthy as a ship, but also that she is reasonably fit to carry the goods or other moveables to the destination contemplated by the policy.

41   Warranty of legality

There is an implied warranty that the adventure insured is a lawful one, and that, so far as the assured can control the matter, the adventure shall be carried out in a lawful manner.

The voyage

42   Implied condition as to commencement of risk

(1) Where the subject-matter is insured by a voyage policy 'at and from' or 'from' a particular place, it is not necessary that the ship should be at that place when the contract is concluded, but there is an implied condition that the adventure shall be commenced within a reasonable time, and that if the adventure be not so commenced the insurer may avoid the contract.

(2) The implied condition may be negatived by showing that the delay was caused by circumstances known to the insurer before the contract was concluded, or by showing that he waived the condition.

43   Alteration of port of departure

Where the place of departure is specified by the policy, and the ship instead of sailing from that place sails from any other place, the risk does not attach.

44   Sailing for different destination

Where the destination is specified in the policy, and the ship, instead of sailing for that destination, sails for any other destination, the risk does not attach.

45   Change of voyage

(1) Where, after the commencement of the risk, the destination of the ship is voluntarily changed from the destination contemplated by the policy, there is said to be a change of voyage.

(2) Unless the policy otherwise provides, where there is a change of voyage, the insurer is discharged from liability as from the time of the change, that it to say, as from the time when the determination to change it is manifested; and it is immaterial that the ship may not have left the course of voyage contemplated by the policy when the loss occurs.

46 Deviation

(1) Where a ship, without lawful excuse, deviates from the voyage contemplated by the policy, the insurer is discharged from liability as from the time of deviation, and it is immaterial that the ship may have regained her route before any loss occurs.

(2) There is a deviation from the voyage contemplated by the policy—

(a) Where the course of the voyage is specifically designated by the policy, and that course is departed from; or

(b) Where the course of the voyage is not specifically designated by the policy, but the usual and customary course is departed from.

(3) The intention to deviate is immaterial; there must be a deviation in fact to discharge the insurer from his liability under the contract.

47 Several ports of discharge

(1) Where several ports of discharge are specified by the policy, the ship may proceed to all or any of them, but, in the absence of any usage or sufficient cause to the contrary, she must proceed to them, or such of them as she goes to, in the order designated by the policy. If she does not there is a deviation.

(2) Where the policy is to 'ports of discharge', within a given area, which are not named, the ship must, in the absence of any usage or sufficient cause to the contrary, proceed to them, or such of them as she goes to, in their geographical order. If she does not there is a deviation.

48 Delay in voyage

In the case of a voyage policy, the adventure insured must be prosecuted throughout its course with reasonable dispatch, and, if without lawful excuse it is not so prosecuted, the insurer is discharged from liability as from the time when the delay becomes unreasonable.

49 Excuses for deviation or delay

(1) Deviation or delay in prosecuting the voyage contemplated by the policy is excused—

(a) Where authorised by any special term in the policy; or

(b) Where caused by circumstances beyond the control of the master and his employer; or

(c) Where reasonably necessary in order to comply with an express or implied warranty; or

(d) Where reasonably necessary for the safety of the ship or subject-matter insured; or

(e) For the purpose of saving human life, or aiding a ship in distress where human life may be in danger; or

(f) Where reasonably necessary for the purpose of obtaining medical or surgical aid for any person on board the ship; or

(g) Where caused by the barratrous conduct of the master or crew, if barratry be one of the perils insured against.

(2) When the cause excusing the deviation or delay ceases to operate, the ship must resume her course, and prosecute her voyage, with reasonable dispatch.

Assignment of policy

50 When and how policy is assignable

(1) A marine policy is assignable unless it contains terms expressly prohibiting assignment. It may be assigned either before or after loss.

(2) Where a marine policy has been assigned so as to pass the beneficial interest in such policy, the assignee of the policy is entitled to sue thereon in his own name; and the defendant is entitled to make any defence arising out of the contract which he would have been entitled to make if the action had been brought in the name of the person by or on behalf of whom the policy was effected.

(3) A marine policy may be assigned by indorsement thereon or in other customary manner.

51   Assured who has no interest cannot assign

Where the assured has parted with or lost his interest in the subject-matter insured, and has not, before or at the time of so doing, expressly or impliedly agreed to assign the policy, any subsequent assignment of the policy is inoperative:

   Provided that nothing in this section affects the assignment of a policy after loss.

The premium

52   When premium payable

Unless otherwise agreed, the duty of the assured or his agent to pay the premium, and the duty of the insurer to issue the policy to the assured or his agent, are concurrent conditions, and the insurer is not bound to issue the policy until payment or tender of the premium.

53   Policy effected through broker

   (1) Unless otherwise agreed, where a marine policy is effected on behalf of the assured by a broker, the broker is directly responsible to the insurer for the premium, and the insurer is directly responsible to the assured for the amount which may be payable in respect of losses, or in respect of returnable premium.

   (2) Unless otherwise agreed, the broker has, as against the assured, a lien upon the policy for the amount of the premium and his charges in respect of effecting the policy; and, where he has dealt with the person who employs him as a principal, he has also a lien on the policy in respect of any balance on any insurance account which may be due to him from such person, unless when the debt was incurred he had reason to believe that such person was only an agent.

54   Effect of receipt on policy

Where a marine policy effected on behalf of the assured by a broker acknowledges the receipt of the premium, such acknowledgement is, in the absence of fraud, conclusive as between the insurer and the assured, but not as between the insurer and broker.

Loss and abandonment

55   Included and excluded losses

   (1) Subject to the provisions of this Act, and unless the policy otherwise provides, the insurer is liable for any loss proximately caused by a peril insured against, but, subject as aforesaid, he is not liable for any loss which is not proximately caused by a peril insured against.

   (2) In particular,—

   (a) The insurer is not liable for any loss attributable to the wilful misconduct of the assured, but, unless the policy otherwise provides, he is liable for any loss proximately caused by a peril insured against, even though the loss would not have happened but for the misconduct or negligence of the master or crew;

   (b) Unless the policy otherwise provides, the insurer on ship or goods is not liable for any loss proximately caused by delay, although the delay be caused by a peril insured against.

   (c) Unless the policy otherwise provides, the insurer is not liable for ordinary wear and tear, ordinary leakage and breakage, inherent vice or nature of the subject-matter insured, or for any loss proximately caused by rats or vermin, or for any injury to machinery not proximately caused by maritime perils.

56   Partial and total loss

   (1) A loss may be either total or partial. Any loss other than a total loss, as herein-after defined, is a partial loss.

   (2) A total loss may be either an actual total loss, or a constructive total loss.

   (3) Unless a different intention appears from the terms of the policy, an insurance against total loss includes a constructive, as well as an actual, total loss.

   (4) Where the assured brings an action for a total loss and the evidence proves only a partial loss, he may, unless the policy otherwise provides, recover for a partial loss.

(5) Where goods reach their destination in specie, but by reason of obliteration of marks, or otherwise, they are incapable of identification, the loss, if any, is partial, and not total.

57   Actual total loss

(1) Where the subject-matter insured is destroyed, or so damaged as to cease to be a thing of the kind insured, or where the assured is irretrievably deprived thereof, there is an actual total loss.

(2) In the case of an actual total loss no notice of abandonment need be given.

58   Missing ship

Where the ship concerned in the adventure is missing, and after the lapse of a reasonable time no news of her has been received, an actual total loss may be presumed.

59   Effect of transhipment, etc.

Where, by a peril insured against, the voyage is interrupted at any intermediate port or place, under such circumstances as apart from any special stipulation in the contract of affreightment, to justify the master in landing and re-shipping the goods or other moveables, or in transhipping them, and sending them on to their destination, the liability of the insurer continues, notwithstanding the landing or transhipment.

60   Constructive total loss defined

(1) Subject to any express provision in the policy, there is a constructive total loss where the subject-matter insured is reasonably abandoned on account of its total loss appearing to be unavoidable, or because it could not be preserved from actual total loss without an expenditure which would exceed its value when the expenditure had been incurred.

(2) In particular, there is a constructive total loss—

  (i)   Where the assured is deprived of the possession of his ship or goods by a peril insured against, and (a) it is unlikely that he can recover the ship or goods, as the case may be, or (b) the cost of recovering the ship or goods, as the case may be, would exceed their value when recovered; or

  (ii) In the case of damage to a ship, where she is so damaged by a peril insured against that the cost of repairing the damage would exceed the value of the ship when repaired.

      In estimating the cost of repairs, no deduction is to be made in respect of general average contributions to those repairs payable by other interests, but account is to be taken of the expense of future salvage operations and of any future general average contributions to which the ship would be liable if repaired; or

  (iii) In the case of damage to goods, where the cost of repairing the damage and forwarding the goods to their destination would exceed their value on arrival.

61   Effect of constructive total loss

Where there is a constructive total loss the assured may either treat the loss as a partial loss, or abandon the subject-matter insured to the insurer and treat the loss as if it were an actual total loss.

62   Notice of abandonment

(1) Subject to the provisions of this section, where the assured elects to abandon the subject-matter insured to the insurer, he must give notice of the abandonment. If he fails to do so the loss can only be treated as a partial loss.

(2) Notice of abandonment may be given in writing, or by word of mouth, or partly in writing and partly by word of mouth, and may be given in terms which indicate the intention of the assured to abandon his insured interest in the subject-matter insured unconditionally to the insurer.

(3) Notice of abandonment must be given with reasonable diligence after the receipt of reliable information of the loss, but where the information is of a doubtful character the assured is entitled to a reasonable time to make inquiry.

(4) Where notice of abandonment is properly given, the rights of the assured are not prejudiced by the fact that the insurer refuses to accept the abandonment.

(5) The acceptance of an abandonment may be either express or implied from the conduct of the insurer. The mere silence of the insurer after notice is not an acceptance.

(6) Where a notice of abandonment is accepted the abandonment is irrevocable. The acceptance of the notice conclusively admits liability for the loss and the sufficiency of the notice.

(7) Notice of abandonment is unnecessary where, at the time when the assured receives information of the loss, there would be no possibility of benefit to the insurer if notice were given to him.

(8) Notice of abandonment may be waived by the insurer.

(9) Where an insurer has re-insured his risk, no notice of abandonment need be given by him.

63 Effect of abandonment

(1) Where there is a valid abandonment the insurer is entitled to take over the interest of the assured in whatever may remain of the subject-matter insured, and all proprietary rights incidental thereto.

(2) Upon the abandonment of a ship, the insurer thereof is entitled to any freight in course of being earned, and which is earned by her subsequent to the casualty causing the loss, less the expenses of earning it incurred after the casualty; and, where a ship is carrying the owner's goods, the insurer is entitled to a reasonable remuneration for the carriage of them subsequent to the casualty causing the loss.

Partial losses (including salvage and general average and particular charges)

64 Particular average loss

(1) A particular average loss is a partial loss of the subject-matter insured, caused by a peril insured against, and which is not a general average loss.

(2) Expenses incurred by or on behalf of the assured for the safety or preservation of the subject-matter insured, other than general average and salvage charges, are called particular charges. Particular charges are not included in particular average.

65 Salvage charges

(1) Subject to any express provision in the policy, salvage charges incurred in preventing a loss by perils insured against may be recovered as a loss by those perils.

(2) 'Salvage charges' means the charges recoverable under maritime law by a salvor independently of contract. They do not include the expenses of services in the nature of salvage rendered by the assured or his agents, or any person employed for hire by them, for the purpose of averting a peril insured against. Such expenses, where properly incurred, may be recovered as particular charges or as a general average loss, according to the circumstances under which they were incurred.

66 General average loss

(1) A general average loss is a loss caused by or directly consequential on a general average act. It includes a general average expenditure as well as a general average sacrifice.

(2) There is a general average act where any extraordinary sacrifice or expenditure is voluntarily and reasonably made or incurred in the time of peril for the purpose of preserving the property imperilled in the common adventure.

(3) Where there is a general average loss, the party on whom it falls is entitled, subject to the conditions imposed by maritime law, to a rateable contribution from the other parties interested, and such contribution is called a general average contribution.

(4) Subject to any express provision in the policy, where the assured has incurred a general average expenditure, he may recover from the insurer in respect of the proportion of the loss which falls upon him; and, in the case of a general average sacrifice, he may recover from the insurer in respect of the whole loss without having enforced his right of contribution from the other parties liable to contribute.

(5) Subject to any express provision in the policy, where the assured has paid, or is liable to pay, a general average contribution in respect of the subject insured, he may recover therefor from the insurer.

(6) In the absence of express stipulation, the insurer is not liable for any general average loss or contribution where the loss was not incurred for the purpose of avoiding, or in connexion with the avoidance of, a peril insured against.

(7) Where ship, freight, and cargo, or any two of those interests, are owned by the same assured, the liability of the insurer in respect of general average losses or contributions is to be determined as if those subjects were owned by different persons.

Measure of indemnity

67   Extent of liability of insurer for loss

(1) The sum which the assured can recover in respect of a loss on a policy by which he is insured, in the case of an unvalued policy to the full extent of the insurable value, or in the case of a valued policy to the full extent of the value fixed by the policy, is called the measure of indemnity.

(2) Where there is a loss recoverable under the policy, the insurer, or each insurer if there be more than one, is liable for such proportion of the measure of indemnity as the amount of his sub-scription bears to the value fixed by the policy in the case of a valued policy, or to the insurable value in the case of an unvalued policy.

68   Total loss

Subject to the provisions of this Act and to any express provision in the policy, where there is a total loss of the subject-matter insured,—

(1) If the policy be a valued policy, the measure of indemnity is the sum fixed by the policy:

(2) If the policy be an unvalued policy, the measure of indemnity is the insurable value of the subject-matter insured.

69   Partial loss of ship

Where a ship is damaged, but not totally lost, the measure of indemnity, subject to any express provision in the policy, is as follows:—

(1) Where the ship has been repaired, the assured is entitled to the reasonable cost of the repairs, less the customary deductions, but not exceeding the sum insured in respect of any one casualty:

(2) Where the ship has been only partially repaired, the assured is entitled to the reasonable cost of such repairs, computed as above, and also to be indemnified for the reasonable depreciation, if any, arising from the unrepaired damage, provided that the aggregate amount shall not exceed the cost of repairing the whole damage, computed as above:

(3) Where the ship has not been repaired, and has not been sold in her damaged state during the risk, the assured is entitled to be indemnified for the reasonable depreciation arising from the unrepaired damage, but not exceeding the reasonable cost of repairing such damage, computed as above.

70   Partial loss of freight

Subject to any express provision in the policy, where there is a partial loss of freight, the measure of indemnity is such proportion of the sum fixed by the policy in the case of a valued policy, or of the insurable value in the case of an unvalued policy, as the proportion of freight lost by the assured bears to the whole freight at the risk of the assured under the policy.

71   Partial loss of goods, merchandise, etc.

Where there is a partial loss of goods, merchandise, or other moveables, the measure of indemnity, subject to any express provision in the policy, is as follows:—

(1) Where part of the goods, merchandise, or other moveables insured by a valued policy is totally lost, the measure of indemnity is such proportion of the sum fixed by the policy as the

insurable value of the part lost bears to the insurable value of the whole, ascertained as in the case of an unvalued policy:

(2) Where part of the goods, merchandise, or other moveables insured by an unvalued policy is totally lost, the measure of indemnity is the insurable value of the part lost, ascertained as in the case of total loss:

(3) Where the whole or any part of the goods or merchandise insured has been delivered damaged at its destination, the measure of indemnity is such proportion of the sum fixed by the policy in the case of a valued policy, or of the insurable value in the case of an unvalued policy, as the difference between the gross sound and damaged values at the place of arrival bears to the gross sound value:

(4) 'Gross value' means the wholesale price or, if there be no such price, the estimated value, with, in either case, freight, landing charges, and duty paid before-hand; provided that, in the case of goods or merchandise customarily sold in bond, the bonded price is deemed to be the gross value. 'Gross proceeds' means the actual price obtained at a sale where all charges on sale are paid by the sellers.

72   Apportionment of valuation

(1) Where different species of property are insured under a single valuation, the valuation must be apportioned over the different species in proportion to their respective insurable values, as in the case of an unvalued policy. The insured value of any part of a species is such proportion of the total insured value of the same as the insurable value of the part bears to the insurable value of the whole, ascertained in both cases as provided by this Act.

(2) Where a valuation has to be apportioned, and particulars of the prime cost of each separate species, quality, or description of goods cannot be ascertained, the division of the valuation may be made over the net arrived sound values of the different species, qualities, or descriptions of goods.

73   General average contributions and salvage charges

(1) Subject to any express provision in the policy, where the assured has paid, or is liable for, any general average contribution, the measure of indemnity is the full amount of such contribution, if the subject-matter liable to contribution is insured for its full contributory value; but, if such subject-matter be not insured for its full contributory value, or if only part of it be insured, the indemnity payable by the insurer must be reduced in proportion to the under insurance, and where there has been a particular average loss which constitutes a deduction from the contributory value, and for which the insurer is liable, that amount must be deducted from the insured value in order to ascertain what the insurer is liable to contribute.

(2) Where the insurer is liable for salvage charges the extent of his liability must be determined on the like principle.

74   Liabilities to third parties

Where the assured has effected an insurance in express terms against any liability to a third party, the measure of indemnity, subject to any express provision in the policy, is the amount paid or payable by him to such third party in respect of such liability.

75   General provisions as to measure of indemnity

(1) Where there has been a loss in respect of any subject-matter not expressly provided for in the foregoing provisions of this Act, the measure of indemnity shall be ascertained, as nearly as may be, in accordance with those provisions, in so far as applicable to the particular case.

(2) Nothing in the provisions of this Act relating to the measure of indemnity shall affect the rules relating to double insurance, or prohibit the insurer from disproving interest wholly or in part, or from showing that at the time of the loss the whole or any part of the subject-matter insured was not at risk under the policy.

76 Particular average warranties

(1) Where the subject-matter insured is warranted free from particular average, the assured cannot recover for a loss of part, other than a loss incurred by a general average sacrifice, unless the contract contained in the policy be apportionable; but, if the contract be apportionable, the assured may recover for a total loss of any apportionable part.

(2) Where the subject-matter insured is warranted free from particular average, either wholly or under a certain percentage, the insurer is nevertheless liable for salvage charges, and for particular charges and other expenses properly incurred pursuant to the provisions of the suing and labouring clause in order to avert a loss insured against.

(3) Unless the policy otherwise provides, where the subject-matter is warranted free from particular average under a specified percentage, a general average loss cannot be added to a particular average loss to make up the specified percentage.

(4) For the purpose of ascertaining whether the specified percentage has been reached, regard shall be had only to the actual loss suffered by the subject-matter insured. Particular charges and the expenses of and incidental to ascertaining and proving the loss must be excluded.

77 Successive losses

(1) Unless the policy otherwise provides, and subject to the provisions of this Act, the insurer is liable for successive losses, even though the total amount of such losses may exceed the sum insured.

(2) Where, under the same policy, a partial loss, which has not been repaired or otherwise made good, is followed by a total loss, the assured can only recover in respect of the total loss:

Provided that nothing in this section shall affect the liability of the insurer under the suing and labouring clause.

78 Suing and labouring clause

(1) Where the policy contains a suing and labouring clause, the engagement thereby entered into is deemed to be supplementary to the contract of insurance, and the assured may recover from the insurer any expenses properly incurred pursuant to the clause, notwithstanding that the insurer may have paid for a total loss, or that the subject-matter may have been warranted free from particular average, either wholly or under a certain percentage.

(2) General average losses and contributions and salvage charges, as defined by this Act, are not recoverable under the suing and labouring clause.

(3) Expenses incurred for the purpose of averting or diminishing any loss not covered by the policy are not recoverable under the suing and labouring clause.

(4) It is the duty of the assured and his agents, in all cases, to take such measures as may be reasonable for the purpose of averting or minimising a loss.

Rights of insurer on payment

79 Right of subrogation

(1) Where the insurer pays for a total loss, either of the whole, or in the case of goods of any apportionable part, of the subject-matter insured, he thereupon becomes entitled to take over the interest of the assured in whatever may remain of the subject-matter so paid for, and he is thereby subrogated to all the rights and remedies of the assured in and in respect of that subject-matter as from the time of the casualty causing the loss.

(2) Subject to the foregoing provisions, where the insurer pays for a partial loss, he acquires no title to the subject-matter insured, or such part of it as may remain, but he is thereupon subrogated to all rights and remedies of the assured in and in respect of the subject-matter insured as from the time of the casualty causing the loss, in so far as the assured has been indemnified, according to this Act, by such payment for the loss.

80   Right of contribution

(1) Where the assured is over-insured by double insurance, each insurer is bound, as between himself and the other insurers, to contribute rateably to the loss in proportion to the amount for which he is liable under his contract.

(2) If any insurer pays more than his proportion of the loss, he is entitled to maintain an action for contribution against the other insurers, and is entitled to the like remedies as a surety who has paid more than his proportion of the debt.

81   Effect of under insurance

Where the assured is insured for an amount less than the insurable value or, in the case of a valued policy, for an amount less than the policy valuation, he is deemed to be his own insurer in respect of the uninsured balance.

Return of premium

82   Enforcement of return

Where the premium or a proportionate part thereof is, by this Act, declared to be returnable,—

    (a) If already paid, it may be recovered by the assured from the insurer; and

    (b) If unpaid, it may be retained by the assured or his agent.

83   Return by agreement

Where the policy contains a stipulation for the return of the premium, or a proportionate part thereof, on the happening of a certain event, and that event happens, the premium, or, as the case may be, the proportionate part thereof, is thereupon returnable to the assured.

84   Return for failure of consideration

(1) Where the consideration for the payment of the premium totally fails, and there has been no fraud or illegality on the part of the assured or his agents, the premium is thereupon returnable to the assured.

(2) Where the consideration for the payment of the premium is apportionable and there is a total failure of any apportionable part of the consideration, a proportionate part of the premium is, under the like conditions, thereupon returnable to the assured.

(3) In particular—

    (a) Where the policy is void, or is avoided by the insurer as from the commencement of the risk, the premium is returnable, provided that there has been no fraud or illegality on the part of the assured; but if the risk is not apportionable, and has once attached, the premium is not returnable;

    (b) Where the subject-matter insured, or part thereof, has never been imperilled, the premium, or, as the case may be, a proportionate part thereof, is returnable: Provided that where the subject-matter has been insured 'lost or not lost' and has arrived in safety at the time when the contract is concluded, the premium is not returnable unless, at such time, the insurer knew of the safe arrival.

    (c) Where the assured has no insurable interest throughout the currency of the risk, the premium is returnable, provided that this rule does not apply to a policy effected by way of gaming or wagering;

    (d) Where the assured has a defeasible interest which is terminated during the currency of the risk, the premium is not returnable;

    (e) Where the assured has over-insured under an unvalued policy, a proportionate part of the premium is returnable;

    (f) Subject to the foregoing provisions, where the assured has over-insured by double insurance, a proportionate part of the several premiums is returnable:

Provided that, if the policies are effected at different times, and any earlier policy has at any time borne the entire risk, or if a claim has been paid on the policy in respect of the full sum insured thereby, no premium is returnable in respect of that policy, and when the double insurance is effected knowingly by the assured no premium is returnable.

Mutual insurance

85   Modification of Act in case of mutual insurance

(1) Where two or more persons mutually agree to insure each other against marine losses there is said to be a mutual insurance.

(2) The provisions of this Act relating to the premium do not apply to mutual insurance, but a guarantee, or such other arrangement as may be agreed upon, may be substituted for the premium.

(3) The provisions of this Act, in so far as they may be modified by the agreement of the parties, may in the case of mutual insurance be modified by the terms of the policies issued by the association, or by the rules and regulations of the association.

(4) Subject to the expectations mentioned in this section, the provisions of this Act apply to a mutual insurance.

Supplemental

86   Ratification by assured

Where a contract of marine insurance is in good faith effected by one person on behalf of another, the person on whose behalf it is effected may ratify the contract even after he is aware of a loss.

87   Implied obligations varied by agreement or usage

(1) Where any right, duty, or liability would arise under a contract of marine insurance by implication of law, it may be negatived or varied by express agreement or by usage, if the usage be such as to bind both parties to the contract.

(2) The provisions of this section extend to any right, duty, or liability declared by this Act which may be lawfully modified by agreement.

88   Reasonable time, etc, a question of fact

Where by this Act any reference is made to reasonable time, reasonable premium, or reasonable diligence, the question what is reasonable is a question of fact.

89   Slip as evidence

Where there is a duly stamped policy, reference may be made, as heretofore, to the slip or covering note, in any legal proceeding.

90   Interpretation of terms

In this Act, unless the context or subject-matter otherwise requires,—

'Action' includes counter-claim and set off:

'Freight' includes the profit derivable by a shipowner from the employment of his ship to carry his own goods or moveables, as well as freight payable by a third party, but does not include passage money:

'Moveables' means any moveable tangible property, other than the ship, and includes money, valuable securities, and other documents.

'Policy' means a marine policy.

91   Savings

(1) Nothing in this Act, or in any repeal effected thereby, shall affect—

   (a) The provisions of the Stamp Act 1891, or any enactment for the time being in force relating to the revenue;

   (b) The provisions of the Companies Act 1862, or any enactment amending or substituted for the same;

   (c) The provisions of any statute not expressly repealed by this Act.

(2) The rules of the common law including the law merchant, save in so far as they are inconsistent with the express provisions of this Act, shall continue to apply to contracts of marine insurance.

94   Short title
This Act may be cited as the Marine Insurance Act 1906.

Section 30

SCHEDULE 1

FORM OF POLICY

Lloyd's SG Policy

BE IT KNOWN THAT ... as well in ... own name as for and in the name and names of all and every other person or persons to whom the same doth, may, or shall appertain, in part or in all doth make assurance and cause ... and them, and every of them, to be insured lost or not lost, at and from ...

Upon any kind of goods and merchandise, and also upon the body, tackle, apparel, ordnance, munition, artillery, boat, and other furniture, of and in the good ship or vessel called the ...

whereof is master under God, for this present voyage, ... or whosoever else shall go for master in the said ship, or by whatsoever other name or names the said ship, or the master thereof, is or shall be named or called; beginning the adventure upon the said goods and merchandised from the loading thereof aboard the said ship, ...

upon the said ship, etc ...

and so shall continue and endure, during her abode there, upon the said ship, etc. And further, until the said ship, with all her ordnance, tackle, apparel, etc., and goods and merchandises whatsoever shall be arrived at ...

upon the said ship, etc., until she hath moored at anchor for twenty-four hours in good safety; and upon the goods and merchandises, until the same be there discharged and safely landed. And it shall be lawful for the said ship, etc., in this voyage to proceed and sail to and touch and stay at any ports or places whatsoever ...

without prejudice to this insurance. The said ship, etc., goods and merchandises, etc., for so much as concerns the assured by agreement between the assured and assurers in this policy, are and shall be valued at ...

Touching the adventures and perils which we the assurers are contented to bear and do take upon us in this voyage: they are of the seas, men of war, fire, enemies, pirates, rovers, thieves, jettisons, letters of mart and countermart, surprisals, takings at sea, arrests, restraints, and detainments of all kings, princes, and people, of what nation, condition, or quality soever, barratry of the master and mariners, and of all other perils, losses, and misfortunes, that have or shall come to the hurt, detriment, or damage of the said goods and merchandises, and ship, etc., or any part thereof.

[*Sue and labour clause*] And in case of any loss or misfortune it shall be lawful to the assured, their factors, servants and assigns, to sue, labour, and travel for, in and about the defence, safeguards, and recovery of the said goods and merchandises, and ship, etc., or any part thereof, without prejudice to this insurance; to the charges whereof we, the assurers, will contribute each one according to the rate and quantity of his sum herein assured.

[*Waiver clause*] And it is especially declared and agreed that no acts of the insurer or insured in recovering, saving, or preserving the property insured shall be considered as a waiver, or acceptance of abandonment. And it is agreed by us, the insurers, that this writing or policy of assurance shall be of as much force and effect as the surest writing or policy of assurance heretofore made in Lombard Street, or in the Royal Exchange, or elsewhere in London. And so we, the assurers, are contented, and do hereby promise and bind ourselves, each one for his own part, our heirs, executors, and goods to the assured, their executors, administrators, and assigns, for the true performance of the premises, confessing ourselves paid the consideration due unto us for this assurance by the assured, at and after the rate of ...

IN WITNESS whereof we, the assurers, have subscribed our names and sums assured in London.

[*Memorandum*] *N.B.*—Corn, fish, salt, fruit, flour, and seed are warranted free from average, unless general, or the ship be stranded-sugar, tobacco, hemp, flax, hides and skins are warranted free from average, under five pounds per cent., and all other goods, also the ship and freight, are warranted free from average, under three pounds per cent. unless general, or the ship be stranded.

Rules for construction of policy

The following are the rules referred to by this Act for the construction of a policy in the above or other like form, where the context does not otherwise require:—

1. Where the subject-matter is insured 'lost or not lost,' and the loss has occurred before the contract is concluded, the risk attaches, unless at such time the assured was aware of the loss, and the insurer was not.

2. Where the subject-matter is insured 'from' a particular place, the risk does not attach until the ship starts on the voyage insured.

3. (a) Where a ship is insured 'at and from' a particular place, and she is at that place in good safety when the contract is concluded, the risk attaches immediately.

   (b) If she be not at that place when the contract is concluded, the risk attaches as soon as she arrives there in good safety, and, unless the policy otherwise provides, it is immaterial that she is covered by another policy for a specified time after arrival.

   (c) Where chartered freight is insured 'at and from' a particular place, and the ship is at that place in good safety when the contract is concluded the risk attaches immediately. If she be not there when the contract is concluded, the risk attaches as soon as she arrives there in good safety.

   (d) Where freight, other than chartered freight, is payable without special conditions and is insured 'at and from' a particular place, the risk attaches pro rata as the goods or merchandise are shipped; provided that if there be cargo in readiness which belongs to the shipowner, or which some other person has contracted with him to ship, the risk attaches as soon as the ship is ready to receive such cargo.

4. Where goods or other moveables are insured 'from the loading thereof,' the risk does not attach until such goods or moveables are actually on board, and the insurer is not liable for them while in transit from shore to ship.

5. Where the risk on goods or other moveables continues until they are 'safely landed,' they must be landed in the customary manner and within a reasonable time after arrival at the port of discharge, and if they are not so landed the risk ceases.

6. In the absence of any further licence or usage, the liberty to touch and stay 'at any port or place whatsoever' does not authorise the ship to depart from the course of her voyage from the port of departure to the port of destination.

7. The term 'perils of the seas' refers only to fortuitous accidents or casualties of the seas. It does not include the ordinary action of the winds and waves.

8. The term 'pirates' includes passengers who mutiny and rioters who attack the ship from the shore.

9. The term 'thieves' does not cover clandestine theft or a theft committed by anyone of the ship's company, whether crew or passengers.

10. The term 'arrests, etc., of kings, princes, and people' refers to political or executive acts, and does not include a loss caused by riot or by ordinary judicial process.

11. The term 'barratry' includes every wrongful act wilfully committed by the master or crew to the prejudice of the owner, or, as the case may be, the charterer.

12. The term 'all other perils' includes only perils similar in kind to the perils specifically mentioned in the policy.

13. The term 'average unless general' means a partial loss of the subject-matter insured other than a general average loss, and does not include 'particular charges.'

14. Where the ship has stranded, the insurer is liable for the excepted losses, although the loss is not attributable to the stranding, provided that when the stranding takes place the risk has attached and, if the policy be on goods, that the damaged goods are on board.

15. The term 'ship' includes the hull, materials and outfit, stores and provisions for the officers and crew, and, in the case of vessels engaged in a special trade, the ordinary fittings requisite for the trade, and also, in the case of a steamship, the machinery, boilers, and coals and engine stores, if owned by the assured.

16. The term 'freight' includes the profit derivable by a shipowner from the employment of his ship to carry his own goods or moveables, as well as freight payable by a third party, but does not include passage money.

17. The term 'goods' means goods in the nature of merchandise, and does not include personal effects or provisions and stores for use on board.

In the absence of any usage to the contrary, deck cargo and living animals must be insured specifically, and not under the general denomination of goods.

Marine Insurance (Gambling Policies) Act 1909

(9 Edw. 7, c. 12)

1   Prohibition of gambling on loss by maritime perils

(1) If—

(a) any person effects a contract of marine insurance without having any bonâ fide interest, direct or indirect, either in the safe arrival of the ship in relation to which the contract is made or in the safety or preservation of the subject-matter insured, or a bonâ fide expectation of acquiring such an interest; or

(b) any person in the employment of the owner of a ship, not being a part owner of the ship, effects a contract of marine insurance in relation to the ship, and the contract is made 'interest or no interest,' or 'without further proof of interest than the policy itself,' or 'without benefit of salvage to the insurer,' or subject to any other like term,

the contract shall be deemed to be a contract by way of gambling on loss by maritime perils, and the person effecting it shall be guilty of an offence, and shall be liable, on summary conviction, to imprisonment [...] for a term not exceeding six months or to a fine not exceeding [level 3 on the standard scale], and in either case to forfeit to the Crown any money he may receive under the contract.

(2) Any broker or other person through whom, and any insurer with whom, any such contract is effected shall be guilty of an offence and liable on summary conviction to the like penalties if he acted knowing that the contract was by way of gambling on loss by maritime perils within the meaning of this Act.

(3) Proceedings under this Act shall not be instituted without the consent in England of the Attorney-General, in Scotland of the Lord Advocate, and in Ireland of the [Attorney-General for Northern Ireland.]

(4) Proceedings shall not be instituted under this Act against a person (other than a person in the employment of the owner of the ship in relation to which the contract was made) alleged to have effected a contract by way of gambling on loss by maritime perils until an opportunity has been afforded him of showing that the contract was not such a contract as aforesaid, and any information given by that person for that purpose shall not be admissible in evidence against him in any prosecution under this Act.

(5) If proceedings under this Act are taken against any person (other than a person in the employment of the owner of the ship in relation to which the contract was made) for effecting such a contract, and the contract was made 'interest or no interest,' or 'without further proof of interest than the policy itself,' or 'without benefit of salvage to the insurer,' or subject to any other like term, the contract shall be deemed to be a contract by way of gambling on loss by maritime perils unless the contrary is proved.

(6) For the purpose of giving jurisdiction under this Act, every offence shall be deemed to have been committed either in the place in which the same actually was committed or in any place in which the offender may be.

(7) Any person aggrieved by an order or decision of a court of summary jurisdiction under this Act, may appeal to [the Crown Court].

(8) For the purposes of this Act the expression 'owner' includes charterer.

(9) Subsection (7) of this section shall not apply to Scotland.

2   Short title

This Act may be cited as the Marine Insurance (Gambling Policies) Act 1909, and the Marine Insurance Act 1906, and this Act may be cited together as the Marine Insurance Acts 1906 and 1909.

Law of Property Act 1925

(15 Geo. 5, c. 20)

136   Legal assignments of things in action

(1) Any absolute assignment by writing under the hand of the assignor (not purporting to be by way of charge only) of any debt or other legal thing in action, of which express notice in writing has been given to the debtor, trustee or other person from whom the assignor would have been entitled to claim such debt or thing in action, is effectual in law (subject to equities having priority over the right of the assignee) to pass and transfer from the date of such notice—

(a) the legal right to such debt or thing in action;

(b) all legal and other remedies for the same; and

(c) the power to give a good discharge for the same without the concurrence of the assignor:

Provided that, if the debtor, trustee or other person liable in respect of such debt or thing in action has notice—

(a) that the assignment is disputed by the assignor or any person claiming under him; or

(b) of any other opposing or conflicting claims to such debt or thing in action; he may, if he thinks fit, either call upon the persons making claim thereto to inter-plead concerning the same, or pay the debt or other thing in action into court under the provisions of the Trustee Act, 1925.

(2) This section does not affect the provisions of the Policies of Assurance Act, 1867.

Law Reform (Frustrated Contracts) Act 1943

(6 & 7 Geo. VI, c. 40)

1   Adjustment of rights and liabilities of parties to frustrated contracts

(1) Where a contract governed by English law has become impossible of performance or been otherwise frustrated, and the parties thereto have for that reason been discharged from the further performance of the contract, the following provisions of this section shall, subject to the provisions of section two of this Act, have effect in relation thereto.

(2) All sums paid or payable to any party in pursuance of the contract before the time when the parties were so discharged (in this Act referred to as 'the time of discharge') shall, in the case of sums so paid, be recoverable from him as money received by him for the use of the party by whom the sums were paid, and, in the case of sums so payable, cease to be so payable: Provided that, if the party to whom the sums were so paid or payable incurred expenses before the time of discharge in, or for the purpose of, the performance of the contract, the court may, if it considers it just to do so having regard

to all the circumstances of the case, allow him to retain or, as the case may be, recover the whole or any part of the sums so paid or payable, not being an amount in excess of the expenses so incurred.

(3) Where any party to the contract has, by reason of anything done by any other party thereto in, or for the purpose of, the performance of the contract, obtained a valuable benefit (other than a payment of money to which the last foregoing subsection applies) before the time of discharge there shall be recoverable from him by the said other party such sum (if any), not exceeding the value of the said benefit to the party obtaining it, as the court considers just, having regard to all the circumstances of the case and, in particular,—

   (a) the amount of any expenses incurred before the time of discharge by the benefited party in, or for the purpose of, the performance of the contract, including any sums paid or payable by him to any other party in pursuance of the contract and retained or recoverable by that party under the last foregoing subsection, and

   (b) the effect, in relation to the said benefit, of the circumstances giving rise to the frustration of the contract.

(4) In estimating, for the purposes of the foregoing provisions of this section, the amount of any expenses incurred by any party to the contract, the court may, without prejudice to the generality of the said provisions, include any sum as appears to be reasonable in respect of overhead expenses and in respect of any work or services performed personally by the said party.

(5) In considering whether any sum ought to be recovered or retained under the foregoing provisions of this section by any party to the contract, the court shall not take into account any sums which have, by reason of the circumstances giving rise to the frustration of the contract, become payable to that party under any contract of insurance unless there was an obligation to insure imposed by an express term of the frustrated contract or by or under any enactment.

(6) Where any person has assumed obligations under the contract in consideration of the conferring of a benefit by any other party to the contract upon any other person, whether a party to the contract or not, the court may, if in all the circumstances of the case it considers it just to do so, treat for the purposes of subsection (3) of this section any benefit so conferred as a benefit obtained by the person who has assumed the obligations as aforesaid.

2   Provision as to application of this Act

(1) This Act shall apply to contracts, whether made before or after the commencement of this Act, as respects which the time of discharge is on or after the first day of July, nineteen hundred and forty-three, but not to contracts as respects which the time of discharge is before the said date.

(2) This Act shall apply to contracts to which the Crown is a party in like manner as to contracts between subjects.

(3) Where any contract to which this Act applies contains any provision which, upon the true construction of the contract, is intended to have effect in the event of circumstances arising which operate, or would but for the said provision operate, to frustrate the contract, or is intended to have effect whether such circumstances arise or not, the court shall give effect to the said provision and shall only give effect to the foregoing section of this Act to such extent, if any, as appears to the court to be consistent with the said provision.

(4) Where it appears to the court that a part of any contract to which this Act applies can be properly severed from the remainder of the contract, being a part wholly performed before the time of discharge, or so performed except for the payment in respect of that part of the contract of sums which are or can be ascertained under the contract, the court shall treat that part of the contract as if it were a separate contract and had not been frustrated and shall treat the foregoing section of this Act as only applicable to the remainder of that contract.

(5) This Act shall not apply—

   (a) to any charterparty, except a time charterparty or a charterparty by way of demise, or to any contract (other than a charterparty) for the carriage of goods by sea; or

   (b) to any contract of insurance, save as is provided by subsection (5) of the foregoing section; or

(c) to any contract to which [section 7 of the Sale of Goods Act 1979] (which avoids contracts for the sale of specific goods which perish before the risk has passed to the buyer) applies, or to any other contract for the sale, or for the sale and delivery, of specific goods, where the contract is frustrated by reason of the fact that the goods have perished.

3   Short title and interpretation

(2) In this Act the expression 'court' means, in relation to any matter, the court or arbitrator by or before whom the matter falls to be determined.

Cheques Act 1957

(5 & 6 Eliz. 2, c. 36)

1   Protection of bankers paying unindorsed or irregularly indorsed cheques, etc.

(1) Where a banker in good faith and in the ordinary course of business pays a cheque drawn on him which is not indorsed or is irregularly indorsed, he does not in doing so, incur any liability by reason only of the absence of, or irregularity in indorsement, and he is deemed to have paid it in due course.

(2) Where a banker in good faith and in the ordinary course of business pays any such instrument as the following namely—

(a) a document issued by a customer of his which, though not a bill of exchange, is intended to enable a person to obtain payment from him of the sum mentioned in the document;

(b) a draft payable on demand drawn by him upon himself, whether payable at the head office or some other office of his bank; he does not, in so doing, incur any liability by reason only of the absence of, or irregularity in, indorsement, and the payment discharges the instrument.

2   Rights of bankers collecting cheques not indorsed by holders

A banker who gives value for, or has a lien on, a cheque payable to order which the holder delivers to him for collection without indorsing it, has such (if any) rights as he would have had if, upon delivery, the holder had indorsed it in blank.

3   Unindorsed cheques as evidence of payment

[(1)] An unindorsed cheque which appears to have been paid by the banker on whom it is drawn is evidence of the receipt by the payee of the sum payable by the cheque.

[(2) For the purposes of subsection (1) above, a copy of a cheque to which that subsection applies is evidence of the cheque if—

(a) the copy is made by the banker in whose possession the cheque is after presentment and,

(b) it is certified by him to be a true copy of the original.]

4   Protection of bankers collecting payment of cheques, &c.

(1) Where a banker, in good faith and without negligence—

(a) receives payment for a customer of an instrument to which this section applies; or

(b) having credited a customer's account with the amount of such an instrument, receives payment thereof for himself;

and the customer has no title, or a defective title, to the instrument, the banker does not incur any liability to the true owner of the instrument by reason only of having received payment thereof.

(2) This section applies to the following instruments, namely:—

(a) cheques [(including cheques which under section 81A(1) of the Bills of Exchange Act 1882 or otherwise are not transferable)];

(b) any document issued by a customer of a banker which, though not a bill of exchange, is intended to enable a person to obtain payment from that banker of the sum mentioned in the document;

(c) any document issued by a public officer is intended to enable a person to obtain payment from the Paymaster General or the Queen's and Lord Treasurer's Remembrancer of the sum mentioned in the document but is not a bill of exchange;

(d) any draft payable on demand drawn by a banker upon himself whether payable at the head office or some other office of his bank.

(3) A banker is not to be treated for the purposes of this section as having been negligent by reason only of his failure to concern himself with absence of, or irregularity in, indorsement of an instrument.

5   Application of certain provisions of Bills of Exchange Act, 1882, to instruments not being bills of exchange

The provisions of the Bills of Exchange Act, 1882, relating to crossed cheques shall, so far as applicable, have effect in relation to instruments (other than cheques) to which the last foregoing section applies as they have effect in relation to cheques.

6   Construction, saving and repeal

(1) This Act shall be construed as one with the Bills of Exchange Act, 1882.

(2) The foregoing provisions of this Act do not make negotiable any instrument which, apart from them, is not negotiable.

Hire-Purchase Act 1964

(1964, c. 53)

[PART III TITLE TO MOTOR VEHICLES ON HIRE-PURCHASE OR CONDITIONAL SALE]

[27   Protection of purchasers of motor vehicles

(1) This section applies where a motor vehicle has been bailed or (in Scotland) hired under a hire-purchase agreement, or has been agreed to be sold under a conditional sale agreement, and, before the property in the vehicle has become vested in the debtor, he disposes of the vehicle to another person.

(2) Where the disposition referred to in subsection (1) above is to a private purchaser, and he is a purchaser of the motor vehicle in good faith without notice of the hire-purchase or conditional sale agreement (the 'relevant agreement') that disposition shall have effect as if the creditor's title to the vehicle has been vested in the debtor immediately before that disposition.

(3) Where the person to whom the disposition referred to in subsection (1) above is made (the 'original purchaser') is a trade or finance purchaser, then if the person who is the first private purchaser of the motor vehicle after that disposition (the 'first private purchaser') is a purchaser of the vehicle in good faith without notice of the relevant agreement, the disposition of the vehicle to the first private purchaser shall have effect as if the title of the creditor to the vehicle had been vested in the debtor immediately before he disposed of it to the original purchaser.

(4) Where, in a case within subsection (3) above—

(a) the disposition by which the first private purchaser becomes a purchaser of the motor vehicle in good faith without notice of the relevant agreement is itself a bailment or hiring under a hire-purchase agreement, and

(b) the person who is the creditor in relation to that agreement disposes of the vehicle to the first private purchaser, or a person claiming under him, by transferring to him the property in the vehicle in pursuance of a provision in the agreement in that behalf, the disposition referred to in paragraph (b) above (whether or not the person to whom it is made is a purchaser in good faith without notice of the relevant agreement) shall as well as the disposition referred to in paragraph (a) above, have effect as mentioned in subsection (3) above.

(5) The preceding provisions of this section apply—

    (a) notwithstanding anything in [section 21 of the Sale of Goods Act 1979] (sale of goods by a person not the owner), but

    (b) without prejudice to the provisions of the Factors Acts (as defined by [section 61(1) of the said Act of 1979)] or any other enactment enabling the apparent owner of goods to dispose of them as if he were the true owner.

(6) Nothing in this section shall exonerate the debtor from any liability (whether criminal or civil) to which he would be subject apart from this section; and, in a case where the debtor disposes of the motor vehicle to a trade or finance purchaser, nothing in this section shall exonerate—

    (a) that trade or finance purchaser, or

    (b) any other trade or finance purchaser who becomes a purchaser of the vehicle and is not a person claiming under the first private purchaser,

from any liability (whether criminal or civil) to which he would be subject apart from this section.]

[28 Presumptions relating to dealings with motor vehicles

(1) Where in any proceedings (whether criminal or civil) relating to a motor vehicle it is proved—

    (a) that the vehicle was bailed or (in Scotland) hired under a hire-purchase agreement, or was agreed to be sold under a conditional sale agreement and

    (b) that a person (whether a party to the proceedings or not) became a private purchaser of the vehicle in good faith without notice of the hire-purchase or conditional sale agreement (the 'relevant agreement'), this section shall have effect for the purposes of the operation of section 27 of this Act in relation to those proceedings.

(2) It shall be presumed for those purposes unless the contrary is proved, that the disposition of the vehicle to the person referred to in subsection (1)(b) above (the 'relevant purchaser') was made by the debtor.

(3) If it is proved that that disposition was not made by the debtor, then it shall be presumed for those purposes, unless the contrary is proved—

    (a) that the debtor disposed of the vehicle to a private purchaser purchasing in good faith without notice of the relevant agreement, and

    (b) that the relevant purchaser is or was a person claiming under the person to whom the debtor so disposed of the vehicle.

(4) If it is proved that the disposition of the vehicle to the relevant purchaser was not made by the debtor, and that the person to whom the debtor disposed of the vehicle (the 'original purchaser') was a trade or finance purchaser, then it shall be presumed for those purposes, unless the contrary is proved,

    (a) that the person who, after the disposition of the vehicle to the original purchaser, first became a private purchaser of the vehicle was a purchaser in good faith without notice of the relevant agreement, and

    (b) that the relevant purchaser is or was a person claiming under the original purchaser.

(5) Without prejudice to any other method of proof, where in any proceedings a party thereto admits a fact, that fact shall, for the purposes of this section, be taken as against him to be proved in relation to those proceedings.]

[29 Interpretation of Part III

(1) In this Part of this Act—

'conditional sale agreement' means an agreement for the sale of goods under which the purchase price or part of it is payable by instalments, and the property in the goods is to remain in the seller (notwithstanding that the buyer is to be in possession of the goods) until such conditions as to the payment of instalments or otherwise as may be specified in the agreement are fulfilled;

'creditor' means the person by whom goods are bailed or (in Scotland) hired under a hire-purchase agreement or as the case may be, the seller under a conditional sale agreement, or the person to whom his rights and duties have passed by assignment or operation of law;

'disposition' means any sale or contract of sale (including a conditional sale agreement), any bailment or (in Scotland) hiring under a hire-purchase agreement and any transfer of the property of goods in pursuance of a provision in that behalf contained in a hire-purchase agreement, and includes any transaction purporting to be a disposition (as so defined), and 'dispose of' shall be construed accordingly:

'hire-purchase agreement' means an agreement, other than a conditional sale agreement, under which—

   (a) goods are bailed or (in Scotland) hired in return for periodical payments by the person to whom they are bailed or hired, and

   (b) the property in the goods will pass to that person if the terms of the agreement are complied with and one or more of the following occurs—

      (i)   the exercise of an option to purchase by that person,

      (ii) the doing of any other specified act by any party to the agreement,

      (iii) the happening of any other specified events; and

'motor vehicle' means a mechanically propelled vehicle intended or adapted for use on roads to which the public has access.

(2) In this Part of this Act 'trade or finance purchaser' means a purchaser who, at the time of the disposition made to him, carries on a business which consists, wholly or partly—

   (a) of purchasing motor vehicles for the purpose of offering or exposing them for sale, or

   (b) of providing finance by purchasing motor vehicles for the purpose of bailing or (in Scotland) hiring them under hire-purchase agreements or agreeing to sell them under conditional sale agreements,

and 'private purchaser' means a purchaser who, at the time of the disposition made to him, does not carry on any such business.

(3) For the purposes of this Part of this Act a person becomes a purchaser of a motor vehicle if, and at the time when, a disposition of the vehicle is made to him; and a person shall be taken to be a purchaser of a motor vehicle without notice of a hire-purchase agreement or conditional sale agreement if, at the time of the disposition made to him, he has no actual notice that the vehicle is or was the subject of any such agreement.

(4) In this Part of this Act the 'debtor' in relation to a motor vehicle which has been bailed or hired under a hire-purchase agreement, or, as the case may be, agreed to be sold under a conditional sale agreement, means the person who at the material time (whether the agreement has before that time been terminated or not) either—

   (a) is the person to whom the vehicle is bailed or hired under that agreement, or

   (b) is, in relation to the agreement, the buyer, including a person who at that time is, by virtue of section 130(4) of the Consumer Credit Act 1974 treated as a bailee or (in Scotland) a custodier of the vehicle.

(5) In this Part of this Act any reference to the title of the creditor to a motor vehicle which has been bailed or (in Scotland) hired under a hire-purchase agreement or agreed to be sold under a conditional sale agreement, and is disposed of by the debtor, is a reference to such title (if any) to the vehicle as, immediately before that disposition, was vested in the person who then was the creditor in relation to the agreement.]

Misrepresentation Act 1967

(1967, c. 7)

1   Removal of certain bars to rescission for innocent misrepresentation

Where a person has entered into a contract after a misrepresentation has been made to him, and—

    (a) the misrepresentation has become a term of the contract, or

    (b) the contract has been performed;

or both, then, if otherwise he would be entitled to rescind the contract without alleging fraud, he shall be so entitled, subject to the provisions of this Act, notwithstanding the matters mentioned in paragraphs (a) and (b) of this section.

2   Damages for misrepresentation

(1)   Where a person has entered into a contract after a misrepresentation has been made to him by another party thereto and as a result thereof he has suffered loss, then, if the person making the misrepresentation would be liable to damages in respect thereof had the misrepresentation been made fraudulently, that person shall be so liable notwithstanding that the misrepresentation was not made fraudulently, unless he proves that he had reasonable ground to believe and did believe up to the time the contract was made that the facts represented were true.

(2)   Where a person has entered into a contract after a misrepresentation has been made to him otherwise than fraudulently, and he would be entitled, by reason of the misrepresentation, to rescind the contract, then, if it is claimed, in any proceedings arising out of the contract, that the contract ought to be or has been rescinded, the court or arbitrator may declare the contract subsisting and award damages in lieu of rescission, if of opinion that it would be equitable to do so having regard to the nature of the misrepresentation and the loss that would be caused by it if the contract were upheld, as well as to the loss that rescission would cause to the other party.

(3)   Damages may be awarded against a person under subsection (2) of this section whether or not he is liable to damages under subsection (1) thereof, but where he is so liable any award under the said subsection (2) shall be taken into account in assessing his liability under the said subsection (1).

[(4)   This section does not entitle a person to be paid damages in respect of a misrepresentation if the person has a right to redress under Part 4A of the Consumer Protection from Unfair Trading Regulations 2008 (SI 2008/1277) in respect of the conduct constituting the misrepresentation.

(5)   Subsection (4) does not prevent a debtor from bringing a claim under section 75(1) of the Consumer Credit Act 1974 against a creditor under a debtor-creditor-supplier agreement in a case where, but for subsection (4), the debtor would have a claim against the supplier in respect of a misrepresentation (and, where section 75 of that Act would otherwise apply, it accordingly applies as if the debtor had a claim against the supplier).]

[3   Avoidance of provision excluding liability for misrepresentation

(1)   If a contract contains a term which would exclude or restrict—

    (a) any liability to which a party to a contract may be subject by reason of any misrepresentation made by him before the contract was made; or

    (b) any remedy available to another party to the contract by reason of such a misrepresentation,

that term shall be of no effect except in so far as it satisfies the requirement of reasonableness as stated in section 11(1) of the Unfair Contract Terms Act 1977; and it is for those claiming that the term satisfies that requirement to show that it does.

(2)   This section does not apply to a term in a consumer contract within the meaning of Part 2 of the Consumer Rights Act 2015 (but see the provision made about such contracts in section 62 of that Act).]

Trade Descriptions Act 1968

(1968, c. 29)

Prohibition of false trade descriptions

1 Prohibition of false trade descriptions

[(2) Sections 2 to 4 shall have effect for the interpretation of expressions used in this Act.]

2 Trade description

(1) A trade description is an indication, direct or indirect, and by whatever means given, of any of the following matters with respect to any goods or parts of goods, that is to say—

(a) quantity, size or gauge;

(b) method of manufacture, production, processing or reconditioning;

(c) composition;

(d) fitness for purpose, strength, performance, behaviour or accuracy;

(e) any physical characteristics not included in the preceding paragraphs;

(f) testing by any person and results thereof;

(g) approval by any person or conformity with a type approved by any person;

(h) place or date of manufacture, production, processing or reconditioning;

(i) person by whom manufactured, produced, processed or reconditioned;

(j) other history, including previous ownership or use.

(2) The matters specified in subsection (1) of this section shall be taken—

(a) in relation to any animal, to include sex, breed or cross, fertility and soundness;

(b) in relation to any semen, to include the identity and characteristics of the animal from which it was taken and measure of dilution.

(3) In this section 'quantity' includes length, width, height, area, volume, capacity, weight and number.

(4) Notwithstanding anything in the preceding provisions of this section, the following shall be deemed not to be trade descriptions, that is to say, any description or mark applied in pursuance of—

(a) [...]

(b) section 2 of the Agricultural Produce (Grading and Marking) Act 1928 (as amended by the Agricultural Produce (Grading and Marking) Amendment Act 1931) or any corresponding enactment of the Parliament of Northern Ireland;

(c) the Plant Varieties and Seeds Act 1964;

(d) the Agriculture and Horticulture Act 1964 or any Community grading rules within the meaning of Part III of that Act;

(e) the Seeds Act (Northern Ireland) 1965;

(f) the Horticulture Act (Northern Ireland) 1966;

[(g) the Consumer Protection Act 1987];

[(h) the Plant Varieties Act 1997];

[any statement made in respect of, or mark applied to, any material in pursuance of Part IV of the Agriculture Act 1970, any name or expression to which a meaning has been assigned under section 70 of that Act when applied to any material in the circumstances specified in that section] [...] any mark prescribed by a system of classification compiled under section 5 of the Agriculture Act 1967 [and any designation, mark or description applied in pursuance of a scheme brought into force under section 6(1) or an order made under section 25(1) of the Agriculture Act 1970.]

(5) Notwithstanding anything in the preceding provisions of this section,

[(a)] where provision is made under [the Food Safety Act 1990] or the [Food Safety (Northern Ireland) Order 1991 or the Consumer Protection Act 1987] prohibiting the application of a description except to goods in the case of which the requirements specified in that provision are complied with, that description, when applied to such goods, shall be deemed not to be a trade description.

[(b) where by virtue of any provision made under Part V of the Medicines Act 1968 (or made under any provisions of the said Part V as applied by an order made under section 104 or section 105 of that Act) anything which in accordance with this Act, constitutes the application of a trade description to goods is subject to any requirements or restrictions imposed by that provision, any particular description specified in that provision, when applied to goods in circumstances to which those requirements or restrictions are applicable, shall be deemed not to be a trade description.]

3　False trade description

(1) A false trade description is a trade description which is false to a material degree.

(2) A trade description which, though not false, is misleading, that is to say, likely to be taken for such an indication of any of the matters specified in section 2 of this Act as would be false to a material degree, shall be deemed to be a false trade description.

(3) Anything which, though not a trade description, is likely to be taken for an indication of any of those matters and, as such an indication, would be false to a material degree, shall be deemed to be a false trade description.

(4) A false indication, or anything likely to be taken as an indication which would be false, that any goods comply with a standard specified or recognised by any person or implied by the approval of any person shall be deemed to be a false trade description, if there is no such person or no standard so specified, recognised or implied.

4　Applying a trade description to goods

(1) A person applies a trade description to goods if he—

(a) affixes or annexes it to or in any manner marks it on or incorporates it with—
  (i)　the goods themselves, or
  (ii)　anything in, on or with which the goods are supplied; or

(b) places the goods in, on or with anything which the trade description has been affixed or annexed to, marked on or incorporated with, or places any such thing with the goods; or

(c) uses the trade description in any manner likely to be taken as referring to the goods.

(2) An oral statement may amount to the use of a trade description.

(3) Where goods are supplied in pursuance of a request in which a trade description is used and the circumstances are such as to make it reasonable to infer that the goods are supplied as goods corresponding to that trade description, the person supplying the goods shall be deemed to have applied the trade description to the goods.

Misstatements other than false trade descriptions

12　False representations as to royal approval or award, etc.

(1) If any person in the course of any trade or business, gives, by whatever means, any false indication, direct or indirect, that any goods or services supplied by him or any methods adopted by him are or are of a kind supplied to or approved by Her Majesty or any member of the Royal Family, he shall, subject to the provisions of this Act be guilty of an offence.

(2) If any person, in the course of any trade or business, uses, without the authority of Her Majesty, any device or emblem signifying the Queen's Award to Industry or anything so nearly resembling such a device or emblem as to be likely to deceive, he shall, subject to the provisions of this Act, be guilty of an offence.

[(3) A person shall not be guilty of an offence under subsection (1) or (2) by reason of doing anything that is a commercial practice unless the commercial practice is unfair.

In this subsection 'commercial practice' and 'unfair' have the same meaning as in the Consumer Protection from Unfair Trading Regulations 2008.]

Prohibition of importation of certain goods

16   Prohibition of importation of goods bearing false indication of origin

Where a false trade description is applied to any goods outside the United Kingdom and the false indication, or one of the false indications, given, or likely to be taken as given, thereby is an indication of the place of manufacture, production, processing or reconditioning of the goods or any part thereof, the goods shall not be imported into the United Kingdom.

Provisions as to offences

18   Penalty for offences

A person guilty of an offence under this Act for which no other penalty is specified shall be liable—

  (a) on summary conviction, to a fine not exceeding [the prescribed sum]; and

  (b) on conviction on indictment, to a fine or imprisonment for a term not exceeding two years or both.

19   Time limit for prosecutions

  (1) No prosecution for an offence under this Act shall be commenced after the expiration of three years from the commission of the offence or one year from its discovery by the prosecutor, whichever is the earlier.

  (2) Not withstanding anything in [section 127(1) of the Magistrates' Courts Act 1980], a magistrates' court may try an information for an offence under this Act if the information was laid at any time within twelve months from the commission of the offence.

  (3) Notwithstanding anything in section 23 of the Summary jurisdiction (Scotland) Act 1954 (limitation of time for proceedings in statutory offences) summary proceedings in Scotland for an offence under this section may be commenced at any time within twelve months from the time when the offence was committed, and subsection (2) of the said section 23 shall apply for the purposes of this subsection as it applies for the purposes of that section.

  (4) Subsections (2) and (3) of this section do not apply where—

  (a) the offence was committed by the making of an oral statement; or [...]

20   Offences by corporations

  (1) Where an offence under this Act which has been committed by a body corporate is proved to have been committed with the consent and connivance of, or to be attributable to any neglect on the part of, any director, manager, secretary or other similar officer of the body corporate, or any person who was purporting to act in any such capacity, he as well as the body corporate shall be liable to be proceeded against and punished accordingly.

  (2) In this section 'director', in relation to any body corporate established by or under any enactment for the purpose of carrying on under national ownership any industry or part of an industry or undertaking, being a body corporate whose affairs are managed by the members thereof, means a member of that body corporate.

21   Accessories to offences committed abroad

  (3) Any person who, in the United Kingdom, assists in or induces the commission outside the United Kingdom of an act which if committed in the United Kingdom, would be an offence under section 12 of this Act shall be guilty of an offence.

23   Offences due to fault of other person

Where the commission by any person of an offence under this Act is due to the act or default of some other person that other person shall be guilty of the offence, and a person may be charged with and convicted of the offence by virtue of this section whether or not proceedings are taken against the first-mentioned person.

Defences

24 Defence of mistake, accident, etc.

(1) In any proceedings for an offence under this Act it shall, subject to subsection (2) of this section, be a defence for the person charged to prove—

(a) that the commission of the offence was due to a mistake or to reliance on information supplied to him or to the act or default of another person, an accident or some other cause beyond his control; and

(b) that he took all reasonable precautions and exercised all due diligence to avoid the commission of such an offence by himself or any person under his control.

(2) If in any case the defence provided by the last foregoing subsection involves the allegation that the commission of the offence was due to the act or default of another person or to reliance on information supplied by another person, the person charged shall not, without leave of the court, be entitled to rely on that defence unless, within a period ending seven clear days before the hearing, he has served on the prosecutor a notice in writing giving such information identifying or assisting in the identification of that other person as was then in his possession.

25 Innocent publication of advertisement

In proceedings for an offence under this Act committed by the publication of an advertisement it shall be a defence for the person charged to prove that he is a person whose business it is to publish or arrange for the publication of advertisements and that he received the advertisement for publication in the ordinary course of business and did not know and had no reason to suspect that its publication would amount to an offence under this Act.

Enforcement

26 Enforcing authorities

(1) It shall be the duty of every local weights and measures authority [as defined in section 69(3) of the Weights and Measures Act 1985] to enforce within their area the provisions of this Act and of any order made under this Act [...]

[(1A) For the investigatory powers available to a local weights and measures authority for the purposes of the duty in subsection (1), see Schedule 5 to the Consumer Rights Act 2015.]

(2) Every local weights and measures authority shall, whenever the Board of Trade so direct, make to the Board a report on the exercise of their functions under this Act in such form and containing such particulars as the Board may direct.

(5) Nothing in this section shall be taken as authorising a local weights and measures authority in Scotland to institute proceedings for an offence.

31 Evidence by certificate

(1) The Board of Trade may by regulations provide that certificates issued by such persons as may be specified by the regulations in relation to such matters as may be so specified shall, subject to the provisions of this section be received in evidence of those matters in any proceedings under this Act.

(2) Such a certificate shall not be received in evidence—

(a) unless the party against whom it is to be given in evidence has been served with a copy thereof not less than seven days before the hearing; or

(b) if that party has, not less than three days before the hearing, served on the other party a notice requiring the attendance of the person issuing the certificate.

(3) In any proceedings under this Act in Scotland, a certificate received in evidence by virtue of this section or, where the attendance of a person issuing a certificate is required under subsection (2)(b) of this section, the evidence of that person, shall be sufficient evidence of the matters stated in the certificate.

(4) For the purposes of this section any document purporting to be such a certificate as is mentioned in this section shall be deemed to be such a certificate unless the contrary is shown.

(5) Regulations under this section shall be made by statutory instrument which shall be subject to annulment in pursuance of a resolution of either House of Parliament.

Miscellaneous and supplemental

34   Trade marks containing trade descriptions

The fact that a trade description is a trade mark, or part of a trade mark, [...] does not prevent it from being a false trade description when applied to any goods, except where the following conditions are satisfied, that is to say—

(a) that it could have been lawfully applied to the goods if this Act had not been passed; and

(b) that on the day this Act is passed the trade mark either is registered under the Trade Marks Act 1938 or is in use to indicate a connection in the course of trade between such goods and the proprietor of the trade mark; and

(c) that the trade mark as applied is used to indicate such a connection between the goods and the proprietor of the trade mark or [, in the case of a registered trade mark, a person licensed to use it]; and

(d) that the person who is the proprietor of the trade mark is the same person as, or a successor in title of, the proprietor on the day this Act is passed.

35   Saving for civil rights

A contract for the supply of any goods shall not be void or unenforceable by reason only of a contravention of any provision of this Act.

36   Country of origin

(1) For the purposes of this Act goods shall be deemed to have been manufactured or produced in the country in which they last underwent a treatment or process resulting in a substantial change.

(2) The Board of Trade may by order specify—

(a) in relation to any description of goods, what treatment or process is to be regarded for the purposes of this section as resulting or not resulting in a substantial change;

(b) in relation to any description of goods different parts of which were manufactured or produced in different countries, or of goods assembled in a country different from that in which their parts were manufactured or produced, in which of those countries the goods are to be regarded for the purposes of this Act as having been manufactured or produced.

38   Orders

(1) Any power to make an order under the preceding provisions of this Act shall be exercisable by statutory instrument, which shall be subject to annulment in pursuance of a resolution of either House of Parliament, and includes power to vary or revoke such an order by a subsequent order.

(2) Any order under the preceding provisions of this Act which relates to [...] fertilisers or any goods used as pesticides or for similar purposes shall be made by the Board of Trade acting jointly with the following Ministers, that is to say, if the order extends to England and Wales, the Minister of Agriculture, Fisheries and Food, and if it extends to Scotland or Northern Ireland, the Secretary of State concerned.

(3) The following provisions shall apply to the making of an order under [section 36 of this Act], except in the case mentioned in section 10(2) thereof, that is to say—

(a) before making the order the Board of Trade shall consult with such organisations as appear to them to be representative of interests substantially affected by it and shall publish, in such manner as the Board think appropriate, notice of their intention to make the order and of the place where copies of the proposed order may be obtained; and

(b) the order shall not be made until the expiration of a period of twenty-eight days from the publication of the notice and may then be made with such modifications (if any) as the Board of Trade think appropriate having regard to any representations received by them.

39 Interpretation

(1) The following provisions shall have effect in addition to sections [2 to 4] of this Act, for the interpretation in this Act of expressions used therein, that is to say,—

'advertisement' includes a catalogue, a circular and a price list;

'goods' includes ships and aircraft, things attached to land and growing crops;

'premises' includes any place and any stall, vehicle, ship or aircraft; and

'ship' includes any boat and any other description of vessel used in navigation.

Carriage of Goods by Sea Act 1971

(1971, c. 19)

1 Application of Hague Rules as amended

(1) In this Act, 'the Rules' means the International Convention for the unification of certain rules of law relating to bills of lading signed at Brussels on 25th August 1924, as amended by the Protocol signed at Brussels on 23rd February 1968 [and by the protocol signed at Brussels on 21 December 1979].

(2) The provisions of the Rules, as set out in the Schedule to this Act, shall have the force of law.

(3) Without prejudice to subsection (2) above, the said provisions shall have effect (and have the force of law) in relation to and in connection with the carriage of goods by sea in ships where the port of shipment is a port in the United Kingdom, whether or not the carriage is between ports in two different States within the meaning of Article X of the Rules.

(4) Subject to subsection (6) below, nothing in this section shall be taken as applying anything in the Rules to any contract for the carriage of goods by sea, unless the contract expressly or by implication provides for the issue of a bill of lading or any similar document of title.

(5) [...]

(6) Without prejudice to Article X (c) of the Rules, the Rules shall have the force of law in relation to—

(a) any bill of lading if the contract contained in or evidenced by it expressly provides that the Rules shall govern the contract, and

(b) any receipt which is a non-negotiable document marked as such if the contract contained in or evidenced by it is a contract for the carriage of goods by sea which expressly provides that the Rules are to govern the contract as if the receipt were a bill of lading,

but subject, where paragraph (b) applies, to any necessary modifications and in particular with the omission in Article III of the Rules of the second sentence of paragraph 4 and of paragraph 7.

(7) If and so far as the contract contained in or evidenced by a bill of lading or receipt within paragraph (a) or (b) of subsection (6) above applies to deck cargo or live animals, the Rules as given the force of law by that subsection shall have effect as if Article I(c) did not exclude deck cargo and live animals.

In this subsection 'deck cargo' means cargo which by the contract of carriage is stated as being carried on deck and is so carried.

[1A Conversion of special drawing rights into sterling

(1) For the purposes of Article IV of the Rules the value on a particular day of one special drawing right shall be treated as equal to such a sum in sterling as the International Monetary Fund have fixed as being the equivalent of one special drawing right—

(a) for that day; or

(b) if no sum has been so fixed for that day, for the last day before that day for which a sum has been so fixed.

(2) A certificate given by or on behalf of the Treasury stating—

    (a) that a particular sum in sterling has been fixed as aforesaid for a particular day; or

    (b) that no sum has been so fixed for a particular day and that a particular sum in sterling has been so fixed for a day which is the last day for which a sum has been so fixed before the particular day,

shall be conclusive evidence of those matters for the purposes of subsection (1) above; and a document purporting to be such a certificate shall in any proceedings be received in evidence and, unless the contrary is proved, be deemed to be such a certificate.

(3) The Treasury may charge a reasonable fee for any certificate given in pursuance of subsection (2) above, and any fee received by the Treasury by virtue of this subsection shall be paid into the Consolidated Fund.]

2   Contracting States, etc.

(1) If Her Majesty by Order in Council certifies to the following effect, that is to say, that for the purposes of the Rules—

    (a) a State specified in the Order is a contracting State, or is a contracting State in respect of any place or territory so specified; or

    (b) any place or territory specified in the Order forms part of a State so specified (whether a contracting State or not),

the Order shall, except so far as it has been superseded by a subsequent Order, be conclusive evidence of the matters so certified.

(2) An Order in Council under this section may be varied or revoked by a subsequent Order in Council.

3   Absolute warranty of seaworthiness not to be implied in contracts to which Rules apply

There shall not be implied in any contract for the carriage of goods by sea to which the Rules apply by virtue of this Act any absolute undertaking by the carrier of the goods to provide a seaworthy ship.

4   Application of Act to British possessions, etc.

(1) Her Majesty may by Order in Council direct that this Act shall extend, subject to such exceptions, adaptations and modifications as may be specified in the Order, to all or any of the following territories, that is—

    (a) any colony (not being a colony for whose external relations a country other than the United Kingdom is responsible),

    (b) any country outside Her Majesty's dominions in which Her Majesty has jurisdiction in right of Her Majesty's Government of the United Kingdom.

(2) An Order in Council under this section may contain such transitional and other consequential and incidental provisions as appear to Her Majesty to be expedient, including provisions amending or repealing any legislation about the carriage of goods by sea forming part of the law of any of the territories mentioned in paragraphs (a) and (b) above.

(3) An Order in Council under this section may be varied or revoked by a subsequent Order in Council.

5   Extension of application of Rules to carriage from ports in British possessions, etc.

(1) Her Majesty may by Order in Council provide that section 1(3) of this Act shall have effect as if the reference therein to the United Kingdom included a reference to all or any of the following territories, that is—

    (a) the Isle of Man;

    (b) any of the Channel Islands specified in the Order;

(c) any colony specified in the Order (not being a colony for whose external relations a country other than the United Kingdom is responsible);

[...]

(e) any country specified in the Order, being a country outside Her Majesty's dominions in which Her Majesty has jurisdiction in right of Her Majesty's Government of the United Kingdom.

(2) An Order in Council under this section may be varied or revoked by a subsequent Order in Council.

6 Supplemental

(1) This Act may be cited as the Carriage of Goods by Sea Act 1971.

(2) It is hereby declared that this Act extends to Northern Ireland.

(3) The following enactments shall be repealed, that is—

(a) the Carriage of Goods by Sea Act 1924,

(b) section 12(4)(a) of the Nuclear Installations Act 1965, and without prejudice to section [17(2)(a) of the Interpretation Act 1978], the reference to the said Act of 1924 in section 1(1)(i)(ii) of the Hovercraft Act 1968 shall include a reference to this Act.

[(4) It is hereby declared that for the purposes of Article VIII of the Rules [section 186 of the Merchant Shipping Act 1985 (which] entirely exempts shipowners and others in certain circumstances from liability for loss of, or damage to, goods) is a provision relating to limitation of liability.]

(5) This Act shall come into force on such day as Her Majesty may by Order in Council appoint, and, for the purposes of the transition from the law in force immediately before the day appointed under this subsection to the provisions of this Act, the Order appointing the day may provide that those provisions shall have effect subject to such transitional provisions as may be contained in the Order.

SCHEDULE

THE HAGUE RULES AS AMENDED BY THE BRUSSELS PROTOCOL 1968

Article I

In these Rules the following words are employed, with the meanings set out below:—

(a) 'Carrier' includes the owner or the charterer who enters into a contract of carriage with a shipper.

(b) 'Contract of carriage' applies only to contracts of carriage covered by a bill of lading or any similar document of title, in so far as such document relates to the carriage of goods by sea, including any bill of lading or any similar document as aforesaid issued under or pursuant to a charter party from the moment at which such bill of lading or similar document of title regulates the relations between a carrier and a holder of the same.

(c) 'Goods' includes goods, wares, merchandise, and articles of every kind whatsoever except live animals and cargo which by the contract of carriage is stated as being carried on deck and is so carried.

(d) 'Ship' means any vessel used for the carriage of goods by sea.

(e) 'Carriage of goods' covers the period from the time when the goods are loaded on to the time they are discharged from the ship.

Article II

Subject to the provisions of Article VI, under every contract of carriage of goods by sea the carrier, in relation to the loading, handling, stowage, carriage, custody, care and discharge of such goods, shall be subject to the responsibilities and liabilities, and entitled to the rights and immunities hereinafter set forth.

Article III

(1) The carrier shall be bound before and at the beginning of the voyage to exercise due diligence to—

(a) Make the ship seaworthy.

(b) Properly man, equip and supply the ship.

(c) Make the holds, refrigerating and cool chambers, and all other parts of the ship in which goods are carried, fit and safe for their reception, carriage and preservation.

(2) Subject to the provisions of Article IV, the carrier shall properly and carefully load, handle, stow, carry, keep, care for, and discharge the goods carried.

(3) After receiving the goods into his charge the carrier or the master or agent of the carrier shall, on demand of the shipper, issue to the shipper a bill of lading showing among other things—

(a) The leading marks necessary for identification of the goods as the same are furnished in writing by the shipper before the loading of such goods starts, provided such marks are stamped or otherwise shown clearly upon the goods if uncovered, or on the cases or coverings in which such goods are contained, in such a manner as should ordinarily remain legible until the end of the voyage.

(b) Either the number of packages or pieces, or the quantity, or weight, as the case may be, as furnished in writing by the shipper.

(c) The apparent order and condition of the goods. Provided that no carrier, master or agent of the carrier shall be bound to state or show in the bill of lading any marks, number, quantity, or weight which he has reasonable ground for suspecting not accurately to represent the goods actually received, or which he has had no reasonable means of checking.

(4) Such a bill of lading shall be prima facie evidence of the receipt by the carrier of the goods as therein described in accordance with paragraph 3(a), (b) and (c). However, proof to the contrary shall not be admissible when the bill of lading has been transferred to a third party acting in good faith.

(5) The shipper shall be deemed to have guaranteed to the carrier the accuracy at the time of shipment of the marks, number, quantity and weight, as furnished by him, and the shipper shall indemnify the carrier against all loss, damages and expenses arising or resulting from inaccuracies in such particulars. The right of the carrier to such indemnity shall in no way limit his responsibility and liability under the contract of carriage to any person other than the shipper.

(6) Unless notice of loss or damage and the general nature of such loss or damage be given in writing to the carrier or his agent at the port of discharge before or at the time of the removal of the goods into the custody of the person entitled to delivery thereof under the contract of carriage, or, if the loss or damage be not apparent, within three days, such removal shall be prima facie evidence of the delivery by the carrier of the goods as described in the bill of lading.

The notice in writing need not be given if the state of the goods has, at the time of their receipt, been the subject of joint survey or inspection.

Subject to paragraph 6*bis* the carrier and the ship shall in any event be discharged from all liability whatsoever in respect of the goods, unless suit is brought within one year of their delivery or of the date when they should have been delivered. This period may, however, be extended if the parties so agree after the cause of action has arisen.

In the case of any actual or apprehended loss or damage the carrier and the receiver shall give all reasonable facilities to each other for inspecting and tallying the goods.

(6bis) An action for indemnity against a third person may be brought even after the expiration of the year provided for in the preceding paragraph if brought within the time allowed by the law of the Court seized of the case. However, the time allowed shall be not less than three months, commencing from the day when the person bringing such action for indemnity has settled the claim or has been served with process in the action against himself.

(7) After the goods are loaded the bill of lading to be issued by the carrier, master, or agent of the carrier, to the shipper shall, if the shipper so demands, be a 'shipped' bill of lading, provided that if the shipper shall have previously taken up any document of title to such goods, he shall surrender the same as against the issue of the 'shipped' bill of lading, but at the option of the carrier such document of title may be noted at the port of shipment by the carrier, master, or agent with the name or names of the ship or ships upon which the goods have been shipped and the date or dates of shipment, and when so noted if it shows the particulars mentioned in paragraph 3 of Article III, shall for the purpose of this article be deemed to constitute a 'shipped' bill of lading.

(8) Any clause, covenant, or agreement in a contract of carriage relieving the carrier or the ship from liability for loss or damage to, or in connection with, goods arising from negligence, fault, or failure in the duties and obligations provided in this article or lessening such liability otherwise than as provided in these Rules, shall be null and void and of no effect. A benefit of insurance in favour of the carrier or similar clause shall be deemed to be a clause relieving the carrier from liability.

Article IV

(1) Neither the carrier nor the ship shall be liable for loss or damage arising or resulting from unseaworthiness unless caused by want of due diligence on the part of the carrier to make the ship seaworthy, and to secure that the ship is properly manned, equipped and supplied, and to make the holds, refrigerating and cool chambers and all other parts of the ship in which goods are carried fit and safe for their reception, carriage and preservation in accordance with the provisions of paragraph 1 of Article III. Whenever loss or damage has resulted from unseaworthiness the burden of proving the exercise of due diligence shall be on the carrier or other person claiming exemption under this article.

(2) Neither the carrier nor the ship shall be responsible for loss or damage arising or resulting from—

- (a) Act, neglect, or default of the master, mariner, pilot, or the servants of the carrier in the navigation or in the management of the ship.
- (b) Fire, unless caused by the actual fault or privity of the carrier.
- (c) Perils, dangers and accidents of the sea or other navigable waters.
- (d) Act of God.
- (e) Act of war.
- (f) Act of public enemies.
- (g) Arrest or restraint of princes, rulers or people, or seizure under legal process.
- (h) Quarantine restrictions.
- (i) Act or omission of the shipper or owner of the goods, his agent or representative.
- (j) Strikes or lockouts or stoppage or restraint of labour from whatever cause, whether partial or general.
- (k) Riots and civil commotions.
- (l) Saving or attempting to save life or property at sea.
- (m) Wastage in bulk or weight or any other loss or damage arising from inherent defect, quality or vice of the goods.
- (n) Insufficiency of packing.
- (o) Insufficiency or inadequacy of marks.
- (p) Latent defects not discoverable by due diligence.
- (q) Any other cause arising without the actual fault or privity of the carrier, or without the fault or neglect of the agents or servants of the carrier, but the burden of proof shall be on the person claiming the benefit of this exception to show that neither the actual fault or privity of the carrier nor the fault or neglect of the agents or servants of the carrier contributed to the loss or damage.

(3) The shipper shall not be responsible for the loss or damage sustained by the carrier or the ship arising or resulting from any cause without the act, fault or neglect of the shipper, his agents or his servants.

(4) Any deviation in saving or attempting to save life or property at sea or any reasonable deviation shall not be deemed to be an infringement or breach of these Rules or of the contract of carriage,
and the carrier shall not be liable for any loss or damage resulting therefrom.

(5) (a) Unless the nature and value of such goods have been declared by the shipper before
shipment and inserted in the bill of lading, neither the carrier nor the ship shall in any
event be or become liable for any loss or damage to or in connection with the goods
in an amount exceeding [666.67 units of account] per package or unit or [2 units of
account per kilogramme] of gross weight of the goods lost or damaged, whichever is
the higher.

(b) The total amount recoverable shall be calculated by reference to the value of such
goods at the place and time at which the goods are discharged from the ship in accordance with the contract or should have been so discharged.

  The value of the goods shall be fixed according to the commodity exchange price,
or, if there be no such price, according to the current market price, or, if there be no
commodity exchange price or current market price, by reference to the normal value
of goods of the same kind and quality.

(c) Where a container, pallet or similar article of transport is used to consolidate goods, the
number of packages or units enumerated in the bill of lading as packed in such article of
transport shall be deemed the number of packages or units for the purpose of this paragraph as far as these packages or units are concerned. Except as aforesaid such article
of transport shall be considered the package or unit.

[(d) The unit of account mentioned in this Article is the special drawing right as defined
by the International Monetary Fund. The amounts mentioned in sub-paragraph (a) of
this paragraph shall be converted into national currency on the basis of the value of
that currency on a date to be determined by the law of the court seised of the case.]

(e) Neither the carrier nor the ship shall be entitled to the benefit of the limitation of liability provided for in this paragraph if it is proved that the damage resulted from an act or
omission of the carrier done with intent to cause damage, or recklessly and with knowledge that damage would probably result.

(f) The declaration mentioned in sub-paragraph (a) of this paragraph, if embodied in the
bill of lading, shall be prima facie evidence, but shall not be binding or conclusive on the
carrier.

(g) By agreement between the carrier, master or agent of the carrier and the shipper other
maximum amounts than those mentioned in sub-paragraph (a) of this paragraph may
be fixed, provided that no maximum amount so fixed shall be less than the appropriate
maximum mentioned in that sub-paragraph.

(h) Neither the carrier nor the ship shall be responsible in any event for loss or damage to,
or in connection with, goods if the nature or value thereof has been knowingly mis-
stated by the shipper in the bill of lading.

(6) Goods of an inflammable, explosive or dangerous nature to the shipment whereof the carrier,
master or agent of the carrier has not consented with knowledge of their nature and character, may
at any time before discharge be landed at any place, or destroyed or rendered innocuous by the carrier without compensation and the shipper of such goods shall be liable for all damages and expenses
directly or indirectly arising out of or resulting from such shipment. If any such goods shipped with
such knowledge and consent shall become a danger to the ship or cargo, they may in like manner be
landed at any place, or destroyed or rendered innocuous by the carrier without liability on the part of
the carrier except to general average, if any.

Article IV bis

(1) The defences and limits of liability provided for in these Rules shall apply in any action
against the carrier in respect of loss or damage to goods covered by a contract of carriage whether
the action be founded in contract or in tort.

(2) If such an action is brought against a servant or agent of the carrier (such servant or agent not being an independent contractor), such servant or agent shall be entitled to avail himself of the defences and limits of liability which the carrier is entitled to invoke under these Rules.

(3) The aggregate of the amounts recoverable from the carrier, and such servants and agents, shall in no case exceed the limit provided for in these Rules.

(4) Nevertheless, a servant or agent of the carrier shall not be entitled to avail himself of the provisions of this article, if it is proved that the damage resulted from an act or omission of the servant or agent done with intent to cause damage or recklessly and with knowledge that damage would probably result.

Article V

A carrier shall be at liberty to surrender in whole or in part all or any of his rights and immunities or to increase any of his responsibilities and obligations under these Rules, provided such surrender or increase shall be embodied in the bill of lading issued to the shipper. The provisions of the Rules shall not be applicable to charter parties, but if bills of lading are issued in the case of a ship under a charter party they shall comply with the terms of these Rules. Nothing in these Rules shall be held to prevent the insertion in a bill of lading of any lawful provisions regarding general average.

Article VI

Notwithstanding the provisions of the preceding articles, a carrier, master or agent of the carrier and a shipper shall in regard to any particular goods be at liberty to enter into any agreement in any terms as to the responsibility and liability of the carrier for such goods, and as to the rights and immunities of the carrier in respect of such goods, or his obligation as to seaworthiness, so far as this stipulation is not contrary to public policy, or the care or diligence of his servants or agents in regard to the loading, handling, stowage, carriage, custody, care and discharge of the goods carried by sea, provided that in this case no bill of lading has been or shall be issued and that the terms agreed shall be embodied in a receipt which shall be a non-negotiable document and shall be marked as such.

Any agreement so entered into shall have full legal effect.

Provided that this article shall not apply to ordinary commercial shipment made in the ordinary course of trade, but only to other shipments where the character or condition of the property to be carried or the circumstances, terms and conditions under which the carriage is to be performed are such as reasonably to justify a special agreement.

Article VII

Nothing herein contained shall prevent a carrier or a shipper from entering into any agreement, stipulation, condition, reservation or exemption as to the responsibility and liability of the carrier or the ship for the loss or damage to, or in connection with, the custody and care and handling of goods prior to the loading on, and subsequent to the discharge from, the ship on which the goods are carried by sea.

Article VIII

The provisions of these Rules shall not affect the rights and obligations of the carrier under any statute for the time being in force relating to the limitation of the liability of owners of sea-going vessels.

Article IX

These rules shall not affect the provisions of any international Convention or national law governing liability for nuclear damage.

Article X

The provisions of these Rules shall apply to every bill of lading relating to the carriage of goods between ports in two different States if:

    (a) the bill of lading is issued in a contracting State, or

    (b) the carriage is from a port in a contracting State, or

(c) the contract contained in or evidenced by the bill of lading provides that these Rules or legislation of any State giving effect to them are to govern the contract, whatever may be the nationality of the ship, the carrier, the shipper, the consignee, or any other interested person.

[Note: The last two paragraphs of this article are not reproduced. They require contracting States to apply the Rules to bills of lading mentioned in the article and authorise them to apply the Rules to other bills of lading.]

[Note: Articles 11 to 16 of the international Convention for the unification of certain rules of law relating to bills of lading signed at Brussels on August 25 1974 are not reproduced. They deal with the coming into force of the Convention, procedure for ratification, accession and denunciation and the right to call for a fresh conference to consider amendments to the Rules contained in the Convention.]

Unsolicited Goods and Services Act 1971

(1971, c. 30)

2 Demands and threats regarding payment

(1) A person who, not having reasonable cause to believe there is a right to payment, in the course of any trade or business makes a demand for payment, or asserts a present or prospective right to payment, for what he knows are unsolicited goods sent (after the commencement of this Act) to another person with a view to his acquiring them [for the purposes of his trade or business], shall be guilty of an offence and on summary conviction shall be liable to a fine not exceeding [level 4 on the standard scale].

(2) A person who, not having reasonable cause to believe there is a right to payment in the course of any trade or business and with a view to obtaining any payment for what he knows are unsolicited goods sent as aforesaid—

(a) threatens to bring any legal proceedings; or
(b) places or causes to be placed the name of any person on a list of defaulters or debtors or threatens to do so; or
(c) invokes or causes to be invoked any other collection procedure or threatens to do so,

shall be guilty of an offence and shall be liable on summary conviction to a fine not exceeding [level 5 on the standard scale].

3 Directory entries

[(1) A person ('the purchaser') shall not be liable to make any payment, and shall be entitled to recover any payment made by him, by way of charge for including or arranging for the inclusion in a directory of an entry relating to that person or his trade or business, unless—

(a) there has been signed by the purchaser or on his behalf an order complying with this section,
(b) there has been signed by the purchaser or on his behalf a note complying with this section of his agreement to the charge and before the note was signed, a copy of it was supplied, for retention by him, to him or a person acting on his behalf, or
(c) there has been transmitted by the purchaser or a person acting on his behalf an electronic communication which includes a statement that the purchaser agrees to the charge and the relevant condition is satisfied in relation to that communication, or
(d) the charge arises under a contract in relation to which the conditions in section 3B(1) (renewed and extended contracts) are met.]

(2) A person shall be guilty of an offence punishable on summary conviction with a fine not exceeding £400 if, in a case where a payment in respect of a charge would [...] be recoverable from him in accordance with the terms of subsection (1) above, he demands payment, or asserts a present

or prospective right to payment, of the charge or any part of it, without knowing or having reasonable cause to believe [that—

    (a) the entry to which the charge relates was ordered in accordance with this section,

    (b) a proper note of the agreement has been duly signed, or

    (c) the requirements set out in subsection (1)(c) or (d) above have been met.]

  (3) For the purposes of [this section—

    (a) an order for an entry in a directory must be made by means of an order form or other stationery belonging to the purchaser, which may be sent electronically but which must bear his name and address (or one or more of his addresses); and

    (b) the note of a person's agreement to a charge must—

      (i) specify the particulars set out in Part 1 of the Schedule to the Regulatory Reform (Unsolicited Goods and Services Act 1971) (Directory Entries and Demands for Payment) Order 2005, and

      (ii) give reasonable particulars of the entry in respect of which the charge would be payable.]

  [(3A) In relation to an electronic communication which includes a statement that the purchaser agrees to a charge for including or arranging the inclusion in a directory of any entry, the relevant condition is that—

    (a) before the electronic communication was transmitted the information referred to in subsection (3B) below was communicated to the purchaser, and

    (b) the electronic communication can readily be produced and retained in a visible and legible form.

  (3B) that information is—

    (a) the following particulars—

      (i)   the amount of the charge;

      (ii) the name of the directory or proposed directory;

      (iii) the name of the person producing the directory;

      (iv) the geographic address at which that person is established;

      (v) if the directory is or is to be available in printed form, the proposed date of publication of the directory or of the issue in which the entry is to be included;

      (vi) if the directory or the issue in which the entry is to be included is to be put on sale, the price at which it is to be offered for sale and the minimum number of copies which are to be available for sale;

      (vii) if the directory or the issue in which the entry is to be included is to be distributed free of charge (whether or not it is also to be put on sale), the minimum number of copies which are to be so distributed;

      (viii) if the directory is or is to be available in a form other than in printed form, adequate details of how it may be accessed; and

    (b) reasonable particulars of the entry in respect of which the charge would be payable.

  (3C) In this section 'electronic communication' has the same meaning as in the Electronic Communications Act 2000.]

[3B   Renewed and extended contracts

  (1) The conditions referred to in section 3(1)(d) above are met in relation to a contract ('the new contract') if—

    (a) a person ('the purchaser') has entered into an earlier contract ('the earlier contract') for including or arranging for the inclusion in a particular issue or version of a directory ('the earlier directory') of an entry ('the earlier entry') relating to him or his trade or business;

    (b) the purchaser was liable to make a payment by way of a charge arising under the earlier contract for including or arranging for the inclusion of the earlier entry in the earlier directory;

    (c) the new contract is a contract for including or arranging for the inclusion in a later issue or version of a directory ('the later directory') of an entry ('the later entry') relating to the purchaser or his trade or business;

    (d) the form, content and distribution of the later directory is materially the same as the form, content and distribution of the earlier directory;

    (e) the form and content of the later entry is materially the same as the form and content of the earlier entry;

    (f) if the later directory is published other than in electronic form—

        (i)   the earlier directory was the last, or the last but one, issue or version of the directory to be published before the later directory, and

        (ii) the date of publication of the later directory is not more than 13 months after the date of publication of the earlier directory;

    (g) if the later directory is published in electronic form, the first date on which the new contract requires the later entry to be published is not more than the relevant period after the last date on which the earlier contract required the earlier entry to be published;

    (h) if it was a term of the earlier contract that the purchaser renew or extend the contract—

        (i)   before the start of the new contract the relevant publisher has given notice in writing to the purchaser containing the information set out in Part 3 of the Schedule to the Regulatory Reform (Unsolicited Goods and Services Act 1971) (Directory Entries and Demands for Payment) Order 2005; and

        (ii) the purchaser has not written to the relevant publisher withdrawing his agreement to the renewal or extension of the earlier contract within the period of 21 days starting when he receives the notice referred to in sub-paragraph (i); and

    (i) if the parties to the earlier contract and the new contract are different—

        (i)   the parties to both contracts have entered into a novation agreement in respect of the earlier contract; or

        (ii) the relevant publisher has given the purchaser the information set out in Part 4 of the Schedule to the Regulatory Reform (Unsolicited Goods and Services Act 1971) (Directory Entries and Demands for Payment) Order 2005.

  (2) For the purposes of subsection (1)(d) and (e), the form, content or distribution of the later directory, or the form or content of the later entry, shall be taken to be materially the same as that of the earlier directory or the earlier entry (as the case may be), if a reasonable person in the position of the purchaser would—

    (a) view the two as being materially the same; or

    (b) view that of the later directory or the later entry as being an improvement on that of the earlier directory or the earlier entry.

  (3) For the purposes of subsection (1)(g) 'the relevant period' means the period of 13 months or (if shorter) the period of time between the first and last dates on which the earlier contract required the earlier entry to be published.

  (4) For the purposes of subsection (1)(h) and (i) 'the relevant publisher' is the person with whom the purchaser has entered into the new contract.

  (5) The information referred to in subsection (1)(i)(ii) must be given to the purchaser prior to the conclusion of the new contract.]

4 Unsolicited publications

(1) A person shall be guilty of an offence if he sends or causes to be sent to another person any book, magazine or leaflet (or advertising material for any such publication which he knows or ought reasonably to know is unsolicited and which describes or illustrates human sexual techniques.

(2) A person found guilty of an offence under this section shall be liable on summary conviction to a fine not exceeding [level 5 on the standard scale] for a first offence and to a fine not exceeding [level 5 on the standard scale] for any subsequent offence.

(3) A prosecution for an offence under this section shall not in England and Wales be instituted except by, or with the consent of, the Director of Public Prosecutions.

5 Offences by corporations

(1) Where an offence under this Act which has been committed by a body corporate is proved to have been committed with the consent or connivance of, or to be attributable to any neglect on the part of, any director, manager, secretary, or other similar officer of the body corporate, or of any person who was purporting to act in any such capacity, he as well as the body corporate shall be guilty of that offence and shall be liable to be proceeded against and punished accordingly.

(2) Where the affairs of a body corporate are managed by its members, this section shall apply in relation to the acts or defaults of a member in connection with his functions of management as if he were a director of the body corporate.

6 Interpretation

(1) In this Act, unless the context or subject matter otherwise requires,—

'acquire' includes hire;

'send' includes deliver, and 'sender' shall be construed accordingly;

'unsolicited' means, in relation to goods sent to any person, that they are sent without any prior request made by him or on his behalf.

[(2) For the purposes of the Act, any invoice or similar document stating the amount of any payment shall be regarded as asserting a right to the payment unless it complies with the conditions set out in Part 2 of the Schedule to the Regulatory Reform (Unsolicited Goods and Services Act 1971) (Directory Entries and Demands for Payment) Order 2005.]

[(3) Nothing in section 3 or 3B affects the rights of any consumer under the Consumer Contracts (Information, Cancellation and Additional Charges) Regulations 2013.]

Supply of Goods (Implied Terms) Act 1973

(1973, c. 13)

8 Implied terms as title

[(1) In every relevant hire-purchase agreement, other than one to which subsection (2) below applies, there is—

(a) an implied term on the part of the creditor that he will have a right to sell the goods at the time when the property is to pass; and

(b) an implied term that—

(i) the goods are free, and will remain free until the time when the property is to pass, from any charge or encumbrance not disclosed or known to the person to whom the goods are bailed or (in Scotland) hired before the agreement is made, and

(ii) that person will enjoy quiet possession of the goods except so far as it may be disturbed by any person entitled to the benefit of any charge or encumbrance so disclosed or known.

(2) In a relevant hire-purchase agreement, in the case of which there appears from the agreement or is to be inferred from the circumstances of the agreement an intention that the creditor should transfer only such title as he or a third person may have, there is—

(a) an implied term that all charges or encumbrances known to the creditor and not known to the person to whom the goods are bailed or hired have been disclosed to that person before the agreement is made; and

(b) an implied term that neither—

(i) the creditor; nor

(ii) in a case where the parties to the agreement intend that any title which may be transferred shall be only such title as a third person may have, that person; nor

(iii) anyone claiming through or under the creditor or that third person not otherwise than under a charge or encumbrance disclosed or known to the person to whom the goods are bailed or hired, before the agreement is made; will disturb the quiet possession of the person to whom the goods are bailed or hired.

(3) As regards England and Wales and Northern Ireland, the term implied by subsection (1)(a) above is a condition and the terms implied by subsections (1)(b), (2)(a) and (2)(b) above are warranties.]

9   Bailing or hiring by description

[(1) Where under a relevant hire-purchase agreement goods are bailed or (in Scotland) hired by description, there is an implied term that the goods will correspond with the description, and if under the agreement the goods are bailed or hired by reference to a sample as well as a description, it is not sufficient that the bulk of the goods corresponds with the sample if the goods do not also correspond with the description.

(1A) As regards England and Wales and Northern Ireland, the term implied by subsection (1) above is a condition.

(2) Goods shall not be prevented from being bailed or hired by description by reason only that, being exposed for sale, bailment or hire, they are selected by the person to whom they are bailed or hired.]

10   Implied undertakings as to quality or fitness

[(1) Except as provided by this section and section 11 below and subject to the provisions of any other enactment, including any enactment of the Parliament of Northern Ireland or the Northern Ireland Assembly, there is no implied term as to the quality or fitness for any particular purpose of goods bailed or (in Scotland) hired under a relevant hire-purchase agreement.

(2) Where the creditor bails or hires goods under a relevant hire-purchase agreement in the course of a business, there is an implied term that the goods supplied under the agreement are of satisfactory quality.

(2A) For the purposes of this Act, goods are of satisfactory quality if they meet the standard that a reasonable person would regard as satisfactory, taking account of any description of the goods, the price (if relevant) and all the other relevant circumstances.

(2B) For the purposes of this Act, the quality of goods includes their state and condition and the following (among others) are in appropriate cases aspects of the quality of goods—

(a) fitness for all the purposes for which goods of the kind in question are commonly supplied,

(b) appearance and finish.

(c)　freedom from minor defects,

(d)　safety, and

(e)　durability.

(2C)　The term implied by subsection (2) above does not extend to any matter making the quality of goods unsatisfactory—

(a)　which is specifically drawn to the attention of the person to whom the goods are bailed or hired before the agreement is made,

(b)　where that person examines the goods before the agreement is made, which that examination ought to reveal, or

(c)　where the goods are bailed or hired by reference to a sample, which would have been apparent on a reasonable examination of the sample.

(3)　Where the creditor bails or hires goods under a [relevant hire-purchase agreement] in the course of a business and the person to whom the goods are bailed or hired, expressly or by implication, makes known—

(a)　to the creditor in the course of negotiations conducted by the creditor in relation to the making of the [relevant hire-purchase agreement], or

(b)　to a credit-broker in the course of negotiations conducted by that broker in relation to goods sold by him to the creditor before forming the subject matter of the [relevant hire-purchase agreement],

any particular purpose for which the goods are being bailed or hired, there is an implied term that the goods supplied under the agreement are reasonably fit for that purpose, whether or not that is a purpose for which such goods are commonly supplied, except where the circumstances show that the person to whom the goods are bailed or hired does not rely, or that it is unreasonable for him to rely, on the skill or judgment of the creditor or credit-broker.

(4)　An implied term as to quality or fitness for a particular purpose may be annexed to a [relevant hire-purchase agreement] by usage.

(5)　The preceding provisions of this section apply to a [relevant hire-purchase agreement] made by a person who in the course of a business is acting as agent for the creditor as they apply to an agreement made by the creditor in the course of a business, except where the creditor is not bailing or hiring in the course of a business and either the person to whom the goods are bailed or hired knows that fact or reasonable steps are taken to bring it to the notice of that person before the agreement is made.

(6)　In subsection (3) above and this subsection—

(a)　'credit-broker' means a person acting in the course of a business of credit brokerage;

(b)　'credit brokerage' means the effecting of introductions of individuals desiring to obtain credit—

(i)　to persons carrying on any business so far as it relates to the provision of credit, or

(ii)　to other persons engaged in credit brokerage.

(7)　As regards England and Wales and Northern Ireland, the terms implied by subsections (2) and (3) above are conditions.]

11　Samples

[(1)　Where under a relevant hire-purchase agreement goods are bailed or (in Scotland) hired by reference to a sample, there is an implied term—

(a)　that the bulk will correspond with the sample in quality; and

(b)　that the person to whom the goods are bailed or hired will have a reasonable opportunity of comparing the bulk with the sample; and

(c)　that the goods will be free from any defect, making their quality unsatisfactory, which would not be apparent on reasonable examination of the sample.

(2) As regards England and Wales and Northern Ireland, the term implied by subsection (1) above is a condition.]

[11A   Modification of remedies for breach of statutory condition in non-consumer cases

(1) Where in the case of a relevant hire-purchase agreement—

    (a) the person to whom goods are bailed would, apart from this subsection, have the right to reject them by reason of a breach on the part of the creditor of a term implied by section 9, 10 or 11(1)(a) or (c) above, but

    (b) the breach is so slight that it would be unreasonable for him to reject them, the breach is not to be treated as a breach of condition but may be treated as a breach of warranty.

(2) This section applies unless a contrary intention appears in, or is to be implied from, the agreement.

(3) It is for the creditor to show—

    (a) that a breach fell within subsection (1)(b) above, and

    (b) that the agreement was a relevant hire-purchase agreement.]

[12   Exclusion of implied terms

An express term does not negative a term implied by this Act unless inconsistent with it.]

15   Supplementary

[(1) In sections 8 to 14 above and this section—

'business' includes a profession and the activities of any government department (including a Northern Ireland department), [or local or public authority];

'buyer' and 'seller' includes a person to whom rights and duties under a conditional sale agreement have passed by assignment or operation of law;

'conditional sale agreement' means an agreement for the sale of goods under which the purchase price or part of it is payable by instalments, and the property in the goods is to remain in the seller (notwithstanding that the buyer is to be in possession of the goods) until such conditions as to the payment of instalments or otherwise as may be specified in the agreement are fulfilled;

['consumer sale' has the same meaning as in section 55 of the Sale of Goods Act 1979 (as set out in paragraph 11 of Schedule 1 to that Act)];

'creditor' means the person by whom the goods are bailed or (in Scotland) hired under a hire-purchase agreement or the person to whom his rights and duties under the agreement have passed by assignment or operation of law; and

'hire-purchase agreement' means an agreement, other than conditional sale agreement, under which—

    (a) goods are bailed or (in Scotland) hired in return for periodical payments by the person to whom they are bailed or hired, and

    (b) the property in the goods will pass to that person if the terms of the agreement are complied with and one or more of the following occurs—

        (i)   the exercise of an option to purchase by that person,

        (ii)   the doing of any other specified act by any party to the agreement,

        (iii)   the happening of any other specified event

[and a hire-purchase agreement is relevant if it is not a contract to which Chapter 2 of Part 1 of the Consumer Rights Act 2015 applies;]

(4) Nothing in sections 8 to 13 above shall prejudice the operation of any other enactment including any enactment of the Parliament of Northern Ireland or the Northern Ireland Assembly or any rule of law whereby any term, other than one relating to quality or fitness, is to be implied in any relevant hire-purchase agreement.]

Consumer Credit Act 1974

(1974, c. 39)

PART II CREDIT AGREEMENTS, HIRE AGREEMENTS AND LINKED TRANSACTIONS

8 Consumer credit agreements

(1) A [consumer] credit agreement is an agreement between an individual ('the debtor') and any other person ('the creditor') by which the creditor provides the debtor with credit of any amount.

[(3) A consumer credit agreement is a regulated agreement within the meaning of this Act if it—

(a) is a regulated credit agreement for the purposes of Chapter 14A of Part 2 of the Regulated Activities Order; and

(b) if entered into on or after 21st March 2016, is not an agreement the purpose of which is the acquisition or retention, by an individual acting for purposes outside those of any trade, business or profession carried on by the individual, of property rights in land or in an existing or projected building.]

[(3A) A reference in paragraph (3)(b) to any land or building—

(a) in relation to an agreement entered into before IP completion day, is a reference to any land or building in the United Kingdom or within the territory of an EEA State;

(b) in relation to an agreement entered into on or after IP completion day, is a reference to any land or building in the United Kingdom.]

[(4) Subsection (1) does not apply in relation to an agreement that is a green deal plan (see instead section 189B).]

9 Meaning of credit

(1) In this Act 'credit' includes a cash loan, and any other form of financial accommodation.

(2) Where credit is provided otherwise than in sterling it shall be treated for the purposes of this Act as provided in sterling of an equivalent amount.

(3) Without prejudice to the generality of subsection (1), the person by whom goods are bailed or (in Scotland) hired to an individual under a hire-purchase agreement shall be taken to provide him with fixed-sum credit to finance the transaction of an amount equal to the total price of the goods less the aggregate of the deposit (if any) and the total charge for credit.

(4) For the purposes of this Act, an item entering into the total charge for credit shall not be treated as credit even though time is allowed for its payment.

10 Running-account credit and fixed-sum credit

(1) For the purposes of this Act—

(a) running-account credit is a facility under a [consumer] credit agreement whereby the debtor is enabled to receive from time to time (whether in his own person, or by another person) from the creditor or a third party cash, goods and services (or any of them) to an amount or value such that, taking into account payments made by or to the credit of the debtor, the credit limit (if any) is not at any time exceeded; and

(b) fixed-sum credit is any other facility under a [consumer] credit agreement whereby the debtor is enabled to receive credit (whether in one amount or by instalments).

(2) In relation to running-account credit, 'credit limit' means, as respects any period, the maximum debit balance which, under the credit agreement, is allowed to stand on the account during that period, disregarding any term of the agreement allowing that maximum to be exceeded merely temporarily.

(3) For the purposes of [any provision of this Act that specifies an amount of credit (except section 17(1)(a))], running-account credit shall be taken not to exceed the amount specified in [that provision] ('the specified amount') if—

(a) the credit limit does not exceed the specified amount; or

(b) whether or not there is a credit limit, and if there is, notwithstanding that it exceeds the specified amount,—

    (i) the debtor is not enabled to draw at any one time an amount which, so far as (having regard to section 9(4)) it represents credit, exceeds the specified amount, or

    (ii) the agreement provides that, if the debit balance rises above a given amount (not exceeding the specified amount), the rate of the total charge for credit increases or any other condition favouring the creditor or his associate comes into operation, or

    (iii) at the time the agreement is made it is probable, having regard to the terms of the agreement and any other relevant considerations, that the debit balance will not at any time rise above the specified amount.

11 Restricted-use credit and unrestricted-use credit

(1) A restricted-use credit agreement is a regulated consumer credit agreement—

(a) to finance a transaction between the debtor and the creditor, whether forming part of that agreement or not, or

(b) to finance a transaction between the debtor and a person (the 'supplier') other than the creditor, or

(c) to refinance any existing indebtedness of the debtor's, whether to the creditor or another person, and 'restricted-use credit' shall be construed accordingly.

(2) An unrestricted-use credit agreement is a regulated consumer credit agreement not falling within subsection (1), and 'unrestricted-use credit' shall be construed accordingly.

(3) An agreement does not fall within subsection (1) if the credit is in fact provided in such a way as to leave the debtor free to use it as he chooses, even though certain uses would contravene that or any other agreement.

(4) An agreement may fall within subsection (1)(b) although the identity of the supplier is unknown at the time the agreement is made.

12 Debtor-creditor supplier agreements

A debtor-creditor-supplier agreement is a regulated consumer credit agreement being—

(a) a restricted-use credit agreement which falls within section 11(1)(a), or

(b) a restricted-use credit agreement which falls within section 11(1)(b) and is made by the creditor under pre-existing arrangements, or in contemplation of future arrangements, between himself and the supplier, or

(c) an unrestricted-use credit agreement which is made by the creditor under pre-existing arrangements between himself and a person (the 'supplier') other than the debtor in the knowledge that the credit is to be used to finance a transaction between the debtor and the supplier.

13 Debtor-creditor agreements

A debtor-creditor agreement is a regulated consumer credit agreement being—

(a) a restricted-use credit agreement which falls within section 11(1)(b) but is not made by the creditor under pre-existing arrangements, or in contemplation of future arrangements, between himself and the supplier, or

(b) a restricted-use credit agreement which falls within section 11(1)(c), or

(c) an unrestricted-use credit agreement which is not made by the creditor under pre-existing arrangements between himself and a person (the 'supplier') other than the debtor in the knowledge that the credit is to be used to finance a transaction between the debtor and the supplier.

14 Credit-token agreements

(1) A credit-token is a card, check, voucher, coupon, stamp, form, booklet or other document or thing given to an individual by a person carrying on a consumer credit business, who undertakes—

(a) that on the production of it (whether or not some other action is also required) he will supply cash, goods and services (or any of them) on credit, or

(b) that where, on the production of it to a third party (whether or not any other action is also required), the third party supplies cash, goods and services (or any of them), he will pay the third party for them (whether or not deducting any discount or commission), in return for payment to him by the individual.

(2) A credit-token agreement is a regulated agreement for the provision of credit in connection with the use of a credit-token.

(3) Without prejudice to the generality of section 9(1), the person who gives to an individual an undertaking falling within subsection (1)(b) shall be taken to provide him with credit drawn on whenever a third party supplies him with cash, goods or services.

(4) For the purposes of subsection (1), use of an object to operate a machine provided by the person giving the object or a third party shall be treated as the production of the object to him.

15   Consumer hire agreements

(1) A consumer hire agreement is an agreement made by a person with an individual (the 'hirer') for the bailment or (in Scotland) the hiring of goods to the hirer, being an agreement which—

> (a) is not a hire-purchase agreement, and
> (b) is capable of subsisting for more than three months, [...].

[(2) A consumer hire agreement is a regulated agreement with the meaning of this Act if it is a regulated consumer hire agreement for the purposes of Chapter 14B of Part 2 of the Regulated Activities Order.]

17   Small agreements

(1) A small agreement is—

> (a) a regulated consumer credit agreement for credit not exceeding [£50], other than a hire-purchase or conditional sale agreement; or
> (b) a regulated consumer hire agreement which does not require the hirer to make payments exceeding [£50],

being an agreement which is either unsecured or secured by a guarantee or indemnity only (whether or not the guarantee or indemnity is itself secured).

[(2) For the purposes of paragraph (a) of subsection (1), running-account credit shall be taken not to exceed the amount specified in that paragraph if the credit limit does not exceed that amount.]

(3) Where—

> (a) two or more small agreements are made at or about the same time between the same parties, and
> (b) it appears probable that they would instead have been made as a single agreement but for the desire to avoid the operation of provisions of this Act which would have applied to that single agreement but, apart from this subsection, are not applicable to the small agreements,

this Act applies to the small agreements as if they were regulated agreements other than small agreements.

(4) If, apart from this subsection, subsection (3) does not apply to any agreements but would apply if, for any party or parties to any of the agreements, there were substituted an associate of that party, or associates of each of those parties, as the case may be, then subsection (3) shall apply to the agreements.

18   Multiple agreements

(1) This section applies to an agreement (a 'multiple agreement') if its terms are such as—

> (a) to place a part of it within one category of agreement mentioned in this Act, and another part of it within a different category of agreement so mentioned, or within a category of agreement not so mentioned, or
> (b) to place it, or a part of it, within two or more categories of agreement so mentioned.

(2) Where a part of an agreement falls within subsection (1), that part shall be treated for the purposes of this Act as a separate agreement.

(3) Where an agreement falls within subsection (1)(b), it shall be treated as an agreement in each of the categories in question, and this Act shall apply to it accordingly.

(4) Where under subsection (2) a part of a multiple agreement is to be treated as a separate agreement, the multiple agreement shall (with any necessary modifications) be construed accordingly; and any sum payable under the multiple agreement, if not apportioned by the parties, shall for the purposes of proceedings in any court relating to the multiple agreement be apportioned by the court as may be requisite.

(5) In the case of an agreement for running-account credit, a term of the agreement allowing the credit limit to be exceeded merely temporarily shall not be treated as a separate agreement or as providing fixed-sum credit in respect of the excess.

(6) This Act does not apply to a multiple agreement so far as the agreement relates to goods if under the agreement payments are to be made in respect of the goods in the form of rent (other than a rentcharge) issuing out of land.

19 Linked transactions

(1) A transaction entered into by the debtor or hirer, or a relative of his, with any other person ('the other party'), except one for the provision of security, is a linked transaction in relation to an actual or prospective regulated agreement (the 'principal agreement') of which it does not form part if—

    (a) the transaction is entered into in compliance with a term of the principal agreement; or

    (b) the principal agreement is a debtor-creditor-supplier agreement and the transaction is financed, or to be financed, by the principal agreement; or

    (c) the other party is a person mentioned in subsection (2), and a person so mentioned initiated the transaction by suggesting it to the debtor or hirer, or his relative, who enters into it—

        (i) to induce the creditor or owner to enter into the principal agreement, or

        (ii) for another purpose related to the principal agreement, or

        (iii) where the principal agreement is a restricted-use credit agreement, for a purpose related to a transaction financed, or to be financed, by the principal agreement.

(2) The persons referred to in subsection (1)(c) are—

    (a) the creditor or owner, or his associate;

    (b) a person who, in the negotiation of the transaction, is represented by a credit-broker who is also a negotiator in antecedent negotiations for the principal agreement;

    (c) a person who, at the time the transaction is initiated, knows that the principal agreement has been made or contemplates that it might be made.

(3) A linked transaction entered into before the making of the principal agreement has no effect until such time (if any) as that agreement is made.

(4) Regulations may exclude linked transactions of the prescribed description from the operation of subsection (3).

[20 Total charge for credit

In this Act, 'the total charge for credit' has the meaning given by the Regulated Activities Order for the purposes of Chapter 14A of Part 2 of that Order.]

PART IV SEEKING BUSINESS

Canvassing, etc.

48 Definition of canvassing off trade premises (regulated agreements)

(1) An individual (the 'canvasser') canvasses a regulated agreement off trade premises if he solicits the entry (as debtor or hirer) of another individual (the 'consumer') into the agreement by making oral representations to the consumer, or any other individual, during a visit by the canvasser to any place (not excluded by subsection (2)) where the consumer, or that other individual, as the case may be, is, being a visit—

    (a) carried out for the purpose of making such oral representations to individuals who are at that place, but

(b) not carried out in response to a request made on a previous occasion.

(2) A place is excluded from subsection (1) if it is a place where a business is carried on (whether on a permanent or temporary basis) by—

(a) the creditor or owner, or

(b) a supplier, or

(c) the canvasser, or the person whose employee or agent the canvasser is, or

(d) the consumer.

49 Prohibition of canvassing debtor-creditor agreements off trade premises

(1) It is an offence to canvass debtor-creditor agreements off trade premises.

(2) It is also an offence to solicit the entry of an individual (as debtor) into a debtor-creditor agreement during a visit carried out in response to a request made on a previous occasion, where—

(a) the request was not in writing signed by or on behalf of the person making it, and

(b) if no request for the visit had been made, the soliciting would have constituted the canvassing of a debtor-creditor agreement off trade premises.

(3) Subsections (1) and (2) do not apply to any soliciting for an agreement enabling the debtor to overdraw on a current account of any description kept with the creditor, where—

(a) the [FCA] has determined that current accounts of that description kept with the creditor are excluded from subsections (1) and (2), and

(b) the debtor already keeps an account with the creditor (whether a current account or not).

(4) A determination under subsection (3)(a)—

(a) may be made subject to such conditions as the [FCA] thinks fit, and

(b) shall be made only where the [FCA] is of opinion that it is not against the interests of debtors.

(5) If soliciting is done in breach of a condition imposed under subsection (4)(a), the determination under subsection (3)(a) does not apply to it.

50 Circulars to minors

(1) A person commits an offence who, with a view to financial gain, sends to a minor any document inviting him to—

(a) borrow money, or

(b) obtain goods on credit or hire, or

(c) obtain services on credit, or

(d) apply for information or advice on borrowing money or otherwise obtaining credit, or hiring goods.

(2) In proceedings under subsection (1) in respect of the sending of a document to a minor, it is a defence for the person charged to prove that he did not know, and had no reasonable cause to suspect, that he was a minor.

(3) Where a document is received by a minor at any school or other educational establishment for minors, a person sending it to him at that establishment knowing or suspecting it to be such an establishment shall be taken to have reasonable cause to suspect that he is a minor.

PART V ENTRY INTO CREDIT OR HIRE AGREEMENTS

Preliminary matters

55 Disclosure of information

(1) Regulations may require specified information to be disclosed in the prescribed manner to the debtor or hirer before a regulated agreement is made.

[(2) If regulations under subsection (1) are not complied with, the agreement is enforceable against the debtor or hirer on an order of the court only (and for these purposes a retaking of goods or land to which the agreement relates is an enforcement of the agreement).]

[55C   Copy of draft consumer credit agreement

(1) Before a regulated consumer credit agreement, other than an excluded agreement, is made, the creditor must, if requested, give to the debtor without delay a copy of the prospective agreement (or such of its terms as have at that time been reduced to writing).

(2) Subsection (1) does not apply if at the time the request is made, the creditor is unwilling to proceed with the agreement.

(3) A breach of the duty imposed by subsection (1) is actionable as a breach of statutory duty.

(4) For the purposes of this section an agreement is an excluded agreement if it is—

(a) an agreement secured on land,

(b) an agreement under which a person takes an article in pawn,

(c) an agreement under which the creditor provides the debtor with credit which exceeds £60, 260 and which is not a residential renovation agreement, or

(d) an agreement entered into by the debtor wholly or predominantly for the purposes of a business carried on, or intended to be carried on, by him.

(5) Article 60C(5) and (6) of the Regulated Activities Order applies for the purposes of subsection (4)(d).]

56   Antecedent negotiations

(1) In this Act 'antecedent negotiations' means any negotiations with the debtor or hirer—

(a) conducted by the creditor or owner in relation to the making of any regulated agreement, or

(b) conducted by a credit-broker in relation to goods sold or proposed to be sold by the credit-broker to the creditor before forming the subject-matter of a debtor-creditor-supplier agreement within section 12(a), or

(c) conducted by the supplier in relation to a transaction financed or proposed to be financed by a debtor-creditor-supplier agreement within section 12(b) or (c), and 'negotiator' means the person by whom negotiations are so conducted with the debtor or hirer.

(2) Negotiations with the debtor in a case falling within subsection (1)(b) or (c) shall be deemed to be conducted by the negotiator in the capacity of agent of the creditor as well as in his actual capacity.

(3) An agreement is void if, and to the extent that, it purports in relation to an actual or prospective regulated agreement—

(a) to provide that a person acting as, or on behalf of, a negotiator is to be treated as the agent of the debtor or hirer, or

(b) to relieve a person from liability for acts or omissions of any person acting as, or on behalf of, a negotiator.

(4) For the purposes of this Act, antecedent negotiations shall be taken to begin when the negotiator and the debtor or hirer first enter into communication (including communication by advertisement), and to include any representations made by the negotiator to the debtor or hirer and any other dealings between them.

57   Withdrawal from prospective agreement

(1) The withdrawal of a party from a prospective regulated agreement shall operate to apply this Part to the agreement, any linked transaction and any other thing done in anticipation of the making of the agreement as it would apply if the agreement were made and then cancelled under section 69.

(2) The giving to a party of a written or oral notice which, however expressed, indicates the intention of the other party to withdraw from a prospective regulated agreement operates as a withdrawal from it.

(3) Each of the following shall be deemed to be the agent of the creditor or owner for the purpose of receiving a notice under subsection (2)—

(a) a credit-broker or supplier who is the negotiator in antecedent negotiations,

(b) any person who, in the course of a business carried on by him, acts on behalf of the debtor or hirer in any negotiations for the agreement.

(4) Where the agreement, if made, would not be a cancellable agreement, subsection (1) shall nevertheless apply as if the contrary were the case.

58 Opportunity for withdrawal from prospective land mortgage

(1) Before sending to the debtor or hirer, for his signature, an unexecuted agreement in a case where the prospective regulated agreement is to be secured on land (the 'mortgaged land'), the creditor or owner shall give the debtor or hirer a copy of the unexecuted agreement which contains a notice in the prescribed form indicating the right of the debtor or hirer to withdraw from the prospective agreement, and how and when the right is exercisable, together with a copy of any other document referred to in the unexecuted agreement.

(2) Subsection (1) does not apply to—

(a) a restricted-use credit agreement to finance the purchase of the mortgaged land, or

(b) an agreement for a bridging loan in connection with the purchase of the mortgaged land or other land.

59 Agreement to enter future agreement void

(1) An agreement is void if, and to the extent that, it purports to bind a person to enter as debtor or hirer into a prospective regulated agreement.

(2) Regulations may exclude from the operation of subsection (1) agreements such as are described in the regulations.

Making the agreement

60 Form and content of agreements

(1) The [Treasury] shall make regulations as to the form and content of documents embodying regulated agreements, and the regulations shall contain such provisions as appear to [them] appropriate with a view to ensuring that the debtor or hirer is made aware of—

(a) the rights and duties conferred or imposed on him by the agreement,

(b) the amount and rate of the total charge for credit (in the case of a consumer credit agreement),

(c) the protection and remedies available to him under this Act, and

(d) any other matters which, in the opinion of the [Treasury], it is desirable for him to know about in connection with the agreement.

(2) Regulations under subsection (1) may in particular—

(a) require specified information to be included in the prescribed manner in documents, and other specified material to be excluded;

(b) contain requirements to ensure that specified information is clearly brought to the attention of the debtor or hirer, and that one part of a document is not given insufficient or excessive prominence compared with another.

(3) If, on an application made to the [FCA] by a person carrying on a consumer credit business or a consumer hire business, it appears to the [FCA] impracticable for the applicant to comply with any requirement of regulations under subsection (1) in a particular case, [it] may, by notice to the applicant direct that the requirement be waived or varied in relation to such agreements, and subject to such conditions (if any), as [it] may specify, and this Act and the regulations shall have effect accordingly.

(4) The [FCA] shall give a notice under subsection (3) only if [it] is satisfied that to do so would not prejudice the interests of debtors or hirers'.

[(5) An application may be made under subsection (3) only if it relates to—

(a) a consumer credit agreement secured on land,

(b) a consumer credit agreement under which a person takes an article in pawn,

(c) a consumer credit agreement under which the creditor provides the debtor with credit which exceeds £60,260 and which is not a residential renovation agreement,

(d) a consumer credit agreement entered into by the debtor wholly or predominantly for the purposes of a business carried on, or intended to be carried on, by him, or

(e) a consumer hire agreement.]

[(6) Article 60C(5) and (6) of the Regulated Activities Order applies for the purposes of subsection (5)(d).]

61   Signing of agreement

(1) A regulated agreement is not properly executed unless—

    (a) a document in the prescribed form itself containing all the prescribed terms and conforming to regulations under section 60(1) is signed in the prescribed manner both by the debtor or hirer and by or on behalf of the creditor or owner, and

    (b) the document embodies all the terms of the agreement, other than implied terms, and

    (c) the document is, when presented or sent to the debtor or hirer for signature, in such a state that all its terms are readily legible.

(2) In addition, where the agreement is one to which section 58(1) applies, it is not properly executed unless—

    (a) the requirements of section 58(1) were complied with, and

    (b) the unexecuted agreement was sent, for his signature, to the debtor or hirer by an appropriate method not less than seven days after a copy of it was given to him under section 58(1), and

    (c) during the consideration period, the creditor or owner refrained from approaching the debtor or hirer (whether in person, by telephone or letter, or in any other way) except in response to a specific request made by the debtor or hirer after the beginning of the consideration period, and

    (d) no notice of withdrawal by the debtor or hirer was received by the creditor or owner before the sending of the unexecuted agreement.

(3) In subsection (2)(c), 'the consideration period' means the period beginning with the giving of the copy under section 58(1) and ending—

    (a) at the expiry of seven days after the day on which the unexecuted agreement is sent, for his signature, to the debtor or hirer, or

    (b) on its return by the debtor or hirer after signature by him, whichever first occurs.

(4) Where the debtor or hirer is a partnership or an unincorporated body of persons, subsection (1)(a) shall apply with the substitution for 'by the debtor or hirer' of 'by or on behalf of the debtor or hirer's'.

[61A   Duty to supply copy of executed consumer credit agreement

(1) Where a regulated consumer credit agreement, other than an excluded agreement, has been made, the creditor must give a copy of the executed agreement, and any other document referred to in it, to the debtor.

(2) Subsection (1) does not apply if—

    (a) a copy of the unexecuted agreement (and of any other document referred to in it) has already been given to the debtor, and

    (b) the unexecuted agreement is in identical terms to the executed agreement.

(3) In a case referred to in subsection (2), the creditor must inform the debtor in writing—

    (a) that the agreement has been executed,

    (b) that the executed agreement is in identical terms to the unexecuted agreement a copy of which has already been given to the debtor, and

    (c) that the debtor has the right to receive a copy of the executed agreement if the debtor makes a request for it at any time before the end of the period referred to in section 66A(2).

(4) Where a request is made under subsection (3)(c) the creditor must give a copy of the executed agreement to the debtor without delay.

(5) If the requirements of this section are not observed, the agreement is not properly executed.

(6) For the purposes of this section, an agreement is an excluded agreement if it is—

    (a) a cancellable agreement, or

(b) an agreement—
    (i)   secured on land,
    (ii) under which the creditor provides the debtor with credit which exceeds £60,260, or
    (iii) entered into by the debtor wholly or predominantly for the purposes of a business carried on, or intended to be carried on, by him,
    unless the creditor or a credit intermediary has complied with or purported to comply with regulation 3(2) of the Consumer Credit (Disclosure of Information) Regulations 2010.

(6A) An agreement is not an excluded agreement by virtue of subsection (6)(b)(ii) if it is a residential renovation agreement.

(7) Article 60C(5) and (6) of the Regulated Activities Order applies for the purposes of subsection (6)(b)(iii).

(8) In this section, 'credit intermediary' means a person who in the course of business—
    (a) carries on any of the activities specified in article 36A(1)(d) to (f) of the Regulated Activities Order for a consideration that is or includes a financial consideration, and
    (b) does not do so as a creditor.]

[61B Duty to supply copy of overdraft agreement

(1) Where an authorised business overdraft agreement or an authorised non-business overdraft agreement has been made, a document containing the terms of the agreement must be given to the debtor.

(2) The creditor must provide the document referred to in subsection (1) to the debtor before or at the time the agreement is made unless—
    (a) the creditor has provided the debtor with the information referred to in regulation 10(3) of the Consumer Credit (Disclosure of Information) Regulations 2010, in which case it must be provided after the agreement is made,
    (b) the creditor has provided the debtor with the information referred to in regulation 10(3)(c), (e), (f), (h) and (k) of those Regulations, in which case it must be provided immediately after the agreement is made, or
    (c) the agreement is an agreement of a description referred to in regulation 10(4)(b) of those Regulations, in which case it must be provided immediately after the agreement is made.

(3) If the requirements of this section are not observed, the agreement is enforceable against the debtor on an order of the court only (and for these purposes a retaking of goods or land to which the agreement relates is an enforcement of the agreement).]

62 Duty to supply copy of unexecuted agreement[: excluded agreements]

(1) If [in the case of a regulated agreement which is an excluded agreement] the unexecuted agreement is presented personally to the debtor or hirer for his signature, but on the occasion when he signs it the document does not become an executed agreement, a copy of it, and of any other document referred to in it, must be there and then delivered to him.

(2) If the unexecuted agreement is sent to the debtor or hirer for his signature, a copy of it, and of any other document referred to in it, must be sent to him at the same time.

(3) A regulated agreement [which is an excluded agreement] is not properly executed if the requirements of this section are not observed.

[(4) In this section, 'excluded agreement' has the same meaning as in section 61A.]

63 Duty to supply copy of executed agreement[: excluded agreements]

(1) If [in the case of a regulated agreement which is an excluded agreement] the unexecuted agreement is presented personally to the debtor or hirer for his signature, and on the occasion when he signs it the document becomes an executed agreement, a copy of the executed agreement, and of any other document referred to in it, must be there and then delivered to him.

(2) A copy of the executed agreement, and of any other document referred to in it, must be given to the debtor or hirer within the seven days following the making of the agreement unless—
    (a) subsection (1) applies, or
    (b) the unexecuted agreement was sent to the debtor or hirer for his signature and, on the occasion of his signing it, the document became an executed agreement.

(3) In the case of a cancellable agreement, a copy under subsection (2) must be sent by an appropriate method.

(4) In the case of a credit-token agreement, a copy under subsection (2) need not be given within the seven days following the making of the agreement if it is given before or at the time when the credit-token is given to the debtor.

(5) A regulated agreement [which is an excluded agreement] is not properly executed if the requirements of this section are not observed.

[(6) In this section, 'excluded agreement' has the same meaning as in section 61A.]

64   Duty to give notice of cancellation rights

(1) In the case of a cancellable agreement, a notice in the prescribed form indicating the right of the debtor or hirer to cancel the agreement, how and when that right is exercisable, and the name and address of a person to whom notice of cancellation may be given,—

(a) must be included in every copy given to the debtor or hirer under section 62 or 63, and

(b) except where section 63(2) applied, must also be sent [by an appropriate method] to the debtor or hirer within the seven days following the making of the agreement.

(2) In the case of a credit-token agreement, a notice under subsection (1)(b) need not be sent [by an appropriate method] within the seven days following the making of the agreement if either—

(a) it is sent [by an appropriate method] to the debtor or hirer before the credit-token is given to him, or

(b) it is sent [by an appropriate method] to him together with the credit-token.

(3) Regulations may provide that except where section 63(2) applied a notice sent under subsection (1)(b) shall be accompanied by a further copy of the executed agreement, and of any other document referred to in it.

(4) Regulations may provide that subsection (1)(b) is not to apply in the case of agreements such as are described in the regulations, being agreements made by a particular person, if—

(a) on an application by that person to the [FCA], the [FCA] has determined that, having regard to—

(i) the manner in which antecedent negotiations for agreements with the applicant of that description are conducted, and

(ii) the information provided to debtors or hirers before such agreements are made, the requirement imposed by subsection (1)(b) can be dispensed with without prejudicing the interests of debtors or hirers, and

(b) any conditions imposed by the [FCA] in making the determination are complied with.

(5) A cancellable agreement is not properly executed if the requirements of this section are not observed.

65   Consequences of improper execution

(1) An improperly-executed regulated agreement is enforceable against the debtor or hirer on an order of the court only.

(2) A retaking of goods or land to which a regulated agreement relates is an enforcement of the agreement.

66   Acceptance of credit-tokens

(1) The debtor shall not be liable under a credit-token agreement for use made of the credit-token by any person unless the debtor had previously accepted the credit-token, or the use constituted an acceptance of it by him.

(2) The debtor accepts a credit-token when—

(a) it is signed, or

(b) a receipt for it is signed, or

(c) it is first used, either by the debtor himself or by a person who, pursuant to the agreement, is authorised by him to use it.

[Withdrawal from certain agreements]

[66A   Withdrawal from consumer credit agreement

(1) The debtor under a regulated consumer credit agreement, other than an excluded agreement, may withdraw from the agreement, without giving any reason, in accordance with this section.

(2) To withdraw from an agreement under this section the debtor must give oral or written notice of the withdrawal to the creditor before the end of the period of 14 days beginning with the relevant day.

(3) For the purposes of subsection (2) the relevant day is whichever is the latest of the following—

  (a) the day on which the agreement is made;

  (b) where the creditor is required to inform the debtor of the credit limit under the agreement, the day on which the creditor first does so;

  (c) in the case of an agreement to which section 61A (duty to supply copy of executed consumer credit agreement) applies, the day on which the debtor receives a copy of the agreement under that section or on which the debtor is informed as specified in subsection (3) of that section;

  (d) in the case of an agreement to which section 63 (duty to supply copy of executed agreement: excluded agreements) applies, the day on which the debtor receives a copy of the agreement under that section.

(4) Where oral notice under this section is given to the creditor it must be given in a manner specified in the agreement.

(5) Where written notice under this section is given by facsimile transmission or electronically—

  (a) it must be sent to the number or electronic address specified for the purpose in the agreement, and

  (b) where it is so sent, it is to be regarded as having been received by the creditor at the time it is sent (and section 176A does not apply).

(6) Where written notice under this section is given in any other form—

  (a) it must be sent by post to, or left at, the postal address specified for the purpose in the agreement, and

  (b) where it is sent by post to that address, it is to be regarded as having been received by the creditor at the time of posting (and section 176 does not apply).

(7) Subject as follows, where the debtor withdraws from a regulated consumer credit agreement under this section—

  (a) the agreement shall be treated as if it had never been entered into, and

  (b) where an ancillary service relating to the agreement is or is to be provided by the creditor, or by a third party on the basis of an agreement between the third party and the creditor, the ancillary service contract shall be treated as if it had never been entered into.

(8) In the case referred to in subsection (7)(b) the creditor must without delay notify any third party of the fact that the debtor has withdrawn from the agreement.

(9) Where the debtor withdraws from an agreement under this section—

  (a) the debtor must repay to the creditor any credit provided and the interest accrued on it (at the rate provided for under the agreement), but

  (b) the debtor is not liable to pay to the creditor any compensation, fees or charges except any non-returnable charges paid by the creditor to a public administrative body.

(10) An amount payable under subsection (9) must be paid without undue delay and no later than the end of the period of 30 days beginning with the day after the day on which the notice of withdrawal was given (and if not paid by the end of that period may be recovered by the creditor as a debt).

(11) Where a regulated consumer credit agreement is a conditional sale, hire-purchase or credit-sale agreement and—

  (a) the debtor withdraws from the agreement under this section after the credit has been provided, and

  (b) the sum payable under subsection (9)(a) is paid in full by the debtor, title to the goods purchased or supplied under the agreement is to pass to the debtor on the same terms as would have applied had the debtor not withdrawn from the agreement.

(12) In subsections (2), (4), (5), (6) and (9)(a) references to the creditor include a person specified by the creditor in the agreement.

(13) In subsection (7)(b) the reference to an ancillary service means a service that relates to the provision of credit under the agreement and includes in particular an insurance or payment protection policy.

(14) For the purposes of this section, an agreement is an excluded agreement if it is—

    (a) an agreement for credit exceeding £60,260,

    (b) an agreement secured on land,

    (c) a restricted-use credit agreement to finance the purchase of land, or

    (d) an agreement for a bridging loan in connection with the purchase of land.]

Cancellation of certain agreements within cooling-off period

67   Cancellable agreements

[(1) Subject to subsection (2)] A regulated agreement may be cancelled by the debtor or hirer in accordance with this Part if the antecedent negotiations included oral representations made when in the presence of the debtor or hirer by an individual acting as, or on behalf of, the negotiator, unless—

    (a) the agreement is secured on land, or is a restricted-use credit agreement to finance the purchase of land or is an agreement for a bridging loan in connection with the purchase of land, or

    (b) the unexecuted agreement is signed by the debtor or hirer at premises at which any of the following is carrying on any business (whether on a permanent or temporary basis)—

        (i)   the creditor or owner;

        (ii) any party to a linked transaction (other than the debtor or hirer or a relative of his);

        (iii) the negotiator in any antecedent negotiations.

[(2) This section does not apply where section 66A applies.]

68   Cooling-off period

The debtor or hirer may serve notice of cancellation of a cancellable agreement between his signing of the unexecuted agreement and—

    (a) the end of the fifth day following the day on which he received a copy under section 63(2) or a notice under section 64(1)(b), or

    (b) if (by virtue of regulations made under section 64(4) section 64(1)(b) does not apply, the end of the fourteenth day following the day on which he signed the unexecuted agreement.

69   Notice of cancellation

(1) If within the period specified in section 68 the debtor or hirer under a cancellable agreement serves on—

    (a) the creditor or owner, or

    (b) the person specified in the notice under section 64(1), or

    (c) a person who (whether by virtue of subsection (6) or otherwise) is the agent of the creditor or owner, a notice (a 'notice of cancellation') which, however expressed and whether or not conforming to the notice given under section 64(1), indicates the intention of the debtor or hirer to withdraw from the agreement, the notice shall operate—

        (i)   to cancel the agreement, and any linked transaction, and

        (ii) to withdraw any offer by the debtor or hirer, or his relative, to enter into a linked transaction.

(2) In the case of a debtor-creditor-supplier agreement for restricted-use credit financing—

    (a) the doing of work or supply of goods to meet an emergency, or

(b) the supply of goods which, before service of the notice of cancellation, had by the act of the debtor or his relative become incorporated in any land or thing not comprised in the agreement or any linked transaction, subsection (1) shall apply with the substitution of the following for paragraph (i)—

'(i) to cancel only such provisions of the agreement and any linked transaction as—

(aa) relate to the provision of credit, or

(bb) require the debtor to pay an item in the total charge for credit, or

(cc) subject the debtor to any obligation other than to pay for the doing of the said work, or the supply of the said goods'.

(3) Except so far as is otherwise provided, references in this Act to the cancellation of an agreement or transaction do not include a case within subsection (2).

(4) Except as otherwise provided by or under this Act, an agreement or transaction cancelled under subsection (1) shall be treated as if it had never been entered into.

(5) Regulations may exclude linked transactions of the prescribed description from subsection (1)(i) or (ii).

(6) Each of the following shall be deemed to be the agent of the creditor or owner for the purpose of receiving a notice of cancellation—

(a) a credit-broker or supplier who is the negotiator in antecedent negotiations,

(b) any person who, in the course of a business carried on by him, acts on behalf of the debtor or hirer in any negotiations for the agreement.

[(7) Whether or not it is actually received by him, a notice of cancellation sent to a person shall be deemed to be served on him—

(a) in the case of a notice sent by post, at the time of posting, and

(b) in the case of a notice transmitted in the form of an electronic communication in accordance with section 176A(1), at the time of the transmission.]

70 Cancellation: recovery of money paid by debtor or hirer

(1) On the cancellation of a regulated agreement, and of any linked transaction,—

(a) any sum paid by the debtor or hirer, or his relative, under or in contemplation of the agreement or transaction, including any item in the total charge for credit, shall become repayable, and

(b) any sum, including any item in the total charge for credit, which but for the cancellation is, or would or might become, payable by the debtor or hirer, or his relative, under the agreement or transaction shall cease to be, or shall not become, so payable, and

(c) in the case of a debtor-creditor-supplier agreement falling within section 12(b), any sum paid on the debtor's behalf by the creditor to the supplier shall become repayable to the creditor.

(2) If, under the terms of a cancelled agreement or transaction, the debtor or hirer, or his relative, is in possession of any goods, he shall have a lien on them for any sum repayable to him under subsection (1) in respect of that agreement or transaction, or any other linked transaction.

(3) A sum repayable under subsection (1) is repayable by the person to whom it was originally paid, but in the case of a debtor-creditor-supplier agreement falling within section 12(b) the creditor and the supplier shall be under a joint and several liability to repay sums paid by the debtor, or his relative, under the agreement or under a linked transaction falling within section 19(1)(b) and accordingly, in such a case, the creditor shall be entitled, in accordance with rules of court, to have the supplier made a party to any proceedings brought against the creditor to recover any such sums.

(4) Subject to any agreement between them, the creditor shall be entitled to be indemnified by the supplier for loss suffered by the creditor in satisfying his liability under subsection (3), including costs reasonably incurred by him in defending proceedings instituted by the debtor.

(5) Subsection (1) does not apply to any sum which, if not paid by a debtor, would be payable by virtue of section 71, and applies to a sum paid or payable by a debtor for the issue of a credit-token only where the credit-token has been returned to the creditor or surrendered to a supplier.

(6) If the total charge for credit includes an item in respect of a fee or commission charged by a credit-broker, the amount repayable under subsection (1) in respect of that item shall be the excess over [£5] of the fee or commission.

(7) If the total charge for credit includes any sum payable or paid by the debtor to a credit-broker otherwise than in respect of a fee or commission charged by him, that sum shall for the purposes of subsection (6) be treated as if it were such a fee or commission.

(8) So far only as is necessary to give effect to section 69(2), this section applies to an agreement or transaction within that subsection as it applies to a cancelled agreement or transaction.

71 Cancellation: repayment of credit

(1) Notwithstanding the cancellation of a regulated consumer credit agreement, other than a debtor-creditor-supplier agreement for restricted-use credit, the agreement shall continue in force so far as it relates to repayment of credit and payment of interest.

(2) If, following the cancellation of a regulated consumer credit agreement, the debtor repays the whole or a portion of the credit—

(a) before the expiry of one month following service of the notice of cancellation, or

(b) in the case of a credit repayable by instalments, before the date on which the first instalment is due,

no interest shall be payable on the amount repaid.

(3) If the whole of a credit repayable by instalments is not repaid on or before the date specified in subsection (2)(b), the debtor shall not be liable to repay any of the credit except on receipt of a request in writing in the prescribed form, signed by or on behalf of the creditor, stating the amounts of the remaining instalments (recalculated by the creditor as nearly as may be in accordance with the agreement and without extending the repayment period), but excluding any sum other than principal and interest.

(4) Repayment of a credit, or payment of interest, under a cancelled agreement shall be treated as duly made if it is made to any person on whom, under section 69, a notice of cancellation could have been served, other than a person referred to in section 69(6)(b).

72 Cancellation: return of goods

(1) This section applies where any agreement or transaction relating to goods, being—

(a) a restricted-use debtor-creditor-supplier agreement, a consumer hire agreement, or a linked transaction to which the debtor or hirer under any regulated agreement is a party, or

(b) a linked transaction to which a relative of the debtor or hirer under any regulated agreement is a party,

is cancelled after the debtor or hirer (in a case within paragraph (a)) or the relative (in a case within paragraph (b)) has acquired possession of the goods by virtue of the agreement or transaction.

(2) In this section—

(a) 'the possessor' means the person who has acquired possession of the goods as mentioned in subsection (1),

(b) 'the other party' means the person from whom the possessor acquired possession, and

(c) 'the pre-cancellation period' means the period beginning when the possessor acquired possession and ending with the cancellation.

(3) The possessor shall be treated as having been under a duty throughout the pre-cancellation period—

(a) to retain possession of the goods, and

(b) to take reasonable care of them.

(4) On the cancellation, the possessor shall be under a duty, subject to any lien, to restore the goods to the other party in accordance with this section, and meanwhile to retain possession of the goods and take reasonable care of them.

(5) The possessor shall not be under any duty to deliver the goods except at his own premises and in pursuance of a request in writing signed by or on behalf of the other party and served on the possessor either before, or at the time when, the goods are collected from those premises.

(6) If the possessor—
- (a) delivers the goods (whether at his own premises or elsewhere) to any person on whom, under section 69, a notice of cancellation could have been served (other than a person referred to in section 69(6)(b), or
- (b) sends the goods at his own expense to such a person, he shall be discharged from any duty to retain the goods or deliver them to any person.

(7) Where the possessor delivers the goods as mentioned in subsection (6)(a), his obligation to take care of the goods shall cease: and if he sends the goods as mentioned in subsection (6)(b), he shall be under a duty to take reasonable care to see that they are received by the other party and not damaged in transit, but in other respects his duty to take care of the goods shall cease.

(8) Where, at any time during the period of 21 days following the cancellation, the possessor receives such a request as is mentioned in subsection (5), and unreasonably refuses or unreasonably fails to comply with it, his duty to take reasonable care of the goods shall continue until he delivers or sends the goods as mentioned in subsection (6), but if within that period he does not receive such a request his duty to take reasonable care of the goods shall cease at the end of that period.

(9) The preceding provisions of this section do not apply to—
- (a) perishable goods, or
- (b) goods which by their nature are consumed by use and which, before the cancellation, were so consumed, or
- (c) goods supplied to meet an emergency, or
- (d) goods which, before the cancellation, had become incorporated in any land or thing not comprised in the cancelled agreement or a linked transaction.

(10) Where the address of the possessor is specified in the executed agreement, references in this section to his own premises are to that address and no other.

(11) Breach of a duty imposed by this section is actionable as a breach of statutory duty.

73   Cancellation: goods given in part-exchange

(1) This section applies on the cancellation of a regulated agreement where, in antecedent negotiations, the negotiator agreed to take goods in part-exchange (the 'part-exchange goods') and those goods have been delivered to him.

(2) Unless, before the end of the period of ten days beginning with the date of cancellation, the part-exchange goods are returned to the debtor or hirer in a condition substantially as good as when they were delivered to the negotiator, the debtor or hirer shall be entitled to recover from the negotiator a sum equal to the part-exchange allowance (as defined in subsection (7)(b)).

(3) In the case of a debtor-creditor-supplier agreement within section 12(b), the negotiator and the creditor shall be under a joint and several liability to pay to the debtor a sum recoverable under subsection (2).

(4) Subject to any agreement between them, the creditor shall be entitled to be indemnified by the negotiator for loss suffered by the creditor in satisfying his liability under subsection (3), including costs reasonably incurred by him in defending proceedings instituted by the debtor.

(5) During the period of ten days beginning with the date of cancellation, the debtor or hirer, if he is in possession of goods to which the cancelled agreement relates, shall have a lien on them for—
- (a) delivery of the part-exchange goods, in a condition substantially as good as when they were delivered to the negotiator, or
- (b) a sum equal to the part-exchange allowance; and if the lien continues to the end of that period it shall thereafter subsist only as a lien for a sum equal to the part-exchange allowance.

(6) Where the debtor or hirer recovers from the negotiator or creditor, or both of them jointly, a sum equal to the part-exchange allowance, then, if the title of the debtor or hirer to the part-exchange goods has not vested in the negotiator, it shall so vest on the recovery of that sum.

(7) For the purposes of this section—

   (a) the negotiator shall be treated as having agreed to take goods in part-exchange if, in pursuance of the antecedent negotiations, he either purchased or agreed to purchase those goods or accepted or agreed to accept them as part of the consideration for the cancelled agreement, and

   (b) the part-exchange allowance shall be the sum agreed as such in the antecedent negotiations or, if no such agreement was arrived at, such sum as it would have been reasonable to allow in respect of the part-exchange goods if no notice of cancellation had been served.

(8) In an action brought against the creditor for a sum recoverable under subsection (2), he shall be entitled, in accordance with rules of court, to have the negotiator made a party to the proceedings.

Exclusion of certain agreements from Part V

74   Exclusion of certain agreements from Part V

[(1) Except as provided in subsections (1A) to (2), this Part does not apply to—

   (a) a non-commercial agreement,

   (b) a debtor-creditor agreement enabling the debtor to overdraw on a current account,

   (c) a debtor-creditor agreement to finance the making of such payments arising on, or connected with, the death of a person as may be prescribed, or

   (d) a small debtor-creditor-supplier agreement for restricted-use credit.

(1A) Section 56 (antecedent negotiations) applies to a non-commercial agreement.

(1B) Where an agreement that falls within subsection (1)(b) is an authorised business overdraft agreement the following provisions apply—

   (b) section 56 (antecedent negotiations);

   (c) section 60 (regulations on form and content of agreements);

   (d) section 61B (duty to supply copy of overdraft agreement).

(1C) Where an agreement that falls within subsection (1)(b) is an authorised non-business overdraft agreement the following provisions apply—

   (a) section 55 (regulations on disclosure of information);

   (c) section 55C (copy of draft consumer credit agreement);

   (d) section 56 (antecedent negotiations);

   (e) section 60 (regulations on form and content of agreements);

   (f) section 61B (duty to supply copy of overdraft agreement).

(1D) Where an agreement that falls within subsection (1)(b) would be an authorised non-business overdraft agreement but for the fact that the credit is not repayable on demand or within three months the following provisions apply—

   (a) section 55 (regulations on disclosure of information);

   (d) section 55C (copy of draft consumer credit agreement);

   (e) section 56 (antecedent negotiations);

   (f) section 60 (regulations on form and content of agreements);

   (g) section 61 (signing of agreement);

   (h) section 61A (duty to supply copy of executed agreement);

   (i) section 66A (withdrawal from consumer credit agreement).

(1E) In the case of an agreement that falls within subsection (1)(b) but does not fall within subsection (1B), (1C) or (1D), section 56 (antecedent negotiations) applies.

(1F) The following provisions apply to a debtor-creditor agreement to finance the making of such payments arising on, or connected with, the death of a person as may be prescribed—

   (a) section 55 (regulations on disclosure of information);

   (d) section 55C (copy of draft consumer credit agreement);

   (e) section 56 (antecedent negotiations);

   (f) section 60 (regulations on form and content of agreements);

   (g) section 61 (signing of agreement);

(h) section 61A (duty to supply copy of executed agreement);

(i) section 66A (withdrawal from consumer credit agreement).

(2) The following provisions apply to a small debtor-creditor-supplier agreement for restricted-use credit—

(a) section 55 (regulations on disclosure of information);

(b) section 56 (antecedent negotiations);

(c) section 66A (withdrawal from consumer credit agreement).]

(3) [Subsection (1)(c) applies] only where the [FCA] so determines, and such a determination—

(a) may be made subject to such conditions as the [FCA] thinks fit, and

(b) shall be made only if the [FCA] is of opinion that it is not against the interests of debtors.

(4) If any term of an agreement falling within subsection [1(d)] is expressed in writing, regulations under section 60(1) shall apply to that term (subject to section 60(3)) as if the agreement were a regulated agreement not falling within subsection [1(d)].

PART VI MATTERS ARISING DURING CURRENCY OF CREDIT OR HIRE AGREEMENTS

75 Liability of creditor for breaches by supplier

(1) If the debtor under a debtor-creditor-supplier agreement falling within section 12(b) or (c) has, in relation to a transaction financed by the agreement, any claim against the supplier in respect of a misrepresentation or breach of contract, he shall have a like claim against the creditor, who, with the supplier, shall accordingly be jointly and severally liable to the debtor.

(2) Subject to any agreement between them, the creditor shall be entitled to be indemnified by the supplier for loss suffered by the creditor in satisfying his liability under subsection (1), including costs reasonably incurred by him in defending proceedings instituted by the debtor.

(3) Subsection (1) does not apply to a claim—

(a) under a non-commercial agreement, [...]

(b) so far as the claim relates to any single item to which the supplier has attached a cash price not exceeding [£100] or more than [£30,000][, or.

(c) under a debtor-creditor-supplier agreement for running-account credit—

(i) which provides for the making of payments by the debtor in relation to specified periods which, in the case of an agreement which is not secured on land, do not exceed three months, and

(ii) which requires that the number of payments to be made by the debtor in repayments of the whole amount of the credit provided in each such period shall not exceed one.].

(4) This section applies notwithstanding that the debtor, in entering into the transaction, exceeded the credit limit or otherwise contravened any term of the agreement.

(5) In an action brought against the creditor under subsection (1) he shall be entitled, in accordance with rules of court, to have the supplier made a party to the proceedings.

[75A Further provision for liability of creditor for breaches by supplier

(1) If the debtor under a linked credit agreement has a claim against the supplier in respect of a breach of contract the debtor may pursue that claim against the creditor where any of the conditions in subsection (2) are met.

(2) The conditions in subsection (1) are—

(a) that the supplier cannot be traced,

(b) that the debtor has contacted the supplier but the supplier has not responded,

(c) that the supplier is insolvent, or

(d) that the debtor has taken reasonable steps to pursue his claim against the supplier but has not obtained satisfaction for his claim.

(3) The steps referred to in subsection (2)(d) need not include litigation.

(4) For the purposes of subsection (2)(d) a debtor is to be deemed to have obtained satisfaction where he has accepted a replacement product or service or other compensation from the supplier in settlement of his claim.

(5) In this section 'linked credit agreement' means a regulated consumer credit agreement which serves exclusively to finance an agreement for the supply of specific goods or the provision of a specific service and where—

  (a) the creditor uses the services of the supplier in connection with the preparation or making of the credit agreement, or

  (b) the specific goods or provision of a specific service are explicitly specified in the credit agreement.

(6) This section does not apply where—

  (a) the cash value of the goods or service is £30, 000 or less,

  (b) the linked credit agreement is for credit which exceeds £60, 260 and is not a residential renovation agreement, or

  (c) the linked credit agreement is entered into by the debtor wholly or predominantly for the purposes of a business carried on, or intended to be carried on, by him.

(7) Article 60C(5) and (6) of the Regulated Activities Order applies for the purposes of subsection (6)(c).]

76 Duty to give notice before taking certain action

(1) The creditor or owner is not entitled to enforce a term of a regulated agreement by—

  (a) demanding earlier payment of any sum, or

  (b) recovering possession of any goods or land, or

  (c) treating any right conferred on the debtor or hirer by the agreement as terminated, restricted or deferred,

except by or after giving the debtor or hirer not less than seven days' notice of his intention to do so.

(2) Subsection (1) applies only where—

  (a) a period for the duration of the agreement is specified in the agreement, and

  (b) that period has not ended when the creditor or owner does an act mentioned in subsection (1),

but so applies notwithstanding that, under the agreement, any party is entitled to terminate it before the end of the period so specified.

(3) A notice under subsection (1) is ineffective if not in the prescribed form.

(4) Subsection (1) does not prevent a creditor from treating the right to draw on any credit as restricted or deferred and taking such steps as may be necessary to make the restriction or deferment effective.

(5) Regulations may provide that subsection (1) is not to apply to agreements described by the regulations.

(6) Subsection (1) does not apply to a right of enforcement arising by reason of any breach by the debtor or hirer of the regulated agreement.

77 Duty to give information to debtor under fixed-sum credit agreement

(1) The creditor under a regulated agreement for fixed-sum credit, within the prescribed period after receiving a request in writing to that effect from the debtor and payment of a fee of [£1], shall give the debtor a copy of the executed agreement (if any) and of any other document referred to in it, together with a statement signed by or on behalf of the creditor showing, according to the information to which it is practicable for him to refer,—

  (a) the total sum paid under the agreement by the debtor;

  (b) the total sum which has become payable under the agreement by the debtor but remains unpaid, and the various amounts comprised in that total sum, with the date when each became due; and

  (c) the total sum which is to become payable under the agreement by the debtor, and the various amounts comprised in that total sum, with the date, or mode of determining the date, when each becomes due.

[(1A) Where a request under subsection (1) also amounts to a request under regulation 49 of the Payment Services Regulations 2017 (information during period of contract), subsection (1) applies as if the words 'and payment of a fee of £1' were omitted.]

(2) If the creditor possesses insufficient information to enable him to ascertain the amounts and dates mentioned in subsection (1)(c), he shall be taken to comply with that paragraph if his statement under subsection (1) gives the basis on which, under the regulated agreement, they would fall to be ascertained.

[(2A) Subsection (2B) applies if the regulated agreement is a green deal plan.

(2B) The duty imposed on the creditor by subsection (1) may be discharged by another person acting on the creditor's behalf.]

(3) Subsection (1) does not apply to—

    (a) an agreement under which no sum is, or will or may become, payable by the debtor, or

    (b) a request made less than one month after a previous request under that subsection relating to the same agreement was complied with.

(4) If the creditor under an agreement fails to comply with subsection (1)—

    (a) he is not entitled, while the default continues, to enforce the agreement; [...].

(5) This section does not apply to a non-commercial agreement.

[77A   Statements to be provided in relation to fixed-sum credit agreements

(1) The creditor under a regulated agreement for fixed-sum credit must give the debtor statements under this section.

(1A) The statements must relate to consecutive periods.

(1B) The first such period must begin with either—

    (a) the day on which the agreement is made, or

    (b) the day the first movement occurs on the debtor's account with the creditor relating to the agreement.

(1C) No such period may exceed a year.

(1D) For the purposes of subsection (1C), a period of a year which expires on a non-working day may be regarded as expiring on the next working day.

(1E) Each statement under this section must be given to the debtor before the end of the period of thirty days beginning with the day after the end of the period to which the statement relates.

(2) Regulations may make provision about the form and content of statements under this section.

[(2A) Subsection (2B) applies if the regulated agreement is a green deal plan.

(2B) Any duty imposed on the creditor by this section may be discharged by another person acting on the creditor's behalf.]

(3) The debtor shall have no liability to pay any sum in connection with the preparation or the giving to him of a statement under this section.

(4) The creditor is not required to give the debtor any statement under this section once the following conditions are satisfied—

    (a) that there is no sum payable under the agreement by the debtor; and

    (b) that there is no sum which will or may become so payable.

(5) Subsection (6) applies if at a time before the conditions mentioned in subsection (4) are satisfied the creditor fails to give the debtor—

    (a) a statement under this section within the period mentioned in subsection (1E);

(6) Where this subsection applies in relation to a failure to give a statement under this section to the debtor—

    (a) the creditor shall not be entitled to enforce the agreement during the period of non-compliance;

    (b) the debtor shall have no liability to pay any sum of interest to the extent calculated by reference to the period of non-compliance or to any part of it; and

    (c) the debtor shall have no liability to pay any default sum which (apart from this paragraph)—

        (i) would have become payable during the period of non-compliance; or

(ii) would have become payable after the end of that period in connection with a breach of the agreement which occurs during that period (whether or not the breach continues after the end of that period).

(7) In this section 'the period of non-compliance' means, in relation to a failure to give a statement under this section to the debtor, the period which—

(a) begins immediately after the end of the period mentioned in subsection (5); and

(b) ends at the end of the day on which the statement is given to the debtor or on which the conditions mentioned in subsection (4) are satisfied, whichever is earlier.

(8) This section does not apply in relation to a non-commercial agreement or to a small agreement.]

[(9) This section does not apply where the holder of a current account overdraws on the account without a pre-arranged overdraft or exceeds a pre-arranged overdraft limit.]

[77B   Fixed-sum credit agreement: statement of account to be provided on request

(1) This section applies to a regulated consumer credit agreement—

(a) which is for fixed-sum credit,

(b) which is of fixed duration,

(c) where the credit is repayable in instalments by the debtor, and

(d) which is not an excluded agreement.

(2) Upon a request from the debtor, the creditor must as soon as reasonably practicable give to the debtor a statement in writing which complies with subsections (3) to (5).

(3) The statement must include a table showing the details of each instalment owing under the agreement as at the date of the request.

(4) Details to be provided under subsection (3) must include—

(a) the date on which the instalment is due,

(b) the amount of the instalment,

(c) any conditions relating to payment of the instalment, and

(d) a breakdown of the instalment showing how much of it is made up of capital repayment, interest payment and other charges.

(5) Where the rate of interest is variable or the charges under the agreement may be varied, the statement must also indicate clearly and concisely that the information in the table is valid only until the rate of interest or charges are varied.

(6) The debtor may make a request under subsection (2) at any time that the agreement is in force unless a previous request has been made less than a month before and has been complied with.

(7) The debtor shall have no liability to pay any sum in connection with the preparation or the giving of a statement under this section.

[(7A) Subsection (7B) applies if the regulated agreement is a green deal plan.

(7B) The duty imposed on the creditor by this section may be discharged by another person acting on the creditor's behalf.]

(8) A breach of the duty imposed by this section is actionable as a breach of statutory duty.

(9) For the purposes of this section, an agreement is an excluded agreement if it is—

(a) an agreement secured on land,

(b) an agreement under which a person takes an article in pawn,

(c) an agreement under which the creditor provides the debtor with credit which exceeds £60, 260 and is not a residential renovation agreement, or

(d) an agreement entered into by the debtor wholly or predominantly for the purpose of a business carried on, or intended to be carried on, by him.

(10) Article 60C(5) and (6) of the Regulated Activities Order applies for the purposes of subsection (9)(d).]

78   Duty to give information to debtor under running-account credit agreement

(1) The creditor under a regulated agreement for running-account credit, within the prescribed period after receiving a request in writing to that effect from the debtor and payment of a fee of [£1],

shall give the debtor a copy of the executed agreement (if any) and of any other document referred to in it, together with a statement signed by or on behalf of the creditor showing, according to the information to which it is practicable for him to refer,—

(a) the state of the account, and

(b) the amount, if any, currently payable under the agreement by the debtor to the creditor, and

(c) the amounts and due dates of any payments which, if the debtor does not draw further on the account, will later become payable under the agreement by the debtor to the creditor.

[(1A) Where a request under subsection (1) also amounts to a request under regulation 49 of the Payment Services Regulations 2017 (information during period of contract), subsection (1) applies as if the words 'and payment of a fee of £1' were omitted.]

(2) If the creditor possesses insufficient information to enable him to ascertain the amounts and dates mentioned in subsection (1)(c), he shall be taken to comply with that paragraph if his statement under subsection (1) gives the basis on which, under the regulated agreement, they would fall to be ascertained.

(3) Subsection (1) does not apply to—

(a) an agreement under which no sum is, or will or may become, payable by the debtor, or

(b) a request made less than one month after a previous request under that subsection relating to the same agreement was complied with.

(4) Where running-account credit is provided under a regulated agreement, the creditor shall give the debtor statements in the prescribed form, and with the prescribed contents—

(a) showing according to the information to which it is practicable for him to refer, the state of the account at regular intervals of not more than twelve months, and

(b) where the agreement provides, in relation to specified periods, for the making of payments by the debtor, or the charging against him of interest or any other sum, showing according to the information to which it is practicable for him to refer the state of the account at the end of each of those periods during which there is any movement in the account.

[(4A) Regulations may require a statement under subsection (4) to contain also information in the prescribed terms about the consequences of the debtor—

(a) failing to make payments as required by the agreement; or

(b) only making payments of a prescribed description in prescribed circumstances.]

(5) A statement under subsection (4) shall be given within the prescribed period after the end of the period to which the statement relates.

(6) If the creditor under an agreement fails to comply with subsection (1)—

(a) he is not entitled, while the default continues, to enforce the agreement; [. . .].

(7) This section does not apply to a non-commercial agreement, and subsections [(4) to (5)] do not apply to a small agreement.

[**78A   Duty to give information to debtor on change of rate of interest**

(1) Where the rate of interest charged under a regulated consumer credit agreement, other than an excluded agreement, is to be varied, the creditor must inform the debtor in writing of the matters mentioned in subsection (3) before the variation can take effect.

(2) But subsection (1) does not apply where—

(a) the agreement provides that the creditor is to inform the debtor in writing periodically of the matters mentioned in subsection (3) in relation to any variation, at such times as may be provided for in the agreement,

(b) the agreement provides that the rate of interest is to vary according to a reference rate,

(c) the reference rate is publicly available,

(d) information about the reference rate is available on the premises of the creditor, and

(e) the variation of the rate of interest results from a change to the reference rate.

(3) The matters referred to in subsections (1) and (2)(a) are—

(a) the variation in the rate of interest,

(b) the amount of any payments that are to be made after the variation has effect, if different, expressed as a sum of money where practicable, and

(c) if the number or frequency of payments changes as a result of the variation, the new number or frequency.

(4) In the case of an agreement mentioned in subsection (5) this section applies as follows—

    (a) the obligation in subsection (1) only applies if the rate of interest increases, and

    (b) subsection (3) is to be read as if paragraphs (b) and (c) were omitted.

(5) The agreements referred to in subsection (4) are—

    (a) an authorised business overdraft agreement,

    (b) an authorised non-business overdraft agreement, or

    (c) an agreement which would be an authorised non-business overdraft agreement but for the fact that the credit is not repayable on demand or within three months.

(6) For the purposes of this section an agreement is an excluded agreement if it is—

    (a) a debtor-creditor agreement arising where the holder of a current account overdraws on the account without a pre-arranged overdraft or exceeds a pre-arranged overdraft limit, or

    (b) an agreement secured on land.]

79   Duty to give hirer information

(1) The owner under a regulated consumer hire agreement, within the prescribed period after receiving a request in writing to that effect from the hirer and payment of a fee of [£1], shall give to the hirer a copy of the executed agreement and of any other document referred to in it, together with a statement signed by or on behalf of the owner showing, according to the information to which it is practicable for him to refer, the total sum which has become payable under the agreement by the hirer but remains unpaid and the various amounts comprised in that total sum, with the date when each became due.

(2) Subsection (1) does not apply to—

    (a) an agreement under which no sum is, or will or may become, payable by the hirer, or

    (b) a request made less than one month after a previous request under that subsection relating to the same agreement was complied with.

(3) If the owner under an agreement fails to comply with subsection (1)—

    (a) he is not entitled, while the default continues, to enforce the agreement; [...].

(4) This section does not apply to a non-commercial agreement.

80   Debtor or hirer to give information about goods

(1) Where a regulated agreement, other than a non-commercial agreement, requires the debtor or hirer to keep goods to which the agreement relates in his possession or control, he shall, within seven working days after he has received a request in writing to that effect from the creditor or owner, tell the creditor or owner where the goods are.

(2) If the debtor or hirer fails to comply with subsection (1), and the default continues for 14 days, he commits an offence.

82   Variation of agreements

(1) Where, under a power contained in a regulated agreement, the creditor or owner varies the agreement, the variation shall not take effect before notice of it is given to the debtor or hirer in the prescribed manner.

[(1A) Subsection (1) does not apply to a variation in the rate of interest charged under an agreement not secured on land (see section 78A).

(1B) Subsection (1) does not apply to a variation in the rate of interest charged under an agreement secured on land if—

    (a) the agreement falls within subsection (1D), and

    (b) the variation is a reduction in the rate.

(1C) Subsection (1) does not apply to a variation in any other charge under an agreement if—

    (a) the agreement falls within subsection (1D), and

    (b) the variation is a reduction in the charge.

(1D) The agreements referred to in subsections (1B) and (1C) are—

    (a) an authorised business overdraft agreement,

(b) an authorised non-business overdraft agreement, or

(c) an agreement which would be an authorised non-business overdraft agreement but for the fact that the credit is not repayable on demand or within three months.

(1E) Subsection (1) does not apply to a debtor-creditor agreement arising where the holder of a current account overdraws on the account without a pre-arranged overdraft or exceeds a pre-arranged overdraft limit.]

(2) Where an agreement (a 'modifying agreement') varies or supplements an earlier agreement, the modifying agreement shall for the purposes of this Act be treated as—

(a) revoking the earlier agreement, and

(b) containing provisions reproducing the combined effect of the two agreements, and obligations outstanding in relation to the earlier agreement shall accordingly be treated as outstanding instead in relation to the modifying agreement.

[(2A) Subsection (2) does not apply if the earlier agreement or the modifying agreement is an exempt agreement.]

[(2B) Subsection (2) does not apply if the modifying agreement varies—

(a) the amount of the repayment to be made under the earlier agreement, or

(b) the duration of the agreement,

as a result of the discharge of part of the debtor's indebtedness under the earlier agreement by virtue of section 94(3).]

(3) If the earlier agreement is a regulated agreement but (apart from this subsection) the modifying agreement is not then, [unless the modifying agreement is—

(a) for running account credit; or

(b) is an exempt agreement,

it shall be treated as a regulated agreement.]

(4) If the earlier agreement is a regulated agreement for running-account credit, and by the modifying agreement the creditor allows the credit limit to be exceeded but intends the excess to be merely temporary, Part V (except section 56) shall not apply to the modifying agreement.

(5) If—

(a) the earlier agreement is a cancellable agreement, and

(b) the modifying agreement is made within the period applicable under section 68 to the earlier agreement,

then, whether or not the modifying agreement would, apart from this subsection, be a cancellable agreement, it shall be treated as a cancellable agreement in respect of which a notice may be served under section 68 not later than the end of the period applicable under that section to the earlier agreement.

[(5A) Subsection 5 does not apply where the modifying agreement is an exempt agreement.]

(6) Except under subsection (5), a modifying agreement shall not be treated as a cancellable agreement.

[(6A) If—

(a) the earlier agreement is an agreement to which section 66A (right of withdrawal) applies, and

(b) the modifying agreement is made within the period during which the debtor may give notice of withdrawal from the earlier agreement (see section 66A(2)),

then, whether or not the modifying agreement would, apart from this subsection, be an agreement to which section 66A applies, it shall be treated as such an agreement in respect of which notice may be given under subsection (2) of that section within the period referred to in paragraph (b) above.

(6B) Except as provided for under subsection (6A) section 66A does not apply to a modifying agreement.]

(7) This section does not apply to a non-commercial agreement.

[(8) In this section, an 'exempt agreement' means an agreement which is an exempt agreement for the purposes of Chapter 14A of Part 2 of the Regulated Activities Order by virtue of article 60C(2) (regulated mortgage contracts and regulated home purchase plans) or article 60D (exemption relating to the purchase of land for non-residential purposes) of that Order.]

83   Liability for misuse of credit facilities

(1) The debtor under a regulated consumer credit agreement shall not be liable to the creditor for any loss arising from use of the credit facility by another person not acting, or to be treated as acting, as the debtor's agent.

(2) This section does not apply to a non-commercial agreement, or to any loss in so far as it arises from misuse of an instrument to which section 4 of the Cheques Act 1957 applies.

84   Misuse of credit-tokens

(1) Section 83 does not prevent the debtor under a credit-token agreement from being made liable to the extent of [£35] (or the credit limit if lower) for loss to the creditor arising from use of the credit-token by other persons during a period beginning when the credit-token ceases to be in the possession of any authorized person and ending when the credit-token is once more in the possession of an authorised person.

(2) Section 83 does not prevent the debtor under a credit-token agreement from being made liable to any extent for loss to the creditor from use of the credit-token by a person who acquired possession of it with the debtor's consent.

(3) Subsection (1) and (2) shall not apply to any use of the credit-token after the creditor has been given oral or written notice that it is lost or stolen, or is for any other reason liable to misuse.

[(3A) Subsections (1) and (2) shall not apply to any use, in connection with a distance contract (other than an excepted contract), of a card which is a credit-token.

(3B) In subsection (3A), 'distance contract' and 'excepted contract' have the meanings given in the Consumer Protection (Distance Selling) Regulations 2000.]

[(3C) Subsections (1) and (2) shall not apply to any use, in connection with a distance contract within the meaning of the Financial Services (Distance Marketing) Regulations 2004, of a card which is a credit-token.]

(4) Subsections (1) and (2) shall not apply unless there are contained in the credit-token agreement in the prescribed manner particulars of the name, address and telephone number of a person stated to be the person to whom notice is to be given under subsection (3).

(5) Notice under subsection (3) takes effect when received, but where it is given orally, and the agreement so requires, it shall be treated as not taking effect if not confirmed in writing within seven days.

(6) Any sum paid by the debtor for the issue of the credit-token to the extent (if any) that it has not been previously offset by use made of the credit-token, shall be treated as paid towards satisfaction of any liability under subsection (1) or (2).

(7) The debtor, the creditor, and any person authorised by the debtor to use the credit-token, shall be authorised persons for the purposes of subsection (1).

(8) Where two or more credit-tokens are given under one credit-token agreement, the preceding provisions of this section apply to each credit-token separately.

85   Duty on issue of new credit-tokens

(1) Whenever, in connection with a credit-token agreement, a credit-token (other than the first) is given by the creditor to the debtor, the creditor shall give the debtor a copy of the executed agreement (if any) and of any other document referred to in it.

(2) If the creditor fails to comply with this section—

   (a) he is not entitled, while the default continues, to enforce the agreement, [...].

(3) This section does not apply to a small agreement.

86   Death of debtor or hirer

(1) The creditor or owner under a regulated agreement is not entitled, by reason of the death of the debtor or hirer, to do an act specified in paragraphs (a) to (e) of section 87(1) if at the death the agreement is fully secured.

(2) If at the death of the debtor or hirer a regulated agreement is only partly secured or is unsecured, the creditor or owner is entitled, by reason of the death of the debtor or hirer, to do an act specified in paragraphs (a) to (e) of section 87(1) on an order of the court only.

(3) This section applies in relation to the termination of an agreement only where—

(a) a period for its duration is specified in the agreement, and

(b) that period has not ended when the creditor or owner purports to terminate the agreement,

but so applies notwithstanding that, under the agreement, any party is entitled to terminate it before the end of the period so specified.

(4) This section does not prevent the creditor from treating the right to draw on any credit as restricted or deferred, and taking such steps as may be necessary to make the restriction or deferment effective.

(5) This section does not affect the operation of any agreement providing for payment of sums—

(a) due under the regulated agreement, or

(b) becoming due under it on the death of the debtor or hirer, out of the proceeds of a policy of assurance on his life.

(6) For the purposes of this section an act is done by reason of the death of the debtor or hirer if it is done under a power conferred by the agreement which is—

(a) exercisable on his death, or

(b) exercisable at will and exercised at any time after his death.

PART VII DEFAULT AND TERMINATION

[Information sheets]

[86A   FCA to prepare information sheets on arrears and default

(1) The FCA shall prepare, and give general notice of, an arrears information sheet and a default information sheet.

(2) The arrears information sheet shall include information to help debtors and hirers who receive notices under section 86B or 86C.

(3) The default information sheet shall include information to help debtors and hirers who receive default notices.

(4) Regulations may make provision about the information to be included in an information sheet.

(5) An information sheet takes effect for the purposes of this Part at the end of the period of three months beginning with the day on which it is issued or on such later date as the FCA may specify in relation to the information sheet.

(6) If the FCA revises an information sheet after it has been issued, it shall issue the revised information sheet.

(7) A revised information sheet takes effect for the purposes of this Part at the end of the period of three months beginning with the day on which it is issued or on such later date as the FCA may specify in relation to the information sheet.]

[Sums in arrears and default sums]

[86B   Notice of sums in arrears under fixed-sum credit agreements etc.

(1) This section applies where at any time the following conditions are satisfied—

(a) that the debtor or hirer under an applicable agreement is required to have made at least two payments under the agreement before that time;

(b) that the total sum paid under the agreement by him is less than the total sum which he is required to have paid before that time;

    (c) that the amount of the shortfall is no less than the sum of the last two payments which he is required to have made before that time;

    (d) that the creditor or owner is not already under a duty to give him notices under this section in relation to the agreement; and

    (e) if a judgment has been given in relation to the agreement before that time, that there is no sum still to be paid under the judgment by the debtor or hirer.

(2) The creditor or owner—

    (a) shall, within the period of 14 days beginning with the day on which the conditions mentioned in subsection (1) are satisfied, give the debtor or hirer a notice under this section; and

    (b) after the giving of that notice, shall give him further notices under this section at intervals of not more than six months.

(3) The duty of the creditor or owner to give the debtor or hirer notices under this section shall cease when either of the conditions mentioned in subsection (4) is satisfied; but if either of those conditions is satisfied before the notice required by subsection (2)(a) is given, the duty shall not cease until that notice is given.

(4) The conditions referred to in subsection (3) are—

    (a) that the debtor or hirer ceases to be in arrears;

    (b) that a judgment is given in relation to the agreement under which a sum is required to be paid by the debtor or hirer.

(5) For the purposes of subsection (4)(a) the debtor or hirer ceases to be in arrears when—

    (a) no payments, which he has ever failed to make under the agreement when required, are still owing;

    (b) no default sum, which has ever become payable under the agreement in connection with his failure to pay any sum under the agreement when required, is still owing;

    (c) no sum of interest, which has ever become payable under the agreement in connection with such a default sum, is still owing; and

    (d) no other sum of interest, which has ever become payable under the agreement in connection with his failure to pay any sum under the agreement when required, is still owing.

(6) A notice under this section shall include a copy of the current arrears information sheet under section 86A.

(7) The debtor or hirer shall have no liability to pay any sum in connection with the preparation or the giving to him of a notice under this section.

(8) Regulations may make provision about the form and content of notices under this section.

(9) In the case of an applicable agreement under which the debtor or hirer must make all payments he is required to make at intervals of one week or less, this section shall have effect as if in subsection (1)(a) and (c) for 'two' there were substituted 'four'.

(10) If an agreement mentioned in subsection (9) was made before the beginning of the relevant period, only amounts resulting from failures by the debtor or hirer to make payments he is required to have made during that period shall be taken into account in determining any shortfall for the purposes of subsection (1)(c).

(11) In subsection (10) 'relevant period' means the period of 20 weeks ending with the day on which the debtor or hirer is required to have made the most recent payment under the agreement.]

[(12) In this section 'applicable agreement' means an agreement which falls within subsection (12A) or (12B).

(12A) An agreement falls within this subsection if—

    (a) it is a regulated agreement for fixed-sum credit; and

    (b) it is not—

        (i) a non-commercial agreement;

    (ii) a small agreement; or

    (iii) a green deal plan.

(12B) An agreement falls within this subsection if—

    (a) it is a regulated consumer hire agreement; and

    (b) it is neither a non-commercial agreement nor a small agreement.]

[(13) In this section—

    (a) 'payments' in relation to an applicable agreement which is a regulated agreement for fixed-sum credit means payments to be made at predetermined intervals provided for under the terms of the agreement; and

    (b) 'payments' in relation to an applicable agreement which is a regulated consumer hire agreement means any payments to be made by the hirer in relation to any period in consideration of the bailment or hiring to him of goods under the agreement.]

[86C   Notice of sums in arrears under running-account credit agreements

(1) This section applies where at any time the following conditions are satisfied—

    (a) that the debtor under an applicable agreement is required to have made at least two payments under the agreement before that time;

    (b) that the last two payments which he is required to have made before that time have not been made;

    (c) that the creditor has not already been required to give a notice under this section in relation to either of those payments; and

    (d) if a judgment has been given in relation to the agreement before that time, that there is no sum still to be paid under the judgment by the debtor.

(2) The creditor shall, no later than the end of the period within which he is next required to give a statement under section 78(4) in relation to the agreement, give the debtor a notice under this section.

(3) The notice shall include a copy of the current arrears information sheet under section 86A.

(4) The notice may be incorporated in a statement or other notice which the creditor gives the debtor in relation to the agreement by virtue of another provision of this Act.

(5) The debtor shall have no liability to pay any sum in connection with the preparation or the giving to him of the notice.

(6) Regulations may make provision about the form and content of notices under this section.

(7) In this section 'applicable agreement' means an agreement which—

    (a) is a regulated agreement for running-account credit; and

    (b) is neither a non-commercial agreement nor a small agreement.

(8) In this section 'payments' means payments to be made at predetermined intervals provided for under the terms of the agreement.]

[86D   Failure to give notice of sums in arrears

(1) This section applies where the creditor or owner under an agreement is under a duty to give the debtor or hirer notices under section 86B but fails to give him such a notice—

    (a) within the period mentioned in subsection (2)(a) of that section; or

    (b) within the period of six months beginning with the day after the day on which such a notice was last given to him.

(2) This section also applies where the creditor under an agreement is under a duty to give the debtor a notice under section 86C but fails to do so before the end of the period mentioned in subsection (2) of that section.

(3) The creditor or owner shall not be entitled to enforce the agreement during the period of non-compliance.

(4) The debtor or hirer shall have no liability to pay—

    (a) any sum of interest to the extent calculated by reference to the period of non-compliance or to any part of it; or

    (b) any default sum which (apart from this paragraph)—

        (i)   would have become payable during the period of non-compliance; or

        (ii) would have become payable after the end of that period in connection with a breach of the agreement which occurs during that period (whether or not the breach continues after the end of that period).

(5) In this section 'the period of non-compliance' means, in relation to a failure to give a notice under section 86B or 86C to the debtor or hirer, the period which—

    (a) begins immediately after the end of the period mentioned in (as the case may be) subsection (1)(a) or (b) or (2); and

    (b) ends at the end of the day mentioned in subsection (6).

(6) That day is—

    (a) in the case of a failure to give a notice under section 86B as mentioned in subsection (1)(a) of this section, the day on which the notice is given to the debtor or hirer;

    (b) in the case of a failure to give a notice under that section as mentioned in subsection (1)(b) of this section, the earlier of the following—

        (i)   the day on which the notice is given to the debtor or hirer;

        (ii) the day on which the condition mentioned in subsection (4)(a) of that section is satisfied;

    (c) in the case of a failure to give a notice under section 86C, the day on which the notice is given to the debtor.]

[86E   Notice of default sums

(1) This section applies where a default sum becomes payable under a regulated agreement by the debtor or hirer.

(2) The creditor or owner shall, within the prescribed period after the default sum becomes payable, give the debtor or hirer a notice under this section.

(3) The notice under this section may be incorporated in a statement or other notice which the creditor or owner gives the debtor or hirer in relation to the agreement by virtue of another provision of this Act.

(4) The debtor or hirer shall have no liability to pay interest in connection with the default sum to the extent that the interest is calculated by reference to a period occurring before the 29th day after the day on which the debtor or hirer is given the notice under this section.

(5) If the creditor or owner fails to give the debtor or hirer the notice under this section within the period mentioned in subsection (2), he shall not be entitled to enforce the agreement until the notice is given to the debtor or hirer.

(6) The debtor or hirer shall have no liability to pay any sum in connection with the preparation or the giving to him of the notice under this section.

(7) Regulations may—

    (a) provide that this section does not apply in relation to a default sum which is less than a prescribed amount;

    (b) make provision about the form and content of notices under this section.

(8) This section does not apply in relation to a non-commercial agreement or to a small agreement.]

[86F Interest on default sums

(1) This section applies where a default sum becomes payable under a regulated agreement by the debtor or hirer.

(2) The debtor or hirer shall only be liable to pay interest in connection with the default sum if the interest is simple interest.]

Default notices

87 Need for default notice

(1) Service of a notice on the debtor or hirer in accordance with section 88 (a 'default notice') is necessary before the creditor or owner can become entitled, by reason of any breach by the debtor or hirer of a regulated agreement,—

    (a) to terminate the agreement, or

    (b) to demand earlier payment of any sum, or

    (c) to recover possession of any goods or land, or

    (d) to treat any right conferred on the debtor or hirer by the agreement as terminated, restricted or deferred, or

    (e) to enforce any security.

(2) Subsection (1) does not prevent the creditor from treating the right to draw upon any credit as restricted or deferred, and taking such steps as may be necessary to make the restriction or deferment effective.

(3) The doing of an act by which a floating charge becomes fixed is not enforcement of a security.

(4) Regulations may provide that section (1) is not to apply to agreements described by the regulations.

[(5) Subsection (1)(d) does not apply in a case referred to in section 98A(4) (termination or suspension of debtor's right to draw on credit under open-end agreement).]

88 Contents and effect of default notice

(1) The default notice must be in the prescribed form and specify—

    (a) the nature of the alleged breach;

    (b) if the breach is capable of remedy, what action is required to remedy it and the date before which that action is to be taken;

    (c) if the breach is not capable of remedy, the sum (if any) required to be paid as compensation for the breach, and the date before which it is to be paid.

(2) A date specified under subsection (1) must not be less than [14] days after the date of service of the default notice, and the creditor or owner shall not take action such as is mentioned in section 87(1) before the date so specified or (if no requirement is made under subsection (1)) before those [14] days have elapsed.

(3) The default notice must not treat as a breach failure to comply with a provision of the agreement which becomes operative only on breach of some other provision, but if the breach of that other provision is not duly remedied or compensation demanded under subsection (1) is not duly paid, or (where no requirement is made under subsection (1)) if the seven days mentioned in subsection (2) have elapsed, the creditor or owner may treat the failure as a breach and section 87(1) shall not apply to it.

(4) The default notice must contain information in the prescribed terms about the consequences of failure to comply with it and any other prescribed matters relating to the agreement.

[(4A) The default notice must also include a copy of the current default information sheet under section 86A.]

(5) A default notice making a requirement under subsection (1) may include a provision for the taking of action such as is mentioned in section 87(1) at any time after the restriction imposed by subsection (2) will cease, together with a statement that the provision will be ineffective if the breach is duly remedied or the compensation duly paid.

89 Compliance with default notice

If before the date specified for that purpose in the default notice the debtor or hirer takes the action specified under section 88(1)(b) or (c) the breach shall be treated as not having occurred.

Further restriction of remedies for default

90   Retaking of protected hire-purchase etc. goods

(1) At any time when—

(a) the debtor is in breach of a regulated hire-purchase or a regulated conditional sale agreement relating to goods, and

(b) the debtor has paid to the creditor one-third or more of the total price of the goods and

(c) the property in the goods remains in the creditor, the creditor is not entitled to recover possession of the goods from the debtor except on an order of the court.

(2) Where under a hire-purchase or conditional sale agreement the creditor is required to carry out any installation and the agreement specifies, as part of the total price, the amount to be paid in respect of the installation (the 'installation charge') the reference in subsection (1)(b) to one-third of the total price shall be construed as a reference to the aggregate of the installation charge and one-third of the remainder of the total price.

(3) In a case where—

(a) subsection (1)(a) is satisfied, but not subsection (1)(b), and

(b) subsection (1)(b) was satisfied on a previous occasion in relation to an earlier agreement, being a regulated hire-purchase or regulated conditional sale agreement, between the same parties, and relating to any of the goods comprised in the later agreement (whether or not other goods were also included),

subsection (1) shall apply to the later agreement with the omission of paragraph (b).

(4) If the later agreement is a modifying agreement, subsection (3) shall apply with the substitution, for the second reference to the later agreement, of a reference to the modifying agreement.

(5) Subsection (1) shall not apply, or shall cease to apply, to an agreement if the debtor has terminated, or terminates, the agreement.

(6) Where subsection (1) applies to an agreement at the death of the debtor, it shall continue to apply (in relation to the possessor of the goods) until the grant of probate or administration, or (in Scotland) confirmation (on which the personal representative would fall to be treated as the debtor).

(7) Goods falling within this section are in this Act referred to as 'protected goods'.

91   Consequences of breach of s. 90

If goods are recovered by the creditor in contravention of section 90—

(a) the regulated agreement, if not previously terminated, shall terminate, and

(b) the debtor shall be released from all liability under the agreement, and shall be entitled to recover from the creditor all sums paid by the debtor under the agreement.

92   Recovery of possession of goods or land

(1) Except under an order of the court, the creditor or owner shall not be entitled to enter any premises to take possession of goods subject to a regulated hire-purchase agreement, regulated conditional sale agreement or regulated consumer hire agreement.

(2) At any time when the debtor is in breach of a regulated conditional sale agreement relating to land, the creditor is entitled to recover possession of the land from the debtor, or any person claiming under him, on an order of the court only.

(3) An entry in contravention of section (1) or (2) is actionable as a breach of statutory duty.

93   Interest not to be increased on default

The debtor under a regulated consumer credit agreement shall not be obliged to pay interest on sums which, in breach of the agreement, are unpaid by him at a rate—

(a) where the total charge for credit includes an item in respect of interest, exceeding the rate of that interest, or

(b) in any other case, exceeding what would be the rate of the total charge for credit if any items included in the total charge for credit by virtue of [rules made by the FCA under paragraph (2)(d) of article 60M of the Regulated Activities Order] were disregarded.

Early payment by debtor

94 Right to complete payments ahead of time

(1) The debtor under a regulated consumer credit agreement is entitled at any time, by notice to the creditor and the payment to the creditor of all amounts payable by the debtor to him under the agreement [and any amount which the creditor claims under section 95A(2) or section 95B(2)] (less any rebate allowable under section 95), to discharge the debtor's indebtedness under the agreement.

(2) A notice under subsection (1) may embody the exercise by the debtor of any option to purchase goods conferred on him by the agreement, and deal with any other matter arising on, or in relation to, the termination of the agreement.

[(3) The debtor under a regulated consumer credit agreement, other than an agreement secured on land, is entitled at any time to discharge part of his indebtedness by taking the steps in subsection (4).

(4) The steps referred to in subsection (3) are as follows—
  (a) he provides notice to the creditor,
  (b) he pays to the creditor some of the amount payable by him to the creditor under the agreement before the time fixed by the agreement, and
  (c) he makes the payment—
    (i) before the end of the period of 28 days beginning with the day following that on which notice under paragraph (a) was received by the creditor, or
    (ii) on or before any later date specified in the notice.

(5) Where a debtor takes the steps in subsection (4) his indebtedness shall be discharged by an amount equal to the sum of the amount paid and any rebate allowable under section 95 less any amount which the creditor claims under section 95A(2) or section 95B(2).

(6) A notice—
  (a) under subsection (1), other than a notice relating to a regulated consumer credit agreement secured on land, or
  (b) under subsection (4)(a),
need not be in writing.]

95 Rebate on early settlement

(1) Regulations may provide for the allowance of a rebate of charges for credit to the debtor under a regulated consumer credit agreement where, under section 94, on refinancing, on breach of the agreement, or for any other reason, his indebtedness is discharged [or is discharged in part] or becomes payable before the time fixed by the agreement, or any sum becomes payable by him before the time so fixed.

(2) Regulations under subsection (1) may provide for calculation of the rebate by reference to any sums paid or payable by the debtor or his relative under or in connection with the agreement (whether to the creditor or some other person), including sums under linked transactions and other items in the total charge for credit.

[95A Compensatory amount

(1) This section applies where—
  (a) a regulated consumer credit agreement, other than an agreement secured on land, provides for the rate of interest on the credit to be fixed for a period of time, and
  (b) under section 94 the debtor discharges all or part of his indebtedness during that period.

(2) The creditor may claim an amount equal to the cost which the creditor has incurred as a result only of the debtor's indebtedness being discharged during that period if—
  (a) the amount of the payment under section 94 exceeds £8,000 or, where more than one such payment is made in any 12 month period, the total of those payments exceeds £8,000,

(b) the agreement is not a debtor-creditor agreement enabling the debtor to overdraw on a current account, and

(c) the amount of the payment under section 94 is not paid from the proceeds of a contract of payment protection insurance.

(3) The amount in subsection (2)—

(a) must be fair,

(b) must be objectively justified, and

(c) must not exceed whichever is the lower of—

(i) the relevant percentage of the amount of the payment under section 94, and

(ii) the total amount of interest that would have been paid by the debtor under the agreement in the period from the date on which the debtor makes the payment under section 94 to the date fixed by the agreement for the discharge of the indebtedness of the debtor.

(4) In subsection (3)(c)(i) 'relevant percentage' means—

(a) 1%, where the period from the date on which the debtor makes the payment under section 94 to the date fixed by the agreement for the discharge of the indebtedness of the debtor is more than one year, or

(b) 0.5%, where that period is equal to or less than one year.]

[95B   Compensatory amount: green deal finance

(1) This section applies where—

(a) a regulated consumer credit agreement provides for the rate of interest on the credit to be fixed for a period of time ('the fixed rate period'),

(b) the agreement is a green deal plan which is of a duration specified for the purposes of this section in regulations, and

(c) under section 94 the debtor discharges all or part of his indebtedness during the fixed rate period.

(2) The creditor may claim an amount equal to the cost which the creditor has incurred as a result only of the debtor's indebtedness being discharged during the fixed rate period if—

(a) the amount of the payment under section 94 is not paid from the proceeds of a contract of payment protection insurance, and

(b) such other conditions as may be specified for the purposes of this section in regulations are satisfied.

(3) The amount in subsection (2)—

(a) must be fair,

(b) must be objectively justified,

(c) must be calculated by the creditor in accordance with provision made for the purposes of this section in regulations, and

(d) must not exceed the total amount of interest that would have been paid by the debtor under the agreement in the period from the date on which the debtor makes the payment under section 94 to the date fixed by the agreement for the discharge of the indebtedness of the debtor.

(4) If a creditor could claim under either section 95A or this section, the creditor may choose under which section to claim.]

96   Effect on linked transactions

(1) Where for any reason the indebtedness of the debtor under a regulated consumer credit agreement is discharged before the time fixed by the agreement, he, and any relative of his, shall at the same time be discharged from any liability under a linked transaction, other than a debt which has already become payable.

(2) Subsection (1) does not apply to a linked transaction which is itself an agreement providing the debtor or his relative with credit.

(3) Regulations may exclude linked transactions of the prescribed description from the operation of subsection (1).

97 Duty to give information

(1) The creditor under a regulated consumer credit agreement, within the prescribed period after he has received a request [...] to that effect from the debtor, shall give the debtor a statement in the prescribed form indicating, according to the information to which it is practicable for him to refer, the amount of the payment required to discharge the debtor's indebtedness under the agreement, together with the prescribed particulars showing how the amount is arrived at.

(2) Subsection (1) does not apply to a request made less than one month after a previous request under that subsection relating to the same agreement was complied with.

[(2A) A request under subsection (1) need not be in writing unless the agreement is secured on land.]

(3) If the creditor fails to comply with subsection (1)—

(a) he is not entitled, while the default continues, to enforce the agreement; [...].

[97A Duty to give information on partial repayment

(1) Where a debtor under a regulated consumer credit agreement—

(a) makes a payment by virtue of which part of his indebtedness is discharged under section 94, and

(b) at the same time or subsequently requests the creditor to give him a statement concerning the effect of the payment on the debtor's indebtedness,

the creditor must give the statement to the debtor before the end of the period of seven working days beginning with the day following that on which the creditor receives the request.

(2) The statement shall be in writing and shall contain the following particulars—

(a) a description of the agreement sufficient to identify it,

(b) the name, postal address and, where appropriate, any other address of the creditor and the debtor,

(c) where the creditor is claiming an amount under section 95A(2) or section 95B(2), that amount and the method used to determine it,

(d) the amount of any rebate to which the debtor is entitled—

(i) under the agreement, or

(ii) by virtue of section 95 where that is higher,

(e) where the amount of the rebate mentioned in paragraph (d)(ii) is given, a statement indicating that this amount has been calculated having regard to the Consumer Credit (Early Settlement) Regulations 2004,

(f) where the debtor is not entitled to any rebate, a statement to this effect,

(g) any change to—

(i) the number, timing or amount of repayments to be made under the agreement, or

(ii) the duration of the agreement, which results from the partial discharge of the indebtedness of the debtor, and

(h) the amount of the debtor's indebtedness remaining under the agreement at the date the creditor gives the statement.]

Termination of agreements

98 Duty to give notice of termination (non-default cases)

(1) The creditor or owner is not entitled to terminate a regulated agreement except by or after giving the debtor or hirer not less than seven days' notice of the termination.

(2) Subsection (1) applies only where—

(a) a period for the duration of the agreement is specified in the agreement, and

(b) that period has not ended when the creditor or owner does an act mentioned in subsection (1),

but so applies notwithstanding that, under the agreement, any party is entitled to terminate it before the end of the period so specified.

(3) A notice under subsection (1) is ineffective if not in the prescribed form.

(4) Subsection (1) does not prevent a creditor from treating the right to draw on any credit as restricted or deferred and taking such steps as may be necessary to make the restriction or deferment effective.

(5) Regulations may provide that subsection (1) is not to apply to agreements described by the regulations.

(6) Subsection (1) does not apply to the termination of a regulated agreement by reason of any breach by the debtor or hirer of the agreement.

[98A   Termination etc of open-end consumer credit agreements

(1) The debtor under a regulated open-end consumer credit agreement, other than an excluded agreement, may by notice terminate the agreement, free of charge, at any time, subject to any period of notice not exceeding one month provided for by the agreement.

(2) Notice under subsection (1) need not be in writing unless the creditor so requires.

(3) Where a regulated open-end consumer credit agreement, other than an excluded agreement, provides for termination of the agreement by the creditor—

(a) the termination must be by notice served on the debtor, and

(b) the termination may not take effect until after the end of the period of two months, or such longer period as the agreement may provide, beginning with the day after the day on which notice is served.

(4) Where a regulated open-end consumer credit agreement, other than an excluded agreement, provides for termination or suspension by the creditor of the debtor's right to draw on credit—

(a) to terminate or suspend the right to draw on credit the creditor must serve a notice on the debtor before the termination or suspension or, if that is not practicable, immediately afterwards,

(b) the notice must give reasons for the termination or suspension, and

(c) the reasons must be objectively justified.

(5) Subsection (4)(a) and (b) does not apply where giving the notice—

(a) is prohibited by a retained EU obligation, or

(b) would, or would be likely to, prejudice—

(i)   the prevention or detection of crime,

(ii) the apprehension or prosecution of offenders, or

(iii) the administration of justice.

(6) An objectively justified reason under subsection (4)(c) may, for example, relate to—

(a) the unauthorised or fraudulent use of credit, or

(b) a significantly increased risk of the debtor being unable to fulfil his obligation to repay the credit.

(7) Subsections (1) and (3) do not affect any right to terminate an agreement for breach of contract.

(8) For the purposes of this section an agreement is an excluded agreement if it is—

(a) an authorised non-business overdraft agreement,

(b) an authorised business overdraft agreement,

(c) a debtor-creditor agreement arising where the holder of a current account overdraws on the account without a pre-arranged overdraft or exceeds a pre-arranged overdraft limit, or

(d) an agreement secured on land.]

99   Right to terminate hire-purchase etc. agreements

(1) At any time before the final payment by the debtor under a regulated hire-purchase or regulated conditional sale agreement falls due, the debtor shall be entitled to terminate the agreement by giving notice to any person entitled or authorised to receive the sums payable under the agreement.

(2) Termination of an agreement under subsection (1) does not affect any liability under the agreement which has accrued before the termination.

(3) Subsection (1) does not apply to a conditional sale agreement relating to land after the title to the land has passed to the debtor.

(4) In the case of a conditional sale agreement relating to goods, where the property in the goods, having become vested in the debtor, is transferred to a person who does not become the debtor under the agreement, the debtor shall not thereafter be entitled to terminate the agreement under subsection (1).

(5) Subject to subsection (4), where a debtor under a conditional sale agreement relating to goods terminates the agreement under this section after the property in the goods has become vested in him, the property in the goods shall thereupon vest in the person (the 'previous owner') in whom it was vested immediately before it became vested in the debtor:

Provided that if the previous owner has died, or any other event has occurred whereby that property, if vested in him immediately before that event, would thereupon have vested in some other person, the property shall be treated as having devolved as if it had been vested in the previous owner immediately before his death or immediately before that event, as the case may be.

100   Liability of debtor on termination of hire-purchase etc. agreement

(1) Where a regulated hire-purchase or regulated conditional sale agreement is terminated under section 99 the debtor shall be liable, unless the agreement provides for a smaller payment, or does not provide for any payment, to pay to the creditor the amount (if any) by which one-half of the total price exceeds the aggregate of the sums paid and the sums due in respect of the total price immediately before the termination.

(2) Where under a hire-purchase or conditional sale agreement the creditor is required to carry out any installation and the agreement specifies, as part of the total price, the amount to be paid in respect of the installation (the 'installation charge') the reference in subsection (1) to one-half of the total price shall be construed as a reference to the aggregate of the installation charge and one-half of the remainder of the total price.

(3) If in any action the court is satisfied that a sum less than the amount specified in subsection (1) would be equal to the loss sustained by the creditor in consequence of the termination of the agreement by the debtor, the court may make an order for the payment of that sum in lieu of the amount specified in subsection (1).

(4) If the debtor has contravened an obligation to take reasonable care of the goods or land, the amount arrived at under subsection (1) shall be increased by the sum required to recompense the creditor for that contravention, and subsection (2) shall have effect accordingly.

(5) Where the debtor, on the termination of the agreement, wrongfully retains possession of goods to which the agreement relates, then, in any action brought by the creditor to recover possession of the goods from the debtor, the court, unless it is satisfied that having regard to the circumstances it would not be just to do so, shall order the goods to be delivered to the creditor without giving the debtor an option to pay the value of the goods.

101   Right to terminate hire agreement

(1) The hirer under a regulated consumer hire agreement is entitled to terminate the agreement by giving notice to any person entitled or authorised to receive the sums payable under the agreement.

(2) Termination of an agreement under subsection (1) does not affect any liability under the agreement which has accrued before the termination.

(3) A notice under subsection (1) shall not expire earlier than eighteen months after the making of the agreement, but apart from that the minimum period of notice to be given under subsection (1), unless the agreement provides for a shorter period, is as follows.

(4) If the agreement provides for the making of payments by the hirer to the owner at equal intervals, the minimum period of notice is the length of one interval or three months, whichever is less.

(5) If the agreement provides for the making of such payments at differing intervals, the minimum period of notice is the length of the shortest interval or three months, whichever is less.

(6) In any other case, the minimum period of notice is three months.

(7) This section does not apply to—

    (a) any agreement which provides for the making by the hirer of payments which in total (and without breach of the agreement) exceed [£1,500] in any year, or

    (b) any agreement where—

        (i) goods are bailed or (in Scotland) hired to the hirer for the purposes of a business carried on by him, or the hirer holds himself out as requiring the goods for those purposes, and

        (ii) the goods are selected by the hirer, and acquired by the owner for the purposes of the agreement at the request of the hirer from any person other than the owner's associate, or

    (c) any agreement where the hirer requires, or holds himself out as requiring, the goods for the purpose of bailing or hiring them to other persons in the course of a business carried on by him.

(8) If, on an application made to the [FCA] by a person carrying on a consumer hire business, it appears to the [FCA] that it would be in the interest of hirers to do so, [it] may [...] direct that[, subject to such conditions (if any) as it may specify, this section shall not apply to consumer hire agreements made by the applicant; and this Act shall have effect accordingly].

[(8A) If it appears to the FCA that it would be in the interests of hirers to do so, it may ... direct that, subject to such conditions (if any) as it may specify, this section shall not apply to a consumer hire agreement if the agreement falls within a specified description; and this Act shall have effect accordingly.]

(9) In the case of a modifying agreement, subsection (3) shall apply with the substitution for 'the making of the agreement' of 'the making of the original agreement'.

102 Agency for receiving notice of rescission

(1) Where the debtor or hirer under a regulated agreement claims to have a right to rescind the agreement, each of the following shall be deemed to be the agent of the creditor or owner for the purpose of receiving any notice rescinding the agreement which is served by the debtor or hirer—

    (a) a credit-broker or supplier who was the negotiator in antecedent negotiations, and

    (b) any person who, in the course of a business carried on by him, acted on behalf of the debtor or hirer in any negotiations for the agreement.

(2) In subsection (1) 'rescind' does not include—

    (a) service of a notice of cancellation, or

    (b) termination of an agreement under section 99 or 101 or by the exercise of a right or power in that behalf expressly conferred by the agreement.

103 Termination statements

(1) If an individual (the 'customer') serves on any person (the 'trader') a notice—

    (a) stating that—

        (i) the customer was the debtor or hirer under a regulated agreement described in the notice, and the trader was the creditor or owner under the agreement, and

        (ii) the customer has discharged his indebtedness to the trader under the agreement, and

        (iii) the agreement has ceased to have any operation; and

    (b) requiring the trader to give the customer a notice, signed by or on behalf of the trader, confirming that those statements are correct, the trader shall, within the prescribed period after receiving the notice, either comply with it or serve on the customer a counter-notice stating that, as the case may be, he disputes the correctness of the notice or asserts that the customer is not indebted to him under the agreement.

(2) Where the trader disputes the correctness of the notice he shall give particulars of the way in which he alleges it to be wrong.

(3) Subsection (1) does not apply in relation to any agreement if the trader has previously complied with that subsection on the service of a notice under it with respect to that agreement.

(4) Subsection (1) does not apply to a non-commercial agreement.

[(6) A breach of the duty imposed by subsection (1) is actionable as a breach of statutory duty.]

104 Goods not to be treated as subject to landlord's hypothec in Scotland

Goods comprised in a hire-purchase agreement or goods comprised in a conditional sale agreement which have not become vested in the debtor shall not be treated in Scotland as subject to the landlord's hypothec—

(a) during the period between the service of a default notice in respect of the goods and the date on which the notice expires or is earlier complied with; or

(b) if the agreement is enforceable on an order of the court only, during the period between the commencement and termination of an action by the creditor to enforce the agreement.

PART VIII SECURITY

General

105 Form and content of securities

(1) Any security provided in relation to a regulated agreement shall be expressed in writing.

(2) Regulations may prescribe the form and content of documents ('security instruments') to be made in compliance with subsection (1).

(3) Regulations under subsection (2) may in particular—

(a) require specified information to be included in the prescribed manner in documents, and other specified material to be excluded;

(b) contain requirements to ensure that specified information is clearly brought to the attention of the surety, and that one part of a document is not given insufficient or excessive prominence compared with another.

(4) A security instrument is not properly executed unless—

(a) a document in the prescribed form, itself containing all the prescribed terms and conforming to regulations under subsection (2), is signed in the prescribed manner by or on behalf of the surety, and

(b) the document embodies all the terms of the security, other than implied terms, and

(c) the document, when presented or sent for the purpose of being signed by or on behalf of the surety, is in such state that its terms are readily legible, and

(d) when the document is presented or sent for the purpose of being signed by or on behalf of the surety there is also presented or sent a copy of the document.

(5) A security instrument is not properly executed unless—

(a) where the security is provided after, or at the time when, the regulated agreement is made, a copy of the executed agreement, together with a copy of any other document referred to in it, is given to the surety at the time the security is provided, or

(b) where the security is provided before the regulated agreement is made, a copy of the executed agreement, together with a copy of any other document referred to in it, is given to the surety within seven days after the regulated agreement is made.

(6) Subsection (1) does not apply to a security provided by the debtor or hirer.

(7) If—

(a) in contravention of subsection (1) a security is not expressed in writing, or

(b) a security instrument is improperly executed, the security, so far as provided in relation to a regulated agreement, is enforceable against the surety on an order of the court only.

(8) If an application for an order under subsection (7) is dismissed (except on technical grounds only) section 106 (ineffective securities) shall apply to the security.

(9) Regulations under section 60(1) shall include provision requiring documents embodying regulated agreements also to embody any security provided in relation to a regulated agreement by the debtor or hirer.

106   Ineffective securities

Where, under any provision of this Act, this section is applied to any security provided in relation to a regulated agreement, then, subject to section 177 (saving for registered charges)—

(a) the security, so far as it is so provided, shall be treated as never having effect;

(b) any property lodged with the creditor or owner solely for the purposes of the security as so provided shall be returned by him forthwith;

(c) the creditor or owner shall take any necessary action to remove or cancel an entry in any register, so far as the entry relates to the security as so provided; and

(d) any amount received by the creditor or owner on realisation of the security shall, so far as it is referable to the agreement, be repaid to the surety.

107   Duty to give information to surety under fixed-sum credit agreement

(1) The creditor under a regulated agreement for fixed-sum credit in relation to which security is provided, within the prescribed period after receiving a request in writing to that effect from the surety and payment of a fee of [£1], shall give to the surety (if a different person from the debtor)—

(a) a copy of the executed agreement (if any) and of any other document referred to in it;

(b) a copy of the security instrument (if any); and

(c) a statement signed by or on behalf of the creditor showing, according to the information to which it is practicable for him to refer,—

   (i)   the total sum paid under the agreement by the debtor,

   (ii) the total sum which has become payable under the agreement by the debtor but remains unpaid, and the various amounts comprised in that total sum, with the date when each became due, and

   (iii) the total sum which is to become payable under the agreement by the debtor, and the various amounts comprised in that total sum, with the date, or mode of determining the date, when each becomes due.

(2) If the creditor possesses insufficient information to enable him to ascertain the amounts and dates mentioned in subsection (1)(c)(iii), he shall be taken to comply with that sub-paragraph if his statement under subsection (1)(c) gives the basis on which, under the regulated agreement, they would fall to be ascertained.

(3) Subsection (1) does not apply to—

(a) an agreement under which no sum is, or will or may become, payable by the debtor, or

(b) a request made less than one month after a previous request under that subsection relating to the same agreement was complied with.

(4) If the creditor under an agreement fails to comply with subsection (1)—

(a) he is not entitled, while the default continues, to enforce the security, so far as provided in relation to the agreement; [...].

(5) This section does not apply to a non-commercial agreement.

108   Duty to give information to surety under running-account credit agreement

(1) The creditor under a regulated agreement for running-account credit in relation to which security is provided, within the prescribed period after receiving a request in writing to that effect

from the surety and payment of a fee of [£1], shall give to the surety (if a different person from the debtor)—

    (a) a copy of the executed agreement (if any) and of any other document referred to in it;

    (b) a copy of the security instrument (if any); and

    (c) a statement signed by or on behalf of the creditor showing, according to the information to which it is practicable for him to refer,—

        (i) the state of the account, and

        (ii) the amount, if any, currently payable under the agreement by the debtor to the creditor, and

        (iii) the amounts and due dates of any payments which, if the debtor does not draw further on the account, will later become payable under the agreement by the debtor to the creditor.

(2) If the creditor possesses insufficient information to enable him to ascertain the amounts and dates mentioned in subsection (1)(c)(iii), he shall be taken to comply with that sub-paragraph if his statement under subsection (1)(c) gives the basis on which, under the regulated agreement, they would fall to be ascertained.

(3) Subsection (1) does not apply to—

    (a) an agreement under which no sum is, or will or may become, payable by the debtor, or

    (b) a request made less than one month after a previous request under that subsection relating to the same agreement was complied with.

(4) If the creditor under an agreement fails to comply with subsection (1)—

    (a) he is not entitled, while the default continues, to enforce the security, so far as provided in relation to the agreement; […].

(5) This section does not apply to a non-commercial agreement.

109 Duty to give information to surety under consumer hire agreement

(1) The owner under a regulated consumer hire agreement in relation to which security is provided, within the prescribed period after receiving a request in writing to that effect from the surety and payment of a fee of [£1], shall give to the surety (if a different person from the hirer)—

    (a) a copy of the executed agreement and of any other document referred to in it;

    (b) a copy of the security instrument (if any); and

    (c) a statement signed by or on behalf of the owner showing, according to the information to which it is practicable for him to refer, the total sum which has become payable under the agreement by the hirer but remains unpaid and the various amounts comprised in that total sum, with the date when each became due.

(2) Subsection (1) does not apply to—

    (a) an agreement under which no sum is, or will or may become, payable by the hirer, or

    (b) a request made less than one month after a previous request under that subsection relating to the same agreement was complied with.

(3) If the owner under an agreement fails to comply with subsection (1)—

    (a) he is not entitled, while the default continues, to enforce the security, so far as provided in relation to the agreement; […].

(4) This section does not apply to a non-commercial agreement.

110 Duty to give information to debtor or hirer

(1) The creditor or owner under a regulated agreement, within the prescribed period after receiving a request in writing to that effect from the debtor or hirer and payment of a fee of [£1], shall give the debtor or hirer a copy of any security instrument executed in relation to the agreement after the making of the agreement.

(2) Subsection (1) does not apply to—

    (a) a non-commercial agreement, or

    (b) an agreement under which no sum is, or will or may become, payable by the debtor or hirer, or

(c) a request made less than one month after a previous request under subsection (1) relating to the same agreement was complied with.

(3) If the creditor or owner under an agreement fails to comply with subsection (1)—

(a) he is not entitled, while the default continues, to enforce the security (so far as provided in relation to the agreement); [...].

111   Duty to give surety copy of default etc. notice

(1) When a default notice or a notice under section 76(1) or 98(1) is served on a debtor or hirer, a copy of the notice shall be served by the creditor or owner on any surety (if a different person from the debtor or hirer).

(2) If the creditor or owner fails to comply with subsection (1) in the case of any surety, the security is enforceable against the surety (in respect of the breach or other matter to which the notice relates) on an order of the court only.

113   Act not to be evaded by use of security

(1) Where a security is provided in relation to an actual or prospective regulated agreement, the security shall not be enforced so as to benefit the creditor or owner, directly or indirectly, to an extent greater (whether as respects the amount of any payment or the time or manner of its being made) than would be the case if the security were not provided and any obligations of the debtor or hirer, or his relative, under or in relation to the agreement were carried out to the extent (if any) to which they would be enforced under this Act.

(2) In accordance with subsection (1), where a regulated agreement is enforceable on an order of the court or the [FCA] only, any security provided in relation to the agreement is enforceable (so far as provided in relation to the agreement) where such an order has been made in relation to the agreement, but not otherwise.

(3) Where—

(a) a regulated agreement is cancelled under section 69(1) or becomes subject to section 69(2), or

(b) a regulated agreement is terminated under section 91, or

(c) in relation to any agreement an application for an order under section [65(1) or 124(1) or a notice under section 28A of the Financial Services and Markets Act 2000] is dismissed (except on technical grounds only), or

(d) a declaration is made by the court under section 142(1) (refusal of enforcement order) as respects any regulated agreement,

section 106 shall apply to any security provided in relation to the agreement.

(4) Where subsection (3)(d) applies and the declaration relates to a part only of the regulated agreement, section 106 shall apply to the security only so far as it concerns that part.

(5) In the case of a cancelled agreement, the duty imposed on the debtor or hirer by section 71 or 72 shall not be enforceable before the creditor or owner has discharged any duty imposed on him by section 106 (as applied by subsection (3)(a)).

(6) If the security is provided in relation to a prospective agreement or transaction, the security shall be enforceable in relation to the agreement or transaction only after the time (if any) when the agreement is made; and until that time the person providing the security shall be entitled, by notice to the creditor or owner, to require that section 106 shall thereupon apply to the security.

(7) Where an indemnity [or guarantee] is given in a case where the debtor or hirer is a minor, or [an indemnity is given in a case where he is] otherwise not of full capacity, the reference in subsection (1) to the extent to which his obligations would be enforced shall be read in relation to the indemnity [or guarantee] as a reference to the extent to which [those obligations] would be enforced if he were of full capacity.

(8) Subsections (1) and (3) also apply where a security is provided in relation to an actual or prospective linked transaction, and in that case—

(a) references to the agreement shall be read as references to the linked transaction, and

(b) references to the creditor or owner shall be read as references to any person (other than the debtor or hirer, or his relative) who is a party, or prospective party, to the linked transaction.

Pledges

114 Pawn-receipts

(1) At the time he receives the article, a person who takes any article in pawn under a regulated agreement shall give to the person from whom he receives it a receipt in the prescribed form (a 'pawn-receipt').

(2) A person who takes any article in pawn from an individual whom he knows to be, or who appears to be and is, a minor commits an offence.

(3) This section and sections [117] to 122 do not apply to—

(a) a pledge of documents of title [or of bearer bonds], or

(b) a non-commercial agreement.

116 Redemption period

(1) A pawn is redeemable at any time within six months after it was taken.

(2) Subject to subsection (1), the period within which a pawn is redeemable shall be the same as the period fixed by the parties for the duration of the credit secured by the pledge, or such longer period as they may agree.

(3) If the pawn is not redeemed by the end of the period laid down by subsections (1) and (2) (the 'redemption period'), it nevertheless remains redeemable until it is realised by the pawnee under section 121 except where under section 120(1)(a) the property in it passes to the pawnee.

(4) No special charge shall be made for redemption of a pawn after the end of the redemption period, and charges in respect of the safe keeping of the pawn shall not be at a higher rate after the end of the redemption period than before.

117 Redemption procedure

(1) On surrender of the pawn-receipt, and payment of the amount owing, at any time when the pawn is redeemable, the pawnee shall deliver the pawn to the bearer of the pawn-receipt.

(2) Subsection (1) does not apply if the pawnee knows or has reasonable cause to suspect that the bearer of the pawn-receipt is neither the owner of the pawn nor authorised by the owner to redeem it.

(3) The pawnee is not liable to any person in tort or delict for delivering the pawn where subsection (1) applies, or refusing to deliver it where the person demanding delivery does not comply with subsection (1) or, by reason of subsection (2), subsection (1) does not apply.

118 Loss etc. of pawn-receipt

(1) A person (the 'claimant') who is not in possession of the pawn-receipt but claims to be the owner of the pawn, or to be otherwise entitled or authorised to redeem it, may do so at any time when it is redeemable by tendering to the pawnee in place of the pawn-receipt—

(a) a statutory declaration made by the claimant in the prescribed form, and with the prescribed contents, or

(b) where the pawn is security for fixed-sum credit not exceeding [£75] or running-account credit on which the credit limit does not exceed [£75], and the pawnee agrees, a statement in writing in the prescribed form, and with the prescribed contents, signed by the claimant.

(2) On compliance by the claimant with subsection (1), section 117 shall apply as if the declaration or statement were the pawn-receipt, and the pawn-receipt itself shall become inoperative for the purposes of section 117.

119   Unreasonable refusal to deliver pawn

(1) If a person who has taken a pawn under a regulated agreement refuses without reasonable cause to allow the pawn to be redeemed, he commits an offence.

(2) On the conviction in England and Wales of a pawnee under subsection (1) where the offence does not amount to theft, [Chapter 3 of Part 7 of the Sentencing Code (restitution orders)] shall apply as if the pawnee had been convicted of stealing the pawn.

(3) On the conviction in Northern Ireland of a pawnee under subsection (1) where the offence does not amount to theft, section 27 (orders for restitution) of the Theft Act (Northern Ireland) 1969, and any provision of the Theft Act (Northern Ireland) 1969 relating to that section, shall apply as if the pawnee had been convicted of stealing the pawn.

120   Consequence of failure to redeem

(1) If at the end of the redemption period the pawn has not been redeemed—

    (a) notwithstanding anything in section 113, the property in the pawn passes to the pawnee where

        [(i)   the redemption period is six months,

        (ii)   the pawn is security for fixed-sum credit not exceeding £75 or running-account credit on which the credit limit does not exceed £75, and

        (iii)   the pawn was not immediately before the making of the regulated consumer credit agreement a pawn under another regulated consumer credit agreement in respect of which the debtor has discharged his indebtedness in part under section 94(3); or]

    (b) in any other case the pawn becomes realisable by the pawnee.

(2) Where the debtor or hirer is entitled to apply to the court for a time order under section 129, subsection (1) shall apply with the substitution, for 'at the end of the redemption period' of 'after the expiry of five days following the end of the redemption period'.

121   Realisation of pawn

(1) When a pawn has become realisable by him, the pawnee may sell it, after giving to the pawnor (except in such cases as may be prescribed) not less than the prescribed period of notice of the intention to sell, indicating in the notice the asking price and such other particulars as may be prescribed.

(2) Within the prescribed period after the sale takes place, the pawnee shall give the pawnor the prescribed information in writing as to the sale, its proceeds and expenses.

(3) Where the net proceeds of sale are not less than the sum which, if the pawn had been redeemed on the date of the sale, would have been payable for its redemption, the debt secured by the pawn is discharged and any surplus shall be paid by the pawnee to the pawnor.

(4) Where subsection (3) does not apply, the debt shall be treated as from the date of sale as equal to the amount by which the net proceeds of sale fall short of the sum which would have been payable for the redemption of the pawn on that date.

(5) In this section the 'net proceeds of sale' is the amount realised (the 'gross amount') less the expenses (if any) of the sale.

(6) If the pawnor alleges that the gross amount is less than the true market value of the pawn on the date of sale, it is for the pawnee to prove that he and any agents employed by him in the sale used reasonable care to ensure that the true market value was obtained, and if he fails to do so subsections (3) and (4) shall have effect as if the reference in subsection (5) to the gross amount were a reference to the true market value.

(7) If the pawnor alleges that the expenses of the sale were unreasonably high, it is for the pawnee to prove that they were reasonable, and if he fails to do so subsections (3) and (4) shall have effect as if the reference in subsection (5) to expenses were a reference to reasonable expenses.

Negotiable instruments

123   Restrictions on taking and negotiating instruments

(1) A creditor or owner shall not take a negotiable instrument, other than a bank note or cheque, in discharge of any sum payable—

(a) by the debtor or hirer under a regulated agreement, or

(b) by any person as surety in relation to the agreement.

(2) The creditor or owner shall not negotiate a cheque taken by him in discharge of a sum payable as mentioned in subsection (1) except to a banker (within the meaning of the Bills of Exchange Act 1882).

(3) The creditor or owner shall not take a negotiable instrument as security for the discharge of any sum payable as mentioned in subsection (1).

(4) A person takes a negotiable instrument as security for the discharge of a sum if the sum is intended to be paid in some other way, and the negotiable instrument is to be presented for payment only if the sum is not paid in that way.

(5) This section does not apply where the regulated agreement is a non-commercial agreement.

(6) The [Treasury] may by order provide that this section shall not apply where the regulated agreement has a connection with a country outside the United Kingdom.

124   Consequences of breach of s. 123

(1) After any contravention of section 123 has occurred in relation to a sum payable as mentioned in section 123(1)(a), the agreement under which the sum is payable is enforceable against the debtor or hirer on an order of the court only.

(2) After any contravention of section 123 has occurred in relation to a sum payable by any surety, the security is enforceable on an order of the court only.

(3) Where an application for an order under subsection (2) is dismissed (except on technical grounds only) section 106 shall apply to the security.

125   Holders in due course

(1) A person who takes a negotiable instrument in contravention of section 123(1) or (3) is not a holder in due course, and is not entitled to enforce the instrument.

(2) Where a person negotiates a cheque in contravention of section 123(2), his doing so constitutes a defect in his title within the meaning of the Bills of Exchange Act 1882.

(3) If a person mentioned in section 123(1)(a) and (b) ('the protected person') becomes liable to a holder in due course of an instrument taken from the protected person in contravention of section 123(1) or (3), or taken from the protected person and negotiated in contravention of section 123(2), the creditor or owner shall indemnify the protected person in respect of that liability.

(4) Nothing in this Act affects the rights of the holder in due course of any negotiable instrument.

Land mortgages

126   Enforcement of land mortgages

[(1) A land mortgage securing a regulated agreement or a regulated mortgage contract (within the meaning of the Regulated Activities Order) is enforceable (so far as provided in relation to the agreement) on an order of the court only.]

[(2) Subject to section 140A(5) (unfair relationships between creditors and debtors), for the purposes of subsection (1) and Part 9 (judicial control), a regulated mortgage contract which would, but for article 60C(2) of the Financial Services and Markets Act 2000 (Regulated Activities) Order 2001, be a regulated agreement is to be treated as if it were a regulated agreement.]

PART IX JUDICIAL CONTROL

Enforcement of certain regulated agreements and securities

127 Enforcement orders in cases of infringement

(1) In the case of an application for an enforcement order under—

    [(za) section 55(2) (disclosure of information), or]

    [(zb) section 61B(3) (duty to supply copy of overdraft agreement), or]

    (a)   section 65(1) (improperly executed agreements), or

    (b)   section 105(7)(a) or (b) (improperly executed security instruments), or

    (c)   section 111(2) (failure to serve copy of notice on surety), or

    (d)   section 124(1) or (2) (taking of negotiable instrument in contravention of section 123),

the court shall dismiss the application if, but [. . .] only if, it considers it just to do so having regard to—

        (i) prejudice caused to any person by the contravention in question, and the degree of culpability for it; and

       (ii) the powers conferred on the court by subsection (2) and sections 135 and 136.

(2) If it appears to the court just to do so, it may in an enforcement order reduce or discharge any sum payable by the debtor or hirer, or any surety, so as to compensate him for prejudice suffered as a result of the contravention in question.

128 Enforcement orders on death of debtor or hirer

The court shall make an order under section 86(2) if, but only if, the creditor or owner proves that he has been unable to satisfy himself that the present and future obligations of the debtor or hirer under the agreement are likely to be discharged.

Extension of time

129 Time orders

(1) [Subject to subsection (3) below,] If it appears to the court just to do so—

    (a)   on an application for an enforcement order; or

    (b)   on an application made by a debtor or hirer under this paragraph after service on him of—

        (i) a default notice, or

       (ii) a notice under section 76(1) or 98(1);

    [(ba) on an application made by a debtor or hirer under this paragraph after he has been given a notice under section 86B or 86c; or]

    (c)   in an action brought by a creditor or owner to enforce a regulated agreement or any security, or recover possession of any goods or land to which a regulated agreement relates,

the court may make an order under this section (a 'time order').

(2) A time order shall provide for one or both of the following, as the court considers just—

    (a) the payment by the debtor or hirer or any surety of any sum owed under a regulated agreement or a security by such instalments, payable at such times, as the court having regard to the means of the debtor or hirer and any surety, considers reasonable;

    (b) the remedying by the debtor or hirer of any breach of a regulated agreement (other than non-payment of money) within such period as the court may specify.

    [(3) Where in Scotland a time to pay direction or a time order has been made in relation to a debt, it shall not thereafter be competent to make a time order in relation to the same debt.]

[129A Debtor or hirer to give notice of intent etc. to creditor or owner

(1) A debtor or hirer may make an application under section 129(1)(ba) in relation to a regulated agreement only if—

    (a) following his being given the notice under section 86B or 86C, he gave a notice within subsection (2) to the creditor or owner; and

    (b) a period of at least 14 days has elapsed after the day on which he gave that notice to the creditor or owner.

(2) A notice is within this subsection if it—
   (a) indicates that the debtor or hirer intends to make the application;
   (b) indicates that he wants to make a proposal to the creditor or owner in relation to his making of payments under the agreement; and
   (c) gives details of that proposal.]

130 Supplemental provisions about time orders

(1) Where in accordance with rules of court an offer to pay any sum by instalments is made by the debtor or hirer and accepted by the creditor or owner, the court may in accordance with rules of court make a time order under section 129(2)(a) giving effect to the offer without hearing evidence of means.

(2) In the case of a hire-purchase or conditional sale agreement only, a time order under section 129(2)(a) may deal with sums which, although not payable by the debtor at the time the order is made, would if the agreement continued in force become payable under it subsequently.

(3) A time order under section 129(2)(a) shall not be made where the regulated agreement is secured by a pledge if, by virtue of regulations made under section 76(5), 87(4) or 98(5), service of a notice is not necessary for enforcement of the pledge.

(4) Where, following the making of a time order in relation to a regulated hire-purchase or conditional sale agreement or a regulated consumer hire agreement, the debtor or hirer is in possession of the goods, he shall be treated (except in the case of a debtor to whom the creditor's title has passed) as a bailee or (in Scotland) a custodier of the goods under the terms of the agreement, notwithstanding that the agreement has been terminated.

(5) Without prejudice to anything done by the creditor or owner before the commencement of the period specified in a time order made under section 129(2)(b) ('the relevant period'),—
   (a) he shall not while the relevant period subsists take in relation to the agreement any action such as is mentioned in section 87(1);
   (b) where—
      (i) a provision of the agreement ('the secondary provision') becomes operative only on breach of another provision of the agreement ('the primary provision'), and
      (ii) the time order provides for the remedying of such a breach of the primary provision within the relevant period,
      he shall not treat the secondary provision as operative before the end of that period;
   (c) if while the relevant period subsists the breach to which the order relates is remedied it shall be treated as not having occurred.

(6) On the application of any person affected by a time order, the court may vary or revoke the order.

[Interest]

[130A Interest payable on judgment debts etc.

(1) If the creditor or owner under a regulated agreement wants to be able to recover from the debtor or hirer post-judgment interest in connection with a sum that is required to be paid under a judgment given in relation to the agreement (the 'judgment sum'), he—
   (a) after the giving of that judgment, shall give the debtor or hirer a notice under this section (the 'first required notice'); and
   (b) after the giving of the first required notice, shall give the debtor or hirer further notices under this section at intervals of not more than six months.

(2) The debtor or hirer shall have no liability to pay post-judgment interest in connection with the judgment sum to the extent that the interest is calculated by reference to a period occurring before the day on which he is given the first required notice.

(3) If the creditor or owner fails to give the debtor or hirer a notice under this section within the period of six months beginning with the day after the day on which such a notice was last given to the debtor or hirer, the debtor or hirer shall have no liability to pay post-judgment interest in

connection with the judgment sum to the extent that the interest is calculated by reference to the whole or to a part of the period which—

    (a) begins immediately after the end of that period of six months; and

    (b) ends at the end of the day on which the notice is given to the debtor or hirer.

    (4) The debtor or hirer shall have no liability to pay any sum in connection with the preparation or the giving to him of a notice under this section.

    (5) A notice under this section may be incorporated in a statement or other notice which the creditor or owner gives the debtor or hirer in relation to the agreement by virtue of another provision of this Act.

    (6) Regulations may make provision about the form and content of notices under this section.

    (7) This section does not apply in relation to post-judgment interest which is required to be paid by virtue of any of the following—

    (a) section 4 of the Administration of Justice (Scotland) Act 1972;

    (b) Article 127 of the Judgments Enforcement (Northern Ireland) Order 1981;

    (c) section 74 of the County Courts Act 1984.

    (8) This section does not apply in relation to a non-commercial agreement or to a small agreement.

    (9) In this section 'post-judgment interest' means interest to the extent calculated by reference to a period occurring after the giving of the judgment under which the judgment sum is required to be paid.]

Protection of property pending proceedings

131 Protection orders

The court, on application of the creditor or owner under a regulated agreement, may make such orders as it thinks just for protecting any property of the creditor or owner, or property subject to any security, from damage or depreciation pending the determination of any proceedings under this Act, including orders restricting or prohibiting use of the property or giving directions as to its custody.

Hire and hire-purchase etc. agreements

132 Financial relief for hirer

    (1) Where the owner under a regulated consumer hire agreement recovers possession of goods to which the agreement relates otherwise than by action, the hirer may apply to the court for an order that—

    (a) the whole or part of any sum paid by the hirer to the owner in respect of the goods shall be repaid, and

    (b) the obligation to pay the whole or part of any sum owed by the hirer to the owner in respect of the goods shall cease,

and if it appears to the court just to do so, having regard to the extent of the enjoyment of the goods by the hirer, the court shall grant the application in full or in part.

    (2) Where in proceedings relating to a regulated consumer hire agreement the court makes an order for the delivery to the owner of goods to which the agreement relates the court may include in the order the like provision as may be made in an order under subsection (1).

133 Hire-purchase etc. agreements: special powers of court

    (1) If, in relation to a regulated hire-purchase or conditional sale agreement, it appears to the court just to do so—

    (a) on an application for an enforcement order or time order; or

    (b) in an action brought by the creditor to recover possession of goods to which the agreement relates,

the court may—

    (i) make an order (a 'return order') for the return to the creditor of goods to which the agreement relates;

    (ii) make an order (a 'transfer order') for the transfer to the debtor of the creditor's title to certain goods to which the agreement relates ('the transferred goods'), and the return to the creditor of the remainder of the goods.

(2) In determining for the purposes of this section how much of the total price has been paid ('the paid-up sum'), the court may—

    (a) treat any sum paid by the debtor, or owed by the creditor, in relation to the goods as part of the paid-up sum;

    (b) deduct any sum owed by the debtor in relation to the goods (otherwise than as part of the total price) from the paid-up sum,

and make corresponding reductions in amounts so owed.

(3) Where a transfer order is made, the transferred goods shall be such of the goods to which the agreement relates as the court thinks just; but a transfer order shall be made only where the paid-up sum exceeds the part of the total price referable to the transferred goods by an amount equal to at least one-third of the unpaid balance of the total price.

(4) Notwithstanding the making of a return order or transfer order, the debtor may at any time before the goods enter the possession of the creditor, on payment of the balance of the total price and the fulfilment of any other necessary conditions, claim the goods ordered to be returned to the creditor.

(5) When, in pursuance of a time order or under this section, the total price of goods under a regulated hire-purchase agreement or regulated conditional sale agreement is paid and any other necessary conditions are fulfilled, the creditor's title to the goods vests in the debtor.

(6) If, in contravention of a return order or transfer order, any goods to which the order relates are not returned to the creditor, the court, on the application of the creditor, may—

    (a) revoke so much of the order as relates to those goods, and

    (b) order the debtor to pay the creditor the unpaid portion of so much of the total price as is referable to those goods.

(7) For the purposes of this section, the part of the total price referable to any goods is the part assigned to those goods by the agreement or (if no such assignment is made) the part determined by the court to be reasonable.

134 Evidence of adverse detention in hire-purchase etc. cases

(1) Where goods are comprised in a regulated hire-purchase agreement, regulated conditional sale agreement or regulated consumer hire agreement, and the creditor or owner—

    (a) brings an action or makes an application to enforce a right to recover possession of the goods from the debtor or hirer and

    (b) proves that a demand for the delivery of the goods was included in the default notice under section 88(5), or that, after the right to recover possession of the goods accrued but before the action was begun or the application was made, he made a request in writing to the debtor or hirer to surrender the goods,

then, for the purposes of the claim of the creditor or owner to recover possession of the goods, the possession of them by the debtor or hirer shall be deemed to be adverse to the creditor or owner.

(2) In subsection (1) 'the debtor or hirer' includes a person in possession of the goods at any time between the debtor's or hirer's death and the grant of probate or administration, or (in Scotland) confirmation.

(3) Nothing in this section affects a claim for damages for conversion or (in Scotland) for delict.

Supplemental provisions as to orders

135 Power to impose conditions, or suspend operation of order

(1) If it considers it just to do so, the court may in an order made by it in relation to a regulated agreement include provisions—

    (a) making the operation of any term of the order conditional on the doing of specified acts by any party to the proceedings;

    (b) suspending the operation of any term of the order either—

        (i) until such time as the court subsequently directs, or

        (ii) until the occurrence of a specified act or omission.

(2) The court shall not suspend the operation of a term requiring the delivery up of goods by any person unless satisfied that the goods are in his possession or control.

(3) In the case of a consumer hire agreement, the court shall not so use its powers under subsection (1)(b) as to extend the period for which, under the terms of the agreement, the hirer is entitled to possession of the goods to which the agreement relates.

(4) On the application of any person affected by a provision included under subsection (1), the court may vary the provision.

136 Power to vary agreements and securities

(1) The court may in an order made by it under this Act include such provision as it considers just for amending any agreement or security in consequence of a term of the order.

[Unfair relationships]

[140A Unfair relationships between creditors and debtors

(1) The court may make an order under section 140B in connection with a credit agreement if it determines that the relationship between the creditor and the debtor arising out of the agreement (or the agreement taken with any related agreement) is unfair to the debtor because of one or more of the following—

    (a) any of the terms of the agreement or of any related agreement;

    (b) the way in which the creditor has exercised or enforced any of his rights under the agreement or any related agreement;

    (c) any other thing done (or not done) by, or on behalf of, the creditor (either before or after the making of the agreement or any related agreement).

(2) In deciding whether to make a determination under this section the court shall have regard to all matters it thinks relevant (including matters relating to the creditor and matters relating to the debtor).

(3) For the purposes of this section the court shall (except to the extent that it is not appropriate to do so) treat anything done (or not done) by, or on behalf of, or in relation to, an associate or a former associate of the creditor as if done (or not done) by, or on behalf of, or in relation to, the creditor.

(4) A determination may be made under this section in relation to a relationship notwithstanding that the relationship may have ended.

(5) An order under section 140B shall not be made in connection with a credit agreement which is an exempt agreement for the purposes of Chapter 14A of Part 2 of the Regulated Activities Order by virtue of article 60C(2) of that Order (regulated mortgage contracts and regulated home purchase plans).

(6) An order under section 140B shall not be made in connection with a credit agreement entered into under the Bounce Back Loan Scheme.

(7) In subsection (6) 'the Bounce Back Loan Scheme' means the scheme of that name operated from 4 May 2020 by the British Business Bank Plc on behalf of the Secretary of State.]

[140B Powers of court in relation to unfair relationships

(1) An order under this section in connection with a credit agreement may do one or more of the following—

    (a) require the creditor, or any associate or former associate of his, to repay (in whole or in part) any sum paid by the debtor or by a surety by virtue of the agreement or any related agreement (whether paid to the creditor, the associate or the former associate or to any other person);

    (b) require the creditor, or any associate or former associate of his, to do or not to do (or to cease doing) anything specified in the order in connection with the agreement or any related agreement;

    (c) reduce or discharge any sum payable by the debtor or by a surety by virtue of the agreement or any related agreement;

    (d) direct the return to a surety of any property provided by him for the purposes of a security;

    (e) otherwise set aside (in whole or in part) any duty imposed on the debtor or on a surety by virtue of the agreement or any related agreement;

    (f) alter the terms of the agreement or of any related agreement;

(g) direct accounts to be taken, or (in Scotland) an accounting to be made, between any persons.

(2) An order under this section may be made in connection with a credit agreement only—

(a) on an application made by the debtor or by a surety;

(b) at the instance of the debtor or a surety in any proceedings in any court to which the debtor and the creditor are parties, being proceedings to enforce the agreement or any related agreement; or

(c) at the instance of the debtor or a surety in any other proceedings in any court where the amount paid or payable under the agreement or any related agreement is relevant.

(3) An order under this section may be made notwithstanding that its effect is to place on the creditor, or any associate or former associate of his, a burden in respect of an advantage enjoyed by another person.

(4) An application under subsection (2)(a) may only be made—

(a) in England and Wales, to the county court;

(b) in Scotland, to the sheriff court;

(c) in Northern Ireland, to the High Court (subject to subsection (6)).

(5) In Scotland such an application may be made in the sheriff court for the district in which the debtor or surety resides or carries on business.

(6) In Northern Ireland such an application may be made to the county court if the credit agreement is an agreement under which the creditor provides the debtor with—

(a) fixed-sum credit not exceeding £15,000; or

(b) running-account credit on which the credit limit does not exceed £15,000.

(7) Without prejudice to any provision which may be made by rules of court made in relation to county courts in Northern Ireland, such rules may provide that an application made by virtue of subsection (6) may be made in the county court for the division in which the debtor or surety resides or carries on business.

(8) A party to any proceedings mentioned in subsection (2) shall be entitled, in accordance with rules of court, to have any person who might be the subject of an order under this section made a party to the proceedings.

(9) If, in any such proceedings, the debtor or a surety alleges that the relationship between the creditor and the debtor is unfair to the debtor, it is for the creditor to prove to the contrary.]

[140C   Interpretation of ss. 140A and 140B

(1) In this section and in sections 140A and 140B 'credit agreement' means any agreement between an individual (the 'debtor') and any other person (the 'creditor') by which the creditor provides the debtor with credit of any amount.

(2) References in this section and in sections 140A and 140B to the creditor or to the debtor under a credit agreement include—

(a) references to the person to whom his rights and duties under the agreement have passed by assignment or operation of law;

(b) where two or more persons are the creditor or the debtor, references to any one or more of those persons.

(3) The definition of 'court' in section 189(1) does not apply for the purposes of sections 140A and 140B.

(4) References in sections 140A and 140B to an agreement related to a credit agreement (the 'main agreement') are references to—

(a) a credit agreement consolidated by the main agreement;

(b) a linked transaction in relation to the main agreement or to a credit agreement within paragraph (a);

(c) a security provided in relation to the main agreement, to a credit agreement within paragraph (a) or to a linked transaction within paragraph (b).

(5) In the case of a credit agreement which is not a regulated consumer credit agreement, for the purposes of subsection (4) a transaction shall be treated as being a linked transaction in relation to that agreement if it would have been such a transaction had that agreement been a regulated consumer credit agreement.

(6) For the purposes of this section and section 140B the definitions of 'security' and 'surety' in section 189(1) apply (with any appropriate changes) in relation to—

(a) a credit agreement which is not a consumer credit agreement as if it were a consumer credit agreement; and

(b) a transaction which is a linked transaction by virtue of subsection (5).

(7) For the purposes of this section a credit agreement (the 'earlier agreement') is consolidated by another credit agreement (the 'later agreement') if—

(a) the later agreement is entered into by the debtor (in whole or in part) for purposes connected with debts owed by virtue of the earlier agreement; and

(b) at any time prior to the later agreement being entered into the parties to the earlier agreement included—

(i)   the debtor under the later agreement; and

(ii) the creditor under the later agreement or an associate or a former associate of his.

(8) Further, if the later agreement is itself consolidated by another credit agreement (whether by virtue of this subsection or subsection (7)), then the earlier agreement is consolidated by that other agreement as well.]

Miscellaneous

141   Jurisdiction and parties

(1) In England and Wales the county court shall have jurisdiction to hear and determine—

(a) any action by the creditor or owner to enforce a regulated agreement or any security relating to it;

(b) any action to enforce any linked transaction against the debtor or hirer or his relative,

and such an action shall not be brought in any other court.

(2) Where an action or application is brought in the High Court which, by virtue of this Act, ought to have been brought in the county court it shall not be treated as improperly brought, but shall be transferred to the county court.

[(3) In Scotland the sheriff court shall have jurisdiction to hear and determine any action falling within subsection (1) and such an action shall not be brought in any other court.]

[(3A) Subject to subsection (3B) an action which is brought in the sheriff court by virtue of subsection (3) shall be brought only in one of the following courts, namely—

(a) the court for the place where the debtor or hirer is domiciled (within the meaning of section 41 or 42 of the Civil Jurisdiction and Judgments Act 1982);

(b) the court for the place where the debtor or hirer carries on business; and

(c) where the purpose of the action is to assert, declare or determine proprietary or possessory rights, or rights of security, in or over movable property, or to obtain authority to dispose of movable property, the court for the place where the property is situated.

(3B) Subsection (3A) shall not apply—

(a) where Rule 3 of Schedule 8 to the said Act of 1982 applies; or

(b) where the jurisdiction of another court has been prorogated by an agreement entered into after the dispute has arisen.]

(4) In Northern Ireland the county court shall have jurisdiction to hear and determine any action or application falling within subsection (1).

(5) Except as may be provided by rules of court, all the parties to a regulated agreement, and any surety, shall be made parties to any proceedings relating to the agreement.

142   Power to declare rights of parties

(1) Where under any provision of this Act a thing can be done by a creditor or owner on an enforcement order only, and either—

(a) the court dismisses (except on technical grounds only) an application for an enforcement order, or

(b) where no such application has been made or such an application has been dismissed on technical grounds only an interested party applies to the court for a declaration under this subsection,

the court may if it thinks just make a declaration that the creditor or owner is not entitled to do that thing, and thereafter no application for an enforcement order in respect of it shall be entertained.

(2) Where—

(a) a regulated agreement or linked transaction is cancelled under section 69(1), or becomes subject to section 69(2), or

(b) a regulated agreement is terminated under section 91, and an interested party applies to the court for a declaration under this subsection, the court may make a declaration to that effect.

PART X ANCILLARY CREDIT BUSINESSES

Definitions

145   Types of ancillary credit business

(1) An ancillary credit business is any business so far as it comprises or relates to—

(a)   credit brokerage,

(b)   debt-adjusting,

(c)   debt-counselling,

(d)   debt-collecting,

[(da) debt administration,]

[(db) the provision of credit information services, or]

(e)   the operation of a credit reference agency.

[(2) 'Credit brokerage' means the carrying on of an activity of the kind specified by article 36A(1)(a) to (c) of the Regulated Activities Order (credit broking), disregarding the effect of paragraph (2) of that article.]

[(5) 'Debt adjusting' means the carrying on of an activity of the kind specified by article 39D of that Order (debt adjusting).]

[(6) 'Debt-counselling' means the carrying on of an activity of the kind specified by article 39E of that Order (debt-counselling).]

[(7) 'Debt-collecting' means the carrying on of an activity of the kind specified by article 39F of that Order (debt-collecting).]

[(7A) 'Debt administration' means the carrying on of an activity of the kind specified by article 39G of that Order (debt administration), disregarding the effect of paragraph (3) of that article.]

[(7B) A person ('P') provides credit information services if P carries on, by way of business, an activity of the kind specified by article 89A(1) or (2) of that Order (providing credit information services).]

[(8) A person ('P') operates a credit reference agency if P carries on, by way of business, an activity of the kind specified by article 89B of that Order (providing credit references).]

Seeking business

153   Definition of canvassing off trade premises (agreements for ancillary credit services)

(1) An individual (the 'canvasser') canvasses off trade premises the services of a person carrying on an ancillary credit business if he solicits the entry of another individual (the 'consumer') into an agreement for the provision to the consumer of those services by making oral representations to the consumer, or any other individual, during a visit by the canvasser to any place (not excluded by subsection (2)) where the consumer, or that other individual as the case may be, is, being a visit—

(a) carried out for the purpose of making such oral representations to individuals who are at that place, but

(b) not carried out in response to a request made on a previous occasion.

(2) A place is excluded from subsection (1) if it is a place where (whether on a permanent or temporary basis)—

(a) the ancillary credit business is carried on, or

(b) any business is carried on by the canvasser or the person whose employee or agent the canvasser is, or by the consumer.

154   Prohibition of canvassing certain ancillary credit services off trade premises

It is an offence to canvass off trade premises the services of a person carrying on a business of credit-brokerage, debt-adjusting [, debt-counselling or the provision of credit information services].

155   Right to recover brokerage fees

(1) [Subject to subsection (2A),] The excess over [£5] of a fee or commission for his services charged by a credit-broker to an individual to whom this subsection applies shall cease to be payable or, as the case may be, shall be recoverable by the individual if the introduction does not result in his entering into a relevant agreement within the six months following the introduction (disregarding any agreement which is cancelled under section 69(1) or becomes subject to section 69(2)).

(2) Subsection (1) applies to an individual who sought an introduction for a purpose which would have been fulfilled by his entry into—

(a) a regulated agreement, or

(b) in the case of an individual [desiring to obtain credit to finance the acquisition or provision of a dwelling occupied or to be occupied by that individual or a relative of that individual], an agreement for credit secured on land,

[(c) a credit agreement which is an exempt agreement for the purposes of Chapter 14A of Part 2 of the Regulated Activities Order, or

(d) an agreement which is not a regulated credit agreement or a regulated consumer hire agreement but which would be such an agreement if the law applicable to the agreement were the law of a part of the United Kingdom].

[(2A) But subsection (1) does not apply where—

(a) the fee or commission relates to the effecting of an introduction of a kind mentioned in article 36E of the Regulated Activities Order (activities in relation to certain agreements relating to land); and

(b) the person charging that fee or commission is an authorised person or an appointed representative, within the meaning of the Financial Services and Markets Act 2000.]

(3) An agreement is a relevant agreement for the purposes of subsection (1) in relation to an individual if it is an agreement such as is referred to in subsection (2) in relation to that individual.

(4) In the case of an individual desiring to obtain credit under a consumer credit agreement, any sum payable or paid by him to a credit-broker otherwise than as a fee or commission for the credit-broker's services shall for the purposes of subsection (1) be treated as such a fee or commission if it enters, or would enter, into the total charge for credit.

Credit reference agencies

157   Duty to disclose name etc. of agency

[(A1) Where a creditor under a prospective regulated agreement, other than an excluded agreement, decides not to proceed with it on the basis of information obtained by the creditor from a credit reference agency, the creditor must, when informing the debtor of the decision—

(a) inform the debtor that this decision has been reached on the basis of information from a credit reference agency, and

(b) provide the debtor with the particulars of the agency including its name, address and telephone number.]

(1) [In any other case,] A creditor, owner or negotiator, within the prescribed period after receiving a request in writing to that effect from the debtor or hirer, shall give him notice of the name

and address of any credit reference agency from which the creditor, owner or negotiator has, during the antecedent negotiations, applied for information about his financial standing.

(2) Subsection (1) does not apply to a request received more than 28 days after the termination of the antecedent negotiations, whether on the making of the regulated agreement or otherwise.

[(2A) A creditor is not required to disclose information under this section if such disclosure—

    (a) contravenes [the UK GDPR],

    (b) is prohibited by a retained EU obligation,

    (c) would create or be likely to create a serious risk that any person would be subject to violence or intimidation, or

    (d) would, or would be likely to, prejudice—

        (i) the prevention or detection of crime,

        (ii) the apprehension or prosecution of offenders, or

        (iii) the administration of justice.]

(3) If the creditor, owner or negotiator fails to comply with subsection [(A1) or] (1) he commits an offence.

[(4) For the purposes of subsection (A1) an agreement is an excluded agreement if it is—

    (a) a consumer hire agreement, or

    (b) an agreement secured on land.]

158 Duty of agency to disclose filed information

(1) A credit reference agency, within the prescribed period after receiving,—

    [(a) a request in writing to that effect from a consumer,] and

    (b) such particulars as the agency may reasonably require to enable them to identify the file, and

    (c) a fee of [£2],

shall give the consumer a copy of the file relating to [it] kept by the agency.

(2) When giving a copy of the file under subsection (1), the agency shall also give the consumer a statement in the prescribed form of [the consumer's] rights under section 159.

(3) If the agency does not keep a file relating to the consumer it shall give [the consumer] notice of that fact, but need not return any money paid.

(4) If the agency contravenes any provision of this section it commits an offence.

[(4A) In this section 'consumer' means—

    (a) a partnership consisting of two or three persons not all of whom are bodies corporate; or

    (b) an unincorporated body of persons which does not consist entirely of bodies corporate and is not a partnership.]

(5) In this Act 'file', in relation to an individual, means all the information about him kept by a credit reference agency, regardless of how the information is stored, and 'copy of the file', as respects information not in plain English, means a transcript reduced into plain English.

159 Correction of wrong information

[(1) Any individual (the 'objector') given—

    (a) information under Article 15(1) to (3) of the UK GDPR (confirmation of processing, access to data and safeguards for third country transfers) by a credit reference agency, or

    (b) information under section 158,

who considers that an entry in his file is incorrect, and that if it is not corrected he is likely to be prejudiced, may give notice to the agency requiring it either to remove the entry from the file or amend it.]

(2) Within 28 days after receiving a notice under subsection (1), the agency shall by notice inform the [objector] that it has—

    (a) removed the entry from the file, or

    (b) amended the entry, or

    (c) taken no action, and if the notice states that the agency has amended the entry it shall include a copy of the file so far as it comprises the amended entry.

(3) Within 28 days after receiving a notice under subsection (2), or where no such notice was given, within 28 days after the expiry of the period mentioned in subsection (2), the [objector] may, unless he has been informed by the agency that it has removed the entry from his file, serve a further notice on the agency requiring it to add to the file an accompanying notice of correction (not exceeding 200 words) drawn up by the [objector], and include a copy of it when furnishing information included in or based on that entry.

(4) Within 28 days after receiving a notice under subsection (3), the agency, unless it intends to apply to the [the relevant authority] under subsection (5), shall by notice inform the [objector] that it has received the notice under subsection (3) and intends to comply with it.

(5) If—

   (a) the [objector] has not received a notice under subsection (4) within the time required, or
   (b) it appears to the agency that it would be improper for it to publish a notice of correction because it is incorrect, or unjustly defames any person, or is frivolous or scandalous, or is for any other reason unsuitable,

the [objector] or, as the case may be, the agency may, in the prescribed manner and on payment of [the prescribed fee], apply to [the relevant authority], who may make such order on the application as he thinks fit.

(6) If a person to whom an order under this section is directed fails to comply with it within the period specified in the order he commits an offence.

[(7) The Information Commissioner may vary or revoke any order made by him under this section.

(8) In this section 'the relevant authority' means

   (a) where the objector is a partnership or other unincorporated body of persons, the FCA, and
   (b) in any other case, the Information Commissioner.]

160 Alternative procedure for business consumers

(1) The [FCA], on an application made by a credit reference agency, may direct that this section shall apply to the agency if [it] is satisfied—

   (a) that compliance with section 158 in the case of consumers who carry on a business would adversely affect the service provided to its customers by the agency, and
   (b) that, having regard to the methods employed by the agency and to any other relevant facts, it is probable that consumers carrying on a business would not be prejudiced by the making of the direction.

(2) Where an agency to which this section applies receives a request, particulars and a fee under section 158(1) from a consumer who carries on a business and section 158(3) does not apply, the agency, instead of complying with section 158, may elect to deal with the matter under the following subsections.

(3) Instead of giving the consumer a copy of the file, the agency shall within the prescribed period give notice to the consumer that it is proceeding under this section, and by notice give the consumer such information included in or based on entries in the file as the [FCA] may direct, together with a statement in the prescribed form of the consumer's rights under subsections (4) and (5).

(4) If within 28 days after receiving the information given to [the consumer] under subsection (3), or such longer period as the [FCA] may allow, the consumer—

   (a) gives notice to the [FCA] that [the consumer] is dissatisfied with the information, and
   (b) satisfies the [FCA] that the [consumer] has taken such steps in relation to the agency as may be reasonable with a view to removing the cause of [the consumer's] dissatisfaction, and
   (c) pays the [FCA the prescribed fee], the [FCA] may direct the agency to give the [FCA] a copy of the file, and the [FCA] may disclose to the consumer such of the information on the file as the [FCA] thinks fit.

(5) Section 159 applies with any necessary modifications to information given to the consumer under this section as it applies to information given under section 158.

(6) If an agency making an election under subsection (2) fails to comply with subsection (3) or (4) it commits an offence.

[(7) In this section 'consumer' has the same meaning as in section 158.]

PART XI ENFORCEMENT OF ACT

161 Enforcement authorities

(1) The following authorities ('enforcement authorities') have a duty to enforce this Act and regulations made under it—

[...]

(b) in Great Britain, the local weights and measures authority,

(c) In Northern Ireland, the Department of Commerce for Northern Ireland.

[(1A) Subsection (1) does not limit any function of the FCA in relation to the enforcement of this Act or regulations made under it.]

[(1B) For the investigatory powers available to a local weights and measures authority or the Department of Enterprise, Trade and Investment in Northern Ireland for the purposes of the duty in subsection (1), see Schedule 5 to the Consumer Rights Act 2015.]

(3) Every local weights and measures authority shall, whenever the [FCA] requires, report to [it] in such form and with such particulars as [it] requires on the exercise of their functions under this Act.

166 Notification of convictions and judgments to [FCA]

Where a person is convicted of an offence or has a judgment given against him by or before any court in the United Kingdom and it appears to the court—

(a) having regard to the functions of the [FCA under the Financial Services and Markets Act 2000 or] this Act, that the conviction or judgment should be brought to the [FCA's] attention, and

(b) that it may not be brought to [its] attention unless arrangements for that purpose are made by the court,

the court may make such arrangements notwithstanding that the proceedings have been finally disposed of.

167 Penalties

(1) An offence under a provision of this Act specified in column 1 of Schedule 1 is triable in the mode or modes indicated in column 3, and on conviction is punishable as indicated in column 4 (where a period of time indicates the maximum term of imprisonment, and a monetary amount indicates the maximum fine, for the offence in question).

168 Defences

(1) In any proceedings for an offence under this Act it is a defence for the person charged to prove—

(a) that his act or omission was due to a mistake, or to reliance on information supplied to him, or to an act or omission by another person, or to an accident or some other cause beyond his control, and

(b) that he took all reasonable precautions and exercised all due diligence to avoid such an act or omission by himself or any person under his control.

(2) If in any case the defence provided by subsection (1) involves the allegation that the act or omission was due to an act or omission by another person or to reliance on information supplied by another person, the person charged shall not, without leave of the court, be entitled to rely on

that defence unless, within a period ending seven clear days before the hearing, he has served on the prosecutor a notice giving such information identifying or assisting in the identification of that other person as was then in his possession.

169 Offences by bodies corporate

Where at any time a body corporate commits an offence under this Act with the consent or connivance of, or because of neglect by, any individual, the individual commits the like offence if at that time—

(a) he is a director, manager, secretary or similar officer of the body corporate, or

(b) he is purporting to act as such an officer, or

(c) the body corporate is managed by its members of whom he is one.

170 No further sanctions for breach of Act

(1) A breach of any requirement made (otherwise than by any court) by or under this Act shall incur no civil or criminal sanction as being such a breach, except to the extent (if any) expressly provided by or under this Act [or by or under the Financial Services and Markets Act 2000 by virtue of an order made under section 107 of the Financial Services Act 2012].

(2) In exercising its functions under this Act the [FCA] may take account of any matter appearing to [it] to constitute a breach of a requirement made by or under this Act, whether or not any sanction for that breach is provided by or under this Act and, if it is so provided, whether or not proceedings have been brought in respect of the breach.

(3) Subsection (1) does not prevent the grant of an injunction, or the making of an order of certiorari, mandamus or prohibition or as respects Scotland the grant of an interdict or of an order under section 91 of the Court of Session Act 1868 (order for specific performance of statutory duty).

171 Onus of proof in various proceedings

(1) If an agreement contains a term signifying that in the opinion of the parties section 10(3)(b)(iii) does not apply to the agreement, it shall be taken not to apply unless the contrary is proved.

(2) It shall be assumed in any proceedings, unless the contrary is proved, that when a person initiated a transaction as mentioned in section 19(1)(c) he knew the principal agreement had been made, or contemplated that it might be made.

(4) In proceedings brought by the creditor under a credit-token agreement—

(a) it is for the creditor to prove that the credit-token was lawfully supplied to the debtor, and was accepted by him, and

(b) if the debtor alleges that any use made of the credit-token was not authorised by him, it is for the creditor to prove either—

(i) that the use was so authorised, or

(ii) that the use occurred before the creditor had been given notice under section 84(3).

(5) In proceedings under section 50(1) in respect of a document received by a minor at any school or other educational establishment for minors, it is for the person sending it to him at that establishment to prove that he did not know or suspect it to be such an establishment.

(6) In proceedings under section 119(1) it is for the pawnee to prove that he had reasonable cause to refuse to allow the pawn to be redeemed.

172 Statements by creditor or owner to be binding

(1) A statement by a creditor or owner is binding on him if given under—

section 77(1),

section 78(1),

section 79(1),

section 97(1),

section 107(1)(c),

section 108(1)(c), or

section 109(1)(c).

(2) Where a trader—

    (a) gives a customer a notice in compliance with section 103(1)(b), or

    (b) gives a customer a notice under section 103(1) asserting that the customer is not indebted to him under an agreement,

the notice is binding on the trader.

(3) Where in proceedings before any court—

    (a) it is sought to rely on a statement or notice given as mentioned in subsection (1) or (2), and

    (b) the statement or notice is shown to be incorrect,

the court may direct such relief (if any) to be given to the creditor or owner from the operation of subsection (1) or (2) as appears to the court to be just.

173 Contracting-out forbidden

(1) A term contained in a regulated agreement or linked transaction, or in any other agreement relating to an actual or prospective regulated agreement or linked transaction, is void if, and to the extent that, it is inconsistent with a provision for the protection of the debtor or hirer or his relative or any surety contained in this Act or in any regulation made under this Act.

(2) Where a provision specifies the duty or liability of the debtor or hirer or his relative or any surety in certain circumstances, a term is inconsistent with that provision if it purports to impose, directly or indirectly, an additional duty or liability on him in those circumstances.

(3) Notwithstanding subsection (1), a provision of this Act under which a thing may be done in relation to any person on an order of the court or the [FCA] only shall not be taken to prevent its being done at any time with that person's consent given at that time, but the refusal of such consent shall not give rise to any liability.

PART XII SUPPLEMENTAL

[174A Powers to require provision of information or documents etc.

(1) Every power conferred on a relevant authority by or under this Act (however expressed) to require the provision or production of information or documents includes the power—

    (a) to require information to be provided or produced in such form as the authority may specify, including, in relation to information recorded otherwise than in a legible form, in a legible form;

    (b) to take copies of, or extracts from, any documents provided or produced by virtue of the exercise of the power;

    (c) to require the person who is required to provide or produce any information or document by virtue of the exercise of the power—

        (i) to state, to the best of his knowledge and belief, where the information or document is

        (ii) to give an explanation of the information or document;

        (iii) to secure that any information provided or produced, whether in a document or otherwise, is verified in such manner as may be specified by the authority;

        (iv) to secure that any document provided or produced is authenticated in such manner as may be so specified;

    (d) to specify a time at or by which a requirement imposed by virtue of paragraph (c) must be complied with.

(2) Every power conferred on a relevant authority by or under this Act (however expressed) to inspect or to seize documents at any premises includes the power to take copies of, or extracts from, any documents inspected or seized by virtue of the exercise of the power.

(3) But a relevant authority has no power under this Act—

(a) to require another person to provide or to produce,

(b) to seize from another person, or

(c) to require another person to give access to premises for the purposes of the inspection of,

any information or document which the other person would be entitled to refuse to provide or produce in proceedings in the High Court on the grounds of legal professional privilege or (in Scotland) in proceedings in the Court of Session on the grounds of confidentiality of communications.

(4) In subsection (3) 'communications' means—

(a) communications between a professional legal adviser and his client;

(b) communications made in connection with or in contemplation of legal proceedings and for the purposes of those proceedings.

(5) In this section 'relevant authority' means an enforcement authority or an officer of an enforcement authority.]

175 Duty of persons deemed to be agents

Where under this Act a person is deemed to receive a notice or payment as agent of the creditor or owner under regulated agreement, he shall be deemed to be under a contractual duty to the creditor or owner to transmit the notice, or remit the payment, to him forthwith.

176 Service of documents

(1) A document to be served under this Act by one person ('the server') on another person ('the subject') is to be treated as properly served on the subject if dealt with as mentioned in the following subsections.

(2) The document may be delivered or sent [by an appropriate method] to the subject, or addressed to him by name and left at his proper address.

(3) For the purposes of this Act, a document sent [by an appropriate method] to, or left at, the address last known to the server as the address of a person shall be treated as sent by post to, or left at, his proper address.

(4) Where the document is to be served on the subject as being the person having any interest in land, and it is not practicable after reasonable inquiry to ascertain the subject's name or address, the document may be served by—

(a) addressing it to the subject by the description of the person having that interest in the land (naming it), and

(b) delivering the document to some responsible person on the land or affixing it, or a copy of it, in a conspicuous position on the land.

(5) Where a document to be served on the subject as being a debtor, hirer or surety, or as having any other capacity relevant for the purposes of this Act, is served at any time on another person who—

(a) is the person last known to the server as having that capacity, but

(b) before that time had ceased to have it, the document shall be treated as having been served at that time on the subject.

(6) Anything done to a document in relation to a person who (whether to the knowledge of the server or not) has died shall be treated for the purposes of subsection (5) as service of the document on that person if it would have been so treated had he not died.

[(7) The following enactments shall not be construed as authorising service on the Public Trustee (in England and Wales) or the Probate Judge (in Northern Ireland) of any document which is to be served under this Act—

section 9 of the Administration of Estates Act 1925;

section 3 of the Administration of Estates Act (Northern Ireland) 1955.]

(8) References in the preceding subsections to the serving of a document on a person include the giving of the document to that person.

[176A   Electronic transmission of documents

(1) A document is transmitted in accordance with this subsection if—

    (a) the person to whom it is transmitted agrees that it may be delivered to him by being transmitted to a particular electronic address in a particular electronic form,

    (b) it is transmitted to that address in that form, and

    (c) the form in which the document is transmitted is such that any information in the document which is addressed to the person to whom the document is transmitted is capable of being stored for future reference for an appropriate period in a way which allows the information to be reproduced without change.

(2) A document transmitted in accordance with subsection (1) shall, unless the contrary is proved, be treated for the purposes of this Act, except section 69, as having been delivered on the working day immediately following the day on which it is transmitted.

(3) In this section, 'electronic address' includes any number or address used for the purposes of receiving electronic communications.]

177   Saving for registered charges

(1) Nothing in this Act affects the rights of a proprietor of a registered charge (within the meaning of the [Land Registration Act 2002]), who—

    (a) became the proprietor under a transfer for valuable consideration without notice of any defect in the title arising (apart from this section) by virtue of this Act, or

    (b) derives title from such a proprietor.

(2) Nothing in this Act affects the operation of section 104 of the Law of Property Act 1925 (protection of purchaser where mortgagee exercises power of sale).

(3) Subsection (1) does not apply to a proprietor carrying on a business of debt-collecting.

(4) Where, by virtue of subsection (1), a land mortgage is enforced which apart from this section would be treated as never having effect, the original creditor or owner shall be liable to indemnify the debtor or hirer against any loss thereby suffered by him.

(5) In the application of this section to Scotland for subsections (1) to (3) there shall be substituted the following subsections—

'(1) Nothing in this Act affects the rights of a creditor in a heritable security who—

    (a) became the creditor under a transfer for value without notice of any defect in the title arising (apart from this section) by virtue of this Act; or

    (b) derives title from such a creditor.

(2) Nothing in this Act affects the operation of section 41 of the Conveyancing (Scotland) Act 1924 (protection of purchasers), or of that section as applied to standard securities by section 32 of the Conveyancing and Feudal Reform (Scotland) Act 1970.

(3) Subsection (1) does not apply to a creditor carrying on [a consumer credit business, a consumer hire business or a business of debt-collecting or debt administration].'

(6) In the application of this section to Northern Ireland—

    (a) any reference to the proprietor of a registered charge (within the meaning of the [Land Registration Act 2002]) shall be construed as a reference to the registered owner of a charge under the Local Registration of Title (Ireland) Act 1891 or Part IV of the Land Registration Act (Northern Ireland) 1970, and

    (b) for the reference to section 104 of the Law Property Act 1925 there shall be substituted a reference to section 21 of the Conveyancing and Law Property Act 1881 and section 5 of the Conveyancing Act 1911.

178   Local Acts

The [Treasury] or the Department of Commerce for Northern Ireland may by order make such amendments or repeals of any provision of any local Act as appears to the [Treasury] or, as the case may be, the Department, necessary or expedient in consequence of the replacement by this Act of the enactments relating to pawnbrokers and moneylenders.

Regulations, orders, etc.

179 Power to prescribe form etc. of secondary documents

(1) Regulations may be made as to the form and content of credit-cards, trading-checks, receipts, vouchers and other documents or things issued by creditors, owners or suppliers under or in connection with regulated agreements or by other persons in connection with linked transactions, and may in particular—

    (a) require specified information to be included in the prescribed manner in documents, and other specified material to be excluded;

    (b) contain requirements to ensure that specified information is clearly brought to the attention of the debtor or hirer, or his relative, and that one part of a document is not given insufficient or excessive prominence compared with another.

(2) If a person issues any document or thing in contravention of regulations under subsection (1) then, as from the time of the contravention but without prejudice to anything done before it, this Act shall apply as if the regulated agreement had been improperly executed by reason of a contravention of regulations under section 60(1).

180 Power to prescribe form etc. of copies

(1) Regulations may be made as to the form and content of documents to be issued as copies of any executed agreement, security instrument or other document referred to in this Act, and may in particular—

    (a) require specified information to be included in the prescribed manner in any copy, and contain requirements to ensure that such information is clearly brought to the attention of a reader of the copy;

    (b) authorise the omission from a copy of certain material contained in the original, or the inclusion of such material in condensed form.

(2) A duty imposed by any provision of this Act [. . .] to supply a copy of any document—

    (a) is not satisfied unless the copy supplied is in the prescribed form and conforms to the prescribed requirements;

    (b) is not infringed by the omission of any material, or its inclusion in condensed form, if that is authorised by regulations;

and references in this Act to copies shall be construed accordingly.

(3) Regulations may provide that a duty imposed by this Act to supply a copy of a document referred to in an unexecuted agreement or an executed agreement shall not apply to documents of a kind specified in the regulations.

181 Power to alter monetary limits etc.

(1) The [Treasury] may by order made by statutory instrument amend, or further amend, any of the following provisions of this Act so as to reduce or increase a sum mentioned in that provision, namely, sections [. . .], 17(1), [. . .], 70(6), 75(3)(b), 77(1), 78(1), 79(1), 84(1), 101(7)(a), 107(1), 108(1), 109(1), 110(1), [140B(6),] 155(1) and 158(1).

(2) An order under subsection (1) amending section [. . .] 17(1), [. . .] 75(3)(b) [or 140B(6)] shall be of no effect unless a draft of the order has been laid before and approved by each House of Parliament.

182 Regulations and orders

(1) Any power of the [Treasury] to make regulations or orders under this Act, except the power conferred by sections [. . .] 181 and 192 shall be exercisable by statutory instrument subject to annulment in pursuance of a resolution of either House of Parliament.

(2) Where a power to make regulations or orders [. . .] is exercisable by the [Treasury] by virtue of this Act, regulations or orders [. . .] made in the exercise of that power may—

    (a) make different provision in relation to different cases or classes of case, and

(b) exclude certain cases or classes of case, and

(c) contain such transitional provision as the [Treasury] thinks fit.

(3) Regulations may provide that specified expressions, when used as described by the regulations, are to be given the prescribed meaning, notwithstanding that another meaning is intended by the person using them.

(4) Any power conferred on the [Treasury] by this Act to make orders includes power to vary or revoke an order so made.

[183   Determinations etc. by FCA

(1) The FCA may vary or revoke any determination made, or direction given, by it under this Act.]

Interpretation

184   Associates

[(1) A person is an associate of an individual if that person is—

(a) the individual's husband or wife or civil partner,

(b) a relative of—

(i)   the individual, or

(ii) the individual's husband or wife or civil partner, or

(c) the husband or wife or civil partner of a relative of—

(i)   the individual, or

(ii) the individual's husband or wife or civil partner.]

(2) A person is an associate of any person with whom he is in partnership, and of the husband or wife [or civil partner] or a relative of any individual with whom he is in partnership.

(3) A body corporate is an associate of another body corporate—

(a) if the same person is a controller of both, or a person is a controller of one and persons who are his associates, or he and persons who are his associates, are controllers of the other; or

(b) if a group of two or more persons is controller of each company, and the groups either consist of the same persons or could be regarded as consisting of the same persons by treating (in one or more cases) a member of either group as replaced by a person of whom he is an associate.

(4) A body corporate is an associate of another person if that person is a controller of it or if that person and persons who are his associates together are controllers of it.

(5) In this section 'relative' means brother, sister, uncle, aunt, nephew, niece, lineal ancestor or lineal descendant, [...] references to a husband or wife include a former husband or wife and a reputed husband [or wife, and references to a civil partner include a former civil partner and a reputed civil partner;] and for the purposes of this subsection a relationship shall be established as if any illegitimate child, step-child or adopted child of a person [were the legitimate child of the relationship in question].

185   Agreement with more than one debtor or hirer

(1) Where an actual or prospective regulated agreement has two or more debtors or hirers (not being a partnership or an unincorporated body of persons)—

(a) anything required by or under this Act to be done to or in relation to the debtor or hirer shall be done to or in relation to each of them; and

(b) anything done under this Act by or on behalf of one of them shall have effect as if done by or on behalf of all of them.

[(2) Notwithstanding subsection (1)(a), where credit is provided under an agreement to two or more debtors jointly, in performing his duties—

(a) in the case of fixed-sum credit, under section 77A, or

(b) in the case of running-account credit, under section 78(4), the creditor need not give statements to any debtor who has signed and given to him a notice (a 'dispensing notice') authorising him not to comply in the debtor's case with section 77A or (as the case may be) 78(4).

(2A) A dispensing notice given by a debtor is operative from when it is given to the creditor until it is revoked by a further notice given to the creditor by the debtor.

(2B) But subsection (2) does not apply if (apart from this subsection) dispensing notices would be operative in relation to all of the debtors to whom the credit is provided.

(2C) Any dispensing notices operative in relation to an agreement shall cease to have effect if any of the debtors dies.

(2D) A dispensing notice which is operative in relation to an agreement shall be operative also in relation to any subsequent agreement which, in relation to the earlier agreement, is a modifying agreement.]

(3) Subsection (1)(b) does not apply for the purposes of section 61(1)(a) [...].

(4) Where a regulated agreement has two or more debtors or hirers (not being a partnership or an unincorporated body of persons), section 86 applies to the death of any of them.

(5) An agreement for the provision of credit, or the bailment or (in Scotland) the hiring of goods, to two or more persons jointly where—

(a) one or more of those persons is an individual, and

(b) one or more of them is [not an individual],

is a consumer credit agreement or consumer hire agreement if it would have been one had they all been individuals; and [each person within paragraph (b)] shall accordingly be included among the debtors or hirers under the agreement.

(6) Where subsection (5) applies, references in this Act to the signing of any document by the debtor or hirer shall be construed in relation to a body corporate [within paragraph (b) of that sub-section] as referring to a signing on behalf of the body corporate.

186   Agreement with more than one creditor or owner

Where an actual or prospective regulated agreement has two or more creditors or owners, anything required by or under this Act to be done to, or in relation to, or by, the creditor or owner shall be effective if done to, or in relation to, or by, any one of them.

187   Arrangements between creditor and supplier

(1) A consumer credit agreement shall be treated as entered into under pre-existing arrangements between a creditor and a supplier if it is entered into in accordance with, or in furtherance of, arrangements previously made between persons mentioned in subsection (4)(a), (b) or (c).

(2) A consumer credit agreement shall be treated as entered into in contemplation of future arrangements between a creditor and a supplier if it is entered into in the expectation that arrangements will subsequently be made between persons mentioned in subsection (4)(a), (b) or (c) for the supply of cash, goods and services (or any of them) to be financed by the consumer credit agreement.

(3) Arrangements shall be disregarded for the purposes of subsection (1) or (2) if—

(a) they are arrangements for the making, in specified circumstances, of payments to the supplier by the creditor, and

(b) the creditor holds himself out as willing to make, in such circumstances, payments of the kind to suppliers generally.

[(3A) Arrangements shall also be disregarded for the purposes of subsections (1) and (2) if they are arrangements for the electronic transfer of funds from a current account at a bank within the meaning of the Bankers' Book Evidence Act 1879.]

(4) The persons referred to in subsections (1) and (2) are—

(a) the creditor and the supplier;

(b) one of them and an associate of the other's;

(c) an associate of one and an associate of the other's.

(5) Where the creditor is an associate of the supplier's. the consumer credit agreement shall be treated, unless the contrary is proved, as entered into under pre-existing arrangements between the creditor and the supplier.

[187A   Definition of 'default sum'

(1) In this Act 'default sum' means, in relation to the debtor or hirer under a regulated agreement, a sum (other than a sum of interest) which is payable by him under the agreement in connection with a breach of the agreement by him.

(2) But a sum is not a default sum in relation to the debtor or hirer simply because, as a consequence of his breach of the agreement, he is required to pay it earlier than he would otherwise have had to.]

188   Examples of use of new terminology

(1) Schedule 2 shall have effect for illustrating the use of terminology employed in this Act.

(2) The examples given in Schedule 2 are not exhaustive.

(3) In the case of conflict between Schedule 2 and any other provision of this Act, that other provision shall prevail.

(4) The [Treasury] may by order amend Schedule 2 by adding further examples or in any other way.

189   Definitions

(1) In this Act, unless the context otherwise requires—

'advertisement' includes every form of advertising, whether in a publication, by television or radio, by display of notices, signs, labels, showcards or goods, by distribution of samples, circulars, catalogues, price lists or other material, by exhibition of pictures, models or films, or in any other way, and references to the publishing of advertisements shall be construed accordingly;

'ancillary credit business' has the meaning given by section 145(1);

'antecedent negotiations' has the meaning given by section 56;

['appropriate method' means—

(a) post, or

(b) transmission in the form of an electronic communication in accordance with section 176A(1);]

'assignment', in relation to Scotland, means assignation;

'associate' shall be construed in accordance with section 184;

['authorised business overdraft agreement' means a debtor-creditor agreement which provides authorisation in advance for the debtor to overdraw on a current account, where the agreement is entered into by the debtor wholly or predominantly for the purposes of the debtor's business (see subsection (2A));]

['authorised non-business overdraft agreement' means a debtor-creditor agreement which provides authorisation in advance for the debtor to overdraw on a current account where—

(a) the credit must be repaid on demand or within three months, and

(b) the agreement is not entered into by the debtor wholly or predominantly for the purposes of the debtor's business (see subsection (2A));]

['authorised institution' means an institution authorised under the Banking Act 1987;]

'bill of sale' has the meaning given by section 4 of the Bills of Sale Act 1878 or, for Northern Ireland, by section 4 of the Bills of Sale (Ireland) Act 1879;

['building society' means a building society within the meaning of the Building Societies Act 1986;]

'business' includes profession or trade, and references to a business apply subject to subsection (2);

'cancellable agreement' means a regulated agreement which, by virtue of section 67, may be cancelled by the debtor or hirer;

'canvass' shall be construed in accordance with sections 48 and 153;

'cash' includes money in any form;

'charity' means as respects England and Wales a charity registered under [the Charities Act 2011] or an exempt charity (within the meaning of that Act), [as respects] Northern Ireland an institution or other organization established for charitable purposes only ('organisation' including any persons administering a trust and 'charitable' being construed in the same way as if it were contained in the Income Tax Acts) [and as respects Scotland a body entered in the Scottish Charity Register];

'conditional sale agreement' means an agreement for the sale of goods or land under which the purchase price or part of it is payable by instalments, and the property in the goods or land is to remain in the seller (notwithstanding that the buyer is to be in possession of the goods or land) until such conditions as to the payment of instalments or otherwise as may be specified in the agreement are fulfilled;

'consumer credit agreement' has the meaning given by section 8, and includes a consumer credit agreement which is cancelled under section 69(1), or becomes subject to section 69(2), so far as the agreement remains in force;

['consumer credit business' means any business being carried on by a person so far as it comprises or relates to—

    (a) the provision of credit by him, or

    (b) otherwise his being a creditor,

under regulated consumer credit agreements;]

'consumer hire agreement' has the meaning given by section 15;

['consumer hire business' means any business being carried on by a person so far as it comprises or relates to—

    (a) the bailment or (in Scotland) the hiring of goods by him, or

    (b) otherwise his being an owner,

under regulated consumer hire agreements;]

'controller', in relation to a body corporate, means a person—

    (a) in accordance with whose directions or instructions the directors of the body corporate or of another body corporate which is its controller (or any of them) are accustomed to act, or

    (b) who, either alone or with any associate or associates, is entitled to exercise, or control the exercise of, one third or more of the voting power at any general meeting of the body corporate or of another body corporate which is its controller;

'copy' shall be construed in accordance with section 180;

'court' means in relation to England and Wales the county court, in relation to Scotland the sheriff court and in relation to Northern Ireland the High Court or the county court;

'credit' shall be construed in accordance with section 9;

'credit-broker' means a person carrying on a business of credit-brokerage;

'credit-brokerage' has the meaning given by section 145(2);

['credit information services' is to be read in accordance with section 145(7B);]

['credit intermediary' has the meaning given by section 160A;]

'credit limit' has the meaning given by section 10(2);

'creditor' means [(except in relation to green deal plans: see instead section 189B(2))] the person providing credit under a consumer credit agreement or the person to whom his rights and duties under the agreement have passed by assignment or operation of law, and in relation to a prospective consumer agreement, includes the prospective creditor;

'credit reference agency' [is to be read in accordance with] section 145(8);

'credit-sale agreement' means an agreement for the sale of goods, under which the purchase price or part of it is payable by instalments, but which is not a conditional sale agreement;

'credit-token' has the meaning given by section 14(1);

'credit-token agreement' means a regulated agreement for the provision of credit in connection with the use of a credit-token;

'debt-adjusting' has the meaning given by section 145(5);

['debt administration' has the meaning given by section 145(7A);]

'debt-collecting' has the meaning given by section 145(7);

'debt-counselling' has the meaning given by section 145(6);

'debtor' means [[except in relation to green deal plans: see instead section 189B(3))]] the individual receiving credit under a consumer credit agreement or the person to whom his rights and duties under the agreement have passed by assignment or operation of law, and in relation to a prospective consumer credit agreement includes the prospective debtor;

'debtor-creditor agreement' has the meaning given by section 13;

'debtor-creditor-supplier agreement' has the meaning given by section 12;

'default notice' has the meaning given by section 87(1);

['default sum' has the meaning given by section 187A;]

'deposit' means [. . .] any sum payable by a debtor or hirer by way of deposit or downpayment, or credited or to be credited to him on account of any deposit or downpayment, whether the sum is to be or has been paid to the creditor or owner or any other person, or is to be or has been discharged by a payment of money or a transfer or delivery of goods or by any other means;

['documents' includes information recorded in any form;]

'electric line' has the meaning given by [the Electricity Act 1989] or, for Northern Ireland the Electricity Supply (Northern Ireland) Order 1972;

['electronic communication' means an electronic communication within the meaning of the Electronic Communications Act 2000 (c.7);]

'embodies' and related words shall be construed in accordance with subsection (4);

'enforcement authority' has the meaning given by section 161(1);

'enforcement order' means an order under section 65(1), 105(7)(a) or (b), 111(2) or 124(1) or (2);

'executed agreement' means a document, signed by or on behalf of the parties, embodying the terms of a regulated agreement, or such of them as have been reduced to writing;

['FCA' means the Financial Conduct Authority;]

'finance' means to finance wholly or partly, and 'financed' and 'refinanced' shall be construed accordingly;

'file' and 'copy of the file' have the meanings given by section 158(5);

'fixed-sum credit' has the meaning given by section 10(1)(b);

'friendly society' means a society registered [or treated as registered under the Friendly Societies Act 1974 or the Friendly Societies Act 1992];

'future arrangements' shall be construed in accordance with section 187;

'give' means deliver or send [by an appropriate method] to;

'goods' has the meaning given by [section 61(1) of the Sale of Goods Act 1979];

['green deal plan' has the meaning given by section 1 of the Energy Act 2011;]

'High Court' means Her Majesty's High Court of Justice, or the Court of Session in Scotland or the High Court of Justice in Northern Ireland;

'hire-purchase agreement' means an agreement, other than a conditional sale agreement, under which—

    (a) goods are bailed or (in Scotland) hired in return for periodical payments by the person to whom they are bailed or hired, and

    (b) the property in the goods will pass to that person if the terms of the agreement are complied with and one or more of the following occurs—

        (i) the exercise of an option to purchase by that person,

        (ii) the doing of any other specified act by any party to the agreement,

        (iii) the happening of any other specified event;

'hirer' means the individual to whom goods are bailed or (in Scotland) hired under a consumer hire agreement, or the person to whom his rights and duties under the agreement have passed by assignment or operation of law, and in relation to a prospective consumer hire agreement includes the prospective hirer;

['individual' includes—

    (a) a partnership consisting of two or three persons not all of whom are bodies corporate; and

    (b) an unincorporated body of persons which does not consist entirely of bodies corporate and is not a partnership;]

'installation' means—

    (a) the installing of any electric line or any gas or water pipe,

    (b) the fixing of goods to the premises where they are to be used, and the alteration of premises to enable goods to be used on them,

    (c) where it is reasonably necessary that goods should be constructed or erected on the premises where they are to be used, any work carried out for the purpose of constructing or erecting them on those premises;

'judgment' includes an order or decree made by any court;

'land' includes an interest in land, and in relation to Scotland includes heritable subjects of whatever description;

'land improvement company' means an improvement company as defined by section 7 of the improvement of Land Act 1899;

'land mortgage' includes any security charged on land;

'linked transaction' has the meaning given by section 19(1);

'local authority', in relation to England and Wales, means the Greater London Council, a county council, a London borough council, a district council, the Common Council of the City of London, or the Council of the Isles of Scilly, [in relation to Wales means a county council or a county borough council,] and in relation to Scotland, means a [council constituted under section 2 of the Local Government etc. (Scotland) Act 1994], and, in relation to Northern Ireland, means a district council;

'modifying agreement' has the meaning given by section 82(2);

'mortgage', in relation to Scotland, includes any heritable security;

'multiple agreement' has the meaning given by section 18(1);

'negotiator' has the meaning given by section 56(1);

'non-commercial agreement' means a consumer credit agreement or a consumer hire agreement not made by the creditor or owner in the course of a business carried on by him;

'notice' means notice in writing;

'notice of cancellation' has the meaning given by section 69(1);

['open-end' in relation to a consumer credit agreement, means of no fixed duration;]

'owner' means a person who bails or (in Scotland) hires out goods under a consumer hire agreement or the person to whom his rights and duties under the agreement have passed by assignment or operation of law, and in relation to a prospective consumer hire agreement, includes the prospective bailor or person from whom the goods are to be hired;

'pawn' means any article subject to a pledge;

'pawn-receipt' has the meaning given by section 114;

'pawnee' and 'pawnor' include any person to whom the rights and duties of the original pawnee or the original pawnor, as the case may be, have passed by assignment or operation of law;

'payment' includes tender;

'pledge' means the pawnee's rights over an article taken in pawn;

'prescribed' means prescribed by regulations made by the Secretary of State;

'pre-existing arrangements' shall be construed in accordance with section 187;

'principal agreement' has the meaning given by section 19(1);

'protected goods' has the meaning given by section 90(7);

'redemption period' has the meaning given by section 116(3);

['Regulated Activities Order' means the Financial Services and Markets Act 2000 (Regulated Activities) Order 2001;]

['regulated agreement' means a consumer credit agreement which is a regulated agreement (within the meaning of section 8(3)) or a consumer hire agreement which is a regulated agreement (within the meaning of section 15(2));]

'regulations' means regulations made by the [Treasury];

'relative', except in section 184, means a person who is an associate by virtue of section 184(1);

'representation' includes any condition or warranty, and any other statement or undertaking, whether oral or in writing;

['residential renovation agreement' means a consumer credit agreement entered into on or after 21st March 2016—

(a) which is unsecured; and

(b) the purpose of which is the renovation of residential property, as described in Article 2(2a) of Directive 2008/48/EC of the European Parliament and of the Council of 23rd April 2008 on credit agreements for consumers.]

'restricted-use credit agreement' and 'restricted-use credit' have the meanings given by section 11(1);

'rules of court', in relation to Northern Ireland means, in relation to the High Court, rules made under section 7 of the Northern Ireland Act 1962, and, in relation to any other court, rules made by the authority having for the time being power to make rules regulating the practice and procedure in that court;

'running-account credit' shall be construed in accordance with section 10;

'security', in relation to an actual or prospective consumer credit agreement or consumer hire agreement, or any linked transaction, means a mortgage, charge, pledge, bond, debenture, indemnity, guarantee, bill, note or other right provided by the debtor or hirer, or at his request (express or implied), to secure the carrying out of the obligations of the debtor or hirer under the agreement;

'security instrument' has the meaning given by section 105(2);

'serve on' means deliver or send [by an appropriate method] to;

'signed' shall be construed in accordance with subsection (3);

'small agreement' has the meaning given by section 17(1), and 'small' in relation to an agreement within any category shall be construed accordingly;

'supplier' has the meaning given by section 11(1)(b) or 12(c) or 13(c) or, in relation to an agreement failing within section 11(1)(a), means the creditor, and includes a person to whom the rights and duties of a supplier (as so defined) have passed by assignment or operation of law, or (in relation to a prospective agreement) the prospective supplier;

'surety' means the person by whom any security is provided, or the person to whom his rights and duties in relation to the security have passed by assignment or operation of law;

'technical grounds' shall be construed in accordance with subsection (5);

'time order' has the meaning given by section 129(1);

['total charge for credit' has the meaning given by section 20;]

'total price' means the total sum payable by the debtor under a hire-purchase agreement or a conditional sale agreement, including any sum payable on the exercise of an option to purchase, but excluding any sum payable as a penalty or as compensation or damages for a breach of the agreement;

['the UK GDPR' has the same meaning as in Parts 5 to 7 of the Data Protection Act 2018 (see section 3(10) and (14) of that Act);]

'unexecuted agreement' means a document embodying the terms of a prospective regulated agreement, or such of them as it is intended to reduce to writing;

'unrestricted-use credit agreement' and 'unrestricted-use credit' have the meanings given by section 11(2);

'working day' means any day other than—

    (a) Saturday or Sunday,

    (b) Christmas Day or Good Friday,

    (c) a bank holiday within the meaning given by section 1 of the Banking and Financial Dealings Act 1971.

[(1A) In sections . . . 70(4), 73(4) and 75(2) and . . . 'costs', in relation to proceedings in Scotland, means expenses.]

(2) A person is not to be treated as carrying on a particular type of business merely because occasionally he enters into transactions belonging to a business of that type.

[(2A) For the purpose of the definitions of 'authorised business overdraft agreement' and 'authorised non-business overdraft agreement' article 60C(5) and (6) of the Regulated Activities Order applies.]

(3) Any provision of this Act requiring a document to be signed is complied with by a body corporate if the document is sealed by that body.

(4) A document embodies a provision if the provision is set out either in the document itself or in another document referred to in it.

(5) An application dismissed by the court [. . .] shall, if the court [. . .] so certifies, be taken to be dismissed on technical grounds only.

(6) Except in so far as the context otherwise requires, any reference in this Act to an enactment shall be construed as a reference to that enactment as amended by or under any other enactment, including this Act.

(7) In this Act, except where otherwise indicated—

    (a) a reference to a numbered Part, section or Schedule is a reference to the Part or section of, or the Schedule to, this Act so numbered, and

    (b) a reference in a section to a numbered subsection is a reference to the subsection of that section so numbered, and

    (c) a reference in a section, subsection or Schedule to a numbered paragraph is a reference to the paragraph of that section, subsection or Schedule so numbered.

[189B   Green deal plans

(1) A green deal plan is to be treated as a consumer credit agreement for the purposes of this Act if (and only if)—

    (a) the property in relation to the plan is a domestic property at the time when the plan is commenced, or

    (b) if paragraph (a) does not apply, the occupier or owner of the property who makes the arrangement for the plan is an individual.

(2) In the application of this Act to a green deal consumer credit agreement—

    (a) the creditor is to be treated as being—

        (i) the green deal provider (within the meaning of Chapter 1 of Part 1 of the Energy Act 2011) for the plan, or

(ii) the person to whom the provider's rights and duties under the plan have passed by assignment or operation of law,

(b) credit is to be treated as advanced under the agreement of an amount equal to the amount of the improvement costs, and

(c) the advance of credit is to be treated as made on the completion of the installation of the energy efficiency improvements to the property (but this paragraph is subject to any term of the green deal plan providing that part of the advance is to be treated as made on completion of any part of the installation).

(3) A reference in a provision of this Act listed in the first column of the table in Schedule 2A to the debtor is, in the application of the provision in relation to a green deal consumer credit agreement, to be read as a reference to—

(a) a person who at the relevant time falls (or fell) within the description or descriptions specified in the corresponding entry in the second column of the table, or

(b) if more than one description is specified and at the relevant time different persons fall (or fell) within the descriptions, each of those persons,

and except as provided by this subsection, a person is not and is not to be treated as the debtor in relation to the agreement.

(4) Where by virtue of subsection (3) a reference to the debtor in a listed provision is to be read as a reference to the improver, it is to be assumed in applying the provision in relation to the green deal consumer credit agreement that the improver is provided with credit on the terms of the green deal plan.

(5) Where by virtue of subsection (3) a reference to the debtor in a listed provision is to be read as a reference to a person who is not the improver, it is to be assumed in applying the provision in relation to the green deal consumer credit agreement—

(a) if the provision in question is any of sections 94 to 97A (which together make provision about early payment by the debtor), that the person is provided with credit on terms that the person is liable to pay all the instalments under the green deal plan;

(b) in any other case, that the person is provided with credit on those terms of the green deal plan that bind or benefit the person for any period by virtue of regulations under section 6(2)(b) of the Energy Act 2011.

(6) References in this section and in Schedule 2A to the 'improver', 'first bill payer', 'current bill payer' and 'previous bill payer' are to be read as follows—

(a) a person is the 'improver' if the person—

(i) is the owner or occupier of the property, and

(ii) is the person who makes (or has made or proposes to make) the arrangement for the green deal plan,

but this is subject to section 189C(4) in cases where the person is not an individual;

(b) a person is the 'first bill payer' if the person is liable to pay the energy bills for the property at the time when the green deal plan is commenced;

(c) a person is the 'current bill payer' if the person is liable by virtue of section 1(6)(a) of the Energy Act 2011 to pay instalments under the plan as a result of being for the time being liable to pay the energy bills for the property;

(d) a person is a 'previous bill payer' if, as a result of previously falling within paragraph (c) for an earlier period, the person has an outstanding payment liability under the plan in respect of that period.

(7) References in this Act to a prospective consumer credit agreement, and references to the creditor and debtor in relation to such an agreement, are to be read in accordance with this section in the case of prospective green deal consumer credit agreements.

(8) In this section and in section 189C—

'domestic property' means a building or part of a building that is occupied as a dwelling or (if not occupied) is intended to be occupied as a dwelling;

'energy bill' has the same meaning as in section 1 of the Energy Act 2011;

'energy efficiency improvements' has the meaning given by section 2(4) of the Energy Act 2011;

'green deal consumer credit agreement' means a green deal plan that is to be treated as a consumer credit agreement for the purposes of this Act by virtue of subsection (1);

'improvement costs', in relation to a green deal plan, are the costs of the energy efficiency improvements to the property which are to be paid by instalments under the plan after the time when credit is to be treated as being advanced by virtue of subsection (2) (but ignoring any interest or other charges for credit in determining those costs);

'listed provision' means a provision of this Act listed in the first column of Schedule 2A;

'occupier' and 'owner' have the same meanings as in Chapter 1 of Part 1 of the Energy Act 2011;

'property', in relation to a green deal plan, means the property to which the energy efficiency improvements under the plan are or are intended to be made.]

[189C   Section 189B: supplementary provision

(1) A green deal consumer credit agreement is to be treated—

(a) as an agreement for fixed-sum credit within the meaning of section 10(1)(b);

(b) as a credit agreement for the purposes of sections 140A and 140B (and section 140C(1) is to be read accordingly).

(2) Where a green deal consumer credit agreement is a regulated agreement within the meaning of this Act (see section 8(3)), it is to be treated as a restricted-use agreement that falls within section 11(1)(a).

(3) Sections 81, 140C(2) and 176(5) do not apply in the case of a green deal consumer credit agreement.

(4) A person who is not an individual is to be treated as the improver in relation to any listed provision in the first column of the table in Schedule 2A only if the corresponding entry in the second column of the table so specifies.

(5) For the purposes of section 189B—

(a) a green deal plan is commenced when—

(i) the occupier or owner of the property signs in the prescribed manner a document in relation to the plan in accordance with section 61(1) (requirements as to form and content of regulated agreements), or

(ii) if the occupier or owner of the property does not sign such a document, the green deal plan is made;

(b) a person is liable to pay the energy bills for a property at any time if the person would be treated as the bill payer for the property at that time for the purposes of Chapter 1 of Part 1 of the Energy Act 2011 (see section 2(3) and (10)).]

190   Financial provisions

(1) There shall be defrayed out of money provided by Parliament—

(a) all expenses incurred by the Secretary of State in consequence of the provisions of this Act;

(b) any expenses incurred in consequence of those provisions by any other Minister of the Crown or Government department;

(c) any increase attributable to this Act in the sums payable out of money so provided under the Superannuation Act 1972 or the Fair Trading Act 1973.

SCHEDULE 1

PROSECUTION AND PUNISHMENT OF OFFENCES

Section 167

1 Section	2 Offence	3 Mode of prosecution	4 Imprisonment or fine
49(1) …	Canvassing debtor-creditor agreements off trade premises.	(a) Summarily.	[The prescribed sum.]
		(b) On indictment.	2 years or a fine or both.
49(2) …	Soliciting debtor-creditor agreements during visits made in response to previous oral requests.	(a) Summarily.	[The prescribed sum.]
		(b) On indictment.	2 years or a fine or both.
50(1) …	Sending circulars to minors.	(a) Summarily.	[The prescribed sum.]
		(b) On indictment.	2 years or a fine or both.
114(2) …	Taking pledges from minors.	(a) Summarily.	[The prescribed sum.]
		(b) On indictment.	1 year or a fine or both.
119(1) …	Unreasonable refusal to allow pawn to be redeemed.	(a) Summarily.	[Level 4 on the standard scale.]
154 …	Canvassing ancillary credit services off trade premises.	(a) Summarily.	[The prescribed sum.]
		(b) On indictment.	1 year or a fine or both.
157(3) …	Refusal to give name etc. of credit reference agency.	(a) Summarily.	[Level 4 on the standard scale.]
158(4) …	Failure of credit reference agency to disclose filed information.	(a) Summarily.	[Level 4 on the standard scale.]
159(6) …	Failure of credit reference agency to correct information.	(a) Summarily.	[Level 4 on the standard scale.]
160(6) …	Failure of credit reference agency to comply with section 160(3) or (4).	(a) Summarily.	[Level 4 on the standard scale.]
		(b) On indictment.	[1 year or a fine or both.]

SCHEDULE 2

EXAMPLES OF USE OF NEW TERMINOLOGY

PART I LIST OF TERMS

Term	Defined in section	Illustrated by example(s)
Advertisement	189(1)	2
Antecedent negotiations	56	1, 2, 3, 4
Cancellable agreement	67	4
Consumer credit agreement ...	8	5, 6, 7, 15, 19, 21
Consumer hire agreement ...	15	20, 24
Credit	9	16, 19, 21
Credit-broker	189(1)	2
Credit limit	10(2)	6, 7, 19, 22, 23
Creditor	189(1)	1, 2, 3, 4
Credit-sale agreement	189(1)	5
Credit-token	14	3, 14, 16
Credit-token agreement ...	14	3, 14, 16, 21
Debtor-creditor agreement ...	13	8, 16, 17, 18
Debtor-creditor-supplier agreement...	12	8, 16
Fixed-sum credit	10	9, 10, 17, 23
Hire-purchase agreement ...	189(1)	10
Individual	189(1)	19, 24
Linked transaction	19	11
Modifying agreement	82(2)	24
Multiple agreement	18	16, 18
Negotiator	56(1)	1, 2, 3, 4
Pre-existing arrangements	187	8, 21
Restricted-use credit	11	10, 12, 13, 14, 16
Running-account credit ...	10	15, 16, 18, 23
Small agreement	17	16, 17, 22
Supplier	189(1)	3, 14
Total charge for credit	20	5, 10
Total price	189(1)	10
Unrestricted-use credit	11	8, 12, 16, 17, 18

PART II EXAMPLES

Example 1

Facts Correspondence passes between an employee of a money-lending company (writing on behalf of the company) and an individual about the terms on which the company would grant him a loan under a regulated agreement.

Analysis The correspondence constitutes antecedent negotiations falling within section 56(1)(a), the money-lending company being both creditor and negotiator.

Example 2

Facts Representations are made about goods in a poster displayed by a shopkeeper near the goods, the goods being selected by a customer who has read the poster and then sold by the shopkeeper to a finance company introduced by him (with whom he has a business relationship). The goods are disposed of by the finance company to the customer under a regulated hire-purchase agreement.

Analysis The representations in the poster constitute antecedent negotiations falling within section 56(1)(b), the shopkeeper being the credit-broker and negotiator and the finance company being the creditor. The poster is an advertisement and the shopkeeper is the advertiser.

Example 3

Facts Discussions take place between a shopkeeper and a customer about goods the customer wishes to buy using a credit-card issued by the D Bank under a regulated agreement.

Analysis The discussions constitute antecedent negotiations falling within section 56(1)(c), the shopkeeper being the supplier and negotiator and the D Bank the creditor. The credit-card is a credit-token as defined in section 14(1), and the regulated agreement under which it was issued is a credit-token agreement as defined in section 14(2).

Example 4

Facts Discussions take place and correspondence passes between a secondhand car dealer and a customer about a car, which is then sold by the dealer to the customer under a regulated conditional sale agreement. Subsequently, on a revocation of that agreement by consent, the car is resold by the dealer to a finance company introduced by him (with whom he has a business relationship), who in turn dispose of it to the same customer under a regulated hire-purchase agreement.

Analysis The discussions and correspondence constitute antecedent negotiations in relation both to the conditional sale agreement and the hire-purchase agreement. They fall under section 56(1)(a) in relation to the conditional sale agreement, the dealer being the creditor and the negotiator. In relation to the hire-purchase agreement they fall within section 56(1)(b), the dealer continuing to be treated as the negotiator but the finance company now being the creditor. Both agreements are cancellable if the discussions took place when the individual conducting the negotiations (whether the 'negotiator' or his employee or agent) was in the presence of the debtor, unless the unexecuted agreement was signed by the debtor at trade premises (as defined in section 67(b)). If the discussions all took place by telephone however, or the unexecuted agreement was signed by the debtor on trade premises (as so defined) the agreements are not cancellable.

Example 5

Facts E agrees to sell to F (an individual) an item of furniture in return for 24 monthly instalments of £10 payable in arrear. The property in the goods passes to F immediately.

Analysis This is a credit-sale agreement (see definition of 'credit-sale agreement' in section 189(1)). The credit provided amounts to £240 less the amount which, [constitutes the total charge for credit (within the meaning given by section 20)]. (This amount is required to be deducted by section 9(4).) Accordingly the agreement falls within section 8(2) and is a consumer credit agreement.

Example 6

Facts The G Bank grants H (an individual) an unlimited overdraft, with an increased rate of interest on so much of any debit balance as exceeds £2,000.

Analysis Although the overdraft purports to be unlimited, the stipulation for increased interest above £2,000 brings the agreement within section 10(3)(b)(ii) and it is a consumer credit agreement.

Example 7

Facts J is an individual who owns a small shop which usually carries a stock worth about £1,000. K makes a stocking agreement under which he undertakes to provide on short-term credit the stock needed from time to time by J without any specified limit.

Analysis Although the agreement appears to provide unlimited credit, it is probable, having regard to the stock usually carried by J, that his indebtedness to K will not at any time rise above £5,000. Accordingly the agreement falls within section 10(3)(b)(iii) and is a consumer credit agreement.

Example 8

Facts U, a moneylender, lends £500 to V (an individual) knowing he intends to use it to buy office equipment from W. W introduced V to U, it being his practice to introduce customers needing finance to him. Sometimes U gives W a commission for this and sometimes not. U pays the £500 direct to V.

Analysis Although this appears to fall under section 11(1)(b), it is excluded by section 11(3) and is therefore (by section 11(2)) an unrestricted-use credit agreement. Whether it is a debtor-creditor agreement (by section 13(c)) or a debtor-creditor-supplier agreement (by section 12(c)) depends on whether the previous dealings between U and W amount to 'pre-existing arrangements', that is whether the agreement can be taken to have been entered into 'in accordance with, or in furtherance of' arrangements previously made between U and W, as laid down in section 187(1).

Example 9

Facts A agrees to lend B (an individual) £4,500 in nine monthly instalments of £500.

Analysis This is a cash loan and is a form of credit (see section 9 and definition of 'cash' in section 189(1)). Accordingly it falls within section 10(1)(b) and is fixed-sum credit amounting to £4,500.

Example 10

Facts C (in England) agrees to bail goods to D (an individual) in return for periodical payments. The agreement provides for the property in the goods to pass to D on payment of a total of £7,500 and the exercise by D of an option to purchase. The sum of £7,500 includes a down-payment of £1,000. It also includes an amount which, according to regulations made under section 20(1), constitutes a total charge for credit of £1,500.

Analysis This is a hire-purchase agreement with a deposit of £1,000 and a total price of £7,500 (see definitions of 'hire-purchase agreement', 'deposit' and 'total price' in section 189(1)). By section 9(3), it is taken to provide credit amounting to £7,500−(£1,500+£1,000), which equals £5,000. Under section 8(2), the agreement is therefore a consumer credit agreement, and under sections 9(3) and 11(1) it is a restricted-use credit agreement for fixed-sum credit. A similar result would follow if the agreement by C had been a hiring agreement in Scotland.

Example 11

Facts X (an individual) borrows £500 from Y (Finance). As a condition of the granting of the loan X is required—

      (a) to execute a second mortgage on his house in favour of Y (Finance), and

      (b) to take out a policy of insurance on his life with Y (Insurances).

In accordance with the loan agreement, the policy is charged to Y (Finance) as collateral security for the loan. The two companies are associates within the meaning of section 184(3).

Analysis The second mortgage is a transaction for the provision of security and accordingly does not fall within section 19(1), but the taking out of the insurance policy is a linked transaction falling within section 19(1)(a). The charging of the policy is a separate transaction (made between different parties) for the provision of security and again is excluded from section 19(1). The only linked transaction is therefore the taking out of the insurance policy. If X had not been required by the loan agreement to take out the policy, but it had been done at the suggestion of Y (Finance) to induce them to enter into the loan agreement, it would have been a linked transaction under section 19(1)(c)(i) by virtue of section 19(2)(a).

Example 12

Facts The N Bank agrees to lend 0 (an individual) £2,000 to buy a car from P. To make sure the loan is used as intended, the N Bank stipulates that the money must be paid by it direct to P.

Analysis The agreement is a consumer credit agreement by virtue of section 8(2). Since it falls within section 11(1)(b), it is a restricted-use credit agreement, P being the supplier. If the N Bank had not stipulated for direct payment to the supplier, section 11(3) would have operated and made the agreement into one for unrestricted-use credit.

Example 13

Facts Q, a debt-adjuster, agrees to pay off debts owed by R (an individual) to various money-lenders. For this purpose the agreement provides for the making of a loan by Q to R in return for R's agreeing to repay the loan by instalments with interest. The loan money is not paid over to R but retained by Q and used to pay off the money lenders.

Analysis This is an agreement to refinance existing indebtedness of the debtor's, and if the loan by Q does not exceed £5,000 is a restricted-use credit agreement falling within section 11(1)(c).

Example 14

Facts On payment of £1, S issues to T (an individual) a trading check under which T can spend up to £20 at any shop which has agreed, or in future agrees, to accept S's trading checks.

Analysis The trading check is a credit-token falling within section 14(1)(b). The credit-token agreement is a restricted-use credit agreement within section 11(1)(b), any shop in which the credit-token is used being the 'supplier'. The fact that further shops may be added after the issue of the credit-token is irrelevant in view of section 11(4).

Example 15

Facts A retailer L agrees with M (an individual) to open an account in M's name and, in return for M's promise to pay a specified minimum sum into the account each month and to pay a monthly charge for credit, agrees to allow to be debited to the account, in respect of purchases made by M from L, such sums as will not increase the debit balance at any time beyond the credit limit, defined in the agreement as a given multiple of the specified minimum sum.

Analysis This agreement provides credit falling within the definition of running-account credit in section 10(1)(a). Provided the credit limit is not over £5,000, the agreement falls within section 8(2) and is a consumer credit agreement for running-account credit.

Example 16

Facts Under an unsecured agreement, A (Credit), an associate of the A Bank, issues to B (an individual) a credit-card for use in obtaining cash on credit from A (Credit), to be paid by branches of the A Bank (acting as agent of A (Credit)), or goods or cash from suppliers or banks who have agreed to honour credit-cards issued by A (Credit). The credit limit is £30.

Analysis This is a credit-token agreement falling within section 14(1)(a) and (b). It is a regulated consumer credit agreement for running-account credit. Since the credit limit does not exceed £30, the agreement is a small agreement. So far as the agreement relates to goods it is a debtor-creditor-supplier agreement within section 12(b), since it provides restricted-use credit under section 11(1)(b). So far as it relates to cash it is a debtor-creditor agreement within section 13(c) and the credit it provides is unrestricted-use credit. This is therefore a multiple agreement. In that the whole agreement falls within several of the categories of agreement mentioned in this Act, it is, by section 18(3), to be treated as an agreement in each of those categories. So far as it is a debtor-creditor-supplier agreement providing restricted-use credit it is, by section 18(2), to be treated as a separate agreement; and similarly so far as it is a debtor-creditor agreement providing unrestricted-use credit. (See also Example 22.)

Example 17

Facts The manager of the C Bank agrees orally with D (an individual) to open a current account in D's name. Nothing is said about overdraft facilities. After maintaining the account in credit for some weeks, D draws a cheque in favour of E for an amount exceeding D's credit balance by £20. E presents the cheque and the Bank pay it.

Analysis In drawing the cheque D, by implication, requests the Bank to grant him an overdraft of £20 on its usual terms as to interest and other charges. In deciding to honour the cheque, the Bank by implication accept the offer. This constitutes a regulated small consumer credit agreement for unrestricted-use, fixed sum credit. It is a debtor-creditor agreement, and falls within section 74(1)(b) if covered by a determination under section 74(3). (Compare Example 18.)

Example 18

Facts F (an individual) has had a current account with the G Bank for many years. Although usually in credit, the account has been allowed by the Bank to become overdrawn from time to time. The maximum such overdraft has been is about £1,000. No explicit agreement has ever been made about overdraft facilities. Now, with a credit balance of £500, F draws a cheque for £1,300.

Analysis It might well be held that the agreement with F (express or implied) under which the Bank operate his account includes an implied term giving him the right to overdraft facilities up to say £1,000. If so, the agreement is a regulated consumer credit agreement for unrestricted-use, running-account credit. It is a debtor-creditor agreement, and falls within section 74(1)(b) if covered by a direction under section 74(3). It is also a multiple agreement, part of which (i.e. the part not dealing with the overdraft), as referred to in section 18(1)(a), falls within a category of agreement not mentioned in this Act. (Compare Example 17.)

Example 19

Facts H (a finance house) agrees with J (a partnership of individuals) to open an unsecured loan account in J's name on which the debit balance is not to exceed £7,500 (having regard to payments into the account made from time to time by J). Interest is to be payable in advance on this sum, with provision for yearly adjustments. H is entitled to debit the account with interest, a 'setting-up' charge, and other charges. Before J has an opportunity to draw on the account it is initially debited with £2,250 for advance interest and other charges.

Analysis This is a personal running-account credit agreement (see sections 8(1) and 10(1)(a), and definition of 'individual' in section 189(1)). By section 10(2) the credit limit is £7,000. By section 9(4) however the initial debit of £2,250, and any other charges later debited to the account by H, are not to be treated as credit even though time is allowed for their payment. Effect is given to this by section 10(3). Although the credit limit of £7,000 exceeds the amount (£5,000) specified in section 8(2) as the maximum for a consumer credit agreement, so that the agreement is not within section

10(3)(a), it is caught by section 10(3)(b)(i). At the beginning J can effectively draw (as credit) no more than £4,750, so the agreement is a consumer credit agreement.

Example 20

Facts K (in England) agrees with L (an individual) to bail goods to L for a period of three years certain at £2,200 a year, payable quarterly. The agreement contains no provision for the passing of the property in the goods to L.

Analysis This is not a hire-purchase agreement (see paragraph (b) of the definition of that term in section 189(1)), and is capable of subsisting for more than three months. Paragraphs (a) and (b) of section 15(1) are therefore satisfied, but paragraph (c) is not. The payments by L must exceed £5,000 if he conforms to the agreement. It is true that under section 101 L has a right to terminate the agreement on giving K three months' notice expiring not earlier than eighteen months after the making of the agreement, but that section applies only where the agreement is a regulated consumer hire agreement apart from the section (see subsection (1)). So the agreement is not a consumer hire agreement, though it would be if the hire charge were say £1,500 a year, or there were a 'break' clause in it operable by either party before the hire charges exceeded £5,000. A similar result would follow if the agreement by K had been a hiring agreement in Scotland.

Example 21

Facts The P Bank decides to issue cheque cards to its customers under a scheme whereby the bank undertakes to honour cheques of up to £30 in every case where the payee has taken the cheque in reliance on the cheque card, whether the customer has funds in his account or not. The P Bank writes to the major retailers advising them of this scheme and also publicises it by advertising. The Bank issues a cheque card to Q (an individual), who uses it to pay by cheque for goods costing £20 bought by Q from R, a major retailer. At the time, Q has £500 in his account at the P Bank.

Analysis The agreement under which the cheque card is issued to Q is a consumer credit agreement even though at all relevant times Q has more than £30 in his account. This is because Q is free to draw out his whole balance and then use the cheque card, in which case the Bank has bound itself to honour the cheque. In other words the cheque card agreement provides Q with credit, whether he avails himself of it or not. Since the amount of the credit is not subject to any express limit, the cheque card can be used any number of times. It may be presumed however that section 10(3)(b)(iii) will apply. The agreement is an unrestricted-use debtor-creditor agreement (by section 13(c)). Although the P Bank wrote to R informing R of the P Bank's willingness to honour any cheque taken by R in reliance on a cheque card, this does not constitute pre-existing arrangements as mentioned in section 13(c) because section 187(3) operates to prevent it. The agreement is not a credit-token agreement within section 14(1)(b) because payment by the P Bank to R, would be a payment of the cheque and not a payment for the goods.

Example 22

Facts The facts are as in Example 16. On one occasion B uses the credit-card in a way which increases his debit balance with A (Credit) to £40. A (Credit) writes to B agreeing to allow the excess on that occasion only, but stating that it must be paid off within one month.

Analysis In exceeding his credit limit B, by implication, requests A (Credit) to allow him a temporary excess (compare Example 17). A (Credit) is thus faced by B's action with the choice of treating it as a breach of contract or granting his implied request. He does the latter. If he had done the former, B would be treated as taking credit to which he was not entitled (see section 14(3)) and, subject to the terms of his contract with A (Credit), would be liable to damages for breach of contract. As it is, the agreement to allow the excess varies the original credit-token agreement by adding a new term. Under section 10(2), the new term is to be disregarded in arriving at the credit limit, so that the credit-token agreement at no time ceases to be a small agreement. By section 82(2) the later agreement is deemed to revoke the original agreement and contain provisions reproducing the combined effect of the two agreements. By section 82(4), this later agreement is exempted from Part V (except section 56).

Example 23

Facts Under an oral agreement made on 10th January, X (an individual) has an overdraft on his current account at the Y bank with a credit limit of £100. On 15th February, when his overdraft stands at £90, X draws a cheque for £25. It is the first time that X has exceeded his credit limit, and on 16th February the bank honours the cheque.

Analysis The agreement of 10th January is a consumer credit agreement for running-account credit. The agreement of 15th–16th February varies the earlier agreement by adding a term allowing the credit limit to be exceeded merely temporarily. By section 82(2) the later agreement is deemed to revoke the earlier agreement and reproduce the combined effect of the two agreements. By section 82(4), Part V of this Act (except section 56) does not apply to the later agreement. By section 18(5), a term allowing a merely temporary excess over the credit limit is not to be treated as a separate agreement, or as providing fixed-sum credit. The whole of the £115 owed to the bank by X on 16th February is therefore running-account credit.

Example 24

Facts On 1st March 1975 Z (in England) enters into an agreement with A (an unincorporated body of persons) to bail to A equipment consisting of two components (component P and component Q). The agreement is not a hire-purchase agreement and is for a fixed term of 3 years, so paragraphs (a) and (b) of section 15(1) are both satisfied. The rental is payable monthly at a rate of £2,400 a year, but the agreement provides that this is to be reduced to £1,200 a year for the remainder of the agreement if at any time during its currency A returns component Q to the owner Z. On 5th May 1976 A is incorporated as A Ltd., taking over A's assets and liabilities. On 1st March 1977, A Ltd. returns component Q. On 1st January 1978, Z and A Ltd. agree to extend the earlier agreement by one year, increasing the rental for the final year by £250 to £1,450.

Analysis When entered into on 1st March 1975, the agreement is a consumer hire agreement. A falls within the definition of 'individual' in section 189(1) and if A returns component Q before 1st May 1976 the total rental will not exceed £5,000 (see section 15(1)(c)). When this date is passed without component Q having been returned it is obvious that the total rental must now exceed £5,000. Does this mean that the agreement then ceases to be a consumer hire agreement? The answer is no, because there has been no change in the terms of the agreement, and without such a change the agreement cannot move from one category to the other. Similarly, the fact that A's rights and duties under the agreement pass to a body corporate on 5th May 1976 does not cause the agreement to cease to be a consumer hire agreement (see definition of 'hirer' in section 189(1)).

The effect of the modifying agreement of 1st January 1978 is governed by section 82(2), which requires it to be treated as containing provisions reproducing the combined effect of the two actual agreements, that is to say as providing that—

    (a) obligations outstanding on 1st January 1978 are to be treated as outstanding under the modifying agreement;

    (b) the modifying agreement applies at the old rate of hire for the months of January and February 1978, and

    (c) for the year beginning 1st March 1978 A Ltd. will be the bailee of component P at a rental of £1,450.

The total rental under the modifying agreement is £1,850. Accordingly the modifying agreement is a regulated agreement. Even if the total rental under the modifying agreement exceeded £5,000 it would still be regulated because of the provisions of section 82(3).

[SCHEDULE 2A

MEANING OF 'DEBTOR' IN RELATION TO GREEN DEAL AGREEMENTS

Section of this Act	References to 'debtor' are to be read as references to the...
Section 19	- improver
Section 55	- improver
Section 55C	- improver - first bill payer
Section 56	- improver - first bill payer
Section 57	- improver
Section 59	- improver
Sections 60 and 61	- improver (including an improver who is not an individual)
Section 61A	- improver
Sections 62, 63, 64	- improver
Section 65	- improver - current bill payer - previous bill payer
Section 66A	- improver
Sections 67, 68, 69, 70, 71, 72, 73	- improver
Section 75A	- improver
Sections 76 and 77	- current bill payer - previous bill payer
Section 77A	- current bill payer
Section 77B	- improver - current bill payer
Section 78A	- improver - current bill payer
Section 80	- improver
Section 82	- improver - current bill payer - previous bill payer
Section 86	- current bill payer - previous bill payer
Section 86E	- current bill payer - previous bill payer
Section 86F	- current bill payer - previous bill payer

Section of this Act	*References to 'debtor' are to be read as references to the...*
Section 87	- current bill payer
	- previous bill payer
Section 89	- current bill payer
	- previous bill payer
Section 93	- current bill payer
	- previous bill payer
Sections 94, 95, 95A, 95B, 96, 97, 97A	- improver
	- current bill payer
Section 98	- current bill payer
	- previous bill payer
Sections 102, 103, 105, 107, 110, 113	- improver
Sections 123, 124	- current bill payer
	- previous bill payer
Section 127	- improver
	- current bill payer
	- previous bill payer
Sections 128, 129, 130, 130A	- current bill payer
	- previous bill payer
Sections 140A, 140B, 140C	- improver
	- current bill payer
	- previous bill payer
Section 141(1), (2), (3A), (3B)	- improver
	- current bill payer
	- previous bill payer
Section 157	- improver
	- first bill payer
Section 173	- improver
	- current bill payer
	- previous bill payer
Section 179	- improver
	- first bill payer
	- current bill payer
	- previous bill payer
Section 185(1), (2), (2A), (2B), (2C), (2D), (4)	- current bill payer
Section 187A	- current bill payer
	- previous bill payer
Section 189(1), so far as relating to definition of 'security'	- improver]

Torts (Interference with Goods) Act 1977

(1977, c. 32)

1 Definition of 'wrongful interference with goods'

In this Act 'wrongful interference', or 'wrongful interference with goods', means—

  (a) conversion of goods (also called trover),

  (b) trespass to goods,

  (c) negligence so far as it results in damage to goods or to an interest in goods,

  (d) subject to section 2, any other tort so far as it results in damage to goods or to an interest in goods

[and references in this Act (however worded) to proceedings for wrongful interference or to a claim or right to claim for wrongful interference shall include references to proceedings by virtue of Part I of the Consumer Protection Act 1987 (product liability) in respect of any damage to goods and to the interest in goods or, as the case may be, to a claim or right to claim by virtue of that Part in respect of any such damage].

2 Abolition of detinue

  (1) Detinue is abolished.

  (2) An action lies in conversion for loss or destruction of goods which a bailee has allowed to happen in breach of his duty to his bailor (that is to say it lies in a case which is not otherwise conversion, but would have been detinue before detinue was abolished).

3 Forms of judgment where goods are detained

  (1) In proceedings for wrongful interference against a person who is in possession or in control of the goods relief may be given in accordance with this section, so far as appropriate.

  (2) The relief is—

  (a) an order for delivery of goods, and for payment of any consequential damages, or

  (b) an order for delivery of the goods, but giving the defendant the alternative of paying damages by reference to the value of the goods, together in either alternative with payment of any consequential damages, or

  (c) damages.

  (3) Subject to rules of court—

  (a) relief shall be given under only one of paragraphs (a), (b) and (c) of subsection (2),

  (b) relief under paragraph (a) of subsection (2) is at the discretion of the court, and the claimant may choose between the others.

  (4) If it is shown to the satisfaction of the court that an order under subsection (2)(a) had not been complied with, the court may—

  (a) revoke the order, or the relevant part of it, and

  (b) make an order for payment of damages by reference to the value of the goods.

  (5) Where an order is made under subsection (2)(b) the defendant may satisfy the order by returning the goods at any time before execution of judgment, but without prejudice to liability to pay any consequential damages.

  (6) An order for delivery of the goods under subsection (2)(a) or (b) may impose such conditions as may be determined by the court, or pursuant to rules of court, and in particular, where damages by reference to the value of the goods would not be the whole of the value of the goods, may require an allowance to be made by the claimant to reflect the difference.

  For example, a bailor's action against the bailee may be one in which the measure of damages is not the full value of the goods, and then the court may order delivery of the goods, but require the bailor to pay the bailee a sum reflecting the difference.

  (7) Where under subsection (1) or subsection (2) of section 6 an allowance is to be made in respect of an improvement of the goods, and an order is made under subsection (2)(a) or (b), the

court may assess the allowance to be made in respect of the improvement, and by the order require, as a condition for delivery of the goods, that allowance to be made by the claimant.

(8) This section is without prejudice—

(a) to the remedies afforded by section 133 of the Consumer Credit Act, or

...

(c) to any jurisdiction to afford ancillary or incidental relief.

4 Interlocutory relief where goods are detained

(1) In this section 'proceedings' means proceedings for wrongful interference.

(2) On the application of any person in accordance with rules of court, the High Court shall, in such circumstances as may be specified in the rules, have power to make an order providing for the delivery up of any goods which are or may become subject matter of subsequent proceedings in the court, or as to which any question may arise in proceedings.

(3) Delivery shall be, as the order may provide, to the claimant or to a person appointed by the court for the purpose, and shall be on such terms and conditions as may be specified in the order.

5 Extinction of title on satisfaction of claim for damages

(1) Where damages for wrongful interference are, or would fall to be, assessed on the footing that the claimant is being compensated—

(a) for the whole of his interest in the goods, or

(b) for the whole of his interest in the goods subject to a reduction for contributory negligence,

payment of the assessed damages (under all heads), or as the case may be settlement of a claim for damages for the wrong (under all heads), extinguishes the claimant's title to that interest.

(2) In subsection (1) the reference to the settlement of the claim includes—

(a) where the claim is made in court proceedings, and the defendant has paid a sum into court to meet the whole claim, the taking of that sum by the claimant, and

(b) where the claim is made in court proceedings, and the proceedings are settled or compromised, the payment of what is due in accordance with the settlement or compromise, and

(c) where the claim is made out of court and is settled or compromised, the payment of what is due in accordance with the settlement or compromise.

(3) It is hereby declared that subsection (1) does not apply where damages are assessed on the footing that the claimant is being compensated for the whole of his interest in the goods, but the damages paid are limited to some lesser amount by virtue of any enactment or rule of law.

(4) Where under section 7(3) the claimant accounts over to another person (the 'third party') so as to compensate (under all heads) the third party for the whole of his interest in the goods, the third party's title to that interest is extinguished.

(5) This section has effect subject to any agreement varying the respective rights of the parties to the agreement, and where the claim is made in court proceedings has effect subject to any court.

6 Allowance for improvement of the goods

(1) If in proceedings for wrongful interference against a person (the 'improver') who has improved the goods, it is shown that the improver acted in the mistaken but honest belief that he had a good title to them, an allowance shall be made for the extent to which, at the time as at which the goods fall to be valued in assessing damages, the value of the goods is attributable to the improvement.

(2) If, in proceedings for wrongful interference against a person ('the purchaser') who has purported to purchase the goods—

(a) from the improver, or

    (b) where after such a purported sale the goods passed by a further purported sale on one or more occasions, on any such occasion,

it is shown that the purchaser acted in good faith, an allowance shall be made on the principle set out in subsection (1).

    For example, where a person in good faith buys a stolen car from the improver and is sued in conversion by the true owner the damages may be reduced to reflect the improvement, but if the person who bought the stolen car from the improver sues the improver for failure of consideration, and the improver acted in good faith, subsection (3) below will ordinarily make a comparable reduction in the damages he recovers from the improver.

    (3) If in a case within subsection (2) the person purporting to sell the goods acted in good faith, then in proceedings by the purchaser for recovery of the purchase price because of failure of consideration, or in any other proceedings founded on that failure of consideration, an allowance shall, where appropriate, be made on the principle set out in subsection (1).

    (4) This section applies, with the necessary modifications, to a purported bailment or other disposition of goods as it applies to a purported sale of goods.

7 Double liability

    (1) In this section 'double liability' means the double liability of the wrongdoer which can arise—

        (a) where one of two or more rights of action for wrongful interference is founded on a possessory title, or

        (b) where the measure of damages in an action for wrongful interference founded on a proprietary title is or includes the entire value of the goods, although the interest is one of two or more interests in the goods.

    (2) In proceedings to which any two or more claimants are parties, the relief shall be such as to avoid double liability of the wrongdoer as between those claimants.

    (3) On satisfaction, in whole or in part, of any claim for an amount exceeding that recoverable if subsection (2) applied, the claimant is liable to account over to the other person having a right to claim to such extent as will avoid double liability.

    (4) Where, as the result of enforcement of a double liability, any claimant is unjustly enriched to an extent, he shall be liable to reimburse the wrongdoer to that extent.

    For example, if a converter of goods pays damages first to a finder of the goods, and then to the true owner, the finder is unjustly enriched unless he accounts over to the true owner under subsection (3); and then the true owner is unjustly enriched and becomes liable to reimburse the converter of the goods.

8 Competing rights to the goods

    (1) The defendant in an action for wrongful interference shall be entitled to show, in accordance with rules of court, that a third party has a better right than the plaintiff as respects all or any part of the interest claimed by the plaintiff, or in right of which he sues, and any rule of law (sometimes called jus tertii) to the contrary is abolished.

    (2) Rules of court relating to proceedings for wrongful interference may—

        (a) require the plaintiff to give particulars of his title,

        (b) require the plaintiff to identify any person who, to his knowledge, has or claims any interest in the goods,

        (c) authorise the defendant to apply for directions as to whether any person should be joined with a view to establishing whether he has a better right than the plaintiff, or has a claim of a result of which the defendant might be doubly liable,

        (d) where a party fails to appear on an application within paragraph (c), or to comply with any direction given by the court on such an application, authorise the court to deprive him of any right of action against the defendant for the wrong either unconditionally, or subject to such terms or conditions as may be specified.

    (3) Subsection (2) is without prejudice to any power of making rules of court.

9 Concurrent actions

...

10 Co-owners

(1) Co-ownership is no defence to an action founded on conversion or trespass to goods where the defendant without the authority of the other co-owner—

(a) destroys the goods, or disposes of the goods in a way giving a good title to the entire property in the goods, or otherwise does anything equivalent to the destruction of the other's interest in the goods, or

(b) purports to dispose of the goods in a way which would give a good title to the entire property in the goods if he was acting with the authority of all co-owners of the goods.

(2) Subsection (1) shall not affect the law concerning execution or enforcement of judgments, or concerning any form of distress.

(3) Subsection (1)(a) is by the way of restatement of existing law so far as it relates to conversion.

11 Minor amendments

(1) Contributory negligence is no defence in proceedings founded on conversion, or on intentional trespass to goods.

(2) Receipt of goods by way of pledge is conversion if the delivery of the goods is conversion.

(3) Denial of title is not of itself conversion.

12 Bailee's power of sale

(1) This section applies to goods in the possession or under the control of a bailee where—

(a) the bailor is in breach of an obligation to take delivery of the goods or, if the terms of the bailment so provide, to give directions as to their delivery, or

(b) the bailee could impose such an obligation by giving notice to the bailor, but is unable to trace or communicate with the bailor, or

(c) the bailee can reasonably expect to be relieved of any duty to safeguard the goods on giving notice to the bailor, but is unable to trace or communicate with the bailor.

(2) In the cases of Part I of Schedule 1 to this Act a bailee may, for the purposes of subsection (1), impose an obligation on the bailor to take delivery of the goods, or as the case may be to give directions as to their delivery, and in those cases the said Part I sets out the method of notification.

(3) If the bailee—

(a) has in accordance with Part II of Schedule 1 to this Act given notice to the bailor of his intention to sell the goods under this subsection, or

(b) has failed to trace or communicate with the bailor with a view to giving him such a notice, after having taken reasonable steps for the purpose, and is reasonably satisfied that the bailor owns the goods, he shall be entitled, as against the bailor, to sell the goods.

(4) Where subsection (3) applies but the bailor did not in fact own the goods, a sale under this section, or under section 13, shall not give a good title as against the owner, or as against a person claiming under the owner.

(5) A bailee exercising his powers under subsection (3) shall be liable to account to the bailor for the proceeds of sale, less any cost of sale, and—

(a) the account shall be taken on the footing that the bailee should have adopted the best method of sale reasonably available in the circumstances, and

(b) where subsection (3)(a) applies, any sum payable in respect of the goods by the bailor to the bailee which accrued due before the bailee gave notice of intention to sell the goods shall be deductible from the proceeds of sale.

(6) A sale duly made under this section gives a good title to the purchaser as against the bailor.

(7) In this section, section 13, and Schedule 1 to the Act,

(a) 'bailor' and 'bailee' include their respective successors in title, and

(b) references to what is payable, paid or due to the bailee in respect of the goods include references to what would be payable by the bailor to the bailee as a condition of delivery of the goods at the relevant time.

(8) This section, and Schedule 1 to this Act, have effect subject to the terms of the bailment.

(9) this section shall not apply where the goods were bailed before the commencement of this Act.

13   Sale authorised by the court

(1) If a bailee of the goods to which section 12 applies satisfies the court that he is entitled to see the goods under section 12, or that he would be so entitled if he had given any notice required in accordance with Schedule 1 to this Act, the court—

(a) may authorise the sale of the goods subject to such terms and conditions, if any, as may be specified in the order and,

(b) may authorise the bailee to deduct from the proceeds of sale any costs of sale and any amount due from the bailor to the bailee in respect of the goods, and

(c) may direct the payment into court of the net proceeds of sale, less any amount deducted under paragraph (b), to be held to the credit of the bailor.

(2) A decision of the court authorising a sale under this section shall, subject to any right of appeal, be conclusive, as against the bailor, of the bailee's entitlement to sell the goods, and gives a good title to the purchaser as against the bailor.

(3) [In this section 'the court', in relation to England and Wales, means the High Court or the county court and, in relation to Northern Ireland, means the High Court or a county court, save that a county court in Northern Ireland has jurisdiction in the proceedings only if] the value of the goods does not exceed the county court limit.

14   Interpretation

(1) In this Act, unless the context otherwise requires—

...

'goods' includes all chattels personal other than things in action and money.

...

16   Extent and application to the Crown

(3) This Act shall bind the Crown, but as regards the Crown's liability in tort shall not bind the Crown further than the Crown is made liable in tort by the Crown Proceedings Act 1947.

Section 12   SCHEDULE 1

UNCOLLECTED GOODS

PART I POWER TO IMPOSE OBLIGATION TO
COLLECT GOODS

1.—(1) For the purposes of section 12(1) a bailee may, in the circumstances specified in this Part of this Schedule, by notice given to the bailor impose on him an obligation to take delivery of the goods.

(2) The notice shall be in writing, and may be given either—

(a) by delivering it to the bailor, or

(b) by leaving it at his proper address, or

(c) by post.

(3) The notice shall—

(a) specify the name and address of the bailee, and give sufficient particulars of the goods and the address or place where they are held, and

(b) state that the goods are ready for delivery to the bailor, or where combined with a notice terminating the contract of bailment, will be ready for delivery when the contract is terminated, and

(c) specify the amount, if any, which is payable by the bailor to the bailee in respect of the goods and which became due before the giving of the notice.

(4) Where the notice is sent by post it may be combined with a notice under Part II of this Schedule if the notice is sent by post in a way complying with paragraph 6(4).

(5) References in this Part of this Schedule to taking delivery of the goods include, where the terms of the bailment admit, references to giving directions as to their delivery.

(6) This Part of this Schedule is without prejudice to the provisions of any contract requiring the bailor to take delivery of the goods.

Goods accepted for repair or other treatment

2. If a bailee has accepted goods for repair or other treatment on the terms (expressed or implied) that they will be re-delivered to the bailor when the repair or other treatment has been carried out, the notice may be given at any time after the repair or other treatment has been carried out.

Goods accepted for valuation or appraisal

3. If a bailee has accepted goods in order to value or appraise them, the notice may be given at any time after the bailee has carried out the valuation or appraisal.

Storage, warehousing, etc.

4.—(1) If a bailee is in possession of goods which he has held as custodian, and his obligation as custodian has come to an end, the notice may be given at any time after the ending of the obligation, or may be combined with any notice terminating his obligation as custodian.

(2) This paragraph shall not apply to goods held by a person as mercantile agent, that is to say by a person having in the customary course of his business as a mercantile agent authority either to sell goods or to consign goods for the purpose of sale, or to buy goods, or to raise money on the security of goods.

Supplemental

5. Paragraphs 2, 3 and 4 apply whether or not the bailor has paid any amount due to the bailee in respect of the goods, and whether or not the bailment is for reward, or in the course of business, or gratuitous.

PART II NOTICE OF INTENTION TO SELL GOODS

6.—(1) A notice under section 12(3) shall—
   (a) specify the name and address of the bailee, and give sufficient particulars of the goods and the address or place where they are held, and
   (b) specify the date on or after which the bailee proposes to sell the goods, and
   (c) specify the amount, if any, which is payable by the bailor to the bailee in respect of the goods, and which became due before giving of the notice.

(2) The period between giving of the notice and the date specified in the notice as that on or after which the bailee proposes to exercise the power of sale shall be such as will afford the bailor a reasonable opportunity of taking delivery of the goods.

(3) If any amount is payable in respect of the goods by the bailor to the bailee, and become due before giving of the notice, the said period shall be not less than three months.

(4) The notice shall be in writing and shall be sent by post in a registered letter, or by the recorded delivery service.

7.—(1) The bailee shall not give a notice under section 12(3), or exercise his right to send the goods pursuant to such a notice, at a time when he has notice that, because of a dispute concerning the goods, the bailor is questioning or refusing to pay all or any part of what the bailee claims to be due to him in respect of the goods.

(2) This paragraph shall be left out of account in determining under section 13(1) whether a bailee of goods is entitled to see the goods under section 12, or would be so entitled if he had given any notice required in accordance with this Schedule.

Unfair Contract Terms Act 1977

(1977, c. 50)

PART I AMENDMENT OF LAW FOR ENGLAND AND WALES AND NORTHERN IRELAND

1 Scope of Part I

(1) For the purposes of this Part of this Act, 'negligence' means the breach—

    (a) of any obligation, arising from the express or implied terms of a contract, to take reasonable care or exercise reasonable skill in the performance of the contract;

    (b) of any common law duty to take reasonable care or exercise reasonable skill (but not any stricter duty);

    (c) of the common duty of care imposed by the Occupiers' Liability Act 1957 or the Occupier's Liability Act (Northern Ireland) 1957.

(2) This Part of the Act is subject to Part III; and in relation to contracts, the operation of sections 2[, 3] and 7 is subject to the exceptions made by Schedule I.

(3) In the case of both contract and tort, sections 2 to 7 apply (except where the contrary is stated in section 6(4)) only to business liability, that is liability to breach of obligations or duties arising—

    (a) from things done or to be done by a person in the course of a business (whether his own business or another's); or

    (b) from the occupation of premises used for business purposes of the occupier;

and references to liability are to be read accordingly [but liability of an occupier of premises for breach of an obligation or duty towards a person obtaining access to the premises for recreational or educational purposes, being liability for loss or damage suffered by reason of the dangerous state of the premises, is not a business liability of the occupier unless granting that person such access for the purposes concerned falls within the business purposes of the occupier.]

(4) In relation to any breach of duty or obligation, it is immaterial for any purpose of this Part of this Act whether the breach was inadvertent or intentional, or whether liability for it arises directly or vicariously.

2 Negligence liability

(1) A person cannot by reference to any contract term or to a notice given to persons generally or to particular persons exclude or restrict his liability for death or personal injury resulting from negligence.

(2) In the case of other loss or damage, a person cannot so exclude or restrict his liability for negligence except in so far as the term or notice satisfies the requirement of reasonableness.

(3) Where a contract term or notice purports to exclude or restrict liability for negligence a person's agreement to or awareness of it is not of itself to be taken as indicating his voluntary acceptance of any risk.

[(4) This section does not apply to—

    (a) a term in a consumer contract, or

    (b) a notice to the extent that it is a consumer notice,

(but see the provision made about such contracts and notices in sections 62 and 65 of the Consumer Rights Act 2015).]

3 Liability arising in contract

(1) This section applies as between contracting parties where one of them deals [...] on the other's written standard terms of business.

(2) As against that party, the other cannot by reference to any contract term—

(a) when himself in breach of contract, exclude or restrict any liability of his in respect of the breach; or

(b) claim to be entitled—

(i)   to render a contractual performance substantially different from that which was reasonably expected of him, or

(ii)   in respect of the whole of any part of his contractual obligation, to render no performance at all,

except in so far as (in any of the cases mentioned above in this subsection) the contract term satisfies the requirement of reasonableness.

[(3) This section does not apply to a term in a consumer contract (but see the provision made about such contracts in section 62 of the Consumer Rights Act 2015).]

6   Sale and hire-purchase

(1) Liability for breach of the obligations arising from—

(a) [section 12 of the Sale of Goods Act 1979] (seller's implied undertakings as to title, etc.);

(b) section 8 of the Supply of Goods (Implied Terms) Act 1973 (the corresponding thing in relation to hire-purchase),

cannot be excluded or restricted by reference to any contract term.

[(1A) Liability for breach of the obligations arising from—

(a) section 13, 14 or 15 of the 1979 Act (seller's implied undertakings as to conformity of goods with description or sample, or as to their quality or fitness for a particular purpose);

(b) section 9, 10 or 11 of the 1973 Act (the corresponding things in relation to hire purchase),

cannot be excluded or restricted by reference to a contract term except in so far as the term satisfies the requirement of reasonableness.]

(4) The liabilities referred to in this section are not only the business liabilities defined by section 1(3), but include those arising under any contract of sale of goods or hire-purchase agreement.

[(5) This section does not apply to a consumer contract (but see the provision made about such contracts in section 31 of the Consumer Rights Act 2015).]

7   Miscellaneous contracts under which goods pass

(1) Where the possession or ownership of goods passes under or in pursuance of a contract not governed by the law of sale of goods or hire-purchase, subsections (2) to (4) below apply as regards the effect (if any) to be given to contract terms excluding or restricting liability for breach of obligation arising by implication of law from the nature of the contract.

[(1A) Liability in respect of the goods' correspondence with description or sample, or their quality or fitness for any particular purpose, cannot be excluded or restricted by reference to such a term except in so far as the term satisfies the requirement of reasonableness.]

[(3A) Liability for breach of the obligations arising under section 2 of the Supply of Goods and Services Act 1982 (implied terms about title etc. in certain contracts for the transfer of the property in goods) cannot be excluded or restricted by reference to any such term.]

(4) Liability in respect of—

(a) the right to transfer ownership of the goods, or give possession; or

(b) the assurance of quiet possession to a person taking goods in pursuance of the contract,

cannot [(in a case to which subsection (3A) above does not apply)] be excluded or restricted by reference to any such term except in so far as the term satisfies the requirement of reasonableness.

[(4A) This section does not apply to a consumer contract (but see the provision made about such contracts in section 31 of the Consumer Rights Act 2015).]

10   Evasion by means of secondary contract

A person is not bound by any contract term prejudicing or taking away rights of his which arise under, or in connection with the performance of, another contract, so far as those rights extend to the enforcement of another's liability which this Part of this Act prevents that other from excluding or restricting.

11   The 'reasonableness' test

(1) In relation to a contract term, the requirement of reasonableness for the purposes of this Part of this Act, section 3 of the Misrepresentation Act 1967 and section 3 of the Misrepresentation Act (Northern Ireland) 1967 is that the term shall have been a fair and reasonable one to be included having regard to the circumstances which were, or ought reasonably to have been, known to or in the contemplation of the parties when the contract was made.

(2) In determining for the purposes of section 6 or 7 above whether a contract term satisfies the requirement of reasonableness, regard shall be had in particular to the matters specified in Schedule 2 to this Act; but this subsection does not prevent the court or arbitrator from holding, in accordance with any rule of law, that a term which purports to exclude or restrict any relevant liability is not a term of the contract.

(3) In relation to a notice (not being a notice having contractual effect), the requirement of reasonableness under this Act is that it should be fair and reasonable to allow reliance on it, having regard to all the circumstances obtaining when the liability arose or (but for the notice) would have arisen.

(4) Where by reference to a contract term or notice a person seeks to restrict liability to a specified sum of money, and the question arises (under this or any other Act) whether the term or notice satisfies the requirement of reasonableness, regard shall be had in particular (but without prejudice to subsection (2) above in the case of contract terms) to—

(a) the resources which he could expect to be available to him for the purpose of meeting the liability should it arise; and

(b) how far it was open to him to cover himself by insurance.

(5) It is for those claiming that a contract term or notice satisfies the requirement of reasonableness to show that it does.

13   Varieties of exemption clause

(1) To the extent that this Part of this Act prevents the exclusion or restriction of any liability it also prevents—

(a) making the liability or its enforcement subject to restrictive or onerous conditions;

(b) excluding or restricting any right or remedy in respect of the liability, or subjecting a person to any prejudice in consequence of his pursuing any such right or remedy;

(c) excluding or restricting rules of evidence or procedure; and (to that extent) sections 2[, 6 and] 7 also prevent excluding or restricting liability by reference to terms and notices which exclude or restrict the relevant obligation or duty.

(2) But an agreement in writing to submit present or future differences to arbitration is not to be treated under this Part of this Act as excluding or restricting any liability.

14   Interpretation of Part I

In this Part of the Act—

'business' includes a profession and the activities of any government department or local or public authority;

['consumer contract' has the same meaning as in the Consumer Rights Act 2015 (see section 61);]

['consumer notice' has the same meaning as in the Consumer Rights Act 2015 (see section 61);]

'goods' has the same meaning as in [the Sales of Goods Act 1979];

'hire-purchase agreement' has the same meaning as in the Consumer Credit Act 1974;

'negligence' has the meaning given by section 1(1);

'notice' includes an announcement, whether or not in writing, and any other communication or pretended communication; and

'personal injury' includes any disease and any impairment of physical or mental condition.

PART III PROVISIONS APPLYING TO WHOLE OF UNITED KINGDOM

26 International supply contracts

(1) The limits imposed by this Act on the extent to which a person may exclude or restrict liability by reference to a contract term do not apply to liability arising under such a contract as is described in subsection (3) below.

(2) The terms of such a contract are not subject to any requirement of reasonableness under section 3 [. . .]: and nothing in Part II of this Act should require the incorporation of the terms of such a contract to be fair and reasonable for them to have effect.

(3) Subject to subsection (4), that description of contract is one whose characteristics are the following—

    (a) either it is a contract of sale of goods or it is one under or in pursuance of which the possession of ownership of goods passes, and

    (b) it is made by parties whose places of business (or, if they have none, habitual residences) are in the territories of different States (the Channel Islands and the Isle of Man being treated for this purpose as different States from the United Kingdom).

(4) A contract falls within subsection (3) above only if either—

    (a) the goods in question are, at the time of the conclusion of the contract, in the course of carriage, or will be carried, from the territory of one State to the territory of another; or

    (b) the acts constituting the offer and acceptance have been done in the territories of different States; or

    (c) the contract provides for the goods to be delivered to the territory of a state other than that within whose territory those acts were done.

27 Choice of law clauses

(1) Where the [law applicable to] a contract is the law of any part of the United Kingdom only by choice of the parties (and apart from that choice would be the law of some country outside the United Kingdom) sections 2 to 7 and 16 to 21 of this Act do not operate as part [of the law applicable to the contract.]

(2) This Act has effect notwithstanding any contract term which applies or purports to apply the law of some country outside the United Kingdom, where [. . .]—

    (a) the term appears to the court, or arbitrator or arbiter to have been imposed wholly or mainly for the purpose of enabling the party imposing it to evade the operation of this Act; [. . .]

29 Saving for other relevant legislation

(1) Nothing in this Act removes or restricts the effect of, or prevents reliance upon, any contractual provision which—

    (a) is authorised or required by the express terms or necessary implication of an enactment; or

    (b) being made with a view to compliance with an international agreement to which the United Kingdom is a party, does not operate more restrictively than is contemplated by the agreement.

(2) A contract term is to be taken—

    (a) for the purposes of Part I of this Act, as satisfying the requirement of reasonableness; and

    (b) for those of Part II, to have been fair and reasonable to incorporate,

if it is incorporated or approved by, or incorporated pursuant to a decision or ruling of, a competent authority acting in the exercise of any statutory jurisdiction or function and is not a term in a contract to which the competent authority is itself a party.

(3) In this section—

'competent authority' means any court, arbitrator or arbiter, government department or public authority;

'enactment' means any legislation (including subordinate legislation) of the United Kingdom or Northern Ireland and any instrument having effect by virtue of such legislation; and

'statutory' means conferred by an enactment.

Section 1(2)   **SCHEDULE 1**

SCOPE OF SECTIONS 2[, 3] AND 7

1. Sections 2 [and 3] of this Act do not extend to—
    (a) any contract of insurance (including a contract to pay an annuity on human life);
    (b) any contract so far as it relates to the creation or transfer of an interest in land, or to the termination of such an interest, whether by extinction, merger, surrender, forfeiture or otherwise;
    (c) any contract so far as it relates to the creation or transfer of a right or interest in any patent, trade mark, copyright [or design right];
    (d) any contract so far as it relates—
        (i)   to the formation or dissolution of a company (which means any body corporate or unincorporated association and includes a partnership), or
        (ii) to its constitution or the rights or obligations of its corporators or members;
    (e) any contract so far as it relates to the creation or transfer of securities or of any right or interest in securities
    [(f) anything that is governed by Article 6 of Regulation (EU) No 181/2011 of the European Parliament and of the Council of 16 February 2011 concerning the rights of passengers in bus and coach transport and amending Regulation (EC) No 2006/2004.]
2. Section 2(1) extends to—
    (a) any contract of marine salvage or towage;
    (b) any charterparty of a ship or hovercraft; and
    (c) any contract for the carriage of goods by ship or hovercraft;
but subject to this sections 2[, 3] and 7 do not extend to any such contract [. . .].
3. Where goods are carried by ship or hovercraft in pursuance of a contract which either—
    (a) specifies that as the means of carriage over part of the journey to be covered, or
    (b) makes no provision as to the means of carriage and does not exclude that means,
then sections 2(2) [and 3] do not [. . .] extend to the contract as it operates for and in relation to the carriage of the goods by that means.
4. Section 2(1) and (2) do not extend to a contract of employment, except in favour of the employee.
5. Section 2(1) does not affect the validity of any discharge and indemnity given by a person, on or in connection with an award to him of compensation for pneumoconiosis attributable to employment in the coal industry, in respect of any further claim arising from his contracting the disease.

Sections 11(2) and 24(2)   **SCHEDULE 2**

'GUIDELINES' FOR APPLICATION OF REASONABLENESS TEST

The matters to which regard is to be had in particular for the purposes of sections [6(1A), 7(1A) and (4),] 20 and 21 are any of the following which appear to be relevant—
    (a) the strength of the bargaining positions of the parties relative to each other, taking into account (among other things) alternative means by which the customer's requirements could have been met;

    (b) whether the customer received an inducement to agree to the term, or in accepting it had an opportunity of entering into a similar contract with other persons, but without having to accept a similar term;

    (c) whether the customer knew or ought reasonably to have known of the existence and extent of the term (having regard, among other things, to any custom of the trade and any previous course of dealing between the parties);

    (d) where the term excludes or restricts any relevant liability if some condition is not complied with, whether it was reasonable at the time of the contract to expect that compliance with that condition would be practicable;

    (e) whether the goods were manufactured, processed or adapted to the special order of the customer.

Sale of Goods Act 1979

(1979, c. 54)

PART I CONTRACTS TO WHICH ACT APPLIES

1 Contracts to which Act applies

(1) This Act applies to contracts of sale of goods made on or after (but not to those made before) 1 January 1894.

(2) In relation to contracts made on certain dates, this Act applies subject to the modification of certain of its sections as mentioned in Schedule 1 below.

(3) Any such modification is indicated in the section concerned by a reference to Schedule 1 below.

(4) Accordingly, where a section does not contain such a reference, this Act applies in relation to the contract concerned without such modification of the section.

[(5) Certain sections or subsections of this Act do not apply to a contract to which Chapter 2 of Part 1 of the Consumer Rights Act 2015 applies.

(6) Where that is the case it is indicated in the section concerned.]

PART II FORMATION OF THE CONTRACT

Contract of sale

2 Contract of sale

(1) A contract of sale of goods is a contract by which the seller transfers or agrees to transfer the property in goods to the buyer for a money consideration, called the price.

(2) There may a contract of sale between one part owner and another.

(3) A contract of sale may be absolute or conditional.

(4) Where under a contract of sale the property in the goods is transferred from the seller to the buyer the contact is called a sale.

(5) Where under a contract of sale the transfer of the property in the goods is to take place at a future time or subject to some condition later to be fulfilled the contract is called an agreement to sell.

(6) An agreement to sell becomes a sale when the time elapses or the conditions are fulfilled subject to which the property in the goods is to be transferred.

3 Capacity to buy and sell

(1) Capacity to buy and sell is regulated by the general law concerning capacity to contract and to transfer and acquire property.

(2) Where necessaries are sold and delivered to a minor or to a person who by reason of [. . .] drunkenness is incompetent to contract, he must pay a reasonable price for them.

(3) In subsection (2) above 'necessaries' means goods suitable to the condition in life of the minor or other person concerned and to his actual requirements at the time of the sale and delivery.

Formalities of contract

4 How contract of sale is made

(1) Subject to this and any other Act, a contract of sale may be made in writing (either with or without seal), or by word of mouth, or partly in writing and partly by word of mouth, or may be implied from the conduct of the parties.

(2) Nothing in this section affects the law relating to corporations.

Subject matter of contract

5 Existing or future goods

(1) The goods which form the subject of a contract of sale may be either existing goods, owned or possessed by the seller, or goods to be manufactured or acquired by him after the making of the contract of sale, in this Act called future goods.

(2) There may be a contract for the sale of goods the acquisition of which by the seller depends on a contingency which may or may not happen.

(3) Where by a contract of sale the seller purports to effect a present sale of future goods, the contract operates as an agreement to sell the goods.

6 Goods which have perished

Where there is a contract for the sale of specific goods, and the goods without the knowledge of the seller have perished at the time when a contract is made, the contract is void.

7 Goods perishing before sale but after agreement to sell

Where there is an agreement to sell specific goods and subsequently the goods, without any fault on the part of the seller or buyer, perish before the risk passes to the buyer, the agreement is avoided.

The price

8 Ascertainment of price

(1) The price in a contract of sale may be fixed by the contract, or may be left to be fixed in a manner agreed by the contract, or may be determined by the course of dealing between the parties.

(2) Where the price is not determined as mentioned in subsection (1) above the buyer must pay a reasonable price.

(3) What is a reasonable price is a question of fact dependent on the circumstances of each particular case.

9 Agreement to sell at valuation

(1) Where there is an agreement to sell goods on the terms that the price is to be fixed by the valuation of a third party, and he cannot or does not make the valuation, the agreement is avoided; but if the goods or any part of them have been delivered to and appropriated by the buyer he must pay a reasonable price for them.

(2) Where the third party is prevented from making the valuation by the fault of the seller or buyer, the party not at fault may maintain an action for damages against the party at fault.

[Implied terms etc.]

10 Stipulations about time

(1) Unless a different intention appears from the terms of the contract, stipulations as to time of payment are not of the essence of a contract of sale.

(2) Whether any other stipulation as to time is or is not of the essence of the contract depends on the terms of the contract.

(3) In a contract of sale 'month' prima facie means calendar month.

11 When condition to be treated as warranty

[(1) This section does not apply to Scotland.]

(2) Where a contract of sale is subject to a condition to be fulfilled by the seller, the buyer may waive the condition, or may elect to treat the breach of the condition as a breach of warranty and not as a ground for treating the contract as repudiated.

(3) Whether a stipulation in a contract of sale is a condition, the breach of which may give rise to a right to treat the contract as repudiated, or a warranty, the breach of which may give rise to a claim for damages but not to a right to reject the goods and treat the contract as repudiated, depends in each case on the construction of the contract; and a stipulation may be a condition, though called a warranty in the contract.

(4) [Subject to section 35A below] Where a contract of sale is not severable and the buyer has accepted the goods or part of them, the breach of a condition to be fulfilled by the seller can only be treated as a breach of warranty, and not as a ground for rejecting the goods and treating the contract as repudiated, unless there is an express or implied term of the contract to that effect.

[(4A) Subsection (4) does not apply to a contract to which Chapter 2 of Part 1 of the Consumer Rights Act 2015 applies (but see the provision made about such contracts in sections 19 to 22 of that Act).]

(6) Nothing in this section affects a condition or warranty whose fulfilment is excused by law by reason of impossibility or otherwise.

12 Implied terms about title, etc.

(1) In a contract of sale, other than one to which subsection (3) below applies, there is an implied [term] on the part of the seller that in the case of a sale he has a right to sell the goods, and in the case of an agreement to sell he will have such a right at the time when the property is to pass.

(2) In a contract of sale, other than one to which subsection (3) below applies, there is also an implied [term] that—

    (a) the goods are free, and will remain free until the time when the property is to pass, from any charge or encumbrance not disclosed or known to the buyer before the contract is made, and

    (b) the buyer will enjoy quiet possession of the goods except so far as it may be disturbed by the owner or other person entitled to the benefit of any charge or encumbrance so disclosed or known.

(3) This subsection applies to a contract of sale in the case of which there appears from the contract or is to be inferred from its circumstances an intention that the seller should transfer only such title as he or a third person may have.

(4) In a contract to which subsection (3) above applies there is an implied [term] that all charges or encumbrances known to the seller and not known to the buyer have been disclosed to the buyer before the contract is made.

(5) In a contract to which subsection (3) above applies there is also an implied [term] that none of the following will disturb the buyer's quiet possession of the goods, namely—

    (a) the seller;

    (b) in a case where the parties to the contract intend that the seller should transfer only such title as a third person may have, that person;

    (c) anyone claiming through or under the seller or that third person otherwise than under a charge or encumbrance disclosed or known to the buyer before the contract is made.

[(5A) As regards England and Wales and Northern Ireland, the term implied by subsection (1) above is a condition and the terms implied by subsections (2), (4) and (5) above are warranties.]

(6) Paragraph 3 of Schedule 1 below applies in relation to a contract made before 18 May 1973.

[(7) This section does not apply to a contract to which Chapter 2 of Part 1 of the Consumer Rights Act 2015 applies (but see the provision made about such contracts in section 17 of that Act).]

13   Sale by description

(1) Where there is a contract for the sale of goods by description, there is an implied [term] that the goods will correspond with the description.

[(1A) As regards England and Wales and Northern Ireland, the term implied by subsection (1) above is a condition.]

(2) If the sale is by sample as well as by description it is not sufficient that the bulk of the goods corresponds with the sample if the goods do not also correspond with the description.

(3) A sale of goods is not prevented from being a sale by description by reason only that, being exposed for sale or hire, they are selected by the buyer.

(4) Paragraph 4 of Schedule 1 below applies in relation to a contract made before 18 May 1973.

[(5) This section does not apply to a contract to which Chapter 2 of Part 1 of the Consumer Rights Act 2015 applies (but see the provision made about such contracts in section 11 of that Act).]

14   Implied terms about quality or fitness

(1) Except as provided by this section and section 15 below and subject to any other enactment, there is no implied [term] about the quality or fitness for any particular purpose of goods supplied under a contract of sale.

[(2) Where the seller sells goods in the course of a business, there is an implied term that the goods supplied under the contract are of satisfactory quality.

(2A) For the purposes of this Act, goods are of satisfactory quality if they meet the standard that a reasonable person would regard as satisfactory, taking account of any description of the goods, the price (if relevant) and all the other relevant circumstances.

(2B) For the purposes of this Act, the quality of goods includes their state and condition and the following (among others) are in appropriate cases aspects of the quality of goods—

    (a) fitness for all the purposes for which goods of the kind in question are commonly supplied,

    (b) appearance and finish,

    (c) freedom from minor defects,

    (d) safety, and

    (e) durability.

(2C) The term implied by subsection (2) above does not extend to any matter making the quality of goods unsatisfactory—

    (a) which is specifically drawn to the buyer's attention before the contract is made,

    (b) where the buyer examines the goods before the contract is made, which that examination ought to reveal, or

    (c) in the case of a contract for sale by sample, which would have been apparent on a reasonable examination of the sample.]

(3) Where the seller sells goods in the course of a business and the buyer, expressly or by implication, makes known—

    (a) to the seller, or

    (b) where the purchase price of part of it is payable by instalments and the goods were previously sold by a credit-broker to the seller, to that credit-broker,

any particular purpose for which the goods are being bought, there is an implied [term] that the goods supplied under the contract are reasonably fit for that purpose, whether or not that is a purpose for which such goods are commonly supplied, except where the circumstances show that the buyer does not rely, or that it is unreasonable for him to rely, on the skill or judgment of the seller or credit-broker.

(4) An implied [term] about quality or fitness for a particular purpose may be annexed to a contract of sale by usage.

(5) The preceding provisions of this section apply to a sale by a person who in the course of a business is acting as agent for another as they apply to a sale by a principal in the course of a business, except where that other is not selling in the course of a business and either the buyer knows that fact or reasonable steps are taken to bring it to the notice of the buyer before the contract is made.

[(6) As regards England and Wales and Northern Ireland, the terms implied by subsections (2) and (3) above are conditions.]

(7) Paragraph 5 of Schedule 1 below applies in relation to a contract made on or after 18 May 1973 and before the appointed day, and paragraph 6 in relation to one made before 18 May 1973.

(8) In subsection (7) above and paragraph 5 of Schedule 1 below references to the appointed day are to the day appointed for the purposes of those provisions by an order of the Secretary of State made by statutory instrument.

[(9) This section does not apply to a contract to which Chapter 2 of Part 1 of the Consumer Rights Act 2015 applies (but see the provision made about such contracts in sections 9, 10 and 18 of that Act).]

Sale by sample

15   Sale by sample

(1) A contract of sale is a contract for sale by sample where there is an express or implied term to that effect in the contract.

(2) In the case of a contract for sale by sample there is an implied [term]—

   (a) that the bulk will correspond with the sample in quality;

   [. . .]

   (c) that the goods will be free from any defect, [making their quality unsatisfactory], which would not be apparent on reasonable examination of the sample.

[(3) As regards England and Wales and Northern Ireland, the term implied by subsection (2) above is a condition.]

(4) Paragraph 7 of Schedule 1 below applies in relation to a contract made before 18 May 1973.

[(5) This section does not apply to a contract to which Chapter 2 of Part 1 of the Consumer Rights Act 2015 applies (but see the provision made about such contracts in sections 13 and 18 of that Act).]

Miscellaneous

[15A   Modification of remedies for breach of condition in non-consumer cases

(1) Where in the case of a contract of sale—

   (a) the buyer would, apart from this subsection, have the right to reject goods by reason of a breach on the part of the seller of a term implied by section 13, 14 or 15 above, but

   (b) the breach is so slight that it would be unreasonable for him to reject them, the breach is not to be treated as a breach of condition but may be treated as a breach of warranty.

(2) This section applies unless a contrary intention appears in, or is to be implied from, the contract.

(3) It is for the seller to show that a breach fell within subsection (1)(b) above.

(4) This section does not apply to Scotland.]

[15B   Remedies for breach of contract as respects Scotland

(1) Where in a contract of sale the seller is in breach of any term of the contract (express or implied), the buyer shall be entitled—

   (a) to claim damages, and

   (b) if the breach is material, to reject any goods delivered under the contract and treat it as repudiated.

(1A) Subsection (1) does not apply to a contract to which Chapter 2 of Part 1 of the Consumer Rights Act 2015 applies (but see the provision made about such contracts in sections 19 to 22 of that Act).

(3) This section applies to Scotland only.]

PART III EFFECTS OF THE CONTRACT

Transfer of property as between seller and buyer

16 Goods must be ascertained

[Subject to section 20A below] Where there is a contract for the sale of unascertained goods no property in the goods is transferred to the buyer unless and until the goods are ascertained.

17 Property passes when intended to pass

(1) Where there is a contract for the sale of specific or ascertained goods the property in them is transferred to the buyer at such time as the parties to the contract intend it to be transferred.

(2) For the purpose of ascertaining the intention of the parties regard shall be had to the terms of the contract, the conduct of the parties and the circumstances of the case.

18 Rules for ascertaining intention

Unless a different intention appears, the following are rules for ascertaining the intention of the parties as to the time at which the property in the goods is to pass to the buyer.

Rule 1.—Where there is an unconditional contract for the sale of specific goods in a deliverable state the property in the goods passes to the buyer when the contract is made, and it is immaterial whether the time of payment or the time of delivery, or both, be postponed.

Rule 2.—Where there is a contract for the sale of specific goods and the seller is bound to do something to the goods for the purpose of putting them into a deliverable state, the property does not pass until the thing is done and the buyer has notice that it has been done.

Rule 3.—Where there is a contract for the sale of specific goods in a deliverable state but the seller is bound to weigh, measure, test, or do some other act or thing with reference to the goods for the purpose of ascertaining the price, the property does not pass until the act or thing is done and the buyer has notice that it has been done.

Rule 4.—When goods are delivered to the buyer on approval or on sale or return or other similar terms the property in the goods passes to the buyer:—

(a) when he signifies his approval or acceptance to the seller or does any other act adopting the transaction;

(b) if he does not signify his approval or acceptance to the seller but retains the goods without giving notice of rejection, then, if a time has been fixed for the return of the goods, on the expiration of that time, and, if no time has been fixed, on the expiration of a reasonable time.

Rule 5.—(1) Where there is a contract for the sale of unascertained or future goods by description, and goods of that description and in a deliverable state are unconditionally appropriated to the contract, either by the seller with the assent of the buyer or by the buyer with the assent of the seller, the property in the goods then passes to the buyer; and the assent may be express or implied, and may be given either before or after the appropriation is made.

(2) Where, in pursuance of the contract, the seller delivers the goods to the buyer or to a carrier or other bailee or custodier (whether named by the buyer or not) for the purpose of transmission to the buyer, and does not reserve the right of disposal, he is to be taken to have unconditionally appropriated the goods to the contract.

[(3) Where there is a contract for the sale of a specified quantity of unascertained goods in a deliverable state forming part of a bulk which is identified either in the contract or by subsequent agreement between the parties and the bulk is reduced to (or to less than) that quantity, then, if the buyer under that contract is the only buyer to whom goods are then due out of the bulk—

(a) the remaining goods are to be taken as appropriated to that contract at the time when the bulk is so reduced; and

(b) the property in those goods then passes to that buyer.

(4) Paragraph (3) above applies also (with the necessary modifications) where a bulk is reduced to (or to less than) the aggregate of the quantities due to a single buyer under separate contracts relating to that bulk and he is the only buyer to whom goods are then due out of that bulk.]

19 Reservation of right of disposal

(1) Where there is a contract for the sale of specific goods or where goods are subsequently appropriated to the contract, the seller may, by the terms of the contract or appropriation, reserve the right of disposal of the goods until certain conditions are fulfilled; and in such a case, notwithstanding the delivery of the goods to the buyer, or to a carrier or other bailee or custodier for the purpose of transmission to the buyer, the property in the goods does not pass to the buyer until the conditions imposed by the seller are fulfilled.

(2) Where goods are shipped, and by the bill of lading the goods are deliverable to the order of the seller or his agent, the seller is prima facie to be taken to reserve the right of disposal.

(3) Where the seller of goods draws on the buyer for the price, and transmits the bill of exchange and bill of lading to the buyer together to secure acceptance or payment of the bill of exchange, the buyer is bound to return the bill of lading if he does not honour the bill of exchange, and if he wrongfully retains the bill of lading the property in the goods does not pass to him.

20 [Passing of risk]

(1) Unless otherwise agreed, the goods remain at the seller's risk until the property in them is transferred to the buyer, but when the property in them is transferred to the buyer the goods are at the buyer's risk whether delivery has been made or not.

(2) But where delivery has been delayed through the fault of either buyer or seller the goods are at the risk of the party at fault as regards any loss which might not have occurred but for such fault.

(3) Nothing in this section affects the duties or liabilities of either seller or buyer as a bailee or custodier of the goods of the other party.

[(4) This section does not apply to a contract to which Chapter 2 of Part 1 of the Consumer Rights Act 2015 applies (but see the provision made about such contracts in section 29 of that Act).]

[20A Undivided shares in goods forming part of a bulk

(1) This section applies to a contract for the sale of a specified quantity of unascertained goods if the following conditions are met—

    (a) the goods or some of them form part of a bulk which is identified either in the contract or by subsequent agreement between the parties; and

    (b) the buyer has paid the price for some or all of the goods which are the subject of the contract and which form part of the bulk.

(2) Where this section applies, then (unless the parties agree otherwise), as soon as the conditions specified in paragraphs (a) and (b) of subsection (1) above are met or at such later time as the parties may agree—

    (a) property in an undivided share in the bulk is transferred to the buyer; and

    (b) the buyer becomes an owner in common of the bulk.

(3) Subject to subsection (4) below, for the purposes of this section, the undivided share of a buyer in a bulk at any time shall be such share as the quantity of goods paid for and due to the buyer out of the bulk bears to the quantity of goods in the bulk at that time.

(4) Where the aggregate of the undivided shares of buyers in a bulk determined under subsection (3) above would at any time exceed the whole of the bulk at that time, the undivided share in the bulk of each buyer shall be reduced proportionately so that the aggregate of the undivided shares is equal to the whole bulk.

(5) Where a buyer has paid the price for only some of the goods due to him out of a bulk, any delivery to the buyer out of the bulk shall, for the purposes of this section, be ascribed in the first place to the goods in respect of which payment has been made.

(6) For the purpose of this section payment of part of the price for any goods shall be treated as payment for a corresponding part of the goods.]

[20B   Deemed consent by co-owner to dealings in bulk goods

(1) A person who has become an owner in common of a bulk by virtue of section 20A above shall be deemed to have consented to—

(a) any delivery of goods out of the bulk to any other owner in common of the bulk, being goods which are due to him under his contract;

(b) any removal, dealing with, delivery or disposal of goods in the bulk by any other person who is an owner in common of the bulk in so far as the goods fall within that co-owner's undivided share in the bulk at the time of the removal, dealing, delivery or disposal.

(2) No cause of action shall accrue to anyone against a person by reason of that person having acted in accordance with paragraph (a) or (b) of subsection (1) above in reliance on any consent deemed to have been given under that subsection.

(3) Nothing in this section or section 20A above shall—

(a) impose an obligation on a buyer of goods out of a bulk to compensate any other buyer of goods out of that bulk for any shortfall in the goods received by that other buyer;

(b) affects any contractual arrangement between buyers of goods out of a bulk for adjustments between themselves; or

(c) affect the rights of any buyer under his contract.]

Transfer of title

21   Sale by person not the owner

(1) Subject to this Act, where goods are sold by a person who is not their owner, and who does not sell them under the authority or with the consent of the owner, the buyer acquires no better title to the goods than the seller had, unless the owner of the goods is by his conduct precluded from denying the seller's authority to sell.

(2) Nothing in this Act affects—

(a) the provisions of the Factors Acts or any enactment enabling the apparent owner of goods to dispose of them as if he were their true owner;

(b) the validity of any contract of sale under any special common law or statutory power of sale or under the order of a court of competent jurisdiction.

22   Market overt

[. . .]

23   Sale under voidable title

When the seller of goods has a voidable title to them, but his title has not been avoided at the time of the sale, the buyer acquires a good title to the goods, provided he buys them in good faith and without notice of the seller's defect of title.

24   Seller in possession after sale

Where a person having sold goods continues or is in possession of the goods, or of the documents of title to the goods, the delivery or transfer by that person, or by a mercantile agent acting for him, of the goods or documents of title under any sale, pledge, or other disposition thereof, to any person receiving the same in good faith and without notice of the previous sale, has the same effect as if the person making the delivery or transfer were expressly authorised by the owner of the goods to make the same.

25   Buyer in possession after sale

(1) Where a person having bought or agreed to buy goods obtains, with the consent of the seller, possession of the goods or the documents of title to the goods, the delivery or transfer by that person, or by a mercantile agent acting for him, of the goods or documents of title, under any sale, pledge, or other disposition thereof, to any person receiving the same in good faith and without

notice of any lien or other right of the original seller in respect of the goods, has the same effect as if the person making the delivery or transfer were a mercantile agent in possession of the goods or documents of title with the consent of the owner.

(2) For the purposes of subsection (1) above—

(a) the buyer under a conditional sale agreement is to be taken not to be a person who has bought or agreed to buy goods, and

(b) 'conditional sale agreement' means an agreement for the sale of goods which is a consumer credit agreement within the meaning of the Consumer Credit Act 1974 under which the purchase price or part of it is payable by instalments, and the property in the goods is to remain in the seller (notwithstanding that the buyer is to be in possession of the goods) until such conditions as to the payment of instalments or otherwise as may be specified in the agreement are fulfilled.

(3) Paragraph 9 of Schedule 1 below applies in relation to a contract under which a person buys or agrees to buy goods and which is made before the appointed day.

(4) In subsection (3) above and paragraph 9 of Schedule 1 below references to the appointed day are to the day appointed for the purposes of those provisions by an order of the Secretary of State made by statutory instrument.

26   Supplementary to sections 24 and 25

In sections 24 and 25 above 'mercantile agent' means a mercantile agent having in the customary course of his business as such agent authority either—

(a) to sell goods, or

(b) to consign goods for the purpose of sale, or

(c) to buy goods, or

(d) to raise money on the security of goods.

PART IV PERFORMANCE OF THE CONTRACT

27   Duties of seller and buyer

It is the duty of the seller to deliver the goods, and of the buyer to accept and pay for them, in accordance with the terms of the contract of sale.

28   Payment and delivery are concurrent conditions

Unless otherwise agreed, delivery of the goods and payment of the price are concurrent conditions, that is to say, the seller must be ready and willing to give possession of the goods to the buyer in exchange for the price and the buyer must be ready and willing to pay the price in exchange for possession of the goods.

29   Rules about delivery

(1) Whether it is for the buyer to take possession of the goods or for the seller to send them to the buyer is a question depending in each case on the contract, express or implied, between the parties.

(2) Apart from any such contract, express or implied, the place of delivery is the seller's place of business if he has one, and if not, his residence; except that, if the contract is for the sale of specific goods, which to the knowledge of the parties when the contract is made are in some other place, then that place is the place of delivery.

(3) Where under the contract of sale the seller is bound to send the goods to the buyer, but no time for sending them is fixed, the seller is bound to send them within a reasonable time.

[(3A) Subsection (3) does not apply to a contract to which Chapter 2 of Part 1 of the Consumer Rights Act 2015 applies (but see the provision made about such contracts in section 28 of that Act).]

(4) Where the goods at the time of sale are in the possession of a third person, there is no delivery by seller to buyer unless and until the third person acknowledges to the buyer that he holds the goods on his behalf; but nothing in this section affects the operation of the issue or transfer of any document of title to goods.

(5) Demand or tender of delivery may be treated as ineffectual unless made at a reasonable hour; and what is a reasonable hour is a question of fact.

(6) Unless otherwise agreed, the expenses of and incidental to putting the goods into a deliverable state must be borne by the seller.

30   Delivery of wrong quantity

(1) Where the seller delivers to the buyer a quantity of goods less than he contracted to sell, the buyer may reject them, but if the buyer accepts the goods so delivered he must pay for them at the contract rate.

(2) Where the seller delivers to the buyer a quantity of goods larger than he contracted to sell, the buyer may accept the goods included in the contract and reject the rest, or he may reject the whole.

[(2A) A buyer may not—

(a) where the seller delivers a quantity of goods less than he contracted to sell, reject the goods under subsection (1) above, or

(b) where the seller delivers a quantity of goods larger than he contracted to sell, reject the whole under subsection (2) above,

if the shortfall or, as the case may be, excess is so slight that it would be unreasonable for him to do so.

(2B) It is for the seller to show that a shortfall or excess fell within subsection (2A) above.

(2C) Subsections (2A) and (2B) above do not apply to Scotland.]

[(2D) Where the seller delivers a quantity of goods—

(a) less than he contracted to sell, the buyer shall not be entitled to reject the goods under subsection (1) above,

(b) larger than he contracted to sell, the buyer shall not be entitled to reject the whole under subsection (2) above,

unless the shortfall or excess is material.

(2E) Subsection (2D) above applies to Scotland only.]

(3) Where the seller delivers to the buyer a quantity of goods larger than he contracted to sell and the buyer accepts the whole of the goods so delivered he must pay for them at the contract rate.

(5) This section is subject to any usage of trade, special agreement, or course of dealing between the parties.

[(6) This section does not apply to a contract to which Chapter 2 of Part 1 of the Consumer Rights Act 2015 applies (but see the provision made about such contracts in section 25 of that Act).]

31   Instalment deliveries

(1) Unless otherwise agreed, the buyer of goods is not bound to accept delivery of them by instalments.

(2) Where there is a contract for the sale of goods to be delivered by stated instalments, which are to be separately paid for, and the seller makes defective deliveries in respect of one or more instalments, or the buyer neglects or refuses to take delivery of or pay for one or more instalments, it is a question in each case depending on the terms of the contract and the circumstances of the case whether the breach of contract is a repudiation of the whole contract or whether it is a severable breach giving rise to a claim for compensation but not to a right to treat the whole contract as repudiated.

[(3) This section does not apply to a contract to which Chapter 2 of Part 1 of the Consumer Rights Act 2015 applies (but see the provision made about such contracts in section 26 of that Act).]

32   Delivery to carrier

(1) Where, in pursuance of a contract of sale, the seller is authorised or required to send the goods to the buyer, delivery of the goods to a carrier (whether named by the buyer or not) for the purpose of transmission to the buyer is prima facie deemed to be delivery of the goods to the buyer.

(2) Unless otherwise authorised by the buyer, the seller must make such contact with the carrier on behalf of the buyer as may be reasonable having regard to the nature of the goods and the

other circumstances of the case; and if the seller omits to do so, and the goods are lost or damaged in course of transit, the buyer may decline to treat the delivery to the carrier as a delivery to himself or may hold the seller responsible in damages.

(3) Unless otherwise agreed, where goods are sent by the seller to the buyer by a route involving sea transit, under circumstances in which it is usual to insure, the seller must give such notice to the buyer as may enable him to insure them during their sea transit, and if the seller fails to do so, the goods are at his risk during such sea transit.

[(4) This section does not apply to a contract to which Chapter 2 of Part 1 of the Consumer Rights Act 2015 applies (but see the provision made about such contracts in section 29 of that Act).]

33   Risk where goods are delivered at distant place

[(1)] Where the seller of goods agrees to deliver them at his own risk at a place other than that where they are when sold, the buyer must nevertheless (unless otherwise agreed) take any risk of deterioration in the goods necessarily incident to the course of transit.

[(2) This section does not apply to a contract to which Chapter 2 of Part 1 of the Consumer Rights Act 2015 applies (but see the provision made about such contracts in section 29 of that Act).]

34   Buyer's right of examining the goods

[(1)] Unless otherwise agreed, when the seller tenders delivery of goods to the buyer, he is bound on request to afford the buyer a reasonable opportunity of examining the goods for the purpose of ascertaining whether they are in conformity with the contract [and, in the case of a contract for sale by sample, of comparing the bulk with the sample.]

[(2) Nothing in this section affects the operation of section 22 (time limit for short-term right to reject) of the Consumer Rights Act 2015.]

35   Acceptance

(1) The buyer is deemed to have accepted the goods [subject to subsection (2) below—
  (a) when he intimates to the seller that he has accepted them, or
  (b) when the goods have been delivered to him and he does any act in relation to them which is inconsistent with the ownership of the seller.

(2) Where goods are delivered to the buyer, and he has not previously examined them, he is not deemed to have accepted them under subsection (1) above until he has had a reasonable opportunity of examining them for the purpose—
  (a) of ascertaining whether they are in conformity with the contract, and
  (b) in the case of a contract for sale by sample, of comparing the bulk with the sample.

(4) The buyer is also deemed to have accepted the goods when after the lapse of a reasonable time he retains the goods without intimating to the seller that he has rejected them.

(5) The questions that are material in determining for the purposes of subsection (4) above whether a reasonable time has elapsed include whether the buyer has had a reasonable opportunity of examining the goods for the purpose mentioned in subsection (2) above.

(6) The buyer is not by virtue of this section deemed to have accepted the goods merely because—
  (a) he asks for, or agrees to, their repair by or under an arrangement with the seller, or
  (b) the goods are delivered to another under a sub-sale or other disposition.

(7) Where the contract is for the sale of goods making one or more commercial units, a buyer accepting any goods included in a unit is deemed to have accepted all the goods making the unit; and in this subsection 'commercial unit' means a unit division of which would materially impair the value of the goods or the character of the unit.]

[(9) This section does not apply to a contract to which Chapter 2 of Part 1 of the Consumer Rights Act 2015 applies (but see the provision made about such contracts in section 21 of that Act).]

[35A   Right of partial rejection

(1) If the buyer—
  (a) has the right to reject the goods by reason of a breach on the part of the seller that affects some or all of them, but

(b) accepts some of the goods, including, where there are any goods unaffected by the breach, all such goods,

he does not by accepting them lose his right to reject the rest.

(2) In the case of a buyer having the right to reject an instalment of goods, subsection (1) above applies as if references to the goods were references to the goods comprised in the instalment.

(3) For the purposes of subsection (1) above, goods are affected by a breach if by reason of the breach they are not in conformity with the contract.

(4) This section applies unless a contrary intention appears in, or is to be implied from, the contract.]

36   Buyer not bound to return rejected goods

[(1)] Unless otherwise agreed, where goods are delivered to the buyer, and he refuses to accept them, having the right to do so, he is not bound to return them to the seller, but it is sufficient if he intimates to the seller that he refuses to accept them.

[(2) This section does not apply to a contract to which Chapter 2 of Part 1 of the Consumer Rights Act 2015 applies (but see the provision made about such contracts in section 20 of that Act).]

37   Buyer's liability for not taking delivery of goods

(1) When the seller is ready and willing to deliver the goods, and requests the buyer to take delivery, and the buyer does not within a reasonable time after such request take delivery of the goods, he is liable to the seller for any loss occasioned by his neglect or refusal to take delivery, and also for a reasonable charge for the care and custody of the goods.

(2) Nothing in this section affects the rights of the seller where the neglect or refusal of the buyer to take delivery amounts to a repudiation of the contract.

PART V   RIGHTS OF UNPAID SELLER AGAINST THE GOODS

Preliminary

38   Unpaid seller defined

(1) The seller of goods is an unpaid seller within the meaning of this Act—

(a) when the whole of the price has not been paid or tendered;

(b) when a bill of exchange or other negotiable instrument has been received as conditional payment, and the condition on which it was received has not been fulfilled by reason of the dishonour of the instrument or otherwise.

(2) In this Part of this Act 'seller' includes any person who is in the position of a seller, as, for instance, an agent of the seller to whom the bill of lading has been indorsed, or a consignor or agent who has himself paid (or is directly responsible for) the price.

39   Unpaid seller's rights

(1) Subject to this and any other Act, notwithstanding that the property in the goods may have passed to the buyer, the unpaid seller of goods, as such, has by implication of law—

(a) a lien on the goods or right to retain them for the price while he is in possession of them;

(b) in the case of the insolvency of the buyer, a right of stopping the goods in transit after he has parted with the possession of them;

(c) a right of re-sale as limited by this Act.

(2) Where the property in goods has not passed to the buyer, the unpaid seller has (in addition to his other remedies) a right of withholding delivery similar to and coextensive with his rights of lien or retention and stoppage in transit where the property has passed to the buyer.

Unpaid seller's lien

41   Seller's lien

(1) Subject to this Act, the unpaid seller of goods who is in possession of them is entitled to retain possession of them until payment or tender of the price in the following cases:—

(a) where the goods have been sold without any stipulation as to credit;

(b) where the goods have been sold on credit but the term of credit has expired;

(c) where the buyer becomes insolvent.

(2) The seller may exercise his lien or right of retention notwithstanding that he is in possession of the goods as agent or bailee or custodier for the buyer.

42 Part delivery

Where an unpaid seller has made part delivery of the goods, he may exercise his lien or right of retention on the remainder, unless such part delivery has been made under such circumstances as to show an agreement to waive the lien or right of retention.

43 Termination of lien

(1) The unpaid seller of goods loses his lien or right of retention in respect of them—

(a) when he delivers the goods to a carrier or other bailee or custodier for the purpose of transmission to the buyer without reserving the right of disposal of the goods;

(b) when the buyer or his agent lawfully obtains possession of the goods;

(c) by waiver of the lien or right of retention.

(2) An unpaid seller of goods who has a lien or right of retention in respect of them does not lose his lien or right of retention by reason only that he has obtained judgment or decree for the price of the goods.

Stoppage in transit

44 Right of stoppage in transit

Subject to this Act, when the buyer of goods becomes insolvent the unpaid seller who has parted with the possession of the goods has the right of stopping them in transit, that is to say, he may resume possession of the goods as long as they are in course of transit, and may retain them until payment or tender of the price.

45 Duration of transit

(1) Goods are deemed to be in course of transit from the time when they are delivered to a carrier or other bailee or custodier for the purpose of transmission to the buyer, until the buyer or his agent in that behalf takes delivery of them from the carrier or other bailee or custodier.

(2) If the buyer or his agent in that behalf obtains delivery of the goods before their arrival at the appointed destination, the transit is at an end.

(3) If, after the arrival of the goods at the appointed destination, the carrier or other bailee or custodier acknowledges to the buyer or his agent that he holds the goods on his behalf and continues in possession of them as bailee or custodier for the buyer or his agent, the transit is at an end, and it is immaterial that a further destination for the goods may have been indicated by the buyer.

(4) If the goods are rejected by the buyer, and the carrier or other bailee or custodier continues in possession of them, the transit is not deemed to be at an end, even if the seller has refused to receive them back.

(5) When goods are delivered to a ship chartered by the buyer it is a question depending on the circumstances of the particular case whether they are in the possession of the master as a carrier or as agent to the buyer.

(6) Where the carrier or other bailee or custodier wrongfully refuses to deliver the goods to the buyer or his agent in that behalf, the transit is deemed to be at an end.

(7) Where part delivery of the goods has been made to the buyer or his agent in that behalf, the remainder of the goods may be stopped in transit, unless such part delivery has been made under such circumstances as to show an agreement to give up possession of the whole of the goods.

46 How stoppage in transit is effected

(1) The unpaid seller may exercise his right of stoppage in transit either by taking actual possession of the goods or by giving notice of his claim to the carrier or other bailee or custodier in whose possession the goods are.

(2) The notice may be given either to the person in actual possession of the goods or to his principal.

(3) If given to the principal, the notice is ineffective unless given at such time and under such circumstances that the principal, by the exercise of reasonable diligence, may communicate it to his servant or agent in time to prevent a delivery to the buyer.

(4) When notice of stoppage in transit is given by the seller to the carrier or other bailee or custodier in possession of the goods, he must re-deliver the goods to, or according to the directions of, the seller; and the expenses of the re-delivery must be borne by the seller.

Re-sale etc. by buyer

47   Effect of sub-sale etc. by buyer

(1) Subject to this Act, the unpaid seller's right of lien or retention or stoppage in transit is not affected by any sale or other disposition of the goods which the buyer may have made, unless the seller has assented to it.

(2) Where a document of title to goods has been lawfully transferred to any person as buyer or owner of the goods, and that person transfers the document to a person who takes it in good faith and for valuable consideration, then—

    (a) if the last-mentioned transfer was by way of sale the unpaid seller's right of lien or retention or stoppage in transit is defeated; and

    (b) if the last-mentioned transfer was made by way of pledge or other disposition for value, the unpaid seller's right of lien or retention of stoppage in transit can only be exercised subject to the rights of the transferee.

Rescission: and re-sale by seller

48   Rescission: and re-sale by seller

(1) Subject to this section, a contract of sale is not rescinded by the mere exercise by an unpaid seller of his right of lien or retention or stoppage in transit.

(2) Where an unpaid seller who has exercised his right of lien or retention or stoppage in transit re-sells the goods, the buyer acquires a good title to them as against the original buyer.

(3) Where the goods are of a perishable nature, or where the unpaid seller gives notice to the buyer of his intention to re-sell, and the buyer does not within a reasonable time pay or tender the price, the unpaid seller may re-sell the goods and recover from the original buyer damages for any loss occasioned by his breach of contract.

(4) Where the seller expressly reserves the right of re-sale in case the buyer should make default, and on the buyer making default re-sells the goods, the original contract of sale is rescinded but without prejudice to any claim the seller may have for damages.

PART VI ACTIONS FOR BREACH OF THE CONTRACT

Seller's remedies

49   Action for price

(1) Where, under a contract of sale, the property in the goods has passed to the buyer and he wrongfully neglects or refuses to pay for the goods according to the terms of the contract, the seller may maintain an action against him for the price of the goods.

(2) Where, under a contract of sale, the price is payable on a day certain irrespective of delivery and the buyer wrongfully neglects or refuses to pay such price, the seller may maintain an action for the price, although the property in the goods has not passed and the goods have not been appropriated to the contract.

(3) Nothing in this section prejudices the right of the seller in Scotland to recover interest on the price from the date of tender of the goods, or from the date on which the price was payable, as the case may be.

50   Damages for non-acceptance

(1) Where the buyer wrongfully neglects or refuses to accept and pay for the goods, the seller may maintain an action against him for damages for non-acceptance.

(2) The measure of damages is the estimated loss directly and naturally resulting in the ordinary course of events, from the buyer's breach of contract.

(3) Where there is an available market for the goods in question the measure of damages is prima facie to be ascertained by the difference between the contract price and the market or current price at the time or times when the goods ought to have been accepted or (if no time was fixed for acceptance) at the time of the refusal to accept.

Buyer's remedies

51   Damages for non-delivery

(1) Where the seller wrongfully neglects or refuses to deliver the goods to the buyer, the buyer may maintain an action against the seller for damages for non-delivery.

(2) The measure of damages is the estimated loss directly and naturally resulting, in the ordinary course of events, from the seller's breach of contract.

(3) Where there is an available market for the goods in question the measure of damages is prima facie to be ascertained by the difference between the contract price and the market or current price of the goods at the time or times when they ought to have been delivered or (if no time was fixed) at the time of the refusal to deliver.

[(4) This section does not apply to a contract to which Chapter 2 of Part 1 of the Consumer Rights Act 2015 applies (but see the provision made about such contracts in section 19 of that Act).]

52   Specific performance

(1) If any action for breach of contract to deliver specific or ascertained goods the court may, if it thinks fit, on the plaintiff s application, by its judgment or decree direct that the contract shall be performed specifically, without giving the defendant the option of retaining the goods on payment of damages.

(2) The plaintiff s application may be made at any time before judgment or decree.

(3) The judgment or decree may be unconditional, or on such terms and conditions as to damages, payment of the price and otherwise as seem just to the court.

(4) The provisions of this section shall be deemed to be supplementary to, and not in derogation of, the right of specific implement in Scotland.

[(5) This section does not apply to a contract to which Chapter 2 of Part 1 of the Consumer Rights Act 2015 applies (but see the provision made about such contracts in section 19 of that Act).]

53   Remedy for breach of warranty

(1) Where there is a breach of warranty by the seller, or where the buyer elects (or is compelled) to treat any breach of a condition on the part of the seller as a breach of warranty, the buyer is not by reason only of such breach of warranty entitled to reject the goods; but he may—

(a) set up against the seller the breach of warranty in diminution of extinction of the price, or

(b) maintain an action against the seller for damages for the breach of warranty.

(2) The measure of damages for breach of warranty is the estimated loss directly and naturally resulting, in the ordinary course of events, from the breach of warranty.

(3) In the case of breach of warranty of quality such loss is prima facie the difference between the value of the goods at the time of delivery to the buyer and the value they would have had if they had fulfilled the warranty.

(4) The fact that the buyer has set up the breach of warranty in diminution or extinction of the price does not prevent him from maintaining an action for the same breach of warranty if he has suffered further damage.

[(4A) This section does not apply to a contract to which Chapter 2 of Part 1 of the Consumer Rights Act 2015 applies (but see the provision made about such contracts in section 19 of that Act).]

Interest, etc.

54 Interest, etc.

[(1)] Nothing in this Act affects the right of the buyer or the seller to recover interest or special damages in any case where by law interest or special damages may be recoverable, or to recover money paid where the consideration for the payment of it has failed.

[(2) This section does not apply to a contract to which Chapter 2 of Part 1 of the Consumer Rights Act 2015 applies (but see the provision made about such contracts in section 19 of that Act).]

PART VII SUPPLEMENTARY

55 Exclusion of implied terms

(1) Where a right duty or liability would arise under a contract of sale of goods by implication of law, it may (subject to the Unfair Contract Terms Act 1977) be negatived or varied by express agreement, or by the course of dealing between the parties, or by such usage as binds both parties to the contract.

[(1A) Subsection (1) does not apply to a contract to which Chapter 2 of Part 1 of the Consumer Rights Act 2015 applies (but see the provision made about such contracts in section 31 of that Act).]

(2) An express [term] does not negative a [term] implied by this Act unless inconsistent with it.

57 Auction sales

(1) Where goods are put up for sale by auction in lots, each lot is prima facie deemed to be the subject of a separate contract of sale.

(2) A sale by auction is complete when the auctioneer announces its completion by the fall of the hammer, or in other customary manner; and until the announcement is made any bidder may retract his bid.

(3) A sale by auction may be notified to be subject to a reserve or upset price, and a right to bid may also be reserved expressly by or on behalf of the seller.

(4) Where a sale by auction is not notified to be subject to a right to bid by or on behalf of the seller, it is not lawful for the seller to bid himself or to employ any person to bid at the sale, or for the auctioneer knowingly to take any bid from the seller or any such person.

(5) A sale contravening subsection (4) above may be treated as fraudulent by the buyer.

(6) Where, in respect of a sale by auction, a right to bid is expressly reserved (but not otherwise) the seller or any one person on his behalf may bid at the auction.

59 Reasonable time a question of fact

Where a reference is made in this Act to a reasonable time the question what is a reasonable time is a question of fact.

60 Rights, etc. enforceable by action

Where a right, duty or liability is declared by this Act, it may (unless otherwise provided by this Act) be enforced by action.

61 Interpretation

(1) In this Act, unless the context or subject matter otherwise requires,— 'action' includes counterclaim and set-off, and in Scotland condescendence and claim and compensation;

['bulk' means a mass or collection of goods of the same kind which—

(a) is contained in a defined space or area; and

(b) is such that any goods in the bulk are interchangeable with any other goods therein of the same number or quantity;]

'business' includes a profession and the activities of any government department (including a Northern Ireland department) or local or public authority;

'buyer' means a person who buys or agrees to buy goods;

'contract of sale' includes an agreement to sell as well as a sale, 'credit-broker' means a person acting in the course of a business of credit brokerage carried on by him, that is a business of effecting introductions of individuals desiring to obtain credit—

>   (a) to persons carrying on any business so far as it relates to the provision of credit, or

>   (b) to other persons engaged in credit brokerage;

'defendant' includes in Scotland defender, respondent, and claimant in a multiple-poinding;

'delivery' means voluntary transfer of possession from one person to another; [except that in relation to sections 20A and 20B above it includes such appropriation of goods to the contract as results in property in the goods being transferred to the buyer;]

'document of title to goods' has the same meaning as it has in the Factors Acts;

'Factors Acts' means the Factors Act 1889, the Factors (Scotland) Act 1890, and any enactment amending or substituted for the same;

'fault' means wrongful act or default;

'future goods' means goods to be manufactured or acquired by the seller after the making of the contract of sale;

'goods' includes all personal chattels other than things in action and money, and in Scotland all corporeal moveables except money; and in particular 'goods' includes emblements, industrial growing crops, and things attached to or forming part of the land which are agreed to be severed before sale or under the contract of sale; [and includes an undivided share in goods;]

'plaintiff' includes pursuer, complainer, claimant in a multiplepoinding and defendant or defender counter-claiming;

'property' means the general property in goods, and not merely a special property;

'sale' includes a bargain and sale as well as a sale and delivery;

'seller' means a person who sells or agrees to sell goods;

'specific goods' means goods identified and agreed on at the time a contract of sale is made; [and includes an undivided share, specified as a fraction or percentage, of goods identified and agreed on as aforesaid;]

'warranty' (as regards England and Wales and Northern Ireland) means an agreement with reference to goods which are the subject of a contract of sale, but collateral to the main purpose of such contract, the breach of which gives rise to a claim for damages, but not to a right to reject the goods and treat the contract as repudiated.

(3) A thing is deemed to be done in good faith within the meaning of this Act when it is in fact done honestly, whether it is done negligently or not.

(4) A person is deemed to be insolvent within the meaning of this Act if he has either ceased to pay his debts in the ordinary course of business or he cannot pay his debts as they become due, [. . .]

(5) Goods are in a deliverable state within the meaning of this Act when they are in such a state that the buyer would under the contract be bound to take delivery of them.

(6) As regards the definition of 'business' in subsection (1) above, paragraph 14 of Schedule 1 below applies in relation to a contract made on or after 18 May 1973 and before 1 February 1978, and paragraph 15 in relation to one made before 18 May 1973.

62   Savings: rules of law, etc.

(1) The rules in bankruptcy relating to contracts of sale apply to those contracts, notwithstanding anything in this Act.

(2) The rules of the common law, including the law merchant, except in so far as they are inconsistent with the provisions of [legislation including this Act and the Consumer Rights Act 2015], and in particular the rules relating to the law of principal and agent and the effect of fraud, misrepresentation, duress or coercion, mistake, or other invalidating cause, apply to contracts for the sale of goods.

(3) Nothing in this Act or the Sale of Goods Act 1893 affects the enactments relating to bills of sale, or any enactment relating to the sale of goods which is not expressly repealed or amended by this Act or that.

(4) The provisions of this Act about contracts of sale do not apply to a transaction in the form of a contract of sale which is intended to operate by way of mortgage, pledge, charge, or other security.

Limitation Act 1980

(1980, c. 58)

[**33B   Extension of time limits because of alternative dispute resolution in certain cross border or domestic contractual disputes**

(1) In this section—

[(g) 'sales contract' means a contract under which a trader transfers, or agrees to transfer, the ownership of goods to a consumer and the consumer pays, or agrees to pay, the price, including any contract that has both goods and services as its object;

(h) 'service contract' means a contract, other than a sales contract, under which a trader supplies, or agrees to supply, a service to a consumer and the consumer pays, or agrees to pay, the price;

(i) 'trader' means a person acting for purposes relating to that person's trade, business, craft or profession, whether acting personally or through another person acting in the trader's name or on the trader's behalf.]

Civil Jurisdiction and Judgments Act 1982

(1982, c. 27)

[**3D   The 2005 Hague Convention to have the force of law**

(1) The 2005 Hague Convention shall have the force of law in the United Kingdom.

(2) For the purposes of this Act the 2005 Hague Convention is to be read together with any reservations or declarations made by the United Kingdom at the time of the approval of the Convention.

(3) For convenience of reference the English text of the 2005 Hague Convention is set out in Schedule 3F.]

[SCHEDULE 3F

TEXT OF THE 2005 HAGUE CONVENTION

CONVENTION ON CHOICE OF COURT AGREEMENTS

(Concluded 30 June 2005)

The States Parties to the present Convention,

Desiring to promote international trade and investment through enhanced judicial co-operation,

Believing that such co-operation can be enhanced by uniform rules on jurisdiction and on recognition and enforcement of foreign judgments in civil or commercial matters,

Believing that such enhanced co-operation requires in particular an international legal regime that provides certainty and ensures the effectiveness of exclusive choice of court agreements between parties to commercial transactions and that governs the recognition and enforcement of judgments resulting from proceedings based on such agreements,

Have resolved to conclude this Convention and have agreed upon the following provisions—

Chapter I Scope and definitions

Article 1   Scope

(1) This Convention shall apply in international cases to exclusive choice of court agreements concluded in civil or commercial matters.

(2) For the purposes of Chapter II, a case is international unless the parties are resident in the same Contracting State and the relationship of the parties and all other elements relevant to the dispute, regardless of the location of the chosen court, are connected only with that State.

(3) For the purposes of Chapter III, a case is international where recognition or enforcement of a foreign judgment is sought.

Article 2 Exclusions from scope

(1) This Convention shall not apply to exclusive choice of court agreements—

    (a) to which a natural person acting primarily for personal, family or household purposes (a consumer) is a party;

    (b) relating to contracts of employment, including collective agreements.

(2) This Convention shall not apply to the following matters—

    (a) the status and legal capacity of natural persons;

    (b) maintenance obligations;

    (c) other family law matters, including matrimonial property regimes and other rights or obligations arising out of marriage or similar relationships;

    (d) wills and succession;

    (e) insolvency, composition and analogous matters;

    (f) the carriage of passengers and goods;

    (g) marine pollution, limitation of liability for maritime claims, general average, and emergency towage and salvage;

    (h) anti-trust (competition) matters;

    (i) liability for nuclear damage;

    (j) claims for personal injury brought by or on behalf of natural persons;

    (k) tort or delict claims for damage to tangible property that do not arise from a contractual relationship;

    (l) rights *in rem* in immovable property, and tenancies of immovable property;

    (m) the validity, nullity, or dissolution of legal persons, and the validity of decisions of their organs;

    (n) the validity of intellectual property rights other than copyright and related rights;

    (o) infringement of intellectual property rights other than copyright and related rights, except where infringement proceedings are brought for breach of a contract between the parties relating to such rights, or could have been brought for breach of that contract;

    (p) the validity of entries in public registers.

(3) Notwithstanding paragraph 2, proceedings are not excluded from the scope of this Convention where a matter excluded under that paragraph arises merely as a preliminary question and not as an object of the proceedings. In particular, the mere fact that a matter excluded under paragraph 2 arises by way of defence does not exclude proceedings from the Convention, if that matter is not an object of the proceedings.

(4) This Convention shall not apply to arbitration and related proceedings.

(5) Proceedings are not excluded from the scope of this Convention by the mere fact that a State, including a government, a governmental agency or any person acting for a State, is a party thereto.

(6) Nothing in this Convention shall affect privileges and immunities of States or of international organisations, in respect of themselves and of their property.

Article 3 Exclusive choice of court agreements

For the purposes of this Convention—

    (a) 'exclusive choice of court agreement' means an agreement concluded by two or more parties that meets the requirements of paragraph (c) and designates, for the purpose of deciding disputes which have arisen or may arise in connection with a particular legal relationship, the courts of one Contracting State or one or more specific courts of one Contracting State to the exclusion of the jurisdiction of any other courts;

    (b) a choice of court agreement which designates the courts of one Contracting State or one or more specific courts of one Contracting State shall be deemed to be exclusive unless the parties have expressly provided otherwise;

    (c) an exclusive choice of court agreement must be concluded or documented—

        (i) in writing; or

        (ii) by any other means of communication which renders information accessible so as to be usable for subsequent reference;

(d) an exclusive choice of court agreement that forms part of a contract shall be treated as an agreement independent of the other terms of the contract. The validity of the exclusive choice of court agreement cannot be contested solely on the ground that the contract is not valid.

Article 4   Other definitions

(1) In this Convention, 'judgment' means any decision on the merits given by a court, whatever it may be called, including a decree or order, and a determination of costs or expenses by the court (including an officer of the court), provided that the determination relates to a decision on the merits which may be recognised or enforced under this Convention. An interim measure of protection is not a judgment.

(2) For the purposes of this Convention, an entity or person other than a natural person shall be considered to be resident in the State—

    (a) where it has its statutory seat;

    (b) under whose law it was incorporated or formed;

    (c) where it has its central administration; or

    (d) where it has its principal place of business.

Chapter II   Jurisdiction

Article 5   Jurisdiction of the chosen court

(1) The court or courts of a Contracting State designated in an exclusive choice of court agreement shall have jurisdiction to decide a dispute to which the agreement applies, unless the agreement is null and void under the law of that State.

(2) A court that has jurisdiction under paragraph 1 shall not decline to exercise jurisdiction on the ground that the dispute should be decided in a court of another State.

(3) The preceding paragraphs shall not affect rules—

    (a) on jurisdiction related to subject matter or to the value of the claim;

    (b) on the internal allocation of jurisdiction among the courts of a Contracting State.

However, where the chosen court has discretion as to whether to transfer a case, due consideration should be given to the choice of the parties.

Article 6   Obligations of a court not chosen

A court of a Contracting State other than that of the chosen court shall suspend or dismiss proceedings to which an exclusive choice of court agreement applies unless—

    (a) the agreement is null and void under the law of the State of the chosen court;

    (b) a party lacked the capacity to conclude the agreement under the law of the State of the court seised;

    (c) giving effect to the agreement would lead to a manifest injustice or would be manifestly contrary to the public policy of the State of the court seised;

    (d) for exceptional reasons beyond the control of the parties, the agreement cannot reasonably be performed; or

    (e) the chosen court has decided not to hear the case.

Article 7   Interim measures of protection

Interim measures of protection are not governed by this Convention. This Convention neither requires nor precludes the grant, refusal or termination of interim measures of protection by a court of a Contracting State and does not affect whether or not a party may request or a court should grant, refuse or terminate such measures.

Chapter III   Recognition and enforcement

Article 8   Registration and enforcement

(1) A judgment given by a court of a Contracting State designated in an exclusive choice of court agreement shall be recognised and enforced in other Contracting States in accordance with this Chapter. Recognition or enforcement may be refused only on the grounds specified in this Convention.

(2) Without prejudice to such review as is necessary for the application of the provisions of this Chapter, there shall be no review of the merits of the judgment given by the court of origin. The court addressed shall be bound by the findings of fact on which the court of origin based its jurisdiction, unless the judgment was given by default.

(3) A judgment shall be recognised only if it has effect in the State of origin, and shall be enforced only if it is enforceable in the State of origin.

(4) Recognition or enforcement may be postponed or refused if the judgment is the subject of review in the State of origin or if the time limit for seeking ordinary review has not expired. A refusal does not prevent a subsequent application for recognition or enforcement of the judgment.

(5) This Article shall also apply to a judgment given by a court of a Contracting State pursuant to a transfer of the case from the chosen court in that Contracting State as permitted by Article 5, paragraph 3. However, where the chosen court had discretion as to whether to transfer the case to another court, recognition or enforcement of the judgment may be refused against a party who objected to the transfer in a timely manner in the State of origin.

Article 9   Refusal of recognition or enforcement

Recognition or enforcement may be refused if—

(a) the agreement was null and void under the law of the State of the chosen court, unless the chosen court has determined that the agreement is valid;

(b) a party lacked the capacity to conclude the agreement under the law of the requested State;

(c) the document which instituted the proceedings or an equivalent document, including the essential elements of the claim,

  (i) was not notified to the defendant in sufficient time and in such a way as to enable him to arrange for his defence, unless the defendant entered an appearance and presented his case without contesting notification in the court of origin, provided that the law of the State of origin permitted notification to be contested; or

  (ii) was notified to the defendant in the requested State in a manner that is incompatible with fundamental principles of the requested State concerning service of documents;

(d) the judgment was obtained by fraud in connection with a matter of procedure;

(e) recognition or enforcement would be manifestly incompatible with the public policy of the requested State, including situations where the specific proceedings leading to the judgment were incompatible with fundamental principles of procedural fairness of that State;

(f) the judgment is inconsistent with a judgment given in the requested State in a dispute between the same parties; or

(g) the judgment is inconsistent with an earlier judgment given in another State between the same parties on the same cause of action, provided that the earlier judgment fulfils the conditions necessary for its recognition in the requested State.

Article 10   Preliminary questions

(1) Where a matter excluded under Article 2, paragraph 2, or under Article 21, arose as a preliminary question, the ruling on that question shall not be recognised or enforced under this Convention.

(2) Recognition or enforcement of a judgment may be refused if, and to the extent that, the judgment was based on a ruling on a matter excluded under Article 2, paragraph 2.

(3) However, in the case of a ruling on the validity of an intellectual property right other than copyright or a related right, recognition or enforcement of a judgment may be refused or postponed under the preceding paragraph only where—

(a) that ruling is inconsistent with a judgment or a decision of a competent authority on that matter given in the State under the law of which the intellectual property right arose; or

(b) proceedings concerning the validity of the intellectual property right are pending in that State.

(4) Recognition or enforcement of a judgment may be refused if, and to the extent that, the judgment was based on a ruling on a matter excluded pursuant to a declaration made by the requested State under Article 21.

Article 11   Damages

(1) Recognition or enforcement of a judgment may be refused if, and to the extent that, the judgment awards damages, including exemplary or punitive damages, that do not compensate a party for actual loss or harm suffered.

(2) The court addressed shall take into account whether and to what extent the damages awarded by the court of origin serve to cover costs and expenses relating to the proceedings.

Article 12   Judicial settlements (*transactions judiciaires*)

Judicial settlements (*transactions judiciaires*) which a court of a Contracting State designated in an exclusive choice of court agreement has approved, or which have been concluded before that court in the course of proceedings, and which are enforceable in the same manner as a judgment in the State of origin, shall be enforced under this Convention in the same manner as a judgment.

Article 13   Documents to be produced

(1) The party seeking recognition or applying for enforcement shall produce—
  (a) a complete and certified copy of the judgment;
  (b) the exclusive choice of court agreement, a certified copy thereof, or other evidence of its existence;
  (c) if the judgment was given by default, the original or a certified copy of a document establishing that the document which instituted the proceedings or an equivalent document was notified to the defaulting party;
  (d) any documents necessary to establish that the judgment has effect or, where applicable, is enforceable in the State of origin;
  (e) in the case referred to in Article 12, a certificate of a court of the State of origin that the judicial settlement or a part of it is enforceable in the same manner as a judgment in the State of origin.

(2) If the terms of the judgment do not permit the court addressed to verify whether the conditions of this Chapter have been complied with, that court may require any necessary documents.

(3) An application for recognition or enforcement may be accompanied by a document, issued by a court (including an officer of the court) of the State of origin, in the form recommended and published by the Hague Conference on Private International Law.

(4) If the documents referred to in this Article are not in an official language of the requested State, they shall be accompanied by a certified translation into an official language, unless the law of the requested State provides otherwise.

Article 14   Procedure

The procedure for recognition, declaration of enforceability or registration for enforcement, and the enforcement of the judgment, are governed by the law of the requested State unless this Convention provides otherwise. The court addressed shall act expeditiously.

Article 15   Severability

Recognition or enforcement of a severable part of a judgment shall be granted where recognition or enforcement of that part is applied for, or only part of the judgment is capable of being recognised or enforced under this Convention.

Chapter IV   General clauses

Article 16   Transitional provisions

(1) This Convention shall apply to exclusive choice of court agreements concluded after its entry into force for the State of the chosen court.

(2) This Convention shall not apply to proceedings instituted before its entry into force for the State of the court seised.

Article 17   Contracts of insurance and reinsurance

(1) Proceedings under a contract of insurance or reinsurance are not excluded from the scope of this Convention on the ground that the contract of insurance or reinsurance relates to a matter to which this Convention does not apply.

(2) Recognition and enforcement of a judgment in respect of liability under the terms of a contract of insurance or reinsurance may not be limited or refused on the ground that the liability under that contract includes liability to indemnify the insured or reinsured in respect of—
  (a) a matter to which this Convention does not apply; or
  (b) an award of damages to which Article 11 might apply.

Article 23 Uniform interpretation
In the interpretation of this Convention, regard shall be had to its international character and to the need to promote uniformity in its application.

Article 25 Non-unified legal systems
(1) In relation to a Contracting State in which two or more systems of law apply in different territorial units with regard to any matter dealt with in this Convention—
  (a) any reference to the law or procedure of a State shall be construed as referring, where appropriate, to the law or procedure in force in the relevant territorial unit;
  (b) any reference to residence in a State shall be construed as referring, where appropriate, to residence in the relevant territorial unit;
  (c) any reference to the court or courts of a State shall be construed as referring, where appropriate, to the court or courts in the relevant territorial unit;
  (d) any reference to a connection with a State shall be construed as referring, where appropriate, to a connection with the relevant territorial unit.

(2) Notwithstanding the preceding paragraph, a Contracting State with two or more territorial units in which different systems of law apply shall not be bound to apply this Convention to situations which involve solely such different territorial units.

(3) A court in a territorial unit of a Contracting State with two or more territorial units in which different systems of law apply shall not be bound to recognise or enforce a judgment from another Contracting State solely because the judgment has been recognised or enforced in another territorial unit of the same Contracting State under this Convention.

(4) This Article shall not apply to a Regional Economic Integration Organisation.

Article 26 Relationship with other international instruments
(1) This Convention shall be interpreted so far as possible to be compatible with other treaties in force for Contracting States, whether concluded before or after this Convention.

(2) This Convention shall not affect the application by a Contracting State of a treaty, whether concluded before or after this Convention, in cases where none of the parties is resident in a Contracting State that is not a Party to the treaty.

(3) This Convention shall not affect the application by a Contracting State of a treaty that was concluded before this Convention entered into force for that Contracting State, if applying this Convention would be inconsistent with the obligations of that Contracting State to any non-Contracting State. This paragraph shall also apply to treaties that revise or replace a treaty concluded before this Convention entered into force for that Contracting State, except to the extent that the revision or replacement creates new inconsistencies with this Convention.

(4) This Convention shall not affect the application by a Contracting State of a treaty, whether concluded before or after this Convention, for the purposes of obtaining recognition or enforcement of a judgment given by a court of a Contracting State that is also a Party to that treaty. However, the judgment shall not be recognised or enforced to a lesser extent than under this Convention.

(5) This Convention shall not affect the application by a Contracting State of a treaty which, in relation to a specific matter, governs jurisdiction or the recognition or enforcement of judgments, even if concluded after this Convention and even if all States concerned are Parties to this Convention. This paragraph shall apply only if the Contracting State has made a declaration in respect of the treaty under this paragraph. In the case of such a declaration, other Contracting States shall not be obliged to apply this Convention to that specific matter to the extent of any inconsistency, where an exclusive choice of court agreement designates the courts, or one or more specific courts, of the Contracting State that made the declaration.

(6) This Convention shall not affect the application of the rules of a Regional Economic Integration Organisation that is a Party to this Convention, whether adopted before or after this Convention—

    (a) where none of the parties is resident in a Contracting State that is not a Member State of the Regional Economic Integration Organisation;

    (b) as concerns the recognition or enforcement of judgments as between Member States of the Regional Economic Integration Organisation.]

Supply of Goods and Services Act 1982

(1982, c. 29)

PART I SUPPLY OF GOODS

Contracts for the transfer of property in goods

1 The contracts concerned

(1) In this Act [in its application to England and Wales and Northern Ireland] a '[relevant contract for the transfer of goods]' means a contract under which one person transfers or agrees to transfer to another the property in goods, other than an excepted contract[, and other than a contract to which Chapter 2 of Part 1 of the Consumer Rights Act 2015 applies.].

(2) For the purposes of this section an excepted contract means any of the following:—

    (a) a contract of sale of goods;

    (b) a hire-purchase agreement;

    [...]

    (d) a transfer or agreement to transfer which is made by deed and for which there is no consideration other than the presumed consideration imported by the deed;

    (e) a contract intended to operate by way of mortgage, pledge, charge or other security.

(3) For the purposes of this Act [in its application to England and Wales and Northern Ireland] a contract is a [relevant contract for the transfer of goods] whether or not services are also provided or to be provided under the contract, and (subject to subsection (2) above) whatever is the nature of the consideration for the transfer or agreement to transfer.

2 Implied terms about title, etc.

(1) In a [relevant contract for the transfer of goods], other than one to which subsection (3) below applies, there is an implied condition on the part of the transferor that in the case of a transfer of the property in the goods he has a right to transfer the property and in the case of an agreement to transfer the property in the goods he will have such a right at the time when the property is to be transferred.

(2) In a [relevant contract for the transfer of goods], other than one to which subsection (3) below applies, there is also an implied warranty that—

    (a) the goods are free, and will remain free until the time when the property is to be transferred, from any charge or encumbrance not disclosed or known to the transferee before the contract is made, and

    (b) the transferee will enjoy quiet possession of the goods except so far as it may be disturbed by the owner or other person entitled to the benefit of any charge or encumbrance so disclosed or known.

(3) This subsection applies to a [relevant contract for the transfer of goods] in the case of which there appears from the contract or is to be inferred from its circumstances an intention that the transferor should transfer only such title as he or a third person may have.

(4) In a contract to which subsection (3) above applies there is an implied warranty that all charges or encumbrances known to the transferor and not known to the transferee have been disclosed to the transferee before the contract is made.

(5) In a contract to which subsection (3) above applies, there is also an implied warranty that none of the following will disturb the transferee's quiet possession of the goods, namely—

    (a) the transferor;

    (b) in a case where the parties to the contract intend that the transferor should transfer only such title as a third person may have, that person;

    (c) anyone claiming through or under the transferor or that third person otherwise than under a charge or encumbrance disclosed or known to the transferee before the contract is made.

3 Implied terms where transfer is by description

(1) This section applies where, under a [relevant contract for the transfer of goods], the transferor transfers or agrees to transfer the property in the goods by description.

(2) In such case there is an implied condition that the goods will correspond with the description.

(3) If the transferor transfers or agrees to transfer the property in the goods by sample as well as by description it is not sufficient that the bulk of the goods corresponds with the sample if the goods do not also correspond with the description.

(4) A contract is not prevented from falling within subsection (1) above by reason only that, being exposed for supply, the goods are selected by the transferee.

4 Implied terms about quality or fitness

(1) Except as provided by this section and section 5 below and subject to the provision of any other enactment, there is no implied condition or warranty about the quality or fitness for any particular purpose of goods supplied under a [relevant contract for the transfer of goods].

[(2) Where, under such a contract, the transferor transfers the property in goods in the course of a business, there is an implied condition that the goods supplied under the contract are of satisfactory quality.

(2A) For the purposes of this section and section 5 below, goods are of satisfactory quality if they meet the standard that a reasonable person would regard as satisfactory, taking account of any description of the goods, the price (if relevant) and all the other relevant circumstances.]

[(3) The condition implied by subsection (2) above does not extend to any matter making the quality of goods unsatisfactory—

    (a) which is specifically drawn to the transferee's attention before the contract is made,

    (b) where the transferee examines the goods before the contract is made, which that examination ought to reveal, or

    (c) where the property in the goods is transferred by reference to a sample, which would have been apparent on a reasonable examination of the sample.]

(4) Subsection (5) below applies where, under a [relevant contract for the transfer of goods], the transferor transfers the property in goods in the course of a business and the transferee, expressly or by implication, makes known—

    (a) to the transferor, or

    (b) where the consideration or part of the consideration for the transfer is a sum payable by instalments and the goods were previously sold by a credit-broker to the transferor, to that credit-broker,

any particular purpose for which the goods are being acquired.

(5) In that case there is (subject to subsection (6) below) an implied condition that the goods supplied under the contract are reasonably fit for that purpose, whether or not that is a purpose for which such goods are commonly supplied.

(6) Subsection (5) above does not apply where the circumstances show that the transferee does not rely, or that it is unreasonable for him to rely, on the skill or judgment of the transferor or credit-broker.

(7) An implied condition or warranty about quality or fitness for a particular purpose may be annexed by usage to a [relevant contract for the transfer of goods].

(8) The preceding provisions of this section apply to a transfer by a person who in the course of a business is acting as agent for another as they apply to a transfer by a principal in the course of a

business, except where that other is not transferring in the course of a business and either the transferee knows that fact or reasonable steps are taken to bring it to the transferee's notice before the contract concerned is made.

5   Implied terms where transfer is by sample

(1) This section applies where, under a [relevant contract for the transfer of goods], the transferor transfers or agrees to transfer the property in the goods by reference to a sample.

(2) In such a case there is an implied condition—

(a) that the bulk will correspond with the sample in quality; and

(b) that the transferee will have a reasonable opportunity of comparing the bulk with the sample; and

(c) that the goods will be free from any defect, [making their quality unsatisfactory], which would not be apparent on reasonable examination of the sample.

(4) For the purposes of this section a transferor transfers or agrees to transfer the property in goods by reference to a sample where there is an express or implied term to that effect in the contract concerned.

[5A   Modification of remedies for breach of statutory condition in non-consumer cases

(1) Where in the case of a relevant contract for the transfer of goods—

(a) the transferee would, apart from this subsection, have the right to treat the contract as repudiated by reason of a breach on the part of the transferor of a term implied by section 3, 4 or 5(2)(a) or (c) above, but

(b) the breach is so slight that it would be unreasonable for him to do so,

the breach is not to be treated as a breach of condition but may be treated as a breach of warranty.

(2) This section applies unless a contrary intention appears in, or is to be implied from, the contract.

(3) It is for the transferor to show that a breach fell within subsection (1)(b) above.]

Contracts for the hire of goods

6   The contracts concerned

(1) In this Act [in its application to England and Wales and Northern Ireland] a '[relevant contract for the hire of goods]' means a contract under which one person bails or agrees to bail goods to another by way of hire, other than [a hire-purchase agreement, and other than a contract to which Chapter 2 of Part 1 of the Consumer Rights Act 2015 applies.].

[. . .]

(3) For the purposes of this Act [in its application to England and Wales and Northern Ireland] a contract is a [relevant contract for the hire of goods] whether or not services are also provided or to be provided under the contract, and [. . .] whatever is the nature of the consideration for the bailment or agreement to bail by way of hire.

7   Implied terms about right to transfer possession, etc.

(1) In a [relevant contract for the hire of goods] there is an implied condition on the part of the bailor that in the case of a bailment he has a right to transfer possession of the goods by way of hire for the period of the bailment and in the case of an agreement to bail he will have such a right at the time of the bailment.

(2) In a [relevant contract for the hire of goods] there is also an implied warranty that the bailee will enjoy quiet possession of the goods for the period of the bailment except so far as the possession may be disturbed by the owner or other person entitled to the benefit of any charge or encumbrance disclosed or known to the bailee before the contract is made.

(3) The preceding provisions of this section do not affect the right of the bailor to repossess the goods under an express or implied term of contract.

8 Implied terms where hire is by description

(1) This section applies where, under a [relevant contract for the hire of goods], the bailor bails or agrees to bail the goods by description.

(2) In such a case there is an implied condition that the goods will correspond with the description.

(3) If under the contract the bailor bails or agrees to bail the goods by reference to a sample as well as a description it is not sufficient that the bulk of the goods corresponds with the sample if the goods do not also correspond with the description.

(4) A contract is not prevented from falling within subsection (1) above by reason only that, being exposed for supply, the goods are selected by the bailee.

9 Implied terms about quality or fitness

(1) Except as provided by this section and section 10 below and subject to the provisions of any other enactment, there is no implied condition or warranty about the quality or fitness for any particular purpose of goods bailed under a [relevant contract for the hire of goods].

[(2) Where, under such a contract, the bailor bails goods in the course of a business, there is an implied condition that the goods supplied under the contract are of satisfactory quality.

(2A) For the purposes of this section and section 10 below, goods are of satisfactory quality if they meet the standard that a reasonable person would regard as satisfactory, taking account of any description of the goods, the consideration for the bailment (if relevant) and all the other relevant circumstances.]

[(3) The condition implied by subsection (2) above does not extend to any matter making the quality of goods unsatisfactory—

(a) which is specifically drawn to the bailee's attention before the contract is made,

(b) where the bailee examines the goods before the contract is made, which that examination ought to reveal, or

(c) where the goods are bailed by reference to a sample, which would have been apparent on a reasonable examination of the sample.]

(4) Subsection (5) below applies where, under a [relevant contract for the hire of goods], the bailor bails goods in the course of a business and the bailee, expressly or by implication, makes known—

(a) to the bailor in the course of negotiations conducted by him in relation to the making of the contract, or

(b) to a credit-broker in the course of negotiations conducted by that broker in relation to goods sold by him to the bailor before forming the subject matter of the contract,

any particular purpose for which the goods are being bailed.

(5) In that case there is (subject to subsection (6) below) an implied condition that the goods supplied under the contract are reasonably fit for that purpose, whether or not that is a purpose for which such goods are commonly supplied.

(6) Subsection (5) above does not apply where the circumstances show that the bailee does not rely, or that it is unreasonable for him to rely, on the skill or judgment of the bailor or credit-broker.

(7) An implied condition or warranty about quality or fitness for a particular purpose may be annexed by usage to a [relevant contract for the hire of goods].

(8) The preceding provisions of this section apply to a bailment by a person who in the course of a business is acting as agent for another as they apply to a bailment by a principal in the course of a business, except where that other is not bailing in the course of a business and either the bailee knows that fact or reasonable steps are taken to bring it to the bailee's notice before the contract concerned is made.

10 Implied terms where hire is by sample

(1) This section applies where, under a [relevant contract for the hire of goods], the bailor bails or agrees to bail the goods by reference to a sample.

(2) In such a case there is an implied condition—

(a) that the bulk will correspond with the sample in quality; and

(b) that the bailee will have a reasonable opportunity of comparing the bulk with the sample; and

    (c) that the goods will be free from any defect, [making their quality unsatisfactory], which would not be apparent on reasonable examination of the sample.

    (4) For the purposes of this section a bailor bails or agrees to bail goods by reference to a sample where there is an express or implied term to that effect in the contract concerned.

[10A   Modification of remedies for breach of statutory condition in non-consumer cases

    (1) Where in the case of a [relevant contract for the hire of goods]—

        (a) the bailee would, apart from this subsection, have the right to treat the contract as repudiated by reason of a breach on the part of the bailor of a term implied by section 8, 9 or 10(2)(a) or (c) above, but

        (b) the breach is so slight that it would be unreasonable for him to do so,

the breach is not to be treated as a breach of condition but may be treated as a breach of warranty.

    (2) This section applies unless a contrary intention appears in, or is to be implied from, the contract.

    (3) It is for the bailor to show that a breach fell within subsection (1)(b) above.]

Exclusion of implied terms, etc.

11   Exclusion of implied terms, etc.

    (1) Where a right, duty or liability would arise under a [relevant contract for the transfer of goods] or a [relevant contract for the hire of goods] by implication of law, it may (subject to subsection (2) below and the 1977 Act) be negatived or varied by express agreement, or by the course of dealing between the parties, or by such usage as binds both parties to the contract.

    (2) An express condition or warranty does not negative a condition or warranty implied by the preceding provisions of this Act unless inconsistent with it.

    (3) Nothing in the preceding provisions of this Act prejudices the operation of any other enactment or any rule of law whereby any condition or warranty (other than one relating to quality or fitness) is to be implied in a [relevant contract for the transfer of goods] or a [relevant contract for the hire of goods].

PART II SUPPLY OF SERVICES

12   The contracts concerned

    (1) In this Act a '[relevant contract for the supply of a service]' means, subject to subsection (2) below a contract under which a person ('the supplier') agrees to carry out a service[, other than a contract to which Chapter 4 of Part 1 of the Consumer Rights Act 2015 applies.]

    (2) For the purposes of this Act, a contract of service or apprenticeship is not a [relevant contract for the supply of a service].

    (3) Subject to subsection (2) above, a contract is a [relevant contract for the supply of a service] for the purposes of this Act whether or not goods are also—

        (a) transferred or to be transferred, or

        (b) bailed or to be bailed by way of hire, under the contract, and whatever is the nature of the consideration for which the service is to be carried out.

    (4) The Secretary of State may by order provide that one or more of sections 13 to 15 below shall not apply to services of a description specified in the order, and such an order may make different provision for different circumstances.

    (5) The power to make an order under subsection (4) above shall be exercisable by statutory instrument subject to annulment in pursuance of a resolution of either House of Parliament.

13   Implied term about care and skill

In a [relevant contract for the supply of a service] where the supplier is acting in the course of a business, there is an implied term that the supplier will carry out the service with reasonable care and skill.

14 Implied term about time of performance

(1) Where, under a [relevant contract for the supply of a service] by a supplier acting in the course of a business, the time for the service to be carried out is not fixed by the contract, left to be fixed in a manner agreed by the contract or determined by the course of dealing between the parties, there is an implied term that the supplier will carry out the service within a reasonable time.

(2) What is a reasonable time is a question of fact.

15 Implied term about consideration

(1) Where, under a [relevant contract for the supply of a service], the consideration for the service is not determined by the contract, left to be determined in a manner agreed by the contract or determined by the course of dealing between the parties, there is an implied term that the party contracting with the supplier will pay a reasonable charge.

(2) What is a reasonable charge is a question of fact.

16 Exclusion of implied terms, etc.

(1) Where a right, duty or liability would arise under [relevant contract for the supply of a service] by virtue of this Part of this Act, it may (subject to subsection (2) below and the 1977 Act) be negatived or varied by express agreement, or by the course of dealing between the parties, or by such usage as binds both parties to the contract.

(2) An express term does not negative a term implied by this Part of this Act unless inconsistent with it.

(3) Nothing in this Part of this Act prejudices—

    (a) any rule of law which imposes on the supplier a duty stricter than that imposed by section 13 or 14 above; or

    (b) subject to paragraph (a) above, any rule of law whereby any term not inconsistent with this Part of this Act is to be implied in a [relevant contract for the supply of a service].

(4) This Part of this Act has effect to any other enactment which defines or restricts the rights, duties or liabilities arising in connection with a service of any description.

PART III SUPPLEMENTARY

18 Interpretation: general

(1) In the preceding provisions of this Act and this section—

'bailee', in relation to a [relevant contract for the hire of goods] means (depending on the context) a person to whom the goods are bailed under a contract, or a person to whom they are to be so bailed, or a person to whom the rights under the contract of either of those persons have passed;

'bailor', in relation to a [relevant contract for the hire of goods], means (depending on the context) a person who bails the goods under the contract, or a person who agrees to do so, or a person to whom the duties under the contract of either of those persons have passed;

'business' includes a profession and the activities of any government department or local or public authority;

'credit-broker' means a person acting in the course of a business of credit brokerage carried on by him;

'credit brokerage' means the effecting of introductions—

    (a) of individuals desiring to obtain credit to persons carrying on any business so far as it relates to the provision of credit; or

    (b) of individuals desiring to obtain goods on hire to persons carrying on a business which comprises or relates to the bailment [or as regards Scotland the hire] of goods under a [relevant contract for the hire of goods]; or

    (c) of individuals desiring to obtain credit, or to obtain goods on hire, to other credit-brokers;

'enactment' means any legislation (including subordinate legislation) of the United Kingdom or Northern Ireland;

'goods' [includes all personal chattels, other than things in action and money, and as regards Scotland all corporeal moveables; and in particular 'goods' includes] emblements, industrial growing crops, and things attached to or forming part of the land which are agreed to be severed before the transfer [bailment or hire] concerned or under the contract concerned [. . .];

'hire-purchase agreement' has the same meaning as in the 1974 Act;

'property', in relation to goods, means the general property in them and not merely a special property;

'transferee', in relation to a contract for the transfer of goods, means (depending on the context) a person to whom the property in the goods is transferred under the contract, or a person to whom the property is to be so transferred, or a person to whom the rights under the contract of either of those persons have passed;

'transferor', in relation to a contract for the transfer of goods, means (depending on the context) a person who transfers the property in the goods under the contract, or a person who agrees to do so, or a person to whom the duties under the contract of either of those persons have passed.

(2) In subsection (1) above, in the definitions of bailee, bailor, transferee and transferor, a reference to rights or duties passing is to their passing by assignment, [assignation] operation of law or otherwise.

[(3) For the purposes of this Act, the quality of goods includes their state and condition and the following (among others) are in appropriate cases aspects of the quality of goods—

    (a) fitness for all the purposes for which goods of the kind in question are commonly supplied,

    (b) appearance and finish,

    (c) freedom from minor defects,

    (d) safety, and

    (e) durability.]

19   Interpretation: references to Acts

In this Act—

'the 1973 Act' means the Supply of Goods (Implied Terms) Act 1973;

'the 1974 Act' means the Consumer Credit Act 1974;

'the 1977 Act' means the Unfair Contract Terms Act 1977;

and 'the 1979 Act' means the Sale of Goods Act 1979.

Insolvency Act 1986

(1986, c. 45)

[A2   Eligible companies

Schedule ZA1 contains provision for determining whether a company is an eligible company for the purposes of this Part [ss A1–A55].]

[A3   Obtaining a moratorium by filing or lodging documents at court

(1) This section applies to an eligible company that—

    (a) is not subject to an outstanding winding-up petition, and

    (b) is not an overseas company.

(2) The directors of the company may obtain a moratorium for the company by filing the relevant documents with the court (for the relevant documents, see section A6).]

[A4   Obtaining a moratorium for company subject to winding-up petition

(1) This section applies to an eligible company that is subject to an outstanding winding-up petition.

(2) The directors of the company may apply to the court for a moratorium for the company.

(3) The application must be accompanied by the relevant documents (for the relevant documents, see section A6).

(4) On hearing the application the court may—
    (a) make an order that the company should be subject to a moratorium, or
    (b) make any other order which the court thinks appropriate.
(5) The court may make an order under subsection (4)(a) only if it is satisfied that a moratorium for the company would achieve a better result for the company's creditors as a whole than would be likely if the company were wound up (without first being subject to a moratorium).]

[A6   The relevant documents

(1) For the purposes of this Chapter [*ss A3–A8*], the relevant documents are—
    (a) a notice that the directors wish to obtain a moratorium,
    (b) a statement from a qualified person (the proposed monitor) that the person—
        (i)   is a qualified person, and
        (ii)   consents to act as the monitor in relation to the proposed moratorium,
    (c) a statement from the proposed monitor that the company is an eligible company,
    (d) a statement from the directors that, in their view, the company is, or is likely to become, unable to pay its debts, and
    (e) a statement from the proposed monitor that, in the proposed monitor's view, it is likely that a moratorium for the company would result in the rescue of the company as a going concern.]

[A8   Obligations to notify where moratorium comes into force

(1) As soon as reasonably practicable after a moratorium for a company comes into force, the directors must notify the monitor of that fact.
(2) As soon as reasonably practicable after receiving a notice under subsection (1), the monitor must notify the following that a moratorium for the company has come into force—
    (a) the registrar of companies,
    (b) every creditor of the company of whose claim the monitor is aware, ...]

[A16   Company enters into insolvency procedure etc

(1) A moratorium comes to an end at any time at which the company—
    (a) enters into a compromise or arrangement (see subsection (2)), or
    (b) enters into a relevant insolvency procedure (see subsection (3)).]

[A19   Publicity about moratorium

(1) During a moratorium, the company must, in any premises—
    (a) where business of the company is carried on, and
    (b) to which customers of the company or suppliers of goods or services to the company have access,
display, in a prominent position so that it may easily be read by such customers or suppliers, a notice containing the required information.
(2) During a moratorium, any websites of the company must state the required information.
(3) During a moratorium, every business document issued by or on behalf of the company must state the required information.
(4) For the purposes of subsections (1), (2) and (3), the required information is—
    (a) that a moratorium is in force in relation to the company, and
    (b) the name of the monitor.]

[A20   Restrictions on insolvency proceedings etc

(1) During a moratorium—
    (a) no petition may be presented for the winding up of the company, except by the directors,
    (b) no resolution may be passed for the voluntary winding up of the company under section 84(1)(a),
    (c) a resolution for the voluntary winding up of the company under section 84(1)(b) may be passed only if the resolution is recommended by the directors,
    (d) no order may be made for the winding up of the company, except on a petition by the directors,

(e) no administration application may be made in respect of the company, except by the directors,

(f) no notice of intention to appoint an administrator of the company under paragraph 14 or 22(1) of Schedule B1 may be filed with the court,

(g) no administrator of the company may be appointed under paragraph 14 or 22(1) of Schedule B1, and

(h) no administrative receiver of the company may be appointed.]

[**A21   Restrictions on enforcement and legal proceedings**

(1) During a moratorium—

(a) a landlord or other person to whom rent is payable may not exercise a right of forfeiture by peaceable re-entry in relation to premises let to the company, except with the permission of the court,

(c) no steps may be taken to enforce any security over the company's property except—

(i) steps to enforce a collateral security charge (within the meaning of the Financial Markets and Insolvency (Settlement Finality) Regulations 1999 (S.I. 1999/2979)),

(ii) steps to enforce security created or otherwise arising under a financial collateral arrangement (within the meaning of regulation 3 of the Financial Collateral Arrangements (No. 2) Regulations 2003 ..., or

(iii) steps taken with the permission of the court,

(d) no steps may be taken to repossess goods in the company's possession under any hire-purchase agreement, except with the permission of the court, and

(e) no legal process (including legal proceedings, execution, distress or diligence) may be instituted, carried out or continued against the company or its property except—

(i) employment tribunal proceedings or any legal process arising out of such proceedings,

(ii) proceedings, not within sub-paragraph (i), involving a claim between an employer and a worker, or

(iii) a legal process instituted, carried out or continued with the permission of the court.

(2) An application may not be made for permission under subsection (1) for the purposes of enforcing a pre-moratorium debt for which the company has a payment holiday during the moratorium.

(3) An application may not be made for permission under subsection (1)(c), (d) or (e) with a view to obtaining—

(a) the crystallisation of a floating charge, or

(b) the imposition, by virtue of provision in an instrument creating a floating charge, of any restriction on the disposal of any property of the company.

(4) Permission of the court under subsection (1) may be given subject to conditions.]

[**A22   Floating charges**

(1) This section applies where there is an uncrystallised floating charge on the property of a company for which a moratorium is in force.

(2) During the moratorium, the holder of the floating charge may not give any notice which would have the effect of—

(a) causing the floating charge to crystallise, or

(b) causing the imposition, by virtue of provision in the instrument creating the charge, of any restriction on the disposal of property of the company.]

[**A23   Enforcement of security granted during moratorium**

(1) Security granted by a company during a moratorium in relation to the company may be enforced only if the monitor consented to the grant of security under section A26.]

[**A25   Restrictions on obtaining credit**

(1) During a moratorium, the company may not obtain credit to the extent of £500 or more from a person unless the person has been informed that a moratorium is in force in relation to the company.

(2) The reference to the company obtaining credit includes—

    (a) the company entering into a conditional sale agreement in accordance with which goods are to be sold to the company,

    (b) the company entering into any other form of hire-purchase agreement under which goods are to be bailed (in Scotland, hired) to the company, and

    (c) the company being paid in advance (whether in money or otherwise) for the supply of goods or services.]

[A26   Restrictions on grant of security etc

(1) During a moratorium, the company may grant security over its property only if the monitor consents.

(2) The monitor may give consent under subsection (1) only if the monitor thinks that the grant of security will support the rescue of the company as a going concern.]

[A27   Prohibition on entering into market contracts etc

(1) If a company enters into a transaction to which this section applies during a moratorium for the company—

    (a) the company commits an offence, and

    (b) any officer of the company who without reasonable excuse authorised or permitted the company to enter into the transaction commits an offence.

(2) A company enters into a transaction to which this section applies if it—

    (a) enters into a market contract,

    (b) enters into a financial collateral arrangement,

    (c) gives a transfer order,

    (d) grants a market charge or a system-charge, or

    (e) provides any collateral security.]

[A28   Restrictions on payment of certain pre-moratorium debts

(1) During a moratorium, the company may make one or more relevant payments to a person that (in total) exceed the specified maximum amount only if—

    (a) the monitor consents,

    (b) the payment is in pursuance of a court order, or

    (c) the payment is required by section A31(3) or A32(3).

(2) In subsection (1)—

'relevant payments' means payments in respect of pre-moratorium debts for which the company has a payment holiday during the moratorium (see section A18);

'specified maximum amount' means an amount equal to the greater of—

    (a) £5000, and

    (b) 1% of the value of the debts and other liabilities owed by the company to its unsecured creditors when the moratorium began, to the extent that the amount of such debts and liabilities can be ascertained at that time.

(3) The monitor may give consent under subsection (1)(a) only if the monitor thinks that it will support the rescue of the company as a going concern.]

[A29   Restrictions on disposal of property

(1) During a moratorium, the company may dispose of its property only if authorised by sub-section (2) or (5).

(2) In the case of property that is not subject to a security interest, the company may dispose of the property if—

    (a) the disposal is made in the ordinary way of the company's business,

    (b) the monitor consents, or

    (c) the disposal is in pursuance of a court order.

(3) The monitor may give consent under subsection (2)(b) only if the monitor thinks that it will support the rescue of the company as a going concern.]

[A30 Restrictions on disposal of hire-purchase property

(1) During a moratorium, the company may dispose of any goods in the possession of the company under a hire-purchase agreement only if the disposal is in accordance with—

(a) section A32(1), or

(b) the terms of the agreement.]

[A31 Disposal of charged property free from charge

(1) During a moratorium, the company may, with the permission of the court, dispose of property which is subject to a security interest as if it were not subject to the security interest.

(2) The court may give permission under subsection (1) only if the court thinks that it will support the rescue of the company as a going concern.

(3) Where the court gives permission under subsection (1) other than in relation to a floating charge, the company must apply the following towards discharging the sums secured—

(a) the net proceeds of disposal of the property, and

(b) any money required to be added to the net proceeds so as to produce the amount determined by the court as the net amount which would be realised on a sale of the property in the open market by a willing vendor.

(4) Where the permission relates to two or more security interests, the condition in subsection (3) requires the application of money in the order of the priorities of the security interests.

(5) Where property subject to a floating charge is disposed of under subsection (1), the holder of the floating charge has the same priority in respect of acquired property as they had in respect of the property disposed of.

(6) In subsection (5) acquired property means property of the company which directly or indirectly represents the property disposed of.

(7) Where the court makes an order giving permission under subsection (1), the directors must, within the period of 14 days beginning with the date of the order, send a copy of it to the registrar of companies.]

[A32 Disposal of hire-purchase property

(1) During a moratorium, the company may, with the permission of the court, dispose of goods which are in the possession of the company under a hire-purchase agreement as if all of the rights of the owner under the agreement were vested in the company.

(2) The court may give permission under subsection (1) only if the court thinks that it will support the rescue of the company as a going concern.

(3) Where the court gives permission under subsection (1), the company must apply the following towards discharging the sums payable under the hire-purchase agreement—

(a) the net proceeds of disposal of the goods, and

(b) any additional money required to be added to the net proceeds so as to produce the amount determined by the court as the net amount which would be realised on a sale of the goods in the open market by a willing vendor.]

[A33 Contravention of certain requirements imposed under this Chapter [ss A18–A33]

The fact that a company contravenes section A19 or any of sections A25 to A32 does not—

(a) make any transaction void or unenforceable, or

(b) affect the validity of any other thing.

[A34 Status of monitor

The monitor in relation to a moratorium is an officer of the court.]

[A35 Monitoring

(1) During a moratorium, the monitor must monitor the company's affairs for the purpose of forming a view as to whether it remains likely that the moratorium will result in the rescue of the company as a going concern.]

[A42 Challenge to monitor's actions

(1) Any of the persons specified below may apply to the court on the ground that an act, omission or decision of the monitor during a moratorium has unfairly harmed the interests of the applicant.

(2) The persons who may apply are—

(a) a creditor, director or member of the company, or

(b) any other person affected by the moratorium.

(3) An application under subsection (1) may be made during the moratorium or after it has ended.

(4) On an application under subsection (1) the court may—

(a) confirm, reverse or modify any act or decision of the monitor,

(b) give the monitor directions, or

(c) make such other order as it thinks fit (but may not, under this paragraph, order the monitor to pay any compensation).]

[A44 Challenge to directors' actions

(1) A creditor or member of a company may apply to the court for an order under this section on the ground that—

(a) during a moratorium, the company's affairs, business and property are being or have been managed by the directors in a manner which has unfairly harmed the interests of its creditors or members generally or of some part of its creditors or members (including at least the applicant), or

(b) any actual or proposed act or omission of the directors during a moratorium causes or would cause such harm.

(3) On an application under subsection (1) the court may make such order as it thinks fit.]

[A52 Void provisions in floating charge documents

(1) A provision in an instrument creating a floating charge is void if it provides for the obtaining of a moratorium, or anything done with a view to obtaining a moratorium, to be—

(a) an event causing the floating charge to crystallise,

(b) an event causing restrictions which would not otherwise apply to be imposed on the disposal of property by the company, or

(c) a ground for the appointment of a receiver.

(4) Subsection (1) does not apply to a provision in an instrument creating a floating charge that is—

(a) a collateral security (as defined by section A27);

(b) a market charge (as defined by section A27);

(c) a security financial collateral arrangement (within the meaning of regulation 3 of the Financial Collateral Arrangements (No. 2) Regulations 2003 . . .);

(d) a system-charge (as defined by section A27).]

[8 Administration

Schedule B1 to this Act (which makes provision about the administration of companies) shall have effect.]

40 Payment of debts out of assets subject to floating charge

(1) The following applies, in the case of a company, where a receiver is appointed on behalf of the holders of any debentures of the company secured by a charge which, as created, was a floating charge.

(2) If the company is not at the time in course of being wound up, its preferential debts (within the meaning given to that expression by section 386 in Part XII) shall be paid out of the assets coming to the hands of the receiver in priority to any claims for principal or interest in respect of the debentures.

(3) Payments made under this section shall be recouped, as far as may be, out of the assets of the company available for payment of general creditors.

[72A Floating charge holder not to appoint administrative receiver

(1) The holder of a qualifying floating charge in respect of a company's property may not appoint an administrative receiver of the company.

(6) This section is subject to the exceptions specified in sections 72B to 72G.]

127   Avoidance of property dispositions, etc.

[(1)] In a winding up by the court, any disposition of the company's property, and any transfer of shares, or alteration in the status of the company's members, made after the commencement of the winding up is, unless the court otherwise orders, void.

[(2) This section has no effect in respect of anything done by an administrator of a company while a winding-up petition is suspended under paragraph 40 of Schedule B1.]

[(3) This section has no effect in respect of anything done during a moratorium under Part A1, or during a period mentioned in section 5(4)(a) following the end of a moratorium, where the winding-up order was made on a petition presented before the moratorium begins, unless the petition was presented under section 367 of the Financial Services and Markets Act 2000 on the ground mentioned in section 367(3)(b) of that Act.]

175   Preferential debts (general provision)

(1) In a winding up the company's preferential debts [...] shall be paid in priority to all other debts [after the payment of—

(a) any liabilities to which section 174A applies, and

(b) expenses of the winding up.]

[(1A) Ordinary preferential debts rank equally among themselves . . . and shall be paid in full, unless the assets are insufficient to meet them, in which case they abate in equal proportions.]

[(1B) Secondary preferential debts rank equally among themselves after the ordinary preferential debts and shall be paid in full, unless the assets are insufficient to meet them, in which case they abate in equal proportions.]

(2) Preferential debts—

[...]

(b) so far as the assets of the company available for payment of general creditors are insufficient to meet them, have priority over the claims of holders of debentures secured by, or holders of, any floating charge created by the company, and shall be paid accordingly out of any property comprised in or subject to that charge.

[(3) In this section 'preferential debts', 'ordinary preferential debts' and 'secondary preferential debts' each has the meaning given in section 386 in Part 12.]

[176ZA   Payment of expenses of winding up (England and Wales)

(1) The expenses of winding up in England and Wales, so far as the assets of the company available for payment of general creditors are insufficient to meet them, have priority over any claims to property comprised in or subject to any floating charge created by the company and shall be paid out of any such property accordingly.

(2) In subsection (1)—

(a) the reference to assets of the company available for payment of general creditors does not include any amount made available under section 176A(2)(a);

(b) the reference to claims to property comprised in or subject to a floating charge is to the claims of—

(i)   the holders of debentures secured by, or holders of, the floating charge, and

(ii) any preferential creditors entitled to be paid out of that property in priority to them.

(3) Provision may be made by rules restricting the application of subsection (1), in such circumstances as may be prescribed, to expenses authorised or approved—

(a) by the holders of debentures secured by, or holders of, the floating charge and by any preferential creditors entitled to be paid in priority to them, or

(b) by the court.

(4) References in this section to the expenses of the winding up are to all expenses properly incurred in the winding up, including the remuneration of the liquidator.]

[176A   Share of assets for unsecured creditors

(1) This section applies where a floating charge relates to property of a company—

(a) which has gone into liquidation,

    (b) which is in administration,

    (c) of which there is a provisional liquidator, or

    (d) of which there is a receiver.

(2) The liquidator, administrator or receiver—

    (a) shall make a prescribed part of the company's net property available for the satisfaction of unsecured debts, and

    (b) shall not distribute that part to the proprietor of a floating charge except in so far as it exceeds the amount required for the satisfaction of unsecured debts.

(3) Subsection (2) shall not apply to a company if—

    (a) the company's net property is less than the prescribed minimum, and

    (b) the liquidator, administrator or receiver thinks that the cost of making a distribution to unsecured creditors would be disproportionate to the benefits.

(4) Subsection (2) shall also not apply to a company if or in so far as it is disapplied by—

    (a) a voluntary arrangement in respect of the company, or

    (b) a compromise or arrangement agreed under section 425 of the Companies Act (compromise with creditors and members).

(5) Subsection (2) shall also not apply to a company if—

    (a) the liquidator, administrator or receiver applies to the court for an order under this subsection on the ground that the cost of making a distribution to unsecured creditors would be disproportionate to the benefits, and

    (b) the court orders that subsection (2) shall not apply.

(6) In subsections (2) and (3) a company's net property is the amount of its property which would, but for this section, be available for satisfaction of claims of holders of debentures secured by, or holders of, any floating charge created by the company.

(7) An order under subsection (2) prescribing part of a company's net property may, in particular, provide for its calculation—

    (a) as a percentage of the company's net property, or

    (b) as an aggregate of different percentages of different parts of the company's net property.

(8) An order under this section—

    (a) must be made by statutory instrument, and

    (b) shall be subject to annulment pursuant to a resolution of either House of Parliament.

(9) In this section—

'floating charge' means a charge which is a floating charge on its creation and which is created after the first order under subsection (2)(a) comes into force, and

'prescribed' means prescribed by order by the Secretary of State.

(10) An order under this section may include transitional or incidental provision.]

213 Fraudulent trading

(1) If in the course of the winding up of a company it appears that any business of the company has been carried on with intent to defraud creditors of the company or creditors of any other person, or for any fraudulent purpose, the following has effect.

(2) The court, on the application of the liquidator may declare that any persons who were knowingly parties to the carrying on of the business in the manner above-mentioned are to be liable to make such contributions (if any) to the company's assets as the court thinks proper.

238 Transactions at an undervalue (England and Wales)

(1) This section applies in the case of a company where—

    [(a) the company enters administration,]

    (b) the company goes into liquidation;

and 'the office-holder' means the administrator or the liquidator, as the case may be.

(2) Where the company has at a relevant time (defined in section 240) entered into a transaction with any person at an undervalue, the office-holder may apply to the court for an order under this section.

(3) Subject as follows, the court shall, on such an application, make such order as it thinks fit for restoring the position to what it would have been if the company had not entered into that transaction.

(4) For the purposes of this section and section 241, a company enters into a transaction with a person at an undervalue if—

> (a) the company makes a gift to that person or otherwise enters into a transaction with that person on terms that provide for the company to receive no consideration, or
>
> (b) the company enters into a transaction with that person for a consideration the value of which, in money or money's worth, is significantly less than the value, in money or money's worth, of the consideration provided by the company.

(5) The court shall not make an order under this section in respect of a transaction at an undervalue if it is satisfied—

> (a) that the company which entered into the transaction did so in good faith and for the purpose of carrying on its business, and
>
> (b) that at the time it did so there were reasonable grounds for believing that the transaction would benefit the company.

239 Preferences (England and Wales)

(1) This section applies as does section 238.

(2) Where the company has at a relevant time (defined in the next section) given a preference to any person, the office-holder may apply to the court for an order under this section.

(3) Subject as follows, the court shall, on such an application, make such order as it thinks fit for restoring the position to what it would have been if the company had not given that preference.

(4) For the purposes of this section and section 241, a company gives a preference to a person if—

> (a) that person is one of the company's creditors or a surety or guarantor for any of the company's debts or other liabilities, and
>
> (b) the company does anything or suffers anything to be done which (in either case) has the effect of putting that person into a position which, in the event of the company going into insolvent liquidation, will be better than the position he would have been in if that thing had not been done.

(5) The court shall not make an order under this section in respect of a preference given to any person unless the company which gave the preference was influenced in deciding to give it by a desire to produce in relation to that person the effect mentioned in subsection (4)(b).

(6) A company which has given a preference to a person connected with the company (otherwise than by reason only of being its employee) at the time the preference was given is presumed, unless the contrary is shown, to have been influenced in deciding to give it by such a desire as is mentioned in subsection (5).

(7) The fact that something has been done in pursuance of the order of a court does not, without more, prevent the doing or suffering of that thing from constituting the giving of a preference.

240 'Relevant time' under ss. 238, 239

. . .

241 Orders under ss. 238, 239

(1) Without prejudice to the generality of sections 238(3) and 239(3), an order under either of those sections with respect to a transaction or preference entered into or given by a company may (subject to the next subsection)—

> (a) require any property transferred as part of the transaction, or in connection with the giving of the preference, to be vested in the company,
>
> (b) require any property to be so vested if it represents in any person's hands the application either of the proceeds of sale of property so transferred or of money so transferred,
>
> (c) release or discharge (in whole or in part) any security given by the company,
>
> (d) require any person to pay, in respect of benefits received by him from the company, such sums to the office-holder as the court may direct,

(e) provide for any surety or guarantor whose obligations to any person were released or discharged (in whole or in part) under the transaction, or by the giving of the preference, to be under such new or revived obligations to that person as the court thinks appropriate,

(f) provide for security to be provided for the discharge of any obligation imposed by or arising under the order, for such an obligation to be charged on any property and for the security or charge to have the same priority as a security or charge released or discharged (in whole or in part) under the transaction or by the giving of the preference, and

(g) provide for the extent to which any person whose property is vested by the order in the company, or on whom obligations are imposed by the order, is to be able to prove in the winding up of the company for debts or other liabilities which arose from, or were released or discharged (in whole or in part) under or by, the transaction or the giving of the preference.

(2) An order under section 238 or 239 may affect the property of, or impose any obligation on, any person whether or not he is the person with whom the company in question entered into the transaction or (as the case may be) the person to whom the preference was given; but such an order—

(a) shall not prejudice any interest in property which was acquired from a person other than the company and was acquired [in good faith and for value], or prejudice any interest deriving from such an interest, and

(b) shall not require a person who received a benefit from the transaction or preference [in good faith and for value] to pay a sum to the office-holder, except where that person was a party to the transaction or the payment is to be in respect of a preference given to that person at a time when he was a creditor of the company.

[(2A) Where a person has acquired an interest in property from a person other than the company in question, or has received a benefit from the transaction or preference, and at the time of that acquisition or receipt—

(a) he had notice of the relevant surrounding circumstances and of the relevant proceedings, or

(b) he was connected with, or was an associate of, either the company in question or the person with whom that company entered into the transaction or to whom that company gave the preference,

then, unless the contrary is shown, it shall be presumed for the purposes of paragraph (a) or (as the case may be) paragraph (b) of subsection (2) that the interest was acquired or the benefit was received otherwise than in good faith.]

[(3) For the purposes of subsection (2A)(a), the relevant surrounding circumstances are (as the case may require)—

(a) the fact that the company in question entered into the transaction at an under-value; or

(b) the circumstances which amounted to the giving of the preference by the company in question;

and subsections (3A) to (3C) have effect to determine whether, for those purposes, a person has notice of the relevant proceedings.]

[(3A) Where section 238 or 239 applies by reason of a company's entering administration, a person has notice of the relevant proceedings if he has notice that—

(a) an administration application has been made,

(b) an administration order has been made,

(c) a copy of a notice of intention to appoint an administrator under paragraph 14 or 22 of Schedule B1 has been filed, or

(d) notice of the appointment of an administrator has been filed under paragraph 18 or 29 of that Schedule.

(3B) Where section 238 or 239 applies by reason of a company's going into liquidation at the time when the appointment of an administrator of the company ceases to have effect, a person has notice of the relevant proceedings if he has notice that—

(a) an administration application has been made,

(b) an administration order has been made,

(c) a copy of a notice of intention to appoint an administrator under paragraph 14 or 22 of Schedule B1 has been filed,

(d) notice of the appointment of an administrator has been filed under paragraph 18 or 29 of that Schedule, or

(e) the company has gone into liquidation.]

[(3C) In a case where section 238 or 239 applies by reason of the company in question going into liquidation at any other time, a person has notice of the relevant proceedings if he has notice—

(a) where the company goes into liquidation on the making of a winding-up order, of the fact that the petition on which the winding-up order is made has been presented or of the fact that the company has gone into liquidation;

(b) in any other case, of the fact that the company has gone into liquidation.]

(4) The provisions of sections 238 to 241 apply without prejudice to the availability of any other remedy, even in relation to a transaction or preference which the company had no power to enter into or give.

244   Extortionate credit transactions

(1) This section applies as does section 238, and where the company is, or has been, a party to a transaction for, or involving, the provision of credit to the company.

(2) The court may, on the application of the office-holder, make an order with respect to the transaction if the transaction is or was extortionate and was entered into in the period of 3 years ending with [the day on which the company entered administration or went into liquidation.]

(3) For the purposes of this section a transaction is extortionate if, having regard to the risk accepted by the person providing the credit—

(a) the terms of it are or were such as to require grossly exorbitant payments to be made (whether unconditionally or in certain contingencies) in respect of the provision of the credit, or

(b) it otherwise grossly contravened ordinary principles of fair dealing;

and it shall be presumed, unless the contrary is proved, that a transaction with respect to which an application is made under this section is or, as the case may be, was extortionate.

(4) An order under this section with respect to any transaction may contain such one or more of the following as the court thinks fit, that is to say—

(a) provision setting aside the whole or part of any obligation created by the transaction,

(b) provision otherwise varying the terms of the transaction or varying the terms on which any security for the purposes of the transaction is held,

(c) provision requiring any person who is or was a party to the transaction to pay to the office-holder any sums paid to that person, by virtue of the transaction, by the company,

(d) provision requiring any person to surrender to the office-holder any property held by him as security for the purposes of the transaction,

(e) provision directing accounts to be taken between any persons.

(5) The powers conferred by this section are exercisable in relation to any transaction concurrently with any powers exercisable in relation to that transaction as a transaction at an undervalue or under section 242 (gratuitous alienations in Scotland).

245   Avoidance of certain floating charges

(1) This section applies as does section 238, but applies to Scotland as well as to England and Wales.

(2) Subject as follows, a floating charge on the company's undertaking or property created at a relevant time is invalid except to the extent of the aggregate of—

(a) the value of so much of the consideration for the creation of the charge as consists of money paid, or goods or services supplied, to the company at the same time as, or after, the creation of the charge,

(b) the value of so much of that consideration as consists of the discharge or reduction, at the same time as, or after, the creation of the charge, of any debt of the company, and

(c) the amount of such interest (if any) as is payable on the amount falling within paragraph (a) or (b) in pursuance of any agreement under which the money was so paid, the goods or services were so supplied or the debt was so discharged or reduced.

(3) Subject to the next subsection, the time at which a floating charge is created by a company is a relevant time for the purposes of this section if the charge is created—

(a) in the case of a charge which is created in favour of a person who is connected with the company, at a time in the period of 2 years ending with the onset of insolvency,

(b) in the case of a charge which is created in favour of any other person, at a time in the period of 12 months ending with the onset of insolvency,

(c) in either case, at a time between the making of an administration application in respect of the company and the making of an administration order on that application, or

(d) in either case, at a time between the filing with the court of a copy of notice of intention to appoint an administrator under paragraph 14 or 22 of Schedule B1 and the making of an appointment under that paragraph.

(4) Where a company creates a floating charge at a time mentioned in subsection (3)(b) and the person in favour of whom the charge is created is not connected with the company, that time is not a relevant time for the purposes of this section unless the company—

(a) is at that time unable to pay its debts within the meaning of section 123 in Chapter VI of Part IV, or

(b) becomes unable to pay its debts within the meaning of that section in consequence of the transaction under which the charge is created.

(5) For the purposes of subsection (3), the onset of insolvency is—

[(a) in a case where this section applies by reason of an administrator of a company being appointed by administration order, the date on which the administration application is made,

(b) in a case where this section applies by reason of an administrator of a company being appointed under paragraph 14 or 22 of Schedule B1 following filing with the court of a copy of notice of intention to appoint under that paragraph, the date on which the copy of the notice is filed,

(c) in a case where this section applies by reason of an administrator of a company being appointed otherwise than as mentioned in paragraph (a) or (b), the date on which the appointment takes effect, and

(d) in a case where this section applies by reason of a company going into liquidation, the date of the commencement of the winding up.]

(6) For the purposes of subsection (2)(a) the value of any goods or services supplied by way of consideration for a floating charge is the amount in money which at the time they were supplied could reasonably have been expected to be obtained for supplying the goods or services in the ordinary course of business and on the same terms (apart from the consideration) as those on which they were supplied to the company.

251   Expressions used generally

In this Group of Parts, except in so far as the context otherwise requires—. . .

'administrative receiver' means—

(a) an administrative receiver as defined by section 29(2) in Chapter I of Part III, or

(b) a receiver appointed under section 51 in Chapter II of that Part in a case where the whole (or substantially the whole) of the company's property is attached by the floating charge;

['agent' does not include a person's counsel acting as such;]

['books and papers' and 'books or papers' includes accounts, deeds, writing and documents;]

'business day' means any day other than a Saturday, a Sunday, Christmas Day, Good Friday or a day which is a bank holiday in any part of Great Britain;

'chattel leasing agreement' means an agreement for the bailment or, in Scotland, the hiring of goods which is capable of subsisting for more than 3 months;

'contributory' has the meaning given by section 79;

['the court', in relation to a company, means a court having jurisdiction to wind up the company;]

'director' includes any person occupying the position of director, by whatever named called;

['document' includes summons, notice, order and other legal process, and registers;]

'floating charge' means a charge which, as created, was a floating charge and includes a floating charge within section 462 of the Companies Act (Scottish floating charges);

['the Gazette' means—

    (a) as respects companies registered in England and Wales, the London Gazette;

    (b) as respects companies registered in Scotland, the Edinburgh Gazette;]

'office copy', in relation to Scotland, means a copy certified by the clerk of court;

['officer', in relation to a body corporate, includes a director, manager or secretary;]

'the official rate', in relation to interest, means the rate payable under section 189(4);

'prescribed' means prescribed by the rules;

'receiver', in the expression 'receiver or manager', does not include a receiver appointed under section 51 in Chapter II of Part III;

'retention of title agreement' means an agreement for the sale of goods to a company, being an agreement—

    (a) which does not constitute a charge on the goods, but

    (b) under which, if the seller is not paid and the company is wound up, the seller will have priority over all other creditors of the company as respects the goods or any property representing the goods;

'the rules' means rules under section 411 in Part XV; and

'shadow director', in relation to a company, means a person in accordance with whose directions or instructions the directors of the company are accustomed to act (but so that a person is not deemed a shadow director by reason only that the directors act on advice given by him in a professional capacity);

and any expression for whose interpretation provision is made by Part XXVI of the Companies Act, other than an expression defined above in this section, is to be constructed in accordance with that provision.

344 Avoidance of general assignment of book debts

(1) The following applies where a person engaged in any business makes a general assignment to another person of his existing or future book debts, or any class of them, and is subsequently [made] bankrupt.

(2) The assignment is void against the trustee of the bankrupt's estate as regards book debts which were not paid before the [making of the bankruptcy application or (as the case may be) the] presentation of the bankruptcy petition, unless the assignment has been registered under the Bills of Sale Act 1878.

(3) For the purpose of subsections (1) and (2)—

    (a) 'assignment' includes an assignment by way of security or charge on book debts, and

    (b) 'general assignment' does not include—

        (i) an assignment of book debts due at the date of the assignment from specified debtors or of debts becoming due under specified contracts, or

        (ii) an assignment of book debts included either in a transfer of a business made in good faith and for value or in an assignment of assets for the benefit of creditors generally.

(4) For the purposes of registration under the Act of 1878 an assignment of book debts is to be treated as if it were a bill of sale given otherwise than by way of security for the payment of a sum

of money; and the provisions of that Act with respect to the registration of bills of sale apply accordingly with such necessary modifications as may be made by rules under that Act.

423 Transactions defrauding creditors

(1) This section relates to transactions entered into at an undervalue; and a person enters into such a transaction with another person if—

   (a) he makes a gift to the other person or he otherwise enters into a transaction with the other on terms that provide for him to receive no consideration;

   (b) he enters into a transaction with the other in consideration of marriage [or the formation of a civil partnership]; or

   (c) he enters into a transaction with the other for a consideration the value of which, in money or money's worth, is significantly less than the value, in money or money's worth, of the consideration provided by himself.

(2) Where a person has entered into such a transaction, the court may, if satisfied under the next subsection, make such order as it thinks fit for—

   (a) restoring the position to what it would have been if the transaction had not been entered into, and

   (b) protecting the interests of persons who are victims of the transaction.

(3) In the case of a person entering into such a transaction, an order shall only be made if the court is satisfied that it was entered into by him for the purpose—

   (a) of putting assets beyond the reach of a person who is making, or may at some time make, a claim against him, or

   (b) of otherwise prejudicing the interests of such a person in relation to the claim which he is making or may make.

(5) In relation to a transaction at an undervalue, references here and below to a victim of the transaction are to a person who is, or is capable of being, prejudiced by it; and in the following two sections the person entering into the transaction is referred to as 'the debtor'.

425 Provision which may be made by order under s. 423

(1) Without prejudice to the generality of section 423, an order made under that section with respect to a transaction may (subject as follows)—

   (a) require any property transferred as part of the transaction to be vested in any person, either absolutely or for the benefit of all the persons on whose behalf the application for the order is treated as made;

   (b) require any property to be so vested if it represents, in any person's hands, the application either of the proceeds of sale of property so transferred or of money so transferred;

   (c) release or discharge (in whole or in part) any security given by the debtor;

   (d) require any person to pay to any other person in respect of benefits received from the debtor such sums as the court may direct;

   (e) provide for any surety or guarantor whose obligations to any person were released or discharged (in whole or in part) under the transaction to be under such new or revived obligations as the court thinks appropriate;

   (f) provide for security to be provided for the discharge of any obligation imposed by or arising under the order, for such an obligation to be charged on any property and for such security or charge to have the same priority as a security or charge released or discharged (in whole or in part) under the transaction.

(2) An order under section 423 may affect the property of, or impose any obligation on, any person whether or not he is the person with whom the debtor entered into the transaction; but such an order—

   (a) shall not prejudice any interest in property which was acquired from a person other than the debtor and was acquired in good faith, for value and without notice of the relevant circumstances, or prejudice any interest deriving from such an interest, and

   (b) shall not require a person who received a benefit from the transaction in good faith, for value and without notice of the relevant circumstances to pay any sum unless he was a party to the transaction.

   (3) For the purposes of this section the relevant circumstances in relation to a transaction are the circumstances by virtue of which an order under section 423 may be made in respect of the transaction.

   (4) In this section 'security' means any mortgage, charge, lien or other security.

[SCHEDULE B1

ADMINISTRATION

NATURE OF ADMINISTRATION

Administration

1.—(1) For the purposes of this Act 'administrator' of a company means a person appointed under this Schedule to manage the company's affairs, business and property.

   (2) For the purposes of this Act—

   (a) a company is 'in administration' while the appointment of an administrator of the company has effect,

   (b) a company 'enters administration' when the appointment of an administrator takes effect,

   (c) a company ceases to be in administration when the appointment of an administrator of the company ceases to have effect in accordance with this Schedule, and

   (d) a company does not cease to be in administration merely because an administrator vacates office (by reason of resignation, death or otherwise) or is removed from office.

2. A person may be appointed as administrator of a company—

   (a) by administration order of the court under paragraph 10,

   (b) by the holder of a floating charge under paragraph 14, or

   (c) by the company or its directors under paragraph 22.

Purpose of administration

3.—(1) The administrator of a company must perform his functions with the objective of—

   (a) rescuing the company as a going concern, or

   (b) achieving a better result for the company's creditors as a whole than would be likely if the company were wound up (without first being in administration), or

   (c) realising property in order to make a distribution to one or more secured or preferential creditors.

   (2) Subject to sub-paragraph (4), the administrator of a company must perform his functions in the interests of the company's creditors as a whole.

   (3) The administrator must perform his functions with the objective specified in sub-paragraph (1)(a) unless he thinks either—

   (a) that it is not reasonably practicable to achieve that objective, or

   (b) that the objective specified in sub-paragraph (1)(b) would achieve a better result for the company's creditors as a whole.

   (4) The administrator may perform his functions with the objective specified in sub-paragraph (1)(c) only if—

   (a) he thinks that it is not reasonably practicable to achieve either of the objectives specified in sub-paragraph (1)(a) and (b), and

   (b) he does not unnecessarily harm the interests of the creditors of the company as a whole.

4. The administrator of a company must perform his functions as quickly and efficiently as is reasonably practicable.

Status of administrator

5. An administrator is an officer of the court (whether or not he is appointed by the court).

APPOINTMENT OF ADMINISTRATOR BY COURT

Administration order

10. An administration order is an order appointing a person as the administrator of a company.

Conditions for making order

11. The court may make an administration order in relation to a company only if satisfied—
  (a) that the company is or is likely to become unable to pay its debts, and
  (b) that the administration order is reasonably likely to achieve the purpose of administration.

Administration application

12.—(1) An application to the court for an administration order in respect of a company (an 'administration application') may be made only by—
  (a) the company,
  (b) the directors of the company,
  (c) one or more creditors of the company,
  (d) the [designated officer] for a magistrates' court in the exercise of the power conferred by section 87A of the Magistrates' Courts Act 1980 (c. 43)(fine imposed on company), or
  (e) a combination of persons listed in paragraphs (a) to (d).

APPOINTMENT OF ADMINISTRATOR BY HOLDER OF FLOATING CHARGE

Power to appoint

14.—(1) The holder of a qualifying floating charge in respect of a company's property may appoint an administrator of the company.

(2) For the purposes of sub-paragraph (1) a floating charge qualifies if created by an instrument which—
  (a) states that this paragraph applies to the floating charge,
  (b) purports to empower the holder of the floating charge to appoint an administrator of the company,
  (c) purports to empower the holder of the floating charge to make an appointment which would be the appointment of an administrative receiver within the meaning given by section 29(2), or
  (d) purports to empower the holder of a floating charge in Scotland to appoint a receiver who on appointment would be an administrative receiver.

(3) For the purposes of sub-paragraph (1) a person is the holder of a qualifying floating charge in respect of a company's property if he holds one or more debentures of the company secured—
  (a) by a qualifying floating charge which relates to the whole or substantially the whole of the company's property,
  (b) by a number of qualifying floating charges which together relate to the whole or substantially the whole of the company's property, or
  (c) by charges and other forms of security which together relate to the whole or substantially the whole of the company's property and at least one of which is a qualifying floating charge.

Restrictions on power to appoint

16. An administrator may not be appointed under paragraph 14 while a floating charge on which the appointment relies is not enforceable.

17. An administrator of a company may not be appointed under paragraph 14 if—

(a) a provisional liquidator of the company has been appointed under section 135, or

(b) an administrative receiver of the company is in office.

EFFECT OF ADMINISTRATION

Dismissal of pending winding-up petition

40.—(1) A petition for the winding up of a company—

(a) shall be dismissed on the making of an administration order in respect of the company, and

(b) shall be suspended while the company is in administration following an appointment under paragraph 14.

(2) Sub-paragraph (1)(b) does not apply to a petition presented under—

(a)   section 124A (public interest), or

[(aa) section 124B (SEs),]

(b)   section 367 of the Financial Services and Markets Act 2000 (c. 8) (petition by [Financial Conduct Authority or Prudential Regulation Authority]).

(3) Where an administrator becomes aware that a petition was presented under a provision referred to in sub-paragraph (2) before his appointment, he shall apply to the court for directions under paragraph 63.

Dismissal of administrative or other receiver

41.—(1) When an administration order takes effect in respect of a company any administrative receiver of the company shall vacate office.

(2) Where a company is in administration, any receiver of part of the company's property shall vacate office if the administrator requires him to.

Moratorium on insolvency proceedings

42.—(1) This paragraph applies to a company in administration.

(2) No resolution may be passed for the winding up of the company.

(3) No order may be made for the winding up of the company.

(4) Sub-paragraph (3) does not apply to an order made on a petition presented under—

(a)   section 124A (public interest), or

[(aa) section 124B (SEs),]

(b)   section 367 of the Financial Services and Markets Act 2000 (c. 8) (petition by [Financial Conduct Authority or Prudential Regulation Authority]).

(5) If a petition presented under a provision referred to in sub-paragraph (4) comes to the attention of the administrator, he shall apply to the court for directions under paragraph 63.

Moratorium on other legal process

43.—(1) This paragraph applies to a company in administration.

(2) No step may be taken to enforce security over the company's property except—

(a) with the consent of the administrator, or

(b) with the permission of the court.

. . .

Publicity

45.—[(1) While a company is in administration, every business document issued by or on behalf of the company or the administrator, and all the company's websites, must state—

(a) the name of the administrator, and

(b) that the affairs, business and property of the company are being managed by the administrator.]

PROCESS OF ADMINISTRATION

Administrator's proposals

49.—(1) The administrator of a company shall make a statement setting out proposals for achieving the purpose of administration.

FUNCTIONS OF ADMINISTRATOR

General powers

59.—(1) The administrator of a company may do anything necessary or expedient for the management of the affairs, business and property of the company.

(3) A person who deals with the administrator of a company in good faith and for value need not inquire whether the administrator is acting within his powers.

60. The administrator of a company has the powers specified in Schedule 1 to this Act.

Administrator as agent of company

69. In exercising his functions under this Schedule the administrator of a company acts as its agent.

Charged property: floating charge

70.—(1) The administrator of a company may dispose of or take action relating to property which is subject to a floating charge as if it were not subject to the charge.

(2) Where property is disposed of in reliance on sub-paragraph (1) the holder of the floating charge shall have the same priority in respect of acquired property as he had in respect of the property disposed of.

(3) In sub-paragraph (2) 'acquired property' means property of the company which directly or indirectly represents the property disposed of.

Charged property: non-floating charge

71.—(1) The court may by order enable the administrator of a company to dispose of property which is subject to a security (other than a floating charge) as if it were not subject to the security.

(2) An order under sub-paragraph (1) may be made only—

(a) on the application of the administrator, and

(b) where the court thinks that disposal of the property would be likely to promote the purpose of administration in respect of the company.

(3) An order under this paragraph is subject to the condition that there be applied towards discharging the sums secured by the security—

(a) the net proceeds of disposal of the property, and

(b) any additional money required to be added to the net proceeds so as to produce the amount determined by the court as the net amount which would be realised on a sale of the property at market value.

(4) If an order under this paragraph relates to more than one security, application of money under sub-paragraph (3) shall be in the order of the priorities of the securities.

(5) An administrator who makes a successful application for an order under this paragraph shall send a copy of the order to the registrar of companies before the end of the period of 14 days starting with the date of the order.

(6) An administrator commits an offence if he fails to comply with sub-paragraph (5) without reasonable excuse.

Hire-purchase property

72.—(1) The court may by order enable the administrator of a company to dispose of goods which are in the possession of the company under a hire-purchase agreement as if all the rights of the owner under the agreement were vested in the company.

Protection for secured or preferential creditor

73.—(1) An administrator's statement of proposals under paragraph 49 may not include any action which—

(a) affects the right of a secured creditor of the company to enforce his security,

(b) would result in a preferential debt of the company being paid otherwise than in priority to its non-preferential debts, or

(c) would result in one preferential creditor of the company being paid a smaller proportion of his debt than another.

(2) Sub-paragraph (1) does not apply to—

(a) action to which the relevant creditor consents,

(b) a proposal for a voluntary arrangement under Part I of this Act (although this sub-paragraph is without prejudice to section 4(3)), or

(c) a proposal for a compromise or arrangement to be sanctioned under [Part 26 or 26A of the Companies Act 2006 (arrangements and reconstructions)].

Consumer Protection Act 1987

(1987, c. 43)

PART I PRODUCT LIABILITY

1 Purpose and construction of Part I

(1) This Part [was enacted] for the purpose of making such provision as [was] necessary in order to comply with the product liability Directive and shall be construed accordingly.

(2) In this Part, except in so far as the context otherwise requires—

'dependant' and 'relative' have the same meaning as they have in, respectively, the Fatal Accidents Act 1976 and the [Damages (Scotland) Act 2011];

'producer', in relation to a product, means—

(a) the person who manufactured it;

(b) in the case of a substance which has not been manufactured but has been won or abstracted, the person who won or abstracted it;

(c) in the case of a product which has not been manufactured, won or abstracted but essential characteristics of which are attributable to an industrial or other process having been carried out (for example, in relation to agricultural produce), the person who carried out that process;

'product', means any goods or electricity and (subject to subsection (3) below) includes a product which is comprised in another product, whether by virtue of being a component part or raw material or otherwise; and

'the product liability Directive' means the Directive of the Council of the European Communities, dated 25th July 1985, (No. 85/374/EEC) on the approximation of the laws, regulations and administrative provisions of the member States concerning liability for defective products.

(3) For the purposes of this Part a person who supplies any product in which products are comprised, whether by virtue of being component parts or raw materials or otherwise, shall not be treated by reason only of his supply of that product as supplying any of the products so comprised.

2 Liability for defective products

(1) Subject to the following provisions of this Part, where any damage is caused wholly or partly by a defect in a product, every person to whom subsection (2) below applies shall be liable for the damage.

(2) This subsection applies to—

(a) the producer of the product;

    (b) any person who, by putting his name on the product or using a trade mark or other distinguishing mark in relation to the product, has held himself out to be the producer of the product;

    (c) any person who has imported the product into [the United Kingdom] in order, in the course of any business of his, to supply it to another.

(3) Subject as aforesaid, where any damage is caused wholly or partly by a defect in a product, any person who supplied the product (whether to the person who suffered the damage, to the producer of any product in which the product in question is comprised or to any other person) shall be liable for the damage if—

    (a) the person who suffered the damage requests the supplier to identify one or more of the persons (whether still in existence or not) to whom subsection (2) above applies in relation to the product;

    (b) that request is made within a reasonable period after the damage occurs and at a time when it is not reasonably practicable for the person making the request to identify all those persons; and

    (c) the supplier fails, within a reasonable period after receiving the request, either to comply with the request or to identify the person who supplied the product to him.

(5) Where two or more persons are liable by virtue of this Part for the same damage, their liability shall be joint and several.

(6) This section shall be without prejudice to any liability arising otherwise than by virtue of this Part.

3   Meaning of 'defect'

(1) Subject to the following provisions of the section, there is a defect in a product for the purposes of this Part if the safety of the product is not such as persons generally are entitled to expect; and for those purposes 'safety', in relation to a product, shall include safety with respect to products comprised in that product and safety in the context of risks of damage to property, as well as in the context of risks of death or personal injury.

(2) In determining for the purposes of subsection (1) above what persons generally are entitled to expect in relation to a product all the circumstances shall be taken into account, including—

    (a) the manner in which, and purposes for which, the product has been marketed, its get-up, the use of any mark in relation to the product and any instructions for, or warnings with respect to, doing or refraining from doing anything with or in relation to the product;

    (b) what might reasonably be expected to be done with or in relation to the product; and

    (c) the time when the product was supplied by its producer to another;

and nothing in this section shall require a defect to be inferred from the fact alone that the safety of a product which is supplied after that time is greater than the safety of the product in question.

4   Defences

(1) In any civil proceedings by virtue of this Part against any person ('the person proceeded against') in respect of a defect in a product it shall be a defence for him to show—

    (a) that the defect is attributable to compliance with any requirement imposed by or under any enactment or with any [retained EU] obligation; or

    (b) that the person proceeded against did not at any time supply the product to another; or

    (c) that the following conditions are satisfied, that is to say—

        (i) that the only supply of the product to another by the person proceeded against was otherwise than in the course of a business of that person's; and

        (ii) that section 2(2) above does not apply to that person or applies to him by virtue only of things done otherwise than with a view to profit; or

    (d) that the defect did not exist in the product at the relevant time; or

    (e) that the state of scientific and technical knowledge at the relevant time was not such that a producer of products of the same description as the product in question might be expected to have discovered the defect if it had existed in his products while they were under his control; or

(f) that the defect—
   (i) constituted a defect in a product ('the subsequent product') in which the product in question had been comprised; and
   (ii) was wholly attributable to the design of the subsequent product or to compliance by the producer of the product in question with instructions given by the producer of the subsequent product.

(2) In this section 'the relevant time', in relation to electricity, means the time at which it was generated, being a time before it was transmitted or distributed, and in relation to any other product, means—
   (a) if the person proceeded against is a person to whom subsection (2) of section 2 above applies in relation to the product, the time when he supplied the product to another;
   (b) if that subsection does not apply to that person in relation to the product, the time when the product was last supplied by a person to whom that subsection does apply in relation to the product.

5   Damage giving rise to liability

(1) Subject to the following provisions of this section, in this Part 'damages' means death or personal injury or any loss of or damage to any property (including land).

(2) A person shall not be liable under section 2 above in respect of any defect in a product for the loss of or any damage to the product itself or for the loss of or any damage to the whole or any part of any product which has been supplied with the product in question comprised in it.

(3) A person shall not be liable under section 2 above for any loss of or damage to any property which, at the time it is lost or damaged, is not—
   (a) of a description of property ordinarily intended for private use, occupation or consumption; and
   (b) intended by the person suffering the loss or damage mainly for his own private use, occupation or consumption.

(4) No damages shall be awarded to any person by virtue of this Part in respect of any loss of or damage to any property if the amount which would fall to be so awarded to that person, apart from this subsection and any liability for interest, does not exceed £275.

(5) In determining for the purposes of this Part who has suffered any loss of or damage to property and when any such loss or damage occurred, the loss or damage shall be regarded as having occurred at the earliest time at which a person with an interest in the property had knowledge of the material facts about the loss or damage.

(6) For the purposes of subsection (5) above the material facts about any loss of or damage to any property are such facts about the loss or damage as would lead a reasonable person with an interest in the property to consider the loss or damage sufficiently serious to justify his instituting proceedings for damages against a defendant who did not dispute liability and was able to satisfy a judgment.

(7) For the purposes of subsection (5) above a person's knowledge includes knowledge which he might reasonably have been expected to acquire—
   (a) from facts observable or ascertainable by him; or
   (b) from facts ascertainable by him with help of appropriate expert advice which it is reasonable for him to seek;
but a person shall not be taken by virtue of this subsection to have knowledge of a fact ascertainable by him only with the help of expert advice unless he has failed to take all reasonable steps to obtain (and, where appropriate, to act on) that advice.

(8) Subsections (5) to (7) above shall not extend to Scotland.

6   Application of certain enactments etc.

(1) Any damage for which a person is liable under section 2 above shall be deemed to have been caused—
   (a) for the purposes of the Fatal Accidents Act 1976, by that person's wrongful act, neglect or default;

    (b) for the purposes of section 3 of the Law Reform (Miscellaneous Provisions) (Scotland) Act 1940 (contribution among joint wrongdoers), by that person's wrongful act or negligent act or omission; . . .

(2) Where—

    (a) a person's death is caused wholly or partly by a defect in a product, or a person dies after suffering damage which has been so caused;

    (b) a request such as mentioned in paragraph (a) of subsection (3) of section 2 above is made to a supplier of the product by that person's personal representatives or, in the case of a person whose death is caused wholly or partly by the defect, by any dependant or relative of that person; and

    (c) the conditions specified in paragraphs (b) and (c) of that subsection are satisfied in relation to that request,

this Part shall have effect for the purposes of the Law Reform (Miscellaneous Provisions) Act 1934, the Fatal Accidents Acts 1976 and the [Damages (Scotland) Act 2011] as if liability of the supplier to that person under that subsection did not depend on that person having requested the supplier to identify certain persons or on the said conditions having been satisfied in relation to a request made by that person.

(3) Section 1 of the Congenital Disabilities (Civil Liability) Act 1976 shall have effect for the purposes of this Part as if—

    (a) a person were answerable to a child in respect of an occurrence caused wholly or partly by a defect in a product if he is or has been liable under section 2 above in respect of any effect of the occurrence on a parent of the child, or would be so liable if the occurrence caused a parent of the child to suffer damage;

    (b) the provisions of this Part relating to liability under section 2 above applied in relation to liability by virtue of paragraph (a) above under the said section 1; and

    (c) subsection (6) of the said section 1 (exclusion of liability) were omitted.

(4) Where any damage is caused partly by a defect in a product and partly by the fault of the person suffering the damage, the Law Reform (Contributory Negligence) Act 1945 and section 5 of the Fatal Accidents Act 1976 (contributory negligence) shall have effect as if the defect were the fault of every person liable by virtue of this Part for the damage caused by the defect.

(5) In subsection (4) above 'fault' has the same meaning as in the said Act of 1945.

(6) Schedule 1 to this Act shall have effect for the purpose of amending the Limitation Act 1980 and the Prescription and Limitation (Scotland) Act 1973 in their application in relation to the bringing of actions by virtue of this Part.

(7) It is hereby declared that liability by virtue of this Part is to be treated as liability in tort for the purposes of any enactment conferring jurisdiction on any court with respect to any matter.

(8) Nothing in this Part shall prejudice the operation of section 12 of the Nuclear Installations Act 1965 (rights to compensation for certain breaches of duties confined to rights under that Act).

7 Prohibition on exclusions from liability

The liability of a person by virtue of this Part to person who has suffered damage caused wholly or partly by a defect in a product, or to a dependant or relative of such a person, shall not be limited or excluded by any contract term, by any notice or by any other provision.

9 Application of Part I to Crown

(1) Subject to subsection (2) below, this Part shall bind the Crown.

(2) The Crown shall not, as regards the Crown's liability by virtue of this Part, be bound by this Part further than the Crown is made liable in tort or in reparation under the Crown Proceedings Act 1947, as that Act has effect from time to time.

PART II CONSUMER SAFETY

11 Safety regulations

(1) The Secretary of State may by regulations under this section ('safety regulations') make such provision as he considers appropriate [. . .] for the purpose of securing—

(a) that goods to which this section applies are safe;

(b) that goods to which this section applies which are unsafe, or would be unsafe in the hands of persons of a particular description, are not made available to persons generally or, as the case may be, to persons of that description, and

(c) that appropriate information is, and inappropriate information is not, provided in relation to goods to which this section applies.

(2) Without prejudice to the generality of subsection (1) above, safety regulations may contain provision—

(a) with respect to the composition or contents, design, construction, finish or packing of goods to which this section applies, with respect to standards for such goods and with respect to other matters relating to such goods;

(b) with respect to the giving, refusal, alteration or cancellation of approvals of such goods, of descriptions of such goods or of standards for such goods;

(c) with respect to the conditions that may be attached to any approval given under the regulations;

(d) for requiring such fees as may be determined by or under the regulations to be paid on the giving or alteration of any approval under the regulations and on the making of an application for such an approval or alteration;

(e) with respect to appeals against refusals, alterations and cancellations of approvals given under the regulations and against the conditions contained in such approvals;

(f) for requiring goods to which this section applies to be approved under the regulations or to conform to the requirements of the regulations or to descriptions or standards specified in or approved by or under the regulations;

(g) with respect to the testing or inspection of goods to which this section applies (including provision for determining the standards to be applied in carrying out any test or inspection);

(h) with respect to the way of dealing with goods of which some or all do not satisfy a test required by or under the regulations or a standard connected with a procedure so required;

(i) for requiring a mark, warning or instruction or any other information relating to goods to be put on or to accompany the goods or to be used or provided in some other manner in relation to the goods, and for securing that inappropriate information is not given in relation to goods either by means of misleading marks or otherwise;

(j) for prohibiting persons from supplying, or from offering to supply, agreeing to supply, exposing for supply or possessing for supply, goods to which this section applies and component parts and raw materials for such goods;

(k) for requiring information to be given to any such person as may be determined by or under the regulations for the purpose of enabling that person to exercise any function conferred on him by the regulations.

(3) Without prejudice as aforesaid, safety regulations may contain provision—

(a) for requiring persons on whom functions are conferred by or under section 27 below to have regard, in exercising their functions so far as relating to any provision of safety regulations, to matters specified in a direction issued by the Secretary of State with respect to that provision;

(b) for securing that a person shall not be guilty of an offence under section 12 below unless it is shown that the goods in question do not conform to a particular standard;

(c) for securing that proceedings for such an offence are not brought in England and Wales except by or with the consent of the Secretary of State or the Director of Public Prosecutions;

(d) for securing that proceedings for such an offence are not brought in Northern Ireland except by or with consent of the Secretary of State or the Director of Public Prosecutions for Northern Ireland;

(e) for enabling a magistrate's court in England and Wales or Northern Ireland to try an information or, in Northern Ireland, a complaint in respect of such an offence if the information was laid or the complaint made within twelve months from the time when the offence was committed;

(f) for enabling summary proceedings for such an offence to be brought in Scotland at any time within twelve months from the time when the offence was committed; and

(g) for determining the persons by whom, and the manner in which, anything required to be done by or under the regulations is to be done.

(4) Safety regulations shall not provide for any contravention of the regulations to be an offence.

(5) Where the Secretary of State proposes to make safety regulations it shall be his duty before he makes them—

(a) to consult such organisations as appear to him to be representative of interests substantially affected by the proposal;

(b) to consult such other persons as he considers appropriate; and

(c) in the case of proposed regulations relating to goods suitable for use at work to consult [the Health and Safety Executive] in relation to the application of the proposed regulations to Great Britain;

but the preceding provisions of this subsection shall not apply in the case of regulations which provide for the regulations to cease to have effect at the end of a period of not more than twelve months beginning with the day on which they come into force and which contain a statement that it appears to the Secretary of State that the need to protect the public requires that the regulations should be made without delay.

(6) The power to make safety regulations shall be exercisable by statutory instrument subject to annulment in pursuance of a resolution of either House of Parliament and shall include power—

(a) to make different provision for different cases; and

(b) to make such supplemental, consequential and transitional provision as the Secretary of State considers appropriate.

(7) This section applies to any goods other than—

(a) growing crops and things comprised in land by virtue of being attached to it;

(b) water, food, feeding stuff and fertiliser;

(c) gas which is, is to be or has been supplied by a person authorised to supply it by or under [section 7A of the Gas Act 1986 (licensing of gas suppliers and gas shippers) or paragraph 5 of Schedule 2A to that Act (supply to very large customers an exception to prohibition on unlicensed activities)];

(d) controlled drugs and licensed medicinal products.

[(e) medical devices.]

[*Note: s 11(7)(e) was not in force on 1 April 2021.*]

12   Offences against the safety regulations

(1) Where safety regulations prohibit a person from supplying or offering or agreeing to supply any goods or from exposing or possessing any goods for supply that person shall be guilty of an offence if he contravenes the prohibition.

(2) Where safety regulations require a person who makes or processes any goods in the course of carrying on a business—

(a) to carry out a particular test or use a particular procedure in connection with the making or processing of the goods with a view to ascertaining whether the goods satisfy any requirements of such regulations; or

(b) to deal or not to deal in a particular way with a quantity of the goods of which the whole or part does not satisfy such a test or does not satisfy standards connected with such a procedure,

that person shall be guilty of an offence if he does not comply with the requirement.

(3) If a person contravenes a provision of safety regulations which prohibits or requires the provision, by means of a mark or otherwise, of information of a particular kind in relation to goods, he shall be guilty of an offence.

(4) Where safety regulations require any person to give information to another for the purpose of enabling that other to exercise any function, that person shall be guilty of an offence if—

(a) he fails without reasonable cause to comply with the requirement; or

(b) in giving the information which is required of him—

(i) he makes any statement which he knows is false in a material particular; or

(ii) he recklessly makes any statement which is false in a material particular.

(5) A person guilty of an offence under this section shall be liable on summary conviction to imprisonment for a term not exceeding six months or to a fine not exceeding level 5 on the standard scale or to both.

13 Prohibition notices and notices to warn

(1) The Secretary of State may—

(a) serve on any person a notice ('a prohibition notice') prohibiting that person, except with the consent of the Secretary of State, from supplying, or from offering to supply, agreeing to supply or possessing for supply, any relevant goods which the Secretary of State considers are unsafe and which are described in the notice;

(b) serve on any person a notice ('a notice to warn') requiring that person at his own expense to publish, in a form and manner and on occasions specified in the notice, a warning about any relevant goods which the Secretary of State considers are unsafe, which that person supplies or has supplied and which are described in the notice.

(2) Schedule 2 to this Act shall have effect with respect to prohibition notices and notices to warn, and the Secretary of State may by regulations make provision specifying the manner in which information is to be given to any person under that Schedule.

(3) A consent given by the Secretary of State for the purposes of a prohibition notice may impose such conditions on the doing of anything for which the consent is required as the Secretary of State considers appropriate.

(4) A person who contravenes a prohibition notice or a notice to warn shall be guilty of an offence and liable on summary conviction to imprisonment for a term not exceeding [three months] or to a fine not exceeding level 5 on the standard scale or to both.

(5) The power to make regulations under subsection (2) above shall be exercisable by statutory instrument subject to annulment in pursuance of a resolution of either House of Parliament and shall include power—

(a) to make different provision for different cases; and

(b) to make such supplemental, consequential and transitional provision as the Secretary of State considers appropriate.

(6) In this section 'relevant goods' means—

(a) in relation to a prohibition notice, any goods to which section 11 above applies; and

(b) in relation to a notice to warn, any goods to which that section applies or any growing crops or things comprised in land by virtue of being attached to it.

[(7) A notice may not be given under this section in respect of any aspect of the safety of goods, or any risk or category of risk associated with goods, concerning which provision is contained in the General Product Safety Regulations 2005.]

14 Suspension notices

(1) Where an enforcement authority has reasonable grounds for suspecting that any safety provision has been contravened in relation to any goods, the authority may serve a notice ('suspension

notice') prohibiting the person on whom it is served, for such period ending not more than six months after the date of the notice as is specified therein, from doing any of the following things without the consent of the authority, that is to say, supplying the goods, offering to supply them, agreeing to supply them or exposing them for supply.

(2) A suspension notice served by an enforcement authority in respect of any goods shall—

(a) describe the goods in a manner sufficient to identify them;

(b) set out the grounds on which the authority suspects that a safety provision has been contravened in relation to the goods, and

(c) state that, and the manner in which, the person on whom the notice is served may appeal against the notice under section 15 below.

(3) A suspension notice served by an enforcement authority for the purpose of prohibiting a person for any period from doing the things mentioned in subsection (1) above in relation to any goods may also require that person to keep the authority informed of the whereabouts throughout that period of any of those goods in which he has an interest.

(4) Where a suspension notice has been served on any person in respect of any goods, no further such notice shall be served on that person in respect of the same goods unless—

(a) proceedings against that person for an offence in respect of a contravention in relation to the goods of a safety provision (not being an offence under this section); or

(b) proceedings for the forfeiture of the goods under section 16 or 17 below, are pending at the end of the period specified in the first-mentioned notice.

(5) A consent given by an enforcement authority for the purposes of subsection (1) above may impose such conditions on the doing of anything for which the consent is required as the authority considers appropriate.

(6) Any person who contravenes a suspension notice shall be guilty of an offence and liable on summary conviction to imprisonment for a term not exceeding [three months] or to a fine not exceeding level 5 on the standard scale or to both.

(7) Where an enforcement authority serves a suspension notice in respect of any goods, the authority shall be liable to pay compensation to any person having an interest in the goods in respect of any loss or damage caused by reason of the service of the notice if—

(a) there has been no contravention in relation to the goods of any safety provision; and

(b) the exercise of the power is not attributable to any neglect or default by that person.

(8) Any disputed question as to the right to or the amount of any compensation payable under this section shall be determined by arbitration or, in Scotland, by a single arbiter appointed, failing agreement between the parties, by the sheriff.

15   Appeals against suspension notices

(1) Any person having an interest in any goods in respect of which a suspension notice is for the time being in force may apply for an order setting aside the notice.

(2) An application under this section may be made—

(a) to any magistrates' court in which proceedings have been brought in England and Wales or Northern Ireland—

(i)   for an offence in respect of a contravention in relation to the goods of any safety provision; or

(ii) for the forfeiture of the goods under section 16 below;

(b) where no such proceedings have been so brought, by way of complaint to a magistrates' court; or

(c) in Scotland, by summary application to the sheriff.

(3) On an application under this section to a magistrates' court in England and Wales or Northern Ireland the court shall make an order setting aside the suspension notice only if the court is satisfied that there has been no contravention in relation to the goods of any safety provision.

(4) On an application under this section to the sheriff he shall make an order setting aside the suspension notice only if he is satisfied that at the date of making the order—

    (a) proceedings for an offence in respect of a contravention in relation to the goods of any safety provision; or

    (b) proceedings for the forfeiture of the goods under section 17 below, have not been brought or, having been brought, have been concluded.

    (5) Any person aggrieved by an order made under this section by a magistrates' court in England and Wales or Northern Ireland, or by a decision of such a court not to make such an order, may appeal against that order or decision—

    (a) in England and Wales, to the Crown Court;

    (b) in Northern Ireland, to the county court;

and an order so made may contain such provision as appears to the court to be appropriate for delaying the coming into force of the order pending the making and determination of any appeal (including any application under section Ill of the Magistrates' Courts Act 1980 or Article 146 of the Magistrates' Courts (Northern Ireland) Order 1981 (statement of case)).

16   Forfeiture: England and Wales and Northern Ireland

    (1) An enforcement authority in England and Wales or Northern Ireland may apply under this section for an order for the forfeiture of any goods on the grounds that there has been a contravention in relation to the goods of a safety provision.

    (2) An application under this section may be made—

    (a) where proceedings have been brought in a magistrates' court for an offence in respect of a contravention in relation to some or all of the goods of any safety provision, to that court;

    (b) where an application with respect to some or all of the goods has been made to a magistrates' court under section 15 above or section 33 below, to that court; and

    (c) where no application for the forfeiture of the goods has been made under paragraph (a) or (b) above, by way of complaint to a magistrates' court.

    (3) On an application under this section the court shall make an order for the forfeiture of any goods only if it is satisfied that there has been a contravention in relation to the goods of a safety provision.

    (4) For the avoidance of doubt it is declared that a court may infer for the purposes of this section that there has been a contravention in relation to any goods of a safety provision if it is satisfied that any such provision has been contravened in relation to goods which are representative of those goods (whether by reason of being of the same design or part of the same consignment or batch or otherwise).

    (5) Any person aggrieved by an order made under this section by a magistrates' court, or by a decision of such a court not to make such an order, may appeal against that order or decision—

    (a) in England and Wales, to the Crown Court;

    (b) in Northern Ireland, to the county court;

and an order so made may contain such provision as appears to the court to be appropriate for delaying the coming into force of the order pending the making and determination of any appeal (including any application under section III of the Magistrates' Courts Act 1980 or Article 146 of the Magistrates' Courts (Northern Ireland) Order 1981 (statement of case)).

    (6) Subject to subsection (7) below, where any goods are forfeited under this section they shall be destroyed in accordance with such directions as the court may give.

    (7) On making an order under this section a magistrates' court may, if it considers it appropriate to do so, direct that the goods to which the order relates shall (instead of being destroyed) be released, to such person as the court may specify, on condition that that person—

    (a) does not supply those goods to any person otherwise than as mentioned in section 46(7)(a) or (b) below, and

    (b) complies with any order to pay costs or expenses (including any order under section 35 below) which has been made against that person in the proceedings for the order for forfeiture.

18   Power to obtain information

(1) If the Secretary of State considers that, for the purpose of deciding whether—

   (a) to make, vary or revoke any safety regulations; or

   (b) to serve, vary or revoke a prohibition notice; or

   (c) to serve or revoke a notice to warn,

he requires information which another person is likely to be able to furnish, the Secretary of State may serve on the other person a notice under this section.

(2) A notice served on any person under this section may require that person—

   (a) to furnish to the Secretary of State, within a period specified in the notice, such information as is so specified;

   (b) to produce such records as are specified in the notice at a time and place so specified and to permit a person appointed by the Secretary of State for the purpose to take copies of the records at that time and place.

(3) A person shall be guilty of an offence if he—

   (a) fails, without reasonable cause, to comply with a notice served on him under this section; or

   (b) in purporting to comply with a requirement which by virtue of paragraph (a) of subsection (2) above is contained in such a notice—

      (i) furnishes information which he knows is false in a material particular;

      (ii) recklessly furnishes information which is false in a material particular.

(4) A person guilty of an offence under subsection (3) above shall—

   (a) in the case of an offence under paragraph (a) of that subsection, be liable on summary conviction to a fine not exceeding level 5 on the standard scale; and

   (b) in the case of an offence under paragraph (b) of that subsection be liable—

      (i) on conviction on indictment, to a fine,

      (ii) on summary conviction, to a fine not exceeding the statutory maximum.

19   Interpretation of Part II

(1) In this Part—

'controlled drug' means a controlled drug within the meaning of the Misuse of Drugs Act 1971;

'feeding stuff' and 'fertiliser' have the same meaning as in Part IV of the Agriculture Act 1970;

'food' does not include anything containing tobacco but, subject to that, has the same meaning as in the [Food Safety Act 1990] or, in relation to Northern Ireland, the same meaning as in the [Food Safety (Northern Ireland) Order 1991];

'licensed medicinal product' means—

   (a) any medicinal product within the meaning of the Medicines Act 1968 in respect of which a product licence within the meaning of that Act is for the time being in force; or

   (b) any other article or substance in respect of which any such licence is for the time being in force in pursuance of an order under section 104 or 105 of that Act (application of Act to other articles and substances); [or

   (c) a veterinary medicinal product that has a marketing authorisation under the Veterinary Medicines Regulations 2006.]

['medical device' has the same meaning as in Part 4 of the Medicines and Medical Devices Act 2021;]

'safe', in relation to any goods, means such that there is no risk, or no risk apart from one reduced to a minimum, that any of the following will (whether immediately or after a definite or indefinite period) cause the death of, or any personal injury to, any person whatsoever, that is to say—

   (a) the goods;

   (b) the keeping, use or consumption of the goods;

   (c) the assembly of any of the goods which are, or are to be supplied unassembled;

   (d) any emission or leakage from the goods or, as a result of the keeping, use or consumption of the goods, from anything else; or

   (e) reliance on the accuracy of any measurement, calculation or other reading made by or by means of the goods, and [. . .] 'unsafe' shall be construed accordingly;

'tobacco' includes any tobacco product within the meaning of the Tobacco Products Duty Act 1979 and any article or substance containing tobacco and intended for oral or nasal use.

(2) In the definition of 'safe' in subsection (1) above, references to the keeping, use or consumption of any goods are references to—

(a) the keeping, use or consumption of the goods by the persons by whom, and in all or any of the ways or circumstances in which, they might reasonably be expected to be kept, used or consumed; and

(b) the keeping, use or consumption of the goods either alone or in conjunction with other goods in conjunction with which they might reasonably be expected to be kept, used or consumed.

[*Note: the definition of 'medical device' in s 19(1) was not in force on 1 April 2021.*]

PART IV ENFORCEMENT OF PARTS II AND III

27 Enforcement

(1) Subject to the following provisions of this section—

(a) it shall be the duty of every weights and measures authority in Great Britain to enforce within their area the safety provisions [. . .]; and

(b) it shall be the duty of every district council in Northern Ireland to enforce within their area the safety provisions.

(2) The Secretary of State may by regulations—

(a) wholly or partly transfer any duty imposed by subsection (1) above on a weights and measures authority or a district council in Northern Ireland to such other person who has agreed to the transfer as is specified in the regulations;

(b) relieve such an authority or council of any such duty so far as it is exercisable in relation to such goods as may be described in the regulations.

(3) The power to make regulations under subsection (2) above shall be exercisable by statutory instrument subject to annulment in pursuance of a resolution of either House of Parliament and shall include power—

(a) to make different provision for different cases; and

(b) to make such supplemental, consequential and transitional provision as the Secretary of State considers appropriate.

[(3A) For the investigatory powers available to a person for the purposes of the duty imposed by subsection (1), see Schedule 5 to the Consumer Rights Act 2015 (as well as section 29).]

(4) Nothing in this section shall authorise any weights and measures authority, or any person whom functions are conferred by regulations under subsection (2) above, to bring proceedings in Scotland for an offence.

29 Powers of search etc.

(1) Subject to the following provisions of this Part, a duly authorised officer of an enforcement authority may at any reasonable hour and on production, if required, of his credentials exercise [the power conferred by subsection (4)].

(4) If the officer has reasonable grounds for suspecting that any goods are manufactured or imported goods which have not been supplied in the United Kingdom since they were manufactured or imported he may—

(a) for the purpose of ascertaining whether there has been any contravention of any safety provision in relation to the goods, require any person carrying on a business, or employed in connection with a business, to produce any records relating to the business;

(b) for the purpose of ascertaining (by testing or otherwise) whether there has been any such contravention, seize and detain the goods;

(c) take copies of, or of any entry in, any records produced by virtue of paragraph (a) above.

(7) If and to the extent that it is reasonably necessary to do so to prevent a contravention of any safety provision [...], the officer may, for the purpose of exercising his power under subsection (4) [...] above to seize any goods [...]—

    (a) require any person having authority to do so to open any container or to open any vending machine; and

    (b) himself open or break open any such container or machine where a requirement made under paragraph (a) above in relation to the container or machine has not been complied with.

[(8) The officer may not exercise a power under this section to secure the disclosure by a telecommunications operator or postal operator of communications data without the consent of the operator.]

[(9) In subsection (8) 'communications data', 'postal operator' and 'telecommunications operator' have the same meanings as in the Investigatory Powers Act 2016 (see sections 261 and 262 of that Act).]

30   Provisions supplemental to s. 29

(1) An officer seizing any goods [...] under section [29(4)] above shall inform the following persons that the goods [...] have been so seized, that is to say—

    (a) the person from whom they are seized; and

    (b) in the case of imported goods seized on any premises under the control of the Commissioners of Customs and Excise, the importer of those goods (within the meaning of the Customs and Excise Management Act 1979).

(2) If a justice of the peace—

    (a) is satisfied by any written information on oath that there are reasonable grounds for believing either—

        (i) that any [...] records which any officer has power to inspect under section [29(4)] above are on any premises and that their inspection is likely to disclose evidence that there has been a contravention of any safety provision or of any provision [...]; or

        (ii) that such a contravention has taken place, is taking place or is about to take place on any premises; and

    (b) is also satisfied by any such information either—

        (i) that admission to the premises has been or is likely to be refused and that notice of intention to apply for a warrant under this section has been given to the occupier; or

        (ii) that an application for admission, or the giving of such a notice, would defeat the object of entry or that the premises are unoccupied or that the occupier is temporarily absent and it might defeat the object of the entry to await his return,

the justice may by warrant under his hand, which shall continue in force for a period of one month, authorise any officer of an enforcement authority to enter the premises, if need be by force.

(3) An officer entering any premises by virtue of [...] a warrant under subsection (2) above may take with him such other persons and such equipment as may appear to him necessary.

(4) On leaving any premises which a person is authorised to enter by a warrant under subsection (2) above, that person shall, if the premises are unoccupied or the occupier is temporarily absent, leave the premises as effectively secured against trespassers as he found them.

(5) If any person who is not an officer of an enforcement authority purports to act as such under section [29(4)] above of this section he shall be guilty of an offence and liable on summary conviction to a fine not exceeding level 5 on the standard scale.

(6) Where any goods seized by an officer under section [29(4)] above are submitted to a test, the officer shall inform the persons mentioned in subsection (1) above of the result of the test and, if—

    (a) proceedings are brought for an offence in respect of a contravention in relation to the goods of any safety provision [...] or for the forfeiture of the goods under section 16 or 17 above, or a suspension notice is served in respect of any goods; and

    (b) the officer is requested to do so and it is practicable to comply with the request, the officer shall allow any person who is a party to the proceedings or, as the case may be, has an interest in the goods to which the notice relates to have the goods tested.

(7) The Secretary of State may by regulations provide that any test of goods seized under section [29(4)] above by an officer of an enforcement authority shall—

    (a) be carried out at the expense of the authority in a manner and by a person prescribed by or determined under the regulations; or

    (b) be carried out either as mentioned in paragraph (a) above or by the authority in a manner prescribed by the regulations.

(8) The power to make regulations under subsection (7) above shall be exercisable by statutory instrument subject to annulment in pursuance of a resolution of either House of Parliament and shall include power—

    (a) to make different provision for different cases; and

    (b) to make such supplemental, consequential and transitional provisions as the Secretary of State considers appropriate.

(9) In the application of this section to Scotland, the reference in subsection (2) above to a justice of the peace shall include a reference to a sheriff and the references to written information on oath shall be construed as references to evidence on oath.

(10) In the application of this section to Northern Ireland, the references in subsection (2) above to any information on oath shall be construed as references to any complaint on oath.

31 Power of customs officer to detain goods

(1) A customs officer may, for the purpose of facilitating the exercise by an enforcement authority or officer of such an authority of any functions conferred on the authority or officer by or under Part II of this Act, or by [section 29(4) of this Act or Schedule 5 to the Consumer Rights Act 2015] in its application for the purposes of the safety provisions, seize any imported goods and detain them for not more than two working days.

(2) Anything seized and detained under this section shall be dealt with during the period of its detention in such manner as the Commissioners of Customs and Excise may direct.

(3) In subsection (1) above the reference to two working days is a reference to a period of forty-eight hours calculated from the time when the goods in question are seized but disregarding so much of any period as falls on a Saturday or Sunday or on Christmas Day, Good Friday or a day which is a bank holiday under the Banking and Financial Dealings Act 1971 in the part of the United Kingdom where the goods are seized.

(4) In this section and section 32 below 'customs officer' means any officer within the meaning of the Customs and Excise Management Act 1979.

32 Obstruction of authorised officer

(1) Any person who—

    (a) intentionally obstructs any officer of an enforcement authority who is acting in pursuance of [section 29(4)] or any customs officer who is [acting in pursuance of section 31]; or

    (b) intentionally fails to comply with any requirements made of him by any officer of an enforcement authority under [section 29(4)], or

    (c) without reasonable cause fails to give any officer of an enforcement authority who is so acting any other assistance or information which the officer may reasonably require of him for the purposes of the exercise of the officer's functions under [section 29(4)],

shall be guilty of an offence and liable on summary conviction to a fine not exceeding level 5 on the standard scale.

(2) A person shall be guilty of an offence if, in giving any information which is required of him by virtue of subsection (1)(c) above—

    (a) he makes any statement which he knows is false in a material particular, or

    (b) he recklessly makes a statement which is false in a material particular.

(3) A person guilty of an offence under subsection (2) above shall be liable—

(a) on conviction on indictment to a fine;

(b) on summary conviction, to a fine not exceeding the statutory maximum.

33   Appeals against detention of goods

(1) Any person having an interest in any goods which are for the time being detained under [section 29(4)] by an enforcement authority or by an officer of such an authority may apply for an order requiring the goods to be released to him or to another person.

(2) An application under this section may be made—

(a) to any magistrates' court in which proceedings have been brought in England and Wales or Northern Ireland—

(i) for an offence in respect of a contravention in relation to the goods of any safety provision [. . .]; or

(ii) for the forfeiture of the goods under section 16 above;

(b) where no such proceedings have been so brought, by way of complaint to a magistrates' court; or

(c) makes an order under section 16 or 17 above for the forfeiture of any goods.

34   Compensation for seizure and detention

(1) Where an officer of an enforcement authority exercises any power under section [29(4)] above to seize and detain goods, the enforcement authority shall be liable to pay compensation to any person having an interest in the goods in respect of any loss or damage caused by reason of the exercise of the power if—

(a) there has been no contravention in relation to the goods of any safety provision [. . .]; and

(b) the exercise of the power is not attributable to any neglect or default by that person.

(2) Any disputed question as to the right to or the amount of any compensation payable under this section shall be determined by arbitration . . .

35   Recovery of expenses of enforcement

(2) The court may (in addition to any other order it may make as to costs or expenses) order the person convicted or, as the case may be, any person having an interest in the goods to reimburse an enforcement authority for any expenditure which has been or may be incurred by that authority—

(a) in connection with any seizure or detention of the goods by or on behalf of the authority; or

(b) in connection with any compliance by the authority with directions given by the court for the purposes of any order for the forfeiture of the goods.

PART V MISCELLANEOUS AND SUPPLEMENTAL

37   [Power of Commissioners for Revenue and Customs to disclose information]

(1) If they think it appropriate to do so for the purpose of facilitating the exercise by any person to whom subsection (2) below applies of any function conferred on that person by or under Part II of this Act, or by or under Part IV of this Act in its application for the purposes of the safety provisions, [the Commissioners for Her Majesty's Revenue and Customs] may authorise the disclosure to that person of any information obtained [or held] for the purposes of the exercise [by Her Majesty's Revenue and Customs] of their functions in relation to imported goods.

(2) This subsection applies to an enforcement authority and to any officer of an enforcement authority.

(3) A disclosure of information made to any person under subsection (1) above shall be made in such manner as may be directed by [the Commissioners for Her Majesty's Revenue and Customs] and may be through such persons acting on behalf of that person as may be so directed.

(4) Information may be disclosed to a person under subsection (1) above whether or not the disclosure of the information has been requested by or on behalf of that person.

39   Defence of due diligence

(1) Subject to the following provisions of this section, in proceedings against any person for an offence to which this section applies it shall be a defence for that person to show that he took all reasonable steps and exercised all due diligence to avoid committing the offence.

(2) Where in any proceedings against any person for such an offence the defence provided by subsection (1) above involves an allegation that the commission of the offence was due—

   (a) to the act or default of another; or

   (b) to reliance on information given by another,

that person shall not, without the leave of the court, be entitled to rely on the defence unless, not less than seven clear days before the hearing of the proceedings, he has served a notice under subsection (3) below on the person bringing the proceedings.

(3) A notice under this subsection shall give such information identifying or assisting in the identification of the person who committed the act or default or gave the information as is in the possession of the person serving the notice at the time he serves it.

(4) It is hereby declared that a person shall not be entitled to rely on the defence provided by subsection (1) above by reason of his reliance on information supplied by another, unless he shows that it was reasonable in all the circumstances for him to have relied on the information, having regard in particular—

   (a) to the steps which he took, and those which might reasonably have been taken, for the
       purpose of verifying the information, and

   (b) to whether he had any reason to disbelieve the information.

(5) This section shall apply to an offence under section [. . .] 12(1), (2) or (3), 13(4) [or 14(6)] above.

40   Liability of persons other than principal offender

(1) Where the commission by any person of an offence to which section 39 above applies is due to an act or default committed by some other person in the course of any business of his, the other person shall be guilty of the offence and may be proceeded against and punished by virtue of this subsection whether or not proceedings are taken against the first-mentioned person.

(2) Where a body corporate is guilty of an offence under this Act (including where it is so guilty by virtue of subsection (1) above) in respect of any act or default which is shown to have been committed with the consent or connivance of, or to be attributable to any neglect on the part of, any director, manager, secretary or other similar officer of the body corporate or any person who was purporting to act in any such capacity he, as well as the body corporate, shall be guilty of that offence and shall be liable to be proceeded against and punished accordingly.

(3) Where the affairs of a body corporate are managed by its members, subsection (2) above shall apply in relation to the acts and defaults of a member in connection with his functions of management as if he were a director of the body corporate.

41   Civil proceedings

(1) An obligation imposed by safety regulations shall be a duty owed to any person who may be affected by a contravention of the obligation and, subject to any provisions to the contrary in the regulations and to the defences and other incidents applying to actions for breach of statutory duty, a contravention of any such obligation shall be actionable accordingly.

(2) This Act shall not be construed as conferring any other right of action in civil proceedings, apart from the right conferred by virtue of Part I of this Act, in respect of any loss or damage suffered in consequence of a contravention of a safety provision [. . .].

(3) Subject to any provision to the contrary in the agreement itself, an agreement shall not be void or unenforceable by reason only of a contravention of a safety provision [. . .].

(4) Liability by virtue of subsection (1) above shall not be limited or excluded by any contract term, by any notice or (subject to the power contained in subsection (1) above to limit or exclude it in safety regulations) by any other provision.

(5) Nothing in subsection (1) above shall prejudice the operation of section 12 of the Nuclear Installations Act 1965 (rights to compensation for certain breaches of duties confined to rights under that Act).

(6) In this section 'damage' includes personal injury and death.

42 Reports etc.

(1) It shall be the duty of the Secretary of State at least once in every five years to lay before each House of Parliament a report on the exercise during the period to which the report relates of the functions which under Part II of this Act, or under Part IV of this Act in its application for the purposes of the safety provisions, are exercisable by the Secretary of State, weights and measures authorities, district councils in Northern Ireland and persons on whom functions are conferred by regulations made under section 27(2) above.

(2) The Secretary of State may from time to time prepare and lay before each House of Parliament such other reports on the exercise of those functions as he considers appropriate.

(3) Every weights and measures authority, every district council in Northern Ireland and every person on whom functions are conferred by regulations under subsection (2) of section 27 above shall, whenever the Secretary of State so directs, make a report to the Secretary of State on the exercise of the functions exercisable by that authority or council under that section or by that person by virtue of any such regulations.

(4) A report under subsection (3) above shall be in such form and shall contain such particulars as are specified in the direction of the Secretary of State.

(5) The first report under subsection (1) above shall be laid before each House of Parliament not more than five years after the laying of the last report under section 8(2) of the Consumer Safety Act 1978.

43 Financial provisions

(1) There shall be paid out of money provided by Parliament—

(a) any expenses incurred or compensation payable by a Minister of the Crown or Government department in consequence of any provision of this Act; and

(b) any increase attributable to this Act in the sums payable out of money so provided under any other Act.

(2) Any sums received by a Minister of the Crown or Government department by virtue of this Act shall be paid into the Consolidated Fund.

44 Service of documents etc.

(1) Any documents required or authorised by virtue of this Act to be served on a person may be so served—

(a) by delivering it to him or by leaving it at his proper address or by sending it by post to him at that address; or

(b) if the person is a body corporate, by serving it in accordance with paragraph (a) above on the secretary or clerk of that body; or

(c) if the person is a partnership, by serving it in accordance with that paragraph on a partner or on a person having control or management of the partnership business.

(2) For the purposes of subsection (1) above, and for the purposes of section 7 of the Interpretation Act 1978 (which relates to the service of documents by post) in its application to that subsection, the proper address of any person on whom a document is to be served by virtue of this Act shall be his last known address except that—

(a) in the case of service on a body corporate or its secretary or clerk, it shall be the address of the registered or principal office of the body corporate;

(b) in the case of service on a partnership or a partner or a person having the control or management of a partnership business, it shall be the principal office of the partnership;

and for the purposes of this subsection the principal office of a company registered outside the United Kingdom or of a partnership carrying on business outside the United Kingdom is its principal office within the United Kingdom.

(3) The Secretary of State may by regulations make provision for the manner in which any information is to be given to any person under any provision of Part IV of this Act.

(4) Without prejudice to the generality of subsection (3) above regulations made by the Secretary of State may prescribe the person, or manner of determining the person, who is to be treated for the purposes of section [...] 30 above as the person from whom goods were [...] seized where the goods were [...] seized from a vending machine.

(5) The power to make regulations under subsection (3) or (4) above shall be exercisable by statutory instrument subject to annulment in pursuance of a resolution of either House of Parliament and shall include power—

    (a) to make different provision for different cases; and

    (b) to make such supplemental, consequential and transitional provision as the Secretary of State considers appropriate.

45 Interpretation

(1) In this Act, expect in so far as the context otherwise requires—

'aircraft' includes gliders, balloons and hovercraft;

'business' includes a trade or profession and the activities of a professional or trade association or of a local authority or other public authority;

'conditional sale agreement', 'credit-sale agreement' and 'hire-purchase agreement' have the same meanings as in the Consumer Credit Act 1974 but as if in the definitions in that Act 'goods' had the same meaning as in this Act;

'contravention' includes a failure to comply and cognate expressions shall be construed accordingly;

'enforcement authority' means the Secretary of State, any other Minister of the Crown in charge of a Government department, any such department and any authority, council or other person on whom functions under this Act are conferred by or under section 27 above;

'gas' has the same meaning as in Part I of the Gas Act 1986;

'goods' includes substances, growing crops and things comprised in land by virtue of being attached to it and any ship, aircraft or vehicle;

'information' includes accounts, estimates and returns;

'magistrates' court', in relation to Northern Ireland, means a court of summary jurisdiction;

'modifications' includes additions, alterations and omissions, and cognate expressions shall be construed accordingly;

'motor vehicle' has the same meaning as in [the Road Traffic Act 1988];

'notice' means a notice in writing;

'notice to warn' means a notice under section 13(1)(b) above;

'officer', in relation to an enforcement authority, means a person authorised in writing to assist the authority in carrying out its functions under or for the purposes of the enforcement of any of the safety provisions or of any of the provisions made by or under Part III of this Act;

'personal injury' includes any disease and any other impairment of a person's physical or mental condition;

'premises' includes any place and any ship, aircraft or vehicle;

'prohibition notice' means a notice under section 13(1)(a) above;

'records' includes any books or documents and any records in non-documentary form;

'safety provision' means [...] any provision of safety regulations, a prohibition notice or a suspension notice;

'safety regulations' means regulations under section 11 above;

'ship' includes any boat and any other description of vessel used in navigation;

'subordinate legislation' has the same meaning as in the Interpretation Act 1978;

'substance' means any natural or artificial substance, whether in solid, liquid or gaseous form or in the form of a vapour, and includes substances that are comprised in or mixed with other goods;

'supply' and cognate expressions shall be construed in accordance with section 46 below;

'suspension notice' means a notice under section 14 above.

(2) Except in so far as the context otherwise requires, references in this Act to a contravention of a safety provision shall, in relation to any goods, include references to anything which would constitute such a contravention if the goods were supplied to any person.

(3) References in this Act to any goods in relation to which any safety provision has been or may have been contravened shall include references to any goods which it is not reasonably practicable to separate from any such goods.

(5) In Scotland, any reference in this Act to things comprised in land by virtue of being attached to it is a reference to moveables which have become heritable by accession to heritable property.

46 Meaning of 'supply'

(1) Subject to the following provisions of this section, references in this Act to supplying goods shall be construed as references to doing any of the following, whether as principal or agent, that is to say—

(a) selling, hiring out or lending the goods;

(b) entering into a hire-purchase agreement to furnish the goods;

(c) the performance of any contract for work and materials to furnish the goods;

(d) providing the goods in exchange for any consideration [. . .] other than money;

(e) providing the goods in or in connection with the performance of any statutory function; or

(f) giving the goods as a prize or otherwise making a gift of the goods;

and, in relation to gas or water, those references shall be construed as including references to providing the service by which the gas or water is made available for use.

(2) For the purposes of any reference in this Act to supplying goods, where a person ('the ostensible supplier') supplies goods to another person ('the customer') under a hire-purchase agreement, conditional sale agreement or credit-sale agreement or under an agreement for the hiring of goods (other than a hire-purchase agreement) and the ostensible supplier—

(a) carries on the business of financing the provision of goods for others by means of such agreements; and

(b) in the course of that business acquired his interest in the goods supplied to the customer as a means of financing the provision of them for the customer by a further person ('the effective supplier'),

the effective supplier and not the ostensible supplier shall be treated as supplying the goods to the customer.

(3) Subject to subsection (4) below, the performance of any contract by the erection of any building or structure on any land or by the carrying out of any other building works shall be treated for the purposes of this Act as a supply of goods in so far as, but only in so far as, it involves the provision of any goods to any person by means of their incorporation into the building, structure or works.

(4) Except for the purposes of, and in relation to, notices to warn [. . .], references in this Act to supplying goods shall not include references to supplying goods comprised in land where the supply is effected by the creation or disposal of an interest in the land.

(5) Except in Part I of this Act references in this Act to a person's supplying goods shall be confined to references to that person's supplying goods in the course of a business of his, but for the purposes of this subsection it shall be immaterial whether the business is a business of dealing in the goods.

(6) For the purposes of subsection (5) above goods shall not be treated as supplied in the course of a business if they are supplied, in pursuance of an obligation arising under or in connection with the insurance of the goods, to the person with whom they were insured.

(7) Except for the purposes of, and in relation to, prohibition notices or suspension notices, references in [Part 2 or Part 4] of this Act to supplying goods shall not include—

(a) references to supplying goods where the person supplied carries on a business of buying goods of the same description as those goods and repairing or reconditioning them,

(b) references to supplying goods by a sale of articles as scrap (that is to say, for the value of materials included in the articles rather that for the value of the articles themselves).

(8) Where any goods have at any time been supplied by being hired out or lent to any person, neither a continuation or renewal of the hire or loan (whether on the same or different terms) nor any transaction for the transfer after that time of any interest in the goods to the person to whom they were hired or lent shall be treated for the purposes of this Act as a further supply of the goods to that person.

(9) A ship, aircraft or motor vehicle shall not be treated for the purposes of this Act as supplied to any person by reason only that services consisting in the carriage of goods or passengers in that ship, aircraft or vehicle, or in its use for any other purpose, are provided to that person in pursuance of an agreement relating to the use of the ship, aircraft or vehicle for a particular period or for particular voyages, flights or journeys.

47   Savings for certain privileges

(1) Nothing in this Act shall be taken as requiring any person to produce any records if he would be entitled to refuse to produce those records in any proceedings in any court on the ground that they are the subject of legal professional privilege or, in Scotland, that they contain a confidential communication made by or to an advocate or solicitor in that capacity, or as authorising any person to take possession of any records which are in the possession of a person who would be so entitled.

(2) Nothing in this Act shall be construed as requiring a person to answer any question or give any information if to do so would incriminate that person or that person's spouse [or civil partner].

Section 13   **SCHEDULE 2**

PROHIBITION NOTICES AND NOTICES TO WARN

PART I PROHIBITION NOTICES

1. A prohibition notice in respect of any goods shall—
   (a) state that the Secretary of State considers that the goods are unsafe;
   (b) set out the reasons why the Secretary of State considers that the goods are unsafe;
   (c) specify the day on which the notice is to come into force; and
   (d) state that the trader may at any time make representations in writing to the Secretary of State for the purpose of establishing that the goods are safe.

2.—(1) If representations in writing about a prohibition notice are made by the trader to the Secretary of State, it shall be the duty of the Secretary of State to consider whether to revoke the notice and—
   (a) if he decides to revoke it, to do so;
   (b) in any other case, to appoint a person to consider those representations, any further representations made (whether in writing or orally) by the trader about the notice and the statements of any witnesses examined under this Part of this Schedule.

(2) Where the Secretary of State has appointed a person to consider representations about a prohibition notice, he shall serve a notification on the trader which—
   (a) states that the trader may make oral representations to the appointed person for the purpose of establishing that the goods to which the notice relates are safe; and
   (b) specifies the place and time at which the oral representations may be made.

(3) The time specified in a notification served under sub-paragraph (2) above shall not be before the end of the period of twenty-one days beginning with the day on which the notification is served, unless the trader otherwise agrees.

(4) A person on whom a notification has been served under sub-paragraph (2) above or his representative may, at the place and time specified in the notification—
   (a) make oral representations to the appointed person for the purpose of establishing that the goods in question are safe; and
   (b) call and examine witnesses in connection with representations.

3.—(1) Where representations in writing about a prohibition notice are made by the trader to the Secretary of State at any time after a person has been appointed to consider representations about that notice, then, whether or not the appointed person has made a report to the Secretary of State, the following provisions of this paragraph shall apply instead of paragraph 2 above.

(2) The Secretary of State shall, before the end of the period of one month beginning with the day on which he receives the representations, serve a notification on the trader which states—

> (a) that the Secretary of State has decided to revoke the notice, has decided to vary it or, as the case may be, has decided neither to revoke nor to vary it; or
>
> (b) that, a person having been appointed to consider representations about the notice, the trader may, at a place and time specified in the notification, make oral representations to the appointed person for the purpose of establishing that the goods to which the notice relates are safe.

(3) The time specified in a notification served for the purposes of sub-paragraph (2)(b) above shall not be before the end of the period of twenty-one days beginning with the day on which the notification is served, unless the trader otherwise agrees or the time is the time already specified for the purposes of paragraph 2(2)(b) above.

(4) A person on whom a notification has been served for the purposes of sub-paragraph (2)(b) above or his representative may, at the place and time specified in the notification—

> (a) make oral representations to the appointed person for the purpose of establishing that the goods in question are safe; and
>
> (b) call and examine witnesses in connection with the representations.

4.—(1) Where a person is appointed to consider representations about a prohibition notice, it shall be his duty to consider—

> (a) any written representations made by the trader about the notice, other than those in respect of which a notification is served under paragraph 3(2)(a) above;
>
> (b) any oral representations made under paragraph 2(4) or 3(4) above; and
>
> (c) any statements made by witnesses in connection with the oral representations,

and, after considering any matters under this paragraph, to make a report (including recommendations) to the Secretary of State about the matters considered by him and the notice.

(2) It shall be the duty of the Secretary of State to consider any report made to him under sub-paragraph (1) above and, after considering the report, to inform the trader of his decision with respect to the prohibition notice to which the report relates.

5.—(1) The Secretary of State may revoke or vary a prohibition notice by serving on the trader a notification stating that the notice is revoked or, as the case may be, is varied as specified in the notification.

(2) The Secretary of State shall not vary a prohibition notice so as to make the effect of the notice more restrictive for the trader.

(3) Without prejudice to the power conferred by section 13(2) of this Act, the service of a notification under sub-paragraph (1) above shall be sufficient to satisfy the requirement of paragraph 4(2) above that the trader shall be informed of the Secretary of State's decision.

PART II NOTICES TO WARN

6.—(1) If the Secretary of State proposes to serve a notice to warn on any person in respect of any goods, the Secretary of State, before he serves the notice shall serve on that person a notification which—

> (a) contains a draft of the proposed notice;
>
> (b) states that the Secretary of State proposes to serve a notice in the form of the draft on that person;
>
> (c) states that the Secretary of State considers that the goods described in the draft are unsafe;
>
> (d) sets out the reasons why the Secretary of State considers that those goods are unsafe; and
>
> (e) states that that person may make representations to the Secretary of State for the purpose of establishing that the goods are safe if, before the end of the period of fourteen days beginning with the day on which the notification is served, he informs the Secretary of State—

     (i) of his intention to make representations; and

     (ii) whether the representations will be made only in writing or both in writing and orally.

  (2) Where the Secretary of State has served a notification containing a draft of a proposed notice to warn on any person, he shall not serve a notice to warn on that person in respect of the goods to which the proposed notice relates unless—

     (a) the period of fourteen days beginning with the day on which the notification was served expires without the Secretary of State being informed as mentioned in sub-paragraph (1)(e) above;

     (b) the period of twenty-eight days beginning with that day expires without any written representations being made by that person to the Secretary of State about the proposed notice; or

     (c) the Secretary of State has considered a report about the proposed notice by a person appointed under paragraph 7(1) below.

  7.—(1) Where a person on whom a notification containing a draft of a proposed notice to warn has been served—

     (a) informs the Secretary of State as mentioned in paragraph 6(1)(e) above before the end of the period of fourteen days beginning with the day on which the notification was served; and

     (b) makes written representations to the Secretary of State about the proposed notice before the end of the period of twenty-eight days beginning with that day,

the Secretary of State shall appoint a person to consider those representations, any further representations made by that person about the draft notice and the statements of any witnesses examined under this Part of this Schedule.

  (2) Where—

     (a) the Secretary of State has appointed a person to consider representations about a proposed notice to warn; and

     (b) the person whose representations are to be considered has informed the Secretary of State for the purposes of paragraph 6(1)(e) above that the representations he intends to make will include oral representations,

the Secretary of State shall inform the person intending to make the representations of the place and time at which oral representations may be made to the appointed person.

  (3) Where a person on whom a notification containing a draft of a proposed notice to warn has been served is informed of a time for the purposes of sub-paragraph (2) above, that time shall not be—

     (a) before the end of the period of twenty-eight days beginning with the day on which the notification was served; or

     (b) before the end of the period of seven days beginning with the day on which that person is informed of the time.

  (4) A person who has been informed of a place and time for the purposes of sub-paragraph (2) above or his representative may, at that place and time—

     (a) make oral representations to the appointed person for the purpose of establishing that the goods to which the proposed notice relates are safe; and

     (b) call and examine witnesses in connection with the representations.

  8.—(1) Where a person is appointed to consider representations about a proposed notice to warn, it shall be his duty to consider—

     (a) any written representations made by the person on whom it is proposed to serve the notice; and

     (b) in a case where a place and time has been appointed under paragraph 7(2) above for oral representations to be made by that person or his representative, any representations so made and any statements made by witnesses in connection with those representations,

and, after considering those matters to make a report (including recommendations) to the Secretary of State about the matters considered by him and the proposal to serve the notice.

(2) It shall be the duty of the Secretary of State to consider any report made to him under sub-paragraph (1) above, and after considering the report, to inform the person on whom it was proposed that a notice to warn should be served of his decision with respect to the proposal.

(3) If at any time after serving a notification on a person under paragraph 6 above the Secretary of State decides not to serve on that person either the proposed notice to warn or that notice with modifications, the Secretary of State shall inform that person of the decision, and nothing done for the purposes of any of the preceding provisions of this Part
of this Schedule before that person was so informed shall—

    (a) entitle the Secretary of State subsequently to serve the proposed notice or the notice with modifications; or

    (b) require the Secretary of State, or any person appointed to consider representations about the proposed notice, subsequently to do anything in respect of, or in consequence of, any such representations.

(4) Where a notification containing a draft of a proposed notice to warn is served on a person in respect of any goods, a notice to warn served on him in consequence of a decision made under sub-paragraph (2) above shall either be in the form of the draft or shall be less onerous than the draft.

9. The Secretary of State may revoke a notice to warn by serving on the person on whom the notice was served a notification stating that the notice is revoked.

PART III GENERAL

10.—(1) Where in a notification served on any person under this Schedule the Secretary of State has appointed a time for the making of oral representations or the examination of witnesses, he may, by giving that person such notification as the Secretary of State considers appropriate, change that time to a later time or appoint further times at which further representations may be made or the examination of witnesses may be continued; and paragraphs 2(4), 3(4) and 7(4) above shall have effect accordingly.

(2) For the purposes of this Schedule the Secretary of State may appoint a person (instead of the appointed person) to consider any representations or statements, if the person originally appointed, or last appointed under this sub-paragraph, to consider those representations or statements has died or appears to the Secretary of State to be otherwise unable to act.

11. In this Schedule—

'the appointed person' in relation to a prohibition notice or a proposal to serve a notice to warn, means the person for the time being appointed under this Schedule to consider representations about the notice or, as the case may be, about the proposed notice;

'notification' means a notification in writing;

'trader', in relation to a prohibition notice, means the person on whom the notice is or was served.

Carriage of Goods by Sea Act 1992

(1992, c. 50)

1 Shipping documents etc. to which Act applies

    (1) This Act applies to the following documents, that is to say—

        (a) any bill of lading;

        (b) any sea waybill; and

        (c) any ship's delivery order.

    (2) References in this Act to a bill of lading—

        (a) do not include references to a document which is incapable of transfer either by indorsement or, as a bearer bill, by delivery without indorsement; but

    (b) subject to that, do include references to a received for shipment bill of lading.

    (3) References in this Act to a sea waybill are references to any document which is not a bill of lading but—

        (a) is such a receipt for goods as contains or evidences a contract for the carriage of goods by sea; and

        (b) identifies the person to whom delivery of the goods is to be made by the carrier in accordance with that contract.

    (4) References in this Act to a ship's delivery order are references to any document which is neither a bill of lading nor a sea waybill but contains an undertaking which—

        (a) is given under or for the purposes of a contract for the carriage by sea of the goods to which the document relates, or of goods which include those goods; and

        (b) is an undertaking by the carrier to a person identified in the document to deliver the goods to which the document relates to that person.

    (5) The Secretary of State may by regulations make provision for the application of this Act to cases where [an electronic communications network] or any other information technology is used for effecting transactions corresponding to—

        (a) the issue of a document to which this Act applies;

        (b) the indorsement, delivery or other transfer of such a document; or

        (c) the doing of anything else in relation to such a document.

    (6) Regulations under subsection (5) above may—

        (a) make such modifications of the following provisions of this Act as the Secretary of State considers appropriate in connection with the application of this Act to any case mentioned in that subsection; and

        (b) contain supplemental, incidental, consequential and transitional provision;

and the power to make regulations under that subsection shall be exercisable by statutory instrument subject to annulment in pursuance of a resolution of either House of Parliament.

2 Rights under shipping documents

    (1) Subject to the following provisions of this section, a person who becomes—

        (a) the lawful holder of a bill of lading;

        (b) the person who (without being an original party to the contract of carriage) is the person to whom delivery of the goods to which a sea waybill relates is to be made by the carrier in accordance with that contract; or

        (c) the person to whom delivery of the goods to which a ship's delivery order relates is to be made in accordance with the undertaking contained in the order,

shall (by virtue of becoming the holder of the bill or, as the case may be, the person to whom delivery is to be made) have transferred to and vested in him all rights of suit under the contract of carriage as if he had been a party to that contract.

    (2) Where, when a person becomes the lawful holder of a bill of lading, possession of the bill no longer gives a right (as against the carrier) to possession of the goods to which the bill relates, that person shall not have any rights transferred to him by virtue of subsection (1) above unless he becomes the holder of the bill—

        (a) by virtue of a transaction effected in pursuance of any contractual or other arrangements made before the time when such a right to possession ceased to attach to possession of the bill; or

        (b) as a result of the rejection to that person by another person of goods or documents delivered to the other person in pursuance of any such arrangements.

    (3) The rights vested in any person by virtue of the operation of subsection (1) above in relation to a ship's delivery order—

        (a) shall be so vested subject to the terms of the order; and

        (b) where the goods to which the order relates form a part only of the goods to which the contract of carriage relates, shall be confined to rights in respect of the goods to which the order relates.

(4) Where, in the case of any document to which this Act applies—

    (a) a person with any interest or right in or in relation to goods to which the document relates sustains loss or damage in consequence of a breach of the contract of carriage; but

    (b) subsection (1) above operates in relation to that document so that rights of suit in respect of that breach are vested in another person,

the other person shall be entitled to exercise those rights for the benefit of the person who sustained the loss or damage to the same extent as they could have been exercised if they had been vested in the person for whose benefit they are exercised.

(5) Where rights are transferred by virtue of the operation of subsection (1) above in relation to any document, the transfer for which that subsection provides shall extinguish any entitlement to those rights which derives—

    (a) where that document is a bill of lading, from a person's having been an original party to the contract of carriage; or

    (b) in the case of any document to which this Act applies, from the previous operation of that subsection in relation to that document;

but the operation of that subsection shall be without prejudice to any rights which derive from a person's having been an original party to the contract contained in, or evidenced by, a sea waybill and, in relation to a ship's delivery order, shall be without prejudice to any rights deriving otherwise than from the previous operation of that subsection in relation to that order.

3 Liabilities under shipping documents

(1) Where subsection (1) of section 2 of this Act operates in relation to any document to which this Act applies and the person in whom rights are vested by virtue of that subsection—

    (a) takes or demands delivery from the carrier of any of the goods to which the document relates;

    (b) makes a claim under the contract of carriage against the carrier in respect of any of those goods; or

    (c) is a person who, at a time before those rights were vested in him, took or demanded delivery from the carrier of any of those goods,

that person shall (by virtue of taking or demanding delivery or making the claim or, in a case falling within paragraph (c) above, of having the rights vested in him) become subject to the same liabilities under that contract as if he had been a party to that contract.

(2) Where the goods to which a ship's delivery order relates form a part only of the goods to which the contract of carriage relates, the liabilities to which any person is subject by virtue of the operation of this section in relation to that order shall exclude liabilities in respect of any goods to which the order does not relate.

(3) This section, so far as it imposes liabilities under any contract on any person, shall be without prejudice to the liabilities under the contract of any person as an original party to the contract.

4 Representations in bills of lading

A bill of lading which—

    (a) represents goods to have been shipped on board a vessel or to have been received for shipment on board a vessel; and

    (b) has been signed by the master of the vessel or by a person who was not the master but had the express, implied or apparent authority of the carrier to sign bills of lading,

shall, in favour of a person who has become the lawful holder of the bill, be conclusive evidence against the carrier of the shipment of the goods or, as the case may be, of their receipt for shipment.

5 Interpretation etc.

(1) In this Act—

'bill of lading', 'sea waybill' and 'ship's delivery order' shall be construed in accordance with section 1 above;

'the contract of carriage'—

    (a) in relation to a bill of lading or sea waybill, means the contract contained in or evidenced by that bill or waybill; and

    (b) in relation to a ship's delivery order, means the contract under or for the purposes of which the undertaking contained in the order is given;

'holder', in relation to a bill of lading, shall be construed in accordance with subsection (2) below;

'information technology' includes any computer or other technology by means of which information or other matter may be recorded or communicated without being reduced to documentary form; [. . .].

(2) References in this Act to the holder of a bill of lading are references to any of the following persons, that is to say—

    (a) a person with possession of the bill who, by virtue of being the person identified in the bill, is the consignee of the goods to which the bill relates;

    (b) a person with possession of the bill as a result of the completion, by delivery of the bill, of any indorsement of the bill or, in the case of a bearer bill, of any other transfer of the bill;

    (c) a person with possession of the bill as a result of any transaction by virtue of which he would have become a holder falling within paragraph (a) or (b) above had not the transaction been effected at a time when possession of the bill no longer gave a right (as against the carrier) to possession of the goods to which the bill relates;

and a person shall be regarded for the purposes of this Act as having become the lawful holder of a bill of lading wherever he has become the holder of the bill in good faith.

(3) References in this Act to a person's being identified in a document include references to his being identified by a description which allows for the identity of the person in question to be varied, in accordance with the terms of the document, after its issue; and the reference in section 1(3)(b) of this Act to a document's identifying a person shall be construed accordingly.

(4) Without prejudice to sections 2(2) and 4 above, nothing in this Act shall preclude its operation in relation to a case where the goods to which a document relates—

    (a) cease to exist after the issue of the document; or

    (b) cannot be identified (whether because they are mixed with other goods or for any other reason);

and references in this Act to the goods to which a document relates shall be construed accordingly.

(5) The preceding provisions of this Act shall have effect without prejudice to the application, in relation to any case, of the rules (the Hague-Visby Rules) which for the time being have the force of law by virtue of section 1 of the Carriage of Goods by Sea Act 1971.

6   Short title, repeal, commencement and extent

    (4) This Act extends to Northern Ireland.

Arbitration Act 1996

(1996, c. 23)

PART I ARBITRATION PURSUANT TO AN ARBITRATION AGREEMENT

Introductory

1   General principles

The provisions of this Part are founded on the following principles, and shall be construed accordingly—

(a) the object of arbitration is to obtain the fair resolution of disputes by an impartial tribunal without unnecessary delay or expense;

(b) the parties should be free to agree how their disputes are resolved, subject only to such safeguards as are necessary in the public interest;

(c) in matters governed by this Part the court should not intervene except as provided by this Part.

2   Scope of application of provisions

(1) The provisions of this Part apply where the seat of the arbitration is in England and Wales or Northern Ireland.

(2) The following sections apply even if the seat of the arbitration is outside England and Wales or Northern Ireland or no seat has been designated or determined—

(a) sections 9 to 11 (stay of legal proceedings, &c.), and

(b) section 66 (enforcement of arbitral awards).

(3) The powers conferred by the following sections apply even if the seat of the arbitration is outside England and Wales or Northern Ireland or no seat has been designated or determined—

(a) section 43 (securing the attendance of witnesses), and

(b) section 44 (court powers exercisable in support of arbitral proceedings);

but the court may refuse to exercise any such power if, in the opinion of the court, the fact that the seat of the arbitration is outside England and Wales or Northern Ireland, or that when designated or determined the seat is likely to be outside England and Wales or Northern Ireland, makes it inappropriate to do so.

(4) The court may exercise a power conferred by any provision of this Part not mentioned in subsection (2) or (3) for the purpose of supporting the arbitral process where—

(a) no seat of the arbitration has been designated or determined, and

(b) by reason of a connection with England and Wales or Northern Ireland the court is satisfied that it is appropriate to do so.

(5) Section 7 (separability of arbitration agreement) and section 8 (death of a party) apply where the law applicable to the arbitration agreement is the law of England and Wales or Northern Ireland even if the seat of the arbitration is outside England and Wales or Northern Ireland or has not been designated or determined.

3   The seat of the arbitration

In this Part 'the seat of the arbitration' means the juridical seat of the arbitration designated—

(a) by the parties to the arbitration agreement, or

(b) by any arbitral or other institution or person vested by the parties with powers in that regard, or

(c) by the arbitral tribunal if so authorised by the parties,

or determined, in the absence of any such designation, having regard to the parties' agreement and all the relevant circumstances.

4   Mandatory and non-mandatory provisions

(1) The mandatory provisions of this Part are listed in Schedule 1 and have effect notwithstanding any agreement to the contrary.

(2) The other provisions of this Part (the 'non-mandatory provisions') allow the parties to make their own arrangements by agreement but provide rules which apply in the absence of such agreement.

(3) The parties may make such arrangements by agreeing to the application of institutional rules or providing any other means by which a matter may be decided.

(4) It is immaterial whether or not the law applicable to the parties' agreement is the law of England and Wales or, as the case may be, Northern Ireland.

(5) The choice of a law other than the law of England and Wales or Northern Ireland as the applicable law in respect of a matter provided for by a non-mandatory provision of this Part is equivalent to an agreement making provision about that matter.

For this purpose an applicable law determined in accordance with the parties' agreement, or which is objectively determined in the absence of any express or implied choice, shall be treated as chosen by the parties.

5   Agreements to be in writing

(1) The provisions of this Part apply only where the arbitration agreement is in writing, and any other agreement between the parties as to any matter is effective for the purposes of this Part only if in writing.

The expressions 'agreement', 'agree' and 'agreed' shall be construed accordingly.

(2) There is an agreement in writing—

(a) if the agreement is made in writing (whether or not it is signed by the parties),

(b) if the agreement is made by exchange of communications in writing, or

(c) if the agreement is evidenced in writing.

(3) Where parties agree otherwise than in writing by reference to terms which are in writing, they make an agreement in writing.

(4) An agreement is evidenced in writing if an agreement made otherwise than in writing is recorded by one of the parties, or by a third party, with the authority of the parties to the agreement.

(5) An exchange of written submissions in arbitral or legal proceedings in which the existence of an agreement otherwise than in writing is alleged by one party against another party and not denied by the other party in his response constitutes as between those parties an agreement in writing to the effect alleged.

(6) References in this Part to anything being written or in writing include its being recorded by any means.

6   Definition of arbitration agreement

(1) In this Part an 'arbitration agreement' means an agreement to submit to arbitration present or future disputes (whether they are contractual or not).

(2) The reference in an agreement to a written form of arbitration clause or to a document containing an arbitration clause constitutes an arbitration agreement if the reference is such as to make that clause part of the agreement.

7   Separability of arbitration agreement

Unless otherwise agreed by the parties, an arbitration agreement which forms or was intended to form part of another agreement (whether or not in writing) shall not be regarded as invalid, non-existent or ineffective because that other agreement is invalid, or did not come into existence or has become ineffective, and it shall for that purpose be treated as a distinct agreement.

8   Whether agreement discharged by death of a party

(1) Unless otherwise agreed by the parties, an arbitration agreement is not discharged by the death of a party and may be enforced by or against the personal representatives of that party.

(2) Subsection (1) does not affect the operation of any enactment or rule of law by virtue of which a substantive right or obligation is extinguished by death.

Stay of legal proceedings

9   Stay of legal proceedings

(1) A party to an arbitration agreement against whom legal proceedings are brought (whether by way of claim or counterclaim) in respect of a matter which under the agreement is to be referred to arbitration may (upon notice to the other parties to the proceedings) apply to the court in which the proceedings have been brought to stay the proceedings so far as they concern that matter.

(2) An application may be made notwithstanding that the matter is to be referred to arbitration only after the exhaustion of other dispute resolution procedures.

(3) An application may not be made by a person before taking the appropriate procedural step (if any) to acknowledge the legal proceedings against him or after he has taken any step in those proceedings to answer the substantive claim.

(4) On an application under this section the court shall grant a stay unless satisfied that the arbitration agreement is null and void, inoperative, or incapable of being performed.

(5) If the court refuses to stay the legal proceedings, any provision that an award is a condition precedent to the bringing of legal proceedings in respect of any matter is of no effect in relation to those proceedings.

10   Reference of interpleader issue to arbitration

(1) Where in legal proceedings relief by way of interpleader is granted and any issue between the claimants is one in respect of which there is an arbitration agreement between them, the court granting the relief shall direct that the issue be determined in accordance with the agreement unless the circumstances are such that proceedings brought by a claimant in respect of the matter would not be stayed.

(2) Where subsection (1) applies but the court does not direct that the issue be determined in accordance with the arbitration agreement, any provision that an award is a condition precedent to the bringing of legal proceedings in respect of any matter shall not affect the determination of that issue by the court.

11   Retention of security where Admiralty proceedings stayed

(1) Where Admiralty proceedings are stayed on the ground that the dispute in question should be submitted to arbitration, the court granting the stay may, if in those proceedings property has been arrested or bail or other security has been given to prevent or obtain release from arrest—

    (a) order that the property arrested be retained as security for the satisfaction of any award given in the arbitration in respect of that dispute, or

    (b) order that the stay of those proceedings be conditional on the provision of equivalent security for the satisfaction of any such award.

(2) Subject to any provision made by rules of court and to any necessary modifications, the same law and practice shall apply in relation to property retained in pursuance of an order as would apply if it were held for the purposes of proceedings in the court making the order.

Commencement of arbitral proceedings

12   Power of court to extend time for beginning arbitral proceedings, &c.

(1) Where an arbitration agreement to refer future disputes to arbitration provides that a claim shall be barred, or the claimant's right extinguished, unless the claimant takes within a time fixed by the agreement some step—

    (a) to begin arbitral proceedings, or

    (b) to begin other dispute resolution procedures which must be exhausted before arbitral proceedings can be begun,

the court may by order extend the time for taking that step.

(2) Any party to the arbitration agreement may apply for such an order (upon notice to the other parties), but only after a claim has arisen and after exhausting any available arbitral process for obtaining an extension of time.

(3) The court shall make an order only if satisfied—

    (a) that the circumstances are such as were outside the reasonable contemplation of the parties when they agreed the provision in question, and that it would be just to extend the time, or

    (b) that the conduct of one party makes it unjust to hold the other party to the strict terms of the provision in question.

(4) The court may extend the time for such period and on such terms as it thinks fit, and may do so whether or not the time previously fixed (by agreement or by a previous order) has expired.

(5) An order under this section does not affect the operation of the Limitation Acts (see section 13).

(6) The leave of the court is required for any appeal from a decision of the court under this section.

13   Application of limitation acts

(1) The Limitation Acts apply to arbitral proceedings as they apply to legal proceedings.

(2) The court may order that in computing the time prescribed by the Limitation Acts for the commencement of proceedings (including arbitral proceedings) in respect of a dispute which was the subject matter—

(a) of an award which the court orders to be set aside or declares to be of no effect, or

(b) of the affected part of an award which the court orders to be set aside in part, or declares to be in part of no effect,

the period between the commencement of the arbitration and the date of the order referred to in paragraph (a) or (b) shall be excluded.

(3) In determining for the purposes of the Limitation Acts when a cause of action accrued, any provision that an award is a condition precedent to the bringing of legal proceedings in respect of a matter to which an arbitration agreement applies shall be disregarded.

(4) In this Part 'the Limitation Acts' means—

(a) in England and Wales, the Limitation Act 1980, the Foreign Limitation Periods Act 1984 and any other enactment (whenever passed) relating to the limitation of actions;

(b) in Northern Ireland, the Limitation (Northern Ireland) Order 1989, the Foreign Limitation Periods (Northern Ireland) Order 1985 and any other enactment (whenever passed) relating to the limitation of actions.

14   Commencement of arbitral proceedings

(1) The parties are free to agree when arbitral proceedings are to be regarded as commenced for the purposes of this Part and for the purposes of the Limitation Acts.

(2) If there is no such agreement the following provisions apply.

(3) Where the arbitrator is named or designated in the arbitration agreement, arbitral proceedings are commenced in respect of a matter when one party serves on the other party or parties a notice in writing requiring him or them to submit that matter to the person so named or designated.

(4) Where the arbitrator or arbitrators are to be appointed by the parties, arbitral proceedings are commenced in respect of a matter when one party serves on the other party or parties notice in writing requiring him or them to appoint an arbitrator or to agree to the appointment of an arbitrator in respect of that matter.

(5) Where the arbitrator or arbitrators are to be appointed by a person other than a party to the proceedings, arbitral proceedings are commenced in respect of a matter when one party gives notice in writing to that person requesting him to make the appointment in respect of that matter.

The arbitral tribunal

15   The arbitral tribunal

(1) The parties are free to agree on the number of arbitrators to form the tribunal and whether there is to be a chairman or umpire.

(2) Unless otherwise agreed by the parties, an agreement that the number of arbitrators shall be two or any other even number shall be understood as requiring the appointment of an additional arbitrator as chairman of the tribunal.

(3) If there is no agreement as to the number of arbitrators, the tribunal shall consist of a sole arbitrator.

16   Procedure for appointment of arbitrators

(1) The parties are free to agree on the procedure for appointing the arbitrator or arbitrators, including the procedure for appointing any chairman or umpire.

(2) If or to the extent that there is no such agreement, the following provisions apply.

(3) If the tribunal is to consist of a sole arbitrator, the parties shall jointly appoint the arbitrator not later than 28 days after service of a request in writing by either party to do so.

(4) If the tribunal is to consist of two arbitrators, each party shall appoint one arbitrator not later than 14 days after service of a request in writing by either party to do so.

(5) If the tribunal is to consist of three arbitrators—

    (a) each party shall appoint one arbitrator not later than 14 days after service of a request in writing by either party to do so, and

    (b) the two so appointed shall forthwith appoint a third arbitrator as the chairman of the tribunal.

(6) If the tribunal is to consist of two arbitrators and an umpire—

    (a) each party shall appoint one arbitrator not later than 14 days after service of a request in writing by either party to do so, and

    (b) the two so appointed may appoint an umpire at any time after they themselves are appointed and shall do so before any substantive hearing or forthwith if they cannot agree on a matter relating to the arbitration.

(7) In any other case (in particular, if there are more than two parties) section 18 applies as in the case of a failure of the agreed appointment procedure.

17   Power in case of default to appoint sole arbitrator

(1) Unless the parties otherwise agree, where each of two parties to an arbitration agreement is to appoint an arbitrator and one party ('the party in default') refuses to do so, or fails to do so within the time specified, the other party, having duly appointed his arbitrator, may give notice in writing to the party in default that he proposes to appoint his arbitrator to act as sole arbitrator.

(2) If the party in default does not within 7 clear days of that notice being given—

    (a) make the required appointment, and

    (b) notify the other party that he has done so,

the other party may appoint his arbitrator as sole arbitrator whose award shall be binding on both parties as if he had been so appointed by agreement.

(3) Where a sole arbitrator has been appointed under subsection (2), the party in default may (upon notice to the appointing party) apply to the court which may set aside the appointment.

(4) The leave of the court is required for any appeal from a decision of the court under this section.

18   Failure of appointment procedure

(1) The parties are free to agree what is to happen in the event of a failure of the procedure for the appointment of the arbitral tribunal.

There is no failure if an appointment is duly made under section 17 (power in case of default to appoint sole arbitrator), unless that appointment is set aside.

(2) If or to the extent that there is no such agreement any party to the arbitration agreement may (upon notice to the other parties) apply to the court to exercise its powers under this section.

(3) Those powers are—

    (a) to give directions as to the making of any necessary appointments;

    (b) to direct that the tribunal shall be constituted by such appointments (or any one or more of them) as have been made;

    (c) to revoke any appointments already made;

    (d) to make any necessary appointments itself.

(4) An appointment made by the court under this section has effect as if made with the agreement of the parties.

(5) The leave of the court is required for any appeal from a decision of the court under this section.

19   Court to have regard to agreed qualifications

In deciding whether to exercise, and in considering how to exercise, any of its powers under section 16 (procedure for appointment of arbitrators) or section 18 (failure of appointment procedure), the court shall have due regard to any agreement of the parties as to the qualifications required of the arbitrators.

20   Chairman

(1) Where the parties have agreed that there is to be a chairman, they are free to agree what the functions of the chairman are to be in relation to the making of decisions, orders and awards.

(2) If or to the extent that there is no such agreement, the following provisions apply.

(3) Decisions, orders and awards shall be made by all or a majority of the arbitrators (including the chairman).

(4) The view of the chairman shall prevail in relation to a decision, order or award in respect of which there is neither unanimity nor a majority under subsection (3).

21   Umpire

(1) Where the parties have agreed that there is to be an umpire, they are free to agree what the functions of the umpire are to be, and in particular—

(a) whether he is to attend the proceedings, and

(b) when he is to replace the other arbitrators as the tribunal with power to make decisions, orders and awards.

(2) If or to the extent that there is no such agreement, the following provisions apply.

(3) The umpire shall attend the proceedings and be supplied with the same documents and other materials as are supplied to the other arbitrators.

(4) Decisions, orders and awards shall be made by the other arbitrators unless and until they cannot agree on a matter relating to the arbitration.

In that event they shall forthwith give notice in writing to the parties and the umpire, whereupon the umpire shall replace them as the tribunal with power to make decisions, orders and awards as if he were sole arbitrator.

(5) If the arbitrators cannot agree but fail to give notice of that fact, or if any of them fails to join in the giving of notice, any party to the arbitral proceedings may (upon notice to the other parties and to the tribunal) apply to the court which may order that the umpire shall replace the other arbitrators as the tribunal with power to make decisions, orders and awards as if he were sole arbitrator.

(6) The leave of the court is required for any appeal from a decision of the court under this section.

22   Decision-making where no chairman or umpire

(1) Where the parties agree that there shall be two or more arbitrators with no chairman or umpire, the parties are free to agree how the tribunal is to make decisions, orders and awards.

(2) If there is no such agreement, decisions, orders and awards shall be made by all or a majority of the arbitrators.

23   Revocation of arbitrator's authority

(1) The parties are free to agree in what circumstances the authority of an arbitrator may be revoked.

(2) If or to the extent that there is no such agreement the following provisions apply.

(3) The authority of an arbitrator may not be revoked except—

(a) by the parties acting jointly, or

(b) by an arbitral or other institution or person vested by the parties with powers in that regard.

(4) Revocation of the authority of an arbitrator by the parties acting jointly must be agreed in writing unless the parties also agree (whether or not in writing) to terminate the arbitration agreement.

(5) Nothing in this section affects the power of the court—

(a) to revoke an appointment under section 18 (powers exercisable in case of failure of appointment procedure), or

(b) to remove an arbitrator on the grounds specified in section 24.

24 Power of court to remove arbitrator

(1) A party to arbitral proceedings may (upon notice to the other parties, to the arbitrator concerned and to any other arbitrator) apply to the court to remove an arbitrator on any of the following grounds—

    (a) that circumstances exist that give rise to justifiable doubts as to his impartiality;

    (b) that he does not possess the qualifications required by the arbitration agreement;

    (c) that he is physically or mentally incapable of conducting the proceedings or there are justifiable doubts as to his capacity to do so;

    (d) that he has refused or failed—

        (i)   properly to conduct the proceedings, or

        (ii) to use all reasonable despatch in conducting the proceedings or making an award,

        and that substantial injustice has been or will be caused to the applicant.

(2) If there is an arbitral or other institution or person vested by the parties with power to remove an arbitrator, the court shall not exercise its power of removal unless satisfied that the applicant has first exhausted any available recourse to that institution or person.

(3) The arbitral tribunal may continue the arbitral proceedings and make an award while an application to the court under this section is pending.

(4) Where the court removes an arbitrator, it may make such order as it thinks fit with respect to his entitlement (if any) to fees or expenses, or the repayment of any fees or expenses already paid.

(5) The arbitrator concerned is entitled to appear and be heard by the court before it makes any order under this section.

(6) The leave of the court is required for any appeal from a decision of the court under this section.

25 Resignation of arbitrator

(1) The parties are free to agree with an arbitrator as to the consequences of his resignation as regards—

    (a) his entitlement (if any) to fees or expenses, and

    (b) any liability thereby incurred by him.

(2) If or to the extent that there is no such agreement the following provisions apply.

(3) An arbitrator who resigns his appointment may (upon notice to the parties) apply to the court—

    (a) to grant him relief from any liability thereby incurred by him, and

    (b) to make such order as it thinks fit with respect to his entitlement (if any) to fees or expenses or the repayment of any fees or expenses already paid.

(4) If the court is satisfied that in all the circumstances it was reasonable for the arbitrator to resign, it may grant such relief as is mentioned in subsection (3)(a) on such terms as it thinks fit.

(5) The leave of the court is required for any appeal from a decision of the court under this section.

26 Death of arbitrator or person appointing him

(1) The authority of an arbitrator is personal and ceases on his death.

(2) Unless otherwise agreed by the parties, the death of the person by whom an arbitrator was appointed does not revoke the arbitrator's authority.

27 Filling of vacancy, &c.

(1) Where an arbitrator ceases to hold office, the parties are free to agree—

    (a) whether and if so how the vacancy is to be filled,

    (b) whether and if so to what extent the previous proceedings should stand, and

    (c) what effect (if any) his ceasing to hold office has on any appointment made by him (alone or jointly).

(2) If or to the extent that there is no such agreement, the following provisions apply.

(3) The provisions of sections 16 (procedure for appointment of arbitrators) and 18 (failure of appointment procedure) apply in relation to the filling of the vacancy as in relation to an original appointment.

(4) The tribunal (when reconstituted) shall determine whether and if so to what extent the previous proceedings should stand.

This does not affect any right of a party to challenge those proceedings on any ground which had arisen before the arbitrator ceased to hold office.

(5) His ceasing to hold office does not affect any appointment by him (alone or jointly) of another arbitrator, in particular any appointment of a chairman or umpire.

28   Joint and several liability of parties to arbitrators for fees and expenses

(1) The parties are jointly and severally liable to pay to the arbitrators such reasonable fees and expenses (if any) as are appropriate in the circumstances.

(2) Any party may apply to the court (upon notice to the other parties and to the arbitrators) which may order that the amount of the arbitrators' fees and expenses shall be considered and adjusted by such means and upon such terms as it may direct.

(3) If the application is made after any amount has been paid to the arbitrators by way of fees or expenses, the court may order the repayment of such amount (if any) as is shown to be excessive, but shall not do so unless it is shown that it is reasonable in the circumstances to order repayment.

(4) The above provisions have effect subject to any order of the court under section 24(4) or 25(3)(b) (order as to entitlement to fees or expenses in case of removal or resignation of arbitrator).

(5) Nothing in this section affects any liability of a party to any other party to pay all or any of the costs of the arbitration (see sections 59 to 65) or any contractual right of an arbitrator to payment of his fees and expenses.

(6) In this section references to arbitrators include an arbitrator who has ceased to act and an umpire who has not replaced the other arbitrators.

29   Immunity of arbitrator

(1) An arbitrator is not liable for anything done or omitted in the discharge or purported discharge of his functions as arbitrator unless the act or omission is shown to have been in bad faith.

(2) Subsection (1) applies to an employee or agent of an arbitrator as it applies to the arbitrator himself.

(3) This section does not affect any liability incurred by an arbitrator by reason of his resigning (but see section 25).

Jurisdiction of the arbitral tribunal

30   Competence of tribunal to rule on its own jurisdiction

(1) Unless otherwise agreed by the parties, the arbitral tribunal may rule on its own substantive jurisdiction, that is, as to—

(a) whether there is a valid arbitration agreement,

(b) whether the tribunal is properly constituted, and

(c) what matters have been submitted to arbitration in accordance with the arbitration agreement.

(2) Any such ruling may be challenged by any available arbitral process of appeal or review or in accordance with the provisions of this Part.

31   Objection to substantive jurisdiction of tribunal

(1) An objection that the arbitral tribunal lacks substantive jurisdiction at the outset of the proceedings must be raised by a party not later than the time he takes the first step in the proceedings to contest the merits of any matter in relation to which he challenges the tribunal's jurisdiction.

A party is not precluded from raising such an objection by the fact that he has appointed or participated in the appointment of an arbitrator.

(2) Any objection during the course of the arbitral proceedings that the arbitral tribunal is exceeding its substantive jurisdiction must be made as soon as possible after the matter alleged to be beyond its jurisdiction is raised.

(3) The arbitral tribunal may admit an objection later than the time specified in subsection (1) or (2) if it considers the delay justified.

(4) Where an objection is duly taken to the tribunal's substantive jurisdiction and the tribunal has power to rule on its own jurisdiction, it may—

  (a) rule on the matter in an award as to jurisdiction, or

  (b) deal with the objection in its award on the merits.

If the parties agree which of these courses the tribunal should take, the tribunal shall proceed accordingly.

(5) The tribunal may in any case, and shall if the parties so agree, stay proceedings whilst an application is made to the court under section 32 (determination of preliminary point of jurisdiction).

32   Determination of preliminary point of jurisdiction

(1) The court may, on the application of a party to arbitral proceedings (upon notice to the other parties), determine any question as to the substantive jurisdiction of the tribunal.

A party may lose the right to object (see section 73).

(2) An application under this section shall not be considered unless—

  (a) it is made with the agreement in writing of all the other parties to the proceedings, or

  (b) it is made with the permission of the tribunal and the court is satisfied—

   (i)   that the determination of the question is likely to produce substantial savings in costs,

   (ii) that the application was made without delay, and

   (iii) that there is good reason why the matter should be decided by the court.

(3) An application under this section, unless made with the agreement of all the other parties to the proceedings, shall state the grounds on which it is said that the matter should be decided by the court.

(4) Unless otherwise agreed by the parties, the arbitral tribunal may continue the arbitral proceedings and make an award while an application to the court under this section is pending.

(5) Unless the court gives leave, no appeal lies from a decision of the court whether the conditions specified in subsection (2) are met.

(6) The decision of the court on the question of jurisdiction shall be treated as a judgment of the court for the purposes of an appeal.

But no appeal lies without the leave of the court which shall not be given unless the court considers that the question involves a point of law which is one of general importance or is one which for some other special reason should be considered by the Court of Appeal.

The arbitral proceedings

33   General duty of the tribunal

(1) The tribunal shall—

  (a) act fairly and impartially as between the parties, giving each party a reasonable opportunity of putting his case and dealing with that of his opponent, and

  (b) adopt procedures suitable to the circumstances of the particular case, avoiding unnecessary delay or expense, so as to provide a fair means for the resolution of the matters falling to be determined.

(2) The tribunal shall comply with that general duty in conducting the arbitral proceedings, in its decisions on matters of procedure and evidence and in the exercise of all other powers conferred on it.

34 Procedural and evidential matters

(1) It shall be for the tribunal to decide all procedural and evidential matters, subject to the right of the parties to agree any matter.

(2) Procedural and evidential matters include—

(a) when and where any part of the proceedings is to be held;

(b) the language or languages to be used in the proceedings and whether translations of any relevant documents are to be supplied;

(c) whether any and if so what form of written statements of claim and defence are to be used, when these should be supplied and the extent to which such statements can be later amended;

(d) whether any and if so which documents or classes of documents should be disclosed between and produced by the parties and at what stage;

(e) whether any and if so what questions should be put to and answered by the respective parties and when and in what form this should be done;

(f) whether to apply strict rules of evidence (or any other rules) as to the admissibility, relevance or weight of any material (oral, written or other) sought to be tendered on any matters of fact or opinion, and the time, manner and form in which such material should be exchanged and presented;

(g) whether and to what extent the tribunal should itself take the initiative in ascertaining the facts and the law;

(h) whether and to what extent there should be oral or written evidence or submissions.

(3) The tribunal may fix the time within which any directions given by it are to be complied with, and may if it thinks fit extend the time so fixed (whether or not it has expired).

35 Consolidation of proceedings and concurrent hearings

(1) The parties are free to agree—

(a) that the arbitral proceedings shall be consolidated with other arbitral proceedings, or

(b) that concurrent hearings shall be held,

on such terms as may be agreed.

(2) Unless the parties agree to confer such power on the tribunal, the tribunal has no power to order consolidation of proceedings or concurrent hearings.

36 Legal or other representation

Unless otherwise agreed by the parties, a party to arbitral proceedings may be represented in the proceedings by a lawyer or other person chosen by him.

37 Power to appoint experts, legal advisers or assessors

(1) Unless otherwise agreed by the parties—

(a) the tribunal may—

(i)   appoint experts or legal advisers to report to it and the parties, or

(ii) appoint assessors to assist it on technical matters,

and may allow any such expert, legal adviser or assessor to attend the proceedings; and

(b) the parties shall be given a reasonable opportunity to comment on any information, opinion or advice offered by any such person.

(2) The fees and expenses of an expert, legal adviser or assessor appointed by the tribunal for which the arbitrators are liable are expenses of the arbitrators for the purposes of this Part.

38 General powers exercisable by the tribunal

(1) The parties are free to agree on the powers exercisable by the arbitral tribunal for the purposes of and in relation to the proceedings.

(2) Unless otherwise agreed by the parties the tribunal has the following powers.

(3) The tribunal may order a claimant to provide security for the costs of the arbitration. This power shall not be exercised on the ground that the claimant is—

(a) an individual ordinarily resident outside the United Kingdom, or

(b) a corporation or association incorporated or formed under the law of a country outside the United Kingdom, or whose central management and control is exercised outside the United Kingdom.

(4) The tribunal may give directions in relation to any property which is the subject of the proceedings or as to which any question arises in the proceedings, and which is owned by or is in the possession of a party to the proceedings—

(a) for the inspection, photographing, preservation, custody or detention of the property by the tribunal, an expert or a party, or

(b) ordering that samples be taken from, or any observation be made of or experiment conducted upon, the property.

(5) The tribunal may direct that a party or witness shall be examined on oath or affirmation, and may for that purpose administer any necessary oath or take any necessary affirmation.

(6) The tribunal may give directions to a party for the preservation for the purposes of the proceedings of any evidence in his custody or control.

39 Power to make provisional awards

(1) The parties are free to agree that the tribunal shall have power to order on a provisional basis any relief which it would have power to grant in a final award.

(2) This includes, for instance, making—

(a) a provisional order for the payment of money or the disposition of property as between the parties, or

(b) an order to make an interim payment on account of the costs of the arbitration.

(3) Any such order shall be subject to the tribunal's final adjudication; and the tribunal's final award, on the merits or as to costs, shall take account of any such order.

(4) Unless the parties agree to confer such power on the tribunal, the tribunal has no such power.

This does not affect its powers under section 47 (awards on different issues, &c.).

40 General duty of parties

(1) The parties shall do all things necessary for the proper and expeditious conduct of the arbitral proceedings.

(2) This includes—

(a) complying without delay with any determination of the tribunal as to procedural or evidential matters, or with any order or directions of the tribunal, and

(b) where appropriate, taking without delay any necessary steps to obtain a decision of the court on a preliminary question of jurisdiction or law (see sections 32 and 45).

41 Powers of tribunal in case of party's default

(1) The parties are free to agree on the powers of the tribunal in case of a party's failure to do something necessary for the proper and expeditious conduct of the arbitration.

(2) Unless otherwise agreed by the parties, the following provisions apply.

(3) If the tribunal is satisfied that there has been inordinate and inexcusable delay on the part of the claimant in pursuing his claim and that the delay—

(a) gives rise, or is likely to give rise, to a substantial risk that it is not possible to have a fair resolution of the issues in that claim, or

(b) has caused, or is likely to cause, serious prejudice to the respondent, the tribunal may make an award dismissing the claim.

(4) If without showing sufficient cause a party—

(a) fails to attend or be represented at an oral hearing of which due notice was given, or

(b) where matters are to be dealt with in writing, fails after due notice to submit written evidence or make written submissions, the tribunal may continue the proceedings in the absence of that party or, as the case may be, without any written evidence or submissions on his behalf, and may make an award on the basis of the evidence before it.

(5) If without showing sufficient cause a party fails to comply with any order or directions of the tribunal, the tribunal may make a peremptory order to the same effect, prescribing such time for compliance with it as the tribunal considers appropriate.

(6) If a claimant fails to comply with a peremptory order of the tribunal to provide security for costs, the tribunal may make an award dismissing his claim.

(7) If a party fails to comply with any other kind of peremptory order, then, without prejudice to section 42 (enforcement by court of tribunal's peremptory orders), the tribunal may do any of the following—

    (a) direct that the party in default shall not be entitled to rely upon any allegation or material which was the subject matter of the order;

    (b) draw such adverse inferences from the act of non-compliance as the circumstances justify;

    (c) proceed to an award on the basis of such materials as have been properly provided to it;

    (d) make such order as it thinks fit as to the payment of costs of the arbitration incurred in consequence of the non-compliance.

Powers of court in relation to arbitral proceedings

42   Enforcement of peremptory orders of tribunal

(1) Unless otherwise agreed by the parties, the court may make an order requiring a party to comply with a peremptory order made by the tribunal.

(2) An application for an order under this section may be made—

    (a) by the tribunal (upon notice to the parties),

    (b) by a party to the arbitral proceedings with the permission of the tribunal (and upon notice to the other parties), or

    (c) where the parties have agreed that the powers of the court under this section shall be available.

(3) The court shall not act unless it is satisfied that the applicant has exhausted any available arbitral process in respect of failure to comply with the tribunal's order.

(4) No order shall be made under this section unless the court is satisfied that the person to whom the tribunal's order was directed has failed to comply with it within the time prescribed in the order or, if no time was prescribed, within a reasonable time.

(5) The leave of the court is required for any appeal from a decision of the court under this section.

43   Securing the attendance of witnesses

(1) A party to arbitral proceedings may use the same court procedures as are available in relation to legal proceedings to secure the attendance before the tribunal of a witness in order to give oral testimony or to produce documents or other material evidence.

(2) This may only be done with the permission of the tribunal or the agreement of the other parties.

(3) The court procedures may only be used if—

    (a) the witness is in the United Kingdom, and

    (b) the arbitral proceedings are being conducted in England and Wales or, as the case may be, Northern Ireland.

(4) A person shall not be compelled by virtue of this section to produce any document or other material evidence which he could not be compelled to produce in legal proceedings.

44   Court powers exercisable in support of arbitral proceedings

(1) Unless otherwise agreed by the parties, the court has for the purposes of and in relation to arbitral proceedings the same power of making orders about the matters listed below as it has for the purposes of and in relation to legal proceedings.

(2) Those matters are—

    (a) the taking of the evidence of witnesses;

    (b) the preservation of evidence;

    (c) making orders relating to property which is the subject of the proceedings or as to which any question arises in the proceedings—

        (i) for the inspection, photographing, preservation, custody or detention of the property, or

        (ii) ordering that samples be taken from, or any observation be made of or experiment conducted upon, the property; and for that purpose authorising any person to enter any premises in the possession or control of a party to the arbitration;

    (d) the sale of any goods the subject of the proceedings;

    (e) the granting of an interim injunction or the appointment of a receiver.

(3) If the case is one of urgency, the court may, on the application of a party or proposed party to the arbitral proceedings, make such orders as it thinks necessary for the purpose of preserving evidence or assets.

(4) If the case is not one of urgency, the court shall act only on the application of a party to the arbitral proceedings (upon notice to the other parties and to the tribunal) made with the permission of the tribunal or the agreement in writing of the other parties.

(5) In any case the court shall act only if or to the extent that the arbitral tribunal, and any arbitral or other institution or person vested by the parties with power in that regard, has no power or is unable for the time being to act effectively.

(6) If the court so orders, an order made by it under this section shall cease to have effect in whole or in part on the order of the tribunal or of any such arbitral or other institution or person having power to act in relation to the subject-matter of the order.

(7) The leave of the court is required for any appeal from a decision of the court under this section.

45   Determination of preliminary point of law

(1) Unless otherwise agreed by the parties, the court may on the application of a party to arbitral proceedings (upon notice to the other parties) determine any question of law arising in the course of the proceedings which the court is satisfied substantially affects the rights of one or more of the parties.

An agreement to dispense with reasons for the tribunal's award shall be considered an agreement to exclude the court's jurisdiction under this section.

(2) An application under this section shall not be considered unless—

    (a) it is made with the agreement of all the other parties to the proceedings, or

    (b) it is made with the permission of the tribunal and the court is satisfied—

        (i) that the determination of the question is likely to produce substantial savings in costs, and

        (ii) that the application was made without delay.

(3) The application shall identify the question of law to be determined and, unless made with the agreement of all the other parties to the proceedings, shall state the grounds on which it is said that the question should be decided by the court.

(4) Unless otherwise agreed by the parties, the arbitral tribunal may continue the arbitral proceedings and make an award while an application to the court under this section is pending.

(5) Unless the court gives leave, no appeal lies from a decision of the court whether the conditions specified in subsection (2) are met.

(6) The decision of the court on the question of law shall be treated as a judgment of the court for the purposes of an appeal.

But no appeal lies without the leave of the court which shall not be given unless the court considers that the question is one of general importance, or is one which for some other special reason should be considered by the Court of Appeal.

The award

46 Rules applicable to substance of dispute

(1) The arbitral tribunal shall decide the dispute—

(a) in accordance with the law chosen by the parties as applicable to the substance of the dispute, or

(b) if the parties so agree, in accordance with such other considerations as are agreed by them or determined by the tribunal.

(2) For this purpose the choice of the laws of a country shall be understood to refer to the substantive laws of that country and not its conflict of laws rules.

(3) If or to the extent that there is no such choice or agreement, the tribunal shall apply the law determined by the conflict of laws rules which it considers applicable.

47 Awards on different issues, &c.

(1) Unless otherwise agreed by the parties, the tribunal may make more than one award at different times on different aspects of the matters to be determined.

(2) The tribunal may, in particular, make an award relating—

(a) to an issue affecting the whole claim, or

(b) to a part only of the claims or cross-claims submitted to it for decision.

(3) If the tribunal does so, it shall specify in its award the issue, or the claim or part of a claim, which is the subject matter of the award.

48 Remedies

(1) The parties are free to agree on the powers exercisable by the arbitral tribunal as regards remedies.

(2) Unless otherwise agreed by the parties, the tribunal has the following powers.

(3) The tribunal may make a declaration as to any matter to be determined in the proceedings.

(4) The tribunal may order the payment of a sum of money, in any currency.

(5) The tribunal has the same powers as the court—

(a) to order a party to do or refrain from doing anything;

(b) to order specific performance of a contract (other than a contract relating to land);

(c) to order the rectification, setting aside or cancellation of a deed or other document.

49 Interest

(1) The parties are free to agree on the powers of the tribunal as regards the award of interest.

(2) Unless otherwise agreed by the parties the following provisions apply.

(3) The tribunal may award simple or compound interest from such dates, at such rates and with such rests as it considers meets the justice of the case—

(a) on the whole or part of any amount awarded by the tribunal, in respect of any period up to the date of the award;

(b) on the whole or part of any amount claimed in the arbitration and outstanding at the commencement of the arbitral proceedings but paid before the award was made, in respect of any period up to the date of payment.

(4) The tribunal may award simple or compound interest from the date of the award (or any later date) until payment, at such rates and with such rests as it considers meets the justice of the case, on the outstanding amount of any award (including any award of interest under subsection (3) and any award as to costs).

(5) References in this section to an amount awarded by the tribunal include an amount payable in consequence of a declaratory award by the tribunal.

(6) The above provisions do not affect any other power of the tribunal to award interest.

50   Extension of time for making award

(1) Where the time for making an award is limited by or in pursuance of the arbitration agreement, then, unless otherwise agreed by the parties, the court may in accordance with the following provisions by order extend that time.

(2) An application for an order under this section may be made—

(a) by the tribunal (upon notice to the parties), or

(b) by any party to the proceedings (upon notice to the tribunal and the other parties),

but only after exhausting any available arbitral process for obtaining an extension of time.

(3) The court shall only make an order if satisfied that a substantial injustice would otherwise be done.

(4) The court may extend the time for such period and on such terms as it thinks fit, and may do so whether or not the time previously fixed (by or under the agreement or by a previous order) has expired.

(5) The leave of the court is required for any appeal from a decision of the court under this section.

51   Settlement

(1) If during arbitral proceedings the parties settle the dispute, the following provisions apply unless otherwise agreed by the parties.

(2) The tribunal shall terminate the substantive proceedings and, if so requested by the parties and not objected to by the tribunal, shall record the settlement in the form of an agreed award.

(3) An agreed award shall state that it is an award of the tribunal and shall have the same status and effect as any other award on the merits of the case.

(4) The following provisions of this Part relating to awards (sections 52 to 58) apply to an agreed award.

(5) Unless the parties have also settled the matter of the payment of the costs of the arbitration, the provisions of this Part relating to costs (sections 59 to 65) continue to apply.

52   Form of award

(1) The parties are free to agree on the form of an award.

(2) If or to the extent that there is no such agreement, the following provisions apply.

(3) The award shall be in writing signed by all the arbitrators or all those assenting to the award.

(4) The award shall contain the reasons for the award unless it is an agreed award or the parties have agreed to dispense with reasons.

(5) The award shall state the seat of the arbitration and the date when the award is made.

53   Place where award treated as made

Unless otherwise agreed by the parties, where the seat of the arbitration is in England and Wales or Northern Ireland, any award in the proceedings shall be treated as made there, regardless of where it was signed, despatched or delivered to any of the parties.

54   Date of award

(1) Unless otherwise agreed by the parties, the tribunal may decide what is to be taken to be the date on which the award was made.

(2) In the absence of any such decision, the date of the award shall be taken to be the date on which it is signed by the arbitrator or, where more than one arbitrator signs the award, by the last of them.

55   Notification of award

(1) The parties are free to agree on the requirements as to notification of the award to the parties.

(2) If there is no such agreement, the award shall be notified to the parties by service on them of copies of the award, which shall be done without delay after the award is made.

(3) Nothing in this section affects section 56 (power to withhold award in case of non-payment).

56   Power to withhold award in case of non-payment

(1)   The tribunal may refuse to deliver an award to the parties except upon full payment of the fees and expenses of the arbitrators.

(2)   If the tribunal refuses on that ground to deliver an award, a party to the arbitral proceedings may (upon notice to the other parties and the tribunal) apply to the court, which may order that—

(a)   the tribunal shall deliver the award on the payment into court by the applicant of the fees and expenses demanded, or such lesser amount as the court may specify,

(b)   the amount of the fees and expenses properly payable shall be determined by such means and upon such terms as the court may direct, and

(c)   that out of the money paid into court there shall be paid out such fees and expenses as may be found to be properly payable and the balance of the money (if any) shall be paid out to the applicant.

(3)   For this purpose the amount of fees and expenses properly payable is the amount the applicant is liable to pay under section 28 or any agreement relating to the payment of the arbitrators.

(4)   No application to the court may be made where there is any available arbitral process for appeal or review of the amount of the fees or expenses demanded.

(5)   References in this section to arbitrators include an arbitrator who has ceased to act and an umpire who has not replaced the other arbitrators.

(6)   The above provisions of this section also apply in relation to any arbitral or other institution or person vested by the parties with powers in relation to the delivery of the tribunal's award.

As they so apply, the references to the fees and expenses of the arbitrators shall be construed as including the fees and expenses of that institution or person.

(7)   The leave of the court is required for any appeal from a decision of the court under this section.

(8)   Nothing in this section shall be construed as excluding an application under section 28 where payment has been made to the arbitrators in order to obtain the award.

57   Correction of award or additional award

(1)   The parties are free to agree on the powers of the tribunal to correct an award or make an additional award.

(2)   If or to the extent there is no such agreement, the following provisions apply.

(3)   The tribunal may on its own initiative or on the application of a party—

(a)   correct an award so as to remove any clerical mistake or error arising from an accidental slip or omission or clarify or remove any ambiguity in the award, or

(b)   make an additional award in respect of any claim (including a claim for interest or costs) which was presented to the tribunal but was not dealt with in the award.

These powers shall not be exercised without first affording the other parties a reasonable opportunity to make representations to the tribunal.

(4)   Any application for the exercise of those powers must be made within 28 days of the date of the award or such longer period as the parties may agree.

(5)   Any correction of an award shall be made within 28 days of the date the application was received by the tribunal or, where the correction is made by the tribunal on its own initiative, within 28 days of the date of the award or, in either case, such longer period as the parties may agree.

(6)   Any additional award shall be made within 56 days of the date of the original award or such longer period as the parties may agree.

(7)   Any correction of an award shall form part of the award.

58   Effect of award

(1)   Unless otherwise agreed by the parties, an award made by the tribunal pursuant to an arbitration agreement is final and binding both on the parties and on any persons claiming through or under them.

(2) This does not affect the right of a person to challenge the award by any available arbitral process of appeal or review or in accordance with the provisions of this Part.

Costs of the arbitration

59 Costs of the arbitration

(1) References in this Part to the costs of the arbitration are to—

(a) the arbitrators' fees and expenses,

(b) the fees and expenses of any arbitral institution concerned, and

(c) the legal or other costs of the parties.

(2) Any such reference includes the costs of or incidental to any proceedings to determine the amount of the recoverable costs of the arbitration (see section 63).

60 Agreement to pay costs in any event

An agreement which has the effect that a party is to pay the whole or part of the costs of the arbitration in any event is only valid if made after the dispute in question has arisen.

61 Award of costs

(1) The tribunal may make an award allocating the costs of the arbitration as between the parties, subject to any agreement of the parties.

(2) Unless the parties otherwise agree, the tribunal shall award costs on the general principle that costs should follow the event except where it appears to the tribunal that in the circumstances this is not appropriate in relation to the whole or part of the costs.

62 Effect of agreement or award about costs

Unless the parties otherwise agree, any obligation under an agreement between them as to how the costs of the arbitration are to be borne, or under an award allocating the costs of the arbitration, extends only to such costs as are recoverable.

63 The recoverable costs of the arbitration

(1) The parties are free to agree what costs of the arbitration are recoverable.

(2) If or to the extent there is no such agreement, the following provisions apply.

(3) The tribunal may determine by award the recoverable costs of the arbitration on such basis as it thinks fit.

If it does so, it shall specify—

(a) the basis on which it has acted, and

(b) the items of recoverable costs and the amount referable to each.

(4) If the tribunal does not determine the recoverable costs of the arbitration, any party to the arbitral proceedings may apply to the court (upon notice to the other parties) which may—

(a) determine the recoverable costs of the arbitration on such basis as it thinks fit, or

(b) order that they shall be determined by such means and upon such terms as it may specify.

(5) Unless the tribunal or the court determines otherwise—

(a) the recoverable costs of the arbitration shall be determined on the basis that there shall be allowed a reasonable amount in respect of all costs reasonably incurred, and

(b) any doubt as to whether costs were reasonably incurred or were reasonable in amount shall be resolved in favour of the paying party.

(6) The above provisions have effect subject to section 64 (recoverable fees and expenses of arbitrators).

(7) Nothing in this section affects any right of the arbitrators, any expert, legal adviser or assessor appointed by the tribunal, or any arbitral institution, to payment of their fees and expenses.

64 Recoverable fees and expenses of arbitrators

(1) Unless otherwise agreed by the parties, the recoverable costs of the arbitration shall include in respect of the fees and expenses of the arbitrators only such reasonable fees and expenses as are appropriate in the circumstances.

(2) If there is any question as to what reasonable fees and expenses are appropriate in the circumstances, and the matter is not already before the court on an application under section 63(4), the court may on the application of any party (upon notice to the other parties)—

(a) determine the matter, or

(b) order that it be determined by such means and upon such terms as the court may specify.

(3) Subsection (1) has effect subject to any order of the court under section 24(4) or 25(3)(b) (order as to entitlement to fees or expenses in case of removal or resignation of arbitrator).

(4) Nothing in this section affects any right of the arbitrator to payment of his fees and expenses.

65 Power to limit recoverable costs

(1) Unless otherwise agreed by the parties, the tribunal may direct that the recoverable costs of the arbitration, or of any part of the arbitral proceedings, shall be limited to a specified amount.

(2) Any direction may be made or varied at any stage, but this must be done sufficiently in advance of the incurring of costs to which it relates, or the taking of any steps in the proceedings which may be affected by it, for the limit to be taken into account.

Powers of the court in relation to award

66 Enforcement of the award

(1) An award made by the tribunal pursuant to an arbitration agreement may, by leave of the court, be enforced in the same manner as a judgment or order of the court to the same effect.

(2) Where leave is so given, judgment may be entered in terms of the award.

(3) Leave to enforce an award shall not be given where, or to the extent that, the person against whom it is sought to be enforced shows that the tribunal lacked substantive jurisdiction to make the award.

The right to raise such an objection may have been lost (see section 73).

(4) Nothing in this section affects the recognition or enforcement of an award under any other enactment or rule of law, in particular under Part II of the Arbitration Act 1950 (enforcement of awards under Geneva Convention) or the provisions of Part III of this Act relating to the recognition and enforcement of awards under the New York Convention or by an action on the award.

67 Challenging the award: substantive jurisdiction

(1) A party to arbitral proceedings may (upon notice to the other parties and to the tribunal) apply to the court—

(a) challenging any award of the arbitral tribunal as to its substantive jurisdiction; or

(b) for an order declaring an award made by the tribunal on the merits to be of no effect, in whole or in part, because the tribunal did not have substantive jurisdiction.

A party may lose the right to object (see section 73) and the right to apply is subject to the restrictions in section 70(2) and (3).

(2) The arbitral tribunal may continue the arbitral proceedings and make a further award while an application to the court under this section is pending in relation to an award as to jurisdiction.

(3) On an application under this section challenging an award of the arbitral tribunal as to its substantive jurisdiction, the court may by order—

(a) confirm the award,

(b) vary the award, or

(c) set aside the award in whole or in part.

(4) The leave of the court is required for any appeal from a decision of the court under this section.

68 Challenging the award: serious irregularity

(1) A party to arbitral proceedings may (upon notice to the other parties and to the tribunal) apply to the court challenging an award in the proceedings on the ground of serious irregularity affecting the tribunal, the proceedings or the award.

A party may lose the right to object (see section 73) and the right to apply is subject to the restrictions in section 70(2) and (3).

(2) Serious irregularity means an irregularity of one or more of the following kinds which the court considers has caused or will cause substantial injustice to the applicant—

(a) failure by the tribunal to comply with section 33 (general duty of tribunal);

(b) the tribunal exceeding its powers (otherwise than by exceeding its substantive jurisdiction: see section 67);

(c) failure by the tribunal to conduct the proceedings in accordance with the procedure agreed by the parties;

(d) failure by the tribunal to deal with all the issues that were put to it;

(e) any arbitral or other institution or person vested by the parties with powers in relation to the proceedings or the award exceeding its powers;

(f) uncertainty or ambiguity as to the effect of the award;

(g) the award being obtained by fraud or the award or the way in which it was procured being contrary to public policy;

(h) failure to comply with the requirements as to the form of the award; or

(i) any irregularity in the conduct of the proceedings or in the award which is admitted by the tribunal or by any arbitral or other institution or person vested by the parties with powers in relation to the proceedings or the award.

(3) If there is shown to be serious irregularity affecting the tribunal, the proceedings or the award, the court may—

(a) remit the award to the tribunal, in whole or in part, for reconsideration,

(b) set the award aside in whole or in part, or

(c) declare the award to be of no effect, in whole or in part.

The court shall not exercise its power to set aside or to declare an award to be of no effect, in whole or in part, unless it is satisfied that it would be inappropriate to remit the matters in question to the tribunal for reconsideration.

(4) The leave of the court is required for any appeal from a decision of the court under this section.

69 Appeal on point of law

(1) Unless otherwise agreed by the parties, a party to arbitral proceedings may (upon notice to the other parties and to the tribunal) appeal to the court on a question of law arising out of an award made in the proceedings.

An agreement to dispense with reasons for the tribunal's award shall be considered an agreement to exclude the court's jurisdiction under this section.

(2) An appeal shall not be brought under this section except—

(a) with the agreement of all the other parties to the proceedings, or

(b) with the leave of the court.

The right to appeal is also subject to the restrictions in section 70(2) and (3).

(3) Leave to appeal shall be given only if the court is satisfied—

(a) that the determination of the question will substantially affect the rights of one or more of the parties,

(b) that the question is one which the tribunal was asked to determine,

(c) that, on the basis of the findings of fact in the award—

(i) the decision of the tribunal on the question is obviously wrong, or

(ii) the question is one of general public importance and the decision of the tribunal is at least open to serious doubt, and

(d) that, despite the agreement of the parties to resolve the matter by arbitration, it is just and proper in all the circumstances for the court to determine the question.

(4) An application for leave to appeal under this section shall identify the question of law to be determined and state the grounds on which it is alleged that leave to appeal should be granted.

(5) The court shall determine an application for leave to appeal under this section without a hearing unless it appears to the court that a hearing is required.

(6) The leave of the court is required for any appeal from a decision of the court under this section to grant or refuse leave to appeal.

(7) On an appeal under this section the court may by order—

(a) confirm the award,

(b) vary the award,

(c) remit the award to the tribunal, in whole or in part, for reconsideration in the light of the court's determination, or

(d) set aside the award in whole or in part.

The court shall not exercise its power to set aside an award, in whole or in part, unless it is satisfied that it would be inappropriate to remit the matters in question to the tribunal for reconsideration.

(8) The decision of the court on an appeal under this section shall be treated as a judgment of the court for the purposes of a further appeal.

But no such appeal lies without the leave of the court which shall not be given unless the court considers that the question is one of general importance or is one which for some other special reason should be considered by the Court of Appeal.

70 Challenge or appeal: supplementary provisions

(1) The following provisions apply to an application or appeal under section 67, 68 or 69.

(2) An application or appeal may not be brought if the applicant or appellant has not first exhausted—

(a) any available arbitral process of appeal or review, and

(b) any available recourse under section 57 (correction of award or additional award).

(3) Any application or appeal must be brought within 28 days of the date of the award or, if there has been any arbitral process of appeal or review, of the date when the applicant or appellant was notified of the result of that process.

(4) If on an application or appeal it appears to the court that the award—

(a) does not contain the tribunal's reasons, or

(b) does not set out the tribunal's reasons in sufficient detail to enable the court properly to consider the application or appeal,

the court may order the tribunal to state the reasons for its award in sufficient detail for that purpose.

(5) Where the court makes an order under subsection (4), it may make such further order as it thinks fit with respect to any additional costs of the arbitration resulting from its order.

(6) The court may order the applicant or appellant to provide security for the costs of the application or appeal, and may direct that the application or appeal be dismissed if the order is not complied with.

The power to order security for costs shall not be exercised on the ground that the applicant or appellant is—

(a) an individual ordinarily resident outside the United Kingdom, or

(b) a corporation or association incorporated or formed under the law of a country outside the United Kingdom, or whose central management and control is exercised outside the United Kingdom.

(7) The court may order that any money payable under the award shall be brought into court or otherwise secured pending the determination of the application or appeal, and may direct that the application or appeal be dismissed if the order is not complied with.

(8) The court may grant leave to appeal subject to conditions to the same or similar effect as an order under subsection (6) or (7).

This does not affect the general discretion of the court to grant leave subject to conditions.

71 Challenge or appeal: effect of order of court

(1) The following provisions have effect where the court makes an order under section 67, 68 or 69 with respect to an award.

(2) Where the award is varied, the variation has effect as part of the tribunal's award.

(3) Where the award is remitted to the tribunal, in whole or in part, for reconsideration, the tribunal shall make a fresh award in respect of the matters remitted within three months of the date of the order for remission or such longer or shorter period as the court may direct.

(4) Where the award is set aside or declared to be of no effect, in whole or in part, the court may also order that any provision that an award is a condition precedent to the bringing of legal proceedings in respect of a matter to which the arbitration agreement applies, is of no effect as regards the subject matter of the award or, as the case may be, the relevant part of the award.

Miscellaneous

72 Saving for rights of person who takes no part in proceedings

(1) A person alleged to be a party to arbitral proceedings but who takes no part in the proceedings may question—

    (a) whether there is a valid arbitration agreement,

    (b) whether the tribunal is properly constituted, or

    (c) what matters have been submitted to arbitration in accordance with the arbitration agreement,

by proceedings in the court for a declaration or injunction or other appropriate relief.

(2) He also has the same right as a party to the arbitral proceedings to challenge an award—

    (a) by an application under section 67 on the ground of lack of substantive jurisdiction in relation to him, or

    (b) by an application under section 68 on the ground of serious irregularity (within the meaning of that section) affecting him;

and section 70(2) (duty to exhaust arbitral procedures) does not apply in his case.

73 Loss of right to object

(1) If a party to arbitral proceedings takes part, or continues to take part, in the proceedings without making, either forthwith or within such time as is allowed by the arbitration agreement or the tribunal or by any provision of this Part, any objection—

    (a) that the tribunal lacks substantive jurisdiction,

    (b) that the proceedings have been improperly conducted,

    (c) that there has been a failure to comply with the arbitration agreement or with any provision of this Part, or

    (d) that there has been any other irregularity affecting the tribunal or the proceedings,

he may not raise that objection later, before the tribunal or the court, unless he shows that, at the time he took part or continued to take part in the proceedings, he did not know and could not with reasonable diligence have discovered the grounds for the objection.

(2) Where the arbitral tribunal rules that it has substantive jurisdiction and a party to arbitral proceedings who could have questioned that ruling—

    (a) by any available arbitral process of appeal or review, or

    (b) by challenging the award,

does not do so, or does not do so within the time allowed by the arbitration agreement or any provision of this Part, he may not object later to the tribunal's substantive jurisdiction on any ground which was the subject of that ruling.

74 Immunity of arbitral institutions, &c.

(1) An arbitral or other institution or person designated or requested by the parties to appoint or nominate an arbitrator is not liable for anything done or omitted in the discharge or purported discharge of that function unless the act or omission is shown to have been in bad faith.

(2) An arbitral or other institution or person by whom an arbitrator is appointed or nominated is not liable, by reason of having appointed or nominated him, for anything done or omitted by the arbitrator (or his employees or agents) in the discharge or purported discharge of his functions as arbitrator.

(3) The above provisions apply to an employee or agent of an arbitral or other institution or person as they apply to the institution or the person himself.

75   Charge to secure payment of solicitors' costs

The powers of the court to make declarations and orders under section 73 of the Solicitors Act 1974 or Article 71H of the Solicitors (Northern Ireland) Order 1976 (power to charge property recovered in the proceedings with the payment of solicitors' costs) may be exercised in relation to arbitral proceedings as if those proceedings were proceedings in the court.

Supplementary

76   Service of notices, &c.

(1) The parties are free to agree on the manner of service of any notice or other document required or authorised to be given or served in pursuance of the arbitration agreement or for the purposes of the arbitral proceedings.

(2) If or to the extent that there is no such agreement the following provisions apply.

(3) A notice or other document may be served on a person by any effective means.

(4) If a notice or other document is addressed, pre-paid and delivered by post—

    (a) to the addressee's last known principal residence or, if he is or has been carrying on a trade, profession or business, his last known principal business address, or

    (b) where the addressee is a body corporate, to the body's registered or principal office,

it shall be treated as effectively served.

(5) This section does not apply to the service of documents for the purposes of legal proceedings, for which provision is made by rules of court.

(6) References in this Part to a notice or other document include any form of communication in writing and references to giving or serving a notice or other document shall be construed accordingly.

77   Powers of court in relation to service of documents

(1) This section applies where service of a document on a person in the manner agreed by the parties, or in accordance with provisions of section 76 having effect in default of agreement, is not reasonably practicable.

(2) Unless otherwise agreed by the parties, the court may make such order as it thinks fit—

    (a) for service in such manner as the court may direct, or

    (b) dispensing with service of the document.

(3) Any party to the arbitration agreement may apply for an order, but only after exhausting any available arbitral process for resolving the matter.

(4) The leave of the court is required for any appeal from a decision of the court under this section.

78   Reckoning periods of time

(1) The parties are free to agree on the method of reckoning periods of time for the purposes of any provision agreed by them or any provision of this Part having effect in default of such agreement.

(2) If or to the extent there is no such agreement, periods of time shall be reckoned in accordance with the following provisions.

(3) Where the act is required to be done within a specified period after or from a specified date, the period begins immediately after that date.

(4) Where the act is required to be done a specified number of clear days after a specified date, at least that number of days must intervene between the day on which the act is done and that date.

(5) Where the period is a period of seven days or less which would include a Saturday, Sunday or a public holiday in the place where anything which has to be done within the period falls to be done, that day shall be excluded.

In relation to England and Wales or Northern Ireland, a 'public holiday' means Christmas Day, Good Friday or a day which under the Banking and Financial Dealings Act 1971 is a bank holiday.

79   Power of court to extend time limits relating to arbitral proceedings

(1) Unless the parties otherwise agree, the court may by order extend any time limit agreed by them in relation to any matter relating to the arbitral proceedings or specified in any provision of this Part having effect in default of such agreement.

This section does not apply to a time limit to which section 12 applies (power of court to extend time for beginning arbitral proceedings, &c.).

(2) An application for an order may be made—

(a) by any party to the arbitral proceedings (upon notice to the other parties and to the tribunal), or

(b) by the arbitral tribunal (upon notice to the parties).

(3) The court shall not exercise its power to extend a time limit unless it is satisfied—

(a) that any available recourse to the tribunal, or to any arbitral or other institution or person vested by the parties with power in that regard, has first been exhausted, and

(b) that a substantial injustice would otherwise be done.

(4) The court's power under this section may be exercised whether or not the time has already expired.

(5) An order under this section may be made on such terms as the court thinks fit.

(6) The leave of the court is required for any appeal from a decision of the court under this section.

80   Notice and other requirements in connection with legal proceedings

(1) References in this Part to an application, appeal or other step in relation to legal proceedings being taken 'upon notice' to the other parties to the arbitral proceedings, or to the tribunal, are to such notice of the originating process as is required by rules of court and do not impose any separate requirement.

(2) Rules of court shall be made—

(a) requiring such notice to be given as indicated by any provision of this Part, and

(b) as to the manner, form and content of any such notice.

(3) Subject to any provision made by rules of court, a requirement to give notice to the tribunal of legal proceedings shall be construed—

(a) if there is more than one arbitrator, as a requirement to give notice to each of them; and

(b) if the tribunal is not fully constituted, as a requirement to give notice to any arbitrator who has been appointed.

(4) References in this Part to making an application or appeal to the court within a specified period are to the issue within that period of the appropriate originating process in accordance with rules of court.

(5) Where any provision of this Part requires an application or appeal to be made to the court within a specified time, the rules of court relating to the reckoning of periods, the extending or abridging of periods, and the consequences of not taking a step within the period prescribed by the rules, apply in relation to that requirement.

(6) Provision may be made by rules of court amending the provisions of this Part—

(a) with respect to the time within which any application or appeal to the court must be made,

(b) so as to keep any provision made by this Part in relation to arbitral proceedings in step with the corresponding provision of rules of court applying in relation to proceedings in the court, or

(c) so as to keep any provision made by this Part in relation to legal proceedings in step with the corresponding provision of rules of court applying generally in relation to proceedings in the court.

(7) Nothing in this section affects the generality of the power to make rules of court.

81   Saving for certain matters governed by common law

(1) Nothing in this Part shall be construed as excluding the operation of any rule of law consistent with the provisions of this Part, in particular, any rule of law as to—

(a) matters which are not capable of settlement by arbitration;

(b) the effect of an oral arbitration agreement; or

(c) the refusal of recognition or enforcement of an arbitral award on grounds of public policy.

(2) Nothing in this Act shall be construed as reviving any jurisdiction of the court to set aside or remit an award on the ground of errors of fact or law on the face of the award.

82   Minor definitions

(1) In this Part—

'arbitrator', unless the context otherwise requires, includes an umpire;

'available arbitral process', in relation to any matter, includes any process of appeal to or review by an arbitral or other institution or person vested by the parties with powers in relation to that matter;

'claimant', unless the context otherwise requires, includes a counterclaimant, and related expressions shall be construed accordingly;

'dispute' includes any difference;

'enactment' includes an enactment contained in Northern Ireland legislation;

'legal proceedings' means civil proceedings [in England and Wales in the High Court or the county court or in Northern Ireland] in the High Court or a county court;

'peremptory order' means an order made under section 41(5) or made in exercise of any corresponding power conferred by the parties;

'premises' includes land, buildings, moveable structures, vehicles, vessels, aircraft and hovercraft;

'question of law' means—

(a) for a court in England and Wales, a question of the law of England and Wales, and

(b) for a court in Northern Ireland, a question of the law of Northern Ireland;

'substantive jurisdiction', in relation to an arbitral tribunal, refers to the matters specified in section 30(1)(a) to (c), and references to the tribunal exceeding its substantive jurisdiction shall be construed accordingly.

(2) References in this Part to a party to an arbitration agreement include any person claiming under or through a party to the agreement.

83   Index of defined expressions: Part I

In this Part the expressions listed below are defined or otherwise explained by the provisions indicated—

agreement, agree and agreed	section 5(1)
agreement in writing	section 5(2) to (5)
arbitration agreement	sections 6 and 5(1)
arbitrator	section 82(1)
available arbitral process	section 82(1)
claimant	section 82(1)
commencement (in relation to arbitral proceedings)	section 14
costs of the arbitration	section 59
the court	section 105
dispute	section 82(1)
enactment	section 82(1)
legal proceedings	section 82(1)
Limitation Acts	section 13(4)
notice (or other document)	section 76(6)
party—	
—in relation to an arbitration agreement	section 82(2)
—where section 106(4) or (3) applies	section 106(4)

agreement, agree and agreed	section 5(1)
question of law	section 82(1)
peremptory order	section 82(1) (and see section 41(5))
premises	section 82(1)
question of law	section 82(1)
recoverable costs	sections 63 and 64
seat of the arbitration	section 3
serve and service (of notice or other document)	section 76(6)
substantive jurisdiction (in relation to an arbitral tribunal)	section 82(1) (and see section 30(1)(a) to (c))
upon notice (to the parties or the tribunal)	section 80
written and in writing	section 5(6)

84   Transitional provisions

(1) The provisions of this Part do not apply to arbitral proceedings commenced before the date on which this Part comes into force.

(2) They apply to arbitral proceedings commenced on or after that date under an arbitration agreement whenever made.

(3) The above provisions have effect subject to any transitional provision made by an order under section 109(2) (power to include transitional provisions in commencement order).

PART II OTHER PROVISIONS RELATING TO ARBITRATION

Domestic arbitration agreements

. . .

Consumer arbitration agreements

89   Application of unfair terms regulations to consumer arbitration agreements

(1) The following sections extend the application of [Part 2 (unfair terms) of the Consumer Rights Act 2015] in relation to a term which constitutes an arbitration agreement.

For this purpose 'arbitration agreement' means an agreement to submit to arbitration present or future disputes or differences (whether or not contractual).

[(2) In those sections 'the Part' means Part 2 (unfair terms) of the Consumer Rights Act 2015.]

(3) Those sections apply whatever the law applicable to the arbitration agreement.

[90   Part applies where consumer is a legal person

The Part applies where the consumer is a legal person as it applies where the consumer is an individual.]

91   Arbitration agreement unfair where modest amount sought

(1) A term which constitutes an arbitration agreement is unfair for the purposes of the [Part] so far as it relates to a claim for a pecuniary remedy which does not exceed the amount specified by order for the purposes of this section.

(2) Orders under this section may make different provision for different cases and for different purposes.

(3) The power to make orders under this section is exercisable—

(a) for England and Wales, by the Secretary of State with the concurrence of the Lord Chancellor,

    (b) for Scotland, by the Secretary of State [. . .], and

    (c) for Northern Ireland, by the Department of Economic Development for Northern Ireland with the concurrence of the Lord Chancellor.

(4) Any such order for England and Wales or Scotland shall be made by statutory instrument which shall be subject to annulment in pursuance of a resolution of either House of Parliament.

(5) Any such order for Northern Ireland shall be a statutory rule for the purposes of the Statutory Rules (Northern Ireland) Order 1979 and shall be subject to negative resolution, within the meaning of section 41(6) of the Interpretation Act (Northern Ireland) 1954.

Small claims arbitration in the county court

92　Exclusion of Part I in relation to small claims arbitration in the county court

Nothing in Part I of this Act applies to arbitration under section 64 of the County Courts Act 1984.

Appointment of judges as arbitrators

93　Appointment of judges as arbitrators

(1) [An eligible High Court judge] or an official referee may, if in all the circumstances he thinks fit, accept appointment as a sole arbitrator or as umpire by or by virtue of an arbitration agreement.

(2) [An eligible High Court judge] shall not do so unless the Lord Chief Justice has informed him that, having regard to the state of business in the High Court and the Crown Court, he can be made available.

(3) An official referee shall not do so unless the Lord Chief Justice has informed him that, having regard to the state of official referees' business, he can be made available.

(4) The fees payable for the services of [an eligible High Court judge] or official referee as arbitrator or umpire shall be taken in the High Court.

[(4A) The Lord Chief Justice may nominate a senior judge (as defined in section 109(5) of the Constitutional Reform Act 2005) to exercise functions of the Lord Chief Justice under this section.]

(5) In this section—

'arbitration agreement' has the same meaning as in Part I; [. . .]

['eligible High Court judge' means—

    (a) a puisne judge of the High Court, or

    (b) a person acting as a judge of the High Court under or by virtue of section 9(1) of the Senior Courts Act 1981;]

'official referee' means a person nominated under section 68(1)(a) of [the Senior Courts Act 1981] to deal with official referees' business.

(6) The provisions of Part I of this Act apply to arbitration before a person appointed under this section with the modifications specified in Schedule 2.

Statutory arbitrations

94　Application of Part I to statutory arbitrations

(1) The provisions of Part I apply to every arbitration under an enactment (a 'statutory arbitration'), whether the enactment was passed or made before or after the commencement of this Act, subject to the adaptations and exclusions specified in sections 95 to 98.

(2) The provisions of Part I do not apply to a statutory arbitration if or to the extent that their application—

    (a) is inconsistent with the provisions of the enactment concerned, with any rules or procedure authorised or recognised by it, or

    (b) is excluded by any other enactment.

(3) In this section and the following provisions of this Part 'enactment'—

    (a) in England and Wales, includes an enactment contained in subordinate legislation within the meaning of the Interpretation Act 1978;

    (b) in Northern Ireland, means a statutory provision within the meaning of section 1(f) of the Interpretation Act (Northern Ireland) 1954.

95 General adaptation of provisions in relation to statutory arbitrations

(1) The provisions of Part I apply to a statutory arbitration—

    (a) as if the arbitration were pursuant to an arbitration agreement and as if the enactment were that agreement, and

    (b) as if the persons by and against whom a claim subject to arbitration in pursuance of the enactment may be or has been made were parties to that agreement.

(2) Every statutory arbitration shall be taken to have its seat in England and Wales, or, as the case may be, in Northern Ireland.

96 Specific adaptations of provisions in relation to statutory arbitrations

(1) The following provisions of Part I apply to a statutory arbitration with the following adaptations.

(2) In section 30(1) (competence of tribunal to rule on its own jurisdiction), the reference in paragraph (a) to whether there is a valid arbitration agreement shall be construed as a reference to whether the enactment applies to the dispute or difference in question.

(3) Section 35 (consolidation of proceedings and concurrent hearings) applies only so as to authorise the consolidation of proceedings, or concurrent hearings in proceedings, under the same enactment.

(4) Section 46 (rules applicable to substance of dispute) applies with the omission of subsection (1)(b) (determination in accordance with considerations agreed by parties).

97 Provisions excluded from applying to statutory arbitrations

The following provisions of Part I do not apply in relation to a statutory arbitration—

    (a) section 8 (whether agreement discharged by death of a party);

    (b) section 12 (power of court to extend agreed time limits);

    (c) sections 9(5), 10(2) and 71(4) (restrictions on effect of provision that award condition precedent to right to bring legal proceedings).

98 Power to make further provision by regulations

(1) The Secretary of State may make provision by regulations for adapting or excluding any provision of Part I in relation to statutory arbitrations in general or statutory arbitrations of any particular description.

(2) The power is exercisable whether the enactment concerned is passed or made before or after the commencement of this Act.

(3) Regulations under this section shall be made by statutory instrument which shall be subject to annulment in pursuance of a resolution of either House of Parliament.

PART III RECOGNITION AND ENFORCEMENT OF CERTAIN FOREIGN AWARDS

Enforcement of Geneva Convention awards

99 Continuation of Part II of the Arbitration Act 1950

Part II of the Arbitration Act 1950 (enforcement of certain foreign awards) continues to apply in relation to foreign awards within the meaning of that Part which are not also New York Convention awards.

Recognition and enforcement of New York Convention awards

100 New York Convention awards

(1) In this Part a 'New York Convention award' means an award made, in pursuance of an arbitration agreement, in the territory of a state (other than the United Kingdom) which is a party to the New York Convention.

(2) For the purposes of subsection (1) and of the provisions of this Part relating to such awards—

(a) 'arbitration agreement' means an arbitration agreement in writing, and

(b) an award shall be treated as made at the seat of the arbitration, regardless of where it was signed, despatched or delivered to any of the parties.

In this subsection 'agreement in writing' and 'seat of the arbitration' have the same meaning as in Part I.

(3) If Her Majesty by Order in Council declares that a state specified in the Order is a party to the New York Convention, or is a party in respect of any territory so specified, the Order shall, while in force, be conclusive evidence of that fact.

(4) In this section 'the New York Convention' means the Convention on the Recognition and Enforcement of Foreign Arbitral Awards adopted by the United Nations Conference on International Commercial Arbitration on 10th June 1958.

101 Recognition and enforcement of awards

(1) A New York Convention award shall be recognised as binding on the persons as between whom it was made, and may accordingly be relied on by those persons by way of defence, set-off or otherwise in any legal proceedings in England and Wales or Northern Ireland.

(2) A New York Convention award may, by leave of the court, be enforced in the same manner as a judgment or order of the court to the same effect.

As to the meaning of 'the court' see section 105.

(3) Where leave is so given, judgment may be entered in terms of the award.

102 Evidence to be produced by party seeking recognition or enforcement

(1) A party seeking the recognition or enforcement of a New York Convention award must produce—

(a) the duly authenticated original award or a duly certified copy of it, and

(b) the original arbitration agreement or a duly certified copy of it.

(2) If the award or agreement is in a foreign language, the party must also produce a translation of it certified by an official or sworn translator or by a diplomatic or consular agent.

103 Refusal of recognition or enforcement

(1) Recognition or enforcement of a New York Convention award shall not be refused except in the following cases.

(2) Recognition or enforcement of the award may be refused if the person against whom it is revoked proves—

(a) that a party to the arbitration agreement was (under the law applicable to him) under some incapacity;

(b) that the arbitration agreement was not valid under the law to which the parties subjected it or, failing any indication thereon, under the law of the country where the award was made;

(c) that he was not given proper notice of the appointment of the arbitrator or of the arbitration proceedings or was otherwise unable to present his case;

(d) that the award deals with a difference not contemplated by or not falling within the terms of the submission to arbitration or contains decisions on matters beyond the scope of the submission to arbitration (but see subsection (4))

(e) that the composition of the arbitral tribunal or the arbitral procedure was not in accordance with the agreement of the parties or, failing such arrangement, with the law of the country in which the arbitration took place;

(f) that the award has not yet become binding on the parties, or has been set aside or suspended by a competent authority of the country in which, or under the law of which, it was made.

(3) Recognition or enforcement of the award may also be refused if the award is in respect of a matter which is not capable of settlement by arbitration, or if it would be contrary to public policy to recognise or enforce the award.

(4) An award which contains decisions on matters not submitted to arbitration may be recognised or enforced to the extent that it contains decisions on matters submitted to arbitration which can be separated from those on matters not so submitted.

(5) Where an application for the setting aside or suspension of the award has been made to such a competent authority as is mentioned in subsection (2)(f), the court before which the award is sought to be relied upon may, if it considers it proper, adjourn the decision on the recognition or enforcement of the award.

It may also on the application of the party claiming recognition or enforcement of the award order the other party to give suitable security.

104 Saving for other bases of recognition or enforcement

Nothing in the preceding provisions of this Part affects any right to rely upon or enforce a New York Convention award at common law or under section 66.

PART IV GENERAL PROVISIONS

105 Meaning of 'the court': jurisdiction of High Court and county court

(1) In this Act 'the court' [in relation to England and Wales means the High Court or the county court and in relation to Northern Ireland] means the High Court or a county court, subject to the following provisions.

(2) The Lord Chancellor may by order make provision—

[(za) allocating proceedings under this Act in England and Wales to the High Court or the county court;]

(a) allocating proceedings under this Act [in Northern Ireland] to the High Court or to county courts; or

(b) specifying proceedings under this Act which may be commenced or taken only in the High Court or in [the county court or (as the case may be)] a county court.

(3) The Lord Chancellor may by order make provision requiring proceedings of any specified description under this Act in relation to which a county court [in Northern Ireland] has jurisdiction to be commenced or taken in one or more specified county courts.

Any jurisdiction so exercisable by a specified county court is exercisable throughout [...] Northern Ireland.

[(3A) The Lord Chancellor must consult the Lord Chief Justice of England and Wales or the Lord Chief Justice of Northern Ireland (as the case may be) before making an order under this section.

(3B) The Lord Chief Justice of England and Wales may nominate a judicial office holder (as defined in section 109(4) of the Constitutional Reform Act 2005) to exercise his functions under this section.

(3C) The Lord Chief Justice of Northern Ireland may nominate any of the following to exercise his functions under this section—

(a) the holder of one of the offices listed in Schedule 1 to the Justice (Northern Ireland) Act 2002;

(b) a Lord Justice of Appeal (as defined in section 88 of that Act).]

(4) An order under this section—

(a) may differentiate between categories of proceedings by reference to such criteria as the Lord Chancellor sees fit to specify, and

(b) may make such incidental or transitional provision as the Lord Chancellor considers necessary or expedient.

(5) An order under this section for England and Wales shall be made by statutory instrument which shall be subject to annulment in pursuance of a resolution of either House of Parliament.

(6) An order under this section for Northern Ireland shall be a statutory rule for the purposes of the Statutory Rules (Northern Ireland) Order 1979 which shall be subject to annulment in pursuance of a resolution of either House of Parliament in like manner as a statutory instrument and section 5 of the Statutory Instruments Act 1946 shall apply accordingly.

106   Crown application

(1) Part I of this Act applies to any arbitration agreement to which Her Majesty, either in right of the Crown or of the Duchy of Lancaster or otherwise, or the Duke of Cornwall, is a party.

(2) Where Her Majesty is party to an arbitration agreement otherwise than in right of the Crown, Her Majesty shall be represented for the purposes of any arbitral proceedings—

(a) where the agreement was entered into by Her Majesty in right of the Duchy of Lancaster, by the Chancellor of the Duchy or such person as he may appoint, and

(b) in any other case, by such person as Her Majesty may appoint in writing under the Royal Sign Manual.

(3) Where the Duke of Cornwall is party to an arbitration agreement, he shall be represented for the purposes of any arbitral proceedings by such person as he may appoint.

(4) References in Part I to a party or the parties to the arbitration agreement or to arbitral proceedings shall be construed, where subsection (2) or (3) applies, as references to the person representing Her Majesty or the Duke of Cornwall.

Section 4(1) **SCHEDULE 1**

MANDATORY PROVISIONS OF PART I

sections 9 to 11 (stay of legal proceedings);

section 12 (power of court to extend agreed time limits);

section 13 (application of Limitation Acts);

section 24 (power of court to remove arbitrator);

section 26(1) (effect of death of arbitrator);

section 28 (liability of parties for fees and expenses of arbitrators);

section 29 (immunity of arbitrator);

section 31 (objection to substantive jurisdiction of tribunal);

section 32 (determination of preliminary point of jurisdiction);

section 33 (general duty of tribunal);

section 37(2) (items to be treated as expenses of arbitrators);

section 40 (general duty of parties);

section 43 (securing the attendance of witnesses);

section 56 (power to withhold award in case of non-payment);

section 60 (effectiveness of agreement for payment of costs in any event);

section 66 (enforcement of award);

sections 67 and 68 (challenging the award: substantive jurisdiction and serious irregularity), and sections 70 and 71 (supplementary provisions; effect of order of court) so far as relating to those sections;

section 72 (saving for rights of person who takes no part in proceedings);
section 73 (loss of right to object);
section 74 (immunity of arbitral institutions, &c.);
section 75 (charge to secure payment of solicitors' costs).

SCHEDULE 2

MODIFICATIONS OF PART I IN RELATION TO JUDGE-ARBITRATORS

Introductory

1. In this Schedule 'judge-arbitrator' means [an eligible High Court judge] or official referee appointed as arbitrator or umpire under section 93.

General

2.—(1) Subject to the following provisions of this Schedule, references in Part I to the court shall be construed in relation to a judge-arbitrator, or in relation to the appointment of a judge-arbitrator, as references to the Court of Appeal.

(2) The references in sections 32(6), 45(6) and 69(8) to the Court of Appeal shall in such a case be construed as references to the [Supreme Court].

Arbitrator's fees

3.—(1) The power of the court in section 28(2) to order consideration and adjustment of the liability of a party for the fees of an arbitrator may be exercised by a judge-arbitrator.

(2) Any such exercise of the power is subject to the powers of the Court of Appeal under sections 24(4) and 25(3)(b) (directions as to entitlement to fees or expenses in case of removal or resignation).

Exercise of court powers in support of arbitration

4.—(1) Where the arbitral tribunal consists of or includes a judge-arbitrator the powers of the court under sections 42 to 44 (enforcement of peremptory orders, summoning witnesses, and other court powers) are exercisable by the High Court and also by the judge-arbitrator himself.

(2) Anything done by a judge-arbitrator in the exercise of those powers shall be regarded as done by him in his capacity as judge of the High Court and have effect as if done by that court.

Nothing in this sub-paragraph prejudices any power vested in him as arbitrator or umpire.

Extension of time for making award

5.—(1) The power conferred by section 50 (extension of time for making award) is exercisable by the judge-arbitrator himself.

(2) Any appeal from a decision of a judge-arbitrator under that section lies to the Court of Appeal with the leave of that court.

Withholding award in case of non-payment

6.—(1) The provisions of paragraph 7 apply in place of the provisions of section 56 (power to withhold award in the case of non-payment) in relation to the withholding of an award for non-payment of the fees and expenses of a judge-arbitrator.

(2) This does not affect the application of section 56 in relation to the delivery of such an award by an arbitral or other institution or person vested by the parties with powers in relation to the delivery of the award

7.—(1) A judge-arbitrator may refuse to deliver an award except upon payment of the fees and expenses mentioned in section 56(1).

(2) The judge-arbitrator may, on an application by a party to the arbitral proceedings, order that if he pays into the High Court the fees and expenses demanded, or such lesser amount as the judge-arbitrator may specify—

    (a) the award shall be delivered,

    (b) the amount of the fees and expenses properly payable shall be determined by such means and upon such terms as he may direct, and

    (c) out of the money paid into court there shall be paid out such fees and expenses as may be found to be properly payable and the balance of the money (if any) shall be paid out to the applicant.

(3) For this purpose the amount of fees and expenses properly payable is the amount the applicant is liable to pay under section 28 or any agreement relating to the payment of the arbitrator.

(4) No application to the judge-arbitrator under this paragraph may be made where there is any available arbitral process for appeal or review of the amount of the fees or expenses demanded.

(5) Any appeal from a decision of a judge-arbitrator under this paragraph lies to the Court of Appeal with the leave of that court.

(6) Where a party to arbitral proceedings appeals under sub-paragraph (5), an arbitrator is entitled to appear and be heard.

Correction of award or additional award

8. Subsections (4) to (6) of section 57 (correction of award or additional award: time limit for application or exercise of power) do not apply to a judge-arbitrator.

Costs

9. Where the arbitral tribunal consists of or includes a judge-arbitrator the powers of the court under section 63(4) (determination of recoverable costs) shall be exercised by the High Court.

10.—(1) The power of the court under section 64 to determine an arbitrator's reasonable fees and expenses may be exercised by a judge-arbitrator.

(2) Any such exercise of the power is subject to the powers of the Court of Appeal under sections 24(4) and 25(3)(b) (directions as to entitlement to fees or expenses in case of removal or resignation).

Enforcement of award

11. The leave of the court required by section 66 (enforcement of award) may in the case of an award of a judge-arbitrator be given by the judge-arbitrator himself.

Solicitors' costs

12. The powers of the court to make declarations and orders under the provisions applied by section 75 (power to charge property recovered in arbitral proceedings with the payment of solicitors' costs) may be exercised by the judge-arbitrator.

Powers of court in relation to service of documents

13.—(1) The power of the court under section 77(2) (powers of court in relation to service of documents) is exercisable by the judge-arbitrator.

(2) Any appeal from a decision of a judge-arbitrator under that section lies to the Court of Appeal with the leave of that court.

Powers of court to extend time limits relating to arbitral proceedings

14.—(1) The power conferred by section 79 (power of court to extend time limits relating to arbitral proceedings) is exercisable by the judge-arbitrator himself.

(2) Any appeal from a decision of a judge-arbitrator under that section lies to the Court of Appeal with the leave of that court.

Late Payment of Commercial Debts (Interest) Act 1998

(1998, c. 20)

PART I STATUTORY INTEREST ON QUALIFYING DEBTS

1 Statutory interest

(1) It is an implied term in a contract to which this Act applies that any qualifying debt created by the contract carries simple interest subject to and in accordance with this Part.

(2) Interest carried under that implied term (in this Act referred to as 'statutory interest') shall be treated, for the purposes of any rule of law or enactment (other than this Act) relating to interest on debts, in the same way as interest carried under an express contract term.

(3) This Part has effect subject to Part II (which in certain circumstances permits contract terms to oust or vary the right to statutory interest that would otherwise be conferred by virtue of the term implied by subsection (1)).

2 Contracts to which Act applies

(1) This Act applies to a contract for the supply of goods or services where the purchaser and the supplier are each acting in the course of a business, other than an excepted contract.

(2) In this Act 'contract for the supply of goods or services' means—

(a) a contract of sale of goods; or

(b) a contract (other than a contract of sale of goods) by which a person does any, or any combination, of the things mentioned in subsection (3) for a consideration that is (or includes) a money consideration.

(3) Those things are—

(a) transferring or agreeing to transfer to another the property in goods;

(b) bailing or agreeing to bail goods to another by way of hire or, in Scotland, hiring or agreeing to hire goods to another; and

(c) agreeing to carry out a service

(4) For the avoidance of doubt a contract of service or apprenticeship is nor a contract for the supply of goods or services.

(5) The following are excepted contracts—

(a) a consumer credit agreement;

(b) a contract intended to operate by way of mortgage, pledge, charge or other security; and

(7) In this section—

'business' includes a profession and the activities of any government department or local or public authority;

'consumer credit agreement' has the same meaning as in the Consumer Credit Act 1974;

'contract of sale of goods' and 'goods' have the same meaning as in the Sale of Goods Act 1979;

['government department' includes any part of the Scottish Administration;]

'property in goods' means the general property in them and not merely a special property.

3 Qualifying debts

(1) A debt created by virtue of an obligation under a contract to which this Act applies to pay the whole or any part of the contract price is a 'qualifying debt' for the purposes of this Act, unless (when created) the whole of the debt is prevented from carrying statutory interest by this section.

(2) A debt does not carry statutory interest if or to the extent that it consists of a sum to which a right to interest or to charge interest applies by virtue of any enactment (other than section 1 of this Act).

This subsection does not prevent a sum from carrying statutory interest by reason of the fact that a court, arbitrator or arbiter would, apart from this Act, have power to award interest on it.

(3) A debt does not carry (and shall be treated as never having carried) statutory interest if or to the extent that a right to demand interest on it, which exists by virtue of any rule of law, is exercised.

4 Period for which statutory interest runs

(1) Statutory interest runs in relation to a qualifying debt in accordance with this section (unless section 5 applies).

(2) Statutory interest starts to run on the day after the relevant day for the debt, at the rate prevailing under section 6 at the end of the relevant day.

[(2A) The relevant day for a debt is—

    (a) where there is an agreed payment day, that day, unless a different day is given by subsection (2D), (2E) or (2G);

    (b) where there is not an agreed payment day, the last day of the relevant 30-day period.

(2B) An 'agreed payment day' is a date agreed between the supplier and the purchaser for payment of the debt (that is, the day on which the debt is to be created by the contract).

(2C) A date agreed for payment of a debt may be a fixed date or may depend on the happening of an event or the failure of an event to happen.

(2D) Where—

    (a) the purchaser is a public authority, and

    (b) the last day of the relevant 30-day period falls earlier than the agreed payment day,

the relevant day is the last day of the relevant 30-day period, unless subsection (2G) applies.

(2E) Where—

    (a) the purchaser is not a public authority, and

    (b) the last day of the relevant 60-day period falls earlier than the agreed payment day,

the relevant day is the last day of the relevant 60-day period, unless subsection (2G) applies.

(2F) But subsection (2E) does not apply (and so the relevant day is the agreed payment day, unless subsection (2G) applies) if the agreed payment day is not grossly unfair to the supplier (see subsection (7A)).

(2G) Where the debt relates to an obligation to make an advance payment, the relevant day is the day on which the debt is treated by section 11 as having been created (instead of the agreed payment day or the day given by subsection (2D) or (2E)).

(2H) 'The relevant 30-day period' is the period of 30 days beginning with the later or latest of—

    (a) the day on which the obligation of the supplier to which the debt relates is performed;

    (b) the day on which the purchaser has notice of the amount of the debt or (where that amount is unascertained) the sum which the supplier claims is the amount of the debt;

    (c) where subsection (5A) applies, the day determined under subsection (5B).

(2I) 'The relevant 60-day period' is the period of 60 days beginning with the later or latest of—

    (a) the day on which the obligation of the supplier to which the debt relates is performed;

    (b) the day on which the purchaser has notice of the amount of the debt or (where that amount is unascertained) the sum which the supplier claims is the amount of the debt;

    (c) where subsection (5A) applies, the day determined under subsection (5B).]

[. . .]

[(5A) This subsection applies where—

    (a) there is a procedure of acceptance or verification (whether provided for by an enactment or by the contract), under which the conforming of goods or services with the contract is to be ascertained, and

    (b) the purchaser has notice of the amount of the debt on or before the day on which the procedure is completed.

(5B) For the purposes of subsections (2H)(c) and (2I)(c), the day in question is the day . . . after the day on which the procedure is completed.

(5C) Where, in a case where subsection (5A) applies, the procedure in question is completed after the end of the period of 30 days beginning with the day on which the obligation of the supplier to which the debt relates is performed, the procedure is to be treated for the purposes of subsection (5B) as being completed immediately after the end of that period.

(5D) Subsection (5C) does not apply if—

(a) the supplier and the purchaser expressly agree in the contract a period for completing the procedure in question that is longer than the period mentioned in that subsection, and

(b) that longer period is not grossly unfair to the supplier (see subsection (7A)).]

(6) Where the debt is created by virtue of an obligation to pay a sum due in respect of a period of hire of goods, [subsections (2H)(a) and (2I)(a) have effect as if they] referred to the last day of that period.

(7) Statutory interest ceases to run when the interest would cease to run if it were carried under an express contract term.

[(7A) In determining for the purposes of subsection (2F) or (5D) whether something is grossly unfair, all circumstances of the case shall be considered; and for that purpose, the circumstances of the case include in particular—

(a) anything that is a gross deviation from good commercial practice and contrary to good faith and fair dealing,

(b) the nature of the goods or services in question, and

(c) whether the purchaser has any objective reason to deviate from the result which is provided for by subsection (2E) or (5C).]

[(8) In this section—

'advance payment' has the same meaning as in section 11;

'enactment' includes an enactment contained in subordinate legislation (within the meaning of the Interpretation Act 1978);

'public authority' means a contracting authority (within the meaning of regulation 3 of the Public Contracts Regulations 2006).]

5   Remission of statutory interest

(1) This section applies where, by reason of any conduct of the supplier, the interests of justice require that statutory interest should be remitted in whole or part in respect of a period for which it would otherwise run in relation to a qualifying debt.

(2) If the interests of justice require that the supplier should receive no statutory interest for a period, statutory interest shall not run for that period.

(3) If the interests of justice require that the supplier should receive statutory interest at a reduced rate for a period, statutory interest shall run at such rate as meets the justice of the case for that period.

(4) Remission of statutory interest under this section may be required—

(a) by reason of conduct at any time (whether before or after the time at which the debt is created); and

(b) for the whole period for which statutory interest would otherwise run or for one or more parts of that period.

(5) In this section 'conduct' includes any act or omission.

[5A   Compensation arising out of late payment

(1) Once statutory interest begins to run in relation to a qualifying debt, the supplier shall be entitled to a fixed sum (in addition to the statutory interest on the debt).

(2) That sum shall be—

(a) for a debt less than £1,000, the sum of £40;

(b) for a debt of £1,000 or more, but less than £10,000, the sum of £70;

(c) for a debt of £10,000 or more, the sum of £100.

(2A) If the reasonable costs of the supplier in recovering the debt are not met by the fixed sum, the supplier shall also be entitled to a sum equivalent to the difference between the fixed sum and those costs.

(3) The obligation to pay a sum under this section in respect of a qualifying debt shall be treated as part of the term implied by section 1(1) in the contract creating the debt.

(4) Section 3(2)(b) of the Unfair Contract Terms Act 1977 (no reliance to be placed on certain contract terms) shall apply in cases where a contract term is not contained in written standard terms of the purchaser as well as in cases where the term is contained in such standard terms.

(5) In this section 'contract term' means a term of the contract relating to a sum due to the supplier under this section.]

6   Rate of statutory interest

(1) The Secretary of State shall by order made with the consent of the Treasury set the rate of statutory interest by prescribing—

    (a) a formula for calculating the rate of statutory interest; or

    (b) the rate of statutory interest.

(2) Before making such an order the Secretary of State shall, among other things, consider the extent to which it may be desirable to set the rate so as to—

    (a) protect suppliers whose financial position makes them particularly vulnerable if their qualifying debts are paid late; and

    (b) deter generally the late payment of qualifying debts.

PART II CONTRACT TERMS RELATING TO LATE PAYMENT OF QUALIFYING DEBTS

7   Purpose of Part II

(1) This Part deals with the extent to which the parties to a contract to which this Act applies may by reference to contract terms oust or vary the right to statutory interest that would otherwise apply when a qualifying debt created by the contract (in this Part referred to as 'the debt') is not paid.

(2) This Part applies to contract terms agreed before the debt is created; after that time the parties are free to agree terms dealing with the debt.

(3) This Part has effect without prejudice to any other ground which may affect the validity of a contract term.

8   Circumstances where statutory interest may be ousted or varied

(1) Any contract terms are void to the extent that they purport to exclude the right to statutory interest in relation to the debt, unless there is a substantial contractual remedy for late payment of the debt.

(2) Where the parties agree a contractual remedy for late payment of the debt that is a substantial remedy, statutory interest is not carried by the debt (unless they agree otherwise).

(3) The parties may not agree to vary the right to statutory interest in relation to the debt unless either the right to statutory interest as varied or the overall remedy for late payment of the debt is a substantial remedy.

(4) Any contract terms are void to the extent that they purport to—

    (a) confer a contractual right to interest that is not a substantial remedy for late payment of the debt, or

    (b) vary the right to statutory interest so as to provide for a right to statutory interest that is not a substantial remedy for late payment of the debt,

unless the overall remedy for late payment of the debt is a substantial remedy.

(5) Subject to this section, the parties are free to agree contract terms which deal with the consequences of late payment of the debt.

9 Meaning of 'substantial remedy'

(1) A remedy for the late payment of the debt shall be regarded as a substantial remedy unless—

    (a) the remedy is insufficient either for the purpose of compensating the supplier for late payment or for deterring late payment; and

    (b) it would not be fair or reasonable to allow the remedy to be relied on to oust or (as the case may be) to vary the right to statutory interest that would otherwise apply in relation to the debt.

(2) In determining whether a remedy is not a substantial remedy, regard shall be had to all the relevant circumstances at the time the terms in question are agreed.

(3) In determining whether subsection (1)(b) applies, regard shall be had (without prejudice to the generality of subsection (2)) to the following matters—

    (a) the benefits of commercial certainty;

    (b) the strength of the bargaining positions of the parties relative to each other;

    (c) whether the term was imposed by one party to the detriment of the other (whether by the use of standard terms or otherwise); and

    (d) whether the supplier received an inducement to agree to the term.

10 Interpretation of Part II

(1) In this Part—

'contract term' means a term of the contract creating the debt or any other contract term binding the parties (or either of them);

'contractual remedy' means a contractual right to interest or any contractual remedy other than interest;

'contractual right to interest' includes a reference to a contractual right to charge interest;

'overall remedy', in relation to the late payment of the debt, means any combination of a contractual right to interest, a varied right to statutory interest or a contractual remedy other than interest;

'substantial remedy' shall be construed in accordance with section 9.

(2) In this Part a reference (however worded) to contract terms which vary the right to statutory interest is a reference to terms altering in any way the effect of Part I in relation to the debt (for example by postponing the time at which interest starts to run or by imposing conditions on the right to interest).

(3) In this Part a reference to late payment of the debt is a reference to late payment of the sum due when the debt is created (excluding any part of that sum which is prevented from carrying statutory interest by section 3).

PART III GENERAL AND SUPPLEMENTARY

11 Treatment of advance payments of the contract price

(1) A qualifying debt created by virtue of an obligation to make an advance payment shall be treated for the purposes of this Act as if it was created on the day mentioned in subsection (3), (4) or (5) (as the case may be).

(2) In this section 'advance payment' means a payment falling due before the obligation of the supplier to which the whole contract price relates ('the supplier's obligation') is performed, other than a payment of a part of the contract price that is due in respect of any part performance of that obligation and payable on or after the day on which that part performance is completed.

(3) Where the advance payment is the whole contract price, the debt shall be treated as created on the day on which the supplier's obligation is performed.

(4) Where the advance payment is a part of the contract price, but the sum is not due in respect of any part performance of the supplier's obligation, the debt shall be treated as created on the day on which the supplier's obligation is performed.

(5) Where the advance payment is a part of the contract price due in respect of any part performance of the supplier's obligation, but is payable before that part performance is completed, the debt shall be treated as created on the day on which the relevant part performance is completed.

(6) Where the debt is created by virtue of an obligation to pay a sum due in respect of a period of hire of goods, this section has effect as if—

    (a) references to the day on which the supplier's obligation is performed were references to the last day of that period; and

    (b) references to part performance of that obligation were references to part of that period.

(7) For the purposes of this section an obligation to pay the whole outstanding balance of the contract price shall be regarded as an obligation to pay the whole contract price and not as an obligation to pay a part of the contract price.

12 Conflict of laws

(1) This Act does not have effect in relation to a contract governed by the law of a part of the United Kingdom by choice of the parties if—

    (a) there is no significant connection between the contract and that part of the United Kingdom; and

    (b) but for that choice, the applicable law would be a foreign law.

(2) This Act has effect in relation to a contract governed by a foreign law by choice of the parties if—

    (a) but for that choice, the applicable law would be the law of a part of the United Kingdom; and

    (b) there is no significant connection between the contract and any country other than that part of the United Kingdom.

(3) In this section—

'contract' means a contract falling within section 2(1); and

'foreign law' means the law of a country outside the United Kingdom.

13 Assignments, etc.

(1) The operation of this Act in relation to a qualifying debt is not affected by—

    (a) any change in the identity of the parties to the contract creating the debt; or

    (b) the passing of the right to be paid the debt, or the duty to pay it (in whole or in part) to a person other than the person who is the original creditor or the original debtor when the debt is created.

(2) Any reference in this Act to the supplier or the purchaser is a reference to the person who is for the time being the supplier or the purchaser or, in relation to a time after the debt in question has been created, the person who is for the time being the creditor or the debtor, as the case may be.

(3) Where the right to be paid part of a debt passes to a person other than the person who is the original creditor when the debt is created, any reference in this Act to a debt shall be construed as (or, if the context so requires, as including) a reference to part of a debt.

(4) A reference in this section to the identity of the parties to a contract changing, or to a right or duty passing, is a reference to it changing or passing by assignment or assignation, by operation of law or otherwise.

14 Contract terms relating to the date for payment of the contract price

(1) This section applies to any contract term which purports to have the effect of postponing the time at which a qualifying debt would otherwise be created by a contract to which this Act applies.

(2) Sections 3(2)(b) and 17(1)(b) of the Unfair Contract Terms Act 1977 (no reliance to be placed on certain contract terms) shall apply in cases where such a contract term is not contained in written standard terms of the purchaser as well as in cases where the term is contained in such standard terms.

(3) In this section 'contract term' has the same meaning as in section 10(1).

15 Orders and regulations

(1) Any power to make an order or regulations under this Act is exercisable by statutory instrument.

(2) Any statutory instrument containing an order or regulations under this Act, other than an order under section 17(2), shall be subject to annulment in pursuance of a resolution of either House of Parliament.

16 Interpretation

(1) In this Act—

'contract for the supply of goods or services' has the meaning given in section 2(2);

'contract price' means the price in a contract of sale of goods or the money consideration referred to in section 2(2)(b) in any other contract for the supply of goods or services;

'purchaser' means (subject to section 13(2)) the seller in a contract of sale or the person who contracts with the supplier in any other contract for the supply of goods or services;

'qualifying debt' means a debt falling within section 3(1);

'statutory interest' means interest carried by virtue of the term implied by section 1(1); and

'supplier' means (subject to section 13(2)) the seller in a contract of sale of goods or the person who does one or more of the things mentioned in section 2(3) in any other contract for the supply of goods or services.

(2) In this Act any reference (however worded) to an agreement or to contract terms includes a reference to both express and implied terms (including terms established by a course of dealing or by such usage as binds the parties).

Contracts (Rights of Third Parties) Act 1999

(1999, c. 31)

1 Right of third party to enforce contractual term

(1) Subject to the provisions of this Act, a person who is not a party to a contract (a 'third party') may in his own right enforce a term of the contract if—

(a) the contract expressly provides that he may, or

(b) subject to subsection (2), the term purports to confer a benefit on him.

(2) Subsection (1)(b) does not apply if on a proper construction of the contract it appears that the parties did not intend the term to be enforceable by the third party.

(3) The third party must be expressly identified in the contract by name, as a member of a class or as answering a particular description but need not be in existence when the contract is entered into.

(4) This section does not confer a right on a third party to enforce a term of a contract otherwise than subject to and in accordance with any other relevant terms of the contract.

(5) For the purpose of exercising his right to enforce a term of the contract, there shall be available to the third party any remedy that would have been available to him in an action for breach of contract if he had been a party to the contract (and the rules relating to damages, injunctions, specific performance and other relief shall apply accordingly).

(6) Where a term of a contract excludes or limits liability in relation to any matter references in this Act to the third party enforcing the term shall be construed as references to his availing himself of the exclusion or limitation.

(7) In this Act, in relation to a term of a contract which is enforceable by a third party—

'the promisor' means the party to the contract against whom the term is enforceable by the third party, and

'the promisee' means the party to the contract by whom the term is enforceable against the promisor.

2 Variation and rescission of contract

(1) Subject to the provisions of this section, where a third party has a right under section 1 to enforce a term of the contract, the parties to the contract may not, by agreement, rescind the contract, or vary it in such a way as to extinguish or alter his entitlement under that right, without his consent if—

    (a) the third party has communicated his assent to the term to the promisor,

    (b) the promisor is aware that the third party has relied on the term, or

    (c) the promisor can reasonably be expected to have foreseen that the third party would rely on the term and the third party has in fact relied on it.

(2) The assent referred to in subsection (1)(a)—

    (a) may be by words or conduct, and

    (b) if sent to the promisor by post or other means, shall not be regarded as communicated to the promisor until received by him.

(3) Subsection (1) is subject to any express term of the contract under which—

    (a) the parties to the contract may by agreement rescind or vary the contract without the consent of the third party, or

    (b) the consent of the third party is required in circumstances specified in the contract instead of those set out in subsection (1)(a) to (c).

(4) Where the consent of a third party is required under subsection (1) or (3), the court or arbitral tribunal may, on the application of the parties to the contract, dispense with his consent if satisfied—

    (a) that his consent cannot be obtained because his whereabouts cannot reasonably be ascertained, or

    (b) that he is mentally incapable of giving his consent.

(5) The court or arbitral tribunal may, on the application of the parties to a contract, dispense with any consent that may be required under subsection (1)(c) if satisfied that it cannot reasonably be ascertained whether or not the third party has in fact relied on the term.

(6) If the court or arbitral tribunal dispenses with a third party's consent, it may impose such conditions as it thinks fit, including a condition requiring the payment of compensation to the third party.

(7) The jurisdiction conferred on the court by subsections (4) to (6) is exercisable [in England and Wales by both the High Court and the county court and in Northern Ireland] by both the High Court and a county court.

3 Defences etc. available to promisor

(1) Subsections (2) to (5) apply where, in reliance on section 1, proceedings for the enforcement of a term of a contract are brought by a third party.

(2) The promisor shall have available to him by way of defence or set-off any matter that—

    (a) arises from or in connection with the contract and is relevant to the term, and

    (b) would have been available to him by way of defence or set-off if the proceedings had been brought by the promisee.

(3) The promisor shall also have available to him by way of defence or set-off any matter if—

    (a) an express term of the contract provides for it to be available to him in proceedings brought by the third party, and

    (b) it would have been available to him by way of defence or set-off if the proceedings had been brought by the promisee.

(4) The promisor shall also have available to him—

    (a) by way of defence or set-off any matter, and

    (b) by way of counterclaim any matter not arising from the contract,

that would have been available to him by way of defence or set-off or, as the case may be, by way of counterclaim against the third party if the third party had been a party to the contract.

(5) Subsections (2) and (4) are subject to any express term of the contract as to the matters that are not available to the promisor by way of defence, set-off or counterclaim.

(6) Where in any proceedings brought against him a third party seeks in reliance on section 1 to enforce a term of a contract (including, in particular, a term purporting to exclude or limit liability), he may not do so if he could not have done so (whether by reason of any particular circumstances relating to him or otherwise) had he been a party to the contract.

4 Enforcement of contract by promisee

Section 1 does not affect any right of the promisee to enforce any term of contract.

5 Protection of promisor from double liability

Where under section 1 a term of a contract is enforceable by a third party, and the promisee has recovered from the promisor a sum in respect of—

(a) the third party's loss in respect of the term, or

(b) the expense to the promisee of making good to the third party the default of the promisor,

then, in any proceedings brought in reliance on that section by the third party, the court or arbitral tribunal shall reduce any award to the third party to such extent as it thinks appropriate to take account of the sum recovered by the promisee.

6 Exceptions

(1) Section 1 confers no rights on a third party in the case of a contract on a bill of exchange, promissory note or other negotiable instrument.

(2) Section 1 confers no rights on a third party in the case of any contract binding on a company and its members under [section 33 of the Companies Act 2006 (effect of company's constitution)].

[(2A) Section 1 confers no rights on a third party in the case of any incorporation document of a limited liability partnership or any agreement (express or implied) between the members of a limited liability partnership, or between a limited liability partnership and its members, that determines the mutual rights and duties of the members and their rights and duties in relation to the limited liability partnership.]

(3) Section 1 confers no right on a third party to enforce—

(a) any term of a contract of employment against an employee,

(b) any term of a worker's contract against a worker (including a home worker), or

(c) any term of a relevant contract against an agency worker.

(4) In subsection (3)—

(a) 'contract of employment', 'employee', 'worker's contract', and 'worker' have the meaning given by section 54 of the National Minimum Wage Act 1998,

(b) 'home worker' has the meaning given by section 35(2) of that Act

(c) 'agency worker' has the same meaning as in section 34(1) of that Act, and

(d) 'relevant contract' means a contract entered into, in a case where section 34 of that Act applies, by the agency worker as respects work falling within subsection (1)(a) of that section.

(5) Section 1 confers no rights on a third party in the case of—

(a) a contract for the carriage of goods by sea, or

(b) a contract for the carriage of goods by rail or road, or for the carriage of cargo by air, which is subject to the rules of the appropriate international transport convention,

except that a third party may in reliance on that section avail himself of an exclusion or limitation of liability in such a contract.

(6) In subsection (5) 'contract for the carriage of goods by sea' means a contract of carriage—

(a) contained in or evidenced by a bill of lading, sea waybill or a corresponding electronic transaction, or

(b) under or for the purposes of which there is given an undertaking which is contained in a ship's delivery order or a corresponding electronic transaction.

(7) For the purposes of subsection (6)—

(a) 'bill of lading', 'sea waybill' and 'ship's delivery order' have the same meaning as in the Carriage of Goods by Sea Act 1992, and

(b) a corresponding electronic transaction is a transaction within section 1(5) of that Act which corresponds to the issue, indorsement, delivery or transfer of a bill of lading, sea waybill or ship's delivery order.

(8) In subsection (5) 'the appropriate international transport convention' means—

    (a) in relation to a contract for the carriage of goods by rail, the Convention which has the force of law in the United Kingdom under [regulation 3 of the Railways (Convention on International Carriage by Rail) Regulations 2005,]

    (b) in relation to a contract for the carriage of goods by road, the Convention which has the force of law in the United Kingdom under section 1 of the Carriage of Goods by Road Act 1965, and

    (c) in relation to a contract for the carriage of cargo by air—

        (i) the Convention which has the force of law in the United Kingdom under section 1 of the Carriage by Air act 1961, or

        (ii) the Convention which has the force of law under section 1 of the Carriage by Air (Supplementary Provisions) Act 1962, or

        (iii) either of the amended Conventions set out in Part B of Schedule 2 or 3 to the Carriage by Air Acts (Application of Provisions) Order 1967.

7 Supplementary provisions relating to third party

(1) Section 1 does not affect any right or remedy of a third party that exists or is available from this Act.

(2) Section 2(2) of the Unfair Contract Terms Act 1977 (restriction on exclusion etc. of liability for negligence) shall not apply where the negligence consists of the breach of an obligation arising from a term of a contract and the person seeking to enforce it is a third party acting in reliance on section 1.

(3) In sections 5 and 8 of the Limitation Act 1980 the references to an action founded on a simple contract and an action upon a specialty shall respectively include references to an action brought in reliance on section 1 relating to a simple contract and an action brought in reliance on that section relating to a specialty.

(4) A third party shall not, by virtue of section 1(5) or 3(4) or (6), be treated as a party to the contract for the purposes of any other Act (or any instrument made under any other Act).

8 Arbitration provisions

(1) Where—

    (a) a right under section 1 to enforce a term ('the substantive term') is subject to a term providing for the submission of disputes to arbitration ('the arbitration agreement'), and

    (b) the arbitration agreement is an agreement in writing for the purposes of Part I of the Arbitration Act 1996,

the third party shall be treated for the purposes of that Act as a party to the arbitration agreement as regards disputes between himself and the promisor relating to the enforcement of the substantive term by the third party.

(2) Where—

    (a) a third party has a right under section 1 to enforce a term providing for one or more descriptions of dispute between the third party and the promisor to be submitted to arbitration ('the arbitration agreement'),

    (b) the arbitration agreement is an agreement in writing for the purposes of Part I of the Arbitration Act 1996, and

    (c) the third party does not fall to be treated under subsection (1) as a party to the arbitration agreement,

the third party shall, if he exercises the right, be treated for the purposes of that Act as a party to the arbitration agreement in relation to the matter with respect to which the right is exercised, and be treated as having been so immediately before the exercise of the right.

Financial Services and Markets Act 2000

(2000, c. 8)

[1A   The Financial Conduct Authority

(1) The body corporate previously known as the Financial Services Authority is renamed as the Financial Conduct Authority.

(2) The Financial Conduct Authority is in this Act referred to as 'the FCA'.

(3) The FCA is to have the functions conferred on it by or under this Act.

(4) The FCA must comply with the requirements as to its constitution set out in Schedule 1ZA.

(5) Schedule 1ZA also makes provision about the status of the FCA and the exercise of certain of its functions.

(6) References in this Act or any other enactment to functions conferred on the FCA by or under this Act include references to functions conferred on the FCA by or under—

   (a)   the Insolvency Act 1986,
   (b)   the Banking Act 2009,
   (c)   the Financial Services Act 2012,
   (cza) the Financial Guidance and Claims Act 2018,
   (czb) the Civil Liability Act 2018,
   [(ca) the Alternative Investment Fund Managers Regulations 2013, or]
   (d)   a [qualifying provision] that is specified, or of a description specified, for the purposes of this subsection by the Treasury by order, or
   (e)   regulations made by the Treasury under section 8 of the European Union (Withdrawal) Act 2018.]

[1B   The FCA's general duties

(1) In discharging its general functions the FCA must, so far as is reasonably possible, act in a way which—

   (a) is compatible with its strategic objective, and
   (b) advances one or more of its operational objectives.

(2) The FCA's strategic objective is: ensuring that the relevant markets (see section 1F) function well.

(3) The FCA's operational objectives are—

   (a) the consumer protection objective (see section 1C);
   (b) the integrity objective (see section 1D);
   (c) the competition objective (see section 1E).

(4) The FCA must, so far as is compatible with acting in a way which advances the consumer protection objective or the integrity objective, discharge its general functions in a way which promotes effective competition in the interests of consumers.

(5) In discharging its general functions the FCA must have regard to—

   (a) the regulatory principles in section 3B, and
   (b) the importance of taking action intended to minimise the extent to which it is possible for a business carried on—
      (i)   by an authorised person or a recognised investment exchange, or
      (ii) in contravention of the general prohibition,
      to be used for a purpose connected with financial crime.

(6) For the purposes of this Chapter, the FCA's general functions are—

   (a) its function of making rules under this Act (considered as a whole),
   (aa) its function of making technical standards in accordance with Chapter 2A of Part 9A,
   (b) its function of preparing and issuing codes under this Act (considered as a whole),
   (c) its functions in relation to the giving of general guidance under this Act (considered as a whole), and

(d) its function of determining the general policy and principles by reference to which it performs particular functions under this Act.

(7) Except to the extent that an order under section 50 of the Financial Services Act 2012 (orders relating to mutual societies functions) so provides, the FCA's general functions do not include functions that are transferred functions within the meaning of section 52 of that Act.

(8) 'General guidance' has the meaning given in section 139B(5).]

[1C The consumer protection objective

(1) The consumer protection objective is: securing an appropriate degree of protection for consumers.

(2) In considering what degree of protection for consumers may be appropriate, the FCA must have regard to—

(a) the differing degrees of risk involved in different kinds of investment or other transaction;

(b) the differing degrees of experience and expertise that different consumers may have;

(c) the needs that consumers may have for the timely provision of information and advice that is accurate and fit for purpose;

(d) the general principle that consumers should take responsibility for their decisions;

(e) the general principle that those providing regulated financial services should be expected to provide consumers with a level of care that is appropriate having regard to the degree of risk involved in relation to the investment or other transaction and the capabilities of the consumers in question;

(f) the differing expectations that consumers may have in relation to different kinds of investment or other transaction;

[. . .]

(h) any information which the scheme operator of the ombudsman scheme has provided to the FCA pursuant to section 232A.]

[1D The integrity objective

(1) The integrity objective is: protecting and enhancing the integrity of the UK financial system.

(2) The 'integrity' of the UK financial system includes—

(a) its soundness, stability and resilience,

(b) its not being used for a purpose connected with financial crime,

(c) its not being affected by behaviour that amounts to market abuse,

(d) the orderly operation of the financial markets, and

(e) the transparency of the price formation process in those markets.]

[1E The competition objective

(1) The competition objective is: promoting effective competition in the interests of consumers in the markets for—

(a) regulated financial services, or

(b) services provided by a recognised investment exchange in carrying on regulated activities in respect of which it is by virtue of section 285(2) exempt from the general prohibition.

(2) The matters to which the FCA may have regard in considering the effectiveness of competition in the market for any services mentioned in subsection (1) include—

(a) the needs of different consumers who use or may use those services, including their need for information that enables them to make informed choices,

(b) the ease with which consumers who may wish to use those services, including consumers in areas affected by social or economic deprivation, can access them,

(c) the ease with which consumers who obtain those services can change the person from whom they obtain them,

(d) the ease with which new entrants can enter the market, and

(e) how far competition is encouraging innovation.]

[1EA   Continuity objective

(1) In relation to the matters mentioned in subsection (2), the continuity objective is: protecting the continuity of the provision in the United Kingdom of core services (see section 142C).

(2) Those matters are—

(a) Part 9B (ring-fencing);

(b) ring-fenced bodies (see section 142A);

(c) any body corporate incorporated in the United Kingdom that has a ring-fenced body as a member of its group;

(d) applications under Part 4A which, if granted, would result, or would be capable of resulting, in a person becoming a ring-fenced body.

(3) The FCA's continuity objective is to be advanced primarily by—

(a) seeking to ensure that the business of ring-fenced bodies is carried on in a way that avoids any adverse effect on the continuity of the provision in the United Kingdom of core services,

(b) seeking to ensure that the business of ring-fenced bodies is protected from risks (arising in the United Kingdom or elsewhere) that could adversely affect the continuity of the provision in the United Kingdom of core services, and

(c) seeking to minimise the risk that the failure of a ring-fenced body or of a member of a ring-fenced body's group could adversely affect the continuity of the provision in the United Kingdom of core services.

(4) In subsection (3)(c), 'failure' is to be read in accordance with section 2J(3) to (4).]

[*Note: s 1EA has effect in accordance with s 1IA, below.*]

[1F   Meaning of 'relevant markets' in strategic objective

In section 1B(2) 'the relevant markets' means—

(a) the financial markets,

(b) the markets for regulated financial services (see section 1H(2)), and

(c) the markets for services that are provided by persons other than authorised persons in carrying on regulated activities but are provided without contravening the general prohibition.]

[1G   Meaning of 'consumer'

(1) In sections 1B to 1E 'consumers' means persons who—

(a) use, have used or may use—

(i)   regulated financial services, or

(ii) services that are provided by persons other than authorised persons but are provided in carrying on regulated activities,

(b) have relevant rights or interests in relation to any of those services,

(c) have invested, or may invest, in financial instruments, [. . .]

(d) have relevant rights or interests in relation to financial instruments[, or

(e) have rights, interests or obligations that are affected by the level of a regulated benchmark].

(2) A person ('P') has a 'relevant right or interest' in relation to any services within subsection (1)(a) if P has a right or interest—

(a) which is derived from, or is otherwise attributable to, the use of the services by others, or

(b) which may be adversely affected by the use of the services by persons acting on P's behalf or in a fiduciary capacity in relation to P.

(3) If a person is providing a service within subsection (1)(a) as trustee, the persons who are, have been or may be beneficiaries of the trust are to be treated as persons who use, have used or may use the service.

(4) A person who deals with another person ('B') in the course of B providing a service within subsection (1)(a) is to be treated as using the service.

(5) A person ('P') has a 'relevant right or interest' in relation to any financial instrument if P has—

(a) a right or interest which is derived from, or is otherwise attributable to, investment in the instrument by others, or

(b) a right or interest which may be adversely affected by the investment in the instrument by persons acting on P's behalf or in a fiduciary capacity in relation to P.]

[1H Further interpretative provisions for sections 1B to 1G

(1) The following provisions have effect for the interpretation of sections 1B to 1G.

(2) 'Regulated financial services' means services provided—

(a) by authorised persons in carrying on regulated activities;

(c) by authorised persons in communicating, or approving the communication by others of, invitations to engage in investment activity or to engage in claims management activity;

(d) by authorised persons who are investment firms, or qualifying credit institutions, in providing relevant ancillary services;

(e) by persons acting as appointed representatives;

(f) by payment service providers in providing payment services;

(g) by electronic money issuers in issuing electronic money;

(h) by sponsors to issuers of securities;

(i) by primary information providers to persons who issue financial instruments.

(3) 'Financial crime' includes any offence involving—

(a) fraud or dishonesty,

(b) misconduct in, or misuse of information relating to, a financial market,

(c) handling the proceeds of crime, or

(d) the financing of terrorism.

(4) 'Offence' includes an act or omission which would be an offence if it had taken place in the United Kingdom.

(5) 'Issuer', except in the expression 'electronic money issuer', has the meaning given in section 102A(6).

(6) 'Financial instrument' has the meaning given in section 102A(4).

(7) 'Securities' has the meaning given in section 102A(2).

[(7A) 'Regulated benchmark' means a benchmark, as defined in section 22(6A), in relation to which any provision made under section 22(1A)(c) has effect.]

(8) In this section—

'electronic money' has the same meaning as in the Electronic Money Regulations 2011;

'electronic money issuer' means a person who is an electronic money issuer as defined in regulation 2(1) of the Electronic Money Regulations 2011 other than a person falling within paragraph (f), (g) or (j) of the definition;

'engage in claims management activity' has the meaning given in section 21;

'engage in investment activity' has the meaning given in section 21;

'financial instrument' has the meaning given in section 102A(4);

'payment services' has the same meaning as in the Payment Services Regulations 2017;

'payment service provider' means a person who is a payment service provider as defined in regulation 2(1) of the Payment Services Regulations 2017 other than a person falling within paragraph (i) or (j) of the definition;

'primary information provider' has the meaning given in section 89P(2);

'relevant ancillary service' means any service of a kind mentioned in Part 3A of Schedule 2 to the Financial Services and Markets Act 2000 (Regulated Activities) Order 2001 the provision of which does not involve the carrying on of a regulated activity;

'sponsor' has the meaning given in section 88(2).]

[1I Meaning of 'the UK financial system'

In this Act 'the UK financial system' means the financial system operating in the United Kingdom and includes—

(a) financial markets and exchanges,

(b) regulated activities, and

(c) other activities connected with financial markets and exchanges.]

[1IA   Modifications applying if core activity not regulated by PRA

(1) If and so long as any regulated activity is a core activity (see section 142B) without also being a PRA-regulated activity (see section 22A), the provisions of this Chapter are to have effect subject to the following modifications.

(2) Section 1B is to have effect as if—

(a) in subsection (3), after paragraph (c) there were inserted—

'(d) in relation to the matters mentioned in section 1EA(2), the continuity objective (see section 1EA)', and

(b) in subsection (4), for 'or the integrity objective,' there were substituted ', the integrity objective or (in relation to the matters mentioned in section 1EA(2)) the continuity objective,'.]

(3) After section 1E there is to be taken to be inserted—[s 1EA].

[Note: s 1EA has been inserted above.]

[1J   Power to amend objectives

The Treasury may by order amend any of the following provisions—

(a) in section 1E(1), paragraphs (a) and (b),

(b) section 1G, and

(c) section 1H(2) and (5) to (8).]

[1JA   Recommendations by Treasury in connection with general duties

(1) The Treasury may at any time by notice in writing to the FCA make recommendations to the FCA about aspects of the economic policy of Her Majesty's Government to which the FCA should have regard when considering—

(a) how to act in a way which is compatible with its strategic objective,

(b) how to advance one or more of its operational objectives,

(c) how to discharge the duty in section 1B(4) (duty to promote effective competition in the interests of consumers),

(d) the application of the regulatory principles in section 3B, and

(e) the matter mentioned in section 1B(5)(b) (importance of taking action to minimise the extent to which it is possible for a business to be used for a purpose connected with financial crime).

(2) The Treasury must make recommendations under subsection (1) at least once in each Parliament.

(3) The Treasury must—

(a) publish in such manner as they think fit any notice given under subsection (1), and

(b) lay a copy of it before Parliament.]

[1K   Guidance about objectives

(1) The general guidance given by the FCA under section 139A must include guidance about how it intends to advance its operational objectives in discharging its general functions in relation to different categories of authorised person or regulated activity.

(2) Before giving or altering any guidance complying with subsection (1), the FCA must consult the PRA.]

[1L   Supervision, monitoring and enforcement

(1) The FCA must maintain arrangements for supervising authorised persons.

(2) The FCA must maintain arrangements designed to enable it to determine whether persons other than authorised persons are complying—

(a) with requirements imposed on them by or under this Act, in cases where the FCA is the appropriate regulator for the purposes of Part 14 (disciplinary measures),

[(aa) with requirements imposed on them by the Alternative Investment Fund Managers Regulations 2013, or]

(b) with requirements imposed on them by any qualifying provision that is specified, or of a description specified, for the purposes of this subsection by the Treasury by order.

(3) The FCA must also maintain arrangements for enforcing compliance by persons other than authorised persons with relevant requirements, within the meaning of Part 14, in cases where the FCA is the appropriate regulator for the purposes of any provision of that Part.]

[1M   The FCA's general duty to consult

The FCA must make and maintain effective arrangements for consulting practitioners and consumers on the extent to which its general policies and practices are consistent with its general duties under section 1B.]

[1N   The FCA Practitioner Panel

(1) Arrangements under section 1M must include the establishment and maintenance of a panel of persons (to be known as 'the FCA Practitioner Panel') to represent the interests of practitioners.

(2) The FCA must appoint one of the members of the FCA Practitioner Panel to be its chair.

(3) The Treasury's approval is required for the appointment or dismissal of the chair.

(4) The FCA must appoint to the FCA Practitioner Panel such—

(a) persons representing authorised persons, and

(b) persons representing recognised investment exchanges,

as it considers appropriate.

(5) The FCA may appoint to the FCA Practitioner Panel such other persons as it considers appropriate.]

[1O   The Smaller Business Practitioner Panel

(1) Arrangements under section 1M must include the establishment and maintenance of a panel of persons (to be known as 'the Smaller Business Practitioner Panel') to represent the interests of eligible practitioners.

(2) 'Eligible practitioners' means authorised persons of a description specified in a statement maintained by the FCA.

(3) The FCA must appoint one of the members of the Smaller Business Practitioner Panel to be its chair.

(4) The Treasury's approval is required for the appointment or dismissal of the chair.

(5) The FCA must appoint to the Smaller Business Practitioner Panel such—

(a) individuals who are eligible practitioners, and

(b) persons representing eligible practitioners,

as it considers appropriate.

(6) The FCA may appoint to the Smaller Business Practitioner Panel such other persons as it considers appropriate.

(7) In making the appointments, the FCA must have regard to the desirability of ensuring the representation of eligible practitioners carrying on a range of regulated activities.

(8) The FCA may revise the statement maintained under subsection (2).

(9) The FCA must—

(a) give the Treasury a copy of the statement or revised statement without delay, and

(b) publish the statement as for the time being in force in such manner as it thinks fit.]

[1P   The Markets Practitioner Panel

(1) Arrangements under section 1M must include the establishment and maintenance of a panel of persons (to be known as 'the Markets Practitioner Panel') to represent the interests of practitioners who are likely to be affected by the exercise by the FCA of its functions relating to markets, including its functions under Parts 6, 8A and 18.

(2) The FCA must appoint one of the members of the Markets Practitioner Panel to be its chair.

(3) The Treasury's approval is required for the appointment or dismissal of the chair.

(4) The FCA must appoint to the Markets Practitioner Panel such persons to represent the interests of persons within subsection (5) as it considers appropriate.

(5) The persons within this subsection are—

(a) authorised persons,

(b) persons who issue financial instruments,

(c) sponsors, as defined in section 88(2),

(d) recognised investment exchanges, and

(e) primary information providers, as defined in section 89P(2).

(6) The FCA may appoint to the Markets Practitioner Panel such other persons as it considers appropriate.]

[1Q The Consumer Panel

(1) Arrangements under section 1M must include the establishment and maintenance of a panel of persons (to be known as 'the Consumer Panel') to represent the interests of consumers.

(2) The FCA must appoint one of the members of the Consumer Panel to be its chair.

(3) The Treasury's approval is required for the appointment or dismissal of the chair.

(4) The FCA may appoint to the Consumer Panel such consumers, or persons representing the interests of consumers, as it considers appropriate.

(5) The FCA must secure that membership of the Consumer Panel is such as to give a fair degree of representation to those who are using, or are or may be contemplating using, services otherwise than in connection with businesses carried on by them.

(5A) If it appears to the Consumer Panel that any matter being considered by it is relevant to the extent to which the general policies and practices of the PRA are consistent with the PRA's general duties under sections 2B to 2H, it may communicate to the PRA any views relating to that matter.

(5B) The PRA may arrange to meet any of the FCA's expenditure on the Consumer Panel which is attributable to the Panel's functions under subsection (5A).

(6) Sections 425A and 425B (meaning of 'consumers') apply for the purposes of this section, but the references to consumers in this section do not include consumers who are authorised persons.]

[1R Duty to consider representations made by the Panels

(1) The FCA must consider representations that are made to it in accordance with arrangements made under section 1M.

(2) The FCA must from time to time publish in such manner as it thinks fit responses to the representations.]

[1S Reviews

(1) The Treasury may appoint an independent person to conduct a review of the economy, efficiency and effectiveness with which the FCA has used its resources in discharging its functions.]

[2A The Prudential Regulation Authority

(1) The 'Prudential Regulation Authority' is the Bank of England.

(2) The Bank's functions as the Prudential Regulation Authority—

(a) are to be exercised by the Bank acting through its Prudential Regulation Committee (see Part 3A of the Bank of England Act 1998), and

(b) are not exercisable by the Bank in any other way.

(3) References in this Act or any other enactment to the Prudential Regulation Authority do not include the Bank of England acting otherwise than in its capacity as the Prudential Regulation Authority.

(4) References in this Act to the Bank of England do not (unless otherwise provided) include the Bank acting in its capacity as the Prudential Regulation Authority.

(5) Subsections (3) and (4) do not apply to this section.

(6) Subsection (4) does not apply for the interpretation of references to the court of directors of the Bank of England, or to a Deputy Governor or committee of the Bank.

(7) The Prudential Regulation Authority is referred to in this Act as the PRA.]

[2AB Functions of the PRA

(1) The PRA is to have the functions conferred on it by or under this Act.

(2) Schedule 1ZB makes provision about functions of the PRA.

(3) References in this Act or any other enactment to functions conferred on the PRA by or under this Act include references to functions conferred on the PRA by or under—

    (a) the Insolvency Act 1986,

    (b) the Banking Act 2009,

    (c) the Financial Services Act 2012,

    (d) a qualifying provision that is specified, or of a description specified, for the purposes of this subsection by the Treasury by order, or

    (e) regulations made by the Treasury under section 8 of the European Union (Withdrawal) Act 2018.]

[2B   The PRA's general objective

(1) In discharging its general functions the PRA must, so far as is reasonably possible, act in a way which advances its general objective.

(2) The PRA's general objective is: promoting the safety and soundness of PRA-authorised persons.

(3) That objective is to be advanced primarily by—

    (a) seeking to ensure that the business of PRA-authorised persons is carried on in a way which avoids any adverse effect on the stability of the UK financial system,

    (b) seeking to minimise the adverse effect that the failure of a PRA-authorised person could be expected to have on the stability of the UK financial system, and

    (c) discharging its general functions in relation to the matters mentioned in subsection (4A) in a way that seeks to—

        (i) ensure that the business of ring-fenced bodies is carried on in a way that avoids any adverse effect on the continuity of the provision in the United Kingdom of core services,

        (ii) ensure that the business of ring-fenced bodies is protected from risks (arising in the United Kingdom or elsewhere) that could adversely affect the continuity of the provision in the United Kingdom of core services, and

        (iii) minimise the risk that the failure of a ring-fenced body or of a member of a ring-fenced body's group could affect the continuity of the provision in the United Kingdom of core services.

(4) The adverse effects mentioned in subsection (3)(a) and (b) may, in particular, result from the disruption of the continuity of financial services.

(4A) The matters referred to in subsection (3)(c) are—

    (a) Part 9B (ring-fencing);

    (b) ring-fenced bodies (see section 142A);

    (c) any body corporate incorporated in the United Kingdom that has a ring-fenced body as a member of its group;

    (d) applications under Part 4A which, if granted, would result, or would be capable of resulting, in a person becoming a ring-fenced body.

(5) In this Act 'PRA-authorised person' means an authorised person who has permission—

    (a) given under Part 4A, or

    (b) resulting from any other provision of this Act,

to carry on regulated activities that consist of or include one or more PRA-regulated activities (see section 22A).

(6) Subsection (1) is subject to sections 2C and 2D.]

[2C   Insurance objective

(1) In discharging its general functions so far as relating to a PRA-regulated activity relating to the effecting or carrying out of contracts of insurance or PRA-authorised persons carrying on that activity, the PRA must, so far as is reasonably possible, act in a way—

(a) which is compatible with its general objective and its insurance objective, and

(b) which the PRA considers most appropriate for the purpose of advancing those objectives.

(2) The PRA's insurance objective is: contributing to the securing of an appropriate degree of protection for those who are or may become policyholders.

(3) This section applies only if the effecting or carrying out of contracts of insurance as principal is to any extent a PRA-regulated activity.]

[2D Power to provide for additional objectives

(1) Subsection (2) applies to an order under section 22A which—

(a) is made at any time after the coming into force of the first order under that section, and

(b) contains a statement by the Treasury that, in their opinion, the effect (or one of the effects) of the proposed order is that an activity would become a PRA-regulated activity.

(2) An order to which this subsection applies may specify an additional objective ('the specified objective') in relation to specified activities that become PRA-regulated activities by virtue of the order ('the additional activities').

(3) In discharging its general functions so far as relating to the additional activities or PRA-authorised persons carrying on those activities, the PRA must, so far as is reasonably possible, act in a way—

(a) which is compatible with its general objective and the specified objective, and

(b) which the PRA considers most appropriate for the purpose of advancing those objectives.]

[2E Strategy

(1) The PRA must—

(a) determine its strategy in relation to its objectives, and

(b) from time to time review, and if necessary revise, the strategy.

(2) Before determining or revising its strategy, the PRA must consult the court of directors of the Bank of England about a draft of the strategy or of the revisions.

(4) The PRA must carry out and complete a review of its strategy before the end of each relevant period.

(5) The relevant period is 12 months beginning with the date on which the previous review was completed, except that in the case of the first review the relevant period is the period of 12 months beginning with the date on which the strategy was determined under subsection (3).

(6) The PRA must publish its strategy.

(7) If the strategy is revised the PRA must publish the revised strategy.]

[2F Interpretation of references to objectives

In this Act, a reference, in relation to any function of the PRA, to the objectives of the PRA is a reference to its general objective but—

(a) so far as the function is exercisable in relation to the activity of effecting or carrying out contracts of insurance, or PRA-authorised persons carrying on that activity, is a reference to its general objective and its insurance objective;

(b) so far as the function is exercisable in relation to an activity to which an objective specified by order by virtue of section 2D(2) relates, or PRA-authorised persons carrying on that activity, is a reference to its general objective and the objective specified by the order.]

[2G Limit on effect of sections 2B to 2D

Nothing in sections 2B to 2D is to be regarded as requiring the PRA to ensure that no PRA-authorised person fails.]

[2H Secondary competition objective and duty to have regard to regulatory principles

(1) When discharging its general functions in a way that advances its objectives (see section 2F), the PRA must so far as is reasonably possible act in a way which, as a secondary objective, facilitates

effective competition in the markets for services provided by PRA-authorised persons in carrying on regulated activities.

(2) In discharging its general functions, the PRA must also have regard to the regulatory principles in section 3B.]

[2I   Guidance about objectives

(1) The PRA must give, and from time to time review, guidance about how it intends to advance its objectives in discharging its general functions in relation to different categories of PRA-authorised person or PRA-regulated activity.

(2) Before giving or altering any guidance complying with subsection (1), the PRA must consult the FCA.

(3) The PRA must publish the guidance as for the time being in force.]

[2J   Interpretation of Chapter 2

(1) For the purposes of this Chapter, the PRA's general functions are—

- (a)   its function of making rules under this Act (considered as a whole),
- (aa) its function of making technical standards in accordance with Chapter 2A of Part 9A,
- (b)   its function of preparing and issuing codes under this Act (considered as a whole), and
- (c)   its function of determining the general policy and principles by reference to which it performs particular functions under this Act.

(3) For the purposes of this Chapter, the cases in which an authorised person ('P') is to be regarded as failing include those where—

- (a) P enters insolvency,
- (b) any of the stabilisation options in Part 1 of the Banking Act 2009 is achieved in relation to P, or
- (c) P falls to be taken for the purposes of the compensation scheme to be unable, or likely to be unable, to satisfy claims against P.

(3A) For the purposes of this Chapter, the cases in which a person ('P') other than an authorised person is to be regarded as failing include any case where P enters insolvency.

(4) In subsections (3)(a) and (3A) 'insolvency' includes—

- (a) bankruptcy,
- (b) liquidation,
- (c) bank insolvency,
- (d) administration,
- (e) bank administration,
- (f) receivership,
- (g) a composition between P and P's creditors, and
- (h) a scheme of arrangement of P's affairs.]

[2K   Arrangements for supervision of PRA-authorised persons

The PRA must maintain arrangements for supervising PRA-authorised persons.]

[2L   The PRA's general duty to consult

The PRA must make and maintain effective arrangements for consulting PRA-authorised persons or, where appropriate, persons appearing to the PRA to represent the interests of such persons on the extent to which its general policies and practices are consistent with its general duties under sections 2B to 2H.]

[2M   The PRA Practitioner Panel

(1) Arrangements under section 2L must include the establishment and maintenance of a panel of persons (to be known as 'the PRA Practitioner Panel') to represent the interests of practitioners.

(2) The PRA must appoint one of the members of the PRA Practitioner Panel to be its chair.

(3) The Treasury's approval is required for the appointment or dismissal of the chair.

(4) The PRA must appoint to the PRA Practitioner Panel such persons representing PRA-authorised persons as it considers appropriate.

(5) The PRA may appoint to the PRA Practitioner Panel such other persons as it considers appropriate.]

[2N Duty to consider representations

(1) The PRA must consider representations that are made to it in accordance with arrangements made under section 2L.

(2) The PRA must from time to time publish in such manner as it thinks fit responses to the representations.]

[3A Meaning of 'regulator'

(1) This section has effect for the interpretation of this Act.

(2) The FCA and the PRA are the 'regulators', and references to a regulator are to be read accordingly.]

[3B Regulatory principles to be applied by both regulators

(1) In relation to the regulators, the regulatory principles referred to in section 1B(5)(a) and 2H(2) are as follows—

    (a) the need to use the resources of each regulator in the most efficient and economic way;

    (b) the principle that a burden or restriction which is imposed on a person, or on the carrying on of an activity, should be proportionate to the benefits, considered in general terms, which are expected to result from the imposition of that burden or restriction;

    (c) the desirability of sustainable growth in the economy of the United Kingdom in the medium or long term;

    (d) the general principle that consumers should take responsibility for their decisions;

    (e) the responsibilities of the senior management of persons subject to requirements imposed by or under this Act, including those affecting consumers, in relation to compliance with those requirements;

    (f) the desirability where appropriate of each regulator exercising its functions in a way that recognises differences in the nature of, and objectives of, businesses carried on by different persons (including different kinds of person such as mutual societies and other kinds of business organisation) subject to requirements imposed by or under this Act;

    (g) the desirability in appropriate cases of each regulator publishing information relating to persons on whom requirements are imposed by or under this Act, or requiring such persons to publish information, as a means of contributing to the advancement by each regulator of its objectives;

    (h) the principle that the regulators should exercise their functions as transparently as possible.

(2) 'Consumer' has the meaning given in section 1G.

(3) 'Objectives', in relation to the FCA, means operational objectives.

(3A) 'Mutual society' has the same meaning as in section 138K.

(4) The Treasury may by order amend subsection (2).]

[3C Duty to follow principles of good governance

In managing its affairs, each regulator must have regard to such generally accepted principles of good corporate governance as it is reasonable to regard as applicable to it.]

[3D Duty of FCA and PRA to ensure co-ordinated exercise of functions

(1) The regulators must co-ordinate the exercise of their respective functions conferred by or under this Act with a view to ensuring—

    (a) that each regulator consults the other regulator (where not otherwise required to do so) in connection with any proposed exercise of a function in a way that may have a material adverse effect on the advancement by the other regulator of any of its objectives;

    (b) that where appropriate each regulator obtains information and advice from the other regulator in connection with the exercise of its functions in relation to matters of common regulatory interest in cases where the other regulator may be expected to have relevant information or relevant expertise;

(c) that where either regulator exercises functions in relation to matters of common regulatory interest, both regulators comply with their respective duties under section 1B(5)(a) or 2H(1)(a), so far as relating to the regulatory principles in section 3B(1)(a) and (b).

(2) The duty in subsection (1) applies only to the extent that compliance with the duty—

(a) is compatible with the advancement by each regulator of any of its objectives, and

(b) does not impose a burden on the regulators that is disproportionate to the benefits of compliance.

(3) A function conferred on either regulator by or under this Act relates to matters of common regulatory interest if—

(a) the other regulator exercises similar or related functions in relation to the same persons,

(b) the other regulator exercises functions which relate to different persons but relate to similar subject-matter, or

(c) its exercise could affect the advancement by the other regulator of any of its objectives.

(4) 'Objectives', in relation to the FCA, means operational objectives.]

[3E Memorandum of understanding

(1) The regulators must prepare and maintain a memorandum which describes in general terms—

(a) the role of each regulator in relation to the exercise of functions conferred by or under this Act which relate to matters of common regulatory interest, and

(b) how the regulators intend to comply with section 3D in relation to the exercise of such functions.

(2) The memorandum may in particular contain provisions about how the regulators intend to comply with section 3D in relation to—

(a) applications for Part 4A permission;

(b) the variation of permission;

(c) the imposition of requirements;

(d) the obtaining and disclosure of information;

(e) cases where a PRA-authorised person is a member of a group whose other members include one or more other authorised persons (whether or not PRA-authorised persons);

(g) the making of rules;

(h) directions under section 138A (modification or waiver of rules);

(i) powers to appoint competent persons under Part 11 (information gathering and investigations) to conduct investigations on their behalf;

(j) functions under Part 12 (control over authorised persons);

(k) functions under Part 13 (incoming firms: intervention by regulator);

(l) functions under Part 19 (Lloyd's);

(m) functions under section 347 (record of authorised persons etc.);

(n) functions under Part 24 (insolvency);

(o) fees payable to either regulator.

(3) The memorandum must contain provision about the co-ordination by the regulators of—

(b) their relations with regulatory bodies outside the United Kingdom, and

(c) the exercise of their functions in relation to the compensation scheme.

(4) The regulators must review the memorandum at least once in each calendar year.

(5) The regulators must give the Treasury a copy of the memorandum and any revised memorandum.

(6) The Treasury must lay before Parliament a copy of any document received by them under this section.

(7) The regulators must ensure that the memorandum as currently in force is published in the way appearing to them to be best calculated to bring it to the attention of the public.

(8) The memorandum need not relate to any aspect of compliance with section 3D if the regulators consider—

(a) that publication of information about that aspect would be against the public interest, or

(b) that that aspect is a technical or operational matter not affecting the public.

(9) The reference in subsection (1)(a) to matters of common regulatory interest is to be read in accordance with section 3D(3).]

[3F   With-profits insurance policies

. . .]

[3G   Power to establish boundary between FCA and PRA responsibilities

(1) The Treasury may by order specify matters that, in relation to the exercise by either regulator of its functions relating to PRA-authorised persons, are to be, or are to be primarily, the responsibility of one regulator rather than the other.]

[3H   Parliamentary control of orders under section 3G

(1) No order may be made under section 3G unless—

(a) a draft of the order has been laid before Parliament and approved by a resolution of each House, or

(b) subsection (3) applies.

(2) Subsection (3) applies if an order under section 3G contains a statement that the Treasury are of the opinion that, by reason of urgency, it is necessary to make the order without a draft being so laid and approved.]

[3I   Power of PRA to require FCA to refrain from specified action

(1) Where the first, second and third conditions are met, the PRA may give a direction under this section to the FCA.

(2) The first condition is that the FCA is proposing—

(a) to exercise any of its regulatory powers in relation to PRA-authorised persons generally, a class of PRA-authorised persons or a particular PRA-authorised person, or

(b) to exercise any of its insolvency powers in relation to—

(i) a PRA-authorised person,

(ii) an appointed representative whose principal, or one of whose principals, is a PRA-authorised person, or

(iii) a person who is carrying on a PRA-regulated activity in contravention of the general prohibition.

(3) In subsection (2)—

(a) 'regulatory powers', in relation to the FCA, means its powers in relation to the regulation of authorised persons, other than its powers in relation to consent for the purposes of section 55F or 55I or its powers under Part 24;

(b) 'insolvency powers', in relation to the FCA, means its powers under Part 24.

(4) The second condition is that the PRA is of the opinion that the exercise of the power in the manner proposed may—

(a) threaten the stability of the UK financial system,

(b) result in the failure of a PRA-authorised person in a way that would adversely affect the UK financial system, or

(c) threaten the continuity of core services provided in the United Kingdom.

(5) The third condition is that the PRA is of the opinion that the giving of the direction is necessary in order to avoid the possible consequence falling within subsection (4).

(6) A direction under this section is a direction requiring the FCA not to exercise the power or not to exercise it in a specified manner.

(7) The direction may be expressed to have effect during a specified period or until revoked.

(8) The FCA is not required to comply with a direction under this section if or to the extent that in the opinion of the FCA compliance would be incompatible with any international obligation of the United Kingdom.

(9) The reference in subsection (4)(b) person is to be read in accordance with section 2J(3) and (4).]

[3J   Power of PRA in relation to with-profits policies
. . .]

[3K   Revocation of directions under section 3I or 3J

(1) The PRA may at any time by notice to the FCA revoke a direction under section 3I or 3J.

(2) The revocation of a direction under section 3I or 3J does not affect the validity of anything previously done in accordance with it.]

[3L   Further provisions about directions under section 3I or 3J

(1) Before giving a direction under section 3I or 3J, the PRA must consult the FCA.

(2) A direction under section 3I or 3J must be given or confirmed in writing, and must be accompanied by a statement of the reasons for giving it.

(3) A notice revoking a direction under section 3I or 3J must be given or confirmed in writing.

(4) The PRA must—
    (a) publish the direction and statement, or the notice, in such manner as it thinks fit, and
    (b) where the direction or notice relates to a particular authorised person or a particular with-profits insurer, give a copy of the direction and statement, or the notice, to that person.

(5) The PRA must give the Treasury a copy of—
    (a) a direction under section 3I;
    (b) a statement relating to such a direction;
    (c) a notice revoking such a direction.

(6) The Treasury must lay before Parliament any document received by them under subsection (5).

(7) Subsection (4) does not apply where the PRA, after consulting the Treasury, decides that compliance with that subsection would be against the public interest, and at any time when this subsection excludes the application of subsection (4) in relation to a direction under section 3I, subsection (6) also does not apply.

(8) Where the PRA decides that compliance with subsection (4) would be against the public interest, it must from time to time review that decision and if it subsequently decides that compliance is no longer against the public interest it must—
    (a) comply with that subsection, and
    (b) in the case of a direction under section 3I, notify the Treasury for the purposes of subsection (6).]

[3M   Directions relating to consolidated supervision of groups

(1) This section applies where one of the regulators ('the supervising regulator'), but not the other, is the competent authority for the purpose of consolidated supervision that is required in relation to some or all of the members of a group ('the relevant group') in pursuance of—
    (a) any implementing provision contained in subordinate legislation (within the meaning of the Interpretation Act 1978) made otherwise than by any of the following—
        (i) statutory instrument, . . .
        . . .; or
    (b) any other implementing provision (as amended from time to time).

(2) 'Consolidated supervision' includes supplementary supervision.

(2A) 'Implementing provision' means an enactment that immediately before exit day implemented provisions of any of the relevant directives.

(3) The 'relevant directives' are—

    (a) the capital requirements directive;

    (b) Directive 2002/87/EC of the European Parliament and of the Council on the supplementary supervision of credit institutions, insurance undertakings and investment firms in a financial conglomerate;

    (d) Directive 2009/138/EC of the European Parliament and the Council of 25 November 2009 on the taking-up and pursuit of the business of Insurance and Reinsurance (Solvency II);

    (e) Directive 2014/59/EU of the European Parliament and of the Council of 15th May 2014 establishing a framework for the recovery and resolution of credit institutions and investment firms.

(4) The supervising regulator may, if it considers it necessary to do so for the effective consolidated supervision of the relevant group, give the other regulator a direction under this section.

(5) A direction under this section is a direction requiring the other regulator to exercise, or not to exercise, a relevant function in a specified manner in relation to authorised persons who are members of the relevant group.

(6) The direction may relate to members of the relevant group other than the members in respect of which consolidated supervision is required.

(7) A 'relevant function', in relation to either regulator, is a function conferred by or under this Act which relates to the regulation of authorised persons, but does not include—

    (a) the regulator's function of making rules under this Act;

    (b) its function of preparing and issuing codes under this Act;

    (c) its function of determining the general policy and principles by reference to which it performs particular functions;

    (d) the FCA's functions in relation to the giving of general guidance;

    (e) the PRA's functions in relation to the giving of guidance under section 2I;

    (f) the FCA's functions in relation to consent for the purposes of section 55F or 55I.

(8) The direction may not require the regulator to which it is given ('the directed regulator') to do anything that it has no power to do, but the direction is relevant to the exercise of any discretion conferred on the directed regulator.

(9) The directed regulator must comply with the direction as soon as practicable, but this is subject to subsections (10) and (11).

(10) The directed regulator is not required to comply with a direction under this section if or to the extent that in its opinion compliance would be incompatible with any international obligation of the United Kingdom.

(11) Directions given by the FCA under this section are subject to any directions given to the FCA under section 3I or 3J.]

[3N Revocation of directions under section 3M

(1) The supervising regulator may at any time by notice to the other regulator revoke a direction under section 3M.

(2) The revocation of the direction does not affect the validity of anything previously done in accordance with it.]

[3O Further provisions about directions under section 3M

(1) Before giving a direction under section 3M, the supervising regulator must consult the other regulator.

(2) A direction under section 3M must be given or confirmed in writing, and must be accompanied by a statement of the reasons for giving it.

(3) A notice revoking a direction under section 3M must be given or confirmed in writing.

(4) The regulator to which a direction under section 3M is given must give a copy of the direction and statement to each of the authorised persons to whom the direction relates.

(5) The supervising regulator must publish the direction and statement, or the notice, in such manner as it thinks fit.

(6) But subsection (4) or (5) does not apply in a case where the regulator on which the duty is imposed considers that compliance with that subsection would be against the public interest.

(7) In a case where a regulator decides that compliance with subsection (4) or (5) would be against the public interest, the regulator must from time to time review that decision and if it subsequently decides that compliance is no longer against the public interest it must comply with the subsection.]

[3P   Consultation by regulator complying with direction

(1) If the directed regulator is required by this Act to consult any person other than the supervising regulator before exercising the relevant function to which the direction relates, the directed regulator must give the supervising regulator copies of any written representations received from the persons consulted.]

[3Q   Co-operation by FCA . . . with Bank of England

(1) The FCA must take such steps as it considers appropriate to cooperate with the Bank of England in connection with—

    (a) the pursuit by the Bank of its Financial Stability Objective, and

    (b) the Bank's compliance with its duties under sections 58 and 59 of the Financial Services Act 2012 (duty to notify Treasury of possible need for public funds and of subsequent changes).]

[3R   Arrangements for provision of services

(1) The regulators may enter into arrangements with each other for the provision of services by one of them to the other.

(2) The FCA may enter into arrangements with the Bank of England for the provision of services—

    (a) by the Bank to the FCA, or

    (b) by the FCA to the Bank.

(3) Either regulator may enter into arrangements with any of the bodies specified in subsection (4) for the provision of services by the regulator to that body.

(4) Those bodies are—

    (a) the single financial guidance body (see Part 1 of the Financial Guidance and Claims Act 2018 and the consumer financial education body (see section 3S(2)),

    (b) the scheme manager (see section 212(1)), and

    (c) the scheme operator (see section 225(2)).

(5) The FCA may enter into arrangements with—

    (a) a local weights and measures authority in England, Wales or Scotland . . .

for the provision by the authority or department to the FCA of services which relate to activities to which this subsection applies.

(7) Arrangements under this section are to be on such terms as may be agreed by the parties.]

19   The general prohibition

(1) No person may carry on a regulated activity in the United Kingdom, or purport to do so, unless he is—

(a) an authorised person; or

(b) an exempt person.

(2) The prohibition is referred to in this Act as the general prohibition.

21   Restrictions on financial promotion

(1) [A person ('A') must not, in the course of business, communicate an invitation or inducement

(a) to engage in investment activity, or

(b) to engage in claims management activity.]

(2) But subsection (1) does not apply if—

(a) A is an authorised person; or

(b) the content of the communication is approved for the purposes of this section by an authorised person.

(3) In the case of a communication originating outside the United Kingdom, subsection (1) applies only if the communication is capable of having an effect in the United Kingdom.

(4) The Treasury may by order specify circumstances in which a person is to be regarded for the purposes of subsection (1) as—

(a) acting in the course of business;

(b) not acting in the course of business.

(5) The Treasury may by order specify circumstances (which may include compliance with financial promotion rules) in which subsection (1) does not apply.

(6) An order under subsection (5) may, in particular, provide that subsection (1) does not apply in relation to communications—

(a) of a specified description;

(b) originating in a specified country or territory outside the United Kingdom;

(c) originating in a country or territory which falls within a specified description of country or territory outside the United Kingdom; or

(d) originating outside the United Kingdom.

(7) The Treasury may by order repeal subsection (3).

(8) 'Engaging in investment activity' means—

(a) entering or offering to enter into an agreement the making or performance of which by either party constitutes a controlled activity; or

(b) exercising any rights conferred by a controlled investment to acquire, dispose of, underwrite or convert a controlled investment.

(9) An activity is a controlled activity if—

(a) it is an activity of a specified kind or one which falls within a specified class of activity; and

(b) it relates to an investment of a specified kind, or to one which falls within a specified class of investment.

(10) An investment is a controlled investment if it is an investment of a specified kind or one which falls within a specified class of investment.

[(10A) 'Engaging in claims management activity' means entering into or offering to enter into an agreement the making or performance of which by either party constitutes a controlled claims management activity.

(10B) An activity is a 'controlled claims management activity' if—

(a) it is an activity of a specified kind,

(b) it is, or relates to, claims management services, and

(c) it is carried on in Great Britain.]

22   [Regulated activities]

(1) An activity is a regulated activity for the purposes of this Act if it is an activity of a specified kind which is carried on by way of business and—

(a) relates to an investment of a specified kind; or

(b) in the case of an activity of a kind which is also specified for the purposes of this paragraph, is carried on in relation to property of any kind.

[22A Designation of activities requiring prudential regulation by PRA

(1) The Treasury may by order specify the regulated activities that are 'PRA-regulated activities' for the purposes of this Act.]

26 Agreements made by unauthorised persons

(1) An agreement made by a person in the course of carrying on a regulated activity in contravention of the general prohibition is unenforceable against the other party.

(2) The other party is entitled to recover—

(a) any money or other property paid or transferred by him under the agreement; and

(b) compensation for any loss sustained by him as a result of having parted with it.

(3) 'Agreement' means an agreement—

(a) made after this section comes into force; and

(b) the making or performance of which constitutes, or is part of, the regulated activity in question.

[26A Agreements relating to credit

(1) An agreement that is made by an authorised person in contravention of section 20 is unenforceable against the other party if the agreement is entered into in the course of carrying on a credit-related regulated activity involving matters falling within section 23(1C)(a).

(2) The other party is entitled to recover—

(a) any money or other property paid or transferred by that party under the agreement, and

(b) compensation for any loss sustained by that party as a result of having parted with it.

(3) In subsections (1) and (2) 'agreement' means an agreement— . . .

(b) the making or performance of which constitutes, or is part of, the credit-related regulated activity.

(4) If the administration of an agreement involves the carrying on of a credit-related regulated activity, the agreement may not be enforced by a person for the time being exercising the rights of the lender under the agreement unless that person

(a) has permission, given under Part 4A or resulting from any other provision of this Act, in relation to that activity

(b) is an appointed representative in relation to that activity,

(c) is an exempt person in relation to that activity, or

(d) is a person to whom, as a result of Part 20, the general prohibition does not apply in relation to that activity.

(5) If the taking of steps to procure payment of debts due under an agreement involves the carrying on of a credit-related regulated activity, the agreement may not be enforced by a person for the time being exercising the rights of the lender under the agreement

(a) unless the agreement is enforced in accordance with permission—

(i)　given under Part 4A to the person enforcing the agreement, or

(ii)　resulting from any other provision of this Act

(b) that person is an appointed representative in relation to that activity,

(c) that person is an exempt person in relation to that activity, or

(d) that person is a person to whom, as a result of Part 20, the general prohibition does not apply in relation to that activity.]

[55A Application for permission

(1) An application for permission to carry on one or more regulated activities may be made to the appropriate regulator by—

(a) an individual,

(b) a body corporate,

(c) a partnership, or

(d) an unincorporated association.

(2) 'The appropriate regulator', in relation to an application under this section, means (subject to subsection (2B))—

(a) the PRA, in a case where—

(i) the regulated activities to which the application relates consist of or include a PRA-regulated activity, or

(ii) the applicant is a PRA-authorised person otherwise than by virtue of a Part 4A permission;

(b) the FCA, in any other case.]

56 Prohibition orders

[(1) The FCA may make a prohibition order if it appears to it that an individual is not a fit and proper person to perform functions in relation to a regulated activity carried on by—

(a) an authorised person,

(b) a person who is an exempt person in relation to that activity, or

(c) a person to whom, as a result of Part 20, the general prohibition does not apply in relation to that activity.

(1A) The PRA may make a prohibition order if it appears to it that an individual is not a fit and proper person to perform functions in relation to a regulated activity carried on by—

(a) a PRA-authorised person, or

(b) a person who is an exempt person in relation to a PRA-regulated activity carried on by the person.]

(2) [A 'prohibition order' is an order] prohibiting the individual from performing a specified function, any function falling within a specified description or any function.

[(3A) A person falls within this subsection if the person is—

(a) an authorised person,

(b) an exempt person, or

(c) a person to whom, as a result of Part 20, the general prohibition does not apply in relation to a regulated activity.]

(4) An individual who performs or agrees to perform a function in breach of a prohibition order is guilty of an offence and liable on summary conviction to a fine not exceeding level 5 on the standard scale.

(5) In proceedings for an offence under subsection (4) it is a defence for the accused to show that he took all reasonable precautions and exercised all due diligence to avoid committing the offence.

(6) [A person falling within subsection (3A)] must take reasonable care to ensure that no function of his, in relation to the carrying on of a regulated activity, is performed by a person who is prohibited from performing that function by a prohibition order.

[64A Rules of conduct

(1) If it appears to the FCA to be necessary or expedient for the purpose of advancing one or more of its operational objectives, the FCA may make rules about the conduct of the following persons—

(a) persons in relation to whom either regulator has given its approval under section 59;

(b) persons who are employees of relevant authorised persons (see section 71A)

(c) persons who are directors of authorised persons.

(2) If it appears to the PRA to be necessary or expedient for the purpose of advancing any of its objectives, the PRA may make rules about the conduct of the following persons—

(a) persons in relation to whom it has given its approval under section 59;

(b) persons in relation to whom the FCA has given its approval under section 59 in respect of the performance by them of a relevant senior management function in relation to the carrying on by a PRA-authorised person of a regulated activity;

(c) persons who are employees of relevant PRA-authorised persons

(d) persons who are directors of PRA-authorised persons.

(3) In subsection (2)—

'relevant PRA-authorised person' means a PRA-authorised person that is a relevant authorised person (see section 71A), and

'relevant senior management function' means a function which the PRA is satisfied is a senior management function as defined in section 59ZA (whether or not the function has been designated as such by the FCA).

(4) Rules made under this section must relate to the conduct of persons in relation to the performance by them of qualifying functions.

(5) In subsection (4) 'qualifying function', in relation to a person, means a function relating to the carrying on of activities (whether or not regulated activities) by—

(a) in the case of an approved person, the person on whose application approval was given,

(ab) in the case of a person who is a director of an authorised person but is not an approved person, that authorised person, and

(b) in any other case, the person's employer.

(7) In this section 'director', in relation to an authorised person, means a member of the board of directors, or if there is no such board, the equivalent body responsible for the management of the authorised person concerned.]

[64B   Rules of conduct: responsibilities of relevant authorised persons

(1) This section applies where a regulator makes rules under section 64A ('conduct rules').

(2) Every relevant authorised person must—

(a) notify all relevant persons of the conduct rules that apply in relation to them, and

(b) take all reasonable steps to secure that those persons understand how those rules apply in relation to them.

(3) The steps which a relevant authorised person must take to comply with subsection (2)(b) include, in particular, the provision of suitable training.

(4) In this section 'relevant person', in relation to an authorised person, means—

(a) any person in relation to whom an approval is given under section 59 on the application of the authorised person,

(b) any employee of the authorised person, and

(c) any person who is a director of the authorised person.

(6A) In this section 'director', in relation to an authorised person, has the same meaning as in section 64A.]

[64C   Requirement for . . . authorised persons to notify regulator of disciplinary action

(1) If—

(a) an authorised person takes disciplinary action in relation to a relevant person, and

(b) the reason, or one of the reasons, for taking that action is a reason specified in rules made by the appropriate regulator for the purposes of this section,

the . . . authorised person must notify that regulator of that fact.]

90   [Compensation for statements in listing particulars or prospectus]

(1) Any person responsible for listing particulars is liable to pay compensation to a person who has—

(a) acquired securities to which the particulars apply; and

(b) suffered loss in respect of them as a result of—
  (i)   any untrue or misleading statement in the particulars; or
  (ii) the omission from the particulars of any matter required to be included by section 80 or 81.

[137A   The FCA's general rules

(1) The FCA may make such rules applying to authorised persons—
  (a) with respect to the carrying on by them of regulated activities, or
  (b) with respect to the carrying on by them of activities which are not regulated activities,
as appear to the FCA to be necessary or expedient for the purpose of advancing one or more of its operational objectives.]

[137C   FCA general rules: cost of credit and duration of credit agreements

(1) The power of the FCA to make general rules includes power to make rules prohibiting authorised persons from—
  (a) entering into a regulated credit agreement that provides for—
    (i)   the payment by the borrower of charges of a specified description, or
    (ii) the payment by the borrower over the duration of the agreement of charges that, taken with the charges paid under one or more other agreements which are treated by the rules as being connected with it, exceed, or are capable of exceeding, a specified amount;
  (b) imposing charges of a specified description or exceeding a specified amount on a person who is the borrower under a regulated credit agreement;
  (c) entering into a regulated credit agreement that—
    (i)   is capable of remaining in force after the end of a specified period,
    (ii) when taken with one or more other regulated credit agreements which are treated by the rules as being connected with it, would be capable of remaining in force after the end of a specified period, or
    (iii) is treated by the rules as being connected with a number of previous regulated credit agreements that exceeds a specified maximum;
  (d) exercising the rights of the lender under a regulated credit agreement (as a person for the time being entitled to exercise them) in a way that enables the agreement to remain in force after the end of a specified period or enables the imposition on the borrower of charges within paragraph (a)(i) or (ii).

(1A) The FCA must make rules by virtue of subsection (1)(a)(ii) and (b) in relation to one or more specified descriptions of regulated credit agreement appearing to the FCA to involve the provision of high-cost short-term credit, with a view to securing an appropriate degree of protection for borrowers against excessive charges.

(1B) Before the FCA publishes a draft of any rules to be made by virtue of subsection (1)(a)(ii) or (b), it must consult the Treasury.

(2) 'Charges' means charges payable, by way of interest or otherwise, in connection with the provision of credit under the regulated credit agreement, whether or not the agreement itself makes provision for them and whether or not the person to whom they are payable is a party to the regulated credit agreement or an authorised person.

(3) 'The borrower' includes—
  (a) any person providing a guarantee or indemnity under the regulated credit agreement, and
  (b) a person to whom the rights and duties of the borrower under the regulated credit agreement or a person falling within paragraph (a) have passed by assignment or operation of law.

(4) In relation to an agreement entered into or obligation imposed in contravention of the rules, the rules may—
  (a) provide for the agreement or obligation to be unenforceable against any person or specified person;

(b) provide for the recovery of any money or other property paid or transferred under the agreement or other obligation by any person or specified person;

(c) provide for the payment of compensation for any loss sustained by any person or specified person as a result of paying or transferring any money or other property under the agreement or obligation.

(5) The provision that may be made as a result of subsection (4) includes provision corresponding to that made by section 30 (enforceability of agreements resulting from unlawful communications).

(6) A credit agreement is a contract of the kind mentioned in paragraph 23 of Schedule 2, other than one under which the obligation of the borrower to repay is secured on land: and a credit agreement is a 'regulated credit agreement' if any of the following is a regulated activity—

(a) entering into or administering the agreement;

(b) exercising or being able to exercise the rights of the lender under the agreement.]

[137D　FCA general rules: product intervention

(1) The power of the FCA to make general rules includes power to make such rules ('product intervention rules') prohibiting authorised persons from doing anything mentioned in subsection (2) as appear to it to be necessary or expedient for the purpose of advancing—

(a) the consumer protection objective or the competition objective, or

(b) if the Treasury by order provide for this paragraph to apply, the integrity objective.

(2) Those prohibited things are—

(a) entering into specified agreements with any person or specified person;

(b) entering into specified agreements with any person or specified person unless requirements specified in the rules have been satisfied;

(c) doing anything that would or might result in the entering into of specified agreements by persons or specified persons, or the holding by them of a beneficial or other kind of economic interest in specified agreements;

(d) doing anything within paragraph (c) unless requirements specified in the rules have been satisfied.]

[234C　Complaints by consumer bodies

(1) A designated consumer body may make a complaint to the FCA that a feature, or combination of features, of a market in the United Kingdom for financial services or of a market in Great Britain for claims management services is, or appears to be, significantly damaging the interests of consumers.

(1A) But a complaint may not be made to the FCA under this section if it is a complaint which could be made to the Payment Systems Regulator by a designated representative body under section 68 of the Financial Services (Banking Reform) Act 2013 (complaints by representative bodies).

'Designated representative body' and 'the Payment Systems Regulator' have the same meaning in this subsection as they have in that section.

(2) 'Designated consumer body' means a body designated by the Treasury by order.

(3) The Treasury—

(a) may designate a body only if it appears to them to represent the interests of consumers of any description, and

(b) must publish in such manner as they think fit (and may from time to time vary) criteria to be applied by them in determining whether to make or revoke a designation.

(4) Sections 425A and 425B (meaning of 'consumers') apply for the purposes of this section, but the references to consumers in this section do not include consumers who are authorised persons.]

[333S　Financial assistance for action against illegal money lending

(1) The Treasury may make grants or loans, or give any other form of financial assistance, to any person for the purpose of taking action against illegal money lending.]

380   Injunctions

(1) If, on the application of the [appropriate regulator] or the Secretary of State, the court is satisfied—

    (a) that there is a reasonable likelihood that any person will contravene a relevant requirement, or

    (b) that any person has contravened a relevant requirement and that there is a reasonable likelihood that the contravention will continue or be repeated,

the court may make an order restraining (or in Scotland an interdict prohibiting) the contravention.

(2) If on the application of the [appropriate regulator] or the Secretary of State the court is satisfied—

    (a) that any person has contravened a relevant requirement, and

    (b) that there are steps which could be taken for remedying the contravention,

the court may make an order requiring that person, and any other person who appears to have been knowingly concerned in the contravention, to take such steps as the court may direct to remedy it.

381   Injunctions in cases of market abuse

(1) If, on the application of the [FCA], the court is satisfied—

    (a) that there is a reasonable likelihood that any person will engage in market abuse, or

    (b) that any person is or has engaged in market abuse and that there is a reasonable likelihood that the market abuse will continue or be repeated,

the court may make an order restraining (or in Scotland an interdict prohibiting) the market abuse.

(2) If on the application of the [FCA] the court is satisfied—

    (a) that any person is or has engaged in market abuse, and

    (b) that there are steps which could be taken for remedying the market abuse,

the court may make an order requiring him to take such steps as the court may direct to remedy it.

382   Restitution orders

(1) The court may, on the application of the [appropriate regulator] or the Secretary of State, make an order under subsection (2) if it is satisfied that a person has contravened a relevant requirement, or been knowingly concerned in the contravention of such a requirement, and—

    (a) that profits have accrued to him as a result of the contravention; or

    (b) that one or more persons have suffered loss or been otherwise adversely affected as a result of the contravention.

(2) The court may order the person concerned to pay to the [regulator concerned] such sum as appears to the court to be just having regard—

    (a) in a case within paragraph (a) of subsection (1), to the profits appearing to the court to have accrued;

    (b) in a case within paragraph (b) of that subsection, to the extent of the loss or other adverse effect;

    (c) in a case within both of those paragraphs, to the profits appearing to the court to have accrued and to the extent of the loss or other adverse effect.

(3) Any amount paid to the [regulator concerned] in pursuance of an order under subsection (2) must be paid by it to such qualifying person or distributed by it among such qualifying persons as the court may direct.

(8) 'Qualifying person' means a person appearing to the court to be someone—

    (a) to whom the profits mentioned in subsection (1)(a) are attributable; or

    (b) who has suffered the loss or adverse effect mentioned in subsection (1)(b).

[Note: subss (11)–(15) define in detail 'appropriate regulator'.]

[404   Consumer redress schemes

(1) This section applies if—

    (a) it appears to the [FCA] that there may have been a widespread or regular failure by relevant firms to comply with requirements applicable to the carrying on by them of any activity;

(b) it appears to it that, as a result, consumers have suffered (or may suffer) loss or damage in respect of which, if they brought legal proceedings, a remedy or relief would be available in the proceedings; and

(c) it considers that it is desirable to make rules for the purpose of securing that redress is made to the consumers in respect of the failure (having regard to other ways in which consumers may obtain redress).

(2) 'Relevant firms' means—

(a) authorised persons; [. . .]

(b) payment service providers [or

(c) electronic money issuers].

(3) The [FCA] may make rules requiring each relevant firm (or each relevant firm of a specified description) which has carried on the activity on or after the specified date to establish and operate a consumer redress scheme.

(4) A 'consumer redress scheme' is a scheme under which the firm is required to take one or more of the following steps in relation to the activity.

(5) The firm must first investigate whether, on or after the specified date, it has failed to comply with the requirements mentioned in subsection (1)(a) that are applicable to the carrying on by it of the activity.

(6) The next step is for the firm to determine whether the failure has caused (or may cause) loss or damage to consumers.

(7) If the firm determines that the failure has caused (or may cause) loss or damage to consumers, it must then—

(a) determine what the redress should be in respect of the failure; and

(b) make the redress to the consumers.

(8) A relevant firm is required to take the above steps in relation to any particular consumer even if, after the rules are made, a defence of limitation becomes available to the firm in respect of the loss or damage in question.

(9) Before making rules under this section, the [FCA] must consult the scheme operator of the ombudsman scheme.

(10) For the meaning of consumers, see section 404E.]

[404A   Rules under s. 404: supplementary

(1) Rules under section 404 may make provision—

(a) specifying the activities and requirements in relation to which relevant firms are to carry out investigations under consumer redress schemes;

(b) setting out, in relation to any specified description of case, examples of things done, or omitted to be done, that are to be regarded as constituting a failure to comply with a requirement;

(c) setting out, in relation to any specified description of case, matters to be taken into account, or steps to be taken, by relevant firms for the purpose of—

(i) assessing evidence as to a failure to comply with a requirement; or

(ii) determining whether such a failure has caused (or may cause) loss or damage to consumers;

(d) as to the kinds of redress that are, or are not, to be made to consumers in specified descriptions of case and the way in which redress is to be determined in specified descriptions of case;

(e) as to the things that relevant firms are, or are not, to do in establishing and operating consumer redress schemes;

(f) securing that relevant firms are not required to investigate anything occurring after a specified date;

(g) specifying the times by which anything required to be done under any consumer redress scheme is to be done;

(h)   requiring relevant firms to provide information to the [FCA];

(i)   authorising one or more competent persons to do anything for the purposes of, or in connection with, the establishment or operation of any consumer redress scheme;

(j)   for the nomination or approval by the [FCA] of persons authorised under paragraph (i);

(k)   as to the circumstances in which, instead of a relevant firm, the [FCA] (or one or more competent persons acting on the [FCA's] behalf) may carry out the investigation and take the other relevant steps under any consumer redress scheme;

(l)   as to the powers to be available to those carrying out an investigation by virtue of paragraph (k);

(m) as to the enforcement of any redress (for example, in the case of a money award, as a debt owed by a relevant firm).

(2) The only examples that may be set out in the rules as a result of subsection (1)(b) are examples of things done, or omitted to be done, that have been, or would be, held by a court or tribunal to constitute a failure to comply with a requirement.

(3) Matters may not be set out in the rules as a result of subsection (1)(c) if they have not been, or would not be, taken into account by a court or tribunal for the purpose mentioned there.

(4) The [FCA] must exercise the power conferred as a result of subsection (1)(d) so as to secure that, in relation to any description of case, the only kinds of redress to be made are those which it considers to be just in relation to that description of case.

(5) In acting under subsection (4), the [FCA] must have regard (among other things) to the nature and extent of the losses or damage in question.

(7) The reference in subsection (1)(k) to the other relevant steps under any consumer redress scheme is a reference to the [FCA] making the determinations mentioned in section 404(6) and (7) (with the firm still required to make the redress).

(8) If the rules include provision under subsection (1)(k), they must also include provision for—

(a) giving warning and decision notices, and

(b) conferring rights on relevant firms to refer matters to the Tribunal,

in relation to any determination mentioned in section 404(6) and (7) made by the [FCA].

(9) Nothing in this section is to be taken as limiting the power conferred by section 404.]

[404B   Complaints to the ombudsman scheme

(1) If—

(a) a consumer makes a complaint under the ombudsman scheme in respect of an act or omission of a relevant firm, and

(b) at the time the complaint is made, the subject-matter of the complaint falls to be dealt with (or has been dealt with) under a consumer redress scheme,

the way in which the complaint is to be determined by the ombudsman is to be as mentioned in subsection (4).

(1A) Subsection (1) does not apply if the consumer and the relevant firm agree that it should not apply.

(2) If a consumer—

(a) is not satisfied with a determination made by a relevant firm under a consumer redress scheme, or

(b) considers that a relevant firm has failed to make a determination in accordance with a consumer redress scheme,

the consumer may, in respect of that determination or failure, make a complaint under the ombudsman scheme.

(2A) The way in which a complaint mentioned in subsection (2) is to be determined by the ombudsman is to be as mentioned in subsection (4).

(2B) Subsection (2A) does not apply if the consumer and the relevant firm agree that it should not apply.

(3) In the following provisions of this section 'relevant complaint' means—

    (a) a complaint mentioned in subsection (1) other than one in relation to which subsection (1A) applies, or

    (b) a complaint mentioned in subsection (2) other than one in relation to which subsection (2B) applies.

(4) A relevant complaint is to be determined by reference to what, in the opinion of the ombudsman, the determination under the consumer redress scheme should be or should have been (subject to subsection (5)).

(5) If, in determining a relevant complaint, the ombudsman determines that the firm should make (or should have made) a payment of an amount to the consumer, the amount awarded by the ombudsman (a 'money award') must not exceed the monetary limit (within the meaning of section 229).

(6) But the ombudsman may recommend that the firm pay a larger amount.

(7) A money award—

    (a) may specify the date by which the amount awarded is to be paid;

    (b) may provide for interest to be payable, at a rate specified in the award, on any amount which is not paid by that date; and

    (c) is enforceable by the consumer in accordance with Part 3 or 3A of Schedule 17 (as the case may be).

(8) If, in determining a relevant complaint, the ombudsman determines that the firm should take (or should have taken) particular action in relation to the consumer, the ombudsman may direct the firm to take that action.

(9) Compliance with a direction under subsection (8) is enforceable, on the application of the consumer, by an injunction . . .

(11) The compulsory jurisdiction of the ombudsman scheme is to include the jurisdiction resulting from this section.]

[404E   Meaning of 'consumers'

(1) For the purposes of sections 404 to 404B 'consumers' means persons—

    (a) who have used, or may have contemplated using, any of the services within subsection (2);

    (b) who have relevant rights or interests in relation to any of the services within that subsection;

    (c) in respect of whom a person carries on an activity which is specified in article 89G of the Financial Services and Markets Act 2000 (Regulated Activities) Order 2001 (seeking out etc claims) whether that activity, as carried on by that person, is a regulated activity or is, by reason of an exclusion provided for under the 2001 Order or the 2000 Act, not a regulated activity.

(2) The services within this subsection are services provided by—

    (a) authorised persons in carrying on regulated activities;

    (c) authorised persons in communicating, or approving the communication by others of, invitations or inducements

        (i)   to engage in investment activity; or

        (ii) to engage in claims management activity;

    (d) authorised persons who are investment firms, or credit institutions, in providing relevant ancillary services;

    (e) persons acting as appointed representatives; [. . .]

    (f) payment service providers in providing payment services[; or

    (g) electronic money issuers].

(3) A person ('P') has a 'relevant right or interest' in relation to any services within subsection (2) if P has a right or interest—

    (a) which is derived from, or is otherwise attributable to, the use of the services by others; or

    (b) which may be adversely affected by the use of the services by persons acting on P's behalf or in a fiduciary capacity in relation to P.

(4) If a person is providing a service within subsection (2) as a trustee, the persons who have been, or may have been, beneficiaries of the trust are to be treated as persons who have used, or may have contemplated using, the service.

(5) A person who deals with another person ('B') in the course of B providing a service within subsection (2) is to be treated as using the service.

(6) In this section—

'engage in investment activity' has the meaning given by section 21;

['electronic money' has the same meaning as in the Electronic Money Regulations 2011 and any reference to issuing electronic money must be read accordingly;]

'payment services' has the same meaning as in the [Payment Services Regulations 2017];

'payment service provider' means a person who is a payment service provider for the purposes of those regulations as a result of falling within any of paragraphs (a) to (g) of the definition in regulation 2(1);

'relevant ancillary services' has the meaning given by section 138(1C).]

[404F   Other definitions etc

(1) For the purposes of sections 404 to 404B—

'redress' includes—

(a) interest; and

(b) a remedy or relief which could not be awarded in legal proceedings;

'specified' means specified in rules made under section 404.

(2) In determining for the purposes of those sections whether an authorised person has failed to comply with a requirement, anything which an appointed representative has done or omitted as respects business for which the authorised person has accepted responsibility is to be treated as having been done or omitted by the authorised person.

(3) References in those sections to the failure by a relevant firm to comply with a requirement applicable to the carrying on by it of any activity include anything done, or omitted to be done, by it in carrying on the activity—

(a) which is in breach of a duty or other obligation, prohibition or restriction; or

(b) which otherwise gives rise to the availability of a remedy or relief in legal proceedings.]

[404G   Power to widen the scope of consumer redress schemes

(1) The Treasury may by order amend the definition of 'relevant firms' in section 404 or the definition of 'consumers' in section 404E (or both).

(2) An order under this section may make consequential amendments of any provision of sections 404 to 404F.]

[415A   Powers under the Act

Any power which the [FCA, the PRA or the Bank of England] has under any provision of this Act is not limited in any way by any other power which it has under any other provision of this Act.]

417   Definitions

(1) In this Act—

['market abuse regulation' means Regulation (EU) No 596/2014 of the European Parliament and of the Council of 16 April 2014 on market abuse (market abuse regulation) and repealing Directive 2003/6/EC of the European Parliament and of the Council and Commission Directives 2003/124/EC, 2003/125/EC and 2004/72/EC, as it forms part of retained EU law;]

[425A   Consumers: regulated activities etc carried on by authorised persons

(1) This section has effect for the purposes of the provisions of this Act which apply this section.

(2) 'Consumers' means persons—

(a) who use, have used or may use any of the services within subsection (3);

(b) who have relevant rights or interests in relation to any of those services;

    (c) whose rights, interests or obligations are affected by the level of a regulated benchmark; or

    (d) in respect of whom a person carries on an activity which is specified in article 89G of the Financial Services and Markets Act 2000 (Regulated Activities) Order 2001 (seeking out etc claims) whether that activity, as carried on by that person, is a regulated activity or is, by reason of an exclusion provided for under the 2001 Order or the 2000 Act, not a regulated activity.

  (3) The services within this subsection are services provided by—

    (a) authorised persons in carrying on regulated activities;

    (b) authorised persons who are investment firms, or credit institutions, in providing relevant ancillary services; or

    (c) persons acting as appointed representatives.

  (4) A person ('P') has a 'relevant right or interest' in relation to any services within subsection (3) if P has a right or interest—

    (a) which is derived from, or is otherwise attributable to, the use of the services by others; or

    (b) which may be adversely affected by the use of the services by persons acting on P's behalf or in a fiduciary capacity in relation to P.

  (5) If a person is providing a service within subsection (3) as a trustee, the persons who are, have been or may be beneficiaries of the trust are to be treated as persons who use, have used or may use the service.

  (6) A person who deals with another person ('A') in the course of A providing a service within subsection (3) is to be treated as using the service.

  (7) In this section—

'regulated benchmark' means a benchmark, as defined in section 22(6) or (6A), in relation to which any provision made under section 22(1A)(b) or (c) has effect.

'relevant ancillary service' means any service of a kind mentioned in Section B of Annex I to the markets in financial instruments directive the provision of which does not involve the carrying on of a regulated activity.]

[425B   Consumers: regulated activities carried on by others

  (1) This section has effect for the purposes of the provisions of this Act which apply this section.

  (2) 'Consumers' means persons who, in relation to regulated activities carried on otherwise than by authorised persons, would be consumers as defined by section 425A if the activities were carried on by authorised persons.]

Enterprise Act 2002

(2002, c. 40)

PART 1 [GENERAL FUNCTIONS OF THE CMA]

General functions of [the CMA]

5   Acquisition of information etc

  (1) The [CMA] has the function of obtaining, compiling and keeping under review information about matters relating to the carrying out of its functions.

  (2) That function is to be carried out with a view to (among other things) ensuring that the [CMA] has sufficient information to take informed decisions and to carry out its other functions effectively.

  (3) In carrying out that function the [CMA] may carry out, commission or support (financially or otherwise) research.

6 Provision of information etc. to the public

(1) The [CMA] has the function of—

    (a) making the public aware of the ways in which competition may benefit consumers in, and the economy of, the United Kingdom; and

    (b) giving information or advice in respect of matters relating to any of its functions to the public.

(2) In carrying out those functions the [CMA] may—

    (a) publish educational materials or carry out other educational activities; or

    (b) support (financially or otherwise) the carrying out by others of such activities or the provision by others of information or advice.

7 Provision of information and advice to Ministers etc.

(1) The [CMA] has the function of—

    (a) making proposals, or

    (b) giving other information or advice,

on matters relating to any of its functions to any Minister of the Crown or other public authority (including proposals, information or advice as to any aspect of the law or a proposed change in the law).

[(1A) The CMA may, in particular, carry out the function under subsection (1)(a) by making a proposal in the form of a recommendation to a Minister of the Crown about the potential effect of a proposal for Westminster legislation on competition within any market or markets in the United Kingdom for goods or services.

(1B) The CMA must publish such a recommendation in such manner as the CMA considers appropriate for bringing the subject matter of the recommendation to the attention of those likely to be affected by it.]

(2) A Minister of the Crown may request the [CMA] to make proposals or give other information or advice on any matter relating to any of its functions; and the [CMA] shall, so far as is reasonably practicable and consistent with its other functions, comply with the request.

[(3) In this section—

'market in the United Kingdom' includes—

    (a) so far as it operates in the United Kingdom or a part of the United Kingdom, any market which operates there and in another country or territory or in a part of another country or territory; and

    (b) any market which operates only in a part of the United Kingdom;

and the reference to a market for goods or services includes a reference to a market for goods and services; and

'Westminster legislation' means—

    (a) an Act of Parliament, or

    (b) subordinate legislation (within the meaning given by section 21 of the Interpretation Act 1978).]

[8A Exclusion of public consumer advice scheme

The CMA may not under this Part support a public consumer advice scheme, where that support of a scheme consists of providing, or securing the provision of, an arrangement for giving advice without charge to individual consumers on matters personal to them.]

Miscellaneous

11 Super-complaints to [CMA]

(1) This section applies where a designated consumer body makes a complaint to the [CMA] that any feature, or combination of features, of a market in the United Kingdom for goods or services is or appears to be significantly harming the interests of consumers.

(2) The [CMA] must, within 90 days after the day on which it receives the complaint, publish a response stating how it proposes to deal with the complaint, and in particular—

    (a) whether it has decided to take any action, or to take no action, in response to the complaint, and

(b) if it has decided to take action, what action it proposes to take.

(3) The response must state the [CMA's] reasons for its proposals.

(4) The Secretary of State may by order amend subsection (2) by substituting any period for the period for the time being specified there.

(5) 'Designated consumer body' means a body designated by the Secretary of State by order.

(6) The Secretary of State—

(a) may designate a body only if it appears to him to represent the interests of consumers of any description, and

(b) must publish (and may from time to time vary) other criteria to be applied by him in determining whether to make or revoke a designation.

(7) The [CMA]—

(a) must issue guidance as to the presentation by the complainant of a reasoned case for the complaint, and

(b) may issue such other guidance as appears to it to be appropriate for the purposes of this section.

(8) An order under this section—

(a) shall be made by statutory instrument, and

(b) shall be subject to annulment in pursuance of a resolution of either House of Parliament.

(9) In this section—

(a) references to a feature of a market in the United Kingdom for goods or services have the same meaning as if contained in Part 4, and

(b) 'consumer' means an individual who is a consumer within the meaning of that Part.

PART 8 ENFORCEMENT OF CERTAIN CONSUMER LEGISLATION

Introduction

210 Consumers

(1) In this Part references to consumers must be construed in accordance with this section.

(2) In relation to a domestic infringement a consumer is an individual in respect of whom the first and second conditions are satisfied.

(3) The first condition is that—

(a) goods are or are sought to be supplied to the individual (whether by way of sale or otherwise) in the course of a business carried on by the person supplying or seeking to supply them, or

(b) services are or are sought to be supplied to the individual in the course of a business carried on by the person supplying or seeking to supply them.

(4) The second condition is that—

(a) the individual receives or seeks to receive the goods or services otherwise than in the course of a business carried on by him, or

(b) the individual receives or seeks to receive the goods or services with a view to carrying on a business but not in the course of a business carried on by him.

(6) In relation to a [Schedule 13 infringement] a consumer is a person who is a consumer for the purposes of [the listed enactment concerned.]

[(6A) An enactment is a listed enactment if it is specified in Schedule 13 or to the extent that it is so specified.

(6B) References to an enactment include— . . .]

(8) A business includes—

(a) a professional practice;

(b) any other undertaking carried on for gain or reward;

(c) any undertaking in the course of which goods or services are supplied otherwise than free of charge.

(9) The Secretary of State may by order modify Schedule 13.

(10) An order under this section must be made by statutory instrument subject to annulment in pursuance of a resolution of either House of Parliament.

211 Domestic infringements

(1) In this Part a domestic infringement is an act or omission which—

    (a) is done or made by a person in the course of a business,

    (b) falls within subsection (2), and

    (c) harms the collective interests of consumers [. . .].

[(1A) But an act or omission which satisfies the conditions in subsection (1) is a domestic infringement only if at least one of the following is satisfied—

    (a) the person supplying (or seeking to supply) goods or services has a place of business in the United Kingdom, or

    (b) the goods or services are supplied (or sought to be supplied) to or for a person in the United Kingdom (see section 232).]

(2) An act or omission falls within this subsection if it is of a description specified by the Secretary of State by order and consists of any of the following—

    (a) a contravention of an enactment which imposes a duty, prohibition or restriction enforceable by criminal proceedings;

    (b) an act done or omission made in breach of contract;

    (c) an act done or omission made in breach of a non-contractual duty owed to a person by virtue of an enactment or rule of law and enforceable by civil proceedings;

    (d) an act or omission in respect of which an enactment provides for a remedy or sanction enforceable by civil proceedings;

    (e) an act done or omission made by a person supplying or seeking to supply goods or services as a result of which an agreement or security relating to the supply is void or unenforceable to any extent;

    (f) an act or omission by which a person supplying or seeking to supply goods or services purports or attempts to exercise a right or remedy relating to the supply in circumstances where the exercise of the right or remedy is restricted or excluded under or by virtue of an enactment;

    (g) an act or omission by which a person supplying or seeking to supply goods or services purports or attempts to avoid (to any extent) liability relating to the supply in circumstances where such avoidance is restricted or prevented under an enactment.

(3) But an order under this section may provide that any description of act or omission falling within subsection (2) is not a domestic infringement.

(4) For the purposes of subsection (2) it is immaterial—

    (a) whether or not any duty, prohibition or restriction exists in relation to consumers as such;

    (b) whether or not any remedy or sanction is provided for the benefit of consumers as such;

    (c) whether or not any proceedings have been brought in relation to the act or omission;

    (d) whether or not any person has been convicted of an offence in respect of the contravention mentioned in subsection (2)(a);

    (e) whether or not there is a waiver in respect of the breach of contract mentioned in subsection (2)(b).

(5) References to an enactment include references to subordinate legislation (within the meaning of the Interpretation Act 1978 (c. 30)).

(6) The power to make an order under this section must be exercised by statutory instrument.

(7) But no such order may be made unless a draft of it has been laid before Parliament and approved by a resolution of each House.

[212   Schedule 13 infringements

(1) In this Part a Schedule 13 infringement is an act or omission which contravenes a listed enactment and which harms the collective interests of consumers.

(2) References to a listed enactment must be construed in accordance with section 210.]

213   Enforcers

(1) Each of the following is a general enforcer—

(a) the [CMA];

(b) every local weights and measures authority in Great Britain;

(c) the Department of Enterprise, Trade and Investment in Northern Ireland.

(2) A designated enforcer is any person or body (whether or not incorporated) which the Secretary of State—

(a) thinks has as one of its purposes the protection of the collective interests of consumers, and

(b) designates by order.

(3) The Secretary of State may designate a public body only if he is satisfied that it is independent.

(4) The Secretary of State may designate a person or body which is not a public body only if the person or body (as the case may be) satisfies such criteria as the Secretary of State specifies by order.

[(5A) Each of the following is a Schedule 13 enforcer—

(a) the CMA;

(b) the Civil Aviation Authority;

(c) the Financial Conduct Authority;

(d) the Secretary of State for Health and Social Care;

(e) the Department of Health, Social Services and Public Safety in Northern Ireland;

(f) the Office of Communications;

(g) the Department of Enterprise, Trade and Investment in Northern Ireland;

(h) every local weights and measures authority in Great Britain;

(i) an enforcement authority within the meaning of section 120(15) of the Communications Act 2003 (regulation of premium rate services);

(j) the Information Commissioner;

(k) the Department for Infrastructure;

(l) the Maritime and Coastguard Agency;

(m) the Office of Rail and Road;

(n) the Office for the Traffic Commissioner].

(6) An order under this section may designate an enforcer in respect of—

(a) all infringements;

(b) infringements of such descriptions as are specified in the order.

(7) An order under this section may make different provision for different purposes.

(8) The designation of a body by virtue of subsection (3) is conclusive evidence for the purposes of any question arising under this Part that the body is a public body.

(9) An order under this section must be made by statutory instrument subject to annulment in pursuance of a resolution of either House of Parliament.

[Enforcement orders and interim enforcement orders]

214   Consultation

[(1) An enforcer must not make an application for an enforcement order unless—

(a) the enforcer has engaged in appropriate consultation with the person against whom the enforcement order would be made, and

(b) if the enforcer is not the CMA, the enforcer has given notice to the CMA of the enforcer's intention to apply for the enforcement order, and the appropriate minimum period has elapsed.

(1A) The appropriate minimum period is—

(a) in the case of an enforcement order, 14 days beginning with the day on which notice under subsection (1)(b) is given;

(b) in the case of an interim enforcement order, seven days beginning with the day on which notice under subsection (1)(b) is given.]

(2) Appropriate consultation is consultation for the purpose of—

    (a) achieving the cessation of the infringement in a case where an infringement is occurring;

    (b) ensuring that there will be no repetition of the infringement in a case where the infringement has occurred;

    (c) ensuring that there will be no repetition of the infringement in a case where the cessation of the infringement is achieved under paragraph (a);

    (d) ensuring that the infringement does not take place in the case of a [Schedule 13 infringement] which the enforcer believes is likely to take place.

(3) Subsection (1) does not apply if the CMA thinks that an application for an enforcement order should be made without delay.

(4) [Subsection (1)(a)] ceases to apply—

    (a) for the purposes of an application for an enforcement order at the end of the period of 14 days [or, where subsection (4A) applies, 28 days] beginning with the day after the person against whom the enforcement order would be made receives a request for consultation from the enforcer;

    (b) for the purposes of an application for an interim enforcement order at the end of the period of seven days beginning with the day after the person against whom the interim enforcement order would be made receives a request for consultation from the enforcer.

[(4A) This subsection applies where the person against whom the enforcement order would be made is a member of, or is represented by, a representative body, and that body operates a consumer code which has been approved by—

    (a) an enforcer, other than a designated enforcer which is not a public body,

    (b) a body which represents an enforcer mentioned in paragraph (a),

    (c) a group of enforcers mentioned in paragraph (a), or

    (d) a community interest company whose objects include the approval of consumer codes.

(4B) In subsection (4A)—

'consumer code' means a code of practice or other document (however described) intended, with a view to safeguarding or promoting the interests of consumers, to regulate by any means the conduct of persons engaged in the supply of goods or services to consumers (or the conduct of their employees or representatives), and

'representative body' means an organisation established to represent the interests of two or more businesses in a particular sector or area, and for this purpose 'business' has the meaning it bears in section 210.]

(5) The Secretary of State may by order make rules in relation to consultation under this section.

(6) Such an order must be made by statutory instrument subject to annulment in pursuance of a resolution of either House of Parliament.

(7) In this section [(except subsections (1A) and (4))] and in sections 215 and 216 references to an enforcement order include references to an interim enforcement order.

215 Applications

(1) An application for an enforcement order must name the person the enforcer thinks—

    (a) has engaged or is engaging in conduct which constitutes a domestic or a [Schedule 13 infringement], or

    (b) is likely to engage in conduct which constitutes a [Schedule 13 infringement].

(2) A general enforcer may make an application for an enforcement order in respect of any infringement.

(3) A designated enforcer may make an application for an enforcement order in respect of any infringement to which his designation relates.

[(4A) A Schedule 13 enforcer may make an application for an enforcement order in respect of a Schedule 13 infringement.]

(5) The following courts have jurisdiction to make an enforcement order—

[(za) the High Court or the county court if the person against whom the order is sought carries on business or has a place of business in England and Wales;]

    (a) the High Court or a county court if the person against whom the order is sought carries on business or has a place of business in [. . .] Northern Ireland;

    (b) the Court of Session or the sheriff if the person against whom the order is sought carries on business or has a place of business in Scotland.

(9) An enforcer which is not the [CMA] must notify the [CMA] of the result of an application under this section.

216 Applications: directions by [CMA]

(1) This section applies if the [CMA] believes that an enforcer other than the [CMA] intends to apply for an enforcement order.

(2) In such a case the [CMA] may direct that if an application in respect of a particular infringement is to be made it must be made—

    (a) only by the [CMA], or

    (b) only by such other enforcer as the [CMA] directs.

(3) If the [CMA] directs that only it may make an application that does not prevent—

    (a) the [CMA] or any enforcer from accepting an undertaking under section 219, or

    (b) the [CMA] from taking such other steps it thinks appropriate (apart from making an application) for the purpose of securing that the infringement is not committed, continued or repeated.

(4) The [CMA] may vary or withdraw a direction given under this section.

(5) The [CMA] must take such steps as it thinks appropriate to bring a direction (or a variation or withdrawal of a direction) to the attention of enforcers it thinks may be affected by it.

217 Enforcement orders

(1) This section applies if an application for an enforcement order is made under section 215 and the court finds that the person named in the application has engaged in conduct which constitutes the infringement.

(2) This section also applies if such an application is made in relation to a [Schedule 13 infringement] and the court finds that the person named in the application is likely to engage in conduct which constitutes the infringement.

(3) If this section applies the court may make an enforcement order against the person.

(4) In considering whether to make an enforcement order the court must have regard to whether the person named in the application—

    (a) has given an undertaking under section 219 in respect of conduct such as is mentioned in subsection (3) of that section;

    (b) has failed to comply with the undertaking.

(5) An enforcement order must—

    (a) indicate the nature of the conduct to which the finding under subsection (1) or (2) relates, and

    (b) direct the person to comply with subsection (6).

(6) A person complies with this subsection if he—

    (a) does not continue or repeat the conduct;

    (b) does not engage in such conduct in the course of his business or another business;

    (c) does not consent to or connive in the carrying out of such conduct by a body corporate with which he has a special relationship (within the meaning of section 222(3)).

(7) But subsection (6)(a) does not apply in the case of a finding under subsection (2).

(8) An enforcement order may require a person against whom the order is made to publish in such form and manner and to such extent as the court thinks appropriate for the purpose of eliminating any continuing effects of the infringement—

    (a) the order;

    (b) a corrective statement.

(9) If the court makes a finding under subsection (1) or (2) it may accept an undertaking by the person—

    (a) to comply with subsection (6), or

    (b) to take steps which the court believes will secure that he complies with subsection (6).

(10) An undertaking under subsection (9) may include a further undertaking by the person to publish in such form and manner and to such extent as the court thinks appropriate for the purpose of eliminating any continuing effects of the infringement—

    (a) the terms of the undertaking;

    (b) a corrective statement.

[(10A) An enforcement order may require a person against whom the order is made to take enhanced consumer measures (defined in section 219A) within a period specified by the court.

(10B) An undertaking under subsection (9) may include a further undertaking by the person to take enhanced consumer measures within a period specified in the undertaking.

(10C) Subsections (10A) and (10B) are subject to section 219C in a case where the application for the enforcement order was made by a designated enforcer which is not a public body.

(10D) Where a person is required by an enforcement order or an undertaking under this section to take enhanced consumer measures, the order or undertaking may include requirements as to the provision of information or documents to the court by the person in order that the court may determine if the person is taking those measures.]

(11) If the court—

    (a) makes a finding under subsection (1) or (2), and

    (b) accepts an undertaking under subsection (9),

it must not make an enforcement order in respect of the infringement to which the undertaking relates.

[(12) An enforcement order made in a part of the United Kingdom by a court specified in relation to that part in the second or third column of the table has effect in another part of the United Kingdom as if made by a court specified in relation to that other part in the same column of the table—

England and Wales	The High Court	The county court
Scotland	The Court of Session	The sheriff
Northern Ireland	The High Court	A county court.]

218 Interim enforcement order

(1) The court may make an interim enforcement order against a person named in the application for the order if it appears to the court—

    (a) that it is alleged that the person is engaged in conduct which constitutes a domestic or [Schedule 13 infringement] or is likely to engage in conduct which constitutes a [Schedule 13 infringement],

    (b) that if the application had been an application for an enforcement order it would be likely to be granted,

    (c) that it is expedient that the conduct is prohibited or prevented (as the case may be) immediately, and

    (d) if no notice of the application has been given to the person named in the application that it is appropriate to make an interim enforcement order without notice.

(2) An interim enforcement order must—

    (a) indicate the nature of the alleged conduct, and

    (b) direct the person to comply with subsection (3).

(3) A person complies with this subsection if he—

    (a) does not continue or repeat the conduct;

    (b) does not engage in such conduct in the course of his business or another business;

    (c) does not consent to or connive in the carrying out of such conduct by a body corporate with which he has a special relationship (within the meaning of section 222(3)).

(4) But subsection (3)(a) does not apply in so far as the application is made in respect of an allegation that the person is likely to engage in conduct which constitutes a [Schedule 13 infringement].

(5) An application for an interim enforcement order against a person may be made at any time before an application for an enforcement order against the person in respect of the same conduct is determined.

(6) An application for an interim enforcement order must refer to all matters—

(a) which are known to the applicant, and

(b) which are material to the question whether or not the application is granted.

(7) If an application for an interim enforcement order is made without notice the application must state why no notice has been given.

(8) The court may vary or discharge an interim enforcement order on the application of—

(a) the enforcer who applied for the order;

(b) the person against whom it is made.

(9) An interim enforcement order against a person is discharged on the determination of an application for an enforcement order made against the person in respect of the same conduct.

(10) If it appears to the court as mentioned in subsection (1)(a) to (c) the court may instead of making an interim enforcement order accept an undertaking from the person named in the application—

(a) to comply with subsection (3), or

(b) to take steps which the court believes will secure that he complies with subsection (3).

[(11) An interim enforcement order made in a part of the United Kingdom by a court specified in relation to that part in the second or third column of the table has effect in another part of the United Kingdom as if made by a court specified in relation to that other part in the same column of the table—

England and Wales	The High Court	The county court
Scotland	The Court of Session	The sheriff
Northern Ireland	The High Court	A county court.]

[Enforcement procedure: supplementary]

[218A   Unfair commercial practices: substantiation of claims

(1) This section applies where an application for an enforcement order, an interim enforcement order, an online interface order or an interim online interface order is made in respect of a Schedule 13 infringement involving a contravention of the Consumer Protection from Unfair Trading Regulations 2008.

(2) For the purposes of considering the application the court may require the relevant person to provide evidence as to the accuracy of any factual claim made as part of a commercial practice of that person if, taking into account the legitimate interests of that person and any other party to the proceedings, it appears appropriate in the circumstances.

(2A) In subsection (2), 'the relevant person', in relation to an application, means—

(a) where the application is for an enforcement order or an interim enforcement order, the person named in the application under section 215(1);

(b) where the application is for an online interface order or an interim online interface order, the person alleged by the CMA to have engaged, be engaging or be likely to engage in conduct which constitutes the Community infringement, provided that person is either the person against whom the order is sought or otherwise a party to the proceedings.

(3) If, having been required under subsection (2) to provide evidence as to the accuracy of a factual claim, a person—

(a) fails to provide such evidence, or

(b) provides evidence as to the accuracy of the factual claim that the court considers inadequate,

the court may consider that the factual claim is inaccurate.

(4) In this section 'commercial practice' has the meaning given by regulation 2 of the Consumer Protection from Unfair Trading Regulations 2008.]

219 Undertakings

(1) This section applies if an enforcer has power to make an application [for an enforcement order or an interim enforcement order under section 215 or for an online interface order or an interim online interface order under section 218ZA].

(2) In such a case the enforcer may accept from a person to whom subsection (3) applies an undertaking that the person will comply with subsection (4).

(3) This subsection applies to a person who the enforcer believes—

    (a) has engaged in conduct which constitutes an infringement;

    (b) is engaging in such conduct;

    (c) is likely to engage in conduct which constitutes a [Schedule 13 infringement].

(4) A person complies with this subsection if he—

    (a) does not continue or repeat the conduct;

    (b) does not engage in such conduct in the course of his business or another business;

    (c) does not consent to or connive in the carrying out of such conduct by a body corporate with which he has a special relationship (within the meaning of section 222(3)).

(5) But subsection (4)(a) does not apply in the case of an undertaking given by a person in so far as subsection (3) applies to him by virtue of paragraph (c).

[(5ZA) An undertaking under this section may include a further undertaking by the person—

    (a) to take enhanced consumer measures (defined in section 219A) within a period specified in the undertaking, and

    (b) where such measures are included, to provide information or documents to the enforcer in order that the enforcer may determine if the person is taking those measures.

(5ZB) Subsection (5ZA) is subject to section 219C in a case where the enforcer is a designated enforcer which is not a public body.]

[(5A) A Schedule 13 enforcer who has accepted an undertaking under this section may—

    (a) accept a further undertaking from the person concerned to publish the terms of the undertaking; or

    (b) take steps itself to publish the undertaking.

(5B) In each case the undertaking shall be published in such form and manner and to such extent as the Schedule 13 enforcer thinks appropriate for the purpose of eliminating any continuing effects of the Schedule 13 infringement.]

(6) If an enforcer accepts an undertaking under this section it must notify the [CMA]—

    (a) of the terms of the undertaking;

    (b) of the identity of the person who gave it.

[219A Definition of enhanced consumer measures

(1) In this Part, enhanced consumer measures are measures (not excluded by subsection (5)) falling within—

    (a) the redress category described in subsection (2),

    (b) the compliance category described in subsection (3), or

    (c) the choice category described in subsection (4).

(2) The measures in the redress category are—

    (a) measures offering compensation or other redress to consumers—

        (i) who have suffered loss as a result of the conduct which has given rise to the enforcement order or undertaking, or

        (ii) where that conduct constitutes a Community infringement, who have been affected in any other way by that conduct.

    (b) where the conduct which has given rise to the enforcement order or undertaking relates to a contract, measures offering consumers falling within paragraph (a)(i) or (ii) the option to terminate (but not vary) that contract,

    (c) where consumers falling within paragraph (a)(i) or (ii) cannot be identified, or cannot be identified without disproportionate cost to the subject of the enforcement order or undertaking, measures intended to be in the collective interests of consumers.

(3) The measures in the compliance category are measures intended to prevent or reduce the risk of the occurrence or repetition of the conduct to which the enforcement order or undertaking relates (including measures with that purpose which may have the effect of improving compliance with consumer law more generally).

(4) The measures in the choice category are measures intended to enable consumers to choose more effectively between persons supplying or seeking to supply goods or services.

(5) The following are not enhanced consumer measures—

    (a) a publication requirement included in an enforcement order as described in section 217(8),

    (b) a publication requirement included in an undertaking accepted by the court as described in section 217(10), or

    (c) a publication requirement included in an undertaking accepted by a Schedule 13 enforcer as described in section 219(5A)(a).]

[219B   Inclusion of enhanced consumer measures etc.

(1) An enforcement order or undertaking may include only such enhanced consumer measures as the court or enforcer (as the case may be) considers to be just and reasonable.

(2) For the purposes of subsection (1) the court or enforcer must in particular consider whether any proposed enhanced consumer measures are proportionate, taking into account—

    (a) the likely benefit of the measures to consumers,

    (b) the costs likely to be incurred by the subject of the enforcement order or undertaking, and

    (c) the likely cost to consumers of obtaining the benefit of the measures.

(3) The costs referred to in subsection (2)(b) are—

    (a) the cost of the measures, and

    (b) the reasonable administrative costs associated with taking the measures.

(4) Where the conduct which has given rise to an enforcement order or undertaking constitutes a domestic infringement and not a Community infringement, the enforcement order or undertaking may include enhanced consumer measures in the redress category—

    (a) only in a loss case, and

    (b) only if the court or enforcer (as the case may be) is satisfied that the cost of such measures to the subject of the enforcement order or undertaking is unlikely to be more than the sum of the losses suffered by consumers as a result of the conduct which has given rise to the enforcement order or undertaking.

(4A) Where the conduct which has given rise to an enforcement order or undertaking constitutes a Community infringement, the enforcement order or undertaking may include enhanced consumer measures in the redress category for the benefit of consumers who have been affected by that conduct.

(5) The cost referred to in subsection (4)(b) does not include the administrative costs associated with taking the measures.

(6) Subsection (7) applies if an enforcement order or undertaking includes enhanced consumer measures offering compensation and a settlement agreement is entered into in connection with the payment of compensation.

(7) A waiver of a person's rights in the settlement agreement is not valid if it is a waiver of the right to bring civil proceedings in respect of conduct other than the conduct which has given rise to the enforcement order or undertaking.

(8) The following definitions apply for the purposes of subsection (4)(a).

(9) In the case of an enforcement order or undertaking under section 217, 'a loss case' means a case in which—

    (a) subsection (1) of that section applies (a finding that a person has engaged in conduct which constitutes an infringement), and

    (b) consumers have suffered loss as a result of that conduct.

(10) In the case of an undertaking under section 219, 'a loss case' means a case in which—

    (a) subsection (3)(a) or (b) of that section applies (a belief that a person has engaged or is engaging in conduct which constitutes an infringement), and

(b) consumers have suffered loss as a result of that conduct.]

[219C Availability of enhanced consumer measures to private enforcers

(1) An enforcement order made on the application of a designated enforcer which is not a public body may require a person to take enhanced consumer measures only if the following conditions are satisfied.

(2) An undertaking given under section 217(9) following an application for an enforcement order made by a designated enforcer which is not a public body, or an undertaking given to such an enforcer under section 219, may include a further undertaking by a person to take enhanced consumer measures only if the following conditions are satisfied.

(3) The first condition is that the enforcer is specified for the purposes of this section by order made by the Secretary of State.

(4) The second condition is that the enhanced consumer measures do not directly benefit the enforcer or an associated undertaking.

(5) Enhanced consumer measures which directly benefit an enforcer or an associated undertaking include, in particular, measures which—

(a) require a person to pay money to the enforcer or associated undertaking,

(b) require a person to participate in a scheme which is designed to recommend persons supplying or seeking to supply goods or services to consumers and which is administered by the the enforcer or associated undertaking, or

(c) would give the enforcer or associated undertaking a commercial advantage over any of its competitors.

(6) The Secretary of State may make an order under subsection (3) specifying an enforcer only if the Secretary of State is satisfied that to do so is likely to—

(a) improve the availability to consumers of redress for infringements to which the enforcer's designation relates,

(b) improve the availability to consumers of information which enables them to choose more effectively between persons supplying or seeking to supply goods or services, or

(c) improve compliance with consumer law.

(7) The Secretary of State may make an order under subsection (3) specifying an enforcer only if the functions of the enforcer under this Part have been specified under section 24 of the Legislative and Regulatory Reform Act 2006 (functions to which principles under section 21 and code of practice under section 22 apply), to the extent that they are capable of being so specified.

(8) The power to make an order under subsection (3)—

(a) is exercisable by statutory instrument subject to annulment in pursuance of a resolution of either House of Parliament;

(b) includes power to make incidental, supplementary, consequential, transitional, transitory or saving provision.

(9) Subsection (10) applies if—

(a) an enforcer exercises a function in relation to a person by virtue of subsection (1) or (2),

(b) that function is a relevant function for the purposes of Part 2 (co-ordination of regulatory enforcement) of the Regulatory Enforcement and Sanctions Act 2008, and

(c) a primary authority (within the meaning of that Part) has given advice or guidance under section 27(1) of that Act—

(i) to that person in relation to that function, or

(ii) to other local authorities (within the meaning of that Part) with that function as to how they should exercise it in relation to that person.

(10) The enforcer must, in exercising the function in relation to that person, act consistently with that advice or guidance.

(11) In this section 'associated undertaking', in relation to a designated enforcer, means—

(a) a parent undertaking or subsidiary undertaking of the enforcer, or

(b) a subsidiary undertaking of a parent undertaking of the enforcer, and for this purpose 'parent undertaking' and 'subsidiary undertaking' have the meanings given by section 1162 of the Companies Act 2006.]

220   Further proceedings

(1) This section applies if the court—

   (a) makes an enforcement order under section 217,

   (b) makes an interim enforcement order under section 218, [...]

   (c) accepts an undertaking under either of those sections[, or

   (d) makes an online interface order under section 218ZB or an interim online interface order under section 218ZC.]

[(1A) This section does not apply in the case of a failure to comply with an order or undertaking which consists only of a failure to provide information or documents required by the order or undertaking as described in section 217(10D).]

(2) [Any Schedule 13 enforcer] has the same right to apply to the court in respect of a failure to comply with [an order (apart from an online interface order or an interim online interface order)] or undertaking as the enforcer who made the application for the order.

(3) An application to the court in respect of a failure to comply with an undertaking may include an application for [an enforcement order, an interim enforcement order, an online interface order or an interim online interface order].

(4) If the court finds that an undertaking is not being complied with it may make [an enforcement order, an interim enforcement order, an online interface order or an interim online interface order] (instead of making any other order it has power to make).

(5) In the case of an application for an enforcement order or for an interim enforcement order as mentioned in subsection (3) sections 214 and 216 must be ignored and [sections 215, 217 or 218 (as the case may be) and 219A, 219B and 219C] apply subject to the following modifications—

   (a) section 215(1)(b) must be ignored;

   (b) section 215(5) must be ignored and the application must be made to the court which accepted the undertaking;

   [(c) section 217(9), (10), (10B) and (11) must be ignored, and section 217(10C) and (10D) must be ignored to the extent that they relate to an undertaking under section 217(9);]

   (d) section 218(10) must be ignored

   [(e) sections 219A, 219B and 219C must be ignored to the extent that they relate to an undertaking under section 217(9) or 219.]

[(5A) In the case of an application for an online interface order or an interim online interface order as mentioned in subsection (3), section 218ZA applies subject to the following modifications—

   (a) in section 218ZA(1), the words 'or is likely to be' must be ignored;

   (b) in section 218ZA(2), the reference to the person the CMA thinks has engaged, is engaging or is likely to engage in conduct which constitutes the Community infringement is to be read as a reference to the person the CMA thinks has engaged or is engaging in such conduct;

   (c) section 218ZA(3) must be ignored and the application must be made to the court which accepted the undertaking.]

(6) If an enforcer which is not the [CMA] makes an application in respect of the failure of a person to comply with an enforcement order, an interim enforcement order or an undertaking given under section 217 or 218 the enforcer must notify the [CMA]—

   (a) of the application;

   (b) of any order made by the court on the application.

222   Bodies corporate: accessories

(1) This section applies if the person whose conduct constitutes a domestic infringement or a [Schedule 13 infringement] is a body corporate.

(2) If the conduct takes place with the consent or connivance of a person (an accessory) who has a special relationship with the body corporate, the consent or connivance is also conduct which constitutes the infringement.

(3) A person has a special relationship with a body corporate if he is—

(a) a controller of the body corporate, or

(b) a director, manager, secretary or other similar officer of the body corporate or a person purporting to act in such a capacity.

(4) A person is a controller of a body corporate if—

(a) the directors of the body corporate or of another body corporate which is its controller are accustomed to act in accordance with the person's directions or instructions, or

(b) either alone or with an associate or associates he is entitled to exercise or control the exercise of one third or more of the voting power at any general meeting of the body corporate or of another body corporate which is its controller.

(5) [An enforcement order, an interim enforcement order, an online interface order or an interim online interface order] may be made against an accessory in respect of an infringement whether or not such an order is made against the body corporate.

(6) The court may accept an undertaking under section 217(9) or 218(10) from an accessory in respect of an infringement whether or not it accepts such an undertaking from the body corporate.

(7) An enforcer may accept an undertaking under section 219 from an accessory in respect of an infringement whether or not it accepts such an undertaking from the body corporate.

(8) Subsection (9) applies if—

(a) [an enforcement order or an interim enforcement order] is made as mentioned in subsection (5), or

(b) an undertaking is accepted as mentioned in subsection (6) or (7).

(9) In such a case for subsection (6) of section 217, subsection (3) of section 218 or subsection (4) of section 219 (as the case may be) there is substituted the following subsection—

'() A person complies with this subsection if he—

(a) does not continue or repeat the conduct;

(b) does not in the course of any business carried on by him engage in conduct such as that which constitutes the infringement committed by the body corporate mentioned in section 222(1);

(c) does not consent to or connive in the carrying out of such conduct by another body corporate with which he has a special relationship (within the meaning of section 222(3)).'

(10) A person is an associate of an individual if—

(a) he is the spouse [or civil partner] of the individual;

(b) he is a relative of the individual;

(c) he is a relative of the individual's spouse [or civil partner];

(d) he is the spouse [or civil partner] of a relative of the individual;

(e) he is the spouse [or civil partner] of a relative of the individual's spouse;

(f) he lives in the same household as the individual otherwise than merely because he or the individual is the other's employer, tenant, lodger or boarder;

(g) he is a relative of a person who is an associate of the individual by virtue of paragraph (f);

(h) he has at some time in the past fallen within any of paragraphs (a) to (g).

(11) A person is also an associate of—

(a) an individual with whom he is in partnership;

(b) an individual who is an associate of the individual mentioned in paragraph (a);

(c) a body corporate if he is a controller of it or he is an associate of a person who is a controller of the body corporate.

(12) A body corporate is an associate of another body corporate if—

(a) the same person is a controller of both;

(b) a person is a controller of one and persons who are his associates are controllers of the other;

(c) a person is a controller of one and he and persons who are his associates are controllers of the other;

(d) a group of two or more persons is a controller of each company and the groups consist of the same persons;

(e) a group of two or more persons is a controller of each company and the groups may be regarded as consisting of the same persons by treating (in one or more cases) a member of either group as replaced by a person of whom he is an associate.

(13) A relative is a brother, sister, uncle, aunt, nephew, niece, lineal ancestor or lineal descendant.

223 Bodies corporate: orders

(1) This section applies if a court makes [an enforcement order, an interim enforcement order, an online interface order or an interim online interface order] against a body corporate and—

(a) at the time the order is made the body corporate is a member of a group of interconnected bodies corporate,

(b) at any time when the order is in force the body corporate becomes a member of a group of interconnected bodies corporate, or

(c) at any time when the order is in force a group of interconnected bodies corporate of which the body corporate is a member is increased by the addition of one or more further members.

(2) The court may direct that the order is binding upon all of the members of the group as if each of them were the body corporate against which the order is made.

(3) A group of interconnected bodies corporate is a group consisting of two or more bodies corporate all of whom are interconnected with each other.

(4) Any two bodies corporate are interconnected—

(a) if one of them is a subsidiary of the other, or

(b) if both of them are subsidiaries of the same body corporate.

[(5) In this section 'subsidiary' has the meaning given by section 1159 of the Companies Act 2006.]

Miscellaneous

[223A Investigatory powers

For the investigatory powers available to enforcers for the purposes of enforcers' functions under this Part, see Schedule 5 to the Consumer Rights Act 2015.]

228 Evidence

(1) Proceedings under this Part are civil proceedings for the purposes of—

(a) section 11 of the Civil Evidence Act 1968 (c. 64) (convictions admissible as evidence in civil proceedings); . . .

(2) In proceedings under this Part any finding by a court in civil proceedings that an act or omission mentioned in section 211(2)(b), (c) or (d) or 212(1) has occurred—

(a) is admissible as evidence that the act or omission occurred;

(b) unless the contrary is proved, is sufficient evidence that the act or omission occurred.

(3) But subsection (2) does not apply to any finding—

(a) which has been reversed on appeal;

(b) which has been varied on appeal so as to negative it.

229 Advice and information

(1) [The CMA] must prepare and publish advice and information with a view to—

(a) explaining the provisions of this Part to persons who are likely to be affected by them, and

(b) indicating how the [CMA] expects such provisions to operate.

[(1A) As soon as is reasonably practicable after the commencement of Schedule 5 to the Consumer Rights Act 2015 (investigatory powers etc.) the CMA must prepare and publish advice and information with a view to—

(a) explaining the provisions of that Schedule, so far as they relate to investigatory powers exercised for the purposes set out in paragraphs 13(2) and (3) and 19 of that Schedule, to persons who are likely to be affected by them, and

(b) indicating how the CMA expects such provisions to operate.]

(2) The [CMA] may at any time publish revised or new advice or information.

(3) Advice or information published in pursuance of subsection (1)(b) may include advice or information about the factors which the [CMA] may take into account in considering how to exercise the functions conferred on it by this Part.

(4) Advice or information published by the [CMA] under this section is to be published in such form and in such manner as it considers appropriate.

(5) In preparing advice or information under this section the [CMA] must consult such persons as it thinks are representative of persons affected by this Part.

(6) If any proposed advice or information relates to a matter in respect of which another [enforcer] may act the persons to be consulted must include that enforcer.

230   Notice to OFT [*now CMA*] of intended prosecution

(1) This section applies if a local weights and measures authority in England and Wales intends to start proceedings for an offence under an enactment or subordinate legislation specified by the Secretary of State by order for the purposes of this section.

(2) The authority must give the [CMA]—
(a) notice of its intention to start the proceedings; [. . .]

(3) The authority must not start the proceedings until whichever is the earlier of the following—
(a) the end of the period of 14 days starting with the day on which the authority gives the notice;
(b) the day on which it is notified by the [CMA] that the [CMA] has received the notice [. . .] given under subsection (2).

(4) The authority must also notify the [CMA] of the outcome of the proceedings after they are finally determined.

(5) But such proceedings are not invalid by reason only of the failure of the authority to comply with this section.

(6) Subordinate legislation has the same meaning as in section 21(1) of the Interpretation Act 1978 (c. 30).

(7) An order under this section must be made by statutory instrument subject to annulment in pursuance of a resolution of either House of Parliament.

231   Notice of convictions and judgments to [CMA]

(1) This section applies if—
(a) a person is convicted of an offence by or before a court in the United Kingdom, or
(b) a judgment is given against a person by a court in civil proceedings in the United Kingdom.

(2) The court may make arrangements to bring the conviction or judgment to the attention of the [CMA] if it appears to the court—
(a) having regard to the functions of the [CMA] under this Part [. . .] that it is expedient for the conviction or judgment to be brought to the attention of the [CMA], and
(b) without such arrangements the conviction or judgment may not be brought to the attention of the [CMA].

(3) For the purposes of subsection (2) it is immaterial that the proceedings have been finally disposed of by the court.

(4) Judgment includes an order or decree and references to the giving of the judgment must be construed accordingly.

Interpretation

232   Goods and services

(1) References in this Part to goods and services must be construed in accordance with this section.

(2) Goods include—
(a) buildings and other structures;

  (b) ships, aircraft and hovercraft.
(3) The supply of goods includes—
  (a) supply by way of sale, lease, hire or hire purchase;
  (b) in relation to buildings and other structures, construction of them by one person for another.
(4) Goods or services which are supplied wholly or partly outside the United Kingdom must be taken to be supplied to or for a person in the United Kingdom if they are supplied in accordance with arrangements falling within subsection (5).
(5) Arrangements fall within this subsection if they are made by any means and—
  (a) at the time the arrangements are made the person seeking the supply is in the United Kingdom, or
  (b) at the time the goods or services are supplied (or ought to be supplied in accordance with the arrangements) the person responsible under the arrangements for effecting the supply is in or has a place of business in the United Kingdom.

233 Person supplying goods

(1) This section has effect for the purpose of references in this Part to a person supplying or seeking to supply goods under—
  (a) a hire-purchase agreement;
  (b) a credit-sale agreement;
  (c) a conditional sale agreement.
(2) The references include references to a person who conducts any antecedent negotiations relating to the agreement.
(3) The following expressions must be construed in accordance with section 189 of the Consumer Credit Act 1974 (c. 39)—
  (a) hire-purchase agreement;
  (b) credit-sale agreement;
  (c) conditional sale agreement;
  (d) antecedent negotiations.

234 Supply of services

(1) References in this Part to the supply of services must be construed in accordance with this section.
(2) The supply of services does not include the provision of services under a contract of service or of apprenticeship whether it is express or implied and (if it is express) whether it is oral or in writing.
(3) The supply of services includes—
  (a) performing for gain or reward any activity other than the supply of goods;
  (b) rendering services to order;
  (c) the provision of services by making them available to potential users.
(4) The supply of services includes making arrangements for the use of computer software or for granting access to data stored in any form which is not readily accessible.
(5) The supply of services includes making arrangements by means of a relevant agreement [(within the meaning of paragraph 17 of Schedule 3A to the Communications Act 2003 (the electronic communications code)) for sharing the use of electronic communications apparatus].
(6) The supply of services includes permitting or making arrangements to permit the use of land in such circumstances as the Secretary of State specifies by order.
(7) The power to make an order under subsection (6) must be exercised by statutory instrument.
(8) But no such order may be made unless a draft of it has been laid before Parliament and approved by a resolution of each House.

Crown

[236 Crown

(1) This Part binds the Crown.]

PART 11 SUPPLEMENTARY

273   Interpretation
In this Act—
['the CMA' means the Competition and Markets Authority;]

[Sections 210 and 243(12)(c)] [SCHEDULE 13

LISTED ENACTMENTS

1. Sections 9 to 11 of the Supply of Goods (Implied Terms) Act 1973(5), to the extent that those sections continue to apply to a contract for a trader to supply goods to a consumer by virtue of the saving made, in connection with their amendment by the Consumer Rights Act 2015(6), by article 6 of the Consumer Rights Act 2015 (Commencement No. 3, Transitional Provisions, Savings and Consequential Amendments) Order 2015.

2. The Consumer Credit Act 1974 and secondary legislation made under that Act excluding requirements relating to consumer hire agreements.

3. Sections 6(2), 7(1), 7(2), 20(2), 21 and 27(2) of the Unfair Contract Terms Act 1977, to the extent that those sections remain in force, or continue to apply to a consumer contract, by virtue of the saving made, in connection with their repeal or disapplication by the Consumer Rights Act 2015, by article 6 of the Consumer Rights Act 2015 (Commencement No. 3, Transitional Provisions, Savings and Consequential Amendments) Order 2015.

4. Sections 13 to 15, 15B, 20 and 32 of the Sale of Goods Act 1979, to the extent that those sections continue to apply to a contract for a trader to supply goods to a consumer by virtue of the saving made, in connection with their amendment by the Consumer Rights Act 2015, by article 6 of the Consumer Rights Act 2015 (Commencement No. 3, Transitional Provisions, Savings and Consequential Amendments) Order 2015.

5. Sections 48A to 48F of the Sale of Goods Act 1979, to the extent that those sections remain in force by virtue of the saving made, in connection with their repeal by the Consumer Rights Act 2015, by article 6 of the Consumer Rights Act 2015 (Commencement No. 3, Transitional Provisions, Savings and Consequential Amendments) Order 2015.

6. Sections 3 to 5, 11C to 11E and 13 of the Supply of Goods and Services Act 1982, and any rule of law in Scotland which provides comparable protection to section 13, to the extent that those sections continue to apply to a contract for a trader to supply goods or, in the case of section 13, a contract for a trader to supply a service, to a consumer by virtue of the saving made, in connection with their amendment by the Consumer Rights Act 2015, by article 6 of the Consumer Rights Act 2015 (Commencement No. 3, Transitional Provisions, Savings and Consequential Amendments) Order 2015.

7. Sections 11M to 11S of the Supply of Goods and Services Act 1982 to the extent that those sections remain in force by virtue of the saving made, in connection with their repeal by the Consumer Rights Act 2015, by article 6 of the Consumer Rights Act 2015 (Commencement No. 3, Transitional Provisions, Savings and Consequential Amendments) Order 2015.

8. The Package Travel, Package Holidays and Package Tours Regulations 1992, to the extent that those Regulations remain in force by virtue of the saving made, in connection with their revocation, by regulation 37(2) of the Package Travel and Linked Travel Arrangements Regulations 2018.

9. The Unfair Terms in Consumer Contracts Regulations 1999, to the extent that those Regulations remain in force by virtue of the saving made, in connection with their revocation by the Consumer Rights Act 2015, by article 6 of the Consumer Rights Act 2015 (Commencement No. 3, Transitional Provisions, Savings and Consequential Amendments) Order 2015.

10. The Consumer Protection (Distance Selling) Regulations 2000, to the extent that those Regulations remain in force for contracts entered into prior to their disapplication by virtue of regulation 2(a) of the Consumer Contracts (Information, Cancellation and Additional Charges) Regulations 2013.

11. Regulations 6, 7, 8, 9 and 11 of the Electronic Commerce (EC Directive) Regulations 2002.

12. Regulation 15 of the Sale and Supply of Goods to Consumers Regulations 2002, to the extent that regulation 15 remains in force by virtue of the saving made, in connection with its revocation by the Consumer Rights Act 2015, by article 6 of the Consumer Rights Act 2015 (Commencement No. 3, Transitional Provisions, Savings and Consequential Amendments) Order 2015.

13. Regulations 19 to 26, 30 and 32 of the Privacy and Electronic Communications (EC Directive) Regulations 2003.

14. The Price Marking Order 2004.

15. Regulation (EC) No 261/2004 of the European Parliament and of the Council of 11 February 2004 establishing common rules on compensation and assistance to air passengers in the event of denied boarding and of cancellation or long delay of flights.

16. The Financial Services (Distance Marketing) Regulations 2004 and rules corresponding to any provisions of those Regulations made by the Financial Conduct Authority or a designated professional body within the meaning of section 326(2) of the Financial Services and Markets Act 2000.

17. The Price Marking Order (Northern Ireland) 2004.

18. The Civil Aviation (Denied Boarding, Compensation and Assistance) Regulations 2005.

19. The Consumer Protection from Unfair Trading Regulations 2008.

20. The Cancellation of Contracts made in a Consumer's Home or Place of Work etc. Regulations 2008, to the extent that those Regulations remain in force for contracts entered into prior to their disapplication by regulation 2(b) of the Consumer Contracts (Information, Cancellation and Additional Charges) Regulations 2013.

21. The Provision of Services Regulations 2009.

22. The Timeshare, Holiday Products, Resale and Exchange Contracts Regulations 2010.

23. Chapters 1 and 2 of Part 14 of the Human Medicines Regulations 2012.

24. Regulations 4 and 6A to 10 of the Consumer Rights (Payment Surcharges) Regulations 2012.

25. The Consumer Contracts (Information, Cancellation and Additional Charges) Regulations 2013.

26. Regulation 19(1) and (2) of the Alternative Dispute Resolution for Consumer Disputes (Competent Authorities and Information) Regulations 2015.

27. Sections 2, 3, 5, 9 to 15, 19, 23, 24, 28 to 32, 36(3) and (4), 37, 38, 42, 50, 54, 58, 59, 61 to 64, 67 to 70, 72 to 74 of, and Schedules 2 and 3 and Part 3 of Schedule 5 to, the Consumer Rights Act 2015.

28. Article 10(4) of Regulation (EU) 2015/751 of the European Parliament and of the Council of 29 April 2015 on interchange fees for card-based payment transactions.

29. The Package Travel and Linked Travel Arrangements Regulations 2018.]

Companies Act 2006

(2006, c. 46)

17   A company's constitution
Unless the context otherwise requires, references in the Companies Acts to a company's constitution include—

    (a) the company's articles, and

    (b) any resolutions and agreements to which Chapter 3 applies (see section 29).

31   Statement of company's objects

    (1) Unless a company's articles specifically restrict the objects of the company, its objects are unrestricted.

33   Effect of company's constitution

    (1) The provisions of a company's constitution bind the company and its members to the same extent as if there were covenants on the part of the company and of each member to observe those provisions.

39   A company's capacity

(1) The validity of an act done by a company shall not be called into question on the ground of lack of capacity by reason of anything in the company's constitution.

40   Power of directors to bind the company

(1) In favour of a person dealing with a company in good faith, the power of the directors to bind the company, or authorise others to do so, is deemed to be free of any limitation under the company's constitution.

(2) For this purpose—

    (a) a person 'deals with' a company if he is a party to any transaction or other act to which the company is a party,

    (b) a person dealing with a company—

        (i)   is not bound to enquire as to any limitation on the powers of the directors to bind the company or authorise others to do so,

        (ii) is presumed to have acted in good faith unless the contrary is proved, and

        (iii) is not to be regarded as acting in bad faith by reason only of his knowing that an act is beyond the powers of the directors under the company's constitution.

41   Constitutional limitations: transactions involving directors or their associates

(1) This section applies to a transaction if or to the extent that its validity depends on section 40 (power of directors deemed to be free of limitations under company's constitution in favour of person dealing with company in good faith).

Nothing in this section shall be read as excluding the operation of any other enactment or rule of law by virtue of which the transaction may be called in question or any liability to the company may arise.

(2) Where—

    (a) a company enters into such a transaction, and

    (b) the parties to the transaction include—

        (i) a director of the company or of its holding company, or

        (ii) a person connected with any such director,

the transaction is voidable at the instance of the company.

(3) Whether or not it is avoided, any such party to the transaction as is mentioned in subsection (2)(b)(i) or (ii), and any director of the company who authorised the transaction, is liable—

    (a) to account to the company for any gain he has made directly or indirectly by the transaction, and

    (b) to indemnify the company for any loss or damage resulting from the transaction.

(4) The transaction ceases to be voidable if—

    (a) restitution of any money or other asset which was the subject matter of the transaction is no longer possible, or

    (b) the company is indemnified for any loss or damage resulting from the transaction, or

    (c) rights acquired bona fide for value and without actual notice of the directors' exceeding their powers by a person who is not party to the transaction would be affected by the avoidance, or

    (d) the transaction is affirmed by the company.

(5) A person other than a director of the company is not liable under subsection (3) if he shows that at the time the transaction was entered into he did not know that the directors were exceeding their powers.

(6) Nothing in the preceding provisions of this section affects the rights of any party to the transaction not within subsection (2)(b)(i) or (ii).

But the court may, on the application of the company or any such party, make an order affirming, severing or setting aside the transaction on such terms as appear to the court to be just.

(7) In this section—

    (a) 'transaction' includes any act; and

(b) the reference to a person connected with a director has the same meaning as in Part 10 (company directors).

43   Company contracts

(1) Under the law of England and Wales or Northern Ireland a contract may be made—

(a) by a company, by writing under its common seal, or

(b) on behalf of a company, by a person acting under its authority, express or implied.

(2) Any formalities required by law in the case of a contract made by an individual also apply, unless a contrary intention appears, to a contract made by or on behalf of a company.

51   Pre-incorporation contracts, deeds and obligations

(1) A contract that purports to be made by or on behalf of a company at a time when the company has not been formed has effect, subject to any agreement to the contrary, as one made with the person purporting to act for the company or as agent for it, and he is personally liable on the contract accordingly.

(2) Subsection (1) applies—

(a) to the making of a deed under the law of England and Wales or Northern Ireland, and

(b) to the undertaking of an obligation under the law of Scotland, as it applies to the making of a contract.

82   Requirement to disclose company name etc.

(1) The Secretary of State may by regulations make provision requiring companies—

(a) to display specified information in specified locations,

(b) to state specified information in specified descriptions of document or communication, and

(c) to provide specified information on request to those they deal with in the course of their business.

83   Civil consequences of failure to make required disclosure

(1) This section applies to any legal proceedings brought by a company to which section 82 applies (requirement to disclose company name etc) to enforce a right arising out of a contract made in the course of a business in respect of which the company was, at the time the contract was made, in breach of regulations under that section.

(2) The proceedings shall be dismissed if the defendant (in Scotland, the defender) to the proceedings shows—

(a) that he has a claim against the claimant (pursuer) arising out of the contract that he has been unable to pursue by reason of the latter's breach of the regulations, or

(b) that he has suffered some financial loss in connection with the contract by reason of the claimant's (pursuer's) breach of the regulations,

unless the court before which the proceedings are brought is satisfied that it is just and equitable to permit the proceedings to continue.

(3) This section does not affect the right of any person to enforce such rights as he may have against another person in any proceedings brought by that person.

161   Validity of acts of directors

(1) The acts of a person acting as a director are valid notwithstanding that it is afterwards discovered—

(a) that there was a defect in his appointment;

(b) that he was disqualified from holding office;

(c) that he had ceased to hold office;

(d) that he was not entitled to vote on the matter in question.

170   Scope and nature of general duties

(1) The general duties specified in sections 171 to 177 are owed by a director of a company to the company.

(2) A person who ceases to be a director continues to be subject—

    (a) to the duty in section 175 (duty to avoid conflicts of interest) as regards the exploitation of any property, information or opportunity of which he became aware at a time when he was a director, and

    (b) to the duty in section 176 (duty not to accept benefits from third parties) as regards things done or omitted by him before he ceased to be a director.

To that extent those duties apply to a former director as to a director, subject to any necessary adaptations.

(3) The general duties are based on certain common law rules and equitable principles as they apply in relation to directors and have effect in place of those rules and principles as regards the duties owed to a company by a director.

(4) The general duties shall be interpreted and applied in the same way as common law rules or equitable principles, and regard shall be had to the corresponding common law rules and equitable principles in interpreting and applying the general duties.

171 Duty to act within powers

A director of a company must—

    (a) act in accordance with the company's constitution, and

    (b) only exercise powers for the purposes for which they are conferred.

174 Duty to exercise reasonable care, skill and diligence

(1) A director of a company must exercise reasonable care, skill and diligence.

(2) This means the care, skill and diligence that would be exercised by a reasonably diligent person with—

    (a) the general knowledge, skill and experience that may reasonably be expected of a person carrying out the functions carried out by the director in relation to the company, and

    (b) the general knowledge, skill and experience that the director has.

175 Duty to avoid conflicts of interest

(1) A director of a company must avoid a situation in which he has, or can have, a direct or indirect interest that conflicts, or possibly may conflict, with the interests of the company.

(4) This duty is not infringed—

    (a) if the situation cannot reasonably be regarded as likely to give rise to a conflict of interest; or

    (b) if the matter has been authorised by the directors.

(7) Any reference in this section to a conflict of interest includes a conflict of interest and duty and a conflict of duties.

176 Duty not to accept benefits from third parties

(1) A director of a company must not accept a benefit from a third party conferred by reason of—

    (a) his being a director, or

    (b) his doing (or not doing) anything as director.

(5) Any reference in this section to a conflict of interest includes a conflict of interest and duty and a conflict of duties.

177 Duty to declare interest in proposed transaction or arrangement

. . .

178 Civil consequences of breach of general duties

(1) The consequences of breach (or threatened breach) of sections 171 to 177 are the same as would apply if the corresponding common law rule or equitable principle applied.

(3) The duties in those sections (with the exception of section 174 (duty to exercise reasonable care, skill and diligence)) are, accordingly, enforceable in the same way as any other fiduciary duty owed to a company by its directors.

180   Consent, approval or authorisation by members

(1) In a case where—

(a) section 175 (duty to avoid conflicts of interest) is complied with by authorisation by the directors, or

(b) section 177 (duty to declare interest in proposed transaction or arrangement) is complied with,

the transaction or arrangement is not liable to be set aside by virtue of any common law rule or equitable principle requiring the consent or approval of the members of the company.

754   Priorities where debentures secured by floating charge

(1) This section applies where debentures of a company registered in England and Wales or Northern Ireland are secured by a charge that, as created, was a floating charge.

(2) If possession is taken, by or on behalf of the holders of the debentures, of any property comprised in or subject to the charge, and the company is not at that time in the course of being wound up, the company's preferential debts shall be paid out of assets coming to the hands of the persons taking possession in priority to any claims for principal or interest in respect of the debentures.

(3) 'Preferential debts' means the categories of debts listed in Schedule 6 to the Insolvency Act 1986 (c. 45) . . .

For the purposes of those Schedules 'the relevant date' is the date of possession being taken as mentioned in subsection (2).

(4) Payments under this section shall be recouped, as far as may be, out of the assets of the company available for payment of general creditors.

[Chapter A1   Registration of company charges]

[859A   Charges created by a company

(1) Subject to subsection (6), this section applies where a company creates a charge.

(2) The registrar must register the charge if, before the end of the period allowed for delivery, the company or any person interested in the charge delivers to the registrar for registration a section 859D statement of particulars.

(3) Where the charge is created or evidenced by an instrument, the registrar is required to register it only if a certified copy of the instrument is delivered to the registrar with the statement of particulars.

(4) 'The period allowed for delivery' is 21 days beginning with the day after the date of creation of the charge (see section 859E), unless an order allowing an extended period is made under section 859F(3).

(5) Where an order is made under section 859F(3) a copy of the order must be delivered to the registrar with the statement of particulars.

(6) This section does not apply to—

(a) a charge in favour of a landlord on a cash deposit given as a security in connection with the lease of land;

(b) a charge created by a member of Lloyd's (within the meaning of the Lloyd's Act 1982) to secure its obligations in connection with its underwriting business at Lloyd's;

(c) a charge excluded from the application of this section by or under any other Act.

(7) In this Part—

'cash' includes foreign currency,

'charge' includes—

(a) a mortgage;

(b) a standard security, assignation in security, and any other right in security constituted under the law of Scotland, including any heritable security, but not including a pledge, and

'company' means a UK-registered company.]

[859B Charge in series of debentures

(1) This section applies where—

(a) a company creates a series of debentures containing a charge, or giving a charge by reference to another instrument, and

(b) debenture holders of that series are entitled to the benefit of the charge pari passu.

(2) The registrar must register the charge if, before the end of the period allowed for delivery, the company or any person interested in the charge delivers to the registrar for registration, a section 859D statement of particulars which also contains the following—

(a) either—

(i) the name of each of the trustees for the debenture holders, or

(ii) where there are more than four such persons, the names of any four persons listed in the charge instrument as trustees for the debenture holders, and a statement that there are other such persons;

(b) the dates of the resolutions authorising the issue of the series;

(c) the date of the covering instrument (if any) by which the series is created or defined.

(3) Where the charge is created or evidenced by an instrument, the registrar is required to register it only if a certified copy of the instrument is delivered to the registrar with the statement of particulars.

(4) Where the charge is not created or evidenced by an instrument, the registrar is required to register it only if a certified copy of one of the debentures in the series is delivered to the registrar with the statement of particulars.

(5) For the purposes of this section a statement of particulars is taken to be a section 859D statement of particulars even if it does not contain the names of the debenture holders.

(6) 'The period allowed for delivery' is—

(a) if there is a deed containing the charge, 21 days beginning with the day after the date on which the deed is executed;

(b) if there is no deed containing the charge, 21 days beginning with the day after the date on which the first debenture of the series is executed.

(7) Where an order is made under section 859F(3) a copy of the order must be delivered to the registrar with the statement of particulars.

(8) In this section 'deed' means—

(a) a deed governed by the law of England and Wales or Northern Ireland, or

(b) an instrument governed by a law other than the law of England and Wales or Northern Ireland which requires delivery under that law in order to take effect.]

[859C Charges existing on property or undertaking acquired

(1) This section applies where a company acquires property or undertaking which is subject to a charge of a kind which would, if it had been created by the company after the acquisition of the property or undertaking, have been capable of being registered under section 859A.

(2) The registrar must register the charge if the company or any person interested in the charge delivers to the registrar for registration a section 859D statement of particulars.

(3) Where the charge is created or evidenced by an instrument, the registrar is required to register it only if a certified copy of the instrument is delivered to the registrar with the statement of particulars.]

[859D Particulars to be delivered to registrar

(1) A statement of particulars relating to a charge created by a company is a 'section 859D statement of particulars' if it contains the following particulars—

(a) the registered name and number of the company;

(b) the date of creation of the charge and (if the charge is one to which section 859C applies) the date of acquisition of the property or undertaking concerned;

(c) where the charge is created or evidenced by an instrument, the particulars listed in subsection (2);

(d) where the charge is not created or evidenced by an instrument, the particulars listed in subsection (3).

(2) The particulars referred to in subsection (1)(c) are—

(a) any of the following—

(i) the name of each of the persons in whose favour the charge has been created or of the security agents or trustees holding the charge for the benefit of one or more persons; or,

(ii) where there are more than four such persons, security agents or trustees, the names of any four such persons, security agents or trustees listed in the charge instrument, and a statement that there are other such persons, security agents or trustees;

(b) whether the instrument is expressed to contain a floating charge and, if so, whether it is expressed to cover all the property and undertaking of the company;

(c) whether any of the terms of the charge prohibit or restrict the company from creating further security that will rank equally with or ahead of the charge;

(d) whether (and if so, a short description of) any land, ship, aircraft or intellectual property that is registered or required to be registered in the United Kingdom, is subject to a charge (which is not a floating charge) or fixed security included in the instrument;

(e) whether the instrument includes a charge (which is not a floating charge) or fixed security over—

(i) any tangible or corporeal property, or

(ii) any intangible or incorporeal property,

not described in paragraph (d).

(3) The particulars referred to in subsection (1)(d) are—

(a) a statement that there is no instrument creating or evidencing the charge;

(b) the names of each of the persons in whose favour the charge has been created or the names of any security agents or trustees holding the charge for the benefit of one or more persons;

(c) the nature of the charge;

(d) a short description of the property or undertaking charged;

(e) the obligations secured by the charge.

(4) In this section 'fixed security' has the meaning given in section 486(1) of the Companies Act 1985.

(5) In this section 'intellectual property' includes—

(a) any patent, trade mark, registered design, copyright or design right;

(b) any licence under or in respect of any such right.]

[859E   Date of creation of charge

(1) For the purposes of this Part, a charge of the type described in column 1 of the Table below is taken to be created on the date given in relation to it in column 2 of that Table.

1. Type of charge	2. When charge created
Standard security	The date of its recording in the Register of Sasines or its registration in the Land Register of Scotland
Charge other than a standard security, where created or evidenced by an instrument	Where the instrument is a deed that has been executed and has immediate effect on execution and delivery, the date of delivery
	Where the instrument is a deed that has been executed and held in escrow, the date of delivery into escrow
	Where the instrument is a deed that has been executed and held as undelivered, the date of delivery
	Where the instrument is not a deed and has immediate effect on execution, the date of execution
	Where the instrument is not a deed and does not have immediate effect on execution, the date on which the instrument takes effect
Charge other than a standard security, where not created or evidenced by an instrument	The date on which the charge comes into effect.

(3) This section applies for the purposes of this Chapter even if further forms, notices, registrations or other actions or proceedings are necessary to make the charge valid or effectual for any other purposes.

(4) For the purposes of this Chapter, the registrar is entitled without further enquiry to accept a charge as created on the date given as the date of creation of the charge in a section 859D statement of particulars.

(5) In this section 'deed' means—

(a) a deed governed by the law of England and Wales or Northern Ireland, or

(b) an instrument governed by a law other than the law of England and Wales or Northern Ireland which requires delivery under that law in order to take effect.

(6) References in this section to delivery, in relation to a deed, include delivery as a deed where required.]

[859F   Extension of period allowed for delivery

(1) Subsection (3) applies if the court is satisfied that—

(a) neither the company nor any other person interested in the charge has delivered to the registrar the documents required under section 859A or (as the case may be) 859B before the end of the period allowed for delivery under the section concerned, and

(b) the requirement in subsection (2) is met.

(2) The requirement is—

(a) that the failure to deliver those documents—

(i)   was accidental or due to inadvertence or to some other sufficient cause, or

(ii)   is not of a nature to prejudice the position of creditors or shareholders of the company, or

(b) that on other grounds it is just and equitable to grant relief.

(3) The court may, on the application of the company or a person interested, and on such terms and conditions as seem to the court just and expedient, order that the period allowed for delivery be extended.]

[859G   Personal information etc in certified copies

(1) The following are not required to be included in a certified copy of an instrument or debenture delivered to the registrar for the purposes of any provision of this Chapter—

(a) personal information relating to an individual (other than the name of an individual);

(b) the number or other identifier of a bank or securities account of a company or individual;

(c) a signature.

(2) The registrar is entitled without further enquiry, to accept the certified copy of an instrument whether or not any of the information in subsection (1) is contained within the instrument.]

[859H   Consequence of failure to deliver charges

(1) This section applies if—

(a) a company creates a charge to which section 859A or 859B applies, and

(b) the documents required by section 859A or (as the case may be) 859B are not delivered to the registrar by the company or another person interested in the charge before the end of the relevant period allowed for delivery.

(2) 'The relevant period allowed for delivery' is—

(a) the period allowed for delivery under the section in question, or

(b) if an order under section 859F(3) has been made, the period allowed by the order.

(3) Where this section applies, the charge is void (so far as any security on the company's property or undertaking is conferred by it) against—

(a) a liquidator of the company,

(b) an administrator of the company, and

(c) a creditor of the company.

(4) Subsection (3) is without prejudice to any contract or obligation for repayment of the money secured by the charge; and when a charge becomes void under this section, the money secured by it immediately becomes payable.]

[859I Entries on the register

(1) This section applies where a charge is registered in accordance with a provision of this Chapter.

(2) The registrar must—

(a) allocate to the charge a unique reference code and place a note in the register recording that reference code; and

(b) include in the register any documents delivered under section 859A(3) or (5), 859B(3), (4) or (7), or 859C(3).

(3) The registrar must give a certificate of the registration of the charge to the person who delivered to the registrar a section 859D statement of particulars relating to the charge.

(4) The certificate must state—

(a) the registered name and number of the company in respect of which the charge was registered; and

(b) the unique reference code allocated to the charge.

(5) The certificate must be signed by the registrar or authenticated by the registrar's official seal.

(6) In the case of registration under section 859A or 859B, the certificate is conclusive evidence that the documents required by the section concerned were delivered to the registrar before the end of the relevant period allowed for delivery.

(7) 'The relevant period allowed for delivery' is—

(a) the period allowed for delivery under the section in question, or

(b) if an order under section 859F(3) has been made, the period allowed by the order.]

[859J Company holding property or undertaking as trustee

(1) Where a company is acting as trustee of property or undertaking which is the subject of a charge delivered for registration under this Chapter, the company or any person interested in the charge may deliver to the registrar a statement to that effect.

(2) A statement delivered after the delivery for registration of the charge must include—

(a) the registered name and number of the company; and

(b) the unique reference code allocated to the charge.]

[859K Registration of enforcement of security

(1) Subsection (2) applies where a person—

(a) obtains an order for the appointment of a receiver or manager of a company's property or undertaking, or

(b) appoints such a receiver or manager under powers contained in an instrument.

(2) The person must, within 7 days of the order or of the appointment under those powers—

(a) give notice to the registrar of that fact, and

(b) if the order was obtained, or the appointment made, by virtue of a registered charge held by the person give the registrar a notice containing—

(i) in the case of a charge created before 6th April 2013, the information specified in subsection (4);

(ii) in the case of a charge created on or after 6th April 2013, the unique reference code allocated to the charge.

(3) Where a person appointed receiver or manager of a company's property or undertaking under powers contained in an instrument ceases to act as such a receiver or manager, the person must, on so ceasing—

(a) give notice to the registrar of that fact, and

(b) give the registrar a notice containing—

(i) in the case of a charge created before 6th April 2013, the information specified in subsection (4), or

(ii)   in the case of a charge created on or after 6th April 2013, the unique reference code allocated to the charge.

(4) The information referred to in subsections (2)(b)(i) and (3)(b)(i) is—

(a) the date of the creation of the charge;

(b) a description of the instrument (if any) creating or evidencing the charge;

(c) short particulars of the property or undertaking charged.

(5) The registrar must include in the register—

(a) a fact of which notice is given under subsection (2)(a), and

(b) a fact of which notice is given under subsection (3)(a).

(6) A person who makes default in complying with the requirements of subsections (2) or (3) of this section commits an offence.

(8) This section applies only to a receiver or manager appointed—

(a) by a court in England and Wales or Northern Ireland, or

(b) under an instrument governed by the law of England and Wales or Northern Ireland.]

[**859L   Entries of satisfaction and release**

(1) Subsection (5) applies if the statement set out in subsection (2) and the particulars set out in subsection (4) are delivered to the registrar with respect to a registered charge.

(2) The statement referred to in subsection (1) is a statement to the effect that—

(a) the debt for which the charge was given has been paid or satisfied in whole or in part, or

(b) all or part of the property or undertaking charged—

(i)   has been released from the charge, or

(ii)   has ceased to form part of the company's property or undertaking.

(3) Where a statement within subsection (2)(b) relates to part only of the property or undertaking charged, the statement must include a short description of that part.

(4) The particulars referred to in subsection (1) are—

(a) the name and address of the person delivering the statement and an indication of their interest in the charge;

(b) the registered name and number of the company that—

(i)   created the charge (in a case within section 859A or 859B), or

(ii)   acquired the property or undertaking subject to the charge (in a case within section 859C);

(c) in respect of a charge created before 6th April 2013—

(i)   the date of creation of the charge;

(ii)   a description of the instrument (if any) by which the charge is created or evidenced;

(iii)   short particulars of the property or undertaking charged;

(d) in respect of a charge created on or after 6th April 2013, the unique reference code allocated to the charge.

(5) The registrar must include in the register—

(a) a statement of satisfaction in whole or in part, or

(b) a statement of the fact that all or part of the property or undertaking has been released from the charge or has ceased to form part of the company's property or undertaking (as the case may be).]

[**859M   Rectification of register**

(1) Subsection (3) applies if the court is satisfied that—

(a) there has been an omission or mis-statement in any statement or notice delivered to the registrar in accordance with this Chapter, and

(b) the requirement in subsection (2) is met.

(2) The requirement is that the court is satisfied—

(a) that the omission or mis-statement—

(i)   was accidental or due to inadvertence or to some other sufficient cause, or

(ii) is not of a nature to prejudice the position of creditors or shareholders of the company, or

(b) that on other grounds it is just and equitable to grant relief.

(3) The court may, on the application of the company or a person interested, and on such terms and conditions as seem to the court just and expedient, order that the omission or mis-statement be rectified.

(4) A copy of the court's order must be sent by the applicant to the registrar for registration.]

[859N　Replacement of instrument or debenture

(1) Subsection (2) applies if the court is satisfied that—

(a) a copy of an instrument or debenture delivered to the registrar under this Chapter contains material which could have been omitted under section 859G;

(b) the wrong instrument or debenture was delivered to the registrar; or

(c) the copy was defective.

(2) The court may, on the application of the company or a person interested, and on such terms and conditions as seem to the court just and expedient, order that the copy of the instrument or debenture be removed from the register and replaced.

(3) A copy of the court's order must be sent by the applicant to the registrar for registration.]

[859O　Notification of addition to or amendment of charge

(1) This section applies where, after the creation of a charge, the charge is amended by adding or amending a term that—

(a) prohibits or restricts the creation of any fixed security or any other charge having priority over, or ranking pari passu with, the charge; or

(b) varies, or otherwise regulates the order of, the ranking of the charge in relation to any fixed security or any other charge.

(2) Either the company that created the charge or the person taking the benefit of the charge (or another charge referred to in subsection (1)(b)) may deliver to the registrar for registration—

(a) a certified copy of the instrument effecting the amendment, variation or regulation, and

(b) a statement of the particulars set out in subsection (3).

(3) The particulars to be included in the statement are—

(a) the registered name and number of the company;

(b) in the case of a charge created before 6th April 2013—

(i) the date of creation of the charge;

(ii) a description of the instrument (if any) by which the charge was created or evidenced;

(iii) short particulars of the property or undertaking charged as set out when the charge was registered;

(c) in the case of a charge created on or after 6th April 2013, (where allocated) the unique reference code allocated to the charge.

(5) In this section 'fixed security' has the meaning given in section 486(1) of the Companies Act 1985.]

[859P　Companies to keep copies of instruments creating and amending charges

(1) A company must keep available for inspection a copy of every—

(a) instrument creating a charge capable of registration under this Chapter, and

(b) instrument effecting any variation or amendment of such a charge.

(2) In the case of a charge contained in a series of uniform debentures, a copy of one of the debentures of the series is sufficient for the purposes of subsection (1)(a).

(3) If the particulars referred to in section 859D(1) or the particulars of the property or undertaking charged are not contained in the instrument creating the charge, but are instead contained

in other documents which are referred to in or otherwise incorporated into the instrument, then the company must also keep available for inspection a copy of those other documents.]

[**859Q   Instruments creating charges to be available for inspection**

(1) This section applies to documents required to be kept available for inspection under section 859P (copies of instruments creating and amending charges).

(2) The documents must be kept available for inspection—

(a) at the company's registered office, or

(b) at a place specified in regulations under section 1136.

(3) The company must give notice to the registrar—

(a) of the place at which the documents are kept available for inspection, and

(b) of any change in that place,

unless they have at all times been kept at the company's registered office.

(4) The documents must be open to the inspection—

(a) of any creditor or member of the company, without charge, and

(b) of any other person, on payment of such fee as may be prescribed.

(5) If default is made for 14 days in complying with subsection (3) or an inspection required under subsection (4) is refused, an offence is committed by—

(a) the company, and

(b) every officer of the company who is in default.

(6) A person guilty of an offence under this section is liable on summary conviction to a fine not exceeding level 3 on the standard scale and, for continued contravention, a daily default fine not exceeding one-tenth of level 3 on the standard scale.

(7) If an inspection required under subsection (4) is refused the court may by order compel an immediate inspection.

(8) Where the company and a person wishing to carry out an inspection under subsection (4) agree, the inspection may be carried out by electronic means.]

Third Parties (Rights against Insurers) Act 2010

(2010, c. 10)

Transfer of rights to third parties

1   Rights against insurer of insolvent person etc

(1) This section applies if—

(a) a relevant person incurs a liability against which that person is insured under a contract of insurance, or

(b) a person who is subject to such a liability becomes a relevant person.

(2) The rights of the relevant person under the contract against the insurer in respect of the liability are transferred to and vest in the person to whom the liability is or was incurred (the 'third party').

(3) The third party may bring proceedings to enforce the rights against the insurer without having established the relevant person's liability; but the third party may not enforce those rights without having established that liability.

(4) For the purposes of this Act, a liability is established only if its existence and amount are established; and, for that purpose, 'establish' means establish—

(a) by virtue of a declaration under section 2 or a declarator under section 3,

(b) by a judgment or decree,

(c) by an award in arbitral proceedings or by an arbitration, or

(d) by an enforceable agreement.

(5) In this Act—

    (a) references to an 'insured' are to a person who incurs or who is subject to a liability to a third party against which that person is insured under a contract of insurance;

    (b) references to a 'relevant person' are to a person within sections 4 to 7 [(and see also paragraph 1A of Schedule 3)];

    (c) references to a 'third party' are to be construed in accordance with subsection (2);

    (d) references to 'transferred rights' are to rights under a contract of insurance which are transferred under this section.

2 Establishing liability in England and Wales and Northern Ireland

(1) This section applies where a person (P)—

    (a) claims to have rights under a contract of insurance by virtue of a transfer under section 1, but

    (b) has not yet established the insured's liability which is insured under that contract.

(2) P may bring proceedings against the insurer for either or both of the following—

    (a) a declaration as to the insured's liability to P;

    (b) a declaration as to the insurer's potential liability to P.

(3) In such proceedings P is entitled, subject to any defence on which the insurer may rely, to a declaration under subsection (2)(a) or (b) on proof of the insured's liability to P or (as the case may be) the insurer's potential liability to P.

(4) Where proceedings are brought under subsection (2)(a) the insurer may rely on any defence on which the insured could rely if those proceedings were proceedings brought against the insured in respect of the insured's liability to P.

(5) Subsection (4) is subject to section 12(1).

(6) Where the court makes a declaration under this section, the effect of which is that the insurer is liable to P, the court may give the appropriate judgment against the insurer.

(7) Where a person applying for a declaration under subsection (2)(b) is entitled or required, by virtue of the contract of insurance, to do so in arbitral proceedings, that person may also apply in the same proceedings for a declaration under subsection (2)(a).

(8) In the application of this section to arbitral proceedings, subsection (6) is to be read as if 'tribunal' were substituted for 'court' and 'make the appropriate award' for 'give the appropriate judgment'.

(9) When bringing proceedings under subsection (2)(a), P may also make the insured a defendant to those proceedings.

(10) If (but only if) the insured is a defendant to proceedings under this section (whether by virtue of subsection (9) or otherwise), a declaration under subsection (2) binds the insured as well as the insurer.

(11) In this section, references to the insurer's potential liability to P are references to the insurer's liability in respect of the insured's liability to P, if established.

Relevant persons

4 Individuals

(1) An individual is a relevant person if any of the following is in force in respect of that individual in England and Wales—

    [. . .]

    (b) an administration order made under Part 6 of the County Courts Act 1984,

    (c) an enforcement restriction order made under Part 6A of that Act,

    (d) subject to subsection (4), a debt relief order made under Part 7A of the Insolvency Act 1986,

    (e) a voluntary arrangement approved in accordance with Part 8 of that Act, or

    (f) a bankruptcy order made under Part 9 of that Act.

(4) If an individual is a relevant person by virtue of subsection (1)(d) [or (3)(ba)], that person is a relevant person for the purposes of section 1(1)(b) only.

5 Individuals who die insolvent

(1) An individual who dies insolvent is a relevant person for the purposes of section 1(1)(b) only.

(2) For the purposes of this section an individual (D) is to be regarded as having died insolvent if, following D's death—

> (a) D's estate falls to be administered in accordance with an order under section 421 of the Insolvency Act 1986 . . .

(3) Where a transfer of rights under section 1 takes place as a result of an insured person being a relevant person by virtue of this section, references in this Act to an insured are, where the context so requires, to be read as references to the insured's estate.

6 Corporate bodies etc

[(1) A body corporate or unincorporated body is a relevant person if a compromise or arrangement between the body and its creditors (or a class of them) is in force, having been sanctioned in accordance with section 899 or 901F of the Companies Act 2006.]

(2) A body corporate or an unincorporated body is a relevant person if, in England and Wales or Scotland—

> (a) a voluntary arrangement approved in accordance with Part 1 of the Insolvency Act 1986 is in force in respect of it,
>
> [(b) the body is in administration under Schedule B1 to that Act,]
>
> (c) there is a person appointed in accordance with Part 3 of that Act who is acting as receiver or manager of the body's property (or there would be such a person so acting but for a temporary vacancy),
>
> (d) the body is, or is being, wound up voluntarily in accordance with Chapter 2 of Part 4 of that Act,
>
> (e) there is a person appointed under section 135 of that Act who is acting as provisional liquidator in respect of the body (or there would be such a person so acting but for a temporary vacancy), or
>
> (f) the body is, or is being, wound up by the court following the making of a winding-up order under Chapter 6 of Part 4 of that Act or Part 5 of that Act.

[(4A) A body corporate or unincorporated body is a relevant person if it is in insolvency under Part 2 of the Banking Act 2009.]

[(4B) A body corporate or unincorporated body is a relevant person if it is in administration under relevant sectoral legislation as defined in Schedule A1.]

(5) A body within [subsection (1)] is not a relevant person in relation to a liability that is transferred to another body by the order sanctioning the compromise or arrangement.

(6) Where a body is a relevant person by virtue of [subsection (1)], section 1 has effect to transfer rights only to a person on whom the compromise or arrangement is binding.

(9) In this section—

> (a) a reference to a person appointed in accordance with Part 3 of the Insolvency Act 1986 includes a reference to a person appointed under section 101 of the Law of Property Act 1925;
>
> (b) a reference to a receiver or manager of a body's property includes a reference to a receiver or manager of part only of the property and to a receiver only of the income arising from the property or from part of it; . . .

[6A Corporate bodies etc that are dissolved

(1)   A body corporate or unincorporated body is a relevant person if the body has been dissolved, subject to the exceptions in subsections (2) and (3).

(2)   The body is not a relevant person by virtue of subsection (1) if, since it was dissolved (or, if it has been dissolved more than once, since it was last dissolved), something has happened which has the effect that the body is treated as not having been dissolved or as no longer being dissolved.

(3)   Subsection (1) applies to a partnership only if it is a body corporate.

(4)   For the purposes of this section, 'dissolved' means dissolved under the law of England and Wales, Scotland or Northern Ireland (whether or not by a process referred to as dissolution).]

Transferred rights: supplemental

8   Limit on rights transferred

Where the liability of an insured to a third party is less than the liability of the insurer to the insured (ignoring the effect of section 1), no rights are transferred under that section in respect of the difference.

9   Conditions affecting transferred rights

(1)   This section applies where transferred rights are subject to a condition (whether under the contract of insurance from which the transferred rights are derived or otherwise) that the insured has to fulfil.

(2)   Anything done by the third party which, if done by the insured, would have amounted to or contributed to fulfilment of the condition is to be treated as if done by the insured.

(3)   The transferred rights are not subject to a condition requiring the insured to provide information or assistance to the insurer if that condition cannot be fulfilled because the insured is—

    (a)   an individual who has died, [...]

    (b)   a body corporate that has been dissolved[, or

    (c)   an unincorporated body, other than a partnership, that has been dissolved.]

(4)   A condition requiring the insured to provide information or assistance to the insurer does not include a condition requiring the insured to notify the insurer of the existence of a claim under the contract of insurance.

(5)   The transferred rights are not subject to a condition requiring the prior discharge by the insured of the insured's liability to the third party.

(6)   In the case of a contract of marine insurance, subsection (5) applies only to the extent that the liability of the insured is a liability in respect of death or personal injury.

(7)   In this section—

'contract of marine insurance' has the meaning given by section 1 of the Marine Insurance Act 1906;

    [...]

'personal injury' includes any disease and any impairment of a person's physical or mental condition.

    [(8)   For the purposes of this section—

    (a)   'dissolved' means dissolved under the law of England and Wales, Scotland or Northern Ireland (whether or not by a process referred to as dissolution), and

    (b)   a body has been dissolved even if, since it was dissolved, something has happened which has the effect that (but for this paragraph) the body is treated as not having been dissolved or as no longer being dissolved.]

10   Insurer's right of set off

(1)   This section applies if—

    (a)   rights of an insured under a contract of insurance have been transferred to a third party under section 1,

    (b)   the insured is under a liability to the insurer under the contract ('the insured's liability'), and

    (c)   if there had been no transfer, the insurer would have been entitled to set off the amount of the insured's liability against the amount of the insurer's own liability to the insured.

(2) The insurer is entitled to set off the amount of the insured's liability against the amount of the insurer's own liability to the third party in relation to the transferred rights.

Provision of information etc

11   Information and disclosure for third parties
Schedule 1 (information and disclosure for third parties) has effect.

Enforcement of transferred rights

12   Limitation and prescription
(1) Subsection (2) applies where a person brings proceedings for a declaration under section 2(2)(a) ... and the proceedings are started ...

    (a) after the expiry of a period of limitation applicable to an action against the insured to enforce the insured's liability, or of a period of prescription applicable to that liability, but

    (b) while such an action is in progress.

(2) The insurer may not rely on the expiry of that period as a defence unless the insured is able to rely on it in the action against the insured.

(3) For the purposes of subsection (1), an action is to be treated as no longer in progress if it has been concluded by a judgment or decree, or by an award, even if there is an appeal or a right of appeal.

(4) Where a person who has already established an insured's liability to that person brings proceedings under this Act against the insurer, nothing in this Act is to be read as meaning—

    (a) that, for the purposes of the law of limitation in England and Wales, that person's cause of action against the insurer arose otherwise than at the time when that person established the liability of the insured, ...

13   Jurisdiction within the United Kingdom
(1) Where a person (P) domiciled in a part of the United Kingdom is entitled to bring proceedings under this Act against an insurer domiciled in another part, P may do so in the part where P is domiciled or in the part where the insurer is domiciled (whatever the contract of insurance may stipulate as to where proceedings are to be brought).

Enforcement of insured's liability

14   Effect of transfer on insured's liability
(1) Where rights in respect of an insured's liability to a third party are transferred under section 1, the third party may enforce that liability against the insured only to the extent (if any) that it exceeds the amount recoverable from the insurer by virtue of the transfer.

(2) Subsection (3) applies if a transfer of rights under section 1 occurs because the insured person is a relevant person by virtue of—

    (a) section 4(1)(a) or (e), (2)(b) or (3)(b) or (c),

    (b) section [6(1)], (2)(a), (3)(c) or (4)(a), or

    (c) section 7(1)(b).

(3) If the liability is subject to the arrangement, trust deed or compromise by virtue of which the insured is a relevant person, the liability is to be treated as subject to that arrangement, trust deed or compromise only to the extent that the liability exceeds the amount recoverable from the insurer by virtue of the transfer.

(6) For the purposes of this section the amount recoverable from the insurer does not include any amount that the third party is unable to recover as a result of—

    (a) a shortage of assets on the insurer's part, in a case where the insurer is a relevant person, or

    (b) a limit set by the contract of insurance on the fund available to meet claims in respect of a particular description of liability of the insured.

(7) Where a third party is eligible to make a claim in respect of the insurer's liability under or by virtue of rules made under Part 15 of the Financial Services and Markets Act 2000 (the Financial Services Compensation Scheme)—

(a) subsection (6)(a) applies only if the third party has made such a claim, and

(b) the third party is to be treated as being able to recover from the insurer any amount paid to, or due to, the third party as a result of the claim.

Application of Act

15 Reinsurance

This Act does not apply to a case where the liability referred to in section 1(1) is itself a liability incurred by an insurer under a contract of insurance.

16 Voluntarily-incurred liabilities

It is irrelevant for the purposes of section 1 whether or not the liability of the insured is or was incurred voluntarily.

17 Avoidance

(1) A contract of insurance to which this section applies is of no effect in so far as it purports, whether directly or indirectly, to avoid or terminate the contract or alter the rights of the parties under it in the event of the insured—

(a) becoming a relevant person, or

(b) dying insolvent (within the meaning given by section 5(2)).

(2) A contract of insurance is one to which this section applies if the insured's rights under it are capable of being transferred under section 1.

18 Cases with a foreign element

Except as expressly provided, the application of this Act does not depend on whether there is a connection with a part of the United Kingdom; and in particular it does not depend on—

(a) whether or not the liability (or the alleged liability) of the insured to the third party was incurred in, or under the law of, England and Wales, Scotland or Northern Ireland;

(b) the place of residence or domicile of any of the parties;

(c) whether or not the contract of insurance (or a part of it) is governed by the law of England and Wales, Scotland or Northern Ireland;

(d) the place where sums due under the contract of insurance are payable.

[19 Power to change the meaning of 'relevant person'

(1) The Secretary of State may by regulations make provision adding or removing circumstances in which a person is a 'relevant person' for the purposes of this Act, subject to subsection (2).

(2) Regulations under this section may add circumstances only if, in the Secretary of State's opinion, the additional circumstances—

(a) involve actual or anticipated dissolution of a body corporate or an unincorporated body,

(b) involve actual or anticipated insolvency or other financial difficulties for an individual, a body corporate or an unincorporated body, or

(c) are similar to circumstances for the time being described in sections 4 to 7.

(3) Regulations under this section may make provision about—

(a) the persons to whom, and the extent to which, rights are transferred under section 1 in the circumstances added or removed by the regulations (the 'affected circumstances'),

(b) the re-transfer of rights transferred under section 1 where the affected circumstances change, and

(c) the effect of a transfer of rights under section 1 on the liability of the insured in the affected circumstances.

(4) Regulations under this section which add or remove circumstances involving actual or anticipated dissolution of a body corporate or unincorporated body may change the cases in which the following provisions apply so that they include or exclude cases involving that type of dissolution or any other type of dissolution of a body—

(a) section 9(3) (cases in which transferred rights are not subject to a condition requiring the insured to provide information or assistance to the insurer), and

    (b) paragraph 3 of Schedule 1 (notices requiring disclosure).

    (5) Regulations under this section which add circumstances may provide that section 1 of this Act applies in cases involving those circumstances in which either or both of the following occurred in relation to a person before the day on which the regulations come into force—

      (a) the circumstances arose in relation to the person;

      (b) a liability against which the person was insured under an insurance contract was incurred.

    (6) Regulations under this section which—

      (a) add circumstances, and

      (b) provide that section 1 of this Act applies in a case involving those circumstances in which both of the events mentioned in subsection (5)(a) and (b) occurred in relation to a person before the day on which the regulations come into force,

must provide that, in such a case, the person is to be treated for the purposes of this Act as not having become a relevant person until that day or a later day specified in the regulations.

    (7) Regulations under this section which remove circumstances may provide that section 1 of this Act does not apply in cases involving those circumstances in which one of the events mentioned in subsection (5)(a) and (b) (but not both) occurred in relation to a person before the day on which the regulations come into force.

    (8) Regulations under this section may—

      (a) include consequential, incidental, supplementary, transitional, transitory or saving provision,

      (b) make different provision for different purposes, and

      (c) make provision by reference to an enactment as amended, extended or applied from time to time,

(and subsections (3) to (7) are without prejudice to the generality of this subsection).

    (9) Regulations under this section may amend an enactment, whenever passed or made, including this Act.

    (10) Regulations under this section are to be made by statutory instrument.

    (11) Regulations under this section may not be made unless a draft of the statutory instrument containing the regulations has been laid before, and approved by a resolution of, each House of Parliament.]

[19A Interpretation

    (1) The references to enactments in sections 4 to 7 [...] and 14(4)[, Schedule A1 and paragraph 3(2)(b)] of Schedule 1 are to be treated as including references to those enactments as amended, extended or applied by another enactment, whenever passed or made, unless the contrary intention appears.

    (2) In this Act, 'enactment' means an enactment contained in, or in an instrument made under, any of the following—

      (a) an Act;

      (b) an Act or Measure of the National Assembly for Wales;

      (c) an Act of the Scottish Parliament;

      (d) Northern Ireland legislation.]

Section 11

SCHEDULES

SCHEDULE 1
INFORMATION AND DISCLOSURE
FOR THIRD PARTIES

1 Notices requesting information

    (1) If a person (A) reasonably believes that—

      (a) another person (B) has incurred a liability to A, and

      (b) B is a relevant person,

A may, by notice in writing, request from B such information falling within sub-paragraph (3) as the notice specifies.

(2) If a person (A) reasonably believes that—

(a) a liability has been incurred to A,

(b) the person who incurred the liability is insured against it under a contract of insurance,

(c) rights of that person under the contract have been transferred to A under section 1, and

(d) there is a person (C) who is able to provide information falling within sub-paragraph (3),

A may, by notice in writing, request from C such information falling within that sub-paragraph as the notice specifies.

(3) The following is the information that falls within this sub-paragraph—

(a) whether there is a contract of insurance that covers the supposed liability or might reasonably be regarded as covering it;

(b) if there is such a contract—

(i) who the insurer is;

(ii) what the terms of the contract are;

(iii) whether the insured has been informed that the insurer has claimed not to be liable under the contract in respect of the supposed liability;

(iv) whether there are or have been any proceedings between the insurer and the insured in respect of the supposed liability and, if so, relevant details of those proceedings;

(v) in a case where the contract sets a limit on the fund available to meet claims in respect of the supposed liability and other liabilities, how much of it (if any) has been paid out in respect of other liabilities;

(vi) whether there is a fixed charge to which any sums paid out under the contract in respect of the supposed liability would be subject.

(4) For the purpose of sub-paragraph (3)(b)(iv), relevant details of proceedings are—

(a) in the case of court proceedings—

(i) the name of the court;

(ii) the case number;

(iii) the contents of all documents served in the proceedings in accordance with rules of court or orders made in the proceedings, and the contents of any such orders;

(b) in the case of arbitral proceedings or, in Scotland, an arbitration—

(i) the name of the arbitrator;

(ii) information corresponding with that mentioned in paragraph (a)(iii).

(6) A notice given by a person under this paragraph must include particulars of the facts on which that person relies as entitlement to give the notice.

2 Provision of information where notice given under paragraph 1

(1) A person (R) who receives a notice under paragraph 1 must, within the period of 28 days beginning with the day of receipt of the notice—

(a) provide to the person who gave the notice any information specified in it that R is able to provide;

(b) in relation to any such information that R is not able to provide, notify that person why R is not able to provide it.

(2) Where—

(a) a person (R) receives a notice under paragraph 1,

(b) there is information specified in the notice that R is not able to provide because it is contained in a document that is not in R's control,

(c) the document was at one time in R's control, and

(d) R knows or believes that it is now in another person's control,

R must, within the period of 28 days beginning with the day of receipt of the notice, provide the person who gave the notice with whatever particulars R can as to the nature of the information and the identity of that other person.

(3) If R fails to comply with a duty imposed on R by this paragraph, the person who gave R the notice may apply to court for an order requiring R to comply with the duty.

(4) No duty arises by virtue of this paragraph in respect of information as to which a claim to legal professional privilege . . . could be maintained in legal proceedings.

3 Notices requiring disclosure: [bodies that have been dissolved]

(1) If—

(a) a person (P) has started proceedings under this Act against an insurer in respect of a liability [. . .], and

[(b) P claims the liability has been incurred to P by—

(i) a body corporate, or

(ii) an unincorporated body other than a partnership, and

(c) the body has been dissolved],

P may by notice in writing require a person to whom sub-paragraph (2) applies to disclose to P any documents that are relevant to that liability.

(2) This sub-paragraph applies to a person if—

(a) immediately before the time of the alleged transfer under section 1, that person was an officer or employee of the body, or

(b) immediately before the body [was dissolved (or, if it has been dissolved more than once, immediately before it was last dissolved)], that person was—

(i) acting as an insolvency practitioner in relation to the body (within the meaning given by section 388(1) of the Insolvency Act 1986 . . . , or

(ii) acting as the official receiver in relation to the winding up of the body.

(3) A notice under this paragraph must be accompanied by—

(a) a copy of the particulars of claim required to be served in connection with the proceedings mentioned in sub-paragraph (1), or

(b) where those proceedings are arbitral proceedings, the particulars of claim that would be required to be so served if they were court proceedings.

[(6) For the purposes of this paragraph—

(a) 'dissolved' means dissolved under the law of England and Wales, Scotland or Northern Ireland (whether or not by a process referred to as dissolution), and

(b) a body has been dissolved even if, since it was dissolved, something has happened which has the effect that (but for this paragraph) the body is treated as not having been dissolved or as no longer being dissolved.]

4 Disclosure and inspection where notice given under paragraph 3

(1) Subject to the provisions of this paragraph and to any necessary modifications—

(a) the duties of disclosure of a person who receives a notice under paragraph 3, and

(b) the rights of inspection of the person giving the notice,

are the same as the corresponding duties and rights under Civil Procedure Rules of parties to court proceedings in which an order for standard disclosure has been made.

(3) A person who by virtue of sub-paragraph (1) or (2) has to serve a list of documents must do so within the period of 28 days beginning with the day of receipt of the notice.

(4) A person who has received a notice under paragraph 3 and has served a list of documents in response to it is not under a duty of disclosure by reason of that notice in relation to documents that the person did not have when the list was served.

5 Avoidance

A contract of insurance is of no effect in so far as it purports, whether directly or indirectly—

(a) to avoid or terminate the contract or alter the rights of the parties under it in the event of a person providing information, or giving disclosure, that the person is required to provide or give by virtue of a notice under paragraph 1 or 3, or

(b) otherwise to prohibit, prevent or restrict a person from providing such information or giving such disclosure.

6 Other rights to information etc

Rights to information, or to inspection of documents, that a person has by virtue of paragraph 1 or 3 are in addition to any such rights as the person has apart from that paragraph.

7   Interpretation

For the purposes of this Schedule—

> (a) a person is able to provide information only if—
>
>> (i)   that person can obtain it without undue difficulty from a document that is in that person's control, or
>>
>> (ii) where that person is an individual, the information is within that person's knowledge;
>
> (b) a document is in a person's control if it is in that person's possession or if that person has a right to possession of it or to inspect or take copies of it.

SCHEDULE 3

TRANSITORY, TRANSITIONAL AND SAVING PROVISIONS

1.—(1) Section 1(1)(a) applies where the insured became a relevant person before, as well as when the insured becomes such a person on or after, commencement day.

(2) Section 1(1)(b) applies where the liability was incurred before, as well as where it is incurred on or after, commencement day.

[1A.   Relevant persons

(1) An individual, company or limited liability partnership not within sections 4 to 7 is to be treated as a relevant person for the purposes of this Act in the following cases.

(2) The first case is where an individual—

> (a) became bankrupt before commencement day, and
>
> (b) has not been discharged from that bankruptcy.

(3) The second case is where—

> (a) an individual made a composition or arrangement with his or her creditors before commencement day, and
>
> (b) the composition or arrangement remains in force.

(4) The third case is where—

> (a) a winding-up order was made, or a resolution for a voluntary winding-up was passed, with respect to a company or limited liability partnership before commencement day, and
>
> (b) the company or partnership is still wound up.

(5) The fourth case is where a company or limited liability partnership—

> (a) entered administration before commencement day, and
>
> (b) is still in administration.

(6) The fifth case is where—

> (a) a receiver or manager of the business or undertaking of a company or limited liability partnership was appointed before commencement day, and
>
> (b) the appointment remains in force.

(7) In those cases, the person is a relevant person only in relation to liabilities under a contract of insurance under which the person was insured at the time of the event mentioned in sub-paragraph (2)(a), (3)(a), (4)(a), (5)(a) or (6)(a) (as appropriate).]

Consumer Insurance (Disclosure and Representations) Act 2012

(2012, c. 6)

Main definitions

1   Main definitions

In this Act—

> 'consumer insurance contract' means a contract of insurance between—
>
>> (a) an individual who enters into the contract wholly or mainly for purposes unrelated to the individual's trade, business or profession, and

(b) a person who carries on the business of insurance and who becomes a party to the contract by way of that business (whether or not in accordance with permission for the purposes of the Financial Services and Markets Act 2000);

'consumer' means the individual who enters into a consumer insurance contract, or proposes to do so;

'insurer' means the person who is, or would become, the other party to a consumer insurance contract.

Pre-contract and pre-variation information

2   Disclosure and representations before contract or variation

(1) This section makes provision about disclosure and representations by a consumer to an insurer before a consumer insurance contract is entered into or varied.

(2) It is the duty of the consumer to take reasonable care not to make a misrepresentation to the insurer.

(3) A failure by the consumer to comply with the insurer's request to confirm or amend particulars previously given is capable of being a misrepresentation for the purposes of this Act (whether or not it could be apart from this subsection).

(4) The duty set out in subsection (2) replaces any duty relating to disclosure or representations by a consumer to an insurer which existed in the same circumstances before this Act applied.

[...]

3   Reasonable care

(1) Whether or not a consumer has taken reasonable care not to make a misrepresentation is to be determined in the light of all the relevant circumstances.

(2) The following are examples of things which may need to be taken into account in making a determination under subsection (1)—

(a) the type of consumer insurance contract in question, and its target market,

(b) any relevant explanatory material or publicity produced or authorised by the insurer,

(c) how clear, and how specific, the insurer's questions were,

(d) in the case of a failure to respond to the insurer's questions in connection with the renewal or variation of a consumer insurance contract, how clearly the insurer communicated the importance of answering those questions (or the possible consequences of failing to do so),

(e) whether or not an agent was acting for the consumer.

(3) The standard of care required is that of a reasonable consumer: but this is subject to subsections (4) and (5).

(4) If the insurer was, or ought to have been, aware of any particular characteristics or circumstances of the actual consumer, those are to be taken into account.

(5) A misrepresentation made dishonestly is always to be taken as showing lack of reasonable care.

Qualifying misrepresentations

4   Qualifying misrepresentations: definition and remedies

(1) An insurer has a remedy against a consumer for a misrepresentation made by the consumer before a consumer insurance contract was entered into or varied only if—

(a) the consumer made the misrepresentation in breach of the duty set out in section 2(2), and

(b) the insurer shows that without the misrepresentation, that insurer would not have entered into the contract (or agreed to the variation) at all, or would have done so only on different terms.

(2) A misrepresentation for which the insurer has a remedy against the consumer is referred to in this Act as a 'qualifying misrepresentation'.

(3) The only such remedies available are set out in Schedule 1.

5   Qualifying misrepresentations: classification and presumptions

(1) For the purposes of this Act, a qualifying misrepresentation (see section 4(2)) is either—

    (a) deliberate or reckless, or

    (b) careless.

(2) A qualifying misrepresentation is deliberate or reckless if the consumer—

    (a) knew that it was untrue or misleading, or did not care whether or not it was untrue or misleading, and

    (b) knew that the matter to which the misrepresentation related was relevant to the insurer, or did not care whether or not it was relevant to the insurer.

(3) A qualifying misrepresentation is careless if it is not deliberate or reckless.

(4) It is for the insurer to show that a qualifying misrepresentation was deliberate or reckless.

(5) But it is to be presumed, unless the contrary is shown—

    (a) that the consumer had the knowledge of a reasonable consumer, and

    (b) that the consumer knew that a matter about which the insurer asked a clear and specific question was relevant to the insurer.

Specific issues

6   Warranties and representations

(1) This section applies to representations made by a consumer—

    (a) in connection with a proposed consumer insurance contract, or

    (b) in connection with a proposed variation to a consumer insurance contract.

(2) Such a representation is not capable of being converted into a warranty by means of any provision of the consumer insurance contract (or of the terms of the variation), or of any other contract (and whether by declaring the representation to form the basis of the contract or otherwise).

7   Group insurance

(1) This section applies where—

    (a) a contract of insurance is entered into by a person ('A') in order to provide cover for another person ('C'), or is varied or extended so as to do so,

    (b) C is not a party to the contract,

    (c) so far as the cover for C is concerned, the contract would have been a consumer insurance contract if entered into by C rather than by A, and

    (d) C provided information directly or indirectly to the insurer before the contract was entered into, or before it was varied or extended to provide cover for C.

(2) So far as the cover for C is concerned—

    (a) sections 2 and 3 apply in relation to disclosure and representations by C to the insurer as if C were proposing to enter into a consumer insurance contract for the relevant cover with the insurer, and

    (b) subject to subsections (3) to (5) and the modifications in relation to the insurer's remedies set out in Part 3 of Schedule 1, the remainder of this Act applies in relation to the cover for C as if C had entered into a consumer insurance contract for that cover with the insurer.

(3) Section 4(1)(b) applies as if it read as follows—

    '(b) the insurer shows that without the misrepresentation, that insurer would not have agreed to provide cover for C at all, or would have done so only on different terms.'

(4) If there is more than one C, a breach on the part of one of them of the duty imposed (by virtue of subsection (2)(a)) by section 2(2) does not affect the contract so far as it relates to the others.

(5) Nothing in this section affects any duty owed by A to the insurer, or any remedy which the insurer may have against A for breach of such a duty.

8 Insurance on life of another

(1) This section applies in relation to a consumer insurance contract for life insurance on the life of an individual ('L') who is not a party to the contract.

(2) If this section applies—

(a) information provided to the insurer by L is to be treated for the purposes of this Act as if it were provided by the person who is the party to the contract, but

(b) in relation to such information, if anything turns on the state of mind, knowledge, circumstances or characteristics of the individual providing the information, it is to be determined by reference to L and not the party to the contract.

9 Agents

Schedule 2 applies for determining, for the purposes of this Act only, whether an agent through whom a consumer insurance contract is effected is the agent of the consumer or of the insurer.

10 Contracting out

(1) A term of a consumer insurance contract, or of any other contract, which would put the consumer in a worse position as respects the matters mentioned in subsection (2) than the consumer would be in by virtue of the provisions of this Act is to that extent of no effect.

(2) The matters are—

(a) disclosure and representations by the consumer to the insurer before the contract is entered into or varied, and

(b) any remedies for qualifying misrepresentations (see section 4(2)).

(3) This section does not apply in relation to a contract for the settlement of a claim arising under a consumer insurance contract.

Final provision

12 Short title, commencement, application and extent

(4) This Act applies only in relation to consumer insurance contracts entered into, and variations to consumer insurance contracts agreed, after the Act comes into force.

In the case of group insurance (see section 7), that includes the provision of cover for C by means of an insurance contract entered into by A after the Act comes into force, or varied or extended so as to do so after the Act comes into force.

(5) Nothing in this Act affects the circumstances in which a person is bound by the acts or omissions of that person's agent.

SCHEDULES

Section 4(3)

SCHEDULE 1
INSURERS' REMEDIES FOR QUALIFYING MISREPRESENTATIONS

PART 1   CONTRACTS

1. General

This Part of this Schedule applies in relation to qualifying misrepresentations made in connection with consumer insurance contracts (for variations to them, see Part 2).

2. Deliberate or reckless misrepresentations

If a qualifying misrepresentation was deliberate or reckless, the insurer—

(a) may avoid the contract and refuse all claims, and

(b) need not return any of the premiums paid, except to the extent (if any) that it would be unfair to the consumer to retain them.

Careless misrepresentations—claims

3. If the qualifying misrepresentation was careless, paragraphs 4 to 8 apply in relation to any claim.

4. The insurer's remedies are based on what it would have done if the consumer had complied with the duty set out in section 2(2), and paragraphs 5 to 8 are to be read accordingly.

5. If the insurer would not have entered into the consumer insurance contract on any terms, the insurer may avoid the contract and refuse all claims, but must return the premiums paid.

6. If the insurer would have entered into the consumer insurance contract, but on different terms (excluding terms relating to the premium), the contract is to be treated as if it had been entered into on those different terms if the insurer so requires.

7. In addition, if the insurer would have entered into the consumer insurance contract (whether the terms relating to matters other than the premium would have been the same or different), but would have charged a higher premium, the insurer may reduce proportionately the amount to be paid on a claim.

8. 'Reduce proportionately' means that the insurer need pay on the claim only X% of what it would otherwise have been under an obligation to pay under the terms of the contract (or, if applicable, under the different terms provided for by virtue of paragraph 6), where—

$$X = \frac{\text{Premium actually charged}}{\text{Higher premium}} \times 100$$

9. Careless misrepresentations—treatment of contract for the future

(1) This paragraph—

(a) applies if the qualifying misrepresentation was careless, but

(b) does not relate to any outstanding claim.

(2) Paragraphs 5 and 6 (as read with paragraph 4) apply as they apply where a claim has been made.

(3) Paragraph 7 (as read with paragraph 4) applies in relation to a claim yet to be made as it applies in relation to a claim which has been made.

(4) If by virtue of sub-paragraph (2) or (3), the insurer would have either (or both) of the rights conferred by paragraph 6 or 7, the insurer may—

(a) give notice to that effect to the consumer, or

(b) terminate the contract by giving reasonable notice to the consumer.

(5) But the insurer may not terminate a contract under sub-paragraph (4)(b) if it is wholly or mainly one of life insurance.

(6) If the insurer gives notice to the consumer under sub-paragraph (4)(a), the consumer may terminate the contract by giving reasonable notice to the insurer.

(7) If either party terminates the contract under this paragraph, the insurer must refund any premiums paid for the terminated cover in respect of the balance of the contract term.

(8) Termination of the contract under this paragraph does not affect the treatment of any claim arising under the contract in the period before termination.

(9) Nothing in this paragraph affects any contractual right to terminate the contract.

PART 2   VARIATIONS

10. This Part of this Schedule applies in relation to qualifying misrepresentations made in connection with variations to consumer insurance contracts.

11. If the subject-matter of a variation can reasonably be treated separately from the subject-matter of the rest of the contract, Part 1 of this Schedule applies (with any necessary modifications) in relation to the variation as it applies in relation to a contract.

12. Otherwise, Part 1 applies (with any necessary modifications) as if the qualifying misrepresentation had been made in relation to the whole contract (for this purpose treated as including the variation) rather than merely in relation to the variation.

PART 3   MODIFICATIONS FOR GROUP INSURANCE

13. Part 1 is to be read subject to the following modifications in relation to cover provided for C under a group insurance contract as mentioned in section 7 (and in this Part 'A' and 'C' mean the same as in that section).

14. References to the consumer insurance contract (however described) are to that part of the contract which provides for cover for C.

15. References to claims and premiums are to claims and premiums in relation to that cover.

16. The reference to the consumer is to be read—

    (a) in paragraph 2(b), as a reference to whoever paid the premiums, or the part of them that related to the cover for C,

    (b) in paragraph 9(4) and (6), as a reference to A.

PART 4   SUPPLEMENTARY

17. Section 84 of the Marine Insurance Act 1906 (return of premium for failure of consideration) is to be read subject to the provisions of this Schedule in relation to contracts of marine insurance which are consumer insurance contracts.

Section 9   **SCHEDULE 2**

RULES FOR DETERMINING STATUS OF AGENTS

1. This Schedule sets out rules for determining, for the purposes of this Act only, whether an agent through whom a consumer insurance contract is effected is acting as the agent of the consumer or of the insurer.

2. The agent is to be taken as the insurer's agent in each of the following cases—

    (a) when the agent does something in the agent's capacity as the appointed representative of the insurer for the purposes of the Financial Services and Markets Act 2000 (see section 39 of that Act),

    (b) when the agent collects information from the consumer, if the insurer had given the agent express authority to do so as the insurer's agent,

    (c) when the agent enters into the contract as the insurer's agent, if the insurer had given the agent express authority to do so.

3.—(1) In any other case, it is to be presumed that the agent is acting as the consumer's agent unless, in the light of all the relevant circumstances, it appears that the agent is acting as the insurer's agent.

    (2) Some factors which may be relevant are set out below.

    (3) Examples of factors which may tend to confirm that the agent is acting for the consumer are—

        (a) the agent undertakes to give impartial advice to the consumer,

        (b) the agent undertakes to conduct a fair analysis of the market,

        (c) the consumer pays the agent a fee.

    (4) Examples of factors which may tend to show that the agent is acting for the insurer are—

        (a) the agent places insurance of the type in question with only one of the insurers who provide insurance of that type,

(b) the agent is under a contractual obligation which has the effect of restricting the number of insurers with whom the agent places insurance of the type in question,

(c) the insurer provides insurance of the type in question through only a small proportion of the agents who deal in that type of insurance,

(d) the insurer permits the agent to use the insurer's name in providing the agent's services,

(e) the insurance in question is marketed under the name of the agent,

(f) the insurer asks the agent to solicit the consumer's custom.

4.—(1) If it appears to the Treasury that the list of factors in sub-paragraph (3) or (4) of paragraph 3 has become outdated, the Treasury may by order made by statutory instrument bring the list up to date by amending the subparagraph so as to add, omit or alter any factor.

(2) A statutory instrument containing an order under sub-paragraph (1) may not be made unless a draft of the instrument has been laid before and approved by a resolution of each House of Parliament.

Financial Services Act 2012

(2012, c. 21)

107 Power to make further provision about regulation of consumer credit

(1) Subsection (2) applies on or at any time after the making, after the passing of this Act, of an order under section 22 of FSMA 2000 which has the effect that an activity (a 'transferred activity')—

(a) ceases to be an activity in respect of which a licence under section 21 of CCA 1974 is required or would be required but for the exemption conferred by subsection (2), (3) or (4) of that section or paragraph 15(3) of Schedule 3 to FSMA 2000, and

(b) becomes a regulated activity for the purposes of FSMA 2000.

(2) The Treasury may by order do any one or more of the following—

(a) transfer to the FCA functions of the OFT under any provision of CCA 1974 that remains in force;

(b) provide that any specified provision of FSMA 2000 which relates to the powers or duties of the FCA in connection with the failure of any person to comply with a requirement imposed by or under FSMA 2000 is to apply, subject to any specified modifications, in connection with the failure of any person to comply with a requirement imposed by or under a specified provision of CCA 1974;

(c) require the FCA to issue a statement of policy in relation to the exercise of powers conferred on it by virtue of paragraph (b);

(d) in connection with provision made by virtue of paragraph (b), provide that failure to comply with a specified provision of CCA 1974 no longer constitutes an offence or that a person may not be convicted of an offence under a specified provision of CCA 1974 in respect of an act or omission in a case where the FCA has exercised specified powers in relation to that person in respect of that act or omission;

(e) provide for the transfer to the Treasury of any functions under CCA 1974 previously exercisable by the Secretary of State;

(f) provide that functions of the Secretary of State under CCA 1974 are exercisable concurrently with the Treasury;

(h) enable local weights and measures authorities to institute proceedings in England and Wales for a relevant offence;

(j) provide that references in a specified enactment to the FCA's functions under FSMA 2000 include references to its functions resulting from any order under this section.

(3) If an order under this section makes provision by virtue of subsection (2)(b) enabling the FCA to exercise any of its powers under sections 205 to 206A of FSMA 2000 (disciplinary measures)

by reference to an act or omission that constitutes an offence under CCA 1974, the order must also make provision by virtue of subsection (2)(d) ensuring that a person in respect of whom the power has been exercised cannot subsequently be convicted of the offence by reference to the same act or omission.

(4) In subsection [(2)(h) and (i)]—

    (a) 'relevant regulated activity' means an activity that is a regulated activity for the purposes of FSMA 2000 by virtue of—

        (i)   an order made under section 22(1) of that Act in relation to an investment of a kind falling within paragraph 23 or 23B of Schedule 2 to that Act, or

        (ii) an order made under section 22(1A)(a) of that Act;

    (b) 'relevant offence' means an offence under FSMA 2000 committed in relation to such an activity.

(6) On or at any time after the making of an order under section 22 of FSMA 2000 of the kind mentioned in subsection (1), the Treasury may by order—

    (a) exclude the application of any provision of CCA 1974 in relation to a transferred activity, or

    (b) repeal any provision of CCA 1974 which relates to a transferred activity.

(7) In exercising their powers under this section, the Treasury must have regard to—

    (a) the importance of securing an appropriate degree of protection for consumers, and

    (b) the principle that a burden or restriction which is imposed on a person, or on the carrying on of an activity, should be proportionate to the benefits, considered in general terms, which are expected to result from the imposition of that burden or restriction.

(8) The additional powers conferred by section 115(2) on a person making an order under this Act include power for the Treasury, when making an order under this section—

    (a) to make such consequential provision as the Treasury consider appropriate;

    (b) to amend any enactment, including any provision of, or made under, this Act.

(9) The provisions of this section do not limit—

    (a) the powers conferred by section 118 or by section 22 of FSMA 2000, or

    (b) the powers exercisable under Schedule 21 in connection with the transfer of functions from the OFT.

(10) In this section—

'CCA 1974' means the Consumer Credit Act 1974;

'consumers' has the meaning given in section 1G of FSMA 2000;

'the OFT' means the Office of Fair Trading.

108   Suspension of licences under Part 3 of Consumer Credit Act 1974

(9) Nothing in this section affects the powers conferred by section 22 of FSMA 2000 or section 107 of this Act.

Enterprise and Regulatory Reform Act 2013

(2013, c. 24)

89   Supply of customer data

(1) The Secretary of State may by regulations require a regulated person to provide customer data—

    (a) to a customer, at the customer's request;

    (b) to a person who is authorised by a customer to receive the data, at the customer's request or, if the regulations so provide, at the authorised person's request.

(2) 'Regulated person' means—

    (a) a person who, in the course of a business, supplies gas or electricity to any premises;

    (b) a person who, in the course of a business, provides a mobile phone service;

(c) a person who, in the course of a business, provides financial services consisting of the provision of current account or credit card facilities;

(d) any other person who, in the course of a business, supplies or provides goods or services of a description specified in the regulations.

(3) 'Customer data' means information which—

(a) is held in electronic form by or on behalf of the regulated person, and

(b) relates to transactions between the regulated person and the customer.

(4) Regulations under subsection (1) may make provision as to the form in which customer data is to be provided and when it is to be provided (and any such provision may differ depending on the form in which a request for the data is made).

(5) Regulations under subsection (1)—

(a) may authorise the making of charges by a regulated person for complying with requests for customer data, and

(b) if they do so, must provide that the amount of any such charge—

(i) is to be determined by the regulated person, but

(ii) may not exceed the cost to that person of complying with the request.

(6) Regulations under subsection (1)(b) may provide that the requirement applies only if the authorised person satisfies any conditions specified in the regulations.

(7) In deciding whether to specify a description of goods or services for the purposes of subsection (2)(d), the Secretary of State must (among other things) have regard to the following—

(a) the typical duration of the period during which transactions between suppliers or providers of the goods or services and their customers take place;

(b) the typical volume and frequency of the transactions;

(c) the typical significance for customers of the costs incurred by them through the transactions;

(d) the effect that specifying the goods or services might have on the ability of customers to make an informed choice about which supplier or provider of the goods or services, or which particular goods or services, to use;

(e) the effect that specifying the goods or services might have on competition between suppliers or providers of the goods or services.

(8) The power to make regulations under this section may be exercised—

(a) so as to make provision generally, only in relation to particular descriptions of regulated persons, customers or customer data or only in relation to England, Wales, Scotland or Northern Ireland;

(b) so as to make different provision for different descriptions of regulated persons, customers or customer data;

(d) so as to provide for exceptions or exemptions from any requirement imposed by the regulations, including doing so by reference to the costs to the regulated person of complying with the requirement (whether generally or in particular cases).

(9) For the purposes of this section, a person ('C') is a customer of another person ('R') if—

(a) C has at any time, including a time before the commencement of this section, purchased (whether for the use of C or another person) goods or services supplied or provided by R or received such goods or services free of charge, and

(b) the purchase or receipt occurred—

(i) otherwise than in the course of a business, or

(ii) in the course of a business of a description specified in the regulations.

(10) In this section, 'mobile phone service' means an electronic communications service which is provided wholly or mainly so as to be available to members of the public for the purpose of communicating with others, or accessing data, by mobile phone.

90 Supply of customer data: enforcement

(1) Regulations may make provision for the enforcement of regulations under section 89 ('customer data regulations') by the Information Commissioner or any other person specified in the regulations (and, in this section, 'enforcer' means a person on whom functions of enforcement are conferred by the regulations).

93 Corporate insolvency: power to give further protection to essential supplies

(1) The Secretary of State may by order make provision for insolvency-related terms of a contract for the supply of essential goods or services to a company to cease to have effect where—

(a) the company enters administration or a voluntary arrangement under Part 1 of the Insolvency Act 1986 takes effect in relation to it, and

(b) any conditions specified in the order are met.

(2) The order must include provision for securing that, where an insolvency-related term of a contract ceases to have effect under the order, the contract may be terminated by the supplier if—

(a) an insolvency office-holder consents to the termination,

(b) a court grants permission for the termination, or

(c) any charges in respect of the supply that are incurred after the company enters administration or the voluntary arrangement takes effect are not paid within the period of 28 days beginning with the day on which payment is due.

(3) The order must include provision for securing that, where an insolvency-related term of a contract ceases to have effect under the order, the supplier may terminate the supply unless an insolvency office-holder personally guarantees the payment of any charges in respect of the continuation of the supply.

(5) The order must (in addition to the provision mentioned in subsections (2) and (3)) include such other provision as the Secretary of State considers appropriate for securing that the interests of suppliers are protected.

(7) An insolvency-related term of a contract for the supply of essential goods or services to a company is a provision of the contract under which—

(a) the contract or the supply would terminate, or any other thing would take place, because the company enters administration or the voluntary arrangement takes effect,

(b) the supplier would be entitled to terminate the contract or the supply, or to do any other thing, because the company enters administration or the voluntary arrangement takes effect, or

(c) the supplier would be entitled to terminate the contract or the supply because of an event that occurred before the company enters administration or the voluntary arrangement takes effect.

94 Individual insolvency: power to give further protection to essential supplies

. . .

Consumer Rights Act 2015

(2015, c. 15)

PART 1 CONSUMER CONTRACTS FOR GOODS, DIGITAL CONTENT AND SERVICES

Chapter 1 Introduction

1 Where Part 1 applies

(1) This Part applies where there is an agreement between a trader and a consumer for the trader to supply goods, digital content or services, if the agreement is a contract.

(2) It applies whether the contract is written or oral or implied from the parties' conduct, or more than one of these combined.

(3) Any of Chapters 2, 3 and 4 may apply to a contract—

(a) if it is a contract for the trader to supply goods, see Chapter 2;

(b) if it is a contract for the trader to supply digital content, see Chapter 3 (also, subsection (6));

(c) if it is a contract for the trader to supply a service, see Chapter 4 (also, subsection (6)).

(4) In each case the Chapter applies even if the contract also covers something covered by another Chapter (a mixed contract).

(5) Two or all three of those Chapters may apply to a mixed contract.

(6) For provisions about particular mixed contracts, see—

(a) section 15 (goods and installation);

(b) section 16 (goods and digital content).

(7) For other provision applying to contracts to which this Part applies, see Part 2 (unfair terms).

2 Key definitions

(1) These definitions apply in this Part (as well as the definitions in section 59).

(2) 'Trader' means a person acting for purposes relating to that person's trade, business, craft or profession, whether acting personally or through another person acting in the trader's name or on the trader's behalf.

(3) 'Consumer' means an individual acting for purposes that are wholly or mainly outside that individual's trade, business, craft or profession.

(4) A trader claiming that an individual was not acting for purposes wholly or mainly outside the individual's trade, business, craft or profession must prove it.

(5) For the purposes of Chapter 2, except to the extent mentioned in subsection (6), a person is not a consumer in relation to a sales contract if—

(a) the goods are second hand goods sold at public auction, and

(b) individuals have the opportunity of attending the sale in person.

(6) A person is a consumer in relation to such a contract for the purposes of—

(a) sections 11(4) and (5), 12, 28 and 29, and

(b) the other provisions of Chapter 2 as they apply in relation to those sections.

(7) 'Business' includes the activities of any government department or local or public authority.

(8) 'Goods' means any tangible moveable items, but that includes water, gas and electricity if and only if they are put up for supply in a limited volume or set quantity.

(9) 'Digital content' means data which are produced and supplied in digital form.

Chapter 2 Goods

What goods contracts are covered?

3 Contracts covered by this Chapter

(1) This Chapter applies to a contract for a trader to supply goods to a consumer.

(2) It applies only if the contract is one of these (defined for the purposes of this Part in sections 5 to 8)—

(a) a sales contract;

(b) a contract for the hire of goods;

(c) a hire-purchase agreement;

(d) a contract for transfer of goods.

(3) It does not apply—

(a) to a contract for a trader to supply coins or notes to a consumer for use as currency;

(b) to a contract for goods to be sold by way of execution or otherwise by authority of law;

(c) to a contract intended to operate as a mortgage, pledge, charge or other security;

(d) in relation to England and Wales or Northern Ireland, to a contract made by deed and for which the only consideration is the presumed consideration imported by the deed; . . .

(4) A contract to which this Chapter applies is referred to in this Part as a 'contract to supply goods'.

(5) Contracts to supply goods include—

    (a) contracts entered into between one part owner and another;

    (b) contracts for the transfer of an undivided share in goods;

    (c) contracts that are absolute and contracts that are conditional.

(6) Subsection (1) is subject to any provision of this Chapter that applies a section or part of a section to only some of the kinds of contracts listed in subsection (2).

(7) A mixed contract (see section 1(4)) may be a contract of any of those kinds.

4   Ownership of goods

(1) In this Chapter ownership of goods means the general property in goods, not merely a special property.

(2) For the time when ownership of goods is transferred, see in particular the following provisions of the Sale of Goods Act 1979 (which relate to contracts of sale)—

section 16: goods must be ascertained

section 17: property passes when intended to pass

section 18: rules for ascertaining intention

section 19: reservation of right of disposal

section 20A: undivided shares in goods forming part of a bulk

section 20B: deemed consent by co-owner to dealings in bulk goods

5   Sales contracts

(1) A contract is a sales contract if under it—

    (a) the trader transfers or agrees to transfer ownership of goods to the consumer, and

    (b) the consumer pays or agrees to pay the price.

(2) A contract is a sales contract (whether or not it would be one under subsection (1)) if under the contract—

    (a) goods are to be manufactured or produced and the trader agrees to supply them to the consumer,

    (b) on being supplied, the goods will be owned by the consumer, and

    (c) the consumer pays or agrees to pay the price.

(3) A sales contract may be conditional (see section 3(5)), but in this Part 'conditional sales contract' means a sales contract under which—

    (a) the price for the goods or part of it is payable by instalments, and

    (b) the trader retains ownership of the goods until the conditions specified in the contract (for the payment of instalments or otherwise) are met;

and it makes no difference whether or not the consumer possesses the goods.

6   Contracts for the hire of goods

(1) A contract is for the hire of goods if under it the trader gives or agrees to give the consumer possession of the goods with the right to use them, subject to the terms of the contract, for a period determined in accordance with the contract.

(2) But a contract is not for the hire of goods if it is a hire-purchase agreement.

7   Hire-purchase agreements

(1) A contract is a hire-purchase agreement if it meets the two conditions set out below.

(2) The first condition is that under the contract goods are hired by the trader in return for periodical payments by the consumer (and 'hired' is to be read in accordance with section 6(1)).

(3) The second condition is that under the contract ownership of the goods will transfer to the consumer if the terms of the contract are complied with and—

    (a) the consumer exercises an option to buy the goods,

    (b) any party to the contract does an act specified in it, or

    (c) an event specified in the contract occurs.

(4) But a contract is not a hire-purchase agreement if it is a conditional sales contract.

8 Contracts for transfer of goods

A contract to supply goods is a contract for transfer of goods if under it the trader transfers or agrees to transfer ownership of the goods to the consumer and—

    (a) the consumer provides or agrees to provide consideration otherwise than by paying a price, or

    (b) the contract is, for any other reason, not a sales contract or a hire-purchase agreement.

What statutory rights are there under a goods contract?

9 Goods to be of satisfactory quality

    (1) Every contract to supply goods is to be treated as including a term that the quality of the goods is satisfactory.

    (2) The quality of goods is satisfactory if they meet the standard that a reasonable person would consider satisfactory, taking account of—

    (a) any description of the goods,

    (b) the price or other consideration for the goods (if relevant), and

    (c) all the other relevant circumstances (see subsection (5)).

    (3) The quality of goods includes their state and condition; and the following aspects (among others) are in appropriate cases aspects of the quality of goods—

    (a) fitness for all the purposes for which goods of that kind are usually supplied;

    (b) appearance and finish;

    (c) freedom from minor defects;

    (d) safety;

    (e) durability.

    (4) The term mentioned in subsection (1) does not cover anything which makes the quality of the goods unsatisfactory—

    (a) which is specifically drawn to the consumer's attention before the contract is made,

    (b) where the consumer examines the goods before the contract is made, which that examination ought to reveal, or

    (c) in the case of a contract to supply goods by sample, which would have been apparent on a reasonable examination of the sample.

    (5) The relevant circumstances mentioned in subsection (2)(c) include any public statement about the specific characteristics of the goods made by the trader, the producer or any representative of the trader or the producer.

    (6) That includes, in particular, any public statement made in advertising or labelling.

    (7) But a public statement is not a relevant circumstance for the purposes of subsection (2)(c) if the trader shows that—

    (a) when the contract was made, the trader was not, and could not reasonably have been, aware of the statement,

    (b) before the contract was made, the statement had been publicly withdrawn or, to the extent that it contained anything which was incorrect or misleading, it had been publicly corrected, or

    (c) the consumer's decision to contract for the goods could not have been influenced by the statement.

    (8) In a contract to supply goods a term about the quality of the goods may be treated as included as a matter of custom.

    (9) See section 19 for a consumer's rights if the trader is in breach of a term that this section requires to be treated as included in a contract.

10 Goods to be fit for particular purpose

    (1) Subsection (3) applies to a contract to supply goods if before the contract is made the consumer makes known to the trader (expressly or by implication) any particular purpose for which the consumer is contracting for the goods.

    (2) Subsection (3) also applies to a contract to supply goods if—

    (a) the goods were previously sold by a credit-broker to the trader,

(b) in the case of a sales contract or contract for transfer of goods, the consideration or part of it is a sum payable by instalments, and

(c) before the contract is made, the consumer makes known to the credit-broker (expressly or by implication) any particular purpose for which the consumer is contracting for the goods.

(3) The contract is to be treated as including a term that the goods are reasonably fit for that purpose, whether or not that is a purpose for which goods of that kind are usually supplied.

(4) Subsection (3) does not apply if the circumstances show that the consumer does not rely, or it is unreasonable for the consumer to rely, on the skill or judgment of the trader or credit-broker.

(5) In a contract to supply goods a term about the fitness of the goods for a particular purpose may be treated as included as a matter of custom.

(6) See section 19 for a consumer's rights if the trader is in breach of a term that this section requires to be treated as included in a contract.

11   Goods to be as described

(1) Every contract to supply goods by description is to be treated as including a term that the goods will match the description.

(2) If the supply is by sample as well as by description, it is not sufficient that the bulk of the goods matches the sample if the goods do not also match the description.

(3) A supply of goods is not prevented from being a supply by description just because—

(a) the goods are exposed for supply, and

(b) they are selected by the consumer.

(4) Any information that is provided by the trader about the goods and is information mentioned in paragraph (a) of Schedule 1 or 2 to the Consumer Contracts (Information, Cancellation and Additional Charges) Regulations 2013 (SI 2013/3134) (main characteristics of goods) is to be treated as included as a term of the contract.

(5) A change to any of that information, made before entering into the contract or later, is not effective unless expressly agreed between the consumer and the trader.

(6) See section 2(5) and (6) for the application of subsections (4) and (5) where goods are sold at public auction.

(7) See section 19 for a consumer's rights if the trader is in breach of a term that this section requires to be treated as included in a contract.

12   Other pre-contract information included in contract

(1) This section applies to any contract to supply goods.

(2) Where regulation 9, 10 or 13 of the Consumer Contracts (Information, Cancellation and Additional Charges) Regulations 2013 (SI 2013/3134) required the trader to provide information to the consumer before the contract became binding, any of that information that was provided by the trader other than information about the goods and mentioned in paragraph (a) of Schedule 1 or 2 to the Regulations (main characteristics of goods) is to be treated as included as a term of the contract.

(3) A change to any of that information, made before entering into the contract or later, is not effective unless expressly agreed between the consumer and the trader.

(4) See section 2(5) and (6) for the application of this section where goods are sold at public auction.

(5) See section 19 for a consumer's rights if the trader is in breach of a term that this section requires to be treated as included in the contract.

13   Goods to match a sample

(1) This section applies to a contract to supply goods by reference to a sample of the goods that is seen or examined by the consumer before the contract is made.

(2) Every contract to which this section applies is to be treated as including a term that—

(a) the goods will match the sample except to the extent that any differences between the sample and the goods are brought to the consumer's attention before the contract is made, and

    (b) the goods will be free from any defect that makes their quality unsatisfactory and that would not be apparent on a reasonable examination of the sample.

(3) See section 19 for a consumer's rights if the trader is in breach of a term that this section requires to be treated as included in a contract.

14 Goods to match a model seen or examined

(1) This section applies to a contract to supply goods by reference to a model of the goods that is seen or examined by the consumer before entering into the contract.

(2) Every contract to which this section applies is to be treated as including a term that the goods will match the model except to the extent that any differences between the model and the goods are brought to the consumer's attention before the consumer enters into the contract.

(3) See section 19 for a consumer's rights if the trader is in breach of a term that this section requires to be treated as included in a contract.

15 Installation as part of conformity of the goods with the contract

(1) Goods do not conform to a contract to supply goods if—

    (a) installation of the goods forms part of the contract,

    (b) the goods are installed by the trader or under the trader's responsibility, and

    (c) the goods are installed incorrectly.

(2) See section 19 for the effect of goods not conforming to the contract.

16 Goods not conforming to contract if digital content does not conform

(1) Goods (whether or not they conform otherwise to a contract to supply goods) do not conform to it if—

    (a) the goods are an item that includes digital content, and

    (b) the digital content does not conform to the contract to supply that content (for which see section 42(1)).

(2) See section 19 for the effect of goods not conforming to the contract.

17 Trader to have right to supply the goods etc

(1) Every contract to supply goods, except one within subsection (4), is to be treated as including a term—

    (a) in the case of a contract for the hire of goods, that at the beginning of the period of hire the trader must have the right to transfer possession of the goods by way of hire for that period,

    (b) in any other case, that the trader must have the right to sell or transfer the goods at the time when ownership of the goods is to be transferred.

(2) Every contract to supply goods, except a contract for the hire of goods or a contract within subsection (4), is to be treated as including a term that—

    (a) the goods are free from any charge or encumbrance not disclosed or known to the consumer before entering into the contract,

    (b) the goods will remain free from any such charge or encumbrance until ownership of them is to be transferred, and

    (c) the consumer will enjoy quiet possession of the goods except so far as it may be disturbed by the owner or other person entitled to the benefit of any charge or encumbrance so disclosed or known.

(3) Every contract for the hire of goods is to be treated as including a term that the consumer will enjoy quiet possession of the goods for the period of the hire except so far as the possession may be disturbed by the owner or other person entitled to the benefit of any charge or encumbrance disclosed or known to the consumer before entering into the contract.

(4) This subsection applies to a contract if the contract shows, or the circumstances when they enter into the contract imply, that the trader and the consumer intend the trader to transfer only—

    (a) whatever title the trader has, even if it is limited, or

    (b) whatever title a third person has, even if it is limited.

(5) Every contract within subsection (4) is to be treated as including a term that all charges or encumbrances known to the trader and not known to the consumer were disclosed to the consumer before entering into the contract.

(6) Every contract within subsection (4) is to be treated as including a term that the consumer's quiet possession of the goods—

    (a) will not be disturbed by the trader, and

    (b) will not be disturbed by a person claiming through or under the trader, unless that person is claiming under a charge or encumbrance that was disclosed or known to the consumer before entering into the contract.

(7) If subsection (4)(b) applies (transfer of title that a third person has), the contract is also to be treated as including a term that the consumer's quiet possession of the goods—

    (a) will not be disturbed by the third person, and

    (b) will not be disturbed by a person claiming through or under the third person, unless the claim is under a charge or encumbrance that was disclosed or known to the consumer before entering into the contract.

(8) In the case of a contract for the hire of goods, this section does not affect the right of the trader to repossess the goods where the contract provides or is to be treated as providing for this.

(9) See section 19 for a consumer's rights if the trader is in breach of a term that this section requires to be treated as included in a contract.

18   No other requirement to treat term about quality or fitness as included

(1) Except as provided by sections 9, 10, 13 and 16, a contract to supply goods is not to be treated as including any term about the quality of the goods or their fitness for any particular purpose, unless the term is expressly included in the contract.

(2) Subsection (1) is subject to provision made by any other enactment (whenever passed or made).

What remedies are there if statutory rights under a goods contract are not met?

19   Consumer's rights to enforce terms about goods

(1) In this section and sections 22 to 24 references to goods conforming to a contract are references to—

    (a) the goods conforming to the terms described in sections 9, 10, 11, 13 and 14,

    (b) the goods not failing to conform to the contract under section 15 or 16, and

    (c) the goods conforming to requirements that are stated in the contract.

(2) But, for the purposes of this section and sections 22 to 24, a failure to conform as mentioned in subsection (1)(a) to (c) is not a failure to conform to the contract if it has its origin in materials supplied by the consumer.

(3) If the goods do not conform to the contract because of a breach of any of the terms described in sections 9, 10, 11, 13 and 14, or if they do not conform to the contract under section 16, the consumer's rights (and the provisions about them and when they are available) are—

    (a) the short-term right to reject (sections 20 and 22);

    (b) the right to repair or replacement (section 23); and

    (c) the right to a price reduction or the final right to reject (sections 20 and 24).

(4) If the goods do not conform to the contract under section 15 or because of a breach of requirements that are stated in the contract, the consumer's rights (and the provisions about them and when they are available) are—

    (a) the right to repair or replacement (section 23); and

    (b) the right to a price reduction or the final right to reject (sections 20 and 24).

(5) If the trader is in breach of a term that section 12 requires to be treated as included in the contract, the consumer has the right to recover from the trader the amount of any costs incurred by the consumer as a result of the breach, up to the amount of the price paid or the value of other consideration given for the goods.

(6) If the trader is in breach of the term that section 17(1) (right to supply etc) requires to be treated as included in the contract, the consumer has a right to reject (see section 20 for provisions about that right and when it is available).

(7) Subsections (3) to (6) are subject to section 25 and subsections (3)(a) and (6) are subject to section 26.

(8) Section 28 makes provision about remedies for breach of a term about the time for delivery of goods.

(9) This Chapter does not prevent the consumer seeking other remedies—
- (a) for a breach of a term that this Chapter requires to be treated as included in the contract,
- (b) on the grounds that, under section 15 or 16, goods do not conform to the contract, or
- (c) for a breach of a requirement stated in the contract.

(10) Those other remedies may be ones—
- (a) in addition to a remedy referred to in subsections (3) to (6) (but not so as to recover twice for the same loss), or
- (b) instead of such a remedy, or
- (c) where no such remedy is provided for.

(11) Those other remedies include any of the following that is open to the consumer in the circumstances—
- (a) claiming damages;
- (b) seeking specific performance;
- (c) seeking an order for specific implement;
- (d) relying on the breach against a claim by the trader for the price;
- (e) for breach of an express term, exercising a right to treat the contract as at an end.

(12) It is not open to the consumer to treat the contract as at an end for breach of a term that this Chapter requires to be treated as included in the contract, or on the grounds that, under section 15 or 16, goods do not conform to the contract, except as provided by subsections (3), (4) and (6).

(13) In this Part, treating a contract as at an end means treating it as repudiated.

(14) For the purposes of subsections (3)(b) and (c) and (4), goods which do not conform to the contract at any time within the period of six months beginning with the day on which the goods were delivered to the consumer must be taken not to have conformed to it on that day.

(15) Subsection (14) does not apply if—
- (a) it is established that the goods did conform to the contract on that day, or
- (b) its application is incompatible with the nature of the goods or with how they fail to conform to the contract.

20   Right to reject

(1) The short-term right to reject is subject to section 22.

(2) The final right to reject is subject to section 24.

(3) The right to reject under section 19(6) is not limited by those sections.

(4) Each of these rights entitles the consumer to reject the goods and treat the contract as at an end, subject to subsections (20) and (21).

(5) The right is exercised if the consumer indicates to the trader that the consumer is rejecting the goods and treating the contract as at an end.

(6) The indication may be something the consumer says or does, but it must be clear enough to be understood by the trader.

(7) From the time when the right is exercised—
- (a) the trader has a duty to give the consumer a refund, subject to subsection (18), and
- (b) the consumer has a duty to make the goods available for collection by the trader or (if there is an agreement for the consumer to return rejected goods) to return them as agreed.

(8) Whether or not the consumer has a duty to return the rejected goods, the trader must bear any reasonable costs of returning them, other than any costs incurred by the consumer in returning the goods in person to the place where the consumer took physical possession of them.

(9) The consumer's entitlement to receive a refund works as follows.

(10) To the extent that the consumer paid money under the contract, the consumer is entitled to receive back the same amount of money.

(11) To the extent that the consumer transferred anything else under the contract, the consumer is entitled to receive back the same amount of what the consumer transferred, unless subsection (12) applies.

(12) To the extent that the consumer transferred under the contract something for which the same amount of the same thing cannot be substituted, the consumer is entitled to receive back in its original state whatever the consumer transferred.

(13) If the contract is for the hire of goods, the entitlement to a refund extends only to anything paid or otherwise transferred for a period of hire that the consumer does not get because the contract is treated as at an end.

(14) If the contract is a hire-purchase agreement or a conditional sales contract and the contract is treated as at an end before the whole of the price has been paid, the entitlement to a refund extends only to the part of the price paid.

(15) A refund under this section must be given without undue delay, and in any event within 14 days beginning with the day on which the trader agrees that the consumer is entitled to a refund.

(16) If the consumer paid money under the contract, the trader must give the refund using the same means of payment as the consumer used, unless the consumer expressly agrees otherwise.

(17) The trader must not impose any fee on the consumer in respect of the refund.

(18) There is no entitlement to receive a refund—

    (a) if none of subsections (10) to (12) applies,

    (b) to the extent that anything to which subsection (12) applies cannot be given back in its original state, or

    (c) where subsection (13) applies, to the extent that anything the consumer transferred under the contract cannot be divided so as to give back only the amount, or part of the amount, to which the consumer is entitled.

(19) It may be open to a consumer to claim damages where there is no entitlement to receive a refund, or because of the limits of the entitlement, or instead of a refund.

(20) Subsection (21) qualifies the application in relation to England and Wales and Northern Ireland of the rights mentioned in subsections (1) to (3) where—

    (a) the contract is a severable contract,

    (b) in relation to the final right to reject, the contract is a contract for the hire of goods, a hire-purchase agreement or a contract for transfer of goods, and

    (c) section 26(3) does not apply.

(21) The consumer is entitled, depending on the terms of the contract and the circumstances of the case—

    (a) to reject the goods to which a severable obligation relates and treat that obligation as at an end (so that the entitlement to a refund relates only to what the consumer paid or transferred in relation to that obligation), or

    (b) to exercise any of the rights mentioned in subsections (1) to (3) in respect of the whole contract.

21   Partial rejection of goods

(1) If the consumer has any of the rights mentioned in section 20(1) to (3), but does not reject all of the goods and treat the contract as at an end, the consumer—

    (a) may reject some or all of the goods that do not conform to the contract, but

    (b) may not reject any goods that do conform to the contract.

(2) If the consumer is entitled to reject the goods in an instalment, but does not reject all of those goods, the consumer—

(a) may reject some or all of the goods in the instalment that do not conform to the contract, but

(b) may not reject any goods in the instalment that do conform to the contract.

(3) If any of the goods form a commercial unit, the consumer cannot reject some of those goods without also rejecting the rest of them.

(4) A unit is a 'commercial unit' if division of the unit would materially impair the value of the goods or the character of the unit.

(5) The consumer rejects goods under this section by indicating to the trader that the consumer is rejecting the goods.

(6) The indication may be something the consumer says or does, but it must be clear enough to be understood by the trader.

(7) From the time when a consumer rejects goods under this section—

(a) the trader has a duty to give the consumer a refund in respect of those goods (subject to subsection (10)), and

(b) the consumer has a duty to make those goods available for collection by the trader or (if there is an agreement for the consumer to return rejected goods) to return them as agreed.

(8) Whether or not the consumer has a duty to return the rejected goods, the trader must bear any reasonable costs of returning them, other than any costs incurred by the consumer in returning those goods in person to the place where the consumer took physical possession of them.

(9) Section 20(10) to (17) apply to a consumer's right to receive a refund under this section (and in section 20(13) and (14) references to the contract being treated as at an end are to be read as references to goods being rejected).

(10) That right does not apply—

(a) if none of section 20(10) to (12) applies,

(b) to the extent that anything to which section 20(12) applies cannot be given back in its original state, or

(c) to the extent that anything the consumer transferred under the contract cannot be divided so as to give back only the amount, or part of the amount, to which the consumer is entitled.

(11) It may be open to a consumer to claim damages where there is no right to receive a refund, or because of the limits of the right, or instead of a refund.

(12) References in this section to goods conforming to a contract are to be read in accordance with section 19(1) and (2), but they also include the goods conforming to the terms described in section 17.

(13) Where section 20(21)(a) applies the reference in subsection (1) to the consumer treating the contract as at an end is to be read as a reference to the consumer treating the severable obligation as at an end.

22 Time limit for short-term right to reject

(1) A consumer who has the short-term right to reject loses it if the time limit for exercising it passes without the consumer exercising it, unless the trader and the consumer agree that it may be exercised later.

(2) An agreement under which the short-term right to reject would be lost before the time limit passes is not binding on the consumer.

(3) The time limit for exercising the short-term right to reject (unless subsection (4) applies) is the end of 30 days beginning with the first day after these have all happened—

(a) ownership or (in the case of a contract for the hire of goods, a hire-purchase agreement or a conditional sales contract) possession of the goods has been transferred to the consumer,

(b) the goods have been delivered, and

(c) where the contract requires the trader to install the goods or take other action to enable the consumer to use them, the trader has notified the consumer that the action has been taken.

(4) If any of the goods are of a kind that can reasonably be expected to perish after a shorter period, the time limit for exercising the short-term right to reject in relation to those goods is the end of that shorter period (but without affecting the time limit in relation to goods that are not of that kind).

(5) Subsections (3) and (4) do not prevent the consumer exercising the short-term right to reject before something mentioned in subsection (3)(a), (b) or (c) has happened.

(6) If the consumer requests or agrees to the repair or replacement of goods, the period mentioned in subsection (3) or (4) stops running for the length of the waiting period.

(7) If goods supplied by the trader in response to that request or agreement do not conform to the contract, the time limit for exercising the short-term right to reject is then either—

(a) 7 days after the waiting period ends, or

(b) if later, the original time limit for exercising that right, extended by the waiting period.

(8) The waiting period—

(a) begins with the day the consumer requests or agrees to the repair or replacement of the goods, and

(b) ends with the day on which the consumer receives goods supplied by the trader in response to the request or agreement.

23   Right to repair or replacement

(1) This section applies if the consumer has the right to repair or replacement (see section 19(3) and (4)).

(2) If the consumer requires the trader to repair or replace the goods, the trader must—

(a) do so within a reasonable time and without significant inconvenience to the consumer, and

(b) bear any necessary costs incurred in doing so (including in particular the cost of any labour, materials or postage).

(3) The consumer cannot require the trader to repair or replace the goods if that remedy (the repair or the replacement)—

(a) is impossible, or

(b) is disproportionate compared to the other of those remedies.

(4) Either of those remedies is disproportionate compared to the other if it imposes costs on the trader which, compared to those imposed by the other, are unreasonable, taking into account—

(a) the value which the goods would have if they conformed to the contract,

(b) the significance of the lack of conformity, and

(c) whether the other remedy could be effected without significant inconvenience to the consumer.

(5) Any question as to what is a reasonable time or significant inconvenience is to be determined taking account of—

(a) the nature of the goods, and

(b) the purpose for which the goods were acquired.

(6) A consumer who requires or agrees to the repair of goods cannot require the trader to replace them, or exercise the short-term right to reject, without giving the trader a reasonable time to repair them (unless giving the trader that time would cause significant inconvenience to the consumer).

(7) A consumer who requires or agrees to the replacement of goods cannot require the trader to repair them, or exercise the short-term right to reject, without giving the trader a reasonable time to replace them (unless giving the trader that time would cause significant inconvenience to the consumer).

(8) In this Chapter, 'repair' in relation to goods that do not conform to a contract, means making them conform.

24 Right to price reduction or final right to reject

(1) The right to a price reduction is the right—

    (a) to require the trader to reduce by an appropriate amount the price the consumer is required to pay under the contract, or anything else the consumer is required to transfer under the contract, and

    (b) to receive a refund from the trader for anything already paid or otherwise transferred by the consumer above the reduced amount.

(2) The amount of the reduction may, where appropriate, be the full amount of the price or whatever the consumer is required to transfer.

(3) Section 20(10) to (17) applies to a consumer's right to receive a refund under subsection (1)(b).

(4) The right to a price reduction does not apply—

    (a) if what the consumer is (before the reduction) required to transfer under the contract, whether or not already transferred, cannot be divided up so as to enable the trader to receive or retain only the reduced amount, or

    (b) if anything to which section 20(12) applies cannot be given back in its original state.

(5) A consumer who has the right to a price reduction and the final right to reject may only exercise one (not both), and may only do so in one of these situations—

    (a) after one repair or one replacement, the goods do not conform to the contract;

    (b) because of section 23(3) the consumer can require neither repair nor replacement of the goods; or

    (c) the consumer has required the trader to repair or replace the goods, but the trader is in breach of the requirement of section 23(2)(a) to do so within a reasonable time and without significant inconvenience to the consumer.

(6) There has been a repair or replacement for the purposes of subsection (5)(a) if—

    (a) the consumer has requested or agreed to repair or replacement of the goods (whether in relation to one fault or more than one), and

    (b) the trader has delivered goods to the consumer, or made goods available to the consumer, in response to the request or agreement.

(7) For the purposes of subsection (6) goods that the trader arranges to repair at the consumer's premises are made available when the trader indicates that the repairs are finished.

(8) If the consumer exercises the final right to reject, any refund to the consumer may be reduced by a deduction for use, to take account of the use the consumer has had of the goods in the period since they were delivered, but this is subject to subsections (9) and (10).

(9) No deduction may be made to take account of use in any period when the consumer had the goods only because the trader failed to collect them at an agreed time.

(10) No deduction may be made if the final right to reject is exercised in the first 6 months (see subsection (11)), unless—

    (a) the goods consist of a motor vehicle, or

    (b) the goods are of a description specified by order made by the Secretary of State by statutory instrument.

(11) In subsection (10) the first 6 months means 6 months beginning with the first day after these have all happened—

    (a) ownership or (in the case of a contract for the hire of goods, a hire-purchase agreement or a conditional sales contract) possession of the goods has been transferred to the consumer,

    (b) the goods have been delivered, and

    (c) where the contract requires the trader to install the goods or take other action to enable the consumer to use them, the trader has notified the consumer that the action has been taken.

(12) In subsection (10)(a) 'motor vehicle'—

    (a) in relation to Great Britain, has the same meaning as in the Road Traffic Act 1988 (see sections 185 to 194 of that Act); . . .

(13) But a vehicle is not a motor vehicle for the purposes of subsection (10)(a) if it is constructed or adapted—

    (a) for the use of a person suffering from some physical defect or disability, and

    (b) so that it may only be used by one such person at any one time.

(14) An order under subsection (10)(b)—

    (a) may be made only if the Secretary of State is satisfied that it is appropriate to do so because of significant detriment caused to traders as a result of the application of subsection (10) in relation to goods of the description specified by the order;

    (b) may contain transitional or transitory provision or savings.

(15) No order may be made under subsection (10)(b) unless a draft of the statutory instrument containing it has been laid before, and approved by a resolution of, each House of Parliament.

Other rules about remedies under goods contracts

25 Delivery of wrong quantity

(1) Where the trader delivers to the consumer a quantity of goods less than the trader contracted to supply, the consumer may reject them, but if the consumer accepts them the consumer must pay for them at the contract rate.

(2) Where the trader delivers to the consumer a quantity of goods larger than the trader contracted to supply, the consumer may accept the goods included in the contract and reject the rest, or may reject all of the goods.

(3) Where the trader delivers to the consumer a quantity of goods larger than the trader contracted to supply and the consumer accepts all of the goods delivered, the consumer must pay for them at the contract rate.

(4) Where the consumer is entitled to reject goods under this section, any entitlement for the consumer to treat the contract as at an end depends on the terms of the contract and the circumstances of the case.

(5) The consumer rejects goods under this section by indicating to the trader that the consumer is rejecting the goods.

(6) The indication may be something the consumer says or does, but it must be clear enough to be understood by the trader.

(7) Subsections (1) to (3) do not prevent the consumer claiming damages, where it is open to the consumer to do so.

(8) This section is subject to any usage of trade, special agreement, or course of dealing between the parties.

26 Instalment deliveries

(1) Under a contract to supply goods, the consumer is not bound to accept delivery of the goods by instalments, unless that has been agreed between the consumer and the trader.

(2) The following provisions apply if the contract provides for the goods to be delivered by stated instalments, which are to be separately paid for.

(3) If the trader makes defective deliveries in respect of one or more instalments, the consumer, apart from any entitlement to claim damages, may be (but is not necessarily) entitled—

    (a) to exercise the short-term right to reject or the right to reject under section 19(6) (as applicable) in respect of the whole contract, or

    (b) to reject the goods in an instalment.

(4) Whether paragraph (a) or (b) of subsection (3) (or neither) applies to a consumer depends on the terms of the contract and the circumstances of the case.

(5) In subsection (3), making defective deliveries does not include failing to make a delivery in accordance with section 28.

(6) If the consumer neglects or refuses to take delivery of or pay for one or more instalments, the trader may—

    (a) be entitled to treat the whole contract as at an end, or

(b) if it is a severable breach, have a claim for damages but not a right to treat the whole contract as at an end.

(7) Whether paragraph (a) or (b) of subsection (6) (or neither) applies to a trader depends on the terms of the contract and the circumstances of the case.

Other rules about goods contracts

28   Delivery of goods

(1) This section applies to any sales contract.

(2) Unless the trader and the consumer have agreed otherwise, the contract is to be treated as including a term that the trader must deliver the goods to the consumer.

(3) Unless there is an agreed time or period, the contract is to be treated as including a term that the trader must deliver the goods—

(a) without undue delay, and

(b) in any event, not more than 30 days after the day on which the contract is entered into.

(4) In this section—

(a) an 'agreed' time or period means a time or period agreed by the trader and the consumer for delivery of the goods;

(b) if there is an obligation to deliver the goods at the time the contract is entered into, that time counts as the 'agreed' time.

(5) Subsections (6) and (7) apply if the trader does not deliver the goods in accordance with subsection (3) or at the agreed time or within the agreed period.

(6) If the circumstances are that—

(a) the trader has refused to deliver the goods,

(b) delivery of the goods at the agreed time or within the agreed period is essential taking into account all the relevant circumstances at the time the contract was entered into, or

(c) the consumer told the trader before the contract was entered into that delivery in accordance with subsection (3), or at the agreed time or within the agreed period, was essential,

then the consumer may treat the contract as at an end.

(7) In any other circumstances, the consumer may specify a period that is appropriate in the circumstances and require the trader to deliver the goods before the end of that period.

(8) If the consumer specifies a period under subsection (7) but the goods are not delivered within that period, then the consumer may treat the contract as at an end.

(9) If the consumer treats the contract as at an end under subsection (6) or (8), the trader must without undue delay reimburse all payments made under the contract.

(10) If subsection (6) or (8) applies but the consumer does not treat the contract as at an end—

(a) that does not prevent the consumer from cancelling the order for any of the goods or rejecting goods that have been delivered, and

(b) the trader must without undue delay reimburse all payments made under the contract in respect of any goods for which the consumer cancels the order or which the consumer rejects.

(11) If any of the goods form a commercial unit, the consumer cannot reject or cancel the order for some of those goods without also rejecting or cancelling the order for the rest of them.

(12) A unit is a 'commercial unit' if division of the unit would materially impair the value of the goods or the character of the unit.

(13) This section does not prevent the consumer seeking other remedies where it is open to the consumer to do so.

(14) See section 2(5) and (6) for the application of this section where goods are sold at public auction.

29   Passing of risk

(1) A sales contract is to be treated as including the following provisions as terms.

(2) The goods remain at the trader's risk until they come into the physical possession of—

(a) the consumer, or

(b) a person identified by the consumer to take possession of the goods.

(3) Subsection (2) does not apply if the goods are delivered to a carrier who—

(a) is commissioned by the consumer to deliver the goods, and

(b) is not a carrier the trader named as an option for the consumer.

(4) In that case the goods are at the consumer's risk on and after delivery to the carrier.

(5) Subsection (4) does not affect any liability of the carrier to the consumer in respect of the goods.

(6) See section 2(5) and (6) for the application of this section where goods are sold at public auction.

30   Goods under guarantee

(1) This section applies where—

(a) there is a contract to supply goods, and

(b) there is a guarantee in relation to the goods.

(2) 'Guarantee' here means an undertaking to the consumer given without extra charge by a person acting in the course of the person's business (the 'guarantor') that, if the goods do not meet the specifications set out in the guarantee statement or in any associated advertising—

(a) the consumer will be reimbursed for the price paid for the goods, or

(b) the goods will be repaired, replaced or handled in any way.

(3) The guarantee takes effect, at the time the goods are delivered, as a contractual obligation owed by the guarantor under the conditions set out in the guarantee statement and in any associated advertising.

(4) The guarantor must ensure that—

(a) the guarantee sets out in plain and intelligible language the contents of the guarantee and the essential particulars for making claims under the guarantee,

(b) the guarantee states that the consumer has statutory rights in relation to the goods and that those rights are not affected by the guarantee, and

(c) where the goods are offered within the territory of the United Kingdom, the guarantee is written in English.

(5) The contents of the guarantee to be set out in it include, in particular—

(a) the name and address of the guarantor, and

(b) the duration and territorial scope of the guarantee.

(6) The guarantor and any other person who offers to supply to consumers the goods which are the subject of the guarantee must, on request by the consumer, make the guarantee available to the consumer within a reasonable time, in writing and in a form accessible to the consumer.

(7) What is a reasonable time is a question of fact.

(8) If a person fails to comply with a requirement of this section, the enforcement authority may apply to the court for an injunction . . . against that person requiring that person to comply.

(9) On an application the court may grant an injunction . . . on such terms as it thinks appropriate.

(10) In this section—

'court' means—

(a) in relation to England and Wales, the High Court or the county court, . . .

'enforcement authority' means—

(a) the Competition and Markets Authority,

(b) a local weights and measures authority in Great Britain, . . .

Can a trader contract out of statutory rights and remedies under a goods contract?

31   Liability that cannot be excluded or restricted

(1) A term of a contract to supply goods is not binding on the consumer to the extent that it would exclude or restrict the trader's liability arising under any of these provisions—

(a) section 9 (goods to be of satisfactory quality);

(b) section 10 (goods to be fit for particular purpose);

(c) section 11 (goods to be as described);

(d) section 12 (other pre-contract information included in contract);

(e) section 13 (goods to match a sample);

(f) section 14 (goods to match a model seen or examined);

(g) section 15 (installation as part of conformity of the goods with the contract);

(h) section 16 (goods not conforming to contract if digital content does not conform);

(i) section 17 (trader to have right to supply the goods etc);

(j) section 28 (delivery of goods);

(k) section 29 (passing of risk).

(2) That also means that a term of a contract to supply goods is not binding on the consumer to the extent that it would—

(a) exclude or restrict a right or remedy in respect of a liability under a provision listed in subsection (1),

(b) make such a right or remedy or its enforcement subject to a restrictive or onerous condition,

(c) allow a trader to put a person at a disadvantage as a result of pursuing such a right or remedy, or

(d) exclude or restrict rules of evidence or procedure.

(3) The reference in subsection (1) to excluding or restricting a liability also includes preventing an obligation or duty arising or limiting its extent.

(4) An agreement in writing to submit present or future differences to arbitration is not to be regarded as excluding or restricting any liability for the purposes of this section.

(5) Subsection (1)(i), and subsection (2) so far as it relates to liability under section 17, do not apply to a term of a contract for the hire of goods.

(6) But an express term of a contract for the hire of goods is not binding on the consumer to the extent that it would exclude or restrict a term that section 17 requires to be treated as included in the contract, unless it is inconsistent with that term (and see also section 62 (requirement for terms to be fair)).

(7) See Schedule 3 for provision about the enforcement of this section.

32 [Contracts applying law of a country other than the UK]

(1) If—

(a) the law of a country or territory other than [the United Kingdom or any part of the United Kingdom] is chosen by the parties to be applicable to a sales contract, but

(b) the sales contract has a close connection with the United Kingdom,

this Chapter, except the provisions in subsection (2), applies despite that choice.

(2) The exceptions are—

(a) sections 11(4) and (5) and 12;

(b) sections 28 and 29;

(c) section 31(1)(d), (j) and (k).

(3) For cases where those provisions apply, or where the law applicable has not been chosen [...], see Regulation (EC) No. 593/2008 of the European Parliament and of the Council of 17 June 2008 on the law applicable to contractual obligations [as that Regulation has effect as retained direct EU legislation (including that Regulation as applied by regulation 5 of the Law Applicable to Contractual Obligations (England and Wales and Northern Ireland) Regulations 2009 and regulation 4 of the Law Applicable to Contractual Obligations (Scotland) Regulations 2009), unless the case is one in respect of which Regulation (EC) No. 593/2008 has effect by virtue of Article 66 of the EU withdrawal agreement, in which case see that Regulation as it has effect by virtue of that Article].

Chapter 3 Digital content

What digital content contracts are covered?

33 Contracts covered by this Chapter

(1) This Chapter applies to a contract for a trader to supply digital content to a consumer, if it is supplied or to be supplied for a price paid by the consumer.

(2) This Chapter also applies to a contract for a trader to supply digital content to a consumer, if—

    (a) it is supplied free with goods or services or other digital content for which the consumer pays a price, and

    (b) it is not generally available to consumers unless they have paid a price for it or for goods or services or other digital content.

(3) The references in subsections (1) and (2) to the consumer paying a price include references to the consumer using, by way of payment, any facility for which money has been paid.

(4) A trader does not supply digital content to a consumer for the purposes of this Part merely because the trader supplies a service by which digital content reaches the consumer.

(5) The Secretary of State may by order provide for this Chapter to apply to other contracts for a trader to supply digital content to a consumer, if the Secretary of State is satisfied that it is appropriate to do so because of significant detriment caused to consumers under contracts of the kind to which the order relates.

(6) An order under subsection (5)—

    (a) may, in particular, amend this Act;

    (b) may contain transitional or transitory provision or savings.

(7) A contract to which this Chapter applies is referred to in this Part as a 'contract to supply digital content'.

(8) This section, other than subsection (4), does not limit the application of section 46.

(9) The power to make an order under subsection (5) is exercisable by statutory instrument.

(10) No order may be made under subsection (5) unless a draft of the statutory instrument containing it has been laid before, and approved by a resolution of, each House of Parliament.

What statutory rights are there under a digital content contract?

34   Digital content to be of satisfactory quality

(1) Every contract to supply digital content is to be treated as including a term that the quality of the digital content is satisfactory.

(2) The quality of digital content is satisfactory if it meets the standard that a reasonable person would consider satisfactory, taking account of—

    (a) any description of the digital content,

    (b) the price mentioned in section 33(1) or (2)(b) (if relevant), and

    (c) all the other relevant circumstances (see subsection (5)).

(3) The quality of digital content includes its state and condition; and the following aspects (among others) are in appropriate cases aspects of the quality of digital content—

    (a) fitness for all the purposes for which digital content of that kind is usually supplied;

    (b) freedom from minor defects;

    (c) safety;

    (d) durability.

(4) The term mentioned in subsection (1) does not cover anything which makes the quality of the digital content unsatisfactory—

    (a) which is specifically drawn to the consumer's attention before the contract is made,

    (b) where the consumer examines the digital content before the contract is made, which that examination ought to reveal, or

    (c) where the consumer examines a trial version before the contract is made, which would have been apparent on a reasonable examination of the trial version.

(5) The relevant circumstances mentioned in subsection (2)(c) include any public statement about the specific characteristics of the digital content made by the trader, the producer or any representative of the trader or the producer.

(6) That includes, in particular, any public statement made in advertising or labelling.

(7) But a public statement is not a relevant circumstance for the purposes of subsection (2)(c) if the trader shows that—

    (a) when the contract was made, the trader was not, and could not reasonably have been, aware of the statement,

(b) before the contract was made, the statement had been publicly withdrawn or, to the extent that it contained anything which was incorrect or misleading, it had been publicly corrected, or

(c) the consumer's decision to contract for the digital content could not have been influenced by the statement.

(8) In a contract to supply digital content a term about the quality of the digital content may be treated as included as a matter of custom.

(9) See section 42 for a consumer's rights if the trader is in breach of a term that this section requires to be treated as included in a contract.

35 Digital content to be fit for particular purpose

(1) Subsection (3) applies to a contract to supply digital content if before the contract is made the consumer makes known to the trader (expressly or by implication) any particular purpose for which the consumer is contracting for the digital content.

(2) Subsection (3) also applies to a contract to supply digital content if—

(a) the digital content was previously sold by a credit-broker to the trader,

(b) the consideration or part of it is a sum payable by instalments, and

(c) before the contract is made, the consumer makes known to the credit-broker (expressly or by implication) any particular purpose for which the consumer is contracting for the digital content.

(3) The contract is to be treated as including a term that the digital content is reasonably fit for that purpose, whether or not that is a purpose for which digital content of that kind is usually supplied.

(4) Subsection (3) does not apply if the circumstances show that the consumer does not rely, or it is unreasonable for the consumer to rely, on the skill or judgment of the trader or credit-broker.

(5) A contract to supply digital content may be treated as making provision about the fitness of the digital content for a particular purpose as a matter of custom.

(6) See section 42 for a consumer's rights if the trader is in breach of a term that this section requires to be treated as included in a contract.

36 Digital content to be as described

(1) Every contract to supply digital content is to be treated as including a term that the digital content will match any description of it given by the trader to the consumer.

(2) Where the consumer examines a trial version before the contract is made, it is not sufficient that the digital content matches (or is better than) the trial version if the digital content does not also match any description of it given by the trader to the consumer.

(3) Any information that is provided by the trader about the digital content that is information mentioned in paragraph (a), (j) or (k) of Schedule 1 or paragraph (a), (v) or (w) of Schedule 2 (main characteristics, functionality and compatibility) to the Consumer Contracts (Information, Cancellation and Additional Charges) Regulations 2013 (SI 2013/3134) is to be treated as included as a term of the contract.

(4) A change to any of that information, made before entering into the contract or later, is not effective unless expressly agreed between the consumer and the trader.

(5) See section 42 for a consumer's rights if the trader is in breach of a term that this section requires to be treated as included in a contract.

37 Other pre-contract information included in contract

(1) This section applies to any contract to supply digital content.

(2) Where regulation 9, 10 or 13 of the Consumer Contracts (Information, Cancellation and Additional Charges) Regulations 2013 (SI 2013/3134) required the trader to provide information to the consumer before the contract became binding, any of that information that was provided by the trader other than information about the digital content and mentioned in paragraph (a), (j) or (k) of Schedule 1 or paragraph (a), (v) or (w) of Schedule 2 to the Regulations (main characteristics, functionality and compatibility) is to be treated as included as a term of the contract.

(3) A change to any of that information, made before entering into the contract or later, is not effective unless expressly agreed between the consumer and the trader.

(4) See section 42 for a consumer's rights if the trader is in breach of a term that this section requires to be treated as included in a contract.

38 No other requirement to treat term about quality or fitness as included

(1) Except as provided by sections 34 and 35, a contract to supply digital content is not to be treated as including any term about the quality of the digital content or its fitness for any particular purpose, unless the term is expressly included in the contract.

(2) Subsection (1) is subject to provision made by any other enactment, whenever passed or made.

39 Supply by transmission and facilities for continued transmission

(1) Subsection (2) applies where there is a contract to supply digital content and the consumer's access to the content on a device requires its transmission to the device under arrangements initiated by the trader.

(2) For the purposes of this Chapter, the digital content is supplied—

(a) when the content reaches the device, or

(b) if earlier, when the content reaches another trader chosen by the consumer to supply, under a contract with the consumer, a service by which digital content reaches the device.

(3) Subsections (5) to (7) apply where—

(a) there is a contract to supply digital content, and

(b) after the trader (T) has supplied the digital content, the consumer is to have access under the contract to a processing facility under arrangements made by T.

(4) A processing facility is a facility by which T or another trader will receive digital content from the consumer and transmit digital content to the consumer (whether or not other features are to be included under the contract).

(5) The contract is to be treated as including a term that the processing facility (with any feature that the facility is to include under the contract) must be available to the consumer for a reasonable time, unless a time is specified in the contract.

(6) The following provisions apply to all digital content transmitted to the consumer on each occasion under the facility, while it is provided under the contract, as they apply to the digital content first supplied—

(a) section 34 (quality);

(b) section 35 (fitness for a particular purpose);

(c) section 36 (description).

(7) Breach of a term treated as included under subsection (5) has the same effect as breach of a term treated as included under those sections (see section 42).

40 Quality, fitness and description of content supplied subject to modifications

(1) Where under a contract a trader supplies digital content to a consumer subject to the right of the trader or a third party to modify the digital content, the following provisions apply in relation to the digital content as modified as they apply in relation to the digital content as supplied under the contract—

(a) section 34 (quality);

(b) section 35 (fitness for a particular purpose);

(c) section 36 (description).

(2) Subsection (1)(c) does not prevent the trader from improving the features of, or adding new features to, the digital content, as long as—

(a) the digital content continues to match the description of it given by the trader to the consumer, and

(b) the digital content continues to conform to the information provided by the trader as mentioned in subsection (3) of section 36, subject to any change to that information that has been agreed in accordance with subsection (4) of that section.

(3) A claim on the grounds that digital content does not conform to a term described in any of the sections listed in subsection (1) as applied by that subsection is to be treated as arising at the time when the digital content was supplied under the contract and not the time when it is modified.

41 Trader's right to supply digital content

(1) Every contract to supply digital content is to be treated as including a term—

(a) in relation to any digital content which is supplied under the contract and which the consumer has paid for, that the trader has the right to supply that content to the consumer;

(b) in relation to any digital content which the trader agrees to supply under the contract and which the consumer has paid for, that the trader will have the right to supply it to the consumer at the time when it is to be supplied.

(2) See section 42 for a consumer's rights if the trader is in breach of a term that this section requires to be treated as included in a contract.

What remedies are there if statutory rights under a digital content contract are not met?

42 Consumer's rights to enforce terms about digital content

(1) In this section and section 43 references to digital content conforming to a contract are references to the digital content conforming to the terms described in sections 34, 35 and 36.

(2) If the digital content does not conform to the contract, the consumer's rights (and the provisions about them and when they are available) are—

(a) the right to repair or replacement (see section 43);

(b) the right to a price reduction (see section 44).

(3) Section 16 also applies if an item including the digital content is supplied.

(4) If the trader is in breach of a term that section 37 requires to be treated as included in the contract, the consumer has the right to recover from the trader the amount of any costs incurred by the consumer as a result of the breach, up to the amount of the price paid for the digital content or for any facility within section 33(3) used by the consumer.

(5) If the trader is in breach of the term that section 41(1) (right to supply the content) requires to be treated as included in the contract, the consumer has the right to a refund (see section 45 for provisions about that right and when it is available).

(6) This Chapter does not prevent the consumer seeking other remedies for a breach of a term to which any of subsections (2), (4) or (5) applies, instead of or in addition to a remedy referred to there (but not so as to recover twice for the same loss).

(7) Those other remedies include any of the following that is open to the consumer in the circumstances—

(a) claiming damages;

(b) seeking to recover money paid where the consideration for payment of the money has failed;

(c) seeking specific performance;

(d) seeking an order for specific implement;

(e) relying on the breach against a claim by the trader for the price.

(8) It is not open to the consumer to treat the contract as at an end for breach of a term to which any of subsections (2), (4) or (5) applies.

(9) For the purposes of subsection (2), digital content which does not conform to the contract at any time within the period of six months beginning with the day on which it was supplied must be taken not to have conformed to the contract when it was supplied.

(10) Subsection (9) does not apply if—

(a) it is established that the digital content did conform to the contract when it was supplied, or

(b) its application is incompatible with the nature of the digital content or with how it fails to conform to the contract.

43   Right to repair or replacement

(1) This section applies if the consumer has the right to repair or replacement.

(2) If the consumer requires the trader to repair or replace the digital content, the trader must—

(a) do so within a reasonable time and without significant inconvenience to the consumer; and

(b) bear any necessary costs incurred in doing so (including in particular the cost of any labour, materials or postage).

(3) The consumer cannot require the trader to repair or replace the digital content if that remedy (the repair or the replacement)—

(a) is impossible, or

(b) is disproportionate compared to the other of those remedies.

(4) Either of those remedies is disproportionate compared to the other if it imposes costs on the trader which, compared to those imposed by the other, are unreasonable, taking into account—

(a) the value which the digital content would have if it conformed to the contract,

(b) the significance of the lack of conformity, and

(c) whether the other remedy could be effected without significant inconvenience to the consumer.

(5) Any question as to what is a reasonable time or significant inconvenience is to be determined taking account of—

(a) the nature of the digital content, and

(b) the purpose for which the digital content was obtained or accessed.

(6) A consumer who requires or agrees to the repair of digital content cannot require the trader to replace it without giving the trader a reasonable time to repair it (unless giving the trader that time would cause significant inconvenience to the consumer).

(7) A consumer who requires or agrees to the replacement of digital content cannot require the trader to repair it without giving the trader a reasonable time to replace it (unless giving the trader that time would cause significant inconvenience to the consumer).

(8) In this Chapter, 'repair' in relation to digital content that does not conform to a contract, means making it conform.

44   Right to price reduction

(1) The right to a price reduction is the right to require the trader to reduce the price to the consumer by an appropriate amount (including the right to receive a refund for anything already paid above the reduced amount).

(2) The amount of the reduction may, where appropriate, be the full amount of the price.

(3) A consumer who has that right may only exercise it in one of these situations—

(a) because of section 43(3)(a) the consumer can require neither repair nor replacement of the digital content, or

(b) the consumer has required the trader to repair or replace the digital content, but the trader is in breach of the requirement of section 43(2)(a) to do so within a reasonable time and without significant inconvenience to the consumer.

(4) A refund under this section must be given without undue delay, and in any event within 14 days beginning with the day on which the trader agrees that the consumer is entitled to a refund.

(5) The trader must give the refund using the same means of payment as the consumer used to pay for the digital content, unless the consumer expressly agrees otherwise.

(6) The trader must not impose any fee on the consumer in respect of the refund.

45   Right to a refund

(1) The right to a refund gives the consumer the right to receive a refund from the trader of all money paid by the consumer for the digital content (subject to subsection (2)).

(2) If the breach giving the consumer the right to a refund affects only some of the digital content supplied under the contract, the right to a refund does not extend to any part of the price attributable to digital content that is not affected by the breach.

(3) A refund must be given without undue delay, and in any event within 14 days beginning with the day on which the trader agrees that the consumer is entitled to a refund.

(4) The trader must give the refund using the same means of payment as the consumer used to pay for the digital content, unless the consumer expressly agrees otherwise.

(5) The trader must not impose any fee on the consumer in respect of the refund.

Compensation for damage to device or to other digital content

46 Remedy for damage to device or to other digital content

(1) This section applies if—

(a) a trader supplies digital content to a consumer under a contract,

(b) the digital content causes damage to a device or to other digital content,

(c) the device or digital content that is damaged belongs to the consumer, and

(d) the damage is of a kind that would not have occurred if the trader had exercised reasonable care and skill.

(2) If the consumer requires the trader to provide a remedy under this section, the trader must either—

(a) repair the damage in accordance with subsection (3), or

(b) compensate the consumer for the damage with an appropriate payment.

(3) To repair the damage in accordance with this subsection, the trader must—

(a) repair the damage within a reasonable time and without significant inconvenience to the consumer, and

(b) bear any necessary costs incurred in repairing the damage (including in particular the cost of any labour, materials or postage).

(4) Any question as to what is a reasonable time or significant inconvenience is to be determined taking account of—

(a) the nature of the device or digital content that is damaged, and

(b) the purpose for which it is used by the consumer.

(5) A compensation payment under this section must be made without undue delay, and in any event within 14 days beginning with the day on which the trader agrees that the consumer is entitled to the payment.

(6) The trader must not impose any fee on the consumer in respect of the payment.

(7) A consumer with a right to a remedy under this section may bring a claim in civil proceedings to enforce that right.

(8) The Limitation Act 1980 and the Limitation (Northern Ireland) Order 1989 (SI 1989/1339 (NI 11)) apply to a claim under this section as if it were an action founded on simple contract.

Can a trader contract out of statutory rights and remedies
under a digital content contract?

47 Liability that cannot be excluded or restricted

(1) A term of a contract to supply digital content is not binding on the consumer to the extent that it would exclude or restrict the trader's liability arising under any of these provisions—

(a) section 34 (digital content to be of satisfactory quality),

(b) section 35 (digital content to be fit for particular purpose),

(c) section 36 (digital content to be as described),

(d) section 37 (other pre-contract information included in contract), or

(e) section 41 (trader's right to supply digital content).

(2) That also means that a term of a contract to supply digital content is not binding on the consumer to the extent that it would—

(a) exclude or restrict a right or remedy in respect of a liability under a provision listed in subsection (1),

(b) make such a right or remedy or its enforcement subject to a restrictive or onerous condition,

(c) allow a trader to put a person at a disadvantage as a result of pursuing such a right or remedy, or

(d) exclude or restrict rules of evidence or procedure.

(3) The reference in subsection (1) to excluding or restricting a liability also includes preventing an obligation or duty arising or limiting its extent.

(4) An agreement in writing to submit present or future differences to arbitration is not to be regarded as excluding or restricting any liability for the purposes of this section.

(5) See Schedule 3 for provision about the enforcement of this section.

(6) For provision limiting the ability of a trader under a contract within section 46 to exclude or restrict the trader's liability under that section, see section 62.

Chapter 4   Services

What services contracts are covered?

48   Contracts covered by this Chapter

(1) This Chapter applies to a contract for a trader to supply a service to a consumer.

(2) That does not include a contract of employment or apprenticeship.

[(3A) This Chapter does not apply to anything that is governed by Regulation (EU) No 181/2011 of the European Parliament and of the Council of 16 February 2011 concerning the rights of passengers in bus and coach transport and amending Regulation (EC) No 2006/2004.]

(4) A contract to which this Chapter applies is referred to in this Part as a 'contract to supply a service'.

(5) The Secretary of State may by order made by statutory instrument provide that a provision of this Chapter does not apply in relation to a service of a description specified in the order.

(6) The power in subsection (5) includes power to provide that a provision of this Chapter does not apply in relation to a service of a description specified in the order in the circumstances so specified.

(7) An order under subsection (5) may contain transitional or transitory provision or savings.

(8) No order may be made under subsection (5) unless a draft of the statutory instrument containing it has been laid before, and approved by a resolution of, each House of Parliament.

What statutory rights are there under a services contract?

49   Service to be performed with reasonable care and skill

(1) Every contract to supply a service is to be treated as including a term that the trader must perform the service with reasonable care and skill.

(2) See section 54 for a consumer's rights if the trader is in breach of a term that this section requires to be treated as included in a contract.

50   Information about the trader or service to be binding

(1) Every contract to supply a service is to be treated as including as a term of the contract anything that is said or written to the consumer, by or on behalf of the trader, about the trader or the service, if—

(a) it is taken into account by the consumer when deciding to enter into the contract, or

(b) it is taken into account by the consumer when making any decision about the service after entering into the contract.

(2) Anything taken into account by the consumer as mentioned in subsection (1)(a) or (b) is subject to—

(a) anything that qualified it and was said or written to the consumer by the trader on the same occasion, and

(b) any change to it that has been expressly agreed between the consumer and the trader (before entering into the contract or later).

(3) Without prejudice to subsection (1), any information provided by the trader in accordance with regulation 9, 10 or 13 of the Consumer Contracts (Information, Cancellation and Additional Charges) Regulations 2013 (SI 2013/3134) is to be treated as included as a term of the contract.

(4) A change to any of the information mentioned in subsection (3), made before entering into the contract or later, is not effective unless expressly agreed between the consumer and the trader.

(5) See section 54 for a consumer's rights if the trader is in breach of a term that this section requires to be treated as included in a contract.

51 Reasonable price to be paid for a service

(1) This section applies to a contract to supply a service if—

    (a) the consumer has not paid a price or other consideration for the service,

    (b) the contract does not expressly fix a price or other consideration, and does not say how it is to be fixed, and

    (c) anything that is to be treated under section 50 as included in the contract does not fix a price or other consideration either.

(2) In that case the contract is to be treated as including a term that the consumer must pay a reasonable price for the service, and no more.

(3) What is a reasonable price is a question of fact.

52 Service to be performed within a reasonable time

(1) This section applies to a contract to supply a service, if—

    (a) the contract does not expressly fix the time for the service to be performed, and does not say how it is to be fixed, and

    (b) information that is to be treated under section 50 as included in the contract does not fix the time either.

(2) In that case the contract is to be treated as including a term that the trader must perform the service within a reasonable time.

(3) What is a reasonable time is a question of fact.

(4) See section 54 for a consumer's rights if the trader is in breach of a term that this section requires to be treated as included in a contract.

53 Relation to other law on contract terms

(1) Nothing in this Chapter affects any enactment or rule of law that imposes a stricter duty on the trader.

(2) This Chapter is subject to any other enactment which defines or restricts the rights, duties or liabilities arising in connection with a service of any description.

What remedies are there if statutory rights under a services contract are not met?

54 Consumer's rights to enforce terms about services

(1) The consumer's rights under this section and sections 55 and 56 do not affect any rights that the contract provides for, if those are not inconsistent.

(2) In this section and section 55 a reference to a service conforming to a contract is a reference to—

    (a) the service being performed in accordance with section 49, or

    (b) the service conforming to a term that section 50 requires to be treated as included in the contract and that relates to the performance of the service.

(3) If the service does not conform to the contract, the consumer's rights (and the provisions about them and when they are available) are—

    (a) the right to require repeat performance (see section 55);

    (b) the right to a price reduction (see section 56).

(4) If the trader is in breach of a term that section 50 requires to be treated as included in the contract but that does not relate to the service, the consumer has the right to a price reduction (see section 56 for provisions about that right and when it is available).

(5) If the trader is in breach of what the contract requires under section 52 (performance within a reasonable time), the consumer has the right to a price reduction (see section 56 for provisions about that right and when it is available).

(6) This section and sections 55 and 56 do not prevent the consumer seeking other remedies for a breach of a term to which any of subsections (3) to (5) applies, instead of or in addition to a remedy referred to there (but not so as to recover twice for the same loss).

(7) Those other remedies include any of the following that is open to the consumer in the circumstances—

  (a) claiming damages;
  (b) seeking to recover money paid where the consideration for payment of the money has failed;
  (c) seeking specific performance;
  (d) seeking an order for specific implement;
  (e) relying on the breach against a claim by the trader under the contract;
  (f) exercising a right to treat the contract as at an end.

55 Right to repeat performance

(1) The right to require repeat performance is a right to require the trader to perform the service again, to the extent necessary to complete its performance in conformity with the contract.

(2) If the consumer requires such repeat performance, the trader—

  (a) must provide it within a reasonable time and without significant inconvenience to the consumer; and
  (b) must bear any necessary costs incurred in doing so (including in particular the cost of any labour or materials).

(3) The consumer cannot require repeat performance if completing performance of the service in conformity with the contract is impossible.

(4) Any question as to what is a reasonable time or significant inconvenience is to be determined taking account of—

  (a) the nature of the service, and
  (b) the purpose for which the service was to be performed.

56 Right to price reduction

(1) The right to a price reduction is the right to require the trader to reduce the price to the consumer by an appropriate amount (including the right to receive a refund for anything already paid above the reduced amount).

(2) The amount of the reduction may, where appropriate, be the full amount of the price.

(3) A consumer who has that right and the right to require repeat performance is only entitled to a price reduction in one of these situations—

  (a) because of section 55(3) the consumer cannot require repeat performance; or
  (b) the consumer has required repeat performance, but the trader is in breach of the requirement of section 55(2)(a) to do it within a reasonable time and without significant inconvenience to the consumer.

(4) A refund under this section must be given without undue delay, and in any event within 14 days beginning with the day on which the trader agrees that the consumer is entitled to a refund.

(5) The trader must give the refund using the same means of payment as the consumer used to pay for the service, unless the consumer expressly agrees otherwise.

(6) The trader must not impose any fee on the consumer in respect of the refund.

Can a trader contract out of statutory rights and remedies
under a services contract?

57 Liability that cannot be excluded or restricted

(1) A term of a contract to supply services is not binding on the consumer to the extent that it would exclude the trader's liability arising under section 49 (service to be performed with reasonable care and skill).

(2) Subject to section 50(2), a term of a contract to supply services is not binding on the consumer to the extent that it would exclude the trader's liability arising under section 50 (information about trader or service to be binding).

(3) A term of a contract to supply services is not binding on the consumer to the extent that it would restrict the trader's liability arising under any of sections 49 and 50 and, where they apply, sections 51 and 52 (reasonable price and reasonable time), if it would prevent the consumer in an appropriate case from recovering the price paid or the value of any other consideration. (If it would not prevent the consumer from doing so, Part 2 (unfair terms) may apply.)

(4) That also means that a term of a contract to supply services is not binding on the consumer to the extent that it would —

    (a) exclude or restrict a right or remedy in respect of a liability under any of sections 49 to 52,

    (b) make such a right or remedy or its enforcement subject to a restrictive or onerous condition,

    (c) allow a trader to put a person at a disadvantage as a result of pursuing such a right or remedy, or

    (d) exclude or restrict rules of evidence or procedure.

(5) The references in subsections (1) to (3) to excluding or restricting a liability also include preventing an obligation or duty arising or limiting its extent.

(6) An agreement in writing to submit present or future differences to arbitration is not to be regarded as excluding or restricting any liability for the purposes of this section.

(7) See Schedule 3 for provision about the enforcement of this section.

Chapter 5 General and supplementary provisions

58 Powers of the court

(1) In any proceedings in which a remedy is sought by virtue of section 19(3) or (4), 42(2) or 54(3), the court, in addition to any other power it has, may act under this section.

(2) On the application of the consumer the court may make an order requiring specific performance . . . by the trader of any obligation imposed on the trader by virtue of section 23, 43 or 55.

(3) Subsection (4) applies if—

    (a) the consumer claims to exercise a right under the relevant remedies provisions, but

    (b) the court decides that those provisions have the effect that exercise of another right is appropriate.

(4) The court may proceed as if the consumer had exercised that other right.

(5) If the consumer has claimed to exercise the final right to reject, the court may order that any reimbursement to the consumer is reduced by a deduction for use, to take account of the use the consumer has had of the goods in the period since they were delivered.

(6) Any deduction for use is limited as set out in section 24(9) and (10).

(7) The court may make an order under this section unconditionally or on such terms and conditions as to damages, payment of the price and otherwise as it thinks just.

(8) The 'relevant remedies provisions' are—

    (a) where Chapter 2 applies, sections 23 and 24;

    (b) where Chapter 3 applies, sections 43 and 44;

    (c) where Chapter 4 applies, sections 55 and 56.

59 Interpretation

(1) These definitions apply in this Part (as well as the key definitions in section 2)—

'conditional sales contract' has the meaning given in section 5(3);

'Consumer Rights Directive' means Directive 2011/83/EU of the European Parliament and of the Council of 25 October 2011 on consumer rights, amending Council Directive 93/13/EEC and Directive 1999/44/EC of the European Parliament and of the Council and repealing Council Directive 85/577/EEC and Directive 97/7/EC of the European Parliament and of the Council;

'credit-broker' means a person acting in the course of a business of credit brokerage carried on by that person;

'credit brokerage' means—

    (a) introducing individuals who want to obtain credit to persons carrying on any business so far as it relates to the provision of credit,

    (b) introducing individuals who want to obtain goods on hire to persons carrying on a business which comprises or relates to supplying goods under a contract for the hire of goods, or

    (c) introducing individuals who want to obtain credit, or to obtain goods on hire, to other persons engaged in credit brokerage;

'delivery' means voluntary transfer of possession from one person to another;

'enactment' includes—

    (a) an enactment contained in subordinate legislation within the meaning of the Interpretation Act 1978 . . .;

'producer', in relation to goods or digital content, means—

    (a) the manufacturer,

    (b) the importer into the [United Kingdom], or

    (c) any person who purports to be a producer by placing the person's name, trade mark or other distinctive sign on the goods or using it in connection with the digital content.

(2) References in this Part to treating a contract as at an end are to be read in accordance with section 19(13).

PART 2   UNFAIR TERMS

What contracts and notices are covered by this Part?

61   Contracts and notices covered by this Part

(1) This Part applies to a contract between a trader and a consumer.

(2) This does not include a contract of employment or apprenticeship.

(3) A contract to which this Part applies is referred to in this Part as a 'consumer contract'.

(4) This Part applies to a notice to the extent that it—

    (a) relates to rights or obligations as between a trader and a consumer, or

    (b) purports to exclude or restrict a trader's liability to a consumer.

(5) This does not include a notice relating to rights, obligations or liabilities as between an employer and an employee.

(6) It does not matter for the purposes of subsection (4) whether the notice is expressed to apply to a consumer, as long as it is reasonable to assume it is intended to be seen or heard by a consumer.

(7) A notice to which this Part applies is referred to in this Part as a 'consumer notice'.

(8) In this section 'notice' includes an announcement, whether or not in writing, and any other communication or purported communication.

What are the general rules about fairness of contract terms and notices?

62   Requirement for contract terms and notices to be fair

(1) An unfair term of a consumer contract is not binding on the consumer.

(2) An unfair consumer notice is not binding on the consumer.

(3) This does not prevent the consumer from relying on the term or notice if the consumer chooses to do so.

(4) A term is unfair if, contrary to the requirement of good faith, it causes a significant imbalance in the parties' rights and obligations under the contract to the detriment of the consumer.

(5) Whether a term is fair is to be determined—

    (a) taking into account the nature of the subject matter of the contract, and

    (b) by reference to all the circumstances existing when the term was agreed and to all of the other terms of the contract or of any other contract on which it depends.

(6) A notice is unfair if, contrary to the requirement of good faith, it causes a significant imbalance in the parties' rights and obligations to the detriment of the consumer.

(7) Whether a notice is fair is to be determined—

(a) taking into account the nature of the subject matter of the notice, and

(b) by reference to all the circumstances existing when the rights or obligations to which it relates arose and to the terms of any contract on which it depends.

(8) This section does not affect the operation of—

(a) section 31 (exclusion of liability: goods contracts),

(b) section 47 (exclusion of liability: digital content contracts),

(c) section 57 (exclusion of liability: services contracts), or

(d) section 65 (exclusion of negligence liability).

63 Contract terms which may or must be regarded as unfair

(1) Part 1 of Schedule 2 contains an indicative and non-exhaustive list of terms of consumer contracts that may be regarded as unfair for the purposes of this Part.

(2) Part 1 of Schedule 2 is subject to Part 2 of that Schedule; but a term listed in Part 2 of that Schedule may nevertheless be assessed for fairness under section 62 unless section 64 or 73 applies to it.

(3) The Secretary of State may by order made by statutory instrument amend Schedule 2 so as to add, modify or remove an entry in Part 1 or Part 2 of that Schedule.

(4) An order under subsection (3) may contain transitional or transitory provision or savings.

(5) No order may be made under subsection (3) unless a draft of the statutory instrument containing it has been laid before, and approved by a resolution of, each House of Parliament.

(6) A term of a consumer contract must be regarded as unfair if it has the effect that the consumer bears the burden of proof with respect to compliance by a distance supplier or an intermediary with an obligation under any enactment or rule implementing the Distance Marketing Directive.

(7) In subsection (6)—

'the Distance Marketing Directive' means Directive 2002/65/EC of the European Parliament and of the Council of 23 September 2002 concerning the distance marketing of consumer financial services and amending Council Directive 90/619/EEC and Directives 97/7/EC and 98/27/EC;

'distance supplier' means—

(a) a supplier under a distance contract within the meaning of the Financial Services (Distance Marketing) Regulations 2004 (SI 2004/2095), or

(b) a supplier of unsolicited financial services within the meaning of regulation 15 of those regulations;

'enactment' includes an enactment contained in subordinate legislation within the meaning of the Interpretation Act 1978;

'intermediary' has the same meaning as in the Financial Services (Distance Marketing) Regulations 2004;

'rule' means a rule made by the Financial Conduct Authority or the Prudential Regulation Authority under the Financial Services and Markets Act 2000 or by a designated professional body within the meaning of section 326(2) of that Act.

64 Exclusion from assessment of fairness

(1) A term of a consumer contract may not be assessed for fairness under section 62 to the extent that—

(a) it specifies the main subject matter of the contract, or

(b) the assessment is of the appropriateness of the price payable under the contract by comparison with the goods, digital content or services supplied under it.

(2) Subsection (1) excludes a term from an assessment under section 62 only if it is transparent and prominent.

(3) A term is transparent for the purposes of this Part if it is expressed in plain and intelligible language and (in the case of a written term) is legible.

(4) A term is prominent for the purposes of this section if it is brought to the consumer's attention in such a way that an average consumer would be aware of the term.

(5) In subsection (4) 'average consumer' means a consumer who is reasonably well-informed, observant and circumspect.

(6) This section does not apply to a term of a contract listed in Part 1 of Schedule 2.

65   Bar on exclusion or restriction of negligence liability

(1) A trader cannot by a term of a consumer contract or by a consumer notice exclude or restrict liability for death or personal injury resulting from negligence.

(2) Where a term of a consumer contract, or a consumer notice, purports to exclude or restrict a trader's liability for negligence, a person is not to be taken to have voluntarily accepted any risk merely because the person agreed to or knew about the term or notice.

(3) In this section 'personal injury' includes any disease and any impairment of physical or mental condition.

(4) In this section 'negligence' means the breach of—
  (a) any obligation to take reasonable care or exercise reasonable skill in the performance of a contract where the obligation arises from an express or implied term of the contract,
  (b) a common law duty to take reasonable care or exercise reasonable skill,
  (c) the common duty of care imposed by the Occupiers' Liability Act 1957 or the Occupiers' Liability Act (Northern Ireland) 1957 . . .

(5) It is immaterial for the purposes of subsection (4)—
  (a) whether a breach of duty or obligation was inadvertent or intentional, or
  (b) whether liability for it arises directly or vicariously.

(6) This section is subject to section 66 (which makes provision about the scope of this section).

66   Scope of section 65

(1) Section 65 does not apply to—
  (a) any contract so far as it is a contract of insurance, including a contract to pay an annuity on human life, or
  (b) any contract so far as it relates to the creation or transfer of an interest in land.

(2) Section 65 does not affect the validity of any discharge or indemnity given by a person in consideration of the receipt by that person of compensation in settlement of any claim the person has.

(4) Section 65 does not apply to the liability of an occupier of premises to a person who obtains access to the premises for recreational purposes if—
  (a) the person suffers loss or damage because of the dangerous state of the premises, and
  (b) allowing the person access for those purposes is not within the purposes of the occupier's trade, business, craft or profession.

67   Effect of an unfair term on the rest of a contract

Where a term of a consumer contract is not binding on the consumer as a result of this Part, the contract continues, so far as practicable, to have effect in every other respect.

68   Requirement for transparency

(1) A trader must ensure that a written term of a consumer contract, or a consumer notice in writing, is transparent.

(2) A consumer notice is transparent for the purposes of subsection (1) if it is expressed in plain and intelligible language and it is legible.

69   Contract terms that may have different meanings

(1) If a term in a consumer contract, or a consumer notice, could have different meanings, the meaning that is most favourable to the consumer is to prevail.

(2) Subsection (1) does not apply to the construction of a term or a notice in proceedings on an application for an injunction or interdict under paragraph 3 of Schedule 3.

How are the general rules enforced?

70   Enforcement of the law on unfair contract terms

(1) Schedule 3 confers functions on the Competition and Markets Authority and other regulators in relation to the enforcement of this Part.

(2) For provision about the investigatory powers that are available to those regulators for the purposes of that Schedule, see Schedule 5.

Supplementary provisions

71   Duty of court to consider fairness of term

(1) Subsection (2) applies to proceedings before a court which relate to a term of a consumer contract.

(2) The court must consider whether the term is fair even if none of the parties to the proceedings has raised that issue or indicated that it intends to raise it.

(3) But subsection (2) does not apply unless the court considers that it has before it sufficient legal and factual material to enable it to consider the fairness of the term.

72   Application of rules to secondary contracts

(1) This section applies if a term of a contract ('the secondary contract') reduces the rights or remedies or increases the obligations of a person under another contract ('the main contract').

(2) The term is subject to the provisions of this Part that would apply to the term if it were in the main contract.

(3) It does not matter for the purposes of this section—
  (a) whether the parties to the secondary contract are the same as the parties to the main contract, or
  (b) whether the secondary contract is a consumer contract.

(4) This section does not apply if the secondary contract is a settlement of a claim arising under the main contract.

73   Disapplication of rules to mandatory terms and notices

(1) This Part does not apply to a term of a contract, or to a notice, to the extent that it reflects—
  (a) mandatory statutory or regulatory provisions, or
  (b) the provisions or principles of an international convention to which the United Kingdom [...] is a party.

(2) In subsection (1) 'mandatory statutory or regulatory provisions' includes rules which, according to law, apply between the parties on the basis that no other arrangements have been established.

74   [Contracts applying law of a country other than the UK]

(1) If—
  (a) the law of a country or territory other than [the United Kingdom or any part of the United Kingdom] is chosen by the parties to be applicable to a consumer contract, but
  (b) the consumer contract has a close connection with the United Kingdom,
this Part applies despite that choice.

(2) For cases where the law applicable has not been chosen [...], see Regulation (EC) No. 593/2008 of the European Parliament and of the Council of 17 June 2008 on the law applicable to contractual obligations [as that Regulation has effect as retained direct EU legislation (including that Regulation as applied by regulation 5 of the Law Applicable to Contractual Obligations (England and Wales and Northern Ireland) Regulations 2009 and regulation 4 of the Law Applicable to Contractual Obligations (Scotland) Regulations 2009), unless the case is one in respect of which Regulation (EC) No. 593/2008 has effect by virtue of Article 66 of the EU withdrawal agreement, in which case see that Regulation as it has effect by virtue of that Article].

76   Interpretation of Part 2

(1) In this Part—
'consumer contract' has the meaning given by section 61(3);
'consumer notice' has the meaning given by section 61(7);

'transparent' is to be construed in accordance with sections 64(3) and 68(2).

(2) The following have the same meanings in this Part as they have in Part 1—

'trader' (see section 2(2));

'consumer' (see section 2(3));

'goods' (see section 2(8));

'digital content' (see section 2(9)).

(3) Section 2(4) (trader who claims an individual is not a consumer must prove it) applies in relation to this Part as it applies in relation to Part 1.

PART 3   MISCELLANEOUS AND GENERAL

Chapter 1   Enforcement etc.

77   Investigatory powers etc

(1) Schedule 5 (investigatory powers etc) has effect.

(2) Schedule 6 (investigatory powers: consequential amendments) has effect.

81   Private actions in competition law

Schedule 8 (private actions in competition law) has effect.

Chapter 3 [ss 83–88]   Duty of letting agents to publicise fees etc

. . .

Chapter 5 [ss 90–95]   Secondary ticketing

. . .

Chapter 6   General

96   Power to make consequential provision

(1) The Secretary of State may by order made by statutory instrument make provision in consequence of this Act.

(2) The power conferred by subsection (1) includes power—

(a) to amend, repeal, revoke or otherwise modify any provision made by an enactment or an instrument made under an enactment (including an enactment passed or instrument made in the same Session as this Act);

(b) to make transitional, transitory or saving provision.

(3) A statutory instrument containing (whether alone or with other provision) an order under this section which amends, repeals, revokes or otherwise modifies any provision of primary legislation is not to be made unless a draft of the instrument has been laid before, and approved by a resolution of, each House of Parliament.

(4) A statutory instrument containing an order under this section which does not amend, repeal, revoke or otherwise modify any provision of primary legislation is subject to annulment in pursuance of a resolution of either House of Parliament.

(5) In this section—

'enactment' includes an Act of the Scottish Parliament, a Measure or Act of the National Assembly for Wales and Northern Ireland legislation;

'primary legislation' means—

(a) an Act of Parliament, . . .

97   Power to make transitional, transitory and saving provision

(1) The Secretary of State may by order made by statutory instrument make transitional, transitory or saving provision in connection with the coming into force of any provision of this Act other than the coming into force of Chapter 3 or 4 of this Part in relation to Wales.

99   Extent

(1) The amendment, repeal or revocation of any provision by this Act has the same extent as the provision concerned.

Section 63

SCHEDULE 2

CONSUMER CONTRACT TERMS WHICH MAY BE REGARDED AS UNFAIR

PART 1   LIST OF TERMS

1. A term which has the object or effect of excluding or limiting the trader's liability in the event of the death of or personal injury to the consumer resulting from an act or omission of the trader.

2. A term which has the object or effect of inappropriately excluding or limiting the legal rights of the consumer in relation to the trader or another party in the event of total or partial non-performance or inadequate performance by the trader of any of the contractual obligations, including the option of offsetting a debt owed to the trader against any claim which the consumer may have against the trader.

3. A term which has the object or effect of making an agreement binding on the consumer in a case where the provision of services by the trader is subject to a condition whose realisation depends on the trader's will alone.

4. A term which has the object or effect of permitting the trader to retain sums paid by the consumer where the consumer decides not to conclude or perform the contract, without providing for the consumer to receive compensation of an equivalent amount from the trader where the trader is the party cancelling the contract.

5. A term which has the object or effect of requiring that, where the consumer decides not to conclude or perform the contract, the consumer must pay the trader a disproportionately high sum in compensation or for services which have not been supplied.

6. A term which has the object or effect of requiring a consumer who fails to fulfil his obligations under the contract to pay a disproportionately high sum in compensation.

7. A term which has the object or effect of authorising the trader to dissolve the contract on a discretionary basis where the same facility is not granted to the consumer, or permitting the trader to retain the sums paid for services not yet supplied by the trader where it is the trader who dissolves the contract.

8. A term which has the object or effect of enabling the trader to terminate a contract of indeterminate duration without reasonable notice except where there are serious grounds for doing so.

9. A term which has the object or effect of automatically extending a contract of fixed duration where the consumer does not indicate otherwise, when the deadline fixed for the consumer to express a desire not to extend the contract is unreasonably early.

10. A term which has the object or effect of irrevocably binding the consumer to terms with which the consumer has had no real opportunity of becoming acquainted before the conclusion of the contract.

11. A term which has the object or effect of enabling the trader to alter the terms of the contract unilaterally without a valid reason which is specified in the contract.

12. A term which has the object or effect of permitting the trader to determine the characteristics of the subject matter of the contract after the consumer has become bound by it.

13. A term which has the object or effect of enabling the trader to alter unilaterally without a valid reason any characteristics of the goods, digital content or services to be provided.

14. A term which has the object or effect of giving the trader the discretion to decide the price payable under the contract after the consumer has become bound by it, where no price or method of determining the price is agreed when the consumer becomes bound.

15. A term which has the object or effect of permitting a trader to increase the price of goods, digital content or services without giving the consumer the right to cancel the contract if the final price is too high in relation to the price agreed when the contract was concluded.

16. A term which has the object or effect of giving the trader the right to determine whether the goods, digital content or services supplied are in conformity with the contract, or giving the trader the exclusive right to interpret any term of the contract.

17. A term which has the object or effect of limiting the trader's obligation to respect commitments undertaken by the trader's agents or making the trader's commitments subject to compliance with a particular formality.

18. A term which has the object or effect of obliging the consumer to fulfil all of the consumer's obligations where the trader does not perform the trader's obligations.

19. A term which has the object or effect of allowing the trader to transfer the trader's rights and obligations under the contract, where this may reduce the guarantees for the consumer, without the consumer's agreement.

20. A term which has the object or effect of excluding or hindering the consumer's right to take legal action or exercise any other legal remedy, in particular by—

(a) requiring the consumer to take disputes exclusively to arbitration not covered by legal provisions,

(b) unduly restricting the evidence available to the consumer, or

(c) imposing on the consumer a burden of proof which, according to the applicable law, should lie with another party to the contract.

PART 2   SCOPE OF PART 1

Financial services

21. Paragraph 8 (cancellation without reasonable notice) does not include a term by which a supplier of financial services reserves the right to terminate unilaterally a contract of indeterminate duration without notice where there is a valid reason, if the supplier is required to inform the consumer of the cancellation immediately.

22. Paragraph 11 (variation of contract without valid reason) does not include a term by which a supplier of financial services reserves the right to alter the rate of interest payable by or due to the consumer, or the amount of other charges for financial services without notice where there is a valid reason, if—

(a) the supplier is required to inform the consumer of the alteration at the earliest opportunity, and

(b) the consumer is free to dissolve the contract immediately.

23.   Contracts which last indefinitely

Paragraphs 11 (variation of contract without valid reason), 12 (determination of characteristics of goods etc after consumer bound) and 14 (determination of price after consumer bound) do not include a term under which a trader reserves the right to alter unilaterally the conditions of a contract of indeterminate duration if—

(a) the trader is required to inform the consumer with reasonable notice, and

(b) the consumer is free to dissolve the contract.

24.   Sale of securities, foreign currency etc

Paragraphs 8 (cancellation without reasonable notice), 11 (variation of contract without valid reason), 14 (determination of price after consumer bound) and 15 (increase in price) do not apply to—

(a) transactions in transferable securities, financial instruments and other products or services where the price is linked to fluctuations in a stock exchange quotation or index or a financial market rate that the trader does not control, and

(b) contracts for the purchase or sale of foreign currency, traveller's cheques or international money orders denominated in foreign currency.

25.   Price index clauses

Paragraphs 14 (determination of price after consumer bound) and 15 (increase in price) do not include a term which is a price-indexation clause (where otherwise lawful), if the method by which prices vary is explicitly described.

Section 70

SCHEDULE 3

ENFORCEMENT OF THE LAW ON UNFAIR CONTRACT TERMS AND NOTICES

1. Application of Schedule

This Schedule applies to—

    (a) a term of a consumer contract,

    (b) a term proposed for use in a consumer contract,

    (c) a term which a third party recommends for use in a consumer contract, or

    (d) a consumer notice.

2. Consideration of complaints

(1) A regulator may consider a complaint about a term or notice to which this Schedule applies (a 'relevant complaint').

(2) If a regulator other than the CMA intends to consider a relevant complaint, it must notify the CMA that it intends to do so, and must then consider the complaint.

(3) If a regulator considers a relevant complaint, but decides not to make an application under paragraph 3 in relation to the complaint, it must give reasons for its decision to the person who made the complaint.

3. Application for injunction or interdict

(1) A regulator may apply for an injunction or (in Scotland) an interdict against a person if the regulator thinks that—

    (a) the person is using, or proposing or recommending the use of, a term or notice to which this Schedule applies, and

    (b) the term or notice falls within any one or more of sub-paragraphs (2), (3) or (5).

(2) A term or notice falls within this sub-paragraph if it purports to exclude or restrict liability of the kind mentioned in—

    (a) section 31 (exclusion of liability: goods contracts),

    (b) section 47 (exclusion of liability: digital content contracts),

    (c) section 57 (exclusion of liability: services contracts), or

    (d) section 65(1) (business liability for death or personal injury resulting from negligence).

(3) A term or notice falls within this sub-paragraph if it is unfair to any extent.

(4) A term within paragraph 1(1)(b) or (c) (but not within paragraph 1(1)(a)) is to be treated for the purposes of section 62(4) and (5) (assessment of fairness) as if it were a term of a contract.

(5) A term or notice falls within this sub-paragraph if it breaches section 68 (requirement for transparency).

(6) A regulator may apply for an injunction or interdict under this paragraph in relation to a term or notice whether or not it has received a relevant complaint about the term or notice.

4. Notification of application

(1) Before making an application under paragraph 3, a regulator other than the CMA must notify the CMA that it intends to do so.

(2) The regulator may make the application only if—

    (a) the period of 14 days beginning with the day on which the regulator notified the CMA has ended, or

    (b) before the end of that period, the CMA agrees to the regulator making the application.

5. Determination of application

(1) On an application for an injunction under paragraph 3, the court may grant an injunction on such conditions, and against such of the respondents, as it thinks appropriate.

(2) On an application for an interdict under paragraph 3, the court may grant an interdict on such conditions, and against such of the defenders, as it thinks appropriate.

(3) The injunction or interdict may include provision about—

    (a) a term or notice to which the application relates, or

    (b) any term of a consumer contract, or any consumer notice, of a similar kind or with a similar effect.

(4) It is not a defence to an application under paragraph 3 to show that, because of a rule of law, a term to which the application relates is not, or could not be, an enforceable contract term.

(5) If a regulator other than the CMA makes the application, it must notify the CMA of—

    (a) the outcome of the application, and

    (b) if an injunction or interdict is granted, the conditions on which, and the persons against whom, it is granted.

6.   Undertakings

(1) A regulator may accept an undertaking from a person against whom it has applied, or thinks it is entitled to apply, for an injunction or interdict under paragraph 3.

(2) The undertaking may provide that the person will comply with the conditions that are agreed between the person and the regulator about the use of terms or notices, or terms or notices of a kind, specified in the undertaking.

(3) If a regulator other than the CMA accepts an undertaking, it must notify the CMA of—

    (a) the conditions on which the undertaking is accepted, and

    (b) the person who gave it.

7.   Publication, information and advice

(1) The CMA must arrange the publication of details of—

    (a) any application it makes for an injunction or interdict under paragraph 3,

    (b) any injunction or interdict under this Schedule, and

    (c) any undertaking under this Schedule.

(2) The CMA must respond to a request whether a term or notice, or one of a similar kind or with a similar effect, is or has been the subject of an injunction, interdict or undertaking under this Schedule.

(3) Where the term or notice, or one of a similar kind or with a similar effect, is or has been the subject of an injunction or interdict under this Schedule, the CMA must give the person making the request a copy of the injunction or interdict.

(4) Where the term or notice, or one of a similar kind or with a similar effect, is or has been the subject of an undertaking under this Schedule, the CMA must give the person making the request—

    (a) details of the undertaking, and

    (b) if the person giving the undertaking has agreed to amend the term or notice, a copy of the amendments.

(5) The CMA may arrange the publication of advice and information about the provisions of this Part.

(6) In this paragraph—

    (a) references to an injunction or interdict under this Schedule are to an injunction or interdict granted on an application by the CMA under paragraph 3 or notified to it under paragraph 5, and

    (b) references to an undertaking are to an undertaking given to the CMA under paragraph 6 or notified to it under that paragraph.

8.   Meaning of 'regulator'

(1) In this Schedule 'regulator' means—

    (a) the CMA,

    (b) the Department of Enterprise, Trade and Investment in Northern Ireland,

    (c) a local weights and measures authority in Great Britain,

    (d) the Financial Conduct Authority,

    (e) the Office of Communications,

    (f) the Information Commissioner,

(g) the Gas and Electricity Markets Authority,

(h) the Water Services Regulation Authority,

(i) [the Office of Rail and Road],

(j) the Northern Ireland Authority for Utility Regulation, or

(k) the Consumers' Association.

(2) The Secretary of State may by order made by statutory instrument amend sub-paragraph (1) so as to add, modify or remove an entry.

(3) An order under sub-paragraph (2) may amend sub-paragraph (1) so as to add a body that is not a public authority only if the Secretary of State thinks that the body represents the interests of consumers (or consumers of a particular description).

(4) The Secretary of State must publish (and may from time to time vary) other criteria to be applied by the Secretary of State in deciding whether to add an entry to, or remove an entry from, sub-paragraph (1).

(5) An order under sub-paragraph (2) may make consequential amendments to this Schedule (including with the effect that any of its provisions apply differently, or do not apply, to a body added to sub-paragraph (1)).

(6) An order under sub-paragraph (2) may contain transitional or transitory provision or savings.

(7) No order may be made under sub-paragraph (2) unless a draft of the statutory instrument containing it has been laid before, and approved by a resolution of, each House of Parliament.

(8) In this paragraph 'public authority' has the same meaning as in section 6 of the Human Rights Act 1998.

9. Other definitions

In this Schedule—

'the CMA' means the Competition and Markets Authority;

'injunction' includes an interim injunction;

'interdict' includes an interim interdict.

10. The Financial Conduct Authority

The functions of the Financial Conduct Authority under this Schedule are to be treated as functions of the Authority under the Financial Services and Markets Act 2000.

Section 77

SCHEDULE 5

INVESTIGATORY POWERS ETC.

PART 1   BASIC CONCEPTS

1. Overview

(1) This Schedule confers investigatory powers on enforcers and specifies the purposes for which and the circumstances in which those powers may be exercised.

(2) Part 1 of this Schedule contains interpretation provisions; in particular paragraphs 2 to 6 explain what is meant by an 'enforcer'.

(3) Part 2 of this Schedule explains what is meant by 'the enforcer's legislation'.

(4) Part 3 of this Schedule contains powers in relation to the production of information; paragraph 13 sets out which enforcers may exercise those powers, and the purposes for which they may do so.

(5) Part 4 of this Schedule contains further powers; paragraphs 19 and 20 set out which enforcers may exercise those powers, and the purposes for which they may do so.

(6) Part 5 of this Schedule contains provisions that are supplementary to the powers in Parts 3 and 4 of this Schedule.

(7) Part 6 of this Schedule makes provision about the exercise of functions by certain enforcers outside their area or district and the bringing of proceedings in relation to conduct outside an enforcer's area or district.

2. Enforcers

(1) In this Schedule 'enforcer' means—

  (a) a domestic enforcer,

  (b) an EU enforcer,

  (c) a public designated enforcer, or

  (d) an unfair contract terms enforcer.

(2) But in Part 4 and paragraphs 38 and 41 of this Schedule 'enforcer' means—

  (a) a domestic enforcer, or

  (b) an EU enforcer.

(3) In paragraphs 13, 19 and 20 of this Schedule, a reference to an enforcer exercising a power includes a reference to an officer of the enforcer exercising that power.

3. Domestic enforcers

(1) In this Schedule 'domestic enforcer' means—

  (a) the Competition and Markets Authority,

  (b) a local weights and measures authority in Great Britain,

  (c) a district council in England, . . .

  (f) the Secretary of State,

  (g) the Gas and Electricity Markets Authority,

  [(gc) the Civil Aviation Authority, for the purposes of the Package Travel and Linked Travel Arrangements Regulations 2018 (S.I. 2018/634),]

  (h) the British Hallmarking Council,

  (i) an assay office within the meaning of the Hallmarking Act 1973, or

  (j) any other person to whom the duty in subsection (1) of section 27 of the Consumer Protection Act 1987 (duty to enforce safety provisions) applies by virtue of regulations under subsection (2) of that section.

(2) But the Gas and Electricity Markets Authority is not a domestic enforcer for the purposes of Part 4 of this Schedule.

4. EU enforcers

In this Schedule 'EU enforcer' means—

  (a) the Competition and Markets Authority,

  (b) a local weights and measures authority in Great Britain,

  (c) the Department of Enterprise, Trade and Investment in Northern Ireland,

  (d) the Financial Conduct Authority,

  (e) the Civil Aviation Authority,

  (f) the Secretary of State,

  (g) the Department of Health, Social Services and Public Safety in Northern Ireland,

  (h) the Office of Communications,

  (i) an enforcement authority within the meaning of section 120(15) of the Communications Act 2003 (regulation of premium rate services), or

  (j) the Information Commissioner.

5. Public designated enforcers

In this Schedule 'public designated enforcer' means a person or body which—

  (a) is designated by order under subsection (2) of section 213 of the Enterprise Act 2002, and

  (b) has been designated by virtue of subsection (3) of that section (which provides that the Secretary of State may designate a public body only if satisfied that it is independent).

6. Unfair contract terms enforcer

In this Schedule 'unfair contract terms enforcer' means a person or body which—

- (a) is for the time being listed in paragraph 8(1) of Schedule 3 (persons or bodies that may enforce provisions about unfair contract terms), and
- (b) is a public authority within the meaning of section 6 of the Human Rights Act 1998.

7. Officers

(1) In this Schedule 'officer', in relation to an enforcer, means—

- (a) an inspector appointed by the enforcer to exercise powers under this Schedule, or authorised to do so,
- (b) an officer of the enforcer appointed by the enforcer to exercise powers under this Schedule, or authorised to do so,
- (c) an employee of the enforcer (other than an inspector or officer) appointed by the enforcer to exercise powers under this Schedule, or authorised to do so, or
- (d) a person (other than an inspector, officer or employee of the enforcer) authorised by the enforcer to exercise powers under this Schedule.

(2) But references in this Schedule to an officer in relation to a particular power only cover a person within sub-paragraph (1) if and to the extent that the person has been appointed or authorised to exercise that power.

(3) A person who, immediately before the coming into force of this Schedule, was appointed or authorised to exercise a power replaced by a power in this Schedule is to be treated as having been appointed or authorised to exercise the new power.

(4) In this paragraph 'employee', in relation to the Secretary of State, means a person employed in the civil service of the State.

8. Interpretation of other terms

In this Schedule—

'Community infringement' has the same meaning as in section 212 of the Enterprise Act 2002;

'document' includes information recorded in any form;

'enforcement order' means an order under section 217 of the Enterprise Act 2002;

'interim enforcement order' means an order under section 218 of that Act;

['interim online interface order' means an order under section 218ZC of that Act;

'online interface order' means an order under section 218ZB of that Act;]

'the Regulation on Accreditation and Market Surveillance' means Regulation (EC) No 765/2008 of the European Parliament and of the Council of 9 July 2008 setting out the requirements for accreditation and market surveillance relating to the marketing of products and repealing Regulation (EEC) No 339/93.

PART 2   THE ENFORCER'S LEGISLATION

9. Enforcer's legislation

(1) In this Schedule 'the enforcer's legislation', in relation to a domestic enforcer, means—

- (a) legislation or notices which, by virtue of a provision listed in paragraph 10, the domestic enforcer has a duty or power to enforce, and
- (b) where the domestic enforcer is listed in an entry in the first column of the table in paragraph 11, the legislation listed in the corresponding entry in the second column of that table.

(2) References in this Schedule to a breach of or compliance with the enforcer's legislation include a breach of or compliance with a notice issued under—

- (a) the enforcer's legislation, or
- (b) legislation under which the enforcer's legislation is made.

(3) References in this Schedule to a breach of or compliance with the enforcer's legislation are to be read, in relation to the [Lifts Regulations 2016 (SI 2016/1093)], as references to a breach of or compliance with the Regulations as they apply to [lifts for private use and consumption and safety components for such lifts].

10. Enforcer's legislation: duties and powers mentioned in paragraph 9(1)(a)

The duties and powers mentioned in paragraph 9(1)(a) are those arising under any of the following provisions—...

11. Enforcer's legislation: legislation mentioned in paragraph 9(1)(b)

Here is the table mentioned in paragraph 9(1)(b)—...

12. Powers to amend paragraph 10 or 11

(1) The Secretary of State may by order made by statutory instrument—

    (a) amend paragraph 10 or the table in paragraph 11 by adding, modifying or removing any entry in it;

    (b) in consequence of provision made under paragraph (a), amend, repeal or revoke any other legislation (including this Act) whenever passed or made.

(2) The Secretary of State may not make an order under this paragraph that has the effect that a power of entry, or an associated power, contained in legislation other than this Act is replaced by a power of entry, or an associated power, contained in this Schedule unless the Secretary of State thinks that the condition in sub-paragraph (3) is met.

(3) That condition is that, on and after the changes made by the order, the safeguards applicable to the new power, taken together, provide a greater level of protection than any safeguards applicable to the old power.

(4) In sub-paragraph (2) 'power of entry' and 'associated power' have the meanings given by section 46 of the Protection of Freedoms Act 2012.

(5) An order under this paragraph may contain transitional or transitory provision or savings.

(6) A statutory instrument containing an order under this paragraph that amends or repeals primary legislation may not be made unless a draft of the instrument containing the order has been laid before, and approved by a resolution of, each House of Parliament.

(7) Any other statutory instrument containing an order under this paragraph is subject to annulment in pursuance of a resolution of either House of Parliament.

(8) In this paragraph 'primary legislation' means—

    (a) an Act of Parliament, ...

PART 3   POWERS IN RELATION TO THE PRODUCTION OF INFORMATION

13. Exercise of powers in this Part

(1) An enforcer of a kind mentioned in this paragraph may exercise a power in this Part of this Schedule only for the purposes and in the circumstances mentioned in this paragraph in relation to that kind of enforcer.

(2) The Competition and Markets Authority may exercise the powers in this Part of this Schedule for any of the following purposes—

    (a) to enable the Authority to exercise or to consider whether to exercise any function it has under Part 8 of the Enterprise Act 2002;

    (b) to enable a private designated enforcer to consider whether to exercise any function it has under that Part;

    (c) to enable a Community enforcer to consider whether to exercise any function it has under that Part;

(d) to ascertain whether a person has complied with or is complying with [an enforcement order, an interim enforcement order, an online interface order or an interim online interface order];

(e) to ascertain whether a person has complied with or is complying with an undertaking given under section 217(9), 218(10) or 219 of the Enterprise Act 2002.

(3) A public designated enforcer, a local weights and measures authority in Great Britain, the Department of Enterprise, Trade and Investment in Northern Ireland or an EU enforcer other than the Competition and Markets Authority may exercise the powers in this Part of this Schedule for any of the following purposes—

(a) to enable that enforcer to exercise or to consider whether to exercise any function it has under Part 8 of the Enterprise Act 2002;

(b) to ascertain whether a person has complied with or is complying with an enforcement order or an interim enforcement order made on the application of that enforcer;

(c) to ascertain whether a person has complied with or is complying with an undertaking given under section 217(9) or 218(10) of the Enterprise Act 2002 following such an application;

(d) to ascertain whether a person has complied with or is complying with an undertaking given to that enforcer under section 219 of that Act.

(4) A domestic enforcer may exercise the powers in this Part of this Schedule for the purpose of ascertaining whether there has been a breach of the enforcer's legislation.

(5) But a domestic enforcer may not exercise the power in paragraph 14 (power to require the production of information) for the purpose in sub-paragraph (4) unless an officer of the enforcer reasonably suspects a breach of the enforcer's legislation.

(6) Sub-paragraph (5) does not apply if the enforcer is a market surveillance authority within the meaning of Article 2(18) of the Regulation on Accreditation and Market Surveillance and the power is exercised for the purpose of market surveillance within the meaning of Article 2(17) of that Regulation.

(7) An unfair contract terms enforcer may exercise the powers in this Part of this Schedule for either of the following purposes—

(a) to enable the enforcer to exercise or to consider whether to exercise any function it has under Schedule 3 (enforcement of the law on unfair contract terms and notices);

(b) to ascertain whether a person has complied with or is complying with an injunction or interdict (within the meaning of that Schedule) granted under paragraph 5 of that Schedule or an undertaking given under paragraph 6 of that Schedule.

(8) But an unfair contract terms enforcer may not exercise the power in paragraph 14 for a purpose mentioned in sub-paragraph (7)(a) unless an officer of the enforcer reasonably suspects that a person is using, or proposing or recommending the use of, a contractual term or notice within paragraph 3 of Schedule 3.

(9) A local weights and measures authority in Great Britain [the Department of Enterprise, Trade and Investment in Northern Ireland or the Secretary of State] may exercise the powers in this Part of this Schedule for either of the following purposes—

(a) to enable it to determine whether to make an order under section 3 or 4 of the Estate Agents Act 1979;

(b) to enable it to exercise any of its functions under section 5, 6, 8, 13 or 17 of that Act.

(10) In this paragraph—

'Community enforcer' has the same meaning as in the Enterprise Act 2002 (see section 213(5) of that Act);

'private designated enforcer' means a person or body which—

(a) is designated by order under subsection (2) of section 213 of that Act, and

(b) has been designated by virtue of subsection (4) of that section (which provides that the Secretary of State may designate a person or body which is not a public body only if it satisfies criteria specified by order).

14. Power to require the production of information

An enforcer or an officer of an enforcer may give notice to a person requiring the person to provide the enforcer with the information specified in the notice.

15. Procedure for notice under paragraph 14

(1) A notice under paragraph 14 must be in writing and specify the purpose for which the information is required.

(2) If the purpose is to enable a person to exercise or to consider whether to exercise a function, the notice must specify the function concerned.

(3) The notice may specify—
> (a) the time within which and the manner in which the person to whom it is given must comply with it;
> (b) the form in which information must be provided.

(4) The notice may require—
> (a) the creation of documents, or documents of a description, specified in the notice, and
> (b) the provision of those documents to the enforcer or an officer of the enforcer.

(5) A requirement to provide information or create a document is a requirement to do so in a legible form.

(6) A notice under paragraph 14 does not require a person to provide any information or create any documents which the person would be entitled to refuse to provide or produce—
> (a) in proceedings in the High Court on the grounds of legal professional privilege . . .

(7) In sub-paragraph (6) 'communications' means—
> (a) communications between a professional legal adviser and the adviser's client, or
> (b) communications made in connection with or in contemplation of legal proceedings or for the purposes of those proceedings.

16. Enforcement of notice under paragraph 14

(1) If a person fails to comply with a notice under paragraph 14, the enforcer or an officer of the enforcer may make an application under this paragraph to the court.

(2) If it appears to the court that the person has failed to comply with the notice, it may make an order under this paragraph.

(3) An order under this paragraph is an order requiring the person to do anything that the court thinks it is reasonable for the person to do, for any of the purposes for which the notice was given, to ensure that the notice is complied with.

(4) An order under this paragraph may require the person to meet the costs or expenses of the application.

(5) If the person is a company, partnership or unincorporated association, the court in acting under sub-paragraph (4) may require an official who is responsible for the failure to meet the costs or expenses.

(6) In this paragraph—

'the court' means—
> (a) the High Court,
> (b) in relation to England and Wales, the county court, . . .

'official' means—
> (a) in the case of a company, a director, manager, secretary or other similar officer,
> (b) in the case of a limited liability partnership, a member,
> (c) in the case of a partnership other than a limited liability partnership, a partner, and
> (d) in the case of an unincorporated association, a person who is concerned in the management or control of its affairs.

17. Limitations on use of information provided in response to a notice under paragraph 14

(1) This paragraph applies if a person provides information in response to a notice under paragraph 14.

(2) This includes information contained in a document created by a person in response to such a notice.

(3) In any criminal proceedings against the person—

    (a) no evidence relating to the information may be adduced by or on behalf of the prosecution, and

    (b) no question relating to the information may be asked by or on behalf of the prosecution.

(4) Sub-paragraph (3) does not apply if, in the proceedings—

    (a) evidence relating to the information is adduced by or on behalf of the person providing it, or

    (b) a question relating to the information is asked by or on behalf of that person.

(5) Sub-paragraph (3) does not apply if the proceedings are for—

    (a) an offence under paragraph 36 (obstruction),

    (b) an offence under section 5 of the Perjury Act 1911 (false statutory declarations and other false statements without oath), . . .

18.　Application to Crown

In its application in relation to—

    (a) an enforcer acting for a purpose within paragraph 13(2) or (3), or

    (b) an enforcer acting for the purpose of ascertaining whether there has been a breach of the Consumer Protection from Unfair Trading Regulations 2008 (SI 2008/1277),

this Part binds the Crown.

PART 4　FURTHER POWERS EXERCISABLE BY DOMESTIC ENFORCERS AND EU ENFORCERS

19.　Exercise of powers in this Part: domestic enforcers

(1) A domestic enforcer may exercise a power in this Part of this Schedule only for the purposes and in the circumstances mentioned in this paragraph in relation to that power.

(2) A domestic enforcer may exercise any power in paragraphs 21 to 26 and 31 to 34 for the purpose of ascertaining compliance with the enforcer's legislation.

(3) A domestic enforcer may exercise the power in paragraph 27 (power to require the production of documents) for either of the following purposes—

    (a) subject to sub-paragraph (4), to ascertain compliance with the enforcer's legislation;

    (b) to ascertain whether the documents may be required as evidence in proceedings for a breach of, or under, the enforcer's legislation.

(4) A domestic enforcer may exercise the power in paragraph 27 for the purpose mentioned in sub-paragraph (3)(a) only if an officer of the enforcer reasonably suspects a breach of the enforcer's legislation, unless—

    (a) the power is being exercised in relation to a document that the trader is required to keep by virtue of a provision of the enforcer's legislation, or

    (b) the enforcer is a market surveillance authority within the meaning of Article 2(18) of the Regulation on Accreditation and Market Surveillance and the power is exercised for the purpose of market surveillance within the meaning of Article 2(17) of that Regulation.

(5) A domestic enforcer may exercise the power in paragraph 28 (power to seize and detain goods) in relation to—

    (a) goods which an officer of the enforcer reasonably suspects may disclose (by means of testing or otherwise) a breach of the enforcer's legislation,

    (b) goods which an officer of the enforcer reasonably suspects are liable to forfeiture under that legislation, and

    (c) goods which an officer of the enforcer reasonably suspects may be required as evidence in proceedings for a breach of, or under, that legislation.

(6) A domestic enforcer may exercise the power in paragraph 29 (power to seize documents required as evidence) in relation to documents which an officer of the enforcer reasonably suspects may be required as evidence—

(a) in proceedings for a breach of the enforcer's legislation, or

(b) in proceedings under the enforcer's legislation.

(7) A domestic enforcer may exercise the power in paragraph 30 (power to decommission or switch off fixed installations)—

(a) if an officer of the enforcer reasonably suspects a breach of the Electromagnetic Compatibility Regulations 2006 (SI 2006/3418), and

(b) for the purpose of ascertaining (by means of testing or otherwise) whether there has been such a breach.

(8) For the purposes of the enforcement of the Estate Agents Act 1979—

(a) the references in sub-paragraphs (2) and (3)(a) to ascertaining compliance with the enforcer's legislation include ascertaining whether a person has engaged in a practice mentioned in section 3(1)(d) of that Act (practice in relation to estate agency work declared undesirable by the Secretary of State), and

(b) the references in sub-paragraph (4) and paragraphs 23(6)(a) and 32(3)(a) to a breach of the enforcer's legislation include references to a person's engaging in such a practice.

20. Exercise of powers in this Part: EU enforcers

(1) Any power in this Part of this Schedule which is conferred on an EU enforcer may be exercised by such an enforcer only for the purposes and in the circumstances mentioned in this paragraph in relation to that power.

(2) If the condition in sub-paragraph (3) is met, an EU enforcer may exercise any power conferred on it by [paragraphs 22 to 25] and 31 to 34 for any purpose relating to the functions that the enforcer has under Part 8 of the Enterprise Act 2002 in its capacity as a CPC enforcer under that Part.

(3) The condition is that an officer of the EU enforcer reasonably suspects—

(a) that there has been, or is likely to be, a Community infringement,

(b) a failure to comply with [an enforcement order, an interim enforcement order, an online interface order or an interim online interface order] made on the application of that enforcer,

(c) a failure to comply with an undertaking given under section 217(9) or 218(10) of the Enterprise Act 2002 following such an application, or

(d) a failure to comply with an undertaking given to that enforcer under section 219 of that Act.

[(3A) An EU enforcer may exercise the power in paragraph 21 (power to purchase products) for either of the following purposes—

(a) the purpose mentioned in sub-paragraph (2), if the condition in sub-paragraph (3) is met, or

(b) to obtain a product for use as evidence in proceedings under Part 8 of the Enterprise Act 2002.]

(4) An EU enforcer may exercise the power in paragraph 27 (power to require the production of documents) for either of the following purposes—

(a) the purpose mentioned in sub-paragraph (2), if the condition in sub-paragraph (3) is met;

(b) to ascertain whether the documents may be required as evidence in proceedings under Part 8 of the Enterprise Act 2002.

(5) An EU enforcer may exercise the power in paragraph 28 (power to seize and detain goods) in relation to goods which an officer of the enforcer reasonably suspects—

(a) may disclose (by means of testing or otherwise) a Community infringement or a failure to comply with a measure specified in sub-paragraph (3)(b), (c) or (d), or

(b) may be required as evidence in proceedings under Part 8 of the Enterprise Act 2002.

(6) An EU enforcer may exercise the power in paragraph 29 (power to seize documents required as evidence) in relation to documents which an officer of the enforcer reasonably suspects may be required as evidence in proceedings under Part 8 of the Enterprise Act 2002.

21. Power to purchase products

(1) An officer of an enforcer may—

    (a) make a purchase of a product, or

    (b) enter into an agreement to secure the provision of a product.

(2) For the purposes of exercising the power in sub-paragraph (1), an officer may—

    (a) at any reasonable time, enter premises to which the public has access (whether or not the public has access at that time), and

    (b) inspect any product on the premises which the public may inspect.

(3) The power of entry in sub-paragraph (2) may be exercised without first giving notice or obtaining a warrant.

22. Power to observe carrying on of business etc

(1) An officer of an enforcer may enter premises to which the public has access in order to observe the carrying on of a business on those premises.

(2) The power in sub-paragraph (1) may be exercised at any reasonable time (whether or not the public has access at that time).

(3) The power of entry in sub-paragraph (1) may be exercised without first giving notice or obtaining a warrant.

23. Power to enter premises without warrant

(1) An officer of an enforcer may enter premises at any reasonable time.

(2) Sub-paragraph (1) does not authorise the entry into premises used wholly or mainly as a dwelling.

(3) In the case of a routine inspection, the power of entry in sub-paragraph (1) may only be exercised if a notice has been given to the occupier of the premises in accordance with the requirements in sub-paragraph (4), unless sub-paragraph (5) applies.

(4) Those requirements are that—

    (a) the notice is in writing and is given by an officer of the enforcer,

    (b) the notice sets out why the entry is necessary and indicates the nature of the offence under paragraph 36 (obstruction), and

    (c) there are at least two working days between the date of receipt of the notice and the date of entry.

(5) A notice need not be given if the occupier has waived the requirement to give notice.

(6) In this paragraph 'routine inspection' means an exercise of the power in sub-paragraph (1) other than where—

    (a) the power is exercised by an officer of a domestic enforcer who reasonably suspects a breach of the enforcer's legislation,

    (b) the officer reasonably considers that to give notice in accordance with sub-paragraph (3) would defeat the purpose of the entry,

    (c) it is not reasonably practicable in all the circumstances to give notice in accordance with that sub-paragraph, in particular because the officer reasonably suspects that there is an imminent risk to public health or safety, or

    (d) the enforcer is a market surveillance authority within the meaning of Article 2(18) of the Regulation on Accreditation and Market Surveillance and the entry is for the purpose of market surveillance within the meaning of Article 2(17) of that Regulation.

(7) If an officer of an enforcer enters premises under sub-paragraph (1) otherwise than in the course of a routine inspection, and finds one or more occupiers on the premises, the officer must provide to that occupier or (if there is more than one) to at least one of them a document that—

    (a) sets out why the entry is necessary, and

    (b) indicates the nature of the offence under paragraph 36 (obstruction).

(8) If an officer of an enforcer enters premises under sub-paragraph (1) and finds one or more occupiers on the premises, the officer must produce evidence of the officer's identity and authority to that occupier or (if there is more than one) to at least one of them.

(9) An officer need not comply with sub-paragraph (7) or (8) if it is not reasonably practicable to do so.

(10) Proceedings resulting from the exercise of the power under sub-paragraph (1) are not invalid merely because of a failure to comply with sub-paragraph (7) or (8).

(11) An officer entering premises under sub-paragraph (1) may be accompanied by such persons, and may take onto the premises such equipment, as the officer thinks necessary.

(12) In this paragraph—

'give', in relation to the giving of a notice to the occupier of premises, includes delivering or leaving it at the premises or sending it there by post;

'working day' means a day other than—

(a) Saturday or Sunday,

(b) Christmas Day or Good Friday, or

(c) a day which is a bank holiday under the Banking and Financial Dealings Act 1971 in the part of the United Kingdom in which the premises are situated.

24. Application of paragraphs 25 to 31

Paragraphs 25 to 31 apply if an officer of an enforcer has entered any premises under the power in paragraph 23(1) or under a warrant under paragraph 32.

25. Power to inspect products etc

(1) The officer may inspect any product on the premises.

(2) The power in sub-paragraph (3) is also available to an officer of a domestic enforcer acting pursuant to the duty in section 27(1) of the Consumer Protection Act 1987 or regulation 10(1) of the General Product Safety Regulations 2005 (SI 2005/1803).

(3) The officer may examine any procedure (including any arrangements for carrying out a test) connected with the production of a product.

(4) The powers in sub-paragraph (5) are also available to an officer of a domestic enforcer acting pursuant to—

(a) the duty in regulation 10(1) of the Weights and Measures (Packaged Goods) Regulations 2006 (SI 2006/659) ('the ('2006 Regulations'), or

(b) the duty in regulation 10(1) of the Weights and Measures (Packaged Goods) Regulations (Northern Ireland) 2011 (SR 2011/331) ('the 2011 Regulations').

(5) The officer may inspect and take copies of, or of anything purporting to be—

(a) a record of a kind mentioned in regulation 5(2) or 9(1), or

(b) evidence of a kind mentioned in regulation 9(3).

(6) The references in sub-paragraph (5) to regulations are to regulations in the 2006 Regulations in the case of a domestic enforcer in Great Britain or the 2011 Regulations in the case of a domestic enforcer in Northern Ireland.

(7) The powers in sub-paragraph (8) are also available to an officer of a domestic enforcer acting pursuant to the duty in regulation 37(1)(a)(ii) or (b)(ii) of the Electromagnetic Compatibility Regulations 2006 (SI 2006/3418).

(8) The officer may—

(a) inspect any apparatus or fixed installation (as defined in those Regulations), or

(b) examine any procedure (including any arrangements for carrying out a test) connected with the production of apparatus.

26. Power to test equipment

(1) An officer of a domestic enforcer may test any weighing or measuring equipment—

(a) which is, or which the officer has reasonable cause to believe may be, used for trade or in the possession of any person or on any premises for such use, or

(b) which has been, or which the officer has reasonable cause to believe to have been, passed by an approved verifier, or by a person purporting to act as such a verifier, as fit for such use.

(2) Expressions used in sub-paragraph (1) have the same meaning—

    (a) as in the Weights and Measures Act 1985, in the case of a domestic enforcer in Great Britain;

    (b) as in the Weights and Measures (Northern Ireland) Order 1981 (SI 1981/231 (NI 10)), in the case of a domestic enforcer in Northern Ireland.

(3) The powers in sub-paragraph (4) are available to an officer of a domestic enforcer acting pursuant to—

    (a) the duty in regulation 10(1) of the Weights and Measures (Packaged Goods) Regulations 2006 (SI 2006/659) ('the 2006 Regulations'), ...

(4) The officer may test any equipment which the officer has reasonable cause to believe is used in—

    (a) making up packages (as defined in regulation 2) in the United Kingdom, or

    (b) carrying out a check mentioned in paragraphs (1) and (3) of regulation 9.

(5) The references in sub-paragraph (4) to regulations are to regulations in the 2006 Regulations in the case of a domestic enforcer in Great Britain or the 2011 Regulations in the case of a domestic enforcer in Northern Ireland.

27. Power to require the production of documents

(1) The officer may, at any reasonable time—

    (a) require a trader occupying the premises, or a person on the premises acting on behalf of such a trader, to produce any documents relating to the trader's business to which the trader has access, and

    (b) take copies of, or of any entry in, any such document.

(2) The power in sub-paragraph (1) is available regardless of whether—

    (a) the purpose for which the documents are required relates to the trader or some other person, or

    (b) the proceedings referred to in paragraph 19(3)(b) or 20(4)(b) could be taken against the trader or some other person.

(3) That power includes power to require the person to give an explanation of the documents.

(4) Where a document required to be produced under sub-paragraph (1) contains information recorded electronically, the power in that sub-paragraph includes power to require the production of a copy of the document in a form in which it can easily be taken away and in which it is visible and legible.

(5) This paragraph does not permit an officer to require a person to create a document other than as described in sub-paragraph (4).

(6) This paragraph does not permit an officer to require a person to produce any document which the person would be entitled to refuse to produce—

    (a) in proceedings in the High Court on the grounds of legal professional privilege ...

(7) In sub-paragraph (6) 'communications' means—

    (a) communications between a professional legal adviser and the adviser's client, or

    (b) communications made in connection with or in contemplation of legal proceedings or for the purposes of those proceedings.

(8) In this paragraph 'trader' has the same meaning as in Part 1 of this Act.

28. Power to seize and detain goods

(1) The officer may seize and detain goods other than documents (for which see paragraph 29).

(2) An officer seizing goods under this paragraph from premises which are occupied must produce evidence of the officer's identity and authority to an occupier of the premises before seizing them.

(3) The officer need not comply with sub-paragraph (2) if it is not reasonably practicable to do so.

(4) An officer seizing goods under this paragraph must take reasonable steps to—

    (a) inform the person from whom they are seized that they have been seized, and

    (b) provide that person with a written record of what has been seized.

(5) If, under this paragraph, an officer seizes any goods from a vending machine, the duty in sub-paragraph (4) also applies in relation to—

    (a) the person whose name and address are on the vending machine as the owner of the machine, or

    (b) if there is no such name and address on the machine, the occupier of the premises on which the machine stands or to which it is fixed.

(6) In determining the steps to be taken under sub-paragraph (4), an officer exercising a power under this paragraph in England and Wales or Northern Ireland must have regard to any relevant provision about the seizure of property made by—

    (a) a code of practice under section 66 of the Police and Criminal Evidence Act 1984 . . .

(7) Goods seized under this paragraph (except goods seized for a purpose mentioned in paragraph 19(5)(b)) may not be detained—

    (a) for a period of more than 3 months beginning with the day on which they were seized, or

    (b) where the goods are reasonably required to be detained for a longer period by the enforcer for a purpose for which they were seized, for longer than they are required for that purpose.

29. Power to seize documents required as evidence

(1) The officer may seize and detain documents.

(2) An officer seizing documents under this paragraph from premises which are occupied must produce evidence of the officer's identity and authority to an occupier of the premises before seizing them.

(3) The officer need not comply with sub-paragraph (2) if it is not reasonably practicable to do so.

(4) An officer seizing documents under this paragraph must take reasonable steps to—

    (a) inform the person from whom they are seized that they have been seized, and

    (b) provide that person with a written record of what has been seized.

(5) In determining the steps to be taken under sub-paragraph (4), an officer exercising a power under this paragraph in England and Wales or Northern Ireland must have regard to any relevant provision about the seizure of property made by—

    (a) a code of practice under section 66 of the Police and Criminal Evidence Act 1984 . . .

(6) This paragraph does not confer any power on an officer to seize from a person any document which the person would be entitled to refuse to produce—

    (a) in proceedings in the High Court on the grounds of legal professional privilege . . .

(7) In sub-paragraph (6) 'communications' means—

    (a) communications between a professional legal adviser and the adviser's client, or

    (b) communications made in connection with or in contemplation of legal proceedings or for the purposes of those proceedings.

(8) Documents seized under this paragraph may not be detained—

    (a) for a period of more than 3 months beginning with the day on which they were seized, or

    (b) where the documents are reasonably required to be detained for a longer period by the enforcer for the purposes of the proceedings for which they were seized, for longer than they are required for those purposes.

30. Power to decommission or switch off fixed installations

(1) The power in sub-paragraph (2) is available to an officer of a domestic enforcer acting pursuant to the duty in regulation 37(1)(a)(ii) or (b)(ii) of the Electromagnetic Compatibility Regulations 2006 (SI 2006/3418).

(2) The officer may decommission or switch off any fixed installation (as defined in those Regulations) or part of such an installation.

31. Power to break open container etc

(1) The officer may, for the purpose of exercising any of the powers in paragraphs 28 to 30, require a person with authority to do so to—

  (a) break open any container,

  (b) open any vending machine, or

  (c) access any electronic device in which information may be stored or from which it may be accessed.

(2) Where a requirement under sub-paragraph (1) has not been complied with, the officer may, for the purpose of exercising any of the powers in paragraphs 28 to 30—

  (a) break open the container,

  (b) open the vending machine, or

  (c) access the electronic device.

(3) Sub-paragraph (1) or (2) applies if and to the extent that the exercise of the power in that sub-paragraph is reasonably necessary for the purposes for which that power may be exercised.

(4) In this paragraph 'container' means anything in which goods may be stored.

32. Power to enter premises with warrant

(1) A justice of the peace may issue a warrant authorising an officer of an enforcer to enter premises if satisfied, on written information on oath given by such an officer, that there are reasonable grounds for believing that—

  (a) condition A or B is met, and

  (b) condition C, D or E is met.

(2) Condition A is that on the premises there are—

  (a) products which an officer of the enforcer has power to inspect under paragraph 25, or

  (b) documents which an officer of the enforcer could require a person to produce under paragraph 27.

(3) Condition B is that, on the premises—

  (a) in the case of a domestic enforcer, there has been or is about to be a breach of the enforcer's legislation,

  (b) in the case of an EU enforcer, there has been or is about to be a Community infringement as defined in section 212 of the Enterprise Act 2002, or

  (c) in the case of an EU enforcer, there has been a failure to comply with a measure specified in paragraph 20(3)(b), (c) or (d).

(4) Condition C is that—

  (a) access to the premises has been or is likely to be refused, and

  (b) notice of the enforcer's intention to apply for a warrant under this paragraph has been given to the occupier of the premises.

(5) Condition D is that it is likely that products or documents on the premises would be concealed or interfered with if notice of entry on the premises were given to the occupier of the premises.

(6) Condition E is that—

  (a) the premises are unoccupied, or

  (b) the occupier of the premises is absent, and it might defeat the purpose of the entry to wait for the occupier's return.

33. Entry to premises under warrant

(1) A warrant under paragraph 32 authorises an officer of the enforcer to enter the premises at any reasonable time, using reasonable force if necessary.

(2) A warrant under that paragraph ceases to have effect at the end of the period of one month beginning with the day it is issued.

(3) An officer entering premises under a warrant under paragraph 32 may be accompanied by such persons, and may take onto the premises such equipment, as the officer thinks necessary.

(4) If the premises are occupied when the officer enters them, the officer must produce the warrant for inspection to an occupier of the premises.

(5) Sub-paragraph (6) applies if the premises are unoccupied or the occupier is temporarily absent.

(6) On leaving the premises the officer must—

(a) leave a notice on the premises stating that the premises have been entered under a warrant under paragraph 32, and

(b) leave the premises as effectively secured against trespassers as the officer found them.

34. Power to require assistance from person on premises

(1) If an officer of an enforcer has entered premises under the power in paragraph 23(1) or under a warrant under paragraph 32, the officer may require any person on the premises to provide such assistance or information as the officer reasonably considers necessary.

(2) Sub-paragraph (3) applies if an officer of a domestic enforcer has entered premises under the power in paragraph 23(1) or under a warrant under paragraph 32 for the purposes of the enforcement of—

(a) the Weights and Measures (Packaged Goods) Regulations 2006 (SI 2006/659) . . .

(3) The officer may, in particular, require any person on the premises to provide such information as the person possesses about the name and address of the packer and of any importer of a package which the officer finds on the premises.

(4) In sub-paragraph (3) 'importer', 'package' and 'packer' have the same meaning as in—

(a) the Weights and Measures (Packaged Goods) Regulations 2006 (see regulation 2), in the case of a domestic enforcer in Great Britain . . .

35. Definitions for purposes of this Part

In this Part of this Schedule—

'goods' has the meaning given by section 2(8);

'occupier', in relation to premises, means any person an officer of an enforcer reasonably suspects to be the occupier of the premises;

'premises' includes any stall, vehicle, vessel or aircraft;

'product' means—

(a) goods,

(b) a service,

(c) digital content, as defined in section 2(9),

(d) immovable property, or

(e) rights or obligations.

PART 5   PROVISIONS SUPPLEMENTARY TO PARTS 3 AND 4

36. Offence of obstruction

(1) A person commits an offence if the person—

(a) intentionally obstructs an enforcer or an officer of an enforcer who is exercising or seeking to exercise a power under Part 4 of this Schedule in accordance with that Part,

(b) intentionally fails to comply with a requirement properly imposed by an enforcer or an officer of an enforcer under Part 4 of this Schedule, or

(c) without reasonable cause fails to give an enforcer or an officer of an enforcer any other assistance or information which the enforcer or officer reasonably requires of the person for a purpose for which the enforcer or officer may exercise a power under Part 4 of this Schedule.

(2) A person commits an offence if, in giving information of a kind referred to in sub-paragraph (1)(c), the person—

(a) makes a statement which the person knows is false or misleading in a material respect, or

(b) recklessly makes a statement which is false or misleading in a material respect.

(3) A person who is guilty of an offence under sub-paragraph (1) or (2) is liable on summary conviction to a fine not exceeding level 3 on the standard scale.

(4) Nothing in this paragraph requires a person to answer any question or give any information if to do so might incriminate that person.

37. Offence of purporting to act as officer

(1) A person who is not an officer of an enforcer commits an offence if the person purports to act as such under Part 3 or 4 of this Schedule.

(2) A person who is guilty of an offence under sub-paragraph (1) is liable on summary conviction to a fine not exceeding level 5 on the standard scale.

(3) If section 85(1) of the Legal Aid, Sentencing and Punishment of Offenders Act 2012 comes into force on or before the day on which this Act is passed—

    (a) section 85 of that Act (removal of limit on certain fines on conviction by magistrates' court) applies in relation to the offence in this paragraph as if it were a relevant offence (as defined in section 85(3) of that Act), and

    (b) regulations described in section 85(11) of that Act may amend or otherwise modify sub-paragraph (2).

38. Access to seized goods and documents

(1) This paragraph applies where anything seized by an officer of an enforcer under Part 4 of this Schedule is detained by the enforcer.

(2) If a request for permission to be granted access to that thing is made to the enforcer by a person who had custody or control of it immediately before it was seized, the enforcer must allow that person access to it under the supervision of an officer of the enforcer.

(3) If a request for a photograph or copy of that thing is made to the enforcer by a person who had custody or control of it immediately before it was seized, the enforcer must—

    (a) allow that person access to it under the supervision of an officer of the enforcer for the purpose of photographing or copying it, or

    (b) photograph or copy it, or cause it to be photographed or copied.

(4) Where anything is photographed or copied under sub-paragraph (3), the photograph or copy must be supplied to the person who made the request within a reasonable time from the making of the request.

(5) This paragraph does not require access to be granted to, or a photograph or copy to be supplied of, anything if the enforcer has reasonable grounds for believing that to do so would prejudice the investigation for the purposes of which it was seized.

(6) An enforcer may recover the reasonable costs of complying with a request under this paragraph from the person by whom or on whose behalf it was made.

(7) References in this paragraph to a person who had custody or control of a thing immediately before it was seized include a representative of such a person.

39. Notice of testing of goods

(1) Sub-paragraphs (3) and (4) apply where goods purchased by an officer of a domestic enforcer under paragraph 21 are submitted to a test and as a result—

    (a) proceedings are brought for a breach of, or under, the enforcer's legislation or for the forfeiture of the goods by the enforcer, or

    (b) a notice is served by the enforcer preventing a person from doing any thing.

(2) Sub-paragraphs (3) and (4) also apply where goods seized by an officer of a domestic enforcer under paragraph 28 are submitted to a test.

(3) The enforcer must inform the relevant person of the results of the test.

(4) The enforcer must allow a relevant person to have the goods tested if it is reasonably practicable to do so.

(5) In sub-paragraph (3) 'relevant person' means the person from whom the goods were purchased or seized or, where the goods were purchased or seized from a vending machine—

    (a) the person whose name and address are on the vending machine as the owner of the machine, or

    (b) if there is no such name and address on the machine, the occupier of the premises on which the machine stands or to which it is fixed.

(6) In sub-paragraph (4) 'relevant person' means—

  (a) a person within sub-paragraph (5),

  (b) in a case within sub-paragraph (1)(a), a person who is a party to the proceedings, and

  (c) in a case within sub-paragraph (1)(b), a person with an interest in the goods.

40. Appeals against detention of goods and documents

(1) This paragraph applies where goods or documents are being detained as the result of the exercise of a power in Part 4 of this Schedule.

(2) A person with an interest in the goods or documents may apply for an order requiring them to be released to that or another person.

(3) An application under this paragraph may be made in England and Wales or Northern Ireland—

  (a) to any magistrates' court in which proceedings have been brought for an offence as the result of the investigation in the course of which the goods or documents were seized,

  (b) to any magistrates' court in which proceedings have been brought for the forfeiture of the goods or documents or (in the case of seized documents) any goods to which the documents relate, or

  (c) if no proceedings within paragraph (a) or (b) have been brought, by way of complaint to a magistrates' court.

(5) On an application under this paragraph, the court . . . may make an order requiring goods to be released only if satisfied that condition A or B is met.

(6) Condition A is that—

  (a) no proceedings have been brought—

    (i) for an offence as the result of the investigation in the course of which the goods or documents were seized, or

    (ii) for the forfeiture of the goods or documents or (in the case of seized documents) any goods to which the documents relate, and

  (b) the period of 6 months beginning with the date the goods or documents were seized has expired.

(7) Condition B is that—

  (a) proceedings of a kind mentioned in sub-paragraph (6)(a) have been brought, and

  (b) those proceedings have been concluded without the goods or documents being forfeited.

(8) A person aggrieved by an order made under this paragraph by a magistrates' court, or by the decision of a magistrates' court not to make such an order, may appeal against the order or decision—

  (a) in England and Wales, to the Crown Court; . . .

(9) An order made under this paragraph by a magistrates' court may contain such provision as the court thinks appropriate for delaying its coming into force pending the making and determination of any appeal.

(10) In sub-paragraph (9) 'appeal' includes an application under section 111 of the Magistrates' Courts Act 1980 . . .

41. Compensation

(1) This paragraph applies where an officer of an enforcer has seized and detained goods under Part 4 of this Schedule for a purpose within paragraph 19(5)(a) or 20(5)(a).

(2) The enforcer must pay compensation to any person with an interest in the goods in respect of any loss or damage caused by the seizure and detention, if the condition in sub-paragraph (3) or (4) that is relevant to the enforcer is met.

(3) The condition that is relevant to a domestic enforcer is that—

  (a) the goods have not disclosed a breach of the enforcer's legislation, and

  (b) the power to seize and detain the goods was not exercised as a result of any neglect or default of the person seeking the compensation.

(4) The condition that is relevant to an EU enforcer is that—

    (a) the goods have not disclosed a Community infringement or a failure to comply with a measure specified in paragraph 20(3)(b), (c) or (d), and

    (b) the power to seize and detain the goods was not exercised as a result of any neglect or default of the person seeking the compensation.

(5) Any dispute about the right to or amount of any compensation payable under this paragraph is to be determined—

    (a) in England and Wales or Northern Ireland, by arbitration . . .

42. Meaning of 'goods' in this Part

In this Part of this Schedule 'goods' does not include a document.

PART 6   EXERCISE OF ENFORCEMENT FUNCTIONS BY AREA ENFORCERS

43. Interpretation of this Part

In this Part, 'area enforcer' means—

    (a) a local weights and measures authority in Great Britain,

    (b) a district council in England, . . .

44. Investigatory powers

(1) Sub-paragraphs (3) to (6) apply in relation to an area enforcer's exercise, in accordance with this Schedule, of a power in Part 3 or 4 of this Schedule.

(2) Sub-paragraphs (3) to (6) also apply in relation to an area enforcer's exercise of an investigatory power—

    (a) conferred by legislation which, by virtue of a provision listed in paragraph 10 of this Schedule, the area enforcer has a duty or power to enforce, or conferred by legislation under which such legislation is made, or

    (b) conferred by legislation listed in the second column of the table in paragraph 11 of this Schedule,

for the purpose of ascertaining whether there has been a breach of that legislation or of any notice issued by the area enforcer under that legislation.

(3) A local weights and measures authority in England or Wales may exercise the power in a part of England or Wales which is outside that authority's area.

(5) A district council in England may exercise the power in a part of England which is outside that council's district.

45. Civil proceedings

(1) Sub-paragraphs (4) to (7) apply in relation to civil proceedings which may be brought by an area enforcer under—

    (a) Part 8 of the Enterprise Act 2002,

    (b) Schedule 3 to this Act,

    (c) legislation which, by virtue of a provision listed in paragraph 10 of this Schedule, the area enforcer has a duty or power to enforce,

    (d) legislation under which legislation mentioned in paragraph (c) is made, or

    (e) legislation listed in the second column of the table in paragraph 11 of this Schedule.

(2) Sub-paragraphs (4) to (7) also apply in relation to an application for forfeiture which may be made by an area enforcer, in circumstances where there are no related criminal proceedings,—

    (a) under section 35ZC of the Registered Designs Act 1949,

    (b) under section 16 of the Consumer Protection Act 1987,

    (c) under section 97 of the Trade Marks Act 1994 (including as applied by section 11 of the Olympic Symbol etc (Protection) Act 1995), or

    (d) under legislation which, by virtue of a provision listed in paragraph 10 of this Schedule, the area enforcer has a duty or power to enforce.

(3) In sub-paragraphs (4), (5), (6) and (7), the reference to civil proceedings includes a reference to an application mentioned in sub-paragraph (2).

(4) A local weights and measures authority in England or Wales may bring civil proceedings in respect of conduct in a part of England or Wales which is outside that authority's area.

(6) A district council in England may bring civil proceedings in respect of conduct in a part of England which is outside that council's district.

46. Criminal proceedings

(1) A local weights and measures authority in England or Wales may bring proceedings for a consumer offence allegedly committed in a part of England or Wales which is outside that authority's area.

(2) In sub-paragraph (1) 'a consumer offence' means—

    (a) an offence under legislation which, by virtue of a provision listed in paragraph 10 of this Schedule, a local weights and measures authority in England or Wales has a duty or power to enforce,

    (b) an offence under legislation under which legislation within paragraph (a) is made,

    (c) an offence under legislation listed in the second column of the table in paragraph 11 of this Schedule in relation to which a local weights and measures authority is listed in the corresponding entry in the first column of the table as an enforcer,

    (d) an offence originating from an investigation into a breach of legislation mentioned in paragraph (a), (b) or (c), or

    (e) an offence described in paragraph 36 or 37 of this Schedule.

(3) A district council in England may bring proceedings for a consumer offence allegedly committed in a part of England which is outside that council's district.

(4) In sub-paragraph (3) 'a consumer offence' means—

    (a) an offence under legislation which, by virtue of a provision listed in paragraph 10 of this Schedule, a district council in England has a duty or power to enforce,

    (b) an offence under legislation under which legislation within paragraph (a) is made,

    (c) an offence originating from an investigation into a breach of legislation mentioned in paragraph (a) or (b), or

    (d) an offence described in paragraph 36 or 37 of this Schedule.

Insurance Act 2015

(2015, c. 4)

PART 1   INSURANCE CONTRACTS: MAIN DEFINITIONS

1   Insurance contracts: main definitions

In this Act (apart from Part 6)—

'consumer insurance contract' has the same meaning as in the Consumer Insurance (Disclosure and Representations) Act 2012;

'non-consumer insurance contract' means a contract of insurance that is not a consumer insurance contract;

'insured' means the party to a contract of insurance who is the insured under the contract, or would be if the contract were entered into;

'insurer' means the party to a contract of insurance who is the insurer under the contract, or would be if the contract were entered into;

'the duty of fair presentation' means the duty imposed by section 3(1).

PART 2   THE DUTY OF FAIR PRESENTATION

2 Application and interpretation

(1) This Part applies to non-consumer insurance contracts only.

(2) This Part applies in relation to variations of non-consumer insurance contracts as it applies to contracts, but—

(a) references to the risk are to be read as references to changes in the risk relevant to the proposed variation, and

(b) references to the contract of insurance are to the variation.

3 The duty of fair presentation

(1) Before a contract of insurance is entered into, the insured must make to the insurer a fair presentation of the risk.

(2) The duty imposed by subsection (1) is referred to in this Act as 'the duty of fair presentation'.

(3) A fair presentation of the risk is one—

(a) which makes the disclosure required by subsection (4),

(b) which makes that disclosure in a manner which would be reasonably clear and accessible to a prudent insurer, and

(c) in which every material representation as to a matter of fact is substantially correct, and every material representation as to a matter of expectation or belief is made in good faith.

(4) The disclosure required is as follows, except as provided in subsection (5)—

(a) disclosure of every material circumstance which the insured knows or ought to know, or

(b) failing that, disclosure which gives the insurer sufficient information to put a prudent insurer on notice that it needs to make further enquiries for the purpose of revealing those material circumstances.

(5) In the absence of enquiry, subsection (4) does not require the insured to disclose a circumstance if—

(a) it diminishes the risk,

(b) the insurer knows it,

(c) the insurer ought to know it,

(d) the insurer is presumed to know it, or

(e) it is something as to which the insurer waives information.

(6) Sections 4 to 6 make further provision about the knowledge of the insured and of the insurer, and section 7 contains supplementary provision.

4 Knowledge of insured

(1) This section provides for what an insured knows or ought to know for the purposes of section 3(4)(a).

(2) An insured who is an individual knows only—

(a) what is known to the individual, and

(b) what is known to one or more of the individuals who are responsible for the insured's insurance.

(3) An insured who is not an individual knows only what is known to one or more of the individuals who are—

(a) part of the insured's senior management, or

(b) responsible for the insured's insurance.

(4) An insured is not by virtue of subsection (2)(b) or (3)(b) taken to know confidential information known to an individual if—

(a) the individual is, or is an employee of, the insured's agent; and

(b) the information was acquired by the insured's agent (or by an employee of that agent) through a business relationship with a person who is not connected with the contract of insurance.

(5) For the purposes of subsection (4) the persons connected with a contract of insurance are—

(a) the insured and any other persons for whom cover is provided by the contract, and

(b) if the contract re-insures risks covered by another contract, the persons who are (by virtue of this subsection) connected with that other contract.

(6) Whether an individual or not, an insured ought to know what should reasonably have been revealed by a reasonable search of information available to the insured (whether the search is conducted by making enquiries or by any other means).

(7) In subsection (6) 'information' includes information held within the insured's organisation or by any other person (such as the insured's agent or a person for whom cover is provided by the contract of insurance).

(8) For the purposes of this section—

(a) 'employee', in relation to the insured's agent, includes any individual working for the agent, whatever the capacity in which the individual acts,

(b) an individual is responsible for the insured's insurance if the individual participates on behalf of the insured in the process of procuring the insured's insurance (whether the individual does so as the insured's employee or agent, as an employee of the insured's agent or in any other capacity), and

(c) 'senior management' means those individuals who play significant roles in the making of decisions about how the insured's activities are to be managed or organised.

5 Knowledge of insurer

(1) For the purposes of section 3(5)(b), an insurer knows something only if it is known to one or more of the individuals who participate on behalf of the insurer in the decision whether to take the risk, and if so on what terms (whether the individual does so as the insurer's employee or agent, as an employee of the insurer's agent or in any other capacity).

(2) For the purposes of section 3(5)(c), an insurer ought to know something only if—

(a) an employee or agent of the insurer knows it, and ought reasonably to have passed on the relevant information to an individual mentioned in subsection (1), or

(b) the relevant information is held by the insurer and is readily available to an individual mentioned in subsection (1).

(3) For the purposes of section 3(5)(d), an insurer is presumed to know—

(a) things which are common knowledge, and

(b) things which an insurer offering insurance of the class in question to insureds in the field of activity in question would reasonably be expected to know in the ordinary course of business.

6 Knowledge: general

(1) For the purposes of sections 3 to 5, references to an individual's knowledge include not only actual knowledge, but also matters which the individual suspected, and of which the individual would have had knowledge but for deliberately refraining from confirming them or enquiring about them.

(2) Nothing in this Part affects the operation of any rule of law according to which knowledge of a fraud perpetrated by an individual ('F') either on the insured or on the insurer is not to be attributed to the insured or to the insurer (respectively), where—

(a) if the fraud is on the insured, F is any of the individuals mentioned in section 4(2)(b) or (3), or

(b) if the fraud is on the insurer, F is any of the individuals mentioned in section 5(1).

7 Supplementary

(1) A fair presentation need not be contained in only one document or oral presentation.

(2) The term 'circumstance' includes any communication made to, or information received by, the insured.

(3) A circumstance or representation is material if it would influence the judgement of a prudent insurer in determining whether to take the risk and, if so, on what terms.

(4) Examples of things which may be material circumstances are—

(a) special or unusual facts relating to the risk,

    (b) any particular concerns which led the insured to seek insurance cover for the risk,

    (c) anything which those concerned with the class of insurance and field of activity in question would generally understand as being something that should be dealt with in a fair presentation of risks of the type in question.

  (5) A material representation is substantially correct if a prudent insurer would not consider the difference between what is represented and what is actually correct to be material.

  (6) A representation may be withdrawn or corrected before the contract of insurance is entered into.

8   Remedies for breach

  (1) The insurer has a remedy against the insured for a breach of the duty of fair presentation only if the insurer shows that, but for the breach, the insurer—

    (a) would not have entered into the contract of insurance at all, or

    (b) would have done so only on different terms.

  (2) The remedies are set out in Schedule 1.

  (3) A breach for which the insurer has a remedy against the insured is referred to in this Act as a 'qualifying breach'.

  (4) A qualifying breach is either—

    (a) deliberate or reckless, or

    (b) neither deliberate nor reckless.

  (5) A qualifying breach is deliberate or reckless if the insured —

    (a) knew that it was in breach of the duty of fair presentation, or

    (b) did not care whether or not it was in breach of that duty.

  (6) It is for the insurer to show that a qualifying breach was deliberate or reckless.

PART 3   WARRANTIES AND OTHER TERMS

9   Warranties and representations

  (1) This section applies to representations made by the insured in connection with—

    (a) a proposed non-consumer insurance contract, or

    (b) a proposed variation to a non-consumer insurance contract.

  (2) Such a representation is not capable of being converted into a warranty by means of any provision of the non-consumer insurance contract (or of the terms of the variation), or of any other contract (and whether by declaring the representation to form the basis of the contract or otherwise).

10   Breach of warranty

  (1) Any rule of law that breach of a warranty (express or implied) in a contract of insurance results in the discharge of the insurer's liability under the contract is abolished.

  (2) An insurer has no liability under a contract of insurance in respect of any loss occurring, or attributable to something happening, after a warranty (express or implied) in the contract has been breached but before the breach has been remedied.

  (3) But subsection (2) does not apply if—

    (a) because of a change of circumstances, the warranty ceases to be applicable to the circumstances of the contract,

    (b) compliance with the warranty is rendered unlawful by any subsequent law, or

    (c) the insurer waives the breach of warranty.

  (4) Subsection (2) does not affect the liability of the insurer in respect of losses occurring, or attributable to something happening—

    (a) before the breach of warranty, or

    (b) if the breach can be remedied, after it has been remedied.

  (5) For the purposes of this section, a breach of warranty is to be taken as remedied—

    (a) in a case falling within subsection (6), if the risk to which the warranty relates later becomes essentially the same as that originally contemplated by the parties,

    (b) in any other case, if the insured ceases to be in breach of the warranty.

(6) A case falls within this subsection if—
    (a) the warranty in question requires that by an ascertainable time something is to be done (or not done), or a condition is to be fulfilled, or something is (or is not) to be the case, and
    (b) that requirement is not complied with.

(7) In the Marine Insurance Act 1906—
    (a) in section 33 (nature of warranty), in subsection (3), the second sentence is omitted,
    (b) section 34 (when breach of warranty excused) is omitted.

11   Terms not relevant to the actual loss

(1) This section applies to a term (express or implied) of a contract of insurance, other than a term defining the risk as a whole, if compliance with it would tend to reduce the risk of one or more of the following—
    (a) loss of a particular kind,
    (b) loss at a particular location,
    (c) loss at a particular time.

(2) If a loss occurs, and the term has not been complied with, the insurer may not rely on the non-compliance to exclude, limit or discharge its liability under the contract for the loss if the insured satisfies subsection (3).

(3) The insured satisfies this subsection if it shows that the non-compliance with the term could not have increased the risk of the loss which actually occurred in the circumstances in which it occurred.

(4) This section may apply in addition to section 10.

PART 4   FRAUDULENT CLAIMS

12   Remedies for fraudulent claims

(1) If the insured makes a fraudulent claim under a contract of insurance—
    (a) the insurer is not liable to pay the claim,
    (b) the insurer may recover from the insured any sums paid by the insurer to the insured in respect of the claim, and
    (c) in addition, the insurer may by notice to the insured treat the contract as having been terminated with effect from the time of the fraudulent act.

(2) If the insurer does treat the contract as having been terminated—
    (a) it may refuse all liability to the insured under the contract in respect of a relevant event occurring after the time of the fraudulent act, and
    (b) it need not return any of the premiums paid under the contract.

(3) Treating a contract as having been terminated under this section does not affect the rights and obligations of the parties to the contract with respect to a relevant event occurring before the time of the fraudulent act.

(4) In subsections (2)(a) and (3), 'relevant event' refers to whatever gives rise to the insurer's liability under the contract (and includes, for example, the occurrence of a loss, the making of a claim, or the notification of a potential claim, depending on how the contract is written).

13   Remedies for fraudulent claims: group insurance

(1) This section applies where—
    (a) a contract of insurance is entered into with an insurer by a person ('A'),
    (b) the contract provides cover for one or more other persons who are not parties to the contract ('the Cs'), whether or not it also provides cover of any kind for A or another insured party, and
    (c) a fraudulent claim is made under the contract by or on behalf of one of the Cs ('CF').

(2) Section 12 applies in relation to the claim as if the cover provided for CF were provided under an individual insurance contract between the insurer and CF as the insured; and, accordingly—
    (a) the insurer's rights under section 12 are exercisable only in relation to the cover provided for CF, and

   (b) the exercise of any of those rights does not affect the cover provided under the contract for anyone else.

   (3) In its application by virtue of subsection (2), section 12 is subject to the following particular modifications—

   (a) the first reference to 'the insured' in subsection (1)(b) of that section, in respect of any particular sum paid by the insurer, is to whichever of A and CF the insurer paid the sum to; but if a sum was paid to A and passed on by A to CF, the reference is to CF,

   (b) the second reference to 'the insured' in subsection (1)(b) is to A or CF,

   (c) the reference to 'the insured' in subsection (1)(c) is to both CF and A,

   (d) the reference in subsection (2)(b) to the premiums paid under the contract is to premiums paid in respect of the cover for CF.

[PART 4A   LATE PAYMENT OF CLAIMS]

[13A   Implied term about payment of claims

   (1) It is an implied term of every contract of insurance that if the insured makes a claim under the contract, the insurer must pay any sums due in respect of the claim within a reasonable time.

   (2) A reasonable time includes a reasonable time to investigate and assess the claim.

   (3) What is reasonable will depend on all the relevant circumstances, but the following are examples of things which may need to be taken into account—

   (a) the type of insurance,

   (b) the size and complexity of the claim,

   (c) compliance with any relevant statutory or regulatory rules or guidance,

   (d) factors outside the insurer's control.

   (4) If the insurer shows that there were reasonable grounds for disputing the claim (whether as to the amount of any sum payable, or as to whether anything at all is payable)—

   (a) the insurer does not breach the term implied by subsection (1) merely by failing to pay the claim (or the affected part of it) while the dispute is continuing, but

   (b) the conduct of the insurer in handling the claim may be a relevant factor in deciding whether that term was breached and, if so, when.

   (5) Remedies (for example, damages) available for breach of the term implied by subsection (1) are in addition to and distinct from—

   (a) any right to enforce payment of the sums due, and

   (b) any right to interest on those sums (whether under the contract, under another enactment, at the court's discretion or otherwise).]

PART 5   GOOD FAITH AND CONTRACTING OUT

Good faith

14   Good faith

   (1) Any rule of law permitting a party to a contract of insurance to avoid the contract on the ground that the utmost good faith has not been observed by the other party is abolished.

   (2) Any rule of law to the effect that a contract of insurance is a contract based on the utmost good faith is modified to the extent required by the provisions of this Act and the Consumer Insurance (Disclosure and Representations) Act 2012.

   (3) Accordingly—

   (a) in section 17 of the Marine Insurance Act 1906 (marine insurance contracts are contracts of the utmost good faith), the words from ', and' to the end are omitted, and

   (b) the application of that section (as so amended) is subject to the provisions of this Act and the Consumer Insurance (Disclosure and Representations) Act 2012.

   (4) In section 2 of the Consumer Insurance (Disclosure and Representations) Act 2012 (disclosure and representations before contract or variation), subsection (5) is omitted.

Contracting out

15   Contracting out: consumer insurance contracts

(1) A term of a consumer insurance contract, or of any other contract, which would put the consumer in a worse position as respects any of the matters provided for in Part 3 or 4 of this Act than the consumer would be in by virtue of the provisions of those Parts (so far as relating to consumer insurance contracts) is to that extent of no effect.

(2) In subsection (1) references to a contract include a variation.

(3) This section does not apply in relation to a contract for the settlement of a claim arising under a consumer insurance contract.

16   Contracting out: non-consumer insurance contracts

(1) A term of a non-consumer insurance contract, or of any other contract, which would put the insured in a worse position as respects representations to which section 9 applies than the insured would be in by virtue of that section is to that extent of no effect.

(2) A term of a non-consumer insurance contract, or of any other contract, which would put the insured in a worse position as respects any of the other matters provided for in Part 2, 3 or 4 of this Act than the insured would be in by virtue of the provisions of those Parts (so far as relating to non-consumer insurance contracts) is to that extent of no effect, unless the requirements of section 17 have been satisfied in relation to the term.

(3) In this section references to a contract include a variation.

(4) This section does not apply in relation to a contract for the settlement of a claim arising under a non-consumer insurance contract.

[16A   Contracting out of the implied term about payment of claims: consumer and non-consumer insurance contracts

(1) A term of a consumer insurance contract, or of any other contract, which would put the consumer in a worse position as respects any of the matters provided for in section 13A than the consumer would be in by virtue of the provisions of that section (so far as relating to consumer insurance contracts) is to that extent of no effect.

(2) A term of a non-consumer insurance contract, or of any other contract, which would put the insured in a worse position as respects deliberate or reckless breaches of the term implied by section 13A than the insured would be in by virtue of that section is to that extent of no effect.

(3) For the purposes of subsection (2) a breach is deliberate or reckless if the insurer—

(a) knew that it was in breach, or

(b) did not care whether or not it was in breach.

(4) A term of a non-consumer insurance contract, or of any other contract, which would put the insured in a worse position as respects any of the other matters provided for in section 13A than the insured would be in by virtue of the provisions of that section (so far as relating to non-consumer insurance contracts) is to that extent of no effect, unless the requirements of section 17 have been satisfied in relation to the term.

(5) In this section references to a contract include a variation.

(6) This section does not apply in relation to a contract for the settlement of a claim arising under an insurance contract.]

17   The transparency requirements

(1) In this section, 'the disadvantageous term' means such a term as is mentioned in section 16(2) [or 16A(4)].

(2) The insurer must take sufficient steps to draw the disadvantageous term to the insured's attention before the contract is entered into or the variation agreed.

(3) The disadvantageous term must be clear and unambiguous as to its effect.

(4) In determining whether the requirements of subsections (2) and (3) have been met, the characteristics of insured persons of the kind in question, and the circumstances of the transaction, are to be taken into account.

(5) The insured may not rely on any failure on the part of the insurer to meet the requirements of subsection (2) if the insured (or its agent) had actual knowledge of the disadvantageous term when the contract was entered into or the variation agreed.

18   Contracting out: group insurance contracts

(1) This section applies to a contract of insurance referred to in section 13(1)(a); and in this section—

'A' and 'the Cs' have the same meaning as in section 13,

'consumer C' means an individual who is one of the Cs, where the cover provided by the contract for that individual would have been a consumer insurance contract if entered into by that person rather than by A, and

'non-consumer C' means any of the Cs who is not a consumer C.

(2) A term of the contract of insurance, or any other contract, which puts a consumer C in a worse position as respects any matter dealt with in section 13 than that individual would be in by virtue of that section is to that extent of no effect.

(3) A term of the contract of insurance, or any other contract, which puts a non-consumer C in a worse position as respects any matter dealt with in section 13 than that person would be in by virtue of that section is to that extent of no effect, unless the requirements of section 17 have been met in relation to the term.

(4) Section 17 applies in relation to such a term as it applies to a term mentioned in section 16(2), with references to the insured being read as references to A rather than the non-consumer C.

(5) In this section references to a contract include a variation.

(6) This section does not apply in relation to a contract for the settlement of a claim arising under a contract of insurance to which this section applies.

PART 7   GENERAL

21   Provision consequential on Part 2

(2) In the Marine Insurance Act 1906, sections 18 (disclosure by assured), 19 (disclosure by agent effecting insurance) and 20 (representations pending negotiation of contract) are omitted.

(3) Any rule of law to the same effect as any of those provisions is abolished.

22   Application etc of Parts 2 to 5

(1) Part 2 (and section 21) and section 14 apply only in relation to—

(a) contracts of insurance entered into after the end of the relevant period, and

(b) variations, agreed after the end of the relevant period, to contracts of insurance entered into at any time.

(2) Parts 3 and 4 of this Act apply only in relation to contracts of insurance entered into after the end of the relevant period, and variations to such contracts.

(3) In subsections (1) and (2) 'the relevant period' means the period of 18 months beginning with the day on which this Act is passed.

[(3A) Part 4A applies only in relation to contracts of insurance entered into after that Part has come into force, and variations to such contracts.]

(4) Unless the contrary intention appears, references in Parts 2 to 5 to something being done by or in relation to the insurer or the insured include its being done by or in relation to that person's agent.

Section 8(2)   **SCHEDULE 1**

INSURERS' REMEDIES FOR QUALIFYING BREACHES

PART 1   CONTRACTS

1.   General

This Part of this Schedule applies to qualifying breaches of the duty of fair presentation in relation to non-consumer insurance contracts (for variations to them, see Part 2).

2. Deliberate or reckless breaches

If a qualifying breach was deliberate or reckless, the insurer—
> (a) may avoid the contract and refuse all claims, and
> (b) need not return any of the premiums paid.

Other breaches

3. Paragraphs 4 to 6 apply if a qualifying breach was neither deliberate nor reckless.

4. If, in the absence of the qualifying breach, the insurer would not have entered into the contract on any terms, the insurer may avoid the contract and refuse all claims, but must in that event return the premiums paid.

5. If the insurer would have entered into the contract, but on different terms (other than terms relating to the premium), the contract is to be treated as if it had been entered into on those different terms if the insurer so requires.

6. (1) In addition, if the insurer would have entered into the contract (whether the terms relating to matters other than the premium would have been the same or different), but would have charged a higher premium, the insurer may reduce proportionately the amount to be paid on a claim.

(2) In sub-paragraph (1), 'reduce proportionately' means that the insurer need pay on the claim only X% of what it would otherwise have been under an obligation to pay under the terms of the contract (or, if applicable, under the different terms provided for by virtue of paragraph 5), where—

$$X = \frac{\text{Premium actually charged}}{\text{Higher premium}} \times 100$$

PART 2   VARIATIONS

7. General

This Part of this Schedule applies to qualifying breaches of the duty of fair presentation in relation to variations to non-consumer insurance contracts.

8. Deliberate or reckless breaches

If a qualifying breach was deliberate or reckless, the insurer—
> (a) may by notice to the insured treat the contract as having been terminated with effect from the time when the variation was made, and
> (b) need not return any of the premiums paid.

Other breaches

9. (1) This paragraph applies if—
> (a) a qualifying breach was neither deliberate nor reckless, and
> (b) the total premium was increased or not changed as a result of the variation.

(2) If, in the absence of the qualifying breach, the insurer would not have agreed to the variation on any terms, the insurer may treat the contract as if the variation was never made, but must in that event return any extra premium paid.

(3) If sub-paragraph (2) does not apply—
> (a) if the insurer would have agreed to the variation on different terms (other than terms relating to the premium), the variation is to be treated as if it had been entered into on those different terms if the insurer so requires, and
> (b) paragraph 11 also applies if (in the case of an increased premium) the insurer would have increased the premium by more than it did, or (in the case of an unchanged premium) the insurer would have increased the premium.

10. (1) This paragraph applies if—
> (a) a qualifying breach was neither deliberate nor reckless, and
> (b) the total premium was reduced as a result of the variation.

(2) If, in the absence of the qualifying breach, the insurer would not have agreed to the variation on any terms, the insurer may treat the contract as if the variation was never made, and paragraph 11 also applies.

(3) If sub-paragraph (2) does not apply—

    (a) if the insurer would have agreed to the variation on different terms (other than terms relating to the premium), the variation is to be treated as if it had been entered into on those different terms if the insurer so requires, and

    (b) paragraph 11 also applies if the insurer would have increased the premium, would not have reduced the premium, or would have reduced it by less than it did.

11. Proportionate reduction

(1) If this paragraph applies, the insurer may reduce proportionately the amount to be paid on a claim arising out of events after the variation.

(2) In sub-paragraph (1), 'reduce proportionately' means that the insurer need pay on the claim only Y% of what it would otherwise have been under an obligation to pay under the terms of the contract (whether on the original terms, or as varied, or under the different terms provided for by virtue of paragraph 9(3)(a) or 10(3)(a), as the case may be), where—

$$Y = \frac{\text{Total Premium actually charged}}{P} \times 100$$

(3) In the formula in sub-paragraph (2), 'P'—

    (a) in a paragraph 9(3)(b) case, is the total premium the insurer would have charged,

    (b) in a paragraph 10(2) case, is the original premium,

    (c) in a paragraph 10(3)(b) case, is the original premium if the insurer would not have changed it, and otherwise the increased or (as the case may be) reduced total premium the insurer would have charged.

PART 3   SUPPLEMENTARY

12. Relationship with section 84 of the Marine Insurance Act 1906

Section 84 of the Marine Insurance Act 1906 (return of premium for failure of consideration) is to be read subject to the provisions of this Schedule in relation to contracts of marine insurance which are non-consumer insurance contracts.

Small Business, Enterprise and Employment Act 2015

(2015, c. 26)

PART 1   ACCESS TO FINANCE

1 Power to invalidate certain restrictive terms of business contracts

(1) The appropriate authority may by regulations make provision for the purpose of securing that any non-assignment of receivables term of a relevant contract—

    (a) has no effect;

    (b) has no effect in relation to persons of a prescribed description;

    (c) has effect in relation to persons of a prescribed description only for such purposes as may be prescribed.

(2) A 'non-assignment of receivables term' of a contract is a term which prohibits or imposes a condition, or other restriction, on the assignment . . . by a party to the contract of the right to be paid any amount under the contract or any other contract between the parties.

(3) A contract is a relevant contract if—

    (a) it is a contract for goods, services or intangible assets (including intellectual property) which is not an excluded financial services contract, and

    (b) at least one of the parties has entered into it in connection with the carrying on of a business.

(4) An 'excluded financial services contract' is a contract which—

(a) is for financial services (see section 2) or is a regulated agreement within the meaning of the Consumer Credit Act 1974 (see section 189 of that Act); and

(b) is of a prescribed description.

(5) 'Prescribed' means prescribed by the regulations.

(6) The 'appropriate authority' means—

(a) in relation to contracts to which the law of Scotland applies, the Scottish Ministers, and

(b) in relation to other contracts, the Secretary of State.

(10) Regulations under this section—

(b) if made by the Secretary of State, are subject to affirmative resolution procedure.

2   Section 1(4)(a): meaning of 'financial services'

(1) In section 1(4)(a) 'financial services' means any service of a financial nature, including (but not limited to)—

(a) insurance-related services consisting of—

(i)   direct life assurance;

(ii) direct insurance other than life assurance;

(iii) reinsurance and retrocession;

(iv) insurance intermediation, such as brokerage and agency;

(v)   services auxiliary to insurance, such as consultancy, actuarial, risk assessment and claim settlement services;

(b) banking and other financial services consisting of—

(i)   accepting deposits and other repayable funds;

(ii) lending (including consumer credit, mortgage credit, factoring and financing of commercial transactions);

(iii) financial leasing;

(iv) payment and money transmission services (including credit, charge and debit cards, travellers' cheques and bankers' drafts);

(v)   providing guarantees or commitments;

(vi) financial trading (as defined in subsection (2));

(vii) participating in issues of any kind of securities (including underwriting and place-ment as an agent, whether publicly or privately) and providing services related to such issues;

(viii) money brokering;

(ix) asset management, such as cash or portfolio management, all forms of collective in-vestment management, pension fund management, custodial, depository and trust services;

(x)   settlement and clearing services for financial assets (including securities, deriva-tive products and other negotiable instruments);

(xi) providing or transferring financial information, and financial data processing or related software (but only by suppliers of other financial services);

(xii) providing advisory and other auxiliary financial services in respect of any activity listed in sub-paragraphs (i) to (xi) (including credit reference and analysis, in-vestment and portfolio research and advice, advice on acquisitions and on cor-porate restructuring and strategy).

(2) In subsection (1)(b)(vi) 'financial trading' means trading for own account or for account of customers, whether on an investment exchange, in an over-the-counter market or otherwise, in—

(a) money market instruments (including cheques, bills and certificates of deposit);

(b) foreign exchange;

(c) derivative products (including futures and options);

(d) exchange rate and interest rate instruments (including products such as swaps and for-ward rate agreements);

(e) transferable securities;

(f) other negotiable instruments and financial assets (including bullion).

3   Companies: duty to publish report on payment practices and performance

(1) The Secretary of State may by regulations impose a requirement, on such descriptions of companies as may be prescribed, to publish, at such intervals and in such manner as may be prescribed, prescribed information about—

(a) the company's payment practices and policies relating to relevant contracts of a prescribed description, and

(b) the company's performance by reference to those practices and policies.

4   Small and medium sized businesses: information to credit reference agencies

(1) The Treasury may make regulations that impose—

(a) a duty on designated banks to provide information about their small and medium sized business customers to designated credit reference agencies, and

(b) a duty on designated credit reference agencies to provide information about small and medium sized businesses to finance providers.

(2) The regulations must provide that the duty in subsection (1)(a) only applies where—

(a) a credit reference agency makes a request to a bank, and

(b) the business customer to whom the information relates has agreed to the information being provided to a credit reference agency.

(3) The regulations must provide that the duty in subsection (1)(b) only applies where—

(a) a finance provider makes a request to a credit reference agency, and

(b) the business to whom the information relates has agreed to the information being provided to the finance provider.

7   Sections 4 to 6: interpretation

(1) For the purposes of sections 4 to 6, a business is a small or medium sized business if—

(a) it has an annual turnover of less than £25 million,

(b) it carries out commercial activities,

(c) it does not carry out regulated activities as its principal activity, and

(d) it is not owned or controlled by a public authority.

8   Disclosure of VAT registration information

(1) The Commissioners for Her Majesty's Revenue and Customs may disclose to a person ('P') any of the information included in the VAT registration of another person ('V') if the disclosure is for the purpose of enabling or assisting P to assess—

(a) V's creditworthiness,

(b) V's compliance with regulatory requirements relating to financial matters, or

(c) the risk of fraud by V.

PART 2   REGULATORY REFORM

33   Definitions of small and micro business

(1) This section applies where any subordinate legislation made by a Minister of the Crown (the 'underlying provision')—

(a) uses the term 'small business' or 'micro business', and

(b) defines that term by reference to this section.

(2) In the underlying provision 'small business' means an undertaking other than a micro business (see subsection (3)) which meets the following conditions ('the small business size conditions')—

(a) it has a headcount of staff of less than 50, and

(b) it has—

(i)   a turnover, or

(ii) a balance sheet total,

of an amount less than or equal to the small business threshold.

(3) In the underlying provision 'micro business' means an undertaking which meets the following conditions ('the micro business size conditions')—

(a) it has a headcount of staff of less than 10, and

(b) it has—

(i) a turnover, or

(ii) a balance sheet total,

of an amount less than or equal to the micro business threshold.

(4) The Secretary of State may by regulations (referred to as 'the small and micro business regulations') make further provision about the meanings of 'small business' and 'micro business'.

Enterprise Act 2016

(2016, c. 12)

1   Small Business Commissioner

(1) A Small Business Commissioner is established.

(2) The Commissioner's principal functions are—

(a) to provide general advice and information to small businesses (see section 3), and

(b) to consider complaints from small businesses relating to payment matters in connection with the supply of goods and services to larger businesses, and make recommendations (see sections 4 to 8).

2   Small businesses in relation to which the Commissioner has functions

(1) In this Part 'small business' means a relevant undertaking which—

(a) has a headcount of staff of less than 50,

(b) if the business threshold condition applies to the relevant undertaking, meets that condition, and

(c) is not a public authority.

(2) The Secretary of State may by regulations ('SBC scope regulations') make further provision about the meaning of 'small business' in this Part.

(3) For the purposes of subsection (1)(b), the business threshold condition applies to a relevant undertaking if—

(a) SBC scope regulations provide for that condition to apply in relation to all relevant undertakings, or

(b) the relevant undertaking falls within a description of undertakings to which SBC scope regulations apply that condition.

(4) A relevant undertaking meets the business threshold condition if it has a turnover, or balance sheet total, of an amount less than or equal to the small business threshold.

3   General advice and information

(1) The Commissioner may publish, or give to small businesses, general advice or information that the Commissioner considers may be useful to small businesses in connection with their supply relationships with larger businesses.

Financial Guidance and Claims Act 2018

(2018, c. 10)

1   The single financial guidance body

(1) A body corporate with functions relating to financial guidance is established (the 'single financial guidance body').

(3) The name of the new body is to be determined by regulations made by the Secretary of State.

2   Objectives

(1) The objectives of the single financial guidance body are—

(a) to improve the ability of members of the public to make informed financial decisions,

(b) to support the provision of information, guidance and advice in areas where it is lacking,

(c) to secure that information, guidance and advice is provided to members of the public in the clearest and most cost-effective way (including having regard to information provided by other organisations),

(d) to ensure that information, guidance and advice is available to those most in need of it (and to allocate its resources accordingly), bearing in mind in particular the needs of people in vulnerable circumstances, and

(e) to work closely with the devolved authorities as regards the provision of information, guidance and advice to members of the public in Scotland, Wales and Northern Ireland.

(2) The single financial guidance body must have regard to its objectives when it exercises its functions.

(3) In this section 'information, guidance and advice' means—

(a) information and guidance on matters relating to occupational and personal pensions,

(b) information and advice on debt, and

(c) information and guidance designed to enhance people's understanding and knowledge of financial matters and their ability to manage their own financial affairs.

3 Functions

(1) The single financial guidance body has the following functions—

(a) the pensions guidance function;

(b) the debt advice function;

(c) the money guidance function;

(d) the consumer protection function;

(e) the strategic function.

(2) The single financial guidance body also has the function of providing—

(a) advice and assistance to the Secretary of State on matters relating to the functions listed in subsection (1), and

(b) advice to the Secretary of State on the establishment of a debt respite scheme (see section 6).

(3) The single financial guidance body may do anything that is incidental or conducive to the exercise of its functions.

(4) The pensions guidance function is to provide, to members of the public, free and impartial information and guidance on matters relating to occupational and personal pensions.

(5) The debt advice function is to provide, to members of the public in England, free and impartial information and advice on debt.

(6) The money guidance function is to provide, to members of the public, free and impartial information and guidance designed to enhance people's understanding and knowledge of financial matters and their ability to manage their own financial affairs.

(7) The consumer protection function is—

(a) to notify the FCA where, in the exercise of its other functions, the single financial guidance body becomes aware of practices carried out by FCA-regulated persons (within the meaning of section 139A of the Financial Services and Markets Act 2000) which it considers to be detrimental to consumers, and

(b) to consider the effect of unsolicited direct marketing on consumers of financial products and services, and, in particular—

(i) from time to time publish an assessment of whether unsolicited direct marketing is, or may be, having a detrimental effect on consumers, and

(ii) advise the Secretary of State whether to make regulations under section 22 (unsolicited direct marketing: other consumer financial products etc).

(8) Where the single financial guidance body provides information, guidance or advice to a person in pursuance of one of the functions mentioned in subsection (1)(a) to (c), it must consider whether the person would benefit from receiving information, guidance or advice in pursuance of any other of those functions (and it must ensure that SFGB delivery partners are under a similar duty).

(9) The strategic function is to develop and co-ordinate a national strategy to improve—

(a) the financial capability of members of the public,

(b) the ability of members of the public to manage debt, and

(c) the provision of financial education to children and young people.

(10) In developing and co-ordinating the national strategy, the single financial guidance body must work with others, such as those in the financial services industry, the devolved authorities and the public and voluntary sectors.

6   Debt respite scheme: advice to the Secretary of State

(1) The Secretary of State must, within three months of the establishment of the single financial guidance body, seek advice from the body on the establishment of a debt respite scheme.

(2) A debt respite scheme is a scheme designed to do one or more of the following—

(a) protect individuals in debt from the accrual of further interest or charges on their debts during the period specified by the scheme,

(b) protect individuals in debt from enforcement action from their creditors during that period, and

(c) help individuals in debt and their creditors to devise a realistic plan for the repayment of some or all of the debts.

7   Debt respite scheme: regulations

(1) As soon as reasonably practicable after receiving advice from the single financial guidance body under section 6, the Secretary of State must consider whether to make regulations under this section.

(2) After receiving advice from the single financial guidance body under section 6, the Secretary of State may make regulations establishing a debt respite scheme.

9   Setting standards

(1) The single financial guidance body must from time to time set standards to be complied with by—

(a) persons providing information or guidance in pursuance of the body's pensions guidance function,

(b) persons providing information or advice in pursuance of the body's debt advice function, and

(c) persons providing information or guidance in pursuance of the body's money guidance function.

(2) Before finalising the standards, the single financial guidance body must obtain the approval of the FCA.

(3) In determining whether to approve the standards, the FCA must have regard to the needs of people who are receiving, or who may seek to receive, the information, guidance or advice to which the standards will apply.

(4) The single financial guidance body must publish the standards.

21   Unsolicited direct marketing: pensions

(1) The Secretary of State may make regulations prohibiting unsolicited direct marketing relating to pensions.

22   Unsolicited direct marketing: other consumer financial products etc

(1) The Secretary of State must keep under review whether a prohibition on unsolicited direct marketing in relation to consumer financial products and services other than pensions would be appropriate.

(2) If the Secretary of State considers that such a prohibition would be appropriate, the Secretary of State may make regulations applying regulations made under section 21 to other consumer financial products and services (with or without modifications).

(3) In considering whether to make such regulations, the Secretary of State must take into account any advice received from the single financial guidance body under section 3(7)(b)(ii) (consumer protection function: advice on effect on consumers of unsolicited direct marketing).

23 Power to dissolve the single financial guidance body

(1) The Secretary of State must keep under review the question of whether the single financial guidance body should be dissolved.

(2) If the Secretary of State considers that the single financial guidance body should be dissolved, he or she must carry out a public consultation.

Sanctions and Anti-Money Laundering Act 2018

(2018, c. 13)

60   Meaning of 'funds', 'economic resources' and 'freeze'

(1) In this Act 'funds' means financial assets and benefits of every kind, including (but not limited to)—

   (a) cash, cheques, claims on money, drafts, money orders and other payment instruments;

   (b) deposits, balances on accounts, debts and debt obligations;

   (c) publicly and privately traded securities and debt instruments, including stocks and shares, certificates representing securities, bonds, notes, warrants, debentures and derivative products;

   (d) interest, dividends and other income on or value accruing from or generated by assets;

   (e) credit, rights of set-off, guarantees, performance bonds and other financial commitments;

   (f) letters of credit, bills of lading and bills of sale;

   (g) documents providing evidence of an interest in funds or financial resources;

   (h) any other instrument of export financing.

(2) In this Act 'economic resources' means assets of every kind, whether tangible or intangible, movable or immovable, which are not funds but can be used to obtain funds, goods or services.

(3) In this Act references to 'freezing' funds are to preventing funds from being dealt with; and for the purposes of this subsection funds are 'dealt with' if—

   (a) they are used, altered, moved, or transferred or access is allowed to them,

   (b) they are dealt with in any other way that would result in any change in volume, amount, location, ownership, possession, character or destination, or

   (c) any other change is made that would enable their use, including portfolio management.

(4) In this Act references to 'freezing' economic resources are to preventing economic resources from being dealt with; and for the purposes of this subsection economic resources are 'dealt with' if—

   (a) they are exchanged for funds, goods or services, or

   (b) they are used in exchange for funds, goods or services (whether by being pledged as security or otherwise).

61   Meaning of 'financial services' and 'financial products'

(1) In this Act 'financial services' means any service of a financial nature, including (but not limited to)—

   (a) insurance-related services consisting of—

      (i)   direct life assurance;

      (ii)   direct insurance other than life assurance;

      (iii)   reinsurance and retrocession;

      (iv)   insurance intermediation, such as brokerage and agency;

    (v)   services auxiliary to insurance, such as consultancy, actuarial, risk assessment and claim settlement services;

  (b) banking and other financial services consisting of—

    (i)   accepting deposits and other repayable funds;

    (ii)   lending (including consumer credit, mortgage credit, factoring and financing of commercial transactions);

    (iii)   financial leasing;

    (iv)   payment and money transmission services (including credit, charge and debit cards, travellers' cheques and bankers' drafts);

    (v)   providing guarantees or commitments;

    (vi)   financial trading (as defined in subsection (2));

    (vii) participating in issues of any kind of securities (including underwriting and placement as an agent, whether publicly or privately) and providing services related to such issues;

    (viii) money brokering;

    (ix)   asset management, such as cash or portfolio management, all forms of collective investment management, pension fund management, custodial, depository and trust services;

    (x)   settlement and clearing services for financial assets (including securities, derivative products and other negotiable instruments);

    (xi)   providing or transferring financial information, and financial data processing or related software (but only by suppliers of other financial services);

    (xii) providing advisory and other auxiliary financial services in respect of any activity listed in sub-paragraphs (i) to (xi) (including credit reference and analysis, investment and portfolio research and advice, advice on acquisitions and on corporate restructuring and strategy).

    (2) In subsection (1)(b)(vi), 'financial trading' means trading for own account or for account of customers, whether on an investment exchange, in an over-the-counter market or otherwise, in financial products.

    (3) In this Act 'financial products' means—

  (a) money market instruments (including cheques, bills and certificates of deposit);

  (b) foreign exchange;

  (c) derivative products (including futures and options);

  (d) exchange rate and interest rate instruments (including products such as swaps and forward rate agreements);

  (e) transferable securities;

  (f) other negotiable instruments and financial assets (including bullion).

United Kingdom Internal Market Act 2020

(2020, c. 27)

PART 1   UK MARKET ACCESS: GOODS

15   Interpretation of references to 'sale' in Part 1

    (1) This section explains the meaning in this Part of references to the sale of goods (however expressed).

    (2) 'Sale' does not include a sale which—

  (a) is not made in the course of a business, or

  (b) is made in the course of a business but only for the purpose of performing a function of a public nature.

(3) Subsection (2)(b) does not exclude a sale which is—

(a) made by a public body or authority for commercial purposes, and

(b) not made for the purpose of performing a function of a public nature (other than a function relating to the carrying on of commercial activities).

(4) 'Sale' includes—

(a) agreement to sell,

(b) offering or exposing for sale, or

(c) having in possession or holding for sale.

(5) This Part applies in relation to a supply of goods other than a sale as it applies in relation to a sale (and any reference to 'sale', outside this subsection, is to be read accordingly).

(6) For this purpose 'supply of goods' means the transfer of possession or property in goods (whether or not under or by virtue of a contract), and includes, for example, supply by way of—

(a) barter or exchange,

(b) the leasing or hiring out of goods, hire-purchase, or bailment of goods, or

(c) gift (or anything else done free of charge).

16   Interpretation of other expressions used in Part 1

(2) 'Goods' means any tangible movable, or corporeal moveable, thing (including any packaging or label), but not water or gas that is not offered for sale in a limited volume or set quantity.

Financial Services Act 2021

(2021, c. 22)

29   FCA rules about level of care provided to consumers by authorised persons

(1) The Financial Conduct Authority must carry out a public consultation about whether it should make general rules providing that authorised persons owe a duty of care to consumers.

(2) The consultation must include consultation about—

(a) whether the Financial Conduct Authority should make other provision in general rules about the level of care that must be provided to consumers by authorised persons, either instead of or in addition to a duty of care,

(b) whether a duty of care should be owed, or other provision should apply, to all consumers or to particular classes of consumer, and

(c) the extent to which a duty of care, or other provision, would advance the Financial Conduct Authority's consumer protection objective (see section 1C of the Financial Services and Markets Act 2000).

(3) The Financial Conduct Authority—

(a) must carry out the consultation, and publish its analysis of the responses, before 1 January 2022, and

(b) must, before 1 August 2022, make such general rules about the level of care that must be provided to consumers, or particular classes of consumer, by authorised persons as it considers appropriate, having regard to that analysis.

(4) The duties to consult under this section may be satisfied by consultation carried out after 1 January 2021 but before this section comes into force (as well as by consultation carried out after this section comes into force).

(5) In this section—

'authorised person' has the same meaning as in the Financial Services and Markets Act 2000 (see section 31 of that Act);

'consumer' has the meaning given in section 1G of that Act;

'general rules' means rules made under section 137A of that Act.

Part II

Proposed Statutes

(Draft) Goods Mortgages Bill

(Law Com. No. 376)

Draft of a Bill to make provision for a new form of non-possessory security that may be created over goods owned by individuals; to repeal the Bills of Sale Acts 1878 and 1882; and for connected purposes. [2017]

PART 2 CREATION OF GOODS MORTGAGES

Goods mortgages

2 Goods mortgages

(1) An individual who owns qualifying goods (see section 4) may in accordance with subsection (2) create a charge over the goods as security for the discharge of an obligation.

(2) The following requirements must be met—

(a) the goods exist, and are owned by the individual concerned, at the time when the charge is created;

(b) the charge is created by a written instrument complying with section 5;

(c) the obligation is not an excluded obligation (see section 6).

(3) A person whose only interest in goods is an equitable interest is not to be regarded for the purposes of this Act as 'owning' the goods.

(4) In this Act 'goods mortgage' means a charge created in accordance with this section or section 3.

3 Goods mortgages: co-owners

(1) Where qualifying goods are owned jointly by two or more individuals, those individuals may in accordance with subsection (3) together create a charge over the goods as security for the discharge of an obligation.

(2) Where qualifying goods are owned in common by two or more persons, any of those persons who is an individual may in accordance with subsection (3) create a charge over his or her undivided share in the goods as security for the discharge of an obligation.

(3) The following requirements must be met—

(a) the goods exist, and are owned by the person or persons concerned, at the time when the charge is created;

(b) the charge is created by a written instrument complying with section 5;

(c) the obligation is not an excluded obligation (see section 6).

(4) References to ownership jointly or in common with others by an individual include references to ownership jointly or in common with others by an individual as a member of a partnership (other than a limited liability partnership).

4 Qualifying goods

(1) This section applies for the interpretation of this Act.

(2) 'Goods' means tangible moveable property.

(3) 'Qualifying goods' means goods other than—

(a) excluded items, or

(b) goods that are outside England and Wales at the time when the charge is created.

(4) In subsection (3) 'excluded items' means—

(a) aircraft registered in the United Kingdom;

(b) anything that is by virtue of provision made under subsection (2)(f) of section 86 of the Civil Aviation Act 1982 included in a mortgage registered by virtue of that section;

(c) a ship as defined by section 313(1) of the Merchant Shipping Act 1995;

(d) currency notes or coins that (in either case) are legal tender in the United Kingdom or elsewhere.

5 Requirements to be met in relation to instrument

(1) The instrument creating a goods mortgage must—

(a) contain prescribed provisions, and

(b) be signed or otherwise authenticated by the prescribed persons and in the prescribed manner.

(2) The Treasury must by regulations require the inclusion in the instrument of statements in such form as the Treasury consider appropriate for the purpose of warning the mortgagor—

(a) that the mortgagor risks losing the goods if the obligation secured by the goods mortgage is not discharged, and

(b) that the mortgagor may commit an offence under the Fraud Act 2006 if, while the goods remain subject to the goods mortgage, the mortgagor makes a disposition of the goods without previously disclosing to the purchaser the existence of the goods mortgage.

(3) Subsection (2) does not apply in the case of an exempt goods mortgage (see section 26).

(4) Nothing in the Consumer Credit Act 1974 enables a court to enforce, or allow the enforcement of, a security that purports to be a goods mortgage but is created by an instrument not complying with this section.

6 Excluded obligations

(1) References in this Part to an 'excluded obligation' are to be read in accordance with this section.

(2) An obligation is an excluded obligation if it—

(a) is an obligation of the intended mortgagor as employee under a contract of employment, or

(b) requires the intended mortgagor to do or perform personally any work or services.

(3) A guarantee is an excluded obligation unless—

(a) the high net worth conditions (see section 7(2)) are met, and

(b) the instrument creating the goods mortgage includes the appropriate declaration (see subsection (5)).

(4) The obligation of the debtor under an agreement for running-account credit is an excluded obligation unless—

(a) the high net worth conditions (see section 7(2)) or the business credit conditions (see section 7(3)) are met, and

(b) the instrument creating the goods mortgage includes the appropriate declaration (see subsection (5)).

(5) In this section 'the appropriate declaration' means a declaration by the mortgagor which—

(a) acknowledges that the mortgagor will not have available the protection and remedies that would be available to the mortgagor under sections 19(1) and 23(2) in the case of a goods mortgage other than an exempt goods mortgage (see section 26), and

(b) complies with prescribed requirements.

(6) In this Act 'guarantee' includes an indemnity given by a person in respect of the obligations of another.

(7) Schedule 1 makes provision for the purposes of this section about the meaning of 'running-account credit' and related matters.

7 'The high net worth conditions' and 'the business credit conditions'

(1) This section applies for the interpretation of this Act.

(2) 'The high net worth conditions', in relation to a goods mortgage, are—

    (a) that a statement complying with prescribed requirements has been made in relation to the income or assets of the mortgagor,

    (b) that the connection between the statement and the goods mortgage complies with prescribed requirements, and

    (c) that a copy of the statement was provided to the mortgagee before the goods mortgage was created.

(3) 'The business credit conditions', in relation to a goods mortgage, are—

    (a) that the obligation to which the goods mortgage relates arises from the provision of credit exceeding the prescribed amount, and

    (b) that the obligation was incurred wholly or predominantly for the purposes of a business carried on, or intended to be carried on, by the mortgagor.

Other non-possessory security on goods

8 Other non-possessory security on goods

(1) This section applies to any agreement or arrangement which—

    (a) is entered into by an individual,

    (b) is neither a goods mortgage (as defined by section 2(4)) nor a security excluded by subsection (4), and

    (c) would (apart from this section) have the effect of—

        (i) creating a mortgage or charge over qualifying goods owned by the individual, or subsequently to be acquired by the individual, as security for the discharge of an obligation, or

        (ii) creating a mortgage or charge over an undivided share in qualifying goods owned by the individual in common with other persons, or subsequently to be acquired by the individual in common with other persons, as security for the discharge of an obligation.

(2) If the goods remain in the possession of, or under the custody of, the individual who provides the goods as security, the agreement or arrangement is void to the extent that it would (apart from this section) have the effect mentioned in subsection (1)(c).

(3) If, before the obligation being secured is discharged, the person to whom the obligation is owed passes custody of the goods to the individual who provided the goods as security, the agreement or arrangement becomes void to the extent that it would (apart from this section) have the effect mentioned in subsection (1)(c).

(4) The securities excluded by this subsection are—

    (a) a pledge, lien or other security under which the individual creating the pledge, lien or other security is not entitled to possession of the goods until the obligation is discharged;

    (b) an agricultural charge under Part 2 of the Agricultural Credits Act 1928;

    (c) a mortgage capable of being registered by virtue of section 86 of the Civil Aviation Act 1982;

    (d) an international interest as defined by regulation 5 of the International Interests in Aircraft Equipment (Cape Town Convention) Regulations 2015 (S.I. 2015/912).

(5) Nothing in this section—

    (a) affects the validity of the obligation whose discharge the agreement or arrangement purports to secure,

    (b) affects any lien or charge arising under an enactment or otherwise by operation of law, or

    (c) affects the validity of any hire-purchase agreement or conditional sale agreement.

PART 3 REGISTRATION AND RIGHTS OF THIRD PARTIES

Registration

9 Registration of goods mortgages

(1) A register of goods mortgages is to be kept by the Secretary of State in accordance with regulations made by the Treasury or the Secretary of State under this section (referred to in this section as 'registration regulations').

(2) The provision that may be made by registration regulations includes (but is not limited to) provision as to—

(a) the making by mortgagees of applications for the registration of goods mortgages;

(b) steps to be taken on receipt of an application for registration;

(c) the persons to whom, and manner in which, notice of the registration of a goods mortgage is required to be given;

(d) the information to be included on the register;

(e) the circumstances in which, and manner in which, registration is to be discharged;

(f) the amendment or rectification of the register;

(g) the making by any persons of searches of the register;

(h) fees to be payable in respect of the registration of goods mortgages or searches of the register.

(3) Registration regulations may (but need not)—

(a) provide for the register to be kept in the High Court;

(b) confer functions on officers of the High Court.

(4) Where two or more goods mortgages are created over the same goods, those mortgages as between themselves have priority according to the times at which they were registered.

(5) The registration under this section of a goods mortgage expires (if not previously discharged) at the end of the 10 years beginning with the day on which the goods mortgage was registered (or, as the case may be, the registration was last renewed), but registration regulations may make provision enabling registration to be renewed on application.

(6) Registration regulations may restrict or exclude the liability in tort, in respect of things done or omitted in relation to the registration of goods mortgages, of the Secretary of State or any other person on whom functions are conferred by registration regulations.

(7) Registration regulations may provide for the supply (including the supply by way of sale) of relevant registration information—

(a) to such persons as may be determined in accordance with the regulations by a person specified in or determined in accordance with the regulations, and

(b) for such price (if any) and on such other terms, and subject to such restrictions, as may be determined in accordance with the regulations by a person specified in or determined in accordance with the regulations.

(8) In subsection (7) 'relevant registration information' means information which is derived from particulars contained in the register but which does not identify any individual or contain anything enabling any individual to be identified.

(9) In this Act 'registered', in relation to a goods mortgage, means registered in the register kept under this section.

Further advances

10 Tacking and further advances

(1) The mortgagee under a registered goods mortgage may make a further advance on the security of the goods mortgage ranking in priority to any subsequent goods mortgage—

(a) if an arrangement has been made to that effect with the subsequent mortgagee,

(b) if, at the time when the further advance is made, the subsequent goods mortgage is not registered, or

(c) if the prior goods mortgage imposes an obligation on the prior mortgagee to make further advances.

(2) Subsection (1) applies whether or not the prior goods mortgage was made expressly for securing further advances.

(3) If the prior goods mortgage was made expressly for securing a current account or other further advances, the prior mortgagee may also make a further advance ranking in priority to a subsequent goods mortgage if—

(a) the subsequent mortgage was not registered at the time when the prior goods mortgage was registered or when the last search of the register by or on behalf of the prior mortgagee was made, whichever happened last, and

(b) at the time when the further advance is made, the subsequent mortgagee has not given notice to the prior mortgagee of the registration of the subsequent goods mortgage.

(4) Tacking in relation to a goods mortgage is possible only as provided by this section.

(5) 'The register' means the register kept under section 9.

Position of third parties

11 Duty of owner to disclose existence of goods mortgage

(1) This section applies where a person owns goods which are subject to a goods mortgage ('the current mortgage').

(2) If the owner of the goods disposes of the goods to a purchaser without discharging the obligation secured by the current mortgage, the owner is under a duty to disclose to the purchaser the existence of the current mortgage before the disposition.

(3) If the owner of the goods creates a further goods mortgage or other security over the goods without discharging the obligation secured by the current mortgage, the owner is under a duty to disclose to the person to whom the further goods mortgage or other security is provided the existence of the current mortgage, before creating the further goods mortgage or other security.

(4) Where an undivided share in goods is subject to a goods mortgage, references in this section to the goods are to be read as references to the undivided share.

(5) For the meanings of 'disposition' and 'purchaser', see section 32.

12 Effect of change in ownership of goods

(1) This section applies if—

(a) goods are subject to a goods mortgage, and

(b) before the obligation secured by the goods mortgage has been discharged, ownership of the goods—

(i) is transferred to another person, or

(ii) passes by operation of law to another person, otherwise than on the owner's bankruptcy in England and Wales (as to which, see section 14).

(2) If the goods mortgage is not registered at the time of the change of ownership, the goods cease to be subject to the goods mortgage.

(3) If ownership is transferred by a disposition (see section 32) to a purchaser who—

(a) is a private purchaser as defined by section 13,

(b) is a purchaser of the goods in good faith, and

(c) at the time of the disposition made to the purchaser, has no actual notice that the goods are subject to a goods mortgage,

the goods cease to be subject to the goods mortgage.

(4) In any other case, the goods remain subject to the goods mortgage in the hands of the new owner.

(5) Subsections (2) and (3) do not exonerate the mortgagor and if different the person making the disposition or other transfer of ownership from any liability (whether criminal or civil) to which either of them would be subject apart from this section.

(6) Where an undivided share in goods is subject to a goods mortgage, references in this section to goods are to be read as references to the undivided share.

13 Meaning of 'private purchaser' in section 12

(1) This section makes provision about the interpretation of section 12(3)(a).

(2) 'Private purchaser', in relation to goods of any kind, means a purchaser who, at the time of the disposition made to the purchaser, does not carry on a business which consists, wholly or partly—

    (a) of purchasing goods of that kind for the purpose of offering or exposing them for sale, or

    (b) of providing finance by purchasing goods of that kind for the purpose of bailing them under hire-purchase agreements or agreeing to sell them under conditional sale agreements.

(3) For the meanings of 'disposition' and 'purchaser', see section 32.

14 Bankruptcy of owner of goods subject to goods mortgage

(1) This section applies if an individual who owns goods subject to a goods mortgage is made bankrupt under Part 9 of the Insolvency Act 1986.

(2) On the vesting of the bankrupt's estate in the trustee in bankruptcy, the goods cease to be subject to the goods mortgage unless at the relevant time the goods mortgage is registered.

(3) The 'relevant time' is the time when the bankruptcy application is made or the bankruptcy petition is presented.

PART 4 RIGHTS OF MORTGAGORS AND MORTGAGEES

General provisions about taking of possession by mortgagees

15 Right of mortgagee to take possession of goods

(1) The mortgagee under a goods mortgage is entitled to take possession of the goods only if one or more of the following conditions is met.

(2) Those conditions are—

    (a) that any sum whose payment is secured by the goods mortgage has become due and remains unpaid;

    (b) that the mortgagor has failed to comply with a term of the goods mortgage relating to the maintenance or insurance of the goods;

    (c) that the mortgagor has moved the goods in breach of a term of the goods mortgage;

    (d) that the mortgagor has offered the goods for sale without the consent of the mortgagee;

    (e) that, in the case of a goods mortgage that secures an obligation other than an obligation to pay money, the obligation secured has not been discharged at the time when it ought to have been discharged;

    (f) that the goods have become liable to be seized under a warrant or writ of control to satisfy a court judgment;

    (g) that, since the goods mortgage was created, the mortgagor—

        (i) has been made bankrupt (under Part 9 of the Insolvency Act 1986),

        (ii) has been adjudged bankrupt by a court in Northern Ireland,

        (iii) has had his or her estate sequestrated by a court in Scotland, or

        (iv) has been subject to a similar order or judgment made by a court in a territory outside the United Kingdom.

(3) Subsection (1) applies only while the goods remain subject to the goods mortgage and is subject to—

    (a) any provision of the goods mortgage further restricting the mortgagee's right to take possession, and

    (b) in a case where a prior goods mortgage over the goods is registered, the rights of the prior mortgagee in relation to possession and sale.

(4) If the goods remain owned by the mortgagor, subsection (1) is also subject to—

    (a) section 19 (possession notice required while goods owned by mortgagor), and

(b) subsections (3) to (6) of section 20 (which further restrict the mortgagee's right to take possession).

16 Entry onto premises

(1) Except under an order of the court, the mortgagee under a goods mortgage is not entitled to enter any premises to take possession of the goods without the consent of the person entitled to authorise entry on the premises ('the appropriate person').

(2) An entry in contravention of subsection (1) is actionable as a breach of statutory duty.

(3) A mortgagee under a goods mortgage who—

(a) wishes to enter any premises for the purposes of taking possession of the goods, and

(b) does not have the consent of the appropriate person,

may make an application to the court for an order under this subsection ('an access order') against the appropriate person.

(4) On an application under subsection (3), the court may make an access order only if the court is satisfied, at the time when it makes the order, that the applicant is entitled to take possession of the goods.

17 Mortgagee's power of sale

(1) If the mortgagee under a goods mortgage has lawfully taken possession of the goods, the mortgagee has power to sell the goods.

(2) This is subject to the following provisions of this section and to section 18.

(3) If the goods mortgage is not registered but another goods mortgage over the goods is registered, the mortgagee under the unregistered goods mortgage may not sell the goods.

(4) Where two or more goods mortgages are registered in relation to the same goods, a subsequent mortgagee may not, except under an order of the court, sell the goods without the concurrence of every prior mortgagee under a registered goods mortgage.

(5) Section 101 of the Law of Property Act 1925 (which contains provisions relating to mortgages made by deed) does not apply in relation to a goods mortgage.

18 Goods seized not to be sold until five days have passed

(1) If the mortgagee takes possession of the goods to which a goods mortgage relates, the mortgagee must not sell the goods before the end of the fifth working day following the day on which possession is taken.

(2) The appropriate person may before the end of the fifth working day apply to the court and the court, if satisfied that, by reason of the payment of money or otherwise, the condition in section 15(2) has ceased to be met, may—

(a) restrain the mortgagee from removing or selling the goods,

(b) order the return of the goods to the appropriate person, or

(c) make such other order as the court thinks just.

(3) If the appropriate person and any subsequent mortgagees have agreed with the mortgagee that the mortgagee may deal with the goods otherwise than by way of sale, references in subsections (1) and (2) to selling the goods include references to disposing of them in any other way.

(4) 'The appropriate person' means the mortgagor, except that, if the goods have become owned by another person, it means that other person.

(5) 'Working day' means a day other than a Saturday, a Sunday, Good Friday, Christmas Day or a bank holiday under section 1 of the Banking and Financial Dealings Act 1971 in England or Wales.

(6) This section does not apply—

(a) if the mortgagee takes possession under an order of the court, or

(b) in a case where—

(i) the goods mortgage is an exempt goods mortgage,

(ii) the instrument creating the goods mortgage includes a statement that the mortgagor agrees to forgo the protection given by this section, and

(iii) the goods remain owned by the mortgagor.

Protection of mortgagors

19 Possession notice required while goods are owned by mortgagor

(1) The giving to the mortgagor of a notice complying with section 20 ('a possession notice') is necessary before the mortgagee can take possession of the goods while they are owned by the mortgagor.

(2) Subsection (1) does not prevent the mortgagee taking possession without giving a possession notice if—

  (a) the goods mortgage is an exempt goods mortgage (see section 26), or

  (b) in the case of a goods mortgage other than an exempt goods mortgage, the following conditions are met—

  (i)   the obligation secured is one that can be discharged by the payment of money,

  (ii) at the time when the goods mortgage was created, the redemption total could be determined, and

  (iii) at the time when the mortgagee takes possession of the goods, less than one third of the relevant amount has been paid.

(3) 'The redemption total' means the total sum that is to be payable by the mortgagor in order to discharge the obligation secured by the goods mortgage, including interest but excluding any sum payable as a penalty.

(4) Where the obligation can be discharged either by the payment of money or by other means, it is to be assumed for the purposes of subsection (3) that the mortgagor does not discharge it by those other means.

(5) The 'relevant amount' means the redemption total, except in a case within subsection (6).

(6) In a case where—

  (a) the goods mortgage secures a regulated credit agreement as defined by section 8(3) of the Consumer Credit Act 1974, and

  (b) at the time when the mortgagee takes possession of the goods, part of the indebtedness has been discharged early in accordance with subsections (3) and (4) of section 94 of that Act (right to complete payments ahead of time),

'the relevant amount' means the redemption total reduced by the amount by which any rebate allowable under section 94 of that Act exceeds any amount which the creditor claims under section 95A(2) of that Act.

20 Possession notice

(1) A possession notice must be in the prescribed form and contain prescribed information.

(2) Regulations made by virtue of subsection (1) must require a possession notice to—

  (a) state that the mortgagee considers that one or more of the conditions in section 15(2) is met, specifying which condition and why the mortgagee considers that it is met,

  (b) state that the mortgagor may exercise the right conferred by section 23 (mortgagor's right to terminate),

  (c) state that the mortgagor may within a prescribed period ('the notice period')—

  (i)   require the mortgagee not to take possession of the goods unless authorised to do so by an order of the court, or

  (ii) inform the mortgagee of the mortgagor's intention to seek advice,

  (d) indicate the amount of any costs that may become payable by the mortgagor under an order of the court if the mortgagor acts under paragraph (c)(i) and the mortgagee applies for such an order, and

  (e) state that the mortgagee intends to take possession of the goods unless within the notice period the mortgagor—

  (i)   remedies the breach to which the notice relates (if the breach is capable of remedy), or

  (ii) acts under paragraph (c)(i) or (ii) or under section 23.

(3) If the mortgagor informs the mortgagee under subsection (2)(c)(ii), within the notice period, of the mortgagor's intention to seek advice, the mortgagor may within a further prescribed period ('the advice period'), require the mortgagee not to take possession of the goods unless authorised to do so by an order of the court.

(4) Where a possession notice has been given to the mortgagor, the mortgagee is not entitled to take possession of the goods—

    (a) before the end of the notice period, and

    (b) if the mortgagor acts under subsection (2)(c)(ii), during the advice period.

(5) If the mortgagor so requires under subsection (2)(c)(i) or (3), the mortgagee may not take possession of the goods except under an order of the court.

(6) If before the relevant time the mortgagor remedies the breach to which the possession notice relates, the breach is to be treated as not having occurred.

(7) In subsection (6) 'the relevant time' means the end of the notice period or, if the mortgagor acts under subsection (2)(c)(ii), the end of the advice period.

21   Defaults under consumer credit agreements

(1) This section applies if the goods mortgage was given to secure the payment of money under a regulated agreement to which subsection (1) of section 87 of the Consumer Credit Act 1974 (need for default notice) applies.

(2) A possession notice—

    (a) may not be given until the restriction imposed by section 88(2) of that Act has ceased to apply to the goods mortgage, and

    (b) may not be given if, by virtue of section 89 of that Act (compliance with default notice), the default is treated as not having occurred.

(3) If because of section 19(2) no possession notice is required—

    (a) the mortgagee is not entitled to take possession of the goods on the basis that a condition in section 15(2) is met unless the restriction imposed by section 88(2) of the Consumer Credit Act 1974 has ceased to apply to the goods mortgage, and

    (b) section 15(2)(a) to (f) does not apply to a default that is treated by section 89 of that Act as not having occurred.

22   Wrongful taking of possession by mortgagee

(1) If the mortgagee takes possession of the goods to which a goods mortgage relates in contravention of section 15(1), 19 or 20, the mortgagor—

    (a) is entitled to have the goods returned, and

    (b) is released from all further liability under the obligation secured by the goods mortgage.

(2) This section does not apply if the goods have ceased to be owned by the mortgagor.

23   Mortgagor's right to terminate

(1) This section applies to a goods mortgage that is not an exempt goods mortgage.

(2) The mortgagor is entitled to terminate the goods mortgage by—

    (a) informing the mortgagee of the mortgagor's intention to terminate the goods mortgage, and

    (b) as soon as reasonably practicable after doing so, delivering the goods to the mortgagee.

(3) If the mortgagee refuses to accept goods that the mortgagor offers or attempts to deliver to the mortgagee after informing the mortgagee of an intention to terminate the goods mortgage, the goods are to be taken for the purposes of subsection (2) to have been delivered to the mortgagee.

(4) The right given by subsection (2) cannot be exercised in relation to a goods mortgage if another goods mortgage over the goods has been registered and the other mortgagee (or mortgagees) have not agreed to the termination.

(5) The mortgagee may refuse termination under subsection (2) by the mortgagor only if one or more of the following applies—

    (a) the mortgagee has applied to the court for possession of the goods,

    (b) the mortgagee is entitled to take possession of the goods without such an order and has incurred expenditure in attempting to take possession of them,

(c) the state of the goods is affected by damage deliberately caused by any person since the creation of the goods mortgage, or

(d) the goods have suffered damage that—

    (i) is attributable to a failure by the mortgagor to comply with a term of the goods mortgage requiring the mortgagor to take reasonable care of the goods, and

    (ii) has a significant adverse effect on the market value of the goods.

(6) Any refusal under subsection (5) must be communicated to the mortgagor within a reasonable time and in any event before the end of the period of 14 days beginning with the day on which the goods were delivered to the mortgagee.

(7) If the mortgagor terminates the goods mortgage under subsection (2) then, unless the mortgagee is entitled under subsection (5) to refuse termination and does so,—

(a) the mortgagor is released from all further liability under the obligation secured by the goods mortgage, and

(b) property in the goods is to be taken to have passed to the mortgagee when the goods were delivered to the mortgagee.

(8) If the mortgagee refuses termination on any of the grounds in subsection (5), the mortgagee must return the goods to the mortgagor.

24 Additional powers of court where mortgagee seeks possession of goods

(1) This section applies where—

(a) in any proceedings the mortgagee under a goods mortgage seeks possession of the goods, and

(b) the goods mortgage does not secure a regulated agreement within the meaning of the Consumer Credit Act 1974 (see section 129 of that Act for powers available to the court in relation to such an agreement).

(2) The court may exercise any of the powers conferred by this section if it appears to the court that in the event of its exercising the power the mortgagor is likely to be able within a reasonable period—

(a) to pay any sums due under the goods mortgage, or

(b) to remedy a default consisting of a breach of any other obligation arising under or by virtue of the goods mortgage.

(3) The court—

(a) may adjourn the proceedings for such period or periods as the court thinks reasonable, or

(b) on giving judgment, or making an order, for the delivery up of, or the taking possession of, the goods that are subject to the goods mortgage, or at any time before the execution of such a judgment or order, may—

    (i) stay or suspend execution of the judgment or order, or

    (ii) postpone the date for the delivery of possession,

for such period or periods as the court thinks reasonable.

(4) The adjournment, stay, suspension or postponement may be made subject to such conditions with regard to the payment by the mortgagor of any sum secured by the goods mortgage or the remedying of any default as the court thinks fit.

(5) The court may from time to time vary or revoke any condition imposed by virtue of this section.

Taking of possession by mortgagee after change of ownership

25 Order for taking of possession while goods owned by third party

(1) The mortgagee under a registered goods mortgage may apply to the court for an order under this section in relation to goods which are in the ownership of a person other than the mortgagor but which remain subject to the goods mortgage.

(2) The court may order the delivery up of the goods to, or the taking of possession by, the mortgagee.

Supplementary

26   Exempt goods mortgage

(1) A goods mortgage is an 'exempt goods mortgage' for the purposes of this Act in the following cases.

(2) A goods mortgage is an exempt goods mortgage if the obligation secured by it is—

(a) a guarantee (see section 6(3) for the cases in which a goods mortgage may secure a guarantee), or

(b) the obligation of the borrower under an agreement for running-account credit as defined by Schedule 1 (see section 6(4) for the cases in which a goods mortgage may secure such an obligation).

(3) A goods mortgage is also an exempt goods mortgage if—

(a) the high net worth conditions or the business credit conditions are met, and

(b) the instrument creating the goods mortgage includes a declaration by the mortgagor which—

(i)   states that the mortgagor agrees to forgo the protection and remedies given by sections 19(1) and 23(2), and

(ii) complies with prescribed requirements.

27   Contracting-out forbidden

(1) A term contained in a goods mortgage, or in any agreement secured by or related to a goods mortgage, is void if, and to the extent that, it is inconsistent with a provision for the protection of the mortgagor contained in this Act or in any regulations made under this Act.

(2) Where the provision specifies the duty or liability of the mortgagor in certain circumstances, the term is inconsistent with that provision if it purports to impose, directly or indirectly, an additional duty or liability on the mortgagor in those circumstances.

(3) Despite subsection (1), a provision of this Act under which a thing may be done in relation to any person only on an order of the court is not to be taken to prevent its being done at any time with that person's consent given at that time.

(4) The refusal of the consent mentioned in subsection (3) is not to give rise to any liability.

28   Interpretation of Part 4

(1) This section has effect for the interpretation of this Part.

(2) In relation to a goods mortgage 'mortgagor' includes a person to whom the original mortgagor's rights and duties under the goods mortgage have passed by operation of law, except that it does not include a trustee in bankruptcy.

(3) In relation to a goods mortgage over an undivided share in goods, references to goods are to be read, unless the context requires otherwise, as references to the undivided share.

PART 5 REPEALS AND FINAL PROVISIONS

Repeals

29   Repeal of Bills of Sale Acts 1878 and 1882

(1) The Bills of Sale Act 1878 and the Bills of Sale Act (1878) Amendment Act 1882 are repealed.

Final provisions

30   Regulations

(1) Any power of the Treasury or the Secretary of State to make regulations under this Act is exercisable by statutory instrument.

(2) Any such power includes—

(a) power to make different provision for different purposes, and

(b) power to make transitional, transitory or saving provision.

(3) Subsection (2) does not apply in relation to the power conferred by section 35 (but see sub-sections (3) and (4) of that section).

(4) A statutory instrument containing regulations under any provision of this Act other than section 35 is subject to annulment in pursuance of a resolution of either House of Parliament.

31 Meaning of 'credit' and 'credit agreement'

(1) In this Act 'credit' includes a cash loan, and any other form of financial accommodation.

(2) In this Act 'credit agreement' means an agreement between one or more persons ('the debtor') and any other person ('the creditor') by which the creditor provides the debtor with credit of any amount.

(3) Where credit is provided otherwise than in sterling, it is to be treated for the purposes of this Act as provided in sterling of an equivalent amount.

(4) For the purposes of this Act, an item entering into the total charge for credit is not to be treated as credit even though time is allowed for its payment.

(5) In subsection (4) 'the total charge for credit' has the meaning given by rules made by the Financial Conduct Authority under Article 60M of the Financial Services and Markets Act 2000 (Regulated Activities) Order 2001 (S.I. 2001/544), but as if any reference in the rules to a regulated credit agreement were to a credit agreement as defined by subsection (2).

32 Meaning of 'disposition' etc

(1) In this Act 'disposition' means—

(a) a contract of sale, as defined by section 2 of the Sale of Goods Act 1979, or

(b) a contract under which the owner of goods transfers or agrees to transfer ownership of the goods to another person and—

(i) the other person provides or agrees to provide consideration otherwise than by paying a price, or

(ii) the contract is, for any other reason, not a contract of sale or a hire-purchase agreement;

and 'dispose of' is to be read accordingly.

(2) For the purposes of this Act, a person becomes a 'purchaser' of goods if, and at the time when, the person enters into a disposition under which ownership of the goods is or is to be transferred to the person.

33 Further general definitions

In this Act—

'conditional sale agreement' has the meaning given by section 189 of the Consumer Credit Act 1974;

'the court' means the High Court or the county court;

'hire-purchase agreement' has the meaning given by section 189 of the Consumer Credit Act 1974;

'mortgagee', in relation to a goods mortgage, means the person or persons to whom the security is provided in accordance with section 2 or 3 or a person to whom the original mortgagee's rights and duties under the goods mortgage have passed by assignment or operation of law;

'mortgagor', in relation to a goods mortgage, means the individual who creates (or individuals who create) the charge in accordance with section 2 or 3, except that in Part 4 it has the extended meaning given by section 28(2);

'prescribed' means prescribed by regulations made by the Treasury under this Act.

36 Index of defined terms

The following Table sets out expressions defined in this Act for general purposes.

Expression	Provision
business credit conditions	section 7(3)
conditional sale agreement	section 33
the court	section 33
credit, credit agreement	section 31
disposition, dispose of	section 32
excluded obligation (in Part 2)	section 6
exempt goods mortgage	section 26
goods	section 4(2) (see also sections 11(4), 12(6) and 28(3))
goods mortgage	section 2(4)
guarantee	section 6(6)
high net worth conditions	section 7(2)
hire-purchase agreement	section 33
mortgagee	section 33
mortgagor	section 33
to own (and related expressions)	section 2(3)
possession notice	section 19(1)
prescribed	section 33
purchaser	section 32
qualifying goods	section 4(3)
registered (in relation to a goods mortgage)	section 9(9)

SCHEDULE 1

RUNNING-ACCOUNT CREDIT: SUPPLEMENTARY PROVISIONS

Introductory

1. This Schedule has effect for the interpretation of—

    (a) subsection (4) of section 6 (excluded obligations), and

    (b) section 7(3)(a) (the business credit conditions) in its application to section 6(4)(a).

Running-account credit

2. Running-account credit is a facility under a credit agreement under which the debtor is enabled to receive from time to time (whether for the debtor or for another person) from the creditor or a third party cash, goods and services (or any of them) to an amount or value such that, taking into account payments made by or to the credit of the debtor, the credit limit (if any) is not at any time exceeded.

3. In relation to running-account credit, 'credit limit' means, as respects any period, the maximum debit balance which, under the credit agreement, is allowed to stand on the account during that period, disregarding any term of the agreement allowing that maximum to be exceeded merely temporarily.

Determining amount of running-account credit

4.—(1) Running-account credit is to be taken not to exceed the amount prescribed for the purposes of section 7(3)(a) ('the specified amount') if—

    (a) the credit limit does not exceed the specified amount, or

    (b) whether or not there is a credit limit, and if there is, despite the fact that it exceeds the specified amount—

        (i)   the debtor is not enabled to draw at any one time an amount which, so far as (having regard to section 31(4)) it represents credit, exceeds the specified amount,

        (ii) the agreement provides that, if the debit balance rises above a given amount (not exceeding the specified amount), any condition favouring the creditor or the creditor's associate comes into operation, or

        (iii) at the time the agreement is made it is probable, having regard to the terms of the agreement and any other relevant considerations, that the debit balance will not at any time rise above the specified amount.

    (2) In sub-paragraph (1)(b)(ii) 'associate' is to be read in accordance with section 184 of the Consumer Credit Act 1974.

SCHEDULE 2

CONSEQUENTIAL AMENDMENTS

1.   Consumer Credit Act 1974 (c. 39)

In section 189(1) of the Consumer Credit Act 1974 (definitions), omit the definition of 'bill of sale'.

2.   Sale of Goods Act 1979 (c. 54)

In section 62 of the Sale of Goods Act 1979 (savings, rules of law etc), in subsection (3), omit 'the enactments relating to bills of sale, or'.

10.   Insolvency Act 1986 (c. 45)

    (1) Section 344 of the Insolvency Act 1986 (avoidance of general assignment of book debts) is amended as follows.

    (2) In subsection (2), for 'the Bills of Sale Act 1878' substitute 'section 9 of the Goods Mortgages Act 2017'.

    (3) For subsection (4) substitute—

'(4) For the purposes of the registration mentioned in subsection (2) of this section, subsections (1) to (3) and (5) and (6) of section 9 of the Goods Mortgages Act 2017 (which relate to the registration of goods mortgages) apply with any necessary modifications.'

(Draft) Insurable Interest Bill

A Bill to make provision about the law relating to insurable interest.   [2018]

1 Definitions

In this Act—

    'a contract of life-related insurance' means a contract of insurance under which the insured event is the death, injury, ill-health or incapacity of an individual, or the life of an individual continuing;

    'insured' means the party to a contract of insurance who is the insured under the contract;

    'insurer' means the party to a contract of insurance who is the insurer under the contract.

2 Insurable interest

    (1) A contract of life-related insurance is void unless at the time the insured enters into it the insured has an insurable interest for the purposes of the contract.

    (2) An insured has an insurable interest if there is a reasonable prospect that the insured will suffer economic loss if the insured event occurs.

    (3) Other circumstances in which an insured has an insurable interest include, in particular, circumstances where—

   (a) the individual who is the subject of the contract—
      (i) is the insured,
      (ii) is the spouse or civil partner of the insured or lives with the insured as a spouse or civil partner,
      (iii) is, or is treated as, the child or grandchild of the insured;
   (b) the individual who is the subject of the contract is a member of a pension or other group scheme which is administered by the insured (whether as a trustee or otherwise);
   (c) the contract is for the benefit of the individual who is the subject of the contract, or a nominee of that individual.

(4) Where the insured is the trustee of a trust, the insured has an insurable interest for the purposes of a contract in any circumstance where the settlor or truster of the trust would have had an insurable interest for the purposes of that contract.

(5) For the purposes of insurable interest, a contract of life-related insurance may provide that a reference to a category or description of individual includes individuals who do not fall within that category or meet that description at the time the contract is entered into, but who subsequently fall within that category or meet that description (including individuals who are not in existence at that time).

3 Effect of untrue statements

(1) If in entering into a contract which is void by virtue of this Act—
   (a) the insured makes an untrue or misleading statement about the insurable interest concerned, and
   (b) the insured knows the statement is untrue or misleading, or does not care whether or not the statement is true or misleading, the insurer need not return any of the premiums paid.

(2) In the case of a consumer insurance contract subsection (1) does not apply to the extent (if any) that it would be unfair to the insured for the insurer to retain the premiums.

(3) A 'consumer insurance contract' means a contract of insurance between—
   (a) an individual who enters into the contract wholly or mainly for purposes unrelated to the individual's trade, business or profession, and
   (b) a person who carries on the business of insurance and who becomes a party to the contract by way of that business (whether or not in accordance with permission for the purposes of the Financial Services and Markets Act 2000).

4 Relationship with existing law

The provision made by this Act replaces any other rule of law relating to the requirement of an insurable interest for the purposes of a contract of life-related insurance.

5 Exclusion for marine insurance contracts

Nothing in this Act has effect in relation to a contract of marine insurance, as defined by section 1 of the Marine Insurance Act 1906.

6 Repeals and consequential amendments

(1) In the Life Assurance Act 1774—
   (a) section 1 is repealed to the extent that it applies in relation to contracts of life-related insurance, and
   (b) sections 2 and 3 are repealed.

(2) The Marine Insurance Act 1788 and the Marine Insurance (Gambling Policies) Act 1909 are repealed.

7 Short title, commencement, application and extent

(3) This Act applies only in relation to contracts entered into after the Act comes into force.

(4) But in relation to any contract entered into before the commencement of this Act, an insured who would have an insurable interest for the purposes of this Act is deemed to have an insurable interest for the purposes of that contract.

(Draft) Consumer Rights (Transfer of Ownership under Sales Contracts) Bill

(Law Com. No. 398)

A Bill to make provision about when ownership of goods is transferred to consumers under sales contracts. [2021]

1   Transfer of ownership under a sales contract

(1) The Consumer Rights Act 2015 is amended as follows.

(2) In section 4 (ownership of goods), for subsection (2) substitute—

'(2) For the time when ownership of goods is transferred—

  (a) under a sales contract to which section 18A or 18B applies, see those sections, and

  (b) in any other case, see in particular the following provisions of the Sale of Goods Act 1979 (which relate to contracts of sale)—

  section 16: goods must be ascertained

  section 17: property passes when intended to pass

  section 18: rules for ascertaining intention

  section 19: reservation of right of disposal

  section 20A: undivided shares in goods forming part of a bulk

  section 20B: deemed consent by co-owner to dealings in bulk goods

(3) Where a sales contract to which section 18B applies is for goods that are contained in a bulk (within the meaning of the Sale of Goods Act 1979), nothing in this Chapter prevents the consumer from becoming an owner in common of the bulk by virtue of section 20A of that Act.'

(3) After section 18 insert—

'*When is ownership transferred under a sales contract?*

18A   Transfer of ownership: actual goods selected

(1) This section applies to a sales contract for goods, or for an undivided share of goods specified as a fraction or percentage, if—

  (a) the actual goods that are to be used to fulfil the contract have been selected when the contract is made, and

  (b) the contract is not a conditional sales contract.

(2) The contract is to be treated as including a term that ownership of the goods, or the share of the goods, transfers to the consumer when the contract is made.

(3) Any term of the contract that purports to provide for ownership to transfer to the consumer at a time later than that provided by virtue of this section is to that extent of no effect.

18B   Transfer of ownership: actual goods not selected

(1) This section applies to a sales contract for goods, or for an undivided share of goods specified as a fraction or percentage, if—

  (a) the actual goods that are to be used to fulfil the contract have not been selected when the contract is made, and

  (b) the contract is not a conditional sales contract.

(2) If under the contract the goods are to be manufactured or produced to a specification agreed between the trader and the consumer, the contract is to be treated as including a term that ownership of the goods, or the share of the goods, transfers to the consumer when the manufacture or production for the consumer is completed.

(3) In any other case, the contract is to be treated as including a term that ownership of the goods, or the share of the goods, transfers to the consumer when the first of the following occurs—

(a) the goods are physically labelled with the consumer's name in a way that is intended by the trader to be permanent;

(b) the goods are physically set aside for the consumer in a way that is intended by the trader to be permanent;

(c) the alteration of the goods to a specification agreed between the trader and the consumer is completed;

(d) the consumer is told by the trader that goods bearing a unique identifier will be used to fulfil the contract;

(e) on examining the goods the consumer agrees that they are to be used to fulfil the contract;

(f) the goods, identified as being those for delivery to theconsumer, are delivered to a carrier;

(g) the goods are delivered to the consumer;

(h) the goods that are to be used to fulfil the contract are selected by the trader in some other way, and the trader intends the selection to be permanent.

(4) If the trader acts as mentioned in subsection (3)(a), (b) or (h), the action is to be taken to have been intended by the trader to be permanent unless the contrary is proved.

(5) Any term of the contract that purports to provide for ownership to transfer to the consumer at a time later than that provided by virtue of this section is to that extent of no effect.'

2   Consequential amendments of the Sale of Goods Act 1979

(1) The Sale of Goods Act 1979 is amended as follows.

(2) In section 1 (contracts to which Act applies), for subsection (5) substitute—

'(5) Certain provisions of this Act do not apply to—

(a)   a contract to which Chapter 2 of Part 1 of the Consumer Rights Act 2015 applies;

(b)   a contract to which section 18A or 18B of that Act applies.'

(3) In section 16 (goods must be ascertained)—

(a) at the beginning insert '(1)', and

(b) at the end insert—

'(2) This section does not apply to a contract to which section 18B of the Consumer Rights Act 2015 applies.'

(4) In section 17 (property passes when intended to pass), at the end insert—

'(3) This section does not apply to a contract to which section 18A or 18B of the Consumer Rights Act 2015 applies.'

(5) In section 18 (rules for ascertaining intention)—

(a) at the beginning insert '(1)', and

(b) at the end insert—

'(2) This section does not apply to a contract to which section 18A or 18B of the Consumer Rights Act 2015 applies.'

(6) In section 19 (reservation of right of disposal), at the end insert—

'(4) This section does not apply to a contract to which section 18A or 18B of the Consumer Rights Act 2015 applies.'

(7) In section 43 (termination of lien), at the end insert—

'(3) In subsection (1)(a), the words "without reserving the right of disposal of the goods" do not apply to a contract to which section 18A or 18B of the Consumer Rights Act 2015 applies.'

3   Extent, commencement and short title

(1) This Act extends to England and Wales only.

(2) This Act comes into force at the end of the period of two months beginning with the day on which it is passed.

(3) This Act does not apply to a contract made before the day on which this Act comes into force.

(4) This Act may be cited as the Consumer Rights (Transfer of Ownership under Sales Contracts) Act 2021.

(Draft) Electronic Trade Documents Bill

(Law Com. No. 405)

A Bill to make provision about electronic trade documents; and for connected purposes.   [2022]

1 Definitions of 'paper trade document' and 'qualifying electronic document'

(1) A document is a 'paper trade document' for the purposes of this Act if—

    (a) it is in paper form, and

    (b) possession of the document is required as a matter of law or commercial custom, usage or practice for a person to claim performance of an obligation.

(2) The following are examples of documents that, if they fall within subsection (1), will be paper trade documents—

    (a) a bill of exchange;

    (b) a promissory note;

    (c) a bill of lading;

    (d) a ship's delivery order;

    (e) a warehouse receipt;

    (f) a mate's receipt;

    (g) a marine insurance policy

    (h) a cargo insurance certificate.

(3) Where information in electronic form is information that, if contained in a document in paper form, would lead to the document being a paper trade document, that information, together with any other information with which it is logically associated that is also in electronic form, constitutes a 'qualifying electronic document' for the purposes of this Act.

2 Definition of 'electronic trade document'

(1) A qualifying electronic document is an 'electronic trade document' for the purposes of this Act if a reliable system is used to—

    (a) identify the document so that it can be distinguished from any copies,

    (b) protect the document against unauthorised alteration,

    (c) secure that it is not possible for more than one person to exercise control of the document at any one time,

    (d) allow any person who is able to exercise control of the document to demonstrate that the person is able to do so, and

    (e) secure that a transfer of the document has effect to deprive any person who was able to exercise control of the document immediately before the transfer of the ability to do so (except to the extent that the person is able to exercise control by virtue of being a transferee).

(2) For the purposes of subsection (1)—

    (a) a person exercises control of a document when the person uses, transfers or otherwise disposes of the document (whether or not the person has the legal right to do so), and

    (b) persons acting jointly are to be treated as one person.

(3) Reading or viewing a document is not, of itself, sufficient to amount to use of the document for the purposes of subsection (2)(a).

(4) When determining whether a system is reliable for the purposes of subsection (1), the matters that may be taken into account include—

    (a) any rules of the system that apply to its operation;

    (b) any measures taken to secure the integrity of information held on the system;

    (c) any measures taken to prevent unauthorised access to and use of the system;

    (d) the security of the hardware and software used by the system;

    (e) the regularity of and extent of any audit of the system by an independent body;

    (f) any assessment of the reliability of the system made by a body with supervisory or regulatory functions;

    (g) the provisions of any voluntary scheme or industry standard that apply in relation to the system.

3 Possession, indorsement and effect of electronic trade documents

(1) A person may possess, indorse and part with possession of an electronic trade document.

(2) An electronic trade document has the same effect as the equivalent paper trade document.

(3) Anything done in relation to an electronic trade document that corresponds to anything that could be done in relation to the equivalent paper trade document has the same effect in relation to the electronic trade document as it would have in relation to the paper trade document.

4 Change of form

(1) A paper trade document may be converted into an electronic trade document, and an electronic trade document may be converted into a paper trade document, if (and only if)—

    (a) a statement that the document has been converted is included in the document in its new form, and

    (b) any contractual or other requirements relating to the conversion of the document are complied with.

(2) Where a document is converted in accordance with subsection (1)—

    (a) the document in its old form ceases to have effect, and

    (b) all rights and liabilities relating to the document continue to have effect in relation to the document in its new form.

5 Documents and instruments to which sections 1 to 4 do not apply

(1) Sections 1 to 4 of this Act do not apply in relation to a document or instrument listed in subsection (2).

(2) The list is as follows—

    (a) a bearer bond;

    (b) an uncertificated unit of a security that is transferable by means of a relevant system in accordance with the Uncertificated Securities Regulations 2001 (S.I. 2001/3755).

(3) The Secretary of State may by regulations made by statutory instrument add, remove or amend an entry in the list in subsection (2).

(4) Regulations under this section may make incidental, consequential, transitional or saving provision.

(5) A statutory instrument containing regulations under this section may not be made unless a draft of the instrument has been laid before and approved by a resolution of each House of Parliament.

6 Consequential provision

(1) In section 89B(2) of the Bills of Exchange Act 1882 (instruments to which section 89A applies), at the end insert 'or to a bill or note that is an electronic trade document for the purposes of the Electronic Trade Documents Act 2022 (see section 2 of that Act).'

(2) In section 1 of the Carriage of Goods by Sea Act 1992 (shipping documents etc), omit subsections (5) and (6).

7 Extent, commencement and short title

(1) This Act extends to England and Wales only.

(2) This Act comes into force at the end of the period of two months beginning with the day on which it is passed.

(3) This Act does not apply to a document issued before the day on which this Act comes into force

(4) This Act may be cited as the Electronic Trade Documents Act 2022.

Part III

Statutory Instruments

Commercial Agents (Council Directive) Regulations 1993

(SI 1993, No. 3053)

PART I GENERAL

1. Citation, commencement and applicable law

(1) These Regulations may be cited as the Commercial Agents (Council Directive) Regulations 1993 and shall come into force on 1st January 1994.

(2) These Regulations govern the relations between commercial agents and their principals and, subject to paragraph (3), apply in relation to the activities of commercial agents in Great Britain.

[(3) A court or tribunal shall:

(a) apply the law of the other member State concerned in place of regulations 3 to 22 where the parties have agreed that the agency contract is to be governed by the law of that member State;

(b) (whether or not it would otherwise be required to do so) apply these Regulations where the law of another member State corresponding to these Regulations enables the parties to agree that the agency contract is to be governed by the law of a different member State and the parties have agreed that it is to be governed by the law of England and Wales or Scotland.]

2. Interpretation, application and extent

(1) In these Regulations—

'commercial agent' means a self-employed intermediary who has continuing authority to negotiate the sale or purchase of goods on behalf of another person (the 'principal'), or to negotiate and conclude the sale or purchase of goods on behalf of and in the name of that principal; but shall be understood as not including in particular:

(i) a person who, in his capacity as an officer of a company or association, is empowered to enter into commitments binding on that company or association;

(ii) a partner who is lawfully authorised to enter into commitments binding on his partners;

(iii) a person who acts as an insolvency practitioner (as that expression is defined in section 388 of the Insolvency Act 1986) or the equivalent in any other jurisdiction;

'commission' means any part of the remuneration of a commercial agent which varies with the number or value of business transactions;

['EEA Agreement' means the Agreement on the European Economic Area signed at Oporto on 2nd May 1992 as adjusted by the Protocol signed at Brussels on 17th March 1993;

'member State' includes a State which is a contracting party to the EEA Agreement;]

'restraint of trade clause' means an agreement restricting the business activities of a commercial agent following termination of the agency contract.

(2) These Regulations do not apply to—

(a) commercial agents whose activities are unpaid;

(b) commercial agents when they operate on commodity exchanges or in the commodity market;

    (c) the Crown Agents for Overseas Governments and Administrations, as set up under the Crown Agents Act 1979, or its subsidiaries.

    (3) The provisions of the Schedule to these Regulations have effect for the purpose of determining the persons whose activities as commercial agents are to be considered secondary.

    (4) These Regulations shall not apply to the persons referred to in paragraph (3) above.

    (5) These Regulations do not extend to Northern Ireland.

PART II   RIGHTS AND OBLIGATIONS

3. Duties of a commercial agent to his principal

    (1) In performing his activities a commercial agent must look after the interests of his principal and act dutifully and in good faith.

    (2) In particular, a commercial agent must—

      (a) make proper efforts to negotiate and, where appropriate, conclude the transactions he is instructed to take care of;

      (b) communicate to his principal all the necessary information available to him;

      (c) comply with reasonable instructions given by his principal.

4. Duties of a principal to his commercial agent

    (1) In his relations with his commercial agent a principal must act dutifully and in good faith.

    (2) In particular, a principal must—

      (a) provide his commercial agent with the necessary documentation relating to the goods concerned;

      (b) obtain for his commercial agent the information necessary for the performance of the agency contract, and in particular notify his commercial agent within a reasonable period once he anticipates that the volume of commercial transactions will be significantly lower than that which the commercial agent could normally have expected.

    (3) A principal shall, in addition, inform his commercial agent within a reasonable period of his acceptance or refusal of, and of any non-execution by him of, a commercial transaction which the commercial agent has procured for him.

5. Prohibition on derogation from regulations 3 and 4 and consequence of breach

    (1) The parties may not derogate from regulations 3 and 4 above.

    (2) The law applicable to the contract shall govern the consequence of breach of the rights and obligations under regulations 3 and 4 above.

PART III   REMUNERATION

6. Form and amount of remuneration in absence of agreement

    (1) In the absence of any agreement as to remuneration between the parties, a commercial agent shall be entitled to the remuneration that commercial agents appointed for the goods forming the subject of his agency contract are customarily allowed in the place where he carries on his activities and, if there is no such customary practice, a commercial agent shall be entitled to reasonable remuneration taking into account all the aspects of the transaction.

    (2) This regulation is without prejudice to the application of any enactment or rule of law concerning the level of remuneration.

    (3) Where a commercial agent is not remunerated (wholly or in part) by commission, regulations 7 to 12 below shall not apply.

7. Entitlement to commission on transactions concluded during agency contract

    (1) A commercial agent shall be entitled to commission on commercial transactions concluded during the period covered by the agency contract—

    (a) where the transaction has been concluded as a result of his action; or

    (b) where the transaction is concluded with a third party whom he has previously acquired as a customer for transactions of the same kind.

(2) A commercial agent shall also be entitled to commission on transactions concluded during the period covered by the agency contract where he has an exclusive right to a specific geographical area or to a specific group of customers and where the transaction has been entered into with a customer belonging to that area or group.

8. Entitlement to commission on transactions concluded after agency contract has terminated

Subject to regulation 9 below, a commercial agent shall be entitled to commission on commercial transactions concluded after the agency contract has terminated if—

    (a) the transaction is mainly attributable to his efforts during the period covered by the agency contract and if the transaction was entered into within a reasonable period after that contract terminated; or

    (b) in accordance with the conditions mentioned in regulation 7 above, the order of the third party reached the principal or the commercial agent before the agency contract terminated.

9. Apportionment of commission between new and previous commercial agents

(1) A commercial agent shall not be entitled to the commission referred to in regulation 7 above if that commission is payable, by virtue of regulation 8 above, to the previous commercial agent, unless it is equitable because of the circumstances for the commission to be shared between the commercial agents.

(2) The principal shall be liable for any sum due under paragraph (1) above to the person entitled to it in accordance with that paragraph, and any sum which the other commercial agent receives to which he is not entitled shall be refunded to the principal.

10. When commission due and date for payment

(1) Commission shall become due as soon as, and to the extent that, one of the following circumstances occurs:

    (a) the principal has executed the transaction; or

    (b) the principal should, according to his agreement with the third party, have executed the transaction; or

    (c) the third party has executed the transaction.

(2) Commission shall become due at the latest when the third party has executed his part of the transaction or should have done so if the principal had executed his part of the transaction, as he should have.

(3) The commission shall be paid not later than on the last day of the month following the quarter in which it became due, and, for the purposes of these Regulations, unless otherwise agreed between the parties, the first quarter period shall run from the date the agency contract takes effect, and subsequent periods shall run from that date in the third month thereafter or the beginning of the fourth month, whichever is the sooner.

(4) Any agreement to derogate from paragraphs (2) and (3) above to the detriment of the commercial agent shall be void.

11. Extinction of right to commission

(1) The right to commission can be extinguished only if and to the extent that—

    (a) it is established that the contract between the third party and the principal will not be executed; and

    (b) that fact is due to a reason for which the principal is not to blame.

(2) Any commission which the commercial agent has already received shall be refunded if the right to it is extinguished.

(3) any agreement to derogate from paragraph (1) above to the detriment of the commercial agent shall be void.

12. Periodic supply of information as to commission due and right of inspection of principal's books

(1) The principal shall supply his commercial agent with a statement of the commission due, not later than the last day of the month following the quarter in which the commission has become due, and such statement shall set out the main components used in calculating the amount of the commission.

(2) A commercial agent shall be entitled to demand that he be provided with all the information (and in particular an extract from the books) which is available to his principal and which he needs in order to check the amount of the commission due to him.

(3) Any agreement to derogate from paragraphs (1) and (2) above shall be void.

(4) Nothing in this regulation shall remove or restrict the effect of, or prevent reliance upon, any enactment or rule of law which recognises the right of an agent to inspect the books of a principal.

PART IV CONCLUSION AND TERMINATION OF THE AGENCY CONTRACT

13. Right to signed written statement of terms of agency contract

(1) The commercial agent and principal shall each be entitled to receive from the other, on request, a signed written document setting out the terms of the agency contract including any terms subsequently agreed.

(2) Any purported waiver of the right referred to in paragraph (1) above shall be void.

14. Conversion of agency contract after expiry of fixed period

An agency contract for a fixed period which continues to be performed by both parties after that period has expired shall be deemed to be converted into an agency contract for an indefinite period.

15. Minimum periods of notice for termination of agency contract

(1) Where an agency contract is concluded for an indefinite period either party may terminate it by notice.

(2) The period of notice shall be—

    (a) 1 month for the first year of the contract;

    (b) 2 months for the second year commenced;

    (c) 3 months for the third year commenced and for the subsequent years;

and the parties may not agree on any shorter periods of notice.

(3) If the parties agree on longer periods than those laid down in paragraph (2) above, the period of notice to be observed by the principal must not be shorter than that to be observed by the commercial agent.

(4) Unless otherwise agreed by the parties, the end of the period of notice must coincide with the end of a calendar month.

(5) The provisions of this regulation shall also apply to an agency contract for a fixed period where it is converted under regulation 14 above into an agency contract for an indefinite period subject to the proviso that the earlier fixed period must be taken into account in the calculation of the period of notice.

16. Savings with regard to immediate termination

These Regulations shall not affect the application of any enactment or rule of law which provides for the immediate termination of the agency contract—

    (a) because of the failure of one party to carry out all or part of his obligations under that contract; or

    (b) where exceptional circumstances arise.

17. Entitlement of commercial agent to indemnity or compensation on termination of agency contract

(1) This regulation has effect for the purpose of ensuring that the commercial agent is, after termination of the agency contract, indemnified in accordance with paragraphs (3) to (5) below or compensated for damage in accordance with paragraphs (6) and (7) below.

(2) Except where the agency [contract] otherwise provides, the commercial agent shall be entitled to be compensated rather than indemnified.

(3) Subject to paragraph (9) and to regulation 18 below, the commercial agent shall be entitled to an indemnity if and to the extent that—

(a) he has brought the principal new customers or has significantly increased the volume of business with existing customers and the principal continues to derive substantial benefits from the business with such customers; and

(b) the payment of this indemnity is equitable having regard to all the circumstances and, in particular, the commission lost by the commercial agent on the business transacted with such customers.

(4) The amount of the indemnity shall not exceed a figure equivalent to an indemnity for one year calculated from the commercial agent's average annual remuneration over the preceding five years and if the contract goes back less than five years the indemnity shall be calculated on the average for the period in question.

(5) The grant of an indemnity as mentioned above shall not prevent the commercial agent from seeking damages.

(6) Subject to paragraph (9) and to regulation 18 below, the commercial agent shall be entitled to compensation for the damage he suffers as a result of the termination of his relations with his principal.

(7) For the purpose of these Regulations such damage shall be deemed to occur particularly when the termination takes place in either or both of the following circumstances, namely circumstances which—

(a) deprive the commercial agent of the commission which proper performance of the agency contract would have procured for him whilst providing his principal with substantial benefits linked to the activities of the commercial agent; or

(b) have not enabled the commercial agent to amortize the costs and expenses that he had incurred in the performance of the agency contract on the advice of his principal.

(8) Entitlement to the indemnity or compensation for damage as provided for under paragraphs (2) to (7) above shall also arise where the agency contract is terminated as a result of the death of the commercial agent.

(9) The commercial agent shall lose his entitlement to the indemnity or compensation for damage in the instances provided for in paragraphs (2) to (8) above if within one year following termination of his agency contract he has not notified his principal that he intends pursuing his entitlement.

18. Grounds for excluding payment of indemnity or compensation under regulation 17

The [indemnity or] compensation referred to in regulation 17 above shall not be payable to the commercial agent where—

(a) the principal has terminated the agency contract because of default attributable to the commercial agent which would justify immediate termination of the agency contract pursuant to regulation 16 above; or

(b) the commercial agent has himself terminated the agency contract, unless such termination is justified—

(i) by circumstances attributable to the principal, or

(ii) on grounds of the age, infirmity or illness of the commercial agent in consequence of which he cannot reasonably be required to continue his activities; or

(c) the commercial agent, with the agreement of his principal, assigns his rights and duties under the agency contract to another person.

19. Prohibition on derogation from regulations 17 and 18

The parties may not derogate from regulations 17 and 18 to the detriment of the commercial agent before the agency contract expires.

20. Restraint of trade clauses

(1) A restraint of trade clause shall be valid only if and to the extent that—

(a) it is concluded in writing; and

(b) it relates to the geographical area or the group of customers and the geographical area entrusted to the commercial agent and to the kind of goods covered by his agency under the contract.

(2) A restraint of trade clause shall be valid for not more than two years after termination of the agency contract.

(3) Nothing in this regulation shall affect any enactment or rule of law which imposes other restrictions on the validity or enforceability of restraint of trade clauses or which enables a court to reduce the obligations on the parties resulting from such clauses.

PART V MISCELLANEOUS AND SUPPLEMENTAL

21. Disclosure of information
Nothing in these Regulations shall require information to be given where such disclosure would be contrary to public policy.

22. Service of notice etc
(1) Any notice, statement or other document to be given or supplied to a commercial agent or to be given or supplied to the principal under these Regulations may be so given or supplied:

(a) by delivering it to him;

(b) by leaving it at his proper address addressed to him by name;

(c) by sending it by post to him addressed either to his registered address or to the address of his registered or principal office;

or by any other means provided for in the agency contract.

(2) Any such notice, statement or document may—

(a) in the case of a body corporate, be given or served on the secretary or clerk of that body;

(b) in the case of a partnership, be given to or served on any partner or on any person having the control or management of the partnership business.

23. Transitional provisions
(1) Notwithstanding any provision in an agency contract made before 1st January 1994, these Regulations shall apply to that contract after that date and, accordingly any provision which is inconsistent with these Regulations shall have effect subject to them.

(2) Nothing in these Regulations shall affect the rights and liabilities of a commercial agent or a principal which have accrued before 1st January 1994.

Regulation 2(3)   # THE SCHEDULE

1. The activities of a person as a commercial agent are to be considered secondary where it may reasonably be taken that the primary purpose of the arrangement with his principal is other than as set out in paragraph 2 below.

2. An arrangement falls within this paragraph if—

(a) the business of the principal is the sale, or as the case may be purchase, of goods of a particular kind; and

(b) the goods concerned are such that—

(i)   transactions are normally individually negotiated and concluded on a commercial basis, and

(ii) procuring a transaction on one occasion is likely to lead to further transactions in those goods with that customer on future occasions, or to transactions in those goods with other customers in the same geographical area or among the same group of customers, and

that accordingly it is in the commercial interests of the principal in developing the market in those goods to appoint a representative to such customers with a view to the representative devoting effort, skill and expenditure from his own resources to that end.

3. The following are indications that an arrangement falls within paragraph 2 above, and the absence of any of them is an indication to the contrary—

(a) the principal is the manufacturer, importer or distributor of the goods;

(b) the goods are specifically identified with the principal in the market in question rather than, or to a greater extent than, with any other person;

(c) the agent devotes substantially the whole of his time to representative activities (whether for one principal or for a number of principals whose interests are not conflicting);

(d) the goods are not normally available in the market in question other than by means of the agent;

(e) the arrangement is described as one of commercial agency.

4. The following are indications that an arrangement does not fall within paragraph 2 above—

(a) promotional material is supplied direct to potential customers;

(b) persons are granted agencies without reference to existing agents in a particular area or in relation to a particular group;

(c) customers normally select the goods for themselves and merely place their orders through the agent.

5. The activities of the following categories of persons are presumed, unless the contrary is established, not to fall within paragraph 2 above—

Mail order catalogue agents for consumer goods.

Consumer credit agents.

Insolvency Act 1986 (Prescribed Part) Order 2003

(SI 2003, No. 2097)

1.   Citation, Commencement and Interpretation

(2) In this order 'the 1986 Act' means the Insolvency Act 1986.

2.   Minimum value of the company's net property

For the purposes of section 176A(3)(a) of the 1986 Act the minimum value of the company's net property is £10,000.

3.   Calculation of prescribed part

(1) The prescribed part of the company's net property to be made available for the satisfaction of un-secured debts of the company pursuant to section 176A of the 1986 Act shall be calculated as follows—

(a) where the company's net property does not exceed £10,000 in value, 50% of that property;

(b) subject to paragraph (2), where the company's net property exceeds £10,000 in value the sum of—

(i)   50% of the first £10,000 in value; and

(ii) 20% of that part of the company's net property which exceeds £10,000 in value.

(2) The value of the prescribed part of the company's net property to be made available for the satisfaction of unsecured debts of the company pursuant to section 176A shall not exceed [£800,000].

Consumer Credit (Disclosure of Information) Regulations 2004

(SI 2004, No. 1481)

1.   Citation, commencement and interpretation

(2) In these Regulations—

['the Act' means the Consumer Credit Act 1974;]

'the Agreements Regulations' mean the Consumer Credit (Agreements) Regulations 1983;

'distance contract' means any regulated agreement made under an organised distance sales or service-provision scheme run by the creditor or owner or by an intermediary of the creditor or owner who, in any such case, for the purpose of that agreement makes exclusive use of one or more means of distance communication up to and including the time at which the agreement is made and for this purpose any means of communication is a means of distance communication if, without the simultaneous physical presence of the creditor or owner or any intermediary of the creditor or owner and of the debtor or hirer, it may be used for the distance marketing of a regulated agreement between the parties to that agreement;

'durable medium' means any instrument which enables the debtor or hirer to store information addressed personally to him in a way accessible for future reference for a period of time adequate for the purposes of the information and which allows the unchanged reproduction of the information stored.

[**2. Agreements to which these Regulations apply**

(1) Subject to paragraph (3) these Regulations apply in respect of the following regulated agreements—

(a) consumer credit agreements secured on land except those to which section 58 of the Act (opportunity for withdrawal from prospective land mortgage) applies,

(b) consumer hire agreements,

(c) consumer credit agreements under which the creditor provides the debtor with credit which exceeds £60,260,

(d) consumer credit agreements entered into by the debtor wholly or predominantly for the purposes of a business carried on, or intended to be carried on, by him, and

(e) small debtor-creditor-supplier agreements for restricted-use credit,

except to the extent the Consumer Credit (Disclosure of Information) Regulations 2010 apply to such agreements.

(2) Subsections (2) to (5) of section 16B of the Act (declaration by the debtor as to the purposes of the agreement) apply for the purposes of paragraph (1)(d).

(3) These Regulations do not apply to—

(a) a distance contract;

(b) an authorised non-business overdraft agreement;

(c) an agreement which would be an authorised non-business overdraft agreement but for the fact that the credit is not repayable on demand or within three months.]

3. Information to be disclosed to a debtor or hirer before a regulated agreement is made

(1) Before a regulated agreement ('the relevant agreement') is made, the creditor or owner must disclose to the debtor or hirer in the manner set out in regulation 4 the information and statements of protection and remedies that are required to be given—

(a) in the case of a regulated consumer credit agreement, under regulation 2 of the Agreements Regulations;

(b) in the case of a regulated consumer hire agreement, under regulation 3 of the Agreements Regulations;

(c) in the case of a modifying agreement which is, or is treated as, a regulated consumer credit agreement, under regulations 2(3) and 7(2) of the Agreements Regulations;

(d) in the case of a modifying agreement which is or is treated as a regulated consumer hirer agreement, under regulations 3(3) and 7(9) of the Agreements Regulations.

[(1A) In the case of an agreement falling within regulation 2(1)(c), (d) or (e), the creditor shall provide, in addition to the information specified in paragraph (1), a statement in accordance with section 157(A1) of the Act that if the creditor decides not to proceed with a prospective regulated consumer credit agreement he must, when informing the debtor of this decision, inform the debtor that this decision has been reached on the basis of information from a credit reference agency and of the particulars of that agency.]

(2) The information and statements of protection required to be disclosed under paragraph (1) shall be the information and statements that will be included in the document embodying the

relevant agreement save that, where any of the information is not known at the time of disclosure, the creditor or owner shall disclose estimated information based on such assumptions as he may reasonably make in all the circumstances of the case.

4. Manner of disclosure

The information and statements of protection and remedies required to be disclosed under regulation 3 must be—

    (a) easily legible and, where applicable, of a colour which is readily distinguishable from the background medium upon which they are displayed;

    (b) not interspersed with any other information or wording apart from subtotals of total amounts and cross references to the terms of the agreement;

    (c) of equal prominence except that headings may be afforded more prominence whether by capital letters, underlining, larger or bold print or otherwise; and

    (d) contained in a document which:

        (i) is separate from the document embodying the relevant agreement (within the meaning of regulation 3) and any other document referred to in the document embodying that agreement;

        (ii) is headed with the words 'Pre-contract Information';

        (iii) does not contain any other information or wording apart from the heading referred to in sub-paragraph (ii);

        (iv) is on paper or on another durable medium which is available and accessible to the debtor or hirer; and

        (v) is of a nature that enables the debtor or hirer to remove it from the place where it is disclosed to him.

General Product Safety Regulations 2005

(SI 2005, No. 1803)

PART 1 GENERAL

2. Interpretation

In these Regulations:—

'the 1987 Act' means the Consumer Protection Act 1987;

'contravention' includes a failure to comply and cognate expressions shall be construed accordingly;

'dangerous product' means a product other than a safe product;

'distributor' means a professional in the supply chain whose activity does not affect the safety properties of a product;

'enforcement authority' means the Secretary of State, any other Minister of the Crown in charge of a government department, any such department and any authority or council mentioned in regulation 10;

'general safety requirement' means the requirement that only safe products should be placed on the market;

'magistrates' court' in relation to Northern Ireland, means a court of summary jurisdiction;

['the market' means the United Kingdom market;]

'notice' means a notice in writing;

'officer', in relation to an enforcement authority, means a person authorised in writing to assist the authority in carrying out its functions under or for the purposes of the enforcement of these Regulations and safety notices, except in relation to an enforcement authority which is a government department where it means an officer of that department;

'producer' means—

    (a) the manufacturer of a product, when he is established in [the United Kingdom] and any other person presenting himself as the manufacturer by affixing to the product his name, trade mark or other distinctive mark, or the person who reconditions the product;

    (b) when the manufacturer is not established in [the United Kingdom]—

        (i) if he has a representative established in [the United Kingdom], the representative,

        (ii) in any other case, the [person established in the United Kingdom that places a product from a country outside the United Kingdom on the market];

    (c) other professionals in the supply chain, insofar as their activities may affect the safety properties of a product;

'product' means a product which is intended for consumers or likely, under reasonably foreseeable conditions, to be used by consumers even if not intended for them and which is supplied or made available, whether for consideration or not, in the course of a commercial activity and whether it is new, used or reconditioned and includes a product that is supplied or made available to consumers for their own use in the context of providing a service. 'product' does not include equipment used by service providers themselves to supply a service to consumers, in particular equipment on which consumers ride or travel which is operated by a service provider;

'recall' means any measure aimed at achieving the return of a dangerous product that has already been supplied or made available to consumers;

'recall notice' means a notice under regulation 15;

'record' includes any book or document and any record in any form;

['relevant enactment' means any retained EU law derived from an EU instrument harmonising the conditions for the marketing of products in the EU but does not include Regulation (EC) No 765/2008 of the European Parliament and the Council setting out the requirements for accreditation and market surveillance relating to the marketing of products and repealing Regulation (EEC) No 339/93];

'requirement to mark' means a notice under regulation 12;

'requirement to warn' means a notice under regulation 13;

'safe product' means a product which, under normal or reasonably foreseeable conditions of use including duration and, where applicable, putting into service, installation and maintenance requirements, does not present any risk or only the minimum risks compatible with the product's use, considered to be acceptable and consistent with a high level of protection for the safety and health of persons. In determining the foregoing, the following shall be taken into account in particular—

    (a) the characteristics of the product, including its composition, packaging, instructions for assembly and, where applicable, instructions for installation and maintenance,

    (b) the effect of the product on other products, where it is reasonably foreseeable that it will be used with other products,

    (c) the presentation of the product, the labelling, any warnings and instructions for its use and disposal and any other indication or information regarding the product, and

    (d) the categories of consumers at risk when using the product, in particular children and the elderly.

The feasibility of obtaining higher levels of safety or the availability of other products presenting a lesser degree of risk shall not constitute grounds for considering a product to be a dangerous product;

'safety notice' means a suspension notice, a requirement to mark, a requirement to warn, a withdrawal notice or a recall notice;

'serious risk' means a serious risk, including one the effects of which are not immediate, requiring rapid intervention;

'supply' in relation to a product includes making it available, in the context of providing a service, for use by consumers;

'suspension notice' means a notice under regulation 11;

'withdrawal' means any measure aimed at preventing the distribution, display or offer of a dangerous product to a consumer;

'withdrawal notice' means a notice under regulation 14.

3. Application

(1) Each provision of these Regulations applies to a product in so far as there are no specific provisions with the same objective in [any relevant enactment] governing the safety of the product [. . .].

(2) Where a product is subject to specific safety requirements imposed by [any relevant enactment . . .], these Regulations shall apply only to the aspects and risks or category of risks not covered by those requirements. This means that:

    (a) the definition of 'safe product' and 'dangerous product' in regulation 2 and regulations 5 and 6 shall not apply to such a product in so far as concerns the risks or category of risks covered by the specific [provisions of the enactment], and

    (b) the remainder of these Regulations shall apply except where there are specific provisions governing the aspects covered by those regulations with the same objective.

4. These Regulations do not apply to a second-hand product supplied as a product to be repaired or reconditioned prior to being used, provided the supplier clearly informs the person to whom he supplies the product to that effect.

PART 2 OBLIGATIONS OF PRODUCERS AND DISTRIBUTORS

5. General safety requirement

(1) No producer shall place a product on the market unless the product is a safe product.

(2) No producer shall offer or agree to place a product on the market or expose or possess a product for placing on the market unless the product is a safe product.

(3) No producer shall offer or agree to supply a product or expose or possess a product for supply unless the product is a safe product.

(4) No producer shall supply a product unless the product is a safe product.

6. Presumption of conformity

(1) Where, in the absence of specific provisions in [any relevant enactment] governing the safety of a product, the product conforms to the specific rules of [any other law] of part of the United Kingdom laying down the health and safety requirements which the product must satisfy in order to be marketed in the United Kingdom, the product shall be deemed safe so far as concerns the aspects covered by such rules.

(2) Where a product conforms to a [standard ('S') which—

    (a) is a voluntary national standard of the United Kingdom or a standard adopted by an international standardising body, and

    (b) meets the conditions in paragraph (2A),

the product] shall be presumed to be a safe product so far as concerns the risks and categories of risk covered by [S].

    [(2A) The conditions referred to in paragraph (2) are that—

    (a) the Secretary of State considers S appropriate for the purposes of giving rise to the presumption of conformity; and

    (b) the Secretary of State has published the reference to S in a manner the Secretary of State considers appropriate.]

(3) In circumstances other than those referred to in paragraphs (1) and (2), the conformity of a product to the general safety requirement shall be assessed taking into account—

    (b) [. . .] national standards drawn up in the United Kingdom,

    (c) recommendations of the [Secretary of State] setting guidelines on product safety assessment,

    (d) product safety codes of good practice in the sector concerned,

    (e) the state of the art and technology, and

    (f) reasonable consumer expectations concerning safety.

(4) Conformity of a product with the criteria designed to ensure the general safety requirement is complied with, in particular the provisions mentioned in paragraphs (1) to (3), shall not bar an enforcement authority from exercising its powers under these Regulations in relation to that product where there is evidence that, despite such conformity, it is dangerous.

[(5) In this regulation 'international standardising body' has the same meaning as it has for the purposes of the Agreement on Technical Barriers to Trade, part of Annex 1A to the agreement establishing the World Trade Organisation signed at Marrakesh on 15 April 1994 (as modified from time to time).]

7. Other obligations of producers

(1) Within the limits of his activities, a producer shall provide consumers with the relevant information to enable them—

    (a) to assess the risks inherent in a product throughout the normal or reasonably foreseeable period of its use, where such risks are not immediately obvious without adequate warnings, and

    (b) to take precautions against those risks.

(2) The presence of warnings does not exempt any person from compliance with the other requirements of these Regulations.

(3) Within the limits of his activities, a producer shall adopt measures commensurate with the characteristics of the products which he supplies to enable him to—

    (a) be informed of the risks which the products might pose, and

    (b) take appropriate action including, where necessary to avoid such risks, withdrawal, adequately and effectively warning consumers as to the risks or, as a last resort, recall.

(4) The measures referred to in paragraph (3) include—

    (a) except where it is not reasonable to do so, an indication by means of the product or its packaging of—

        (i)   the name and address of the producer, and

        (ii) the product reference or where applicable the batch of products to which it belongs; and

    (b) where and to the extent that it is reasonable to do so—

        (i)   sample testing of marketed products,

        (ii) investigating and if necessary keeping a register of complaints concerning the safety of the product, and

        (iii) keeping distributors informed of the results of such monitoring where a product presents a risk or may present a risk.

8. Obligations of distributors

(1) A distributor shall act with due care in order to help ensure compliance with the applicable safety requirements and in particular he—

    (a) shall not expose or possess for supply or offer or agree to supply, or supply, a product to any person which he knows or should have presumed, on the basis of the information in his possession and as a professional, is a dangerous product; and

    (b) shall, within the limits of his activities, participate in monitoring the safety of a product placed on the market, in particular by—

        (i)   passing on information on the risks posed by the product,

        (ii) keeping the documentation necessary for tracing the origin of the product,

        (iii) producing the documentation necessary for tracing the origin of the product, and cooperating in action taken by a producer or an enforcement authority to avoid the risks.

(2) Within the limits of his activities, a distributor shall take measures enabling him to co-operate efficiently in the action referred to in paragraph (1)(b)(iii).

9. Obligations of producers and distributors

(1) Subject to paragraph (2), where a producer or a distributor knows that a product he has placed on the market or supplied poses risks to the consumer that are incompatible with the general

safety requirement, he shall forthwith notify an enforcement authority in writing of that information and—

   (a) the action taken to prevent risk to the consumer; [. . .].

(2) Paragraph (1) shall not apply—

   (a) in the case of a second-hand product supplied as an antique or as a product to be repaired or reconditioned prior to being used, provided the supplier clearly informed the person to whom he supplied the product to that effect,

   (b) in conditions concerning isolated circumstances or products.

(3) In the event of a serious risk the notification under paragraph (1) shall include the following—

   (a) information enabling a precise identification of the product or batch of products in question,

   (b) a full description of the risks that the product presents,

   (c) all available information relevant for tracing the product, and

   (d) a description of the action undertaken to prevent risks to the consumer.

(4) Within the limits of his activities, a person who is a producer or a distributor shall co-operate with an enforcement authority (at the enforcement authority's request) in action taken to avoid the risks posed by a product which he supplies or has supplied. Every enforcement authority shall maintain procedures for such co-operation, including procedures for dialogue with the producers and distributors concerned on issues related to product safety.

PART 3 ENFORCEMENT

10. Enforcement

(1) It shall be the duty of every authority to which paragraph (4) applies to enforce within its area these Regulations and safety notices.

(2) An authority in England or Wales to which paragraph (4) applies shall have the power to investigate and prosecute for an alleged contravention of any provision imposed by or under these Regulations which was committed outside its area in any part of England and Wales.

(3) A district council in Northern Ireland shall have the power to investigate and prosecute for an alleged contravention of any provision imposed by or under these Regulations which was committed outside its area in any part of Northern Ireland.

(4) The authorities to which this paragraph applies are:

   (a) in England, a county council, district council, London Borough Council, the Common Council of the City of London in its capacity as a local authority and the Council of the Isles of Scilly,

   (b) in Wales, a county council or a county borough council,

   (c) in Scotland, a council constituted under section 2 of the Local Government etc. (Scotland) Act 1994,

   (d) in Northern Ireland any district council.

(5) An enforcement authority shall in enforcing these Regulations act in a manner proportionate to the seriousness of the risk and shall take due account of the precautionary principle. In this context, it shall encourage and promote voluntary action by producers and distributors. Notwithstanding the foregoing, an enforcement authority may take any action under these Regulations urgently and without first encouraging and promoting voluntary action if a product poses a serious risk.

11. Suspension notices

(1) Where an enforcement authority has reasonable grounds for suspecting that a requirement of these Regulations has been contravened in relation to a product, the authority may, for the period needed to organise appropriate safety evaluations, checks and controls, serve a notice ('a suspension notice') prohibiting the person on whom it is served from doing any of the following things without the consent of the authority, that is to say—

   (a) placing the product on the market, offering to place it on the market, agreeing to place it on the market or exposing it for placing on the market, or

(b) supplying the product, offering to supply it, agreeing to supply it or exposing it for supply.

(2) A suspension notice served by an enforcement authority in relation to a product may require the person on whom it is served to keep the authority informed of the whereabouts of any such product in which he has an interest.

(3) A consent given by the enforcement authority for the purposes of paragraph (1) may impose such conditions on the doing of anything for which the consent is required as the authority considers appropriate.

12. Requirements to mark

(1) Where an enforcement authority has reasonable grounds for believing that a product is a dangerous product in that it could pose risks in certain conditions, the authority may serve a notice ('a requirement to mark') requiring the person on whom the notice is served at his own expense to undertake either or both of the following, as specified in the notice—

> (a) to ensure that the product is marked in accordance with requirements specified in the notice with warnings as to the risks it may present,
>
> (b) to make the marketing of the product subject to prior conditions as specified in the notice so as to ensure the product is a safe product.

(2) The requirements referred to in paragraph (1)(a) shall be such as to ensure that the product is marked with a warning which is suitable, clearly worded and easily comprehensible.

13. Requirements to warn

Where an enforcement authority has reasonable grounds for believing that a product is a dangerous product in that it could pose risks for certain persons, the authority may serve a notice ('a requirement to warn') requiring the person on whom the notice is served at his own expense to undertake one or more of the following, as specified in the notice—

> (a) where and to the extent it is practicable to do so, to ensure that any person who could be subject to such risks and who has been supplied with the product be given warning of the risks in good time and in a form specified in the notice,
>
> (b) to publish a warning of the risks in such form and manner as is likely to bring those risks to the attention of any such person,
>
> (c) to ensure that the product carries a warning of the risks in a form specified in the notice.

14. Withdrawal notices

(1) Where an enforcement authority has reasonable grounds for believing that a product is a dangerous product, the authority may serve a notice ('a withdrawal notice') prohibiting the person on whom it is served from doing any of the following things without the consent of the authority, that is to say—

> (a) placing the product on the market, offering to place it on the market, agreeing to place it on the market or exposing it for placing on the market, or
>
> (b) supplying the product, offering to supply it, agreeing to supply it or exposing it for supply.

(2) A withdrawal notice may require the person on whom it is served to take action to alert consumers to the risks that the product presents.

(3) In relation to a product that is already on the market, a withdrawal notice may only be served by an enforcement authority where the action being undertaken by the producer or the distributor concerned in fulfilment of his obligations under these Regulations is unsatisfactory or insufficient to prevent the risks concerned to the health and safety of persons.

(4) Paragraph (3) shall not apply in the case of a product posing a serious risk requiring, in the view of the enforcement authority, urgent action.

(5) A withdrawal notice served by an enforcement authority in relation to a product may require the person on whom it is served to keep the authority informed of the whereabouts of any such product in which he has an interest.

(6) A consent given by the enforcement authority for the purposes of paragraph (1) may impose such conditions on the doing of anything for which the consent is required as the authority considers appropriate.

15. Recall notices

(1) Subject to paragraph (4), where an enforcement authority has reasonable grounds for believing that a product is a dangerous product and that it has already been supplied or made available to consumers, the authority may serve a notice ('a recall notice') requiring the person on whom it is served to use his reasonable endeavours to organise the return of the product from consumers to that person or to such other person as is specified in the notice.

(2) A recall notice may require—

(a) the recall to be effected in accordance with a code of practice applicable to the product concerned, or

(b) the recipient of the recall notice to—

(i) contact consumers who have purchased the product in order to inform them of the recall, where and to the extent it is practicable to do so,

(ii) publish a notice in such form and such manner as is likely to bring to the attention of purchasers of the product the risk the product poses and the fact of the recall, or

(iii) make arrangements for the collection or return of the product from consumers who have purchased it or for its disposal,

and may impose such additional requirements on the recipient of the notice as are reasonable and practicable with a view to achieving the return of the product from consumers to the person specified in the notice or its disposal.

(3) In determining what requirements to include in a recall notice, the enforcement authority shall take into consideration the need to encourage distributors, users and consumers to contribute to its implementation.

(4) A recall notice may only be issued by an enforcement authority where—

(a) other action which it may require under these Regulations would not suffice to prevent the risks concerned to the health and safety of persons,

(b) the action being undertaken by the producer or the distributor concerned in fulfilment of his obligations under these Regulations is unsatisfactory or insufficient to prevent the risks concerned to the health and safety of persons, and

(c) the authority has given not less than [ten] days notice to the person on whom the recall notice is to be served of its intention to serve such a notice and where that person has before the expiry of that period by notice required the authority to seek the advice of such person as the Institute determines on the questions of—

(i) whether the product is a dangerous product,

(ii) whether the issue of a recall notice is proportionate to the seriousness of the risk, and

the authority has taken account of such advice.

(5) Paragraphs (4)(b) and (c) shall not apply in the case of a product posing a serious risk requiring, in the view of the enforcement authority, urgent action.

(6) Where a person requires an enforcement authority to seek advice as referred to in paragraph (4)(c), that person shall be responsible for the fees, costs and expenses of the Institute and of the person appointed by the Institute to advise the authority.

(7) In paragraphs 4(c) and (6) 'the Institute' means the charitable organisation with registered number 803725 and known as the Chartered Institute of Arbitrators.

(8) A recall notice served by an enforcement authority in relation to a product may require the person on whom it is served to keep the authority informed of the whereabouts of any such product to which the recall notice relates, so far as he is able to do so.

(9) Where the conditions in paragraph (1) for serving a recall notice are satisfied and either the enforcement authority has been unable to identify any person on whom to serve a recall notice, or the person on whom such a notice has been served has failed to comply with it, then the authority may itself take such action as could have been required by a recall notice.

(10) Where—

(a) an authority has complied with the requirements of paragraph (4); and

(b) the authority has exercised its powers under paragraph (9) to take action following the failure of the person on whom the recall notice has been served to comply with that notice,

then the authority may recover from the person on whom the notice was served summarily as a civil debt, any costs or expenses reasonably incurred by it in undertaking the action referred to in sub-paragraph (b).

(11) A civil debt recoverable under the preceding paragraph may be recovered—

(a) in England and Wales by way of complaint (as mentioned in section 58 of the Magistrates' Courts Act 1980,

(b) in Northern Ireland in proceedings under Article 62 of the Magistrate's Court (Northern Ireland) Order 1981.

16.   Supplementary provisions relating to safety notices

(1) Whenever feasible, prior to serving a safety notice the authority shall give an opportunity to the person on whom the notice is to be served to submit his views to the authority. Where, due to the urgency of the situation, this is not feasible the person shall be given an opportunity to submit his views to the authority after service of the notice.

(2) A safety notice served by an enforcement authority in respect of a product shall—

(a) describe the product in a manner sufficient to identify it;

(b) state the reasons on which the notice is based;

(c) indicate the rights available to the recipient of the notice under these Regulations and (where applicable) the time limits applying to their exercise; and

(d) in the case of a suspension notice, state the period of time for which it applies.

(3) A safety notice shall have effect throughout the United Kingdom.

(4) Where an enforcement authority serves a suspension notice in respect of a product, the authority shall be liable to pay compensation to a person having an interest in the product in respect of any loss or damage suffered by reason of the notice if—

(a) there has been no contravention of any requirement of these Regulations in relation to the product; and

(b) the exercise by the authority of the power to serve the suspension notice was not attributable to any neglect or default by that person.

(5) Where an enforcement authority serves a withdrawal notice in respect of a product, the authority shall be liable to pay compensation to a person having an interest in the product in respect of any loss or damage suffered by reason of the notice if—

(a) the product was not a dangerous product; and

(b) the exercise by the authority of the power to serve the withdrawal notice was not attributable to any neglect or default by that person.

(6) Where an enforcement authority serves a recall notice in respect of a product, the authority shall be liable to pay compensation to the person on whom the notice was served in respect of any loss or damage suffered by reason of the notice if—

(a) the product was not a dangerous product; and

(b) the exercise by the authority of the power to serve the recall notice was not attributable to any neglect or default by that person.

(7) An enforcement authority may vary or revoke a safety notice which it has served provided that the notice is not made more restrictive for the person on whom it is served or more onerous for that person to comply with.

(8) Wherever feasible prior to varying a safety notice the authority shall give an opportunity to the person on whom the original notice was served to submit his views to the authority.

17.   Appeals against safety notices

(1) A person on whom a safety notice has been served and a person having an interest in a product in respect of which a safety notice (other than a recall notice) has been served may, before the end of the period of 21 days beginning with the day on which the notice was served, apply for an order to vary or set aside the terms of the notice.

(2) On an application under paragraph (1) the court or the sheriff, as the case may be, shall make an order setting aside the notice only if satisfied that—

- (a) in the case of a suspension notice, there has been no contravention in relation to the product of any requirement of these Regulations,
- (b) in the case of a requirement to mark or a requirement to warn, the product is not a dangerous product,
- (c) in the case of a withdrawal notice—
    - (i) the product is not a dangerous product, or
    - (ii) where applicable, regulation 14(3) has not been complied with by the enforcement authority concerned,
- (d) in the case of a recall notice—
    - (i) the product is not a dangerous product, or
    - (ii) regulation 15(4) has not been complied with,
- (e) in any case, the serving of the safety notice concerned was not proportionate to the seriousness of the risk.

(3) On an application concerning the period of time specified in a suspension notice as the period for which it applies, the court or the sheriff, as the case may be, may reduce the period to such period as it considers sufficient for organising appropriate safety evaluations, checks and controls.

(4) On an application to vary the terms of a notice, the court or the sheriff, as the case may be, may vary the requirements specified in the notice as it considers appropriate.

(5) A person on whom a recall notice has been served and who proposes to make an application under paragraph (1) in relation to the notice may, before the end of the period of seven days beginning with the day on which the notice was served, apply to the court or the sheriff for an order suspending the effect of the notice and the court or the sheriff may, in any case where it considers it appropriate to do so, make an order suspending the effect of the notice.

(6) If the court or the sheriff makes an order suspending the effect of a recall notice under paragraph (5) in the absence of the enforcement authority, the enforcement authority may apply for the revocation of such order.

(7) An order under paragraph (5) shall take effect from the time it is made until—

- (a) it is revoked under paragraph (6),
- (b) where no application is made under paragraph (1) in respect of the recall notice within the time specified in that paragraph, the expiration of that time,
- (c) where such an application is made but is withdrawn or dismissed for want of prosecution, the date of dismissal or withdrawal of the application, or
- (d) where such an application is made and is not withdrawn or dismissed for want of prosecution, the determination of the application.

(8) Subject to paragraph (6), in Scotland the sheriff's decision under paragraph (5) shall be final.

(9) An application under this regulation may be made—

- (a) by way of complaint to any magistrates' court in which proceedings have been brought in England and Wales or Northern Ireland—
    - (i) in respect of a contravention in relation to the product of a requirement imposed by or under these Regulations; or
    - (ii) for the forfeiture of the product under regulation 18;
- (b) where no such proceedings have been brought, by way of complaint to any magistrates' court; or
- (c) in Scotland, by summary application to the sheriff.

(10) A person aggrieved by an order made pursuant to an application under paragraph (1) by a magistrates' court in England, Wales or Northern Ireland, or by a decision of such a court not to make such an order, may appeal against that order or decision—

- (a) in England and Wales, to the Crown Court;
- (b) in Northern Ireland, to the county court.

18. Forfeiture: England and Wales and Northern Ireland

(1) An enforcement authority in England and Wales or Northern Ireland may apply for an order for the forfeiture of a product on the grounds that the product is a dangerous product.

(2) An application under paragraph (1) may be made—

(a) where proceedings have been brought in a magistrates' court for an offence in respect of a contravention in relation to the product of a requirement imposed by or under these Regulations, to that court,

(b) where an application with respect to the product has been made to a magistrates' court under regulation 17 (appeals against safety notices) or 25 (appeals against detention of products and records) to that court, and

(c) otherwise, by way of complaint to a magistrates' court.

(3) An enforcement authority making an application under paragraph (1) shall serve a copy of the application on any person appearing to it to be the owner of, or otherwise to have an interest in, the product to which the application relates, together with a notice giving him the opportunity to appear at the hearing of the application to show cause why the product should not be forfeited.

(4) A person on whom notice is served under paragraph (3) and any other person claiming to be the owner of, or otherwise to have an interest in, the product to which the application relates shall be entitled to appear at the hearing of the application and show cause why the product should not be forfeited.

(5) The court shall not make an order for the forfeiture of a product—

(a) if any person on whom notice is served under paragraph (3) does not appear, unless service of the notice on that person is proved, or

(b) if no notice under paragraph (3) has been served, unless the court is satisfied that in the circumstances it was reasonable not to serve notice on any person.

(6) The court may make an order for the forfeiture of a product only if it is satisfied that the product is a dangerous product.

(7) Any person aggrieved by an order made by a magistrates' court for the forfeiture of a product, or by a decision of such a court not to make such an order, may appeal against that order or decision—

(a) in England and Wales, to the Crown Court;

(b) in Northern Ireland, to the county court.

(8) An order for the forfeiture of a product shall not take effect until the later of—

(i) the end of the period within which an appeal under paragraph (7) may be brought or within which an application under section 111 of the Magistrates' Courts Act 1980 or article 146 of the Magistrates' Courts (Northern Ireland) Order 1981 (statement of case) may be made, or

(ii) if an appeal or an application is so made, when the appeal or application is determined or abandoned.

(9) Subject to the following paragraph, where a product is forfeited it shall be destroyed in accordance with such directions as the court may give.

(10) On making an order for forfeiture of a product a magistrates' court may, if it considers it appropriate to do so, direct that the product shall (instead of being destroyed) be delivered up to such person as the court may specify, on condition that the person—

(a) does not supply the product to any person otherwise than as mentioned in paragraph (11), and

(b) on condition, if the court considers it appropriate, that he complies with any order to pay costs or expenses (including any order under regulation 28) which has been made against him in the proceedings for the order for forfeiture.

(11) The supplies which may be permitted under the preceding paragraph are—

(a) a supply to a person who carries on a business of buying products of the same description as the product concerned and repairing or reconditioning them,

(b) a supply to a person as scrap (that is to say, for the value of materials included in the product rather than for the value of the product itself),

(c) a supply to any person, provided that being so supplied the product is repaired by or on behalf of the person to whom the product was delivered up by direction of the court and that following such repair it is not a dangerous product.

20. Offences

(1) A person who contravenes regulations 5 or 8(1)(a) shall be guilty of an offence and liable on conviction on indictment to imprisonment for a term not exceeding 12 months or to a fine not exceeding £20,000 or to both, or on summary conviction to imprisonment for a term not exceeding three months or to a fine not exceeding the statutory maximum or to both.

(2) A person who contravenes regulation 7(1), 7(3) (by failing to take any of the measures specified in regulation 7(4)), 8(1)(b)(i), (ii) or (iii) or 9(1) shall be guilty of an offence and liable on summary conviction to imprisonment for a term not exceeding three months or to a fine not exceeding level 5 on the standard scale or to both.

(3) A producer or distributor who does not give notice to an enforcement authority under regulation 9(1) in respect of a product he has placed on the market or supplied commits an offence where it is proved that he ought to have known that the product poses risks to consumers that are incompatible with the general safety requirement and he shall be liable on summary conviction to imprisonment for a term not exceeding three months or to a fine not exceeding level 5 on the standard scale or to both.

(4) A person who contravenes a safety notice shall be guilty of an offence and liable on conviction on indictment to imprisonment for a term not exceeding 12 months or to a fine not exceeding £20,000 or to both, or on summary conviction to imprisonment for a term not exceeding three months or to a fine not exceeding the statutory maximum or to both.

27. Recovery of expenses of enforcement

(1) This regulation shall apply where a court—
(a) convicts a person of an offence in respect of a contravention in relation to a product of any requirement imposed by or under these Regulations, or
(b) makes an order under regulation 18 or 19 for the forfeiture of a product.

(2) The court may (in addition to any other order it may make as to costs or expenses) order the person convicted or, as the case may be, any person having an interest in the product to reimburse an enforcement authority for any expenditure which has been or may be incurred by that authority—
(a) in connection with any seizure or detention of the product by or on behalf of the authority, or
(b) in connection with any compliance by the authority with directions given by the court for the purposes of any order for the forfeiture of the product.

28. Power of Secretary of State to obtain information

(1) If the Secretary of State considers that, for the purposes of deciding whether to serve a safety notice, or to vary or revoke a safety notice which he has already served, he requires information or a sample of a product he may serve on a person a notice requiring him:
(a) to furnish to the Secretary of State, within a period specified in the notice, such information as is specified;
(b) to produce such records as are specified in the notice at a time and place so specified (and to produce any such records which are stored in any electronic form in a form in which they are visible and legible) and to permit a person appointed by the Secretary of State for that purpose to take copies of the records at that time and place;
(c) to produce such samples of a product as are specified in the notice at a time and place so specified.

(2) A person shall be guilty of an offence if he—
(a) fails, without reasonable cause, to comply with a notice served on him under paragraph (1); or
(b) in purporting to comply with a requirement which by virtue of paragraph (1)(a) or (b) is contained in such a notice—

      (i)   furnishes information or records which he knows are false in a material particular, or

      (ii) recklessly furnishes information or records which are false in a material particular.

  (3) A person guilty of an offence under paragraph (2) shall—

    (a) in the case of an offence under sub-paragraph (a) of that paragraph, be liable on summary conviction to a fine not exceeding level 5 on the standard scale; and

    (b) in the case of an offence under sub-paragraph (b) of that paragraph, be liable—

      (i)   on conviction on indictment, to a fine;

      (ii) on summary conviction, to a fine not exceeding the statutory maximum.

29. Defence of due diligence

  (1) Subject to the following provisions of this regulation, in proceedings against a person for an offence under these Regulations it shall be a defence for that person to show that he took all reasonable steps and exercised all due diligence to avoid committing the offence.

  (2) Where in any proceedings against any person for such an offence the defence provided by paragraph (1) involves an allegation that the commission of the offence was due—

    (a) to the act or default of another, or

    (b) to reliance on information given by another,

that person shall not, without the leave of the court, be entitled to rely on the defence unless, not less than seven clear days before, in England, Wales and Northern Ireland, the hearing of the proceedings or, in Scotland, the trial diet, he has served a notice under paragraph (3) on the person bringing the proceedings.

  (3) A notice under this paragraph shall give such information identifying or assisting in the identification of the person who—

    (a) committed the act or default, or

    (b) gave the information,

as is in the possession of the person serving the notice at the time he serves it.

  (4) A person may not rely on the defence provided by paragraph (1) by reason of his reliance on information supplied by another, unless he shows that it was reasonable in all the circumstances to have relied on the information, having regard in particular—

    (a) to the steps which he took, and those which might reasonably have been taken, for the purpose of verifying the information; and

    (b) to whether he had any reason to disbelieve the information.

30. Defence in relation to antiques

  (1) This regulation shall apply in proceedings against any person for an offence under regulation 20(1) in respect of the supply, offer or agreement to supply or exposure or possession for supply of second hand products supplied as antiques.

  (2) It shall be a defence for that person to show that the terms on which he supplied the product or agreed or offered to supply the product or, in the case of a product which he exposed or possessed for supply, the terms on which he intended to supply the product, contemplated the acquisition of an interest in the product by the person supplied or to be supplied.

  (3) Paragraph (2) applies only if the producer or distributor clearly informed the person to whom he supplied the product, or offered or agreed to supply the product or, in the case of a product which he exposed or possessed for supply, he intended to so inform that person, that the product is an antique.

31. Liability of person other than principal offender

  (1) Where the commission by a person of an offence under these Regulations is due to an act or default committed by some other person in the course of a commercial activity of his, the other person shall be guilty of the offence and may be proceeded against and punished by virtue of this paragraph whether or not proceedings are taken against the first-mentioned person.

(2) Where a body corporate is guilty of an offence under these Regulations (including where it is so guilty by virtue of paragraph (1)) in respect of any act or default which is shown to have been committed with the consent or connivance of, or to be attributable to any neglect on the part of, any director, manager, secretary or other similar officer of the body corporate or any person who was purporting to act in any such capacity he, as well as the body corporate, shall be guilty of that offence and shall be liable to be proceeded against and punished accordingly.

(3) Where the affairs of a body corporate are managed by its members, paragraph (2) shall apply in relation to the acts and defaults of a member in connection with his functions of management as if he were a director of the body corporate.

(4) Where a Scottish partnership is guilty of an offence under these Regulations (including where it is so guilty by virtue of paragraph (1)) in respect of any act or default which is shown to have been committed with the consent or connivance of, or to be attributable to any neglect on the part of, a partner in the partnership, he, as well as the partnership, shall be guilty of that offence and shall be liable to be proceeded against and punished accordingly.

PART 4 MISCELLANEOUS

32. Reports

(1) It shall be the duty of the Secretary of State to lay before each House of Parliament a report on the exercise during the period to which the report relates of the functions which are exercisable by enforcement authorities under these Regulations.

(2) The first such report shall relate to the period beginning on the day on which these Regulations come into force and ending on 31 March 2008 and subsequent reports shall relate to a period of not more than five years beginning on the day after the day on which the period to which the previous report relates ends.

(3) The Secretary of State may from time to time prepare and lay before each House of Parliament such other reports on the exercise of those functions as he considers appropriate.

(4) The Secretary of State may direct an enforcement authority to report at such intervals as he may specify in the direction on the discharge by that authority of the functions exercisable by it under these Regulations.

(5) A report under paragraph (4) shall be in such form and shall contain such particulars as are specified in the direction of the Secretary of State.

33. Duty to notify Secretary of State [. . .]

[(A1) The Secretary of State must establish and operate a database containing information relating to market surveillance and product safety.]

[(B1) The database referred to in paragraph (A1) must be designed so as to enable notifications required under paragraph (1), (2) or (4), or under Article 22 of Regulation (EC) 765/2008 of the European Parliament and of the Council setting out the requirements for accreditation and market surveillance relating to the marketing of products and repealing Regulation (EEC) No 339/93, to be made to the Secretary of State through the database.]

[(1) An enforcement authority which has received a notification of a risk under regulation 9(1) shall immediately notify the Secretary of State of the risk through the database referred to in paragraph (A1).]

(2) Where an enforcement authority takes a measure which restricts the placing on the market of a product, or requires its withdrawal or recall, it shall immediately notify the Secretary of State [of the action taken through the database referred to in paragraph (A1)], specifying its reasons for taking the action. It shall also immediately notify the Secretary of State of any modification or lifting of such a measure.

(4) Where an enforcement authority adopts or decides to adopt, recommend or agree with producers and distributors, whether on a compulsory or voluntary basis, a measure or action to prevent,

restrict or impose specific conditions on the possible marketing or use of a product (other than a [medicinal] product) by reason of a serious risk, it shall immediately notify the Secretary of State [of the measure or action taken through the database referred to in paragraph (A1)]. It shall also immediately notify the Secretary of State of any modification or withdrawal of any such measure or action [through the database referred to in paragraph (A1)].

(10) In this regulation—

(a) references to a product excludes a second hand product supplied as an antique or as a product to be repaired or reconditioned prior to being used, provided the supplier clearly informs the person to whom he supplies the product to that effect;

[(b) 'medicinal product' has the meaning given to it in regulation 2 of the Human Medicines Regulations 2012.]

34. Provisions supplemental to regulation 33

(1) A notification under regulation 33(2) to [or (4)] to the Secretary of State [. . .] shall [. . .] provide all available details and at least the following information—

(a) information enabling the product to be identified,

(b) a description of the risk involved, including a summary of the results of any test or analysis and of their conclusions which are relevant to assessing the level of risk,

(c) the nature and the duration of the measures or action taken or decided on, if applicable,

(d) information on supply chains and distribution of the product, in particular on destination countries.

37. Complaints procedures

An enforcement authority shall maintain and publish a procedure by which complaints may be submitted by any person on product safety and on surveillance and control activities, which complaints shall be followed up as appropriate.

39. Information

(1) An enforcement authority shall in general make available to the public such information as is available to it on the following matters relating to the risks to consumer health and safety posed by a product—

(a) the nature of the risk,

(b) the product identification,

and the measures taken in respect of the risk, without prejudice to the need not to disclose information for effective monitoring and investigation activities.

(2) Paragraph (1) shall not apply to any information obtained by an enforcement authority for the purposes of these Regulations which, by its nature, is covered by professional secrecy, unless the circumstances require such information to be made public in order to protect the health and safety of consumers.

40. Service of documents

(1) A document required or authorised by virtue of these Regulations to be served on a person may be so served—

(a) on an individual by delivering it to him or by leaving it at his proper address or by sending it by post to him at that address;

(b) on a body corporate other than a limited liability partnership, by serving it in accordance with sub-paragraph (a) on the secretary of the body;

(c) on a limited liability partnership, by serving it in accordance with sub-paragraph (a) on a member of the partnership; or

(d) on a partnership, by serving it in accordance with sub-paragraph (a) on a partner or a person having the control or management of the partnership business;

(e) on any other person by leaving it at his proper address or by sending it by post to him at that address.

(2) For the purposes of paragraph (1), and for the purposes of section 7 of the Interpretation Act 1978 (which relates to the service of documents by post) in its application to that paragraph, the proper address of a person on whom a document is to be served by virtue of these Regulations shall be his last known address except that—

(a) in the case of a body corporate (other than a limited liability partnership) or its secretary, it shall be the address of the registered or principal office of the body;

(b) in the case of a limited liability partnership or a member of the partnership, it shall be the address of the registered or principal office of the partnership;

(c) in the case of a partnership or a partner or a person having the control or management of a partnership business, it shall be the address of the principal office of the partnership,

and for the purposes of this paragraph the principal officer of a company constituted under the law of a country or territory outside the United Kingdom or of a partnership carrying on business outside the United Kingdom is its principal office within the United Kingdom.

(3) A document required or authorised by virtue of these Regulations to be served on a person may also be served by transmitting the request by any means of electronic communication to an electronic address (which includes a fax number and an e-mail address) being an address which the person has held out as an address at which he or it can be contacted for the purposes of receiving such documents.

(4) A document transmitted by any means of electronic communication in accordance with the preceding paragraph is, unless the contrary is proved, deemed to be received on the business day after the notice was transmitted over a public electronic communications network.

41. Extension of time for bringing summary proceedings

(1) Notwithstanding section 127 of the Magistrates' Courts Act 1980 or article 19 of the Magistrates' Courts (Northern Ireland) Order 1981, in England, Wales and Northern Ireland a magistrates' court may try an information (in the case of England and Wales) or a complaint (in the case of Northern Ireland) in respect of an offence under these Regulations if (in the case of England and Wales) the information is laid or (in the case of Northern Ireland) the complaint is made within three years from the date of the offence or within one year from the discovery of the offence by the prosecutor whichever is the earlier.

(2) Notwithstanding section 136 of the Criminal Procedure (Scotland) Act 1995, in Scotland summary proceedings for an offence under these Regulations may be commenced within three years from the date of the offence or within one year from the discovery of the offence by the prosecutor whichever is the earlier.

(3) For the purposes of paragraph (2), section 136(3) of the Criminal Procedure (Scotland) Act 1995 shall apply as it applies for the purposes of that section.

42. Civil proceedings

These Regulations shall not be construed as conferring any right of action in civil proceedings in respect of any loss or damage suffered in consequence of a contravention of these Regulations.

43. Privileged information

(1) Nothing in these Regulations shall be taken as requiring a person to produce any records if he would be entitled to refuse to produce those records in any proceedings in any court on the grounds that they are the subject of legal professional privilege or, in Scotland, that they contain a confidential communication made by or to an advocate or solicitor in that capacity, or as authorising a person to take possession of any records which are in the possession of a person who would be so entitled.

(2) Nothing in these Regulations shall be construed as requiring a person to answer any question or give any information if to do so would incriminate that person or that person's spouse or civil partner.

44. Evidence in proceedings for offence relating to regulation 9(1)

(1) This regulation applies where a person has given a notification to an enforcement authority pursuant to regulation 9(1).

(2) No evidence relating to that statement may be adduced and no question relating to it may be asked by the prosecution in any criminal proceedings (other than proceedings in which that person is charged with an offence under regulation 20 for a contravention of regulation 9(1)), unless evidence relating to it is adduced, or a question relating to it is asked, in the proceedings by or on behalf of that person.

Business Protection from Misleading Marketing Regulations 2008

(SI 2008, No. 1276)

2. Interpretation

(1) In these Regulations—

'advertising' means any form of representation which is made in connection with a trade, business, craft or profession in order to promote the supply or transfer of a product and 'advertiser' shall be construed accordingly;

['CMA' means the Competition and Markets Authority;]

'code owner' means a trader or a body responsible for—

(a) the formulation and revision of a code of conduct; or

(b) monitoring compliance with the code by those who have undertaken to be bound by it;

'comparative advertising' means advertising which in any way, either explicitly or by implication, identifies a competitor or a product offered by a competitor;

'court', in relation to England and Wales and Northern Ireland, means a county court or the High Court, and, in relation to Scotland, the sheriff or the Court of Session;

['DETINI' means the Department of Enterprise, Trade and Investment in Northern Ireland;]

['enforcement authority' means the CMA, every local weights and measures authority, DETINI and GEMA];

['GEMA' means the Gas and Electricity Markets Authority;]

'goods' includes ships, aircraft, animals, things attached to land and growing crops;

['local weights and measures authority' means a local weights and measures authority in Great Britain (within the meaning of section 69 of the Weights and Measures Act 1985);]

'premises' includes any place and any stall, vehicle, ship or aircraft;

'product' means any goods or services and includes immovable property, rights and obligations;

'ship' includes any boat and any other description of vessel used in navigation; and

'trader' means any person who is acting for purposes relating to his trade, craft, business or profession and anyone acting in the name of or on behalf of a trader.

(2) In the application of these Regulations to Scotland for references to an 'injunction' or an 'interim injunction' there shall be substituted references to an 'interdict' or an 'interim interdict' respectively.

3. Prohibition of advertising which misleads traders

(1) Advertising which is misleading is prohibited.

(2) Advertising is misleading which—

(a) in any way, including its presentation, deceives or is likely to deceive the traders to whom it is addressed or whom it reaches; and by reason of its deceptive nature, is likely to affect their economic behaviour; or

(b) for those reasons, injures or is likely to injure a competitor.

(3) In determining whether advertising is misleading, account shall be taken of all its features, and in particular of any information it contains concerning—

(a) the characteristics of the product (as defined in paragraph (4));

    (b) the price or manner in which the price is calculated;

    (c) the conditions on which the product is supplied or provided; and

    (d) the nature, attributes and rights of the advertiser (as defined in paragraph (5)).

(4) In paragraph (3)(a) the 'characteristics of the product' include—

    (a)   availability of the product;

    (b) nature of the product;

    (c) execution of the product;

    (d) composition of the product;

    (e) method and date of manufacture of the product;

    (f) method and date of provision of the product;

    (g) fitness for purpose of the product;

    (h) uses of the product;

    (i)   quantity of the product;

    (j)   specification of the product;

    (k) geographical or commercial origin of the product;

    (l)   results to be expected from use of the product; or

    (m) results and material features of tests or checks carried out on the product.

(5) In paragraph (3)(d) the 'nature, attributes and rights' of the advertiser include the advertiser's—

    (a) identity;

    (b) assets;

    (c) qualifications;

    (d) ownership of industrial, commercial or intellectual property rights; or

    (e) awards and distinctions.

4. Comparative advertising

Comparative advertising shall, as far as the comparison is concerned, be permitted only when the following conditions are met—

    (a) it is not misleading under regulation 3;

    (b) it is not a misleading action under regulation 5 of the Consumer Protection from Unfair Trading Regulations 2008 or a misleading omission under regulation 6 of those Regulations;

    (c) it compares products meeting the same needs or intended for the same purpose;

    (d) it objectively compares one or more material, relevant, verifiable and representative features of those products, which may include price;

    (e) it does not create confusion among traders—

        (i)   between the advertiser and a competitor, or

        (ii) between the trade marks, trade names, other distinguishing marks or products of the advertiser and those of a competitor;

    (f) it does not discredit or denigrate the trade marks, trade names, other distinguishing marks, products, activities, or circumstances of a competitor;

    (g) for products with designation of origin, it relates in each case to products with the same designation;

    (h) it does not take unfair advantage of the reputation of a trade mark, trade name or other distinguishing marks of a competitor or of the designation of origin of competing products;

    (i)   it does not present products as imitations or replicas of products bearing a protected trade mark or trade name.

5. Promotion of misleading advertising and comparative advertising which is not permitted

A code owner shall not promote in a code of conduct—

    (a) advertising which is misleading under regulation 3; or

    (b) comparative advertising which is not permitted under regulation 4.

6. Misleading advertising

A trader is guilty of an offence if he engages in advertising which is misleading under regulation 3.

7. Penalty for offence under regulation 6

A person guilty of an offence under regulation 6 shall be liable—

(a) on summary conviction, to a fine not exceeding the statutory maximum; or

(b) on conviction on indictment, to a fine or imprisonment for a term not exceeding two years or both.

8. Offences committed by bodies of persons

(1) Where an offence under these Regulations committed by a body corporate is proved—

(a) to have been committed with the consent or connivance of an officer of the body, or

(b) to be attributable to any neglect on his part,

the officer as well as the body corporate is guilty of the offence and liable to be proceeded against and punished accordingly.

(2) In paragraph (1) a reference to an officer of a body corporate includes a reference to—

(a) a director, manager, secretary or other similar officer; and

(b) a person purporting to act as a director, manager, secretary or other similar officer.

(3) Where an offence under these Regulations committed by a Scottish partnership is proved—

(a) to have been committed with the consent or connivance of a partner, or

(b) to be attributable to any neglect on his part,

the partner as well as the partnership is guilty of the offence and liable to be proceeded against and punished accordingly.

(4) In paragraph (3) a reference to a partner includes a person purporting to act as a partner.

9. Offence due to the default of another person

(1) This regulation applies where a person 'X'—

(a) commits an offence under regulation 6, or

(b) would have committed an offence under regulation 6 but for a defence under regulation 11 or 12,

and the commission of the offence, or of what would have been an offence but for X being able to rely on a defence under regulations 11 or 12, is due to the act or default of some other person 'Y'.

(2) Where this regulation applies Y shall be guilty of the offence subject to regulations 11 and 12 whether or not Y is a trader and whether or not Y's act or default is advertising.

(3) Y may be charged with and convicted of the offence by virtue of paragraph (2) whether or not proceedings are taken against X.

10. Time limit for prosecution

(1) No proceedings for an offence under these Regulations shall be commenced after—

(a) the end of the period of three years beginning with the date of the commission of the offence; or

(b) the end of the period of one year beginning with the date of discovery of the offence by the prosecutor,

whichever is earlier.

11. Due diligence defence

(1) In any proceedings against a person for an offence under regulation 6 it is a defence for that person to prove—

(a) that the commission of the offence was due to—

(i)   a mistake;

(ii) reliance on information supplied to him by another person;

(iii) the act or default of another person;

(iv) an accident; or

(v)   another cause beyond his control; and
(b) that he took all reasonable precautions and exercised all due diligence to avoid the commission of such an offence by himself or any person under his control.

(2) A person shall not be entitled to rely on the defence provided by paragraph (1) by reason of the matters referred to in paragraph (ii) or (iii) of paragraph (1)(a) without the leave of the court unless—

(a) he has served on the prosecutor a notice in writing giving such information identifying or assisting in the identification of that other person as was in his possession; and
(b) the notice is served on the prosecutor at least seven clear days before the date of the hearing.

12.   Innocent publication defence

In any proceedings against a person for an offence under regulation 6 committed by the publication of advertising it is a defence for that person to prove that—

(a) he is a person whose business it is to publish or to arrange for the publication of advertising;
(b) he received the advertising for publication in the ordinary course of business; and
(c) he did not know and had no reason to suspect that its publication would amount to an offence under regulation 6.

PART 3   ENFORCEMENT

13.   [Duty and power to enforce]

(4) [In determining how to comply with paragraph (1), or as the case may be, paragraph (1A)] every enforcement authority shall have regard to the desirability of encouraging control of advertising which is misleading under regulation 3 and comparative advertising which is not permitted under regulation 4 by such established means as it considers appropriate having regard to all the circumstances of the particular case.

14.   Notice to [CMA] of intended prosecution

(1) Where an enforcement authority is a local weights and measures authority in England and Wales it may bring proceedings for an offence under regulation 6 only if—

(a) it has notified the [CMA] of its intention to bring proceedings at least fourteen days before the date on which proceedings are brought; or
(b) the [CMA] consents to proceedings being brought in a shorter period.

(2) The enforcement authority must also notify the [CMA] of the outcome of the proceedings after they are finally determined.

(3) Such proceedings are not invalid by reason only of the failure to comply with this regulation.

15.   Injunctions to secure compliance with the Regulations

(1) This regulation applies where an enforcement authority considers that there has been or is likely to be a breach of regulation 3, 4 or 5.

(2) Where this regulation applies an enforcement authority may, subject to paragraph (3), if it thinks it appropriate to do so, bring proceedings for an injunction (in which proceedings it may also apply for an interim injunction) against any person appearing to it to be concerned or likely to be concerned with the breach.

(3) Where the enforcement authority is a local weights and measures authority in Great Britain [or GEMA] it may apply for an injunction only if—

(a) it has notified the [CMA] of its intention to apply for an injunction at least fourteen days before the date on which the application is made; or
(b) the [CMA] consents to the application for an injunction being made within a shorter period.

(4) Proceedings referred to in paragraph (2) are not invalid by reason only of the failure to comply with paragraph (3).

16. Undertakings

Where an enforcement authority considers that there has been or is likely to be a breach of regulation 3, 4 or 5 it may accept from the person concerned or likely to be concerned with the breach an undertaking that he will comply with those regulations.

17. Co-ordination

[(1) If more than one enforcement authority in Great Britain is contemplating bringing proceedings under regulation 15 in any particular case, the CMA may direct which enforcement authority is to bring the proceedings or decide that only it may do so.]

(2) Where the [CMA] directs that only it may bring such proceedings it may take into account whether compliance with regulation 3, 4 or 5 could be achieved by other means in deciding whether to bring proceedings.

18. Powers of the court

(1) The court on an application by an enforcement authority may grant an injunction on such terms as it may think fit to secure compliance with regulation 3, 4 or 5.

(2) Before granting an injunction the court shall have regard to all the interests involved and in particular the public interest.

(3) An injunction may relate not only to particular advertising but to any advertising in similar terms or likely to convey a similar impression.

(4) The court may also require any person against whom an injunction (other than an interim injunction) is granted to publish in such form and manner and to such extent as the court thinks appropriate for the purpose of eliminating any continuing effects of the advertising—

    (a) the injunction; and

    (b) a corrective statement.

(5) In considering an application for an injunction the court may require the person named in the application to provide evidence as to the accuracy of any factual claim made as part of the advertising of that person if, taking into account the legitimate interests of that person and any other party to the proceedings, it appears appropriate in the circumstances.

(6) If, having been required under paragraph (5) to provide evidence as to the accuracy of a factual claim, a person—

    (a) fails to provide such evidence, or

    (b) provides evidence as to the accuracy of the factual claim that the court considers inadequate,

the court may consider that the factual claim is inaccurate.

(7) The court may grant an injunction even where there is no evidence of proof of actual loss or damage or of intention or negligence on the part of the advertiser.

19. Notifications of undertakings and orders to the [CMA]

An enforcement authority, other than the [CMA], shall notify the [CMA]—

    (a) of any undertaking given to it under regulation 16;

    (b) of the outcome of any application made by it under regulation 15 and the terms of any order made by the court; and

    (c) of the outcome of any application made by it to enforce a previous order of the court.

20. Publication, information and advice

(1) The [CMA] must arrange for the publication, in such form and manner as it considers appropriate, of—

    (a) details of any undertaking or order notified to it under regulation 19;

    (b) details of any undertaking given to it under regulation 16;

    (c) details of any application made by it under regulation 15 and of the terms of any undertaking given to, or order made by, the court;

    (d) details of any application made by it to enforce a previous order of the court.

(2) [An enforcement authority] may arrange for the dissemination, in such form and manner as it considers appropriate, of such information and advice concerning the operation of these Regulations as appear to it to be expedient to give to the public and to all persons likely to be affected by these Regulations.

PART 4   INVESTIGATION POWERS

28.   Crown

(2) The Crown is not criminally liable as a result of any provision of these Regulations.

(3) Paragraph (2) does not affect the application of any provision of these Regulations in relation to a person in the public service of the Crown.

29.   Validity of agreements

An agreement shall not be void or unenforceable by reason only of a breach of these Regulations.

Consumer Protection from Unfair Trading Regulations 2008

(SI 2008, No. 1277)

PART 1   GENERAL

2.   Interpretation

(1) In these Regulations—

'average consumer' shall be construed in accordance with paragraphs (2) to (6);

'business' includes[—

    (a)] a trade, craft or profession[, and

    (b) the activities of any government department or local or public authority];

['CMA' means the Competition and Markets Authority;]

'code of conduct' means an agreement or set of rules (which is not imposed by legal or administrative requirements), which defines the behaviour of traders who undertake to be bound by it in relation to one or more commercial practices or business sectors;

'code owner' means a trader or a body responsible for—

    (a) the formulation and revision of a code of conduct; or

    (b) monitoring compliance with the code by those who have undertaken to be bound by it;

'commercial practice' means any act, omission, course of conduct, representation or commercial communication (including advertising and marketing) by a trader, which is directly connected with the promotion, sale or supply of a product to or from consumers, whether occurring before, during or after a commercial transaction (if any) in relation to a product;

['consumer' means an individual acting for purposes that are wholly or mainly outside that individual's business;]

['DETINI' means the Department of Enterprise, Trade and Investment in Northern Ireland;]

['digital content' means data which are produced and supplied in digital form;]

['enforcement authority' means the CMA, every local weights and measures authority and DETINI;]

['goods' means any tangible moveable items, but that includes water, gas and electricity if and only if they are put up for sale in a limited volume or set quantity;]

'invitation to purchase' means a commercial communication which indicates characteristics of the product and the price in a way appropriate to the means of that commercial communication and thereby enables the consumer to make a purchase;

['local weights and measures authority' means a local weights and measures authority in Great Britain (within the meaning of section 69 of the Weights and Measures Act 1985);]

'materially distort the economic behaviour' means in relation to an average consumer, appreciably to impair the average consumer's ability to make an informed decision thereby causing him to take a transactional decision that he would not have taken otherwise;

'premises' includes any place and any stall, vehicle, ship or aircraft;

['product' means—

    (a) goods,

    (b) a service,

    (c) digital content,

    (d) immoveable property,

    (e) rights or obligations, or

    (f) a product of the kind mentioned in paragraphs (1A) and (1B),

but the application of this definition to Part 4A is subject to regulations 27C and 27D;]

'professional diligence' means the standard of special skill and care which a trader may reasonably be expected to exercise towards consumers which is commensurate with either—

    (a) honest market practice in the trader's field of activity, or

    (b) the general principle of good faith in the trader's field of activity;

'ship' includes any boat and any other description of vessel used in navigation;

['trader'—

    (a) means a person acting for purposes relating to that person's business, whether acting personally or through another person acting in the trader's name or on the trader's behalf, and

    (b) except in Part 4A, includes a person acting in the name of or on behalf of a trader;]

'transactional decision' means any decision taken by a consumer, whether it is to act or to refrain from acting, concerning—

    (a) whether, how and on what terms to purchase, make payment in whole or in part for, retain or dispose of a product; or

    (b) whether, how and on what terms to exercise a contractual right in relation to a product [(but the application of this definition to regulations 5 and 7 as they apply for the purposes of Part 4A is subject to regulation 27B(2))].

[(1A) A trader ('T') who demands payment from a consumer ('C') in full or partial settlement of C's liabilities or purported liabilities to T is to be treated for the purposes of these Regulations as offering to supply a product to C.

(1B) In such a case the product that T offers to supply comprises the full or partial settlement of those liabilities or purported liabilities.]

(2) In determining the effect of a commercial practice on the average consumer where the practice reaches or is addressed to a consumer or consumers account shall be taken of the material characteristics of such an average consumer including his being reasonably well informed, reasonably observant and circumspect.

(3) Paragraphs (4) and (5) set out the circumstances in which a reference to the average consumer shall be read as in addition referring to the average member of a particular group of consumers.

(4) In determining the effect of a commercial practice on the average consumer where the practice is directed to a particular group of consumers, a reference to the average consumer shall be read as referring to the average member of that group.

(5) In determining the effect of a commercial practice on the average consumer—

    (a) where a clearly identifiable group of consumers is particularly vulnerable to the practice or the underlying product because of their mental or physical infirmity, age or credulity in a way which the trader could reasonably be expected to foresee, and

    (b) where the practice is likely to materially distort the economic behaviour only of that group,

a reference to the average consumer shall be read as referring to the average member of that group.

(6) Paragraph (5) is without prejudice to the common and legitimate advertising practice of making exaggerated statements which are not meant to be taken literally.

PART 2 PROHIBITIONS

3. Prohibition of unfair commercial practices

(1) Unfair commercial practices are prohibited.

(2) Paragraphs (3) and (4) set out the circumstances when a commercial practice is unfair.

(3) A commercial practice is unfair if—

(a) it contravenes the requirements of professional diligence; and

(b) it materially distorts or is likely to materially distort the economic behaviour of the average consumer with regard to the product.

(4) A commercial practice is unfair if—

(a) it is a misleading action under the provisions of regulation 5;

(b) it is a misleading omission under the provisions of regulation 6;

(c) it is aggressive under the provisions of regulation 7; or

(d) it is listed in Schedule 1.

4. Prohibition of the promotion of unfair commercial practices

The promotion of any unfair commercial practice by a code owner in a code of conduct is prohibited.

5. Misleading actions

(1) A commercial practice is a misleading action if it satisfies the conditions in either paragraph (2) or paragraph (3).

(2) A commercial practice satisfies the conditions of this paragraph—

(a) if it contains false information and is therefore untruthful in relation to any of the matters in paragraph (4) or if it or its overall presentation in any way deceives or is likely to deceive the average consumer in relation to any of the matters in that paragraph, even if the information is factually correct; and

(b) it causes or is likely to cause the average consumer to take a transactional decision he would not have taken otherwise.

(3) A commercial practice satisfies the conditions of this paragraph if—

(a) it concerns any marketing of a product (including comparative advertising) which creates confusion with any products, trade marks, trade names or other distinguishing marks of a competitor; or

(b) it concerns any failure by a trader to comply with a commitment contained in a code of conduct which the trader has undertaken to comply with, if—

(i) the trader indicates in a commercial practice that he is bound by that code of conduct, and

(ii) the commitment is firm and capable of being verified and is not aspirational,

and it causes or is likely to cause the average consumer to take a transactional decision he would not have taken otherwise, taking account of its factual context and of all its features and circumstances.

(4) The matters referred to in paragraph (2)(a) are—

(a) the existence or nature of the product;

(b) the main characteristics of the product (as defined in paragraph 5);

(c) the extent of the trader's commitments;

(d) the motives for the commercial practice;

(e) the nature of the sales process;

(f) any statement or symbol relating to direct or indirect sponsorship or approval of the trader or the product;

(g) the price or the manner in which the price is calculated;

(h) the existence of a specific price advantage;

(i) the need for a service, part, replacement or repair;

(j) the nature, attributes and rights of the trader (as defined in paragraph 6);

(k) the consumer's rights or the risks he may face.

(5) In paragraph (4)(b), the 'main characteristics of the product' include—

    (a) availability of the product;
    (b) benefits of the product;
    (c) risks of the product;
    (d) execution of the product;
    (e) composition of the product;
    (f) accessories of the product;
    (g) after-sale customer assistance concerning the product;
    (h) the handling of complaints about the product;
    (i) the method and date of manufacture of the product;
    (j) the method and date of provision of the product;
    (k) delivery of the product;
    (l) fitness for purpose of the product;
    (m) usage of the product;
    (n) quantity of the product;
    (o) specification of the product;
    (p) geographical or commercial origin of the product;
    (q) results to be expected from use of the product; and
    (r) results and material features of tests or checks carried out on the product.

    (6) In paragraph (4)(j), the 'nature, attributes and rights' as far as concern the trader include the trader's—

    (a) identity;
    (b) assets;
    (c) qualifications;
    (d) status;
    (e) approval;
    (f) affiliations or connections;
    (g) ownership of industrial, commercial or intellectual property rights; and
    (h) awards and distinctions.

    (7) In paragraph (4)(k) 'consumer's rights' include rights the consumer may have under [sections 19 and 23 or 24 of the Consumer Rights Act 2015].

6. Misleading omissions

    (1) A commercial practice is a misleading omission if, in its factual context, taking account of the matters in paragraph (2)—

    (a) the commercial practice omits material information,
    (b) the commercial practice hides material information,
    (c) the commercial practice provides material information in a manner which is unclear, unintelligible, ambiguous or untimely, or
    (d) the commercial practice fails to identify its commercial intent, unless this is already apparent from the context,

and as a result it causes or is likely to cause the average consumer to take a transactional decision he would not have taken otherwise.

    (2) The matters referred to in paragraph (1) are—

    (a) all the features and circumstances of the commercial practice;
    (b) the limitations of the medium used to communicate the commercial practice (including limitations of space or time); and
    (c) where the medium used to communicate the commercial practice imposes limitations of space or time, any measures taken by the trader to make the information available to consumers by other means.

    (3) In paragraph (1) 'material information' means—

    (a) the information which the average consumer needs, according to the context, to take an informed transactional decision; and

    (b) any information requirement which applies in relation to a commercial communication as a result of a Community obligation.

    (4) Where a commercial practice is an invitation to purchase, the following information will be material if not already apparent from the context in addition to any other information which is material information under paragraph (3)—

        (a) the main characteristics of the product, to the extent appropriate to the medium by which the invitation to purchase is communicated and the product;

        (b) the identity of the trader, such as his trading name, and the identity of any other trader on whose behalf the trader is acting;

        (c) the geographical address of the trader and the geographical address of any other trader on whose behalf the trader is acting;

        (d) either—

            (i)   the price, including any taxes; or

            (ii) where the nature of the product is such that the price cannot reasonably be calculated in advance, the manner in which the price is calculated;

        (e) where appropriate, either—

            (i)   all additional freight, delivery or postal charges; or

            (ii) where such charges cannot reasonably be calculated in advance, the fact that such charges may be payable;

        (f) the following matters where they depart from the requirements of professional diligence—

            (i)   arrangements for payment,

            (ii) arrangements for delivery,

            (iii) arrangements for performance,

            (iv) complaint handling policy;

        (g) for products and transactions involving a right of withdrawal or cancellation, the existence of such a right.

7. Aggressive commercial practices

    (1) A commercial practice is aggressive if, in its factual context, taking account of all of its features and circumstances—

        (a) it significantly impairs or is likely significantly to impair the average consumer's freedom of choice or conduct in relation to the product concerned through the use of harassment, coercion or undue influence; and

        (b) it thereby causes or is likely to cause him to take a transactional decision he would not have taken otherwise.

    (2) In determining whether a commercial practice uses harassment, coercion or undue influence account shall be taken of—

        (a) its timing, location, nature or persistence;

        (b) the use of threatening or abusive language or behaviour;

        (c) the exploitation by the trader of any specific misfortune or circumstance of such gravity as to impair the consumer's judgment, of which the trader is aware, to influence the consumer's decision with regard to the product;

        (d) any onerous or disproportionate non-contractual barrier imposed by the trader where a consumer wishes to exercise rights under the contract, including rights to terminate a contract or to switch to another product or another trader; and

        (e) any threat to take any action which cannot legally be taken.

    (3) In this regulation—

        (a) 'coercion' includes the use of physical force; and

        (b) 'undue influence' means exploiting a position of power in relation to the consumer so as to apply pressure, even without using or threatening to use physical force, in a way which significantly limits the consumer's ability to make an informed decision.

PART 3 OFFENCES

Offences relating to unfair commercial practices

8.—(1) A trader is guilty of an offence if—

(a) he knowingly or recklessly engages in a commercial practice which contravenes the requirements of professional diligence under regulation 3(3)(a); and

(b) the practice materially distorts or is likely to materially distort the economic behaviour of the average consumer with regard to the product under regulation 3(3)(b).

(2) For the purposes of paragraph (1)(a) a trader who engages in a commercial practice without regard to whether the practice contravenes the requirements of professional diligence shall be deemed recklessly to engage in the practice, whether or not the trader has reason for believing that the practice might contravene those requirements.

9. A trader is guilty of an offence if he engages in a commercial practice which is a misleading action under regulation 5 otherwise than by reason of the commercial practice satisfying the condition in regulation 5(3)(b).

10. A trader is guilty of an offence if he engages in a commercial practice which is a misleading omission under regulation 6.

11. A trader is guilty of an offence if he engages in a commercial practice which is aggressive under regulation 7.

12. A trader is guilty of an offence if he engages in a commercial practice set out in any of paragraphs 1 to 10, 12 to 27 and 29 to 31 of Schedule 1.

13. Penalty for offences

A person guilty of an offence under regulation 8, 9, 10, 11 or 12 shall be liable—

(a) on summary conviction, to a fine not exceeding the statutory maximum; or

(b) on conviction on indictment, to a fine or imprisonment for a term not exceeding two years or both.

14. Time limit for prosecution

(1) No proceedings for an offence under these Regulations shall be commenced after—

(a) the end of the period of three years beginning with the date of the commission of the offence, or

(b) the end of the period of one year beginning with the date of discovery of the offence by the prosecutor,

whichever is earlier.

(2) For the purposes of paragraph (1)(b) a certificate signed by or on behalf of the prosecutor and stating the date on which the offence was discovered by him shall be conclusive evidence of that fact and a certificate stating that matter and purporting to be so signed shall be treated as so signed unless the contrary is proved.

(3) Notwithstanding anything in section 127(1) of the Magistrates' Courts Act 1980, an information relating to an offence under these Regulations which is triable by a magistrates' court in England and Wales may be so tried if it is laid at any time before the end of the period of twelve months beginning with the date of the commission of the offence.

(4) Notwithstanding anything in section 136 of the Criminal Procedure (Scotland) Act 1995 summary proceedings in Scotland for an offence under these Regulations may be commenced at any time before the end of the period of twelve months beginning with the date of the commission of the offence.

(5) For the purposes of paragraph (4), section 136(3) of the Criminal Procedure (Scotland) Act 1995 shall apply as it applies for the purposes of that subsection.

(6) Notwithstanding anything in Article 19(1) of the Magistrates' Courts (Northern Ireland) Order 1981 a complaint charging an offence under these Regulations which is triable by a magistrates' court in Northern Ireland may be so tried if it is made at any time before the end of the period of twelve months beginning with the date of the commission of the offence.

15.   Offences committed by bodies of persons

(1) Where an offence under these Regulations committed by a body corporate is proved—

    (a) to have been committed with the consent or connivance of an officer of the body, or

    (b) to be attributable to any neglect on his part,

the officer as well as the body corporate is guilty of the offence and liable to be proceeded against and punished accordingly.

(2) In paragraph (1) a reference to an officer of a body corporate includes a reference to—

    (a) a director, manager, secretary or other similar officer; and

    (b) a person purporting to act as a director, manager, secretary or other similar officer.

(3) Where an offence under these Regulations committed by a Scottish partnership is proved—

    (a) to have been committed with the consent or connivance of a partner, or

    (b) to be attributable to any neglect on his part,

the partner as well as the partnership is guilty of the offence and liable to be proceeded against and punished accordingly.

(4) In paragraph (3) a reference to a partner includes a person purporting to act as a partner.

16.   Offence due to the default of another person

(1) This regulation applies where a person 'X'—

    (a) commits an offence under regulation 9, 10, 11 or 12, or

    (b) would have committed an offence under those regulations but for a defence under regulation 17 or 18,

and the commission of the offence, or of what would have been an offence but for X being able to rely on a defence under regulation 17 or 18, is due to the act or default of some other person 'Y'.

(2) Where this regulation applies Y is guilty of the offence, subject to regulations 17 and 18, whether or not Y is a trader and whether or not Y's act or default is a commercial practice.

(3) Y may be charged with and convicted of the offence by virtue of paragraph (2) whether or not proceedings are taken against X.

17.   Due diligence defence

(1) In any proceedings against a person for an offence under regulation 9, 10, 11 or 12 it is a defence for that person to prove—

    (a) that the commission of the offence was due to—

        (i)   a mistake;

        (ii)   reliance on information supplied to him by another person;

        (iii) the act or default of another person;

        (iv)   an accident; or

        (v)   another cause beyond his control; and

    (b) that he took all reasonable precautions and exercised all due diligence to avoid the commission of such an offence by himself or any person under his control.

(2) A person shall not be entitled to rely on the defence provided by paragraph (1) by reason of the matters referred to in paragraph (ii) or (iii) of paragraph (1)(a) without leave of the court unless—

    (a) he has served on the prosecutor a notice in writing giving such information identifying or assisting in the identification of that other person as was in his possession; and

    (b) the notice is served on the prosecutor at least seven clear days before the date of the hearing.

18.   Innocent publication of advertisement defence

(1) In any proceedings against a person for an offence under regulation 9, 10, 11 or 12 committed by the publication of an advertisement it shall be a defence for a person to prove that—

    (a) he is a person whose business it is to publish or to arrange for the publication of advertisements;

    (b) he received the advertisement for publication in the ordinary course of business; and

(c) he did not know and had no reason to suspect that its publication would amount to an offence under the regulation to which the proceedings relate.

(2) In paragraph (1) 'advertisement' includes a catalogue, a circular and a price list.

PART 4 ENFORCEMENT

19.   [Duty and power to enforce]

[(1) It shall be the duty of every local weights and measures authority and DETINI to enforce these Regulations [(other than Part 4A)].

(1A) The CMA may also enforce these Regulations.]

(2) Where the enforcement authority is a local weights and measures authority the duty referred to in paragraph (1) shall apply to the enforcement of these Regulations within the authority's area.

(3) Where the enforcement authority is [DETINI] the duty referred to in paragraph (1) shall apply to the enforcement of these Regulations within Northern Ireland.

(4) [In determining how to comply with paragraph (1), or as the case may be, paragraph (1A),] every enforcement authority shall have regard to the desirability of encouraging control of unfair commercial practices by such established means as it considers appropriate having regard to all the circumstances of the particular case.

(5) Nothing in this regulation shall authorise any enforcement authority to bring proceedings in Scotland for an offence.

[PART 4A CONSUMERS' RIGHTS TO REDRESS]

[27A. When does a consumer have a right to redress?

(1) A consumer has a right to redress under this Part if—
  (a) the conditions in this regulation are met, and
  (b) the conditions (if any) in the following provisions of this Part for the availability of that right are met.

(2) The first condition is that—
  (a) the consumer enters into a contract with a trader for the sale or supply of a product by the trader (a 'business to consumer contract'),
  (b) the consumer enters into a contract with a trader for the sale of goods to the trader (a 'consumer to business contract'), or
  (c) the consumer makes a payment to a trader for the supply of a product (a 'consumer payment').

(3) Paragraph (2)(b) does not apply if, under the contract, the trader supplies or agrees to supply a product to the consumer as well as paying or agreeing to pay the consumer.

(4) The second condition is that—
  (a) the trader engages in a prohibited practice in relation to the product, or
  (b) in a case where a consumer enters into a business to consumer contract for goods or digital content—
    (i)   a producer engages in a prohibited practice in relation to the goods or digital content, and
    (ii) when the contract is entered into, the trader is aware of the commercial practice that constitutes the prohibited practice or could reasonably be expected to be aware of it.

(5) In paragraph (4)(b) 'producer' means—
  (a) a manufacturer of the goods or digital content,
  (b) an importer of the goods or digital content into the [United Kingdom], or

(c) a person who purports to be a producer by placing the person's name, trade mark or other distinctive sign on the goods or using it in connection with the digital content,

and includes a producer acting personally or through another person acting in the producer's name or on the producer's behalf.

(6) The third condition is that the prohibited practice is a significant factor in the consumer's decision to enter into the contract or make the payment.]

[27B.   What does 'prohibited practice' mean in this Part?

(1) In this Part 'prohibited practice' means a commercial practice that—

(a) is a misleading action under regulation 5, or

(b) is aggressive under regulation 7.

(2) Regulations 5 and 7 apply for the purposes of this Part as if for the definition of 'transactional decision' in regulation 2(1) there were substituted—

''transactional decision' means any decision taken by a consumer to enter into a contract with a trader for the sale or supply of a product by the trader, or for the sale of goods to the trader, or to make a payment to a trader for the supply of a product.']

[27C.   What immoveable property is covered by this Part?

(1) In this Part 'product' does not include immoveable property other than a relevant lease.

(2) In this regulation 'relevant lease' in relation to England [. . .] means—

(a) an assured tenancy within the meaning of Part 1 of the Housing Act 1988, or

(b) a lease under which accommodation is let as holiday accommodation.

(3) But none of the following are relevant leases for the purposes of paragraph (2)(a)—

(a) a lease granted by—

(i) a private registered provider of social housing, or

(ii) a registered social landlord within the meaning of Part 1 of the Housing Act 1996;

(b) a lease of a dwelling-house or part of a dwelling-house—

(i) granted on payment of a premium calculated by reference to a percentage of the value of the dwelling-house or part or of the cost of providing it, or

(ii) under which the lessee (or the lessee's personal representatives) will or may be entitled to a sum calculated by reference, directly or indirectly, to the value of the dwelling-house or part;

(c) a lease granted to a person as a result of the exercise by a local housing authority within the meaning of the Housing Act 1996 of its functions under Part 7 (homelessness) of that Act.]

[(7) In this regulation 'relevant lease' in relation to Wales means—

(a) a standard contract, within the meaning given by the Renting Homes (Wales) Act 2016 (see section 8 of that Act), or

(b) a lease under which accommodation is let as holiday accommodation.

(8) But none of the following are relevant leases for the purposes of paragraph (7)(a)—. . .]

[27D.   What financial services are covered by this Part?

(1) In this Part 'product' does not include a service provided in the course of carrying on a regulated activity within the meaning of section 22 of the Financial Services and Markets Act 2000, other than a service to which paragraph (2) applies.

(2) This paragraph applies to a service consisting of the provision of credit under an agreement which is a restricted-use credit agreement within paragraph (a) or (b) of the definition of that term in article 60L(1) of the Financial Services and Markets Act 2000 (Regulated Activities) Order 2001.

(3) But paragraph (2) does not apply to an agreement under which the obligation of the borrower to repay is secured by a legal or equitable mortgage on land (other than timeshare accommodation).

(4) In paragraph (3)—

'mortgage' includes a charge and (in Scotland) a heritable security;

'timeshare accommodation' means overnight accommodation which is the subject of a timeshare contract within the meaning of the Timeshare, Holiday Products, Resale and Exchange Contracts Regulations 2010.

(5) The fact that the supply of a product within regulation 2(1A) and (1B) may constitute an activity within article 39F (debt-collecting) of the Financial Services and Markets Act 2000 (Regulated Activities) Order 2001 does not prevent this Part from applying in relation to that supply.]

[27E. When does the right to unwind apply to a business to consumer contract?

(1) A consumer has the right to unwind in respect of a business to consumer contract if the consumer indicates to the trader that the consumer rejects the product, and does so—

    (a) within the relevant period, and

    (b) at a time when the product is capable of being rejected.

(2) An indication under paragraph (1) may be something that the consumer says or does, but it must be clear.

(3) In paragraph (1)(a) 'the relevant period' means the period of 90 days beginning with the later of—

    (a) the day on which the consumer enters into the contract, and

    (b) the relevant day.

(4) In this Part 'the relevant day' means the day on which—

    (a) the goods are first delivered,

    (b) the performance of the service begins,

    (c) the digital content is first supplied,

    (d) the lease begins, or

    (e) the right is first exercisable,

(as the case may be).

(5) But in the case of a mixed contract, 'the relevant day' means the latest of the days mentioned in paragraph (4) that is relevant to the contract.

(6) In this Part 'mixed contract' means a contract relating to a product which consists of any two or more of goods, a service, digital content, immoveable property or rights.

(7) For the purposes of this Part, where the consumer's access to digital content on a device requires its transmission to the device under arrangements initiated by the trader, the day on which the digital content is first provided is—

    (a) the day on which it reaches the device, or

    (b) if earlier, the day on which it reaches another trader chosen by the consumer to supply, under a contract with the consumer, a service by which digital content reaches the device.

(8) For the purposes of paragraph (1)(b), a product remains capable of being rejected only if—

    (a) the goods have not been fully consumed,

    (b) the service has not been fully performed,

    (c) the digital content has not been fully consumed,

    (d) the lease has not expired, or

    (e) the right has not been fully exercised,

(as the case may be).

(9) For the purposes of paragraph (8)—

    (a) goods have been fully consumed only if nothing is left of them, and

    (b) digital content has been fully consumed only if the digital content was available to the consumer for a fixed period and that period has expired.

(10) A consumer does not have the right to unwind in respect of a business to consumer contract if the consumer has exercised the right to a discount in respect of that contract and the same prohibited practice.]

[27F. How does the right to unwind work in the case of a business to consumer contract?

  (1) Where a consumer has the right to unwind in respect of a business to consumer contract—

   (a) the contract comes to an end so that the consumer and the trader are released from their obligations under it,

   (b) the trader has a duty to give the consumer a refund (subject as follows), and

   (c) if the contract was wholly or partly for the sale or supply of goods the consumer must make the goods available for collection by the trader.

  (2) The consumer's entitlement to a refund works as follows.

  (3) To the extent that the consumer paid money under the contract, the consumer is entitled to receive back the same amount of money (but see paragraphs (7) to (10)).

  (4) To the extent that the consumer transferred anything else under the contract, the consumer is entitled to receive back the same amount of what the consumer transferred, unless paragraph (5) applies.

  (5) To the extent that the consumer transferred under the contract something for which the same amount of the same thing cannot be substituted—

   (a) the consumer is entitled to receive back in its original state whatever the consumer transferred, or

   (b) if it cannot be given back in its original state, the consumer is entitled to be paid its market price as at the time when the product was rejected.

  (6) There is no entitlement to a refund if none of paragraphs (3) to (5) applies.

  (7) The consumer's entitlement to receive back the same amount of money as the consumer paid is qualified by paragraphs (8) to (10) if—

   (a) the contract was for the sale or supply of a product on a regular or continuous basis, and

   (b) the period beginning with the relevant day and ending with the day on which the consumer rejected the product exceeds one month.

  (8) In that case the consumer is only entitled to receive back the amount (if any) found by deducting the market price, when the consumer rejected the product, of the product supplied up to that time from the amount the consumer paid for it.

  (9) But paragraph (8) does not apply if it is not appropriate to apply that deduction having regard to—

   (a) the behaviour of the person who engaged in the prohibited practice, and

   (b) the impact of the practice on the consumer.

  (10) Where the product supplied up to the time when the consumer rejected it consists wholly or partly of goods, their market price is only to be taken into account under paragraph (8) to the extent that they have been consumed.]

[27G. How does the right to unwind work in the case of a consumer to business contract?

  (1) A consumer who has a right to redress in respect of a consumer to business contract has the right to unwind in respect of that contract.

  (2) Where paragraph (1) applies—

   (a) the consumer has the right to treat the contract as at an end so that the trader and the consumer are released from their obligations under it, and

   (b) the consumer has the right within paragraph (5) or (6).

  (3) To treat the contract as at an end, the consumer must indicate to the trader that the contract is ended.

  (4) An indication under paragraph (3) may be something that the consumer says or does, but it must be clear.

  (5) If the trader is able to return the goods to the consumer in the condition they were in when sold by the consumer—

   (a) the consumer has a right to the return of the goods, and

(b) the consumer must repay to the trader the amount (if any) that the trader has paid for the goods.

(6) If paragraph (5) does not apply, the consumer has a right to a payment from the trader of the amount (if any) by which the market price of the goods when the trader paid for them exceeds what the trader paid for them.]

[27H. How does the right to unwind work if payments are demanded which are not due?

(1) A consumer has the right to unwind in respect of a consumer payment for a product within regulation 2(1A) and (1B) if the consumer was not required to make all or part of the payment.

(2) Where paragraph (1) applies, the consumer has the right to receive back from the trader—

(a) the same amount of money as the consumer paid to the trader, or

(b) in a case where the consumer was required to make part of the payment, an amount equal to the part of the payment the consumer was not required to make.]

[27I. How does the right to a discount work?

(1) A consumer has the right to a discount in respect of a business to consumer contract if—

(a) the consumer has made one or more payments for the product to the trader or one or more payments under the contract have not been made, and

(b) the consumer has not exercised the right to unwind in respect of the contract.

(2) If the consumer has made one or more payments, the consumer has the right to receive back from the trader the relevant percentage of the payment or payments.

(3) If one or more payments have not been made, the consumer has the right—

(a) to reduce by the relevant percentage as many of those payments as is appropriate having regard to the seriousness of the prohibited practice, or

(b) in a case within paragraph (6), to reduce all of those payments by the relevant percentage.

(4) Subject to paragraph (6), the relevant percentage is as follows—

(a) if the prohibited practice is more than minor, it is 25%,

(b) if the prohibited practice is significant, it is 50%,

(c) if the prohibited practice is serious, it is 75%, and

(d) if the prohibited practice is very serious, it is 100%.

(5) The seriousness of the prohibited practice is to be assessed by reference to—

(a) the behaviour of the person who engaged in the practice,

(b) the impact of the practice on the consumer, and

(c) the time that has elapsed since the prohibited practice took place.

(6) [Paragraph (4)] does not apply if—

(a) the amount payable for the product under the contract exceeds £5,000,

(b) the market price of the product, at the time that the consumer entered into the contract, is lower than the amount payable for it under the contract, and

(c) there is clear evidence of the difference between the market price of the product and the amount payable for it under the contract.

(7) In such a case, the relevant percentage is the percentage difference between the market price of the product and the amount payable for it under the contract.

(8) The application of this regulation does not affect any of the other rights and liabilities under the contract.]

[27J. How does the right to damages work?

(1) Subject as follows, a consumer has the right to damages if the consumer—

(a) has incurred financial loss which the consumer would not have incurred if the prohibited practice in question had not taken place, or

(b) has suffered alarm, distress or physical inconvenience or discomfort which the consumer would not have suffered if the prohibited practice in question had not taken place.

(2) The right to damages is the right to be paid damages by the trader for the loss or the alarm, distress or physical inconvenience or discomfort in question.

(3) The right to be paid damages for financial loss does not include the right to be paid damages in respect of the difference between the market price of a product and the amount payable for it under a contract.

(4) The right to be paid damages under this regulation is a right to be paid only damages in respect of loss that was reasonably foreseeable at the time of the prohibited practice.

(5) A consumer does not have the right to damages if the trader proves that—

  (a) the occurrence of the prohibited practice in question was due to—

    (i) a mistake,

    (ii) reliance on information supplied to the trader by another person,

    (iii) the act or default of a person other than the trader,

    (iv) an accident, or

    (v) another cause beyond the trader's control, and

  (b) the trader took all reasonable precautions and exercised all due diligence to avoid the occurrence of the prohibited practice.]

[27K. How can a consumer enforce the rights to redress?

(1) A consumer with a right to redress under this Part may bring a claim in civil proceedings to enforce that right.

(3) Paragraph (4) applies if in proceedings under this regulation the consumer establishes that the consumer has—

  (a) the right to unwind,

  (b) the right to a discount, or

  (c) the right to damages.

(4) The court must make an order that gives effect to—

  (a) that right, and

  (b) any associated obligations of the consumer under this Part.

(5) The Limitation Act 1980 applies to a claim under this regulation in England and Wales as if it were an action founded on simple contract.]

[27L. How does this Part relate to the existing law?

(1) Nothing in this Part affects the ability of a consumer to make a claim under a rule of law or equity, or under an enactment, in respect of conduct constituting a prohibited practice.

(2) But a consumer may not—

  (a) make a claim to be compensated under a rule of law or equity, or under an enactment, in respect of such conduct if the consumer has been compensated under this Part in respect of the conduct, or

  (b) make a claim to be compensated under this Part in respect of such conduct if the consumer has been compensated under a rule of law or equity, or under an enactment, in respect of the conduct.

(3) In this regulation 'enactment' includes—

  (a) an enactment contained in subordinate legislation within the meaning of the Interpretation Act 1978,

  (b) an enactment contained in, or in an instrument made under, a Measure or Act of the National Assembly for Wales,]

[27M. Inertia selling

(1) This regulation applies where a trader engages in the unfair commercial practice described in paragraph 29 of Schedule 1 (inertia selling).

(2) The consumer is exempted from any obligation to provide consideration for the products supplied by the trader.

(3) The absence of a response from the consumer following the supply does not constitute consent to the provision of consideration for, or the return or safekeeping of, the products.

(4) In the case of an unsolicited supply of goods, the consumer may, as between the consumer and the trader, use, deal with or dispose of the goods as if they were an unconditional gift to the consumer.]

PART 5 SUPPLEMENTARY

28. Crown

(2) The Crown is not criminally liable as a result of any provision of these Regulations.

(3) Paragraph (2) does not affect the application of any provision of these Regulations in relation to a person in the public service of the Crown.

29. Validity of agreements

[Except as provided by Part 4A,] An agreement shall not be void or unenforceable by reason only of a breach of these Regulations.

Regulation 3(4)(d)   ### SCHEDULE 1

COMMERCIAL PRACTICES WHICH ARE IN ALL CIRCUMSTANCES CONSIDERED UNFAIR

1. Claiming to be a signatory to a code of conduct when the trader is not.

2. Displaying a trust mark, quality mark or equivalent without having obtained the necessary authorisation.

3. Claiming that a code of conduct has an endorsement from a public or other body which it does not have.

4. Claiming that a trader (including his commercial practices) or a product has been approved, endorsed or authorised by a public or private body when the trader, the commercial practices or the product have not or making such a claim without complying with the terms of the approval, endorsement or authorisation.

5. Making an invitation to purchase products at a specified price without disclosing the existence of any reasonable grounds the trader may have for believing that he will not be able to offer for supply, or to procure another trader to supply, those products or equivalent products at that price for a period that is, and in quantities that are, reasonable having regard to the product, the scale of advertising of the product and the price offered (bait advertising).

6. Making an invitation to purchase products at a specified price and then—

    (a) refusing to show the advertised item to consumers,

    (b) refusing to take orders for it or deliver it within a reasonable time, or

    (c) demonstrating a defective sample of it,

with the intention of promoting a different product (bait and switch).

7. Falsely stating that a product will only be available for a very limited time, or that it will only be available on particular terms for a very limited time, in order to elicit an immediate decision and deprive consumers of sufficient opportunity or time to make an informed choice.

8. Undertaking to provide after-sales service to consumers with whom the trader has communicated prior to a transaction in a language which is not [English (in the case of a trader located in the United Kingdom) or not] an official language of the EEA State where the trader is located and then making such service available only in another language without clearly disclosing this to the consumer before the consumer is committed to the transaction.

9. Stating or otherwise creating the impression that a product can legally be sold when it cannot.

10. Presenting rights given to consumers in law as a distinctive feature of the trader's offer.

11. Using editorial content in the media to promote a product where a trader has paid for the promotion without making that clear in the content or by images or sounds clearly identifiable by the consumer (advertorial).

12. Making a materially inaccurate claim concerning the nature and extent of the risk to the personal security of the consumer or his family if the consumer does not purchase the product.

13. Promoting a product similar to a product made by a particular manufacturer in such a manner as deliberately to mislead the consumer into believing that the product is made by that same manufacturer when it is not.

14. Establishing, operating or promoting a pyramid promotional scheme where a consumer gives consideration for the opportunity to receive compensation that is derived primarily from the introduction of other consumers into the scheme rather than from the sale or consumption of products.

15. Claiming that the trader is about to cease trading or move premises when he is not.

16. Claiming that products are able to facilitate winning in games of chance.

17. Falsely claiming that a product is able to cure illnesses, dysfunction or malformations.

18. Passing on materially inaccurate information on market conditions or on the possibility of finding the product with the intention of inducing the consumer to acquire the product at conditions less favourable than normal market conditions.

19. Claiming in a commercial practice to offer a competition or prize promotion without awarding the prizes described or a reasonable equivalent.

20. Describing a product as 'gratis', 'free', 'without charge' or similar if the consumer has to pay anything other than the unavoidable cost of responding to the commercial practice and collecting or paying for delivery of the item.

21. Including in marketing material an invoice or similar document seeking payment which gives the consumer the impression that he has already ordered the marketed product when he has not.

22. Falsely claiming or creating the impression that the trader is not acting for purposes relating to his trade, business, craft or profession, or falsely representing oneself as a consumer.

23. Creating the false impression that after-sales service in relation to a product is available in [the United Kingdom (if the product is sold there) or in] an EEA State other than the one in which the product is sold.

24. Creating the impression that the consumer cannot leave the premises until a contract is formed.

25. Conducting personal visits to the consumer's home ignoring the consumer's request to leave or not to return, except in circumstances and to the extent justified to enforce a contractual obligation.

26. Making persistent and unwanted solicitations by telephone, fax, e-mail or other remote media except in circumstances and to the extent justified to enforce a contractual obligation.

27. Requiring a consumer who wishes to claim on an insurance policy to produce documents which could not reasonably be considered relevant as to whether the claim was valid, or failing systematically to respond to pertinent correspondence, in order to dissuade a consumer from exercising his contractual rights.

28. Including in an advertisement a direct exhortation to children to buy advertised products or persuade their parents or other adults to buy advertised products for them.

29. Demanding immediate or deferred payment for or the return or safekeeping of products supplied by the trader, but not solicited by the consumer [. . .].

30. Explicitly informing a consumer that if he does not buy the product or service, the trader's job or livelihood will be in jeopardy.

31. Creating the false impression that the consumer has already won, will win, or will on doing a particular act win, a prize or other equivalent benefit, when in fact either—

    (a) there is no prize or other equivalent benefit, or

    (b) taking any action in relation to claiming the prize or other equivalent benefit is subject to the consumer paying money or incurring a cost.

[EXPLANATORY NOTE

[to the Consumer Protection (Amendment)
Regulations 2014]

(This note is not part of the Regulations)]

The table below sets out the rights to redress which are available to the consumer if the conditions in regulation 27A are met:

Consumer transaction	Right to redress
Business to consumer contract	The right to unwind (regulation 27F)
	The right to a discount (regulation 27I)
	The right to damages (regulation 27J)
Consumer to business contract	The right to unwind (regulation 27G)
	The right to damages (regulation 27J)
Consumer payment for product within regulation 2(1A) and (1B)	The right to unwind (regulation 27H)
	The right to damages (regulation 27J)
Consumer payment for any other type of product	The right to damages

Consumer Credit (Disclosure of Information) Regulations 2010

(SI 2010, No. 1013)

1. Citation, commencement and interpretation

(2) In these Regulations—

'the Act' means the Consumer Credit Act 1974;

'advance payment' includes any deposit and in relation to a regulated consumer credit agreement includes also any part-exchange allowance in respect of any goods agreed in antecedent negotiations [. . .] to be taken by the creditor in part exchange but does not include a repayment of credit or any insurance premium or any amount entering into the total charge for credit;

'ancillary service' means a service that relates to the provision of credit under the agreement and includes in particular an insurance or payment protection policy;

'the APR' means the annual percentage rate of charge for credit determined in accordance with Schedule 2 to these Regulations and the [total charge for credit rules];

'cash price' in relation to any goods, services, land or other things means the price or charge at which the goods, services, land or other things may be purchased by, or supplied to, the debtor for cash account being taken of any discount generally available from the dealer or supplier in question;

'credit intermediary' has the same meaning as in [section 61A] of the Act;

'distance contract' means any regulated agreement made under an organised distance sales or service-provision scheme run by or on behalf of the creditor who, in any such case, for the purpose of that agreement makes exclusive use of one or more means of distance communication up to and including the time at which the agreement is made. For this purpose, 'means of distance communication' means any means which, without the simultaneous physical presence of the creditor or a person acting on behalf of the creditor and of the debtor, may be used for the making of a regulated agreement between the parties to that agreement;

'excluded pawn agreement' means a pawn agreement—
  (a) where the debtor is not a new customer of the creditor ([paragraph (6)]), and
  (b) where, before the agreement is made, the creditor has not received a request from the debtor for the pre-contract credit information (see regulation 9);
'linked credit agreement' means a regulated consumer credit agreement which—
  (a) serves exclusively to finance an agreement for the supply of specific goods or the provision of a specific service or land, and
  (b) (i) where the supplier or service provider himself finances the credit for the debtor, or if it is financed by a third party, where the creditor uses the services of the supplier or service provider in connection with the preparation or making of the credit agreement, or
       (ii) where the specific goods or land or the provision of a specific service are explicitly specified in the credit agreement;
'pawn agreement' means a consumer credit agreement under which the creditor takes an article in pawn;
'pre-contract credit information' means the information specified in regulation 3(4);
'total amount of credit' means the credit limit or the total sums made available under a consumer credit agreement;
'total amount payable' means the sum of the total charge for credit and the total amount of credit payable under the agreement as well as any advance payment;
'total charge for credit' means the total charge for credit determined in accordance with the [total charge for credit rules] and the Schedule to these Regulations;
['the total charge for credit rules' means rules made by the Financial Conduct Authority under article 60M of the Financial Services and Markets Act 2000 (Regulated Activities) Order 2001 for the purposes of Chapter 14A of Part 2 of that Order].
  (3) In these Regulations, a reference to a repayment is a reference to—
  (a) a repayment of the whole or any part of the credit,
  (b) a payment of the whole or any part of the total charge for credit, or
  (c) a combination of such repayments and payments.
  (4) In these Regulations, a reference to rate of interest is a reference to the interest rate expressed as a fixed or variable percentage applied on an annual basis to the amount of credit drawn down.
  (5) In these Regulations, a reference to an agreement includes a reference to a prospective agreement.
  (6) For the purposes of the definition of 'excluded pawn agreement' and regulation 8 the debtor is a new customer if the debtor has not entered into a pawn agreement with the creditor in the three years preceding the start of the negotiations antecedent to the agreement.

2.   Agreements to which these Regulations apply
  (1) These Regulations apply in respect of a regulated consumer credit agreement, except as provided for in paragraphs (2) to (4).
  (2) These regulations do not apply to an agreement to which section 58 of the Act (opportunity for withdrawal from prospective land mortgage) applies.
  (3) These Regulations do not apply to an authorised non-business overdraft agreement which is—
  (a) for credit which exceeds £60,260 [unless it is a residential renovation agreement], or
  (b) secured on land.
  (4) Except as provided for in paragraph (5) these Regulations do not apply to an agreement—
  (a) under which the creditor provides the debtor with credit exceeding £60,260 [unless it is a residential renovation agreement],
  (b) secured on land,

(c)   entered into by the debtor wholly or predominantly for the purposes of a business also carried on, or intended to be carried on, by him, or

(d)   made before 1st February 2011.

(5)   These Regulations apply to an agreement mentioned in paragraph (4) (which is not also an agreement mentioned in paragraph (2) or (3)) where a creditor or, where applicable a credit intermediary, discloses or purports to disclose the pre-contract credit information in accordance with these Regulations rather than in accordance with the Consumer Credit (Disclosure of Information) Regulations 2004 or the Financial Services (Distance Marketing) Regulations 2004 (as the case may be).

[(6)   Article 60C(5) and (6) of the Financial Services and Markets Act 2000 (Regulated Activities) Order 2001 applies for the purposes of paragraph (4)(c).]

3.   Information to be disclosed: agreements other than telephone contracts, non-telephone distance contracts, excluded pawn agreements and overdraft agreements

(1)   This regulation applies to an agreement other than—

[(a)   an agreement made by voice telephone communication where it is a distance contract and the debtor consents to the disclosure of the information referred to in regulation 4(2);

(aa)   an agreement made by voice telephone communication where it is not a distance contract (see regulation 4(3));]

(b)   an agreement made using a means of distance communication other than a voice telephone communication, which does not enable the provision of the pre-contract credit information before the agreement is made (see regulation 5);

(c)   an excluded pawn agreement;

(d)   an authorised non-business overdraft agreement (see regulations 10 and 11).

(2)   In good time before the agreement is made, the creditor must disclose to the debtor, in the manner set out in regulation 8, the pre-contract credit information.

(3)   Paragraph (2) does not require a creditor to disclose the pre-contract credit information where it has already been disclosed to the debtor by a credit intermediary in a manner which complies with paragraph (2).

(4)   For the purposes of these Regulations, the pre-contract credit information comprises—

(a)   the type of credit,

(b)   the identity and geographical address of the creditor and, where applicable, of the credit intermediary,

(c)   the total amount of credit to be provided under the agreement and the conditions governing the draw down of credit. In the case of an agreement for running-account credit, the total amount of credit may be expressed as a statement indicating the manner in which the credit limit will be determined where it is not practicable to express the limit as a sum of money,

(d)   the duration or minimum duration of the agreement or a statement that the agreement has no fixed or minimum duration,

(e)   in the case of—

(i)   credit in the form of deferred payment for specific goods, services or land, or

(ii)   a linked credit agreement,

a description of the goods, services or land and the cash price of each and the total cash price,

(f)   the rate of interest charged, any conditions applicable to that rate, where available, any reference rate on which that rate is based and any information on any changes to the rate of interest (including the periods that the rate applies, and any conditions or procedure applicable to changing the rate),

(g)   where different rates of interest are charged in different circumstances the creditor must provide the information in paragraph (f) in respect of each rate,

(h)   the APR and the total amount payable under the agreement illustrated (if not known) by way of a representative example mentioning all the assumptions used in order to calculate that rate and amount,

(i)   the amount (expressed as a sum of money), number (if applicable) and frequency of repayments to be made by the debtor and, where appropriate, the order in which repayments will be allocated to different outstanding balances charged at different rates of interest,

(j)   in the case of an agreement for running-account credit, the amount of each repayment is to be expressed as (a) a sum of money; (b) a specified proportion of a specified amount; (c) a combination of (a) or (b); or (d) in a case where the amount of any repayment cannot be expressed in accordance with (a), (b) or (c), a statement indicating the manner in which the amount will be determined,

(k)   if applicable, any charges for maintaining an account recording both payment transactions and draw downs, unless the opening of an account is optional, and any charge payable for using a method of payment in respect of payment transactions or draw downs,

(l)   any other charges payable deriving from the credit agreement and the conditions under which those charges may be changed,

(m)   if applicable, a statement that fees will be payable by the debtor to a notary on conclusion of the credit agreement,

(n)   the obligation, if any, to enter into a contract for ancillary services relating to the consumer credit agreement, in particular insurance services, where the conclusion of such a contract is compulsory in order to obtain the credit or to obtain it on the terms and conditions marketed,

(o)   the rate of interest applicable in the case of late payments and the arrangements for its adjustment, and, where applicable, any charges payable for default,

(p)   a warning regarding the consequences of missing payments (for example, the possibility of legal proceedings and the possibility that the debtor's home may be repossessed),

(q)   where applicable, any security to be provided by the debtor or on behalf of the debtor,

(r)   the existence or absence of a right of withdrawal,

(s)   the debtor's right of early repayment under section 94 of the Act, and where applicable, information concerning the creditor's right to compensation and the way in which that compensation will be determined,

(t)   the requirement for a creditor to inform a debtor in accordance with section 157(A1) of the Act that a decision not to proceed with a prospective regulated consumer credit agreement has been reached on the basis of information from a credit reference agency and of the particulars of that agency,

(u)   the debtor's right to be supplied under section 55C of the Act on request and free of charge, with a copy of the draft agreement except where—

    (i)   the creditor is at the time of the request unwilling to proceed to the making of the agreement, or

    (ii)   the agreement is an agreement referred to in regulation 2(4)(a) to (c) or a pawn agreement, and

(v)   if applicable, the period of time during which the creditor is bound by the pre-contract credit information[, and

(w)   where the agreement references a benchmark, as defined in point 3 of Article 3(1) of Regulation EU 2016/1011(2) of the European Parliament and of the Council of 8 June 2016 on indices used as benchmarks in financial instruments and financial contracts or to measure the performance of investment funds and amending Directives 2008/48/EC(3) and 2014/17/EU(4) and Regulation (EU) No 596/2014(5), the name of the benchmark and of its administrator and the potential implications on the debtor.]

(5) For the purpose of the representative example referred to in paragraph (4)(h)—

    (a) (i)   where the debtor has informed the creditor or credit intermediary of one or more components of his preferred credit, such as the duration of the consumer credit agreement or the total amount of credit, and

        (ii) where the creditor would in principle agree to offer credit on such terms,

       the creditor or credit intermediary must take those components into account when calculating the representative APR and the total amount payable;

    (b) where the creditor uses the assumption set out in [the total charge for credit rules] the creditor must indicate that other draw down mechanisms for this type of consumer credit agreement may result in a higher APR;

    (c) subject to paragraph (a), in the case of an agreement for running-account credit, where the credit limit is not known at the date on which the pre-contract credit information is disclosed, the total amount of credit is to be assumed to be £1,200 or in a case where credit is to be provided subject to a maximum credit limit of less than £1,200, an amount equal to that maximum limit.

(6) In the case of a consumer credit agreement under which repayments do not give rise to an immediate reduction in the total amount of credit advanced but are used to constitute capital as provided for under the agreement or under an ancillary agreement, the creditor or credit intermediary must provide a clear and concise statement that such agreements do not provide for a guarantee of repayment of the total amount of credit drawn down under the credit agreement unless such a guarantee is given.

4.   Information to be disclosed: telephone contracts

(1) This regulation applies to an agreement (other than an authorised non-business overdraft agreement) made by way of a voice telephone communication (whether or not it is a distance contract).

(2) Where the agreement is a distance contract and where the debtor explicitly consents, the creditor must disclose the following information before the agreement is made—

    (a) the identity of the person in contact with the debtor and that person's link with the creditor,

    (b) a description of the main characteristics of the credit agreement which includes the information set out in regulation 3(4)(c), (d), (e), (f), (g), (h), [(j) and (w)],

    (c) the total price to be paid by the debtor to the creditor for the credit including all taxes paid via the creditor or, if an exact price cannot be indicated, the basis for the calculation of the price enabling the debtor to verify it,

    (d) notice of the possibility that other taxes or costs may exist that are not paid via the creditor or imposed by the creditor,

    (e) whether or not there is—

        (i) a right to withdraw under section 66A of the Act, or

        (ii) a right to cancel under regulation 9 of the Financial Services (Distance Marketing) Regulations 2004 and, where there is such a right, its duration and the conditions for exercising it, including information on the amount which the consumer may be required to pay in accordance with regulation 13 of those Regulations, as well as the consequences of not exercising that right,

    (f) that other information is available on request and the nature of that information.

(3) Where the agreement is not a distance contract the creditor must disclose the information in paragraph (2)(b) before the agreement is made.

(4) The creditor must disclose the pre-contract credit information in the manner set out in regulation 8 immediately after the agreement is made.

5.   Information to be disclosed: non-telephone distance contracts

(1) This regulation applies to an agreement (other than an authorised non-business overdraft agreement) made—

(a) at the debtor's request, and

(b) using a means of distance communication other than a voice telephone communication which does not enable the provision before the agreement is made of the pre-contract credit information.

(2) The creditor must disclose the pre-contract credit information in the manner set out in regulation 8 immediately after the agreement is made.

6. Information to be disclosed: distance contracts for the purpose of a business

(1) This regulation applies to an agreement that is a distance contract entered into by the debtor wholly or predominantly for the purposes of a business carried on, or intended to be carried on by him.

(2) Where the agreement is an agreement to which [regulations 3, 4 or 5] would otherwise apply the creditor may comply with those regulations by disclosing the pre-contract credit information immediately after the agreement is entered into.

[(3) Article 60C(5) and (6) of the Financial Services and Markets Act 2000 (Regulated Activities) Order 2001 applies for the purposes of paragraph (1).]

7. Information about contractual terms and conditions: [regulations 3, 4 and 5]

(1) This regulation applies to an agreement which is—

(a) a distance contract to which [regulation 3, 4 or 5] applies, and

(b) which is not entered into by the debtor wholly or predominantly for the purposes of a business carried on, or intended to be carried on, by him.

(2) The creditor must ensure that—

(a) the information provided to the debtor pursuant to [regulation 3, 4 or 5] includes the contractual terms and conditions, and

(b) the information provided to the debtor in relation to the contractual obligations which would arise if the distance contract were made accurately reflects the contractual obligations which would arise under the law presumed to be applicable to that contract.

[(3) Article 60C(5) and (6) of the Financial Services and Markets Act 2000 (Regulated Activities) Order 2001 applies for the purposes of paragraph (1).]

8. Manner of disclosure

(1) The pre-contract credit information must be disclosed by means of the form contained in Schedule 1.

(2) The form must be—

(a) in writing, and

(b) of a nature that enables the debtor to remove it from the place where it is disclosed to him.

(3) The form must be completed as specified in this paragraph—

(a) the relevant pre-contract credit information is to be provided in the appropriate row,

(b) the form is to be completed in accordance with the notes to that form,

(c) the asterisks and notes may be deleted,

(d) gridlines and boxes may be omitted, and

(e) any information contained in the form must be clear and easily legible.

(4) Any additional information relating to the credit which is provided in writing by the creditor to the debtor must be provided in a separate document to the form.

(5) Where a consumer credit agreement is a multiple agreement containing more than one part for the purposes of section 18 of the Act, the pre-contract credit information in respect of each part may be provided in the same form provided that—

(a) information that is not common to each part of the agreement is disclosed separately within the relevant section of the form, and

(b) it is clear which information relates to which part.

[(6) Where a consumer credit agreement references a benchmark, the name of the benchmark and of its administrator and the potential implications for the debtor shall be provided by the creditor, or where applicable, by the credit intermediary, to the debtor in a separate document, which may be annexed to the form in Schedule 1.]

9. Information to be disclosed: pawn agreements

(1) This Regulation applies to a pawn agreement.

(2) In good time before a pawn agreement is made (unless the debtor is a new customer), the creditor must inform the debtor of his right to receive the pre-contract credit information in the form contained in Schedule 1, free of charge, on request.

Information to be disclosed: overdraft agreements

10.—(1) This regulation applies to an agreement which is an authorised non-business overdraft agreement.

(2) In good time before an authorised non-business overdraft agreement is made, the creditor must disclose to the debtor, the information in paragraph (3) in the manner set out in regulation 11.

(3) The information referred to in paragraph (2) is as follows—

(a) the type of credit,

(b) the identity and geographical address of the creditor and, where applicable, of the credit intermediary,

(c) the total amount of credit,

(d) the duration of the agreement,

(e) the rate of interest charged, any conditions applicable to that rate, any reference rate on which that rate is based and any information on any changes to the rate of interest (including the periods that the rate applies, and any conditions or procedure applicable to changing the rate),

(f) where different rates of interest are charged in different circumstances the creditor must provide the information in paragraph (e) in respect of each rate,

(g) the conditions and procedure for terminating the agreement,

(h) where applicable, an indication that the debtor may be requested to repay the amount of credit in full on demand at any time,

(i) the rate of interest applicable in the case of late payments and the arrangements for its adjustment, and, where applicable, any charges payable for default,

(j) the requirement for a creditor to inform a debtor in accordance with section 157(A1) of the Act that a decision not to proceed with a prospective regulated consumer credit agreement has been reached on the basis of information from a credit reference agency and of the particulars of that agency,

(k) the charges, other than the rates of interest, payable by the debtor under the agreement (and the conditions under which those charges may be varied),

(l) if applicable, the period of time during which the creditor is bound by the information set out in this paragraph.

(4) Paragraph (2) does not apply to—

(a) an agreement made by a voice telephone communication (whether or not it is a distance contract),

(b) an agreement made at the debtor's request using a means of distance communication, other than a voice telephone communication, which does not enable the provision of the information required by paragraph (2) before the agreement is made, or

(c) an agreement that does not come within sub-paragraph (a) or (b) but where the debtor requests the overdraft be made available with immediate effect.

(5) In the case of an agreement that falls within paragraph (4)(a) that is also a distance contract, where the debtor explicitly consents the creditor must disclose the following information before the agreement is made—

(a) the identity of the person in contact with the debtor and that person's link with the creditor,

(b) a description of the main characteristics of the financial service including at least the information in paragraph (3)(c), (e), (f), (h) and (k),

(c) the total price to be paid by the debtor to the creditor for the credit including all taxes paid via the creditor or, if an exact price cannot be indicated, the basis for the calculation of the price enabling the debtor to verify it,

(d) notice of the possibility that other taxes or costs may exist that are not paid via the creditor or imposed by the creditor,

(e) whether or not there is a right to cancel under regulation 9 of the Financial Services (Distance Marketing) Regulations 2004 and where there is such a right, its duration and the conditions for exercising it including information on the amount which the consumer may be required to pay in accordance with regulation 13 of those regulations, as well as the consequences of not exercising that right, and

(f) that other information is available on request and the nature of that information.

[(5A) In the case of an agreement that falls within paragraph (4)(a) that is also a distance contract, where the debtor does not explicitly consent to the disclosure of the information in paragraph (5), the creditor must disclose the information in paragraph (3) to the debtor before the agreement is made.]

(6) In the case of an agreement that falls within paragraph (4)(a) that is not a distance contract the creditor must disclose the information in paragraph (5)(b) before the agreement is made.

(7) In the case of an agreement that is a distance contract to which this regulation applies the creditor must ensure that the information he provides to the debtor pursuant to this regulation regarding the contractual obligations which would arise if the distance contract were concluded, accurately reflects the contractual obligations which would arise under the law presumed to be applicable to that contract.

(8) In the case of an agreement that falls within paragraph (4)(c), the creditor must disclose the information in paragraph (3)(c), (e), (f), (h), and (k) to the debtor before the agreement is made in the manner set out in regulation 11.

(9) Where a current account is an agreement for two or more debtors jointly the creditor may comply with paragraphs (5), [(5A),] (6) or (8) by disclosing the information to one debtor provided that each of the debtors have given the creditor their consent that the creditor may not comply in each debtor's case with the relevant paragraph.

11.—(1) Where regulation 10(2) applies, the creditor must comply with that regulation by—

(a) disclosing the information by means of the [. . .] form set out in Schedule 3 to these Regulations and as specified in paragraph (2), or

(b) disclosing the information in writing so that all information is equally prominent.

(2) The specifications referred to in paragraph (1)(a) are that—

(a) the relevant information must be provided in the appropriate row,

(b) the form must be completed in accordance with the notes to that form,

(c) the asterisks and notes may be deleted,

(d) gridlines and boxes may be omitted, and

(e) any information contained in the form must be clear and easily legible.

(3) Where regulation 10(8) applies, the creditor may provide the information orally.

12. Modifying agreements

(1) Subject to paragraphs (2) to (4), these Regulations apply to a modifying agreement which varies or supplements an earlier agreement and which is, or is treated under section 82(3) of the Act as, a regulated agreement.

[(2) Where a modifying agreement modifies an earlier consumer credit agreement, the requirements of regulations 3, 4 and 10 will be deemed to be satisfied if—

(a) in good time before the modifying agreement is made—

(i) the information specified by regulations 3(4) and 10(3) is disclosed to the debtor in respect of any provision of the earlier agreement which is varied or supplemented, and

(ii) the creditor informs the debtor in writing that the other information in the earlier agreement remains unchanged, and

(b) where the Financial Services (Distance Marketing) Regulations 2004 apply, the creditor complies with regulations 7 and 8 of those Regulations.]

(3) Where a modifying agreement is made in a manner that does not allow the creditor to comply with the requirement in [paragraph (2)(a)(ii)], the creditor is deemed to have complied with that requirement if—

(a) before the agreement is made the creditor informs the debtor orally that the other information in the earlier agreement remains unchanged, and

(b) this is confirmed to the debtor in writing immediately after the agreement is made.

(4) This regulation does not apply to an excluded pawn agreement.

Regulation 8(1)

SCHEDULE 1

PRE-CONTRACT CREDIT INFORMATION

(Standard European Consumer Credit Information)

1. Contact details

Creditor.	[Identity.]
Address.	[Geographical address of the creditor
Telephone number(s).*	to be used by the debtor.]
E-mail address.*	
Fax number.*	
Web address.*	
If applicable	
Credit intermediary.	[Identity.]
Address.	[Geographical address of the credit
Telephone number(s).*	intermediary to be used by the debtor.]
E-mail address.*	
Fax number.*	
Web address.*	

* This information is optional for the creditor. The row may be deleted if the information is not provided.

Wherever 'if applicable' is indicated, the creditor must give the information relevant to the credit product or, if the information is not relevant for the type of credit considered, delete the respective information or the entire row, or indicate that the information is not applicable.

Indications between square brackets provide explanations for the creditor and must be replaced with the corresponding information.

2. Key features of the credit product

[The type of credit].	
The total amount of credit. This means the amount of credit to be provided under the proposed credit agreement or the credit limit.	[The amount is to be expressed as a sum of money. In the case of running-account credit, the total amount may be expressed as a statement indicating the manner in which the credit limit will be determined where it is not practicable to express the limit as a sum of money.]
How and when credit would be provided.	[Details of how and when any credit being advanced is to be drawn down.]
The duration of the credit agreement.	[The duration or minimum duration of the agreement or a statement that the agreement has no fixed or minimum duration.]
Repayments. If applicable: Your repayments will pay off what you owe in the following order.	[The amount (expressed as a sum of money), number (if applicable) and frequency of repayments to be made by the debtor. In the case of an agreement for running-account credit, the amount may be expressed as a sum of money or a specified proportion of a specified amount or both, or in a case where the amount of any repayment cannot be expressed as a sum of money or a specified proportion, a statement indicating the manner in which the amount will be determined.] [The order in which repayments will be allocated to different outstanding balances charged at different rates of interest.]
The total amount you will have to pay. This means the amount you have borrowed plus interest and other costs.	[The amount payable by the debtor under the agreement (where necessary, illustrated by means of a representative example). The total amount payable will be the sum of the total amount of credit and the total charge for credit payable under the agreement as well as any advance payment where required. In the case of running account credit, where it is not practicable to express the limit as a sum of money, a credit limit of £1200 should be assumed. In a case where credit is to be provided subject to a maximum credit limit of less than £1200, an amount equal to that maximum limit. The total charge for credit is to be calculated using the relevant APR assumptions set out in Schedule 2 to the Consumer Credit (Disclosure of Information) Regulations 2010 and the [total charge for credit rules], and where appropriate the relevant components of the debtor's preferred credit.]
If applicable The proposed credit will be granted in the form of a deferred payment for goods or service.] or [The proposed credit will be linked to the supply of specific goods or the provision of a service.] Description of goods/services/land (as applicable). Cash price.	[A list or other description] [Cash price of goods or service.] [Total cash price.]

If applicable Security required. This is a description of the security to be provided by you in relation to the credit agreement.	[Description of any security to be provided by or on behalf of the debtor.]
If applicable Repayments will not immediately reduce the amount you owe.	[In the case of a credit agreement under which repayments do not give rise to an immediate reduction in the total amount of credit advanced but are used to constitute capital as provided by the agreement (or an ancillary agreement a clear and concise statement) where applicable, that the agreement does not provide for a guarantee of the repayment of the total amount of credit drawn down under the credit agreement.]

3. Costs of the credit

The rates of interest which apply to the credit agreement	[Details of the rate of interest charged, any conditions applicable to that rate, where available, any reference rate on which that rate is based and any information on changes to the rate of interest (including the periods that the rate applies, and any conditions or procedure applicable to changing the rate). Where different rates of interest are charged in different circumstances, the creditor must provide the above information in respect of each rate.]
Annual Percentage Rate of Charge (APR). This is the total cost expressed as an annual percentage of the total amount of credit. The APR is there to help you compare different offers.	[% if known. If the APR is not known a representative example (expressed as a %) mentioning all the necessary assumptions used for calculating the rate (as set out in Schedule 2 to the Consumer Credit (Disclosure of Information) Regulations 2010, the [total charge for credit rules] and, where appropriate, the relevant components of the debtor's preferred credit). Where the creditor uses the assumption set out in [. . .] the [total charge for credit rules], the creditor shall indicate that other draw down mechanisms for this type of agreement may result in a higher APR.]
If applicable In order to obtain the credit or to obtain it on the terms and conditions marketed, you must take out: — an insurance policy securing the credit, or — another ancillary service contract. If we do not know the costs of these services they are not included in the APR.	[Nature and description of any insurance or other ancillary service contract required.]
Related costs	
If applicable You must have a separate account for recording both payment transactions and drawdowns.	[Details of any account or accounts that the creditor requires to be set up in order to obtain the credit together with the amount of any charge for this.]
If applicable Charge for using a specific payment method.	[Specify means of payment and the amount of charge.]

If applicable Any other costs deriving from the credit agreement.	[Description and amount of any other charges not otherwise referred to in this form.]
If applicable Conditions under which the above charges can be changed.	[Details of the conditions under which any of the charges mentioned above can be changed.]
If applicable You will be required to pay notarial fees.	[Description and amount of any fee.]
Costs in the case of late payments.	Either [A statement that there are no charges for late or missed payments.] Or [Applicable rate of interest in the case of late payments and arrangements for its adjustment and, where applicable any charges payable for default.]
Consequences of missing payments.	[A statement warning about the consequences of missing payments, including: — a reference to possible legal proceedings and repossession of the debtor's home where this is a possibility, and — the possibility of missing payments making it more difficult to obtain credit in the future.]

4.   Other important legal aspects
If applicable

Right of withdrawal.	Either: [A statement that the debtor has the right to withdraw from the credit agreement before the end of 14 days beginning with the day after the day on which the agreement is made, or if information is provided after the agreement is made, the day on which the debtor receives a copy of the executed agreement under sections 61A or 63 of the Consumer Credit Act 1974, the day on which the debtor receives the information required in section 61A(3) of that Act or the day on which the creditor notifies the debtor of the credit limit, the first time it is provided, whichever is the latest.] Or [There is no right to withdraw from this agreement—if there is a right to cancel the agreement this should be stated.] [If the right to cancel is under the Financial Services (Distance Marketing) Regulations 2004 refer to section 5 of the form.]
Early repayment. If applicable Compensation payable in the case of early repayment.	[A statement that the debtor has the right to repay the credit early at any time in full or partially.] [Determination of the compensation (calculation method) in accordance with section 95A (and, where applicable, section 95B) of the Consumer Credit Act 1974.]
Consultation with a Credit Reference Agency.	[A statement that if the creditor decides not to proceed with a prospective regulated consumer credit agreement on the basis of information from a credit reference agency the creditor must, when informing the debtor of the decision, inform the debtor that it has been reached on the basis of information from a credit reference agency and of the particulars of that agency.]

Right to a draft credit agreement.	[A statement that the debtor has the right, upon request, to obtain a copy of the draft credit agreement free of charge, unless the creditor is unwilling at the time of the request to proceed to the conclusion of the credit agreement.]
If applicable The period of time during which the creditor is bound by the pre-contractual information.	[This information is valid from [—] until [—].] or [Period of time during which the information on this form is valid.]

5. Additional information in the case of distance marketing of financial services

(a) concerning the creditor	
If applicable The creditor's representative in [the United Kingdom]. Address. Telephone number(s). E-mail address.* Fax number.* Web address.*	[i.e. where different from section 1.] [Identity.] [Geographical address to be used by the debtor.]
If applicable Registration number.	[Consumer credit licence number and any other relevant registration number of the creditor. (For 90 days, starting on the day that a creditor is given an FRN, either the FRN or any Interim Permission Number valid immediately before the start of this 90 day period may be provided.)]
If applicable The supervisory authority.	[The Financial Conduct Authority or any other relevant supervisory authority or both.]
(b) concerning the credit agreement	
If applicable Right to cancel the credit agreement.	[Practical instructions for exercising the right to cancel indicating, amongst other things, the period for exercising the right, the address to which notification of exercise of the right to cancel should be sent and the consequences of non-exercise of that right.]
If applicable The law taken by the creditor as a basis for the establishment of relations with you before the conclusion of the credit agreement.	[English/other law]
If applicable The law applicable to the credit agreement and/or the competent court.	[A statement concerning the law which governs the contract and the courts to which disputes may be referred.]
If applicable Language to be used in connection with the credit agreement.	[Details of the language that the information and contractual terms will be supplied in and used, with your consent, for communication during the duration of the credit agreement.]

(c) concerning redress	
Access to out-of-court complaint and redress mechanism.	[Whether or not there is an out-of-court complaint and redress mechanism for the debtor and, if so, the methods of access to it.]

* This information is optional for the creditor. The row may be deleted if the information is not provided.

Regulation 1(2)
SCHEDULE 2

PROVISIONS RELATING TO CALCULATION AND DISCLOSURE OF THE TOTAL CHARGE FOR CREDIT AND APR

1. Assumptions about running-account credit
  (a) In the case of an agreement for running-account credit, the assumption in paragraph (b) shall have effect for the purpose of calculating the total charge for credit and any APR in place of any assumptions in [the total charge for credit rules] that might otherwise apply—
  (b) in a case where the credit limit applicable to the credit is not known at the time the pre-contract credit information is disclosed but it is known that it will be subject to a maximum limit of less than £1,200, the credit limit shall be assumed to be an amount equal to that maximum limit.

2. Permissible tolerances in disclosure of an APR
For the purposes of these Regulations, it shall be sufficient compliance with the requirement to show an APR if there is included in the pre-contract credit information—
  (a) a rate which exceeds the APR by not more than one,
  (b) a rate which falls short of the APR by not more than 0.1, or
  (c) in a case to which paragraph 3 or 4 of this Schedule applies, a rate determined in accordance with those paragraphs or whichever of them applies to that case.

3. Tolerance where repayments are nearly equal
In the case of an agreement under which all repayments but one are equal and that one repayment does not differ from any other repayment by more whole pence than there are repayments of credit, there may be included in the pre-contract credit information a rate found under [the total charge for credit rules] as if that one repayment were equal to the other repayments to be made under the agreement.

4. Tolerance where interval between relevant date and first repayment is greater than interval between repayments
In the case of an agreement under which—
  (a) three or more repayments are to be made at equal intervals, and
  (b) the interval between the relevant date and the first repayment is greater than the interval between the repayments,
there may be included in the pre-contract credit information a rate found under [the total charge for credit rules] as if the interval between the relevant date and the first repayment were shortened so as to be equal to the interval between repayments.

Consumer Rights (Payment Surcharges) Regulations 2012

(SI 2012, No. 3110)

2.   'Consumer' and 'trader'

In these Regulations—

'consumer' means an individual acting for purposes which are wholly or mainly outside that individual's trade, business, craft or profession;

['trader' means a person acting for purposes relating to that person's trade, business, craft or profession, whether acting personally or through another person acting in the trader's name or on the trader's behalf].

3.   Other definitions

In these Regulations—

['business' includes the activities of any government department or local or public authority;]

['CMA' means the Competition and Markets Authority;]

'court' in relation to England and Wales and Northern Ireland means a county court or the High Court, and in relation to Scotland means the sheriff or the Court of Session;

'digital content' means data which are produced and supplied in digital form;

'district heating' means the supply of heat (in the form of steam or hot water or otherwise) from a central source of production through a transmission and distribution system to heat more than one building;

'goods' means any tangible movable items, but that includes water, gas and electricity if and only if they are put up for sale in a limited volume or a set quantity;

['payee', 'payer', 'payment instrument', 'payment service' and 'payment service provider' have the meanings given in regulation 2(1) of the Payment Services Regulations 2017;]

'sales contract' means a contract under which a trader transfers or agrees to transfer the ownership of goods to a consumer and the consumer pays or agrees to pay the price[, including any contract that has both goods and services as its object];

'service contract' means a contract, other than a sales contract, under which a trader supplies or agrees to supply a service to a consumer and the consumer pays or agrees to pay the price.

4.   [Fees a trader must not charge a consumer]

A trader must not charge consumers, in respect of the use of a given means of payment, fees that exceed the cost borne by the trader for the use of that means.

5.   Contracts where [regulation 4] applies

(1) Regulation 4 applies only if the use is as a means for the consumer to make payments for the purposes of a contract with the trader, and only to the extent that that contract—

(a) is a sales or service contract, or a contract (other than a sales or service contract) for the supply of water, gas, electricity, district heating or digital content, and

(b) is not an excluded contract.

(2) An excluded contract is a contract—

(a) for social services, including social housing, childcare and support of families and persons permanently or temporarily in need, including long-term care;

(b) for health services provided, whether or not via healthcare facilities, by health professionals to patients to assess, maintain or restore their state of health, including the prescription, dispensation and provision of medicinal products and medical devices (and 'health professionals' has the meaning given by Article 3(f) of Directive 2011/24/EU of the European Parliament and of the Council on the application of patients' rights in cross-border healthcare [as it had effect immediately before exit day]);

(c) for gambling within the meaning of the Gambling Act 2005 (which includes gaming, betting and participating in a lottery);

(d) for services of a banking, credit, insurance, personal pension, investment or payment nature;

(e) for the creation of immovable property or of rights in immovable property;

(f) for rental of accommodation for residential purposes;

(g) for the construction of new buildings, or the construction of substantially new buildings by the conversion of existing buildings;

(h) which is a regulated contract within the meaning of the Timeshare, Holiday Products, Resale and Exchange Contracts Regulations 2010;]

(i) for the supply of foodstuffs, beverages or other goods intended for current consumption in the household, and which are supplied by a trader on frequent and regular rounds to the consumer's home, residence or workplace;

(j) concluded by means of automatic vending machines or automated commercial premises;

(k) concluded with a telecommunications operator through a public telephone for the use of the telephone;

(l) concluded for the use of one single connection, by telephone, internet or fax, established by a consumer;

(m) under which goods are sold by way of execution or otherwise by authority of law.

[6A. Fees any payee must not charge any payer

(1) A payee must not charge a payer any fee in respect of payment by means of—

(a) a payment instrument which—

(i) is a card-based payment instrument as defined in Article 2(20) of Regulation (EU) 2015/751 of the European Parliament and of the Council of 29th April 2015 on interchange fees for card-based payment transactions; and

(ii) is not a commercial card as defined in Article 2(6) of that Regulation; or

(b) a payment instrument which—

(i) is not a card-based payment instrument as defined in Article 2(20) of that Regulation; and

(ii) would not fall within the definition of commercial card at Article 2(6) of that Regulation if, in that definition, the reference to any card-based payment instrument were to any payment instrument and the reference to such cards were to such payment instruments; or

(c) a payment service to which Regulation (EU) 260/2012 of the European Parliament and of the Council of 14th March 2012 establishing technical and business requirements for credit transfers and direct debits in euro applies.

(2) A payee receiving a payment by means of a payment instrument must not charge the payer, in respect of such payment, a fee which exceeds the costs borne by the payee for the use of that specific payment instrument.]

[6B. Application of regulation 6A

(1) Regulation 6A applies only if the payment service provider of the payer or the payment service provider of the payee is located in the United Kingdom.

(2) Where the payment service providers of both the payee and the payer are located in the United Kingdom, regulation 6A(1) and (2) apply.

(3) Where the payment service provider of either the payer or the payee, but not both, is located in the United Kingdom, regulation 6A(2) applies but regulation 6A(1) does not apply.]

7. Complaints

(1) It is the duty of an enforcement authority to consider any complaint made to it about a contravention of regulation 4 [or 6A] unless—

(a) the complaint appears to the authority to be frivolous or vexatious; or

(b) another enforcement authority has notified the OFT that it agrees to consider the complaint.

(2) If an enforcement authority has notified the OFT as mentioned in paragraph (1)(b), that authority is under a duty to consider the complaint.

(3) An enforcement authority which is under a duty to consider a complaint must—

(a) decide whether or not to make an application under regulation 8, and

(b) give reasons for its decision.

(4) In deciding whether or not to make an application, an enforcement authority may, if it considers it appropriate to do so, have regard to any undertaking given to it or another enforcement authority by or on behalf of any person as to compliance with regulation 4 [or 6A].

(5) The following are enforcement authorities for the purposes of these Regulations—

(a) every local weights and measures authority in Great Britain (within the meaning of section 69 of the Weights and Measures Act 1985);

(b) the Department of Enterprise, Trade and Investment in Northern Ireland.

8.   Orders to secure compliance

(1) An enforcement authority may apply for an injunction, or in Scotland an interdict or any other appropriate relief or remedy, against any person who appears to the authority to be responsible for a contravention of regulation 4 [or 6A].

(2) The court on an application under this regulation may grant an injunction, interdict or order on such terms as it thinks fit to secure compliance with regulation 4 [or 6A].

9.   Notification of undertakings and orders to the [CMA]

An enforcement authority must notify the [CMA]—

(a) of any undertaking given to it by or on behalf of any person who appears to it to be responsible for a contravention of regulation 4;

(b) of the outcome of any application made by it under regulation 8, and of the terms of any undertaking given to the court or of any order made by the court;

(c) of the outcome of any application made by it to enforce a previous order of the court.

10.   [Right] of redress

Where a trader charges a fee in contravention of regulation 4 [or any payee charges a fee in contravention of regulation 6A]—

(a) any provision of a contract requiring the [payment of] the fee is unenforceable to the extent [that the charging of the fee contravenes regulation 4 or 6A], and

(b) the contract for the purposes of which the payment is made is to be treated as providing for the [fee to be repaid to the extent that the charging of the fee contravenes regulation 4 or 6A].

Consumer Contracts (Information, Cancellation and Additional Charges) Regulations 2013

(SI 2013, No. 3134)

PART 1   GENERAL

3.   Review

(1) The Secretary of State must before the end of each review period—

(a) carry out a review of these Regulations,

(b) set out the conclusions of the review in a report, and

(c) publish the report.

(3) The report must in particular—

(a) set out the objectives intended to be achieved by these Regulations,

(b) assess the extent to which those objectives have been achieved, and

(c) assess whether those objectives remain appropriate and, if so, the extent to which they could be achieved in a way that imposes less regulation.

(4) A review period is—

    (a) the period of 5 years beginning with the day on which these Regulations come into force, and

    (b) each successive period of 5 years.

4. 'Consumer' and 'trader'

In these Regulations—

'consumer' means an individual acting for purposes which are wholly or mainly outside that individual's trade, business, craft or profession;

'trader' means a person acting for purposes relating to that person's trade, business, craft or profession, whether acting personally or through another person acting in the trader's name or on the trader's behalf.

5. Other definitions

In these Regulations—

'business' includes the activities of any government department or local or public authority;

'business premises' in relation to a trader means—

    (a) any immovable retail premises where the activity of the trader is carried out on a permanent basis, or

    (b) any movable retail premises where the activity of the trader is carried out on a usual basis;

'CMA' means the Competition and Markets Authority;

'commercial guarantee', in relation to a contract, means any undertaking by the trader or producer to the consumer (in addition to the trader's duty to supply goods that are in conformity with the contract) to reimburse the price paid or to replace, repair or service goods in any way if they do not meet the specifications or any other requirements not related to conformity set out in the guarantee statement or in the relevant advertising available at the time of the contract or before it is entered into;

'court'—

    (a) in relation to England and Wales, means the county court or the High Court, . . .

'delivery' means voluntary transfer of possession from one person to another;

'digital content' means data which are produced and supplied in digital form;

'distance contract' means a contract concluded between a trader and a consumer under an organised distance sales or service-provision scheme without the simultaneous physical presence of the trader and the consumer, with the exclusive use of one or more means of distance communication up to and including the time at which the contract is concluded;

'district heating' means the supply of heat (in the form of steam or hot water or otherwise) from a central source of production through a transmission and distribution system to heat more than one building;

'durable medium' means paper or email, or any other medium that—

    (a) allows information to be addressed personally to the recipient,

    (b) enables the recipient to store the information in a way accessible for future reference for a period that is long enough for the purposes of the information, and

    (c) allows the unchanged reproduction of the information stored;

'functionality' in relation to digital content includes region coding, restrictions incorporated for the purposes of digital rights management, and other technical restrictions;

'goods' means any tangible moveable items, but that includes water, gas and electricity if and only if they are put up for sale in a limited volume or a set quantity;

'off-premises contract' means a contract between a trader and a consumer which is any of these—

    (a) a contract concluded in the simultaneous physical presence of the trader and the consumer, in a place which is not the business premises of the trader;

    (b) a contract for which an offer was made by the consumer in the simultaneous physical presence of the trader and the consumer, in a place which is not the business premises of the trader;

    (c) a contract concluded on the business premises of the trader or through any means of distance communication immediately after the consumer was personally and individually addressed in a place which is not the business premises of the trader in the simultaneous physical presence of the trader and the consumer;

    (d) a contract concluded during an excursion organised by the trader with the aim or effect of promoting and selling goods or services to the consumer;

'on-premises contract' means a contract between a trader and a consumer which is neither a distance contract nor an off-premises contract;

'public auction' means a method of sale where—

    (a) goods or services are offered by a trader to consumers through a transparent, competitive bidding procedure run by an auctioneer,

    (b) the consumers attend or are given the possibility to attend in person, and

    (c) the successful bidder is bound to purchase the goods or services;

'sales contract' means a contract under which a trader transfers or agrees to transfer the ownership of goods to a consumer and the consumer pays or agrees to pay the price, including any contract that has both goods and services as its object;

'service' includes—

    (a) the supply of water, gas or electricity if they are not put up for sale in a limited volume or a set quantity, and

    (b) the supply of district heating;

'service contract' means a contract, other than a sales contract, under which a trader supplies or agrees to supply a service to a consumer and the consumer pays or agrees to pay the price.

6. Limits of application: general

    (1) These Regulations do not apply to a contract, to the extent that it is—

        (a) for—

            (i) gambling within the meaning of the Gambling Act 2005 (which includes gaming, betting and participating in a lottery); [. . . or]

            [(iii) participating in a lottery which forms part of the National Lottery within the meaning of the National Lottery etc. Act 1993]

        (b) for services of a banking, credit, insurance, personal pension, investment or payment nature;

        (c) for the creation of immovable property or of rights in immovable property;

        (d) for rental of accommodation for residential purposes;

        (e) for the construction of new buildings, or the construction of substantially new buildings by the conversion of existing buildings;

        (f) for the supply of foodstuffs, beverages or other goods intended for current consumption in the household and which are supplied by a trader on frequent and regular rounds to the consumer's home, residence or workplace;

        [(g) which is a package travel contract within the meaning of the Package Travel and Linked Travel Arrangements Regulations 2018;]

        [(h) which is a regulated contract within the meaning of the Timeshare, Holiday Products, Resale and Exchange Contracts Regulations 2010.]

    (2) These Regulations do not apply to contracts—

        (a) concluded by means of automatic vending machines or automated commercial premises;

        (b) concluded with a telecommunications operator through a public telephone for the use of the telephone;

        (c) concluded for the use of one single connection, by telephone, internet or fax, established by a consumer;

        (d) under which goods are sold by way of execution or otherwise by authority of law.

    (3) Paragraph (1)(b) is subject to regulations 38(4) (ancillary contracts) and 40(3) (additional payments).

PART 2 INFORMATION REQUIREMENTS

Chapter 1 Provision of information

7. Application of Part 2

(1) This Part applies to on-premises, off-premises and distance contracts, subject to paragraphs (2), (3) and (4) and regulation 6.

(2) This Part does not apply to contracts to the extent that they are—

(a) for the supply of a medicinal product by administration by a prescriber, or under a prescription or directions given by a prescriber;

(b) for the supply of a product by a health care professional or a person included in a relevant list, under arrangements for the supply of services as part of the health service, where the product is one that, at least in some circumstances is available under such arrangements free or on prescription.

(3) This Part, except for regulation 14(1) to (5), does not apply to contracts to the extent that they are for passenger transport services.

(4) This Part does not apply to off-premises contracts under which the payment to be made by the consumer is not more than £42.

(5) In paragraph (2)—

'health care professional' and 'prescriber' have the meaning given by regulation 2(1) of the National Health Service (Pharmaceutical and Local Pharmaceutical Services) Regulations 2013;

'health service' means—

(a) the health service as defined by section 275(1) of the National Health Service Act 2006 or section 206(1) of the National Health Service (Wales) Act 2006, . . .

'medicinal product' has the meaning given by regulation 2(1) of the Human Medicines Regulations 2012;

'relevant list' means—

(d) a relevant list for the purposes of the National Health Service (Pharmaceutical and Local Pharmaceutical Services) Regulations 2013, or

(e) a list maintained under those Regulations.

8. Making information etc available to a consumer

For the purposes of this Part, something is made available to a consumer only if the consumer can reasonably be expected to know how to access it.

9. Information to be provided before making an on-premises contract

(1) Before the consumer is bound by an on-premises contract, the trader must give or make available to the consumer the information described in Schedule 1 in a clear and comprehensible manner, if that information is not already apparent from the context.

(2) Paragraph (1) does not apply to a contract which involves a day-to-day transaction and is performed immediately at the time when the contract is entered into.

[(3) If the contract is for the supply of digital content other than for a price paid by the consumer—

(a) any information that the trader gives the consumer as required by this regulation is to be treated as included as a term of the contract, and

(b) a change to any of that information, made before entering into the contract or later, is not effective unless expressly agreed between the consumer and the trader].

10. Information to be provided before making an off-premises contract

(1) Before the consumer is bound by an off-premises contract, the trader—

(a) must give the consumer the information listed in Schedule 2 in a clear and comprehensible manner, and

(b) if a right to cancel exists, must give the consumer a cancellation form as set out in part B of Schedule 3.

(2) The information and any cancellation form must be given on paper or, if the consumer agrees, on another durable medium and must be legible.

(3) The information referred to in paragraphs (l), (m) and (n) of Schedule 2 may be provided by means of the model instructions on cancellation set out in part A of Schedule 3; and a trader who has supplied those instructions to the consumer, correctly filled in, is to be treated as having complied with paragraph (1) in respect of those paragraphs.

(4) If the trader has not complied with paragraph (1) in respect of paragraph (g), (h) or (m) of Schedule 2, the consumer is not to bear the charges or costs referred to in those paragraphs.

[(5) If the contract is for the supply of digital content other than for a price paid by the consumer—

- (a) any information that the trader gives the consumer as required by this regulation is to be treated as included as a term of the contract, and
- (b) a change to any of that information, made before entering into the contract or later, is not effective unless expressly agreed between the consumer and the trader].

(7) This regulation is subject to regulation 11.

11. Provision of information in connection with repair or maintenance contracts

(1) If the conditions in paragraphs (2), (3) and (4) are met, regulation 10(1) does not apply to an off-premises contract where—

- (a) the contract is a service contract,
- (b) the consumer has explicitly requested the trader to supply the service for the purpose of carrying out repairs or maintenance,
- (c) the obligations of the trader and the consumer under the contract are to be performed immediately, and
- (d) the payment to be made by the consumer is not more than £170.

(2) The first condition is that, before the consumer is bound by the contract, the trader gives or makes available to the consumer on paper or, if the consumer expressly agrees, on another durable medium—

- (a) the information referred to in paragraphs (b) to (d), (f) and (g) of Schedule 2,
- (b) an estimate of the total price, where it cannot reasonably be calculated in advance, and
- (c) where a right to cancel exists, a cancellation form as set out in part B of Schedule 3.

(3) The second condition is that, before the consumer is bound by the contract, the trader gives or makes available to the consumer the information referred to in paragraphs (a), (l) and (o) of Schedule 2, either on paper or another durable medium or otherwise if the consumer expressly agrees.

(4) The third condition is that the confirmation of the contract provided in accordance with regulation 12 contains the information required by regulation 10(1).

(5) For the right to cancel where this regulation applies, see in particular—

- (a) regulation 28(1)(e) and (2) (cases where cancellation excluded: visit requested for urgent work);
- (b) regulation 36 (form of consumer's request, and consequences).

12. Provision of copy or confirmation of off-premises contracts

(1) In the case of an off-premises contract, the trader must give the consumer—

- (a) a copy of the signed contract, or
- (b) confirmation of the contract.

(2) The confirmation must include all the information referred to in Schedule 2 unless the trader has already provided that information to the consumer on a durable medium prior to the conclusion of the off-premises contract.

(3) The copy or confirmation must be provided on paper or, if the consumer agrees, on another durable medium.

(4) The copy or confirmation must be provided within a reasonable time after the conclusion of the contract, but in any event—

    (a) not later than the time of the delivery of any goods supplied under the contract, and

    (b) before performance begins of any service supplied under the contract.

(5) If the contract is for the supply of digital content not on a tangible medium and the consumer has given the consent and acknowledgement referred to in regulation 37(1)(a) and (b), the copy or confirmation must include confirmation of the consent and acknowledgement.

13. Information to be provided before making a distance contract

(1) Before the consumer is bound by a distance contract, the trader—

    (a) must give or make available to the consumer the information listed in Schedule 2 in a clear and comprehensible manner, and in a way appropriate to the means of distance communication used, and

    (b) if a right to cancel exists, must give or make available to the consumer a cancellation form as set out in part B of Schedule 3.

(2) In so far as the information is provided on a durable medium, it must be legible.

(3) The information referred to in paragraphs (l), (m) and (n) of Schedule 2 may be provided by means of the model instructions on cancellation set out in part A of Schedule 3; and a trader who has supplied those instructions to the consumer, correctly filled in, is to be treated as having complied with paragraph (1) in respect of those paragraphs.

(4) Where a distance contract is concluded through a means of distance communication which allows limited space or time to display the information—

    (a) the information listed in paragraphs (a), (b), (f), (g), (h), (l) and (s) of Schedule 2 must be provided on that means of communication in accordance with paragraphs (1) and (2), but

    (b) the other information required by paragraph (1) may be provided in another appropriate way.

(5) If the trader has not complied with paragraph (1) in respect of paragraph (g), (h) or (m) of Schedule 2, the consumer is not to bear the charges or costs referred to in those paragraphs.

[(6) If the contract is for the supply of digital content other than for a price paid by the consumer—

    (a) any information that the trader gives the consumer as required by this regulation is to be treated as included as a term of the contract, and

    (b) a change to any of that information, made before entering into the contract or later, is not effective unless expressly agreed between the consumer and the trader].

14. Requirements for distance contracts concluded by electronic means

(1) This regulation applies where a distance contract is concluded by electronic means.

(2) If the contract places the consumer under an obligation to pay, the trader must make the consumer aware in a clear and prominent manner, and directly before the consumer places the order, of the information listed in paragraphs (a), (f), (g), (h), (s) and (t) of Schedule 2.

(3) The trader must ensure that the consumer, when placing the order, explicitly acknowledges that the order implies an obligation to pay.

(4) If placing an order entails activating a button or a similar function, the trader must ensure that the button or similar function is labelled in an easily legible manner only with the words 'order with obligation to pay' or a corresponding unambiguous formulation indicating that placing the order entails an obligation to pay the trader.

(5) If the trader has not complied with paragraphs (3) and (4), the consumer is not bound by the contract or order.

(6) The trader must ensure that any trading website through which the contract is concluded indicates clearly and legibly, at the latest at the beginning of the ordering process, whether any delivery restrictions apply and which means of payment are accepted.

15.   Telephone calls to conclude a distance contract

If the trader makes a telephone call to the consumer with a view to concluding a distance contract, the trader must, at the beginning of the conversation with the consumer, disclose—

(a)   the trader's identity,

(b)   where applicable, the identity of the person on whose behalf the trader makes the call, and

(c)   the commercial purpose of the call.

16.   Confirmation of distance contracts

(1)   In the case of a distance contract the trader must give the consumer confirmation of the contract on a durable medium.

(2)   The confirmation must include all the information referred to in Schedule 2 unless the trader has already provided that information to the consumer on a durable medium prior to the conclusion of the distance contract.

(3)   If the contract is for the supply of digital content not on a tangible medium and the consumer has given the consent and acknowledgment referred to in regulation 37(1)(a) and (b), the confirmation must include confirmation of the consent and acknowledgement.

(4)   The confirmation must be provided within a reasonable time after the conclusion of the contract, but in any event—

(a)   not later than the time of delivery of any goods supplied under the contract, and

(b)   before performance begins of any service supplied under the contract.

(5)   For the purposes of paragraph (4), the confirmation is treated as provided as soon as the trader has sent it or done what is necessary to make it available to the consumer.

17.   Burden of proof in relation to off-premises and distance contracts

(1)   In case of dispute about the trader's compliance with any provision of regulations 10 to 16, it is for the trader to show that the provision was complied with.

(2)   That does not apply to proceedings—

(a)   for an offence under regulation 19, or

(b)   relating to compliance with an injunction, interdict or order under regulation 45.

18.   Effect on contract of failure to provide information

Every contract to which this Part applies is to be treated as including a term that the trader has complied with the provisions of—

(a)   regulations 9 to 14, and

(b)   regulation 16.

Chapter 2   Offences

19.   Offence relating to the failure to give notice of the right to cancel

(1)   A trader is guilty of an offence if the trader enters into an off-premises contract to which regulation 10 applies but fails to give the consumer the information listed in paragraph (l), (m) or (n) of Schedule 2 in accordance with that regulation.

(2)   A person who is guilty of an offence under paragraph (1) is liable on summary conviction to a fine not exceeding level 5 on the standard scale.

20.   Defence of due diligence

(1)   In any proceedings against a person (A) for an offence under regulation 19 it is a defence for A to prove—

(a)   that the commission of the offence was due to—

(i)   the act or default of another, or

(ii)   reliance on information given by another, and

(b)   that A took all reasonable precautions and exercised all due diligence to avoid the commission of such an offence by A or any person under A's control.

(2) A person is not entitled to rely on the defence provided by paragraph (1) without leave of the court unless—

  (a) that person has served on the prosecutor a notice in writing giving such information as was in that person's possession identifying or assisting in the identification of the other person; and

  (b) the notice is served on the prosecutor not less than 7 days before the hearing of the proceedings or, in Scotland, 7 days before the intermediate diet or 14 days before the trial diet, whichever is earlier.

21. Liability of persons other than the principal offender

Where the commission by a person of an offence under regulation 19 is due to the act or default of another person, that other person is guilty of the offence and may be proceeded against and punished whether or not proceedings are taken against the first person.

22. Offences committed by bodies of persons

(1) Where an offence under regulation 19 committed by a body corporate is proved—

  (a) to have been committed with the consent or connivance of an officer of the body corporate or

  (b) to be attributable to any neglect on the part of an officer of the body corporate,

the officer, as well as the body corporate, is guilty of the offence and liable to be proceeded against and punished accordingly.

(2) In paragraph (1) a reference to an officer of a body corporate includes a reference to—

  (a) a director, manager, secretary or other similar officer; and

  (b) a person purporting to act as a director, manager, secretary or other similar officer.

(3) Where an offence under regulation 19 committed in Scotland by a Scottish partnership is proved—

  (a) to have been committed with the consent or connivance of a partner, or

  (b) to be attributable to any neglect on the part of a partner,

that partner, as well as the partnership shall be guilty of the offence and liable to be proceeded against and punished accordingly.

(4) In paragraph (3) a reference to a partner includes a person purporting to act as a partner.

23. Duty to enforce

(1) Subject to paragraphs (2) and (3)—

  (a) it is the duty of every weights and measures authority in Great Britain to enforce regulation 19 within its area; and

  (b) it is the duty of the Department of Enterprise, Trade and Investment in Northern Ireland to enforce regulation 19 within Northern Ireland.

(2) No proceedings for an offence under regulation 19 may be instituted in England and Wales except by or on behalf of an enforcement authority.

PART 3 RIGHT TO CANCEL

27. Application of Part 3

(1) This Part applies to distance and off-premises contracts between a trader and a consumer, subject to paragraphs (2) and (3) and regulations 6 and 28.

(2) This Part does not apply to contracts to the extent that they are—

  (a) for the supply of a medicinal product by administration by a prescriber, or under a prescription or directions given by a prescriber;

  (b) for the supply of a product by a health care professional or a person included in a relevant list, under arrangements for the supply of services as part of the health service, where the product is one that, at least in some circumstances is available under such arrangements free or on prescription;

(c) for passenger transport services.

(3) This Part does not apply to off-premises contracts under which the payment to be made by the consumer is not more than £42.

(4) In paragraph (2)(a) and (b), expressions defined in regulation 7(5) have the meaning given there.

28. Limits of application: circumstances excluding cancellation

(1) This Part does not apply as regards the following—

(a) the supply of—

    (i) goods, or

    (ii) services, other than supply of water, gas, electricity or district heating,

for which the price is dependent on fluctuations in the financial market which cannot be controlled by the trader and which may occur within the cancellation period;

(b) the supply of goods that are made to the consumer's specifications or are clearly personalised;

(c) the supply of goods which are liable to deteriorate or expire rapidly;

(d) the supply of alcoholic beverages, where—

    (i) their price has been agreed at the time of the conclusion of the sales contract,

    (ii) delivery of them can only take place after 30 days, and

    (iii) their value is dependent on fluctuations in the market which cannot be controlled by the trader;

(e) contracts where the consumer has specifically requested a visit from the trader for the purpose of carrying out urgent repairs or maintenance;

(f) the supply of a newspaper, periodical or magazine with the exception of subscription contracts for the supply of such publications;

(g) contracts concluded at a public auction;

(h) the supply of accommodation, transport of goods, vehicle rental services, catering or services related to leisure activities, if the contract provides for a specific date or period of performance.

(2) Sub-paragraph (e) of paragraph (1) does not prevent this Part applying to a contract for—

(a) services in addition to the urgent repairs or maintenance requested, or

(b) goods other than replacement parts necessarily used in making the repairs or carrying out the maintenance,

if the trader supplies them on the occasion of a visit such as is mentioned in that sub-paragraph.

(3) The rights conferred by this Part cease to be available in the following circumstances—

(a) in the case of a contract for the supply of sealed goods which are not suitable for return due to health protection or hygiene reasons, if they become unsealed after delivery;

(b) in the case of a contract for the supply of sealed audio or sealed video recordings or sealed computer software, if the goods become unsealed after delivery;

(c) in the case of any sales contract, if the goods become mixed inseparably (according to their nature) with other items after delivery.

29. Right to cancel

(1) The consumer may cancel a distance or off-premises contract at any time in the cancellation period without giving any reason, and without incurring any liability except under these provisions—

(a) regulation 34(3) (where enhanced delivery chosen by consumer);

(b) regulation 34(9) (where value of goods diminished by consumer handling);

(c) regulation 35(5) (where goods returned by consumer);

(d) regulation 36(4) (where consumer requests early supply of service).

(2) The cancellation period begins when the contract is entered into and ends in accordance with regulation 30 or 31.

(3) Paragraph (1) does not affect the consumer's right to withdraw an offer made by the consumer to enter into a distance or off-premises contract, at any time before the contract is entered into, without giving any reason and without incurring any liability.

30.   Normal cancellation period

(1) The cancellation period ends as follows, unless regulation 31 applies.

(2) If the contract is—

(a) a service contract, or

(b) a contract for the supply of digital content which is not supplied on a tangible medium,

the cancellation period ends at the end of 14 days after the day on which the contract is entered into.

(3) If the contract is a sales contract and none of paragraphs (4) to (6) applies, the cancellation period ends at the end of 14 days after the day on which the goods come into the physical possession of—

(a) the consumer, or

(b) a person, other than the carrier, identified by the consumer to take possession of them.

(4) If the contract is a sales contract under which multiple goods are ordered by the consumer in one order but some are delivered on different days, the cancellation period ends at the end of 14 days after the day on which the last of the goods come into the physical possession of—

(a) the consumer, or

(b) a person, other than the carrier, identified by the consumer to take possession of them.

(5) If the contract is a sales contract under which goods consisting of multiple lots or pieces of something are delivered on different days, the cancellation period ends at the end of 14 days after the day on which the last of the lots or pieces come into the physical possession of—

(a) the consumer, or

(b) a person, other than the carrier, identified by the consumer to take possession of them.

(6) If the contract is a sales contract for regular delivery of goods during a defined period of more than one day, the cancellation period ends at the end of 14 days after the day on which the first of the goods come into the physical possession of—

(a) the consumer, or

(b) a person, other than the carrier, identified by the consumer to take possession of them.

31.   Cancellation period extended for breach of information requirement

(1) This regulation applies if the trader does not provide the consumer with the information on the right to cancel required by paragraph (l) of Schedule 2, in accordance with Part 2.

(2) If the trader provides the consumer with that information in the period of 12 months beginning with the first day of the 14 days mentioned in regulation 30(2) to (6), but otherwise in accordance with Part 2, the cancellation period ends at the end of 14 days after the consumer receives the information.

(3) Otherwise the cancellation period ends at the end of 12 months after the day on which it would have ended under regulation 30.

32.   Exercise of the right to withdraw or cancel

(1) To withdraw an offer to enter into a distance or off-premises contract, the consumer must inform the trader of the decision to withdraw it.

(2) To cancel a contract under regulation 29(1), the consumer must inform the trader of the decision to cancel it.

(3) To inform the trader under paragraph (2) the consumer may either—

(a) use a form following the model cancellation form in part B of Schedule 3, or

(b) make any other clear statement setting out the decision to cancel the contract.

(4) If the trader gives the consumer the option of filling in and submitting such a form or other statement on the trader's website—

(a) the consumer need not use it, but

(b) if the consumer does, the trader must communicate to the consumer an acknowledgement of receipt of the cancellation on a durable medium without delay.

(5) Where the consumer informs the trader under paragraph (2) by sending a communication, the consumer is to be treated as having cancelled the contract in the cancellation period if the communication is sent before the end of the period.

(6) In case of dispute it is for the consumer to show that the contract was cancelled in the cancellation period in accordance with this regulation.

33. Effect of withdrawal or cancellation

(1) If a contract is cancelled under regulation 29(1)—

(a) the cancellation ends the obligations of the parties to perform the contract, and

(b) regulations 34 to 38 apply.

(2) Regulations 34 and 38 also apply if the consumer withdraws an offer to enter into a distance or off-premises contract.

34. Reimbursement by trader in the event of withdrawal or cancellation

(1) The trader must reimburse all payments, other than payments for delivery, received from the consumer, subject to paragraph (10).

(2) The trader must reimburse any payment for delivery received from the consumer, unless the consumer expressly chose a kind of delivery costing more than the least expensive common and generally acceptable kind of delivery offered by the trader.

(3) In that case, the trader must reimburse any payment for delivery received from the consumer up to the amount the consumer would have paid if the consumer had chosen the least expensive common and generally acceptable kind of delivery offered by the trader.

(4) Reimbursement must be without undue delay, and in any event not later than the time specified in paragraph (5) or (6).

(5) If the contract is a sales contract and the trader has not offered to collect the goods, the time is the end of 14 days after—

(a) the day on which the trader receives the goods back, or

(b) if earlier, the day on which the consumer supplies evidence of having sent the goods back.

(6) Otherwise, the time is the end of 14 days after the day on which the trader is informed of the consumer's decision to withdraw the offer or cancel the contract, in accordance with [regulation 32].

(7) The trader must make the reimbursement using the same means of payment as the consumer used for the initial transaction, unless the consumer has expressly agreed otherwise.

(8) The trader must not impose any fee on the consumer in respect of the reimbursement.

(9) If (in the case of a sales contract) the value of the goods is diminished by any amount as a result of handling of the goods by the consumer beyond what is necessary to establish the nature, characteristics and functioning of the goods, the trader may recover that amount from the consumer, up to the contract price.

(10) An amount that may be recovered under paragraph (9)—

(a) may be deducted from the amount to be reimbursed under paragraph (1);

(b) otherwise, must be paid by the consumer to the trader.

(11) Paragraph (9) does not apply if the trader has failed to provide the consumer with the information on the right to cancel required by paragraph (l) of Schedule 2, in accordance with Part 2.

(12) For the purposes of paragraph (9) handling is beyond what is necessary to establish the nature, characteristics and functioning of the goods if, in particular, it goes beyond the sort of handling that might reasonably be allowed in a shop.

(13) Where the provisions of this regulation apply to cancellation of a contract, the contract is to be treated as including those provisions as terms.

35. Return of goods in the event of cancellation

(1) Where a sales contract is cancelled under regulation 29(1), it is the trader's responsibility to collect the goods if—

(a) the trader has offered to collect them, or

(b) in the case of an off-premises contract, the goods were delivered to the consumer's home when the contract was entered into and could not, by their nature, normally be returned by post.

(2) If it is not the trader's responsibility under paragraph (1) to collect the goods, the consumer must—

(a) send them back, or

(b) hand them over to the trader or to a person authorised by the trader to receive them.

(3) The address to which goods must be sent under paragraph (2)(a) is—

(a) any address specified by the trader for sending the goods back;

(b) if no address is specified for that purpose, any address specified by the trader for the consumer to contact the trader;

(c) if no address is specified for either of those purposes, any place of business of the trader.

(4) The consumer must send off the goods under paragraph (2)(a), or hand them over under paragraph (2)(b), without undue delay and in any event not later than 14 days after the day on which the consumer informs the trader as required by regulation 32(2).

(5) The consumer must bear the direct cost of returning goods under paragraph (2), unless—

(a) the trader has agreed to bear those costs, or

(b) the trader failed to provide the consumer with the information about the consumer bearing those costs, required by paragraph (m) of Schedule 2, in accordance with Part 2.

(6) The contract is to be treated as including a term that the trader must bear the direct cost of the consumer returning goods under paragraph (2) where paragraph (5)(b) applies.

(7) The consumer is not required to bear any other cost of returning goods under paragraph (2).

(8) The consumer is not required to bear any cost of collecting goods under paragraph (1) [unless the trader has offered to collect the goods and the consumer has agreed to bear the costs of the trader doing so.]

36. Supply of service in cancellation period

(1) The trader must not begin the supply of a service before the end of the cancellation period provided for in regulation 30(1) unless the consumer—

(a) has made an express request, and

(b) in the case of an off-premises contract, has made the request on a durable medium.

(2) In the case of a service other than supply of water, gas, electricity or district heating, the consumer ceases to have the right to cancel a service contract under regulation 29(1) if the service has been fully performed, and performance of the service began—

(a) after a request by the consumer in accordance with paragraph (1), and

(b) with the acknowledgement that the consumer would lose that right once the contract had been fully performed by the trader.

(3) Paragraphs (4) to (6) apply where a contract is cancelled under regulation 29(1) and a service has been supplied in the cancellation period.

(4) Where the service is supplied in response to a request in accordance with paragraph (1), the consumer must (subject to paragraph (6)) pay to the trader an amount—

(a) for the supply of the service for the period for which it is supplied, ending with the time when the trader is informed of the consumer's decision to cancel the contract, in accordance with regulation 32(2), and

(b) which is in proportion to what has been supplied, in comparison with the full coverage of the contract.

(5) The amount is to be calculated—
  (a) on the basis of the total price agreed in the contract, or
  (b) if the total price is excessive, on the basis of the market value of the service that has been supplied, calculated by comparing prices for equivalent services supplied by other traders.

(6) The consumer bears no cost for supply of the service, in full or in part, in the cancellation period, if—
  (a) the trader has failed to provide the consumer with the information on the right to cancel required by paragraph (l) of Schedule 2, or the information on payment of that cost required by paragraph (n) of that Schedule, in accordance with Part 2, or
  (b) the service is not supplied in response to a request in accordance with paragraph (1).

37. Supply of digital content in cancellation period

(1) Under a contract for the supply of digital content not on a tangible medium, the trader must not begin supply of the digital content before the end of the cancellation period provided for in regulation 30(1), unless—
  (a) the consumer has given express consent, and
  (b) the consumer has acknowledged that the right to cancel the contract under regulation 29(1) will be lost.

(2) The consumer ceases to have the right to cancel such a contract under regulation 29(1) if, before the end of the cancellation period, supply of the digital content has begun after the consumer has given the consent and acknowledgement required by paragraph (1).

(3) Paragraph (4) applies where a contract is cancelled under regulation 29(1) and digital content has been supplied, not on a tangible medium, in the cancellation period.

(4) The consumer bears no cost for supply of the digital content, in full or in part, in the cancellation period, if—
  (a) the consumer has not given prior express consent to the beginning of the performance of the digital content before the end of the 14-day period referred to in regulation 30,
  (b) the consumer gave that consent but did not acknowledge when giving it that the right to cancel would be lost, or
  (c) the trader failed to provide confirmation required by regulation 12(5) or 16(3).

38. Effects of withdrawal or cancellation on ancillary contracts

(1) If a consumer withdraws an offer to enter into a distance or off-premises contract, or cancels such a contract under regulation 29(1), any ancillary contracts are automatically terminated, without any costs for the consumer, other than any costs under these provisions—
  (a) regulation 34(3) (where enhanced delivery chosen by consumer);
  (b) regulation 34(9) (where value of goods diminished by consumer handling);
  (c) regulation 35(5) (where goods returned by consumer);
  (d) regulation 36(4) (where consumer requests early supply of service).

(2) When a trader is informed by a consumer under regulation 32(1) or (2) of a decision to withdraw an offer or cancel a contract, the trader must inform any other trader with whom the consumer has an ancillary contract that is terminated by paragraph (1).

(3) An 'ancillary contract', in relation to a distance or off-premises contract (the 'main contract'), means a contract by which the consumer acquires goods or services related to the main contract, where those goods or services are provided—
  (a) by the trader, or
  (b) by a third party on the basis of an arrangement between the third party and the trader.

(4) Regulation 6(1)(b) (exclusion of financial services contracts) does not limit the contracts that are ancillary contracts for the purposes of this regulation.

PART 4 PROTECTION FROM INERTIA SELLING AND ADDITIONAL CHARGES

40. Additional payments under a contract

(1) Under a contract between a trader and a consumer, no payment is payable in addition to the remuneration agreed for the trader's main obligation unless, before the consumer became bound by the contract, the trader obtained the consumer's express consent.

(2) There is no express consent (if there would otherwise be) for the purposes of this paragraph if consent is inferred from the consumer not changing a default option (such as a pre-ticked box on a website).

(3) This regulation does not apply if the trader's main obligation is to supply services within regulation 6(1)(b), but in any other case it applies even if an additional payment is for such services.

(4) Where a trader receives an additional payment which, under this regulation, is not payable under a contract, the contract is to be treated as providing for the trader to reimburse the payment to the consumer.

41. Help-line charges over basic rate

(1) Where a trader operates a telephone line for the purpose of consumers contacting the trader by telephone in relation to contracts entered into with the trader, a consumer contacting the trader must not be bound to pay more than the basic rate.

(2) If in those circumstances a consumer who contacts a trader in relation to a contract is bound to pay more than the basic rate, the contract is to be treated as providing for the trader to pay to the consumer any amount by which the charge paid by the consumer for the call is more than the basic rate.

PART 6 ENFORCEMENT

44. Complaints

(1) It is the duty of an enforcement authority to consider any complaint made to it about a contravention of these Regulations, unless—

    (a) the complaint appears to the authority to be frivolous or vexatious, or

    (b) another enforcement authority has notified the CMA that it agrees to consider the complaint.

(2) If an enforcement authority has notified the CMA as mentioned in paragraph (1)(b), that authority is under a duty to consider the complaint.

(3) The following are enforcement authorities for the purposes of these Regulations—

    (a) every local weights and measures authority in Great Britain;

    (b) the Department of Enterprise, Trade and Investment in Northern Ireland.

45. Orders to secure compliance

(1) An enforcement authority may apply for an injunction, or in Scotland an interdict or order of specific implement, against any person who appears to the authority to be responsible for a contravention of these Regulations.

(2) The court on an application under this regulation may grant an injunction, interdict or order on such terms as it thinks fit to secure compliance with these Regulations.

46. Notification of undertakings and orders to the CMA

An enforcement authority must notify the CMA—

    (a) of any undertaking given to it by or on behalf of any person who appears to it to be responsible for a contravention of these Regulations;

(b) of the outcome of any application made by it under regulation 45, and of the terms of any undertaking given to the court or of any order made by the court;

(c) of the outcome of any application made by it to enforce a previous order of the court.

Regulation 9(1)   **SCHEDULE 1**

INFORMATION RELATING TO ON-PREMISES CONTRACTS

The information referred to in regulation 9(1) is—

(a) the main characteristics of the [goods, services or digital content], to the extent appropriate to the medium of communication and to the goods or services;

(b) the identity of the trader (such as the trader's trading name), the geographical address at which the trader is established and the trader's telephone number;

(c) the total price of the [goods, services or digital content] inclusive of taxes, or where the nature of the goods or services is such that the price cannot reasonably be calculated in advance, the manner in which the price is to be calculated;

(d) where applicable, all additional delivery charges or, where those charges cannot reasonably be calculated in advance, the fact that such additional charges may be payable;

(e) where applicable, the arrangements for payment, delivery, performance, and the time by which the trader undertakes to deliver the goods[, to perform the service or to supply the digital content];

(f) where applicable, the trader's complaint handling policy;

(g) in the case of a sales contract, a reminder that the trader is under a legal duty to supply goods that are in conformity with the contract;

(h) where applicable, the existence and the conditions of after-sales services and commercial guarantees;

(i) the duration of the contract, where applicable, or, if the contract is of indeterminate duration or is to be extended automatically, the conditions for terminating the contract;

(j) where applicable, the functionality, including applicable technical protection measures, of digital content;

(k) where applicable, any relevant compatibility of digital content with hardware and software that the trader is aware of or can reasonably be expected to have been aware of.

Regulations 10(1) and 13(1)   **SCHEDULE 2**

INFORMATION RELATING TO DISTANCE AND OFF-PREMISES CONTRACTS

The information referred to in regulations 10(1) and 13(1) is (subject to the note at the end of this Schedule)—

(a) the main characteristics of the [goods, services or digital content], to the extent appropriate to the medium of communication and to the goods or services;

(b) the identity of the trader (such as the trader's trading name);

(c) the geographical address at which the trader is established and, where available, the trader's telephone number, fax number and e-mail address, to enable the consumer to contact the trader quickly and communicate efficiently;

(d) where the trader is acting on behalf of another trader, the geographical address and identity of that other trader;

(e) if different from the address provided in accordance with paragraph (c), the geographical address of the place of business of the trader, and, where the trader acts on behalf of another trader, the geographical address of the place of business of that other trader, where the consumer can address any complaints;

(f) the total price of the [goods, services or digital content] inclusive of taxes, or where the nature of the goods or services is such that the price cannot reasonably be calculated in advance, the manner in which the price is to be calculated,

(g) where applicable, all additional delivery charges and any other costs or, where those charges cannot reasonably be calculated in advance, the fact that such additional charges may be payable;

(h) in the case of a contract of indeterminate duration or a contract containing a subscription, the total costs per billing period or (where such contracts are charged at a fixed rate) the total monthly costs;

(i) the cost of using the means of distance communication for the conclusion of the contract where that cost is calculated other than at the basic rate;

(j) the arrangements for payment, delivery, performance, and the time by which the trader undertakes to deliver the goods[, to perform the services or to supply the digital content.];

(k) where applicable, the trader's complaint handling policy;

(l) where a right to cancel exists, the conditions, time limit and procedures for exercising that right in accordance with regulations 27 to 38;

(m) where applicable, that the consumer will have to bear the cost of returning the goods in case of cancellation and, for distance contracts, if the goods, by their nature, cannot normally be returned by post, the cost of returning the goods;

(n) that, if the consumer exercises the right to cancel after having made a request in accordance with regulation 36(1), the consumer is to be liable to pay the trader reasonable costs in accordance with regulation 36(4);

(o) where under regulation 28, 36 or 37 there is no right to cancel or the right to cancel may be lost, the information that the consumer will not benefit from a right to cancel, or the circumstances under which the consumer loses the right to cancel;

(p) in the case of a sales contract, a reminder that the trader is under a legal duty to supply goods that are in conformity with the contract;

(q) where applicable, the existence and the conditions of after-sale customer assistance, after-sales services and commercial guarantees;

(r) the existence of relevant codes of conduct, as defined in regulation 5(3)(b) of the Consumer Protection from Unfair Trading Regulations 2008, and how copies of them can be obtained, where applicable;

(s) the duration of the contract, where applicable, or, if the contract is of indeterminate duration or is to be extended automatically, the conditions for terminating the contract;

(t) where applicable, the minimum duration of the consumer's obligations under the contract;

(u) where applicable, the existence and the conditions of deposits or other financial guarantees to be paid or provided by the consumer at the request of the trader;

(v) where applicable, the functionality, including applicable technical protection measures, of digital content;

(w) where applicable, any relevant compatibility of digital content with hardware and software that the trader is aware of or can reasonably be expected to have been aware of;

(x) where applicable, the possibility of having recourse to an out-of-court complaint and redress mechanism, to which the trader is subject, and the methods for having access to it.

Note: In the case of a public auction, the information listed in paragraphs (b) to (e) may be replaced with the equivalent details for the auctioneer.

Regulations 10 and 13   **SCHEDULE 3**

INFORMATION ABOUT THE EXERCISE OF THE RIGHT TO CANCEL

. . .

Financial Services Act 2012 (Consumer Credit) Order 2013

(SI 2013, No. 1882)

1. Citation, commencement and interpretation

(2) In this Order, 'the 1974 Act' means the Consumer Credit Act 1974.

4. Statements of policy

(1) The FCA must prepare and issue a statement of its policy with respect to—

(a) the imposition of penalties, suspensions[, conditions, limitations] or restrictions imposed under sections 66 (disciplinary powers), 205 (public censure), 206 (financial penalties) and 206A (suspending permission to carry on regulated activities etc.) of FSMA 2000 as applied by article 3;

(b) the amount of penalties imposed under sections 66 and 206 of FSMA 2000 as so applied;

(c) the period for which suspensions[, conditions, limitations] or restrictions imposed under sections 66 and 206A of FSMA 2000 as so applied are to have effect.

(2) The FCA's policy in determining what the amount of a penalty should be, or what the period for which a suspension[, condition, limitation] or restriction is to have effect should be, must include having regard to—

(a) the seriousness of the failure in question in relation to the nature of the requirement concerned;

(b) the extent to which that failure was deliberate or reckless; and

(c) whether the person against whom the action is to be taken is an individual.

(3) The FCA may at any time alter or replace a statement issued by it under this article.

(4) If a statement issued under this article is altered or replaced by the FCA, the FCA must issue the altered or replacement statement.

(5) The FCA must, without delay, give the Treasury a copy of any statement which it publishes under this article.

(6) A statement by the FCA issued under this article must be published by the FCA in the way appearing to the FCA to be best calculated to bring it to the attention of the public.

(7) In exercising, or deciding whether to exercise, its powers under section 66, 205, 206 or 206A of FSMA 2000 as applied by article 3 in the case of any particular contravention, the FCA must have regard to any statement published by it under this article and in force at the time when the contravention in question occurred.

5.   Statements of policy: procedure

(1) Before the FCA issues a statement under article 4, the FCA must publish a draft of the proposed statement in the way appearing to it to be best calculated to bring it to the attention of the public.

(2) The draft must be accompanied by notice that representations about the proposal may be made to the FCA within a specified time.

(3) Before issuing the proposed statement, the FCA must have regard to any representations made in accordance with paragraph (2).

(4) If the FCA issues the proposed statement it must publish an account, in general terms, of—

(a) the representations made to it in accordance with paragraph (2); and

(b) its response to them.

(5) If the statement differs from the draft published under paragraph (1) in a way which is, in the opinion of the FCA, significant, the FCA must (in addition to complying with paragraph (4)) publish details of the difference.

(6) This article also applies to a proposal to alter or replace a statement.

6.   Disciplinary measures: criminal proceedings and conviction under the 1974 Act

A person may not be convicted of an offence under the 1974 Act in respect of an act or omission in a case where the FCA has exercised its powers under section 66, 205, 206 or 206A of FSMA 2000 in relation to that person in respect of that act or omission.

8.   Application of provisions of the 1974 Act in relation to failure to comply with FSMA 2000

(1) The following provisions of the 1974 Act apply in relation to the commission or suspected commission of a relevant offence with the modifications specified.

(2) Section 162 (powers of entry and inspection) applies as if a reference to 'a breach of any provision of or under this Act' included a reference to a relevant offence.

(3) Section 163 (compensation for loss) applies in connection with the powers of a duly appointed officer of an enforcement authority as if the reference to 'an offence under this Act' in subsection (1) included a reference to a relevant offence.

(4) Section 164 (power to make test purchases etc.) applies as if—

(a) in subsection (1), the reference to 'determining whether any provisions made by or under this Act are being complied with' included a reference to determining whether a relevant offence is being committed;

(b) in subsection (4), the reference to 'proceedings under this Act' included a reference to proceedings for a relevant offence.

(5) Section 165 (obstruction of authorised persons) applies as if—

(a) in subsection (1)(a), the reference to 'acting in pursuance of this Act' included a reference to acting in pursuance of FSMA 2000 so far as relating to a relevant offence;

(b) in subsection (1)(c), the reference to 'performing his functions under this Act' included a reference to performing functions under FSMA 2000 in relation to a relevant offence.

(6) Section 174A (powers to require provision of information or documents etc.) applies where a relevant authority (as defined in subsection (5)) is performing functions under FSMA 2000 in relation to a relevant offence.

9.   Functions of local weights and measures ... under FSMA 2000

(1) Local weights and measures authorities may institute proceedings in England and Wales for a relevant offence.

Financial Services and Markets Act 2000 (Regulated Activities) (Amendment) (No. 2) Order 2013

(SI 2013, No. 1881)

1.   Citation, commencement and interpretation

(7) In this Order—

'the Act' means the Financial Services and Markets Act 2000;

'the Regulated Activities Order' means the Financial Services and Markets Act 2000 (Regulated Activities) Order 2001.

12.   Obligations of certain [persons who carry on credit broking]

[[(1) This article applies to a person ('P') who is within the description in paragraph (1A) or the description in paragraph (1B).

(1A) A person is within the description in this paragraph if the person—

    (a) is not an authorised person,

    (b) carries on an activity of the kind specified by article 36A(1)(d) to (f) of the Regulated Activities Order (credit broking), and

    (c) is not exempt from the general prohibition in relation to the carrying on of that activity by virtue of section 327(1) of the Act (exemption from the general prohibition for members of a designated professional body).

(1B) A person is within the description in this paragraph if the person would be carrying on an activity of the kind specified by article 36A(1)(d) to (f) (credit broking) of the Regulated Activities Order but for article 36B(1)(a) (introducing by individuals in the course of canvassing off trade premises), 36F (activities carried on by members of the legal profession etc) or 72G (local authorities) of that Order.]

(2) P must indicate in advertising and documentation intended for borrowers or those who may become a borrower the extent of P's powers, in particular whether P works exclusively for one or more lenders or does not work for any lender.

(3) P must disclose to the borrower or any person who may become a borrower the fee, if any, payable by the borrower to P for P's services.

(4) Any fee to be paid by the borrower to P must be agreed between the borrower and P and that agreement must be recorded in writing or other durable medium before the credit agreement is entered into.

(5) P must disclose to the lender the fee, if any, payable by the borrower to P for P's services for the purpose of enabling the lender to calculate the annual percentage rate of charge in relation to the credit agreement.

(6) In this article, 'borrower' and 'lender' have the meanings given by Article 60L of the Regulated Activities Order.

(7) A contravention by P of a provision of this article is actionable at the suit of a private person who suffers loss as a result of the contravention, subject to the defences and other incidents applying to actions for breach of statutory duties.

(8) 'Private person' has the meaning prescribed for the purposes of section 138D of the Act (action for damages).

(9) Sections 165 (regulator's power to require information: authorised persons etc.) and 167 (appointment of persons to carry out general investigations) apply as if each reference to an authorised person (except in section 165(11) and 167(2)) included a reference to a person who falls within paragraph (1).

(10) Part 14 of the Act (disciplinary measures) applies to the requirements imposed by this article as if each reference to an authorised person included a reference to a person who, at the time of the contravention of the requirement, fell within paragraph (1).

Enterprise Act 2002 (Part 8 Domestic Infringements) Order 2015

(SI 2015, No. 1727)

2. Specified infringements

Acts or omissions in respect of any provision of Parts 1 and 2 and Chapter 5 of Part 3 of the Consumer Rights Act 2015 are specified for the purposes of section 211(2) of the Enterprise Act 2002.

Money Laundering, Terrorist Financing and Transfer of Funds (Information on the Payer) Regulations 2017

(SI 2017, No. 692)

4. Meaning of business relationship

(1) For the purpose of these Regulations, 'business relationship' means a business, professional or commercial relationship between a relevant person and a customer, which—

(a) arises out of the business of the relevant person, and

(b) is expected by the relevant person, at the time when contact is established, to have an element of duration.

(2) A relationship where the relevant person is asked to form a company for its customer is to be treated as a business relationship for the purpose of these Regulations, whether or not the formation of the company is the only transaction carried out for that customer.

(3) For the purposes of these Regulations, an estate agent is to be treated as entering into a business relationship with a purchaser (as well as with a seller), at the point when the purchaser's offer is accepted by the seller.

Payment Services Regulations 2017

(SI 2017, No. 752)

PART 1 INTRODUCTORY PROVISIONS

2. Interpretation

(1) In these Regulations—

'the 2000 Act' means the Financial Services and Markets Act 2000;

'account information service' means an online service to provide consolidated information on one or more payment accounts held by the payment service user with another payment service provider or with more than one payment service provider, and includes such a service whether information is provided—

(a) in its original form or after processing;

(b) only to the payment service user or to the payment service user and to another person in accordance with the payment service user's instructions;

'account information service provider' means a payment service provider which provides account information services;

'account servicing payment service provider' means a payment service provider providing and maintaining a payment account for a payer;

'acquiring of payment transactions' means a payment service provided by a payment service provider contracting with a payee to accept and process payment transactions which result in a transfer of funds to the payee;

'agent' means a person who acts on behalf of an [authorised payment institution, a small payment institution or a registered account information service provider] in the provision of payment services;

'authentication' means a procedure which allows a payment service provider to verify the identity of a payment service user or the validity of the use of a specific payment instrument, including the use of the user's personalised security credentials;

'authorised payment institution' means—

    (a) a person authorised as a payment institution pursuant to regulation 6 (conditions for authorisation as a payment institution) and included by the FCA in the register as an authorised payment institution pursuant to regulation 4(1)(a) (the register of certain payment service providers); or

    (b) a person included by the FCA in the register pursuant to regulation 150 or 152, and regulation 153(1) (transitional provisions);

'the FCA' means the Financial Conduct Authority;

'branch' means a place of business, other than the head office, of—

    (a) an authorised payment institution;

    (b) a small payment institution; [or]

    (c) a registered account information service provider;

which forms a legally dependent part of such a payment service provider and which carries out directly all or some of the services inherent in the business of such a payment service provider; [. . .]

'business day' means any day on which the relevant payment service provider is open for business as required for the execution of a payment transaction;

['the capital requirements regulation' means Regulation (EU) 575/2013 of the European Parliament and of the Council of 26th June 2013 on prudential requirements for credit institutions and investment firms;]

'charity', in Parts 6 (information requirements for payment services) and 7 (rights and obligations in relation to the provision of payment services), means a body whose annual income is less than £1 million and is—

    (a) in England and Wales, a charity as defined by section 1(1) of the Charities Act 2011 (meaning of 'charity'); . . .

'co-badged', in relation to a payment instrument, refers to an instrument on which is included two or more payment brands, or two or more payment applications of the same payment brand;

'the Commissioners' means the Commissioners for Her Majesty's Revenue and Customs;

'consumer' means an individual who, in contracts for payment services to which these Regulations apply, is acting for purposes other than a trade, business or profession;

'credit institution' has the meaning given in Article 4(1)(1) of the capital requirements regulation;

'credit transfer' means a payment service for crediting a payee's payment account with a payment transaction or a series of payment transactions from a payer's payment account by the payment service provider which holds the payer's payment account, based on an instruction given by the payer;

'designated system' has the meaning given in regulation 2(1) of the Financial Markets and Insolvency (Settlement Finality) Regulations 1999 (interpretation);

'digital content' means goods or services which are produced and supplied in digital form, the use or consumption of which is restricted to a technical device and which do not include in any way the use or consumption of physical goods or services;

'direct debit' means a payment service for debiting the payer's payment account where a payment transaction is initiated by the payee on the basis of consent given by the payer to the payee, to the payee's payment service provider or to the payer's own payment service provider;

'durable medium' means any instrument which enables the payment service user to store information addressed personally to them in a way accessible for future reference for a period of time adequate for the purposes of the information and which allows the unchanged reproduction of the information stored;

['electronic communications network' means transmission systems and, where applicable, switching or routing equipment and other resources which permit the conveyance of signals by wire, by radio, by optical or by other electromagnetic means, including satellite networks, fixed (circuit- and packet-switched, including Internet) and mobile terrestrial networks, electricity cable systems, to the extent that they are used for the purpose of transmitting signals, networks used for radio and television broadcasting, and cable television networks, irrespective of the type of information conveyed;]

['electronic communications service' means a service normally provided for remuneration which consists wholly or mainly in the conveyance of signals on electronic communications networks, including telecommunications services and transmission services in networks used for broadcasting, but exclude services providing, or exercising editorial control over, content transmitted using electronic communications networks and services; it does not include information society services, as defined in (Article 1 of Directive (EU) 2015/1535 of the European Parliament and of the Council of 9 September 2015) laying down a procedure for the provision of information in the field of technical regulations and of rules on Information Society services, which do not consist wholly or mainly in the conveyance of signals on electronic communications networks;]

'electronic money' has the meaning given in [regulation 2(1) of the Electronic Money Regulations 2011];

'electronic money institution' has the meaning given in [regulation 2(1) of the Electronic Money Regulations 2011];

'excluded provider' means a provider of services falling within paragraphs 2(k)(i) to (iii), (l) or (o) of Schedule 1 (limited network, electronic communications and cash withdrawal exclusions);

'framework contract' means a contract for payment services which governs the future execution of individual and successive payment transactions and which may contain the obligation and conditions for setting up a payment account;

'funds' means banknotes and coins, scriptural money and electronic money;

'group' means a group of—

    (a) undertakings linked to each other by a relationship referred to in Article 22(1), (2) or (7) of Directive 2013/34/EU of the European Parliament and of the Council of 26th June 2013 on the annual financial statements, consolidated financial statements and related reports of certain types of undertakings, amending Directive 2006/43/EC of the European Parliament and of the Council and repealing Council Directives 78/660/EEC and 83/349/EEC; or

    (b) undertakings as defined in Articles 4 to 7 of Commission Delegated Regulation (EU) No. 241/2014 of 7th January 2014 supplementing Regulation (EU) 575/2013 of the European Parliament and of the Council with regard to regulatory technical standards for Own Funds requirements for institutions, which are linked to each other by a relationship referred to in Article 10(1) or [113(6)] of the capital requirements regulation;

'interchange fee regulation' means Regulation (EU) 2015/751 of the European Parliament and of the Council of 29th April 2015 on interchange fees for card-based payment transactions;

'issuing of payment instruments' means a payment service by a payment service provider contracting with a payer to provide a payment instrument to initiate payment orders and to process the payer's payment transactions;

'means of distance communication' means a method which, without the simultaneous physical presence of the payment service provider and the payment service user, may be used for the conclusion of a contract for payment services between those parties;

'micro-enterprise' means an enterprise which, at the time at which the contract for payment services is entered into, is an enterprise as defined in Article 1 and Article 2(1) and (3) of the Annex to Recommendation 2003/361/EC of 6th May 2003 concerning the definition of micro, small and medium-sized enterprises;

'money remittance' means a service for the transmission of money (or any representation of monetary value), without any payment accounts being created in the name of the payer or the payee, where—

> (a) funds are received from a payer for the sole purpose of transferring a corresponding amount to a payee or to another payment service provider acting on behalf of the payee; or
>
> (b) funds are received on behalf of, and made available to, the payee;

'notice' means a notice in writing;

'own funds' means own funds as defined in Article 4(1)(118) of the capital requirements regulation, and 'Common Equity Tier 1 capital', 'Tier 1 capital' and 'Tier 2 capital' have the same meanings as in that regulation;

'parent undertaking' has the same meaning as in the Companies Acts, as defined by section 1162 of, and Schedule 7 to, the Companies Act 2006 (parent and subsidiary undertakings);

'participant' has the meaning given in regulation 2(1) of the Financial Markets and Insolvency (Settlement Finality) Regulations 1999 (interpretation);

'payee' means a person who is the intended recipient of funds which have been the subject of a payment transaction;

'payer' means—

> (a) a person who holds a payment account and initiates, or consents to the initiation of, a payment order from that payment account; or
>
> (b) where there is no payment account, a person who gives a payment order;

'payment account' means an account held in the name of one or more payment service users which is used for the execution of payment transactions;

'payment brand' means any material or digital name, term, sign or symbol, or combination of them, capable of denoting under which payment card scheme card-based payment transactions are carried out;

'payment initiation service' means an online service to initiate a payment order at the request of the payment service user with respect to a payment account held at another payment service provider;

'payment initiation service provider' means a payment service provider which provides payment initiation services;

'payment instrument' means any—

> (a) personalised device; or
>
> (b) personalised set of procedures agreed between the payment service user and the payment service provider,

used by the payment service user in order to initiate a payment order;

'payment order' means any instruction by a payer or a payee to their respective payment service provider requesting the execution of a payment transaction;

'payment service' means any of the activities specified in Part 1 of Schedule 1 (payment services) when carried out as a regular occupation or business activity, other than any of the activities specified in Part 2 of that Schedule (activities which do not constitute payment services);

'payment services directive' means Directive 2015/2366/EU of the European Parliament and of the Council of 25th November 2015 on payment services in the internal market, amending Directives 2002/65/EC, 2009/110/EC and 2013/36/EU and Regulation (EU) No. 1093/2010, and repealing Directive 2007/64/EC;

'payment service provider' means any of the following when they carry out payment services—

> (a) authorised payment institutions;
>
> (b) small payment institutions;
>
> (c) registered account information service providers;
>
> (f) electronic money institutions, including branches located in the [United Kingdom] of such institutions whose head office is outside the [United Kingdom], in so far as the

payment services provided by those branches are linked to the issuance of electronic money;

(g) credit institutions, including branches located in the EEA;

(h) the Post Office Limited;

(i) the Bank of England, [other than when acting in its] capacity as a monetary authority or carrying out other functions of a public nature; and

(j) government departments and local authorities, other than when carrying out functions of a public nature,

and in Part 9 (the FCA) and Schedule 6 (application and modification of legislation), includes agents of payment service providers and excluded providers;

'payment service user' means a person when making use of a payment service in the capacity of payer, payee, or both;

'payment system' means a funds transfer system with formal and standardised arrangements and common rules for the processing, clearing and settlement of payment transactions;

'the Payment Systems Regulator' means the body established under section 40 of the Financial Services (Banking Reform) Act 2013 (the Payment Systems Regulator);

'payment transaction' means an act initiated by the payer or payee, or on behalf of the payer, of placing, transferring or withdrawing funds, irrespective of any underlying obligations between the payer and payee;

'personalised security credentials' means personalised features provided by a payment service provider to a payment service user for the purposes of authentication;

'qualifying holding' has the meaning given in Article 4(1)(36) of the capital requirements regulation;

'reference exchange rate' means the exchange rate which is used as the basis to calculate any currency exchange and which is made available by the payment service provider or comes from a publicly available source;

'reference interest rate' means the interest rate which is used as the basis for calculating any interest to be applied and which comes from a publicly available source which can be verified by both parties to a contract for payment services;

'the register' means the register maintained by the FCA under regulation 4 (the register of certain payment service providers);

'registered account information service provider' means an account information service provider registered pursuant to regulation 18 and included by the FCA on the register pursuant to regulation 4(1)(c) (the register of certain payment service providers);

'regulated agreement' has the meaning given by section 189(1) of the Consumer Credit Act 1974 (definitions);

'remote payment transaction' means a payment transaction initiated through the internet or otherwise initiated through a device that can be used for distance communication;

'sensitive payment data' means information, including personalised security credentials, which could be used to carry out fraud; but in relation to account information services and payment initiation services does not include the name of an account holder or an account number;

['the SEPA regulation' means Regulation (EU) No 260/2012 of the European Parliament and of the Council of 14 March 2012 establishing technical and business requirements for credit transfers and direct debits in euro and amending Regulation (EC) No 924/2009;]

'single payment service contract' means a contract for a single payment transaction not covered by a framework contract;

'small payment institution' means—

(a) a person registered as a small payment institution pursuant to regulation 14 and included by the FCA in the register pursuant to regulation 4(1)(b) (the register of certain payment service providers); or

(b) a person included by the FCA in the register pursuant to regulations 151 and 153(1) (transitional provisions);

'strong customer authentication' means authentication based on the use of two or more elements that are independent, in that the breach of one element does not compromise the reliability of any other element, and designed in such a way as to protect the confidentiality of the authentication data, with the elements falling into two or more of the following categories—

    (a) something known only by the payment service user ('knowledge');

    (b) something held only by the payment service user ('possession');

    (c) something inherent to the payment service user ('inherence');

'subsidiary undertaking' has the same meaning as in the Companies Acts (see section 1162 of, and Schedule 7 to, the Companies Act 2006 (parent and subsidiary undertakings));

'transfer order' has the meaning given in regulation 2(1) of the Financial Markets and Insolvency (Settlement Finality) Regulations 1999 (interpretation);

'unique identifier' means a combination of letters, numbers or symbols specified to the payment service user by the payment service provider and to be provided by the payment service user in relation to a payment transaction in order to identify unambiguously one or both of—

    (a) another payment service user who is a party to the payment transaction;

    (b) the other payment service user's payment account;

'value date' means a reference time used by a payment service provider for the calculation of interest on the funds debited from or credited to a payment account.

(2) In these Regulations references to amounts in euros include references to equivalent amounts in pounds sterling.

(4) Expressions used in a modification to a provision in primary or secondary legislation applied by these Regulations have the same meaning as in these Regulations.

3.   Exemption for certain bodies

(1) Subject to paragraph (2) and regulation 4(1)(f), these Regulations do not apply to the following persons—

    (a) credit unions;

    (b) municipal banks; and

    (c) the National Savings Bank.

(2) Where municipal banks provide or propose to provide payment services they must give notice to the FCA.

(3) In this regulation—

'credit union' means a credit union within the meaning of—

    (a) the Credit Unions Act 1979;

    (b) the Credit Unions (Northern Ireland) Order 1985;

'municipal bank' means a company which, immediately before 1st December 2001, fell within the definition of a municipal bank in section 103 of the Banking Act 1987 (municipal banks).

PART 2 REGISTRATION

The register

4.   The register of certain payment service providers

(1) The FCA must maintain a register of—

    (a) authorised payment institutions [. . .];

    (b) small payment institutions;

    (c) registered account information service providers;

    (d) persons providing a service falling within paragraph 2(k)(i) to (iii) or (l) of Schedule 1 who have notified the FCA under regulation 38 or 39 (notification of use of limited network or electronic communications exclusion);

    (e) agents of authorised payment institutions, small payment institutions and registered account information service providers, registered under regulation 34 (use of agents); and

(f) the persons specified in regulation 3(1) (exemption for certain bodies) where they provide payment services.

(2) The FCA may include on the register any of the persons mentioned in paragraphs (f) to (i) of the definition of a payment service provider in regulation 2(1) (interpretation) where such persons provide payment services.

(3) Where a person mentioned in paragraph (h), (i) or (j) of the definition of a payment service provider in regulation 2(1)—

(a) is not included on the register; and

(b) provides, or proposes to provide, payment services,

the person must give notice to the FCA.

(4) The FCA may—

(a) keep the register in any form it thinks fit;

(b) include on it such information as the FCA considers appropriate, provided that the register identifies the payment services for which an institution is authorised or registered under this Part; and

(c) exploit commercially the information contained in the register, or any part of that information.

(5) The FCA must—

(a) publish the register online and make it available for public inspection;

(b) enter in the register any cancellation of an authorisation or registration;

(c) enter in the register a description of the service provided by a person included on the register by virtue of paragraph (1)(d);

(d) update the register without delay; and

(e) provide a certified copy of the register, or any part of it, to any person who asks for it—

(i)   on payment of the fee (if any) fixed by the FCA; and

(ii) in a form (either written or electronic) in which it is legible to the person asking for it.

Authorisation as a payment institution

5. Application for authorisation as a payment institution or variation of an existing authorisation

(1) An application for authorisation as a payment institution must contain or be accompanied by the information specified in Schedule 2 (information to be included in or with an application for authorisation).

(2) An application for the variation of an authorisation as a payment institution must—

(a) contain a statement of the proposed variation;

(b) contain a statement of the payment services which the applicant proposes to carry on if the authorisation is varied; and

(c) contain, or be accompanied by, such other information as the FCA may reasonably require.

(3) An application under paragraph (1) or (2) must be made in such manner as the FCA may direct.

(4) At any time after receiving an application and before determining it, the FCA may require the applicant to provide it with such further information as it reasonably considers necessary to enable it to determine the application.

(5) Different directions may be given, and different requirements imposed, in relation to different applications or categories of application.

6. Conditions for authorisation as a payment institution

(1) The FCA may refuse to grant all or part of an application for authorisation as a payment institution only if any of the conditions set out in paragraphs (2) to (9) is not met.

(2) The application must comply with the requirements of, and any requirements imposed under, regulations 5 (application for authorisation) and 20 (duty to notify changes).

(3) The applicant must immediately before the time of authorisation hold the amount of initial capital specified in Part 1 of Schedule 3 (capital requirements).

(4) The applicant must be a body corporate constituted under the law of a part of the United Kingdom having—

(a) its head office, and

(b) if it has a registered office, that office,

in the United Kingdom.

(5) The applicant carries on, or will carry on, at least part of its payment service business in the United Kingdom.

(6) The applicant must satisfy the FCA that, taking into account the need to ensure the sound and prudent conduct of the affairs of the institution, it has—

(a) robust governance arrangements for its payment service business, including a clear organisational structure with well-defined, transparent and consistent lines of responsibility;

(b) effective procedures to identify, manage, monitor and report any risks to which it might be exposed;

(c) adequate internal control mechanisms, including sound administrative, risk management and accounting procedures,

which are comprehensive and proportionate to the nature, scale and complexity of the payment services to be provided by the institution.

(7) The applicant must satisfy the FCA that—

(a) any persons having a qualifying holding in it are fit and proper persons having regard to the need to ensure the sound and prudent conduct of the affairs of an authorised payment institution;

(b) the directors and persons responsible for the management of the institution and, where relevant, the persons responsible for the management of payment services, are of good repute and possess appropriate knowledge and experience to provide payment services;

(c) it has a business plan (including, for the first three years, a forecast budget calculation) under which appropriate and proportionate systems, resources and procedures will be employed by the institution to operate soundly;

(d) it has taken adequate measures for the purpose of safeguarding payment service users' funds in accordance with regulation 23 (safeguarding requirements);

(e) in the case of an applicant which proposes to carry on payment initiation services, it holds professional indemnity insurance or a comparable guarantee, which covers—

(i) the territories in which the applicant proposes to offer payment initiation services; and

(ii) the applicant's potential liability under regulations 76 (payment service provider's liability for unauthorised payment transactions) and 91 to 95 (non-execution or defective or late execution of transactions, liability for charges and interest and right of recourse), up to such amount as the FCA may direct; and

(f) in the case of an applicant which proposes to carry on account information services, it holds professional indemnity insurance or a comparable guarantee, which covers—

(i) the territories in which the applicant proposes to offer account information services; and

(ii) the applicant's potential liability to account servicing payment service providers and payment service users resulting from unauthorised or fraudulent access to, or use of, payment account information, up to such amount as the FCA may direct.

(8) The applicant must comply with a requirement of the Money Laundering, Terrorist Financing and Transfer of Funds (Information on the Payer) Regulations 2017 to be included in a register maintained under those Regulations where such a requirement applies to the applicant.

(9) If the applicant has close links with another person ('CL') the applicant must satisfy the FCA—

(a) that those links are not likely to prevent the FCA's effective supervision of the applicant; and

(b) if it appears to the FCA that CL is subject to the laws, regulations or administrative provisions of a territory [outside the United Kingdom] ('the foreign provisions'), that neither the foreign provisions, nor any deficiency in their enforcement, would prevent the FCA's effective supervision of the applicant.

(10) For the purposes of paragraph (9), an applicant has close links with CL if—

(a) CL is a parent undertaking of the applicant;

(b) CL is a subsidiary undertaking of the applicant;

(c) CL is a parent undertaking of a subsidiary undertaking of the applicant;

(d) CL is a subsidiary undertaking of a parent undertaking of the applicant;

(e) CL owns or controls 20% or more of the voting rights or capital of the applicant; or

(f) the applicant owns or controls 20% or more of the voting rights or capital of CL.

7. Imposition of requirements

(1) The FCA may include in an authorisation such requirements as it considers appropriate.

(2) A requirement may, in particular, be imposed so as to require the person concerned to—

(a) take a specified action;

(b) refrain from taking a specified action.

(3) A requirement may be imposed by reference to the person's relationship with its group or other members of its group.

(4) Where—

(a) an applicant for authorisation as a payment institution intends to carry on business activities other than the provision of payment services; and

(b) the FCA considers that the carrying on of such other business activities will impair, or is likely to impair—

(i)   the financial soundness of the applicant, or

(ii) the FCA's effective supervision of the applicant,

the FCA may require the applicant to establish a separate body corporate to carry on the payment service business.

(5) A requirement expires at the end of such period as the FCA may specify in the authorisation.

(6) Paragraph (5) does not affect the FCA's powers under regulation 8 or 12 (variation of authorisation).

8. Variation etc. at request of authorised payment institution

The FCA may, on the application of an authorised payment institution, vary that person's authorisation by—

(a) adding a payment service to those for which it has granted authorisation;

(b) removing a payment service from those for which it has granted authorisation;

(c) imposing a requirement such as may, under regulation 7 (imposition of requirements), be included in an authorisation;

(d) cancelling a requirement included in the authorisation or previously imposed under paragraph (c); or

(e) varying such a requirement,

provided that the FCA is satisfied that the conditions set out in regulation 6(4) to (9) (conditions for authorisation) and, if applicable, the requirement in regulation 22(1) (capital requirements) to maintain own funds, are being or are likely to be met.

9. Determination of application for authorisation or variation of authorisation

(1) The FCA must determine an application for authorisation or the variation of an authorisation before the end of the period of three months beginning with the date on which it received the completed application.

(2) The FCA may determine an incomplete application if it considers it appropriate to do so, and it must in any event determine any such application within 12 months beginning with the date on which it received the application.

(3) The applicant may withdraw its application, by giving the FCA notice, at any time before the FCA determines it.

(4) The FCA may grant authorisation to carry out the payment services to which the application relates or such of them as may be specified in the grant of the authorisation.

(5) If the FCA decides to grant an application for authorisation, or for the variation of an authorisation, it must give the applicant notice of its decision specifying—

    (a) the payment services for which authorisation has been granted; or

    (b) the variation granted,

described in such manner as the FCA considers appropriate.

(6) The notice must state the date on which the authorisation or variation takes effect.

(7) If the FCA proposes to refuse an application or to impose a requirement it must give the applicant a warning notice.

(8) The FCA must, having considered any representations made in response to the warning notice—

    (a) if it decides to refuse the application or to impose a requirement, give the applicant a decision notice; or

    (b) if it grants the application without imposing a requirement, give the applicant notice of its decision, stating the date on which the authorisation or variation takes effect.

(9) If the FCA decides to refuse the application or to impose a requirement the applicant may refer the matter to the Upper Tribunal.

(10) If the FCA decides to authorise the applicant, or vary its authorisation, it must update the register as soon as practicable.

10. Cancellation of authorisation

(1) The FCA may cancel a person's authorisation and enter such cancellation in the register where—

    (a) the person does not provide payment services within 12 months beginning with the date on which the authorisation took effect;

    (b) the person requests, or consents to, the cancellation of the authorisation;

    (c) the person ceases to engage in business activity for more than six months;

    (d) the person has obtained authorisation through false statements or any other irregular means;

    (e) the person no longer meets, or is unlikely to continue to meet, any of the conditions set out in regulation 6(4) to (9) (conditions for authorisation) or, if applicable, the requirement in regulation 22(1) (capital requirements) to maintain own funds, or does not inform the FCA of a major change in circumstances which is relevant to its meeting those conditions or that requirement, as required by regulation 37 (duty to notify change in circumstance);

    (f) the person has provided payment services other than in accordance with the authorisation granted to it;

    (g) the person would constitute a threat to the stability of, or trust in, a payment system by continuing its payment services business;

    (h) the cancellation is desirable in order to protect the interests of consumers; or

    (i) the person's provision of payment services is otherwise unlawful, including where such provision of services is unlawful because the person's registration in a register maintained under regulation 54 or 55 of the Money Laundering, Terrorist Financing and Transfer of Funds (Information on the Payer) Regulations 2017 (duty and power to maintain registers) has been cancelled under regulation 60 of those Regulations (cancellation and suspension of registration).

(2) Where the FCA proposes to cancel a person's authorisation, other than at the person's request, it must give the person a warning notice.

(3) The FCA must, having considered any representations made in response to the warning notice—

    (a) if it decides to cancel the authorisation, give the person a decision notice; or

    (b) if it decides not to cancel the authorisation, give the person notice of its decision.

(4) If the FCA decides to cancel the authorisation, other than at the person's request, the person may refer the matter to the Upper Tribunal.

(5) Where the period for a reference to the Upper Tribunal has expired without a reference being made, the FCA must as soon as practicable update the register accordingly.

11. Request for cancellation of authorisation

(1) A request for cancellation of a person's authorisation under regulation 10(1)(b) (cancellation of authorisation) must be made in such manner as the FCA may direct.

(2) At any time after receiving a request and before determining it, the FCA may require the person making the request to provide it with such further information as it reasonably considers necessary to enable it to determine the request.

(3) Different directions may be given and different requirements imposed, in relation to different requests or categories of request.

12. Variation of authorisation on FCA's own initiative

(1) The FCA may vary a person's authorisation in any of the ways mentioned in regulation 8 if it appears to the FCA that—

    (a) the person no longer meets, or is unlikely to continue to meet, any of the conditions set out in regulation 6(4) to (9) (conditions for authorisation) or, if applicable, the requirement in regulation 22(1) (capital requirements) to maintain own funds, or does not inform the FCA of a major change in circumstances which is relevant to its meeting those conditions or that requirement, as required by regulation 37 (duty to notify change in circumstance);

    (b) the person has provided a particular payment service or payment services other than in accordance with the authorisation granted to it;

    (c) the person would constitute a threat to the stability of, or trust in, a payment system by continuing to provide a particular payment service or payment services;

    (d) the variation is desirable in order to protect the interests of consumers; or

    (e) the person's provision of a particular payment service or payment services is otherwise unlawful, including where such provision of services is unlawful because the person's registration in a register maintained under regulation 54 or 55 of the Money Laundering, Terrorist Financing and Transfer of Funds (Information on the Payer) Regulations 2017 (duty and power to maintain registers) has been cancelled under regulation 60 of those Regulations (cancellation and suspension of registration).

(2) A variation under this regulation takes effect—

    (a) immediately, if the notice given under paragraph (6) states that that is the case;

    (b) on such date as may be specified in the notice; or

    (c) if no date is specified in the notice, when the matter to which the notice relates is no longer open to review.

(3) A variation may be expressed to take effect immediately or on a specified date only if the FCA, having regard to the ground on which it is exercising the power under paragraph (1), reasonably considers that it is necessary for the variation to take effect immediately or, as the case may be, on that date.

(4) The FCA must as soon as practicable after the variation takes effect update the register accordingly.

(5) A person who is aggrieved by the variation of their authorisation under this regulation may refer the matter to the Upper Tribunal.

(6) Where the FCA proposes to vary a person's authorisation under this regulation, it must give the person notice.

(7) The notice must—

(a) give details of the variation;

(b) state the FCA's reasons for the variation and for its determination as to when the variation takes effect;

(c) inform the person that they may make representations to the FCA within such period as may be specified in the notice (whether or not the person has referred the matter to the Upper Tribunal);

(d) inform the person of the date on which the variation takes effect; and

(e) inform the person of their right to refer the matter to the Upper Tribunal and the procedure for such a reference.

(8) The FCA may extend the period allowed under the notice for making representations.

(9) If, having considered any representations made by the person, the FCA decides—

(a) to vary the authorisation in the way proposed, or

(b) if the authorisation has been varied, not to rescind the variation,

it must give the person notice.

(10) If, having considered any representations made by the person, the FCA decides—

(a) not to vary the authorisation in the way proposed,

(b) to vary the authorisation in a different way, or

(c) to rescind a variation which has taken effect,

it must give the person notice.

(11) A notice given under paragraph (9) must inform the person of their right to refer the matter to the Upper Tribunal and the procedure for such a reference.

(12) A notice under paragraph (10)(b) must comply with paragraph (7).

(13) For the purposes of paragraph (2)(c), paragraphs (a) to (d) of section 391(8) of the 2000 Act (publication) apply to determine whether a matter is open to review.

Registration as a small payment institution

13. Application for registration as a small payment institution or variation of an existing registration

(1) An application for registration as a small payment institution must contain, or be accompanied by, such information as the FCA may reasonably require.

(2) An application for the variation of a registration as a small payment institution must—

(a) contain a statement of the proposed variation;

(b) contain a statement of the payment services which the applicant proposes to carry on if the registration is varied; and

(c) contain, or be accompanied by, such other information as the FCA may reasonably require.

(3) An application under paragraph (1) or (2) must be made in such manner as the FCA may direct.

(4) At any time after receiving an application and before determining it, the FCA may require the applicant to provide it with such further information as it reasonably considers necessary to enable it to determine the application.

(5) Different directions may be given, and different requirements imposed, in relation to different applications or categories of application.

14. Conditions for registration as a small payment institution

(1) The FCA may refuse to register an applicant as a small payment institution only if any of the conditions set out in paragraphs (2) to (11) is not met.

(2) The application must comply with the requirements of, and any requirements imposed under, regulations 13 and 20.

(3) The monthly average over the period of 12 months preceding the application of the total amount of payment transactions executed by the applicant, including any of its agents in the United Kingdom, must not exceed 3 million euros.

(4) The business to which the application relates must not include the provision of account information services or payment initiation services.

(5) None of the individuals responsible for the management or operation of the business has been convicted of—

(a) an offence under Part 7 of the Proceeds of Crime Act 2002 (money laundering) or under the Money Laundering, Terrorist Financing and Transfer of Funds (Information on the Payer) Regulations 2017;

(b) an offence under section 15 (fund-raising), 16 (use and possession), 17 (funding arrangements), 18 (money laundering) or 63 (terrorist finance: jurisdiction) of the Terrorism Act 2000;

(c) an offence under the 2000 Act;

[(ca) an offence under any of regulations 11 to 16 of the Counter-Terrorism (Sanctions) (EU Exit) Regulations 2019;]

(d) an offence under regulation 3, 4 or 6 of the Al-Qaida and Taliban (Asset-Freezing) Regulations 2010, or regulation 10 of the ISIL (Da'esh) and Al-Qaida (Asset-Freezing) Regulations 2011 (contravention and circumvention of prohibitions);

[(da) an offence under regulations 8 to 13, 25 or 26 of the ISIL (Da'esh) and Al-Qaida (United Nations Sanctions) (EU Exit) Regulations 2019 or regulations 11 to 16 of the Counter-Terrorism (International Sanctions) (EU Exit) Regulations 2019;]

(e) an offence under section 11, 12, 13, 14, 15 or 18 of the Terrorist Asset-Freezing etc Act 2010 (offences relating to the freezing of funds etc. of designated persons);

(f) an offence under these Regulations or the Electronic Money Regulations 2011; or

(g) any other financial crimes.

(6) Where the applicant is a partnership, an unincorporated association or a body corporate, the applicant must satisfy the FCA that any persons having a qualifying holding in it are fit and proper persons having regard to the need to ensure the sound and prudent conduct of the affairs of a small payment institution.

(7) The applicant must satisfy the FCA that—

(a) where the applicant is a body corporate, the directors;

(b) the persons responsible for the management of the institution; and

(c) where relevant, the persons responsible for the management of payment services,

are of good repute and possess appropriate knowledge and experience to provide payment services.

(8) If the applicant is a body corporate which has close links with another person ('CL') the applicant must satisfy the FCA—

(a) that those links are not likely to prevent the FCA's effective supervision of the applicant; and

(b) if it appears to the FCA that CL is subject to the laws, regulations or administrative provisions of a territory [outside the United Kingdom] ('the foreign provisions'), that neither the foreign provisions, nor any deficiency in their enforcement, would prevent the FCA's effective supervision of the applicant.

(9) Regulation 6(10) (conditions for authorisation: definition of close links) applies for the purposes of paragraph (8) of this regulation as it applies for the purposes of regulation 6(9).

(10) The applicant's head office, registered office or place of residence, as the case may be, must be in the United Kingdom.

(11) The applicant must comply with a requirement of the Money Laundering, Terrorist Financing and Transfer of Funds (Information on the Payer) Regulations 2017 to be included in a register maintained under those Regulations where such a requirement applies to the applicant.

(12) For the purposes of paragraph (3) where the applicant has yet to commence the provision of payment services, or has been providing payment services for less than 12 months, the monthly

average may be based on the projected total amount of payment transactions over a 12 month period.

(13) In paragraph (5) 'financial crime' includes any offence involving fraud or dishonesty and, for this purpose, 'offence' includes any act or omission which would be an offence if it had taken place in the United Kingdom.

[*Note: reg 14(5)(e) is due to be revoked on a day to be appointed.*]

15. Supplementary provisions

Regulations 7 to 12 apply to registration as a small payment institution as they apply to authorisation as a payment institution as if—

    (a) references to authorisation were references to registration;

    (b) in regulation 7 (imposition of requirements), paragraph (4) were omitted;

    (c) in regulation 8 (variation at request of authorised payment institution)—

        (i) for 'an authorised payment institution' there were substituted 'small payment institution'; and

        (ii) for 'provided that' to the end there were substituted—

            'provided that the FCA is satisfied that the conditions set out in regulation 14(4) to (11) are being or are likely to be met and that the monthly average over any period of 12 months of the total amount of payment transactions executed by the institution, including any of its agents in the United Kingdom, continues not to exceed 3 million euros ('the financial limit').';

    (d) in regulation 10(1) (cancellation of authorisation) for sub-paragraph (e) there were substituted—

        '(e) the person does not meet, or is unlikely to meet, any of the conditions set out in regulation 14(4) to (11) (conditions for registration as small payment institution) or the financial limit referred to in regulation 8 or does not inform the FCA of a major change in circumstances which is relevant to its meeting those conditions or that requirement, as required by regulation 37 (duty to notify change in circumstance);'

        ; and

    (e) in regulation 12(1) (variation of authorisation on FCA's own initiative) for sub-paragraph (a) there were substituted—

        '(a) the person does not meet, or is unlikely to meet, any of the conditions set out in regulation 14(4) to (11) or the financial limit referred to in regulation 8;'.

16. Application for authorisation or registration if requirements cease to be met

If a small payment institution no longer meets a condition in regulation 14(3), (5) or (10) (conditions for registration as small payment institution) or intends to provide services other than those permitted by regulation 32 (additional activities), the institution concerned must, within 30 days of becoming aware of the change in circumstances, apply for authorisation as a payment institution under regulation 5 or registration as an account information service provider under regulation 17, as appropriate, if it intends to continue providing payment services in the United Kingdom.

Registration as an account information service provider

17. Application for registration as an account information service provider or variation of an existing registration

(1) An application for registration as an account information service provider or for the variation of a registration as an account information service provider must—

    (a) contain or be accompanied by the information specified in paragraphs 1, 2, 5 to 8, 10, 12, 14 and 16 to 19 of Schedule 2 (information to be provided in or with an application for authorisation); and

    (b) be made in such manner as the FCA may direct.

(2) At any time after receiving an application and before determining it, the FCA may require the applicant to provide it with such further information as it reasonably considers necessary to enable it to determine the application.

(3) Different directions may be given, and different requirements imposed, in relation to different applications or categories of application.

18. Conditions for registration as an account information service provider

(1) The FCA may refuse to register an applicant as an account information service provider if—

(a) any of the conditions set out in paragraphs (2) to (4) is not met; or

(b) any of the grounds in regulation 10(1) (as applied by regulation 19) would be met if the applicant were registered.

(2) The application must comply with the requirements of, and any requirements imposed under, regulations 17 (application for registration as an account information service provider) and 20 (duty to notify changes).

(3) The business to which the application relates must not include the provision of any payment service other than account information services.

(4) The applicant must hold professional indemnity insurance or a comparable guarantee, which covers—

(a) the territories in which the applicant proposes to offer account information services; and

(b) the applicant's potential liability to account servicing payment service providers and payment service users resulting from unauthorised or fraudulent access to, or use of, payment account information, up to such amount as the FCA may direct.

19. Supplementary provisions

Regulations 7 to 12 apply to registration as an account information service provider as they apply to authorisation as a payment institution, but as if—

(a) references to authorisation were references to registration;

(b) in regulation 7 (imposition of requirements), paragraph (4) were omitted;

(c) in regulation 8 (variation at request of authorised payment institution)—

(i) for 'an authorised payment institution' there were substituted 'registered account information service provider';

(ii) paragraphs (a) and (b) were omitted; and

(iii) for 'provided that' to the end there were substituted 'provided that the conditions set out in regulation 18(3) and (4) are being or are likely to be met.';

(d) in regulation 10(1) (cancellation of authorisation) for sub-paragraph (e) there were substituted—

'(e) the person does not meet, or is unlikely to meet, the conditions set out in regulation 18(3) and (4);'

; and

(e) in regulation 12(1) (variation of authorisation on FCA's own initiative) for sub-paragraph (a) there were substituted—

'(a) the person does not meet, or is unlikely to meet, the conditions set out in regulation 18(3) and (4);'.

Common provisions

20. Duty to notify changes

(1) If at any time after an applicant has provided the FCA with any information under regulation 5(1), (2), or (4) (application for authorisation or variation of authorisation), 13(1), (2) or (4) (application for registration as a small payment institution or variation of registration) or 17(1) or (2) (application for registration as an account information service provider or variation of registration) and before the FCA has determined the application—

(a) there is, or is likely to be, a material change affecting any matter contained in that information; or

(b) it becomes apparent to the applicant that the information is incomplete or contains a material inaccuracy,

the applicant must provide the FCA with details of the change, the complete information or a correction of the inaccuracy (as the case may be) without undue delay, or, in the case of a material change which has not yet taken place, the applicant must provide details of the likely change as soon as the applicant is aware of such change.

(2) The obligation in paragraph (1) also applies to material changes or significant inaccuracies affecting any matter contained in any supplementary information provided pursuant to that paragraph.

(3) Any information to be provided to the FCA under this regulation must be in such form or verified in such manner as it may direct.

21. Authorised payment institutions, small payment institutions and registered account information service providers acting without permission

If an authorised payment institution, a small payment institution or a registered account information service provider carries on a payment service in the United Kingdom, or purports to do so, other than in accordance with an authorisation or registration granted to it by the FCA, it is to be taken to have contravened a requirement imposed on it under these Regulations.

PART 3 AUTHORISED PAYMENT INSTITUTIONS

22. Capital requirements

(1) An authorised payment institution must maintain at all times own funds equal to or in excess of the greater of—

(a) the amount of initial capital specified in Part 1 of Schedule 3 (capital requirements), or

(b) in the case of an authorised payment institution which does not fall within paragraph (2), the amount of own funds calculated in accordance with Part 2 of Schedule 3.

(2) An authorised payment institution falls within this paragraph if—

(a) it does not offer payment services specified in paragraph 1(a) to (f) of Schedule 1 (payment services other than payment initiation services or account information services); or

(b) (i) it is included in the consolidated supervision of a parent credit institution [in accordance with the capital requirements regulation and CRR rules (as defined in section 144A of the 2000 Act)]; and

(ii) all of the conditions specified in Article 7(1) of the capital requirements regulation are met in respect of it.

(3) The own funds maintained must meet the following requirements—

(a) the amount of Tier 2 capital must be equal to or less than one third of the amount of Tier 1 capital;

(b) at least 75% of the amount of Tier 1 capital must be in the form of Common Equity Tier 1 capital.

(4) An authorised payment institution must not include in its own funds calculation any item—

(a) used in an equivalent calculation by an authorised payment institution, credit institution, investment firm, asset management company or insurance undertaking in the same group; or

(b) in the case of an authorised payment institution which carries out activities other than providing payment services, is used in carrying out those activities.

23. Safeguarding requirements

(1) For the purposes of this regulation 'relevant funds' comprise the following—

(a) sums received from, or for the benefit of, a payment service user for the execution of a payment transaction; and

(b) sums received from a payment service provider for the execution of a payment transaction on behalf of a payment service user.

(2) Where—

    (a) only a portion of the sums referred to in paragraph (1)(a) or (b) is to be used for the execution of a payment transaction (with the remainder being used for non-payment services); and

    (b) the precise portion attributable to the execution of the payment transaction is variable or unknown in advance,

the relevant funds are such amount as may be reasonably estimated, on the basis of historical data and to the satisfaction of the FCA, to be representative of the portion attributable to the execution of the payment transaction.

(3) An authorised payment institution must safeguard relevant funds in accordance with either—

    (a) paragraphs (5) to (11); or

    (b) paragraphs (12) and (13).

(4) An authorised payment institution may safeguard certain relevant funds in accordance with paragraphs (5) to (11) and the remaining relevant funds in accordance with paragraphs (12) and (13).

(5) An authorised payment institution must keep relevant funds segregated from any other funds that it holds.

(6) Where the authorised payment institution continues to hold the relevant funds at the end of the business day following the day on which they were received it must—

    (a) place them in a separate account that it holds with an authorised credit institution or the Bank of England; or

    (b) invest the relevant funds in such secure, liquid assets as the FCA may approve ('relevant assets') and place those assets in a separate account with an authorised custodian.

(7) An account in which relevant funds or relevant assets are placed under paragraph (6) must—

    (a) be designated in such a way as to show that it is an account which is held for the purpose of safeguarding relevant funds or relevant assets in accordance with this regulation; and

    (b) be used only for holding those funds or assets[, or for holding those funds or assets together with proceeds of an insurance policy or guarantee held in accordance with paragraph (12)(b)].

(8) No person other than the authorised payment institution may have any interest in or right over the relevant funds or relevant assets placed in an account in accordance with paragraph (6)(a) or (b) except as provided by this regulation.

(9) Notwithstanding paragraphs (5), (6), (7)(b) and (8), where an authorised payment institution is a participant in a designated system and the institution holds an account at the Bank of England for the purposes of completing the settlement of transfer orders that have been entered into the designated system on behalf of payment service users—

    (a) funds held in the account pending settlement in accordance with the rules or default arrangements of the designated system, in respect of transfer orders that have been entered into the designated system on behalf of payment service users, may continue to be held in the account with relevant funds;

    (b) the account, or a specified amount of funds in the account, may be subject to an interest or right in favour of the Bank of England in order to ensure the availability of funds to complete the settlement of transfer orders in accordance with the rules or default arrangements of the designated system;

    (c) subject to paragraph (10), funds received into the account by the authorised payment institution upon settlement are to be considered as having been appropriately safeguarded in accordance with this regulation from the time of receipt in the designated system until the time of receipt into the account.

(10) The FCA may direct that paragraph (9)(c) does not apply in relation to a designated system if, in the FCA's view, the rules and default arrangements of that system do not adequately insulate

the funds of payment service users from the claims of other creditors of authorised payment institutions which are participants in the system.

(11) The authorised payment institution must keep a record of—

(a) any relevant funds segregated in accordance with paragraph (5);

(b) any relevant funds placed in an account in accordance with paragraph (6)(a);

(c) any relevant assets placed in an account in accordance with paragraph (6)(b);

(d) any funds held in an account as permitted by paragraph (9)(a);

(e) any funds expected to be received into an account as described in paragraph (9)(c) in respect of transfer orders that have been entered into the designated system;

(f) any funds received into an account as described in paragraph (9)(c).

(12) The authorised payment institution must ensure that—

(a) any relevant funds are covered by—

(i) an insurance policy with an authorised insurer;

(ii) a comparable guarantee given by an authorised insurer; or

(iii) a comparable guarantee given by an authorised credit institution; and

(b) the proceeds of any such insurance policy or guarantee are payable upon an insolvency event into a separate account held by the authorised payment institution which must—

(i) be designated in such a way as to show that it is an account which is held for the purpose of safeguarding relevant funds in accordance with this regulation; and

(ii) be used only for holding such proceeds[, or for holding those proceeds together with funds or assets held in accordance with paragraph (7)].

(13) No person other than the authorised payment institution may have any interest in or right over the proceeds placed in an account in accordance with paragraph (12)(b) except as provided by this regulation.

(14) Subject to paragraph (15), where there is an insolvency event—

(a) the claims of payment service users are to be paid from the asset pool in priority to all other creditors; and

(b) until all the claims of payment service users have been paid, no right of set-off or security right may be exercised in respect of the asset pool except to the extent that the right of set-off relates to fees and expenses in relation to operating an account held in accordance with paragraph (6)(a) or (b), (9) or (12)(b).

(15) The claims referred to in paragraph (14)(a) shall not be subject to the priority of expenses of an insolvency proceeding except in respect of the costs of distributing the asset pool.

(16) Paragraphs (14) and (15) apply to any relevant funds which a small payment institution voluntarily safeguards in accordance with either paragraphs (5) to (11) or paragraphs (12) and (13).

(17) An authorised payment institution (and any small payment institution which voluntarily safeguards relevant funds) must maintain organisational arrangements sufficient to minimise the risk of the loss or diminution of relevant funds or relevant assets through fraud, misuse, negligence or poor administration.

(18) In this regulation—

'asset pool' means—

(a) any relevant funds segregated in accordance with paragraph (5);

(b) any relevant funds held in an account in accordance with paragraph (6)(a);

(c) where paragraph (9) applies, any funds that are received into the account held at the Bank of England upon settlement in respect of transfer orders that have been entered into the designated system on behalf of payment service users, whether settlement occurs before or after the insolvency event;

(d) any relevant assets held in an account in accordance with paragraph (6)(b); and

(e) any proceeds of an insurance policy or guarantee held in an account in accordance with paragraph (12)(b);

'authorised insurer' means a person authorised for the purposes of the 2000 Act to effect and carry out a contract of general insurance as principal [. . .], other than a person in the same group as the authorised payment institution;

'authorised credit institution' means a person authorised for the purposes of the 2000 Act to accept deposits [or an approved foreign credit institution (see paragraph (19)), but does not include] a person in the same group as the authorised payment institution;

'authorised custodian' means a person authorised for the purposes of the 2000 Act to safeguard and administer investments [. . .];

'default arrangements' has the meaning given in regulation 2(1) of the Financial Markets and Insolvency (Settlement Finality) Regulations 1999 (interpretation);

'insolvency event' means any of the following procedures in relation to an authorised payment institution or small payment institution—

    (a) the making of a winding-up order;

    (b) the passing of a resolution for voluntary winding-up;

    (c) the entry of the institution into administration;

    (d) the appointment of a receiver or manager of the institution's property;

    (e) the approval of a proposed voluntary arrangement (being a composition in satisfaction of debts or a scheme of arrangement);

    (f) the making of a bankruptcy order;

    (g) in Scotland, the award of sequestration;

    (h) the making of any deed of arrangement for the benefit of creditors or, in Scotland, the execution of a trust deed for creditors;

    (i) the conclusion of any composition contract with creditors; or

    (j) the making of an insolvency administration order or, in Scotland, sequestration, in respect of the estate of a deceased person;

'insolvency proceeding' means—

    (a) winding-up, administration, receivership, bankruptcy or, in Scotland, sequestration;

    (b) a voluntary arrangement, deed of arrangement or trust deed for the benefit of creditors; or

    (c) the administration of the insolvent estate of a deceased person;

'rules' has the meaning given in regulation 2(1) of the Financial Markets and Insolvency (Settlement Finality) Regulations 1999 (interpretation);

'security right' means—

    (a) security for a debt owed by an authorised payment institution or a small payment institution and includes any charge, lien, mortgage or other security over the asset pool or any part of the asset pool; and

    (b) any charge arising in respect of the expenses of a voluntary arrangement;

'settlement' and 'system' have the same meanings as in the Financial Markets and Insolvency (Settlement Finality) Regulations 1999.

    [(19)   In paragraph (18), 'approved foreign credit institution' means—

    (a) the central bank of a State that is a member of the Organisation for Economic Co-operation and Development ('an OECD state'),

    (b) a credit institution that is supervised by the central bank or other banking regulator of an OECD state,

    (c) any credit institution that—

        (i) is subject to regulation by the banking regulator of a State that is not an OECD state,

        (ii) is required by the law of the country or territory in which it is based to provide audited accounts,

        (iii) has minimum net assets of £5 million (or its equivalent in any other currency at the relevant time),

        (iv) has a surplus of revenue over expenditure for the last two financial years, and

        (v) has an annual report which is not materially qualified.]

[23A Insolvency Regulations

Sections 93(4) and 233 to 236 of the Banking Act 2009 apply to authorised payment institutions and small payment institutions with the modifications set out in Schedule 3A.]

24. Accounting and statutory audit

(1) Where an authorised payment institution carries on activities other than the provision of payment services, it must provide to the FCA separate accounting information in respect of its provision of payment services.

(2) Such accounting information must be subject, where relevant, to an auditor's report prepared by the institution's [statutory auditor].

(3) A statutory auditor [. . .] ('the auditor') must, in any of the circumstances referred to in paragraph (4), communicate to the FCA information on, or its opinion on, matters—

    (a) of which it has become aware in its capacity as auditor of an authorised payment institution or of a person with close links to an authorised payment institution; and

    (b) which relate to payment services provided by that institution.

(4) The circumstances are that—

    (a) the auditor reasonably believes that—

        (i) there is or has been, or may be or may have been, a contravention of any requirement imposed on the authorised payment institution by or under these Regulations; and

        (ii) the contravention may be of material significance to the FCA in determining whether to exercise, in relation to that institution, any functions conferred on the FCA by these Regulations;

    (b) the auditor reasonably believes that the information on, or his opinion on, those matters may be of material significance to the FCA in determining whether the institution meets or will continue to meet the conditions set out in regulation 6(4) to (9) (conditions for authorisation) and, if applicable, the requirement in regulation 22(1) (capital requirements) to maintain own funds;

    (c) the auditor reasonably believes that the institution is not, may not be or may cease to be, a going concern;

    (d) the auditor is precluded from stating in his report that the annual accounts have been properly prepared in accordance with the Companies Act 2006;

    (e) the auditor is precluded from stating in his report, where applicable, that the annual accounts give a true and fair view of the matters referred to in section 495 of the Companies Act 2006 (auditor's report on company's annual accounts) including as it is applied and modified by regulation 39 of the Limited Liability Partnerships (Accounts and Audit) (Application of Companies Act 2006) Regulations 2008 ('the LLP Regulations') (auditor's report); or

    (f) the auditor is required to state in his report in relation to the person concerned any of the facts referred to in subsection (2), (3) or (5) of section 498 of the Companies Act 2006 (duties of auditor) or, in the case of limited liability partnerships, subsection (2), (3) or (4) of section 498 as applied and modified by regulation 40 of the LLP Regulations (duties and rights of auditors).

(5) In this regulation a person has close links with an authorised payment institution ('A') if that person is—

    (a) a parent undertaking of A;

    (b) a subsidiary undertaking of A;

    (c) a parent undertaking of a subsidiary undertaking of A; or

    (d) a subsidiary undertaking of a parent undertaking of A.

[(6) In this regulation 'statutory auditor' has the same meaning as in Part 42 of the Companies Act 2006 (see section 1210 of that Act).]

25. Outsourcing

(1) An authorised payment institution must notify the FCA of its intention to enter into a contract with another person under which that other person will carry out any operational function relating to its provision of payment services ('outsourcing').

(2) Where an authorised payment institution intends to outsource any important operational function, including the provision of an information technology system, all of the following conditions must be met—

(a) the outsourcing is not undertaken in such a way as to impair—
  (i) the quality of the authorised payment institution's internal control; or
  (ii) the ability of the FCA to monitor and retrace the authorised payment institution's compliance with these Regulations;
(b) the outsourcing does not result in any delegation by the senior management of the authorised payment institution of responsibility for complying with the requirements imposed by or under these Regulations;
(c) the relationship and obligations of the authorised payment institution towards its payment service users under these Regulations is not substantially altered;
(d) compliance with the conditions which the authorised payment institution must observe in order to be authorised and remain so is not adversely affected; and
(e) none of the conditions of the payment institution's authorisation requires removal or variation.

(3) For the purposes of paragraph (2), an operational function is important if a defect or failure in its performance would materially impair—
  (a) compliance by the authorised payment institution with these Regulations and any requirements of its authorisation;
  (b) the financial performance of the authorised payment institution; or
  (c) the soundness or continuity of the authorised payment institution's payment services.

(4) An authorised payment institution must notify the FCA without undue delay of any change in outsourced functions or the persons to which functions are outsourced.

PART 4 PROVISIONS APPLICABLE TO AUTHORISED PAYMENT INSTITUTIONS AND SMALL PAYMENT INSTITUTIONS

31. Record keeping

(1) An authorised payment institution or small payment institution must maintain relevant records and keep them for at least five years from the date on which the record was created.

(2) For the purposes of paragraph (1), records are relevant where they relate to compliance with obligations imposed by or under Parts 2 to 5 and, in particular, would enable the FCA to supervise effectively such compliance.

32. Additional activities

(1) Authorised payment institutions and small payment institutions may, in addition to providing payment services, engage in the following activities—
  (a) the provision of operational and closely related ancillary services, including—
    (i) ensuring the execution of payment transactions;
    (ii) foreign exchange services;
    (iii) safe-keeping activities; and
    (iv) the storage and processing of data;
  (b) the operation of payment systems; and
  (c) business activities other than the provision of payment services, subject to any relevant provision of [. . .] or national law.

(2) Authorised payment institutions and small payment institutions may grant credit in relation to the provision of the payment services specified in paragraph 1(d) or (e) of Schedule 1 (execution of payment transactions where funds are covered by a credit line, issuing payment instruments or acquiring payment transactions) only if—
  (a) such credit is ancillary and granted exclusively in connection with the execution of a payment transaction;
  (b) such credit is not granted from the funds received or held for the purposes of executing payment transactions; [and]

(d) in relation to an authorised payment institution, in the opinion of the FCA the institution's own funds are, and continue to be, adequate in the light of the overall amount of credit granted.

33.   Payment accounts and sums received for the execution of payment transactions

Any payment account held by an authorised payment institution or a small payment institution must be used only in relation to payment transactions.

34.   Use of agents

(1) Authorised payment institutions[, small payment institutions and registered account information service providers] may not provide payment services in the United Kingdom through an agent unless the agent is included on the register.

(3) An application for an agent to be included on the register must—
    (a) contain, or be accompanied by, the following information—
        (i)   the name and address of the agent;
        (ii) where relevant, a description of the internal control mechanisms that will be used by the agent to comply with the provisions of the [Money Laundering, Terrorist Financing and Transfer of Funds (Information on the Payer) Regulations 2017];
        (iii) the identity of the directors and persons responsible for the management of the agent and, if the agent is not a payment service provider, evidence that they are fit and proper persons;
        (iv) the payment services for which the agent is appointed;
        (v)   the unique identification code or number of the agent, if any; and
        (vi) such other information as the FCA may reasonably require; and
    (b) be made in such manner as the FCA may direct.

(4) Different directions may be given, and different requirements imposed, in relation to different applications or categories of application.

(5) At any time after receiving an application and before determining it, the FCA may require the applicant to provide it with such further information as it reasonably considers necessary to enable it to determine the application.

(7) The FCA may refuse to include the agent on the register only if—
    (a) it has not received the information referred to in paragraph (3)(a), or is not satisfied that such information is correct;
    (b) it is not satisfied that the directors and persons responsible for the management of the agent are fit and proper persons;
    (c) it has reasonable grounds to suspect that, in connection with the provision of services through the agent—
        (i)   money laundering or terrorist financing within the meaning of the [Money Laundering, Terrorist Financing and Transfer of Funds (Information on the Payer) Regulations 2017] is taking place, has taken place, or has been attempted; or
        (ii) the risk of such activities taking place would be increased.

(8) If the FCA proposes to refuse to include the agent on the register, it must give the authorised payment institution[, the small payment institution or the registered account information service provider], as the case may be, a warning notice.

(9) The FCA must, having considered any representations made in response to the warning notice—
    (a) if it decides not to include the agent on the register, give the applicant a decision notice; or
    (b) if it decides to include the agent on the register, give the applicant notice of its decision, stating the date on which the registration takes effect.

[(11) The FCA must give any notice required by paragraph (9) within a period of two months beginning on the date on which the FCA received the completed application.]

(12) If the FCA decides not to include the agent on the register the applicant may refer the matter to the Upper Tribunal.

(13) If the FCA decides to include the agent on the register, it must update the register as soon as practicable.

(15) An application under paragraph (3) may be combined with an application under [regulation 5, 13 or 17], in which case the application must be determined in the manner set out in regulation 9 (determination of application for authorisation) (if relevant, as applied by regulation 15 [or 19] (supplementary provisions relating to applications for registration as a small payment institution [or account information service provider]).

(16) An authorised payment institution[, a small payment institution or a registered account information service provider] must ensure that agents acting on its behalf inform payment service users of the agency arrangement.

(17) An authorised payment institution[, a small payment institution or a registered account information service provider] must notify the FCA without undue delay if there is any change in the information provided under paragraph (3) or (5).

35. Removal of agent from register

(1) The FCA may remove an agent of an authorised payment institution[, small payment institution or registered account information service provider] from the register where—

(a) the authorised payment institution[, small payment institution or registered account information service provider] requests, or consents to, the agent's removal from the register;

(b) the authorised payment institution[, small payment institution or registered account information service provider] has obtained registration through false statements or any other irregular means;

(c) regulation 34(7)(b) or (c) (use of agents) applies;

(d) the removal is desirable in order to protect the interests of consumers; or

(e) the agent's provision of payment services is otherwise unlawful.

(2) Where the FCA proposes to remove an agent from the register, other than at the request of the authorised payment institution[, small payment institution or registered account information service provider], it must give the authorised payment institution[, small payment institution or registered account information service provider] a warning notice.

(3) The FCA must, having considered any representations made in response to the warning notice—

(a) if it decides to remove the agent, give the authorised payment institution[, small payment institution or registered account information service provider] a decision notice; or

(b) if it decides not to remove the agent, give the authorised payment institution[, small payment institution or registered account information service provider] notice of its decision.

(4) If the FCA decides to remove the agent, other than at the request of the authorised payment institution[, small payment institution or registered account information service provider], the [authorised payment institution, small payment institution or registered account information service provider] may refer the matter to the Upper Tribunal.

(5) Where the period for a reference to the Upper Tribunal has expired without a reference being made, the FCA must as soon as practicable update the register accordingly.

36. Reliance

(1) Where an authorised payment institution[, a small payment institution or a registered account information service provider] relies on a third party for the performance of operational functions it must take all reasonable steps to ensure that these Regulations are complied with.

(2) Without prejudice to paragraph (1), an authorised payment institution[, a small payment institution or a registered account information service provider] is responsible, to the same extent

as if it had expressly permitted it, for anything done or omitted by any of its employees, any agent or branch providing payment services on its behalf, or any entity to which activities are outsourced.

37. Duty to notify change in circumstance

(1) Where it becomes apparent to an authorised payment institution[, a small payment institution or a registered account information service provider] that there is, or is likely to be, a significant change in circumstances which is relevant to—

    (a)   in the case of an authorised payment institution—

        (i)   its fulfilment of any of the conditions set out in regulation 6(4) to (9) (conditions for authorisation) and, if applicable, the requirement in regulation 22(1) (capital requirements) to maintain own funds; [. . .]

        (ii) the payment services which it seeks to carry on in exercise of its passport rights;

    (b)   in the case of a small payment institution, its fulfilment of any of the conditions set out in regulation 14(5) to (11) (conditions for registration as a small payment institution) and compliance with the financial limit referred to in regulation 8 (as modified by regulation 15) (variation of registration at request of small payment institution); [. . .]

    [(ba) in the case of a registered account information service provider, its fulfilment of any of the conditions set out in regulation 18(3) and (4) (conditions for registration); and]

    (c)   in the case of the use of an agent to provide payment services, the matters referred to in regulation 34(7)(b) and (c) (use of agents),

it must provide the FCA with details of the change without undue delay, or, in the case of a substantial change in circumstances which has not yet taken place, details of the likely change a reasonable period before it takes place.

(2) Any information to be provided to the FCA under this regulation must be in such form or verified in such manner as it may direct.

PART 5 REQUIREMENTS FOR PROVIDERS OF CERTAIN SERVICES WHICH ARE NOT PAYMENT SERVICES

38. Notification of use of limited network exclusion

(1) If a person ('service provider') provides services of the type falling within paragraph 2(k)(i) to (iii) of Schedule 1 (limited network exclusion) and the total value of the payment transactions executed through such services provided by the service provider in any period of 12 months exceeds 1 million euros, the service provider must notify the FCA.

(2) The period of 12 months referred to in paragraph (1) does not include any period in respect of which a notification has already been made under paragraph (1).

(3) A notification under paragraph (1) must—

    (a) include a description of the services offered; and

    (b) specify the exclusion by virtue of which the services are not payment services.

(4) Notifications and information provided to the FCA under this regulation must be given—

    (a) within such time as the FCA may direct after the end of the period of 12 months referred to in paragraph (1); and

    (b) in such form or verified in such manner as the FCA may direct,

and different directions may be given in relation to different notifications or information or categories of notification or information.

(5) When the FCA receives a notification under this regulation, the FCA must assess whether the notified services fall within paragraph 2(k)(i) to (iii) of Schedule 1.

(6) If the FCA considers that any part of the notified services does not fall within paragraph 2(k)(i) to (iii) of Schedule 1—

    (a) the FCA must notify the service provider, and

    (b) the service provider may refer the matter to the Upper Tribunal.

39. Notification of use of electronic communications exclusion

(1) If a person ('service provider') provides, or intends to provide, a service for payment transactions falling within paragraph 2(l) of Schedule 1 (electronic communications exclusion), the service provider must—

(a) notify the FCA, and

(b) include with such notification a description of the service.

(2) The service provider must provide a notification under paragraph (1)—

(a) if the service provider starts to provide the service before 13th January 2018, on or before that date, or

(b) otherwise, before the service provider starts to provide the service.

(3) The service provider must also provide to the FCA, at such times as the FCA may direct, an annual audit opinion testifying that the transactions for which the service is provided comply with the limits mentioned in paragraph 2(l) of Schedule 1.

(4) Information provided to the FCA under this regulation must be in such form or verified in such manner as the FCA may direct.

(5) Different directions may be given under paragraph (3) and (4) in relation to different service providers or different categories of service provider.

PART 6 INFORMATION REQUIREMENTS FOR PAYMENT SERVICES

Application

40. Application of Part 6

(1) This Part applies to payment services where—

(a) the services are provided from an establishment maintained by a payment service provider or its agent in the United Kingdom; and

(b) the services are provided in one of the following circumstances—

(i) the payment service providers of both the payer and the payee are located within [the United Kingdom] and the service relates to a transaction in [sterling];

[(ia) the payment service providers of both the payer and the payee are located within the qualifying area and the service relates to a transaction in euro executed under a payment scheme which operates across the qualifying area;]

(ii) the payment service providers of both the payer and the payee are located within [the United Kingdom] and the service relates to a transaction in a currency other than [sterling]; or

(iii) the payment service provider of either the payer or the payee, but not both, is located within [the United Kingdom and the case does not fall within paragraph (ia)].

[(1A) In paragraph (1)(b)(ia)—

(a) 'payment service provider' includes any person who is a PSP as defined in Article 2(8B) of the SEPA regulation;

(b) 'the qualifying are' means the area of the United Kingdom and the EEA States.]

(2) In the circumstances mentioned at paragraph (1)(b)(ii)—

(a) this Part applies only in respect of those parts of a transaction which are carried out in the [United Kingdom]; and

(b) regulations 43(2)(b) and 52(a) and paragraph 2(e) of Schedule 4 (maximum execution time) do not apply.

(3) In the circumstances mentioned at paragraph (1)(b)(iii)—

(a) this Part applies only in respect of those parts of a transaction which are carried out in the [United Kingdom]; and

(b) regulations 43(2)(b) and 52(a) and paragraphs 2(e) and 5(g) of Schedule 4 (maximum execution time and conditions for refund of direct debits) do not apply.

(4) This Part does not apply to registered account information service providers [. . .], except for regulations 59 (burden of proof on payment service provider) and 60 (information requirements for account information service providers).

(5) Regulations 43 to 47 apply to payment services provided under a single payment service contract.

(6) Regulations 48 to 54 apply to payment services provided under a framework contract.

(7) If the payment service user is not a consumer, a micro-enterprise or a charity, the parties to a contract for payment services may agree that any or all of the provisions of this Part do not apply.

(8) Paragraph (1) applies to cash withdrawal services falling within paragraph 2(o) of Schedule 1 as if—

(a) references to payment services were references to cash withdrawal services falling within paragraph 2(o) of Schedule 1;

(b) references to payment service providers were references to providers of cash withdrawal services falling within paragraph 2(o) of Schedule 1; and

(c) references to this Part were references to regulation 61 (information on ATM withdrawal charges).

PART 6   INFORMATION REQUIREMENTS FOR PAYMENT SERVICES

Application

41.   Application of this Part in the case of consumer credit agreements

(1) This regulation applies where a payment service is provided in relation to payment transactions that consist of the placing, transferring or withdrawal of funds covered by a credit line provided under a regulated agreement.

(2) Regulations 50 (changes in contractual information) and 51 (termination of framework contract) do not apply.

(3) Where a payment service provider is required to provide the same information to a payment service user by a provision in this Part and by a provision in the Consumer Credit Act 1974 or subordinate legislation made under that Act ('a CCA provision'), information which has been provided in compliance with the CCA provision, and which was provided in a manner which complies with the requirements of the provision in this Part, need not be provided again in order to comply with the provision in this Part.

42.   Disapplication of certain regulations in the case of low-value payment instruments

(1) This regulation applies in respect of payment instruments which, under the framework contract governing their use—

(a) can be used only to execute individual payment transactions of 30 euros or less, or in relation to payment transactions executed wholly within the United Kingdom, 60 euros or less;

(b) have a spending limit of 150 euros or, where payment transactions must be executed wholly within the United Kingdom, 300 euros; or

(c) store funds that do not exceed 500 euros at any time.

(2) Where this regulation applies—

(a) regulations 48 and 52 do not apply and the payment service provider is only required to provide the payer with information about the main characteristics of the payment service, including—

    (i)   the way in which the payment instrument can be used;

    (ii) the liability of the payer, as set out in regulation 77 (payer or payee's liability for unauthorised payment transactions);

    (iii) charges levied;

    (iv) any other material information the payer might need to take an informed decision; and

    (v)   an indication of where the information specified in Schedule 4 (prior general information for framework contracts) is made available in an easily accessible manner;

  (b) the parties may agree that regulations 53 and 54 do not apply and instead—

    (i)   the payment service provider must provide or make available a reference enabling the payment service user to identify the payment transaction, the amount of the payment transaction and any charges payable in respect of the payment transaction;

    (ii) in the case of several payment transactions of the same kind made to the same payee, the payment service provider must provide or make available to the payment service user information about the total amount of the payment transactions and any charges for those payment transactions; or

    (iii) where the payment instrument is used anonymously or the payment service provider is not otherwise technically able to provide or make available the information specified in paragraph (i) or (ii), the payment service provider must enable the payer to verify the amount of funds stored; and

  (c) the parties may agree that regulation 55(1) does not apply to information provided or made available in accordance with regulation 50.

Single payment service contracts

43. Information required prior to the conclusion of a single payment service contract

(1) A payment service provider must provide or make available to the payment service user the information specified in paragraph (2) in relation to the service, whether by supplying a copy of the draft single payment service contract or supplying a copy of the draft payment order or otherwise, either—

  (a) before the payment service user is bound by the single payment service contract; or

  (b) immediately after the execution of the payment transaction, where the contract is concluded at the payment service user's request using a means of distance communication which does not enable provision of such information in accordance with sub-paragraph (a).

(2) The information referred to in paragraph (1) is—

  (a) the information or unique identifier that has to be provided by the payment service user in order for a payment order to be properly initiated or executed;

  (b) the maximum time in which the payment service will be executed;

  (c) the charges payable by the payment service user to the user's payment service provider and, where applicable, a breakdown of such charges;

  (d) where applicable, the actual or reference exchange rate to be applied to the payment transaction; and

  (e) such of the information specified in Schedule 4 (prior general information for framework contracts) as is relevant to the single payment service contract in question.

(3) Where a payment order is to be initiated through a payment initiation service provider, the payment initiation service provider must also provide or make available to the payer, before the payment is initiated, clear and comprehensive information as follows—

  (a) the name of the payment initiation service provider;

  (b) the address of the head office of the payment initiation service provider;

(c) where applicable, the address of the head office of the agent or branch through which the payment initiation service provider provides services in the United Kingdom;

(d) other contact details relevant for communication with the payment initiation service provider, including an electronic mail address; and

(e) the contact details of the FCA.

44. Information required after the initiation of a payment order

(1) Where a payment order is initiated through a payment initiation service provider, immediately after the initiation of the payment order the payment initiation service provider must provide or make available to the payer and, where applicable, to the payee—

(a) confirmation of the successful initiation of the payment order with the payer's account servicing payment service provider;

(b) a reference enabling the payer and the payee, to identify the payment transaction and, where appropriate, the payee to identify the payer, and any information transferred with the payment order;

(c) the amount of the payment transaction;

(d) where applicable, the amount of any charges payable to the payment initiation service provider in relation to the payment transaction, and where applicable a breakdown of the amounts of such charges.

(2) Where a payment order is initiated through a payment initiation service provider, the payment initiation service provider must provide or make available to the payer's account servicing payment service provider the reference for the payment transaction.

45. Information required after receipt of the payment order

(1) The payer's payment service provider must, immediately after receipt of the payment order, provide or make available to the payer the information specified in paragraph (2) in relation to the service to be provided by the payer's payment service provider.

(2) The information referred to in paragraph (1) is—

(a) a reference enabling the payer to identify the payment transaction and, where appropriate, information relating to the payee;

(b) the amount of the payment transaction in the currency used in the payment order;

(c) the amount of any charges for the payment transaction payable by the payer and, where applicable, a breakdown of the amounts of such charges;

(d) where an exchange rate is used in the payment transaction and the actual rate used in the payment transaction differs from the rate provided in accordance with regulation 43(2)(d), the actual rate used or a reference to it, and the amount of the payment transaction after that currency conversion; and

(e) the date on which the payment service provider received the payment order.

46. Information for the payee after execution

(1) The payee's payment service provider must, immediately after the execution of the payment transaction, provide or make available to the payee the information specified in paragraph (2) in relation to the service provided by the payee's payment service provider.

(2) The information referred to in paragraph (1) is—

(a) a reference enabling the payee to identify the payment transaction and, where appropriate, the payer and any information transferred with the payment transaction;

(b) the amount of the payment transaction in the currency in which the funds are at the payee's disposal;

(c) the amount of any charges for the payment transaction payable by the payee and, where applicable, a breakdown of the amount of such charges;

(d) where applicable, the exchange rate used in the payment transaction by the payee's payment service provider, and the amount of the payment transaction before that currency conversion; and

(e) the credit value date.

47.   Avoidance of duplication of information

Where a payment order for a single payment transaction is transmitted by way of a payment instrument issued under a framework contract, the payment service provider in respect of that single payment transaction need not provide or make available under regulations 43 to 46 information which has been provided or made available, or will be provided or made available, under regulations 48 to 53 by another payment service provider in respect of the framework contract.

Framework contracts

48.   Prior general information for framework contracts

(1) A payment service provider must provide to the payment service user the information specified in Schedule 4 (prior general information for framework contracts), either—

(a) in good time before the payment service user is bound by the framework contract; or

(b) where the contract is concluded at the payment service user's request using a means of distance communication which does not enable provision of such information in accordance with sub-paragraph (a), immediately after the conclusion of the contract.

(2) The payment service provider may discharge the duty under paragraph (1) by providing a copy of the draft framework contract provided that such contract includes the information specified in Schedule 4 (prior general information for framework contracts).

49.   Information during period of contract

If the payment service user so requests at any time during the contractual relationship, the payment service provider must provide the information specified in Schedule 4 (prior general information for framework contracts) and the terms of the framework contract.

50.   Changes in contractual information

(1) Subject to paragraph (4), any proposed changes to—

(a) the existing terms of the framework contract; or

(b) the information specified in Schedule 4 (prior general information for framework contracts),

must be provided by the payment service provider to the payment service user no later than two months before the date on which they are to take effect.

(2) The framework contract may provide for any such proposed changes to be made unilaterally by the payment service provider where the payment service user does not, before the proposed date of entry into force of the changes, notify the payment service provider to the contrary.

(3) Where paragraph (2) applies, the payment service provider must inform the payment service user that

(a) the payment service user will be deemed to have accepted the changes in the circumstances referred to in that paragraph; and

(b) the payment service user has the right to terminate the framework contract without charge at any time before the proposed date of their entry into force.

(4) Changes in the interest or exchange rates may be applied immediately and without notice where—

(a) such a right is agreed under the framework contract and any such changes in interest or exchange rates are based on the reference interest or exchange rates information which has been provided to the payment service user in accordance with this Part; or

(b) the changes are more favourable to the payment service user.

(5) The payment service provider must inform the payment service user of any change to the interest rate as soon as possible unless the parties have agreed on a specific frequency or manner in which the information is to be provided or made available.

(6) Any change in the interest or exchange rate used in payment transactions must be implemented and calculated in a neutral manner that does not discriminate against payment service users.

51. Termination of framework contract

(1) The payment service user may terminate the framework contract at any time unless the parties have agreed on a period of notice not exceeding one month.

(2) Any charges for the termination of the contract must reasonably correspond to the actual costs to the payment service provider of termination.

(3) The payment service provider may not charge the payment service user for the termination of a framework contract after the expiry of 6 months of the contract.

(4) The payment service provider may terminate a framework contract concluded for an indefinite period by giving at least two months' notice, if the contract so provides.

(5) Notice of termination given in accordance with paragraph (4) must be provided in the same way as information is required by regulation 55(1) (communication of information) to be provided or made available.

(6) Where charges for the payment service are levied on a regular basis, such charges must be apportioned up until the time of the termination of the contract and any charges paid in advance must be reimbursed proportionally.

(7) This regulation does not affect any right of a party to the framework contract to treat it, in accordance with the general law of contract, as unenforceable, void or discharged.

52. Information prior to execution of individual payment transaction

Where an individual payment transaction under a framework contract is initiated by the payer, at the payer's request the payer's payment service provider must inform the payer of—

    (a) the maximum execution time;

    (b) the charges payable by the payer in respect of the payment transaction; and

    (c) where applicable, a breakdown of the amounts of such charges.

53. Information for the payer on individual payment transactions

(1) The payer's payment service provider under a framework contract must provide to the payer the information specified in paragraph (2) in respect of each payment transaction on paper or on another durable medium at least once per month free of charge.

(2) The information is—

    (a) a reference enabling the payer to identify the payment transaction and, where appropriate, information relating to the payee;

    (b) the amount of the payment transaction in the currency in which the payer's payment account is debited or in the currency used for the payment order;

    (c) the amount of any charges for the payment transaction and, where applicable, a breakdown of the amounts of such charges, or the interest payable by the payer;

    (d) where applicable, the exchange rate used in the payment transaction by the payer's payment service provider and the amount of the payment transaction after that currency conversion; and

    (e) the debit value date or the date of receipt of the payment order.

(3) A framework contract may include a condition that the payer may require the information specified in paragraph (2) be provided or made available periodically at least once a month, free of charge and in an agreed manner which enables the payer to store and reproduce the information unchanged.

(4) Paragraph (1) does not require a payment service provider to provide information where—

    (a) the information has been, or is to be, provided or made available as required by the payer under a condition of the type referred to in paragraph (3); or

    (b) more than one month has passed since information was last provided, but there are no payment transactions in respect of which the payment service provider has not previously provided or made available information in accordance with paragraph (1) or as required by the payer under a condition of the type referred to in paragraph (3).

54. Information for the payee on individual payment transactions

(1) The payee's payment service provider under a framework contract must provide to the payee the information specified in paragraph (2) in respect of each payment transaction on paper or on another durable medium at least once per month free of charge.

(2) The information is—
- (a) a reference enabling the payee to identify the payment transaction and the payer, and any information transferred with the payment transaction;
- (b) the amount of the payment transaction in the currency in which the payee's payment account is credited;
- (c) the amount of any charges for the payment transaction and, where applicable, a break-down of the amounts of such charges, or the interest payable by the payee;
- (d) where applicable, the exchange rate used in the payment transaction by the payee's pay-ment service provider, and the amount of the payment transaction before that currency conversion; and
- (e) the credit value date.

(3) A framework contract may include a condition that the information specified in paragraph (2) is to be provided or made available periodically at least once a month and in an agreed manner which enables the payee to store and reproduce the information unchanged.

(4) Paragraph (1) does not require a payment service provider to provide information where—
- (a) the information has been, or is to be, provided or made available in accordance with a condition of the type referred to in paragraph (3); or
- (b) more than one month has passed since information was last provided, but there are no payment transactions in respect of which the payment service provider has not previ-ously provided or made available information in accordance with paragraph (1) or in accordance with a condition of the type referred to in paragraph (3).

Common provisions

55. Communication of information

(1) Subject to regulation 42(2)(c) (disapplication of certain regulations in the case of low-value payment transactions), any information provided or made available in accordance with this Part must be provided or made available—
- (a) in the case of single payment service contracts, in an easily accessible manner;
- (b) subject to paragraph (2), on paper or on another durable medium;
- (c) in easily understandable language and in a clear and comprehensible form; and
- (d) in English or in the language agreed by the parties.

(2) Paragraph (1)(b)—
- (a) in the case of single payment service contracts, only applies where the payment service user so requests; and
- (b) in the case of framework contracts, is subject to any agreement in accordance with regu-lation 53(3) or 54(3) (information for the payer or payee on individual payment transac-tions) as to the manner in which information is to be provided or made available.

56. Charges for information

(1) A payment service provider may not charge for providing or making available information which is required to be provided or made available by this Part.

(2) The payment service provider and the payment service user may agree on charges for any information which is provided at the request of the payment service user where such information is—
- (a) additional to the information required to be provided or made available by this Part;
- (b) provided more frequently than is specified in this Part; or
- (c) transmitted by means of communication other than those specified in the framework contract.

(3) Any charges imposed under paragraph (2) must reasonably correspond to the payment ser-vice provider's actual costs.

57. Currency and currency conversion

(1) Payment transactions must be executed in the currency agreed between the parties.

(2) Where a currency conversion service is offered before the initiation of the payment transaction—

(a) at an automatic teller machine or the point of sale; or

(b) by the payee,

the party offering the currency conversion service to the payer must disclose to the payer all charges as well as the exchange rate to be used for converting the payment transaction.

58. Information on additional charges or reductions

(1) The payee must inform the payer of any charge requested or reduction offered by the payee for the use of a particular payment instrument before the initiation of the payment transaction.

(2) The payment service provider, or any relevant other party involved in the transaction, must inform the payment service user of any charge requested by the payment service provider or other party, as the case may be, for the use of a particular payment instrument before the initiation of the payment transaction.

(3) A payer or payment service user is not obliged to pay a charge of the type referred to in paragraph (1) or (2) if the payer or payment service user was not informed of the full amount of the charge in accordance with the relevant paragraph.

59. Burden of proof on payment service provider

Where a payment service provider is alleged to have failed to provide information in accordance with this Part, it is for the payment service provider to prove that it provided the information in accordance with this Part.

Other information requirements

60. Information requirements for account information service providers

(1) A registered account information service provider [. . .] must provide to the payment service user—

(a) such information specified in Schedule 4 (prior general information for framework contracts) as is relevant to the service provided;

(b) all charges payable by the payment service user to the account information service provider and, where applicable, a breakdown of those charges.

61. Information on ATM withdrawal charges

A provider of cash withdrawal services falling within paragraph 2(o) of Schedule 1 must ensure that a customer using such services is provided with information on withdrawal charges falling within regulations 43 (information required prior to the conclusion of a single payment service contract), 45 (information required after receipt of the payment order), 46 (information for the payee after execution) and 57 (currency and currency conversion), before the withdrawal and on receipt of the cash.

62. Provision of information leaflet

[(A1) The FCA must—

(a) produce a user-friendly electronic document listing in a clear and easily comprehensible manner the rights of consumers under these Regulations,

(b) make the document available in an easily accessible manner on its website, and

(c) inform associations of payment service providers and associations of consumers of its publication.]

(1) A payment service provider must make available free of charge in an easily accessible manner the document produced by the [FCA under paragraph (A1)]—

(a) in electronic form on its website (if any);

(b) in paper form at any branches and through any agent it uses or any entity to which activities are outsourced.

(3) Payment service providers and the FCA must also make the information contained in the document available by alternative means or in alternative formats so as to be accessible to persons with disabilities.

PART 7 RIGHTS AND OBLIGATIONS IN RELATION TO THE PROVISION OF PAYMENT SERVICES

Application

63. Application of Part 7

(1) This Part applies to payment services where—

(a) the services are provided from an establishment maintained by a payment service provider or its agent in the United Kingdom; and

(b) the services are provided in one of the following circumstances—

(i) the payment service providers of both the payer and the payee are located within [the United Kingdom] and the service relates to a transaction in [sterling];

[(ia) the payment service providers of both the payer and the payee are located within the qualifying area and the service relates to a transaction in euro executed under a payment scheme which operates across the qualifying area;]

(ii) the payment service providers of both the payer and the payee are located within [the United Kingdom] and the service relates to a transaction in a currency other than [sterling or euro]; or

(iii) the payment service provider of either the payer or the payee, but not both, is located within the [United Kingdom and the case does not fall within paragraph (ia)].

[(1A) In paragraph (1)(b)(ia)—

(a) 'payment service provider' includes any person who is a PSP as defined in Article 2(8B) of the SEPA regulation;

(b) 'the qualifying area' means the area of the United Kingdom and the EEA States.]

(2) In the circumstances mentioned at paragraph (1)(b)(ii)—

(a) this Part applies only in respect of those parts of a transaction which are carried out in the [United Kingdom]; and

(b) regulations 84 to 88 (amounts transferred and received and execution time) do not apply.

(3) In the circumstances mentioned at paragraph (1)(b)(iii)—

(a) this Part applies only in respect of those parts of a transaction which are carried out in the [United Kingdom]; and

(b) regulations 66(2) (responsibility for charges), 79 (refunds for direct debits), 80 (requests for direct debit refunds), 84 (amounts transferred and received), 86(1) to (3) (execution time for transactions to a payment account), 91 (defective execution of payer-initiated transactions), 92 (defective execution of payee-initiated transactions), 94 (liability for charges and interest) and 95 (right of recourse) do not apply.

(4) This Part does not apply to registered account information service providers [. . .], except for regulations 70 (access to payment accounts for account information services), 71(7) to (10) (denial of access to payment accounts), 72(3) (payment service user's obligation to keep personalised security credentials safe) and 98 to 100 (risk management, incident reporting, authentication and dispute resolution).

(5) Where the payment service user is not a consumer, a micro-enterprise or a charity, the payment service user and the payment service provider may agree that—

(a) any or all of regulations 66(1) (charges), 67(3) and (4) (withdrawal of consent), 75 (evidence on authentication and execution), 77 (payer or payee's liability for unauthorised transactions), 79 (refunds for direct debits), 80 (requests for direct debit refunds), 83 (revocation of a payment order), 91 (defective execution of payer-initiated transactions), 92 (defective execution of payee-initiated transactions) and 94 (liability for charges and interest) do not apply;

(b) a different time period applies for the purposes of regulation 74(1) (notification of unauthorised or incorrectly executed payment transactions).

64. Application of this Part in the case of consumer credit agreements

(1) This regulation applies where a payment service is provided in relation to payment transactions that consist of the placing, transferring or withdrawal of funds covered by a credit line provided under a regulated agreement.

(2) Regulation 71(2) to (5) (limits on the use of payment instruments) do not apply where section 98A(4) of the Consumer Credit Act 1974 (termination etc of open-end consumer credit agreements) applies.

(3) Regulations 76(1) to (4) and 77(1) to (5) (rectification of and liability for unauthorised transactions), and regulation 74 (notification and rectification of unauthorised or incorrectly executed payment transactions) as it applies in relation to regulation 76, do not apply.

(4) Regulations 76(5) and 77(6) apply as if—

    (a) in regulation 76(5), the references to an unauthorised payment transaction were to a payment transaction initiated by use of a credit facility in the circumstances described in section 83(1) of the Consumer Credit Act 1974 (liability for misuse of credit facilities);

    (b) the references to complying with regulation 76(1) were to compensating the payer for loss arising as described in section 83(1) of the Consumer Credit Act 1974.

65. Disapplication of certain regulations in the case of low value payment instruments

(1) This regulation applies in respect of payment instruments which, under the framework contract governing their use—

    (a) can be used only to execute individual payment transactions of 30 euros or less, or in relation to payment transactions executed wholly within the United Kingdom, 60 euros or less;

    (b) have a spending limit of 150 euros, or where payment transactions must be executed wholly within the United Kingdom, 300 euros; or

    (c) store funds that do not exceed 500 euros at any time.

(2) Where this regulation applies the parties may agree that—

    (a) regulations 72(1)(b) (obligation to notify loss or misuse of instrument), 73(1)(c), (d) and (e) (means of notifying loss) and 77(4) (payer not liable for certain losses) do not apply where the payment instrument does not allow for the stopping or prevention of its use;

    (b) regulations 75 (evidence on authentication and execution), 76 (payment service provider's liability for unauthorised transactions) and 77(1) and (2) (payer's liability for unauthorised transactions) do not apply where the payment instrument is used anonymously or the payment service provider is not in a position, for other reasons concerning the payment instrument, to prove that a payment transaction was authorised;

    (c) despite regulation 82(1) (refusal of payment orders), the payment service provider is not required to notify the payment service user of the refusal of a payment order if the non-execution is apparent from the context;

    (d) the payer may not revoke the payment order under regulation 83 after transmitting the payment order or giving their consent to execute the payment transaction to the payee;

    (e) execution periods other than those provided by regulations 86 (payment transactions to payment account) and 87 (absence of payment account) apply.

(3) Subject to paragraph (2)(b), regulations 76 (payment service provider's liability for unauthorised transactions) and 77(1) and (2) (payer's liability for unauthorised transactions) apply to electronic money unless the payer's payment service provider does not have the ability under the contract to—

    (a) freeze the payment account on which the electronic money is stored; or

    (b) stop the use of the payment instrument.

Charges

66. Charges

(1) The payment service provider may only charge the payment service user for the fulfilment of any of its obligations under this Part—

    (a) in accordance with regulation 82(3) (refusal of payment orders), 83(6) (revocation of a payment order) or 90(2)(b) (incorrect unique identifiers);

    (b) where agreed between the parties; and

    (c) where such charges reasonably correspond to the payment service provider's actual costs.

(2) Where both the payer's and the payee's payment service providers, or the only payment service provider, in respect of a payment transaction are within the [United Kingdom], the respective payment service providers must ensure that—

    (a) the payee pays any charges levied by the payee's payment service provider; and

    (b) the payer pays any charges levied by the payer's payment service provider.

[(2A) Where, in respect of payment transaction in euro executed under a payment scheme which operates across the qualifying area, both the payer's and the payee's payment service providers are, or the only payment service provider is, in the United Kingdom the respective payment service providers must ensure that—

    (a) the payee pays any charges levied by the payee's payment service provider; and

    (b) the payer pays any charges levied by the payer's payment service provider.]

(3) The payee's payment service provider may not prevent the payee from—

    (a) requesting payment of a charge by the payer for the use of a particular payment instrument;

    (b) offering a reduction to the payer for the use of a particular payment instrument; or

    (c) otherwise steering the payer towards the use of a particular payment instrument.

[(4) In paragraph (2A)—

    (a) 'payment service provider' includes any person who is a PSP as defined in Article 2(8B) of the SEPA regulation;

    (b) 'the qualifying area' means the area of the United Kingdom and the EEA States.]

Authorisation of payment transactions

67. Consent and withdrawal of consent

(1) A payment transaction is to be regarded as having been authorised by the payer for the purposes of this Part only if the payer has given its consent to—

    (a) the execution of the payment transaction; or

    (b) the execution of a series of payment transactions of which that payment transaction forms part.

(2) Such consent—

    (a) may be given before or, if agreed between the payer and its payment service provider, after the execution of the payment transaction;

    (b) must be given in the form, and in accordance with the procedure, agreed between the payer and its payment service provider; and

    (c) may be given via the payee or a payment initiation service provider.

(3) The payer may withdraw its consent to a payment transaction at any time before the point at which the payment order can no longer be revoked under regulation 83 (revocation of a payment order).

(4) Subject to regulation 83(3) to (5), the payer may withdraw its consent to the execution of a series of payment transactions at any time with the effect that any future payment transactions are not regarded as authorised for the purposes of this Part.

68.   Confirmation of availability of funds for card-based payment transactions

(1) This regulation does not apply to payment transactions initiated through card-based payment instruments on which electronic money is stored.

(2) Where the conditions in paragraph (3) are met, a payment service provider which issues card-based payment instruments may request that an account servicing payment service provider confirm whether an amount necessary for the execution of a card-based payment transaction is available on the payment account of the payer.

(3) The conditions are that—

(a) the payer has given explicit consent to the payment service provider to request the confirmation;

(b) the payer has initiated a payment transaction for the amount in question using a card-based payment instrument issued by the payment service provider making the request;

(c) the payment service provider making the request complies, for each request, with the authentication and secure communication requirements set out in the [technical standards made under regulation 106A] in its communications with the account servicing payment service provider.

(4) If the conditions in paragraph (5) are met, an account servicing payment service provider which receives a request under paragraph (2) must provide the requested confirmation, in the form of a 'yes' or 'no' answer, to the requesting payment service provider immediately.

(5) The conditions are that—

(a) the payment account is accessible online when the account servicing payment service provider receives the request; and

(b) before the account servicing payment service provider receives the first request under paragraph (2) from the requesting payment service provider in relation to the payer's payment account, the payer has given the account servicing payment service provider explicit consent to provide confirmation in response to such requests by that payment service provider.

(6) If the payer so requests, the account servicing payment service provider must also inform the payer of the payment service provider which made the request under paragraph (2) and the answer provided under paragraph (4).

(7) An account servicing payment service provider must not—

(a) include with a confirmation provided under paragraph (4) a statement of the account balance; or

(b) block funds on a payer's payment account as a result of a request under paragraph (2).

(8) The payment service provider which makes a request under paragraph (2) must not—

(a) store any confirmation received under paragraph (4); or

(b) use the confirmation received for a purpose other than the execution of the card-based payment transaction for which the request was made.

69.   Access to payment accounts for payment initiation services

(1) This regulation applies only in relation to a payment account which is accessible online.

(2) Where a payer gives explicit consent in accordance with regulation 67 (consent and withdrawal of consent) for a payment to be executed through a payment initiation service provider, the payer's account servicing payment service provider must—

(a) communicate securely with the payment initiation service provider in accordance with the [technical standards made under regulation 106A];

(b) immediately after receipt of the payment order from the payment initiation service provider, provide or make available to the payment initiation service provider all information on the initiation of the payment transaction and all information accessible to the account servicing payment service provider regarding the execution of the payment transaction;

    (c) treat the payment order in the same way as a payment order received directly from the payer, in particular in terms of timing, priority or charges, unless the account servicing payment service provider has objective reasons for treating the payment order differently;

    (d) not require the payment initiation service provider to enter into a contract before complying with the preceding sub-paragraphs.

  (3) A payment initiation service provider must—

    (a) not hold a payer's funds in connection with the provision of the payment initiation service at any time;

    (b) ensure that a payer's personalised security credentials are—

      (i) not accessible to other parties, with the exception of the issuer of the credentials; and

      (ii) transmitted through safe and efficient channels;

    (c) ensure that any other information about a payer is not provided to any person except a payee, and is provided to the payee only with the payer's explicit consent;

    (d) each time it initiates a payment order, identify itself to the account servicing payment service provider and communicate with the account servicing payment service provider, the payer and the payee in a secure way in accordance with the [technical standards made under regulation 106A];

    (e) not store sensitive payment data of the payment service user;

    (f) not request any information from a payer except information required to provide the payment initiation service;

    (g) not use, access or store any information for any purpose except for the provision of a payment initiation service explicitly requested by a payer;

    (h) not change the amount, the payee or any other feature of a transaction notified to it by the payer.

70. Access to payment accounts for account information services

  (1) This regulation applies only in relation to a payment account which is accessible online.

  (2) Where a payment service user uses an account information service, the payment service user's account servicing payment service provider must—

    (a) communicate securely with the account information service provider in accordance with the [technical standards made under regulation 106A];

    (b) treat a data request from the account information service provider in the same way as a data request received directly from the payer, unless the account servicing payment service provider has objective reasons for treating the request differently;

    (c) not require the account information service provider to enter into a contract before complying with the preceding sub-paragraphs.

  (3) An account information service provider must—

    (a) not provide account information services without the payment service user's explicit consent;

    (b) ensure that the payment service user's personalised security credentials are—

      (i) not accessible to other parties, with the exception of the issuer of the credentials; and

      (ii) transmitted through safe and efficient channels;

    (c) for each communication session, identify itself to the account servicing payment service provider and communicate securely with the account servicing payment service provider and the payment service user in accordance with the [technical standards made under regulation 106A];

    (d) not access any information other than information from designated payment accounts and associated payment transactions;

    (e) not request sensitive payment data linked to the payment accounts accessed;

    (f) not use, access or store any information for any purpose except for the provision of the account information service explicitly requested by the payment service user.

71. Limits on the use of payment instruments and access to payment accounts

(1) Where a specific payment instrument is used for the purpose of giving consent to the execution of a payment transaction, the payer and its payment service provider may agree on spending limits for any payment transactions executed through that payment instrument.

(2) A framework contract may provide for the payment service provider to have the right to stop the use of a payment instrument on reasonable grounds relating to—

(a) the security of the payment instrument;

(b) the suspected unauthorised or fraudulent use of the payment instrument; or

(c) in the case of a payment instrument with a credit line, a significantly increased risk that the payer may be unable to fulfil its liability to pay.

(3) The payment service provider must, in the manner agreed between the payment service provider and the payer and before carrying out any measures to stop the use of the payment instrument—

(a) inform the payer that it intends to stop the use of the payment instrument; and

(b) give its reasons for doing so.

(4) Where the payment service provider is unable to inform the payer in accordance with paragraph (3) before carrying out any measures to stop the use of the payment instrument, it must do so immediately after.

(5) Paragraphs (3) and (4) do not apply where provision of the information in accordance with paragraph (3) would compromise reasonable security measures or is otherwise unlawful.

(6) The payment service provider must allow the use of the payment instrument or replace it with a new payment instrument as soon as practicable after the reasons for stopping its use cease to exist.

(7) An account servicing payment service provider may deny an account information service provider or a payment initiation service provider access to a payment account for reasonably justified and duly evidenced reasons relating to unauthorised or fraudulent access to the payment account by that account information service provider or payment initiation service provider, including the unauthorised or fraudulent initiation of a payment transaction.

(8) If an account servicing payment service provider denies access to a payment account under paragraph (7)—

(a) the account servicing payment service provider must notify the payment service user of the denial of access and the reason for the denial of access, in the form agreed with the payment service user;

(b) the notification under sub-paragraph (a) must be provided before the denial of access if possible, or otherwise immediately after the denial of access;

(c) the account servicing payment service provider must immediately report the incident to the FCA in such form as the FCA may direct, and such report must include the details of the case and the reasons for taking action;

(d) the account servicing payment service provider must restore access to the account once the reasons for denying access no longer justify such denial of access.

(9) Paragraph (8)(a) and (b) do not apply if notifying the payment service user—

(a) would compromise reasonably justified security reasons; or

(b) is unlawful.

(10) When the FCA receives a report under paragraph (8)(c), it must assess the case and take such measures as it considers appropriate.

72. Obligations of the payment service user in relation to payment instruments and personalised security credentials

(1) A payment service user to whom a payment instrument has been issued must—

(a) use the payment instrument in accordance with the terms and conditions governing its issue and use; and

(b) notify the payment service provider in the agreed manner and without undue delay on becoming aware of the loss, theft, misappropriation or unauthorised use of the payment instrument.

(2) Paragraph (1)(a) applies only in relation to terms and conditions that are objective, non-discriminatory and proportionate.

(3) The payment service user must take all reasonable steps to keep safe personalised security credentials relating to a payment instrument or an account information service.

73. Obligations of the payment service provider in relation to payment instruments

(1) A payment service provider issuing a payment instrument must—

(a) ensure that the personalised security credentials are not accessible to persons other than the payment service user to whom the payment instrument has been issued;

(b) not send an unsolicited payment instrument, except where a payment instrument already issued to a payment service user is to be replaced;

(c) ensure that appropriate means are available at all times to enable the payment service user to notify the payment service provider in accordance with regulation 72(1)(b) (notification of loss or unauthorised use of payment instrument) or to request that, in accordance with regulation 71(6), the use of the payment instrument is no longer stopped;

(d) on request, provide the payment service user at any time during a period of 18 months after the alleged date of notification under regulation 72(1)(b) with the means to prove that such notification to the payment service provider was made;

(e) provide the payment service user with an option to make a notification under regulation 72(1)(b) free of charge, and ensure that any costs charged are directly attributed to the replacement of the payment instrument;

(f) prevent any use of the payment instrument once notification has been made under regulation 72(1)(b).

(2) The payment service provider bears the risk of sending to the payment service user a payment instrument or any personalised security credentials relating to it.

74. Notification and rectification of unauthorised or incorrectly executed payment transactions

(1) A payment service user is entitled to redress under regulation 76, 91, 92, 93 or 94 (liability for unauthorised transactions, non-execution or defective or late execution of transactions, or charges and interest), only if it notifies the payment service provider without undue delay, and in any event no later than 13 months after the debit date, on becoming aware of any unauthorised or incorrectly executed payment transaction.

(2) Where the payment service provider has failed to provide or make available information concerning the payment transaction in accordance with Part 6 of these Regulations (information requirements for payment services), the payment service user is entitled to redress under the regulations referred to in paragraph (1) notwithstanding that the payment service user has failed to notify the payment service provider as mentioned in that paragraph.

75. Evidence on authentication and execution of payment transactions

(1) Where a payment service user—

(a) denies having authorised an executed payment transaction; or

(b) claims that a payment transaction has not been correctly executed,

it is for the payment service provider to prove that the payment transaction was authenticated, accurately recorded, entered in the payment service provider's accounts and not affected by a technical breakdown or some other deficiency in the service provided by the payment service provider.

(2) If a payment transaction was initiated through a payment initiation service provider, it is for the payment initiation service provider to prove that, within its sphere of competence, the payment transaction was authenticated, accurately recorded and not affected by a technical breakdown or other deficiency linked to the payment initiation service.

(3) Where a payment service user denies having authorised an executed payment transaction, the use of a payment instrument recorded by the payment service provider, including a payment initiation service provider where appropriate, is not in itself necessarily sufficient to prove either that—

    (a) the payment transaction was authorised by the payer; or

    (b) the payer acted fraudulently or failed with intent or gross negligence to comply with regulation 72 (user's obligations in relation to payment instruments and personalised security credentials).

(4) If a payment service provider, including a payment initiation service provider where appropriate, claims that a payer acted fraudulently or failed with intent or gross negligence to comply with regulation 72, the payment service provider must provide supporting evidence to the payer.

76. Payment service provider's liability for unauthorised payment transactions

(1) Subject to regulations 74 and 75, where an executed payment transaction was not authorised in accordance with regulation 67 (consent and withdrawal of consent), the payment service provider must—

    (a) refund the amount of the unauthorised payment transaction to the payer; and

    (b) where applicable, restore the debited payment account to the state it would have been in had the unauthorised payment transaction not taken place.

(2) The payment service provider must provide a refund under paragraph (1)(a) as soon as practicable, and in any event no later than the end of the business day following the day on which it becomes aware of the unauthorised transaction.

(3) Paragraph (2) does not apply where the payment service provider has reasonable grounds to suspect fraudulent behaviour by the payment service user and notifies a person mentioned in section 333A(2) of the Proceeds of Crime Act 2002 (tipping off: regulated sector) of those grounds in writing.

(4) When crediting a payment account under paragraph (1)(b), a payment service provider must ensure that the credit value date is no later than the date on which the amount of the unauthorised payment transaction was debited.

(5) Where an unauthorised payment transaction was initiated through a payment initiation service provider—

    (a) the account servicing payment service provider must comply with paragraph (1);

    (b) if the payment initiation service provider is liable for the unauthorised payment transaction (in relation to which see regulation 75(2)) the payment initiation service provider must, on the request of the account servicing payment service provider, compensate the account servicing payment service provider immediately for the losses incurred or sums paid as a result of complying with paragraph (1), including the amount of the unauthorised transaction.

77. Payer or payee's liability for unauthorised payment transactions

(1) Subject to paragraphs (2), (3) and (4), a payment service provider which is liable under regulation 76(1) may require that the payer is liable up to a maximum of £35 for any losses incurred in respect of unauthorised payment transactions arising from the use of a lost or stolen payment instrument, or from the misappropriation of a payment instrument.

(2) Paragraph (1) does not apply if—

    (a) the loss, theft or misappropriation of the payment instrument was not detectable by the payer prior to the payment, except where the payer acted fraudulently; or

    (b) the loss was caused by acts or omissions of an employee, agent or branch of a payment service provider or of an entity which carried out activities on behalf of the payment service provider.

(3) The payer is liable for all losses incurred in respect of an unauthorised payment transaction where the payer—

(a) has acted fraudulently; or

(b) has with intent or gross negligence failed to comply with regulation 72 (obligations of the payment service user in relation to payment instruments and personalised security credentials).

(4) Except where the payer has acted fraudulently, the payer is not liable for any losses incurred in respect of an unauthorised payment transaction—

(a) arising after notification under regulation 72(1)(b);

(b) where the payment service provider has failed at any time to provide, in accordance with regulation 73(1)(c) (obligations of the payment service provider in relation to payment instruments), appropriate means for notification;

(c) where regulation 100 (authentication) requires the application of strong customer authentication, but the payer's payment service provider does not require strong customer authentication; or

(d) where the payment instrument has been used in connection with a distance contract (other than an excepted contract).

(5) In paragraph (4)(d)—

'distance contract' means a distance contract as defined by regulation 5 of the Consumer Contracts (Information, Cancellation and Additional Charges) Regulations 2013 (other definitions);

'excepted contract' means a contract that—

(a) falls to any extent within regulation 6(1) of those Regulations (limits of application: general); or

(b) falls within regulation 6(2) of those Regulations.

(6) Where regulation 100 requires the application of strong customer authentication, but the payee or the payee's payment service provider does not accept strong customer authentication, the payee or the payee's payment service provider, or both (as the case may be), must compensate the payer's payment service provider for the losses incurred or sums paid as a result of complying with regulation 76(1).

78. Payment transactions where the transaction amount is not known in advance

Where a card-based payment transaction is initiated by or through the payee and the amount of the transaction is not known when the payer authorises the transaction—

(a) the payer's payment service provider may not block funds on the payer's payment account unless the payer has authorised the exact amount of the funds to be blocked; and

(b) the payer's payment service provider must release the blocked funds without undue delay after becoming aware of the amount of the payment transaction, and in any event immediately after receipt of the payment order.

79. Refunds for payment transactions initiated by or through a payee

(1) Where the conditions in paragraph (2) and the requirement in regulation 80(1) are satisfied, the payer is entitled to a refund from its payment service provider of the full amount of any authorised payment transaction initiated by or through the payee.

(2) The conditions are that—

(a) the authorisation did not specify the exact amount of the payment transaction when the authorisation was given in accordance with regulation 67 (consent and withdrawal of consent); and

(b) the amount of the payment transaction exceeded the amount that the payer could reasonably have expected taking into account the payer's previous spending pattern, the conditions of the framework contract and the circumstances of the case.

(3) The payer is entitled to an unconditional refund from its payment service provider of the full amount of any direct debit transactions of the type referred to in Article 1 of Regulation (EU) 260/2012 of the European Parliament and of the Council of 14th March 2012 establishing technical and business requirements for credit transfers and direct debits in euro and amending Regulation (EC) No 924/2009.

(4) When crediting a payment account under paragraph (1), a payment service provider must ensure that the credit value date is no later than the date on which the amount of the unauthorised payment transaction was debited.

(5) For the purposes of paragraph (2)(b), the payer cannot rely on currency exchange fluctuations where the reference exchange rate provided under regulation 43(2)(d) or paragraph 3(b) of Schedule 4 was applied.

(6) The payer and payment service provider may agree in the framework contract that the right to a refund does not apply where—

    (a) the payer has given consent directly to the payment service provider for the payment transaction to be executed; and

    (b) if applicable, information on the payment transaction was provided or made available in an agreed manner to the payer for at least four weeks before the due date by the payment service provider or by the payee.

80. Requests for refunds for payment transactions initiated by or through a payee

(1) The payer must request a refund under regulation 79 from its payment service provider within 8 weeks from the date on which the funds were debited.

(2) The payment service provider may require the payer to provide such information as is reasonably necessary to prove that the conditions in regulation 79(2) are satisfied.

(3) The payment service provider must either—

    (a) refund the full amount of the payment transaction; or

    (b) provide justification for refusing to refund the payment transaction, indicating the bodies to which the payer may refer the matter if the payer does not accept the justification provided.

(4) Any refund or justification for refusing a refund must be provided within 10 business days of receiving a request for a refund or, where applicable, within 10 business days of receiving any further information requested under paragraph (2).

(5) If the payment service provider requires further information under paragraph (2), it may not refuse the refund until it has received further information from the payer.

Execution of payment transactions

81. Receipt of payment orders

(1) A payer's payment service provider must not debit the payment account before receipt of a payment order.

(2) Subject to paragraphs (3) to (6), for the purposes of these Regulations the time of receipt of a payment order is the time at which the payment order is received by the payer's payment service provider.

(3) If the time of receipt of a payment order does not fall on a business day for the payer's payment service provider, the payment order is deemed to have been received on the first business day thereafter.

(4) The payment service provider may set a time towards the end of a business day after which any payment order received will be deemed to have been received on the following business day.

(5) Where the payment service user initiating a payment order agrees with its payment service provider that execution of the payment order is to take place—

    (a) on a specific day;

    (b) on the last day of a certain period; or

    (c) on the day on which the payer has put funds at the disposal of its payment service provider,

the time of receipt is deemed to be the day so agreed.

(6) If the day agreed under paragraph (5) is not a business day for the payer's payment service provider, the payment order is deemed to have been received on the first business day thereafter.

82. Refusal of payment orders

(1) Subject to paragraph (4), where a payment service provider refuses to execute a payment order or to initiate a payment transaction, it must notify the payment service user of—

   (a) the refusal;

   (b) if possible, the reasons for such refusal; and

   (c) where it is possible to provide reasons for the refusal and those reasons relate to factual matters, the procedure for rectifying any factual errors that led to the refusal.

(2) Any notification under paragraph (1) must be given or made available in an agreed manner and at the earliest opportunity, and in any event within the periods specified in regulation 86.

(3) The framework contract may provide for the payment service provider to charge the payment service user for such refusal where the refusal is reasonably justified.

(4) The payment service provider is not required to notify the payment service user under paragraph (1) where such notification would be otherwise unlawful.

(5) Where all the conditions set out in the payer's framework contract with the account servicing payment service provider have been satisfied, the account servicing payment service provider may not refuse to execute an authorised payment order irrespective of whether the payment order is initiated by the payer, through a payment initiation service provider, or by or through a payee, unless such execution is otherwise unlawful.

(6) For the purposes of regulations 86, 91 and 92 (payment transactions to a payment account and non-execution or defective or late execution of a payment transaction) a payment order of which execution has been refused is deemed not to have been received.

83. Revocation of a payment order

(1) Subject to paragraphs (2) to (5), a payment service user may not revoke a payment order after it has been received by the payer's payment service provider.

(2) In the case of a payment transaction initiated by a payment initiation service provider, or by or through the payee, the payer may not revoke the payment order after giving consent to the payment initiation service provider to initiate the payment transaction or giving consent to execute the payment transaction to the payee.

(3) In the case of a direct debit, the payer may not revoke the payment order after the end of the business day preceding the day agreed for debiting the funds.

(4) Where a day is agreed under regulation 81(5) (receipt of payment orders), the payment service user may not revoke a payment order after the end of the business day preceding the agreed day.

(5) At any time after the time limits for revocation set out in paragraphs (1) to (4), the payment order may only be revoked if the revocation is—

   (a) agreed between the payment service user and the relevant payment service provider or providers; and

   (b) in the case of a payment transaction initiated by or through the payee, including in the case of a direct debit, also agreed with the payee.

(6) A framework contract may provide for the relevant payment service provider to charge for revocation under this regulation.

84. Amounts transferred and amounts received

(1) Subject to paragraph (2), the payment service providers of the payer and payee must ensure that the full amount of the payment transaction is transferred and that no charges are deducted from the amount transferred.

(2) The payee and its payment service provider may agree for the relevant payment service provider to deduct its charges from the amount transferred before crediting it to the payee provided that the full amount of the payment transaction and the amount of the charges are clearly stated in the information provided to the payee.

(3) If charges other than those provided for by paragraph (2) are deducted from the amount transferred—

(a) in the case of a payment transaction initiated by the payer, the payer's payment service provider must ensure that the payee receives the full amount of the payment transaction;

(b) in the case of a payment transaction initiated by the payee, the payee's payment service provider must ensure that the payee receives the full amount of the payment transaction.

Execution time and value date

85. Application of regulations 86 to 88

(1) Regulations 86 to 88 apply to any payment transaction—

[(a) executed wholly within the qualifying area in euro under a payment scheme which operates across the qualifying area];

(b) executed wholly within the United Kingdom in sterling; or

(c) [executed wholly under a payment scheme which operates across the qualifying area and] involving only one currency conversion between the euro and sterling, provided that—

(i) the currency conversion is carried out in the United Kingdom; and

(ii) in the case of cross-border payment transactions, the cross-border transfer takes place in euro.

(2) In respect of any other payment transaction, the payment service user may agree with the payment service provider that regulations 86 to 88 (except regulation 86(3)) do not apply.

[(3) In paragraph (1), 'the qualifying area' means the area of the United Kingdom and the EEA States.]

86. Payment transactions to a payment account

(1) Subject to paragraphs (2) and (3), the payer's payment service provider must ensure that the amount of the payment transaction is credited to the payee's payment service provider's account by the end of the business day following the time of receipt of the payment order.

(2) Where a payment transaction is initiated by way of a paper payment order the reference in paragraph (1) to the end of the business day following the time of receipt of the payment order is to be treated as a reference to the end of the second business day following the time of receipt of the payment order.

(3) Where a payment transaction—

(a) does not fall within paragraphs (a) to (c) of regulation 85(1); but

(b) is to be executed wholly within the [United Kingdom],

the payer's payment service provider must ensure that the amount of the payment transaction is credited to the payee's payment service provider's account by the end of the fourth business day following the time of receipt of the payment order.

(4) The payee's payment service provider must value date and credit the amount of the payment transaction to the payee's payment account following its receipt of the funds.

(5) The payee's payment service provider must transmit a payment order initiated by or through the payee to the payer's payment service provider within the time limits agreed between the payee and its payment service provider, enabling settlement in respect of a direct debit to occur on the agreed due date.

87. Absence of payee's payment account with the payment service provider

(1) Paragraph (2) applies where a payment service provider accepts funds on behalf of a payee who does not have a payment account with that payment service provider.

(2) The payment service provider must make the funds available to the payee immediately after the funds have been credited to that payment service provider's account.

88. Cash placed on a payment account

Where a payment service user places cash on its payment account with a payment service provider in the same currency as that payment account, the payment service provider must—

(a) if the user is a consumer, micro-enterprise or charity, ensure that the amount is made available and value dated immediately after the receipt of the funds;

(b) in any other case, ensure that the amount is made available and value dated no later than the end of the next business day after the receipt of the funds.

89. Value date and availability of funds

(1) The credit value date for the payee's payment account must be no later than the business day on which the amount of the payment transaction is credited to the account of the payee's payment service provider.

(2) Paragraph (3) applies where—

(a) the transaction does not involve a currency conversion [by the payee's payment service provider];

(b) the transaction involves [a currency conversion by the payee's payment service provider] between the euro and pounds sterling [. . .]; or

(c) the transaction involves only one payment service provider.

(3) The payee's payment service provider must ensure that the amount of the payment transaction is at the payee's disposal immediately after that amount has been credited to that payment service provider's account.

(4) The debit value date for the payer's payment account must be no earlier than the time at which the amount of the payment transaction is debited to that payment account.

Liability

90. Incorrect unique identifiers

(1) Where a payment order is executed in accordance with the unique identifier, the payment order is deemed to have been correctly executed by each payment service provider involved in executing the payment order with respect to the payee specified by the unique identifier.

(2) Where the unique identifier provided by the payment service user is incorrect, the payment service provider is not liable under regulation 91 or 92 for non-execution or defective execution of the payment transaction, but the payment service provider—

(a) must make reasonable efforts to recover the funds involved in the payment transaction; and

(b) may, if agreed in the framework contract, charge the payment service user for any such recovery.

(3) The payee's payment service provider must co-operate with the payer's payment service provider in its efforts to recover the funds, in particular by providing to the payer's payment service provider all relevant information for the collection of funds.

(4) If the payer's payment service provider is unable to recover the funds it must, on receipt of a written request, provide to the payer all available relevant information in order for the payer to claim repayment of the funds.

(5) Where the payment service user provides information additional to that specified in regulation 43(2)(a) (information required prior to the conclusion of a single payment service contract) or paragraph 2(b) of Schedule 4 (prior general information for framework contracts), the payment service provider is liable only for the execution of payment transactions in accordance with the unique identifier provided by the payment service user.

91. Non-execution or defective or late execution of payment transactions initiated by the payer

(1) This regulation applies where a payment order is initiated directly by the payer.

(2) The payer's payment service provider is liable to the payer for the correct execution of the payment transaction unless it can prove to the payer and, where relevant, to the payee's payment service provider, that the payee's payment service provider received the amount of the payment transaction in accordance with regulation 86(1) to (3) (payment transactions to a payment account).

(3) Where the payer's payment service provider is liable under paragraph (2), it must without undue delay refund to the payer the amount of the non-executed or defective payment transaction

and, where applicable, restore the debited payment account to the state in which it would have been had the defective payment transaction not taken place.

(4) The credit value date for a credit under paragraph (3) must be no later than the date on which the amount was debited.

(5) If the payer's payment service provider proves that the payee's payment service provider received the amount of the payment transaction in accordance with regulation 86, the payee's payment service provider is liable to the payee for the correct execution of the payment transaction and must—

   (a) immediately make available the amount of the payment transaction to the payee; and

   (b) where applicable, credit the corresponding amount to the payee's payment account.

(6) The credit value date for a credit under paragraph (5)(b) must be no later than the date on which the amount would have been value dated if the transaction had been executed correctly.

(7) Where a payment transaction is executed late, the payee's payment service provider must, on receipt of a request from the payer's payment service provider on behalf of the payer, ensure that the credit value date for the payee's payment account is no later than the date the amount would have been value dated if the transaction had been executed correctly.

(8) Regardless of liability under this regulation, the payer's payment service provider must, on request by the payer, immediately and without charge—

   (a) make efforts to trace any non-executed or defectively executed payment transaction; and

   (b) notify the payer of the outcome.

92.   Non-execution or defective or late execution of payment transactions initiated by the payee

(1) This regulation applies where a payment order is initiated by the payee.

(2) The payee's payment service provider is liable to the payee for the correct transmission of the payment order to the payer's payment service provider in accordance with regulation 86(5) (payment transactions to a payment account).

(3) Where the payee's payment service provider is liable under paragraph (2), it must immediately re-transmit the payment order in question to the payer's payment service provider.

(4) The payee's payment service provider must also ensure that the transaction is handled in accordance with regulation 89 (value date and availability of funds), such that the amount of the transaction—

   (a) is at the payee's disposal immediately after it is credited to the payee's payment service provider's account; and

   (b) is value dated on the payee's payment account no later than the date the amount would have been value dated if the transaction had been executed correctly.

(5) The payee's payment service provider must, on request by the payee and free of charge, make immediate efforts to trace the payment transaction and notify the payee of the outcome.

(6) Subject to paragraph (8), if the payee's payment service provider proves to the payee and, where relevant, to the payer's payment service provider, that it is not liable under paragraph (2) in respect of a non-executed or defectively executed payment transaction, the payer's payment service provider is liable to the payer and must, as appropriate and immediately—

   (a) refund to the payer the amount of the payment transaction; and

   (b) restore the debited payment account to the state in which it would have been had the defective payment transaction not taken place.

(7) The credit value date for a credit under paragraph (6)(b) must be no later than the date on which the amount was debited.

(8) If the payer's payment service provider proves that the payee's service provider has received the amount of the payment transaction, paragraph (6) does not apply and the payee's payment service provider must value date the amount on the payee's payment account no later than the date the amount would have been value dated if the transaction had been executed correctly.

93. Non-execution or defective or late execution of payment transactions initiated through a payment initiation service

(1) This regulation applies where a payment order is initiated by the payer through a payment initiation service.

(2) The account servicing payment service provider must refund to the payer the amount of the non-executed or defective payment transaction and, where applicable, restore the debited payment account to the state in which it would have been had the defective payment transaction not taken place.

(3) Paragraph (4) applies if the payment initiation service provider does not prove to the account servicing payment service provider that—

(a) the payment order was received by the payer's account servicing payment service provider in accordance with regulation 81 (receipt of payment orders); and

(b) within the payment initiation service provider's sphere of influence the payment transaction was authenticated, accurately recorded and not affected by a technical breakdown or other deficiency linked to the non-execution, defective or late execution of the transaction.

(4) On request from the account servicing payment service provider, the payment initiation service provider must immediately compensate the account servicing payment service provider for the losses incurred or sums paid as a result of the refund to the payer.

94. Liability of payment service provider for charges and interest

A payment service provider is liable to its payment service user for—

(a) any charges for which the payment service user is responsible; and

(b) any interest which the payment service user must pay,

as a consequence of the non-execution or defective or late execution of the payment transaction.

95. Right of recourse

Where the liability of a payment service provider ('the first provider') under regulation 76, 91, 92 or 93 (payment service providers' liability for unauthorised or defective payment transactions) is attributable to another payment service provider or an intermediary, including where there is a failure to use strong customer authentication as required by regulation 100 (authentication), the other payment service provider or intermediary must compensate the first provider for any losses incurred or sums paid pursuant to those regulations.

96. Force majeure

(1) A person is not liable for any contravention of a requirement imposed on it by or under this Part where the contravention is due to abnormal and unforeseeable circumstances beyond the person's control, the consequences of which would have been unavoidable despite all efforts to the contrary.

(2) A payment service provider is not liable for any contravention of a requirement imposed on it by or under this Part where the contravention is due to the obligations of the payment service provider under other provisions of [. . .] national law.

Miscellaneous

97. Consent for use of personal data

A payment service provider must not access, process or retain any personal data for the provision of payment services by it, unless it has the explicit consent of the payment service user to do so.

98. Management of operational and security risks

(1) Each payment service provider must establish a framework with appropriate mitigation measures and control mechanisms to manage the operational and security risks, relating to the payment services it provides. As part of that framework, the payment service provider must establish and maintain effective incident management procedures, including for the detection and classification of major operational and security incidents.

(2) Each payment service provider must provide to the FCA an updated and comprehensive assessment of the operational and security risks relating to the payment services it provides and on the adequacy of the mitigation measures and control mechanisms implemented in response to those risks.

(3) Such assessment must—

(a) be provided on an annual basis, or at such shorter intervals as the FCA may direct; and

(b) be provided in such form and manner, and contain such information, as the FCA may direct.

99. Incident reporting

(1) If a payment service provider becomes aware of a major operational or security incident, the payment service provider must, without undue delay, notify the FCA.

(2) A notification under paragraph (1) must be in such form and manner, and contain such information, as the FCA may direct.

(3) If the incident has or may have an impact on the financial interests of its payment service users, the payment service provider must, without undue delay, inform its payment service users of the incident and of all measures that they can take to mitigate the adverse effects of the incident.

(4) Upon receipt of the notification referred to in paragraph (1), the FCA [must notify any other relevant authorities in the United Kingdom].

100. Authentication

(1) A payment service provider must apply strong customer authentication where a payment service user—

(a) accesses its payment account online, whether directly or through an account information service provider;

(b) initiates an electronic payment transaction; or

(c) carries out any action through a remote channel which may imply a risk of payment fraud or other abuses.

(2) Where a payer initiates an electronic remote payment transaction directly or through a payment initiation service provider, the payment service provider must apply strong customer authentication that includes elements which dynamically link the transaction to a specific amount and a specific payee.

(3) A payment service provider must maintain adequate security measures to protect the confidentiality and integrity of payment service users' personalised security credentials.

(4) An account servicing payment service provider must allow a payment initiation service provider or account information service provider to rely on the authentication procedures provided by the account servicing payment service provider to a payment service user in accordance with the preceding paragraphs of this regulation.

(5) Paragraphs (1), (2) and (3) are subject to any exemptions from the requirements in those paragraphs provided for in [. . .] technical standards [made under regulation 106A].

101. Dispute resolution

(1) This regulation applies in relation to complaints from payment service users who are not eligible within the meaning of section 226(6) of the 2000 Act (the ombudsman scheme—compulsory jurisdiction).

(2) A payment service provider must put in place and apply adequate and effective complaint resolution procedures for the settlement of complaints from payment service users about the rights and obligations arising under Parts 6 and 7.

(4) When a payment service provider receives a complaint from a payment service user, the payment service provider must make every possible effort to address all points raised in a reply to the complaint on paper or, if agreed between payment service provider and payment service user, in another durable medium.

(5) Subject to paragraph (6), the reply must be provided to the complainant within an adequate timeframe and at the latest 15 business days after the day on which the payment service provider received the complaint.

(6) In exceptional situations, if a full reply cannot be given in accordance with paragraph (4) for reasons beyond the control of the payment service provider, the payment service provider must send a holding reply, clearly indicating the reasons for the delay in providing a full reply to the complaint and specifying the deadline by which the payment service user will receive a full reply.

(7) The deadline specified under paragraph (6) must not be later than 35 business days after the day on which the payment service provider received the complaint.

(8) The payment service provider must inform the payment service user about the details of one or more providers of dispute resolution services able to deal with disputes concerning the rights and obligations arising under this Part and Part 6 (information requirements for payment services), if the payment service provider uses such services.

(9) The payment service provider must also make available in a clear, comprehensive and easily accessible way—

(a) the information referred to in paragraph (7); and

(b) details of how to access further information about any provider of dispute resolution services referred to in paragraph (8) and the conditions for using such services.

(10) The information to be made available under paragraph (8) must be made available—

(a) on the website of the payment service provider (if any);

(b) at branches of the payment service provider (if any); and

(c) in the general terms and conditions of the contract between the payment service provider and the payment service user.

PART 8 ACCESS TO PAYMENT SYSTEMS AND BANK ACCOUNTS

102. Application of regulation 103

(1) Regulation 103 does not apply to the following kinds of payment systems—

(a) a designated system;

(b) a payment system consisting solely of payment service providers belonging to the same group.

103. Prohibition on restrictive rules on access to payment systems

(1) Rules or conditions governing access to, or participation in, a payment system by authorised or registered payment service providers must—

(a) be objective, proportionate and non-discriminatory; and

(b) not prevent, restrict or inhibit access or participation more than is necessary to—

(i) safeguard against specific risks such as settlement risk, operational risk or business risk; or

(ii) protect the financial and operational stability of the payment system.

(2) Paragraph (1) applies only to such payment service providers as are legal persons.

(3) Rules or conditions governing access to, or participation in, a payment system must not, in respect of payment service providers, payment service users or other payment systems—

(a) restrict effective participation in other payment systems;

(b) discriminate (whether directly or indirectly) between

(i) different authorised payment service providers; or

(ii) different registered payment service providers;

in relation to the rights, obligations or entitlements of participants in the payment system; or

(c) impose any restrictions on the basis of institutional status.

104. Indirect access to designated systems

(1) This regulation applies where a participant in a designated system allows an authorised or registered payment service provider that is not a participant in the system to pass transfer orders through the system.

(2) The participant—

    (a) must treat a request by another authorised or registered payment service provider to pass transfer orders through the system in an objective, proportionate and non-discriminatory manner; and

    (b) must not—

        (i) prevent, restrict or inhibit access to or participation in the system more than is necessary to safeguard against specific risks such as settlement risk, operational risk or business risk, or to protect the financial and operational stability of the participant or the payment system;

        (ii) discriminate (whether directly or indirectly) between different authorised payment service providers or different registered payment service providers in relation to the rights, obligations or entitlements of such providers in relation to access to or participation in the system; or

        (iii) impose any restrictions on the basis of institutional status.

(3) If the participant refuses such a request, it must provide full reasons for the refusal to the payment service provider which made the request.

105.   Access to bank accounts

(1) A credit institution must—

    (a) grant payment service providers of the types referred to in paragraphs (a) to (f) of the definition of 'payment service provider' in regulation 2(1), and applicants for authorisation or registration as such payment service providers, access to payment accounts services on an objective, non-discriminatory and proportionate basis;

    (b) when a payment service provider of a type mentioned in sub-paragraph (a) enquires about such access, include in the response to the enquiry the criteria that the credit institution applies when considering requests for such access; and

    (c) maintain arrangements to ensure that those criteria are applied in a manner which ensures compliance with sub-paragraph (a).

(2) Access to payment accounts services granted to a payment service provider pursuant to paragraph (1) must be sufficiently extensive to allow the payment service provider to provide payment services in an unhindered and efficient manner.

(3) If a credit institution refuses a request for access to such services from a payment service provider of the types mentioned in paragraph (1)(a), or withdraws access to such services for such a payment service provider, it must notify the FCA.

(4) A notification under paragraph (3) must—

    (a) contain duly motivated reasons for the refusal or the withdrawal of access; and

    (b) contain such information, and be provided in such form and manner and within such period following the refusal or withdrawal of access, as the FCA may direct.

(5) The FCA must provide the reasons received under paragraph (4) to the Payment Systems Regulator, unless the Payment Systems Regulator informs the FCA that it does not wish to receive them.

PART 9   THE FINANCIAL CONDUCT AUTHORITY

106.   Functions of the FCA

(1) The FCA [. . .] has the functions and powers conferred on it by these Regulations.

(3) In determining the general policy and principles by reference to which it performs particular functions under these Regulations [. . .] the FCA must have regard to—

    (a) the need to use its resources in the most efficient and economic way;

    (b) the principle that a burden or restriction which is imposed on a person, or on the carrying on of an activity, should be proportionate to the benefits, considered in general terms, which are expected to result from the imposition of that burden or restriction;

    (c) the desirability of sustainable growth in the economy of the United Kingdom in the medium or long term;

    (d) the general principle that consumers should take responsibility for their own decisions;

    (e) the responsibilities of those who manage the affairs of persons subject to requirements imposed by or under these Regulations, including those affecting consumers, in relation to compliance with those requirements;

    (f) the desirability where appropriate of the FCA exercising its functions in a way that recognises differences in the nature of, and objectives of, businesses carried on by different persons subject to requirements imposed by or under these Regulations;

    (g) the desirability in appropriate cases of the FCA publishing information in relation to persons on whom requirements are imposed by or under these Regulations;

    (h) the principle that the FCA should exercise its functions as transparently as possible.

[106A. Technical standards

(1) The FCA may make technical standards specifying—

    (a) requirements that must be met by the strong customer authentication referred to in regulation 100(1) and (2);

    (b) exemptions from the application of regulation 100(1), (2) and (3), based on the criteria specified in paragraph (3) of this regulation;

    (c) the requirements with which security measures have to comply, in accordance with regulation 100(3), in order to protect the confidentiality and integrity of the payment service users' personalised security credentials;

    (d) the requirements for common and secure open standards of communication for the purpose of identification, authentication, notification and information, as well as for the implementation of security measures, between account servicing payment service providers, payment initiation service providers, account information service providers, payers, payees and other payment service providers.

(2) In making technical standards under this regulation, the FCA must have regard to the need to—

    (a) ensure an appropriate level of security for payment service users and payment service providers through the adoption of effective and risk-based requirements;

    (b) ensure the safety of payment service users' funds and personal data;

    (c) secure and maintain fair competition among all payment service providers;

    (d) ensure technology and business-model neutrality;

    (e) allow for the development of user-friendly, accessible and innovative means of payment.

(3) The exemptions referred to in paragraph (1)(b) must be based on—

    (a) the level of risk involved in the service provided;

    (b) the amount of the transaction, its recurrence, or both;

    (c) the payment channel used for the execution of the transaction.

(4) The FCA must review and, if appropriate, update the technical standards on a regular basis in order (among other things) to take account of innovation and technological developments.

(5) Section 138P of the 2000 Act contains provision about the making of technical standards by the FCA.]

107. Application of this Part to requirements of [retained direct EU legislation] and FCA rules

For the purposes of this Part, including the legislation applied by regulation 122 and Schedule 6, but with the exception of regulation 119 and Schedule 5 (credit agreements)—

    (a) the requirements imposed on payment service providers by Articles 8(2), 9(2) and 12 of the interchange fee regulation are to be treated as if they were included in Part 5 of these Regulations (requirements for providers of certain services which are not payment services);

    (b) the requirements imposed on payment service providers by Articles 8(5) and (6), 9(1), 10(1) and (5) and 11 of the interchange fee regulation are to be treated as if they were included in Part 6 of these Regulations (information requirements for payment services); and

(c) requirements imposed on payment service providers by or under [retained direct EU legislation] adopted under the payment services directive, or by rules made by the FCA pursuant to [paragraph 3 of Schedule 6], are to be treated as if they were imposed by or under Part 7 of these Regulations (rights and obligations in relation to the provision of payment services).

Supervision and enforcement

108. Monitoring and enforcement

(1) The FCA must maintain arrangements designed to enable it to determine whether—

(a) persons on whom requirements are imposed by or under Parts 2 to 7 or regulation 105 (access to bank accounts) are complying with them;

(b) there has been any contravention of regulation 138(1) (prohibition on provision of payment services by persons other than payment service providers), 139(1) (false claims to be a payment service provider or exempt) or 142(1)(a) or (2) (misleading a regulator).

(2) The arrangements referred to in paragraph (1) may provide for functions to be performed on behalf of the FCA by any body or person who is, in its opinion, competent to perform them.

(3) The FCA must also maintain arrangements for enforcing the provisions of these Regulations.

(4) Paragraph (2) does not affect the FCA's duty under paragraph (1).

109. Reporting requirements

(1) A person must give the FCA such information as the FCA may direct in respect of its provision of payment services or its compliance with requirements imposed by or under Parts 2 to 7 or regulation 105 (access to bank accounts).

(2) Information required under this regulation must be given at such times and in such form, and verified in such manner, as the FCA may direct.

(3) A direction under paragraph (2) must specify the purpose for which the information is required, as appropriate, and the time within which the information is to be given.

(4) Each [payment service provider in the United Kingdom (but not an agent of such a payment service provider or an excluded provider)] must provide to the FCA statistical data on fraud relating to different means of payment.

(5) Such data must be provided at least once per year, and must be provided in such form as the FCA may direct.

110. Public censure

If the FCA considers that a person has contravened a requirement imposed on them by or under these Regulations, the FCA may publish a statement to that effect.

111. Financial penalties

(1) The FCA may impose a penalty of such amount as it considers appropriate on—

(a) a payment service provider who has contravened a requirement imposed on them by or under these Regulations; or

(b) a person who has contravened regulation 138(1) (prohibition on provision of payment services by persons other than payment service providers), 139(1) (false claims to be a payment service provider or exempt) or 142(1)(a) or (2) (misleading a regulator).

(2) The FCA may not in respect of any contravention both require a person to pay a penalty under this regulation and cancel their authorisation as a payment institution or their registration as a small payment institution or account information service provider (as the case may be).

(3) A penalty under this regulation is a debt due from that person to the FCA, and is recoverable accordingly.

112. Proposal to take disciplinary measures

(1) Where the FCA proposes to publish a statement under regulation 110 or to impose a penalty under regulation 111, it must give the person concerned a warning notice.

(2) The warning notice must set out the terms of the proposed statement or state the amount of the proposed penalty.

(3) If, having considered any representations made in response to the warning notice, the FCA decides to publish a statement under regulation 110 or to impose a penalty under regulation 111, it must without delay give the person concerned a decision notice.

(4) The decision notice must set out the terms of the statement or state the amount of the penalty.

(5) If the FCA decides to publish a statement under regulation 110 or impose a penalty on a person under regulation 111, the person concerned may refer the matter to the Upper Tribunal.

(6) Sections 210 (statements of policy) and 211 (statements of policy: procedure) of the 2000 Act apply in respect of the imposition of penalties under regulation 111 and the amount of such penalties as they apply in respect of the imposition of penalties under Part 14 of the 2000 Act (disciplinary measures) and the amount of penalties under that Part of that Act.

(7) After a statement under regulation 110 is published, the FCA must send a copy of it to the person concerned and to any person to whom a copy of the decision notice was given under section 393(4) of the 2000 Act (third party rights) (as applied by paragraph 10 of Schedule 6 to these Regulations).

113. Injunctions

(1) If, on the application of the FCA, the court is satisfied—

   (a) that there is a reasonable likelihood that any person will contravene a requirement imposed by or under these Regulations; or

   (b) that any person has contravened such a requirement and that there is a reasonable likelihood that the contravention will continue or be repeated,

the court may make an order restraining (or in Scotland an interdict prohibiting) the contravention.

(2) If, on the application of the FCA, the court is satisfied—

   (a) that any person has contravened a requirement imposed by or under these Regulations; and

   (b) that there are steps which could be taken for remedying the contravention,

the court may make an order requiring that person, and any other person who appears to have been knowingly concerned in the contravention, to take such steps as the court may direct to remedy it.

(3) If, on the application of the FCA, the court is satisfied that any person may have—

   (a) contravened a requirement imposed by or under these Regulations; or

   (b) been knowingly concerned in the contravention of such a requirement,

it may make an order restraining (or in Scotland an interdict prohibiting) them from disposing of, or otherwise dealing with, any assets of theirs which it is satisfied they are reasonably likely to dispose of or otherwise deal with.

(4) The jurisdiction conferred by this regulation is exercisable by the High Court and the Court of Session.

(5) In paragraph (2), references to remedying a contravention include references to mitigating its effect.

114. Power of FCA to require restitution

(1) The FCA may exercise the power in paragraph (2) if it is satisfied that a payment service provider (referred to in this regulation and regulation 115 as 'the person concerned') has contravened a requirement imposed by or under these Regulations, or been knowingly concerned in the contravention of such a requirement, and that—

   (a) profits have accrued to the person concerned as a result of the contravention; or

   (b) one or more persons have suffered loss or been otherwise adversely affected as a result of the contravention.

(2) The power referred to in paragraph (1) is a power to require the person concerned, in accordance with such arrangements as the FCA considers appropriate, to pay to the appropriate person or distribute among the appropriate persons such amount as appears to the FCA to be just having regard—

(a) in a case within sub-paragraph (a) of paragraph (1), to the profits appearing to the FCA to have accrued;

(b) in a case within sub-paragraph (b) of that paragraph, to the extent of the loss or other adverse effect;

(c) in a case within both of those paragraphs, to the profits appearing to the FCA to have accrued and to the extent of the loss or other adverse effect.

(3) In paragraph (2) 'appropriate person' means a person appearing to the FCA to be someone—

(a) to whom the profits mentioned in paragraph (1)(a) are attributable; or

(b) who has suffered the loss or adverse effect mentioned in paragraph (1)(b).

115. Proposal to require restitution

(1) If the FCA proposes to exercise the power under regulation 114(2), it must give the person concerned a warning notice.

(2) The warning notice must state the amount which the FCA propose to require the person concerned to pay or distribute as mentioned in regulation 114(2).

(3) If, having considered any representations made in response to the warning notice, the FCA decides to exercise the power under regulation 114(2), it must without delay give the person concerned a decision notice.

(4) The decision notice must—

(a) state the amount that the person concerned is to pay or distribute;

(b) identify the person or persons to whom that amount is to be paid or among whom that amount is to be distributed; and

(c) state the arrangements in accordance with which the payment or distribution is to be made.

(5) If the FCA decides to exercise the power under regulation 114(2), the person concerned may refer the matter to the Upper Tribunal.

116. Restitution orders

(1) The court may, on the application of the FCA, make an order under paragraph (2) if it is satisfied that a person has contravened a requirement imposed by or under these Regulations, or been knowingly concerned in the contravention of such a requirement, and that—

(a) profits have accrued to them as a result of the contravention; or

(b) one or more persons have suffered loss or been otherwise adversely affected as a result of the contravention.

(2) The court may order the person concerned to pay to the FCA such sum as appears to the court to be just having regard—

(a) in a case within sub-paragraph (a) of paragraph (1), to the profits appearing to the court to have accrued;

(b) in a case within sub-paragraph (b) of that paragraph, to the extent of the loss or other adverse effect;

(c) in a case within both of those sub-paragraphs, to the profits appearing to the court to have accrued and to the extent of the loss or other adverse effect.

(3) Any amount paid to the FCA in pursuance of an order under paragraph (2) must be paid by it to such qualifying person or distributed by it among such qualifying persons as the court may direct.

(4) In paragraph (3), 'qualifying person' means a person appearing to the court to be someone—

(a) to whom the profits mentioned in paragraph (1)(a) are attributable; or

(b) who has suffered the loss or adverse effect mentioned in paragraph (1)(b).

(5) On an application under paragraph (1) the court may require the person concerned to supply it with such accounts or other information as it may require for any one or more of the following purposes—

(a) establishing whether any and, if so, what profits have accrued to them as mentioned in sub-paragraph (a) of that paragraph;

(b) establishing whether any person or persons have suffered any loss or adverse effect as mentioned in sub-paragraph (b) of that paragraph; and

(c) determining how any amounts are to be paid or distributed under paragraph (3).

(6) The court may require any accounts or other information supplied under paragraph (5) to be verified in such manner as it may direct.

(7) The jurisdiction conferred by this regulation is exercisable by the High Court and the Court of Session.

(8) Nothing in this regulation affects the right of any person other than the FCA to bring proceedings in respect of the matters to which this regulation applies.

117. Complaints

(1) The FCA must maintain arrangements designed to enable payment service users and other interested parties to submit complaints to it that a requirement imposed by or under Parts 2 to 7 of these Regulations has been breached by a payment service provider.

(2) Where it considers it appropriate, the FCA must include in any reply to a complaint under paragraph (1) details of the ombudsman scheme established under Part 16 of the 2000 Act (the ombudsman scheme).

Miscellaneous

118. Costs of supervision

(1) The functions of the FCA under these Regulations are to be treated for the purposes of paragraph 23 of Schedule 1ZA (fees) to the 2000 Act as functions conferred on the FCA under that Act, with the following modifications—

(a) section 1B(5)(a) of the 2000 Act (FCA's general duties) does not apply to the making of rules under paragraph 23 by virtue of this regulation;

(b) rules made under paragraph 23 by virtue of this regulation are not to be treated as regulating provisions for the purposes of section 140A(1) of the 2000 Act (competition scrutiny);

(c) paragraph 23(7) does not apply.

(2) The FCA must in respect of each of its financial years pay to the Treasury any amounts received by it during the year by way of penalties imposed under regulation 111.

(3) The Treasury may give directions to the FCA as to how the FCA is to comply with its duty under paragraph (2).

(4) The directions may in particular—

(a) specify the time when any payment is required to be made to the Treasury, and

(b) require the FCA to provide the Treasury at specified times with information relating to penalties that the FCA has imposed under regulation 111.

(5) The Treasury must pay into the Consolidated Fund any sums received by them under this regulation.

120. Guidance

(1) The FCA may give guidance consisting of such information and advice as it considers appropriate with respect to—

(a) the operation of these Regulations;

(b) any matters relating to the functions of the FCA under these Regulations;

(c) any other matters about which it appears to the FCA to be desirable to give information or advice in connection with these Regulations.

(2) The FCA may—

(a) publish its guidance;

(b) offer copies of its published guidance for sale at a reasonable price;

(c) if it gives guidance in response to a request made by any person, make a reasonable charge for that guidance.

121. FCA's exemption from liability in damages
The functions of the FCA under these Regulations are to be treated for the purposes of paragraph 25 (exemption from liability in damages) of Part 4 of Schedule 1ZA to the 2000 Act as functions conferred on the FCA under that Act.

122. Application and modification of primary and secondary legislation
The provisions of primary and secondary legislation set out in Schedule 6 apply for the purposes of these Regulations with the modifications set out in that Schedule.

PART 10 THE PAYMENT SYSTEMS REGULATOR

123. Interpretation of Part 10
In this Part—
'the 2013 Act' means the Financial Services (Banking Reform) Act 2013;
'compliance failure' means a failure by a regulated person to comply with—
    (a) a [qualifying] requirement; or
    (b) a direction given under regulation 125;
'general direction' has the meaning given in regulation 125(5);
'general guidance' has the meaning given in regulation 134(2);
['qualifying requirement' means an obligation, prohibition or restriction imposed by regulation 61 (information on ATM withdrawal charges) or Part 8 (access to payment systems and bank accounts), with the exception of the obligation imposed on the FCA by regulation 105(5) (access to bank accounts);]
'regulated person' means a person on whom a [qualifying] requirement is imposed.

124. Functions of the Payment Systems Regulator
(1) The Payment Systems Regulator [has the functions and powers conferred on it by these Regulations].
(2) In determining the general policy and principles by reference to which it performs particular functions under these Regulations [. . .].
(3) The Payment Systems Regulator must maintain arrangements designed to enable it to determine whether regulated persons are complying with [qualifying] requirements, and for enforcing [qualifying] requirements.

125. Directions
(1) The Payment Systems Regulator may give a direction in writing to any regulated person.
(2) A direction may be given for the purpose of—
    (a) obtaining information about—
        (i) compliance with a [qualifying] requirement; or
        (ii) the application of a [qualifying] requirement to a person;
    (b) remedying a failure to comply with a [qualifying] requirement; or
    (c) preventing a failure to comply, or continued non-compliance, with a [qualifying] requirement.
(3) A direction may require or prohibit the taking of specified action.
(4) A direction may apply—
    (a) in relation to all regulated persons or in relation to every regulated person of a specified description; or
    (b) in relation to a specified regulated person or specified regulated persons.
(5) A direction that applies as mentioned in paragraph (4)(a) is referred to in this Part as a 'general direction'.
(6) A direction requiring the provision of information must specify the purpose for which the information is required, as appropriate, and the time within which the information is to be given.
(7) The Payment Systems Regulator must publish any general direction.

126. Publication of compliance failures and penalties

The Payment Systems Regulator may publish details of—

(a) a compliance failure by a regulated person; or

(b) a penalty imposed under regulation 127.

127. Penalties

(1) The Payment Systems Regulator may require a regulated person to pay a penalty in respect of a compliance failure.

(2) A penalty—

(a) must be paid to the Payment Systems Regulator; and

(b) may be enforced by the Payment Systems Regulator as a debt.

(3) The Payment Systems Regulator must prepare a statement of the principles which it will apply in determining—

(a) whether to impose a penalty; and

(b) the amount of a penalty.

(4) The Payment Systems Regulator must—

(a) publish the statement on its website;

(b) send a copy to the Treasury;

(c) review the statement from time to time and revise it if necessary (and sub-paragraphs (a) and (b) apply to a revision); and

(d) in applying the statement to a compliance failure, apply the version in force when the compliance failure occurred.

128. Notice of publication of a compliance failure or of imposition of a penalty

Before publishing details of a compliance failure by a regulated person under regulation 126(a) or imposing a penalty on a regulated person under regulation 127, the Payment Systems Regulator must—

(a) give the person notice in writing of the proposed publication or penalty and reasons for the proposed publication or penalty;

(b) give the person at least 21 days to make representations;

(c) consider any representations made; and

(d) as soon as is reasonably practicable, give the person a notice in writing stating whether or not it intends to publish the details or impose the penalty.

129. Injunctions

(1) If, on the application of the Payment Systems Regulator, the court is satisfied—

(a) that there is a reasonable likelihood that there will be a compliance failure, or

(b) that there has been a compliance failure and there is a reasonable likelihood that it will continue or be repeated,

the court may make an order restraining the conduct constituting the failure.

(2) If, on the application of the Payment Systems Regulator, the court is satisfied—

(a) that there has been a compliance failure by a regulated person; and

(b) that there are steps which could be taken for remedying the failure,

the court may make an order requiring the regulated person, and anyone else who appears to have been knowingly concerned in the failure, to take such steps as the court may direct to remedy it.

(3) The jurisdiction conferred by this regulation is exercisable—

(a) in England and Wales and Northern Ireland, by the High Court; and

(b) in Scotland, by the Court of Session.

(4) In this regulation—

(a) references to an order restraining anything are, in Scotland, to be read as references to an interdict prohibiting that thing; and

(b) references to remedying a failure include mitigating its effect.

130. Appeals: general

(1) A person who is affected by a decision to give a direction under regulation 125 (directions) other than a general direction or a decision to publish details under regulation 126(a) (publication of compliance failures) may appeal against the decision to the Competition Appeal Tribunal in accordance with regulation 131.

(2) A person who is affected by a decision to impose a penalty under regulation 127 (penalties) may appeal against the decision to the Competition Appeal Tribunal in accordance with regulation 132.

131. Appeals against directions and publication of compliance failures

(1) This regulation applies where a person is appealing to the Competition Appeal Tribunal against a decision to give a direction under regulation 125 (directions) or to publish details under regulation 126(a) (publication of compliance failures).

(2) The means of making an appeal is by sending the Competition Appeal Tribunal a notice of appeal in accordance with Tribunal rules.

(3) The notice of appeal must be sent within the period specified, in relation to the decision appealed against, in those rules.

(4) In determining an appeal made in accordance with this regulation, the Competition Appeal Tribunal must apply the same principles as would be applied by a court on an application for judicial review.

(5) The Competition Appeal Tribunal must either—

    (a) dismiss the appeal; or

    (b) quash the whole or part of the decision to which the appeal relates.

(6) If the Competition Appeal Tribunal quashes the whole or part of a decision, it may refer the matter back to the Payment Systems Regulator with a direction to reconsider and make a new decision in accordance with its ruling.

(7) The Competition Appeal Tribunal may not direct the Payment Systems Regulator to take any action which it would not otherwise have the power to take in relation to the decision.

(8) In this regulation and regulation 132 'Tribunal rules' means rules under section 15 of the Enterprise Act 2002.

132. Appeals in relation to penalties

(1) This regulation applies where a person is appealing to the Competition Appeal Tribunal against a decision to impose a penalty under regulation 127 (penalty).

(2) The person may appeal against—

    (a) the imposition of the penalty;

    (b) the amount of the penalty; or

    (c) any date by which the penalty, or any part of it, is required to be paid.

(3) The means of making an appeal is by sending the Competition Appeal Tribunal a notice of appeal in accordance with Tribunal rules.

(4) The notice of appeal must be sent within the period specified, in relation to the decision appealed against, in those rules.

(5) The Competition Appeal Tribunal may do any of the following—

    (a) uphold the penalty;

    (b) set aside the penalty;

    (c) substitute for the penalty a penalty of an amount decided by the Competition Appeal Tribunal;

    (d) vary any date by which the penalty, or any part of it, is required to be paid.

(6) If an appeal is made in accordance with this regulation, the penalty is not required to be paid until the appeal has been determined.

(7) Paragraphs (2), (5) and (6) do not restrict the power to make Tribunal rules; and those paragraphs are subject to Tribunal rules.

(8) Except as provided by this regulation, the validity of the penalty may not be questioned by any legal proceedings whatever.

(9) In the case of an appeal made in accordance with this regulation, a decision of the Competition Appeal Tribunal has the same effect as, and may be enforced in the same manner as, a decision of the Payment Systems Regulator.

133. Complaints

(1) The Payment Systems Regulator must maintain arrangements designed to enable persons to submit complaints to it that a [qualifying] requirement has been breached.

(2) Where it considers it appropriate, the Payment Systems Regulator must include in any reply to a complaint under paragraph (1) details of the ombudsman scheme established under Part 16 of the 2000 Act (the ombudsman scheme).

134. Guidance

(1) The Payment Systems Regulator may give guidance consisting of such information and advice as it considers appropriate in relation to—

(a) the [qualifying] requirements;

(b) its functions under these Regulations;

(c) any related matters about which it appears to the Payment Systems Regulator to be desirable to give information or advice.

(2) In this Part 'general guidance' means guidance given by the Payment Systems Regulator under this regulation which is—

(a) given to persons generally or to a class of persons;

(b) intended to have continuing effect; and

(c) given in writing or other legible form.

(3) The Payment Systems Regulator may publish its guidance.

135. Information and investigation

[*Note: affects the Financial Services (Banking Reform) Act 2013 and the Financial Services (Banking Reform) Act 2013 (Disclosure of Confidential Information) Regulations 2014.*]

136. Application of other provisions of the 2013 Act

[*Note: affects the Financial Services (Banking Reform) Act 2013.*]

PART 11 GENERAL

Contracting out of statutory requirements

137. Prohibition on contracting out of statutory requirement

(1) A payment service provider may not agree with a payment service user that it will not comply with any provision of these Regulations unless—

(a) such agreement is permitted by these Regulations, or

(b) such agreement provides for terms which are more favourable to the payment service user than the relevant provisions of these Regulations.

(2) A contractual term is void if and to the extent that—

(a) the term is agreed in contravention of paragraph (1), or

(b) the term relates to a transaction alleged to have been unauthorised or defectively executed, and purports to—

(i)   impose liability to provide compensation on a different person from the person identified in these Regulations, or

(ii) allocate the burden of proof to a different person from the person identified in these Regulations.

Criminal Offences

138. Prohibition on provision of payment services by persons other than payment service providers

(1) A person may not provide a payment service in the United Kingdom, or purport to do so, unless the person is—

    (a)   an authorised payment institution;

    (b)   a small payment institution;

    (c)   a registered account information service provider;

    (e)   a credit institution authorised in the United Kingdom [. . .];

    [(ea) after IP completion day, a credit institution while it is an exempt person for the purposes of section 19(1)(b) of the Financial Services and Markets Act 2000 by virtue of regulation 47 of the EEA Passport Rights (Amendment, etc., and Transitional Provisions) (EU Exit) Regulations 2018 but only in respect of a payment service specified in paragraph (3);]

    (f)   an electronic money institution which for the purposes of the Electronic Money Regulations 2011 is—

        (i)   registered in the United Kingdom as an authorised electronic money institution or a small electronic money institution; [. . .]

        (ii) an EEA authorised electronic money institution exercising passport rights in the United Kingdom;

    [(fa) after IP completion day, a relevant electronic money institution while it is exempt from the prohibitions in regulation 63(1) of the Electronic Money Regulations 2011 and this regulation by virtue of paragraph 12L of Schedule 3 to the Electronic Money, Payment Services and Payment Systems (Amendment and Transitional Provisions) (EU Exit) Regulations 2018 but only in respect of a payment service specified in paragraph (4);]

    (g)   the Post Office Limited;

    (h)   the Bank of England, [. . .]

    (i)   a government department or a local authority; or

    (j)   exempt under regulation 3 (exemption for certain bodies).

(2) A person who contravenes paragraph (1) is guilty of an offence and is liable—

    (a)   on summary conviction, to imprisonment for a term not exceeding three months or to a fine, which in Scotland or Northern Ireland may not exceed the statutory maximum, or both;

    (b)   on conviction on indictment, to imprisonment for a term not exceeding two years or to a fine, or both.

[(3) A payment service is specified as one that may be provided by a credit institution under paragraph (1)(ea) only to the extent that the credit institution was providing the service in the United Kingdom immediately before IP completion day in accordance with the exercise of an EEA passport right under Title 5 of Directive 2013/36/EU as in force immediately before IP completion day and the service is necessary as specified in paragraph (4).

(4) This paragraph applies where the service is necessary—

    (a)   for the performance of a contract entered into before IP completion day and provided for the purposes of performing such a contract or to redeem outstanding electronic money;

    (b)   for the purpose of reducing the financial risk of a party to a contract entered into before IP completion day or of a third party affected by the performance of such a contract;

    (c)   in order to transfer the property, rights or liabilities under a contract entered into before IP completion day to a person authorised to carry on a regulated activity under section 31(1)(a) of FSMA (other than a person authorised to carry on a regulated activity under that section of FSMA by virtue of the provisions contained in the Financial Services Contracts (Transitional and Saving Provision) (EU Exit) Regulations 2019); or

    (d)   in order to comply with a requirement imposed by or under an enactment.

(5) For the purposes of paragraph (4)(a), the performance of a contract entered into before IP completion day includes the performance of an obligation under the contract which is contingent or conditional.

(6) A payment service is specified as one that may be provided by a relevant electronic money institution under paragraph (1)(fa) only to the extent that—

(a) the relevant electronic money institution was providing the service in the United Kingdom immediately before IP completion day in accordance with the exercise of an EEA passport right under article 3(1) of Directive 2009/110/EC as in force immediately before IP completion day; and

(b) the services are necessary for the performance of a contract entered into before IP completion day and provided for the purposes of performing such a contract.

(7) In this regulation, a 'relevant electronic money institution' is an EEA authorised electronic money institution which was exercising its EEA passport rights in the United Kingdom immediately before IP completion day (other than through an establishment in the United Kingdom maintained by it or its agent) while it is exempt from the prohibitions in regulation 63(1) of the Electronic Money Regulations 2011 and this regulation by virtue of paragraph 12L of Schedule 3 to the Electronic Money, Payment Services and Payment Systems (Amendment and Transitional Provisions) (EU Exit) Regulations 2018.]

139.　False claims to be a payment service provider or exempt

(1) A person who does not fall within any of sub-paragraphs (a) to (f) of regulation 138(1) may not—

(a) describe themselves (in whatever terms) as a person falling within any of those sub-paragraphs; or

(b) behave, or otherwise hold themselves out, in a manner which indicates (or which is reasonably likely to be understood as indicating) that they are such a person.

(2) A person who contravenes paragraph (1) is guilty of an offence and is liable on summary conviction to imprisonment for a term not exceeding three months or to a fine, which in Scotland or Northern Ireland may not exceed level 5 on the standard scale, or both.

140.　Defences

In proceedings for an offence under regulation 138 or 139 it is a defence for the accused to show that they took all reasonable precautions and exercised all due diligence to avoid committing the offence.

141.　Contravention of regulations 57 and 58

(1) A person (not being a payment service provider) who contravenes regulation 57(2) or 58(2) (information on charges and exchange rates) is guilty of an offence and liable on summary conviction to a fine, which in Scotland or Northern Ireland may not exceed level 5 on the standard scale.

(2) No offence is committed if the person took all reasonable steps and exercised all due diligence to ensure that the requirement imposed on the person by regulation 57(2) or 58(2), as the case may be, would be complied with.

142.　Misleading the FCA or the Payment Systems Regulator

(1) A person may not, in purported compliance with any requirement imposed by or under these Regulations, knowingly or recklessly give information which is false or misleading in a material particular to—

(a) the FCA; or

(b) the Payment Systems Regulator.

(2) A person may not—

(a) provide any information to another person, knowing the information to be false or misleading in a material particular, or

      (b) recklessly provide to another person any information which is false or misleading in a material particular,

knowing that the information is to be used for the purpose of providing information to the FCA in connection with its functions under these Regulations.

    (3) A person may not—

      (a) provide any information to another person, knowing the information to be false or misleading in a material particular, or

      (b) recklessly provide to another person any information which is false or misleading in a material particular,

knowing that the information is to be used for the purpose of providing information to the Payment Systems Regulator in connection with its functions under these Regulations.

    (4) A person who contravenes paragraph (1), (2) or (3) is guilty of an offence and is liable—

      (a) on summary conviction, to a fine, which in Scotland or Northern Ireland may not exceed the statutory maximum;

      (b) on conviction on indictment, to a fine.

143.   Restriction on penalties

A person who is convicted of an offence under these Regulations is not liable to a penalty under regulation 111 or 127 (financial penalties) in respect of the same contravention of a requirement imposed by or under these Regulations.

144.   Liability of officers of bodies corporate etc

    (1) If an offence under these Regulations committed by a body corporate is shown—

      (a) to have been committed with the consent or connivance of an officer, or

      (b) to be attributable to any neglect on their part,

the officer as well as the body corporate is guilty of the offence and liable to be proceeded against and punished accordingly.

    (2) If the affairs of a body corporate are managed by its members, paragraph (1) applies in relation to the acts and defaults of a member in connection with such member's functions of management as if the member were a director of the body.

    (3) If an offence under these Regulations committed by a partnership is shown—

      (a) to have been committed with the consent or connivance of a partner, or

      (b) to be attributable to any neglect on their part,

the partner as well as the partnership is guilty of the offence and liable to be proceeded against and punished accordingly.

    (4) If an offence under these Regulations committed by an unincorporated association (other than a partnership) is shown—

      (a) to have been committed with the consent or connivance of an officer, or

      (b) to be attributable to any neglect of such officer,

the officer as well as the association is guilty of the offence and liable to be proceeded against and punished accordingly.

    (5) In this regulation—

'officer'—

      (a) in relation to a body corporate, means a director, manager, secretary, chief executive, member of the committee of management, or a person purporting to act in such a capacity; and

      (b) in relation to an unincorporated association, means any officer of the association or any member of its governing body, or a person purporting to act in such capacity; and

'partner' includes a person purporting to act as a partner.

145.   Prosecution of offences

    (1) Proceedings for an offence under these Regulations may be instituted only—

      (a) in respect of an offence under regulation 138 (prohibition on provision of payment services by persons other than payment service providers), 139 (false claims to be a payment service provider or exempt), 141 (contravention of regulations 57 and 58), or 142(4) in so far as it relates to regulation 142(1)(a) or (2) (misleading the FCA), by the FCA;

   (b) in respect of an offence under regulation 142(4) in so far as it relates to regulation 142(1)(b) or (3) (misleading the Payment Systems Regulator), by the Payment Systems Regulator; or

   (c) by or with the consent of the Director of Public Prosecutions.

(2) Paragraph (1) does not apply to proceedings in Scotland.

146. Proceedings against unincorporated bodies

(1) Proceedings for an offence alleged to have been committed by a partnership or an unincorporated association must be brought in the name of the partnership or association (and not in that of its members).

(2) A fine imposed on the partnership or association on its conviction of an offence is to be paid out of the funds of the partnership or association.

(3) Rules of court relating to the service of documents are to have effect as if the partnership or association were a body corporate.

(4) In proceedings for an offence brought against the partnership or association—

   (a) section 33 of the Criminal Justice Act 1925 (procedure on charge of offence against corporation) and section 46 of and Schedule 3 to the Magistrates' Courts Act 1980 (corporations) apply as they do in relation to a body corporate;

   (b) section 70 of the Criminal Procedure (Scotland) Act 1995 (proceedings against organisations) applies as it does in relation to a body corporate;

   (c) section 18 of the Criminal Justice (Northern Ireland) Act 1945 (procedure on charge) and Schedule 4 to the Magistrates' Courts (Northern Ireland) Order 1981 (corporations) apply as they do in relation to a body corporate.

(5) Summary proceedings for an offence under these Regulations may be taken—

   (a) against a body corporate or unincorporated association at any place at which it has a place of business;

   (b) against an individual at any place where they are for the time being.

(6) Paragraph (5) does not affect any jurisdiction exercisable apart from this regulation.

Miscellaneous

147. Duty to co-operate and exchange of information

(1) The FCA, the Commissioners and the Payment Systems Regulator [may] take such steps as they consider appropriate to co-operate with each other and—

   [(b) the Bank of England; and

   (c) any other public authority exercising functions in the United Kingdom in relation to payment service providers,]

for the purposes of the exercise by those bodies of their functions [under these Regulations and other relevant legislation].

(2) Subject to the requirements of the Data Protection Act 1998, section 348 of the 2000 Act (restrictions on disclosure of confidential information by FCA etc.) (as applied with modifications by paragraph 8 of Schedule 6 to these Regulations), regulation 105 of the Money Laundering, Terrorist Financing and Transfer of Funds (Information on the Payer) Regulations 2017 (disclosure by the Commissioners) and any other applicable restrictions on the disclosure of information, the FCA, the Commissioners and the Payment Systems Regulator may provide information to each other and—

   (a) the bodies mentioned in paragraph [(1)(c)];

   [(b) the Bank of England when acting in its capacity as a monetary and oversight authority;]

   (c) where relevant, other public authorities responsible for the oversight of payment and settlement systems;

for the purposes of the exercise by those bodies of their functions under [these Regulations and other relevant legislation].

(3) Part 9 of the Enterprise Act 2002 (information) does not prohibit disclosure of information under paragraph (2) but a person to whom that Part applies must have regard to the considerations mentioned in section 244 of that Act (specified information: considerations relevant to disclosure) before making any such disclosure.

148. Actions for breach of requirements

(1) A contravention—
- (a) which is to be taken to have occurred by virtue of regulation 21 (authorised payment institutions, small payment institutions and registered account information service providers acting without permission);
- (b) of a requirement imposed by regulation 23 (safeguarding requirements); or
- (c) of a requirement imposed by or under Part 6 (information requirements for payment services) or 7 (rights and obligations in relation to the provision of payment services),

is actionable at the suit of a private person who suffers loss as a result of the contravention, subject to the defences and other incidents applying to actions for breach of statutory duty.

(2) A person acting in a fiduciary or representative capacity may bring an action under paragraph (1) on behalf of a private person if any remedy—
- (a) will be exclusively for the benefit of the private person; and
- (b) cannot be obtained by way of an action brought otherwise than at the suit of the fiduciary or representative.

(3) In this regulation 'private person' means—
- (a) any individual, except where the individual suffers the loss in question in the course of providing payment services; and
- (b) any person who is not an individual, except where that person suffers the loss in question in the course of carrying on business of any kind;

but does not include a government, a local authority (in the United Kingdom or elsewhere) or an international organisation.

(4) Where there has been a contravention of a requirement under regulation 76(5)(b) (payment service provider's liability for unauthorised payment transactions), 77(6) (payer or payee's liability for unauthorised payment transactions), 93(4) (non-execution or defective or late execution of payment transactions initiated through a payment initiation service) or 95 (right of recourse) for a payment service provider to compensate another payment service provider, the payment service provider to which compensation is required to be paid is to be treated for the purposes of this regulation as if it were a private person.

[148A Single Euro Payments Area

(1) If the SEPA Regulation is revoked under regulation 15 of the Credit Transfers and Direct Debits in Euro (Amendment) (EU Exit) Regulations 2018, the Treasury may by regulations make such amendments of regulations 40, 63, 66 and 85 of these Regulations as appear to them to be appropriate in connection with the revocation.

(2) Regulations under this regulation may contain transitional and consequential provisions and savings.

(3) A statutory instrument containing regulations under paragraph (1) is subject to annulment in pursuance of a resolution of either House of Parliament.]

Review

158. Review

(1) The Treasury must from time to time—
- (a) carry out a review of the regulatory provision contained in these Regulations; and
- (b) publish the report setting out the conclusions of the review.

(2) The first report under this regulation must be published on or before 13th January 2023.

(3) Subsequent reports must be published at intervals not exceeding five years.

(5) Section 30(4) of [the Small Business, Enterprise and Employment Act 2015] requires that a report published under this regulation must, in particular—

    (a) set out the objectives intended to be achieved by the regulatory provision referred to in paragraph (1)(a);

    (b) assess the extent to which those objectives are achieved;

    (c) assess whether those objectives remain appropriate; and

    (d) if those objectives remain appropriate, assess the extent to which they could be achieved in another way that imposes less onerous regulatory provision.

(6) In this regulation, 'regulatory provision' has the same meaning as in sections 28 to 32 of the Small Business, Enterprise and Employment Act 2015 (see section 32 of that Act).

Regulation 2(1)

SCHEDULE 1

PAYMENT SERVICES

PART 1 PAYMENT SERVICES

1. Subject to Part 2, the following, when carried out as a regular occupation or business activity, are payment services—

    (a) services enabling cash to be placed on a payment account and all of the operations required for operating a payment account;

    (b) services enabling cash withdrawals from a payment account and all of the operations required for operating a payment account;

    (c) the execution of payment transactions, including transfers of funds on a payment account with the user's payment service provider or with another payment service provider—

        (i) execution of direct debits, including one-off direct debits;

        (ii) execution of payment transactions through a payment card or a similar device;

        (iii) execution of credit transfers, including standing orders;

    (d) the execution of payment transactions where the funds are covered by a credit line for a payment service user—

        (i) execution of direct debits, including one-off direct debits;

        (ii) execution of payment transactions through a payment card or a similar device;

        (iii) execution of credit transfers, including standing orders;

    (e) issuing payment instruments or acquiring payment transactions;

    (f) money remittance;

    (g) payment initiation services;

    (h) account information services.

PART 2 ACTIVITIES WHICH DO NOT CONSTITUTE PAYMENT SERVICES

2. The following do not constitute payment services—

    (a) payment transactions executed wholly in cash and directly between the payer and the payee, without any intermediary intervention;

    (b) payment transactions between the payer and the payee through a commercial agent authorised in an agreement to negotiate or conclude the sale or purchase of goods or services on behalf of either the payer or the payee but not both the payer and the payee;

    (c) the professional physical transport of banknotes and coins, including their collection, processing and delivery;

(d) payment transactions consisting of non-professional cash collection and delivery as part of a not-for-profit or charitable activity;

(e) services where cash is provided by the payee to the payer as part of a payment transaction for the purchase of goods or services following an explicit request by the payer immediately before the execution of the payment transaction;

(f) cash-to-cash currency exchange operations where the funds are not held on a payment account;

(g) payment transactions based on any of the following documents drawn on the payment service provider with a view to placing funds at the disposal of the payee—

    (i) paper cheques of any kind, including traveller's cheques;

    (ii) bankers' drafts;

    (iii) paper-based vouchers;

    (iv) paper postal orders;

(h) payment transactions carried out within a payment or securities settlement system between payment service providers and settlement agents, central counterparties, clearing houses, [central securities depositories,] central banks or other participants in the system;

(i) payment transactions related to securities asset servicing, including dividends, income or other distributions, or redemption or sale, carried out by persons referred to in sub-paragraph (h) or by investment firms, credit institutions, collective investment undertakings or asset management companies providing investment services or by any other entities allowed to have the custody of financial instruments;

(j) services provided by technical service providers, which support the provision of payment services, without the provider entering at any time into possession of the funds to be transferred, excluding payment initiation services or account information services but including—

    (i) the processing and storage of data;

    (ii) trust and privacy protection services;

    (iii) data and entity authentication;

    (iv) information technology;

    (v) communication network provision; and

    (vi) the provision and maintenance of terminals and devices used for payment services;

(k) services based on specific payment instruments that can be used only in a limited way and meet one of the following conditions—

    (i) allow the holder to acquire goods or services only in the issuer's premises;

    (ii) are issued by a professional issuer and allow the holder to acquire goods or services only within a limited network of service providers which have direct commercial agreements with the issuer;

    (iii) may be used only to acquire a very limited range of goods or services; or

    (iv) are valid only in [the United Kingdom], are provided at the request of an undertaking or a public sector entity, and are regulated by a national or regional public authority for specific social or tax purposes to acquire specific goods or services from suppliers which have a commercial agreement with the issuer.

(l) payment transactions resulting from services provided by a provider of electronic communications networks or services, including transactions between persons other than that provider and a subscriber, where those services are provided in addition to electronic communications services for a subscriber to the network or service, and where the additional service is—

    (i) for purchase of digital content and voice-based services, regardless of the device used for the purchase or consumption of the digital content, and charged to the related bill; or

(ii) performed from or via an electronic device and charged to the related bill for the purchase of tickets or for donations to organisations which are registered or recognised as charities by public authorities, whether in the United Kingdom or elsewhere,

provided that the value of any single payment transaction does not exceed £40, and the cumulative value of payment transactions for an individual subscriber in a month does not exceed £240;

(m) payment transactions carried out between payment service providers, or their agents or branches, for their own account;

(n) payment transactions and related services between a parent undertaking and its subsidiary or between subsidiaries of the same parent undertaking, without any intermediary intervention by a payment service provider other than an undertaking belonging to the same group;

(o) cash withdrawal services provided through automatic teller machines, where the provider—

(i) is acting on behalf of one or more card issuers;

(ii) is not party to the framework contract with the customer withdrawing money from a payment account; and

(iii) does not conduct any other payment service.

Regulation 5(1)

SCHEDULE 2

INFORMATION TO BE INCLUDED IN OR WITH AN APPLICATION FOR AUTHORISATION

1. A programme of operations setting out, in particular, the type of payment services envisaged.

2. A business plan including a forecast budget calculation for the first three financial years which demonstrates that the applicant is able to employ appropriate and proportionate systems, resources and procedures to operate soundly.

3. Evidence that the applicant holds initial capital for the purposes of regulation 6(3).

4. Where regulation 23 (safeguarding requirements) applies, a description of the measures taken for safeguarding payment service users' funds in accordance with that regulation.

5. A description of the applicant's governance arrangements and internal control mechanisms, including administrative risk management and accounting procedures, which demonstrates that such arrangements, mechanisms and procedures are proportionate, appropriate, sound and adequate.

6. A description of the applicant's procedure for monitoring, handling and following up security incidents and security-related customer complaints, including an incidents reporting mechanism which takes account of the notification obligations under regulation 99 (incident reporting).

7. A description of the applicant's process for filing, monitoring, tracking and restricting access to sensitive payment data.

8. A description of the applicant's business continuity arrangements, including a clear identification of the critical operations, effective contingency plans, and a procedure for regular testing and reviewing of the adequacy and efficiency of such plans.

9. A description of the principles and definitions used by the applicant in collecting statistical data on performance, transactions and fraud.

10. A statement of the applicant's security policy, including—

(a) a detailed risk assessment in relation to the payment services to be provided, including risks of fraud and illegal use of sensitive and personal data, and

(b) a description of—

(i) the applicant's security control and mitigation measures to provide adequate protection to users against the risks identified,

(ii) how such measures ensure a high level of technical security and data protection, including such security and protection for the software and IT systems used by the applicant and any undertakings to which the applicant outsources any part of its operations, and

(iii) the applicant's measures to comply with regulation 98(1) (management of operational and security risks), [. . .].

11. For an applicant subject to the obligations in relation to money laundering and terrorist financing under the Money Laundering, Terrorist Financing and Transfer of Funds (Information on the Payer) Regulations 2017 and Regulation 2015/847/EU of the European Parliament and of the Council of 20th May 2015 on information accompanying transfers of funds, a description of the internal control mechanisms which the applicant has established in order to comply with those obligations.

12. A description of the applicant's structural organisation, including, where applicable, a description of the intended use of agents and branches and the off-site and on-site checks that the applicant undertakes to perform on them at least annually, a description of outsourcing arrangements, and a description of its participation in any national or international payment system.

13. In relation to each person holding, directly or indirectly, a qualifying holding in the applicant—

(a) the size and nature of their qualifying holding; and

(b) evidence of their suitability taking into account the need to ensure the sound and prudent management of a payment institution.

14. (1) The identity of directors and persons who are or will be responsible for the management of the applicant and, where relevant, persons who are or will be responsible for the management of the payment services activities of the applicant.

(2) Evidence that the persons described in sub-paragraph (1) are of good repute and that they possess appropriate knowledge and experience to perform payment services.

15. The identity of the auditors of the applicant, if any.

16. (1) The legal status of the applicant and, where the applicant is a limited company, its articles.

(2) In this paragraph 'articles' has the meaning given in section 18 of the Companies Act 2006 (articles of association).

17. The address of the head office of the applicant.

18. For the purposes of paragraphs 4, 5, 6 and 12, a description of the audit arrangements of the applicant and of the organisational arrangements the applicant has set up with a view to taking all reasonable steps to protect the interests of its payment service users and to ensure continuity and reliability in the performance of payment services.

19. In the case of an applicant which proposes to provide payment initiation services or account information services, the professional indemnity insurance or comparable guarantee which it holds in relation to such services.

Regulations 6(1), 22

SCHEDULE 3

CAPITAL REQUIREMENTS

PART 1 INITIAL CAPITAL

1. For the purposes of this Part, 'initial capital' comprises one or more of the items specified in Article 26(1)(a) to (e) of the capital requirements regulation.

2. (1) The amount of initial capital referred to in regulations 6(3) (conditions for authorisation) and 22(1)(a) (capital requirements) is the amount specified in the second column of the table, corresponding to the payment services provided or to be provided as specified in the first column.

Payment services	Initial capital requirement (euros)
Services specified in paragraph 1(h) of Schedule 1	None
Services specified in paragraph 1(f) of Schedule 1 (money remittance)	20,000
Services specified in paragraph 1(g) of Schedule 1 (payment initiation services)	50,000
Services specified in paragraph 1(a) to (e) of Schedule 1	125,000

(2) Where payment services in more than one row of the table are provided or to be provided, the amount of initial capital is the greater of the corresponding amounts in the second column.

PART 2 OWN FUNDS

Own funds requirement

3. The amount of own funds referred to in regulation 22(1)(b) is to be calculated in accordance with such of Method A, Method B or Method C (set out in paragraphs 8 to 10) as the FCA may direct.

Adjustment by the FCA

4. The FCA may direct that an authorised payment institution must hold own funds up to 20% higher, or up to 20% lower, than the amount which would result from paragraph 3.

5. A direction made under paragraph 4 must be on the basis of an evaluation of the relevant authorised payment institution including, if available and where the FCA considers it appropriate, any risk-management processes, risk loss database or internal control mechanisms of the authorised payment institution.

6. The FCA may make a reasonable charge for making an evaluation required under paragraph 5.

Provision for start-up payment institutions

7. If an authorised payment institution has not completed a full financial year's business, references to a figure for the preceding financial year are to be read as the equivalent figure projected in the business plan provided in the payment institution's application for authorisation, subject to any adjustment to that plan required by the FCA.

Method A

8. (1) 'Method A' means the calculation method set out in this paragraph.

(2) The own funds requirement is 10% of the authorised payment institution's fixed overheads for the preceding financial year.

(3) If a material change has occurred in an authorised payment institution's business since the preceding financial year, the FCA may direct that the own funds requirement is to be a higher or lower amount than that calculated in accordance with sub-paragraph (2).

Method B

9. (1) 'Method B' means the calculation method set out in this paragraph.

(2) The own funds requirement is the sum of the following elements multiplied by the scaling factor—

(a) 4% of the first 5,000,000 euros of payment volume;

(b) 2.5% of the next 5,000,000 euros of payment volume;

(c) 1% of the next 90,000,000 euros of payment volume;

(d) 0.5% of the next 150,000,000 euros of payment volume; and

(e) 0.25% of any remaining payment volume.

(3) 'Payment volume' means the total amount of payment transactions executed by the authorised payment institution in the preceding financial year divided by the number of months in that year.

(4) The 'scaling factor' is—

    (a) 0.5 for a payment institution that is authorised to provide only the payment service specified in paragraph 1(f) of Schedule 1 (money remittance); and

    (b) 1 for a payment institution that is authorised to provide any other payment service specified in paragraph 1(a) to (e) of Schedule 1.

Method C

10. (1) 'Method C' means the calculation method set out in this paragraph.

(2) The own funds requirement is the relevant indicator multiplied by—

    (a) the multiplication factor; and

    (b) the scaling factor;

subject to the proviso in sub-paragraph (7).

(3) The 'relevant indicator' is the sum of the following elements—

    (a) interest income;

    (b) interest expenses;

    (c) gross commissions and fees received; and

    (d) gross other operating income.

(4) For the purpose of calculating the relevant indicator—

    (a) each element must be included in the sum with its positive or negative sign;

    (b) income from extraordinary or irregular items must not be used;

    (c) expenditure on the outsourcing of services rendered by third parties may reduce the relevant indicator if the expenditure is incurred from a payment service provider;

    (d) the relevant indicator is calculated on the basis of the twelve-monthly observation at the end of the previous financial year;

    (e) the relevant indicator must be calculated over the previous financial year; and

    (f) audited figures must be used unless they are not available in which case business estimates may be used.

(5) The 'multiplication factor' is the sum of—

    (a) 10% of the first 2,500,000 euros of the relevant indicator;

    (b) 8% of the next 2,500,000 euros of the relevant indicator;

    (c) 6% of the next 20,000,000 euros of the relevant indicator;

    (d) 3% of the next 25,000,000 euros of the relevant indicator; and

    (e) 1.5% of any remaining amount of the relevant indicator.

(6) 'Scaling factor' has the meaning given in paragraph 9(4).

(7) The proviso is that the own funds requirement must not be less than 80% of the average of the previous three financial years for the relevant indicator.

Application of accounting standards

11. Except where this Schedule provides for a different method of recognition, measurement or valuation, whenever a provision in this Schedule refers to an asset, liability, equity or income statement item, an authorised payment institution must, for the purpose of that provision, recognise the asset, liability, equity or income statement item and measure its value in accordance with whichever of the following are applicable for the purpose of the institution's external financial reporting—

    (a) Financial Reporting Standards and Statements of Standard Accounting Practice issued or adopted by the Financial Reporting Council Limited;

    (b) Statements of Recommended Practice, issued by industry or sectoral bodies recognised for this purpose by the Financial Reporting Council Limited;

    (c) International Financial Reporting Standards and International Accounting Standards issued or adopted by the International Accounting Standards Board;

    (d) International Standards on Auditing (United Kingdom and Ireland) issued by the Financial Reporting Council Limited or a predecessor body;

    (e) the Companies Act 2006.

SCHEDULE 4

PRIOR GENERAL INFORMATION FOR FRAMEWORK CONTRACTS

1. The following information about the payment service provider—
   (a) the name of the payment service provider;
   (b) the address and contact details of the payment service provider's head office;
   (c) if different from the information under sub-paragraph (b), the address and contact details of the branch or agent from which the payment service is being provided;
   (d) details of the payment service provider's regulators, including any reference or registration number of the payment service provider.

2. The following information about the payment service—
   (a) a description of the main characteristics of the payment service to be provided;
   (b) the information or unique identifier that must be provided by the payment service user in order for a payment order to be properly initiated or executed;
   (c) the form and procedure for giving consent to the initiation of a payment order or execution of a payment transaction and for the withdrawal of consent in accordance with regulation 67 (consent and withdrawal of consent);
   (d) a reference to the time of receipt of a payment order, in accordance with regulation 81 (receipt of payment orders), and the cut-off time, if any, established by the payment service provider;
   (e) the maximum execution time for the payment services to be provided;
   (f) whether spending limits for the use of a payment instrument may be agreed in accordance with regulation 71(1) (limits on the use of payment instruments);
   (g) in the case of co-badged card-based payment instruments, the payment services user's rights under Article 8 of the interchange fee regulation.

3. The following information about charges, interest and exchange rates—
   (a) details of all charges payable by the payment service user to the payment service provider, including those connected to the manner in and frequency with which information is provided or made available and, where applicable, a breakdown of the amounts of any charges;
   (b) where relevant, details of the interest and exchange rates to be applied or, if reference interest and exchange rates are to be used, the method of calculating the actual interest and the relevant date and index or base for determining such reference interest or exchange rates;
   (c) where relevant and if agreed, the immediate application of changes in reference interest or exchange rates and information requirements relating to the changes in accordance with regulation 50(4) (changes in contractual information).

4. The following information about communication—
   (a) the means of communication agreed between the parties for the transmission of information or notifications under these Regulations including, where relevant, any technical requirements for the payment service user's equipment and software for receipt of the information or notifications;
   (b) the manner in which and frequency with which information under these Regulations is to be provided or made available;
   (c) the language or languages in which the framework contract will be concluded and in which any information or notifications under these Regulations will be communicated;
   (d) the payment service user's right to receive the terms of the framework contract and information in accordance with regulation 49 (information during period of contract).

5. The following information about safeguards and corrective measures—

    (a) where relevant, a description of the steps that the payment service user is to take in order to keep safe a payment instrument and how to notify the payment service provider for the purposes of regulation 72(1)(b) (obligations of the payment service user in relation to payment instruments and personalised security credentials);

    (b) the secure procedure by which the payment service provider will contact the payment service user in the event of suspected or actual fraud or security threats;

    (c) where relevant, the conditions under which the payment service provider proposes to reserve the right to stop or prevent the use of a payment instrument in accordance with regulation 71(2) to (6);

    (d) the payer's liability under regulation 77 (payer or payee's liability for unauthorised payment transactions), including details of any limits on such liability;

    (e) how and within what period of time the payment service user is to notify the payment service provider of any unauthorised or incorrectly initiated or executed payment transaction under regulation 74 (notification and rectification of unauthorised or incorrectly executed payment transactions), and the payment service provider's liability for unauthorised payment transactions under regulation 76 (payment service provider's liability for unauthorised payment transactions) or, as the case may be, section 83 of the Consumer Credit Act 1974 (liability for misuse of credit facilities);

    (f) the payment service provider's liability for the initiation or execution of payment transactions under regulation 91 or 92 (non-execution or defective or late execution of payment transactions);

    (g) the conditions for the payment of any refund under regulation 79 (refunds for payment transactions initiated by or through a payee).

6. The following information about changes to and termination of the framework contract—

    (a) where relevant, the proposed terms under which the payment service user will be deemed to have accepted changes to the framework contract in accordance with regulation 50(2) (changes in contractual information), unless they notify the payment service provider that they do not accept such changes before the proposed date of their entry into force;

    (b) the duration of the framework contract;

    (c) where relevant, the right of the payment service user to terminate the framework contract and any agreements relating to termination in accordance with regulation 51 (termination of framework contract).

7. The following information about redress—

    (a) any contractual clause on—

        (i) the law applicable to the framework contract;

        (ii) the competent courts;

    (b) the availability of alternative dispute resolution procedures for the payment service user and the methods for having access to them.

. . .

Business Contract Terms (Assignment of Receivables) Regulations 2018

(SI 2018, No. 1254)

1. Citation, commencement, interpretation and application

    (3) In these Regulations—

'firm' has the same meaning as in the Companies Act 2006;

'intangible assets' includes electricity and data which are produced and supplied in digital form;

'licensee', in relation to a petroleum licence, means the person to whom a petroleum licence is granted, their personal representatives and any person to whom the rights conferred by that licence may lawfully be assigned;

'large group' means a group that is not a small group or a medium-sized group (within the meanings given by the Companies Act 2006 or by that Act as applied with modifications by the Limited Liability Partnerships (Accounts and Audit) (Application of the Companies Act 2006) Regulations 2008);

'LLP' means a limited liability partnership formed under the Limited Liability Partnerships Act 2000;

'petroleum licence' means a licence granted under section 2 of the Petroleum (Production) Act 1934(6) or under section 3 of the Petroleum Act 1998;

'prescribed financial services' means a regulated agreement within the meaning of the Consumer Credit Act 1974 or any financial service within the meaning of section 2 of the Small Business, Enterprise and Employment Act 2015; and

'receivable' is a right (whether or not earned by performance) to be paid any amount under a contract (other than a contract mentioned in regulation 4) for the supply of goods, services or intangible assets (and in relation to a receivable, 'supplier' means the supplier of those goods, services or intangible assets to whom that amount is payable and 'debtor' means the person liable to pay that amount).

(4) These Regulations have effect notwithstanding any contract term which applies or purports to apply the law of Scotland or some country outside the United Kingdom, where the term appears to the court or arbitrator or arbiter to have been imposed wholly or mainly for the purpose of enabling the party imposing it to evade the operation of these Regulations.

2. Effect of a non-assignment of receivables term

(1) Subject to regulations 3 and 4, a term in a contract has no effect to the extent that it prohibits or imposes a condition, or other restriction, on the assignment of a receivable arising under that contract or any other contract between the same parties.

(2) A term in a contract which imposes a condition or other restriction on the assignment of a receivable includes a term which prevents a person to whom a receivable is assigned from determining the validity or value of the receivable or their ability to enforce the receivable.

(3) For the purposes of paragraph (2), a term prevents a person to whom a receivable is assigned from determining the validity or value of the receivable or their ability to enforce the receivable if the condition or other restriction prevents that person from obtaining—

    (a) the names and addresses of the parties to the contract;

    (b) the name and address of the person who on behalf of the debtor can confirm the validity and amount of the receivable;

    (c) the VAT registration number of the debtor and of the supplier;

    (d) the date on which the goods, services or intangible assets that give rise to the receivable are supplied;

    (e) a description sufficient to identify the goods, services or intangible assets that give rise to the receivable (including the quantity of goods or intangible assets, or the extent of services, the unit price, the rate of VAT and the amount payable, excluding VAT);

    (f) the date and number of the invoice for the goods, services or intangible assets that give rise to the receivable and any credit note related to the invoice (and the reason for issuing the credit note);

    (g) the amount, basis or rate of any applicable discount;

    (h) the total amount of VAT chargeable;

    (i) the reason for any VAT zero-rating or VAT exemption;

    (j) details of any term in the contract to which regulation 2(1) applies;

    (k) the credit period for paying the receivable;

(l) evidence of the performance of that part of the contract (or other contract between the parties) which gives rise to the receivable; or

(m) particulars and evidence of any potential defence or set-off by a party to the contract.

3. Exception for suppliers who are large enterprises or special purpose vehicles

(1) Regulation 2 does not apply and accordingly a term mentioned in that regulation does have effect in relation to the assignment of a receivable if at the time of the assignment the supplier is a large enterprise or a special purpose vehicle.

(2) A supplier is a large enterprise unless it satisfies one of the conditions in paragraph (3) and in paragraph (3) 'relevant financial year' means the last financial year (before the date on which the receivable is assigned) in respect of which the supplier has filed accounts.

(3) The conditions in this paragraph are—

(a) the supplier is an individual, a partnership (other than an LLP or a limited partnership) or an unincorporated association;

(b) the supplier is a company to which the small companies regime (within the meaning given by sections 381 to 384 of the Companies Act 2006) applied in the relevant financial year and which was not a member of a large group in the relevant financial year;

(c) the supplier is a company which qualified as medium-sized (within the meaning given by sections 465 to 467 of the Companies Act 2006) in respect of the relevant financial year and which was not a member of a large group in the relevant financial year;

(d) the supplier is a company (other than an unlimited company exempt under section 448 of the Companies Act 2006 from the obligation to file accounts) that has not filed accounts since its incorporation and whose accounts are not overdue and which is not a member of a large group;

(e) the supplier is an unlimited company exempt under section 448 of the Companies Act 2006 from the obligation to file accounts, that has not filed accounts since its incorporation and whose accounts would not be overdue if the exemption under that section did not apply and which is not a member of a large group;

(f) the supplier is an LLP to which the small LLPs regime (within the meaning given by the Companies Act 2006, as applied with modifications by regulation 5 of the Limited Liability Partnerships (Accounts and Audit) (Application of the Companies Act 2006) Regulations 2008), applied in the relevant financial year and which was not a member of a large group in the relevant financial year;

(g) the supplier is an LLP which qualified as medium-sized (within the meaning given by the Companies Act 2006, as applied with modifications by regulation 26 of the Limited Liability Partnerships (Accounts and Audit) (Application of the Companies Act 2006) Regulations 2008) in respect of the relevant financial year and which was not a member of a large group in the relevant financial year;

(h) the supplier is an LLP that has not filed accounts since its incorporation and whose accounts are not overdue and which is not a member of a large group;

(i) the supplier is a body corporate incorporated outside the United Kingdom which, if it were a company formed and registered under the Companies Act 2006, would have been a company to which the small companies regime (within the meaning given by that Act) would have applied in the relevant financial year and which would not have been a member of a large group in the relevant financial year;

(j) the supplier is a body corporate incorporated outside the United Kingdom which, if it were a company formed and registered under the Companies Act 2006, would have qualified as medium-sized (within the meaning given by that Act) in respect of the relevant financial year and which would not have been a member of a large group in the relevant financial year; and

(k) the supplier is a body corporate incorporated outside the United Kingdom that has not filed accounts since its incorporation and whose accounts would not be overdue, and which would not be a member of a large group if it were a company formed and registered under the Companies Act 2006.

(4) A special purpose vehicle is a firm, wherever it is incorporated or established, that carries out a primary purpose in relation to—

(a) the holding of assets (other than trading stock within the meaning of the Income Tax (Trading and Other Income) Act 2005); or

(b) the financing of commercial transactions,

which in either case involves it incurring a liability under an agreement of £10 million or more.

(5) For the purposes of paragraph (4)—

(a) where a liability is a contingent liability under or by virtue of a guarantee or an indemnity or security provided on behalf of another person, the amount of that liability is the full amount of the liability in relation to which the guarantee, indemnity or security is provided;

(b) where the amount of a liability is reduced or recourse in respect of it is limited by reference to the value of the special purpose vehicle's assets at the time the liability is due, the amount of that liability is the full amount of the liability, ignoring that reduction or limit;

(c) the reference to a liability includes—

(i) a present or future liability whether, in either case, it is certain or contingent,

(ii) a reference to a liability to be paid wholly or partly in foreign currency (in which case the sterling equivalent shall be calculated as at the time when the liability was incurred).

4. Other exceptions

Regulation 2 does not apply to a term in a contract which is—

(a) a contract for, or entered into in connection with, prescribed financial services;

(b) a contract which concerns any interest in land;

(c) a contract where one or more of the parties to the contract is acting for purposes which are outside a trade, business or profession;

(d) a contract where none of the parties to the contract has entered into it in the course of carrying on a business in the United Kingdom;

(e) a contract which concerns national security interests (and a certificate provided by the Secretary of State to the effect that a contract concerns national security interests shall be conclusive evidence of that fact);

(f) a contract where one or more parties to the contract is a person designated as a counterparty for a contract for difference under section 7 of the Energy Act 2013 and who has entered into the contract by virtue of that Act;

(g) a petroleum licence;

(h) a contract where one or more parties to the contract is the licensee in respect of a petroleum licence whose terms would prohibit or restrict the assignment of receivables under that contract;

(i) a contract which is entered into for the purposes of, or in connection with, the acquisition, disposal or transfer of an ownership interest in a firm, wherever it is incorporated or established, or of a business or undertaking or part of a business or undertaking, and which includes a statement to that effect;

(j) an option, future, swap, forward, contract for differences or other derivatives contract, not falling within paragraph (a), which may be settled physically or in cash, relating to commodities, energy, emission allowances, climactic variables, freight rates or inflation rates or other official economic statistics that is either—

> > (i)   traded on a regulated market, multilateral trading facility or organised trading fa-
> > cility, or
> > (ii)   is not traded on a regulated market, multilateral trading facility or organised trad-
> > ing facility, but is entered into under a market agreement providing for close-out
> > netting,
> > and 'regulated market', 'multilateral trading facility' and 'organised trading facility'
> > have the same meaning as in Article 4(1) of Directive 2014/65/EU of the European
> > Parliament and of the Council of 15 May 2014 on Markets in Financial Instruments
> > (recast);
> (k)   a contract entered into by the project company of a project which is—
> > (i)   a public-private partnership project;
> > (ii)   a utility project;
> > (iii)   a financed project; or
> > (iv)   designed wholly or mainly to develop land which at the commencement of the pro-
> > ject is wholly or partly in a designated disadvantaged area outside Northern Ireland,
> > and expressions used in this sub-paragraph which are also used in Chapter 4 of Part 3 of
> > the Insolvency Act 1986 have the meaning given in that Chapter, except that 'company'
> > includes a firm, wherever it is incorporated or established;
> (l)   a contract entered into by a trust, fund or other entity, or an arrangement entered, cre-
> > ated by or on behalf of a site operator (within the meaning in the Energy Act 2008) to
> > hold and accumulate assets under the terms of a funding arrangements plan that is part
> > of a funded decommissioning programme submitted to the Secretary of State for ap-
> > proval under section 45 of that Act; or
> (m) a contract, not falling within paragraph (a), entered into wholly or mainly for the pur-
> > pose of granting by one person of a right to possession or control of an object to another
> > person in return for a rental or other payment.

Electronic Presentment of Instruments (Evidence of Payment and Compensation for Loss) Regulations 2018

(SI 2018, No. 832)

3.   Provision of copy of a paid instrument

(1)   A banker who has paid an instrument as a result of presentment under section 89A of the Bills of Exchange Act 1882 must, if requested to do so by the creator of the instrument, provide a copy of the instrument to the creator before the end of the period of 10 working days beginning with the first working day after the banker received the request.

4.   Copy of instrument as evidence of payment

A copy of an instrument and the accompanying information provided in accordance with regulation 3 is evidence of receipt by the payee named in the instrument of the sum payable by the instrument.

5.   Responsible banker to compensate eligible claimants

(1)   Subject to the following provisions of this Part, a responsible banker must compensate a person ('the claimant') for loss incurred by the claimant if—

> (a)   the claimant incurred the loss in connection with electronic presentment or purported
> electronic presentment of an instrument,
> (b)   the claimant is—
> > (i)   the customer of the banker which has paid the instrument, from whose account the
> > payment was debited, or

      (ii) the banker which paid the instrument,
  (c) the loss resulted wholly or in part from a factor other than—
      (i) gross negligence on the part of the claimant, or
      (ii) fraudulent activity in which the claimant was knowingly involved,
  (d) the claimant has notified a banker in accordance with regulation 6(1) and made a claim in accordance with regulation 6(3) and (4), and
  (e) one of the criteria in paragraph (2) is met.

(2) The criteria are—
  (a) the electronic presentment or purported electronic presentment of the instrument was of a type described in section 89E(2)(c), (d) or (e) of the Bills of Exchange Act 1882;
  (b) the instrument was collected for or paid to a person other than the true owner of the instrument.

(3) Paragraph (1) applies irrespective of fault for the loss incurred by the claimant (but regulation 8 makes provision for the reduction in the amount of compensation to be paid in certain circumstances).

(4) In this regulation, references to 'loss' are to loss arising directly from the debiting of funds from the claimant's account and do not include any further loss arising in consequence thereof.

6. Procedure for making and determining claims

(1) Before making a claim for compensation under this Part—
  (a) where the claimant is the customer of the banker which paid the instrument, and from whose account the payment was debited, the claimant must notify that banker in writing of the loss to which the claim relates;
  (b) where the claimant is the banker which paid the instrument, the claimant must notify the responsible banker in writing of the loss to which the claim relates.

(2) Where the banker which paid the instrument has been notified in accordance with paragraph (1)(a), that banker must notify the responsible banker in writing of that notification before the end of the period of 5 working days starting on the first working day after the banker received the notification.

(3) A claim for compensation under this Part must—
  (a) be made to the responsible banker in writing, and
  (b) include all information relating to the claim necessary for the responsible banker to assess whether the conditions in regulation 5 have been met.

(4) A claim for compensation under this Part—
  (a) may be made only if—
      (i) the period of 56 days beginning with the day after the day on which the claimant notified the loss in accordance with paragraph (1) has expired, and
      (ii) compensation for the total loss to which the claim relates has not been paid to the claimant, whether under another scheme or otherwise, and
  (b) must be made before the end of the period of 6 years beginning with the day after the day on which the loss was incurred.

(5) Subject to paragraph (7), the responsible banker must before the end of the period of 15 working days beginning with the first working day after the day on which the responsible banker receives a claim for compensation under this Part, send to the claimant in writing—
  (a) acceptance of the claim, and confirmation of—
      (i) the amount that has been paid in respect of the claim, or
      (ii) the amount that will be paid in respect of the claim and the date by which such amount will be paid, which must be before the end of the period of 10 working days beginning with the first working day after the day on which the acceptance is sent,
  (b) refusal of the claim and the reason for the refusal, or
  (c) a request for further information to enable the responsible banker to assess the claim.

(6) If the responsible banker requests further information under paragraph (5)(c), the responsible banker must in any event send the claimant an acceptance or refusal of the claim as described in paragraph (5)(a) or (b) within the period of 120 days beginning with the day after that on which the responsible banker received the claim.

(7) The responsible banker is not required to give a notification of refusal in accordance with paragraph (5)(b) if—

(a) the responsible banker has reasonable grounds to suspect fraudulent activity in which the claimant was knowingly involved,

(b) the responsible banker has notified the appropriate authority of such suspected fraudulent activity and grounds, and

(c) the responsible banker considers that giving a notification in accordance with paragraph (5)(b) would be likely to prejudice any investigation into the suspected fraudulent activity.

7. Protection of potential claimant by section 80 of the Bills of Exchange Act 1882

Regulation 5 does not require the responsible banker to compensate the claimant if the claimant is entitled to the same rights, and is placed in the same position, as if payment of the instrument had been made to the true owner thereof pursuant to section 80 of the Bills of Exchange Act 1882 (protection to banker and drawer where cheque is crossed).

8. Contributory behaviour by the claimant

Where a claimant incurs a loss in respect of which a responsible banker is liable to pay compensation under regulation 5, and that loss results wholly or in part from an act or omission of the claimant, the amount of the compensation to be paid by the responsible banker to the claimant is reduced in proportion to the contribution of such act or omission to the loss.

9. Action for damages

A failure by a banker to pay the full amount of compensation to be paid to a claimant under this Part is actionable at the suit of the claimant, subject to the defences and other incidents applying to actions for breach of statutory duty.

10. Review

(1) The Treasury must from time to time—

(a) carry out a review of the regulatory provision contained in these Regulations,

. . .

(5) In this regulation, 'regulatory provision' has the same meaning as in sections 28 to 32 of the Small Business, Enterprise and Employment Act 2015 (see section 32 of that Act).

International Conventions

United Nations Convention on Contracts for the International Sale of Goods 1980*

THE STATES PARTIES TO THIS CONVENTION,

BEARING IN MIND the broad objectives in the resolutions adopted by the sixth special session of the General Assembly of the United Nations on the establishment of a New International Economic Order,

CONSIDERING that the development of international trade on the basis of equality and mutual benefit is an important element in promoting friendly relations among States,

BEING OF THE OPINION that the adoption of uniform rules which govern contracts for the international sale of goods and take into account the different social, economic and legal systems would contribute to the removal of legal barriers in international trade and promote the development of international trade,

HAVE AGREED as follows:

PART I SPHERE OF APPLICATION AND GENERAL PROVISIONS

Chapter I Sphere of application

Article 1

1. This Convention applies to contracts of sale of goods between parties whose places of business are in different States:
    (a) when the States are Contracting States; or
    (b) when the rules of private international law lead to the application of the law of a Contracting State.

2. The fact that the parties have their places of business in different States is to be disregarded whenever this fact does not appear either from the contract or from any dealings between, or from information disclosed by, the parties at any time before or at the conclusion of the contract.

3. Neither the nationality of the parties nor the civil or commercial character of the parties or of the contract is to be taken into consideration in determining the application of this Convention.

Article 2

This Convention does not apply to sales:
    (a) of goods bought for personal, family or household use unless the seller, at any time before or at the conclusion of the contract, neither knew nor ought to have known that the goods were bought for any such use;
    (b) by auction;
    (c) on execution or otherwise by authority of law;
    (d) of stocks, shares, investment securities, negotiable instruments or money;
    (e) of ships, vessels, hovercraft or aircraft;
    (f) of electricity.

* Reproduced with permission from the United Nations Commission on International Trade Law (UNCITRAL).

Article 3

1. Contracts for the supply of goods to be manufactured or produced are to be considered sales unless the party who orders the goods undertakes to supply a substantial part of the materials necessary for such manufacture or production.

2. This Convention does not apply to contracts in which the preponderant part of the obligations of the party who furnishes the goods consists in the supply of labour or other services.

Article 4

This Convention governs only the formation of the contract of sale and the rights and obligations of the seller and the buyer arising from such a contract. In particular, except as otherwise expressly provided in this Convention, it is not concerned with:

>   (a) the validity of the contract or of any of its provisions or of any usage;

>   (b) the effect which the contract may have on the property in the goods sold.

Article 5

This Convention does not apply to the liability of the seller for death or personal injury caused by the goods to any person.

Article 6

The parties may exclude the application of this Convention or, subject to article 12, derogate from or vary the effect of any of its provisions.

Chapter II General provisions

Article 7

1. In the interpretation of this Convention, regard is to be had to its international character and to the need to promote uniformity in its application and the observance of good faith in international trade.

2. Questions concerning matters governed by this Convention which are not expressly settled in it are to be settled in conformity with the general principles on which it is based or, in the absence of such principles, in conformity with the law applicable by virtue of the rules of private international law.

Article 8

1. For the purposes of this Convention statements made by and other conduct of a party are to be interpreted according to his intent where the other party knew or could not have been unaware what that intent was.

2. If the preceding paragraph is not applicable, statements made by and other conduct of a party are to be interpreted according to the understanding that a reasonable person of the same kind as the other party would have had in the same circumstances.

3. In determining the intent of a party or the understanding a reasonable person would have had, due consideration is to be given to all relevant circumstances of the case including the negotiations, any practices which the parties have established between themselves, usages and any subsequent conduct of the parties.

Article 9

1. The parties are bound by any usage to which they have agreed and by any practices which they have established between themselves.

2. The parties are considered, unless otherwise agreed, to have impliedly made applicable to their contract or its formation a usage of which the parties knew or ought to have known and which in international trade is widely known to, and regularly observed by, parties to contracts of the type involved in the particular trade concerned.

Article 10

For the purposes of this Convention:

>   (a) if a party has more than one place of business, the place of business is that which has the closest relationship to the contract and its performance, having regard to the

circumstances known to or contemplated by the parties at any time before or at the conclusion of the contract;

(b) if a party does not have a place of business, reference is to be made to his habitual residence.

Article 11

A contract of sale need not be concluded in or evidenced by writing and is not subject to any other requirement as to form. It may be proved by any means, including witnesses.

Article 12

Any provision of article 11, article 29 or Part II of this Convention that allows a contract of sale or its modification or termination by agreement or any offer, acceptance or other indication of intention to be made in any form other than in writing does not apply where any party has his place of business in a Contracting State which has made a declaration under article 96 of this Convention. The parties may not derogate from or vary the effect of this article.

Article 13

For the purposes of this Convention 'writing' includes telegram and telex.

PART II FORMATION OF THE CONTRACT

Article 14

1. A proposal for concluding a contract addressed to one or more specific persons constitutes an offer if it is sufficiently definite and indicates the intention of the offeror to be bound in case of acceptance. A proposal is sufficiently definite if it indicates the goods and expressly or implicitly fixes or makes provision for determining the quantity and the price.

2. A proposal other than one addressed to one or more specific persons is to be considered merely as an invitation to make offers, unless the contrary is clearly indicated by the person making the proposal.

Article 15

1. An offer becomes effective when it reaches the offeree.

2. An offer, even if it is irrevocable, may be withdrawn if the withdrawal reaches the offeree before or at the same time as the offer.

Article 16

1. Until a contract is concluded an offer may be revoked if the revocation reaches the offeree before he has dispatched an acceptance.

2. However, an offer cannot be revoked:

(a) if it indicates, whether by stating a fixed time for acceptance or otherwise, that it is irrevocable; or

(b) if it was reasonable for the offeree to rely on the offer as being irrevocable and the offeree has acted in reliance on the offer.

Article 17

An offer, even if it is irrevocable, is terminated when a rejection reaches the offeror.

Article 18

1. A statement made by or other conduct of the offeree indicating assent to an offer is an acceptance. Silence or inactivity does not itself amount to acceptance.

2. An acceptance of an offer becomes effective at the moment the indication of assent reaches the offeror. An acceptance is not effective if the indication of assent does not reach the offeror within the time he has fixed or, if no time is fixed, within a reasonable time, due account being taken of the circumstances of the transaction, including the rapidity of the means of communication employed by the offeror. An oral offer must be accepted immediately unless the circumstances indicate otherwise.

3. However, if, by virtue of the offer or as a result of practices which the parties have established between themselves or of usage, the offeree may indicate assent by performing an act, such as one relating to the dispatch of the goods or payment of the price, without notice to the offeror, the acceptance is effective at the moment the act is performed, provided that the act is performed within the period of time laid down in the preceding paragraph.

Article 19

1. A reply to an offer which purports to be an acceptance but contains additions, limitations or other modifications is a rejection of the offer and constitutes a counter-offer.

2. However, a reply to an offer which purports to be an acceptance but contains additional or different terms which do not materially alter the terms of the offer constitutes an acceptance, unless the offeror, without undue delay, objects orally to the discrepancy or dispatches a notice to the effect. If he does not so object, the terms of the contract are the terms of the offer with the modifications contained in the acceptance.

3. Additional or different terms relating, among other things, to the price, payment, quality and quantity of the goods, place and time of delivery, extent of one party's liability to the other or the settlement of disputes are considered to alter the terms of the offer materially.

Article 20

1. A period of time for acceptance fixed by the offeror in a telegram or a letter begins to run from the moment the telegram is handed in for dispatch or from the date shown on the letter or, if no such date is shown on the letter or, if no such date is shown, from the date shown on the envelope. A period of time for acceptance fixed by the offeror by telephone, telex or other means of instantaneous communication, begins to run from the moment that the offer reaches the offeree.

2. Official holidays or non-business days occurring during the period for acceptance are included in calculating the period. However, if a notice of acceptance cannot be delivered at the address of the offeror on the last day of the period because that day falls on an official holiday or a non-business day at the place of business of the offeror, the period is extended until the first business day which follows.

Article 21

1. A late acceptance is nevertheless effective as an acceptance if without delay the offeror orally so informs the offeree or dispatches a notice to that effect.

2. If a letter or other writing containing a late acceptance shows that it has been sent in such circumstances that if its transmission had been normal it would have reached the offeror in due time, the late acceptance is effective as an acceptance unless, without delay, the offeror orally informs the offeree that he considers his offer as having lapsed or dispatches a notice to that effect.

Article 22

An acceptance may be withdrawn if the withdrawal reaches the offeror before or at the same time as the acceptance would have become effective.

Article 23

A contract is concluded at the moment when an acceptance of an offer becomes effective in accordance with the provisions of this Convention.

Article 24

For the purposes of this Part of the Convention, an offer, declaration of acceptance or any other indication of intention 'reaches' the addressee when it is made orally to him or delivered by any other means to him personally, to his place of business or mailing address or, if he does not have a place of business or mailing address, to his habitual residence.

PART III SALE OF GOODS

Chapter I General provisions

Article 25

A breach of contract committed by one of the parties is fundamental if it results in such detriment to the other party as substantially to deprive him of what he is entitled to expect under the contract, unless the party in breach did not foresee and a reasonable person of the same kind in the same circumstances would not have foreseen such a result.

Article 26

A declaration of avoidance of the contract is effective only if made by notice to the other party.

Article 27

Unless otherwise expressly provided in this Part of the Convention, if any notice, request or other communication is given or made by a party in accordance with this Part and by means appropriate in the circumstances, a delay or error in the transmission of the communication or its failure to arrive does not deprive that party of the right to rely on the communication.

Article 28

If, in accordance with the provisions of this Convention, one party is entitled to require performance of any obligation by the other party, a court is not bound to enter a judgment for specific performance unless the court would do so under its own law in respect of similar contracts of sale not governed by this Convention.

Article 29

1. A contract may be modified or terminated by the mere agreement of the parties.

2. A contract in writing which contains a provision requiring any modification or termination by agreement to be in writing may not be otherwise modified or terminated by agreement. However, a party may be precluded by his conduct from asserting such a provision to the extent that the other party has relied on that conduct.

Chapter II Obligations of the seller

Article 30

The seller must deliver the goods, hand over any documents relating to them and transfer the property in the goods, as required by the contract and this Convention.

Section I Delivery of the goods and handing over of documents

Article 31

If the seller is not bound to deliver the goods at any other particular place, his obligation to deliver consists:

(a) if the contract of sale involves carriage of the goods—in handing the goods over to the first carrier for transmission to the buyer;

(b) if, in cases not within the preceding sub-paragraph, the contract relates to specific goods, or unidentified goods to be drawn from a specific stock or to be manufactured or produced, and at the time of the conclusion of the contract the parties knew that the goods were at, or were to be manufactured or produced at, a particular place—in placing the goods at the buyer's disposal at that place;

(c) in other cases—in placing the goods at the buyer's disposal at the place where the seller had his place of business at the time of the conclusion of the contract.

Article 32

1. If the seller, in accordance with the contract or this Convention, hands the goods over to a carrier and if the goods are not clearly identified to the contract by markings on the goods, by shipping documents or otherwise, the seller must give the buyer notice of the consignment specifying the goods.

2. If the seller is bound to arrange for carriage of the goods, he must make such contracts as are necessary for carriage to the place fixed by means of transportation appropriate in the circumstances and according to the usual terms for such transportation.

3. If the seller is not bound to effect insurance in respect of the carriage of the goods, he must, at the buyer's request, provide him with all available information necessary to enable him to effect such insurance.

Article 33

The seller must deliver the goods:
   (a) if a date is fixed by or determinable from the contract, on that date;
   (b) if a period of time is fixed by or determinable from the contract, at any time within that period unless circumstances indicate that the buyer is to choose a date; or
   (c) in any other case, within a reasonable time after the conclusion of the contract.

Article 34

If the seller is bound to hand over documents relating to the goods, he must hand them over at the time and place and in the form required by the contract. If the seller has handed over documents before that time, he may, up to that time, cure any lack of conformity in the documents, if the exercise of this right does not cause the buyer unreasonable inconvenience or unreasonable expense. However, the buyer retains any right to claim damages as provided for in this Convention.

Section II Conformity of the goods and third party claims

Article 35

1. The seller must deliver goods which are of the quantity, quality and description required by the contract and which are contained or packaged in the manner required by the contract.

2. Except where the parties have agreed otherwise, the goods do not conform with the contract unless they:
   (a) are fit for the purposes for which goods of the same description would ordinarily be used
   (b) are fit for any particular purpose expressly or impliedly made known to the seller at the time of the conclusion of the contract, except where the circumstances show that the buyer did not rely, or that it was unreasonable for him to rely, on the seller's skill and judgment;
   (c) possess the qualities of goods which the seller has held out to the buyer as a sample or model;
   (d) are contained or packaged in the manner usual for such goods or, where there is no such manner, in a manner adequate to preserve and protect the goods.

3. The seller is not liable under subparagraphs (a) to (d) of the preceding paragraph for any lack of conformity of the goods if at the time of the conclusion of the contract the buyer knew or could not have been unaware of such lack of conformity.

Article 36

1. The seller is liable in accordance with the contract and this Convention for any lack of conformity which exists at the time when the risk passes to the buyer, even though the lack of conformity becomes apparent only after that time.

2. The seller is also liable for any lack of conformity which occurs after the time indicated in the preceding paragraph and which is due to a breach of any of his obligations, including a breach of any guarantee that for a period of time the goods will remain fit for their ordinary purpose or for some particular purpose or will retain specified qualities or characteristics.

Article 37

If the seller has delivered goods before the date for delivery, he may, up to that date, deliver any missing part or make up any deficiency in the quantity of the goods delivered, or deliver goods in replacement of any non-conforming goods delivered or remedy any lack of conformity in the goods delivered, provided that the exercise of this right does not cause the buyer unreasonable inconvenience or unreasonable expense. However, the buyer retains any right to claim damages as provided for in this Convention.

Article 38

1. The buyer must examine the goods, or cause them to be examined, within as short a period as is practicable in the circumstances.

2. If the contract involves carriage of the goods, examination may be deferred until after the goods have arrived at their destination.

3. If the goods are redirected in transit or redispatched by the buyer without a reasonable opportunity for examination by him and at the time of the conclusion of the contract the seller knew or ought to have known of the possibility of such redirection or redispatch, examination may be deferred until after the goods have arrived at the new destination.

Article 39

1. The buyer loses the right to rely on a lack of conformity of the goods if he does not give notice to the seller specifying the nature of the lack of conformity within a reasonable time after he has discovered it or ought to have discovered it.

2. In any event, the buyer loses the right to rely on a lack of conformity of the goods if he does not give the seller notice thereof at the latest within a period of two years from the date on which the goods were actually handed over to the buyer, unless this time-limit is inconsistent with a contractual period of guarantee.

Article 40

The seller is not entitled to rely on the provisions of articles 38 and 39 if the lack of conformity relates to facts of which he knew or could not have been unaware and which he did not disclose to the buyer.

Article 41

The seller must deliver goods which are free from any right or claim of a third party, unless the buyer agreed to take the goods subject to that right or claim. However, if such right or claim is based on industrial property or other intellectual property, the seller's obligation is governed by article 42.

Article 42

1. The seller must deliver goods which are free from any right or claim of a third party based on industrial property or other intellectual property, of which at the time of the conclusion of the contract the seller knew or could not have been unaware, provided that the right or claim is based on industrial property or other intellectual property:

   (a) under the law of the State where the goods will be resold or otherwise used, if it was contemplated by the parties at the time of the conclusion of the contract that the goods would be resold or otherwise used in that State; or

   (b) in any other case, under the law of the State where the buyer has his place of business.

2. The obligation of the seller under the preceding paragraph does not extend to cases where:

   (a) at the time of the conclusion of the contract the buyer knew or could not have been unaware of the right or claim; or

   (b) the right or claim results from the seller's compliance with technical drawings, designs, formulae or other such specifications furnished by the buyer.

Article 43

1. The buyer loses the right to rely on the provisions of article 41 or article 42 if he does not give notice to the seller specifying the nature of the right or claim of the third party within a reasonable time after he has become aware or ought to have become aware of the right or claim.

2. The seller is not entitled to rely on the provisions of the preceding paragraph if he knew of the right or claim of the third party and the nature of it.

Article 44

Notwithstanding the provisions of paragraph 1 of article 39 and paragraph 1 of article 43, the buyer may reduce the price in accordance with article 50 or claim damages, except for loss of profit, if he has a reasonable excuse for his failure to give the required notice.

Section III Remedies for breach of contract by the seller

Article 45

1. If the seller fails to perform any of his obligations under the contract or this Convention, the buyer may:

    (a) exercise the rights provided in articles 46 to 52;

    (b) claim damages as provided in articles 74 to 77.

2. The buyer is not deprived of any right he may have to claim damages by exercising his right to other remedies.

3. No period of grace may be granted to the seller by a court or arbitral tribunal when the buyer resorts to a remedy for breach of contract.

Article 46

1. The buyer may require performance by the seller of his obligations unless the buyer has resorted to a remedy which is inconsistent with this requirement.

2. If the goods do not conform with the contract, the buyer may require delivery of substitute goods only if the lack of conformity constitutes a fundamental breach of contract and a request for substitute goods is made either in conjunction with notice given under article 39 or within a reasonable time thereafter.

3. If the goods do not conform with the contract, the buyer may require the seller to remedy the lack of conformity by repair, unless this is unreasonable having regard to all the circumstances. A request for repair must be made either in conjunction with notice given under article 39 or within a reasonable time thereafter.

Article 47

1. The buyer may fix an additional period of time of reasonable length for performance by the seller of his obligations.

2. Unless the buyer has received notice from the seller that he will not perform within the period so fixed, the buyer may not, during that period, resort to any remedy for breach of contract. However, the buyer is not deprived thereby of any right he may have to claim damages for delay in performance.

Article 48

1. Subject to article 49, the seller may, even after the date for delivery, remedy at his own expense any failure to perform his obligations, if he can do so without unreasonable delay and without causing the buyer unreasonable inconvenience or uncertainty of reimbursement by the seller of expenses advanced by the buyer. However, the buyer retains any right to claim damages as provided for in this Convention.

2. If the seller requests the buyer to make known whether he will accept performance and the buyer does not comply with the request within a reasonable time, the seller may perform within the time indicated in his request. The buyer may not, during that period of time, resort to any remedy which is inconsistent with performance by the seller.

3. A notice by the seller that he will perform within a specified period of time is assumed to include a request, under the preceding paragraph, that the buyer make known his decision.

4. A request or notice by the seller under paragraph 2 or 3 of this article is not effective unless received by the buyer.

Article 49

1. The buyer may declare the contract avoided:

    (a) if the failure by the seller to perform any of his obligations under the contract or this Convention amounts to a fundamental breach of contract; or

(b) in case of non-delivery, if the seller does not deliver the goods within the additional period of time fixed by the buyer in accordance with paragraph 1 of article 47 or declares that he will not deliver within the period so fixed.

2. However, in cases where the seller has delivered the goods, the buyer loses the right to declare the contract avoided unless he does so:

(a) in respect of late delivery, within a reasonable time after he has become aware that delivery has been made;

(b) in respect of any breach other than late delivery, within a reasonable time:

(i) after he knew or ought to have known of the breach;

(ii) after the expiration of any additional period of time fixed by the buyer in accordance with paragraph 1 of article 47, or after the seller has declared that he will not perform his obligations within such an additional period; or

(iii) after the expiration of any additional period of time indicated by the seller in accordance with paragraph 2 of article 48, or after the buyer has declared that he will not accept performance.

Article 50

If the goods do not conform with the contract and whether or not the price has already been paid, the buyer may reduce the price in the same proportion as the value that the goods actually delivered had at the time of the delivery bears to the value that conforming goods would have had at that time. However, if the seller remedies any failure to perform his obligations in accordance with article 37 or article 48 or if the buyer refuses to accept performance by the seller in accordance with those articles, the buyer may not reduce the price.

Article 51

1. If the seller delivers only a part of the goods or if only a part of the goods delivered is in conformity with the contract, articles 46 to 50 apply in respect of the part which is missing or which does not conform.

2. The buyer may declare the contract avoided in its entirety only if the failure to make delivery completely or in conformity with the contract amounts to a fundamental breach of the contract.

Article 52

1. If the seller delivers the goods before the date fixed, the buyer may take delivery or refuse to take delivery.

2. If the seller delivers a quantity of goods greater than that provided for in the contract, the buyer may take delivery or refuse to take delivery of the excess quantity. If the buyer takes delivery of all or part of the excess quantity, he must pay for it at the contract rate.

Chapter III Obligations of the buyer

Article 53

The buyer must pay the price for the goods and take delivery of them as required by the contract and this Convention.

Section I Payment of the price

Article 54

The buyer's obligation to pay the price includes taking such steps and complying with such formalities as may be required under the contract or any laws and regulations to enable payment to be made.

Article 55

Where a contract has been validly concluded but does not expressly or implicitly fix or make provision for determining the price, the parties are considered, in the absence of any indication to the contrary, to have impliedly made reference to the price generally charged at the time of the conclusion of the contract for such goods sold under comparable circumstances in the trade concerned.

Article 56

If the price is fixed according to the weight of the goods, in case of doubt it is to be determined by the net weight.

Article 57

1. If the buyer is not bound to pay the price at any other particular place, he must pay it to the seller:
    (a) at the seller's place of business; or
    (b) if the payment is to be made against the handing over of the goods or of documents, at the place where the handing over takes place.
2. The seller must bear any increase in the expenses incidental to payment which is caused by a change in his place of business subsequent to the conclusion of the contract.

Article 58

1. If the buyer is not bound to pay the price at any other specific time, he must pay it when the seller places either the goods or documents controlling their disposition at the buyer's disposal in accordance with the contract and this Convention. The seller may make such payment a condition for handing over the goods or documents.
2. If the contract involves carriage of the goods, the seller may dispatch the goods on terms whereby the goods, or documents controlling their disposition, will not be handed over to the buyer except against payment of the price.
3. The buyer is not bound to pay the price until he has had an opportunity to examine the goods, unless the procedures for delivery or payment agreed upon by the parties are inconsistent with his having such an opportunity.

Article 59

The buyer must pay the price on the date fixed by or determinable from the contract and this Convention without the need for any request or compliance with any formality on the part of the seller.

Section II Taking delivery

Article 60

The buyer's obligation to take delivery consists:
    (a) in doing all the acts which could reasonably be expected of him in order to enable the seller to make delivery, and
    (b) in taking over the goods.

Section III Remedies for breach of contract by the buyer

Article 61

1. If the buyer fails to perform any of his obligations under the contract or this Convention, the seller may:
    (a) exercise the rights provided in articles 62 to 65;
    (b) claim damages as provided in articles 74 to 77.
2. The seller is not deprived of any right he may have to claim damages by exercising his right to other remedies.
3. No period of grace may be granted to the buyer by a court or arbitral tribunal when the seller resorts to a remedy for breach of contract.

Article 62

The seller may require the buyer to pay the price, take delivery or perform his other obligations, unless the seller has resorted to a remedy which is inconsistent with this requirement.

Article 63

1. The seller may fix an additional period of time of reasonable length for performance by the buyer of his obligations.

2. Unless the seller has received notice from the buyer that he will not perform within the period so fixed, the seller may not, during that period, resort to any remedy for breach of contract. However, the seller is not deprived thereby of any right he may have to claim damages for delay in performance.

Article 64

1. The seller may declare the contract avoided:
    (a) if the failure by the buyer to perform any of his obligations under the contract or this Convention amounts to a fundamental breach of contract, or
    (b) if the buyer does not, within the additional period of time fixed by the seller in accordance with paragraph 1 of article 63, perform his obligation to pay the price or take delivery of the goods, or if he declares that he will not do so within the period so fixed.

2. However, in cases where the buyer has paid the price, the seller loses the right to declare the contract avoided unless he does so:
    (a) in respect of late performance by the buyer, before the seller has become aware that performance has been rendered; or
    (b) in respect of any breach other than late performance by the buyer, within a reasonable time:
        (i) after the seller knew or ought to have known the breach; or
        (ii) after the expiration of any additional period of time fixed by the seller in accordance with paragraph 1 of article 63, or after the buyer has declared that he will not perform his obligations within such an additional period.

Article 65

1. If under the contract the buyer is to specify the form, measurement or other features of the goods and he fails to make such specification either on the date agreed upon or within a reasonable time after receipt of a request from the seller, the seller may, without prejudice to any other rights he may have, make the specification himself in accordance with the requirements of the buyer that may be known to him.

2. If the seller makes the specification himself, he must inform the buyer of the details thereof and must fix a reasonable time within which the buyer may make a different specification. If, after receipt of such a communication, the buyer fails to do so within the time so fixed, the specification made by the seller is binding.

Chapter IV Passing of risk

Article 66

Loss of or damage to the goods after the risk has passed to the buyer does not discharge him from his obligation to pay the price, unless the loss or damage is due to an act or omission of the seller.

Article 67

1. If the contract of sale involves carriage of the goods and the seller is not bound to hand them over at a particular place, the risk passes to the buyer when the goods are handed over to the first carrier for transmission to the buyer in accordance with the contract of sale. If the seller is bound to hand the goods over to a carrier at a particular place, the risk does not pass to the buyer until the goods are handed over to the carrier at that place. The fact that the seller is authorized to retain documents controlling the disposition of the goods does not affect the passage of the risk.

2. Nevertheless, the risk does not pass to the buyer until the goods are clearly identified to the contract, whether by markings on the goods, by shipping documents, by notice given to the buyer or otherwise.

Article 68

The risk in respect of goods sold in transit passes to the buyer from the time of the conclusion of the contract. However, if the circumstances so indicate, the risk is assumed by the buyer from the time the goods were handed over to the carrier who issued the documents embodying the contract of carriage. Nevertheless, if at the time of the conclusion of the contract of sale the seller knew or ought to have known that the goods had been lost or damaged and did not disclose this to the buyer, the loss or damage is at the risk of the seller.

Article 69

1. In cases not within articles 67 and 68, the risk passes to the buyer when he takes over the goods or, if he does not do so in due time, from the time when the goods are placed at his disposal and he commits a breach of contract by failing to take delivery.

2. However, if the buyer is bound to take over the goods at a place other than a place of business of the seller, the risk passes when delivery is due and the buyer is aware of the fact that the goods are placed at his disposal at that place.

3. If the contract relates to goods not then identified, the goods are considered not to be placed at the disposal of the buyer until they are clearly identified to the contract.

Article 70

If the seller has committed a fundamental breach of contract, articles 67, 68 and 69 do not impair the remedies available to the buyer on account of the breach.

Chapter V Provisions common to the obligations of the seller and of the buyer

Section I Anticipatory breach and instalment contracts

Article 71

1. A party may suspend the performance of his obligations if, after the conclusion of the contract, it becomes apparent that the other party will not perform a substantial part of his obligations as a result of:

(a) a serious deficiency in his ability to perform or in is creditworthiness; or

(b) his conduct in preparing to perform or in performing the contract.

2. If the seller has already dispatched the goods before the grounds described in the preceding paragraph become evident, he may prevent the handing over of the goods to the buyer even though the buyer holds a document which entitles him to obtain them. The present paragraph relates only to the rights in the goods as between the buyer and the seller.

3. A party suspending performance, whether before or after dispatch of the goods, must immediately give notice of the suspension to the other party and must continue with performance if the other party provides adequate assurance of his performance.

Article 72

1. If prior to the date for performance of the contract it is clear that one of the parties will commit a fundamental breach of contract, the other party may declare the contract avoided.

2. If time allows, the party intending to declare the contract avoided must give reasonable notice to the other party in order to permit him to provide adequate assurance of his performance.

3. The requirements of the preceding paragraph do not apply if the other party has declared that he will not perform his obligations.

Article 73

1. In the case of a contract for delivery of goods by instalments, if the failure of one party to perform any of his obligations in respect of any instalment constitutes a fundamental breach of contract with respect to that instalment, the other party may declare the contract avoided with respect to that instalment.

2. If one party's failure to perform any of his obligations in respect of any instalment gives the other party good grounds to conclude that a fundamental breach of contract will occur with respect to future instalments, he may declare the contract avoided for the future, provided that he does so within a reasonable time.

3. A buyer who declares the contract avoided in respect of any delivery may, at the same time, declare it avoided in respect of deliveries already made or of future deliveries if, by reason of their interdependence, those deliveries could not be used for the purpose contemplated by the parties at the time of the conclusion of the contract.

Section II Damages

Article 74

Damages for breach of contract by one party consist of a sum equal to the loss, including loss of profit, suffered by the other party as a consequence of the breach. Such damages may not exceed the loss which the party in breach foresaw or ought to have foreseen at the time of the conclusion of the contract, in the light of the facts and matters of which he then knew or ought to have known, as a possible consequence of the breach of contract.

Article 75

If the contract is avoided and if, in a reasonable manner and with a reasonable time after avoidance, the buyer has bought goods in replacement or the seller has resold the goods, the party claiming damages may recover the difference between the contract price and the price in the substitute transaction as well as any further damages recoverable under article 74.

Article 76

1. If the contract is avoided and there is a current price for the goods, the party claiming damages may, if he has not made a purchase or resale under article 75, recover the difference between the price fixed by the contract and the current price at the time of avoidance as well as any further damages recoverable under article 74. If, however, the party claiming damages has avoided the contract after taking over the goods, the current price at the time of such taking over shall be applied instead of the current price at the time of avoidance.

2. For the purposes of the preceding paragraph, the current price is the price prevailing at the place where delivery of the goods should have been made or, if there is no current price at that place, the price at such other place as serves as a reasonable substitute, making due allowance for differences in the cost of transporting the goods.

Article 77

A party who relies on a breach of contract must take such measures as are reasonable in the circumstances to mitigate the loss, including loss of profit, resulting from the breach. If he fails to take such measures, the party in breach may claim a reduction in the damages in the amount by which the loss should have been mitigated.

Section III Interest

Article 78

If a party fails to pay the price or any other sum that is in arrears, the other party is entitled to interest on it, without prejudice to any claim for damages recoverable under article 74.

Section IV Exemptions

Article 79

1. A party is not liable for a failure to perform any of his obligations if he proves that the failure was due to an impediment beyond his control and he could not reasonably be expected to have taken the impediment into account at the time of the conclusion of the contract or to have avoided or overcome it or its consequences.

2. If the party's failure is due to the failure by a third person whom he has engaged to perform the whole or a part of the contract, that party is exempt from liability only if:

    (a) he is exempt under the preceding paragraph; and

    (b) the person whom he has so engaged would be so exempt if the provisions of that paragraph were applied to him.

3. The exemption provided by this article has effect for the period during which the impediment exists.

4. The party who fails to perform must give notice to the other party of the impediment and its effect on his ability to perform. If the notice is not received by the other party within a reasonable time after the party who fails to perform knew or ought to have known of the impediment, he is liable for damages resulting from such non-receipt.

5. Nothing in this article prevents either party from exercising any right other than to claim damages under this Convention.

Article 80

A party may not rely on a failure of the other party to perform, to the extent the such failure was caused by the first party's act or omission.

Section V   Effects of avoidance

Article 81

1. Avoidance of the contract releases both parties from their obligations under it, subject to any damages which may be due. Avoidance does not affect any provision of the contract for the settlement of disputes or any other provision of the contract governing the rights and obligations of the parties consequent upon the avoidance of the contract.

2. A party who has performed the contract either wholly or in part may claim restitution from the other party of whatever the first party has supplied or paid under the contract. If both parties are bound to make restitution, they must do so concurrently.

Article 82

1. The buyer loses the right to declare the contract avoided or to require the seller to deliver substitute goods if it is impossible for him to make restitution of the goods substantially in the condition in which he received them.

2. The preceding paragraph does not apply:

    (a) if the impossibility of making restitution of the goods or of making restitution of the goods substantially in the condition in which the buyer received them is not due to his act or omission;

    (b) if the goods or part of the goods have perished or deteriorated as a result of the examination provided for in article 38; or

    (c) if the goods or part of the goods have been sold in the normal course of business or have been consumed or transformed by the buyer in the course of normal use before he discovered or ought to have discovered the lack of conformity.

Article 83

A buyer who has lost the right to declare the contract avoided or to require the seller to deliver substitute goods in accordance with article 82 retains all other remedies under the contract and this Convention.

Article 84

1. If the seller is bound to refund the price, he must also pay interest on it, from the date on which the price was paid.

2. The buyer must account to the seller for all benefits which he has derived from the goods or part of them:

    (a) if he must make restitution of the goods or part of them; or

    (b) if it is impossible for him to make restitution of all or part of the goods or to make restitution of all or part of the goods substantially in the condition in which he received them, but he has nevertheless declared the contract avoided or required the seller to deliver substitute goods.

Section VI   Preservation of the goods

Article 85

If the buyer is in delay in taking delivery of the goods or, where payment of the price and delivery of the goods are to be made concurrently, if he fails to pay the price, and the seller is either in possession of the goods or otherwise able to control their disposition, the seller must take such steps as are reasonable in the circumstances to preserve them. He is entitled to retain them until he has been reimbursed his reasonable expenses by the buyer.

Article 86

1. If the buyer has received the goods and intends to exercise any right under the contract or this Convention to reject them, he must take such steps to preserve them as are reasonable in the circumstances. He is entitled to retain them until he has been reimbursed his reasonable expenses by the seller.

2. If goods dispatched to the buyer have been placed at his disposal at their destination and he exercises the right to reject them, he must take possession of them on behalf of the seller, provided that this can be done without payment of the price and without unreasonable inconvenience or unreasonable expense. This provision does not apply if the seller or a person authorized to take charge of the goods on his behalf is present at the destination. If the buyer takes possession of the goods under this paragraph, his rights and obligations are governed by the preceding paragraph.

Article 87

A party who is bound to take steps to preserve the goods may deposit them in a warehouse of a third person at the expense of the other party provided that the expense incurred is not unreasonable.

Article 88

1. A party who is bound to preserve the goods in accordance with article 85 or 86 may sell them by an appropriate means if there has been an unreasonable delay by the other party in taking possession of the goods or in taking them back or in paying the price or the cost of preservation, provided that reasonable notice of the intention to sell has been given to the other party.

2. If the goods are subject to rapid deterioration or their preservation would involve unreasonable expense, a party who is bound to preserve the goods in accordance with article 85 or 86 must take reasonable measures to sell them. To the extent possible he must give notice to the other party of his intention to sell.

3. A party selling the goods has the right to retain out of the proceeds of sale an amount equal to the reasonable expenses of preserving the goods and of selling them. He must account to the other party for the balance.

PART IV FINAL PROVISIONS

Article 89

...

Article 90

This Convention does not prevail over any international agreement which has already been or may be entered into and which contains provisions concerning the matters governed by this Convention, provided that the parties have their places of business in States parties to such agreement.

Article 91

...

Article 92

1. A Contracting State may declare at the time of signature, ratification, acceptance, approval or accession that it will not be bound by Part II of this Convention or that it will not be bound by Part III of this Convention.

2. A Contracting State which makes a declaration in accordance with the preceding paragraph in respect of Part II or Part III of this Convention is not to be considered a Contracting State within paragraph 1 of article 1 of this Convention in respect of matters governed by the Part to which the declaration applies.

Article 93

1. If a Contracting State has two or more territorial units in which, according to its constitution, different systems of law are applicable in relation to the matters dealt within this Convention, it may, at the time of signature, ratification, acceptance, approval or accession, declare that this Convention is to extend to all its territorial units or only to one or more of them, and may amend its declaration by submitting another declaration at any time.

...

Article 94

1. Two or more Contracting States which have the same or closely related legal rules on matters governed by this Convention may at any time declare that the Convention is not to apply to contracts of sale or to their formation where the parties have their places of business in those States. Such declaration may be made jointly or by reciprocal unilateral declarations.

2. A Contracting State which has the same or closely related legal rules on matters governed by this Convention as one or more non-Contracting States may at any time declare that the Convention is not to apply to contracts of sale or to their formation where the parties have their places of business in those States.

3. If a State which is the object of a declaration under the preceding paragraph subsequently becomes a Contracting State, the declaration made will, as from the date on which the Convention enters into force in respect of the new Contracting State, have the effect of a declaration made under paragraph 1, provided that the new Contracting State joins in such declaration or makes a reciprocal unilateral declaration.

Article 95

Any State may declare at the time of the deposit of its instrument of ratification, acceptance, approval or accession that it will not be bound by subparagraph 1(b) of article 1 of this Convention.

Article 96

A Contracting State whose legislation requires contracts of sale to be concluded in or evidenced by writing may at any time make a declaration in accordance with article 12 that any provision of article 11, article 29, or Part II of this Convention, that allows a contract of sale or its modification or termination by agreement or any offer, acceptance, or other indication of intention to be made in any form other than in writing, does not apply where any party has his place of business in that State.

Article 98

No reservations are permitted except those expressly authorized in this Convention.

Article 99

1. This Convention enters into force, subject to the provisions of paragraph 6 of this article, on the first day of the month following the expiration of twelve months after the date of deposit of the tenth instrument of ratification, acceptance, approval or accession, including an instrument which contains a declaration made under article 92.

Done at Vienna, this day of eleventh day of April, one thousand nine hundred and eighty, ...

...

United Nations Convention on Contracts for the International Carriage of Goods Wholly or Partly by Sea [2008]*

(The Rotterdam Rules)

[11 December 2008]

The States Parties to this Convention,

Reaffirming their belief that international trade on the basis of equality and mutual benefit is an important element in promoting friendly relations among States,

---

* Reproduced with permission from the United Nations Commission on International Trade Law (UNCITRAL).

Convinced that the progressive harmonization and unification of international trade law, in reducing or removing legal obstacles to the flow of international trade, significantly contributes to universal economic cooperation among all States on a basis of equality, equity and common interest, and to the well-being of all peoples,

Recognizing the significant contribution of the International Convention for the Unification of Certain Rules of Law relating to Bills of Lading, signed in Brussels on 25 August 1924, and its Protocols, and of the United Nations Convention on the Carriage of Goods by Sea, signed in Hamburg on 31 March 1978, to the harmonization of the law governing the carriage of goods by sea,

Mindful of the technological and commercial developments that have taken place since the adoption of those conventions and of the need to consolidate and modernize them,

Noting that shippers and carriers do not have the benefit of a binding universal regime to support the operation of contracts of maritime carriage involving other modes of transport,

Believing that the adoption of uniform rules to govern international contracts of carriage wholly or partly by sea will promote legal certainty, improve the efficiency of international carriage of goods and facilitate new access opportunities for previously remote parties and markets, thus playing a fundamental role in promoting trade and economic development, both domestically and internationally,

Have agreed as follows:

Chapter 1 General provisions

Article 1 Definitions

For the purposes of this Convention:

1. 'Contract of carriage' means a contract in which a carrier, against the payment of freight, undertakes to carry goods from one place to another. The contract shall provide for carriage by sea and may provide for carriage by other modes of transport in addition to the sea carriage.

2. 'Volume contract' means a contract of carriage that provides for the carriage of a specified quantity of goods in a series of shipments during an agreed period of time. The specification of the quantity may include a minimum, a maximum or a certain range.

3. 'Liner transportation' means a transportation service that is offered to the public through publication or similar means and includes transportation by ships operating on a regular schedule between specified ports in accordance with publicly available timetables of sailing dates.

4. 'Non-liner transportation' means any transportation that is not liner transportation.

5. 'Carrier' means a person that enters into a contract of carriage with a shipper.

6. (a) 'Performing party' means a person other than the carrier that performs or undertakes to perform any of the carrier's obligations under a contract of carriage with respect to the receipt, loading, handling, stowage, carriage, keeping, care, unloading or delivery of the goods, to the extent that such person acts, either directly or indirectly, at the carrier's request or under the carrier's supervision or control.

   (b) 'Performing party' does not include any person that is retained, directly or indirectly, by a shipper, by a documentary shipper, by the controlling party or by the consignee instead of by the carrier.

7. 'Maritime performing party' means a performing party to the extent that it performs or undertakes to perform any of the carrier's obligations during the period between the arrival of the goods at the port of loading of a ship and their departure from the port of discharge of a ship. An inland carrier is a maritime performing party only if it performs or undertakes to perform its services exclusively within a port area.

8. 'Shipper' means a person that enters into a contract of carriage with a carrier.

9. 'Documentary shipper' means a person, other than the shipper, that accepts to be named as 'shipper' in the transport document or electronic transport record.

10. 'Holder' means:

    (a) A person that is in possession of a negotiable transport document; and

       (i) if the document is an order document, is identified in it as the shipper or the consignee, or is the person to which the document is duly endorsed; or

     (ii) if the document is a blank endorsed order document or bearer document, is the bearer thereof; or

  (b) The person to which a negotiable electronic transport record has been issued or transferred in accordance with the procedures referred to in article 9, paragraph 1.

11. 'Consignee' means a person entitled to delivery of the goods under a contract of carriage or a transport document or electronic transport record.

12. 'Right of control' of the goods means the right under the contract of carriage to give the carrier instructions in respect of the goods in accordance with chapter 10.

13. 'Controlling party' means the person that pursuant to article 51 is entitled to exercise the right of control.

14. 'Transport document' means a document issued under a contract of carriage by the carrier that:

  (a) Evidences the carrier's or a performing party's receipt of goods under a contract of carriage; and

  (b) Evidences or contains a contract of carriage.

15. 'Negotiable transport document' means a transport document that indicates, by wording such as 'to order' or 'negotiable' or other appropriate wording recognized as having the same effect by the law applicable to the document, that the goods have been consigned to the order of the shipper, to the order of the consignee, or to bearer, and is not explicitly stated as being 'non-negotiable' or 'not negotiable'.

16. 'Non-negotiable transport document' means a transport document that is not a negotiable transport document.

17. 'Electronic communication' means information generated, sent, received or stored by electronic, optical, digital or similar means with the result that the information communicated is accessible so as to be usable for subsequent reference.

18. 'Electronic transport record' means information in one or more messages issued by electronic communication under a contract of carriage by a carrier, including information logically associated with the electronic transport record by attachments or otherwise linked to the electronic transport record contemporaneously with or subsequent to its issue by the carrier, so as to become part of the electronic transport record, that:

  (a) Evidences the carrier's or a performing party's receipt of goods under a contract of carriage; and

  (b) Evidences or contains a contract of carriage.

19. 'Negotiable electronic transport record' means an electronic transport record:

  (a) That indicates, by wording such as 'to order', or 'negotiable', or other appropriate wording recognized as having the same effect by the law applicable to the record, that the goods have been consigned to the order of the shipper or to the order of the consignee, and is not explicitly stated as being 'non-negotiable' or 'not negotiable'; and

  (b) The use of which meets the requirements of article 9, paragraph 1.

20. 'Non-negotiable electronic transport record' means an electronic transport record that is not a negotiable electronic transport record.

21. The 'issuance' of a negotiable electronic transport record means the issuance of the record in accordance with procedures that ensure that the record is subject to exclusive control from its creation until it ceases to have any effect or validity.

22. The 'transfer' of a negotiable electronic transport record means the transfer of exclusive control over the record.

23. 'Contract particulars' means any information relating to the contract of carriage or to the goods (including terms, notations, signatures and endorsements) that is in a transport document or an electronic transport record.

24. 'Goods' means the wares, merchandise, and articles of every kind whatsoever that a carrier undertakes to carry under a contract of carriage and includes the packing and any equipment and container not supplied by or on behalf of the carrier.

25. 'Ship' means any vessel used to carry goods by sea.

26. 'Container' means any type of container, transportable tank or flat, swapbody, or any similar unit load used to consolidate goods, and any equipment ancillary to such unit load.

27. 'Vehicle' means a road or railroad cargo vehicle.

28. 'Freight' means the remuneration payable to the carrier for the carriage of goods under a contract of carriage.

29. 'Domicile' means (a) a place where a company or other legal person or association of natural or legal persons has its (i) statutory seat or place of incorporation or central registered office, whichever is applicable, (ii) central administration or (iii) principal place of business, and (b) the habitual residence of a natural person.

30. 'Competent court' means a court in a Contracting State that, according to the rules on the internal allocation of jurisdiction among the courts of that State, may exercise jurisdiction over the dispute.

Article 2   Interpretation of this Convention
In the interpretation of this Convention, regard is to be had to its international character and to the need to promote uniformity in its application and the observance of good faith in international trade.

Article 3   Form requirements
The notices, confirmation, consent, agreement, declaration and other communications referred to in articles 19, paragraph 2; 23, paragraphs 1 to 4; 36, subparagraphs 1 (b), (c) and (d); 40, subparagraph 4 (b); 44; 48, paragraph 3; 51, subparagraph 1 (b); 59, paragraph 1; 63; 66; 67, paragraph 2; 75, paragraph 4; and 80, paragraphs 2 and 5, shall be in writing. Electronic communications may be used for these purposes, provided that the use of such means is with the consent of the person by which it is communicated and of the person to which it is communicated.

Article 4   Applicability of defences and limits of liability
1. Any provision of this Convention that may provide a defence for, or limit the liability of, the carrier applies in any judicial or arbitral proceeding, whether founded in contract, in tort, or otherwise, that is instituted in respect of loss of, damage to, or delay in delivery of goods covered by a contract of carriage or for the breach of any other obligation under this Convention against:

    (a) The carrier or a maritime performing party;

    (b) The master, crew or any other person that performs services on board the ship; or

    (c) Employees of the carrier or a maritime performing party.

2. Any provision of this Convention that may provide a defence for the shipper or the documentary shipper applies in any judicial or arbitral proceeding, whether founded in contract, in tort, or otherwise, that is instituted against the shipper, the documentary shipper, or their subcontractors, agents or employees.

Chapter 2 Scope of application

Article 5   General scope of application
1. Subject to article 6, this Convention applies to contracts of carriage in which the place of receipt and the place of delivery are in different States, and the port of loading of a sea carriage and the port of discharge of the same sea carriage are in different States, if, according to the contract of carriage, any one of the following places is located in a Contracting State:

    (a) The place of receipt;

    (b) The port of loading;

    (c) The place of delivery; or

    (d) The port of discharge.

2. This Convention applies without regard to the nationality of the vessel, the carrier, the performing parties, the shipper, the consignee, or any other interested parties.

Article 6   Specific exclusions

1. This Convention does not apply to the following contracts in liner transportation:
    (a) Charter parties; and
    (b) Other contracts for the use of a ship or of any space thereon.
2. This Convention does not apply to contracts of carriage in non-liner transportation except when:
    (a) There is no charter party or other contract between the parties for the use of a ship or of any space thereon; and
    (b) A transport document or an electronic transport record is issued.

Article 7   Application to certain parties

Notwithstanding article 6, this Convention applies as between the carrier and the consignee, controlling party or holder that is not an original party to the charterparty or other contract of carriage excluded from the application of this Convention. However, this Convention does not apply as between the original parties to a contract of carriage excluded pursuant to article 6.

Chapter 3   Electronic transport records

Article 8   Use and effect of electronic transport records

Subject to the requirements set out in this Convention:
    (a) Anything that is to be in or on a transport document under this Convention may be recorded in an electronic transport record, provided the issuance and subsequent use of an electronic transport record is with the consent of the carrier and the shipper; and
    (b) The issuance, exclusive control, or transfer of an electronic transport record has the same effect as the issuance, possession, or transfer of a transport document.

Article 9   Procedures for use of negotiable electronic transport records

1. The use of a negotiable electronic transport record shall be subject to procedures that provide for:
    (a) The method for the issuance and the transfer of that record to an intended holder;
    (b) An assurance that the negotiable electronic transport record retains its integrity;
    (c) The manner in which the holder is able to demonstrate that it is the holder; and
    (d) The manner of providing confirmation that delivery to the holder has been effected, or that, pursuant to articles 10, paragraph 2, or 47, subparagraphs 1 (a) (ii) and (c), the electronic transport record has ceased to have any effect or validity.
2. The procedures in paragraph 1 of this article shall be referred to in the contract particulars and be readily ascertainable.

Article 10   Replacement of negotiable transport document or negotiable electronic transport record

1. If a negotiable transport document has been issued and the carrier and the holder agree to replace that document by a negotiable electronic transport record:
    (a) The holder shall surrender the negotiable transport document, or all of them if more than one has been issued, to the carrier;
    (b) The carrier shall issue to the holder a negotiable electronic transport record that includes a statement that it replaces the negotiable transport document; and
    (c) The negotiable transport document ceases thereafter to have any effect or validity.
2. If a negotiable electronic transport record has been issued and the carrier and the holder agree to replace that electronic transport record by a negotiable transport document:
    (a) The carrier shall issue to the holder, in place of the electronic transport record, a negotiable transport document that includes a statement that it replaces the negotiable electronic transport record; and
    (b) The electronic transport record ceases thereafter to have any effect or validity.

Chapter 4 Obligations of the carrier

Article 11 Carriage and delivery of the goods

The carrier shall, subject to this Convention and in accordance with the terms of the contract of carriage, carry the goods to the place of destination and deliver them to the consignee.

Article 12 Period of responsibility of the carrier

1. The period of responsibility of the carrier for the goods under this Convention begins when the carrier or a performing party receives the goods for carriage and ends when the goods are delivered.

2. (a) If the law or regulations of the place of receipt require the goods to be handed over to an authority or other third party from which the carrier may collect them, the period of responsibility of the carrier begins when the carrier collects the goods from the authority or other third party.

   (b) If the law or regulations of the place of delivery require the carrier to hand over the goods to an authority or other third party from which the consignee may collect them, the period of responsibility of the carrier ends when the carrier hands the goods over to the authority or other third party.

3. For the purpose of determining the carrier's period of responsibility, the parties may agree on the time and location of receipt and delivery of the goods, but a provision in a contract of carriage is void to the extent that it provides that:

   (a) The time of receipt of the goods is subsequent to the beginning of their initial loading under the contract of carriage; or

   (b) The time of delivery of the goods is prior to the completion of their final unloading under the contract of carriage.

Article 13 Specific obligations

1. The carrier shall during the period of its responsibility as defined in article 12, and subject to article 26, properly and carefully receive, load, handle, stow, carry, keep, care for, unload and deliver the goods.

2. Notwithstanding paragraph 1 of this article, and without prejudice to the other provisions in chapter 4 and to chapters 5 to 7, the carrier and the shipper may agree that the loading, handling, stowing or unloading of the goods is to be performed by the shipper, the documentary shipper or the consignee. Such an agreement shall be referred to in the contract particulars.

Article 14 Specific obligations applicable to the voyage by sea

The carrier is bound before, at the beginning of, and during the voyage by sea to exercise due diligence to:

(a) Make and keep the ship seaworthy;

(b) Properly crew, equip and supply the ship and keep the ship so crewed, equipped and supplied throughout the voyage; and

(c) Make and keep the holds and all other parts of the ship in which the goods are carried, and any containers supplied by the carrier in or upon which the goods are carried, fit and safe for their reception, carriage and preservation.

Article 15 Goods that may become a danger

Notwithstanding articles 11 and 13, the carrier or a performing party may decline to receive or to load, and may take such other measures as are reasonable, including unloading, destroying, or rendering goods harmless, if the goods are, or reasonably appear likely to become during the carrier's period of responsibility, an actual danger to persons, property or the environment.

Article 16 Sacrifice of the goods during the voyage by sea

Notwithstanding articles 11, 13, and 14, the carrier or a performing party may sacrifice goods at sea when the sacrifice is reasonably made for the common safety or for the purpose of preserving from peril human life or other property involved in the common adventure.

Chapter 5 Liability of the carrier for loss, damage or delay

Article 17   Basis of liability

1. The carrier is liable for loss of or damage to the goods, as well as for delay in delivery, if the claimant proves that the loss, damage, or delay, or the event or circumstance that caused or contributed to it took place during the period of the carrier's responsibility as defined in chapter 4.

2. The carrier is relieved of all or part of its liability pursuant to paragraph 1 of this article if it proves that the cause or one of the causes of the loss, damage, or delay is not attributable to its fault or to the fault of any person referred to in article 18.

3. The carrier is also relieved of all or part of its liability pursuant to paragraph 1 of this article if, alternatively to proving the absence of fault as provided in paragraph 2 of this article, it proves that one or more of the following events or circumstances caused or contributed to the loss, damage, or delay:

(a) Act of God;

(b) Perils, dangers, and accidents of the sea or other navigable waters;

(c) War, hostilities, armed conflict, piracy, terrorism, riots, and civil commotions;

(d) Quarantine restrictions; interference by or impediments created by governments, public authorities, rulers, or people including detention, arrest, or seizure not attributable to the carrier or any person referred to in article 18;

(e) Strikes, lockouts, stoppages, or restraints of labour;

(f) Fire on the ship;

(g) Latent defects not discoverable by due diligence;

(h) Act or omission of the shipper, the documentary shipper, the controlling party, or any other person for whose acts the shipper or the documentary shipper is liable pursuant to article 33 or 34;

(i) Loading, handling, stowing, or unloading of the goods performed pursuant to an agreement in accordance with article 13, paragraph 2, unless the carrier or a performing party performs such activity on behalf of the shipper, the documentary shipper or the consignee;

(j) Wastage in bulk or weight or any other loss or damage arising from inherent defect, quality, or vice of the goods;

(k) Insufficiency or defective condition of packing or marking not performed by or on behalf of the carrier;

(l) Saving or attempting to save life at sea;

(m) Reasonable measures to save or attempt to save property at sea;

(n) Reasonable measures to avoid or attempt to avoid damage to the environment; or

(o) Acts of the carrier in pursuance of the powers conferred by articles 15 and 16.

4. Notwithstanding paragraph 3 of this article, the carrier is liable for all or part of the loss, damage, or delay:

(a) If the claimant proves that the fault of the carrier or of a person referred to in article 18 caused or contributed to the event or circumstance on which the carrier relies; or

(b) If the claimant proves that an event or circumstance not listed in paragraph 3 of this article contributed to the loss, damage, or delay, and the carrier cannot prove that this event or circumstance is not attributable to its fault or to the fault of any person referred to in article 18.

5. The carrier is also liable, notwithstanding paragraph 3 of this article, for all or part of the loss, damage, or delay if:

(a) The claimant proves that the loss, damage, or delay was or was probably caused by or contributed to by

(i)   the unseaworthiness of the ship;

(ii) the improper crewing, equipping, and supplying of the ship; or

      (iii) the fact that the holds or other parts of the ship in which the goods are carried, or any containers supplied by the carrier in or upon which the goods are carried, were not fit and safe for reception, carriage, and preservation of the goods; and

  (b) The carrier is unable to prove either that:

      (i) none of the events or circumstances referred to in subparagraph 5 (a) of this article caused the loss, damage, or delay; or

      (ii) that it complied with its obligation to exercise due diligence pursuant to article 14.

6. When the carrier is relieved of part of its liability pursuant to this article, the carrier is liable only for that part of the loss, damage or delay that is attributable to the event or circumstance for which it is liable pursuant to this article.

Article 18   Liability of the carrier for other persons

The carrier is liable for the breach of its obligations under this Convention caused by the acts or omissions of:

  (a) Any performing party;

  (b) The master or crew of the ship;

  (c) Employees of the carrier or a performing party; or

  (d) Any other person that performs or undertakes to perform any of the carrier's obligations under the contract of carriage, to the extent that the person acts, either directly or indirectly, at the carrier's request or under the carrier's supervision or control.

Article 19   Liability of maritime performing parties

1. A maritime performing party is subject to the obligations and liabilities imposed on the carrier under this Convention and is entitled to the carrier's defences and limits of liability as provided for in this Convention if:

  (a) The maritime performing party received the goods for carriage in a Contracting State, or delivered them in a Contracting State, or performed its activities with respect to the goods in a port in a Contracting State; and

  (b) The occurrence that caused the loss, damage or delay took place:

      (i) during the period between the arrival of the goods at the port of loading of the ship and their departure from the port of discharge from the ship; and either

      (ii) while the maritime performing party had custody of the goods; or

      (iii) at any other time to the extent that it was participating in the performance of any of the activities contemplated by the contract of carriage.

2. If the carrier agrees to assume obligations other than those imposed on the carrier under this Convention, or agrees that the limits of its liability are higher than the limits specified under this Convention, a maritime performing party is not bound by this agreement unless it expressly agrees to accept such obligations or such higher limits.

3. A maritime performing party is liable for the breach of its obligations under this Convention caused by the acts or omissions of any person to which it has entrusted the performance of any of the carrier's obligations under the contract of carriage under the conditions set out in paragraph 1 of this article.

4. Nothing in this Convention imposes liability on the master or crew of the ship or on an employee of the carrier or of a maritime performing party.

Article 20   Joint and several liability

1. If the carrier and one or more maritime performing parties are liable for the loss of, damage to, or delay in delivery of the goods, their liability is joint and several but only up to the limits provided for under this Convention.

2. Without prejudice to article 61, the aggregate liability of all such persons shall not exceed the overall limits of liability under this Convention.

Article 21   Delay

Delay in delivery occurs when the goods are not delivered at the place of destination provided for in the contract of carriage within the time agreed.

Article 22   Calculation of compensation

1. Subject to article 59, the compensation payable by the carrier for loss of or damage to the goods is calculated by reference to the value of such goods at the place and time of delivery established in accordance with article 43.

2. The value of the goods is fixed according to the commodity exchange price or, if there is no such price, according to their market price or, if there is no commodity exchange price or market price, by reference to the normal value of the goods of the same kind and quality at the place of delivery.

3. In case of loss of or damage to the goods, the carrier is not liable for payment of any compensation beyond what is provided for in paragraphs 1 and 2 of this article except when the carrier and the shipper have agreed to calculate compensation in a different manner within the limits of chapter 16.

Article 23   Notice in case of loss, damage or delay

1. The carrier is presumed, in absence of proof to the contrary, to have delivered the goods according to their description in the contract particulars unless notice of loss of or damage to the goods, indicating the general nature of such loss or damage, was given to the carrier or the performing party that delivered the goods before or at the time of the delivery, or, if the loss or damage is not apparent, within seven working days at the place of delivery after the delivery of the goods.

2. Failure to provide the notice referred to in this article to the carrier or the performing party shall not affect the right to claim compensation for loss of or damage to the goods under this Convention, nor shall it affect the allocation of the burden of proof set out in article 17.

3. The notice referred to in this article is not required in respect of loss or damage that is ascertained in a joint inspection of the goods by the person to which they have been delivered and the carrier or the maritime performing party against which liability is being asserted.

4. No compensation in respect of delay is payable unless notice of loss due to delay was given to the carrier within twenty-one consecutive days of delivery of the goods.

5. When the notice referred to in this article is given to the performing party that delivered the goods, it has the same effect as if that notice was given to the carrier, and notice given to the carrier has the same effect as a notice given to a maritime performing party.

6. In the case of any actual or apprehended loss or damage, the parties to the dispute shall give all reasonable facilities to each other for inspecting and tallying the goods and shall provide access to records and documents relevant to the carriage of the goods.

Chapter 6   Additional provisions relating to particular stages of carriage

Article 24   Deviation

When pursuant to applicable law a deviation constitutes a breach of the carrier's obligations, such deviation of itself shall not deprive the carrier or a maritime performing party of any defence or limitation of this Convention, except to the extent provided in article 61.

Article 25   Deck cargo on ships

1. Goods may be carried on the deck of a ship only if:
   (a) Such carriage is required by law;
   (b) They are carried in or on containers or vehicles that are fit for deck carriage, and the decks are specially fitted to carry such containers or vehicles; or
   (c) The carriage on deck is in accordance with the contract of carriage, or the customs, usages or practices of the trade in question.

2. The provisions of this Convention relating to the liability of the carrier apply to the loss of, damage to or delay in the delivery of goods carried on deck pursuant to paragraph 1 of this article, but the carrier is not liable for loss of or damage to such goods, or delay in their delivery, caused by the special risks involved in their carriage on deck when the goods are carried in accordance with subparagraphs 1 (a) or (c) of this article.

3. If the goods have been carried on deck in cases other than those permitted pursuant to paragraph 1 of this article, the carrier is liable for loss of or damage to the goods or delay in their delivery that is exclusively caused by their carriage on deck, and is not entitled to the defences provided for in article 17.

4. The carrier is not entitled to invoke subparagraph 1 (c) of this article against a third party that has acquired a negotiable transport document or a negotiable electronic transport record in good faith, unless the contract particulars state that the goods may be carried on deck.

5. If the carrier and shipper expressly agreed that the goods would be carried under deck, the carrier is not entitled to the benefit of the limitation of liability for any loss of, damage to or delay in the delivery of the goods to the extent that such loss, damage, or delay resulted from their carriage on deck.

Article 26 Carriage preceding or subsequent to sea carriage

When loss of or damage to goods, or an event or circumstance causing a delay in their delivery, occurs during the carrier's period of responsibility but solely before their loading onto the ship or solely after their discharge from the ship, the provisions of this Convention do not prevail over those provisions of another international instrument that, at the time of such loss, damage or event or circumstance causing delay:

(a) Pursuant to the provisions of such international instrument would have applied to all or any of the carrier's activities if the shipper had made a separate and direct contract with the carrier in respect of the particular stage of carriage where the loss of, or damage to goods, or an event or circumstance causing delay in their delivery occurred;

(b) Specifically provide for the carrier's liability, limitation of liability, or time for suit; and

(c) Cannot be departed from by contract either at all or to the detriment of the shipper under that instrument.

Chapter 7 Obligations of the shipper to the carrier

Article 27 Delivery for carriage

1. Unless otherwise agreed in the contract of carriage, the shipper shall deliver the goods ready for carriage. In any event, the shipper shall deliver the goods in such condition that they will withstand the intended carriage, including their loading, handling, stowing, lashing and securing, and unloading, and that they will not cause harm to persons or property.

2. The shipper shall properly and carefully perform any obligation assumed under an agreement made pursuant to article 13, paragraph 2.

3. When a container is packed or a vehicle is loaded by the shipper, the shipper shall properly and carefully stow, lash and secure the contents in or on the container or vehicle, and in such a way that they will not cause harm to persons or property.

Article 28 Cooperation of the shipper and the carrier in providing information and instructions

The carrier and the shipper shall respond to requests from each other to provide information and instructions required for the proper handling and carriage of the goods if the information is in the requested party's possession or the instructions are within the requested party's reasonable ability to provide and they are not otherwise reasonably available to the requesting party.

Article 29 Shipper's obligation to provide information, instructions and documents

1. The shipper shall provide to the carrier in a timely manner such information, instructions and documents relating to the goods that are not otherwise reasonably available to the carrier, and that are reasonably necessary:

(a) For the proper handling and carriage of the goods, including precautions to be taken by the carrier or a performing party; and

(b) For the carrier to comply with law, regulations or other requirements of public authorities in connection with the intended carriage, provided that the carrier notifies the shipper in a timely manner of the information, instructions and documents it requires.

2. Nothing in this article affects any specific obligation to provide certain information, instructions and documents related to the goods pursuant to law, regulations or other requirements of public authorities in connection with the intended carriage.

Article 30 Basis of shipper's liability to the carrier

1. The shipper is liable for loss or damage sustained by the carrier if the carrier proves that such loss or damage was caused by a breach of the shipper's obligations under this Convention.

2. Except in respect of loss or damage caused by a breach by the shipper of its obligations pursuant to articles 31, paragraph 2, and 32, the shipper is relieved of all or part of its liability if the cause or one of the causes of the loss or damage is not attributable to its fault or to the fault of any person referred to in article 34.

3. When the shipper is relieved of part of its liability pursuant to this article, the shipper is liable only for that part of the loss or damage that is attributable to its fault or to the fault of any person referred to in article 34.

Article 31 Information for compilation of contract particulars

1. The shipper shall provide to the carrier, in a timely manner, accurate information required for the compilation of the contract particulars and the issuance of the transport documents or electronic transport records, including the particulars referred to in article 36, paragraph 1; the name of the party to be identified as the shipper in the contract particulars; the name of the consignee, if any; and the name of the person to whose order the transport document or electronic transport record is to be issued, if any.

2. The shipper is deemed to have guaranteed the accuracy at the time of receipt by the carrier of the information that is provided according to paragraph 1 of this article. The shipper shall indemnify the carrier against loss or damage resulting from the inaccuracy of such information.

Article 32 Special rules on dangerous goods

When goods by their nature or character are, or reasonably appear likely to become, a danger to persons, property or the environment:

(a) The shipper shall inform the carrier of the dangerous nature or character of the goods in a timely manner before they are delivered to the carrier or a performing party. If the shipper fails to do so and the carrier or performing party does not otherwise have knowledge of their dangerous nature or character, the shipper is liable to the carrier for loss or damage resulting from such failure to inform; and

(b) The shipper shall mark or label dangerous goods in accordance with any law, regulations or other requirements of public authorities that apply during any stage of the intended carriage of the goods. If the shipper fails to do so, it is liable to the carrier for loss or damage resulting from such failure.

Article 33 Assumption of shipper's rights and obligations by the documentary shipper

1. A documentary shipper is subject to the obligations and liabilities imposed on the shipper pursuant to this chapter and pursuant to article 55, and is entitled to the shipper's rights and defences provided by this chapter and by chapter 13.

2. Paragraph 1 of this article does not affect the obligations, liabilities, rights or defences of the shipper.

Article 34 Liability of the shipper for other persons

The shipper is liable for the breach of its obligations under this Convention caused by the acts or omissions of any person, including employees, agents and subcontractors, to which it has entrusted the performance of any of its obligations, but the shipper is not liable for acts or omissions of the carrier or a performing party acting on behalf of the carrier, to which the shipper has entrusted the performance of its obligations.

Chapter 8   Transport documents and electronic transport records

Article 35   Issuance of the transport document or the electronic transport record

Unless the shipper and the carrier have agreed not to use a transport document or an electronic transport record, or it is the custom, usage or practice of the trade not to use one, upon delivery of the goods for carriage to the carrier or performing party, the shipper or, if the shipper consents, the documentary shipper, is entitled to obtain from the carrier, at the shipper's option:

> (a) A non-negotiable transport document or, subject to article 8, subparagraph (a), a non-negotiable electronic transport record; or
> (b) An appropriate negotiable transport document or, subject to article 8, subparagraph (a), a negotiable electronic transport record, unless the shipper and the carrier have agreed not to use a negotiable transport document or negotiable electronic transport record, or it is the custom, usage or practice of the trade not to use one.

Article 36   Contract particulars

1. The contract particulars in the transport document or electronic transport record referred to in article 35 shall include the following information, as furnished by the shipper:

> (a) A description of the goods as appropriate for the transport;
> (b) The leading marks necessary for identification of the goods;
> (c) The number of packages or pieces, or the quantity of goods; and
> (d) The weight of the goods, if furnished by the shipper.

2. The contract particulars in the transport document or electronic transport record referred to in article 35 shall also include:

> (a) A statement of the apparent order and condition of the goods at the time the carrier or a performing party receives them for carriage;
> (b) The name and address of the carrier;
> (c) The date on which the carrier or a performing party received the goods, or on which the goods were loaded on board the ship, or on which the transport document or electronic transport record was issued; and
> (d) If the transport document is negotiable, the number of originals of the negotiable transport document, when more than one original is issued.

3. The contract particulars in the transport document or electronic transport record referred to in article 35 shall further include:

> (a) The name and address of the consignee, if named by the shipper;
> (b) The name of a ship, if specified in the contract of carriage;
> (c) The place of receipt and, if known to the carrier, the place of delivery; and
> (d) The port of loading and the port of discharge, if specified in the contract of carriage.

4. For the purposes of this article, the phrase 'apparent order and condition of the goods' in subparagraph 2 (a) of this article refers to the order and condition of the goods based on:

> (a) A reasonable external inspection of the goods as packaged at the time the shipper delivers them to the carrier or a performing party; and
> (b) Any additional inspection that the carrier or a performing party actually performs before issuing the transport document or electronic transport record.

Article 37   Identity of the carrier

1. If a carrier is identified by name in the contract particulars, any other information in the transport document or electronic transport record relating to the identity of the carrier shall have no effect to the extent that it is inconsistent with that identification.

2. If no person is identified in the contract particulars as the carrier as required pursuant to article 36, subparagraph 2 (b), but the contract particulars indicate that the goods have been loaded on board a named ship, the registered owner of that ship is presumed to be the carrier, unless it proves that the ship was under a bareboat charter at the time of the carriage and it identifies this bareboat charterer and indicates its address, in which case this bareboat charterer is presumed to be the carrier. Alternatively, the registered owner may rebut the presumption of being the carrier by identifying the carrier and indicating its address. The bareboat charterer may rebut any presumption of being the carrier in the same manner.

3. Nothing in this article prevents the claimant from proving that any person other than a person identified in the contract particulars or pursuant to paragraph 2 of this article is the carrier.

Article 38   Signature

1. A transport document shall be signed by the carrier or a person acting on its behalf.

2. An electronic transport record shall include the electronic signature of the carrier or a person acting on its behalf. Such electronic signature shall identify the signatory in relation to the electronic transport record and indicate the carrier's authorization of the electronic transport record.

Article 39   Deficiencies in the contract particulars

1. The absence or inaccuracy of one or more of the contract particulars referred to in article 36, paragraphs 1, 2 or 3, does not of itself affect the legal character or validity of the transport document or of the electronic transport record.

2. If the contract particulars include the date but fail to indicate its significance, the date is deemed to be:

    (a) The date on which all of the goods indicated in the transport document or electronic transport record were loaded on board the ship, if the contract particulars indicate that the goods have been loaded on board a ship; or

    (b) The date on which the carrier or a performing party received the goods, if the contract particulars do not indicate that the goods have been loaded on board a ship.

3. If the contract particulars fail to state the apparent order and condition of the goods at the time the carrier or a performing party receives them, the contract particulars are deemed to have stated that the goods were in apparent good order and condition at the time the carrier or a performing party received them.

Article 40   Qualifying the information relating to the goods in the contract particulars

1. The carrier shall qualify the information referred to in article 36, paragraph 1 to indicate that the carrier does not assume responsibility for the accuracy of the information furnished by the shipper if:

    (a) The carrier has actual knowledge that any material statement in the transport document or electronic transport record is false or misleading; or

    (b) The carrier has reasonable grounds to believe that a material statement in the transport document or electronic transport record is false or misleading.

2. Without prejudice to paragraph 1 of this article, the carrier may qualify the information referred to in article 36, paragraph 1 in the circumstances and in the manner set out in paragraphs 3 and 4 of this article to indicate that the carrier does not assume responsibility for the accuracy of the information furnished by the shipper.

3. When the goods are not delivered for carriage to the carrier or a performing party in a closed container or vehicle, or when they are delivered in a closed container or vehicle and the carrier or a performing party actually inspects them, the carrier may qualify the information referred to in article 36, paragraph 1, if:

    (a) The carrier had no physically practicable or commercially reasonable means of checking the information furnished by the shipper, in which case it may indicate which information it was unable to check; or

   (b) The carrier has reasonable grounds to believe the information furnished by the shipper to be inaccurate, in which case it may include a clause providing what it reasonably considers accurate information.

4. When the goods are delivered for carriage to the carrier or a performing party in a closed container or vehicle, the carrier may qualify the information referred to in:

   (a) Article 36, subparagraphs 1 (a), (b), or (c), if –
       (i) The goods inside the container or vehicle have not actually been inspected by the carrier or a performing party; and
       (ii) Neither the carrier nor a performing party otherwise has actual knowledge of its contents before issuing the transport document or the electronic transport record; and
   (b) Article 36, subparagraph 1 (d), if –
       (i) Neither the carrier nor a performing party weighed the container or vehicle, and the shipper and the carrier had not agreed prior to the shipment that the container or vehicle would be weighed and the weight would be included in the contract particulars; or
       (ii) There was no physically practicable or commercially reasonable means of checking the weight of the container or vehicle.

Article 41   Evidentiary effect of the contract particulars

Except to the extent that the contract particulars have been qualified in the circumstances and in the manner set out in article 40:

   (a) A transport document or an electronic transport record is prima facie evidence of the carrier's receipt of the goods as stated in the contract particulars;
   (b) Proof to the contrary by the carrier in respect of any contract particulars shall not be admissible, when such contract particulars are included in:
       (i) A negotiable transport document or a negotiable electronic transport record that is transferred to a third party acting in good faith; or
       (ii) A non-negotiable transport document that indicates that it must be surrendered in order to obtain delivery of the goods and is transferred to the consignee acting in good faith.
   (c) Proof to the contrary by the carrier shall not be admissible against a consignee that in good faith has acted in reliance on any of the following contract particulars included in a non-negotiable transport document or a non-negotiable electronic transport record:
       (i) The contract particulars referred to in article 36, paragraph 1, when such contract particulars are furnished by the carrier;
       (ii) The number, type and identifying numbers of the containers, but not the identifying numbers of the container seals; and
       (iii) The contract particulars referred to in article 36, paragraph 2.

Article 42   'Freight prepaid'

If the contract particulars contain the statement 'freight prepaid' or a statement of a similar nature, the carrier cannot assert against the holder or the consignee the fact that the freight has not been paid. This article does not apply if the holder or the consignee is also the shipper.

Chapter 9   Delivery of the goods

Article 43   Obligation to accept delivery

When the goods have arrived at their destination, the consignee that demands delivery of the goods under the contract of carriage shall accept delivery of the goods at the time or within the time period and at the location agreed in the contract of carriage or, failing such agreement, at the time and location at which, having regard to the terms of the contract, the customs, usages or practices of the trade and the circumstances of the carriage, delivery could reasonably be expected.

Article 44   Obligation to acknowledge receipt

On request of the carrier or the performing party that delivers the goods, the consignee shall acknowledge receipt of the goods from the carrier or the performing party in the manner that is customary at the place of delivery. The carrier may refuse delivery if the consignee refuses to acknowledge such receipt.

Article 45   Delivery when no negotiable transport document or negotiable electronic transport record is issued

When neither a negotiable transport document nor a negotiable electronic transport record has been issued:

    (a) The carrier shall deliver the goods to the consignee at the time and location referred to in article 43. The carrier may refuse delivery if the person claiming to be the consignee does not properly identify itself as the consignee on the request of the carrier;

    (b) If the name and address of the consignee are not referred to in the contract particulars, the controlling party shall prior to or upon the arrival of the goods at the place of destination advise the carrier of such name and address;

    (c) Without prejudice to article 48, paragraph 1, if the goods are not deliverable because

        (i) the consignee, after having received a notice of arrival, does not, at the time or within the time period referred to in article 43, claim delivery of the goods from the carrier after their arrival at the place of destination,

        (ii) the carrier refuses delivery because the person claiming to be the consignee does not properly identify itself as the consignee, or

        (iii) the carrier is, after reasonable effort, unable to locate the consignee in order to request delivery instructions,

    the carrier may so advise the controlling party and request instructions in respect of the delivery of the goods. If, after reasonable effort, the carrier is unable to locate the controlling party, the carrier may so advise the shipper and request instructions in respect of the delivery of the goods. If, after reasonable effort, the carrier is unable to locate the shipper, the carrier may so advise the documentary shipper and request instructions in respect of the delivery of the goods;

    (d) The carrier that delivers the goods upon instruction of the controlling party, the shipper or the documentary shipper pursuant to subparagraph (c) of this article is discharged from its obligations to deliver the goods under the contract of carriage.

Article 46   Delivery when a non-negotiable transport document that requires surrender is issued

When a non-negotiable transport document has been issued that indicates that it shall be surrendered in order to obtain delivery of the goods:

    (a) The carrier shall deliver the goods at the time and location referred to in article 43 to the consignee upon the consignee properly identifying itself on the request of the carrier and surrender of the non-negotiable document. The carrier may refuse delivery if the person claiming to be the consignee fails to properly identify itself on the request of the carrier, and shall refuse delivery if the non-negotiable document is not surrendered. If more than one original of the non negotiable document has been issued, the surrender of one original will suffice and the other originals cease to have any effect or validity;

    (b) Without prejudice to article 48, paragraph 1, if the goods are not deliverable because

        (i) the consignee, after having received a notice of arrival, does not, at the time or within the time period referred to in article 43, claim delivery of the goods from the carrier after their arrival at the place of destination,

        (ii) the carrier refuses delivery because the person claiming to be the consignee does not properly identify itself as the consignee or does not surrender the document, or

        (iii) the carrier is, after reasonable effort, unable to locate the consignee in order to request delivery instructions, the carrier may so advise the shipper and request instructions in respect of the delivery of the goods. If, after reasonable effort, the carrier is unable to locate the shipper, the carrier may so advise the documentary shipper and request instructions in respect of the delivery of the goods;

(c) The carrier that delivers the goods upon instruction of the shipper or the documentary shipper pursuant to subparagraph (b) of this article is discharged from its obligation to deliver the goods under the contract of carriage, irrespective of whether the non-negotiable transport document has been surrendered to it.

Article 47 Delivery when a negotiable transport document or negotiable electronic transport record is issued

1. When a negotiable transport document or a negotiable electronic transport record has been issued:

(a) The holder of the negotiable transport document or negotiable electronic transport record is entitled to claim delivery of the goods from the carrier after they have arrived at the place of destination, in which event the carrier shall deliver the goods at the time and location referred to in article 43 to the holder:

  (i) Upon surrender of the negotiable transport document and, if the holder is one of the persons referred to in article 1, subparagraph 10 (a)(i), upon the holder properly identifying itself; or

  (ii) Upon demonstration by the holder, in accordance with the procedures referred to in article 9, paragraph 1, that it is the holder of the negotiable electronic transport record.

(b) The carrier shall refuse delivery if the requirements of subparagraph (a)(i) or (a)(ii) of this paragraph are not met;

(c) If more than one original of the negotiable transport document has been issued, and the number of originals is stated in that document, the surrender of one original will suffice and the other originals cease to have any effect or validity. When a negotiable electronic transport record has been used, such electronic transport record ceases to have any effect or validity upon delivery to the holder in accordance with the procedures required by article 9, paragraph 1.

2. Without prejudice to article 48, paragraph 1, if the negotiable transport document or the negotiable electronic transport record expressly states that the goods may be delivered without the surrender of the transport document or the electronic transport record, the following rule applies:

(a) If the goods are not deliverable because

  (i) the holder, after having received a notice of arrival, does not, at the time or within the time period referred to in article 43, claim delivery of the goods from the carrier after their arrival at the place of destination,

  (ii) the carrier refuses delivery because the person claiming to be a holder does not properly identify itself as one of the persons referred to in article 1, subparagraph 10 (a)(i), or

  (iii) the carrier is, after reasonable effort, unable to locate the holder in order to request delivery instructions,

  the carrier may so advise the shipper and request instructions in respect of the delivery of the goods. If, after reasonable effort, the carrier is unable to locate the shipper, the carrier may so advise the documentary shipper and request instructions in respect of the delivery of the goods;

(b) The carrier that delivers the goods upon instruction of the shipper or the documentary shipper in accordance with subparagraph 2 (a) of this article is discharged from its obligation to deliver the goods under the contract of carriage to the holder, irrespective of whether the negotiable transport document has been surrendered to it, or the person claiming delivery under a negotiable electronic transport record has demonstrated, in accordance with the procedures referred to in article 9, paragraph 1, that it is the holder;

(c) The person giving instructions under subparagraph 2 (a) of this article shall indemnify the carrier against loss arising from its being held liable to the holder under subparagraph 2 (e) of this article. The carrier may refuse to follow those instructions if the person fails to provide adequate security as the carrier may reasonably request;

(d) A person that becomes a holder of the negotiable transport document or the negotiable electronic transport record after the carrier has delivered the goods pursuant to subparagraph 2 (b) of this article, but pursuant to contractual or other arrangements made before such delivery acquires rights against the carrier under the contract of carriage, other than the right to claim delivery of the goods;

(e) Notwithstanding subparagraphs 2 (b) and 2 (d) of this article, a holder that becomes a holder after such delivery, and that did not have and could not reasonably have had knowledge of such delivery at the time it became a holder, acquires the rights incorporated in the negotiable transport document or negotiable electronic transport record. When the contract particulars state the expected time of arrival of the goods, or indicate how to obtain information as to whether the goods have been delivered, it is presumed that the holder at the time that it became a holder had or could reasonably have had knowledge of the delivery of the goods.

Article 48 Goods remaining undelivered

1. For the purposes of this article, goods shall be deemed to have remained undelivered only if, after their arrival at the place of destination:

(a) The consignee does not accept delivery of the goods pursuant to this chapter at the time and location referred to in article 43;

(b) The controlling party, the holder, the shipper or the documentary shipper cannot be found or does not give the carrier adequate instructions pursuant to articles 45, 46 and 47;

(c) The carrier is entitled or required to refuse delivery pursuant to articles 44, 45, 46 and 47;

(d) The carrier is not allowed to deliver the goods to the consignee pursuant to the law or regulations of the place at which delivery is requested; or

(e) The goods are otherwise undeliverable by the carrier.

2. Without prejudice to any other rights that the carrier may have against the shipper, controlling party or consignee, if the goods have remained undelivered, the carrier may, at the risk and expense of the person entitled to the goods, take such action in respect of the goods as circumstances may reasonably require, including:

(a) To store the goods at any suitable place;

(b) To unpack the goods if they are packed in containers or vehicles, or to act otherwise in respect of the goods, including by moving them; and

(c) To cause the goods to be sold or destroyed in accordance with the practices or pursuant to the law or regulations of the place where the goods are located at the time.

3. The carrier may exercise the rights under paragraph 2 of this article only after it has given reasonable notice of the intended action under paragraph 2 of this article to the person stated in the contract particulars as the person, if any, to be notified of the arrival of the goods at the place of destination, and to one of the following persons in the order indicated, if known to the carrier: the consignee, the controlling party or the shipper.

4. If the goods are sold pursuant to subparagraph 2 (c) of this article, the carrier shall hold the proceeds of the sale for the benefit of the person entitled to the goods, subject to the deduction of any costs incurred by the carrier and any other amounts that are due to the carrier in connection with the carriage of those goods.

5. The carrier shall not be liable for loss of or damage to goods that occurs during the time that they remain undelivered pursuant to this article unless the claimant proves that such loss or damage resulted from the failure by the carrier to take steps that would have been reasonable in the circumstances to preserve the goods and that the carrier knew or ought to have known that the loss or damage to the goods would result from its failure to take such steps.

Article 49   Retention of goods

Nothing in this Convention affects a right of the carrier or a performing party that may exist pursuant to the contract of carriage or the applicable law to retain the goods to secure the payment of sums due.

Chapter 10   Rights of the controlling party

Article 50   Exercise and extent of right of control

1. The right of control may be exercised only by the controlling party and is limited to:
   (a) The right to give or modify instructions in respect of the goods that do not constitute a variation of the contract of carriage;
   (b) The right to obtain delivery of the goods at a scheduled port of call or, in respect of inland carriage, any place en route; and
   (c) The right to replace the consignee by any other person including the controlling party.
2. The right of control exists during the entire period of responsibility of the carrier, as provided in article 12, and ceases when that period expires.

Article 51   Identity of the controlling party and transfer of the right of control

1. Except in the cases referred to in paragraphs 2, 3 and 4 of this article:
   (a) The shipper is the controlling party unless the shipper, when the contract of carriage is concluded, designates the consignee, the documentary shipper or another person as the controlling party;
   (b) The controlling party is entitled to transfer the right of control to another person. The transfer becomes effective with respect to the carrier upon its notification of the transfer by the transferor, and the transferee becomes the controlling party; and
   (c) The controlling party shall properly identify itself when it exercises the right of control.
2. When a non-negotiable transport document has been issued that indicates that it shall be surrendered in order to obtain delivery of the goods:
   (a) The shipper is the controlling party and may transfer the right of control to the consignee named in the transport document by transferring the document to that person without endorsement. If more than one original of the document was issued, all originals shall be transferred in order to effect a transfer of the right of control; and
   (b) In order to exercise its right of control, the controlling party shall produce the document and properly identify itself. If more than one original of the document was issued, all originals shall be produced, failing which the right of control cannot be exercised.
3. When a negotiable transport document is issued:
   (a) The holder or, if more than one original of the negotiable transport document is issued, the holder of all originals is the controlling party;
   (b) The holder may transfer the right of control by transferring the negotiable transport document to another person in accordance with article 57. If more than one original of that document was issued, all originals shall be transferred to that person in order to effect a transfer of the right of control; and
   (c) In order to exercise the right of control, the holder shall produce the negotiable transport document to the carrier, and if the holder is one of the persons referred to in article 1, subparagraph 10 (a)(i), the holder shall properly identify itself. If more than one original of the document was issued, all originals shall be produced, failing which the right of control cannot be exercised.
4. When a negotiable electronic transport record is issued:
   (a) The holder is the controlling party;
   (b) The holder may transfer the right of control to another person by transferring the negotiable electronic transport record in accordance with the procedures referred to in article 9, paragraph 1; and

(c) In order to exercise the right of control, the holder shall demonstrate, in accordance with the procedures referred to in article 9, paragraph 1, that it is the holder.

Article 52 Carrier's execution of instructions

1. Subject to paragraphs 2 and 3 of this article, the carrier shall execute the instructions referred to in article 50 if:

(a) The person giving such instructions is entitled to exercise the right of control;

(b) The instructions can reasonably be executed according to their terms at the moment that they reach the carrier; and

(c) The instructions will not interfere with the normal operations of the carrier, including its delivery practices.

2. In any event, the controlling party shall reimburse the carrier for any reasonable additional expense that the carrier may incur and shall indemnify the carrier against loss or damage that the carrier may suffer as a result of diligently executing any instruction pursuant to this article, including compensation that the carrier may become liable to pay for loss of or damage to other goods being carried.

3. The carrier is entitled to obtain security from the controlling party for the amount of additional expense, loss or damage that the carrier reasonably expects will arise in connection with the execution of an instruction pursuant to this article. The carrier may refuse to carry out the instructions if no such security is provided.

4. The carrier's liability for loss of or damage to the goods or for delay in delivery resulting from its failure to comply with the instructions of the controlling party in breach of its obligation pursuant to paragraph 1 of this article shall be subject to articles 17 to 23, and the amount of the compensation payable by the carrier shall be subject to articles 59 to 61.

Article 53 Deemed delivery

Goods that are delivered pursuant to an instruction in accordance with article 52, paragraph 1, are deemed to be delivered at the place of destination, and the provisions of chapter 9 relating to such delivery apply to such goods.

Article 54 Variations to the contract of carriage

1. The controlling party is the only person that may agree with the carrier to variations to the contract of carriage other than those referred to in article 50, subparagraphs 1 (b) and (c).

2. Variations to the contract of carriage, including those referred to in article 50, subparagraphs 1 (b) and (c), shall be stated in a negotiable transport document or in a non-negotiable transport document that requires surrender, or incorporated in a negotiable electronic transport record, or, upon the request of the controlling party, shall be stated in a non-negotiable transport document or incorporated in a non-negotiable electronic transport record. If so stated or incorporated, such variations shall be signed in accordance with article 38.

Article 55 Providing additional information, instructions or documents to carrier

1. The controlling party, on request of the carrier or a performing party, shall provide in a timely manner information, instructions or documents relating to the goods not yet provided by the shipper and not otherwise reasonably available to the carrier that the carrier may reasonably need to perform its obligations under the contract of carriage.

2. If the carrier, after reasonable effort, is unable to locate the controlling party or the controlling party is unable to provide adequate information, instructions or documents to the carrier, the shipper shall provide them. If the carrier, after reasonable effort, is unable to locate the shipper, the documentary shipper shall provide such information, instructions or documents.

Article 56 Variation by agreement

The parties to the contract of carriage may vary the effect of articles 50, subparagraphs 1 (b) and (c), 50, paragraph 2, and 52. The parties may also restrict or exclude the transferability of the right of control referred to in article 51, subparagraph 1 (b).

Chapter 11 Transfer of rights

Article 57 When a negotiable transport document or negotiable electronic transport record is issued

1. When a negotiable transport document is issued, the holder may transfer the rights incorporated in the document by transferring it to another person:

    (a) Duly endorsed either to such other person or in blank, if an order document; or

    (b) Without endorsement, if:

        (i) A bearer document or a blank endorsed document; or

        (ii) A document made out to the order of a named person and the transfer is between the first holder and the named person.

2. When a negotiable electronic transport record is issued, its holder may transfer the rights incorporated in it, whether it be made out to order or to the order of a named person, by transferring the electronic transport record in accordance with the procedures referred to in article 9, paragraph 1.

Article 58 Liability of holder

1. Without prejudice to article 55, a holder that is not the shipper and that does not exercise any right under the contract of carriage does not assume any liability under the contract of carriage solely by reason of being a holder.

2. A holder that is not the shipper and that exercises any right under the contract of carriage assumes any liabilities imposed on it under the contract of carriage to the extent that such liabilities are incorporated in or ascertainable from the negotiable transport document or the negotiable electronic transport record.

3. For the purposes of paragraphs 1 and 2 of this article, a holder that is not the shipper does not exercise any right under the contract of carriage solely because:

    (a) It agrees with the carrier, pursuant to article 10, to replace a negotiable transport document by a negotiable electronic transport record or to replace a negotiable electronic transport record by a negotiable transport document; or

    (b) It transfers its rights pursuant to article 57.

Chapter 12 Limits of liability

Article 59 Limits of liability

1. Subject to articles 60 and 61, paragraph 1, the carrier's liability for breaches of its obligations under this Convention is limited to 875 units of account per package or other shipping unit, or 3 units of account per kilogram of the gross weight of the goods that are the subject of the claim or dispute, whichever amount is the higher, except when the value of the goods has been declared by the shipper and included in the contract particulars, or when a higher amount than the amount of limitation of liability set out in this article has been agreed upon between the carrier and the shipper.

2. When goods are carried in or on a container, pallet or similar article of transport used to consolidate goods, or in or on a vehicle, the packages or shipping units enumerated in the contract particulars as packed in or on such article of transport or vehicle are deemed packages or shipping units. If not so enumerated, the goods in or on such article of transport or vehicle are deemed one shipping unit.

3. The unit of account referred to in this article is the Special Drawing Right as defined by the International Monetary Fund. The amounts referred to in this article are to be converted into the national currency of a State according to the value of such currency at the date of judgement or award or the date agreed upon by the parties. The value of a national currency, in terms of the Special Drawing Right, of a Contracting State that is a member of the International Monetary Fund is to be calculated in accordance with the method of valuation applied by the International Monetary Fund in effect at the date in question for its operations and transactions. The value of a national currency, in terms of the Special Drawing Right, of a Contracting State that is not a member of the International Monetary Fund is to be calculated in a manner to be determined by that State.

Article 60   Limits of liability for loss caused by delay

Subject to article 61, paragraph 2, compensation for loss of or damage to the goods due to delay shall be calculated in accordance with article 22 and liability for economic loss due to delay is limited to an amount equivalent to two and one-half times the freight payable on the goods delayed. The total amount payable pursuant to this article and article 59, paragraph 1 may not exceed the limit that would be established pursuant to article 59, paragraph 1 in respect of the total loss of the goods concerned.

Article 61   Loss of the benefit of limitation of liability

1. Neither the carrier nor any of the persons referred to in article 18 is entitled to the benefit of the limitation of liability as provided in article 59, or as provided in the contract of carriage, if the claimant proves that the loss resulting from the breach of the carrier's obligation under this Convention was attributable to a personal act or omission of the person claiming a right to limit done with the intent to cause such loss or recklessly and with knowledge that such loss would probably result.

2. Neither the carrier nor any of the persons mentioned in article 18 is entitled to the benefit of the limitation of liability as provided in article 60 if the claimant proves that the delay in delivery resulted from a personal act or omission of the person claiming a right to limit done with the intent to cause the loss due to delay or recklessly and with knowledge that such loss would probably result.

Chapter 13   Time for suit

Article 62   Period of time for suit

1. No judicial or arbitral proceedings in respect of claims or disputes arising from a breach of an obligation under this Convention may be instituted after the expiration of a period of two years.

2. The period referred to in paragraph 1 of this article commences on the day on which the carrier has delivered the goods or, in cases in which no goods have been delivered or only part of the goods have been delivered, on the last day on which the goods should have been delivered. The day on which the period commences is not included in the period.

3. Notwithstanding the expiration of the period set out in paragraph 1 of this article, one party may rely on its claim as a defence or for the purpose of set-off against a claim asserted by the other party.

Article 63   Extension of time for suit

The period provided in article 62 shall not be subject to suspension or interruption, but the person against which a claim is made may at any time during the running of the period extend that period by a declaration to the claimant. This period may be further extended by another declaration or declarations.

Article 64   Action for indemnity

An action for indemnity by a person held liable may be instituted after the expiration of the period provided in article 62 if the indemnity action is instituted within the later of:

    (a) The time allowed by the applicable law in the jurisdiction where proceedings are instituted; or

    (b) Ninety days commencing from the day when the person instituting the action for indemnity has either settled the claim or been served with process in the action against itself, whichever is earlier.

Article 65   Actions against the person identified as the carrier

An action against the bareboat charterer or the person identified as the carrier pursuant to article 37, paragraph 2, may be instituted after the expiration of the period provided in article 62 if the action is instituted within the later of:

    (a) The time allowed by the applicable law in the jurisdiction where proceedings are instituted; or

    (b) Ninety days commencing from the day when the carrier has been identified, or the registered owner or bareboat charterer has rebutted the presumption that it is the carrier, pursuant to article 37, paragraph 2.

Chapter 14 Jurisdiction

Article 66   Actions against the carrier

Unless the contract of carriage contains an exclusive choice of court agreement that complies with article 67 or 72, the plaintiff has the right to institute judicial proceedings under this Convention against the carrier:

(a) In a competent court within the jurisdiction of which is situated one of the following places:
   (i) The domicile of the carrier;
   (ii) The place of receipt agreed in the contract of carriage;
   (iii) The place of delivery agreed in the contract of carriage; or
   (iv) The port where the goods are initially loaded on a ship or the port where the goods are finally discharged from a ship; or

(b) In a competent court or courts designated by an agreement between the shipper and the carrier for the purpose of deciding claims against the carrier that may arise under this Convention.

Article 67   Choice of court agreements

1. The jurisdiction of a court chosen in accordance with article 66, paragraph (b), is exclusive for disputes between the parties to the contract only if the parties so agree and the agreement conferring jurisdiction:

(a) Is contained in a volume contract that clearly states the names and addresses of the parties and either (i) is individually negotiated or (ii) contains a prominent statement that there is an exclusive choice of court agreement and specifies the sections of the volume contract containing that agreement; and

(b) Clearly designates the courts of one Contracting State or one or more specific courts of one Contracting State.

2. A person that is not a party to the volume contract is bound by an exclusive choice of court agreement concluded in accordance with paragraph 1 of this article only if:

(a) The court is in one of the places designated in article 66, paragraph (a);

(b) That agreement is contained in the transport document or electronic transport record;

(c) That person is given timely and adequate notice of the court where the action shall be brought and that the jurisdiction of that court is exclusive; and

(d) The law of the court seized recognizes that that person may be bound by the exclusive choice of court agreement.

Article 68   Actions against the maritime performing party

The plaintiff has the right to institute judicial proceedings under this Convention against the maritime performing party in a competent court within the jurisdiction of which is situated one of the following places:

(a) The domicile of the maritime performing party; or

(b) The port where the goods are received by the maritime performing party, the port where the goods are delivered by the maritime performing party or the port in which the maritime performing party performs its activities with respect to the goods.

Article 69   No additional bases of jurisdiction

Subject to articles 71 and 72, no judicial proceedings under this Convention against the carrier or a maritime performing party may be instituted in a court not designated pursuant to articles 66 or 68.

Article 70   Arrest and provisional or protective measures

Nothing in this Convention affects jurisdiction with regard to provisional or protective measures, including arrest. A court in a State in which a provisional or protective measure was taken does not have jurisdiction to determine the case upon its merits unless:

(a) The requirements of this chapter are fulfilled; or

(b) An international convention that applies in that State so provides.

Article 71   Consolidation and removal of actions

1. Except when there is an exclusive choice of court agreement that is binding pursuant to articles 67 or 72, if a single action is brought against both the carrier and the maritime performing party arising out of a single occurrence, the action may be instituted only in a court designated pursuant to both article 66 and article 68. If there is no such court, such action may be instituted in a court designated pursuant to article 68, subparagraph (b), if there is such a court.

2. Except when there is an exclusive choice of court agreement that is binding pursuant to articles 67 or 72, a carrier or a maritime performing party that institutes an action seeking a declaration of non-liability or any other action that would deprive a person of its right to select the forum pursuant to article 66 or 68 shall, at the request of the defendant, withdraw that action once the defendant has chosen a court designated pursuant to article 66 or 68, whichever is applicable, where the action may be recommenced.

Article 72   Agreement after a dispute has arisen and jurisdiction when the defendant has entered an appearance

1. After a dispute has arisen, the parties to the dispute may agree to resolve it in any competent court.

2. A competent court before which a defendant appears, without contesting jurisdiction in accordance with the rules of that court, has jurisdiction.

Article 73   Recognition and enforcement

1. A decision made in one Contracting State by a court having jurisdiction under this Convention shall be recognized and enforced in another Contracting State in accordance with the law of such latter Contracting State when both States have made a declaration in accordance with article 74.

2. A court may refuse recognition and enforcement based on the grounds for the refusal of recognition and enforcement available pursuant to its law.

3. This chapter shall not affect the application of the rules of a regional economic integration organization that is a party to this Convention, as concerns the recognition or enforcement of judgements as between member States of the regional economic integration organization, whether adopted before or after this Convention.

Article 74   Application of chapter 14

The provisions of this chapter shall bind only Contracting States that declare in accordance with article 91 that they will be bound by them.

Chapter 15   Arbitration

Article 75   Arbitration agreements

1. Subject to this chapter, parties may agree that any dispute that may arise relating to the carriage of goods under this Convention shall be referred to arbitration.

2. The arbitration proceedings shall, at the option of the person asserting a claim against the carrier, take place at:

   (a) Any place designated for that purpose in the arbitration agreement; or
   (b) Any other place situated in a State where any of the following places is located:
       (i)   The domicile of the carrier;
       (ii) The place of receipt agreed in the contract of carriage;
       (iii) The place of delivery agreed in the contract of carriage; or
       (iv) The port where the goods are initially loaded on a ship or the port where the goods are finally discharged from a ship.

3. The designation of the place of arbitration in the agreement is binding for disputes between the parties to the agreement if the agreement is contained in a volume contract that clearly states the names and addresses of the parties and either:

   (a) Is individually negotiated; or
   (b) Contains a prominent statement that there is an arbitration agreement and specifies the sections of the volume contract containing the arbitration agreement.

4. When an arbitration agreement has been concluded in accordance with paragraph 3 of this article, a person that is not a party to the volume contract is bound by the designation of the place of arbitration in that agreement only if:

 (a) The place of arbitration designated in the agreement is situated in one of the places referred to in subparagraph 2 (b) of this article;

 (b) The agreement is contained in the transport document or electronic transport record;

 (c) The person to be bound is given timely and adequate notice of the place of arbitration; and

 (d) Applicable law permits that person to be bound by the arbitration agreement.

5. The provisions of paragraphs 1, 2, 3 and 4 of this article are deemed to be part of every arbitration clause or agreement, and any term of such clause or agreement to the extent that it is inconsistent therewith is void.

Article 76 Arbitration agreement in non-liner transportation

1. Nothing in this Convention affects the enforceability of an arbitration agreement in a contract of carriage in non-liner transportation to which this Convention or the provisions of this Convention apply by reason of:

 (a) The application of article 7; or

 (b) The parties' voluntary incorporation of this Convention in a contract of carriage that would not otherwise be subject to this Convention.

2. Notwithstanding paragraph 1 of this article, an arbitration agreement in a transport document or electronic transport record to which this Convention applies by reason of the application of article 7 is subject to this chapter unless such a transport document or electronic transport record:

 (a) Identifies the parties to and the date of the charterparty or other contract excluded from the application of this Convention by reason of the application of article 6; and

 (b) Incorporates by specific reference the clause in the charterparty or other contract that contains the terms of the arbitration agreement.

Article 77 Agreement to arbitrate after a dispute has arisen

Notwithstanding the provisions of this chapter and chapter 14, after a dispute has arisen the parties to the dispute may agree to resolve it by arbitration in any place.

Article 78 Application of chapter 15

The provisions of this chapter shall bind only Contracting States that declare in accordance with article 91 that they will be bound by them.

Chapter 16 Validity of contractual terms

Article 79 General provisions

1. Unless otherwise provided in this Convention, any term in a contract of carriage is void to the extent that it:

 (a) Directly or indirectly excludes or limits the obligations of the carrier or a maritime performing party under this Convention;

 (b) Directly or indirectly excludes or limits the liability of the carrier or a maritime performing party for breach of an obligation under this Convention; or

 (c) Assigns a benefit of insurance of the goods in favour of the carrier or a person referred to in article 18.

2. Unless otherwise provided in this Convention, any term in a contract of carriage is void to the extent that it:

 (a) Directly or indirectly excludes, limits or increases the obligations under this Convention of the shipper, consignee, controlling party, holder or documentary shipper; or

 (b) Directly or indirectly excludes, limits or increases the liability of the shipper, consignee, controlling party, holder or documentary shipper for breach of any of its obligations under this Convention.

Article 80   Special rules for volume contracts

1. Notwithstanding article 79, as between the carrier and the shipper, a volume contract to which this Convention applies may provide for greater or lesser rights, obligations and liabilities than those imposed by this Convention.

2. A derogation pursuant to paragraph 1 of this article is binding only when:

(a) The volume contract contains a prominent statement that it derogates from this Convention;

(b) The volume contract is (i) individually negotiated or (ii) prominently specifies the sections of the volume contract containing the derogations;

(c) The shipper is given an opportunity and notice of the opportunity to conclude a contract of carriage on terms and conditions that comply with this Convention without any derogation under this article; and

(d) The derogation is neither (i) incorporated by reference from another document nor (ii) included in a contract of adhesion that is not subject to negotiation.

3. A carrier's public schedule of prices and services, transport document, electronic transport record or similar document is not a volume contract pursuant to paragraph 1 of this article, but a volume contract may incorporate such documents by reference as terms of the contract.

4. Paragraph 1 of this article does not apply to rights and obligations provided in articles 14, subparagraphs (a) and (b), 29 and 32 or to liability arising from the breach thereof, nor does it apply to any liability arising from an act or omission referred to in article 61.

5. The terms of the volume contract that derogate from this Convention, if the volume contract satisfies the requirements of paragraph 2 of this article, apply between the carrier and any person other than the shipper provided that:

(a) Such person received information that prominently states that the volume contract derogates from this Convention and gave its express consent to be bound by such derogations; and

(b) Such consent is not solely set forth in a carrier's public schedule of prices and services, transport document or electronic transport record.

6. The party claiming the benefit of the derogation bears the burden of proof that the conditions for derogation have been fulfilled.

Article 81   Special rules for live animals and certain other goods

Notwithstanding article 79 and without prejudice to article 80, the contract of carriage may exclude or limit the obligations or the liability of both the carrier and a maritime performing party if:

(a) The goods are live animals, but any such exclusion or limitation will not be effective if the claimant proves that the loss of or damage to the goods, or delay in delivery, resulted from an act or omission of the carrier or of a person referred to in article 18, done with the intent to cause such loss of or damage to the goods or such loss due to delay or done recklessly and with knowledge that such loss or damage or such loss due to delay would probably result; or

(b) The character or condition of the goods or the circumstances and terms and conditions under which the carriage is to be performed are such as reasonably to justify a special agreement, provided that such contract of carriage is not related to ordinary commercial shipments made in the ordinary course of trade and that no negotiable transport document or negotiable electronic transport record is issued for the carriage of the goods.

Chapter 17   Matters not governed by this Convention

Article 82   International conventions governing the carriage of goods by other modes of transport

Nothing in this Convention affects the application of any of the following international conventions in force at the time this Convention enters into force, including any future amendment to such conventions, that regulate the liability of the carrier for loss of or damage to the goods:

(a) Any convention governing the carriage of goods by air to the extent that such convention according to its provisions applies to any part of the contract of carriage;

(b) Any convention governing the carriage of goods by road to the extent that such convention according to its provisions applies to the carriage of goods that remain loaded on a road cargo vehicle carried on board a ship;

(c) Any convention governing the carriage of goods by rail to the extent that such convention according to its provisions applies to carriage of goods by sea as a supplement to the carriage by rail; or

(d) Any convention governing the carriage of goods by inland waterways to the extent that such convention according to its provisions applies to a carriage of goods without trans-shipment both by inland waterways and sea.

Article 83   Global limitation of liability

Nothing in this Convention affects the application of any international convention or national law regulating the global limitation of liability of vessel owners.

Article 84   General average

Nothing in this Convention affects the application of terms in the contract of carriage or provisions of national law regarding the adjustment of general average.

Article 85   Passengers and luggage

This Convention does not apply to a contract of carriage for passengers and their luggage.

Article 86   Damage caused by nuclear incident

No liability arises under this Convention for damage caused by a nuclear incident if the operator of a nuclear installation is liable for such damage:

(a) Under the Paris Convention on Third Party Liability in the Field of Nuclear Energy of 29 July 1960 as amended by the Additional Protocol of 28 January 1964 and by the Protocols of 16 November 1982 and 12 February 2004, the Vienna Convention on Civil Liability for Nuclear Damage of 21 May 1963 as amended by the Joint Protocol Relating to the Application of the Vienna Convention and the Paris Convention of 21 September 1988 and as amended by the Protocol to Amend the 1963 Vienna Convention on Civil Liability for Nuclear Damage of 12 September 1997, or the Convention on Supplementary Compensation for Nuclear Damage of 12 September 1997, including any amendment to these conventions and any future convention in respect of the liability of the operator of a nuclear installation for damage caused by a nuclear incident; or

(b) Under national law applicable to the liability for such damage, provided that such law is in all respects as favourable to persons that may suffer damage as either the Paris or Vienna Conventions or the Convention on Supplementary Compensation for Nuclear Damage.

Chapter 18 Final clauses

Article 87   Depositary

The Secretary-General of the United Nations is hereby designated as the depositary of this Convention.

Article 88   Signature, ratification, acceptance, approval or accession

1. This Convention is open for signature by all States at Rotterdam, the Netherlands, on 23 September 2009 and thereafter at the Headquarters of the United Nations in New York.

2. This Convention is subject to ratification, acceptance or approval by the signatory States.

3. This Convention is open for accession by all States that are not signatory States as from the date it is open for signature.

4. Instruments of ratification, acceptance, approval and accession are to be deposited with the Secretary-General of the United Nations.

Article 89 Denunciation of other conventions

1. A State that ratifies, accepts, approves or accedes to this Convention and is a party to the International Convention for the Unification of certain Rules relating to Bills of Lading signed at Brussels on 25 August 1924; to the Protocol signed on 23 February 1968 to amend the International Convention for the Unification of certain Rules relating to Bills of Lading signed at Brussels on 25 August 1924; or to the Protocol to amend the International Convention for the Unification of certain Rules relating to Bills of Lading as Modified by the Amending Protocol of 23 February 1968, signed at Brussels on 21 December 1979 shall at the same time denounce that Convention and the protocol or protocols thereto to which it is a party by notifying the Government of Belgium to that effect, with a declaration that the denunciation is to take effect as from the date when this Convention enters into force in respect of that State.

2. A State that ratifies, accepts, approves or accedes to this Convention and is a party to the United Nations Convention on the Carriage of Goods by Sea concluded at Hamburg on 31 March 1978 shall at the same time denounce that Convention by notifying the Secretary-General of the United Nations to that effect, with a declaration that the denunciation is to take effect as from the date when this Convention enters into force in respect of that State.

3. For the purposes of this article, ratifications, acceptances, approvals and accessions in respect of this Convention by States parties to the instruments listed in paragraphs 1 and 2 of this article that are notified to the depositary after this Convention has entered into force are not effective until such denunciations as may be required on the part of those States in respect of these instruments have become effective. The depositary of this Convention shall consult with the Government of Belgium, as the depositary of the instruments referred to in paragraph 1 of this article, so as to ensure necessary coordination in this respect.

Article 90 Reservations

No reservation is permitted to this Convention.

Article 91 Procedure and effect of declarations

1. The declarations permitted by articles 74 and 78 may be made at any time. The initial declarations permitted by article 92, paragraph 1, and article 93, paragraph 2, shall be made at the time of signature, ratification, acceptance, approval or accession. No other declaration is permitted under this Convention.

2. Declarations made at the time of signature are subject to confirmation upon ratification, acceptance or approval.

3. Declarations and their confirmations are to be in writing and to be formally notified to the depositary.

4. A declaration takes effect simultaneously with the entry into force of this Convention in respect of the State concerned. However, a declaration of which the depositary receives formal notification after such entry into force takes effect on the first day of the month following the expiration of six months after the date of its receipt by the depositary.

5. Any State that makes a declaration under this Convention may withdraw it at any time by a formal notification in writing addressed to the depositary. The withdrawal of a declaration, or its modification where permitted by this Convention, takes effect on the first day of the month following the expiration of six months after the date of the receipt of the notification by the depositary.

Article 92 Effect in domestic territorial units

1. If a Contracting State has two or more territorial units in which different systems of law are applicable in relation to the matters dealt with in this Convention, it may, at the time of signature, ratification, acceptance, approval or accession, declare that this Convention is to extend to all its territorial units or only to one or more of them, and may amend its declaration by submitting another declaration at any time.

2. These declarations are to be notified to the depositary and are to state expressly the territorial units to which the Convention extends.

3. When a Contracting State has declared pursuant to this article that this Convention extends to one or more but not all of its territorial units, a place located in a territorial unit to which this Convention does not extend is not considered to be in a Contracting State for the purposes of this Convention.

4. If a Contracting State makes no declaration pursuant to paragraph 1 of this article, the Convention is to extend to all territorial units of that State.

Article 93   Participation by regional economic integration organizations

1. A regional economic integration organization that is constituted by sovereign States and has competence over certain matters governed by this Convention may similarly sign, ratify, accept, approve or accede to this Convention. The regional economic integration organization shall in that case have the rights and obligations of a Contracting State, to the extent that that organization has competence over matters governed by this Convention. When the number of Contracting States is relevant in this Convention, the regional economic integration organization does not count as a Contracting State in addition to its member States which are Contracting States.

2. The regional economic integration organization shall, at the time of signature, ratification, acceptance, approval or accession, make a declaration to the depositary specifying the matters governed by this Convention in respect of which competence has been transferred to that organization by its member States. The regional economic integration organization shall promptly notify the depositary of any changes to the distribution of competence, including new transfers of competence, specified in the declaration pursuant to this paragraph.

3. Any reference to a 'Contracting State' or 'Contracting States' in this Convention applies equally to a regional economic integration organization when the context so requires.

Article 94   Entry into force

1. This Convention enters into force on the first day of the month following the expiration of one year after the date of deposit of the twentieth instrument of ratification, acceptance, approval or accession.

2. For each State that becomes a Contracting State to this Convention after the date of the deposit of the twentieth instrument of ratification, acceptance, approval or accession, this Convention enters into force on the first day of the month following the expiration of one year after the deposit of the appropriate instrument on behalf of that State.

3. Each Contracting State shall apply this Convention to contracts of carriage concluded on or after the date of the entry into force of this Convention in respect of that State.

Article 95   Revision and amendment

1. At the request of not less than one third of the Contracting States to this Convention, the depositary shall convene a conference of the Contracting States for revising or amending it.

2. Any instrument of ratification, acceptance, approval or accession deposited after the entry into force of an amendment to this Convention is deemed to apply to the Convention as amended.

Article 96   Denunciation of this Convention

1. A Contracting State may denounce this Convention at any time by means of a notification in writing addressed to the depositary.

2. The denunciation takes effect on the first day of the month following the expiration of one year after the notification is received by the depositary. If a longer period is specified in the notification, the denunciation takes effect upon the expiration of such longer period after the notification is received by the depositary.

DONE at New York, this eleventh day of December two thousand and eight, in a single original, of which the Arabic, Chinese, English, French, Russian and Spanish texts are equally authentic.

IN WITNESS WHEREOF the undersigned plenipotentiaries, being duly authorized by their respective Governments, have signed this Convention.

Part V

Codes

ICC Uniform Customs and Practice for Documentary Credits

(2007 Revision)

(ICC Publication No. 600LF—ISBN 978–92-842-0007-8)

Notes:
Text published by arrangement with ICC through ICC Services-Publications from:
Uniform Customs and Practice for Documentary Credits
ICC Publication N° 600 (E) – ISBN 978–92–842–1257–6
    © 2006 — International Chamber of Commerce (ICC)
    Available from the ICC Store at www.storeiccwbo.org.

Article 1   Application of UCP
The *Uniform Customs and Practice for Documentary Credits, 2007 Revision*, ICC Publication No. 600 ('UCP') are rules that apply to any documentary credit ('credit') (including, to the extent to which they may be applicable, any standby letter of credit) when the text of the credit expressly indicates that it is subject to these rules. They are binding on all parties thereto unless expressly modified or excluded by the credit.

Article 2   Definitions
For the purpose of these rules:

Advising bank means the bank that advises the credit at the request of the issuing bank.

Applicant means the party on whose request the credit is issued.

Banking day means a day on which a bank is regularly open at the place at which an act subject to these rules is to be performed.

Beneficiary means the party in whose favour a credit is issued.

Complying presentation means a presentation that is in accordance with the terms and conditions of the credit, the applicable provisions of these rules and international standard banking practice.

Confirmation means a definite undertaking of the confirming bank, in addition to that of the issuing bank, to honour or negotiate a complying presentation.

Confirming bank means the bank that adds its confirmation to a credit upon the issuing bank's authorization or request.

Credit means any arrangement, however named or described, that is irrevocable and thereby constitutes a definite undertaking of the issuing bank to honour a complying presentation.

Honour means:
  (a) to pay at sight if the credit is available by sight payment.
  (b) to incur a deferred payment undertaking and pay at maturity if the credit is available by deferred payment.
  (c) to accept a bill of exchange ('draft') drawn by the beneficiary and pay at maturity if the credit is available by acceptance.

Issuing bank means the bank that issues a credit at the request of an applicant or on its own behalf.

Negotiation means the purchase by the nominated bank of drafts (drawn on a bank other than the nominated bank) and/or documents under a complying presentation, by advancing or agreeing to advance funds to the beneficiary on or before the banking day on which reimbursement is due to the nominated bank.

Nominated bank means the bank with which the credit is available or any bank in the case of a credit available with any bank.

Presentation means either the delivery of documents under a credit to the issuing bank or nominated bank or the documents so delivered.

Presenter means a beneficiary, bank or other party that makes presentation.

Article 3   Interpretations

For the purpose of these rules:

Where applicable, words in the singular include the plural and in the plural include the singular. A credit is irrevocable even if there is no indication to that effect.

A document may be signed by handwriting, facsimile signature, perforated signature, stamp, symbol or any other mechanical or electronic method of authentication.

A requirement for a document to be legalized, visaed, certified or similar will be satisfied by any signature, mark, stamp or label on the document which appears to satisfy that requirement.

Branches of a bank in different countries are considered to be separate banks.

Terms such as 'first class', 'well known', 'qualified', 'independent', 'official', 'competent' or 'local' used to describe the issuer of a document allow any issuer except the beneficiary to issue that document.

Unless required to be used in a document, words such as 'prompt', 'immediately' or 'as soon as possible' will be disregarded.

The expression 'on or about' or similar will be interpreted as a stipulation that an event is to occur during a period of five calendar days before until five calendar days after the specified date, both start and end dates included.

The words 'to', 'until', 'till', 'form' and 'between' when used to determine a period of shipment include the date or dates mentioned, and the words 'before' and 'after' exclude the date mentioned.

The words 'from' and 'after' when used to determine a maturity date exclude the date mentioned.

The terms 'first half' and 'second half' of a month shall be construed respectively as the 1st to the 15th and the 16th to the last day of the month, all dates inclusive.

The terms 'beginning', 'middle' and 'end' of a month shall be construed respectively as the 1st to the 10th, the 11th to the 20th and the 21st to the last day of the month, all dates inclusive.

Article 4   Credits v. contracts

(a) A credit by its nature is a separate transaction from the sale or other contract on which it may be based. Banks are in no way concerned with or bound by such contract, even if any reference whatsoever to it is included in the credit. Consequently, the undertaking of a bank to honour, to negotiate or to fulfil any other obligation under the credit is not subject to claims or defences by the applicant resulting from its relationships with the issuing bank or the beneficiary.

A beneficiary can in no case avail itself of the contractual relationships existing between banks or between the applicant and the issuing bank.

(b) An issuing bank should discourage any attempt by the applicant to include, as a integral part of the credit, copies of the underlying contract, proforma invoice and the like.

Article 5   Documents v. goods, services or performance

Banks deal with documents and not with goods, services or performance to which the documents may relate.

Article 6   Availability, expiry date and place for presentation

(a) A credit must state the bank with which it is available or whether it is available with any bank. A credit available with a nominated bank is also available with the issuing bank.

(b) A credit must state whether it is available by sight payment, deferred payment, acceptance or negotiation.

(c) A credit must not be issued available by a draft drawn on the applicant.

(d) (i) A credit must state an expiry date for presentation. An expiry date for honour or negotiation will be deemed to be an expiry date for presentation.

(ii) The place of the bank with which the credit is available is the place for presentation. The place for presentation under a credit available with any bank is that of any bank. A place for presentation other than that of the issuing bank is in addition to the place of the issuing bank.

(e) Except as provided in sub-article 29(a), a presentation by or on behalf of the beneficiary must be made on or before the expiry date.

Article 7 Issuing bank undertaking

(a) Provided that the stipulated documents are presented to the nominated bank or to the issuing bank and that they constitute a complying presentation, the issuing bank must honour if the credit is available by:

(i) sight payment, deferred payment or acceptance with the issuing bank;

(ii) sight payment with a nominated bank and that nominated bank does not pay;

(iii) deferred payment with a nominated bank and that nominated bank does not incur its deferred payment undertaking or, having incurred its deferred payment undertaking, does not pay at maturity;

(iv) acceptance with a nominated bank and that nominated bank does not accept a draft drawn on it or, having accepted a draft on it, does not pay at maturity;

(v) negotiation with a nominated bank and that nominated bank does not negotiate.

(b) An issuing bank is irrevocably bound to honour as of the time it issues the credit.

(c) An issuing bank undertakes to reimburse a nominated bank that has honoured or negotiated a complying presentation and forwarded the documents to the issuing bank. Reimbursement for the amount of a complying presentation under a credit available by acceptance or deferred payment is due at maturity, whether or not the nominated bank prepaid or purchased before maturity. An issuing bank's undertaking to reimburse a nominated bank is independent of the issuing bank's undertaking to the beneficiary.

Article 8 Confirming bank undertaking

(a) Provided that the stipulated documents are presented to the confirming bank or to any other nominated bank and that they constitute a complying presentation, the confirming bank must:

(i) honour, if the credit is available by

(a) sight payment, deferred payment or acceptance with the confirming bank;

(b) sight payment with another nominated bank and that nominated bank does not pay;

(c) deferred payment with another nominated bank and that nominated bank does not incur its deferred payment undertaking or, having incurred its deferred payment undertaking, does not pay at maturity;

(d) acceptance with another nominated bank and that nominated bank does not accept a draft drawn on it or, having accepted a draft drawn on it, does not pay at maturity;

(e) negotiation with another nominated bank and that nominated bank does not negotiate.

(ii) negotiate, without recourse, if the credit is available by negotiation with the confirming bank.

(b) A confirming bank is irrevocably bound to honour or negotiate as of the time it adds its confirmation to the credit.

(c) A confirming bank undertakes to reimburse another nominated bank that has honoured or negotiated a complying presentation and forwarded the documents to the confirming bank.

Reimbursement for the amount of a complying presentation under a credit available by acceptance or deferred payment is due at maturity, whether or not another nominated bank prepaid or purchased before maturity. A confirming bank's undertaking to reimburse another nominated bank is independent of the confirming bank's undertaking to the beneficiary.

(d) If a bank is authorized or requested by the issuing bank to confirm a credit but is not prepared to do so, it must inform the issuing bank without delay and may advise the credit without confirmation.

Article 9   Advising of credits and amendments

(a) A credit and any amendment may be advised to a beneficiary through an advising bank. An advising bank that is not a confirming bank advises the credit and any amendment without any undertaking to honour or negotiate.

(b) By advising the credit or amendment, the advising bank signifies that is has satisfied itself as to the apparent authenticity of the credit or amendment and that the advice accurately reflects the terms and conditions of the credit or amendment received.

(c) An advising bank may utilize the services of another bank ('second advising bank') to advise the credit and any amendment to the beneficiary. By advising the credit or amendment, the second advising bank signifies that it has satisfied itself as to the apparent authenticity of the advice it has received and that the advice accurately reflects the terms and conditions of the credit or amendment received.

(d) A bank utilizing the services of an advising bank or second advising bank to advise a credit must use the same bank to advise any amendment thereto.

(e) If a bank is requested to advise a credit or amendment but elects not to do so, it must so inform, without delay, the bank from which the credit, amendment or advice has been received.

(f) If a bank is requested to advise a credit or amendment but cannot satisfy itself as to the apparent authenticity of the credit, the amendment or the advice, it must so inform, without delay, the bank from which the instructions appear to have been received. If the advising bank or second advising bank elects nonetheless to advise the credit or amendment, it must inform the beneficiary or second advising bank that it has not been able to satisfy itself as to the apparent authenticity of the credit, the amendment or the advice.

Article 10   Amendments

(a) Except as otherwise provided by article 38, a credit can neither be amended nor cancelled without the agreement of the issuing bank, the confirming bank, if any, and the beneficiary.

(b) An issuing bank is irrevocably bound by an amendment as of the time it issues the amendment. A confirming bank may extend its confirmation to an amendment and will be irrevocably bound as of the time it advises the amendment. A confirming bank may, however, choose to advise an amendment without extending its confirmation and, if so, it must inform the issuing bank without delay and inform the beneficiary in its advice.

(c) The terms and conditions of the original credit (or a credit incorporating previously accepted amendments) will remain in force for the beneficiary until the beneficiary communicates its acceptance of the amendment to the bank that advised such amendment. The beneficiary should give notification of acceptance or rejection of an amendment. If the beneficiary fails to give such notification, a presentation that complies with the credit and to any not yet accepted amendment will be deemed to be notification of acceptance by the beneficiary of such amendment. As of that moment the credit will be amended.

(d) A bank that advises an amendment should inform the bank from which it received the amendment of any notification of acceptance or rejection.

(e) Partial acceptance of an amendment is not allowed and will be deemed to be notification of rejection of the amendment.

(f) A provision in an amendment to the effect that the amendment shall enter into force unless rejected by the beneficiary within a certain time shall be disregarded.

Article 11   Teletransmitted and pre-advised credits and amendments

(a) A authenticated teletransmission of a credit or amendment will be deemed to be the operative credit or amendment, and any subsequent mail confirmation shall be disregarded.

If a teletransmission states 'full details to follow' (or words of similar effect), or states that the mail confirmation is to be the operative credit or amendment, then the teletransmission will not be deemed to be the operative credit or amendment. The issuing bank must then issue the operative credit or amendment without delay in terms not inconsistent with the teletransmission.

(b) A preliminary advice of the issuance of a credit or amendment ('pre-advice') shall only be sent if the issuing bank is prepared to issue the operative credit or amendment. An issuing bank that sends a pre-advice is irrevocably committed to issue the credit or amendment, without delay, in terms not inconsistent with the pre-advice.

Article 12   Nomination

(a) Unless a nominated bank is the confirming bank, authorization to honour or negotiate does not impose any obligation on that nominated bank to honour or negotiate, except when expressly agreed to by that nominated bank and so communicated to the beneficiary.

(b) By nominating a bank to accept a draft or incur a deferred payment undertaking, an issuing bank authorizes that nominated bank to prepay or purchase a draft accepted or a deferred payment undertaking incurred by that nominated bank.

(c) Receipt or examination and forwarding of documents by a nominated bank that is not a confirming bank does not make that nominated bank liable to honour or negotiate, nor does it constitute honour or negotiation.

Article 13   Bank-to-bank reimbursement arrangements

(a) If a credit states that reimbursement is to be obtained by a nominated bank ('claiming bank') claiming on another party ('reimbursing bank'), the credit must state if the reimbursement is subject to the ICC rules for bank-to-bank reimbursements in effect on the date of issuance of the credit.

(b) If a credit does not state that reimbursement is subject to the ICC rules for bank-to-bank reimbursements, the following apply:

(i)   An issuing bank must provide a reimbursing bank with a reimbursement authorization that conforms with the availability stated in the credit. The reimbursement authorization should not be subject to an expiry date.

(ii) A claiming bank shall not be required to supply a reimbursing bank with a certificate of compliance with the terms and conditions of the credit.

(iii) An issuing bank will be responsible for any loss of interest, together with any expenses incurred, if reimbursement is not provided on first demand by a reimbursing bank in accordance with the terms and conditions of the credit.

(iv) A reimbursing bank's charges are for the account of the issuing bank. However, if the charges are for the account of the beneficiary, it is the responsibility of an issuing bank to so indicate in the credit and in the reimbursement authorization. If a reimbursing bank's charges are for the account of the beneficiary, they shall be deducted from the amount due to a claiming bank when reimbursement is made. If no reimbursement is made, the reimbursing bank's charges remain the obligation of the issuing bank.

(c) An issuing bank is not relieved of any of its obligations to provide reimbursement if reimbursement is not made by a reimbursing bank on first demand.

Article 14   Standard for examination of documents

(a) A nominated bank acting on its nomination, a confirming bank, if any, and the issuing bank must examine a presentation to determine, on the basis of the documents alone, whether or not the documents appear on their face to constitute a complying presentation.

(b) A nominated bank acting on its nomination, a confirming bank, if any, and the issuing bank shall each have a maximum of five banking days following the day of presentation to determine if a presentation is complying. This period is not curtailed or otherwise affected by the occurrence on or after the date of presentation of any expiry date or last day for presentation.

(c) A presentation including one or more original transport documents subject to articles 19, 20, 21, 22, 23, 24 or 25 must be made by or on behalf of the beneficiary not later than 21 calendar days after the date of shipment as described in these rules, but in any event not later than the expiry date of the credit.

(d) Data in a document, when read in context with the credit, the document itself and international standard banking practice, need not be identical to, but must not conflict with, data in that document, any other stipulated document or the credit.

(e) In documents other than the commercial invoice, the description of the goods, services or performance, if stated, may be in general terms not conflicting with their description in the credit.

(f) If a credit requires presentation of a document other than a transport document, insurance document or commercial invoice, without stipulating by whom the document is to be issued or its data content, banks will accept the document as presented if its content appears to fulfil the function of the required document and otherwise complies with sub-article 14(d).

(g) A document presented but not required by the credit will be disregarded and may be returned to the presenter.

(h) If a credit contains a condition without stipulating the document to indicate compliance with the condition, banks will deem such condition as not stated and will disregard it.

(i) A document may be dated prior to the issuance date of the credit, but must not be dated later than its date of presentation.

(j) When the addresses of the beneficiary and the applicant appear in any stipulated document, they need not be same as those stated in the credit or in any other stipulated document, but must be within the same country as the respective addresses mentioned in the credit. Contact details (telefax, telephone, email and the like) stated as part of the beneficiary's and the applicant's address will be disregarded. However, when the address and contact details of the applicant appear as part of the consignee or notify party details on a transport document subject to articles 19, 20, 21, 22, 23, 24 or 25, they must be as stated in the credit.

(k) The shipper or consignor of the goods indicated on any document need not be the beneficiary of the credit.

(l) A transport document may be issued by any party other than a carrier, owner, master or charterer provided that the transport document meets the requirements of articles 19, 20, 21, 22, 23 or 24 of these rules.

Article 15   Complying presentation

(a) When an issuing bank determines that a presentation is complying, it must honour.

(b) When a confirming bank determines that a presentation is complying, it must honour or negotiate and forward the documents to the issuing bank.

(c) When a nominated bank determines that a presentation is complying and honours or negotiates, it must forward the documents to the confirming bank or issuing bank.

Article 16   Discrepant documents, waiver and notice

(a) When a nominated bank acting on its nomination, a confirming bank, if any, or the issuing bank determines that a presentation does not comply, it may refuse to honour or negotiate.

(b) When an issuing bank determines that a presentation does not comply, it may in its sole judgement approach the applicant for a waiver of the discrepancies. This does not, however, extend the period mentioned in sub-article 14(b).

(c) When a nominated bank acting on its nomination, a confirming bank, if any, or the issuing bank decides to refuse to honour or negotiate, it must give a single notice to that effect to the presenter.

The notice must state:

    (i)   that the bank is refusing to honour or negotiate; and

    (ii) each discrepancy in respect of which the bank refuses to honour or negotiate; and

    (iii) (a) that the bank is holding the documents pending further instructions from the presenter; or

(b) that the issuing bank is holding the documents until it receives a waiver from the applicant and agrees to accept it, or receives further instructions from the presenter prior to agreeing to accept a waiver; or

(c) that the bank is returning the documents; or

(d) that the bank is acting in accordance with instructions previously received from the presenter.

(d) The notice required in sub-article 16(c) must be given by telecommunication or, if that is not possible, by other expeditious means no later than the close of the fifth banking day following the day of presentation.

(e) A nominated bank acting on its nomination, a conforming bank, if any, or the issuing bank may, after providing notice required by sub-article 16(c)(iii)(a) or (b), return the documents to the presenter at any time.

(f) If an issuing bank or a confirming bank fails to act in accordance with the provisions of this article, it shall be precluded from claiming that the documents do not constitute a complying presentation.

(g) When an issuing bank refuses to honour or a confirming bank refuses to honour or negotiate and has given notice to that effect in accordance with this article, it shall then be entitled to claim a refund, with interest, of any reimbursement made.

Article 17 Original document and copies

(a) At least one original of each document stipulated in the credit must be presented.

(b) A bank shall treat as an original any document bearing an apparently original signature, mark, stamp, or label the issuer of the document, unless the document itself indicates that it is not an original.

(c) Unless a document indicates otherwise, a bank will also accept a document as original if it:

(i) appears to be written, typed, perforated or stamped by the document issuer's hand; or

(ii) appears to be on the document issuer's original stationery; or

(iii) states that is original, unless the statement appears not to apply to the document presented.

(d) If a credit requires presentation of copies of documents, presentation of either originals or copies is permitted.

(e) If a credit requires presentation of multiple documents by using terms such as 'in duplicated', 'in two fold' or 'in two copies', this will be satisfied by the presentation of at least one original and the remaining number in copies, except when the document itself indicates otherwise.

Article 18 Commercial invoice

(a) A Commercial Invoice:

(i) must appear to have been issued by the beneficiary (except as provided in article 38);

(ii) must be made out in the name of the applicant (except as provided in sub-article 38(g));

(iii) must be made out in the same currency as the credit; and

(iv) need not be signed.

(b) A nominated bank acting on its nomination, a confirming bank, if any, or the issuing bank may accept a commercial invoice issued for an amount in excess of the amount permitted by the credit, and its decision will be binding upon all parties, provided the bank in question has not honoured or negotiated for an amount in excess of that permitted by the credit.

(c) The description of the goods, services or performance in a commercial invoice must correspond with that appearing in the credit

Article 19 Transport document covering at least two different modes of transport

(a) A transport document covering at least two different modes of transport (multimodal or combined transport document), however named, must appear to:

(i) indicate the name of the carrier and be signed by:

- the carrier or a named agent for or on behalf of the carrier, or
- the master or a named agent for or on behalf of the master.

    Any signature by the carrier, master or agent must be identified as that of the carrier, master or agent.

    Any signature by an agent must indicate whether the agent has signed for or on behalf of the carrier or for or on behalf of the master.

  (ii) indicate that the goods have been dispatched, taken in charge or shipped on board at the place stated in the credit, by:

- pre-printed wording, or
- a stamp or notation indicating the date on which the goods have been dispatched, taken in charge or shipped on board.

    The date of issuance of the transport document will be deemed to be the date of dispatch, taking in charge or shipped on board, and the date of shipment. However, if the transport document indicates, by stamp or notation, a date of dispatch, taking in charge or shipped on board, this date will be deemed to be the date of shipment.

  (iii) indicate the place of dispatch, taking in charge or shipment, and the place of final destination stated in the credit, even if:

    (a) the transport document states, in addition, a different place of dispatch, taking in charge or shipment or place of final destination, or

    (b) the transport document contains the indication 'intended' or similar qualification in relation to the vessel, port of loading or port of discharge.

  (iv) be the sole original transport document or, if issued in more than one original, be the full set as indicted on the transport document.

  (v) contain terms and conditions of carriage or make reference to another source containing the terms and conditions of carriage (short form or blank back transport document). Contents of terms and conditions of carriage will not be examined.

  (vi) contain no indication that it is subject to a charter party.

(b) For the purpose of this article, transhipment means unloading from one means of conveyance and reloading to another means of conveyance (whether or not in different modes of transport) during the carriage from the place of dispatch, taking in charge or shipment to the place of final destination stated in the credit.

  (c) (i) A transport document may indicate that the goods will or may be transhipped provided that the entire carriage is covered by one and the same transport document.

    (ii) A transport document indicating that transhipment will or may take place is acceptable, even if the credit prohibits transhipment.

Article 20   Bill of lading

(a) A bill of lading, however named, must appear to:

  (i) indicate the name of the carrier and be signed by:

- the carrier or a named agent for or on behalf of the carrier, or
- the master or a named agent for or on behalf of the master.

    Any signature by the carrier, master or agent must be identified as that of the carrier, master or agent.

    Any signature by an agent must indicate whether the agent has signed for or on behalf of the carrier or for or on behalf of the master.

  (ii) indicate that the goods have been shipped on board a named vessel at the port of loading stated in the credit by:

- pre-printed wording, or
- an on board notation indicating the date on which the goods have been shipped on board.

    The date of issuance of the bill of lading will be deemed to be the date of shipment unless the bill of lading contains an on board notation indicating the date of shipment, in which case the date stated in the on board notation will be deemed to be the date of shipment.

    If the bill of lading contains the indication 'intended vessel' or similar qualification in relation to the name of the vessel, an on board notation indicating the date of shipment and the name of the actual vessel is required.

(iii) indicate shipment from the port of loading to the port of discharge stated in the credit.

    If the bill of lading does not indicate the port of loading stated in the credit as the port of loading, or if it contains the indication 'intended' or similar qualification in relation to the port of loading, an on board notation indicating the port of loading as stated in the credit, the date of shipment and the name of the vessel is required. This provision applies even when loading on board or shipment on a named vessel is indicated by pre-printed wording on the bill of lading.

(iv) be the sole original bill of lading or, if issued in more than one original, be the full set as indicated on the bill of lading.

(v) contain terms and conditions of carriage or make reference to another source containing the terms and conditions of carriage (short form or blank back bill of lading). Contents of terms and conditions of carriage will not be examined.

(vi) contain no indication that it is subject to a charter party.

(b) For the purpose of this article, transhipment means unloading from one vessel and reloading to another vessel during the carriage from the port of loading to the port of discharge stated in the credit.

(c) (i) A bill of lading may indicate that the goods will or may be transhipped provided that the entire carriage is covered by one and the same bill of lading.

(ii) A bill of lading indicating that transhipment will or may take place is acceptable, even if the credit prohibits transhipment, if the goods have been shipped in a container, trailer or LASH barge as evidenced by the bill of lading.

(d) Clauses in a bill of lading stating that the carrier reserves the right to tranship will be disregarded.

Article 21   Non-negotiable sea waybill

(a) A non-negotiable sea waybill, however named, must appear to:

(i) indicate the name of the carrier and be signed by:

- the carrier or a named agent for or on behalf of the carrier, or
- the master or a named agent for or on behalf of the master.

    Any signature by the carrier, master or agent must be identified as that of the carrier, master or agent.

    Any signature by an agent must indicate whether the agent has signed for or on behalf of the master.

(ii) indicate that the goods have been shipped on board a named vessel at the port of loading stated in the credit by:

- pre-printed wording, or
- an on board notation indicating the date on which the goods have been shipped on board.

    The date of issuance of the non-negotiable sea waybill will be deemed to be the date of shipment unless the non-negotiable sea waybill contains an on board notation indicating the date of shipment, in which case the date stated in the on board notation will be deemed to be the date of shipment. If the non-negotiable sea waybill contains the indication 'intended vessel' or similar qualification in relation to the name of the vessel, an on board notation indicating the date of shipment and the name of the actual vessel is required.

(iii) indicate shipment from the port of loading to the port of discharge stated in the credit.

If the non-negotiable sea waybill does not indicate the port of loading stated in the credit as the port of loading, or if it contains the indication 'intended' or similar qualification in relation to the port of loading, an on board notation indicating the port of loading as stated in the credit, the date of shipment and the name of the vessel is required. This provision applies even when loading on board or shipment on a named vessel is indicated by pre-printed wording on the non-negotiable sea waybill.

(iv) be the sole original non-negotiable sea waybill or, if issued in more than one original, be the full set as indicated on the non-negotiable sea waybill.

(v) contain terms and conditions of carriage or make reference to another source containing the terms and conditions of carriage (short form or blank back non-negotiable sea waybill). Contents of terms and conditions of carriage will not be examined.

(vi) contain no indication that it is subject to a charter party.

(b) For the purpose of this article, transhipment means unloading from one vessel and reloading to another vessel during the carriage from the port of loading to the port of discharge stated in the credit.

(c) (i) A non-negotiable sea waybill may indicate that the goods will or may be transhipped provided that the entire carriage is covered by one and the same non-negotiable sea waybill.

(ii) A non-negotiable sea waybill indicating that transhipment will or may take place is acceptable, even if the credit prohibits transhipment, if the goods have been shipped in a container, trailer or LASH barge as evidenced by the non-negotiable sea waybill.

(d) Clauses in a non-negotiable sea waybill stating that the carrier reserves the right to tranship will be disregarded.

Article 22 Charter party bill of lading

(a) A bill of lading, however named, containing an indication that it is subject to a charter party (charter party bill of lading), must appear to:

(i) be signed by:
- the master or a named agent for or on behalf of the master, or
- the owner or a named agent for or on behalf of the owner, or
- the charterer or a named agent for or on behalf of the charterer.

Any signature by the master, owner, charterer or agent must be identified as that of the master, owner, charterer or agent.

Any signature by an agent must indicate whether the agent has signed for or on behalf of the master, owner or charterer.

An agent signing for or on behalf of the owner or charterer must indicate the name of the owner or charterer.

(ii) indicate that the goods have been shipped on board a named vessel at the port of loading stated in the credit by:
- pre-printed wording, or
- an on board notation indicating the date on which the goods have been shipped on board.

The date of issuance of the charter party bill of lading will be deemed to be the date of shipment unless the charter party bill of lading an contains on board notation indicating the date of shipment, in which case the date stated in the on board notation will be deemed to be the date of shipment.

(iii) indicate shipment from the port of the loading to the port of discharge stated in the credit. The port of discharge may also be shown as a range of ports or a geographical area, as stated in the credit.

(iv) be the sole original charter party bill of lading or, if issued in more than one original, be the full set as indicated on the charter party bill of lading.

(b) A bank will not examine charter party contracts, even if they are required to be presented by the terms of the credit.

Article 23   Air transport document

(a) An air transport document, however named, must appear to:

  (i)   indicate the name of the carrier and be signed by:

  - the carrier, or
  - a named agent for or on behalf of the carrier.

       Any signature by the carrier or agent must be identified as that of the carrier or agent.

       Any signature by an agent must indicate that the agent has signed for or on behalf of the carrier.

  (ii) indicate that the goods have been accepted for carriage.

  (iii) indicate the date of issuance. This date will be deemed to be the date of shipment unless the air transport document contains a specific notation of the actual date of shipment, in which case the date stated in the notation will be deemed to be the date of shipment.

       Any other information appearing on the air transport document relative to the flight number and date will not be considered in determining the date of shipment.

  (iv) Indicate the airport of departure and the airport of destination stated in the credit.

  (v)   be the original for consignor or shipper, even if the credit stipulates a full set of originals.

  (vi) contain terms and conditions of carriage or make reference to another source containing the terms and conditions of carriage. Contents of terms and conditions of carriage will not be examined.

(b) For the purpose of this article, transhipment means unloading from one aircraft and reloading to another aircraft during the carriage from the airport of departure to the airport of destination stated in the credit.

(c) (i)   An air transport document may indicate that the goods will or may be transhipped, provided that the entire carriage is covered by one and the same air transport document.

  (ii) An air transport document indicating that transshipment will or may take place is acceptable, even if the credit prohibits transhipment.

Article 24   Road, rail or inland waterway transport documents

(a) A road, rail or inland waterway transport document, however named, must appear to:

  (i)   indicate the name of the carrier and:

  - be signed by the carrier or a named agent for or on behalf of the carrier, or
  - indicate receipt of the goods by signature, stamp or notation by the carrier or a named agent for or on behalf of the carrier.

       Any signature, stamp or notation of receipt of the goods by the carrier or agent must be identified as that of the carrier or agent.

       Any signature, stamp or notation of receipt of the goods by the agent musty indicate that the agent has signed or acted for or an behalf of the carrier. If a rail transport document does not identify the carrier, any signature or stamp of the railway company will be accepted as evidence of the document being signed by the carrier.

  (ii) indicate the date of shipment of the date the goods have been received for shipment, dispatch or carriage at the place stated in the credit. Unless the transport document contains a dated reception stamp, an indication of the date of receipt or a date of shipment, the date of issuance of the transport document will be deemed to be the date of shipment.

  (iii) indicate the place of shipment and the place of destination stated in the credit.

(b) (i) A road transport document must appear to be the original for consignor or shipper or bear no marking indicating for whom the document has been prepared.

(ii) A rail transport document marked 'duplicate' will be accepted as an original.

(iii) A rail or inland waterway transport document will be accepted as an original whether marked as an original or not.

(c) In the absence of an indication on the transport document as to the number of originals issued, the number presented will be deemed to constitute a full set.

(d) For the purpose for this article, transhipment means unloading from one means of conveyance and reloading to another means of conveyance, within the same mode of transport, during the carriage from the place of shipment, dispatch or carriage to the place of destination stated in the credit.

(e) (i) A road, rail or inland waterway transport document may indicate that the goods will or may be transhipped provided that the entire carriage is covered by one and the same transport document.

(ii) A road, rail or inland waterway transport document indicating that transhipment will or may take place is acceptable, even if the credit prohibits transhipment.

Article 25   Courier receipt, post receipt or certificate of posting

(a) A courier receipt, however named, evidencing receipt of goods for transport, must appear to:

(i) indicate the name of the courier service and be stamped or signed by the named courier service at the place from which the credit states the goods are to be shipped; and

(ii) indicate a date of pickup or of receipt or wording to this effect. This date will be deemed to be the date of shipment.

(b) A requirement that courier charges are to be paid or prepaid may be satisfied by a transport document issued by a courier service evidencing that courier charges are for the account of a party other than the consignee.

(c) A post receipt of certificate of posting, however named, evidencing receipt of goods for transport, must appear to be stamped or signed and dated at the place from which the credit states the goods are to be shipped. This date will be deemed to be the date of shipment.

Article 26   'On deck', 'shipper's load and count', 'said by shipper to contain' and charges additional to freight

(a) A transport document must not indicate that the goods are or will be loaded on deck. A clause on a transport document stating that the goods may be loaded on deck is acceptable.

(b) A transport document bearing a clause such as 'shipper's load and count' and 'said by shipper to contain' is acceptable.

(c) A transport document may bear a reference, by stamp or otherwise, to charges additional to the freight.

Article 27   Clean transport document

A bank will only accept a clean transport document. A clean transport document is one bearing no clause or notation expressly declaring a defective condition of the goods or their packaging. The word 'clean' need not appear on a transport document, even if a credit has a requirement for the transport document to be 'clean on board'.

Article 28   Insurance document and coverage

(a) An insurance document, such as an insurance policy, an insurance certificate or a declaration under an open cover, must appear to be issued and signed by an insurance company, an underwriter or their agents or their proxies.

Any signature by an agent or proxy must indicate whether the agent or proxy has signed for or on behalf of the insurance company or underwriter.

(b) When the insurance document indicates that it has been issued in more than one original, all originals must be presented.

(c) Cover notes will not be accepted.

(d) An insurance policy is acceptable in lieu of an insurance certificate or a declaration under an open cover.

(e) The date of the insurance document must be no later than the date of shipment, unless it appears from the insurance document that the cover is effective from a date not later than the date of shipment.

(f) (i) The insurance document must indicate the amount of insurance coverage and be in the same currency as the credit.

   (ii) A requirement in the credit for insurance coverage to be for a percentage of the value of the goods, of the invoice value or similar is deemed to be the minimum amount of coverage required.

If there is no indication in the credit of the insurance coverage required, the amount of insurance coverage must be at least 110% of the CIF or CIP value of the goods.

When the CIF or CIP value cannot be determined from the documents, the amount of insurance coverage must be calculated on the basis of the amount for which honour or negotiation is requested or the gross value of the goods as shown on the invoice, whichever is greater.

   (iii) The insurance document must indicate that risks are covered at least between the place of taking in charge or shipment and the place of discharge or final destination as stated in the credit.

(g) A credit should state the type of insurance required and, if any, the additional risks to be covered. An insurance document will be accepted without regard to any risks that are not covered if the credit uses imprecise terms such as 'usual risks' or 'customary risks'.

(h) When a credit requires insurance against 'all risks' and an insurance document is presented containing any 'all risks' notation or clause, whether or not bearing the heading 'all risks', the insurance document will be accepted without regard to any risks state to be excluded.

(i) An insurance document may contain reference to any exclusion clause.

(j) An insurance document may indicate that the cover is subject to a franchise or excess (deductible).

Article 29   Extension of expiry date or last day for presentation

(a) If the expiry date of a credit or the last day for presentation falls on a day when the bank to which presentation is to be made is closed for reasons other than those referred to in article 36, the expiry date or the last day for presentation, as the case may be, will be extended to the first following banking day.

(b) If presentation is made on the first following banking day, a nominated bank must provide the issuing bank or confirming bank with a statement on its covering schedule that the presentation was made within the time limits extended in accordance with sub-article 29(a).

(c) The latest date for shipment will not be extended as a result of sub-article 29(a).

Article 30   Tolerance in credit amount, quantity and unit prices

(a) The words 'about' or 'approximately' used in connection with the amount of the credit or the quantity or the unit price stated in the credit are to be construed as allowing a tolerance not to exceed 10% more or 10% less than the amount, the quantity or the unit price to which they refer.

(b) A tolerance not to exceed 5% more or 5% less than the quantity of the goods is allowed, provided the credit does not state the quantity in terms of a stipulated number of packing units or individual items and the total amount of the drawings does not exceed the amount of the credit.

(c) Even when partial shipments are not allowed, a tolerance not to exceed 5% less than the amount of the credit is allowed, provided that the quantity of the goods, if stated in the credit, is shipped in full and a unit price, if stated in the credit, is not reduced or that sub-article 30(b) is not applicable. This tolerance does not apply when the credit stipulates a specific tolerance or uses the expressions referred to in sub-article 30(a).

Article 31   Partial drawings or shipments

(a) Partial drawings or shipments are allowed.

(b) A presentation consisting of more than one set of transport documents evidencing shipment commencing on the same means of conveyance and for the same journey, provided they indicate the same destination, will not be regarded as covering a partial shipment, even if they indicate different dates of shipment or different ports or loading, places of taking in charge or dispatch. If the presentation consists of more than one set of transport documents, the latest date of shipment as evidenced on any of the sets of transport documents will be regarded as the date of shipment.

A presentation consisting of one or more sets of transport documents evidencing shipment on more than one means of conveyance within the same mode of transport will be regarded as covering a partial shipment, even if the means of conveyance leave on the same day for the same destination.

(c) A presentation consisting of more than one courier receipt, post receipt or certificate of posting will not be regarded as a partial shipment if the courier receipts, post receipts or certificates of posting appear to have been stamped or signed by the same courier or postal service at the same place and date and for the same destination.

Article 32   Instalment drawings or shipments

If a drawing or shipment by instalments within given periods is stipulated in the credit and any instalment is not drawn or shipped within the period allowed for that instalment, the credit ceases to be available for that and any subsequent instalment.

Article 33   Hours of presentation

A bank has no obligation to accept a presentation outside of its banking hours.

Article 34   Disclaimer on effectiveness of documents

A bank assumes no liability or responsibility for the form, sufficiency, accuracy, genuineness, falsification or legal effect of any document, or for the general or particular conditions stipulated in a document or superimposed thereon; nor does it assume any liability or responsibility for the description, quantity, weight, quality, condition, packing, delivery, value or existence of the goods, services or other performance represented by any document, or for the good faith or acts or omissions, solvency, performance or standing of the consignor, the carrier, the forwarder, the consignee or the insurer of the goods or any other person.

Article 35   Disclaimer on transmission and translation

A bank assumes no liability or responsibility for the consequences arising out of delay, loss in transit, mutilation or other errors arising in the transmission of any messages or delivery of letters or documents, when such messages, letters or documents are transmitted or sent according to the requirements stated in the credit, or when the bank may have taken the initiative in the choice of the delivery service in the absence of such instructions in the credit.

If a nominated bank determines that a presentation is complying and forwards the documents to the issuing bank or confirming bank, whether or not the nominated bank has honoured or negotiated, an issuing bank or confirming bank must honour or negotiate, or reimburse that nominated bank, even when the documents have been lost in transit between the nominated bank and the issuing bank or confirming bank, or between the confirming bank and the issuing bank.

A bank assumes no liability or responsibility for errors in translation or interpretation of technical terms and may transmit credit terms without translating them.

Article 36   Force majeure

A bank assumes no liability or responsibility for the consequences arising out of the interruption of its business by Acts or God, riots, civil commotions, insurrections, wars, acts of terrorism, or by any strikes or lockouts or any other causes beyond its control.

A bank will not, upon resumption of its business, honour or negotiate under a credit that expired during such interruption of its business.

Article 37   Disclaimer for acts of an instructed party

(a) A bank utilizing the services of another bank for the purpose of giving effect to the instruction of the applicant does so for the account and at the risk of the applicant.

(b) An issuing bank or advising bank assumes no liability or responsibility should the instructions it transmits to another bank not be carried out, even if it has taken the initiative in the choice of that other bank.

(c) A bank instructing another bank to perform services is liable for any commissions, fees, costs or expenses ('charges') incurred by that bank in connection with its instructions.

If a credit states that charges are for the account of the beneficiary and charges cannot be collected or deducted from proceeds, the issuing bank remains liable for payment of charges.

A credit or amendment should not stipulate that the advising to a beneficiary is conditional upon the receipt by the advising bank or second advising bank of its charges.

(d) The applicant shall be bound by and liable to indemnify a bank against all obligations and responsibilities imposed by foreign laws and usages.

Article 38   Transferable credits

(a) A bank is under no obligation to transfer a credit except to the extent and in the manner expressly consented to by that bank.

(b) For the purpose of this article:

Transferable credit means a credit that specifically states it is 'transferable'. A transferable credit may be made available in whole or in part to another beneficiary ('second beneficiary') at the request of the beneficiary ('first beneficiary').

Transferring bank means a nominated bank that transfers the credit or, in a credit available with any bank, a bank that is specifically authorized by the issuing bank to transfer and that transfers the credit. An issuing bank may be a transferring bank.

Transferred credit means a credit that has been made available by the transferring bank to a second beneficiary.

(c) Unless otherwise agreed at the time of transfer, all charges (such as commissions, fees, costs or expenses) incurred in respect of a transfer must be paid by the first beneficiary.

(d) A credit may be transferred in part to more than one second beneficiary provided partial drawings or shipments are allowed.

A transferred credit cannot be transferred at the request of a second beneficiary to any subsequent beneficiary. The first beneficiary is not considered to be a subsequent beneficiary.

(e) Any request for transfer must indicate if and under what conditions amendments may be advised to the second beneficiary. The transferred credit must clearly indicate those conditions.

(f) If a credit is transferred to more than one second beneficiary, rejection of an amendment by one or more second beneficiary does not invalidate the acceptance by any other second beneficiary, with respect to which the transferred credit will be amended accordingly. For any second beneficiary that rejected the amendment, the transferred credit will remain unamended.

(g) The transferred credit must accurately reflect the terms and conditions of the credit, including confirmation, if any, with the exception of:

- the amount of the credit,
- any unit price stated therein,
- the expiry date,
- the period for presentation, or
- the latest shipment date or given period for shipment,

any or all of which may be reduced or curtailed.

The percentage for which insurance cover must be effected may be increased to provide the amount of cover stipulated in the credit or these articles.

The name of the first beneficiary may be substituted for that of the applicant in the credit.

If the name of the applicant is specifically required by the credit to appear in any document other than the invoice, such requirement must be reflected in the transferred credit.

(h) The first beneficiary has the right to substitute its own invoice and draft, if any, for those of a second beneficiary for an amount not in excess of that stipulated in the credit, and upon such substitution the first beneficiary can draw under the credit for the difference, if any, between its invoice and the invoice of a second beneficiary.

(i) If the first beneficiary is to present its own invoice and draft, if any, but fails to do so on first demand, or if the invoices presented by the first beneficiary create discrepancies that did not exist in the presentation made by the second beneficiary and the first beneficiary fails to correct them on first demand, the transferring bank has the right to present the documents as received from the second beneficiary to the issuing bank, without further responsibility to the first beneficiary.

(j) The first beneficiary may, in its request for transfer, indicate that honour or negotiation is to be effected to a second beneficiary at the place to which the credit has been transferred, up to and including the expiry date of the credit. This is without prejudice to the right of the first beneficiary in accordance with sub-article 38(h).

(k) Presentation of documents by or on behalf of a second beneficiary must be made to the transferring bank.

Article 39   Assignment of proceeds

The fact that a credit is not stated to be transferable shall not affect the right of the beneficiary to assign any proceeds to which it may be or may become entitled under the credit, in accordance with the provisions of applicable law. This article relates only to the assignment of proceeds and not to the assignment of the right to perform under the credit.

SUPPLEMENT FOR ELECTRONIC PRESENTATION eUCP VERSION 2.0

Preliminary Considerations

The mode of presentation to the nominated bank, confirming bank, if any, or the issuing bank, by or on behalf of the beneficiary, of electronic records alone or in combination with paper documents, is outside the scope of the eUCP.

The mode of presentation to the applicant, by the issuing bank, of electronic records alone or in combination with paper documents, is outside the scope of the eUCP.

Where not defined or modified in the eUCP, definitions given in UCP 600 will continue to apply.

Before agreeing to issue, advise, confirm, amend or transfer an eUCP credit, banks should satisfy themselves that they can examine the required electronic records in a presentation made thereunder.

Article e1   Scope of the eUCP

(a) The eUCP supplements the Uniform Customs and Practice for Documentary Credits (2007 Revision, ICC Publication No. 600) ('UCP') in order to accommodate presentation of electronic records alone or in combination with paper documents.

(b) The eUCP shall apply where the credit indicates that it is subject to the eUCP ('eUCP credit').

(c) This version is Version 2.0. An eUCP credit must indicate the applicable version of the eUCP. If not indicated, it is subject to the latest version in effect on the date the eUCP credit is issued or, if made subject to the eUCP by an amendment accepted by the beneficiary, on the date of that amendment.

(d) An eUCP credit must indicate the physical location of the issuing bank. In addition, it must also indicate the physical location of any nominated bank and, if different to the nominated bank, the physical location of the confirming bank, if any, when such location is known to the issuing bank at the time of issuance. If the physical location of any nominated bank and/or confirming bank is not indicated in the credit, such bank must indicate its physical location to the beneficiary no later than the time of advising or confirming the credit or, in the case of a credit available with any bank, and where another bank willing to act on the nomination to honour or negotiate is not the advising or confirming bank, at the time of agreeing to act on its nomination.

Article e2   Relationship of the eUCP to the UCP

(a) An eUCP credit is also subject to the UCP without express incorporation of the UCP.

(b) Where the eUCP applies, its provisions shall prevail to the extent that they would produce a result different from the application of the UCP.

(c) If an eUCP credit allows the beneficiary to choose between presentation of paper documents or electronic records and it chooses to present only paper documents, the UCP alone shall apply to that presentation. If only paper documents are permitted under an eUCP credit, the UCP alone shall apply.

Article e3   Definitions

(a) Where the following terms are used in the UCP, for the purpose of applying the UCP to an electronic record presented under an eUCP credit, the term:

   (i)   **Appear on their face** and the like shall apply to examination of the data content of an electronic record.

   (ii) **Document** shall include an electronic record.

   (iii) **Place for presentation** of an electronic records means an electronic address of a data processing system.

   (iv) **Presenter** means the beneficiary, or any party acting on behalf of the beneficiary who makes a presentation to a nominated bank, confirming bank, if any, or to the issuing bank directly.

   (v)   **Sign** and the like shall include an electronic signature.

   (vi) **Superimposed, notation** or **stamped** means data content whose supplementary character is apparent in an electronic record.

(b) The following terms used in the eUCP shall have the following meaning:

   (i)   **Data corruption** means any distortion or loss of data that renders the electronic record, as it was presented, unreadable in whole or in part.

   (ii) **Data processing system** means a computerised or an electronic or any other automated means used to process and manipulate date, initiate an action or respond to data messages or performances in whole or in part.

   (iii) **Electronic record** means data created, generated, sent, communicated, received or stored by electronic means, including, where appropriate, all information logically associated with or otherwise linked together so as to become part of the record whether generated contemporaneously or not, that is:

   - capable of being authenticated as to the apparent identity of a sender and the apparent source of the data contained in it, and as to whether it has remained complete and unaltered, and
   - capable of being examined for compliance with terms and conditions of the eUCP credit.

   (iv) **Electronic signature** means a data process attached to or logically associated with an electronic record and executed or adopted by a person in order to identify that person and to indicate that person's authentication of the electronic record.

   (v)   **Format** means the data organisation in which the electronic record is expressed or to which it refers.

   (vi) **Paper document** means a document in a paper form.

   (vii) **Received** means when an electronic record enters a data processing system, at the place for presentation indicated in the eUCP credit, in a format capable of being accepted by that system. Any acknowledgement of receipt generated by that system does not imply that the electronic record has been viewed, examined, accepted or refused under an eUCP credit.

(viii) **Re-present** or **re-presented** means to substitute or replace an electronic record already presented.

Article e4   Electronic Records and Paper Documents v. Goods, Services or Performance

Banks do not deal with the goods, services or performance to which an electronic record or paper document may relate.

Article e5   Format

An eUCP credit must indicate the format of each electronic record. If the format of an electronic record is not indicated, it may be presented in any format.

Article e6   Presentation

(a) (i)   An eUCP credit must indicate a place for presentation of electronic records.

    (ii) An eUCP credit requiring or allowing presentation of both electronic records and paper documents must, in addition to the place for presentation of the electronic records, also indicate a place for presentation of the paper documents.

(b) Electronic records may be presented separately and need not be presented at the same time.

(c) (i)   When one or more electronic records are presented alone or in combination with paper documents, the presenter is responsible for providing a notice of completeness to the nominated bank, confirming bank, if any, or to the issuing bank, where a presentation is made directly. The receipt of the notice of completeness will act as notification that the presentation is complete and that the period for examination of the presentation is to commence.

    (ii) The notice of completeness may be given as an electronic record or paper document and must identify the eUCP credit to which it relates.

    (iii) Presentation is deemed not to have been made if the notice of completeness is not received.

    (iv) When a nominated bank, whether acting on its nomination or not, forwards or makes available electronic records to a confirming bank or issuing bank, a notice of completeness need not be sent.

(d) (i)   Each presentation of an electronic record under an eUCP credit must identify the eUCP credit under which it is presented. This may be by specific reference thereto in the electronic record itself, or in metadata attached or superimposed thereto, or by identification in the covering letter or schedule that accompanies the presentation.

    (ii) Any presentation of an electronic record not so identified may be treated as not received.

(e) (i)   If the bank to which presentation is to be made is open but its system is unable to receive a transmitted electronic record on the stipulated expiry date and/or the last day for presentation, as the case may be, the bank will be deemed to be closed and thet [sic] expiry date and/or last day for presentation shall be extended to the next banking day on which such bank is able to receive an electronic record.

    (ii) In this event, the nominated bank must provide the confirming bank or issuing bank, if any, with a statement on its covering schedule that the presentation of electronic records was made within the time limits extended in accordance with sub-article e6(e)(i).

    (iii) If the only electronic record remaining to be presented is the notice of completeness, it may be given by telecommunication or by paper document and will be deemed timely, provided that it is sent before the bank is able to receive an electronic record[.]

(f) An electronic record that cannot be authenticated is deemed not to have been presented.

Article e7   Examination

(a) (i)   The period for the examination of documents commences on the banking day following the day on which the notice of completeness is received by the nominated bank, confirming bank, if any, or by the issuing bank, where a presentation is made directly.

   (ii)   If the time for presentation of documents or the notice of completeness is extended, as provided in sub-article e6(e)(i), the time for the examination of documents commences on the next banking day following the day on which the bank to which presentation is to be made is able to receive the notice of completeness, at the place for presentation.

(b) (i)   If an electronic record contains a hyperlink to an external system or a presentation indicates that the electronic record may be examined by reference to an external system, the electronic record at the hyperlink or the external system shall be deemed to constitute an integral part of the electronic record to be examined.

   (ii)   The failure of the external system to provide access to the required electronic record at the time of examination shall constitute a discrepancy, except as provided in sub-article e7(d)(ii).

(c)   The inability of a nominated bank acting on its nomination, a confirming bank, if any, or the issuing bank, to examine an electronic record in a format required by an eUCP credit or, if no format is required, to examine it in the format presented is not a basis for refusal.

(d) (i)   The forwarding of electronic records by a nominated bank, whether or not it is acting on its nomination to honour or negotiate, signifies that it has satisfied itself as to the apparent authenticity of the electronic records.

   (ii)   In the event that a nominated bank determines that a presentation is complying and forwards or makes available those electronic records to the confirming bank or issuing bank, whether or not the nominated bank has honoured or negotiated, an issuing bank or confirming bank must honour or negotiate, or reimburse that nominated bank, even when a specified hyperlink or external system does not allow the issuing bank or confirming bank to examine one or more electronic records that have been made available between the nominated bank and the issuing bank or confirming bank, or between the confirming bank and the issuing bank.

Article e8   Notice of Refusal

If a nominated bank acting on its nomination, a confirming bank, if any, or the issuing bank, provides a notice of refusal of a presentation which includes electronic records and does not receive instructions from the party to which notice of refusal is given for the disposition of the electronic records within 30 calendar days from the date the notice of refusal is given, the bank shall return any paper documents not previously returned to that party, but may dispose of the electronic records in any manner deemed appropriate without any responsibility.

Article e9   Originals and Copies

Any requirement for presentation of one or more originals or copies of an electronic record is satisfied by the presentation of one electronic record.

Article e10   Date of Issuance

An electronic record must provide evidence of its date of issuance.

Article e11   Transport

If an electronic record evidencing transport does not indicate a date of shipment or dispatch or taking in charge or a date the goods were accepted for carriage, the date of issuance of the electronic record will be deemed to be the date of shipment or dispatch or taking in charge of the date the goods were accepted for carriage. However, if the electronic record bears a notation that evidences the date of shipment or dispatch or taking in charge or the date the goods were accepted for carriage, the date of the notation will be deemed to be the date of shipment or dispatch or taking in charge or the date the goods were accepted for carriage. Such a notation showing additional data content need not be separately signed or otherwise authenticated.

Article e12 Data Corruption of an Electronic Record

(a) If an electronic record that has been received by a nominated bank acting on its nomination or not, confirming bank, if any, or the issuing bank, appears to have been affected by a data corruption, the bank may inform the presenter and may request it to be re-presented.

(b) If a bank makes such a request:

    (i) the time for examination is suspended and resumes when the electronic record is re-presented; and

    (ii) if the nominated bank is not a confirming bank, it must provide any confirming bank and the issuing bank with notice of the request for the electronic record to be re-presented and inform it of the suspension; but

    (iii) if the same electronic record is not re-presented within 30 calendar days, or on or before the expiry date and/or last day for presentation, whichever occurs first, the bank may treat the electronic record as not presented.

Article e13 Additional Disclaimer of Liability for Presentation of Electronic Records under eUCP

(a) By satisfying itself as to the apparent authenticity of an electronic record, a bank assumes no liability for the identity of the sender, source of the information, or its complete and unaltered character other than that which is apparent in the electronic record received by the use of a data processing system for the receipt, authentication, and identification of electronic records.

(b) A bank assumes no liability or responsibility for the consequences arising out of the unavailability of a data processing system other than its own.

Article e14 Force Majeure

A bank assumes no liability or responsibility for the consequences arising out of the interruption of its business, including but not limited to its inability to access a data processing system, or a failure of equipment, software or communications network, caused by Acts of God, riots, civil commotions, insurrections, wars, acts of terrorism, cyberattacks, or by any strikes or lockouts or any other causes, including failure of equipment, software or communications networks, beyond its control.